edmunds.com℠
where smart car buyers start®

Used Cars & Trucks Buyer's Guide

2005

Where Smart Car Buyers Start®

Table of Contents

Edmunds.com Used Cars & Trucks Buyer's Guide

2005 Edition, Volume U3901 ISBN: 0-87759-687-5 ISSN: 1541-8510

Further copyright information on page 5

Table of Contents

Publisher
Peter Steinlauf

President
Jeremy Anwyl

Chief Operating Officer
Avi Steinlauf

General Manager, Edmunds Media
Matthew Kumin

Editorial Director
Kevin Smith

Editor in Chief
Karl Brauer

Managing Editor
Donna DeRosa

Senior Road Test Editor
Ed Hellwig

Manager of Vehicle Testing
Kelly Toepke

Senior Editor, Content & Syndication
Erin Riches

Senior Consumer Advice Editor
Phil Reed

Photography Editor
Scott Jacobs

Road Test Editors
John DiPietro, Brian Moody, Dan Kahn

New Vehicle Reviews Editor
Jeff Bryan

Content Editor
Warren Clarke

Production Editor
Caroline Pardilla

Vice President, Data Development and Operations
Jane Liu, Ph.D.

Director, Automotive Research
Charles Schiavone

Photographic Data Specialist
Matt Landish

Senior Manager, Vehicle Data
Ken Brown

Used Vehicle Research Supervisor
Dan Orosco

Vehicle Data Editor
Kevin Shapiro

Programmer, Book Automation
John Song

Director, Creative Services
Guy Schackman

Design Manager, Creative Services
Justin Nowlen

Book Designer and Master Layout
Jeff Zugale

Production Layout Artist
Keno Rider

Printed in USA

Introduction

Welcome to the *Edmunds.com Used Cars & Trucks Buyer's Guide*

Ever since we produced our first automotive pricing guide in 1966, the name Edmunds has been associated with timely, accurate and unbiased vehicle information. For over 39 years, Edmunds.com has provided advice on getting the best deal when buying a vehicle; a complete breakdown of used car and truck pricing; straightforward, consumer-friendly explanations of terms like "trade-in" and "wholesale"; and other useful automotive consumer resources.

In 1994, Edmunds took a monumental step forward by offering all this valuable used vehicle content to Internet users…for free! As the first automotive resource to go on-line, we introduced used vehicle buyers and sellers to the concept of "information transparency," which essentially means giving consumers access to the same pricing information available to dealers and manufacturers. No one could match the quality of our on-line content offering in 1994, and 10 years later Edmunds.com continues to be the automotive information leader.

What You'll Find Inside This Book

Our used vehicle pricing and option information is presented in an easy to read format. We've grouped all years of each model together so you can more easily track values as the car ages. And, of course, we still present each vehicle's three True Market Value (TMV®) prices: the dealer trade-in price, the private party price and the dealer retail price. Keep in mind that the Edmunds.com True Market Value® prices are not the "asking" or "suggested" prices. TMV is our exclusive system for determining, and reporting to you, what others are paying and getting for similar used vehicles. Edmunds.com's True Market Value pricing system for new and used vehicles is the industry's best guide to market value pricing and the only pricing system designed with the consumer in mind.

Comprehensive Photography

We have provided at least one photograph for every "generation" of vehicle covered in this book (all non-exotic, U.S.-sold cars and trucks from 1995 to 2004). Most automakers substantially redesign their models about every four to seven years. While some changes are made to many models almost every year, it is during a redesign that a car or truck will often take on an entirely different look. By including over 700 images in this book we have provided you with an accurate visual representation of what each model looks like over the past 10 years.

In-Depth Buying and Selling Advice

You also get a comprehensive advice section with in-depth buying and selling articles, tips on how to use today's technology to research a vehicle's history, information on certified used vehicles and our picks for the "Best Bet" for a smart used car purchase. Specific advice articles include:

10 Steps to Buying and 10 Steps to Selling a Used Car (starts on page 7)

Buying this book is a smart first step on the path to buying or selling a used vehicle, but finding the car or truck that's right for you, and ensuring you get the vehicle at a fair price, can be a daunting process. Conversely, if you're trying to turn a car into cash, you'll want to understand how to properly prepare and accurately price the vehicle. To help you we've created our simple, straightforward "10 Steps" series. These tutorials, written by a former car salesman, will help guide you through the process to ensure you get a fair deal, regardless of whether you're buying or selling.

Vehicle History Reports (starts on page 17)

At one time there was no way to verify a used vehicle's history. But computer technology now allows car shoppers to use the Vehicle Identification Number (VIN) to reveal a car's (possibly) checkered past. As this article explains, vehicle history reports can be a valuable tool whether you are buying or selling a car.

Certified Used Vehicles (starts on page 606)

With so many manufacturers now offering a certified used vehicle program, it makes sense to consider such a vehicle when shopping for your next car or truck. We give you a basic description of each manufacturer's program, as well as some questions to consider when buying a certified used vehicle.

And Much More...

In addition to these features, you'll find a mileage chart (page 605) to further aid you in pricing a used vehicle. And as mentioned earlier, there's also a section devoted to our "Best Bet" used vehicles for 2004 (page 27). These are the cars and trucks we consider the best combination of reliability, safety and value in the used market. You'll also discover a glossary of used vehicle terms (page 22).

Don't Forget Our Web Site

There's no denying that the **Edmunds.com Used Cars & Trucks Buyer's Guide** is a powerful tool you can use in your quest to find the right used vehicle at the right price. As most car shoppers know, the Internet is another powerful tool for car-buying research. Consider this book a portable version of Edmunds.com. Use it to do basic vehicle research and as an easy reference guide (especially the pricing data and "10 Steps" section) when navigating the often treacherous waters that make up the used car buying process.

And don't forget that, despite our efforts to stuff everything you need to know about used cars into one book, you will always benefit from visiting our Web site at Edmunds.com. Once there you'll have access to a full array of new and used vehicle buying tools, including our True Market Value Used Vehicle Appraiser that calculates used vehicle values for specific models and styles based on color, options, mileage, condition and region. You'll also find used vehicle listings for your area, an on-line community of thousands of automotive consumers (some of them talking about the same car you're interested in buying), an on-line maintenance section listing recalls and technical service bulletins and hundreds of vehicle reviews dating back to 1996.

The technology available for researching a used vehicle purchase may have changed, but Edmunds.com's mission is still the same: To inform consumers, striving to give them the benefit of our knowledge, insight into the automotive industry, the experience of owning and driving vehicles and lessons we've learned about owning, buying and selling automobiles. We exist for the consumer, and write for that audience. Everything we publish is designed to make our readers better-educated car owners, buyers and sellers.

Karl Brauer
Editor in Chief
Edmunds.com

How To Use This Book

Our *Used Cars & Trucks Buyer's Guide* makes it easy for you to research used vehicle pricing. Here is a basic explanation of the information provided for each make, model and year.

Make:
Vehicle manufacturer

Model:
Vehicle model name

Year:
This lists the specific year for a used vehicle.

Mileage Category:
Use this code, along with the Mileage Table on page 605, to compute how a specific vehicle's mileage affects its value.

Major Changes:
This text describes the major changes that took place each year for a given model.

Body Styles:
This box lists the various body styles and trims available in a given year

TMV Pricing:
These figures represent the current True Market Value for a vehicle in terms of dealer trade-in, private party sale or dealer sale.

Options:
This box lists the options available during a given model year.

Option Price:
Use these figures to get a customized used car value based on options that may be on the vehicle you are considering.

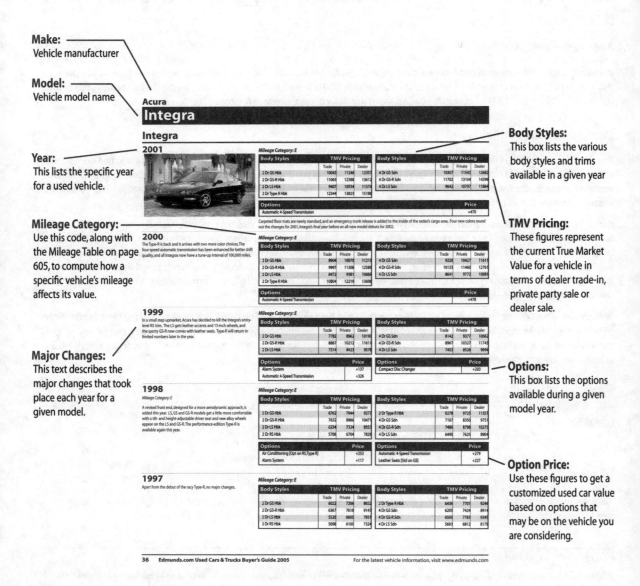

Acura

Integra

Integra

2001

Mileage Category: E

Body Styles	TMV Pricing			Body Styles	TMV Pricing		
	Trade	Private	Dealer		Trade	Private	Dealer
2 Dr GS Hbk	10043	11246	12357	4 Dr GS Sdn	10307	11542	12682
2 Dr GS-R Hbk	11063	12388	13612	4 Dr GS-R Sdn	11702	13104	14398
2 Dr LS Hbk	9407	10534	11574	4 Dr LS Sdn	9642	10797	11864
2 Dr Type R Hbk	12344	13823	15188				

Options	Price
Automatic 4-Speed Transmission	+470

Carpeted floor mats are newly standard, and an emergency trunk release is added to the inside of the sedan's cargo area. Four new colors round out the changes for 2001, Integra's final year before an all-new model debuts for 2002.

2000

The Type-R is back and it arrives with two more color choices. The four-speed automatic transmission has been enhanced for better shift quality, and all Integras now have a tune-up interval of 100,000 miles.

Mileage Category: E

Body Styles	TMV Pricing			Body Styles	TMV Pricing		
	Trade	Private	Dealer		Trade	Private	Dealer
2 Dr GS Hbk	8904	10070	11213	4 Dr GS Sdn	9220	10427	11611
2 Dr GS-R Hbk	9997	11306	12589	4 Dr GS-R Sdn	10133	11460	12761
2 Dr LS Hbk	8472	9581	10666	4 Dr LS Sdn	8641	9772	10881
2 Dr Type R Hbk	10804	12219	13600				

Options	Price
Automatic 4-Speed Transmission	+478

1999

In a small step upmarket, Acura has decided to kill the Integra's entry-level RS trim. The LS gets leather accents and 15-inch wheels, and the sporty GS-R now comes with leather seats. Type-R will return in limited numbers later in the year.

Mileage Category: E

Body Styles	TMV Pricing			Body Styles	TMV Pricing		
	Trade	Private	Dealer		Trade	Private	Dealer
2 Dr GS Hbk	7782	8962	10190	4 Dr GS Sdn	8142	9377	10662
2 Dr GS-R Hbk	8867	10212	11611	4 Dr GS-R Sdn	8967	10327	11743
2 Dr LS Hbk	7314	8423	9576	4 Dr LS Sdn	7403	8526	9694

Options	Price	Options	Price
Alarm System	+137	Compact Disc Changer	+203
Automatic 4-Speed Transmission	+326		

1998

Mileage Category: E

A revised front end, designed for a more aerodynamic approach, is added this year. LS, GS and GS-R models get a little more comfortable with a tilt- and height-adjustable driver seat and new alloy wheels appear on the LS and GS-R. The performance-edition Type-R is available again this year.

Body Styles	TMV Pricing			Body Styles	TMV Pricing		
	Trade	Private	Dealer		Trade	Private	Dealer
2 Dr GS Hbk	6762	7944	9277	2 Dr Type R Hbk	8278	9725	11357
2 Dr GS-R Hbk	7632	8966	10471	4 Dr GS Sdn	7107	8350	9751
2 Dr LS Hbk	6234	7324	8553	4 Dr GS-R Sdn	7489	8798	10275
2 Dr RS Hbk	5706	6704	7828	4 Dr LS Sdn	6490	7625	8904

Options	Price	Options	Price
Air Conditioning [Opt on RS,Type R]	+253	Automatic 4-Speed Transmission	+279
Alarm System	+117	Leather Seats [Std on GS]	+227

1997

Apart from the debut of the racy Type-R, no major changes.

Mileage Category: E

Body Styles	TMV Pricing			Body Styles	TMV Pricing		
	Trade	Private	Dealer		Trade	Private	Dealer
2 Dr GS Hbk	6022	7206	8652	2 Dr Type R Hbk	6436	7701	9246
2 Dr GS-R Hbk	6367	7618	9147	4 Dr GS Sdn	6205	7424	8914
2 Dr LS Hbk	5520	6605	7931	4 Dr GS-R Sdn	6505	7783	9345
2 Dr RS Hbk	5098	6100	7324	4 Dr LS Sdn	5691	6812	8179

For the latest vehicle information, visit www.edmunds.com

For the latest vehicle information, visit www.edmunds.com

10 Steps to Buying a Used Car

The following steps will tell you how to locate, price and negotiate to buy the used car you want. Remember to consult our Glossary (page 22) if you find words here that you don't understand.

1. Starting Out

If you've decided to buy a used car, you've already made a smart decision. You can get a car that's almost as good as a brand-new one, without suffering the depreciation that wallops new car buyers as soon as they drive the car off the lot. Used cars — even those that are only one or two years old — are 20 to 30 percent cheaper than new cars.

But there are other good reasons to buy a used car:

- Buying a used car means you can buy a larger and/or more luxurious vehicle that you normally couldn't afford.
- You'll save money on insurance.
- The glut of cars coming off lease makes it easy to find one in good condition.
- Superior bargains are possible for the smart used car shopper.

Furthermore, the classic reasons to avoid used cars — lack of reliability and the expense of repairs — are less of an issue these days. Consider these related thoughts:

- Some used cars are still covered by the factory warranty.
- Most new carmakers now sell certified used cars, which include warranties.
- The history of a used car can easily be traced using the VIN number.
- Finance rates for used cars have dropped in recent years.
- If you buy from a private party, the negotiation process is usually less stressful.

True, you can't be the first one on the block with the trendiest vehicle. But you'll have the satisfaction of knowing that you got a great deal and made a smart financial decision. So read on, as we guide you along the road to used car happiness.

2. How Much Can You Afford?

The smart shopper will consider how to finance the car at the beginning of the shopping process. This will avoid unpleasant surprises later in the game and help you make an unemotional decision that fits your budget. You will need to estimate three figures that will guide you as you go shopping:

- Monthly payment. If you are going to take out a loan, how much can you afford to pay each month?
- Down payment. How much cash can you put down to reduce your monthly payments?
- Purchase price of the car. Answering the first two questions will provide the answer to this final question.

Once you've determined these amounts, write down the figures. Later, in the heat of the moment, when you are negotiating for a used car and need to stay within your budget, you might need to check your figures to keep yourself from overspending.

3. Locating the Right Used Car

It's possible that you need to expand your horizons when considering what to buy. You might want to think of other vehicles in the same class. For example, if you are considering a Toyota Camry, you should also look at the Honda Accord, Ford Taurus or Mitsubishi Galant. These cars were built for the same market, but they often have different features at lower prices.

It's also important to remember the difference between your needs and your wants. You may want a luxury car or SUV for image purposes, but you really only need a midsize sedan to meet your passenger and cargo requirements. Obviously, you can buy whatever you want, but keep in mind that buying more car than you need is an unnecessary cost, at least in terms of covering your basic transportation goals.

10 Steps to Buying a Used Car

4. Look For Used Car Bargains

The cost of a used car is based on its condition, mileage, reliability, performance and popularity. Of course, you want a car that is reliable and performs well. But do you want the same used car everyone else wants? If so, you will pay a premium for it. In some cases, the only difference is the nameplate.

Some shoppers believe they can get a killer deal by going to police auctions or buying a car with a salvage title (one that has been declared a total loss by an insurance company). True, the initial cost is much lower, but you know little about what you are getting. It could have frame damage, a safety problem or a faulty transmission. For most people, it's better to stick to the more common used car sources: private parties and the used car department of the local dealership. You might even consider buying a certified used car that comes with a factory warranty. Then you get the best of both worlds: a break on the price and peace of mind.

5. Research Your Prospective Used Car

You will find all the information you need to make an informed decision about what to buy in the pages of this book. The major topics are covered, providing you with information on prices, standard features, specs, safety and warranties. If you can visit Edmunds.com, you can broaden your base of knowledge by reading the editorial reviews of the car and by checking out what current owners have to say in our Forums section. With over half a million registered users in Town Hall, you are almost guaranteed to find someone who has experience with the car (or cars) you are considering.

Another essential part of the used car buying process involves the Edmunds.com True Market Value (TMV®) pricing system, which serves as a guideline when car shopping. Again, by visiting Edmunds.com on-line you can get a "Customized Appraisal" that prices the car more accurately. The figures you can get are based upon thousands of similar sales across the country. We will go into more detail about how to use Edmunds.com's TMV later.

One last vital step to getting a great used car deal: you should run a vehicle history report on any used car you are considering. Several companies sell these reports, which are based on the vehicle identification number (VIN), but Carfax (www.carfax.com) seems to be the most comprehensive. With these reports, you will find out the vital information about a used car, including whether it has a salvage title or its odometer has been rolled back.

6. Set Up Financing for Your Used Car

There are three ways to pay for your used car:

1. Cash. Need we say more? Money talks — you-know-what walks.

2. Financing through a bank, on-line lender or credit union. Assuming you can't pay in cash, we highly recommend this route because it will usually save money and give you the most control over the transaction.

3. Financing through the dealer. This can work for some people, depending on their credit scores and the current interest rates offered. Also, by prearranging financing through an independent source, the dealer may sometimes offer to beat the rate with a low-interest loan.

Financing through an independent source (on-line lender, bank or credit union) offers several advantages:

- Keeps negotiations simple in the dealership
- Allows you to shop competitive interest rates ahead of time
- Removes dependency on dealership financing
- Encourages you to stick to your budgeted amount
- Low-interest loans can easily be arranged on-line through banks such as Capital One Auto Finance (http://www.capitaloneautofinance.com)

7. Used Car Markets

The most common places to buy a used car are:

- Private parties
- New car dealerships
- Used car lots

Of these sources, private parties usually have the most reasonable prices. It is also a more relaxed transaction to buy a used car from a private party rather than face a salesman at a dealership.

Still, there are advantages to buying a used car from a new car dealership. Many used cars on these lots are trade-ins. Dealerships usually get these cars at rock-bottom prices. If you make a low offer — but one that gives them some profit — you just might get a great deal. Furthermore, many dealerships offer certified used cars that have been thoroughly inspected and are backed by attractive warranties. Search for your car by using online ads or in the classifieds of your local newspaper. When shopping on the Internet, you'll notice that some sites allow you to search according to specific criteria such as make, model, options and price range. In some cases, you can search the used car inventory of new car dealerships through their Web site.

While the Internet is an amazing resource, you should still try the conventional sources. Ask friends and relatives if they are selling a used car. Keep your eyes peeled for cars with "For Sale" signs in the window. Scan the bulletin boards at supermarkets or local schools and colleges. Finally, don't forget old faithful — the newspaper classifieds, particularly on Friday, Saturday and Sunday.

A lot of time can be saved by calling the selling party before you go see the vehicle. In this way, you can eliminate cars that have problems such as excessive mileage or a salvage title. Here are a few key questions to ask over the phone:

- What is the mileage? Why is it low? High? (12,000 to 15,000 miles a year is average)
- What color is the exterior? Interior? Does it have leather or cloth seats?
- Has it been in an accident?
- Is the engine a four-cylinder, V6 or V8?
- Is the transmission auto? Manual?
- Is the car still under warranty?
- Is there a salvage title?
- What options/add-ons does it have?
- What is the asking price?

If, after talking to the seller, the car still meets your needs, set up an appointment for a test-drive. If possible, make this appointment during the day so you can more accurately determine the car's condition. Also, ask for the VIN number so you can run a Carfax report. This will give you detailed information about the car's history.

8. Test-Driving a Used Car

Used car shopping will involve inspecting the vehicle to determine its condition. This process is simplified if you buy a certified used car that has passed a thorough inspection and is backed by a manufacturer's warranty. But while buying a certified used car removes a lot of the guesswork about the vehicle's mechanical condition, you pay for this service in the form of a higher purchase price.

Most new cars are sold with a minimum three-year/36,000-mile basic warranty. Therefore, if you buy a car that is one to three years old, with less than 36,000 miles on the odometer, it will still be under the factory warranty. If anything goes wrong with the car you just bought, the problem will be fixed for free (provided it's not a wear item like brake pads). Warranties vary from one manufacturer to the next. Always read the restrictions of the warranty before buying the car.

10 Steps to Buying a Used Car

If you are serious about buying a used car but have doubts about its condition, take it to a mechanic you trust. A private party will probably allow you to do this without much resistance. But at a dealership, it might be more difficult. If it is a factory-certified used car, you don't have to take it to a mechanic.

Once you get behind the wheel, your first impression will be the way the car feels when you sit in it. Is it a good fit? Does it offer enough head-room? Legroom? Are the gauges and controls conveniently positioned?

Try to arrange your test-drive so that you start the engine when it is completely cold. Some cars are harder to start after they have been sitting, and starting them up in this condition can reveal chronic problems. If you can have a friend stand behind the car to watch the tailpipe while you start it, even better. A condition to watch for is blue or white smoke emitted from the tailpipe for several seconds (or longer) after the engine starts. If you see steam or water vapor, don't worry about it. Turn off the radio before you start the vehicle — you want to hear the engine and concentrate on the driving experience.

On the test-drive, evaluate these additional points:

- Acceleration from a stop
- Visibility (Check for blind spots)
- Engine noise
- Passing acceleration (Does it downshift quickly and smoothly?)
- Hill-climbing power
- Braking
- Cornering (Do you feel in control when making turns?)
- Suspension (How does it ride?)
- Rattles and squeaks
- Cargo space
- Seat comfort/support
- Wear and tear (Are interior components mostly intact or does it feel like it's falling apart?)

On the test-drive, take your time and be sure to simulate the conditions of your normal driving patterns. If you do a lot of highway driving, be sure to merge and take the car up to 65 mph. If you go into the mountains, test the car on a steep slope. You don't want to find out — after you've bought the car — that it doesn't perform as needed.

After the test-drive, ask the owner if you can see the service records and if receipts are available. If so, note whether the car has had oil changes at regular intervals (at every 5,000 to 7,500 miles). Be cautious of buying a car that has had major repairs such as transmission rebuilds, valve jobs or engine overhauls.

9. Negotiating for a Used Car

Whether you are buying a used car from a dealer or a private party, let them know you have the cash in hand (or financing arranged) to make a deal on the spot. Preface your offer with a statement like, "I'm ready to make a deal now. I can give you cash (or a cashier's check) now. But we need to talk about the price."

At this point, you need to have a persuasive argument for why the price is too high. So let's talk about pricing. The foundation of successful negotiation is information. This is particularly true when buying a used car. Yet, the variable condition of used cars means prices will vary widely as well.

Edmunds.com has removed much of the guesswork in used car pricing by developing True Market Value pricing. After you have gathered information about a car you are considering, look it up in this book. If you can, visit www.edmunds.com and follow the link that gives you a "Customized Appraisal." When you're finished, print out the three TMV prices: Trade-In, Private Party and Dealer Retail.

Dealers have lots of negotiating experience. Most private party sellers do not. Therefore, buying a used car from a dealer or a private party will be two very different experiences. But there is one overriding similarity — they both want to sell the car. In fact, the incentive to sell the car might be greater to the dealer than to the private party owner.

You should, however, follow these guidelines when negotiating:

- Beware of negotiating with a salesperson (or private party seller) who makes you feel uncomfortable or intimidated.
- Make an opening offer that is low, but in the ballpark.
- Decide ahead of time how high you will go and leave when your limit is reached.
- Make it clear that you are prepared to walk away if a deal can't be made — this is your strongest negotiating tool.
- Be patient — plan to spend an hour or more negotiating at a dealership, much less with a private party.
- Leave the dealership if you get tired or hungry — in other words, don't sign the contract just to "get it over with."
- Don't be distracted by pitches for related items such as extended warranties or anti-theft devices.
- Try to keep the deal simple — negotiate the buying price and the trade-in price (if you have a trade-in) separately.
- Expect a closer (a second salesman) to come in during the final negotiations to try and improve the deal before you reach a final price.

Once you have a deal, you need to make sure the transaction is completed properly. The next section, the final step, will tell you what to expect and what you need to do.

10. Closing the Deal

If you are at a dealership, you still have to go through the finance and insurance (F&I) process. If you are buying a car from a private party, you have to pay and make sure the title and registration are properly transferred.

Also, you need to make sure you have insurance for the car you just bought before you drive it away. At a dealership, the F&I person will probably try to sell you a number of additional items: an extended warranty, alarms or anti-theft services such as LoJack, prepaid service plans, fabric protection, rust proofing and emergency roadside kits. Some people swear by extended warranties, so this is something you might want to consider (unless your used car is certified or still under the manufacturer's warranty). However, the other items typically sold in the F&I room are expensive and hold little value for you.

The F&I person may seem like a financial advisor, but he or she is really an experienced salesperson. Some F&I people can become very persistent trying to sell these items. Be firm. Say, "I'm not interested in any aftermarket extras, thank you. I just want the car."

Once the contract is ready, review it thoroughly. In most states, it will contain the cost of the vehicle, a documentation fee, a smog fee, a small charge for a smog certificate, sales tax and license fees (also known as DMV fees). Make sure you understand the charges and question the appearance of any significant, sudden additions to the contract.

Finally, you should inspect the car before you take possession of it. If any repair work is required, and has been promised by the dealer, get it in writing in a "Due Bill." Make sure the temporary registration has been put in the proper place (usually on the lower part of the windshield) — and you're finally on your way.

When you buy a car from a private party, you will probably be asked to pay with a cashier's check or in cash. But before money changes hands, request the title (sometimes called the "pink slip") and have it signed over to you. Rules governing vehicle registration and licensing vary from state to state. Check with the DMV in your state (much of this information is now available on DMV Web sites).

Once all of the paperwork is complete, it is finally time to relax and begin enjoying your new purchase: a good used car.

10 Steps to Buying a Used Car

Checklist

1. Choose the right vehicle for you by making sure the car suits your needs.

2. Consider all cars in the class you have chosen (compact sedan, large SUV, midsize wagon, etc.)

3. Look up the car on Edmunds.com and check its reliability record, editorial reviews and consumer commentary.

4. Check the Edmunds.com TMV price in this book or visit **www.edmunds.com** to get the most accurate price on the car you want to buy (adjusted for mileage, options, color, condition and region).

5. Decide how much you have to spend: down payment, monthly payment and purchase price.

6. Decide how you are going to finance your car. If you are going through a bank, on-line lender or credit union, obtain loan approval before you start shopping.

7. Using the Internet, including Edmunds.com's Used Vehicle Listings, search for the used car you've decided to buy.

8. Call the seller and verify the pertinent information. Get the VIN. Run a Carfax report on the car.

9. Test-drive the car under your normal driving conditions. Take the car to a mechanic if it is not certified by the manufacturer or covered by a comprehensive warranty.

10. Negotiate your best deal.

11. Review the contract carefully before signing and always make sure you get a clean title.

12. Inspect the car for dents, dings and scratches before taking final delivery.

10 Steps to Selling a Used Car

Here are 10 simple steps to turn your used car into cash in the shortest amount of time.

1. Know the Market

Is your car going to be easy to sell? Is it a hot commodity? Or will you have to drop your price and search out additional avenues to sell it?

Here are a few general rules to answer these questions:

- Family sedans, while unexciting to many, are in constant demand by people needing basic, inexpensive transportation.
- SUVs are very popular right now and often move quickly, even older models.
- The sale of convertibles and sports cars is seasonal. Sunny weather brings out the buyers. Fall and winter months will be slow.
- Trucks and vans, used for work, are steady sellers and command competitive prices. Don't underestimate their value.
- Collector cars will take longer to sell and are often difficult to price. However, these cars can have unexpected value if you find the right buyer.

Your first step is to check classified ads in your local newspaper and on-line. See what is for sale and at what price. Edmunds.com and other Internet sites allow you to search with specific criteria. For example, select the year and trim level of your car and see how many similar cars are currently on the market. Take note of their condition, mileage, geographic location and selling price.

2. Price Your Car Competitively

The best way to price your car is to use the information in this book. If you want a more up-to-date price, visit Edmunds.com and look up the car you are selling. You will see a link under the "Used Car Prices, Reviews & Info" heading near the top of the page labeled "Appraise a Car." Click on this and follow the prompts. This will give you an Edmunds.com True Market Value® price that is adjusted for mileage, color, region, options and condition.

There are exceptions to the rules of pricing, so you should follow your intuition. And be sure to leave a little wiggle room in your asking price. You should always ask for more money than you are actually willing to accept. If you want to get $12,000 for the car, you should list the car at $12,500. That way, if you get $12,500 — great! But if you have to go lower, it won't be a terrible loss.

You may have noticed how creative used car dealers get in pricing cars. Their prices usually end in "995," as in $12,995. Are we not supposed to notice that the car basically costs $13,000? There is a lot of psychology in setting prices. A product that doesn't sell well at $20 might jump off the shelf at $19.95.

On the other hand, a private party doesn't want to look like a car dealer. Therefore, you might want to take a simple approach and set your price at a round figure such as $12,750 or $12,500.

3. Give Your Car "Curb Appeal"

When people come to look at your car, they will probably make up their minds to buy it or not within the first few seconds. This is based on their first look at the car. So you want this first look to be positive. You want your car to have "curb appeal."

Before you advertise your car for sale, make sure it looks clean and attractive. This goes beyond just taking it to the car wash. Here is a to-do list that will help you turn your heap into a cream puff:

- Make sure it is washed, waxed and detailed.
- Make sure your car is both mechanically sound and free from dents, dings and scrapes.
- Consider making low-cost repairs yourself rather than selling it "as is."
- Shovel out all the junk from the inside of the car. When prospects go for a test-drive, you don't want them to feel like they've walked into your messy bedroom. Let them visualize the car as theirs.
- Wipe the brake dust off the wheel covers and clean the tires with a product such as Armor All.

10 Steps to Selling a Used Car

- Thoroughly clean the windows (inside and out) and all the mirrored surfaces.
- Wipe down the dashboard and empty the ashtrays.
- Dig out all your maintenance records and have them ready to show buyers.
- If the car needs servicing or even a routine oil change, take care of that ahead of time.
- Have your mechanic check out your car and issue a report about its condition. You can use this to motivate a buyer who is on the fence.
- Order a Carfax report and show it to the buyer to prove the car's title is clean and the odometer reading is accurate.

4. Where to Advertise Your Car

Now that your car is looking great and running well, it's time to advertise it for sale. Traditionally, people advertise in newspaper classified ads. These ads can be expensive, but they get results. However, on-line ads are becoming more popular, particularly with hard-to-find or collector cars.

Here are the main markets for advertising used cars:

- On-line classified ads such as those on Edmunds.com
- Daily newspaper classified ads
- Weekly "shoppers" and giveaway newspapers
- Bulletin boards at your job, a local supermarket or on a college campus
- Word of mouth — tell your friends and family you have a car for sale
- Put a "For Sale" sign in the car window

Creativity is required when it comes to advertising. Think of unusual places to put ads (skywriting is probably too expensive), and you will get results.

One last word of advice about advertising: if you run an expensive classified ad, be sure you are available to take phone calls from possible buyers. Many people won't leave a message for a return call. So answer the phone — and be polite. This is the first hurdle to clear in getting buyers to come and see the car in person.

5. Create Ads That Sell

When creating "For Sale" signs or putting a classified ad in the paper, you have an opportunity to show how eager you are to sell the car. This can be done by inserting the following abbreviations and phrases:

Must Sell!: This often means the seller is leaving town and needs to dump the car at a fire sale price. This shows the seller is as eager as possible without giving the car away.

OBO: This stands for "Or Best Offer" and it indicates that you are willing to entertain offers below the stated price. This usually means you are eager to sell the car.

Asking price: This also communicates the feeling that you will negotiate, but it is one notch below OBO on the eagerness scale.

Firm: This word is used to rebuff attempts to negotiate. It indicates that you aren't in a hurry to sell the car — you are most interested in getting your price.

Think about what you are telling people by the way you phrase your ad. Little words convey a lot.

6. Showing Your Car

Keep in mind that when you sell your car, people will also be evaluating you. They will be thinking something like, "Here's the person who's owned this car for the past few years. Do I trust him/her?" Make the buyers feel comfortable. They will probably be uneasy about making a big decision and spending money. Put them at ease and answer their questions openly.

10 Steps to Selling a Used Car

Potential buyers will want to test-drive the car. Check to make sure they have a driver license. Ride along with them so you can answer any questions about the car's history and performance. Also, they may not know the area, so you might have to guide them.

There are many unexpected bumps in the road that can arise while selling a used car. These will be handled easily if you are dealing with a reasonable person. So, as you are contacted by prospective buyers, use your intuition to evaluate them. If they seem difficult, pushy or even shady, wait for another buyer. With the right person, selling a used car should be simple.

Some sellers feel uncomfortable about having buyers come to their house to see the car. However, you can generally screen buyers on the phone. If they sound suspicious, don't do business with them. If you don't want people knowing where you live, arrange to show the car at a park or shopping center located near your home. However, keep in mind that people will eventually see your address when you sign the title over to them.

Some buyers will want to take the car to a mechanic to have it inspected. If you have an inspection report from your mechanic, this might put their doubts to rest. However, if they still want to take the car to their mechanic, this is a reasonable request. By now, you should have a feeling for the person's trustworthiness. If you feel uncomfortable or have reason to think they will steal the car, decline the offer or go along with them.

Be ready for trick questions such as, "So, what's really wrong with the car?" If you get this, refer them to the mechanic's report or invite them to look over the car more carefully.

7. Negotiate for Your Best Price

If a person comes to look at the car and it passes their approval after a test-drive, you can expect them to make an offer. Most people are uncomfortable negotiating, so their opening offer might take several forms.

"I like the car, but…" This is the softest way to negotiate on the price. They may not even state that the price seems too high. However, if they say, "I like the car, but…" and then lapse into uncomfortable silence, you might consider an appropriate response. If you really want to move the car, you could say, "How much would you be willing to pay?"

"What's your best price?" This is a more direct way to probe the seller to find out how much he or she will come down. If you get this from a prospective buyer, don't seem too eager to reduce your price.

"Would you accept…?" Now we're getting somewhere. This buyer has thought it over and is making an offer. But the offer is being presented in a polite manner designed to allow for a counter offer.

"Take it or leave it." This buyer is making an offer that supposedly leaves no room for a counter offer. In reality, this buyer might be bluffing. Still, they are sending a message that they are close to their final price. The only way to know for sure whether it really is a "take it or leave it" offer is to leave it — and let them leave. They may return tomorrow ready to pay your price.

The above are just a few of the openers you might encounter. Think of your response ahead of time so you won't be caught unprepared. In general, it's a good idea to hold to your price when your car first goes up for sale. If you don't get any buyers right away, you'll know you have to be flexible.

8. Handling Complications

In some cases, you might reach an agreement with a buyer that is contingent on performing repair work on the car. This can lead to misunderstandings down the line, so avoid this if you can. The best thing to do is have your car in good running order while being fully aware of any necessary repairs. If you state clearly in your ads that the car is being sold "as is," you can refer to this statement when it's time to close the deal.

Still, a trip to the prospective buyer's mechanic might turn up a new question about the car's condition. What to do?

This must be handled on a case-by-case basis. If the repair is needed, and you trust the mechanic's assessment, you could propose reducing the agreed-upon price by all, or part, of the amount for the repair. If the repair is questionable, but the buyer is insistent, split the difference, or have the car taken to your mechanic for further evaluation.

Remember, the older the car, the more problems a mechanic is likely to find. At some point, you have to draw the line. You may have to say to the buyer, "True, this work could be done. But the car drives well as it is. And the proposed repair isn't addressing a safety concern." After all, a used car — particularly an elderly one — isn't expected to be perfect.

10 Steps to Selling a Used Car

9. Finalize the Sale

Rules governing the sale of motor vehicles vary from state to state. Make sure you check with the department of motor vehicles (DMV) in your state, and keep in mind that much of the information is now available on DMV Web sites.

When selling your car, it's important to limit your liability. If someone drives away in the car you just sold, and they get into an accident, can you be held responsible? There are two ways to deal with this concern.

Once you have the money from the sale (it's customary to request either cash or a cashier's check) record the odometer reading and sign the car's title over to the buyer. In some states, the license plates go along with the car. A new title will be issued and mailed to the new owner.

But what if you still owe money on the car, and the bank is holding the title? One way to deal with this is to conclude the sale at the bank where the title is held. Call ahead and have the title ready. Then, once money has changed hands and the bank has been paid the balance of the loan, sign the title over to the buyer.

In some cases, however, an out-of-state bank might hold the title. In this instance, it is recommended that you go with the buyer to the DMV and get a temporary operating permit based on a bill of sale. Then, after you pay off the balance of the loan with the proceeds from the car sale, have the title mailed to the new owner. Sign it over to the new owner and the transaction is complete.

Finally, remember to contact your insurance agent to cancel your policy on the vehicle you have sold (or transfer the coverage to your new car).

Before your car drives away for the final time, take a last look through the glove compartment, the trunk and under the seats. You might find some long forgotten treasures you misplaced years ago.

10. After the Sale

In most states, the condition of a used car for sale is considered "as is" and no warranty is provided or implied. Therefore, if the car breaks down after you have sold it you are under no obligation to refund the buyer's money or pay to have it repaired. If you have sold a car to someone who took it for inspection at a garage and the mechanic found nothing wrong with it, you have done all you can to protect yourself and the buyer.

The best way to feel peace of mind after selling your used car is to make sure you did everything correctly. This means being open about the condition of the car before the sale and timely and complete in transferring DMV paperwork after the sale.

When done correctly, selling a used car can be a win-win situation. You have turned your used car into cash and provided reliable transportation for the next owner. Focus on the benefits to both parties and you are likely to have a smooth and successful experience.

Vehicle History Reports

Your Key to a Good Used Car

You're shopping for a used car when you think you've hit pay dirt. It's an '01 import with low miles. It drives great, and the price is right. When you question the owner about the car's history, he says he bought it from a used car lot only two years ago.

You're about to write a check when you have a troubling thought: This deal seems too good to be true. Maybe something's wrong with the car that the seller is keeping hidden. Who owned the car before? Is there any damage or problems you should know about?

At one time there was no way to verify a vehicle's history. Buyers could only examine the evidence in front of them, basing their decision on the mechanical condition of the car. But computer technology now allows car shoppers to use the Vehicle Identification Number (VIN) to reveal a car's possibly checkered past.

Vehicle history reports can be ordered from a number of Internet companies. The first company to offer this service is Carfax (www.carfax.com), which, as the name suggests, began faxing used car reports as early as 1986. Now, the Fairfax, Virginia-based company accesses many different information sources to compile reports that are e-mailed almost instantaneously to customers.

"We literally have every car on the road in our database back to 1981," said a Carfax spokesman. He notes that 1981 was when the U.S. government accepted the VIN as a standard tracking code for a vehicle's history. "Think of the Carfax as the DNA of the car — the Carfax report never forgets."

Vehicle History Reports — A Growing Field

While Carfax seems to be the leader in this new field, there are other companies vying for the consumer's business. Many of these companies draw on similar sources for their information and present the data in a compiled report at competitive prices. Carfax charges $19.99 for a single report and $24.99 for an unlimited number of reports for one month.

Consumer Guide (www.consumerguide.com) has taken the process one step further. Vehicle history information is drawn from the monster database of Experian (with 1.7 billion records) and coupled with Consumer Guide's repair information.

"What we do that is unique is marry the Consumer Guide data to [vehicle history reports] on the fly," said a Consumer Guide spokesman. "We also track trouble spots for the year, make and model of that vehicle." While the information doesn't pertain to that specific vehicle, it gives a buyer a general picture of the car's reliability and the replacement cost of parts, should something go wrong.

"If you are selling your car, you can buy the report and show it to the potential buyer," suggested another Consumer Guide source. "This will show [consumers] there isn't some sort of wreck that they weren't aware of."

Odometer Rollbacks

If you order a report from Carfax, your report is broken into categories: vehicle specifications, title check, odometer rollback check, problem check, registration check and vehicle history details. The different pieces of the report are summarized in a table that may flag problems. Details are listed later in the report.

Most importantly, Carfax provides an independent check of a vehicle's history. While the odometer of a used car might show that it has only 55,000 miles, the Carfax might indicate that the odometer readings at key events in the car's history — emissions tests or title changes — don't match up.

For example, the report might show that a certain vehicle was smog-checked in December 1999 at 55,000 miles. But then, when a change of title was issued two months later, the odometer reading was recorded as being 45,000 miles. Obviously, there was some kind of foul play here.

The number of miles a car is driven directly affects the price of the car. Therefore, a seller has a strong incentive to roll back the odometer. Each excess mile a car is driven — over the expected yearly average of between 12,000 to 15,000 — reduces its value. Therefore, turning back an odometer 10,000 miles can increase the sale price of the car by $600.

In another situation, a person might be ready to return a lease car and be faced with paying $2,000 in mileage penalties to the dealer. A quick trip to a "spinner" — someone who turns back odometers — will save them lots of money. In this way, dealers are defrauded, and so is the next person who buys the car.

"Folks think because [the odometer] is digital, it is harder to roll back," the Carfax spokesman said."But it's not. Anyone with a laptop [and the right software] can plug into the car's computer under the hood and do it." He added that some estimates have shown that 40 percent of lease cars have been involved in some type of scam.

Title Washing and Curb Stoning

Another scam detected by Carfax is called title washing. This occurs when state X might not recognize titles from state Y. People who are unscrupulous will take bad cars and move them into that state.

But a Carfax report tracks the car as it crosses state lines. If a car has been "branded" in another state — with a salvage title, for example — this will be revealed on the report. Salvage titles are assigned to cars that have been considered a total loss by insurance companies. Of course, the car might still run and be drivable, but having a salvage title significantly reduces its value.

"Curb stoning" occurs when a dealer has an inferior or damaged car he can't sell on his lot. He gives the car to a salesperson to sell through the classifieds, as if it were a private party sale. However, a Carfax report will show that the title recently changed hands and may reveal that it is a lemon or an otherwise branded car. Fredericks recommends proceeding with extreme caution if the seller's name is different from the name on the title.

Edmunds Test-Drives Carfax

While we were writing this article, Carfax gave us an account to run a number of vehicle history reports. In many cases, reports were run on cars that were known to have salvage or lemon titles. Carfax reports caught those problems and flagged the pertinent information.

As a test case, we entered a VIN number for a '98 Corvette we knew had been branded as a lemon. Sure enough, the Carfax report clearly flagged the problem by stating:"LEMON LAW VEHICLE repurchased by manufacturer."

In other cases, we ran reports on cars we knew little about. In one instance, the report noted a "potential odometer rollback." Looking closely at the vehicle's file, however, it appeared the source of the rollback alert was probably a clerical error at a smog inspection station. Everything else about the car's history lined up.

In another case, an Edmunds employee was considering buying a '95 Acura. He test-drove the car and felt it was in good mechanical condition. However, after running a Carfax report, it was discovered that the car was given a salvage title in 1996 and, several years later, a junk title (a junk vehicle is one that was reported to the DMV by an individual or a dismantler as having been dismantled). When the seller was confronted with this information, he said, "Oh yeah, I thought I told you about that."

In yet another case, an Edmunds editor ran the VIN number of a car she had owned several years ago. It was the only report that was returned listing an accident. It read, "Accident reported involving left side impact with another motor vehicle." Carfax is beginning to receive information from law enforcement sources reporting accidents. If a car is totaled in an accident, a salvage title is assigned. But prospective buyers will still want to know about minor accidents. In this way, they can find out if the damage was properly repaired.

Consumer Guide said their reports also list accident reports, usually if they were serious enough to cause damage to the car's frame.

What Does the Future Hold?

With the increased speed of data communications, the amount of information about vehicles will increase in the coming years. Both Carfax and Consumer Guide hope to tap into service and repair records in the near future. Then, a consumer can see if a car was maintained according to the manufacturer's requirements before purchasing it.

Frequently Asked Questions

1. Why does it make good financial sense to buy a used car?

A new car depreciates between 20 and 30 percent as soon as you drive it off the lot. In the ensuing years of a car's life, it depreciates only about 5 to 10 percent a year. Therefore, if you buy a one-year-old car, someone else has paid for that steep depreciation. Furthermore, cars are more reliable now than ever before. Buying a yearling with about 12,000 miles on it means you are getting a car that will feel new at a significant savings.

2. What is the best way to check out the condition of a used car?

First, it is important to run a vehicle history report on the car you are considering. You can do this for a reasonable fee through a company such as Carfax (www.carfax.com). This will tell you who has owned the car and if it has a salvage title (that is, it has been declared a "total loss" by an insurance company due to an accident or flooding) or the odometer has been rolled back. If the vehicle history looks clear, consider taking it to your mechanic for an inspection. However, if you are buying a factory-certified used car, this will probably not be necessary. Also, check to see if the used car is still covered by the factory warranty (and make sure it is transferable). Should something go wrong with the car after you buy it, you can have it fixed at no cost if it's still under warranty.

3. I want to pay cash for my used car at the dealership. Do I have an advantage?

Not necessarily. You must remember that no matter how you pay for your car, it's all cash to the dealer. In the old days when dealers carried your note, you could save money by paying cash because there was no risk to the dealer. Today, dealerships finance through one of several lending institutions (banks, credit unions or the automaker's captive financing division) that pay them cash when the contract is presented. In fact, if dealerships do the financing on your behalf, they tend to make more money on your contract in the form of a reserve; anywhere from a one-half to a one-point spread on the interest. For example, if the published rate is 8.75 percent, the lender-to-dealer rate may be discounted to 8 percent. The remaining .75 percent is the reserve held by the dealer as additional profit. This may not sound like much, but it adds up to hundreds of thousands of dollars a year at larger dealerships. This is the reason you should always arrange financing before going to the dealership, and then ask the dealer if they can beat your preapproved rate.

Paying cash is an advantage if you suffer from poor credit or bankruptcy, because it allows you to avoid the higher interest rates charged on loans to people with past credit problems. The bottom line is that if you think you can invest your money at a higher return than the interest rate of the car loan, you could actually save money by not paying cash.

4. Why won't the dealer give me wholesale value for my trade-in?

When a dealership takes a car in on trade, it is responsible for the car. Before the trade-in can be resold, it must be inspected and often repaired. Sometimes, emissions work is necessary. All this inspection and repair work costs the dealership money. If the trade is in good condition and has low miles, the dealer will put the car on the used car lot for retail price. When the car sells, it is rarely for retail price, so the profit margin is shaved. The less a dealer pays for a trade-in, the more room he has to make a deal with a prospective buyer, and the more money the dealer will make due to increased profit margins.

If the car doesn't sell, has high miles or is in poor condition, the dealer will have to wholesale it. The dealer will likely sell the car for below wholesale value at the auction, and therefore expects to recoup some of the money spent reconditioning and inspecting the car on the front end. If the dealer offered you wholesale price when you traded in the car, it wouldn't make the money back in the event that the trade-in went to auction.

Regardless of the condition of your car, the dealer will anticipate taking the car to auction and will leave room to make money in that event. Your best bet is to sell your car on your own to a private party and forget about trading it in.

5. Should I buy an extended factory warranty for my used car?

Some people like the peace of mind an extended factory warranty provides. Other people like to save money and gamble. The decision is up to you. However, you should determine how much of the factory warranty is still in effect on the used car you are buying. The bumper-to-bumper warranty might have expired, but maybe the powertrain (which includes the major components that move the car, such as the engine and transmission) is still covered. Consider how long you expect to have the car. Will you keep it beyond the warranty that is in effect now? Also, keep in mind that extended warranties are negotiable; shop around for your best deal and you could save several hundred dollars.

6. When is the best time to purchase a car from a dealer?

There's as much advice about when to visit a dealer as there are days in a year. Some say that Mondays are good because business is slower on Monday than on the weekend. Some say holidays like Thanksgiving are good for the same reason: nobody else will be there, and the sales team will be hungry for a sale. Others advise to go when it's raining or snowing; after all, who wants to look at a car and get wet? Then there's the advice that the end of the month is the best time because the dealership needs to make its "quota" of car sales and will be more willing to cut a deal. Still others advise not to buy a car until the end of the model year, or in slow months like August or December when people are busy thinking about going back to school or shopping for Christmas gifts rather than buying a new car.

Our advice is don't buy a car until you're ready. That's usually the best time. By then you have had plenty of time to do your research for low-interest financing and you know what make and model best fits your needs.

7. When should a car be considered used?

Technically, a vehicle is considered used if it has been titled. However, some dealers can rack up hundreds or thousands of miles on a new car without titling it. In these cases, the ethical definition of a used car should include any car used for extensive demonstration or personal use by dealership staff members. The only miles a new car should have on the odometer when purchased are those put on during previous test-drives by prospective buyers (at dealerships where demonstrators are not used), and any miles driven during a dealer trade, within a reasonable limit. If the new car you're considering has more than 300 miles on the odometer, you should question how the car accumulated so many miles, and request a discount for the excessive mileage. We think a discount amounting to a dollar a mile up to 500 miles is reasonable. For higher mileage amounts, the cost deducted should be approximately 15 cents a mile for wear and tear inflicted by the dealership.

8. What's the difference between a demo car and a program car?

Both of these types of used cars might be sold at a discount by a new car dealership, so it's important to know what you are buying. A demo car is one used by the dealership for test-drives for potential buyers. Often, dealership personnel will use demo cars as personal transportation.

Program cars have been owned by the manufacturer and given to employees for a short time to use for company business. The idea is to have a Ford employee, for example, drive a late-model Ford to advertise the company's product. These cars are maintained by the factory and usually sent to auction before the odometer turns 10,000 miles. The cars are sold to Ford dealers at closed auctions and then put up for sale on the car lot and advertised as "program cars." Dealers like these cars because they can get them at low prices and then sell them at a good profit. Program cars have been well maintained, so in essence you are buying a nearly new car with no worries about mechanical problems.

9. Is it fair for a dealer to ask if my trade has ever been wrecked or damaged in any way?

Certainly. If you were buying a car from a used car dealer, you'd want to know the same thing, wouldn't you? You can always run a Carfax report on a dealer's used car or ask them to do it for you.

10. How do I determine a fair price for a used car?

Edmunds.com publishes True Market Value (TMV) prices for used cars back to 1980. If you can visit the site on-line, enter the information about the car you are considering into the Used Car Appraiser and you will find the average selling price in your region. Keep in mind that TMV is intended as a "transaction price" for the car — the price at which you actually close the deal — not an "asking price." When setting your price, it is also a good idea to look at used car prices in the local newspaper and through other on-line sources.

Frequently Asked Questions

11. How can I determine what a dealer paid for a used car at auction or in trade?

Unless the dealer discloses this amount, you can't determine the wholesale price. However, by making a low opening offer you will find the point at which the dealer firms up on price. When this happens, you've gotten about as low as you can go; any lower and the dealer figures it would be better to just hang onto the car.

12. Why does Edmunds.com's used car pricing differ from other price guides?

Each guide uses different sources to determine pricing. You must keep in mind that these publications, and Edmunds.com, are to be considered guides. The values contained within are not absolute; they are intended to give the user a range of values to consider when determining a fair price. Used car values depend on mileage, vehicle condition, geographic location, model popularity, seasonal demand and even color.

Also remember that the dealer will use whatever pricing guide works to its advantage in the deal. By providing pricing that favors the dealer, other guides make big bucks on subscriptions to industry personnel. Some even publish two different pricing guides — one for consumers and one for dealers. Rarely do dealers use values found at Edmunds.com. We believe that speaks volumes about the fairness of our published pricing to the consumer.

The most important thing to remember about buying, selling or trading a used car is this: a used car is only worth as much as somebody is willing to pay for it.

13. How often is Edmunds.com's used car pricing updated?

We update our used car pricing information on our Web site every six weeks. Our used car book comes out once a year.

14. Should I consider buying a car with a salvage title?

A salvage title means that the car has been damaged to a level that an insurance company has declared the car a "total loss." The car then is issued a salvage title to alert buyers to the car's history. However, the car may have been repaired, running well and capable of providing reliable transportation to someone. If the car has been thoroughly inspected by a mechanic, it might be a good deal for the right person. But keep in mind that when you try to resell the car, it will bring substantially less because the salvage title will scare away prospective buyers. In a nutshell, proceed with caution.

Glossary of Used Car Buying Terms

Add-ons: Extra items the dealership will try to sell you after you have made a deal on a vehicle. Examples are rust protection, extended warranties and insurance. These are high-profit sources for the dealer and are usually presented by the F&I person.

Advertising Fee: This is a fee that some dealers try to pass along to the buyer. You can try to remove this fee from the contract during negotiations. Or you can threaten to buy your car from a dealer who does not charge this fee.

Bait and Switch: Buyers are often lured into a dealership with the promise of a great deal on a specific car. This is the bait. When they ask to see that car, they are told that the car has already been sold but there is this other great car over here. The buyer has now been switched. This puts buyers at a disadvantage because they are now trying to negotiate a car they don't know much about (and it almost always costs more than the advertised car).

Certified Used Car: Certified used cars present a great option for used car shoppers. A certified car is one that has been thoroughly inspected — and where necessary, repaired — by factory-trained mechanics and is sold at a slightly higher price. The car comes with a limited time/mileage warranty and, in some cases, roadside assistance. The advantage for buyers is that they don't need to take the car to a mechanic for an inspection. They can buy the car with the knowledge that if it breaks down within the warranty period, the repairs will be covered.

Equity: Your car's equity is similar to the equity in your house. The car is worth a certain amount — and you probably owe a certain amount on it. Subtracting these figures will give you your car's equity. For example, if your car is worth $10,000 and you still owe $6,000, you have $4,000 of equity in the car. Unfortunately, it's easy to get "upside down" — the car is worth less than you owe on it — when buying a car. You might still owe $6,000 but the car could only be sold for $5,000. Even if you are upside down, keep in mind that you still have a car you can drive.

F&I Person: This stands for Finance and Insurance person. The F&I person will draw up a contract and present it to you once you have negotiated a deal with the salesperson. It is important to understand that the F&I person is really a "closer" — someone who makes sure you sign the contract. Therefore, the buyer needs to carefully read the contract to make sure it is the deal they reached with the salesman. This is also the person who will try to sell you "add-ons" at this stage of the purchase.

Market Value: This is a general term that defines how much you can get for your car if you sell it to a private party. In other words, if you advertise the car through the classifieds, or put a "For Sale" sign in the car window, the price you eventually sell the car for should theoretically be the market value. (See also "Trade-in Value.")

"No Haggle" or "No Dicker Sticker": When you shop for a TV or dishwasher, you check the price tag on the item assuming that it is not negotiable. Some dealers sell used cars the same way. This doesn't necessarily mean you are getting the best car for the fewest dollars. But it does reduce the time and trauma of haggling with aggressive salespeople over price.

Sticker Price: The sticker price of a new car (posted on the sticker displayed in the car's window) is also known as the MSRP or "Manufacturer's Suggested Retail Price." This translates to the dealer's "hoped for" price. The sticker price for new cars is set by the manufacturer and is as much as 10-percent above what the dealer bought the car for. The sticker price for a used car is set by the dealer. The buyer should, basically, ignore the sticker price. For a used car, begin your negotiations using the Edmunds.com TMV price.

Title: The title of your car is an official document that proves you own it. The title is given to you by your state's department of motor vehicles if you pay the full price for a car. If you buy a vehicle with a loan, a bank or other lending institution holds the title until the loan is paid in full. When you sell a car, you must sign the title over to the new owner.

Trade-in: When you use your old car as part of the purchase price for a new car at a dealership, it is called a "trade-in." You will never get the full market value of your car when you trade it in, because the dealer always leaves room to sell your old car at a profit (either to a private party or at a dealer auction). Despite the hassle of selling your old car on your own, you should consider doing this if you want to get maximum value for it.

Trade-in Value: This is the amount you should expect to get for your car when you use it as a trade-in toward the purchase of a new or newer car. (See also "Market Value.") This is not money in your pocket. It is the amount the dealer is willing to deduct from the purchase price of a new car.

"Turned Over" or T.O.: At some dealerships you are greeted by one salesman on the lot, then "turned over" to a more aggressive, experienced salesman who will actually negotiate the sale. You may then be "turned over" again to the F&I person. Many buyers find this process unpleasant. It is also designed to wear down your resistance and may cause you to take a deal just to get the whole thing over with. Never forget that you can simply walk away from the car lot if you are feeling unduly pressured or abused by these tactics.

Online Used Car Buying

By the Editors at Edmunds.com

Used car shopping is much faster and easier when you know how to use the tools available on the Internet. In this article we'll show you a new route to used car buying that will get you a great deal on good wheels.

In the not-so-good old days of used car shopping, you had to scrutinize columns of fine print in the newspaper classifieds looking for the car you wanted. Now, most classifieds are listed online. Autotrader.com (www.autotrader.com) provides a sophisticated, flexible search engine that allows you to quickly compile a list of cars you may want to look at.

If you are not finding the car of your dreams, you can usually find an "advanced search" feature to click on. Modify the terms of your search, and expand the distance you are searching until you build a list of cars to view. But wait! Before you schlep across town to physically inspect the car, run a Carfax report on the vehicle. A one-month Carfax subscription (www.carfax.com) is $24.99. If the Carfax is "clean" (no odometer rollbacks, serious accidents or salvage titles) then it's time to contact the seller.

Many classified ads include the e-mail address of the seller so you can ask for additional information or photographs. In most cases it's best not to negotiate on the price until you have physically inspected the car. However, you can, perhaps, probe the seller to find out how firm they are on the price.

It's a good idea to ask for comprehensive, high-quality photographs before traveling to look at a vehicle. While an in-person inspection should precede any vehicle purchase, don't underestimate the ability of photos to convey vital information about a vehicle. Look for ads that offer multiple images rather than a single exterior shot. Interior, engine and detailed exterior shots can confirm whether a car matches its description—often without you ever leaving the comfort of your home or office.

When it comes time to price the vehicle, the Internet also makes it easy to find used car prices. Edmunds.com presents True Market Value (TMV®) pricing for used cars (http://www.edmunds.com/tmv/used/index.html). Follow the prompts to select your car, and then adjust for mileage, options, color, region and several other factors. Unlike the "asking prices" presented by some other sites, TMV is a "transaction price." This takes the guesswork out of used car pricing.

Used car shoppers who want to go the dealership route will find that many car lots now post their inventory on their Web sites. Rather than walking up and down rows of cars and enduring the chatter of an eager salesman, you can now scan multiple dealerships at once looking for the car you want to buy. When you find what you are looking for, it is easy to contact the Internet manager at the dealership via e-mail.

Let's not forget about how you're going to pay for that used car. Finance rates offered by online lenders are some of the lowest out there. In most cases, online lenders will have you fill out an online application and then contact you with the interest rate you qualify for. In many cases, they will send you a blank check, with a credit limit, that can be used to pay a private party or dealer.

Remember, as you set out on your used car shopping search that there are many new ways to find and price vehicles—and new and easier ways to contact buyers. Put the Internet to work and you'll be driving a good used car in no time.

Online Used Car Buying

eBay Car Shopping

eBay.com (www.ebaymotors.com) is a great source for used cars. And often, eBay cars can be purchased at below-market rates. Still, you need to know how to make this auction service work for you. If you decide to go the online auction route, here are a few tips from the experts:

- **Narrow the search:** Choose the make, model and year of the car you a searching for. It's easier to perform frequent checks on the auction market by using an exact model in the search field.

- **Don't get an itchy finger:** Watch the auctions for a while before bidding. Search for completed items to determine final sale prices.

- **Check the seller:** Be sure to check feedback from other buyers regarding the seller. Make sure the individual is rated as a seller, not a buyer. Read the auction description carefully and request more photos by e-mail if necessary.

- **Call the seller:** It can be reassuring to develop a rapport with the seller, and sale terms may be more flexible than you think.

- **Look for no-reserve auctions:** Find a seller who doesn't set a minimum winning bid amount, which often is as high as the car's retail value.

- **Make sure you have an out:** Bid only on auctions in which sellers allow you to cancel after you inspect the car.

- **Have the car inspected by a mechanic:** Contact a mechanic in the city where the car is being sold and arrange for an inspection when you arrive. The eBay site offers inspection services in most major metro markets, as well as a free limited warranty for the drive home on many cars.

- **Use Carfax (www.carfax.com):** This company's online vehicle history reports can tell you where the car has been, verify its mileage and whether it has been damaged in a serious accident or a flood.

- **Price the car with True Market Value (TMV):** Visit our Web site at Edmunds.com and get a realistic idea of the private party value of the car.

- **Bid and walk away:** Decide on a fair price for a car, then bid and walk away. Don't get caught up in a bidding war and end up paying too much. Or better yet, subscribe to a "sniping" service that will enter you bid at that last second.

- **Factor in travel or delivery costs:** Remember you have to pick up the vehicle or have it shipped when you win the auction. Include gas, hotels, food, lost work time and plane tickets in your budgeted costs. Buy a round-trip plane ticket — it's often cheaper than a one-way ticket, and gives you flexibility if you decide you don't want the car when you see it.

- **Cash is king:** While the banking industry is getting more creative about financing online purchases, most interstate transactions are cash sales. (Or use an escrow service as described below.)

- **Pay through an escrow site:** Use an online escrow service to transfer money to the seller. This will show that you have paid for the car without releasing the money to the seller. You can then inspect the vehicle and get the title before your money is in the seller's pocket.

Used Car Buying Quiz

Buying a used car should be pretty simple. Right? Well, actually, there are some pitfalls that could be costly. So just to make sure, take our used car buying quiz and see if you are ready.

Give yourself one point for each correct answer. If you score nine or above, you can expect to get a cream puff. If your score is six to eight, memorize your mechanic's home phone number. Scores of five and below, you'll probably be getting a visit from the repo man soon.

1. The best way to judge the mechanical condition of a used car is by pressing the preset radio station buttons on the car's sound system. That way, you can avoid buying a car from a heavy metal headbanger or someone else who would abuse the car. True or false?

2. When you go to inspect a used car, the only thing you need to do is ask for the service records. That tells the whole story of a used car. True or false?

3. A used car should be taken to a mechanic for inspection before you buy it. But there is one time when this isn't necessary. That is when:

  a)   The owner seems trustworthy.
  b)   The car comes with a certified pre-owned factory warranty.
  c)   The asking price is low and you don't want to blow the deal.

4. Name two places where the used cars on a new car dealer's lot come from:

  a)   _____
  b)   _____

5. The dealer makes more on used cars than on new cars. True or false?

6. Establishing the price for a used car is total guesswork. Look at the price, roll the dice and start haggling. True or false?

7. If your credit is weak, the place that will give you the best interest rate is:

  a)   The dealer
  b)   An on-line lender
  c)   A credit union

8. The best strategy in negotiating for a used car is to:

  a)   Try to intimidate the seller by using a lot of technical terms.
  b)   Ask the seller to throw in extras to get a good deal.
  c)   Make a low starting offer and gradually increase your price.

9. Leasing applies strictly to new cars. You can't lease a used car. True or false?

10. In comparison to new cars, interest rates for used cars are almost always higher. True or false?

Answers are on the next page.

Answers:

1. False. There are much better ways to find out about the potentially checkered past of a car's past life. See the next question.

2. False. Asking for service records is important. But the best thing to do is run a vehicle history report on the car you are interested in buying. Companies such as Carfax can reveal odometer rollbacks, salvage titles and, in some cases, accidents. Running a vehicle history report on a used car is essential.

3. B. The car comes with a certified pre-owned factory warranty. A certified used car means it has been thoroughly inspected by factory-trained mechanics. If something goes wrong after you buy it the repair will, for a limited time, be covered under the warranty.

4. Trade-ins and used car auctions, which sell one-year-old rentals and cars coming off lease. See the next answer for more on this subject.

5. True. Dealerships make more money selling used cars than new cars. (And, they make as much money servicing cars and selling parts as they do on both new and used cars combined.) The reason used cars are so lucrative is that there is a higher margin of profit. If you understand why, it might help you get a good deal on a used car.

The used cars on a new car dealership's lot come from trade-ins and auctions. The idea is to buy low and sell high. They buy as low as possible meaning that they will give the lowest possible price for a car that is offered as a trade-in. If they give an $8,000 credit for a car, they might try to sell it for as much as $14,000. This means they can comfortably bargain down to $9,500 or even $9,000 and still make money on the car. So, when you see a used car on a new car dealership, assume it has been marked up — way up. Moral of the story: Know beforehand how much a used car is worth by using Edmunds.com's TMV.

6. False. Several sources list current values for used cars. Edmunds.com has prices for used cars going back to 1980. Once you've looked up the car you want to buy or sell, make sure to click the "Customized Appraisal" bar and be realistic about the condition of the car.

7. B. An on-line lender. If your credit is weak, a dealer will likely mark up the interest rate and claim they are doing you a favor by letting you buy their car. In some cases, "nonprime" borrowers can pay as much as four interest points more than they should. It's a good idea to check your credit before you go to the dealership. Some on-line lenders have become very popular with consumers because they have tried to humanize the process by not humiliating "nonprime" borrowers.

8. C. Make a low starting offer and gradually increase your price. Even though there are pricing guides, such as Edmunds.com's True Market Value, you might be able to get an even lower price. It doesn't hurt to start low (but in the ballpark) and hear them say "no" several times. When they finally do say "yes" you'll know you are getting the lowest possible price. If you are negotiating in a car dealership, however, you might need to threaten to walk out before they will know it is your "take it or leave it" price.

9. False. Leasing is just another way of financing which can be applied to used cars as well as new cars. LeaseCompare.com is a good example of an on-line lender that has streamlined the leasing process.

10. True. Higher interest rates are one of the few bad things about buying a used car. The no-interest and super-low-interest rates offered by manufacturers usually pertain to new cars. However, the amount you save in depreciation when buying a used car will more than offset the higher interest rates.

About Used Car Best Bets

Our editors are often asked what the best used car choices are, so we've decided to present the collective opinions of our editorial staff through our Edmunds.com Used Car Best Bets for 2005. In order to put together this list of our top choices in the used vehicle market, we emphasized the most important criteria that should be considered when researching and deciding on a vehicle: reliability, safety and availability. We also limited the eligible years from 1998 to 2002 for the following reasons: Older vehicles will probably have too many miles on them, and newer ones will suffer the large depreciation hit that typically makes a 2- or 3-year-old car (with low miles) the best value.

First, we looked at a number of sources that report on reliability and longevity, and applied our own experience and judgment to determine a vehicle's reliability. Second, we looked at how these vehicles rated in various crash tests conducted by the National Highway Traffic Safety Administration and the Insurance Institute for Highway Safety. And third, in most instances, we felt that the larger the spread of potential model years a buyer had to choose from the better. This is why one (more abundant) car may have beaten out another (less available one) if the two were otherwise closely matched.

Economy Car: 1998-2003 Honda Civic

For years, it's been the Civic and Toyota's Corolla fighting for the title of best economy car. Both are wise choices from a strictly utilitarian point of view; they're frugal with fuel, require minimal maintenance and are reliable. That said, the Civic gets our vote because it offers a few things that the Corolla line lacks: a sportier driving feel, a coupe body style in addition to a sedan and, in 1999, 2000 and 2002, an Si version that boasts a sizzling 160-horsepower inline four and a taut handling-biased suspension.

Midsize Car: 1998-2003 Toyota Camry

Fine build quality, legendary reliability and a hushed ride characterize the Camry. Though the arch rival Honda Accord may offer a more sporting drive, we picked the Camry based on its more serene cabin and compliant ride, qualities that are typically more appreciated in a family midsize car than apex-strafing proficiency. Furthermore, the Camry was redesigned in 1997 and this generation lasted through the 2001 model year, meaning all of these years are equally strong picks. An all-new Camry bowed for 2002, offering even more refinement and better driving dynamics.

Large Car: 1998-2003 Ford Crown Victoria/Mercury Grand Marquis

Ever wonder why police departments and taxi companies use these "old-tech" V8, rear-wheel-drive sedans? Because they're basically bullet-proof. Really, could a car have a tougher job than serving cab duty in New York City? Or cruiser duty in Los Angeles? Not only that, but these traditional American full-sizers are also very comfortable to ride in, have plenty of luggage capacity and are cheap to keep in light of their low maintenance requirements and commendable fuel efficiency (highway ratings are as high as 25 mpg). They also have very good crash test scores.

Luxury Car: 1998-2003 Lexus ES 300

As with the Camry, the Lexus ES 300 was revamped in 1997 and remained basically unchanged through 2001. Roomier than most entry-level luxury cars, silent and composed even when pushed, and boasting a level of fit and finish that holds up to the toughest scrutiny, the ES 300 doesn't ask for much more than the occasional oil change in return for thousands of miles of comfortable and stress-free motoring. An all-new ES 300 bowed for 2002, offering even more refinement and better driving dynamics.

Sporty Car: 1999-2003 Mazda Miata

Anyone who wonders how car enthusiasts can be so passionate about driving need only take a spin in a Miata. With its ultraresponsive and communicative steering, an exuberant engine and a manual transmission with short, precise throws, Mazda's little two-seater wins over even those who don't know a camshaft from a half shaft. Nothing within the average Joe's means represents affordable all-around automotive athleticism better than a Miata. Factor in great reliability, frugal fuel usage and plenty of aftermarket accessories and it's easy to see why so many Miata owners love their car as much as (maybe even more than) their significant other.

Mini-SUV: 1998-2003 Honda CR-V

It seems that everybody wants an SUV. The reasons for their overwhelming popularity include massive cargo capacity, the ability to traverse rugged and/or slippery terrain and a high seating position that affords a better view of the road ahead. Trouble is, most people who buy them will never come close to using a truck-based SUV's off-road capability, yet will have to endure the mediocre ride and handling and poor fuel mileage that accompany a "real" SUV. For those people who are more practical and less image-conscious, there is a better choice: the Honda CR-V. Combining the most practical attributes of an SUV (such as plenty of luggage capacity and all-wheel-drive traction for dealing with messy weather) with superior ride and handling characteristics, plenty of passenger room, excellent fuel economy and Honda's stout reliability history, the CR-V stands head and shoulders above most other SUVs, be they big or small. And in 2002, a roomier and more powerful CR-V debuted, cementing Honda's place in this segment.

SUV: 1999-2003 Nissan Pathfinder

With their dizzying array of driveline components, SUVs are rather complex beasts. Hence, they tend to be more maintenance-intensive than your everyday sedan. Unfortunately, that means more things that can go wrong. The Japanese SUVs have long enjoyed a big advantage over the American versions in the reliability area, and two of the best examples of this are the Toyota 4Runner and Nissan Pathfinder. We give the Pathfinder the nod because, in addition to matching the Toyota in build quality and dependability, the Pathfinder boasts a more comfortable ride and greater cargo capacity than its chief rival.

Minivan: 1999-2003 Honda Odyssey

Before 1999, the Odyssey couldn't compete with the more powerful V6-powered minivans from Dodge and Toyota. A four-cylinder engine, no matter how refined, isn't going to cut it when the van is loaded up with seven passengers and their belongings. That all changed when Honda brought out the completely revamped Odyssey in 1999. Boasting the most powerful V6 in the segment, along with a huge interior, hide-away third-row seat, top safety scores and Honda's solid reputation for quality and reliability, the Odyssey quickly jumped to the head of the class. You'll probably have to lay out a few more greenbacks for one of these vans, even in the used market, but consider it money well spent.

Small Pickup: 1998-2003 Toyota Tacoma

In addition to the well-known strengths of impressive overall quality and a rock-solid reliability record, the Tacoma offers a pickup for most any need or personality. There's even the PreRunner edition which offers the suspension, ride height and aggressive tires of a 4WD truck without the added complexity and fuel appetite. Whether you're looking for a sporty street truck, an aggressive off-roader or a crew-cab family truck, we're willing to bet that the Tacoma lineup has something with your name on it.

Large Pickup: 1998-2003 Ford F-150

There must be a very good reason that the Ford F-150 has been the top-selling vehicle in America for the last two decades. We can think of many: a huge variety of cab styles and trim levels, a comfortable interior with sound ergonomics, a compliant ride, communicative and precise steering, smooth power plants and best-in-class brakes.

Featured Vehicle Review

2004 Mazda RX-8

What Goes Around Has Come Back Around

By Karl Brauer

With more new models coming out a faster rate than ever, Mazda is well aware of the need to rise above today's growing product noise. The company has touted the virtues of driving passion for decades, and when it released the Miata MX-5 in 1990, followed by the redesigned RX-7 in 1993 (not to mention an overall win at Le Mans in 1991), it seemed the company was serious about having fun. Then came the mid-'90s and a string of not-so-fun vehicles (along with the departure of the RX-7 from American showrooms). Mazda officials now admit to losing their focus during this period. They were trying to build cars for everyone instead of remaining true to the manufacturer's core beliefs.

Zoom-zoom forward to late 2002 and what you'll find is a company in full renaissance mode. The Mazda folks tell us that the plan to reinvent their company, called the "Millennium Plan," began in 1999. The Mazda 6 was the first car to be developed under this new (actually, make that newly rediscovered) philosophy of driving passion. The non-U.S. market Demio model was the second step in the process, while the car presented here, the 2004 RX-8, is the third and, according to company officials, most important.

It would be easy to simply think of the RX-8 as the latest version of Mazda's halo car — an heir to the sports car throne left vacant since the last U.S.-spec RX-7 was sold here almost a decade ago. While the RX-8 will be all of those things, its redesigned rotary engine, reverse-opening rear doors and room for four adults make it far more.

Pulling the RX-8 out of today's ever burbling product blitz starts under the car's sloping hood where an all-new rotary engine resides. Mazda remains the one and only automaker willing to invest the resources necessary to develop and sell a rotary engine in a production car. You might remember that it was increasingly stringent emissions standards (along with poor sales) that killed Mazda's last rotary engine in the U.S. This new power plant, dubbed the Renesis (for rotary engine and genesis), addresses not only emission requirements but also power, efficiency and weight concerns — all key sports car elements.

The most important Renesis change relates to the location of the intake and exhaust ports. Because a rotary engine has no valve train, the location of these ports is crucial to the engine's performance. In the previous engine, these ports were located on the outer edge of the rotary housing, but in Renesis they are on the side of the rotary chamber. Unlike the previous design, this location allows engineers to completely close the exhaust port before the intake port opens, and vice versa. It also allows them to use 30-percent larger intake ports than before, along with a variable intake system that optimizes air flow.

What this design means to the consumer is better fuel efficiency and increased performance. Mazda estimates the RX-8 will get 20-percent better mileage in the city than the RX-7 did. Exact figures are yet to be determined, but current estimates put the engine at 18-19 mpg in the city and 23-24 mpg on the highway. The new design also means far less emissions (the previous rotary's major bugaboo) because the Renesis allows unburned hydrocarbons to be sent back into the engine and ignited again. Despite the reduction in exhaust gasses and increase in fuel mileage, the new engine produces 238 peak horsepower and 160 peak pound-feet of torque while offering a redline of 9,000 rpm. Those figures are for the "high-power" rotary that is mated to a six-speed manual transmission, but a 200-horsepower version of the Renesis, mated to a five-speed automatic, is also offered.

These numbers may seem disappointing at first (the old twin-turbo RX-7's rotary made 255 peak horsepower and 217 pound-feet of twist while offering an 8,000 rpm redline), but keep in mind that the new engine is not turbocharged...at least not yet. Questions about the possibility of one day turbocharging the Renesis were given casual dismissal by Mazda representatives, but it's obvious any company capable of making a rotary work in the 21st century could certainly make it work with forced induction.

In the meantime, the lack of a turbo, and all its associated plumbing, gives the Renesis an 80-pound weight advantage over the previous RX-7's engine. That weight advantage, combined with this rotary's smaller size (approximately two-thirds the size of a comparable inline four-cylinder) also allows the engine to be mounted further back and lower than it was in the turbo-topped RX-7. The result is a 50/50-weight balance between each set of wheels, a low center of gravity and a low hoodline that contributes to the car's sporty style and 0.3 coefficient of drag.

Cradling this high-tech drivetrain is an all-new chassis and suspension that uses a double-wishbone system up front and a multilink design for the rear wheels. Mazda's goal was to provide the handling characteristics of the RX-7 with the fine ride quality and road noise isolation of a premium sedan. The company also wanted to meet current and future safety standards. High-strength crossmembers are strategically located in the engine compartment and along the frame's primary backbone to add chassis stiffness, enhance suspension tuning and improve crash protection. Items like seat-mounted side airbags, head curtain airbags and crushable pedals contribute to passenger protection, as do "built-in" B-pillars within the reverse-opening rear doors. Much like traditional B-pillars, these beams dissipate side-impact crash energy and contribute to body rigidity.

It's these reverse-opening rear doors that differentiate the RX-8 from other sports cars (as much or more than the rotary engine under its hood). The idea of a "four-door sports car" has been bandied about for decades, but Mazda's efforts set a new benchmark in this area. The key is the near seamless integration of these rear doors into an otherwise lithe and lean vehicle. With the exception of its slightly elongated wheelbase and subtly truncated rear window angle, there is little indication that the RX-8 is anything other than a dedicated supercar. Casual observers will likely notice neither characteristic and simply wonder how fast this sleek, low-slung machine is.

When said observers learn that the RX-8 will hold four full-size adults comfortably, they will further appreciate the car's exterior shape. Similar to the design of Saturn's new Ion coupe, or any noncrew-cab four-door truck, the RX-8's rear doors open only after the front doors are released, and they must be closed before the fronts are shut. Amazingly, a full-size adult can be situated in the front driver or passenger seat while another full-size adult hops in back (no front-seat sliding required). That same full-size adult will fit comfortably in either of the rear seats, which are just as heavily bolstered and supportive as the front chairs. That's not to say that the interior feels large or roomy. The RX-8's designers told us they wanted the cabin to fit four comfortably while still having a "cozy" feel. Put four adults in the RX-8 and the word cozy will certainly apply.

From the driver seat, the RX-8 offers an attractive combination of design cues and logical control placement. The seats are low and heavily bolstered with optional contrasting inserts that match the exterior color (this same contrasting color is also found on the steering wheel rim). The gauge cluster uses three pods, with the larger central pod housing a tachometer and a digital speedometer. Fuel level and engine temperature information are housed in the left pod while oil pressure and the odometer/tripmeter are on the right. We liked the optitronic gauge cluster lighting that changes from white to red when the headlights are switched on, but we were disappointed that an analog speedometer was nowhere to be found. We also liked the circular theme that makes up the center stack controls, but we still aren't sold on having the radio display at the top of the center stack, which is a considerable distance from the audio controls (similar to the Mazda 6's setup). However, should you ever forget what type of engine powers the RX-8, you need only glance at the six-speed shift knob or upper seat back design to be reminded that a rotary motor sits under the hood.

Another way to confirm what the RX-8 is all about involves flogging it on a closed course. Mazda let us do just that at the company's Miyoshi Proving Grounds in Japan. Miyoshi comes fully equipped with a long straightaway, sweeping corners and fast transitions. Several of the facility's curves include midcorner bumps that test even the most advanced suspension's ability to sort things out.

After almost a dozen laps around Miyoshi, it was clear that Mazda has again mastered the art of driving passion. The RX-8 features powerful and progressive braking, sublime steering and accurate shift action. It tends to understeer slightly when driven at the limit, but it's nothing a bit of throttle can't fix. We should also note that the steering uses an electric assist system, an increasingly popular design found on such cars as the Honda S2000, BMW Z4 and the Mini Cooper.

2004 Mazda RX-8

The engine will spin to 9,000-rpm faster than you can say "rev limiter" and feels more willing at high rpm than even Honda's S2000 because of the rotary's phenomenal smoothness. Midrange torque is fully adequate and a second burst of power comes on at about 7,000 rpm, giving the RX-8 a larger "sweet zone" than that offered by Honda's roadster or the Toyota Celica GT-S.

But perhaps the Mazda's most impressive characteristic was how stable it felt during fast sweepers and through quick transitions, even when the pavement was of "Detroit quality." Driving the RX-8 at its limit took several laps simply because that limit was quite high and, when it was finally surpassed, the car proved very predictable and easy to reel back in.

It's these characteristics that distinguish the RX-8 from the mass of product available in showrooms these days. The car appeals to a wide array of customers, including both sports car fans and family folks looking for something different.

If you fit into either (or both) of these segments, you'll want to give this Mazda a spin.

Ford's F-150 Makeover

By Brian Moody

Ford has been building trucks for more than 85 years, but the nature of those trucks and of those who buy them has changed dramatically in just the past 10 years. As new car buyers gradually turn into new truck buyers, the battle to build the best and most popular full-size pickup has cranked up considerably. Dodge upped the ante in the mid-1990s and again in 2002 with the bold-looking Ram, and GM has been continually improving its Silverado and Sierra. By comparison, the previous F-150 looked boring and lacked the grunt of the V8-powered GM trucks. So Ford has answered the call with an all-new truck, and in this market there is little room for error.

Right away the surface improvements are obvious. Ford recently pledged to spend more money on its interiors and this new truck pays dividends on that promise. Sporting a more contemporary look and a cleaner design, the exterior now shares styling cues with the recently restyled Expedition.

Our XLT tester looked a little bland inside, but the uncluttered design and simple, easy-to-use controls are a noticeable upgrade from the previous pickup. But it's not just the look that's improved; the quality of the interior materials is vastly improved as well. Knobs and switches lack the cheap feel they previously had and the plastics used on the steering wheel, door panels and the center stack of the dash all have an attractive texture.

This test vehicle on these pages came with cloth seats in a durable woven material and a handy center armrest/storage box that proved very useful. The storage container is large and deep enough to hold items such as a wallet, a cell phone, CDs and other miscellaneous stuff. The seats are wide and accommodating and feel rather firm at first, but on a long trip, they proved to be supportive and soft enough to elicit no complaints from three editors who all took turns driving and riding. We're not sure we'd want to spend a long stint in the backseat of the SuperCab, but it is reasonable for an adult to ride back there for short trips. Of course, if you need more people space than cargo capacity the SuperCrew is probably what you want.

Like other extended cabs, the SuperCab offers a compromise between a four-door family truck and a standard cab work truck. To make the rear area more user-friendly, the seats can fold out of the way in a 60/40-split to allow for multiple configurations. As on most "extra cab" trucks, the F-150's reverse-hinged rear doors only open to 90 degrees, or about halfway. When parked in a lot with cars on both sides, having the front and rear doors open creates an area that sort of traps you. If you have a shopping cart full of stuff, you'll have to continue to open and close one of the doors to gain access to the cargo you want to load into the truck. Nissan's Titan solves this problem by allowing the rear doors to open 180 degrees or all the way until they're flush with the bed. We expect to see more trucks incorporate this feature in the near future, but for now Nissan has the only implementation of the fully opening clamshell rear doors, and not having that feature makes the Ford a little more cumbersome in some cases.

2004 Ford F-150

Sure, interior features and exterior styling are fine, but real truck buyers want a vehicle that performs. Making an impressive 300 horsepower, the new 5.4-liter Triton motor is much improved in terms of refinement and power over the previous version. The extra power is noticeable, but it still feels somewhat lacking compared to GM's Vortec engines — even though the Ford motor does make more horsepower. It's not that the F-150 feels underpowered or slow, it's just that the Silverado with a 5.3-liter V8 feels so much more energetic. Off the line, the F-150 feels fine, but as the rpm climb, the engine seems to get short of breath. Remember, this is the bigger 5.4-liter Triton engine we're talking about — if you were thinking of purchasing an F-150 with the smaller 4.6-liter unit, we suggest you stay with the bigger motor.

But power is just one factor; weight is also a key factor when discussing performance. At more than 5,400 pounds, the F-150 weighs between 500 and 800 pounds more than it did last year. By comparison, the Silverado is about 400 pounds lighter depending on options, and that alone could account for the peppier performance. On paper, the new F-150 outclasses the competition by offering more power and more towing capacity than the competition, but in real-world situations the power feels merely adequate.

Still, in terms of ride and handling the new F-150 is a vast improvement. On the road, the F-150 remains composed and quiet — dare we say, almost sedanlike. Even at speeds of 70 or 80 mph, the truck is a pleasant place to spend time. There is some wind noise from the outside mirrors, but overall road noise is well controlled.

Handling is also improved. The suspension feels tighter, and the truck has a solid feel that was lacking in previous F-150s. As it is a truck, the Ford does exhibit some body roll when cornering, but the handling is very predictable. More forgiving than the Dodge Ram, but not quite as plush as the Silverado, the F-150's ride is fine most of the time.

With regard to safety, we see the F-150 as a mixed bag. It has been designed with collapsible front frame rails, a front passenger-sensing system and has earned five stars for both front-seat occupant protection in side impacts, but the lack of available side airbags seems odd. Not to beat a dead horse, but both the new Nissan Titan and the Dodge Ram offer side-impact airbags. It's not as if Ford didn't give safety any consideration, it's just that the new truck is lacking the one feature that has become quite common in new vehicles, and it seems more important now that many families are buying vehicles like the F-150 as family haulers.

Ultimately, a truck is for hauling stuff, or at least a combination of stuff and people. We found the F-150 to be just as capable as any other truck in terms of what you can fit in the bed. A trip to the city dump showed that Ford's claim of a bed that's 2 inches deeper was not just PR hype. Some pickups seem to have a long shallow bed; not so with this new Ford truck. We're not sure if the extra depth is due to higher side rails or a lower bed floor thanks to reworked suspension. Either way, there is plenty of usable space and we made great use of it by piling various amounts of bricks, old galvanized pipes and rotting fence posts in the back. Accessing that bed is made much easier by the lightweight tailgate. It doesn't sound like much, but having a tailgate that can easily be opened or closed with just one hand is a huge help.

Ford's new truck has much to offer anyone considering the purchase of a full-size pickup. There are plenty of thoughtful touches like the light-weight tailgate, the much improved interior and the more masculine exterior styling. The engine is more refined and more powerful but there's still room for improvement — bottom line is we feel it could use a little more grunt.

While it's not perfect, the F-150 is now a much more serious contender in the full-size pickup segment. With the recent introduction of the Hemi-powered Ram, the all-new Nissan Titan and Ford's complete reworking of the stalwart F-150, the competition is really heating up. As the sales leader in this segment for many years we know the new F-150 will continue to win friends and influence truck buyers.

4A	4 speed automatic	GVWR	gross vehicle weight rating	PRNDL	Park, Reverse, Neutral, Drive, Low
5A	5 speed automatic	GPS	global positioning satellite	RBL	raised black-letter (tire)
6A	6 speed automatic	Hbk.	hatchback	Reg.	regular
2dr	2 door	HD	heavy duty	RH	right hand
4dr	4 door	Hp	horsepower	r/l	right and left
5M	5 speed manual	HUD	heads-up display	rpm	revolutions per minute
6M	6 speed manual	HVAC	heating, ventilation and air	RWD	rear-wheel drive
8V	8-valve		conditioning	SAE	Society of Automotive Engineers
12V	12-valve	I-4	inline four	SB	shortbed
16V	16-valve	I-5	inline five	SBR	steel-belted radial (tire)
24V	24-valve	I-6	inline six	Sdn	sedan
2WD	two-wheel drive	ISRV	inside rearview mirror	SFI	sequential fuel injection
4WD	four-wheel drive	KW	kilowatt	SLA	short/long arm
ABS	antilock braking system	L	liter	SMPI	sequential multi-port injection
A/C	air conditioning	LB	longbed	SOHC	single overhead cam
ALR	automatic locking retractor	lb(s).	pound(s)	SPI	sequential port injection
	(seatbelt)	lb-ft.	pound-feet	SRW	single rear wheels
Amp	ampere		(measurement of torque)	Std.	standard
A/S	all-season (tire)	LCD	liquid crystal display	SULEV	super ultra low emission vehicle
ASR	automatic slip regulation	LED	light emitting diode	SUV	sport utility vehicle
AT	automatic	LEV	low emission vehicle	SWB	short wheelbase
Auto	automatic	LH	left hand	TDI	turbocharged direct injection
AWD	all-wheel drive	LWB	long wheelbase	TMV®	Edmunds.com's True Market
BSW	black sidewall (tire)	mm	millimeter		Value®
Cass.	cassette	mpg	miles per gallon	TOD	torque on demand
CC	cubic centimeter	mph	miles per hour	ULEV	ultra low emission vehicle
CD	compact disc	MPI	multi-port injection	V6	V-type six
CFC	chloroflourocarbon	MSRP	manufacturer's suggested retail	V8	V-type eight
Conv.	convertible		price	V10	V-type ten
Cpe	coupe	N/A	not available OR not applicable	V12	V-type twelve
Cu. Ft.	cubic foot (feet)	NC	no charge	VR	v-rated
Cyl.	cylinder	NHTSA	National Highway and Traffic	VSC	vehicle skid control
DOHC	dual overhead cam		Safety Administration	VTEC	variable valve timing and
DRL	daytime running light(s)	NLEV	National Low Emission Vehicle		lift electronic control
DRW	dual rear wheels	Nm	Newton meters	VVT-i	variable valve timing, intelligence
DSC	dynamic stability control		(measurement of torque)	Wgn.	wagon
DVD	digital video disc	NVH	noise, vibration and harshness	WOL	white outline-letter (tire)
EDL	electronic differential lock	OD	overdrive	WS	work series (truck)
EFI	electronic fuel injection	OHC	overhead cam	WSW	white sidewall (tire)
EPA	Environmental Protection Agency	OHV	overhead valve	W/T	work truck
ETR	electronically-tuned radio	Opt.	option OR optional	X-Cab	extended cab
Ext.	extended	OSRV	outside rearview mirror		
FWD	front-wheel drive	OWL	outline white-letter (tire)		
Gal.	gallon(s)	Pass.	passenger		
GAWR	gross axle weight rating	PIO	Port Installed Option		
GVW	gross vehicle weight	Pkg.	package		

CL

2003

Mileage Category: H

Body Styles	TMV Pricing			Body Styles	TMV Pricing		
	Trade	Private	Dealer		Trade	Private	Dealer
2 Dr 3.2 Cpe	15765	16739	18362	2 Dr 3.2 Type-S Cpe	17559	18644	20452

Options	Price
Navigation System	+1651

Acura has made a number of changes on its already highly competent luxury sport coupe. The biggest news is the availability of a six-speed manual transmission on the Type-S trim. If that doesn't interest you, there's certainly more. On the outside, the CL gains new wheels, updated headlights and taillights, a revised grille and new exhaust tips. Inside, Acura has added LATCH child safety seat attachments, a dual-stage and dual-threshold driver's front airbag and an auto-up driver's window. Cars with the optional navigation system also gain OnStar, the vehicle communications service.

2002

Mileage Category: H

Body Styles	TMV Pricing			Body Styles	TMV Pricing		
	Trade	Private	Dealer		Trade	Private	Dealer
2 Dr 3.2 Cpe	13837	14856	16555	2 Dr 3.2 Type-S Cpe	15331	16460	18342

Options	Price
Navigation System	+1375

Updated last year, the Acura CL is unchanged for 2002.

2001

Mileage Category: H

Body Styles	TMV Pricing			Body Styles	TMV Pricing		
	Trade	Private	Dealer		Trade	Private	Dealer
2 Dr 3.2 Cpe	12310	13727	15035	2 Dr 3.2 Type-S Cpe	13330	14866	16283

Options	Price
Navigation System	+1176

New from the ground up, the CL receives upgraded 3.2-liter V6 engines making up to 260 horsepower (in Type-S form), a five-speed automatic transmission with sequential SportShift and a full load of standard equipment for a bargain-basement price. A new sport-tuned Type-S is worth the extra money if you value performance over ride comfort.

1999

Mileage Category: H

Body Styles	TMV Pricing			Body Styles	TMV Pricing		
	Trade	Private	Dealer		Trade	Private	Dealer
2 Dr 2.3 Cpe	6797	7982	9216	2 Dr 3.0 Cpe	7665	9001	10391

Options	Price	Options	Price
Automatic 4-Speed Transmission [Std on 3.0]	+326	Rear Spoiler	+183

The previously optional Premium package, consisting of leather seats, is now standard.

1998

A new 2.3L engine replaces last year's 2.2L unit. All CL models get a revised grille and new alloy wheels.

Body Styles	TMV Pricing			Body Styles	TMV Pricing		
	Trade	Private	Dealer		Trade	Private	Dealer
2 Dr 2.3 Cpe	5232	6235	7366	2 Dr 3.0 Cpe	6130	7304	8628
2 Dr 2.3 Premium Cpe	5591	6662	7869	2 Dr 3.0 Premium Cpe	6282	7486	8843

Options	Price	Options	Price
Automatic 4-Speed Transmission [Opt on 2.3, 2.3 Premium]	+279	Rear Spoiler	+157

1997

Mileage Category: H

Body Styles	TMV Pricing			Body Styles	TMV Pricing		
	Trade	Private	Dealer		Trade	Private	Dealer
2 Dr 2.2 Cpe	4363	5303	6452	2 Dr 3.0 Cpe	5124	6154	7413
2 Dr 2.2 Premium Cpe	4640	5573	6713	2 Dr 3.0 Premium Cpe	5388	6470	7792

Options	Price	Options	Price
Automatic 4-Speed Transmission [Opt on 2.2]	+243	Rear Spoiler	+137

Like many Acura products, the CL is based on a Honda platform, in this case the Honda Accord. The CL's sights are aimed squarely at BMW's 3 Series coupes.

Integra

2001

Mileage Category: E

Body Styles	TMV Pricing			Body Styles	TMV Pricing		
	Trade	Private	Dealer		Trade	Private	Dealer
2 Dr GS Hbk	8521	9686	10761	4 Dr GS Sdn	8746	9941	11044
2 Dr GS-R Hbk	9388	10671	11855	4 Dr GS-R Sdn	9930	11287	12540
2 Dr LS Hbk	7983	9073	10080	4 Dr LS Sdn	8181	9299	10331
2 Dr Type R Hbk	11451	13016	14461				

Options	Price
Automatic 4-Speed Transmission	+470

Carpeted floor mats are newly standard, and an emergency trunk release is added to the inside of the sedan's cargo area. Four new colors round out the changes for 2001, Integra's final year before an all-new model debuts for 2002.

2000

The Type-R is back, and it arrives with two more color choices. The four-speed automatic transmission has been enhanced for better shift quality, and all Integras now have a tune-up interval of 100,000 miles.

Mileage Category: E

Body Styles	TMV Pricing			Body Styles	TMV Pricing		
	Trade	Private	Dealer		Trade	Private	Dealer
2 Dr GS Hbk	7605	8741	9855	4 Dr GS Sdn	7873	9050	10203
2 Dr GS-R Hbk	8538	9814	11064	4 Dr GS-R Sdn	8654	9947	11214
2 Dr LS Hbk	7236	8317	9377	4 Dr LS Sdn	7381	8483	9563
2 Dr Type R Hbk	10020	11517	12985				

Options	Price
Automatic 4-Speed Transmission	+410

1999

In a small step upmarket, Acura has decided to kill the Integra's entry-level RS trim. The LS gets leather accents and 15-inch wheels, and the sporty GS-R now comes with leather seats. Type-R will return in limited numbers later in the year.

Mileage Category: E

Body Styles	TMV Pricing			Body Styles	TMV Pricing		
	Trade	Private	Dealer		Trade	Private	Dealer
2 Dr GS Hbk	6502	7659	8864	4 Dr GS Sdn	6804	8015	9276
2 Dr GS-R Hbk	7408	8727	10100	4 Dr GS-R Sdn	7495	8829	10217
2 Dr LS Hbk	6112	7200	8333	4 Dr LS Sdn	6186	7287	8433

Options	Price	Options	Price
Alarm System	+137	Compact Disc Changer	+203
Automatic 4-Speed Transmission	+326		

1998

A revised front end, designed for a more aerodynamic approach, is added this year. LS, GS and GS-R models get a little more comfortable with a tilt- and height-adjustable driver seat and new alloy wheels appear on the LS and GS-R. The performance-edition Type-R is available again this year.

Mileage Category: E

Body Styles	TMV Pricing			Body Styles	TMV Pricing		
	Trade	Private	Dealer		Trade	Private	Dealer
2 Dr GS Hbk	5334	6450	7709	2 Dr Type R Hbk	7316	8847	10574
2 Dr GS-R Hbk	6235	7540	9012	4 Dr GS Sdn	5805	7020	8391
2 Dr LS Hbk	5092	6158	7360	4 Dr GS-R Sdn	6119	7400	8844
2 Dr RS Hbk	4661	5637	6738	4 Dr LS Sdn	5302	6412	7663

Options	Price	Options	Price
Air Conditioning [Opt on RS, Type R]	+253	Automatic 4-Speed Transmission	+279
Alarm System	+117	Leather Seats [Std on GS]	+227

1997

Apart from the debut of the racy Type-R, no major changes.

Mileage Category: E

Body Styles	TMV Pricing			Body Styles	TMV Pricing		
	Trade	Private	Dealer		Trade	Private	Dealer
2 Dr GS Hbk	4726	5868	7263	2 Dr Type R Hbk	5722	7124	8837
2 Dr GS-R Hbk	5000	6206	7681	4 Dr GS Sdn	4871	6047	7485
2 Dr LS Hbk	4333	5380	6660	4 Dr GS-R Sdn	5107	6340	7847
2 Dr RS Hbk	4002	4968	6149	4 Dr LS Sdn	4469	5548	6867

Options	Price	Options	Price
AM/FM/Cassette/CD Audio System	+115	Automatic 4-Speed Transmission	+243
Air Conditioning [Opt on RS, Type R]	+221	Leather Seats [Std on GS]	+198

1996

All Integras get new wheel cover and alloy wheel designs this year, as well as green-tinted glass. LS models receive body-colored moldings. Three new colors can be applied to the 1996 Integra: pearls in red, green or black.

Mileage Category: E

Body Styles	TMV Pricing		
	Trade	Private	Dealer
2 Dr GS-R Hbk	4187	5286	6803
2 Dr LS Hbk	3674	4638	5970
2 Dr RS Hbk	3213	4056	5221
2 Dr Special Edition Hbk	4087	5161	6644

Options	Price
Air Conditioning [Opt on RS]	+202
Automatic 4-Speed Transmission	+224

Body Styles	TMV Pricing		
	Trade	Private	Dealer
4 Dr GS-R Sdn	4244	5358	6896
4 Dr LS Sdn	3856	4869	6267
4 Dr RS Sdn	3360	4242	5461
4 Dr Special Edition Sdn	4195	5297	6818

Options	Price
Compact Disc Changer	+140
Leather Seats [Opt on GS-R]	+182

1995

A Special Edition model debuts, sporting leather interior, spoiler and larger tires. All LS models receive a sunroof.

Mileage Category: E

Body Styles	TMV Pricing		
	Trade	Private	Dealer
2 Dr GS-R Hbk	3450	4395	5969
2 Dr LS Hbk	3082	3926	5333
2 Dr RS Hbk	2637	3360	4564
2 Dr Special Edition Hbk	3375	4299	5839

Options	Price
AM/FM/CD Audio System	+78
AM/FM/Cassette/CD Audio System	+91
Air Conditioning [Opt on RS]	+174

Body Styles	TMV Pricing		
	Trade	Private	Dealer
4 Dr GS-R Sdn	3503	4463	6063
4 Dr LS Sdn	3214	4095	5562
4 Dr RS Sdn	2763	3520	4781
4 Dr Special Edition Sdn	3464	4413	5995

Options	Price
Automatic 4-Speed Transmission	+192
Leather Seats [Opt on GS-R]	+156

Legend
1995

Mileage Category: H

Body Styles	TMV Pricing		
	Trade	Private	Dealer
2 Dr L Cpe	4803	5858	7617
2 Dr LS Cpe	5675	6922	8999
4 Dr GS Sdn	5611	6756	8665

Options	Price
Automatic 4-Speed Transmission [Opt on GS,L,LS Cpe]	+192
Compact Disc Changer [Opt on L]	+144

Body Styles	TMV Pricing		
	Trade	Private	Dealer
4 Dr L Sdn	4348	5303	6894
4 Dr LS Sdn	5168	6303	8195
4 Dr SE Sdn	5138	6267	8148

Options	Price
Leather Seats [Opt on L Sdn]	+205

Last year for the Acura flagship, the 1996 replacement will bear Acura's new alphanumeric nomenclature. No changes for this year's model.

MDX
2004

Mileage Category: O

Body Styles	TMV Pricing		
	Trade	Private	Dealer
4 Dr STD AWD SUV	28505	29958	32380

Options	Price
DVD Entertainment System [Opt on Touring]	+1500

Body Styles	TMV Pricing		
	Trade	Private	Dealer
4 Dr Touring AWD SUV	30553	32007	34432

Options	Price
Navigation System [Opt on Touring]	+2200

A number of interior, exterior and mechanical updates were made for 2004. The V6 engine added slightly more power and is now rated at 265 horsepower and 253 pound-feet of torque. Outside, you'll find a restyled front fascia, new chrome trim, dual exhaust tips, a new wheel design for Touring models, updated headlights and taillights and a rear wing spoiler. The interior now features trendy brushed metal-look trim for the center stack, leather armrests, auto-on/off headlights, new ambient foot lighting and enhanced functionality of the second-row seat for third-row access. Touring models get a new version of the Bose premium audio system and power lumbar support for the driver seat. Finally, safety has been improved on all MDXs with the addition of side curtain airbags and a tire-pressure monitoring system.

2003

Further honing its already quite capable MDX, Acura has made a number of key improvements for 2003. First up is a 20-horsepower boost, giving the MDX a total of 260. To support the increased power, there's a revised five-speed automatic transmission, a new stability control system, a strengthened chassis, a retuned suspension and stronger brakes. Inside, the optional navigation system has gained voice recognition capability, enhanced graphics and expanded database coverage. There's also a tailgate-mounted rearview camera this year that transmits its view to the display screen when the vehicle is put in reverse. Lastly, Acura will be offering an optional DVD-based entertainment system as a factory option.

Mileage Category: O

Body Styles	TMV Pricing			Body Styles	TMV Pricing		
	Trade	Private	Dealer		Trade	Private	Dealer
4 Dr STD 4WD SUV	25742	27185	29589	4 Dr Touring 4WD SUV	27393	28928	31486

Options	Price	Options	Price
DVD Entertainment System [Opt on Touring]	+1152	Navigation System [Opt on Touring]	+1689

2002

Introduced last year, Acura's capable SUV receives only minor changes for 2002. There are four new exterior colors, and enhancements have been made to reduce noise, vibration and harshness (NVH) for a quieter, more comfortable ride.

Mileage Category: O

Body Styles	TMV Pricing			Body Styles	TMV Pricing		
	Trade	Private	Dealer		Trade	Private	Dealer
4 Dr STD 4WD SUV	22079	23363	25504	4 Dr Touring 4WD SUV	22897	24229	26450

Options	Price
Navigation System	+1375

2001

Acura brings a new sport-utility vehicle to the marketplace, combining great on-road performance, class-leading fuel economy and outstanding all-weather handling with seven-passenger seating and cavernous cargo capacity.

Mileage Category: O

Body Styles	TMV Pricing			Body Styles	TMV Pricing		
	Trade	Private	Dealer		Trade	Private	Dealer
4 Dr STD 4WD SUV	17972	19694	21284	4 Dr Touring 4WD SUV	18933	20748	22423

Options	Price
Navigation System	+1176

NSX

2004

Mileage Category: R

Body Styles	TMV Pricing		
	Trade	Private	Dealer
2 Dr STD Cpe	71548	74338	78988

Acura's top sports car gains a trunk-mounted CD changer, keyless entry, a restyled transmission shifter knob and new gauge cluster surround trim.

2003

There are no changes in store for Acura's supercar.

Mileage Category: R

Body Styles	TMV Pricing		
	Trade	Private	Dealer
2 Dr STD Cpe	66429	68963	73187

2002

For the first time since the car's introduction in 1991, Acura's midengined supercar receives a variety of styling enhancements. These include new fixed HID headlights, freshened front and rear bumpers and updated exhaust tips. Inside, six new color schemes are available. These schemes can be matched to the car's exterior color for a customized look. The center panel has also been updated with new chrome plating. Mechanically, the NSX remains unchanged, though the suspension has been retuned and larger wheels have been fitted.

Mileage Category: R

Body Styles	TMV Pricing		
	Trade	Private	Dealer
2 Dr STD Cpe	60469	62940	67059

2001

Mileage Category: R

Body Styles	TMV Pricing			Body Styles	TMV Pricing		
	Trade	Private	Dealer		Trade	Private	Dealer
2 Dr STD Cpe	53389	56988	60311	2 Dr T Cpe	55906	59675	63155

Acura's decade-old, aluminum-bodied, midengined supercar carries over for 2001 with no major changes.

2000

Mileage Category: R

Body Styles	TMV Pricing			Body Styles	TMV Pricing		
	Trade	Private	Dealer		Trade	Private	Dealer
2 Dr STD Cpe	46218	49823	53356	2 Dr T Cpe	49610	53480	57273

For 2000 the NSX gets improvements to its six-speed manual transmission, an upgraded perforated leather interior, and a cleaner engine that now qualifies it as a low emission vehicle.

1999

Mileage Category: R

Body Styles	TMV Pricing			Body Styles	TMV Pricing		
	Trade	Private	Dealer		Trade	Private	Dealer
2 Dr STD Cpe	40041	43723	47556	2 Dr T Cpe	43890	47927	52129

An Alex Zanardi Edition of the NSX is new this year, but only 50 will be made for sale in North America. The special-edition car features a fixed roof, lighter rear spoiler and manual steering in its quest to shed nearly 150 pounds. The Zanardi Edition adds BBS alloy wheels, a titanium shifter and softer red-stitched leather seats. And it wouldn't be a tribute to the CART champion without a stiffer suspension and lower height.

1998

Mileage Category: R

Body Styles	TMV Pricing			Body Styles	TMV Pricing		
	Trade	Private	Dealer		Trade	Private	Dealer
2 Dr STD Cpe	36970	40726	44961	2 Dr T Cpe	39091	43062	47540

No changes for 1998.

1997

Mileage Category: R

Body Styles	TMV Pricing			Body Styles	TMV Pricing		
	Trade	Private	Dealer		Trade	Private	Dealer
2 Dr STD Cpe	33059	36623	40978	2 Dr T Cpe	35033	38809	43424

The six-speed NSX comes to us this year with a larger 3.2-liter V6 engine that makes 290 ponies. Automatic NSXs continue with the 3.0-liter, 252-horse V6.

1996

Mileage Category: R

Body Styles	TMV Pricing			Body Styles	TMV Pricing		
	Trade	Private	Dealer		Trade	Private	Dealer
2 Dr STD Cpe	28806	31954	36302	2 Dr T Cpe	30988	34375	39053

Options	Price
Automatic 4-Speed Transmission	+856

The hardtop NSX is reintroduced to the Acura lineup.

1995

Mileage Category: R

Body Styles	TMV Pricing		
	Trade	Private	Dealer
2 Dr T Cpe	26629	29418	34067

Options	Price	Options	Price
AM/FM/Cassette/CD Audio System	+107	Automatic 4-Speed Transmission	+701

Acura offers an open-top version of the NSX, called the NSX-T. The "T" stands for targa (removable) top. Other than the pop-top, the NSX-T is identical to the standard NSX.

RL

2004

Mileage Category: I

Body Styles	TMV Pricing		
	Trade	Private	Dealer
4 Dr 3.5 Sdn	28876	30313	32708

The RL receives only minor changes for the 2004 model year. The dash has been slightly revised to accommodate a newly available XM radio. To accompany the digital-quality sound from XM radio, there's a new Bose audio system with two additional speakers and an in-dash six-disc CD changer. The previously optional navigation system is now standard on the RL, as is driver-side power lumbar adjustment.

2003

For 2003, Acura's RL receives only a few changes, including a new taillight design, restyled wheels and different interior trim colors.

Mileage Category: I

Body Styles	TMV Pricing		
	Trade	Private	Dealer
4 Dr 3.5 Sdn	23263	24473	26489

Options	Price
Navigation System	+1536

2002

The 3.5-liter RL now makes a generous 225 horsepower (up 15 from last year), and 231 pound-feet of torque, but a V8 engine still isn't available. The luxury sedan's double-wishbone suspension has been tuned for sportier handling characteristics this year, and wider, low-profile Michelins shoe the redesigned 16-inch alloy wheels. Noise and vibration should be quelled better by additional insulation material under the hood and dashboard, and the OnStar communications system makes its debut. Outside, the 2002 RL is freshened by new body-colored lower side sills, splash guards and roof strips.

Mileage Category: I

Body Styles	TMV Pricing		
	Trade	Private	Dealer
4 Dr 3.5 Sdn	16546	17635	19451

Options	Price
Navigation System	+1375

2001

Floor mats become standard, leaving the DVD-based navigation system alone on the factory options list. Also new is an emergency trunk release located on the inside of the cargo area.

Mileage Category: I

Body Styles	TMV Pricing		
	Trade	Private	Dealer
4 Dr 3.5 Sdn	14544	15997	17339

Options	Price
Navigation System	+1176

2000

A new Vehicle Stability Assist system keeps the RL pointed straight, a new navigation system offers a larger screen and more information, and the 3.5-liter V6 now meets low-emission vehicle standards.

Mileage Category: I

Body Styles	TMV Pricing		
	Trade	Private	Dealer
4 Dr 3.5 Sdn	12210	13743	15246

Options	Price	Options	Price
AM/FM/Cassette/CD Audio System	+192	Navigation System	+1025

1999

The suspension has been revised for better handling and a firmer ride, brake rotors have added mass, side airbags are standard, styling is more aggressive, and the Premium features have been incorporated into one trim level.

Mileage Category: I

Body Styles	TMV Pricing		
	Trade	Private	Dealer
4 Dr 3.5 Sdn	10388	11715	13097

Options	Price	Options	Price
AM/FM/Cassette/CD Audio System	+153	Navigation System	+650

1998

Slight suspension enhancements provide sportier handling without sacrificing ride.

Mileage Category: I

Body Styles	TMV Pricing			Body Styles	TMV Pricing		
	Trade	Private	Dealer		Trade	Private	Dealer
4 Dr 3.5 Premium Sdn	10715	12237	13954	4 Dr 3.5 Special Edition Sdn	9648	11019	12565
4 Dr 3.5 Sdn	9373	10705	12207				

Options	Price	Options	Price
AM/FM/Cassette/CD Audio System	+131	Navigation System	+558
Compact Disc Changer [Opt on 3.5]	+192		

1997

No changes for the 1997 3.5RL.

Mileage Category: I

Body Styles	TMV Pricing			Body Styles	TMV Pricing		
	Trade	Private	Dealer		Trade	Private	Dealer
4 Dr 3.5 Premium Sdn	7731	9086	10742	4 Dr 3.5 Sdn	7373	8665	10243

Options	Price	Options	Price
AM/FM/Cassette/CD Audio System	+115	Navigation System	+488
Compact Disc Changer [Opt on 3.5]	+168		

1996

Mileage Category: I

Body Styles	TMV Pricing		
	Trade	Private	Dealer
4 Dr 3.5 Premium Sdn	6785	7892	9421

Options	Price
Compact Disc Changer [Opt on 3.5]	+154

Body Styles	TMV Pricing		
	Trade	Private	Dealer
4 Dr 3.5 Sdn	6420	7468	8915

Options	Price
Navigation System	+447

The replacement for the Legend arrives wearing Acura's new alphanumeric naming system: the 3.5 RL. The 3.5 refers to the Acura's engine size. The front wheels of the 3.5 RL are powered by a torquey V6 engine mated to an electronic four-speed automatic transmission. Other changes include 101 ways to isolate bumps, vibrations and road noise.

RSX

2004

Mileage Category: E

Body Styles	TMV Pricing		
	Trade	Private	Dealer
2 Dr STD Hbk	13730	14854	16727

Options	Price
Automatic 5-Speed Transmission [Opt on STD]	+900

Body Styles	TMV Pricing		
	Trade	Private	Dealer
2 Dr Type-S Hbk	16073	17178	19019

Options	Price
Leather Seats [Opt on STD]	+1075

For 2004, the RSX receives heated sideview mirrors as standard equipment.

2003

Mileage Category: E

Body Styles	TMV Pricing		
	Trade	Private	Dealer
2 Dr STD Hbk	13035	14018	15657

Options	Price
Automatic 5-Speed Transmission [Opt on STD]	+691

Body Styles	TMV Pricing		
	Trade	Private	Dealer
2 Dr Type-S Hbk	14802	15831	17546

Options	Price
Leather Seats [Opt on STD]	+826

Other than a new color, Redondo Red Pearl, there are no changes to the RSX in its sophomore year. Available from the dealer, however, is a new "Factory Performance" package that adds high-performance suspension components, better brakes, larger wheels and tires and a body kit.

2002

Mileage Category: E

Body Styles	TMV Pricing		
	Trade	Private	Dealer
2 Dr STD Hbk	12113	13022	14537

Options	Price
Automatic 5-Speed Transmission [Opt on STD]	+619

Body Styles	TMV Pricing		
	Trade	Private	Dealer
2 Dr Type-S Hbk	13629	14634	16308

Options	Price
Leather Seats [Opt on STD]	+687

The sporty RSX is an all-new replacement for the Acura Integra. Highlights include more powerful engines, higher levels of standard equipment and enhanced driving dynamics.

SLX

1999

Mileage Category: O

Body Styles	TMV Pricing		
	Trade	Private	Dealer
4 Dr STD 4WD SUV	7861	9340	10879

The SLX is carried over unchanged from a year ago.

1998

Mileage Category: O

Body Styles	TMV Pricing		
	Trade	Private	Dealer
4 Dr STD 4WD SUV	6082	7429	8949

Acura's rebadged Isuzu Trooper gets more power and torque, a trick new 4WD system and revised styling for 1998.

1997

Mileage Category: O

Body Styles	TMV Pricing		
	Trade	Private	Dealer
4 Dr Premium 4WD SUV	5110	6376	7924

Body Styles	TMV Pricing		
	Trade	Private	Dealer
4 Dr STD 4WD SUV	4809	6001	7457

No changes to Acura's upscale Isuzu Trooper twin.

Acura
SLX/TL

1996

The SLX is one of the first luxury-badged sport-utes to be released in this country. Based on the successful Isuzu Trooper, the SLX is very similar to its twin.

Mileage Category: O

Body Styles	TMV Pricing		
	Trade	Private	Dealer
4 Dr STD 4WD SUV	3548	4425	5635

Options	Price	Options	Price
Leather Seats	+277	Power Moonroof	+307

TL

2004

Mileage Category: H

Body Styles	TMV Pricing		
	Trade	Private	Dealer
4 Dr 3.2 Sdn	27568	29004	31396

Options	Price
Navigation System	+2000

The TL has been completely redesigned for 2004. A 270-horsepower V6 is standard, and both a six-speed manual and a five-speed automatic transmission are available. The level of luxury inside the cabin is up, and driving dynamics are better than ever.

2003

Mileage Category: H

Body Styles	TMV Pricing			Body Styles	TMV Pricing		
	Trade	Private	Dealer		Trade	Private	Dealer
4 Dr 3.2 Sdn	17700	18762	20531	4 Dr 3.2 Type-S Sdn	19366	20528	22464

Options	Price
Navigation System	+1651

For 2003, all TL models equipped with the navigation system receive OnStar as standard equipment.

2002

The TL Type-S makes its debut this year, sporting a 260-horsepower engine, sport-tuned suspension, Vehicle Stability Assist and 17-inch tires. 2002 also sees some styling revisions to the TL's front end and taillights. An in-dash six-disc changer, one-touch-up driver window and two-position memory system for driver seat and mirrors are standard on both the 3.2TL and the Type-S, and Acura has added insulation materials to the doors and reshaped the side mirrors to cut down on wind and road noise inside the cabin. Anthracite Metallic, Aegean Blue Pearl and Eternal Blue Pearl are the new exterior colors.

Mileage Category: H

Body Styles	TMV Pricing			Body Styles	TMV Pricing		
	Trade	Private	Dealer		Trade	Private	Dealer
4 Dr 3.2 Sdn	14760	15763	17434	4 Dr 3.2 Type-S Sdn	16272	17378	19220

Options	Price
Navigation System	+1375

2001

Standard equipment now includes floor mats and an emergency trunk release.

Mileage Category: H

Body Styles	TMV Pricing		
	Trade	Private	Dealer
4 Dr 3.2 Sdn	12789	14162	15429

Options	Price
Navigation System	+1176

2000

A new five-speed sequential SportShift automatic transmission and free-flowing intake manifold debut. A side-airbag system becomes standard as does a dual-stage inflator for the front-passenger airbag. The optional navigation system now features a DVD database.

Mileage Category: H

Body Styles	TMV Pricing		
	Trade	Private	Dealer
4 Dr 3.2 Sdn	10464	11824	13158

Options	Price
Navigation System	+1025

1999

The TL has been redesigned for 1999, with everything just getting better. The 2.5-liter engine is gone, making way for an all-new 3.2-liter V6. The transmission has been refined, the interior design makes better use of space, and the exterior is updated.

Mileage Category: H

Body Styles	TMV Pricing		
	Trade	Private	Dealer
4 Dr 3.2 Sdn	8713	10055	11451

For the latest vehicle information, visit www.edmunds.com

1999 (cont'd)

Options	Price
Chrome Wheels	+457
Compact Disc Changer	+264

Options	Price
Navigation System	+650
Rear Spoiler	+142

1998

Mileage Category: H

Body Styles	TMV Pricing		
	Trade	Private	Dealer
4 Dr 2.5 Sdn	6821	8036	9407

Body Styles	TMV Pricing		
	Trade	Private	Dealer
4 Dr 3.2 Sdn	7112	8379	9807

Options	Price
Rear Spoiler	+122

The premium level is gone, but the TL gets more standard equipment.

1997

The TL is unchanged for 1997.

Mileage Category: H

Body Styles	TMV Pricing		
	Trade	Private	Dealer
4 Dr 2.5 Premium Sdn	5346	6469	7842
4 Dr 2.5 Sdn	5061	6124	7424

Body Styles	TMV Pricing		
	Trade	Private	Dealer
4 Dr 3.2 Premium Sdn	7032	8508	10311
4 Dr 3.2 Sdn	5599	6774	8209

1996

Vigor replacement designed to do battle with new Infiniti I30 and the Lexus ES 300 in the near-luxury segment. Cleanly styled with room for four, the new TL comes with either a 2.5-liter, inline five-cylinder or a smooth 3.2-liter V6.

Mileage Category: H

Body Styles	TMV Pricing		
	Trade	Private	Dealer
4 Dr 2.5 Premium Sdn	4292	5291	6670
4 Dr 2.5 Sdn	4166	5136	6475

Body Styles	TMV Pricing		
	Trade	Private	Dealer
4 Dr 3.2 Premium Sdn	5650	6965	8781
4 Dr 3.2 Sdn	4617	5691	7174

Options	Price
Compact Disc Changer	+182

1995

This "Touring/Luxury" replacement for the Vigor, aimed squarely at the Lexus ES300, offers a choice of either inline-five cylinder power (in the 2.5 TL) or more powerful V6 motivation (in the 3.2 TL). The five puts out 176 horsepower, the six makes 200 ponies. An automatic transmission is the sole gearbox, and, as expected, the 3.2 TL has more standard features to go with its higher price tag.

Mileage Category: H

Body Styles	TMV Pricing		
	Trade	Private	Dealer
4 Dr 2.5 Premium Sdn	3682	4559	6020

Body Styles	TMV Pricing		
	Trade	Private	Dealer
4 Dr 2.5 Sdn	3405	4216	5567

Options	Price
Rear Spoiler	+84

TSX

2004

Mileage Category: H

Body Styles	TMV Pricing		
	Trade	Private	Dealer
4 Dr STD Sdn	21839	23040	25042

Options	Price
Navigation System	+2000

Although based on an existing European Honda, the TSX is an all-new car for the U.S. market.

90

1995

Mileage Category: H

Body Styles	TMV Pricing		
	Trade	Private	Dealer
4 Dr STD Sdn	2309	2970	4072
4 Dr Sport Sdn	2474	3182	4363

Options	Price
Automatic 4-Speed Transmission	+184
Leather Seats	+253

Sport 90 model introduced, featuring lowered suspension.

Body Styles	TMV Pricing		
	Trade	Private	Dealer
4 Dr quattro AWD Sdn	2759	3550	4867

Options	Price
Power Sunroof	+138

A4

2004

The Cabriolet is now available with all-wheel drive, while all A4s now come standard with a tire-pressure monitoring system, revised steering wheels and two-stage airbags. The 1.8T models have been upgraded with 16-inch aluminum wheels and now offer a six-speed manual transmission as an option.

Mileage Category: H

Body Styles	TMV Pricing		
	Trade	Private	Dealer
2 Dr 1.8T Turbo Conv	29101	30598	33093
2 Dr 3.0 Conv	34812	36309	38804
2 Dr 3.0 quattro AWD Conv	36074	37646	40266
4 Dr 1.8T Avant quattro Turbo AWD Wgn	21247	22482	24539
4 Dr 1.8T Turbo Sdn	18925	20160	22217

Options	Price
17 Inch Wheels	+550
18 Inch Wheels [Opt on Sdn, Wgn]	+850
Aero Kit [Opt on Sdn, Wgn]	+1200
Automatic 5-Speed Transmission [Opt on quattro Sdn, Wgn]	+1050
Automatic Dimming Rearview Mirror	+200
Automatic Dimming Sideview Mirror(s) [Opt on 3.0]	+200
Automatic On/Off Headlights	+175
Bose Audio System	+900
Continuously Variable Transmission [Opt on 1.8T Sdn]	+1150
Heated Front Seats	+135
Leather Seats [Opt on 1.8T]	+745
Navigation System [Opt on 3.0]	+1350
OnStar Telematics System [Opt on Sdn, Wgn]	+850

Body Styles	TMV Pricing		
	Trade	Private	Dealer
4 Dr 1.8T quattro Turbo AWD Sdn	20522	21757	23814
4 Dr 3.0 Avant quattro AWD Wgn	25231	26466	28523
4 Dr 3.0 Sdn	23903	25174	27293
4 Dr 3.0 quattro AWD Sdn	25240	26512	28631

Options	Price
Power Driver Seat [Opt on 1.8T Sdn]	+205
Power Driver Seat w/Memory [Opt on 3.0]	+225
Power Moonroof [Opt on Sdn, Wgn]	+950
Power Rear Window Sunshade [Opt on 3.0 Sdn]	+375
Power Retractable Mirrors [Opt on 3.0]	+150
Rear Side Airbag Restraints [Opt on Sdn, Wgn]	+350
Satellite Radio System	+350
Special Factory Paint	+450
Special Leather Seat Trim [Opt on 3.0, 1.8T Conv]	+1000
Sport Seats [Opt on 3.0 Conv]	+1500
Sport Suspension	+200
Xenon Headlamps	+300

2003

The big news is the arrival of the A4 Cabriolet, a fetching drop-top version of the A4 sedan. Initially, the company will offer only one drivetrain choice -- front-wheel drive with the 3.0-liter V6 engine and continuously variable transmission. Expect to see a 1.8T version midway through the model year and a 3.0 quattro Cab by October 2003. No word yet on the possibility of a manual transmission. As if this weren't enough, Audi plans to release a coupe version of the A4 in early 2003. The rest of the A4 lineup benefits from equipment upgrades. Leather is now optional on all 1.8T models, as are 12-way power front seats. All 3.0s will come swathed in leather, with more deluxe leather optional. Previous stand-alone options for the 3.0, including xenons and satellite steering wheel controls, have been swept up into the Premium Package. A new cold weather package includes seat heaters and a ski sack, and 17-inch all-season tires are a stand-alone extra.

Mileage Category: H

Body Styles	TMV Pricing		
	Trade	Private	Dealer
2 Dr 1.8T Turbo Conv	26946	28374	30754
2 Dr 3.0 Conv	30495	32111	34803
4 Dr 1.8T Avant quattro Turbo AWD Wgn	19314	20337	22042
4 Dr 1.8T Turbo Sdn	17345	18263	19794

Options	Price
16 Inch Wheels [Opt on 1.8T]	+342
17 Inch Wheels	+342
Automatic 5-Speed Transmission [Opt on AWD]	+875
Automatic Dimming Sideview Mirror(s) [Opt on 3.0]	+152
Bose Audio System	+494
Continuously Variable Transmission [Opt on FWD]	+875
Heated Front Seats	+247
Leather Seats	+723
Navigation System [Opt on 3.0]	+1027
OnStar Telematics System	+532

Body Styles	TMV Pricing		
	Trade	Private	Dealer
4 Dr 1.8T quattro Turbo AWD Sdn	18917	19919	21590
4 Dr 3.0 Avant quattro AWD Wgn	23058	24279	26315
4 Dr 3.0 Sdn	20996	22108	23961
4 Dr 3.0 quattro AWD Sdn	23018	24237	26268

Options	Price
Power Driver Seat [Opt on 1.8T]	+183
Power Driver Seat w/Memory [Opt on 3.0]	+228
Power Moonroof [Opt on Sdn, Wgn]	+761
Power Passenger Seat [Opt on 3.0]	+183
Power Rear Window Sunshade [Opt on 3.0 Sdn]	+285
Power Retractable Mirrors [Opt on 3.0]	+141
Rear Side Airbag Restraints [Opt on Sdn, Wgn]	+266
Ski Sack [Opt on Sdn, Wgn]	+133
Special Factory Paint	+342
Special Leather Seat Trim [Opt on 3.0]	+761

Options	Price
Sport Seats [Opt on Conv]	+1141
Sport Suspension	+228

Options	Price
Xenon Headlamps	+380

Mileage Category: H

2002

Audi's entry-level sedan and wagon are all new for 2002. Along with a redesigned body structure and new sheet metal, the new A4 receives a variety of changes to make it sportier. It is motivated by either a 170-horsepower 1.8-liter turbocharged four or a completely new 3.0-liter 220-horsepower V6, which can be mated to a six-speed manual transmission. Making its debut this year for non-quattro models is a continuously variable transmission (CVT), also known as multitronic. An in-dash six-disc CD changer and a dual-zone auto climate control top the standard features list.

Body Styles	TMV Pricing		
	Trade	Private	Dealer
4 Dr 1.8T Avant quattro Turbo AWD Wgn	16535	17628	19451
4 Dr 1.8T Turbo Sdn	14555	15518	17122
4 Dr 1.8T quattro Turbo AWD Sdn	15985	17042	18804

Body Styles	TMV Pricing		
	Trade	Private	Dealer
4 Dr 3.0 Avant quattro AWD Wgn	19724	21028	23202
4 Dr 3.0 Sdn	17892	19076	21049
4 Dr 3.0 quattro AWD Sdn	19081	20343	22447

Options	Price
16 Inch Wheels [Opt on 1.8T]	+306
17 Inch Wheels	+306
Automatic 5-Speed Transmission	+714
Automatic Dimming Sideview Mirror(s)	+136
Bose Audio System	+442
Continuously Variable Transmission	+782
Heated Front and Rear Seats	+357
Leather Seats	+626
Metallic Paint	+306
Navigation System	+918

Options	Price
OnStar Telematics System	+577
Park Distance Control (Rear) [Opt on 3.0]	+238
Pearlescent Metallic Paint	+816
Power Driver Seat w/Memory [Opt on 3.0]	+204
Power Moonroof	+599
Power Rear Window Sunshade	+255
Rear Side Airbag Restraints	+238
Ski Sack	+119
Sport Suspension	+204
Xenon Headlamps	+340

Mileage Category: H

2001

The entire Audi lineup receives a new 4-year/50,000-mile limited warranty and no-charge scheduled maintenance, a 12-year limited warranty against corrosion perforation, and 24-hour roadside assistance for four years. All A4s are now equipped with head protection airbags, have lengthier oil change intervals and an optional Electronic Stabilization Program (ESP). The 1.8T engine gets a horsepower boost from 150 to a racy 170 and meets ULEV standards.

Body Styles	TMV Pricing		
	Trade	Private	Dealer
4 Dr 1.8T Avant quattro Turbo AWD Wgn	10945	12104	13174
4 Dr 1.8T Turbo Sdn	9558	10570	11504
4 Dr 1.8T quattro Turbo AWD Sdn	10737	11874	12924

Body Styles	TMV Pricing		
	Trade	Private	Dealer
4 Dr 2.8 Avant quattro AWD Wgn	13763	15220	16566
4 Dr 2.8 Sdn	12694	14038	15280
4 Dr 2.8 quattro AWD Sdn	13099	14487	15768

Options	Price
17 Inch Wheels - Spoke	+261
Automatic 5-Speed Transmission [Std on 2.8 FWD]	+638
Automatic Dimming Sideview Mirror(s)	+116
Automatic Stability Control	+319
Bose Audio System	+377
Compact Disc Changer	+319
Heated Front Seats	+151
Leather Seats	+766

Options	Price
Metallic Paint	+261
Navigation System	+743
Pearlescent Metallic Paint	+261
Power Moonroof	+551
Ski Sack	+138
Sport Seats	+290
Sport Suspension	+232
Xenon Headlamps	+290

Mileage Category: H

2000

All A4 models receive minor updates to the interior, exterior and chassis. The front styling has been changed with new headlights, a new grille, new door handles and new mirror housings. Inside, you'll find a revised instrument cluster and center console, along with other minor interior changes. The rear seats have been modified to improve comfort. There are now optional head airbags and xenon headlights. The chassis has been reworked for improved ride comfort and responsiveness.

Body Styles	TMV Pricing		
	Trade	Private	Dealer
4 Dr 1.8T Avant quattro Turbo AWD Wgn	9387	10642	11871
4 Dr 1.8T Turbo Sdn	7971	9037	10081
4 Dr 1.8T quattro Turbo AWD Sdn	9150	10373	11571

Body Styles	TMV Pricing		
	Trade	Private	Dealer
4 Dr 2.8 Avant quattro AWD Wgn	12044	13654	15232
4 Dr 2.8 Sdn	10491	11894	13269
4 Dr 2.8 quattro AWD Sdn	11592	13142	14662

Options	Price
Automatic 5-Speed Transmission	+548
Bose Audio System	+315
Compact Disc Changer	+267
Front and Rear Head Airbag Restraints	+145
Heated Front Seats	+133
Leather Seats	+530
Navigation System	+620

Options	Price
Power Moonroof	+484
Ski Sack [Opt on Sdn]	+121
Special Factory Paint	+229
Spoke Wheels	+169
Sport Seats	+242
Sport Suspension	+218
Xenon Headlamps	+242

Audi
A4/S4

1999

Audi introduces the 1.8T Avant wagon to its lineup, while other A4 models gain standard equipment and new options.

Mileage Category: H

Body Styles	TMV Pricing		
	Trade	Private	Dealer
4 Dr 1.8T Avant quattro Turbo AWD Wgn	7691	9140	10648
4 Dr 1.8T Turbo Sdn	6866	8161	9508
4 Dr 1.8T quattro Turbo AWD Sdn	7388	8779	10227

Body Styles	TMV Pricing		
	Trade	Private	Dealer
4 Dr 2.8 Avant quattro AWD Wgn	9844	11699	13629
4 Dr 2.8 Sdn	8948	10634	12388
4 Dr 2.8 quattro AWD Sdn	9527	11322	13190

Options	Price
Automatic 5-Speed Transmission	+467
Compact Disc Changer	+205
Leather Seats	+406
Power Moonroof	+371

Options	Price
Special Factory Paint	+195
Spoke Wheels	+130
Sport Seats	+185
Sport Suspension	+167

1998

The 2.8 sedan gets a valve job resulting in 18 more horsepower and additional torque. Side-impact airbags are standard, as is traction control. Opt for the automatic and you'll get the same Tiptronic technology that allows Biff to manually shift Buffy's 911 Cabriolet. A new station wagon called Avant debuts, while the A4 1.8T gets new wheels, a sport package and an ambient temperature gauge. New colors and stereo improvements round out the changes for 1998.

Mileage Category: H

Body Styles	TMV Pricing		
	Trade	Private	Dealer
4 Dr 1.8T Turbo Sdn	5325	6531	7890
4 Dr 1.8T quattro Turbo AWD Sdn	5429	6658	8043
4 Dr 2.8 Avant Wgn	6906	8467	10228

Body Styles	TMV Pricing		
	Trade	Private	Dealer
4 Dr 2.8 Avant quattro AWD Wgn	7420	9097	10989
4 Dr 2.8 Sdn	6607	8102	9787
4 Dr 2.8 quattro AWD Sdn	6764	8293	10018

Options	Price
Automatic 5-Speed Transmission	+374
Bose Audio System	+196
Compact Disc Changer	+163
Leather Seats	+326
Metallic Paint	+137

Options	Price
Power Moonroof	+298
Special Factory Paint	+157
Sport Seats	+149
Sport Suspension	+134

1997

A cheaper Audi A4 1.8T debuts, featuring a 150-horsepower, 20-valve, turbocharged inline four-cylinder engine and a base price in the low 20s. The 2.8 gains a revised deck lid and expanded central locking features. All models have new cloth upholstery, and the console and armrests are trimmed with the same fabric as the seats. Three new colors debut for 1997.

Mileage Category: H

Body Styles	TMV Pricing		
	Trade	Private	Dealer
4 Dr 1.8T Turbo Sdn	4507	5618	6976
4 Dr 1.8T quattro Turbo AWD Sdn	4616	5754	7144

Body Styles	TMV Pricing		
	Trade	Private	Dealer
4 Dr 2.8 Sdn	5048	6292	7812
4 Dr 2.8 quattro AWD Sdn	5269	6568	8156

Options	Price
Automatic 5-Speed Transmission	+267
Bose Audio System	+162
Leather Seats	+269

Options	Price
Power Moonroof	+245
Special Factory Paint	+129
Sport Seats	+116

1996

All new, the A4 replaces the compact 90. This car performs better than the lackluster 90, and features a full load of standard features. Plus, it's drop-dead gorgeous. For the first time, a five-speed automatic transmission is available with the optional Quattro all-wheel-drive system.

Mileage Category: H

Body Styles	TMV Pricing		
	Trade	Private	Dealer
4 Dr 2.8 Sdn	3913	5027	6565

Body Styles	TMV Pricing		
	Trade	Private	Dealer
4 Dr 2.8 quattro AWD Sdn	4362	5605	7321

Options	Price
Automatic 5-Speed Transmission	+236
Bose Audio System	+146
Leather Seats	+250

Options	Price
Metallic Paint	+125
Power Moonroof	+226

S4

2004

Mileage Category: F

Body Styles	TMV Pricing		
	Trade	Private	Dealer
2 Dr quattro AWD Conv	44194	45886	48705
4 Dr Avant quattro AWD Wgn	34121	35859	38756

Body Styles	TMV Pricing		
	Trade	Private	Dealer
4 Dr quattro AWD Sdn	34967	36563	39224

Options	Price
Automatic 6-Speed Transmission	+1150
Automatic On/Off Headlights	+125
Bose Audio System	+500
Carbon Interior Trim [Opt on Conv]	+300

Options	Price
Heated Front Seats	+450
Navigation System	+1350
OnStar Telematics System [Opt on Sdn, Wgn]	+850
Power Driver Seat w/Memory	+250

2004 (cont'd)

Options	Price
Power Moonroof	+425
Power Rear Window Sunshade [Opt on Sdn]	+375
Rear Side Airbag Restraints [Opt on Sdn, Wgn]	+350
Rear Wind Deflector [Opt on Conv]	+150

Options	Price
Satellite Radio System	+500
Special Factory Paint	+450
Steering Wheel Radio Controls	+150

The all-new S4 sports some serious hardware, not the least of which is a 4.2-liter V8 bristling with 340 horsepower. A convertible body style has been added to the lineup.

2002

Mileage Category: F

Body Styles	TMV Pricing		
	Trade	Private	Dealer
4 Dr Avant quattro Turbo AWD Wgn	22971	24517	27094

Options	Price
Aluminum/Alloy Interior Trim	+136
Automatic Dimming Sideview Mirror(s)	+136
Bose Audio System	+442
Compact Disc Changer	+374
Heated Front Seats	+306

Body Styles	TMV Pricing		
	Trade	Private	Dealer
4 Dr quattro Turbo AWD Sdn	19886	21224	23454

Options	Price
Nappa Leather Seat Trim	+136
Navigation System	+918
Pearlescent Metallic Paint	+816
Power Moonroof	+646
Ski Sack	+162

Nothing new for 2002.

2001

Mileage Category: F

Body Styles	TMV Pricing		
	Trade	Private	Dealer
4 Dr Avant quattro Turbo AWD Wgn	20246	22554	24684

Options	Price
Alcantra and Leather Package	+261
Automatic Dimming Sideview Mirror(s)	+116
Bose Audio System	+377
Compact Disc Changer	+319
Heated Front Seats	+145

Body Styles	TMV Pricing		
	Trade	Private	Dealer
4 Dr quattro Turbo AWD Sdn	17818	19849	21723

Options	Price
Navigation System	+743
Pearlescent Metallic Paint	+697
Power Moonroof	+551
Ski Sack	+138

The Electronic Stabilization Program is made standard on the S4 sedan. The S4 Avant debuts for 2001, allowing for more cargo space and family-hauling capabilities. Casablanca White is made available as an exterior color, as are aluminum mirror housings in combination with the Pearl Napa/Alcantara sets and aluminum trim. A new four-year warranty concept is introduced this year.

2000

Mileage Category: F

Body Styles	TMV Pricing		
	Trade	Private	Dealer
4 Dr quattro Turbo AWD Sdn	14528	16627	18685

Options	Price
Bose Audio System	+315
Compact Disc Changer	+267
Heated Front Seats	+121

Options	Price
Navigation System	+620
Power Moonroof	+484

The Audi S4 is a new sport sedan based off the excellent A4 platform introduced in 1996. Highlights include a turbocharged 250-horsepower engine, all-wheel drive and improved handling and braking.

A6

2004

Mileage Category: I

Body Styles	TMV Pricing		
	Trade	Private	Dealer
4 Dr 2.7T S-Line quattro Turbo AWD Sdn	32684	34318	37041
4 Dr 2.7T quattro Turbo AWD Sdn	32309	33943	36667
4 Dr 3.0 Avant quattro AWD Wgn	29904	31490	34133

Options	Price
Automatic Dimming Rearview Mirror [Std on 4.2]	+150
Automatic Dimming Sideview Mirror(s)	+150
Bose Audio System	+600
Forged Alloy Wheels [Opt on 4.2]	+1000
Garage Door Opener [Std on 4.2]	+125
Heated Front and Rear Seats	+500
Heated Steering Wheel [Opt on 4.2]	+200
Navigation System [Opt on 2.7, 4.2]	+1350
OnStar Telematics System	+850

Body Styles	TMV Pricing		
	Trade	Private	Dealer
4 Dr 3.0 Sdn	26753	28355	31025
4 Dr 3.0 quattro AWD Sdn	30558	32227	35009
4 Dr 4.2 quattro AWD Sdn	37641	39431	42413

Options	Price
Park Distance Control (Rear)	+350
Power Driver Seat w/Memory [Std on 4.2]	+250
Power Moonroof [Opt on 3.0 FWD]	+425
Power Rear Window Sunshade [Opt on 2.7, 4.2]	+250
Power Retractable Mirrors	+150
Power Solar Sunroof [Opt on 4.2]	+750
Rear Side Airbag Restraints	+350
Satellite Radio System	+350
Sport Seats [Opt on 2.7, 4.2]	+450

A sport mode is added to the "multitronic" CVT, the center console's retractable cup holder is replaced by a power point and all quattro models now come standard with a sunroof.

2004 (cont'd)

Options	Price
Sport Suspension [Opt on 4.2]	+400

Options	Price
Xenon Headlamps	+200

2003

All 3.0 and 2.7T models get standard leather upholstery. In addition, the 2.7T now comes standard with a firmer sport-tuned suspension and 17-inch wheels and 235/45 high-performance tires (these items were previously available in the sport package). All models can be equipped with a cold weather package that includes front and rear seat heaters (front seats only in 3.0 models); a ski sack; and on the 4.2 sedan only, a heated steering wheel.

Mileage Category: I

Body Styles	TMV Pricing		
	Trade	Private	Dealer
4 Dr 2.7T quattro Turbo AWD Sdn	25758	27140	29443
4 Dr 3.0 Avant quattro AWD Wgn	24302	25605	27777
4 Dr 3.0 Sdn	21839	23010	24961

Body Styles	TMV Pricing		
	Trade	Private	Dealer
4 Dr 3.0 quattro AWD Sdn	24547	25864	28058
4 Dr 4.2 quattro AWD Sdn	30074	31687	34374

Options	Price
17 Inch Wheels	+342
Automatic Dimming Sideview Mirror(s)	+152
Bose Audio System	+571
Heated Front Seats [Opt on 3.0]	+342
Heated Front and Rear Seats [Opt on 2.7T]	+437
Navigation System [Opt on 2.7T,4.2]	+1027
OnStar Telematics System	+532
Park Distance Control (Rear)	+266
Power Driver Seat w/Memory [Std on 4.2]	+228
Power Moonroof	+669

Options	Price
Power Rear Window Sunshade [Opt on 2.7T]	+342
Power Retractable Mirrors	+141
Power Solar Sunroof [Opt on 4.2]	+418
Rear Side Airbag Restraints	+266
Ski Sack	+152
Special Leather Seat Trim [Opt on 2.7T]	+609
Sport Seats [Opt on 2.7T]	+380
Sport Suspension [Opt on 4.2]	+228
Steering Wheel Radio Controls [Opt on 3.0]	+152
Xenon Headlamps	+342

2002

The A6 gets a new 220-horsepower 3.0-liter V6 to replace last year's 2.8-liter. A continuously variable transmission (CVT) is available on front-wheel-drive models with this engine. Other mechanical changes this year include stronger brakes, an improved stability control system and BrakeAssist. OnStar telematics makes its way onto the options list, and you'll be pleased to find a standard six-disc changer in the dashboard. Styling in and around the car, such as the head and taillamps, is slightly modified and new interior and exterior colors expand your choices.

Mileage Category: I

Body Styles	TMV Pricing		
	Trade	Private	Dealer
4 Dr 2.7T quattro Turbo AWD Sdn	21385	22735	24986
4 Dr 3.0 Avant quattro AWD Wgn	20620	21922	24092
4 Dr 3.0 Sdn	19174	20384	22401

Body Styles	TMV Pricing		
	Trade	Private	Dealer
4 Dr 3.0 quattro AWD Sdn	20346	21630	23771
attro AWD Sdn	25918	27555	30282

Options	Price
17 Inch Wheels	+459
17 Inch Wheels - Spoke [Opt on 2.7T]	+459
Automatic Dimming Sideview Mirror(s) [Std on 4.2]	+136
Bose Audio System [Std on 4.2]	+510
Heated Front and Rear Seats	+170
Leather Seats [Std on 4.2]	+626
Navigation System	+918
OnStar Telematics System	+475
Park Distance Control (Rear)	+238
Pearlescent Metallic Paint	+816
Power Driver Seat w/Memory [Std on 4.2]	+204

Options	Price
Power Moonroof [Std on 4.2]	+599
Power Rear Window Sunshade	+238
Power Retractable Mirrors [Std on 4.2]	+126
Power Solar Sunroof	+442
Rear Side Airbag Restraints	+238
Ski Sack	+119
Sport Seats	+221
Sport Suspension	+289
Steering Wheel Radio Controls [Std on 4.2]	+136
Third Seat	+510
Xenon Headlamps	+238

2001

All 2001 Audis receive a new 4-year/50,000-mile limited warranty and no-charge scheduled maintenance, a 12-year limited warranty against corrosion perforation and 24-hour Roadside Assistance for four years. All A6s are now equipped with the high-tech Immobilizer III security system, side-curtain airbags, a 12-millimeter increase in the headrest height adjustment and an optional multifunction steering wheel.

Mileage Category: I

Body Styles	TMV Pricing		
	Trade	Private	Dealer
4 Dr 2.7T quattro Turbo AWD Sdn	16476	18219	19827
4 Dr 2.8 Avant quattro AWD Wgn	14412	15937	17345
4 Dr 2.8 Sdn	13247	14648	15941

Body Styles	TMV Pricing		
	Trade	Private	Dealer
4 Dr 2.8 quattro AWD Sdn	14634	16183	17612
4 Dr 4.2 quattro AWD Sdn	19255	21291	23171

Options	Price
17 Inch Wheels [Opt on 2.7T,4.2]	+435
Automatic Dimming Sideview Mirror(s) [Std on 4.2]	+116
Automatic Stability Control [Opt on 2.8]	+319
Compact Disc Changer	+319
Forged Alloy Wheels	+580
Heated Front and Rear Seats	+193
Leather Seats [Std on 4.2]	+900
Navigation System	+743
Park Distance Control (Rear)	+203
Pearlescent Metallic Paint	+697

Options	Price
Power Driver Seat w/Memory [Opt on 2.7T]	+174
Power Moonroof [Std on 4.2]	+551
Power Rear Window Sunshade [Opt on 2.7T]	+261
Rear Side Airbag Restraints	+203
Ski Sack [Std on 4.2,Avant]	+138
Sport Seats	+276
Sport Suspension	+248
Third Seat	+435
Xenon Headlamps	+276

2000

There are two new models joining the A6 2.8 and A6 2.8 Avant. The first is the A6 2.7T powered by a turbocharged V6 engine. The second model is the A6 4.2 powered by a virile V8.

Mileage Category: I

Body Styles	TMV Pricing		
	Trade	Private	Dealer
4 Dr 2.7T quattro Turbo AWD Sdn	13640	15432	17187
4 Dr 2.8 Avant quattro AWD Wgn	11980	13552	15094
4 Dr 2.8 Sdn	11449	12954	14428

Options	Price
Automatic Stability Control [Opt on 4.2]	+280
Bose Audio System [Std on 4.2]	+320
Compact Disc Changer	+278
Front and Rear Head Airbag Restraints [Opt on 2.7T,2.8]	+145
Heated Front and Rear Seats	+169
Leather Seats [Std on 4.2]	+605
Metallic Paint	+472
Navigation System	+620
Park Distance Control (Rear)	+178
Power Driver Seat w/Memory [Opt on 2.7T,2.8]	+153

Body Styles	TMV Pricing		
	Trade	Private	Dealer
4 Dr 2.8 quattro AWD Sdn	12271	13883	15462
4 Dr 4.2 quattro AWD Sdn	16711	18906	21058

Options	Price
Power Moonroof [Std on 4.2]	+484
Power Rear Window Sunshade	+229
Power Solar Sunroof	+433
Rear Side Airbag Restraints	+178
Ski Sack [Std on 4.2,Avant]	+121
Spoke Wheels	+364
Sport Seats	+242
Sport Suspension	+218
Third Seat	+339
Xenon Headlamps	+242

1999

The A6 continues basically unchanged after last year's redesign.

Mileage Category: I

Body Styles	TMV Pricing		
	Trade	Private	Dealer
4 Dr 2.8 Avant quattro AWD Wgn	10529	12355	14256
4 Dr 2.8 Sdn	9072	10645	12282

Options	Price
Bose Audio System	+245
Compact Disc Changer	+214
Heated Front and Rear Seats	+130
Leather Seats	+464
Metallic Paint	+212
Power Driver Seat w/Memory	+130

Body Styles	TMV Pricing		
	Trade	Private	Dealer
4 Dr 2.8 quattro AWD Sdn	9571	11231	12958

Options	Price
Power Moonroof	+371
Power Rear Window Sunshade	+195
Power Solar Sunroof	+369
Rear Side Airbag Restraints	+152
Third Seat	+260
Xenon Headlamps	+206

1998

Stretch an A4 platform, add rounded styling with plenty of edges for character, toss in a sumptuously comfortable interior available in several "atmosphere" styles, blend it all with traditional Germanic handling and what do you get? The excellent new Audi A6 sedan. Our only quibble is with the taillights, which appear to have been inspired by the Chevrolet S-10 pickup. The wagon is carried over from 1997.

Mileage Category: I

Body Styles	TMV Pricing		
	Trade	Private	Dealer
4 Dr 2.8 Avant Wgn	7002	8412	10003
4 Dr 2.8 Avant quattro AWD Wgn	8092	9721	11559

Options	Price
Bose Audio System	+196
Compact Disc Changer	+171
Leather Seats	+372
Metallic Paint	+169
Power Moonroof	+298

Body Styles	TMV Pricing		
	Trade	Private	Dealer
4 Dr 2.8 Sdn	7142	8580	10202
4 Dr 2.8 quattro AWD Sdn	7126	8560	10178

Options	Price
Power Passenger Seat [Opt on Wgn]	+163
Power Rear Window Sunshade [Opt on Sdn]	+157
Power Solar Sunroof [Opt on Sdn]	+296
Rear Side Airbag Restraints [Opt on Sdn]	+122
Xenon Headlamps [Opt on Sdn]	+165

1997

Mileage Category: I

Body Styles	TMV Pricing		
	Trade	Private	Dealer
4 Dr 2.8 Sdn	5226	6476	8003
4 Dr 2.8 Wgn	5844	7241	8948

Options	Price
Bose Audio System	+162
Leather Seats	+307
Metallic Paint	+140

Body Styles	TMV Pricing		
	Trade	Private	Dealer
4 Dr 2.8 quattro AWD Sdn	5627	6973	8618
4 Dr 2.8 quattro AWD Wgn	6505	8060	9960

Options	Price
Power Moonroof	+245
Power Passenger Seat	+135

A new quattro Value Package is available with a power glass sunroof, larger alloy wheels, bigger tires and, of course, the quattro all-wheel-drive system. Selective unlocking capability expands to the remote keyless entry fob, and the alarm system now features interior monitoring. Jacquard cloth upholstery is new, and three new colors debut: Tornado Red, Volcano Black metallic and Byzantine metallic.

Audi
A6/S6

1996

Traction control systems have been improved this year. Fans of the manual transmission will mourn the loss of it; all 1996 A6 models are saddled with an automatic shifter.

Mileage Category: I

Body Styles	TMV Pricing		
	Trade	Private	Dealer
4 Dr 2.8 Sdn	4592	5762	7377
4 Dr 2.8 Wgn	4915	6169	7900

Options	Price
Bose Audio System	+146
Leather Seats	+285
Metallic Paint	+130

Body Styles	TMV Pricing		
	Trade	Private	Dealer
4 Dr 2.8 quattro AWD Sdn	4868	6109	7823
4 Dr 2.8 quattro AWD Wgn	5654	7095	9086

Options	Price
Power Moonroof	+224
Power Passenger Seat	+119

1995

Subtle restyle of last year's 100 brings a new name. Sedan or wagon available in either front- or all-wheel drive. Wagon comes only with an automatic transmission.

Mileage Category: I

Body Styles	TMV Pricing		
	Trade	Private	Dealer
4 Dr 2.8 Sdn	3082	3922	5323
4 Dr 2.8 Wgn	3824	4867	6604

Options	Price
Automatic 4-Speed Transmission [Std on Wgn]	+184
Bose Audio System	+127
Compact Disc Changer	+161

Body Styles	TMV Pricing		
	Trade	Private	Dealer
4 Dr 2.8 quattro AWD Sdn	3787	4820	6541
4 Dr 2.8 quattro AWD Wgn	3940	5014	6804

Options	Price
Leather Seats	+253
Power Moonroof	+180

S6

2003

Mileage Category: F

Body Styles	TMV Pricing		
	Trade	Private	Dealer
4 Dr Avant quattro AWD Wgn	38400	40806	44815

Options	Price
Heated Front and Rear Seats	+190
Navigation System	+1027
OnStar Telematics System	+532

Options	Price
Park Distance Control (Rear)	+266
Power Solar Sunroof	+571
Rear Side Airbag Restraints	+266

Audi makes no changes to the high-performance S6 in its second year on the U.S. market.

2002

Proving that even those burdened with the yoke of responsibility deserve a little fun, Audi releases a high-performance version of the A6 station wagon. Good for sub-7-second 0-to-60 acceleration runs, the S6 rides on a more muscular suspension structure to temper the 340-horsepower V8.

Mileage Category: F

Body Styles	TMV Pricing		
	Trade	Private	Dealer
4 Dr Avant quattro AWD Wgn	32056	34524	38638

Options	Price
Heated Front and Rear Seats	+170
Navigation System	+918
OnStar Telematics System	+611
Park Distance Control (Rear)	+238

Options	Price
Pearlescent Metallic Paint	+816
Power Solar Sunroof	+510
Rear Side Airbag Restraints	+238

1995

The former S4 is renamed the S6 to match Audi's new naming system. Last year for this model based on the 100 platform.

Mileage Category: F

Body Styles	TMV Pricing		
	Trade	Private	Dealer
4 Dr quattro Turbo AWD Sdn	8458	10018	12618

Options	Price
Compact Disc Changer	+120

RS 6
2003

Body Styles	Mileage Category: F TMV Pricing		
	Trade	Private	Dealer
4 Dr quattro Turbo AWD Sdn	59343	61649	65491

Options	Price	Options	Price
Carbon Interior Trim	+228	Power Solar Sunroof	+418
Navigation System	+1027	Rear Side Airbag Restraints	+266
er Rear Window Sunshade	+342		

The Audi RS 6 sedan is the product of a joint effort between Audi and its tuning division, quattro GmbH, and will be the fastest Audi to reach U.S. shores thus far. It will offer a considerably higher level of performance than the S6 Avant introduced last year, largely because two turbochargers will be affixed to its 4.2-liter V8, resulting in 450 horsepower and 415 pound-feet of torque, slotting it in between the BMW M5 and the 2003 Mercedes-Benz E55 -- just where Audi wants to be. Quattro GmbH also made a number of chassis upgrades to manage all this power -- highlights include the debut of Dynamic Ride Control, which uses hydraulics to adjust damping during cornering, an even stiffer suspension than the S6's, a quicker steering ratio and a new brake system. Indeed, it's a good time to be a wealthy enthusiast.

A8
2004

Body Styles	Mileage Category: I TMV Pricing		
	Trade	Private	Dealer
4 Dr L quattro AWD Sdn	52050	54684	59074

Options	Price	Options	Price
18 Inch Wheels	+1150	Park Distance Control (Front and Rear)	+700
19 Inch Wheels	+1900	Power Rear Window Sunshade	+600
Adaptive Cruise Control	+2100	Power Solar Sunroof	+650
Alcantara and Leather Package	+1500	Power Trunk Closer	+700
Climate Controlled Seats (Rear)	+600	Ski Sack	+150
Heated Front and Rear Seats	+600	Tire Pressure Monitoring System	+600
Heated Steering Wheel	+400	Ventilated Seats (Front)	+800

Audi's flagship is completely revamped and sports a lighter chassis, more powerful V8 and a treasure trove of comfort, safety and suspension upgrades.

2003

Body Styles	TMV Pricing				Body Styles	TMV Pricing		
	Trade	Private	Dealer			Trade	Private	Dealer
4 Dr L quattro AWD Sdn	35669	38009	41910		4 Dr quattro AWD Sdn	34767	37049	40852

Mileage Category: I

Options	Price	Options	Price
17 Inch Wheels	+380	Pearlescent Metallic Paint	+913
18 Inch Wheels [Opt on L quattro]	+685	Power Rear Window Sunshade [Opt on quattro]	+342
Heated Front and Rear Seats [Opt on quattro]	+380	Power Solar Sunroof [Opt on L quattro]	+647
Navigation System	+1027	Ski Sack [Opt on quattro]	+181
OnStar Telematics System	+532	Tire Pressure Monitoring System	+297
Park Distance Control (Front and Rear) [Opt on L quattro]	+533	Xenon Headlamps [Opt on quattro]	+361

A redesigned A8 is coming for the 2004 model year, so 2003 changes are minimal. Premium packages for both the A8 and A8 L now include the navigation system, parking assist system, tire pressure monitoring system and 17-inch wheels with 225/55R17 all-season tires. In addition, this year only the A8 L will be eligible for the optional 18-inch wheels and 245/45R18 performance tires.

2002

Body Styles	TMV Pricing				Body Styles	TMV Pricing		
	Trade	Private	Dealer			Trade	Private	Dealer
4 Dr L quattro AWD Sdn	29736	32016	35816		4 Dr quattro AWD Sdn	28018	30166	33746

Mileage Category: I

Options	Price	Options	Price
17 Inch Wheels	+340	Pearlescent Metallic Paint	+816
18 Inch Wheels - Spoke	+1020	Power Rear Window Sunshade [Std on L]	+306
Alcantara and Leather Package	+2041	Power Solar Sunroof	+578
Heated Front and Rear Seats [Std on L]	+340	Ski Sack	+162
Navigation System	+918	Tire Pressure Monitoring System	+265
OnStar Telematics System	+475	Xenon Headlamps [Std on L]	+323
Park Distance Control (Front and Rear)	+476		

Audi will introduce the second generation of its flagship sedan next year, so 2002 sees only minor changes. Among them is a standard in-dash six-disc CD changer, OnStar telematics system as an option, an improved stability control system and updated navigation system software.

Audi
A8

2001

The Electronic Stabilization Program (ESP) now comes standard, as does a multifunctional steering wheel with audio, telephone and Tiptronic controls. Audi adds an oil level sensor to the A8 and an Office Package consisting of an electrically folding desk and minibar/cold storage for the rear seat is added to the options list.

Mileage Category: I

Body Styles	TMV Pricing		
	Trade	Private	Dealer
4 Dr L quattro AWD Sdn	22881	25861	28612

Options	Price
17 Inch Wheels - Spoke [Opt on quattro]	+580
18 Inch Wheels [Opt on L quattro]	+871
Alcantra and Leather Package	+2032
Heated Front and Rear Seats [Opt on quattro]	+261
Navigation System [Std on L Quattro]	+743
Park Distance Control (Front and Rear)	+406

Body Styles	TMV Pricing		
	Trade	Private	Dealer
4 Dr quattro AWD Sdn	21478	24274	26856

Options	Price
Pearlescent Metallic Paint	+697
Power Rear Window Sunshade [Opt on quattro]	+261
Power Solar Sunroof [Opt on L quattro]	+493
Power Sunroof [Std on L Quattro]	+493
Ski Sack	+138
Xenon Headlamps	+276

2000

Updated styling in the form of a revised grille, enlarged headlights, added chrome and aluminum trim and reshaped bumpers provides a subtle new look. Inside, new interior surfaces and standard Valcona leather intensify an already richly appointed cabin. Revised switchgear makes it easier to pilot the A8, and a new navigation system is available. A new 4.2-liter, 40-valve V8 resides under the hood, and aluminum suspension components reduce unsprung weight and enhance handling. A long wheelbase version (A8L) is now available for increased comfort of rear passengers, and comes standard with an electronic stability control system and navigation system.

Mileage Category: I

Body Styles	TMV Pricing		
	Trade	Private	Dealer
4 Dr L quattro AWD Sdn	17505	20238	22916

Options	Price
17 Inch Wheels - Spoke [Opt on L quattro]	+510
18 Inch Wheels [Opt on L quattro]	+765
Alcantra and Leather Package	+1611
Automatic Stability Control [Opt on quattro]	+280
Heated Front and Rear Seats [Opt on quattro]	+169
Navigation System	+620

Body Styles	TMV Pricing		
	Trade	Private	Dealer
4 Dr quattro AWD Sdn	16793	19415	21986

Options	Price
Park Distance Control (Front and Rear)	+357
Power Rear Window Sunshade [Opt on quattro]	+229
Power Solar Sunroof	+433
Ski Sack	+121
Xenon Headlamps	+242

1999

The A8's warm weather package is modified to improve electronic accessory performance, while dual-pane laminated glass replaces insulated glass. Standard on the A8 is a larger right outside mirror, a first aid kit and a CD changer. A premium leather/Alcantara trim package and a new Volcano Black exterior paint color are optional. A8 prices will remain unchanged from 1998.

Mileage Category: I

Body Styles	TMV Pricing		
	Trade	Private	Dealer
4 Dr STD Sdn	10698	12520	14417

Options	Price
17 Inch Wheels	+434
Alcantra and Leather Package	+1235
Bose Audio System [Opt on STD]	+316
Heated Front and Rear Seats	+130

Body Styles	TMV Pricing		
	Trade	Private	Dealer
4 Dr quattro AWD Sdn	12463	14586	16796

Options	Price
Metallic Paint	+212
Power Rear Window Sunshade	+195
Power Solar Sunroof	+369
Xenon Headlamps	+206

1998

Tiptronic automanual gear shifting is standard, as is a glass sunroof, dual-pane laminated window glass, an improved stereo and an upgraded antilock braking system.

Mileage Category: I

Body Styles	TMV Pricing		
	Trade	Private	Dealer
4 Dr STD Sdn	8726	10410	12308

Options	Price
17 Inch Wheels	+348
Bose Audio System [Opt on STD]	+252
Compact Disc Changer	+160

Body Styles	TMV Pricing		
	Trade	Private	Dealer
4 Dr quattro AWD Sdn	10139	12094	14300

Options	Price
Metallic Paint	+169
Power Rear Window Sunshade	+157
Power Solar Sunroof	+296

1997

Audi revolutionizes luxury sedan construction with the Audi Space Frame, which employs seven new aircraft-grade aluminum alloys to lighten weight and provide a tighter, more crashworthy structure. The new A8 is also the first passenger car equipped with six airbags. The usual accoutrements associated with a premium German sedan are all in place.

Mileage Category: I

Body Styles	TMV Pricing		
	Trade	Private	Dealer
4 Dr STD Sdn	6112	7488	9169

Options	Price
17 Inch Wheels	+287
Bose Audio System [Opt on STD]	+196
Heated Front and Rear Seats	+143

Body Styles	TMV Pricing		
	Trade	Private	Dealer
4 Dr quattro AWD Sdn	8002	9804	12006

Options	Price
Metallic Paint	+140
Power Rear Window Sunshade	+129
Power Solar Sunroof	+244

S8

2003

Mileage Category: I

Body Styles	TMV Pricing		
	Trade	Private	Dealer
4 Dr quattro AWD Sdn	47738	50160	54196

Options	Price	Options	Price
Heated Front and Rear Seats	+190	Power Rear Window Sunshade	+342
Navigation System	+1027	Power Solar Sunroof	+647
OnStar Telematics System	+684	Ski Sack	+183
Park Distance Control (Front and Rear)	+533	Tire Pressure Monitoring System	+297

Changes to Audi's hot-rod version of the A8 flagship are minimal for 2003. Among them are a new set of 18-inch alloys; birch or sycamore wood interior trim; new black dash and door panel trim; and "Audi Exclusive" embossment for the headrests. Also, the premium package now includes the navigation, parking assist and tire pressure monitoring systems. Three limited-edition color combinations will be offered -- a silver exterior with a burgundy interior, a Ming Blue exterior with a platinum interior and a black exterior with a caramel interior -- but the Alcantara leather package has been discontinued.

2002

Mileage Category: I

Body Styles	TMV Pricing		
	Trade	Private	Dealer
4 Dr quattro AWD Sdn	40957	43168	46852

Options	Price	Options	Price
Alcantra and Leather Package	+2381	Pearlescent Metallic Paint	+816
Heated Front and Rear Seats	+170	Power Rear Window Sunshade	+306
Navigation System	+918	Power Sunroof	+578
OnStar Telematics System	+611	Ski Sack	+163
Park Distance Control (Front and Rear)	+476	Tire Pressure Monitoring System	+265

The S8 is Audi's high-performance version of the flagship A8. For 2002, Audi has made an in-dash six-disc CD changer standard, and an OnStar telematics system and a tire-pressure monitor optional fare. It has also improved the stability control system and updated the navigation system software. New exterior and interior colors round out the changes.

2001

Mileage Category: I

Body Styles	TMV Pricing		
	Trade	Private	Dealer
4 Dr quattro AWD Sdn	34914	38223	41277

Options	Price	Options	Price
Alcantra and Leather Package	+2032	Power Rear Window Sunshade	+261
Navigation System	+743	Power Sunroof	+493
Park Distance Control (Front and Rear)	+406	Ski Sack	+138
Pearlescent Metallic Paint	+697		

The S8 is Audi's new high-performance version of the flagship A8. It's armed with more horsepower, a stiffer suspension and more powerful brakes. As with other 2001 A8s, the 2001 S8 has the Electronic Stabilization Program (ESP) and the new multifunctional steering wheel as standard equipment.

allroad quattro

2004

Mileage Category: I

Body Styles	TMV Pricing			Body Styles	TMV Pricing		
	Trade	Private	Dealer		Trade	Private	Dealer
4 Dr 4.2 AWD Wgn	36799	38524	41400	4 Dr Turbo AWD Wgn	29558	31184	33893

Options	Price	Options	Price
Automatic Dimming Rearview Mirror	+200	Park Distance Control (Rear)	+350
Automatic Dimming Sideview Mirror(s)	+200	Power Driver Seat w/Memory [Opt on Turbo]	+450
Bose Audio System	+600	Power Moonroof	+800
Garage Door Opener [Opt on Turbo]	+250	Power Retractable Mirrors	+225
Heated Front and Rear Seats	+500	Power Solar Sunroof [Opt on 4.2]	+750
Heated Steering Wheel [Opt on 4.2]	+200	Rear Side Airbag Restraints	+350
Leather Seats [Opt on Turbo]	+850	Satellite Radio System	+500
Navigation System	+1350	Steering Wheel Radio Controls [Opt on Turbo]	+150
OnStar Telematics System	+850	Xenon Headlamps [Opt on Turbo]	+400

A 4.2-liter V8 version of the allroad debuts, sending 300 horsepower through the tall wagon's quattro AWD system. Other changes include an additional console power point and a satellite radio prep package.

2003

Audi's rugged allroad quattro receives no changes, but the options list has been simplified. Rather than offering various "convenience," "preferred" and "warm weather" packages, a lengthy list of desirable features, including leather, xenons, sunroof and auto-dimming mirrors have been bundled into a handful of premium packages. A cold weather package includes front and rear seat heaters with a ski sack. The Parktronic parking assist system is now a stand-alone extra, and the rear-facing third-row seat has been deleted from the options list. Finally, for those who find the allroad's twin turbo V6 wanting, Audi is expected to introduce its 4.2-liter V8 sometime in the 2003 calendar year.

Mileage Category: I

Body Styles	TMV Pricing		
	Trade	Private	Dealer
4 Dr Turbo AWD Wgn	24420	26098	28895

Options	Price	Options	Price
17 Inch Wheels - Spoke	+723	Park Distance Control (Rear)	+266
Automatic 5-Speed Transmission	+799	Power Driver Seat w/Memory	+228
Automatic Dimming Sideview Mirror(s)	+152	Power Moonroof	+700
Bose Audio System	+571	Power Retractable Mirrors	+141
Heated Front and Rear Seats	+456	Rear Side Airbag Restraints	+266
Leather Seats	+669	Steering Wheel Radio Controls	+152
Navigation System	+1027	Tire Pressure Monitoring System	+297
OnStar Telematics System	+532	Xenon Headlamps	+266

2002

The height-adjustable allroad debuted last year to fill a slot left in Audi's lineup by the lack of an SUV. For 2002, a heated multifunctional steering wheel with Tiptronic is an option, as is an OnStar telematics system. Standard is an in-dash six-disc changer. Brushed aluminum-finish accents spruce up the interior.

Mileage Category: I

Body Styles	TMV Pricing		
	Trade	Private	Dealer
4 Dr Turbo AWD Wgn	22019	23564	26139

Options	Price	Options	Price
17 Inch Wheels	+646	Power Moonroof	+626
Automatic 5-Speed Transmission	+714	Power Retractable Mirrors	+126
Automatic Dimming Sideview Mirror(s)	+136	Power Solar Sunroof	+1088
Bose Audio System	+510	Rear Side Airbag Restraints	+238
Heated Front and Rear Seats	+374	Ski Sack	+119
Leather Seats	+599	Third Seat	+510
Navigation System	+918	Tire Pressure Monitoring System	+265
OnStar Telematics System	+475	Xenon Headlamps	+238
Park Distance Control (Rear)	+238		

2001

Based on the A6 platform, the height-adjustable allroad debuts this year to fill a slot left in Audi's lineup by the lack of an SUV. This luxury-station-wagon-turned-SUV is powered by the A6's 250-horsepower 2.7-liter V6 engine and features Audi's legendary quattro all-wheel-drive system. Audi blends these features in a distinctive vehicle that can handle a wide range of transportation needs.

Mileage Category: I

Body Styles	TMV Pricing		
	Trade	Private	Dealer
4 Dr Turbo AWD Wgn	20368	22550	24564

Options	Price	Options	Price
Automatic 5-Speed Transmission	+580	Power Moonroof	+580
Automatic Dimming Sideview Mirror(s)	+116	Power Passenger Seat w/Memory	+174
Bose Audio System	+435	Power Solar Sunroof	+987
Compact Disc Changer	+319	Rear Side Airbag Restraints	+203
Heated Front and Rear Seats	+261	Steering Wheel Radio Controls	+116
Navigation System	+743	Third Seat	+435
Park Distance Control (Rear)	+203	Xenon Headlamps	+276
Power Driver Seat w/Memory	+174		

Cabriolet

1998

Mileage Category: H

Body Styles	TMV Pricing		
	Trade	Private	Dealer
2 Dr STD Conv	8198	9939	11902

Options	Price	Options	Price
Leather Seats	+382	Special Factory Paint	+137
Metallic Paint	+137	Sport Seats	+134
Power Convertible Top	+348		

Based on the ancient 80/90 platform from the late '80s, the Cabriolet soldiers on with minimal change. A new steering wheel design is standard, and the Audi logo disappears from the side moldings.

1997

Base price drops a couple grand, but at the expense of the power top, burled walnut wood trim and leather seats. Opt for the Premium Equipment Package, and these items magically reappear. Casablanca White and Cactus Green join the list of paint colors, and three new top colors debut. Leather seats can be had in two new shades, too.

Mileage Category: H

Body Styles	TMV Pricing		
	Trade	Private	Dealer
2 Dr STD Conv	6512	8051	9932

Options	Price	Options	Price
Bucket Seats	+292	Power Convertible Top	+287
Leather Seats	+316		

1996

Better acceleration, a new radio, a new color and revised alloy wheels are the only changes.

Mileage Category: H

Body Styles	TMV Pricing		
	Trade	Private	Dealer
2 Dr STD Conv	5524	6927	8865

Options	Price
Bucket Seats	+262

1995

No changes.

Mileage Category: H

Body Styles	TMV Pricing		
	Trade	Private	Dealer
2 Dr STD Conv	4462	5700	7762

TT

2004

A more powerful TT 3.2 joins the lineup with a 250-horsepower V6 and a new "Direct Shift Gearbox," an automanual with technology that promises both smooth automatic operation and quick manual gear changes. A pair of gills at each front corner, a larger rear spoiler, unique wheels and a rear fascia accent distinguish the TT 3.2 from its stablemates. You can get the 3.2 in both coupe and roadster form. Also this year, xenon headlamps are now standard on all models.

Mileage Category: F

Body Styles	TMV Pricing		
	Trade	Private	Dealer
2 Dr 225hp quattro Turbo AWD Conv	29480	30941	33376
2 Dr 225hp quattro Turbo AWD Cpe	27415	28876	31311
2 Dr 250hp quattro Turbo AWD Conv	33393	35042	37789

Body Styles	TMV Pricing		
	Trade	Private	Dealer
2 Dr 250hp quattro Turbo AWD Cpe	31180	32829	35576
2 Dr Turbo Conv	26345	27806	30241
2 Dr Turbo Cpe	24870	26331	28766

Options	Price	Options	Price
18 Inch Wheels [Opt on 225hp, 250hp]	+775	Heated Front Seats	+550
Bose Audio System	+700	Navigation System	+1350
Compact Disc Changer	+400	Power Convertible Top	+800
Forged Alloy Wheels [Opt on 225hp]	+600	Special Factory Paint	+1000
Garage Door Opener	+150	Special Leather Seat Trim	+1000

2003

Never considered hard-edged performance cars in their respective segments, Audi's stylish 2003 TT coupe and roadster finally offer an automatic transmission -- and a six-speed unit at that. Unfortunately, it's available only on the front-drive, 180-horsepower coupe and roadster. In other news, the quattro version of the 180-hp coupe is no longer offered and the remaining cars get a new front grille and revised exterior badging. Cast-alloy wheel designs have been updated, and, this year, you'll be able to get optional 17-inch all-season tires on all TTs (you could only get summer performance tires in this size previously); 18-inch all-season rubber is available on 225-hp models. Finally, the optional Bose sound system gets AudioPilot technology, which uses volume and tonal adjustments to compensate for outside noise.

Mileage Category: F

Body Styles	TMV Pricing		
	Trade	Private	Dealer
2 Dr 225hp quattro Turbo AWD Conv	24258	25896	28625
2 Dr 225hp quattro Turbo AWD Cpe	23354	24931	27558

Body Styles	TMV Pricing		
	Trade	Private	Dealer
2 Dr Turbo Conv	22431	23945	26468
2 Dr Turbo Cpe	20933	22346	24701

Options	Price	Options	Price
18 Inch Wheels [Opt on 225hp]	+590	Navigation System	+1027
Bose Mini Disc Player	+418	Power Convertible Top [Opt on 180hp Conv]	+609
Compact Disc Changer	+361	Special Leather Seat Trim	+761
Heated Front Seats	+342	Xenon Headlamps	+380

2002

Two new colors join the TT palette, Brilliant White and Moro Blue. HomeLink is available as an option, and the navigation system gets an upgrade, as does the stereo. A blue top is available for the roadster, and the trunk gets an interior release. In the spring of 2002, Audi will appeal to collectors and offer the ALMS (American Le Mans Series) Commemorative Edition TT Coupe in a limited run of 1,000 cars. This special TT Coupe will come in two configurations -- a Misano Red exterior with a Silver Silk napa leather interior or an Avus Silver exterior with a Brilliant Red interior. Although the ALMS is essentially a more exquisitely trimmed version of the 225-hp coupe, Audi will fit it with 18-inch wheels and Z-rated 225/40 high-performance tires.

Mileage Category: F

Body Styles	TMV Pricing		
	Trade	Private	Dealer
2 Dr 225hp ALMS Edition quattro Turbo AWD Cpe	21955	23640	26448
2 Dr 225hp quattro Turbo AWD Conv	21259	22890	25608
2 Dr 225hp quattro Turbo AWD Cpe	19467	20960	23449

Options	Price
17 Inch Wheels [Std on 225hp ALMS]	+340
Bose Audio System	+420
Compact Disc Changer	+356
Heated Front Seats	+306

Body Styles	TMV Pricing		
	Trade	Private	Dealer
2 Dr Turbo Conv	18174	19569	21893
2 Dr Turbo Cpe	16974	18252	20381
2 Dr quattro Turbo AWD Cpe	17464	18804	21037

Options	Price
Navigation System	+918
Power Convertible Top [Std on 225hp]	+544
Xenon Headlamps [Std on 225hp ALMS]	+340

2001

For 2001 Audi introduces the TT Roadster, which retains the same interior and chassis as the coupe. Makes sense, as the coupe was designed with the roadster version in mind. There's also a 225-horsepower quattro version for both the coupe and convertible. The entire Audi lineup receives a new 4-year/50,000-mile limited warranty and no-charge scheduled maintenance, a 12-year limited warranty against corrosion perforation and 24-hour roadside assistance for four years.

Mileage Category: F

Body Styles	TMV Pricing		
	Trade	Private	Dealer
2 Dr 225hp quattro Turbo AWD Conv	18457	20935	23222
2 Dr 225hp quattro Turbo AWD Cpe	17078	19364	21474
2 Dr Turbo Conv	15900	18034	20004

Options	Price
17 Inch Wheels - Spoke	+290
6-Speed Transmission	+522
Bose Audio System	+348
Compact Disc Changer	+304

Body Styles	TMV Pricing		
	Trade	Private	Dealer
2 Dr Turbo Cpe	14816	16806	18642
2 Dr quattro Turbo AWD Cpe	15251	17299	19189

Options	Price
Heated Front Seats	+138
Navigation System	+743
Power Convertible Top	+464
Xenon Headlamps	+232

2000

Audi introduces the funky-looking TT Coupe for the 2000 model year. A turbocharged, 1.8-liter engine squeezes out 180 horsepower for this avant-garde sports car.

Mileage Category: F

Body Styles	TMV Pricing		
	Trade	Private	Dealer
2 Dr Turbo Cpe	11350	13201	15015

Options	Price
Bose Audio System	+315
Compact Disc Changer	+267
Heated Front Seats	+121

Body Styles	TMV Pricing		
	Trade	Private	Dealer
2 Dr quattro Turbo AWD Cpe	12564	14613	16622

Options	Price
Performance/Handling Package	+306
Xenon Headlamps	+204

3 Series

Mileage Category: H

Body Styles	TMV Pricing		
	Trade	Private	Dealer
2 Dr 325Ci Conv	30432	32118	34928
2 Dr 325Ci Cpe	22470	23730	25831
2 Dr 330Ci Conv	34427	36235	39249
2 Dr 330Ci Cpe	26674	28135	30570
4 Dr 325i Sdn	22183	23532	25779

Options	Price
18 Inch Wheels [Opt on 330Ci]	+1000
6-Speed Sequential Semi-Manual Transmission [Opt on 325Ci, 330Ci, 325i, 330i]	+1500
Automatic 5-Speed Transmission	+1275
Automatic Dimming Rearview Mirror	+400
Hardtop Roof	+2295
Harman Kardon Audio System [Std on 330Ci, 330i, 330xi]	+675
Headlight Washers	+250
Heated Front Seats	+350
Leather Seats [Std on 330Ci Conv]	+900
Metallic Paint	+475
Navigation System	+1800
Park Distance Control (Rear)	+350
Performance/Handling Package [Opt on 330Ci, 330i]	+3600

Body Styles	TMV Pricing		
	Trade	Private	Dealer
4 Dr 325i Wgn	22584	23882	26044
4 Dr 325xi AWD Sdn	22165	23468	25640
4 Dr 325xi AWD Wgn	23200	24586	26895
4 Dr 330i Sdn	25882	27336	29760
4 Dr 330xi AWD Wgn	26178	27439	29541

Options	Price
Power Convertible Top [Opt on 325Ci Conv]	+1600
Power Driver Seat [Opt on 325Ci, 325i, 325xi]	+995
Power Driver Seat w/Memory [Opt on 325Ci Cpe, 325i, 325xi]	+700
Power Moonroof [Std on 325i, 325xi Wgn]	+700
Power Passenger Seat [Opt on 325Ci Cpe, 325i, 325xi]	+600
Rear Side Airbag Restraints	+385
Ski Sack	+150
Split Folding Rear Seat [Std on Cpe, Wgn]	+300
Sport Package	+600
Telematics System	+750
Trip Computer [Opt on 325i, 325xi]	+300
Wood Interior Trim	+400
Xenon Headlamps	+700

A six-speed SMG (Sequential Manual Gearbox) transmission is now optional on select 3 Series models, while a five-speed Steptronic automatic is now offered with the 330i Performance Package. Rain-sensing wipers, automatic headlights and hands-free wireless cell phone capability are now standard features on the sedan and wagon. There are new alloy wheel designs for the 325i, 325xi and 330xi Sport Package. All 330i sedans get a revised grille -- a new black grille instead of silver, with a lower grille combination of body color and black. All 3 Series coupes and convertibles receive a revised front fascia, plus new front and rear bumper contours, Adaptive headlamps and taillights and new designs for both the standard and optional wheels. Interior changes are limited to a revised climate control panel. Finally, Sirius Satellite Radio is now available as an accessory on all 3 Series models.

Mileage Category: H

Body Styles	TMV Pricing		
	Trade	Private	Dealer
2 Dr 325Ci Conv	28530	30066	32627
2 Dr 325Ci Cpe	20596	21868	23988
2 Dr 330Ci Conv	32588	34239	36991
2 Dr 330Ci Cpe	24672	26196	28737
4 Dr 325i Sdn	18981	20153	22107

Options	Price
18 Inch Wheels [Opt on 330]	+707
Automatic 5-Speed Transmission	+1002
Hardtop Roof [Opt on Conv]	+1803
Harman Kardon Audio System [Opt on 325]	+530
Heated Front Seats	+354
Leather Seats [Opt on 325]	+1139
Metallic Paint	+373
Navigation System	+1414
Park Distance Control (Rear) [Opt on 330]	+275
Power Convertible Top [Opt on 325Ci Conv]	+589

Body Styles	TMV Pricing		
	Trade	Private	Dealer
4 Dr 325i Wgn	20250	21501	23585
4 Dr 325xi AWD Sdn	20333	21589	23683
4 Dr 325xi AWD Wgn	21283	22597	24788
4 Dr 330i Sdn	23133	24563	26945
4 Dr 330xi AWD Sdn	25501	27076	29701

Options	Price
Power Driver Seat w/Memory [Opt on 325i, 325Ci]	+369
Power Moonroof	+825
Power Passenger Seat [Opt on 325]	+236
Rain Sensing Windshield Wipers [Opt on 325]	+118
Rear Side Airbag Restraints	+303
Ski Sack	+157
Split Folding Rear Seat [Opt on Sdn]	+373
Sport Package	+471
Trip Computer [Opt on 325i]	+236
Xenon Headlamps	+550

For 2003, BMW will finally offer a DVD-based navigation system -- meaning that you won't have to give up an in-dash CD player if you opt for the nav system. Other changes include a standard front armrest for all 325 models, as well as a rear center headrest for all sedans and wagons. Additionally, all wagons will come with a moonroof. In terms of options, the Premium Package for all 325s now includes automatic headlights and rain-sensing wipers, and the Sport Package for the 330xi includes double-spoke alloy wheels and run-flat tires.

Mileage Category: H

Body Styles	TMV Pricing		
	Trade	Private	Dealer
2 Dr 325Ci Conv	25657	27258	29925
2 Dr 325Ci Cpe	18876	20054	22018
2 Dr 330Ci Conv	29620	31317	34145
2 Dr 330Ci Cpe	21899	23266	25543
4 Dr 325i Sdn	17306	18386	20185

Options	Price
17 Inch Wheels	+216
18 Inch Wheels	+647

Body Styles	TMV Pricing		
	Trade	Private	Dealer
4 Dr 325i Wgn	18419	19568	21482
4 Dr 325xi AWD Sdn	18859	20036	21998
4 Dr 325xi AWD Wgn	19440	20653	22674
4 Dr 330i Sdn	21111	22429	24626
4 Dr 330xi AWD Sdn	22952	24385	26773

Options	Price
Automatic 5-Speed Transmission	+916
Hardtop Roof	+1649

BMW has seen fit to give the sedans and wagons a facelift for 2002. An in-dash CD player finally makes it onto the standard features list. The center stack has been altered to accommodate the new automatic climate controls. Steptronic automanual operation has been altered so that you move the transmission lever forward for downshifts and backward for upshifts. Bi-xenon headlamps are on the options list so that both low and high beams can glow a cold blue and can be set to automatic operation. Rear side airbags are available for coupes and convertibles. Two new colors, Electric Red and Gray Green (and a Natural Brown interior leather) join the color spectrum.

2002 (cont'd)

Options	Price
Harman Kardon Audio System [Std on 330]	+485
Heated Front Seats	+251
Leather Seats [Std on 330Ci Conv]	+1042
Metallic Paint	+341
Navigation System	+1293
Park Distance Control (Rear)	+251
Power Convertible Top [Std on 330Ci Conv]	+539
Power Driver Seat w/Memory [Std on 330]	+338

Options	Price
Power Moonroof	+754
Power Passenger Seat [Std on 330]	+338
Rear Side Airbag Restraints	+277
Ski Sack	+180
Sport Package	+431
Trip Computer [Opt on 325]	+216
Xenon Headlamps	+503

2001

A boost in engine displacement and technology, plus an available all-wheel-drive system, keeps BMW's venerable 3 Series at the top of its game in the competitive entry-level luxury market. Larger wheels and brakes are part of the engine upgrade. Addressing concerns that their cars are low on feature content, BMW adds automatic climate control, foglights, heated mirrors and cruise control as standard equipment for all 325 models. The 330s get power seats and a premium audio package at no extra cost.

Mileage Category: H

Body Styles	TMV Pricing		
	Trade	Private	Dealer
2 Dr 325Ci Conv	22719	25024	27151
2 Dr 325Ci Cpe	16280	17930	19453
2 Dr 330Ci Conv	25564	27951	30154
2 Dr 330Ci Cpe	18906	20824	22593
4 Dr 325i Sdn	15445	17011	18457

Body Styles	TMV Pricing		
	Trade	Private	Dealer
4 Dr 325i Wgn	16037	17662	19162
4 Dr 325xi AWD Sdn	16274	17924	19447
4 Dr 325xi AWD Wgn	16900	18614	20196
4 Dr 330i Sdn	17780	19585	21251
4 Dr 330xi AWD Sdn	19279	21233	23036

Options	Price
AM/FM/CD Audio System	+126
Automatic 5-Speed Transmission	+802
Hardtop Roof	+1444
Harman Kardon Audio System	+425
Heated Front Seats	+315
Leather Seats	+675
Metallic Paint	+299
Navigation System	+1133
Park Distance Control (Rear)	+220

Options	Price
Power Convertible Top [Opt on 325Ci Conv]	+472
Power Driver Seat w/Memory [Std on 330Ci,Conv]	+296
Power Moonroof	+661
Power Passenger Seat [Std on 330Ci,Conv]	+296
Rear Side Airbag Restraints	+242
Ski Sack	+166
Sport Package	+378
Trip Computer [Std on 330,325Ci]	+189
Xenon Headlamps	+315

2000

For 2000 3 Series coupes, convertibles and wagons are all new; the hatchback has been discontinued. After last year's complete redesign, 2000 sedans see only minor improvements.

Mileage Category: H

Body Styles	TMV Pricing		
	Trade	Private	Dealer
2 Dr 323Ci Conv	17596	19771	21902
2 Dr 323Ci Cpe	13466	15130	16761
2 Dr 328Ci Cpe	15052	16913	18737

Body Styles	TMV Pricing		
	Trade	Private	Dealer
4 Dr 323i Sdn	12619	14178	15706
4 Dr 323iT Wgn	13477	15143	16775
4 Dr 328i Sdn	15049	16908	18731

Options	Price
AM/FM/CD Audio System	+116
AM/FM/Cassette/CD Audio System	+267
Automatic 5-Speed Transmission	+500
Compact Disc Changer	+272
Cruise Control [Opt on 323i,323iT]	+129
Fog Lights [Opt on 323i,323iT]	+121
Hardtop Roof	+961
Harman Kardon Audio System	+314
Heated Front Seats	+140
Leather Seats	+570
Metallic Paint	+221
Navigation System	+838

Options	Price
Park Distance Control (Rear) [Opt on 323iT,328]	+186
Power Driver Seat w/Memory [Opt on 323]	+252
Power Moonroof	+488
Power Passenger Seat [Opt on 323]	+252
Radio Navigation System	+559
Rear Side Airbag Restraints	+205
Ski Sack [Std on 323Ci]	+140
Split Folding Rear Seat [Opt on 323i,328i]	+221
Spoke Wheels	+232
Sport Suspension [Std on 323Ci,328Ci]	+174
Trip Computer [Opt on 323i,323iT]	+123
Xenon Headlamps	+232

1999

The 3 Series sedans redesigned for 1999, offering 5 Series style along with more room for rear-seat passengers. Coupes and convertibles remain on old platform.

Mileage Category: H

Body Styles	TMV Pricing		
	Trade	Private	Dealer
2 Dr 318ti Hbk	8244	9446	10698
2 Dr 323i Conv	14177	16245	18398
2 Dr 323is Cpe	11570	13258	15015
2 Dr 328i Conv	15701	17992	20377

Body Styles	TMV Pricing		
	Trade	Private	Dealer
2 Dr 328is Cpe	12828	14699	16646
4 Dr 323i Sdn	10753	12321	13954
4 Dr 328i Sdn	12889	14769	16726

Options	Price
AM/FM/Cassette/CD Audio System	+217
Alarm System [Opt on 323]	+123
Aluminum/Alloy Wheels [Opt on 323i]	+243
Automatic 4-Speed Transmission	+368
Automatic 5-Speed Transmission [Opt on Sdn]	+454
Compact Disc Changer	+245
Folding Canvas Roof [Opt on 318ti]	+605
Hardtop Roof	+867
Harman Kardon Audio System	+324
Leather Seats	+463
Metallic Paint	+180
Navigation System	+544

Options	Price
Park Distance Control (Rear) [Opt on 328i]	+168
Power Convertible Top	+510
Power Driver Seat w/Memory [Opt on 323i]	+228
Power Moonroof	+397
Power Passenger Seat [Opt on 323i]	+228
Rear Side Airbag Restraints	+185
Rollover Protection System [Opt on Conv]	+696
Split Folding Rear Seat [Opt on Sdn]	+228
Sport Package	+265
Sport Suspension [Std on 318ti]	+142
Xenon Headlamps [Opt on Sdn]	+190

1998

Mileage Category: H

Body Styles	TMV Pricing		
	Trade	Private	Dealer
2 Dr 318ti Hbk	5784	6769	7879
2 Dr 323i Conv	10520	12311	14331
2 Dr 323is Cpe	8047	9416	10960
2 Dr 328i Conv	12963	15170	17658

Body Styles	TMV Pricing		
	Trade	Private	Dealer
2 Dr 328is Cpe	9695	11345	13205
4 Dr 318i Sdn	7013	8206	9552
4 Dr 328i Sdn	9571	11200	13037

Options	Price
AM/FM/Cassette/CD Audio System	+190
Aluminum/Alloy Wheels [Opt on 318i,318ti]	+197
Automatic 4-Speed Transmission	+321
Compact Disc Changer	+213
Folding Canvas Roof [Opt on 318ti]	+527
Front Side Airbag Restraints [Opt on 318ti]	+127
Hardtop Roof	+755
Harman Kardon Audio System	+222

Options	Price
Leather Seats	+403
Limited Slip Differential	+115
Metallic Paint	+157
Power Convertible Top	+444
Power Sunroof	+312
Rollover Protection System	+605
Sport Package	+230
Sport Suspension	+124

BMW swaps out the four-cylinder engine in the 318 coupe and convertible for a 168-horsepower 2.5-liter inline six -- these cars become the 323is coupe and 323i convertible (why it's "323" and not "325," we'll never know). Meanwhile, the 318i sedan and 318ti hatchback continue on unchanged. All cars get standard side airbags this year, except the 318ti, on which they are optional.

1997

Mileage Category: H

Body Styles	TMV Pricing		
	Trade	Private	Dealer
2 Dr 318i Conv	7408	8949	10832
2 Dr 318is Cpe	6132	7408	8967
2 Dr 318ti Hbk	4713	5694	6892
2 Dr 328i Conv	10295	12437	15054

Body Styles	TMV Pricing		
	Trade	Private	Dealer
2 Dr 328is Cpe	7554	9125	11046
4 Dr 318i Sdn	5585	6746	8165
4 Dr 328i Sdn	7420	8963	10849

Options	Price
AM/FM/Cassette/CD Audio System	+170
Aluminum/Alloy Wheels [Opt on 318i,318ti]	+177
Automatic 4-Speed Transmission	+289
Hardtop Roof	+680
Leather Seats [Std on 328i Conv]	+348

Options	Price
Metallic Paint	+141
Power Sunroof	+281
Premium Audio System [Opt on Cpe,Sdn]	+200
Rollover Protection System	+502
Sport Package	+311

Traction control and heated side mirrors are now standard across the line. Additionally, all cars receive minor styling revisions to the grille and rear fascia, as well as in the cockpit.

1996

Mileage Category: H

Body Styles	TMV Pricing		
	Trade	Private	Dealer
2 Dr 318i Conv	6116	7482	9368
2 Dr 318is Cpe	5111	6252	7827
2 Dr 318ti Hbk	4054	4960	6210
2 Dr 328i Conv	8237	10076	12615

Body Styles	TMV Pricing		
	Trade	Private	Dealer
2 Dr 328is Cpe	6748	8254	10334
4 Dr 318i Sdn	4891	5983	7492
4 Dr 328i Sdn	6456	7897	9888

Options	Price
AM/FM/Cassette/CD Audio System	+158
Aluminum/Alloy Wheels [Opt on 318ti,318i]	+165
Automatic 4-Speed Transmission	+298
Hardtop Roof	+631
Leather Seats [Std on 328i Conv]	+323

Options	Price
Metallic Paint	+131
Power Sunroof [Opt on 318ti]	+261
Premium Audio System [Opt on Cpe,Sdn]	+206
Rollover Protection System	+443
Sport Package	+198

BMW's highly acclaimed 3 Series receives new engines across the board. The six-cylinder models drop the 325 designation for 328, thanks to a new 2.8-liter inline six. While the new six offers a negligible gain in horsepower (now 190), acceleration is significantly improved by a 14 percent increase in torque (now up to 207). To go along with the heartier engine, 328 models get vented rear disc brakes to minimize brake fade. The 318 models keep the 318 name despite an increase in engine displacement to 1.9 liters, which yields a slight increase in torque. Automatic climate control is standard across the line, except in the 318ti, and upgraded sound systems are optional on all models.

BMW
3 Series/M3

1995

BMW adds a more compact two-door hatchback called the 318ti to the lineup for 1995. With a chopped tail and the semi-trailing arm rear suspension from the previous-generation 3 Series (E30) aboard, the 318ti is intended to attract entry-level buyers. A 138-horsepower 1.8-liter four-cylinder resides under the hood, and the interior decor is rather austere compared with the increasingly plush innards of other 3 Series cars. Antilock brakes, alloy wheels and a five-speed manual gearbox are standard; a four-speed automatic is optional. Also this year, a couple new option packages (premium and sport) allow buyers to give their cars a distinct luxury or performance flavor.

Mileage Category: H

Body Styles	TMV Pricing		
	Trade	Private	Dealer
2 Dr 318i Conv	4382	5351	6967
2 Dr 318is Cpe	4013	4901	6381
2 Dr 318ti Hbk	3113	3802	4951
2 Dr 325i Conv	5948	7264	9458

Options	Price
AM/FM/Cassette/CD Audio System	+123
Aluminum/Alloy Wheels [Opt on 318i Sdn]	+128
Automatic 4-Speed Transmission	+209
er	+132
Leather Seats [Opt on 318i,318is,318ti]	+252
Limited Slip Differential	+75

Body Styles	TMV Pricing		
	Trade	Private	Dealer
2 Dr 325is Cpe	4859	5934	7726
4 Dr 318i Sdn	3580	4371	5690
4 Dr 325i Sdn	4797	5858	7626

Options	Price
Power Sunroof [Opt on 318ti]	+204
Premium Audio System [Opt on 318]	+145
Rollover Protection System [Opt on Conv]	+345
Sport Package	+154
Sport Suspension	+81
Trip Computer	+75

M3

2004

BMW Assist is now an available option for immediate roadside assistance, and Sirius Satellite Radio is newly available as a dealer-installed accessory.

Mileage Category: F

Body Styles	TMV Pricing		
	Trade	Private	Dealer
2 Dr STD Conv	45373	47809	51869

Options	Price
19 Inch Wheels	+1750
6-Speed Sequential Semi-Manual Transmission	+2400
Aluminum/Alloy Interior Trim	+300
Hardtop Roof [Opt on Conv]	+2295
Harman Kardon Audio System	+675
Heated Front Seats	+450
Metallic Paint	+475
Nappa Leather Seat Trim [Opt on Cpe]	+1200
Navigation System	+1800

Body Styles	TMV Pricing		
	Trade	Private	Dealer
2 Dr STD Cpe	38484	40921	44982

Options	Price
Park Distance Control (Rear)	+350
Power Driver Seat w/Memory [Opt on Cpe]	+700
Power Moonroof [Opt on Cpe]	+700
Power Passenger Seat [Opt on Cpe]	+470
Power Passenger Seat w/Memory [Opt on Coupe]	+700
Rear Side Airbag Restraints	+385
Ski Sack	+200
Telematics System [Std on Conv]	+750
Xenon Headlamps	+700

2003

For 2003, BMW will offer a DVD-based navigation system -- meaning that you won't have to give up an in-dash CD player if you opt for the nav system. Additionally, automatic headlights and rain-sensing wipers are now standard, while aluminum interior trim is a new stand-alone option. The power seat package has been excised from the coupe's option list, so you'll have to spring for the pricey premium package if you want front seats (these come standard on the convertible).

Mileage Category: F

Body Styles	TMV Pricing		
	Trade	Private	Dealer
2 Dr STD Conv	41342	43521	47153

Options	Price
19 Inch Wheels	+1375
6-Speed Sequential Semi-Manual Transmission	+1886
Aluminum/Alloy Interior Trim	+236
Hardtop Roof [Opt on Conv]	+1803
Harman Kardon Audio System	+530
Heated Front Seats	+354
Metallic Paint	+373
Nappa Leather Seat Trim [Opt on Cpe]	+864

Body Styles	TMV Pricing		
	Trade	Private	Dealer
2 Dr STD Cpe	36084	37986	41155

Options	Price
Navigation System	+1414
Park Distance Control (Rear)	+275
Power Driver Seat w/Memory [Opt on Cpe]	+369
Power Moonroof [Opt on Cpe]	+825
Power Passenger Seat [Opt on Cpe]	+236
Rear Side Airbag Restraints	+303
Ski Sack	+157
Xenon Headlamps	+550

2002

An optional sequential manual gearbox makes its way into the M3s, which allows the driver to shift with almost instantaneous precision without a clutch. A CD player becomes standard, the automatic climate control has been revised and rear-seat side airbags are optional for both the coupe and convertible.

Mileage Category: F

Body Styles	TMV Pricing		
	Trade	Private	Dealer
2 Dr STD Conv	35216	37256	40657

Options	Price
6-Speed Sequential Semi-Manual Transmission	+1725
Hardtop Roof	+1649
Harman Kardon Audio System	+485
Heated Front Seats	+251
Metallic Paint	+341
Nappa Leather Seat Trim	+790
Navigation System	+1293

Body Styles	TMV Pricing		
	Trade	Private	Dealer
2 Dr STD Cpe	30591	32364	35319

Options	Price
Park Distance Control (Rear)	+251
Power Driver Seat w/Memory [Opt on Cpe]	+338
Power Moonroof	+754
Power Passenger Seat [Opt on Cpe]	+216
Rear Side Airbag Restraints	+277
Ski Sack	+180
Xenon Headlamps	+503

2001

Powered by a 333-horsepower inline six, the athletic coupe and convertible possess the appeal, functionality and performance to back up their "M" badges.

Mileage Category: F

Body Styles	TMV Pricing		
	Trade	Private	Dealer
2 Dr STD Conv	32908	35783	38437

Options	Price
AM/FM/CD Audio System	+126
Hardtop Roof	+1444
Harman Kardon Audio System	+425
Heated Front Seats	+166
Metallic Paint	+299
Navigation System	+1133
Park Distance Control (Rear)	+220

Body Styles	TMV Pricing		
	Trade	Private	Dealer
2 Dr STD Cpe	27714	30134	32368

Options	Price
Power Driver Seat w/Memory [Opt on Cpe]	+296
Power Moonroof	+661
Power Passenger Seat [Opt on Cpe]	+296
Rear Side Airbag Restraints	+242
Ski Sack	+166
Xenon Headlamps	+315

1999

Mileage Category: F

Body Styles	TMV Pricing		
	Trade	Private	Dealer
2 Dr STD Conv	22126	24812	27608

Options	Price
AM/FM/Cassette/CD Audio System	+269
Automatic 5-Speed Transmission	+477
Compact Disc Changer	+219
Forged Alloy Wheels	+372
Hardtop Roof	+913
Harman Kardon Audio System	+269

Body Styles	TMV Pricing		
	Trade	Private	Dealer
2 Dr STD Cpe	17873	20043	22301

Options	Price
Heated Front Seats	+199
Power Driver Seat	+228
Power Moonroof	+378
Power Passenger Seat	+228
Rear Spoiler	+140
Trip Computer	+147

Production of M3 four-door sedans ends this year as BMW concentrates on selling the M3 coupe and recently introduced M3 convertible. These models go unchanged for 1999.

1998

BMW further expands the M3 lineup by adding a four-seat convertible version for enthusiasts who crave open-air motoring. Like the M3 sedan, the convertible is available with either a manual or automatic transmission. Napa leather upholstery and a rollover protection system are standard. All M3s get standard side airbags this year.

Mileage Category: F

Body Styles	TMV Pricing		
	Trade	Private	Dealer
2 Dr STD Conv	18319	20675	23332
2 Dr STD Cpe	14710	16602	18735

Options	Price
Automatic 5-Speed Transmission [Opt on Conv,Sdn]	+395
Compact Disc Changer	+213
Forged Alloy Wheels	+308
Hardtop Roof [Opt on Conv]	+755
Harman Kardon Audio System [Opt on Cpe,Sdn]	+198

Body Styles	TMV Pricing		
	Trade	Private	Dealer
4 Dr STD Sdn	14215	16043	18104

Options	Price
Metallic Paint	+157
Power Driver Seat	+177
Power Passenger Seat	+177
Power Sunroof [Opt on Cpe,Sdn]	+312
Rear Spoiler [Opt on Cpe,Sdn]	+115

1997

To the delight of sports car enthusiasts who need the practicality of four doors, BMW releases a sedan version of the M3. Identical to the coupe in virtually every respect, the M3 sedan is available with either a five-speed manual or five-speed automatic transmission. Note that the coupe is no longer available with the automatic.

Body Styles	TMV Pricing		
	Trade	Private	Dealer
2 Dr STD Cpe	12285	14039	16183

Options	Price
Automatic 5-Speed Transmission [Opt on Sdn]	+355
Compact Disc Changer [Opt on Sdn]	+192
Forged Alloy Wheels [Opt on Sdn]	+277
Harman Kardon Audio System [Opt on Sdn]	+200

Body Styles	TMV Pricing		
	Trade	Private	Dealer
4 Dr STD Sdn	11033	12608	14534

Options	Price
Metallic Paint	+141
Power Sunroof	+281
Premium Audio System [Opt on Cpe]	+200

1996

The M3's inline six grows to 3.2 liters of displacement and gains 11 extra pound-feet of torque (for a total of 236); peak torque is now accessible at 3,800 rpm as opposed to 4,200. Otherwise, this superb performance coupe is unchanged for 1996.

Mileage Category: F

Body Styles	TMV Pricing		
	Trade	Private	Dealer
2 Dr STD Cpe	10273	11822	13960

Options	Price	Options	Price
Power Sunroof	+261	Premium Audio System	+206

BMW
M3/5 Series

1995

After a three-year hiatus, the high-performance M3 makes its return midway through the life cycle of the E36 generation of BMW's 3 Series line. While its predecessor was a narrowly focused track car, this sophisticated two-door coupe is an exceptional road machine with a flexible 240-horsepower, 3.0-liter inline six and an imperturbable chassis. A limited slip differential and 17-inch wheels with low-profile performance tires are standard; inside, front sport seats come dressed in cloth and suede (Nappa leather is optional). Initially, the M3 is available only with a five-speed manual, but later in the model year, BMW adds an optional five-speed automatic. Additionally, buyers can opt for a luxury package that provides a less aggressive wheel design, power seat adjustments and leather and wood inlays for the door panels and console.

Mileage Category: F

Body Styles	TMV Pricing		
	Trade	Private	Dealer
2 Dr STD Cpe	8574	9747	11701

Options	Price	Options	Price
Automatic 5-Speed Transmission	+257	Power Sunroof	+204
Compact Disc Changer	+132	Rear Spoiler	+75
Power Driver Seat	+77	Trip Computer	+75
Power Passenger Seat	+77		

5 Series

2004

The 5 Series has been completely redesigned for 2004. Along with a new V8 and the iDrive vehicle management system, buyers can expect even greater handling from this premier midsize sedan than before.

Mileage Category: I

Body Styles	TMV Pricing			Body Styles	TMV Pricing		
	Trade	Private	Dealer		Trade	Private	Dealer
4 Dr 525i Sdn	28773	30470	33299	4 Dr 545i Sdn	41060	42945	46086
4 Dr 530i Sdn	33228	34578	36828				

Options	Price	Options	Price
6-Speed Sequential Semi-Manual Transmission [Opt on 525i, 530i]	+1500	Navigation System	+1800
6-Speed Transmission [Opt on 545i]	+3300	Park Distance Control (Front and Rear)	+700
Adaptive Cruise Control	+2200	Power Passenger Seat w/Memory [Opt on 530i, 545i]	+300
Automatic 6-Speed Transmission [Opt on 525i, 530i]	+1275	Power Rear Window Sunshade	+400
Automatic Dimming Rearview Mirror [Opt on 525i, 530i]	+400	Premium Audio System	+1800
Comfort Seats [Opt on 530i, 545i]	+900	Rear Heater	+350
Garage Door Opener [Std on 545i]	+300	Rear Side Airbag Restraints	+385
Headlight Washers	+250	Satellite Radio System	+595
Heads-Up Display	+1000	Split Folding Rear Seat	+400
Heated Front Seats	+350	Sport Package	+3300
Heated Steering Wheel	+150	Xenon Headlamps [Std on 545i]	+800
Leather Seats [Std on 545i]	+1000		

2003

This is your last chance to get a traditionally styled 5 Series -- next year, its styling becomes more closely aligned with the controversial 7 Series. For now, BMW will offer a DVD-based navigation system for the existing 5 Series -- but alas, you must still give up an in-dash CD player if you opt for the nav system. Besides that, rear head protection airbags (optional last year) are now standard across the line. Additionally, all six-cylinder models get a standard moonroof. Standard on the manual-shift 540i (and optional with the automatic) is a new sport package that includes 18-inch wheels, a revised sport suspension, front and rear spoilers, visible exhaust outlets, black side molding, a black headliner, titanium-ringed gauges and an M footrest for the driver. Finally, the 525i gets a new alloy wheel design, and its premium package now includes rain-sensing wipers.

Mileage Category: I

Body Styles	TMV Pricing			Body Styles	TMV Pricing		
	Trade	Private	Dealer		Trade	Private	Dealer
4 Dr 525i Sdn	25052	26558	29069	4 Dr 540i Sdn	31725	33633	36812
4 Dr 525i Wgn	24194	25649	28074	4 Dr 540i Wgn	32032	33958	37169
4 Dr 530i Sdn	26082	27651	30266				

Options	Price	Options	Price
6-Speed Transmission [Opt on 540]	+3143	Park Distance Control (Front and Rear)	+550
Automatic 5-Speed Transmission [Opt on 525,530]	+1002	Power Rear Window Sunshade [Opt on Wgn]	+452
Automatic Load Leveling [Opt on Wgn]	+597	Rear Side Airbag Restraints	+303
Comfort Seats [Opt on 540]	+943	Ski Sack [Opt on Sdn]	+157
Heated Front Seats	+354	Split Folding Rear Seat [Opt on Sdn]	+373
Hi-Fi Audio System	+943	Sport Package	+1572
Leather Seats [Opt on 525,530]	+1061	Trip Computer [Opt on 525,530]	+177
Navigation System	+1414	Xenon Headlamps [Opt on 525,530]	+393

2002

This year a standard CD player, climate control and power seats. The 4.4-liter V8 of the 540 now makes 290 horsepower, up 8 from last year. Rear side-impact airbags are now a no-charge option, rather than standard.

Mileage Category: I

Body Styles	TMV Pricing			Body Styles	TMV Pricing		
	Trade	Private	Dealer		Trade	Private	Dealer
4 Dr 525i Sdn	21676	23061	25370	4 Dr 525i Wgn	20866	22177	24361

Body Styles	TMV Pricing		
	Trade	Private	Dealer
4 Dr 530i Sdn	22650	24073	26444
4 Dr 540i Sdn	28582	30409	33453

Options	Price
17 Inch Wheels	+216
6-Speed Transmission [Opt on 540]	+1940
Automatic 5-Speed Transmission [Std on 540]	+916
Automatic Dimming Rearview Mirror [Std on 540]	+133
Automatic Load Leveling [Std on 540]	+546
Comfort Seats	+862
Digital Audio System	+862
Heated Front Seats	+287
Leather Seats [Std on 540]	+970

Body Styles	TMV Pricing		
	Trade	Private	Dealer
4 Dr 540i Wgn	27987	29776	32756

Options	Price
Navigation System	+1293
Park Distance Control (Front and Rear)	+503
Power Moonroof [Std on 540]	+754
Power Rear Window Sunshade	+395
Rear Head Airbag Restraints [Opt on Sdn]	+119
Rear Side Airbag Restraints	+277
Ski Sack	+144
Sport Package	+1078
Xenon Headlamps [Std on 540]	+359

Mileage Category: I

2001

The former base 2.8-liter engine gets bumped up to 3.0 liters, with an expected horsepower and torque increase to go along with the larger displacement. A new 2.5-liter engine premieres this year, as do rear-seat head airbags and a slightly freshened exterior. BMW also improved some of the optional equipment, including Park Distance Control for both the front and rear of the vehicle, a bigger LCD screen for the navigation system, and an optional in-dash single-disc CD player.

Body Styles	TMV Pricing		
	Trade	Private	Dealer
4 Dr 525i Sdn	18484	20394	22158
4 Dr 525i Wgn	17417	19218	20879
4 Dr 530i Sdn	19301	21295	23135

Options	Price
6-Speed Transmission [Opt on 540]	+1495
AM/FM/CD Audio System	+126
Automatic 5-Speed Transmission [Opt on 525,530]	+802
Automatic Climate Control (2 Zone) - Driver and Passenger [Opt on 525]	+243
Automatic Dimming Rearview Mirror [Std on 540]	+116
Automatic Load Leveling [Opt on 525i Wgn]	+478
Comfort Seats	+755
Heated Front Seats	+189
Leather Seats [Std on 540]	+912

Body Styles	TMV Pricing		
	Trade	Private	Dealer
4 Dr 540i Sdn	24002	26482	28771
4 Dr 540i Wgn	23927	26400	28682

Options	Price
Navigation System	+1133
Park Distance Control (Front and Rear)	+441
Power Moonroof [Std on 540]	+661
Power Passenger Seat [Opt on 525,530]	+252
Power Rear Window Sunshade [Opt on Sdn]	+362
Rear Side Airbag Restraints	+242
Ski Sack [Opt on 530,540]	+299
Sport Package	+944
Xenon Headlamps [Std on 540]	+315

Mileage Category: I

2000

The 5 Series cars carry over from last year with small changes and no price increase.

Body Styles	TMV Pricing		
	Trade	Private	Dealer
4 Dr 528i Sdn	15139	17009	18843
4 Dr 528i Wgn	14737	16558	18343

Options	Price
6-Speed Transmission [Opt on 540]	+1261
Automatic 5-Speed Transmission [Opt on 528]	+478
Automatic Load Leveling [Std on 540i Wgn]	+372
Comfort Seats	+588
Compact Disc Changer	+245
Heated Front Seats	+159
Hi-Fi Audio System	+588
Leather Seats [Std on 540]	+721
Metallic Paint	+233
Navigation System	+882
Park Distance Control (Rear)	+186

Body Styles	TMV Pricing		
	Trade	Private	Dealer
4 Dr 540i Sdn	18673	20981	23243
4 Dr 540i Wgn	19452	21856	24211

Options	Price
Power Moonroof [Std on 540]	+514
Power Rear Window Sunshade [Opt on Sdn]	+306
Rear Side Airbag Restraints	+205
Rear Spoiler	+196
Ski Sack [Opt on 528,540]	+183
Split Folding Rear Seat [Opt on Sdn]	+282
Spoke Wheels	+387
Sport Package	+773
Sport Seats	+233
Sport Suspension	+367
Xenon Headlamps [Std on 540]	+245

Mileage Category: I

1999

New 528i and 540i sport wagons debut, all 5 Series models achieve low emission vehicle (LEV) status, and consumers will find extensive new standard and optional equipment on the cars.

Body Styles	TMV Pricing		
	Trade	Private	Dealer
4 Dr 528i Sdn	12608	14404	16274
4 Dr 528i Wgn	13087	14951	16891

Body Styles	TMV Pricing		
	Trade	Private	Dealer
4 Dr 540i Sdn	16741	19126	21609
4 Dr 540i Wgn	17251	19709	22267

1999 (cont'd)

Options	Price
17 Inch Wheels - Cross-Spoke [Opt on 528]	+349
6-Speed Transmission [Opt on 540]	+1025
Automatic 4-Speed Transmission	+388
Automatic Load Leveling [Opt on 528i Wgn]	+302
Automatic Stability Control [Opt on 528]	+240
Comfort Seats	+477
Compact Disc Changer	+199
Heated Front Seats	+130
Hi-Fi Audio System [Opt on 528]	+477
Leather Seats [Opt on 528]	+547
Metallic Paint	+190
Navigation System	+573

Options	Price
Park Distance Control (Rear)	+168
Power Moonroof [Opt on 528]	+418
Power Rear Window Sunshade [Opt on Sdn]	+276
Premium Audio System	+477
Rear Side Airbag Restraints	+185
Rear Spoiler	+159
Ski Sack [Opt on Sdn]	+149
Split Folding Rear Seat [Opt on Sdn]	+229
Sport Package	+911
Sport Seats	+190
Sport Suspension	+298
Xenon Headlamps	+199

1998

Side-impact airbags are now available for rear-seat passengers, as is break-resistant glass for the windows and moonroof.

Mileage Category: I

Body Styles	TMV Pricing		
	Trade	Private	Dealer
4 Dr 528i Sdn	10657	12299	14150

Body Styles	TMV Pricing		
	Trade	Private	Dealer
4 Dr 540i Sdn	13502	15582	17927

Options	Price
17 Inch Wheels - Cross-Spoke	+304
6-Speed Transmission [Opt on 540]	+892
Automatic 4-Speed Transmission	+338
Comfort Seats	+415
Leather Seats [Opt on 528]	+567
Metallic Paint	+165
Navigation System	+692
Power Moonroof [Opt on 528]	+364
Power Rear Window Sunshade	+240

Options	Price
Premium Audio System	+415
Rear Bench Seat	+200
Rear Side Airbag Restraints	+161
Rear Spoiler	+138
Ski Sack	+130
Sport Package	+438
Sport Seats	+165
Sport Suspension	+203

1997

The 5 Series is redesigned and introduced midway through 1996 as a 1997 model. The Touring wagons are no longer available, and the 3.0-liter V8 is history. New 5 Series models can be had as a six-cylinder 528i or a V8 540i. Both models feature new engines, all-aluminum suspensions, improved brakes and available side-impact airbag protection.

Mileage Category: I

Body Styles	TMV Pricing		
	Trade	Private	Dealer
4 Dr 528i Sdn	8799	10226	11969

Body Styles	TMV Pricing		
	Trade	Private	Dealer
4 Dr 540i Sdn	10348	12026	14076

Options	Price
17 Inch Wheels - Cross-Spoke [Opt on 528]	+277
6-Speed Transmission [Opt on 540]	+726
AM/FM/Cassette/CD Audio System	+148
Automatic 4-Speed Transmission	+289
Comfort Seats	+355
Compact Disc Changer	+148
Leather Seats [Opt on 528]	+408

Options	Price
Metallic Paint	+141
Navigation System	+663
Power Moonroof [Opt on 528]	+299
Power Rear Window Sunshade	+199
Premium Audio System	+355
Rear Spoiler	+118
Sport Suspension	+222

1995

BMW improves its 540i by making a six-speed manual transmission available. That option includes 12-way power sport seats, a sport suspension and beefy antiroll bars. Unfortunately, all models lose their V-rated tires in favor of wimpy H-rated tires in an attempt to improve fuel economy.

Mileage Category: I

Body Styles	TMV Pricing		
	Trade	Private	Dealer
4 Dr 525i Sdn	5310	6285	7909
4 Dr 525i Wgn	5631	6665	8388
4 Dr 530i Sdn	6313	7471	9402

Body Styles	TMV Pricing		
	Trade	Private	Dealer
4 Dr 530i Wgn	6165	7297	9183
4 Dr 540i Sdn	6655	7876	9911

Options	Price
6-Speed Transmission [Opt on 540]	+525
AM/FM/CD Audio System	+75
Automatic 4-Speed Transmission [Std on Wgn]	+209
Compact Disc Changer	+107
Dual Power Sunroofs [Opt on 525i Wgn]	+315

Options	Price
Leather Seats [Opt on 525i]	+295
Metallic Paint	+102
Power Sunroof [Opt on 525i Wgn]	+190
Traction Control System	+107
Trip Computer [Opt on 525i]	+75

M5

Mileage Category: F

Body Styles	TMV Pricing		
	Trade	Private	Dealer
4 Dr STD Sdn	52247	54529	58333

Options	Price	Options	Price
Park Distance Control (Front and Rear)	+550	Split Folding Rear Seat	+373
Power Rear Window Sunshade	+452		

For 2003, BMW will offer a DVD-based navigation system for the M5 -- but alas, you still can't get an in-dash CD player. Besides that, rear head protection airbags (optional last year) are now standard across the line. This is the last year for the current 5 Series -- the M5 being the higher-performance relative of the 540i -- as it will get a full redesign for the 2004 model year. If recent history holds, the M5 is likely to go on hiatus for a couple of years before returning to the welcoming arms and wallets of wealthy enthusiasts. And rumor has it that it will be coming back with a V10 under the hood.

BMW's top performance sedan gets some new exterior colors. Rear side-impact airbags are now a no-charge option, rather than standard.

Mileage Category: F

Body Styles	TMV Pricing		
	Trade	Private	Dealer
4 Dr STD Sdn	44592	46707	50232

Options	Price	Options	Price
Digital Audio System	+647	Power Rear Window Sunshade	+413
Park Distance Control (Front and Rear)	+503	Split Folding Rear Seat	+341

BMW's top-performance sedan, the 394-horsepower M5, gets subtle exterior tweaks and a new head-protection airbag system for rear-seat passengers.

Mileage Category: F

Body Styles	TMV Pricing		
	Trade	Private	Dealer
4 Dr STD Sdn	39697	42718	45506

Options	Price	Options	Price
Park Distance Control (Front and Rear)	+441	Ski Sack	+299
Power Rear Window Sunshade	+362	Split Folding Rear Seat	+299

The M5 is a powerful (nearly 400 horsepower), all-new sport sedan based on the 540i.

Mileage Category: F

Body Styles	TMV Pricing		
	Trade	Private	Dealer
4 Dr STD Sdn	32175	34851	37474

Options	Price	Options	Price
Park Distance Control (Front and Rear)	+372	Rear Side Airbag Restraints	+205
Power Rear Window Sunshade	+306	Split Folding Rear Seat	+252

6 Series

Mileage Category: F

Body Styles	TMV Pricing			Body Styles	TMV Pricing		
	Trade	Private	Dealer		Trade	Private	Dealer
2 Dr 645Ci Conv	68646	71237	75556	2 Dr 645Ci Cpe	61060	63652	67972

Options	Price	Options	Price
Adaptive Cruise Control	+2200	Premium Audio System	+1800
Heated Front Seats	+350	Ski Sack	+150
Heated Steering Wheel	+200	Sport Package	+2800
Park Distance Control (Front and Rear)	+700		

The 6 Series coupe is back after a 14-year hiatus from the BMW lineup. With eight-cylinder power and all the latest technology, it has the necessary ingredients to take on the world's finest luxury two-doors.

7 Series

2004

A regular-wheelbase 760i model has been added to complement the long-wheelbase 760Li -- it features all the power and amenities of the top-line model in a more manageable size. The 745i and 745Li models are freshened with new alloy wheels, and are available with all-season run-flat tires as a no-charge option. All 7 Series models can add adaptive headlights as an option, and Sirius Satellite Radio as a dealer-installed accessory. BMW has made revisions to the iDrive control system to simplify various functions, and the automatic climate control system now has a humidity sensor. Finally, the outside mirrors get a power-fold function this year.

Mileage Category: I

Body Styles	TMV Pricing		
	Trade	Private	Dealer
4 Dr 745Li Sdn	53701	56118	60145
4 Dr 745i Sdn	50937	53354	57381

Options	Price
19 Inch Wheels [Std on 760Li]	+1300
Adaptive Cruise Control	+2200
Automatic Load Leveling [Opt on 745i, 745Li]	+800
Comfort Seats [Opt on 745i, 745Li]	+800
Heated Front Seats [Opt on 745i, 745Li]	+550
Heated Front and Rear Seats [Opt on 745i, 745Li]	+400
Heated Steering Wheel [Opt on 745i, 745Li]	+350
Park Distance Control (Front and Rear) [Opt on 745i, 745Li]	+700
Power Passenger Seat w/Memory [Opt on 745i]	+350

Body Styles	TMV Pricing		
	Trade	Private	Dealer
4 Dr 760Li Sdn	85560	89321	95589
4 Dr 760i Sdn	78855	81834	86799

Options	Price
Power Rear Seat [Opt on 745Li]	+900
Power Rear Window Sunshade [Std on 760Li]	+750
Power Trunk Closer [Std on 760Li]	+500
Premium Audio System [Opt on 745i]	+1800
Rear Side Airbag Restraints	+385
Ski Sack [Opt on 745i, 745Li]	+200
Sport Package [Opt on 745i, 745Li]	+3200
Ventilated Seats (Front and Rear) [Opt on 745i, 745Li]	+1000
Ventilated Seats (Front) [Opt on 745i, 745Li]	+400

2003

The big news for 2003 is the late-fall arrival of the 760Li, which combines all the greatness of the 745 while adding a 6.0-liter V12. BMW has not released U.S. output ratings, but European specs have it at 408 horsepower and 442 pound-feet of torque. The more interesting aspect of the 760Li is that it's the first BMW with direct gasoline injection, which, in combination with the Valvetronic technology already used in the 745 models, allows for stellar performance, and according to BMW, "outstanding fuel economy." We'll wait and see on that one. In other news, all models get rear head-protection airbags, and Active Cruise Control finally makes it to the options list, along with run-flat tires. The Rear Comfort Seat package for the 745Li now includes rear-seat ventilation.

Mileage Category: I

Body Styles	TMV Pricing		
	Trade	Private	Dealer
4 Dr 745Li Sdn	49412	51500	54981
4 Dr 745i Sdn	47323	49323	52655

Options	Price
19 Inch Wheels [Opt on 745]	+1021
AM/FM/CD Changer Audio System [Opt on 745]	+471
Adaptive Cruise Control	+1729
Automatic Load Leveling [Opt on 745]	+550
Comfort Seats [Opt on 745]	+707
Electronic Damping Suspension Control [Opt on 745]	+943
Heated Front and Rear Seats [Opt on 745]	+511
Lexicon Audio System	+943
Park Distance Control (Front and Rear) [Opt on 745]	+550
Power Passenger Seat w/Memory [Opt on 745i]	+393

Body Styles	TMV Pricing		
	Trade	Private	Dealer
4 Dr 760Li Sdn	79930	83586	89679

Options	Price
Power Rear Seat [Opt on 745]	+2750
Power Rear Window Sunshade [Opt on 745]	+589
Power Trunk Closer	+589
Rear Side Airbag Restraints	+303
Security Glass	+2043
Ski Sack [Opt on 745]	+118
Sport Package	+2514
Tire Pressure Monitoring System	+236
Ventilated Seats (Front) [Opt on 745i]	+707

2002

Completely and controversially redesigned, the 2002 BMW 7 Series arrives chock-full of innovative technology and luxury trimmings.

Mileage Category: I

Body Styles	TMV Pricing		
	Trade	Private	Dealer
4 Dr 745Li Sdn	42317	45021	49527

Options	Price
19 Inch Wheels	+934
Automatic Load Leveling	+395
Comfort Seats	+1006
Compact Disc Changer	+431
Digital Audio System	+862
Electronic Damping Suspension Control	+575
Heated Front Seats	+323
Heated Front and Rear Seats	+467
Park Distance Control (Front and Rear)	+503

Body Styles	TMV Pricing		
	Trade	Private	Dealer
4 Dr 745i Sdn	40412	42950	47179

Options	Price
Power Passenger Seat w/Memory [Opt on 745i]	+359
Power Rear Seat	+2084
Power Rear Window Sunshade	+539
Power Trunk Closer	+719
Rear Side Airbag Restraints	+277
Security Glass	+1868
Tire Pressure Monitoring System	+216
Ventilated Seats (Front)	+647

2001

All 7 Series models receive an integrated Motorola StarTAC cell phone with BMW's Mayday function. Body-colored rocker panels and lower-bumper valances, as well as white turn signal lenses, enhance the 7 Series' exterior look. Sport Packages are now available on the 740iL and 750iL models.

Mileage Category: I

Body Styles	TMV Pricing		
	Trade	Private	Dealer
4 Dr 740i Sdn	27337	30162	32770
4 Dr 740iL Protection Sdn	37891	41806	45420
4 Dr 740iL Sdn	28402	31336	34045

Options	Price
Automatic Load Leveling [Opt on 740]	+472
Comfort Seats [Opt on 740]	+315
Electronic Damping Suspension Control [Opt on 740]	+724
Heated Front Seats [Opt on 740]	+315
Park Distance Control (Front and Rear) [Std on 750]	+566

Body Styles	TMV Pricing		
	Trade	Private	Dealer
4 Dr 750iL Protection Sdn	48066	53033	57617
4 Dr 750iL Sdn	30169	33286	36163

Options	Price
Power Rear Window Sunshade [Opt on 740]	+362
Power Security Sunroof [Std on Protection]	+1636
Rear Side Airbag Restraints	+242
Ski Sack [Std on 750]	+189
Sport Package	+1479

2000

The Premium Package is standard on the 740i and 740iL and the Cold Weather Package now includes heated rear seats. Two new "Protection" trim levels are also available that provide light armor, bullet-resistant glass and run-flat tires.

Mileage Category: I

Body Styles	TMV Pricing		
	Trade	Private	Dealer
4 Dr 740i Sdn	21105	23714	26271
4 Dr 740iL Protection Sdn	31855	35791	39649
4 Dr 740iL Sdn	21678	24357	26983

Options	Price
Automatic Load Leveling [Opt on 740]	+399
Comfort Seats [Opt on 740i]	+1010
Electronic Damping Suspension Control [Opt on 740]	+611
Heated Front Seats [Opt on 740]	+245
Park Distance Control (Front and Rear) [Opt on 740]	+478
Power Rear Window Sunshade [Opt on 740]	+393

Body Styles	TMV Pricing		
	Trade	Private	Dealer
4 Dr 750iL Protection Sdn	40045	44993	49844
4 Dr 750iL Sdn	25289	28414	31478

Options	Price
Power Sunroof	+722
Rear Side Airbag Restraints	+205
Security Glass [Std on Protection]	+1063
Ski Sack [Std on 750iL]	+159
Spoke Wheels	+412
Sport Package	+1249

1999

All 7 Series engines achieve low emission vehicle (LEV) status. Revised standard and optional equipment add to the cars' appeal.

Mileage Category: I

Body Styles	TMV Pricing		
	Trade	Private	Dealer
4 Dr 740i Sdn	14827	17144	19555
4 Dr 740iL Sdn	16373	18930	21591

Options	Price
Automatic Load Leveling [Opt on 740iL]	+319
Comfort Seats [Opt on 740i]	+576
Compact Disc Changer [Opt on 740]	+312
Electronic Damping Suspension Control [Opt on 740]	+756
Heated Front Seats [Opt on 740]	+199
Navigation System	+891
Park Distance Control (Front and Rear) [Opt on 740iL]	+432
Power Rear Window Sunshade [Opt on 740]	+355

Body Styles	TMV Pricing		
	Trade	Private	Dealer
4 Dr 750iL Sdn	19041	22015	25111

Options	Price
Power Security Sunroof [Opt on 740iL]	+1034
Power Sunroof	+652
Rear Side Airbag Restraints	+185
Security Glass [Opt on 750iL]	+1034
Ski Sack [Opt on 740]	+130
Sport Package	+1128
Xenon Headlamps	+238

1998

BMW introduces Dynamic Stability Control (DSC). DSC is designed to automatically correct the yaw on all 7 Series cars, preventing plowing and fishtailing.

Body Styles	TMV Pricing		
	Trade	Private	Dealer
4 Dr 740i Sdn	12706	14664	16873
4 Dr 740iL Sdn	14090	16261	18710

Options	Price
Automatic Load Leveling [Opt on 740iL]	+277
Comfort Seats [Opt on 740i]	+501
Compact Disc Changer	+271
Electronic Damping Suspension Control [Opt on 740]	+692
Heated Front Seats [Opt on 740]	+173

Body Styles	TMV Pricing		
	Trade	Private	Dealer
4 Dr 750iL Sdn	16690	19262	22162

Options	Price
Navigation System	+776
Park Distance Control (Front and Rear) [Opt on 740iL]	+376
Power Security Sunroof [Opt on 740iL]	+900
Power Sunroof	+567
Rear Side Airbag Restraints	+161

1997

BMW reintroduces the regular length 740i after the uproar caused over its cancellation for the 1996 model year. Like the rest of the 7 Series, the 740i has a standard equipment list that will leave the Sultan of Brunei drooling with desire.

Mileage Category: I

Body Styles	TMV Pricing		
	Trade	Private	Dealer
4 Dr 740i Sdn	10947	12722	14891
4 Dr 740iL Sdn	12071	14029	16421

Options	Price
Automatic Load Leveling [Opt on 740iL]	+237
Comfort Seats [Opt on 740i]	+416
Compact Disc Changer [Opt on 740]	+225
Electronic Damping Suspension Control [Opt on 740]	+563

Body Styles	TMV Pricing		
	Trade	Private	Dealer
4 Dr 750iL Sdn	14004	16274	19049

Options	Price
Heated Front Seats [Opt on 740]	+148
Navigation System	+628
Park Distance Control (Front and Rear) [Opt on 740iL]	+286

1996

BMW's flagship gets stretched; the only 7 Series models available for 1996 are long-wheelbase models. The 740iL receives a larger V8 that substantially increases torque. BMW's killer 440-watt sound system is now standard on the 750iL and optional on the 740iL. A sophisticated interior-motion theft-deterrent system is now available.

Mileage Category: I

Body Styles	TMV Pricing		
	Trade	Private	Dealer
4 Dr 740iL Sdn	9593	11320	13705

Options	Price
Automatic Load Leveling [Opt on 740iL]	+209
Comfort Seats [Opt on 740iL]	+330
Park Distance Control (Front and Rear) [Opt on 740iL]	+252

Body Styles	TMV Pricing		
	Trade	Private	Dealer
4 Dr 750iL Sdn	11496	13564	16420

Options	Price
Power Rear Window Sunshade [Opt on 740iL]	+226
Premium Audio System [Opt on 740iL]	+443

1995

The big Bimmer is totally redesigned for 1995. The flagship sedan now features sleek styling and a lengthened wheelbase. Three models are available for 1995, including a new 740i regular-wheelbase model. The V12 engine found in the 750iL gains 27 horsepower and 30 pound-feet of torque. New interior refinements include a residual heat system which will continue to heat the car after the power has been turned off, and 14-way power seats.

Mileage Category: I

Body Styles	TMV Pricing		
	Trade	Private	Dealer
4 Dr 740i Sdn	5967	7062	8887
4 Dr 740iL Sdn	7009	8296	10441

Options	Price
Comfort Seats [Opt on 740]	+107
Compact Disc Changer [Opt on 740]	+155
Heated Front Seats [Opt on 740]	+81

Body Styles	TMV Pricing		
	Trade	Private	Dealer
4 Dr 750iL Sdn	8965	10611	13353

Options	Price
Park Distance Control (Front and Rear) [Opt on 740iL]	+196
Premium Audio System [Opt on 740i]	+171

8 Series
1997

Mileage Category: I

Body Styles	TMV Pricing		
	Trade	Private	Dealer
2 Dr 840Ci Cpe	17294	19290	21730

Options	Price
Forged Alloy Wheels	+277

Body Styles	TMV Pricing		
	Trade	Private	Dealer
2 Dr 850Ci Cpe	20999	23423	26385

Engine displacement is bumped up, making the 1997 840Ci and 850Ci a bit stronger than last year's models. BMW's five-speed Steptronic is now standard on both models.

1996

The high-performance 850CSi has been dropped. The remaining 850Ci and 840Ci models now feature the speed-sensitive variable assist steering system previously available only on the 850Ci. The 840Ci gets two upgrades previously exclusive to the V12 model: the Steptronic automatic transmission and bird's eye maple interior trim. A slightly larger displacement for the V8 engine results in more torque (310 lb-ft vs. 295 lb-ft) at lower rpm but horsepower remains at 282. Both models receive a redesigned audio system and automatic-locking retractor seatbelts to better accommodate child seats.

Mileage Category: I

Body Styles	TMV Pricing		
	Trade	Private	Dealer
2 Dr 840Ci Cpe	13655	15190	17309
2 Dr 850CSi Cpe	23582	26084	29539

Options	Price
Aluminum/Alloy Wheels	+343

Body Styles	TMV Pricing		
	Trade	Private	Dealer
2 Dr 850Ci Cpe	18058	20088	22891

Options	Price
Forged Alloy Wheels	+244

1995

No changes for the 8 Series.

Mileage Category: I

Body Styles	TMV Pricing		
	Trade	Private	Dealer
2 Dr 840Ci Cpe	10613	11906	14061
2 Dr 850CSi Cpe	21455	23896	27965

Body Styles	TMV Pricing		
	Trade	Private	Dealer
2 Dr 850Ci Cpe	14155	15880	18755

Options	Price		Options	Price
Aluminum/Alloy Wheels	+86		Forged Alloy Wheels	+190
Electronic Damping Suspension Control	+300			

X3
2004

Mileage Category: O

Body Styles	TMV Pricing				Body Styles	TMV Pricing		
	Trade	Private	Dealer			Trade	Private	Dealer
4 Dr 2.5i AWD SUV	24165	25676	28195		4 Dr 3.0i AWD SUV	29137	30790	33544

Options	Price		Options	Price
18 Inch Wheels [Opt on 3.0i]	+500		Power Moonroof	+1350
Automatic 5-Speed Transmission	+1275		Power Panorama Roof	+800
Automatic Dimming Rearview Mirror	+300		Premium Audio System	+675
Cruise Control [Opt on 2.5i]	+475		Privacy Glass	+350
Fog Lights [Opt on 2.5i]	+150		Rain Sensing Windshield Wipers	+200
Headlight Washers	+250		Rear Side Airbag Restraints	+385
Heated Front Seats	+350		Ski Sack	+150
Leather Seats	+1400		Sport Package	+1500
Metallic Paint	+475		Telematics System	+750
Navigation System	+1800		Trip Computer [Opt on 2.5i]	+300
Park Distance Control (Front and Rear)	+700		Xenon Headlamps	+500
Power Driver Seat [Opt on 2.5i]	+995			

The X3 is an all-new compact sport-utility vehicle from BMW. It is based on the 3 Series sedan and shares many of that car's components and its overall dimensions.

X5
2004

Mileage Category: O

Body Styles	TMV Pricing				Body Styles	TMV Pricing		
	Trade	Private	Dealer			Trade	Private	Dealer
4 Dr 3.0i AWD SUV	32233	33879	36621		4 Dr 4.8i AWD SUV	55761	58157	62149
4 Dr 4.4i AWD SUV	42002	43835	46890					

Options	Price		Options	Price
19 Inch Wheels [Opt on 4.4i]	+950		Park Distance Control (Front and Rear) [Std on 4.8i]	+700
Automatic 5-Speed Transmission [Opt on 3.0i]	+1275		Power Moonroof [Opt on 3.0i, 4.4i]	+1350
Automatic Climate Control [Opt on 3.0i]	+600		Power Panorama Roof [Opt on 3.0i, 4.4i]	+800
Automatic Climate Control (3 Zone) [Opt on 3.0i, 4.4i]	+200		Premium Audio System [Std on 4.8i]	+1200
			Privacy Glass [Std on 4.8i]	+200
Automatic Dimming Rearview Mirror [Std on 4.8i]	+150		Rear Side Airbag Restraints	+385
Automatic Dimming Sideview Mirror(s) [Std on 4.8i]	+200		Ski Sack [Opt on 3.0i, 4.4i]	+150
Automatic Load Leveling [Opt on 3.0i]	+700		Sport Package [Opt on 3.0i, 4.4i]	+1600
Headlight Washers [Std on 4.8i]	+250		Telematics System [Std on 4.8i]	+750
Heated Front Seats [Opt on 3.0i, 4.4i]	+350		Wood Interior Trim [Opt on 3.0i]	+400
Heated Front and Rear Seats [Std on 4.8i]	+350		Xenon Headlamps [Opt on 3.0i]	+800
Leather Seats [Opt on 3.0i]	+1400			
Navigation System	+1800			

The high-performance X5 4.6is is discontinued. The 3.0i and 4.4i receive an exterior update, as well as a new all-wheel-drive system called xDrive. A six-speed manual transmission is now standard on the 3.0i, and a six-speed automatic is standard on the 4.4i. The 4.4i also receives a new 4.4-liter engine with Valvetronic and a fully variable intake system. Both models can add Sirius Satellite Radio and Bluetooth hands-free cell phone capability as dealer-installed accessories.

2003

Mileage Category: O

Body Styles	TMV Pricing				Body Styles	TMV Pricing		
	Trade	Private	Dealer			Trade	Private	Dealer
4 Dr 3.0i AWD SUV	28285	29880	32538		4 Dr 4.6is AWD SUV	47660	50347	54824
4 Dr 4.4i AWD SUV	35479	37480	40814					

Options	Price		Options	Price
19 Inch Wheels [Opt on 4.4i]	+746		Electronic Suspension Control [Std on 4.6is]	+393
Automatic 5-Speed Transmission [Opt on 3.0i]	+1002		Heated Front Seats [Opt on 3.0i]	+354
Automatic Climate Control (2 Zone) - Driver and Passenger [Opt on 3.0i]	+236		Heated Front and Rear Seats [Opt on 4.4i]	+275
			Leather Seats [Opt on 3.0i]	+1139
Automatic Dimming Sideview Mirror(s) [Std on 4.6is]	+138		Navigation System	+1414
Automatic Load Leveling [Std on 4.6is]	+550		Park Distance Control (Front and Rear) [Std on 4.6is]	+550
Comfort Seats [Opt on 4.4i]	+943		Power Moonroof [Std on 4.6is]	+825
Digital Audio System [Std on 4.6is]	+943			

This year, BMW will finally offer a DVD-based navigation system, though you must still give up the in-dash CD player if you opt for nav. Besides that, rear head protection airbags (optional last year) are now standard, as is an interesting new safety item called a brakeforce display -- during emergency braking situations, an extra set of rear brake lights will illuminate to warn motorists behind you. If you order the optional adjustable ride height suspension package, it no longer precludes the addition of the sport package. On the inside, new Dakota leather replaces the familiar Montana leather upholstery (it's optional on the 3.0i model and standard on the 4.4i). Individual model changes include a body-colored tailgate handle for any 3.0i equipped with the sport or premium package, and V-rated tires and an unlimited top speed for any sport package-equipped 4.4i.

2003 (cont'd)

Options	Price
Power Passenger Seat [Opt on 3.0i]	+236
Privacy Glass [Std on 4.6is]	+196
Rain Sensing Windshield Wipers [Std on 4.6is]	+118
Rear Side Airbag Restraints	+303

Options	Price
Sport Package [Std on 4.6is]	+1257
Sport Seats [Std on 4.6is]	+314
Trip Computer [Std on 4.6is]	+236
Xenon Headlamps [Std on 4.6is]	+393

2002

A sports car-quick X5 4.6is makes its debut, boasting a 340-hp 4.6-liter V8 making 350 pound-feet of torque. The 4.4-liter V8 has been upgraded to make 290 horsepower, up from last year's 282. The X5 now offers such goodies as enhanced Hill Descent Control, trailer stability control and a self-leveling suspension. A CD player finally makes its way onto the standard equipment list.

Mileage Category: O

Body Styles	TMV Pricing		
	Trade	Private	Dealer
4 Dr 3.0i AWD SUV	24173	25677	28183
4 Dr 4.4i AWD SUV	30319	32236	35430

Body Styles	TMV Pricing		
	Trade	Private	Dealer
4 Dr 4.6is AWD SUV	42032	44689	49118

Options	Price
19 Inch Wheels [Opt on 4.4i]	+683
Automatic 5-Speed Transmission [Opt on 3.0]	+916
Automatic Climate Control [Opt on 3.0]	+216
Automatic Dimming Rearview Mirror [Std on 4.6is]	+180
Automatic Dimming Sideview Mirror(s) [Std on 4.6is]	+144
Automatic Load Leveling [Opt on 3.0]	+503
Digital Audio System [Std on 4.6is]	+862
Electronic Suspension Control [Std on 4.6is]	+359
Heated Front Seats [Std on 4.6is]	+216
Heated Front and Rear Seats [Std on 4.6is]	+467
Leather Seats [Opt on 3.0]	+1042
Navigation System	+1293

Options	Price
Park Distance Control (Front and Rear) [Std on 4.6is]	+503
Power Moonroof [Std on 4.6is]	+754
Power Passenger Seat [Opt on 3.0]	+216
Rear Head Airbag Restraints	+119
Rear Side Airbag Restraints	+277
Ski Sack [Std on 4.6is]	+180
Sport Package [Std on 4.6is]	+1150
Sport Seats [Opt on 3.0]	+287
Tinted Glass	+287
Trip Computer [Std on 4.6is]	+216
Xenon Headlamps [Std on 4.6is]	+359

2001

A lower-priced X5, with a standard 3.0-liter inline six, is offered for 2001. Other newsworthy items include available sunshades for the back doors, as well as optional heated rear seats. The Sport package includes a sport steering wheel, and 16-way power front seats can be purchased. All X5s come with a self-leveling rear suspension as standard equipment.

Mileage Category: O

Body Styles	TMV Pricing		
	Trade	Private	Dealer
4 Dr 3.0i AWD SUV	21668	23842	25848

Body Styles	TMV Pricing		
	Trade	Private	Dealer
4 Dr 4.4i AWD SUV	27494	30251	32795

Options	Price
AM/FM/CD Audio System	+126
Automatic 5-Speed Transmission [Opt on 3.0i]	+802
Automatic Climate Control [Opt on 3.0i]	+189
Automatic Dimming Rearview Mirror	+189
Automatic Dimming Sideview Mirror(s)	+126
Automatic Load Leveling	+478
Cast Alloy Wheels	+566
Comfort Seats	+755
Heated Front Seats	+189
Heated Front and Rear Seats [Opt on 4.4i]	+409
Leather Seats [Opt on 3.0i]	+912

Options	Price
Navigation System	+1252
Park Distance Control (Rear)	+220
Power Moonroof	+661
Power Passenger Seat [Opt on 3.0i]	+252
Privacy Glass	+173
Rear Side Airbag Restraints	+242
Ski Sack	+122
Sport Seats	+299
Sport Suspension	+427
Trip Computer	+189
Xenon Headlamps	+315

2000

BMW joins the SUV craze with its all-new X5 SAV (sport activity vehicle), powered by the same superb V8 fitted to the 540i.

Mileage Category: O

Body Styles	TMV Pricing		
	Trade	Private	Dealer
4 Dr 4.4i AWD SUV	23271	25711	28102

Options	Price
AM/FM/Cassette/CD Audio System	+282
Compact Disc Changer	+294
Heated Front Seats	+159
Heated Front and Rear Seats	+345
Navigation System	+974
Park Distance Control (Rear)	+186
Power Moonroof	+514

Options	Price
Premium Audio System	+438
Privacy Glass	+137
Rear Side Airbag Restraints	+205
Sport Package	+490
Sport Seats	+258
Sport Suspension	+361
Xenon Headlamps	+245

Z3

Mileage Category: F

Body Styles	TMV Pricing		
	Trade	Private	Dealer
2 Dr 2.5i Conv	18398	19627	21674
2 Dr 3.0i Conv	21383	22838	25262

Options	Price
Aluminum/Alloy Interior Trim [Opt on 2.5 Conv]	+216
Automatic 5-Speed Transmission	+916
Hardtop Roof	+1365
Harman Kardon Audio System [Opt on 2.5 Conv]	+485
Heated Front Seats	+287
Leather Seats [Opt on 2.5 Conv]	+539

Body Styles	TMV Pricing		
	Trade	Private	Dealer
2 Dr 3.0i Cpe	20379	21765	24076

Options	Price
Metallic Paint	+341
Power Convertible Top	+431
Power Moonroof	+216
Special Leather Seat Trim	+862
Sport Package	+431
Trip Computer	+216

A CD player can be found on the standard features list. New hues color the sleek sportster, and aluminum-finish trim replaces maple wood inside the Z3 3.0i coupe.

Engine displacement in the 2.8 Roadster and Coupe is bumped from 2.8 liters to 3.0 liters. Horsepower and torque have been increased to 225 and 214 pound-feet, respectively. Bigger brakes and larger 17-inch wheels and tires accompany the new engine. The base 2.5-liter engine sees a 14-horsepower increase, and will appropriately be called the Z3 2.5i. An optional five-speed automatic with manual shifting capability replaces last year's four-speed automatic transmission.

Body Styles	TMV Pricing		
	Trade	Private	Dealer
2 Dr 2.5i Conv	16764	18464	20034
2 Dr 3.0i Conv	18876	20791	22559

Options	Price
17 Inch Wheels - Cross-Spoke [Opt on 3.0 Cpe]	+189
AM/FM/CD Audio System	+126
Aluminum/Alloy Interior Trim	+189
Automatic 5-Speed Transmission	+802
Hardtop Roof [Opt on Conv]	+1196
Harman Kardon Audio System [Opt on 2.5 Conv]	+425
Heated Front Seats	+205

Body Styles	TMV Pricing		
	Trade	Private	Dealer
2 Dr 3.0i Cpe	18526	20406	22141

Options	Price
Leather Seats [Opt on 2.5 Conv]	+572
Metallic Paint	+299
Power Convertible Top	+472
Power Moonroof	+189
Sport Package	+378
Sport Seats [Opt on Conv]	+252
Trip Computer	+189

Dynamic Stability Control is now standard on all Z3s. The cars also receive freshened exterior and interior styling and appointments.

Mileage Category: F

Body Styles	TMV Pricing		
	Trade	Private	Dealer
2 Dr 2.3 Conv	14178	15757	17304
2 Dr 2.8 Conv	15998	17780	19526

Options	Price
17 Inch Wheels [Opt on 2.8]	+598
AM/FM/CD Audio System	+122
Automatic 4-Speed Transmission	+478
Chrome Wheels [Opt on 2.3 Conv]	+417
Cruise Control [Opt on 2.3 Conv]	+145
Fog Lights [Opt on 2.3 Conv]	+128
Hardtop Roof [Opt on Conv]	+931
Harman Kardon Audio System [Opt on 2.3 Conv]	+331
Heated Front Seats	+171

Body Styles	TMV Pricing		
	Trade	Private	Dealer
2 Dr 2.8 Cpe	13976	15532	17057

Options	Price
Leather Seats [Opt on 2.3 Conv]	+483
Metallic Paint	+233
Power Convertible Top [Opt on Conv]	+367
Power Moonroof [Opt on 2.8 Cpe]	+490
Special Factory Paint [Opt on Conv]	+233
Special Leather Seat Trim [Opt on 2.8]	+638
Spoke Wheels [Opt on 2.3 Conv]	+551
Sport Seats [Opt on Conv]	+196
Trip Computer	+171

The Z3 2.8 Coupe is new, side airbags are now standard on all models and a 2.5-liter inline six replaces the 1.9-liter four-cylinder engine on the entry-level roadster.

Mileage Category: F

Body Styles	TMV Pricing		
	Trade	Private	Dealer
2 Dr 2.3 Conv	11994	13450	14966
2 Dr 2.8 Conv	14002	15702	17471

Options	Price
17 Inch Wheels - Spoke [Opt on 2.8 Cpe]	+540
Automatic 4-Speed Transmission	+388
Chrome Wheels	+338
Cruise Control [Opt on 2.3 Conv]	+118
Hardtop Roof	+756
Harman Kardon Audio System [Opt on 2.3 Conv]	+269

Body Styles	TMV Pricing		
	Trade	Private	Dealer
2 Dr 2.8 Cpe	11993	13449	14964

Options	Price
Heated Front Seats	+140
Leather Seats [Opt on 2.3 Conv]	+436
Metallic Paint	+190
Power Convertible Top	+298
Power Moonroof	+398
Special Factory Paint [Opt on Conv]	+190

1999 (cont'd)

Options	Price
Special Leather Seat Trim [Opt on 2.8]	+576
Spoke Wheels	+447

Options	Price
Sport Seats [Opt on Conv]	+159
Trip Computer	+140

1998

BMW's excellent roadster is now available with a power-operated top.

Mileage Category: F

Body Styles	TMV Pricing		
	Trade	Private	Dealer
2 Dr 1.9 Conv	10071	11366	12827

Options	Price
17 Inch Wheels - Spoke [Opt on 2.8]	+470
Alarm System	+122
Automatic 4-Speed Transmission	+338
Harman Kardon Audio System [Opt on 1.9]	+282
Heated Front Seats	+122
Leather Seats [Opt on 1.9]	+380

Body Styles	TMV Pricing		
	Trade	Private	Dealer
2 Dr 2.8 Conv	12435	14034	15838

Options	Price
Metallic Paint	+165
Power Convertible Top	+260
Special Factory Paint	+165
Special Leather Seat Trim [Opt on 2.8]	+501
Sport Seats	+138
Trip Computer	+122

1997

BMW makes its 190-horsepower six-cylinder engine available in the Z3 2.8.

Mileage Category: F

Body Styles	TMV Pricing		
	Trade	Private	Dealer
2 Dr 1.9 Conv	8490	9703	11185

Options	Price
17 Inch Wheels - Spoke [Opt on 2.8]	+390
Automatic 4-Speed Transmission	+289
Compact Disc Changer	+163
Leather Seats [Opt on 1.9]	+325

Body Styles	TMV Pricing		
	Trade	Private	Dealer
2 Dr 2.8 Conv	10357	11837	13645

Options	Price
lic Paint	+141
Special Factory Paint	+141
Special Leather Seat Trim [Opt on 2.8]	+416
Traction Control System [Opt on 1.9]	+237

1996

BMW follows Mazda's lead and introduces a roadster. This dreamy two-seater made its debut in the James Bond movie, "GoldenEye," and has had enthusiasts across the country drooling over its smart styling and impressive refinement. Featured as the perfect Christmas gift in the 1995 Neiman Marcus Christmas catalog, BMW sold out of Z3s before the first one was released to the public.

Mileage Category: F

Body Styles	TMV Pricing		
	Trade	Private	Dealer
2 Dr 1.9 Conv	7581	8724	10302

Options	Price
Automatic 4-Speed Transmission	+268
Leather Seats	+301
Metallic Paint	+131

Options	Price
Special Factory Paint	+131
Traction Control System	+220

M

2002

Mileage Category: F

Body Styles	TMV Pricing		
	Trade	Private	Dealer
2 Dr STD Conv	26150	27929	30894

Options	Price
Hardtop Roof	+1365

Body Styles	TMV Pricing		
	Trade	Private	Dealer
2 Dr STD Cpe	24744	26428	29234

Options	Price
Power Moonroof	+216

BMW makes a CD player part of the standard equipment list. No other changes are in store for the 2002 model year.

2001

BMW's performance sport coupe and roadster are powered by a new inline six-cylinder engine capable of generating 315 horses. Complementing the increase in power is a more tautly sprung suspension. Standard equipment Dynamic Stability Control keeps overenthusiastic drivers in check, and a new tire-pressure monitoring system alerts you of underinflated rubber.

Mileage Category: F

Body Styles	TMV Pricing		
	Trade	Private	Dealer
2 Dr STD Conv	21913	24136	26188

Options	Price
AM/FM/CD Audio System	+126
Hardtop Roof [Opt on Conv]	+1196

Body Styles	TMV Pricing		
	Trade	Private	Dealer
2 Dr STD Cpe	20954	23079	25041

Options	Price
Power Moonroof [Opt on Cpe]	+189

2000

The M cars carry over for 2000, save for two new exterior colors. Prices remain unchanged.

Mileage Category: F

Body Styles	TMV Pricing		
	Trade	Private	Dealer
2 Dr STD Conv	18800	20893	22945

Options	Price
Hardtop Roof [Opt on Conv]	+837

Body Styles	TMV Pricing		
	Trade	Private	Dealer
2 Dr STD Cpe	16185	17987	19754

Options	Price
Power Moonroof [Opt on Cpe]	+485

1999

These high-performance versions of the Z3 roadster and coupe make 240 M-power ponies.

Mileage Category: F

Body Styles	TMV Pricing		
	Trade	Private	Dealer
2 Dr STD Conv	16911	18965	21102

Options	Price
Hardtop Roof [Opt on Conv]	+756

Body Styles	TMV Pricing		
	Trade	Private	Dealer
2 Dr STD Cpe	14371	16116	17932

Options	Price
Power Moonroof [Opt on Cpe]	+438

1998

BMW's Motorsport division creates a meaner version of the Z3 dubbed the M Roadster. The M comes with 240-horsepower 3.2-liter inline six and rides on a stiffened version of the Z3 chassis with sticky 17-inch rubber mounted at each corner. The result is something like a German translation of an old big-block Cobra.

Mileage Category: F

Body Styles		TMV Pricing		
		Trade	Private	Dealer
2 Dr STD Conv		15395	17375	19607

Z4

2004

Rain-sensing windshield wipers are now standard equipment, while Sirius Satellite Radio is now an available accessory.

Mileage Category: F

Body Styles	TMV Pricing		
	Trade	Private	Dealer
2 Dr 2.5i Conv	24216	25677	28111

Options	Price
6-Speed Sequential Semi-Manual Transmission	+1500
Automatic 5-Speed Transmission	+1275
Automatic Climate Control	+550
Automatic Dimming Rearview Mirror	+150
Automatic Dimming Sideview Mirror(s)	+150
Cruise Control [Opt on 2.5i]	+300
Fog Lights [Opt on 2.5i]	+260
Heated Front Seats	+500
Leather Seats [Opt on 3.0i]	+1100
Metallic Paint	+475

Body Styles	TMV Pricing		
	Trade	Private	Dealer
2 Dr 3.0i Conv	29121	30631	33147

Options	Price
Navigation System	+1800
Power Convertible Top	+1200
Power Driver Seat w/Memory	+700
Power Passenger Seat	+470
Premium Audio System [Opt on 2.5i]	+875
Sport Package	+1200
Telematics System	+750
Trip Computer [Opt on 2.5i]	+200
Wood Interior Trim	+200
Xenon Headlamps	+700

2003

The all-new Z4 roadster picks up where the Z3 left off. Well, sort of. There's no coupe version this time around. And the jury is still out on whether the Z4's "flame-surfaced" body is a welcome replacement for its predecessor's sexy corporate styling. In other respects, the newcomer offers much to like -- a more rigid chassis, a real glass rear window and, starting in the spring of 2003, a Sequential Manual Gearbox (SMG) like the one in the M3. All in all, the driving experience is exhilarating -- so if you can get past the styling and come up with the requisite cash, you know where this one belongs on your test drive list.

Mileage Category: F

Body Styles	TMV Pricing		
	Trade	Private	Dealer
2 Dr 2.5i Conv	22808	24210	26546

Options	Price
6-Speed Sequential Semi-Manual Transmission	+1179
Automatic 5-Speed Transmission	+1002
Automatic Climate Control	+177
Automatic Dimming Sideview Mirror(s)	+161
Cruise Control [Opt on 2.5i]	+373
Fog Lights [Opt on 2.5i]	+204
Heated Front and Rear Seats	+393
Leather Seats [Opt on 3.0i]	+825
Metallic Paint	+373
Navigation System	+1414

Body Styles	TMV Pricing		
	Trade	Private	Dealer
2 Dr 3.0i Conv	26272	27887	30579

Options	Price
Power Convertible Top	+471
Power Driver Seat	+236
Power Passenger Seat	+236
Premium Audio System [Opt on 2.5i]	+688
Rain Sensing Windshield Wipers	+138
Special Interior Trim	+118
Special Leather Interior Trim [Opt on 3.0i]	+943
Sport Package	+943
Trip Computer [Opt on 2.5i]	+157
Xenon Headlamps	+550

Century

2004

While the 2004 Century offers nothing new, revised trim levels make it easier to select the features you want. All models now come with four-wheel disc brakes and an upgraded sound system.

Mileage Category: D

Body Styles	TMV Pricing			Body Styles	TMV Pricing		
	Trade	Private	Dealer		Trade	Private	Dealer
4 Dr Custom Sdn	9897	10910	12599	4 Dr STD Sdn	9556	10575	12272
4 Dr Limited Sdn	10378	11391	13079	4 Dr Special Edition Sdn	11200	12213	13902

Options	Price	Options	Price
AM/FM/Cassette/CD Audio System	+280	OnStar Telematics System	+695
Aluminum/Alloy Wheels [Opt on Custom, Limited]	+425	Power Driver Seat [Opt on STD]	+350
Antilock Brakes [Opt on STD, Custom, Limited]	+300	Traction Control System [Std on Special Edition]	+200
Cruise Control [Opt on STD]	+250		
Driver Side Airbag Restraint [Opt on Limited, Special Edition]	+350		

2003

The deletion of the Century Limited trim level from the 2003 model lineup leaves us with a lone Century this year, and it offers only a short list of updates. Most important to note is that antilock brakes, OnStar and the driver side-impact airbag are now optional, instead of standard equipment. Other standard features moved to the optional equipment list include the rear glass antenna, front bucket seats and accompanying center console, cassette player, split-folding rear seat, sunroof, heated exterior mirrors and the 15-inch aluminum wheels. Other changes remain largely aesthetic; a new exterior appearance package adds revised fascias, updated door moldings and a graphite color grille. Inside, the Century benefits only from new wood switch plates. There's also a new starter for improved cold weather cranking and an impact-absorbing headliner that exceeds new federal requirements.

Mileage Category: D

Body Styles	TMV Pricing		
	Trade	Private	Dealer
4 Dr Custom Sdn	7328	8171	9575

Options	Price	Options	Price
AM/FM/Cassette/CD Audio System	+156	Leather Seats	+387
Aluminum/Alloy Wheels	+237	OnStar Telematics System	+387
Antilock Brakes	+390	Power Driver Seat	+139
Front Side Airbag Restraints	+195	Split Folding Rear Seat	+153

2002

Buick's midsize Century remains relatively unchanged for 2002. LATCH child-seat attachment points are now standard, along with a revised cruise control system. Dark Bronze Mist is added to the color palette and Limited models get wood grain trim on the doors.

Mileage Category: D

Body Styles	TMV Pricing			Body Styles	TMV Pricing		
	Trade	Private	Dealer		Trade	Private	Dealer
4 Dr Custom Sdn	6114	6859	8099	4 Dr Limited Sdn	7323	8214	9700

Options	Price	Options	Price
AM/FM/Cassette/CD Audio System	+135	Power Driver Seat [Opt on Custom]	+121
Chrome Wheels	+121	Power Passenger Seat	+121
OnStar Telematics System [Opt on Custom]	+218	Power Sunroof	+385

2001

New rear-wheel house liners promise a quieter ride on wet roads, a special appearance package is offered and OnStar in-vehicle safety, security and information service is now standard on Limited models.

Mileage Category: D

Body Styles	TMV Pricing			Body Styles	TMV Pricing		
	Trade	Private	Dealer		Trade	Private	Dealer
4 Dr Custom Sdn	4939	5953	6889	4 Dr Limited Sdn	5704	6874	7955

Options	Price	Options	Price
Aluminum/Alloy Wheels	+146	Power Passenger Seat	+125
OnStar Telematics System [Opt on Custom]	+185	Power Sunroof	+270
Power Driver Seat	+119		

2000

Buick's midsize Century heads into the new millennium with a special-edition model commemorating the turn of the century and more horsepower in all three models from a revised 3.1-liter 3100 V6.

Mileage Category: D

Body Styles	TMV Pricing			Body Styles	TMV Pricing		
	Trade	Private	Dealer		Trade	Private	Dealer
4 Dr Custom Sdn	3833	4810	5767	4 Dr Limited Sdn	4264	5350	6415

Options	Price	Options	Price
AM/FM/Cassette/CD Audio System	+141	OnStar Telematics System	+301
Aluminum/Alloy Wheels	+126	Power Moonroof	+233

1999

The year 1999 brings a host of safety improvements, many of them standard. Additionally, the suspension has been retuned for less body roll, the sound systems have been upgraded and one new paint color, called Auburn Nightmist, has been added.

Mileage Category: D

Body Styles	TMV Pricing			Body Styles	TMV Pricing		
	Trade	Private	Dealer		Trade	Private	Dealer
4 Dr Custom Sdn	2935	3770	4638	4 Dr Limited Sdn	3275	4206	5175

1999 (cont'd)

Options	Price
Leather Seats	+157
OnStar Telematics System	+250

Options	Price
Power Moonroof	+174

1998

The addition of second-generation airbags, three new exterior colors, one new interior color and the availability of OnStar mobile communications are this year's changes.

Mileage Category: D

Body Styles	TMV Pricing		
	Trade	Private	Dealer
4 Dr Custom Sdn	2233	3009	3884

Body Styles	TMV Pricing		
	Trade	Private	Dealer
4 Dr Limited Sdn	2748	3703	4780

Options	Price
Leather Seats [Opt on Limited]	+121
OnStar Telematics System	+220

Options	Price
Power Moonroof	+154

1997

Buick redesigns its bread-and-butter midsize sedan, dropping the wagon variant in the process. A 3.1-liter V6 engine, roomier interior, larger trunk and traditional Buick styling cues highlight the new Century.

Mileage Category: D

Body Styles	TMV Pricing		
	Trade	Private	Dealer
4 Dr Custom Sdn	1627	2293	3106

Body Styles	TMV Pricing		
	Trade	Private	Dealer
4 Dr Limited Sdn	2096	2953	4001

Options	Price
Power Moonroof	+128

1996

Mileage Category: D

Body Styles	TMV Pricing		
	Trade	Private	Dealer
4 Dr STD Sdn	1254	1841	2650

Body Styles	TMV Pricing		
	Trade	Private	Dealer
4 Dr STD Wgn	1307	1919	2763

Wagons get the V6 as standard equipment. Power windows, cassette player, rear window defogger and a remote trunk release make the standard equipment list as this ancient A-body rolls into its final year of production.

1995

Instruments have new backlighting, and seats are revised.

Mileage Category: D

Body Styles	TMV Pricing		
	Trade	Private	Dealer
4 Dr Custom Sdn	858	1321	2093
4 Dr Limited Sdn	1096	1687	2673

Body Styles	TMV Pricing		
	Trade	Private	Dealer
4 Dr Special Sdn	835	1285	2036
4 Dr Special Wgn	841	1295	2051

Options	Price
3.1L V6 OHV 12V FI Engine [Opt on Special]	+89

LeSabre

2004

Mileage Category: G

Body Styles	TMV Pricing		
	Trade	Private	Dealer
4 Dr Custom Sdn	12617	13904	16049

Body Styles	TMV Pricing		
	Trade	Private	Dealer
4 Dr Limited Sdn	15808	17121	19310

Options	Price
16 Inch Wheels	+325
16 Inch Wheels - Chrome	+335
AM/FM/Cassette/CD Audio System [Opt on Custom]	+200
Automatic Stability Control [Opt on Limited]	+495
Front Side Airbag Restraints [Opt on Custom]	+350
Heads-Up Display [Opt on Limited]	+325
Heated Front Seats [Opt on Custom]	+295

Options	Price
Leather Seats [Opt on Custom]	+800
OnStar Telematics System [Opt on Custom]	+695
Power Driver Seat w/Memory [Opt on Limited]	+190
Power Moonroof [Opt on Limited]	+1095
Power Passenger Seat [Opt on Custom]	+165
Satellite Radio System	+325
Special Factory Paint [Opt on Limited]	+800

The LeSabre remains largely unchanged, with new colors and a few new options like rain-sensing wipers the only notable differences.

Buick
LeSabre

2003

To recognize the Buick LeSabre's successful 10-year sales record as the best-selling full-size car in America, and to celebrate Buick's centennial anniversary in 2003, Buick has added a new trim option for the LeSabre Limited model. Buick's product planners must have been feeling particularly creative when they named it; it's called the Celebration Edition. It features a new monochrome emblem, a blacked-out grille and license plate pocket and two new premium paints, Crimson Pearl and White Diamond. Additional Celebration exterior bits include body-color lower fascias and rocker moldings, turn-signal indicators in the side mirrors and new 16-inch chrome-plated aluminum wheels. Interior refinements are limited to two-tone leather seating and Black Cherry wood grain trim. It also includes a number of otherwise optional features, such as StabiliTrak. The rest of the LeSabre line is pretty much unchanged, with the exception of XM Satellite Radio, which is a new option on the Limited, and side-impact airbags, formerly standard on all LeSabres, are now optional on Custom models.

Mileage Category: G

Body Styles	TMV Pricing		
	Trade	Private	Dealer
4 Dr Custom Sdn	10412	11321	12836

Options	Price
16 Inch Wheels - Chrome [Opt on Custom]	+220
Aluminum/Alloy Wheels [Opt on Custom]	+164
Automatic Stability Control [Opt on Limited]	+276
Front Side Airbag Restraints [Opt on Custom]	+195
Heads-Up Display [Opt on Limited]	+167
Heated Front Seats [Opt on Custom]	+164

Body Styles	TMV Pricing		
	Trade	Private	Dealer
4 Dr Limited Sdn	13215	14369	16292

Options	Price
Leather Seats [Opt on Custom]	+499
OnStar Telematics System [Opt on Custom]	+387
Power Moonroof [Opt on Limited]	+554
Satellite Radio System [Opt on Limited]	+181
Special Factory Paint [Opt on Limited]	+306

2002

Buick's LeSabre receives only minor trim changes for 2002. Limited models get additional standard features and new 16-inch wheels, while all models get new radios, manual trunk release latches and the LATCH system for securing child safety seats.

Mileage Category: G

Body Styles	TMV Pricing		
	Trade	Private	Dealer
4 Dr Custom Sdn	8900	9831	11383

Options	Price
16 Inch Wheels	+143
AM/FM/Cassette/CD Audio System [Opt on Custom]	+133
Aluminum/Alloy Wheels [Opt on Custom]	+181
Automatic Stability Control	+239
Chrome Wheels	+336
Heads-Up Display	+145

Body Styles	TMV Pricing		
	Trade	Private	Dealer
4 Dr Limited Sdn	10773	11899	13777

Options	Price
Heated Front Seats [Opt on Custom]	+143
Leather Seats [Opt on Custom]	+433
OnStar Telematics System [Opt on Custom]	+230
Power Passenger Seat [Opt on Custom]	+116
Power Sunroof	+435

2001

Changes include dual-stage airbags, standard (on this Limited) OnStar in-vehicle safety, security and information service, and the engine oil change interval has been increased to 10,000 miles.

Mileage Category: G

Body Styles	TMV Pricing		
	Trade	Private	Dealer
4 Dr Custom Sdn	6991	8168	9253

Options	Price
AM/FM/Cassette/CD Audio System	+136
Aluminum/Alloy Wheels [Opt on Custom]	+126
Automatic Stability Control	+193
Compact Disc Changer	+232
Heads-Up Display [Opt on Limited]	+117

Body Styles	TMV Pricing		
	Trade	Private	Dealer
4 Dr Limited Sdn	8397	9810	11114

Options	Price
Heated Front Seats [Opt on Limited]	+115
Leather Seats	+304
OnStar Telematics System [Opt on Custom]	+185
Power Passenger Seat [Opt on Custom]	+128
Power Sunroof	+350

2000

Buick's LeSabre has been totally redesigned for the 2000 model year. Though it looks a lot like a '99, this car has undergone a remarkable transformation, riding on a new platform with mildly tweaked sheet metal and an entirely reworked cabin. Better ride, steering and seats, plus side airbags and integrated seatbelts, make it an even better value than before.

Mileage Category: G

Body Styles	TMV Pricing		
	Trade	Private	Dealer
4 Dr Custom Sdn	5690	6822	7932

Options	Price
Automatic Stability Control	+166
Compact Disc Changer	+200
Leather Seats	+334

Body Styles	TMV Pricing		
	Trade	Private	Dealer
4 Dr Limited Sdn	6416	7693	8944

Options	Price
OnStar Telematics System	+301
Power Moonroof	+334

1999

Mileage Category: G

Body Styles	TMV Pricing		
	Trade	Private	Dealer
4 Dr Custom Sdn	3967	4910	5891

Options	Price
Leather Seats	+185

Body Styles	TMV Pricing		
	Trade	Private	Dealer
4 Dr Limited Sdn	4662	5770	6923

Options	Price
OnStar Telematics System	+250

Buick has made some emissions system improvements for '99, and added two exterior metallic paint choices, Sterling Silver and Dark Bronze Mist.

1998

Mileage Category: G

Body Styles	TMV Pricing		
	Trade	Private	Dealer
4 Dr Custom Sdn	3171	4092	5131

Options	Price
Leather Seats	+121

Body Styles	TMV Pricing		
	Trade	Private	Dealer
4 Dr Limited Sdn	3724	4806	6026

Options	Price
OnStar Telematics System	+220

Cruise control is standard on base models, OnStar Mobile Communications is a dealer-installed option, Limited models get a couple of electrochromic mirrors and new colors are on tap inside and out. Second-generation airbags are made standard.

1997

Mileage Category: G

Body Styles	TMV Pricing		
	Trade	Private	Dealer
4 Dr Custom Sdn	2712	3598	4682

Body Styles	TMV Pricing		
	Trade	Private	Dealer
4 Dr Limited Sdn	3154	4185	5445

Buick freshens the LeSabre with new front and rear styling. Redesigned wheel selections, new seats on Custom models and walnut instrument panel appliques round out the visual changes. Structurally, the LeSabre now meets side-impact standards.

1996

Mileage Category: G

Body Styles	TMV Pricing		
	Trade	Private	Dealer
4 Dr Custom Sdn	2044	2799	3841

Body Styles	TMV Pricing		
	Trade	Private	Dealer
4 Dr Limited Sdn	2374	3250	4460

The Series II engine becomes standard on LeSabre. Order the Gran Touring suspension, and get the same magnetic variable effort steering found on the Park Avenue Ultra. Now standard on the Custom is an electric rear window defogger and storage armrest. Limited trim levels get Twilight Sentinel, dual automatic ComforTemp climate controls and a rear-seat center armrest.

1995

Mileage Category: G

Body Styles	TMV Pricing		
	Trade	Private	Dealer
4 Dr Custom Sdn	1357	1917	2851

Body Styles	TMV Pricing		
	Trade	Private	Dealer
4 Dr Limited Sdn	1511	2136	3177

New climate controls and radios are major changes.

Park Avenue

2004

Mileage Category: H

Body Styles	TMV Pricing		
	Trade	Private	Dealer
4 Dr STD Sdn	18479	19608	21490

Options	Price
16 Inch Wheels - Chrome [Opt on STD]	+350
AM/FM/Cassette/CD Audio System [Opt on STD]	+200
Automatic Dimming Rearview Mirror [Opt on STD]	+200
Automatic Dimming Sideview Mirror(s) [Opt on STD]	+200
Automatic Stability Control [Std on Ultra]	+495
Bucket Seats [Opt on Ultra]	+400
Compact Disc Changer	+350
Garage Door Opener [Opt on STD]	+250
Heads-Up Display	+250
Heated Front Seats [Opt on STD]	+250

Body Styles	TMV Pricing		
	Trade	Private	Dealer
4 Dr Ultra S/C Sdn	21140	22367	24412

Options	Price
OnStar Telematics System [Std on Ultra]	+240
Park Distance Control (Rear)	+295
Power Driver Seat w/Memory [Opt on STD]	+250
Power Moonroof	+885
Premium Audio System [Std on Ultra]	+295
Rain Sensing Windshield Wipers [Std on Ultra]	+250
Special Factory Paint	+750
Tire Pressure Monitoring System [Opt on STD]	+150
Traction Control System [Std on Ultra]	+300

New interior and exterior colors are the only notable changes for the Park Avenue.

2003

Mileage Category: H

Body Styles	TMV Pricing		
	Trade	Private	Dealer
4 Dr STD Sdn	15700	16886	18864

Options	Price
Automatic Stability Control [Std on Ultra]	+276
Chrome Wheels [Std on Ultra]	+423
Compact Disc Changer	+331
Heads-Up Display	+167
OnStar Telematics System [Std on Ultra]	+251
Park Distance Control (Rear)	+164

Body Styles	TMV Pricing		
	Trade	Private	Dealer
4 Dr Ultra S/C Sdn	19634	20926	23079

Options	Price
Power Moonroof	+610
Premium Audio System [Std on Ultra]	+164
Special Factory Paint	+306
Touring Suspension [Std on Ultra]	+159
Traction Control System [Std on Ultra]	+139

A revamped Park Avenue Ultra, chock-full of aesthetic goodies, emerges for 2003. This Ultra model features a new grille, side mirror-mounted turn indicators, 17-inch chrome-plated aluminum wheels and retro-style fender portholes. The three holes on each front fender are meant to link the updated 2003 model to Buick's 40-plus years of design heritage. The Ultra also boasts an improved ride, largely due to the specially-tuned Gran Touring suspension and rear stabilizer bar, both of which are standard Ultra equipment. Inside, faux wood grain trim and a new gauge cluster graphics help define the Ultra's fresh look.

2002

Mileage Category: H

Body Styles	TMV Pricing		
	Trade	Private	Dealer
4 Dr STD Sdn	12631	13812	15779

Body Styles	TMV Pricing		
	Trade	Private	Dealer
4 Dr Ultra S/C Sdn	14355	15555	17554

Buick's top-of-the-line luxury sedan remains virtually unchanged for 2002. Minor updates include wood grain trim on the doors and instrument panel and two new exterior colors.

Park Avenue

2002 (cont'd)

Options	Price
Automatic Stability Control [Opt on STD]	+239
Chrome Wheels	+368
Compact Disc Changer	+288
Heads-Up Display	+145
Heated Front and Rear Seats [Opt on STD]	+143

Options	Price
OnStar Telematics System [Opt on STD]	+206
Park Distance Control (Rear)	+143
Power Sunroof	+530
Premium Audio System [Opt on STD]	+143
Special Factory Paint	+218

2001

Buick's full-size Park Avenue gets minor refinements in the areas of safety, convenience and colors for 2001. The biggest news is the addition of the Ultrasonic Rear Park Assist system, improving safety while backing up.

Mileage Category: H

Body Styles	TMV Pricing		
	Trade	Private	Dealer
4 Dr STD Sdn	9467	10953	12325

Body Styles	TMV Pricing		
	Trade	Private	Dealer
4 Dr Ultra S/C Sdn	11013	12583	14032

Options	Price
Automatic Stability Control	+193
Chrome Wheels	+296
Compact Disc Changer	+232
Heads-Up Display	+117
Heated Front and Rear Seats [Opt on STD]	+115

Options	Price
Park Distance Control (Rear)	+115
Power Sunroof	+426
Premium Audio System [Opt on STD]	+115
Special Factory Paint	+175

2000

Park Avenue gets StabiliTrak, GM's advanced vehicle stability control system.

Mileage Category: H

Body Styles	TMV Pricing		
	Trade	Private	Dealer
4 Dr STD Sdn	6685	8005	9299

Body Styles	TMV Pricing		
	Trade	Private	Dealer
4 Dr Ultra S/C Sdn	7970	9424	10850

Options	Price
Chrome Wheels	+233
Compact Disc Changer	+200
Leather Seats [Opt on STD]	+252

Options	Price
OnStar Telematics System	+301
Power Moonroof	+367
Special Factory Paint	+133

1999

The Park Avenue's taillamps are now similar to those found on the upscale Ultra model. Also new this year is an enhanced eight-speaker audio system dubbed Concert Sound III, a new hood-to-fender seal for improved appearance, an adjustable rubber bumper for the deck lid and four new exterior colors.

Mileage Category: H

Body Styles	TMV Pricing		
	Trade	Private	Dealer
4 Dr STD Sdn	5015	6248	7531

Body Styles	TMV Pricing		
	Trade	Private	Dealer
4 Dr Ultra S/C Sdn	6012	7490	9028

Options	Price
Chrome Wheels	+174
Compact Disc Changer	+149
Leather Seats [Opt on STD]	+188

Options	Price
OnStar Telematics System	+250
Power Moonroof	+275

1998

Exterior mirrors can be folded away, a new optional feature tilts the exterior mirrors down for curb viewing during reversing, dealers can install an OnStar Communications system and new colors are available inside and out. Second-generation airbags are made standard.

Mileage Category: H

Body Styles	TMV Pricing		
	Trade	Private	Dealer
4 Dr STD Sdn	3692	4802	6053

Body Styles	TMV Pricing		
	Trade	Private	Dealer
4 Dr Ultra S/C Sdn	5053	6573	8287

Options	Price
Chrome Wheels	+154
Compact Disc Changer	+132
Leather Seats [Opt on STD]	+133

Options	Price
OnStar Telematics System	+220
Power Moonroof	+220

1997

Buick engineers substantially improve the Park Avenue for 1997 by strengthening the body structure, improving interior ergonomics, and introducing a sleek new look. Powertrains are carried over, and two models are available: base and Ultra.

Mileage Category: H

Body Styles	TMV Pricing		
	Trade	Private	Dealer
4 Dr STD Sdn	2851	3853	5078

Body Styles	TMV Pricing		
	Trade	Private	Dealer
4 Dr Ultra S/C Sdn	3578	4837	6375

Options	Price
Chrome Wheels	+128

Options	Price
Power Moonroof	+184

1996

Mileage Category: H

Body Styles	TMV Pricing			Body Styles	TMV Pricing		
	Trade	Private	Dealer		Trade	Private	Dealer
4 Dr STD Sdn	2281	3165	4385	4 Dr Ultra S/C Sdn	2814	3905	5411

Options	Price
Power Moonroof	+158

Ultra gets new Series II supercharged engine as standard equipment, as well as magnetic variable effort steering gear. Colors and trim are revised, battery rundown protection is added, and long-life engine components keep the Park going longer between maintenance stops.

1995

Mileage Category: H

Body Styles	TMV Pricing			Body Styles	TMV Pricing		
	Trade	Private	Dealer		Trade	Private	Dealer
4 Dr STD Sdn	1657	2420	3692	4 Dr Ultra S/C Sdn	2094	3058	4665

Options	Price	Options	Price
Leather Seats [Opt on STD]	+79	Premium Audio System	+86
Power Moonroof	+131		

Base engine upgraded to 3800 Series II status; makes 35 more horsepower than previous year. Base models get styling tweaks front and rear. New climate controls and radios are added.

Rainier

2004

Mileage Category: M

Body Styles	TMV Pricing			Body Styles	TMV Pricing		
	Trade	Private	Dealer		Trade	Private	Dealer
4 Dr CXL AWD SUV	19027	20294	22406	4 Dr CXL Plus SUV	18586	19743	21671
4 Dr CXL Plus AWD SUV	19552	20819	22931	4 Dr CXL SUV	18060	19218	21146

Options	Price	Options	Price
5.3L V8 OHV 16V FI Engine	+1500	Navigation System	+1200
AM/FM/CD Audio System	+400	Power Adjustable Foot Pedals	+150
AM/FM/CD Changer Audio System [Std on CXL Plus]	+290	Power Moonroof	+885
DVD Entertainment System	+1435	Side Steps	+450
Front Side Airbag Restraints	+350	Special Factory Paint	+165
Heated Front Seats	+275		

The Rainier is an all-new SUV for Buick. It is based on GM's capable midsize SUV architecture which also supports the Chevy TrailBlazer and GMC Envoy. The Rainier is available with a V8 power, but there is no extended-length version.

Regal

2004

Mileage Category: D

Body Styles	TMV Pricing			Body Styles	TMV Pricing		
	Trade	Private	Dealer		Trade	Private	Dealer
4 Dr GS S/C Sdn	13387	14799	17153	4 Dr LS Sdn	11691	12956	15065

Options	Price	Options	Price
AM/FM/Cassette/CD Audio System	+280	Leather Seats [Opt on LS]	+800
Aluminum/Alloy Wheels [Opt on LS]	+650	OnStar Telematics System	+695
Antilock Brakes [Opt on LS]	+200	Power Moonroof	+900
Automatic Climate Control (2 Zone) - Driver and Passenger [Opt on LS]	+500	Power Passenger Seat	+350
Automatic Dimming Rearview Mirror [Opt on LS]	+120	Split Folding Rear Seat [Opt on LS]	+300
Chrome Wheels	+650	Steering Wheel Radio Controls [Opt on LS]	+150
Driver Side Airbag Restraint	+350	Traction Control System [Opt on LS]	+200
Heated Front Seats	+295		

For 2004, the Regal gets only minor cosmetic changes. New wood trim is offered along with a new ETR audio system with speed-sensing volume, RDS and a CD player. The Leather package has been upgraded with dual-zone climate control and a split-folding rear seat. Carpeted floor mats that were standard equipment last year are now part of an options package that must be purchased at additional cost.

Regal

2003

Many features that were on the standard equipment list for 2002 have been deemed optional, or deleted altogether, for the 2003 model. Deleted items are speed variable power-assisted steering, which is being downgraded to a nonspeed dependent system, and heated outside rearview mirrors. Side-impact airbags are now optional instead of standard (and continue to be available with leather seating surfaces only), as is a rear split-folding seat. Safety also comes with a separate price tag, as antilock brakes and traction control are now options on the lower Regal LS, but together with a tire inflation monitor, remain standard on the more upscale GS model. On the upside, all Regals receive an improved starter for cold weather cranking, and a new impact-absorbent headliner, plus two new packages to help Regal buyers group options for a better price. The new Luxury Package includes dual-zone climate control, illuminated visor mirrors, auto-dimming inside and outside rearview mirrors, AM/FM stereo with both cassette and CD player and steering wheel-mounted audio controls. The simpler Leather and Wheel Package includes leather seats, a split-folding rear seat and 15-inch aluminum wheels.

Mileage Category: D

Body Styles	TMV Pricing		
	Trade	Private	Dealer
4 Dr GS S/C Sdn	11545	12743	14739

Options	Price
Aluminum/Alloy Wheels [Opt on LS]	+187
Antilock Brakes [Opt on LS]	+390
Automatic Climate Control (2 Zone) - Driver and Passenger [Opt on LS]	+139
Chrome Wheels	+362
Front Side Airbag Restraints	+195
Heated Front Seats	+164
Leather Seats [Opt on LS]	+362

Body Styles	TMV Pricing		
	Trade	Private	Dealer
4 Dr LS Sdn	9609	10606	12267

Options	Price
Monsoon Audio System	+220
OnStar Telematics System	+387
Power Moonroof	+443
Power Passenger Seat	+195
Special Leather Seat Trim	+195
Split Folding Rear Seat [Opt on LS]	+153

2002

For 2002, the biggest news in the Regal lineup is the continuation of the upscale Joseph Abboud model along with a new Dark Bronze Mist exterior color. Additional wood grain trim will be added to all Regals later in the year and LATCH child seat attachment points are now standard.

Mileage Category: D

Body Styles	TMV Pricing		
	Trade	Private	Dealer
4 Dr GS S/C Sdn	9660	10836	12797

Options	Price
16 Inch Wheels [Opt on LS]	+145
Aluminum/Alloy Wheels [Opt on LS]	+162
Automatic Climate Control (2 Zone) - Driver and Passenger [Opt on LS]	+121
Chrome Wheels	+191
Heated Front and Rear Seats	+143
Leather Seats [Opt on LS]	+314

Body Styles	TMV Pricing		
	Trade	Private	Dealer
4 Dr LS Sdn	8286	9295	10976

Options	Price
Monsoon Audio System	+143
OnStar Telematics System [Opt on LS]	+230
Power Moonroof	+336
Power Sunroof	+385
Touring Suspension	+121

2001

The "Car for the Supercharged Family" gets new rear-wheel house liners for a quieter ride, a standard trunk entrapment release and two new colors, Graphite Metallic and White. An Olympic appearance package is now available and OnStar in-vehicle safety, security and information service is standard on GS models.

Mileage Category: D

Body Styles	TMV Pricing		
	Trade	Private	Dealer
4 Dr GS S/C Sdn	7621	9186	10630

Options	Price
Aluminum/Alloy Wheels [Opt on LS]	+130
Chrome Wheels	+154
Heated Front and Rear Seats	+115
Leather Seats [Opt on LS]	+214

Body Styles	TMV Pricing		
	Trade	Private	Dealer
4 Dr LS Sdn	6493	7825	9055

Options	Price
Monsoon Audio System	+115
OnStar Telematics System [Opt on LS]	+185
Power Moonroof	+270
Power Passenger Seat	+128

2000

New alloy wheels, a standard body-colored grille on the GS and two new colors, Gold Metallic and Sterling Silver debut. Inside, there's now a split-folding rear seat and an optional side airbag for the driver on leather-lined Regals.

Mileage Category: D

Body Styles	TMV Pricing		
	Trade	Private	Dealer
4 Dr GS S/C Sdn	5899	7401	8873
4 Dr LS Sdn	4597	5768	6915

Options	Price
Chrome Wheels	+133
Compact Disc Changer	+184
Leather Seats [Opt on LS]	+218

Body Styles	TMV Pricing		
	Trade	Private	Dealer
4 Dr LSE Sdn	4857	6094	7306

Options	Price
OnStar Telematics System	+301
Power Moonroof	+233

1999

Performance-oriented changes, such as more power, sporty tweaks to the steering and suspension, firmer motor mounts and the addition of a strut tower brace underhood, lead the news for the '99 Regal. Other changes include enhancements to the ABS and traction control systems, as well as the addition of a tire inflation monitor, perimeter lighting and the Concert Sound II audio system to Regal's already long list of standard equipment. New options include a self-dimming electrochromic outside rearview mirror, redesigned 15-inch alloy wheels and the eight-speaker, 220-watt Monsoon audio system. And that's all in addition to a new exterior paint color, Auburn Nightmist.

Mileage Category: D

Body Styles	TMV Pricing		
	Trade	Private	Dealer
4 Dr GS S/C Sdn	4360	5601	6892

Options	Price
Compact Disc Changer	+138
Leather Seats [Opt on LS]	+163

Body Styles	TMV Pricing		
	Trade	Private	Dealer
4 Dr LS Sdn	3576	4595	5655

Options	Price
OnStar Telematics System	+250
Power Moonroof	+174

1998

Mileage Category: D

Body Styles	TMV Pricing		
	Trade	Private	Dealer
4 Dr 25th Anniv Sdn	3688	4969	6414
4 Dr GS S/C Sdn	3650	4918	6349

Options	Price
Compact Disc Changer	+121
Leather Seats [Opt on LS]	+133

Body Styles	TMV Pricing		
	Trade	Private	Dealer
4 Dr LS Sdn	2909	3920	5060

Options	Price
OnStar Telematics System	+220
Power Moonroof	+154

Regal LS gets a new standard four-speed automatic transmission, and three new exterior colors are available. Dealers will install an OnStar Mobile Communications system if the buyer desires, and second-generation airbags are added.

1997

Mileage Category: D

Body Styles	TMV Pricing		
	Trade	Private	Dealer
4 Dr GS S/C Sdn	2915	4106	5563

Options	Price
Power Moonroof	+128

Body Styles	TMV Pricing		
	Trade	Private	Dealer
4 Dr LS Sdn	2386	3361	4553

The complete redesign of the Regal means Buick finally has a viable entry in the midsize sedan marketplace. The standard equipment list is long, including ABS, traction control, dual-zone climate controls, heated exterior mirrors, retained accessory power and battery rundown protection.

1996

Mileage Category: D

Body Styles	TMV Pricing		
	Trade	Private	Dealer
2 Dr Custom Cpe	1505	2208	3179
2 Dr Gran Sport Cpe	1774	2603	3747
4 Dr Custom Sdn	1534	2250	3239

Body Styles	TMV Pricing		
	Trade	Private	Dealer
4 Dr Gran Sport Sdn	1890	2773	3991
4 Dr Limited Sdn	1710	2509	3613
4 Dr Olympic Gold Sdn	1688	2477	3566

The Series II 3.8-liter V6 is standard on Limited and Gran Sport, optional on base Custom models. Standard equipment now includes dual ComforTemp climate controls and a cassette player. Revised wheels, available in chrome, are standard on the Gran Sport. Base V6 is upgraded, and both engines feature long-life engine components.

1995

Mileage Category: D

Body Styles	TMV Pricing		
	Trade	Private	Dealer
2 Dr Custom Cpe	1136	1749	2772
2 Dr Gran Sport Cpe	1212	1868	2960
4 Dr Custom Sdn	1154	1777	2816

Body Styles	TMV Pricing		
	Trade	Private	Dealer
4 Dr Custom Select Sdn	1084	1669	2645
4 Dr Gran Sport Sdn	1207	1859	2945
4 Dr Limited Sdn	1172	1805	2860

Options	Price
Power Moonroof	+92

New interior has dual airbags housed in revised instrument panel. Seats are new, too. Fake wood has been chopped from door panels. Exterior styling is updated.

Rendezvous

2004

Mileage Category: L

Body Styles	TMV Pricing		
	Trade	Private	Dealer
4 Dr CX AWD SUV	14873	15976	17815
4 Dr CX SUV	13304	14398	16223
4 Dr CXL AWD SUV	16738	17852	19710

Body Styles	TMV Pricing		
	Trade	Private	Dealer
4 Dr CXL SUV	15721	16830	18677
4 Dr Ultra AWD SUV	19617	20748	22633

Options	Price
3.6L V6 DOHC 24V FI Engine [Opt on CXL]	+2025
AM/FM/Cassette/CD Audio System [Opt on CX]	+350
Aluminum/Alloy Wheels [Opt on CX]	+325
Antilock Brakes [Opt on CX]	+600
Camper/Towing Package	+325
Captain Chairs (4) [Std on Ultra]	+435
Chrome Wheels [Opt on CXL]	+755
DVD Entertainment System [Opt on CXL, Ultra]	+1100
Front Side Airbag Restraints [Opt on CX FWD]	+350
Heads-Up Display [Opt on CXL]	+325
Heated Front Seats [Opt on CXL]	+275

Options	Price
Leather Seats [Opt on CX]	+800
Navigation System [Opt on CXL, Ultra]	+1100
Power Driver Seat [Std on CXL Plus]	+190
Power Driver Seat w/Memory [Std on Ultra]	+225
Power Moonroof	+885
Power Passenger Seat w/Memory [Opt on CX]	+240
Satellite Radio System [Std on Ultra]	+325
Steering Wheel Radio Controls [Opt on CX]	+125
Third Seat [Std on Ultra]	+465
Traction Control System [Opt on CX]	+175

A luxurious Ultra model has been added to the lineup that features an all-new V6, a monochrome exterior and heavy doses of wood and leather trim inside. A DVD-based navigation system is now on the options list for the CXL and the Ultra, and XM Satellite Radio is now available on all models. GM's head-up display is now available on the CXL as a stand-alone option.

2003

With just one year of production under its belt, Buick is already making some substantial content changes to its Rendezvous model line. Instead of offering standard all-wheel drive on its upscale CXL model, both the lower-level CX and the CXL will now come with front-wheel drive, with Versatrack all-wheel drive available on both models. Other formerly standard items that are now optional this year include: four-wheel disc brakes, ABS, side airbags, all-speed traction control and luggage rack crossbows. On the upside, both models get dual-zone climate control. The CXL also benefits from an optional DVD-based entertainment system and optional XM Satellite Radio for extra enjoyment.

Mileage Category: L

Body Styles	TMV Pricing		
	Trade	Private	Dealer
4 Dr CX AWD SUV	12512	13597	15407
4 Dr CX SUV	11343	12328	13969

Options	Price
16 Inch Wheels - Chrome	+164
AM/FM/CD Changer Audio System [Opt on CXL]	+245
AM/FM/Cassette/CD Audio System [Opt on CX]	+195
Antilock Brakes [Opt on FWD]	+390
Automatic Climate Control (2 Zone) - Driver and Passenger	+125
Camper/Towing Package	+181
Captain Chairs (4)	+242
DVD Entertainment System [Opt on CXL]	+613
Front Side Airbag Restraints [Opt on CXL]	+195
Heads-Up Display [Opt on CXL]	+153

Body Styles	TMV Pricing		
	Trade	Private	Dealer
4 Dr CXL AWD SUV	14023	15241	17270
4 Dr CXL SUV	12686	13787	15623

Options	Price
Heated Front Seats [Opt on CXL]	+125
Leather Seats [Opt on CXL]	+276
OnStar Telematics System [Opt on CXL]	+387
Park Distance Control (Rear) [Opt on CXL]	+164
Power Driver Seat [Opt on CX]	+150
Power Moonroof	+493
Satellite Radio System [Opt on CXL]	+181
Third Seat	+259
Tire Pressure Monitoring System [Opt on CXL]	+120

2002

The Rendezvous is one of a new breed of crossover vehicles that combines the look and utility of an SUV with the comfort of a touring car.

Mileage Category: L

Body Styles	TMV Pricing		
	Trade	Private	Dealer
4 Dr CX AWD SUV	10616	11640	13345
4 Dr CX SUV	9596	10520	12061

Options	Price
16 Inch Wheels [Opt on CX]	+121
AM/FM/CD Changer Audio System	+191
AM/FM/Cassette/CD Audio System [Opt on CX]	+169
Captain Chairs (4)	+121
Heads-Up Display [Opt on CX]	+133
Leather Seats [Opt on CX]	+317
OnStar Telematics System [Opt on CX]	+206

Body Styles	TMV Pricing		
	Trade	Private	Dealer
4 Dr CXL AWD SUV	12345	13534	15515

Options	Price
Park Distance Control (Rear)	+143
Power Driver Seat [Opt on CX]	+145
Power Passenger Seat [Opt on CX]	+145
Power Sunroof	+336
Third Seat	+169
Traction Control System [Opt on CX]	+121

Riviera

1999

Mileage Category: H

Body Styles	TMV Pricing		
	Trade	Private	Dealer
2 Dr S/C Cpe	5834	7266	8757

Options	Price
Chrome Wheels	+174
OnStar Telematics System	+250

Options	Price
Power Moonroof	+275

Traction control is now standard on the Riviera and this year brings the choice of four new paint colors (Sterling Silver, Titanium Blue, Gold Firemist and Dark Bronze Mist). Buick decided to pull the plug on the big coupe so only approximately 2,000 Rivieras were built for the 1999 model year, along with a limited run of 200 special-edition models dubbed "Silver Arrow."

1998

Supercharged power is now standard, OnStar satellite communications system is a new option and depowered airbags debut. Four exterior colors are new, suspension and steering have been massaged and a heated passenger seat with lumbar support has been added to the options list.

Mileage Category: H

Body Styles	TMV Pricing		
	Trade	Private	Dealer
2 Dr S/C Cpe	4593	5974	7531

Options	Price
Chrome Wheels	+154
OnStar Telematics System	+220

Options	Price
Power Moonroof	+220

1997

Upgraded transmissions, several new colors inside and out, additional standard equipment and new options summarize minimal changes to the Riviera.

Mileage Category: H

Body Styles	TMV Pricing		
	Trade	Private	Dealer
2 Dr S/C Cpe	3512	4749	6259

Body Styles	TMV Pricing		
	Trade	Private	Dealer
2 Dr STD Cpe	3274	4426	5834

1997 (cont'd)

Options	Price
Wheels	+128
Leather Seats	+138

Options	Price
Power Moonroof	+202

1996

Series II supercharged engine gives top-of-the-line Riv 240 horsepower. There are new colors inside and out, real wood on the dash and revised climate and radio controls. Chrome wheels are optional.

Mileage Category: H

Body Styles	TMV Pricing		
	Trade	Private	Dealer
2 Dr S/C Cpe	2596	3602	4991

Body Styles	TMV Pricing		
	Trade	Private	Dealer
2 Dr STD Cpe	2514	3489	4836

Options	Price
Power Moonroof	+158

1995

All-new Riviera debuts. Dual airbags and ABS are standard. Base engine is 3800 Series II V6; optional is a supercharged 3.8-liter. Traction control is optional.

Mileage Category: H

Body Styles	TMV Pricing		
	Trade	Private	Dealer
2 Dr S/C Cpe	1924	2810	4288

Body Styles	TMV Pricing		
	Trade	Private	Dealer
2 Dr STD Cpe	1819	2656	4051

Options	Price
Leather Seats	+92

Options	Price
Power Moonroof	+131

Roadmaster

1996

Mileage Category: G

Body Styles	TMV Pricing		
	Trade	Private	Dealer
4 Dr Estate Wgn	3227	4418	6062
4 Dr Limited Sdn	3173	4344	5961

Body Styles	TMV Pricing		
	Trade	Private	Dealer
4 Dr STD Sdn	2768	3789	5199

Options	Price
Leather Seats	+123

Last year for 260-horsepower land yacht. All models are designated Collector's Editions.

1995

New radios and larger rearview mirrors are added. Cassette player is made standard. Wagon gets standard alloy wheels. New options are heated front seats and memory feature for power driver seat.

Mileage Category: G

Body Styles	TMV Pricing		
	Trade	Private	Dealer
4 Dr Estate Wgn	2198	3104	4614
4 Dr Limited Sdn	2347	3315	4928

Body Styles	TMV Pricing		
	Trade	Private	Dealer
4 Dr STD Sdn	2156	3045	4527

Options	Price
Leather Seats	+102

Skylark

1998

Mileage Category: C

Body Styles	TMV Pricing		
	Trade	Private	Dealer
4 Dr Custom Sdn	1744	2531	3417

Skylark was sold strictly to fleets for 1998. If you're buying one used, chances are good that it was once a rental car.

1997

Skylark gets minimal revisions this year. The standard equipment list is expanded.

Mileage Category: C

Body Styles	TMV Pricing		
	Trade	Private	Dealer
2 Dr Custom Cpe	1188	1878	2721
2 Dr Gran Sport Cpe	1488	2353	3410

Body Styles	TMV Pricing		
	Trade	Private	Dealer
4 Dr Custom Sdn	1209	1912	2770
4 Dr Gran Sport Sdn	1424	2252	3263

Buick
Skylark

1996

Styling changes inside and out this year. Dual airbags are new, as are three-point seatbelts mounted to the B-pillar. A new twin-cam engine replaces the 2.3-liter Quad 4, and automatic transmissions include traction control. Air conditioning, a rear window defroster and a tilt wheel are now standard. Long-life engine components round out the long list of improvements.

Mileage Category: C

Body Styles	TMV Pricing		
	Trade	Private	Dealer
2 Dr Custom Cpe	825	1396	2185
4 Dr Custom Sdn	808	1366	2137

Body Styles	TMV Pricing		
	Trade	Private	Dealer
4 Dr Olympic Gold Sdn	864	1462	2286

1995

Rear suspension is revised. New base engine is 150-horsepower Quad 4. GS gets 3.1-liter V6 standard. Power sunroof is a new option.

Mileage Category: C

Body Styles	TMV Pricing		
	Trade	Private	Dealer
2 Dr Custom Cpe	600	1034	1757
2 Dr Gran Sport Cpe	721	1242	2109

Body Styles	TMV Pricing		
	Trade	Private	Dealer
4 Dr Custom Sdn	603	1038	1764
4 Dr Gran Sport Sdn	721	1242	2109

Options	Price
Power Moonroof	+78

Catera

2001

Mileage Category: H

Body Styles	TMV Pricing		
	Trade	Private	Dealer
4 Dr STD Sdn	8081	9390	10598

Options	Price	Options	Price
Bose Audio System	+436	Power Moonroof	+445
Chrome Wheels	+356	Power Rear Window Sunshade	+132
Heated Front Seats	+190	Xenon Headlamps	+224

OnStar 2.6 in-vehicle safety, security and information service, vented rear disc brakes and the Solar Protect windshield are now standard on all models. The Catera Sport receives new seats, and projector beam headlamps are now standard on the base Catera.

2000

Mildly successful front and rear styling enhancements and a revised interior update Catera for 2000. Side airbags are standard on all models, and an optional sport package finally arrives with 17-inch wheels, heated sport seats, a spoiler, rocker panel extensions, xenon HID headlights and brushed-aluminum interior trim. Electronic drive-by-wire throttle control and a revised torque converter improve oomph off the line. Revised suspension tuning better controls ride motions and body roll, while tightened steering improves road feel. Two new colors round out the changes.

Body Styles	TMV Pricing		
	Trade	Private	Dealer
4 Dr STD Sdn	6516	7831	9119

Options	Price
AM/FM/Cassette/CD Audio System	+136
Bose Audio System	+170
Chrome Wheels	+309
Compact Disc Changer	+175
Heated Front Seats [Opt on STD]	+165

Body Styles	TMV Pricing		
	Trade	Private	Dealer
4 Dr Sport Sdn	6586	7914	9216

Options	Price
Heated Front and Rear Seats	+136
OnStar Telematics System	+348
Power Moonroof	+386
Power Rear Window Sunshade	+115

1999

Catera's "black chrome" grille will be darkened this year, while new electronics and emissions systems make the '99 Catera the first Cadillac to meet the federal Low Emissions Vehicle (LEV) standards. There's also a redesigned fuel cap and tether with an instrument cluster light to indicate a loose fuel cap. Up to four remote entry key fobs can now be programmed for separate memory settings, all with enhanced automatic door lock/unlock functions. Cadillac is rumored to be working on a special Sport Edition planned for later in the model year.

Mileage Category: H

Body Styles	TMV Pricing		
	Trade	Private	Dealer
4 Dr STD Sdn	4538	5732	6974

Options	Price	Options	Price
Chrome Wheels	+224	OnStar Telematics System	+279
Compact Disc Changer	+126	Power Moonroof	+279

1998

New radios are available across the board, and a new option is a power rear sunshade. Second-generation airbags arrived during the middle of the model year.

Mileage Category: H

Body Styles	TMV Pricing		
	Trade	Private	Dealer
4 Dr STD Sdn	3181	4244	5443

Options	Price	Options	Price
Chrome Wheels	+181	OnStar Telematics System	+226
Delco/Bose Audio System	+171	Power Moonroof	+226
Leather Seats	+341		

1997

Cadillac leaps into the near luxury segment of the market with a stylish German-engineered sedan that features a 200-horsepower V6, an impressive load of standard equipment and proper rear-wheel drive.

Mileage Category: H

Body Styles	TMV Pricing		
	Trade	Private	Dealer
4 Dr STD Sdn	2415	3288	4355

Options	Price	Options	Price
Chrome Wheels	+154	Power Moonroof	+193
Leather Seats	+290		

Cadillac
CTS/CTS-V/DeVille

CTS

2004

For 2004, the CTS adds a more powerful 3.6-liter V6 in addition to the standard 3.2-liter motor. The base suspension has been modified with new shocks, while the Sport package is now available on all models. The interior receives a slight refresh in the form of a color-keyed center console, additional chrome trim and white lighting. Lastly, an engine water temperature gauge replaces the clock on the dash.

Mileage Category: H

Body Styles	TMV Pricing		
	Trade	Private	Dealer
4 Dr STD Sdn	21157	22491	24715

Options	Price	Options	Price
17 Inch Wheels	+600	Navigation System	+450
3.6L V6 DOHC 24V FI Engine	+2200	Power Driver Seat w/Memory	+350
AM/FM/CD Changer Audio System	+350	Power Moonroof	+800
Alarm System	+200	Power Passenger Seat	+400
Automatic 5-Speed Transmission	+1300	Satellite Radio System	+325
Automatic Load Leveling	+400	Special Factory Paint	+995
Automatic Stability Control	+500	Split Folding Rear Seat	+500
Bose Audio System	+800	Sport Suspension	+400
Garage Door Opener	+150	Wood Gearshift Knob	+200
Headlight Washers	+350	Wood Steering Wheel	+300
Heated Front Seats	+350	Xenon Headlamps	+345

2003

A replacement for the aging Catera sedan, the all-new CTS shares few parts with its German-built predecessor.

Mileage Category: H

Body Styles	TMV Pricing		
	Trade	Private	Dealer
4 Dr STD Sdn	18880	20306	22683

Options	Price	Options	Price
17 Inch Wheels	+363	Navigation System	+939
AM/FM/CD Changer Audio System	+396	Power Driver Seat w/Memory	+148
AM/FM/Cassette/CD Changer Audio System	+379	Power Moonroof	+791
Automatic Load Leveling	+165	Power Passenger Seat	+165
Automatic Stability Control	+326	Special Factory Paint	+494
Bose Audio System	+445	Split Folding Rear Seat	+297
Compact Disc Changer	+396	Sport Suspension	+132
Heated Front Seats	+264	Xenon Headlamps	+280

CTS-V

2004

Mileage Category: F

Body Styles	TMV Pricing		
	Trade	Private	Dealer
4 Dr STD Sdn	32390	34403	37757

Options	Price
Power Moonroof	+1200

Cadillac has given the tuner treatment to the CTS sedan, creating the high-performance CTS V-Series. Equipped with the Corvette Z06 drivetrain and race-ready running gear, the CTS-V is designed to take on the most powerful sport sedans from Europe.

DeVille

2004

Mileage Category: I

Body Styles	TMV Pricing			Body Styles	TMV Pricing		
	Trade	Private	Dealer		Trade	Private	Dealer
4 Dr DHS Sdn	24997	26674	29469	4 Dr STD Sdn	22216	23894	26689
4 Dr DTS Sdn	24997	26674	29469				

Options	Price	Options	Price
17 Inch Wheels - Chrome [Opt on STD]	+795	Compact Disc Changer	+200
AM/FM/Cassette/CD Audio System [Opt on STD]	+150	Garage Door Opener	+150
Automatic Dimming Sideview Mirror(s) [Std on DHS]	+200	Heads-Up Display [Opt on STD]	+700
Automatic Stability Control [Opt on DHS, STD]	+545	Heated Front and Rear Seats [Opt on DTS]	+400
Chrome Wheels [Opt on STD]	+795	Heated Steering Wheel [Opt on STD]	+200

2004 (cont'd)

Options	Price
Navigation System	+1995
Night Vision	+900
Park Distance Control (Rear)	+200
Power Driver Seat w/Memory [Std on DHS]	+350
Power Moonroof	+700
Power Tilt and Telescopic Steering Wheel [Opt on DTS]	+280
Rain Sensing Windshield Wipers [Opt on STD]	+650

Options	Price
Rear Side Airbag Restraints	+295
Satellite Radio System	+325
Special Factory Paint	+995
Ventilated Seats (Front) [Opt on STD]	+350
Wood Gearshift Knob [Opt on DTS]	+150
Wood Steering Wheel [Opt on DTS]	+200

The stately DeVille heads into '04 with few changes. New heated and cooled front seats coupled with a heated steering wheel replace the previously available adaptive front seats. The base DeVille now comes standard with a CD-only stereo while Night Vision has been added to its options list. An electronic parking brake release replaces the manual unit on all models. High-profile customers can now order an armored edition of the DeVille in either standard or stretched wheelbase versions.

2003

Mileage Category: I

Body Styles	TMV Pricing		
	Trade	Private	Dealer
4 Dr DHS Sdn	22032	23322	25471
4 Dr DTS Sdn	22522	23840	26037

Body Styles	TMV Pricing		
	Trade	Private	Dealer
4 Dr STD Sdn	19085	20202	22063

Options	Price
17 Inch Wheels - Chrome [Opt on STD]	+524
Adaptive Seat Package [Opt on DHS,DTS]	+656
Automatic Stability Control [Opt on DHS,STD]	+231
Compact Disc Changer	+392
Heated Front and Rear Seats [Opt on DTS]	+231
Navigation System	+1315
Night Vision [Opt on DHS,DTS]	+1483

Options	Price
Park Distance Control (Rear) [Opt on DHS,STD]	+194
Power Moonroof	+1022
Power Tilt and Telescopic Steering Wheel [Opt on DTS]	+231
Rear Side Airbag Restraints	+194
Satellite Radio System	+214
Special Factory Paint	+656

In an effort to improve its DeVille, Cadillac has made a few changes for 2003. On all models, the side-view mirrors are now fully equipped with turn-signal indicators, and all models also have revised taillamps. A tire-pressure monitoring system is also new. On the inside, base DeVilles can now get the navigation system as an option, and all models can be had with the XM Satellite Radio feature.

2002

Mileage Category: I

Body Styles	TMV Pricing		
	Trade	Private	Dealer
4 Dr DHS Sdn	17713	19029	21221
4 Dr DTS Sdn	18618	20000	22304

Body Styles	TMV Pricing		
	Trade	Private	Dealer
4 Dr STD Sdn	16321	17533	19553

Options	Price
17 Inch Wheels - Chrome	+447
Adaptive Seat Package	+559
Automatic Stability Control [Opt on DHS]	+197
Chrome Wheels [Opt on STD]	+447
Compact Disc Changer	+334
Heated Front and Rear Seats [Opt on STD]	+197
Navigation System	+1121
Night Vision	+1264

Options	Price
Park Distance Control (Rear)	+166
Power Driver Seat w/Memory [Opt on DTS]	+118
Power Moonroof	+871
Power Tilt and Telescopic Steering Wheel [Opt on DTS]	+197
Rear Side Airbag Restraints	+166
Satellite Radio System	+166
Special Factory Paint	+365

For 2002, the DeVille gets a host of minor refinements, many of which won't be available until later in the year. New shocks and strut valving have been added to shore up the ride quality, leather seating is standard on all models and an optional advanced navigation system with voice-recognition capabilities is offered. A Bose 4.0 sound system can now be ordered, while digital satellite radio provisions will be available later in the year. Dual-stage airbag inflators, an increased oil change interval and a new wreath and crest Cadillac badge round out the rest of this year's changes.

2001

Mileage Category: I

Body Styles	TMV Pricing		
	Trade	Private	Dealer
4 Dr DHS Sdn	14935	16787	18496
4 Dr DTS Sdn	15699	17646	19443

Body Styles	TMV Pricing		
	Trade	Private	Dealer
4 Dr STD Sdn	11634	13076	14407

Options	Price
17 Inch Wheels - Chrome [Opt on DTS]	+356
Adaptive Seat Package [Opt on DHS,DTS]	+445
Automatic Stability Control [Std on DTS]	+222
Bose Audio System [Opt on DHS,DTS]	+546
Chrome Wheels	+356
Compact Disc Changer	+266
Heated Front and Rear Seats [Std on DHS]	+157
Leather Seats [Opt on STD]	+351

Options	Price
Navigation System	+893
Night Vision	+1007
Park Distance Control (Rear)	+132
Power Moonroof	+694
Power Tilt and Telescopic Steering Wheel [Opt on DTS]	+157
Rear Side Airbag Restraints	+132
Special Factory Paint	+291

After a complete redesign last year, changes for 2001 are minimal at best. A tire pressure monitoring system is available, Graphite replaces Parisian Blue and Polo Green paint schemes, Dark Gray is added as an interior color and all Devilles are now certified throughout the U.S. as low-emissions vehicles.

Cadillac
DeVille

2000

The 2000 DeVille is all new inside and out and showcases new automotive technologies such as Night Vision, Ultrasonic Rear Parking Assist and the newest generation of GM's StabiliTrak traction-control system. It also boasts improvements to the Northstar V8 that not only improve fuel economy, but make this engine operate even smoother than before.

Mileage Category: I

Body Styles	TMV Pricing		
	Trade	Private	Dealer
4 Dr DHS Sdn	11773	13431	15057
4 Dr DTS Sdn	12319	14054	15755

Options	Price
AM/FM/Cassette/CD Audio System [Opt on STD]	+117
Adaptive Seat Package [Opt on DHS,DTS]	+386
Automatic Stability Control [Opt on DHS,STD]	+186
Chrome Wheels [Opt on DHS,STD]	+309
Compact Disc Changer	+214
Heated Front and Rear Seats [Opt on DHS,STD]	+136
Leather Seats [Opt on STD]	+305
Navigation System [Opt on DHS,DTS]	+775

Body Styles	TMV Pricing		
	Trade	Private	Dealer
4 Dr STD Sdn	9716	11084	12425

Options	Price
Night Vision [Opt on DHS,DTS]	+775
OnStar Telematics System	+348
Park Distance Control (Rear)	+117
Power Moonroof	+602
Power Tilt and Telescopic Steering Wheel [Opt on DTS]	+136
Rear Side Airbag Restraints	+115
Special Factory Paint	+252

1999

Mileage Category: I

Body Styles	TMV Pricing		
	Trade	Private	Dealer
4 Dr Concours Sdn	7232	8386	9588
4 Dr D'elegance Sdn	7182	8329	9522

Options	Price
AM/FM/Cassette/CD Audio System [Opt on STD]	+140
Automatic Stability Control [Opt on Concours,D'elegance]	+155
Chrome Wheels [Std on D'elegance]	+224
Compact Disc Changer	+155

Body Styles	TMV Pricing		
	Trade	Private	Dealer
4 Dr STD Sdn	6662	7725	8832

Options	Price
Leather Seats [Opt on STD]	+220
OnStar Telematics System	+279
Power Moonroof	+436
Special Factory Paint	+183

Comfort is big with Cadillac, so who else would offer massaging lumbar seats? Sure enough, this industry-first option is available on '99 d'Elegance and Concours models. All DeVilles get an electrochromic inside rearview mirror with compass added to the standard equipment list, in addition to an audible theft-deterrent system. There are three new exterior colors this year, and one different shade of leather inside. As if that weren't enough, side airbag deployment now communicates with the optional OnStar communications system, so the outside world will know when you've taken a broadside hit. Comforting, indeed. Look for a limited run of about 2,000 specially badged and optioned Golden Anniversary Edition DeVilles, painted White Diamond with gold trim, to celebrate the model's 50th anniversary.

1998

StabiliTrak, an integrated chassis control system that can prevent four-wheel lateral skids, is available on base and d'Elegance. New radio systems debut, and door lock programmability is enhanced. An idiot light is added to warn about loose fuel caps, and new colors are available inside and out. Heated seats are added to the d'Elegance and Concours while the Concours also gets a much needed alloy wheel redesign. Second-generation airbags debut as standard equipment.

Mileage Category: I

Body Styles	TMV Pricing		
	Trade	Private	Dealer
4 Dr Concours Sdn	5627	7042	8638
4 Dr D'elegance Sdn	5609	7019	8610

Options	Price
Chrome Wheels [Opt on Concours,STD]	+181
Compact Disc Changer	+125
Leather Seats [Opt on STD]	+178

Body Styles	TMV Pricing		
	Trade	Private	Dealer
4 Dr STD Sdn	5143	6436	7895

Options	Price
OnStar Telematics System	+226
Power Moonroof	+352

1997

DeVille undergoes a substantial revamp for 1997, including revised styling, the addition of standard side-impact airbags and a fresh interior that is actually functional. Concours receives stability enhancement and road texture detection as part of its Integrated Chassis Control System (ICCS), while a new d'Elegance model picks up where the defunct Fleetwood left off. Finally, the OnStar Services package provides DeVille owners with security and convenience features that will pinpoint the car's location at any given time or allow you to book a flight to Paris from the comfort of your driver seat.

Mileage Category: I

Body Styles	TMV Pricing		
	Trade	Private	Dealer
4 Dr Concours Sdn	4679	5956	7517
4 Dr D'elegance Sdn	4614	5874	7413

Options	Price
Chrome Wheels	+154
Compact Disc Changer	+128
Leather Seats [Opt on STD]	+152

Body Styles	TMV Pricing		
	Trade	Private	Dealer
4 Dr STD Sdn	3942	5018	6333

Options	Price
OnStar Telematics System	+192
Power Moonroof	+300

1996

Northstar V8 is installed in base DeVille, along with a new transmission, Integrated Chassis Control System and road-sensing suspension. Concours gets 25 horsepower boost to 300, along with a higher final-drive ratio for quicker pickup and an improved continuously variable road-sensing suspension. Automatic windshield wipers and new variable-effort steering are standard on the Concours. Daytime running lights debut on both of these monsters.

Mileage Category: I

Body Styles	TMV Pricing		
	Trade	Private	Dealer
4 Dr Concours Sdn	3722	4809	6310

Body Styles	TMV Pricing		
	Trade	Private	Dealer
4 Dr STD Sdn	2976	3845	5046

1996 (cont'd)

Options	Price
Chrome Wheels	+130
Leather Seats [Opt on STD]	+128
OnStar Telematics System	+162

Options	Price
Power Moonroof	+253
Vinyl Roof	+122

1995

Traction control (which can be shut off) is standard on base DeVille. Headlights come on automatically when windshield wipers are activated. Chrome wheels can be ordered on Concours. Garage door opener is optional on DeVille; standard on Concours.

Mileage Category: I

Body Styles	TMV Pricing		
	Trade	Private	Dealer
4 Dr Concours Sdn	2643	3500	4928

Options	Price
Chrome Wheels	+101
Leather Seats [Opt on STD]	+100

Body Styles	TMV Pricing		
	Trade	Private	Dealer
4 Dr STD Sdn	2346	3107	4375

Options	Price
Power Moonroof	+197

Eldorado

2002

A special Collectors' Series package marks the final 1,600 coupes to come off the assembly line as the Eldorado heads for retirement.

Mileage Category: I

Body Styles	TMV Pricing		
	Trade	Private	Dealer
2 Dr ESC Cpe	18109	19354	21430
2 Dr ETC Collectors Series Cpe	21255	22717	25154

Options	Price
AM/FM/Cassette/CD Audio System [Opt on ESC]	+225
Automatic Stability Control [Opt on ESC]	+197
Bose Audio System [Opt on ESC]	+449
Chrome Wheels	+447

Body Styles	TMV Pricing		
	Trade	Private	Dealer
2 Dr ETC Cpe	19255	20580	22787

Options	Price
Compact Disc Changer	+281
Power Driver Seat w/Memory [Opt on ESC]	+121
Power Moonroof	+871
Special Factory Paint	+365

2001

Only three minor changes grace the Eldorado for 2001: Sequoia is added for an exterior color, Dark Gray is added for the interior and the Bose sound system with mini-disc player goes away.

Mileage Category: I

Body Styles	TMV Pricing		
	Trade	Private	Dealer
2 Dr ESC Cpe	14056	15799	17408

Options	Price
Automatic Stability Control [Opt on ESC]	+222
Bose Audio System [Opt on ESC]	+546
Chrome Wheels	+356

Body Styles	TMV Pricing		
	Trade	Private	Dealer
2 Dr ETC Cpe	15806	17765	19574

Options	Price
Compact Disc Changer	+266
Power Moonroof	+694
Special Factory Paint	+291

2000

The Northstar V8s have been improved, and the standard Eldorado gets a new logo, ESC (for Eldorado Sport Coupe). The racy Eldorado Touring Coupe (ETC) lands exterior enhancements such as body-color fascia moldings and side inserts (replacing chrome), new seven-spoke wheels with Cadillac logos in the center caps and a new ETC deck lid logo.

Mileage Category: I

Body Styles	TMV Pricing		
	Trade	Private	Dealer
2 Dr ESC Cpe	11416	13024	14600

Options	Price
AM/FM/Cassette/CD Audio System [Opt on ESC]	+117
Automatic Stability Control [Opt on ESC]	+192
Bose Audio System [Opt on ESC]	+233
Chrome Wheels	+309

Body Styles	TMV Pricing		
	Trade	Private	Dealer
2 Dr ETC Cpe	12347	14086	15790

Options	Price
Compact Disc Changer	+214
OnStar Telematics System	+348
Power Moonroof	+602
Special Factory Paint	+194

1999

Colors are big each year with Cadillac, and 1999 is no different. Cashmere, Parisian Blue and Sterling Silver replace Frost Beige, Baltic Blue Silver Mist and Shale on Eldorado's exterior color chart. Oatmeal leather replaces Cappuccino Cream as an interior color, while Pewter cloth has been deleted, leaving only Shale and Blue cloth available. In the hardware department, an electrochromic inside rearview mirror with compass and an audible theft-deterrent system are now standard equipment. The Eldorado Touring Coupe (ETC) also gets the Bose four-speaker AM/FM cassette/single-slot CD and Weather Band audio system standard, with the option of adding massaging lumbar seats that provide a gentle back rub as you drive.

Mileage Category: I

Body Styles	TMV Pricing		
	Trade	Private	Dealer
2 Dr STD Cpe	8861	10386	11973

Options	Price
Automatic Stability Control [Opt on STD]	+155
Chrome Wheels	+224
Compact Disc Changer	+155
Delco/Bose Audio System [Opt on STD]	+342

Body Styles	TMV Pricing		
	Trade	Private	Dealer
2 Dr Touring Cpe	9830	11521	13282

Options	Price
Leather Seats [Opt on STD]	+220
OnStar Telematics System	+279
Power Moonroof	+436
Special Factory Paint	+140

Cadillac
Eldorado/Escalade

1998

New radios, a revised interior electrochromic mirror, enhanced programmable features, second-generation airbags and the addition of StabiliTrak to the base model's options list are the major improvements for 1998.

Mileage Category: I

Body Styles	TMV Pricing		
	Trade	Private	Dealer
2 Dr STD Cpe	7009	8397	9963

Options	Price
Chrome Wheels	+181
Compact Disc Changer	+125
Delco/Bose Audio System [Opt on STD]	+277

Body Styles	TMV Pricing		
	Trade	Private	Dealer
2 Dr Touring Cpe	7980	9562	11345

Options	Price
Leather Seats [Opt on STD]	+178
OnStar Telematics System	+226
Power Moonroof	+352

1997

Structural, suspension and brake system enhancements are made across the board. Base models get MagnaSteer variable effort steering, while the Eldorado Touring Coupe (ETC) receives a new Integrated Chassis Control System (ICCS) that includes stability enhancement and road texture detection. All Eldos have slightly revised stereo and climate controls, and the OnStar services package is a slick new option that can notify emergency personnel where your disabled car is located or can allow you to book dinner reservations from the driver seat.

Mileage Category: I

Body Styles	TMV Pricing		
	Trade	Private	Dealer
2 Dr STD Cpe	5655	6946	8523

Options	Price
Chrome Wheels	+154
Delco/Bose Audio System	+236
Leather Seats [Opt on STD]	+152

Body Styles	TMV Pricing		
	Trade	Private	Dealer
2 Dr Touring Cpe	6232	7655	9394

Options	Price
OnStar Telematics System	+192
Power Moonroof	+300

1996

Sea Mist Green is a new interior and exterior color, and daytime running lights are standard. Eldorado gets new seats and revised audio systems. Touring Coupe interior is revised, with a center-stack console, bigger gauges and seamless passenger airbag. Rainsense, an automatic windshield wiper system, is standard on the ETC, as is an updated continuously variable road-sensing suspension.

Mileage Category: I

Body Styles	TMV Pricing		
	Trade	Private	Dealer
2 Dr STD Cpe	4015	5275	7016

Options	Price
Chrome Wheels	+130
Compact Disc Changer	+126
Delco/Bose Audio System	+131

Body Styles	TMV Pricing		
	Trade	Private	Dealer
2 Dr Touring Cpe	4588	6029	8018

Options	Price
Leather Seats [Opt on STD]	+128
OnStar Telematics System	+162
Power Moonroof	+253

1995

Northstar V8 power is increased. Electronic chassis controls now evaluate steering angle when deciding what to do with the Road Sensing Suspension, traction control and ABS. Styling is slightly revised front and rear. Headlights come on automatically when windshield wipers are activated.

Mileage Category: I

Body Styles	TMV Pricing		
	Trade	Private	Dealer
2 Dr STD Cpe	2876	3872	5533

Options	Price
Chrome Wheels	+101
Delco/Bose Audio System	+92

Body Styles	TMV Pricing		
	Trade	Private	Dealer
2 Dr Touring Cpe	3129	4212	6018

Options	Price
Leather Seats [Opt on STD]	+100
Power Moonroof	+197

Escalade

2004

Mileage Category: O

Body Styles	TMV Pricing		
	Trade	Private	Dealer
4 Dr STD AWD SUV	38546	40304	43235

Options	Price
17 Inch Wheels - Chrome	+700
AM/FM/CD Audio System	+500
DVD Entertainment System	+1295

Body Styles	TMV Pricing		
	Trade	Private	Dealer
4 Dr STD SUV	36553	38311	41242

Options	Price
Navigation System	+1100
Power Moonroof	+1000
Special Factory Paint	+995

Although the Escalade remains basically unchanged, there are a few upgrades to the standard equipment list and how some optional equipment can be configured. XM Satellite Radio, a tire-pressure monitoring system, second-row bucket seats and a tow package are all now standard equipment, while a sunroof can now be ordered in conjunction with the rear-seat DVD entertainment system. Blue Chip, Quicksilver and Red E are new exterior colors.

2003

Mileage Category: O

Body Styles	TMV Pricing		
	Trade	Private	Dealer
4 Dr STD AWD SUV	33507	35807	39641

Options	Price
Camper/Towing Package	+125
Chrome Wheels	+524
DVD Entertainment System	+854
Navigation System	+1022

Body Styles	TMV Pricing		
	Trade	Private	Dealer
4 Dr STD SUV	31130	33267	36828

Options	Price
Power Moonroof	+1022
Satellite Radio System	+214
Special Factory Paint	+656

Despite brisk sales of the Escalade in 2002, there are numerous upgrades for 2003 to keep the luxury sport-ute at the top of its game. An improved StabiliTrak stability control system is now standard on both two- and all-wheel-drive models, while all Escalades get an improved braking system, High Intensity Discharge (HID) headlights, exterior mirrors with integrated turn signals and chrome wheels as an option. The interior has also been updated with new features like tri-zone climate control, satellite steering wheel controls and a redesigned instrument cluster and center console. The standard Bose audio system received some minor upgrades while new options include XM Satellite Radio, a DVD entertainment system and second-row captain's chairs. Added safety comes in the way of dual-stage airbags, adjustable pedals, a front-passenger seat sensor and three-point belts for all first- and second-row passengers.

2002

Mileage Category: O

Body Styles	TMV Pricing		
	Trade	Private	Dealer
4 Dr STD AWD SUV	28374	30638	34412

Options	Price
Power Moonroof	+871

Body Styles	TMV Pricing		
	Trade	Private	Dealer
4 Dr STD SUV	26240	28334	31823

Options	Price
Special Factory Paint	+559

No longer a mere Yukon Denali spin-off, the radiant new Escalade bursts onto the luxury SUV scene and attempts to maul its competitors with a monstrous 6.0-liter engine and enough technology to satisfy the target demographic.

2000

Mileage Category: O

Body Styles	TMV Pricing		
	Trade	Private	Dealer
4 Dr STD 4WD SUV	15288	17577	19820

Options	Price
OnStar Telematics System	+348

The big change for 2000 is the availability of vertical-split rear cargo doors in addition to the standard split-tailgate rear-hatch design.

1999

Mileage Category: O

Body Styles	TMV Pricing		
	Trade	Private	Dealer
4 Dr STD 4WD SUV	12899	14935	17054

Options	Price
OnStar Telematics System	+279

The new Cadillac Escalade is really more a 1999 GMC Yukon Denali than it is a Cadillac. (And GMC's Yukon Denali is really more Yukon than anything else -- except, perhaps, a Chevrolet Tahoe, but that's another story). Regardless of its origins, think of the Escalade as a big four-wheel-drive Cadillac limo for well-heeled outdoorsy types. Loaded with luxury touches and every possible convenience (even GM's OnStar mobile communications system), Escalade comes in four special colors and lacks only one thing: an options list. Why? It's got it all.

Escalade ESV

2004

Mileage Category: O

Body Styles	TMV Pricing		
	Trade	Private	Dealer
4 Dr Platinum Edition AWD SUV	47893	49487	52144

Options	Price
17 Inch Wheels - Chrome [Opt on STD AWD]	+700
AM/FM/CD Audio System [Opt on STD AWD]	+500
DVD Entertainment System [Opt on STD AWD]	+1295

Body Styles	TMV Pricing		
	Trade	Private	Dealer
4 Dr STD AWD SUV	40100	41695	44352

Options	Price
Navigation System [Opt on STD AWD]	+1100
Power Moonroof [Opt on STD AWD]	+1000
Special Factory Paint	+995

For 2004, the ESV adds XM Satellite Radio, a tire-pressure monitoring system and a towing package to the standard equipment list. The rear-seat entertainment system and sunroof can now be ordered together. A limited-production Platinum edition ESV will become available in late 2003 that offers a more lavish interior, dual DVD screens for the rear seats, 20-inch chrome wheels and a lowered suspension.

2003

Mileage Category: O

Body Styles	TMV Pricing		
	Trade	Private	Dealer
4 Dr STD AWD SUV	36081	38120	41517

The ESV is an all-new model in the Cadillac lineup. Essentially nothing more than a slightly stretched version of the standard Escalade, the ESV incorporates all of the improvements made to the standard Escalade for 2003.

2003 (cont'd)

Options	Price
Camper/Towing Package	+125
Chrome Wheels	+524
DVD Entertainment System	+854
Navigation System	+1022

Options	Price
Power Moonroof	+1022
Satellite Radio System	+214
Special Factory Paint	+656

Escalade EXT

2004

Mileage Category: O

Body Styles		TMV Pricing	
	Trade	Private	Dealer
4 Dr STD AWD Crew Cab SB	37524	39258	42148

Options	Price
17 Inch Wheels - Chrome	+700
AM/FM/CD Audio System	+500
DVD Entertainment System	+1295

Options	Price
Navigation System	+1100
Power Moonroof	+1000
Special Factory Paint	+995

For 2004, the EXT adds XM Satellite Radio, a tire-pressure monitoring system and a towing package as standard equipment. The rear-seat entertainment system and sunroof can now be ordered together. Quicksilver and Red E are new exterior colors, while Silver Sand and Green Envy are no longer available.

2003

Despite strong sales in 2002, the EXT gets a host of new upgrades for 2003 to help maintain its momentum. An improved StabiliTrak stability control system is now standard along with an upgraded braking system, High Intensity Discharge (HID) headlights, exterior mirrors with integrated turn signals and chrome wheels as an option. The interior also has a number of improvements, including tri-zone climate control, satellite steering wheel controls and a redesigned instrument cluster and center console. The standard Bose audio system receives some minor upgrades while new options include XM Satellite Radio, a DVD entertainment system and bucket seats for the second row. Added safety comes in the way of dual-stage airbags, adjustable pedals, a front-passenger seat sensor and three-point belts for all first- and second-row passengers.

Mileage Category: O

Body Styles		TMV Pricing	
	Trade	Private	Dealer
4 Dr STD AWD Crew Cab SB	32284	34460	38087

Options	Price
Camper/Towing Package	+125
Chrome Wheels	+524
DVD Entertainment System	+854
Navigation System	+1022

Options	Price
Power Moonroof	+1022
Satellite Radio System	+214
Special Factory Paint	+656

2002

In response to Lincoln's new Blackwood pickup, which is little more than a Ford F-150 Super Crew with a Navigator cabin grafted on, Cadillac trots out this Chevrolet Avalanche with an Escalade facelift.

Mileage Category: O

Body Styles		TMV Pricing	
	Trade	Private	Dealer
4 Dr STD AWD Crew Cab SB	27012	29167	32759

Options	Price
Power Moonroof	+871

Options	Price
Special Factory Paint	+559

Fleetwood

1996

Mileage Category: I

Body Styles		TMV Pricing	
	Trade	Private	Dealer
4 Dr STD Sdn	4299	5449	7037

Options	Price
Chrome Wheels	+195
Leather Seats	+128

Options	Price
Power Moonroof	+253
Vinyl Roof	+151

Final year for the longest production car sold in the U.S. Updates are limited to a new audio system, revised center storage armrest and prewiring for Cadillac's Dual Mode cellular phone.

1995

Traction control gets on/off switch. Platinum-tipped spark plugs are added, allowing tune-ups to occur every 100,000 miles. Antilockout feature added. Remote keyless entry, central unlocking and fold-away outside mirrors are added. Garage door opener is new option.

Mileage Category: I

Body Styles		TMV Pricing	
	Trade	Private	Dealer
4 Dr STD Sdn	2965	3927	5530

Options	Price
Chrome Wheels	+152
Leather Seats	+100

Options	Price
Power Moonroof	+197
Vinyl Roof	+118

Seville

Mileage Category: I

Body Styles	TMV Pricing		
	Trade	Private	Dealer
4 Dr SLS Sdn	23281	25380	28877

Options	Price	Options	Price
16 Inch Wheels - Chrome	+300	Power Driver Seat w/Memory	+350
AM/FM/Cassette/CD Audio System	+450	Power Moonroof	+1550
Automatic Dimming Sideview Mirror(s)	+250	Power Tilt and Telescopic Steering Wheel	+380
Bose Audio System	+1100	Rain Sensing Windshield Wipers	+250
Chrome Wheels	+795	Satellite Radio System	+325
Compact Disc Changer	+400	Special Factory Paint	+995
Garage Door Opener	+150	Wood Gearshift Knob	+150
Navigation System	+1995	Wood Steering Wheel	+200

The STS has been dropped from the lineup in anticipation of the all-new version scheduled for release in mid-'04. The remaining SLS gets two new colors and a standard eight-speaker stereo with TheftLock.

2003

The STS now sports standard 17-inch chrome wheels while all Sevilles can now couple XM Satellite Radio with the DVD navigation system. The SLS also gets a new body-colored grille and foglamps for a monochromatic look.

Mileage Category: I

Body Styles	TMV Pricing			Body Styles	TMV Pricing		
	Trade	Private	Dealer		Trade	Private	Dealer
4 Dr SLS Sdn	18438	19811	22098	4 Dr STS Sdn	23055	24772	27633

Options	Price	Options	Price
Chrome Wheels [Opt on SLS]	+524	Rain Sensing Windshield Wipers [Opt on SLS]	+115
Compact Disc Changer	+363	Satellite Radio System	+214
Navigation System	+1187	Special Factory Paint	+656
Power Driver Seat w/Memory [Opt on SLS]	+142	Tire Pressure Monitoring System [Opt on STS]	+165
Power Moonroof	+1022	Xenon Headlamps [Opt on STS]	+330
Power Tilt and Telescopic Steering Wheel [Opt on SLS]	+231		

2002

An advanced navigation system with voice recognition and the Bose 4.0 sound system is new for 2002. Cadillac's restyled wreath and crest ornamentation is also added along with oil change intervals that have been increased from 10,000 to 12,500 miles. Later in the year, Seville gets two new colors, as well as provisions for Digital Satellite radio and a cellular integration package.

Mileage Category: I

Body Styles	TMV Pricing			Body Styles	TMV Pricing		
	Trade	Private	Dealer		Trade	Private	Dealer
4 Dr SLS Sdn	15838	17338	19839	4 Dr STS Sdn	18395	20138	23042

Options	Price	Options	Price
17 Inch Wheels - Chrome	+449	Power Moonroof	+871
AM/FM/Cassette/CD Changer Audio System	+225	Power Tilt and Telescopic Steering Wheel [Opt on SLS]	+197
Chrome Wheels	+447	Satellite Radio System	+166
Compact Disc Changer	+309	Special Factory Paint	+365
Navigation System	+1011	Xenon Headlamps	+281
Power Driver Seat w/Memory [Opt on SLS]	+121		

2001

Tire-pressure monitoring is now available on the STS, as well as an e-mail-capable Infotainment radio, a hands-free integrated cellular phone, 17-inch chrome wheels and high-intensity discharge headlamps. OnStar in-vehicle safety, security and information service is now standard fare on the STS and available on the SLS. Two new SLS and three STS packages round out the changes.

Mileage Category: I

Body Styles	TMV Pricing			Body Styles	TMV Pricing		
	Trade	Private	Dealer		Trade	Private	Dealer
4 Dr SLS Sdn	13810	15971	17967	4 Dr STS Sdn	15394	17804	20028

Options	Price	Options	Price
Adaptive Seat Package	+445	Power Tilt and Telescopic Steering Wheel [Opt on SLS]	+157
Bose Audio System [Opt on SLS]	+425	Premium Audio System	+425
Chrome Wheels	+356	Special Factory Paint	+291
Compact Disc Changer	+246	Xenon Headlamps	+224
Park Distance Control (Rear)	+132		
Power Moonroof	+694		

2000

The Northstar V8s have been improved, and all models get a new airbag suppression system and the revised version of GM's StabiliTrak. A new ultrasonic rear parking assist feature and an advanced navigation system are optional on both STS and SLS. There are also two new exterior colors, Midnight Blue and Bronzemist.

Mileage Category: I

Body Styles	TMV Pricing			Body Styles	TMV Pricing		
	Trade	Private	Dealer		Trade	Private	Dealer
4 Dr SLS Sdn	11255	13298	15300	4 Dr STS Sdn	12813	15138	17417

2000 (cont'd)

Options	Price
Adaptive Seat Package	+466
Bose Audio System [Opt on SLS]	+369
Bose Mini Disc Player [Opt on SLS]	+486
Chrome Wheels	+309
Compact Disc Changer	+214
Navigation System	+775

Options	Price
OnStar Telematics System	+348
Park Distance Control (Rear)	+115
Power Moonroof	+602
Power Tilt and Telescopic Steering Wheel [Opt on SLS]	+136
Special Factory Paint	+252

1999

The Seville sees only minor changes after its successful redesign in 1998. Cadillac's new massaging lumbar seats are offered as an option on the STS. Heated seats become part of the adaptive seat package, which is now available on both SLS and STS trim levels. And the optional OnStar mobile communications system will automatically notify the OnStar customer assistance center in the case of any airbag deployment, front or side, so that the center can dispatch emergency services to the scene. Previously, notification occurred only with a front airbag deployment. There are also three new exterior colors, Cashmere, Parisian Blue and Sterling Silver, and one new interior shade called Oatmeal.

Mileage Category: I

Body Styles	TMV Pricing		
	Trade	Private	Dealer
4 Dr SLS Sdn	9344	11413	13566

Body Styles	TMV Pricing		
	Trade	Private	Dealer
4 Dr STS Sdn	9869	12055	14331

Options	Price
Adaptive Seat Package	+338
Chrome Wheels	+224
Compact Disc Changer	+155
Delco/Bose Audio System [Opt on SLS]	+232

Options	Price
OnStar Telematics System	+279
Power Moonroof	+436
Special Factory Paint	+183

1998

Cadillac redefines the American luxury car by debuting an all-new Seville that boasts the performance, style, refinement and technological innovation necessary to play ball on a global level.

Mileage Category: I

Body Styles	TMV Pricing		
	Trade	Private	Dealer
4 Dr SLS Sdn	6366	7967	9772

Body Styles	TMV Pricing		
	Trade	Private	Dealer
4 Dr STS Sdn	7170	8973	11006

Options	Price
Adaptive Seat Package [Opt on STS]	+273
Chrome Wheels	+181
Compact Disc Changer	+125

Options	Price
Delco/Bose Audio System [Opt on SLS]	+187
OnStar Telematics System	+226
Power Moonroof	+352

1997

Mileage Category: I

Body Styles	TMV Pricing		
	Trade	Private	Dealer
4 Dr SLS Sdn	4571	5819	7345

Body Styles	TMV Pricing		
	Trade	Private	Dealer
4 Dr STS Sdn	5259	6695	8451

Options	Price
Chrome Wheels	+154
Delco/Bose Audio System	+160
Leather Seats [Opt on SLS]	+152

Options	Price
OnStar Telematics System	+192
Power Moonroof	+300

All Sevilles receive body structure, suspension, brake system and interior enhancements. STS models get a new stability enhancement feature designed to correct lateral skids, and road texture detection, which helps modulate the ABS more effectively on rough roads. Enhanced programmable memory systems are new to both models, as is a revised rear seat back and the availability of OnStar, a vehicle information and communications service. SLS models get MagnaSteer variable-effort steering.

1996

All Sevilles get new seats and seat trim, redesigned sound systems, an (optional) integrated voice-activated cellular phone, daytime running lights and programmable door lock functions and seating positions. The STS also receives an updated instrument panel with big gauges and a new center console, the Cadillac-exclusive Rainsense Wiper System (which detects rainfall and turns the wipers on automatically) and a newly improved continuously variable road-sensing suspension. Magnasteer variable-assist steering replaces the old speed-sensitive gear on last year's STS.

Mileage Category: I

Body Styles	TMV Pricing		
	Trade	Private	Dealer
4 Dr SLS Sdn	3794	4901	6430

Body Styles	TMV Pricing		
	Trade	Private	Dealer
4 Dr STS Sdn	4233	5469	7177

Options	Price
Chrome Wheels	+130
Delco/Bose Audio System	+122
Leather Seats	+128

Options	Price
OnStar Telematics System	+162
Power Moonroof	+253

1995

Northstar V8 power is increased. Electronic chassis controls now evaluate steering angle when deciding what to do with the road-sensing suspension, traction control and ABS. Headlights come on automatically when windshield wipers are activated. Chrome wheels are a new option.

Mileage Category: I

Body Styles	TMV Pricing		
	Trade	Private	Dealer
4 Dr SLS Sdn	2922	3871	5452

Body Styles	TMV Pricing		
	Trade	Private	Dealer
4 Dr STS Sdn	3274	4336	6106

Options	Price
Chrome Wheels	+101
Leather Seats [Opt on SLS]	+100

Options	Price
Power Moonroof	+197

SRX
2004

Mileage Category: O

Body Styles	TMV Pricing		
	Trade	Private	Dealer
4 Dr V6 AWD SUV	27706	29302	31961
4 Dr V6 SUV	25037	26633	29292

Options	Price
18 Inch Wheels [Opt on V6 AWD]	+600
Air Conditioning - Front and Rear [Opt on V6 RWD]	+500
Automatic Dimming Sideview Mirror(s) [Opt on V6 RWD]	+150
Bose Audio System	+400
Camper/Towing Package [Opt on V8]	+250
DVD Entertainment System	+1200
Electronic Suspension Control [Opt on V6 AWD]	+1650
Garage Door Opener [Opt on V6 RWD]	+150
Headlight Washers [Opt on AWD]	+150
Heated Front Seats [Opt on V6 RWD]	+350
Navigation System [Opt on AWD]	+600
Polished Aluminum/Alloy Wheels [Opt on V6]	+400

Body Styles	TMV Pricing		
	Trade	Private	Dealer
4 Dr V8 AWD SUV	31906	33616	36466
4 Dr V8 SUV	30629	32337	35184

Options	Price
Power Adjustable Foot Pedals [Opt on V6 RWD]	+250
Power Driver Seat w/Memory [Opt on V6 RWD]	+350
Power Panorama Roof	+1800
Power Passenger Seat [Opt on V6 RWD]	+300
Power Third Seat	+1000
Premium Audio System	+1100
Satellite Radio System	+325
Special Factory Paint	+995
Wood Gearshift Knob [Opt on V6 RWD]	+150
Wood Interior Trim [Opt on V6 RWD]	+200
Wood Steering Wheel [Opt on V6 RWD]	+200
Xenon Headlamps [Opt on AWD]	+250

The SRX is an all-new car-based luxury SUV that shares its styling and platform with the CTS sedan.

XLR
2004

Mileage Category: F

Body Styles	TMV Pricing		
	Trade	Private	Dealer
2 Dr STD Conv	57712	59761	63175

Options	Price
Satellite Radio System	+325

The XLR is an all-new luxury roadster from Cadillac.

Astro

2004

Mechanically unchanged, the Astro now offers a chrome grille.

Mileage Category: P

Body Styles	TMV Pricing			Body Styles	TMV Pricing		
	Trade	Private	Dealer		Trade	Private	Dealer
3 Dr LS AWD Pass Van Ext	13604	14835	16887	3 Dr LT Pass Van Ext	14531	15762	17814
3 Dr LS Pass Van Ext	12628	13859	15911	3 Dr STD AWD Pass Van Ext	12996	14227	16279
3 Dr LT AWD Pass Van Ext	15506	16737	18789	3 Dr STD Pass Van Ext	12021	13252	15304

Options	Price	Options	Price
AM/FM/CD Audio System [Opt on LS]	+205	Overhead Console [Opt on LS]	+250
AM/FM/Cassette/CD Audio System [Opt on LS]	+600	Power Driver Seat [Opt on LS]	+450
Air Conditioning - Front and Rear [Opt on LS]	+525	Rear Audio Controls [Opt on LS]	+125
Camper/Towing Package	+265	Rear Heater	+240
Keyless Entry System [Opt on STD]	+170	Rear Window Defroster [Opt on LS]	+250
Leather Seats [Opt on LT]	+950	Rear Window Wiper [Opt on LS]	+300
Locking Differential	+280	Running Boards [Opt on LS]	+400
Luggage Rack [Opt on LS]	+130	Trip Computer [Opt on LS]	+250

2003

All 2003 Astros have larger 16-inch aluminum wheels and an improved braking system.

Mileage Category: P

Body Styles	TMV Pricing			Body Styles	TMV Pricing		
	Trade	Private	Dealer		Trade	Private	Dealer
3 Dr LS AWD Pass Van Ext	11014	12067	13821	3 Dr LT Pass Van Ext	11464	12559	14385
3 Dr LS Pass Van Ext	10268	11249	12884	3 Dr STD AWD Pass Van Ext	10332	11319	12965
3 Dr LT AWD Pass Van Ext	12202	13368	15311	3 Dr STD Pass Van Ext	9550	10463	11984

Options	Price	Options	Price
AM/FM/CD Audio System [Opt on LS]	+260	Locking Differential	+161
Air Conditioning - Front and Rear [Opt on LS]	+334	Power Driver Seat [Opt on LS]	+153
Camper/Towing Package	+197	Rear Heater	+131
Leather Seats [Opt on LT]	+606	Running Boards [Opt on LS]	+255

2002

A multiport fuel-injection system has been added for smoother operation along with a revised catalytic converter for better emissions control. Synthetic gear oil is now standard in the rear axle for reduced wear during heavy towing.

Mileage Category: P

Body Styles	TMV Pricing			Body Styles	TMV Pricing		
	Trade	Private	Dealer		Trade	Private	Dealer
3 Dr LS AWD Pass Van Ext	9097	10021	11561	3 Dr LT AWD Pass Van Ext	10065	11087	12791
3 Dr LS Pass Van Ext	8263	9102	10501	3 Dr LT Pass Van Ext	9443	10402	12001

Options	Price	Options	Price
AM/FM/Cassette/CD Audio System [Std on LT]	+172	Locking Differential	+145
Air Conditioning - Front and Rear [Std on LT]	+430	Power Driver Seat [Std on LT]	+138
Camper/Towing Package	+177	Rear Heater [Std on LT]	+118
Leather Seats	+545	Running Boards	+229

2001

Performance from Astro's Vortec 4300 V6 is enhanced, compliments of a new powertrain control module. Also new is a low-emission-vehicle (LEV) version. Color choices are expanded to include Light Pewter Metallic and Dark Carmine Red Metallic.

Mileage Category: P

Body Styles	TMV Pricing			Body Styles	TMV Pricing		
	Trade	Private	Dealer		Trade	Private	Dealer
3 Dr LS AWD Pass Van Ext	7209	8655	9989	3 Dr LS Pass Van Ext	6155	7389	8528

Options	Price	Options	Price
AM/FM/Cassette/CD Audio System	+189	Locking Differential	+132
Air Conditioning - Front and Rear	+274	Power Driver Seat	+125
Aluminum/Alloy Wheels	+191	Running Boards	+210
Leather Seats	+498	Trailer Hitch	+162

2000

Retained accessory power and additional warning chimes are added for 2000. Also new are automatic headlights with a flash-to-pass feature, remote keyless entry, battery rundown protection, lockout protection and a tow/haul trailering mode for the transmission. The ABS, engine and exhaust have been improved, and a plastic 27-gallon fuel tank is standard.

Mileage Category: P

Body Styles	TMV Pricing			Body Styles	TMV Pricing		
	Trade	Private	Dealer		Trade	Private	Dealer
3 Dr LS AWD Pass Van Ext	5485	6764	8018	3 Dr LT Pass Van Ext	5538	6829	8095
3 Dr LS Pass Van Ext	4938	6089	7217	3 Dr STD AWD Pass Van Ext	5420	6684	7923
3 Dr LT AWD Pass Van Ext	6263	7724	9156	3 Dr STD Pass Van Ext	4462	5502	6522

Options	Price
7 Passenger Seating	+281
AM/FM/CD Audio System	+190
AM/FM/Cassette/CD Audio System [Opt on LS]	+237
Air Conditioning - Front and Rear [Opt on LS]	+245
Camper/Towing Package	+145
Chrome Wheels [Std on LS]	+159

Options	Price
Leather Seats	+444
Limited Slip Differential	+118
Power Windows [Opt on STD]	+123
Privacy Glass [Opt on STD]	+136
Running Boards	+187
Trailer Hitch	+145

Mileage Category: P

1999

A new all-wheel-drive active transfer case replaces the previous AWD system, and includes a new control module and service light. There are two new interior roof consoles: one with storage is optional on base model, another with trip computer is standard on LS and LT trim. A new LT stripe design comes in three new colors. Dealer-installed running boards are available, as are new optional aluminum wheels. Three exterior paint colors are added for '99, while depowered airbags finally arrive this year. Finally, the outside mirrors are redesigned, available heated and with or without electrochromatic glare reduction.

Body Styles	TMV Pricing		
	Trade	Private	Dealer
3 Dr LS AWD Pass Van Ext	4382	5527	6719
3 Dr LS Pass Van Ext	3726	4698	5710
3 Dr LT AWD Pass Van Ext	5028	6341	7708

Body Styles	TMV Pricing		
	Trade	Private	Dealer
3 Dr LT Pass Van Ext	4460	5625	6837
3 Dr STD AWD Pass Van Ext	4055	5114	6217
3 Dr STD Pass Van Ext	3598	4538	5516

Options	Price
7 Passenger Seating	+224
AM/FM/CD Audio System	+151
AM/FM/Cassette/CD Audio System	+189
Air Conditioning - Front and Rear	+195
Aluminum/Alloy Wheels [Std on LT]	+136

Options	Price
Camper/Towing Package	+115
Chrome Wheels [Std on LS]	+127
Leather Seats	+355
Running Boards	+149

Mileage Category: P

1998

New colors, improved clearcoating, a standard theft-deterrent system and the addition of composite headlights and an uplevel grille to base models are all that's different on this year's Astro. Full-power airbags continue for 1998.

Body Styles	TMV Pricing		
	Trade	Private	Dealer
3 Dr LS AWD Pass Van Ext	3546	4629	5851
3 Dr LS Pass Van Ext	3150	4113	5199
3 Dr LT AWD Pass Van Ext	3711	4845	6123

Body Styles	TMV Pricing		
	Trade	Private	Dealer
3 Dr LT Pass Van Ext	3407	4449	5623
3 Dr STD AWD Pass Van Ext	3124	4079	5156
3 Dr STD Pass Van Ext	2596	3389	4284

Options	Price
7 Passenger Seating	+189
8 Passenger Seating [Opt on STD]	+125
AM/FM/CD Audio System	+128

Options	Price
AM/FM/Cassette/CD Audio System	+160
Air Conditioning - Front and Rear	+165
Leather Seats	+299

Mileage Category: P

1997

Daytime running lights debut, and LT models can be equipped with leather upholstery. Also optional this year is a HomeLink three-channel transmitter. Delayed entry-exit lighting is now standard on all Astro passenger vans. Transmission refinements mean smoother shifts, and electronic variable orifice steering eases steering effort at low speeds.

Body Styles	TMV Pricing		
	Trade	Private	Dealer
3 Dr LS AWD Pass Van Ext	2770	3751	4949
3 Dr LS Pass Van Ext	2523	3415	4506
3 Dr LT AWD Pass Van Ext	3078	4167	5499

Body Styles	TMV Pricing		
	Trade	Private	Dealer
3 Dr LT Pass Van Ext	2879	3898	5143
3 Dr STD AWD Pass Van Ext	2577	3489	4603
3 Dr STD Pass Van Ext	2215	2998	3956

Options	Price
7 Passenger Seating	+171
AM/FM/CD Audio System	+116
AM/FM/Cassette/CD Audio System	+144

Options	Price
Air Conditioning - Front and Rear	+149
Leather Seats	+270

Mileage Category: P

1996

A new interior with dual airbags, new radio systems, an improved V6 and three new paint colors are the changes for this year.

Body Styles	TMV Pricing		
	Trade	Private	Dealer
3 Dr LS AWD Pass Van Ext	2218	3101	4321
3 Dr LS Pass Van Ext	1950	2726	3798
3 Dr LT AWD Pass Van Ext	2456	3434	4784

Body Styles	TMV Pricing		
	Trade	Private	Dealer
3 Dr LT Pass Van Ext	2390	3341	4655
3 Dr STD AWD Pass Van Ext	2171	3035	4229
3 Dr STD Pass Van Ext	1736	2427	3382

Options	Price
7 Passenger Seating	+135
AM/FM/Cassette/CD Audio System	+131

Options	Price
Air Conditioning - Front and Rear	+135

Mileage Category: P

1995

Front sheet metal is restyled. Regular-length versions are dropped from the lineup, leaving only the extended-length model. Multileaf steel springs replace single-leaf plastic springs. One engine is available, the 190-horsepower, 4.3-liter V6. Air conditioning is standard, and remote keyless entry is a new option.

Body Styles	TMV Pricing		
	Trade	Private	Dealer
3 Dr CL AWD Pass Van Ext	1830	2624	3946

Body Styles	TMV Pricing		
	Trade	Private	Dealer
3 Dr CL Pass Van Ext	1561	2239	3369

Chevrolet
Astro/Avalanche

1995 (cont'd)

Body Styles	TMV Pricing		
	Trade	Private	Dealer
3 Dr CS AWD Pass Van Ext	1634	2344	3526
3 Dr CS Pass Van Ext	1414	2028	3052
3 Dr LT AWD Pass Van Ext	1960	2811	4228

Options	Price
7 Passenger Seating	+121
8 Passenger Seating [Std on CL,LT]	+80

Body Styles	TMV Pricing		
	Trade	Private	Dealer
3 Dr LT Pass Van Ext	1830	2624	3948
3 Dr STD AWD Pass Van Ext	1617	2320	3491
3 Dr STD Pass Van Ext	1403	2011	3025

Options	Price
AM/FM/CD Audio System	+91
Air Conditioning - Front and Rear	+121

Avalanche
2004

The North Face package is no longer offered, but an electronic stability control system is now available as part of the Z66 Premium On-Road Suspension package. Hydroboost brakes are now standard on all 1500 series Avalanches and the optional 8.1-liter V8 is now rated at 320 hp and 445 lb-ft of torque.

Mileage Category: K

Body Styles	TMV Pricing		
	Trade	Private	Dealer
4 Dr 1500 4WD Crew Cab SB	23658	25014	27273
4 Dr 1500 Crew Cab SB	21289	22570	24704

Options	Price
Automatic Climate Control (2 Zone) - Driver and Passenger	+200
Camper/Towing Package	+210
DVD Entertainment System	+1295
Front Side Airbag Restraints	+350
Leather Seats	+800
Locking Differential	+295
Luggage Rack	+195
OnStar Telematics System	+200
Power Driver Seat w/Memory	+250

Body Styles	TMV Pricing		
	Trade	Private	Dealer
4 Dr 2500 4WD Crew Cab SB	25289	26719	29101

Options	Price
Power Moonroof	+200
Power Retractable Mirrors	+120
Satellite Radio System	+120
Side Steps	+585
Trailer Hitch	+195
Trip Computer	+150
Z66 Suspension Package [Opt on 1500 RWD]	+1335
Z71 Off-Road Suspension Package [Opt on 1500 4WD]	+1955

2003

The Avalanche gets numerous interior upgrades for '03 in addition to the midyear introduction of a "decladded" version that does without the oft-derided extensive lower body trim. Dual-zone climate control is now standard equipment on all models along with multistage airbags and a passenger airbag sensor. A redesigned instrument panel houses a more comprehensive driver information display; and an optional multifunction steering wheel puts climate, radio and trip computer controls right in the palm of your hands. New entertainment options include a Bose stereo system, XM Satellite Radio and a rear passenger DVD video system. Other new options include the StabiliTrak stability control system on 2WD half-ton models, adjustable pedals, and a fully automatic multizone climate control system.

Mileage Category: K

Body Styles	TMV Pricing		
	Trade	Private	Dealer
4 Dr 1500 4WD Crew Cab SB	21298	22836	25398
4 Dr 1500 Crew Cab SB	19019	20392	22680
4 Dr 1500 North Face Edition 4WD Crew Cab SB	24370	26129	29060

Options	Price
AM/FM/CD Changer Audio System	+255
Automatic Climate Control (2 Zone) - Driver and Passenger	+160
Bose Audio System [Std on North Face]	+249
Bucket Seats [Std on North Face]	+128
Camper/Towing Package	+121
DVD Entertainment System	+827
Front Side Airbag Restraints	+192
Heated Front Seats	+128
Leather Seats [Std on North Face]	+447
Locking Differential [Std on North Face]	+188

Body Styles	TMV Pricing		
	Trade	Private	Dealer
4 Dr 2500 4WD Crew Cab SB	22549	24177	26889
4 Dr 2500 Crew Cab SB	20566	22050	24524

Options	Price
Luggage Rack	+124
OnStar Telematics System	+444
Power Adjustable Foot Pedals	+160
Power Moonroof	+699
Power Passenger Seat	+163
Power Retractable Mirrors	+128
Satellite Radio System	+207
Side Steps	+373
Z66 Suspension Package [Opt on 2WD]	+667
Z71 Off-Road Suspension Package [Opt on 1500 4WD]	+667

2002

The 2002 Chevrolet Avalanche is the newest addition to the Chevy truck lineup. Incorporating a unique convertible cab system, the Avalanche can transform itself from a five-passenger sport-utility with a 5-foot-3-inch bed into a standard cab pickup with a full 8-foot-1-inch utility bed. A 5300 Vortec V8 is standard along with a heavy-duty towing package.

Mileage Category: K

Body Styles	TMV Pricing		
	Trade	Private	Dealer
4 Dr 1500 4WD Crew Cab SB	18073	19584	22101
4 Dr 1500 Crew Cab SB	16418	17791	20078

Options	Price
Automatic Climate Control	+143
Bucket Seats	+172
Heated Front Seats	+115
Leather Seats	+401
Locking Differential [Opt on 2WD]	+163

Body Styles	TMV Pricing		
	Trade	Private	Dealer
4 Dr 2500 4WD Crew Cab SB	19168	20770	23440
4 Dr 2500 Crew Cab SB	17445	18903	21334

Options	Price
Off-Road Suspension Package	+479
OnStar Telematics System	+244
Power Moonroof	+567
Power Passenger Seat	+115
Power Sunroof	+628

For the latest vehicle information, visit www.edmunds.com

Options	Price
Side Steps	+335

Options	Price
Z71 Off-Road Suspension Package	+479

Aveo
2004

Mileage Category: A

Body Styles	TMV Pricing		
	Trade	Private	Dealer
4 Dr LS Hbk	6429	7062	8118
4 Dr LS Sdn	6429	7062	8118
4 Dr STD Hbk	5963	6596	7652

Body Styles	TMV Pricing		
	Trade	Private	Dealer
4 Dr STD Sdn	5963	6596	7652
4 Dr Special Value Hbk	5193	5583	6232
4 Dr Special Value Sdn	5193	5583	6232

Options	Price
AM/FM/CD/MP3 Audio System [Opt on STD]	+300
Aluminum/Alloy Wheels [Opt on LS]	+375
Antilock Brakes [Opt on STD, LS]	+400
Automatic 4-Speed Transmission [Opt on STD, LS]	+850

Options	Price
Keyless Entry System [Opt on STD]	+350
Power Moonroof [Opt on LS]	+725
Premium Audio System [Opt on LS]	+250
Rear Spoiler [Opt on STD Hbk, LS Hbk]	+225

The Aveo is an all-new entry-level car from Chevrolet available as a four-door sedan or five-door hatchback.

Beretta
1996

Mileage Category: C

Body Styles	TMV Pricing		
	Trade	Private	Dealer
2 Dr STD Cpe	955	1624	2547

Body Styles	TMV Pricing		
	Trade	Private	Dealer
2 Dr Z26 Cpe	1138	1935	3036

Options	Price
3.1L V6 OHV 12V FI Engine [Opt on STD]	+329
Automatic 3-Speed Transmission	+143

Options	Price
Automatic 4-Speed Transmission [Opt on STD]	+220
Sunroof	+129

Final year for Beretta. Only change is the addition of long-life coolant to the engine.

1995

Daytime running lights are newly standard. 170-horse Quad 4 engine is dropped, and 3.1-liter V6 loses five horsepower. Platinum-tipped spark plugs are standard on both engines.

Body Styles	TMV Pricing		
	Trade	Private	Dealer
2 Dr STD Cpe	644	1170	2047

Body Styles	TMV Pricing		
	Trade	Private	Dealer
2 Dr Z26 Cpe	815	1484	2598

Options	Price
3.1L V6 OHV 12V FI Engine [Opt on STD]	+295
Automatic 3-Speed Transmission	+128

Options	Price
Automatic 4-Speed Transmission [Opt on STD]	+198
Sunroof	+116

Blazer
2004

Mileage Category: M

Body Styles	TMV Pricing		
	Trade	Private	Dealer
2 Dr LS 4WD SUV	12025	13233	15245
2 Dr LS SUV	10399	11424	13131
2 Dr LS ZR2 4WD SUV	13325	14550	16592
2 Dr LS ZR2 SUV	11833	12858	14566

Body Styles	TMV Pricing		
	Trade	Private	Dealer
2 Dr Xtreme SUV	11457	12482	14190
4 Dr LS 4WD SUV	13660	14923	17027
4 Dr LS SUV	12667	13930	16034

Options	Price
AM/FM/CD Changer Audio System	+395
Alarm System [Opt on Xtreme]	+180
Automatic 4-Speed Transmission [Opt on 2 Dr]	+1000
Bucket Seats [Opt on 4 Dr LS]	+250
Camper/Towing Package [Opt on LS]	+210
Keyless Entry System	+170
Locking Differential	+270
Power Door Locks	+180

Options	Price
Power Driver Seat	+200
Power Heated Mirrors	+120
Power Moonroof	+800
Power Windows	+185
Rear Window Defroster [Opt on LS]	+150
Skid Plates [Opt on 4WD]	+126
Steering Wheel Radio Controls [Opt on 2 Dr]	+125

A deluxe overhead console and the AutoTrac four-wheel-drive system can now be ordered as stand-alone options on any Blazer. The Xtreme model gets revised wheels.

Chevrolet
Blazer

2003

The Blazer gets only a few minor changes for 2003. A new fuel-injection system helps smooth out the aging 4.3-liter V6 while the interior get refreshed with new seat fabrics. Two-door models are now available in a bright yellow exterior color while the Xtreme model gets new quarter-panel graphics.

Mileage Category: M

Body Styles	TMV Pricing		
	Trade	Private	Dealer
2 Dr LS 4WD SUV	10162	11068	12577
2 Dr LS SUV	8644	9415	10699
2 Dr LS ZR2 4WD SUV	11151	12145	13802
2 Dr LS ZR2 SUV	10314	11234	12766

Options	Price
AM/FM/CD Changer Audio System	+252
Automatic 4-Speed Transmission [Opt on 2 Dr]	+638
Camper/Towing Package [Opt on LS]	+134
Cruise Control	+115
Locking Differential	+172

Body Styles	TMV Pricing		
	Trade	Private	Dealer
2 Dr Xtreme SUV	9767	10638	12089
4 Dr LS 4WD SUV	11689	12731	14468
4 Dr LS SUV	10725	11681	13273

Options	Price
Power Door Locks	+118
Power Driver Seat	+153
Power Moonroof	+511
Power Windows	+144

2002

Most new additions for 2002 involve cosmetic enhancements such as new exterior colors and optional sport stripes on the Xtreme model. LS models get a monotone paint scheme along with newly styled wheels.

Mileage Category: M

Body Styles	TMV Pricing		
	Trade	Private	Dealer
2 Dr LS 4WD SUV	8410	9306	10798
2 Dr LS SUV	7188	7954	9230
2 Dr Xtreme SUV	8081	8942	10376

Options	Price
AM/FM/CD Changer Audio System	+169
Automatic 4-Speed Transmission [Opt on 2 Dr]	+573
Bose Audio System	+284
Camper/Towing Package	+120
Compact Disc Changer	+227
Heated Front Seats	+143

Body Styles	TMV Pricing		
	Trade	Private	Dealer
4 Dr LS 4WD SUV	9654	10682	12396
4 Dr LS SUV	8921	9871	11454

Options	Price
Leather Seats	+430
Locking Differential	+155
Power Driver Seat	+138
Power Moonroof	+459
Power Windows	+129
Wide Stance Suspension Package	+1147

2001

Standard OnStar on premium models. Xtreme, a new trim level on the two-wheel-drive two-door that includes a low-riding sport suspension lowered by 2.5 inches, body cladding and special wheels, is now available.

Mileage Category: M

Body Styles	TMV Pricing		
	Trade	Private	Dealer
2 Dr LS 4WD SUV	6844	8023	9112
2 Dr LS SUV	5778	6773	7692
2 Dr Xtreme SUV	6621	7762	8816
4 Dr LS 4WD SUV	8587	10067	11433
4 Dr LS SUV	7795	9139	10378

Options	Price
Automatic 4-Speed Transmission [Opt on 2 Dr]	+525
Bose Audio System	+260
Compact Disc Changer	+207
Heated Front Seats	+131
Leather Seats [Opt on LT]	+446
Locking Differential	+174

Body Styles	TMV Pricing		
	Trade	Private	Dealer
4 Dr LT 4WD SUV	9357	10971	12460
4 Dr LT SUV	8628	10114	11487
4 Dr TrailBlazer 4WD SUV	9551	11197	12716
4 Dr TrailBlazer SUV	9456	11086	12589

Options	Price
Power Driver Seat [Std on LT]	+125
Power Moonroof	+420
Power Passenger Seat [Std on Trailblazer]	+126
Power Windows [Opt on LS]	+137
Wide Stance Suspension Package	+1049

2000

Base models are dropped. The engine, exhaust and ABS are refined for increased durability, and exterior trim on some models is modified. Two new colors are available.

Mileage Category: M

Body Styles	TMV Pricing		
	Trade	Private	Dealer
2 Dr LS 4WD SUV	5054	6191	7305
2 Dr LS SUV	3861	4729	5580
4 Dr LS 4WD SUV	6097	7621	9115
4 Dr LS SUV	5662	6935	8183

Options	Price
AM/FM/CD Audio System [Opt on LS]	+154
Automatic 4-Speed Transmission [Opt on 2 Dr]	+468
Bose Audio System	+232
Compact Disc Changer	+187
Heated Front Seats	+117

Body Styles	TMV Pricing		
	Trade	Private	Dealer
4 Dr LT 4WD SUV	6280	7784	9258
4 Dr LT SUV	5925	7444	8933
4 Dr Trailblazer 4WD SUV	6629	8121	9583
4 Dr Trailblazer SUV	6474	7930	9357

Options	Price
Leather Seats [Opt on LT]	+398
Limited Slip Differential	+126
OnStar Telematics System	+325
Power Moonroof	+351
Power Windows [Opt on LS]	+122

Options	Price
ZR2 Highrider Suspension Package	+865

1999

Blazer gets automatic transmission improvements, new exterior colors and larger outside mirrors, while four-wheel-drive versions can be equipped with GM's AutoTrac active transfer case. Inside, there are new power-seating features, upgraded sound system options and available redundant radio controls in the steering wheel. On the safety side, the '99 Blazer now offers a vehicle content theft alarm, flash-to-pass headlamp feature and a liftgate ajar warning lamp. What's more, a new TrailBlazer trim package is available on four-door versions, featuring monochrome paint with gold accents, unique aluminum wheels, touring suspension and leather-lined interior.

Mileage Category: M

Body Styles	TMV Pricing			Body Styles	TMV Pricing		
	Trade	Private	Dealer		Trade	Private	Dealer
2 Dr LS 4WD SUV	4557	5699	6887	4 Dr LT 4WD SUV	5563	6957	8407
2 Dr LS SUV	3488	4362	5272	4 Dr LT SUV	5460	6828	8252
2 Dr STD 4WD SUV	4154	5195	6279	4 Dr STD 4WD SUV	4845	6059	7323
2 Dr STD SUV	3398	4249	5134	4 Dr STD SUV	4220	5277	6377
4 Dr LS 4WD SUV	5428	6788	8203	4 Dr Trailblazer 4WD SUV	5819	7276	8793
4 Dr LS SUV	4946	6185	7474	4 Dr Trailblazer SUV	5559	6952	8401

Options	Price	Options	Price
AM/FM/CD Audio System [Std on 2 Dr]	+123	Delco/Bose Audio System	+185
Automatic 4-Speed Transmission [Opt on 2 Dr]	+415	Power Moonroof [Opt on LS]	+280
Compact Disc Changer	+149	ZR2 Highrider Suspension Package	+691

1998

Blazer gets a front-end restyle and an interior redesign. New standard equipment includes a theft-deterrent system, automatic headlight control, four-wheel disc brakes and dual airbags incorporating second-generation technology to reduce the bags' inflation force. New radios, colors and a column-mounted automatic shift selector round out the major changes.

Mileage Category: M

Body Styles	TMV Pricing			Body Styles	TMV Pricing		
	Trade	Private	Dealer		Trade	Private	Dealer
2 Dr LS 4WD SUV	3939	5011	6220	4 Dr LS SUV	4170	5305	6585
2 Dr LS SUV	3095	3938	4889	4 Dr LT 4WD SUV	4733	6021	7474
2 Dr STD 4WD SUV	3740	4758	5905	4 Dr LT SUV	4275	5439	6751
2 Dr STD SUV	2975	3784	4697	4 Dr STD 4WD SUV	4081	5192	6445
4 Dr LS 4WD SUV	4245	5400	6703	4 Dr STD SUV	3463	4405	5468

Options	Price	Options	Price
Automatic 4-Speed Transmission [Opt on 2 Dr]	+349	Sport Suspension	+205
Power Moonroof	+218	Wide Stance Suspension Package	+582

1997

Those who prefer a liftgate over a tailgate have that option on 1997 four-door Blazers. A power sunroof is a new option for all Blazers, and models equipped with LT decor are equipped with a HomeLink transmitter that will open your garage, among other things. All-wheel-drive Blazers get four-wheel disc brakes, and automatic transmissions are revised for smoother shifting. Early-production 4WD two-door Blazers could be ordered with a ZR2 suspension package. Base Blazers get a chrome grille, while LT four-door models have body-color grilles in six exterior colors. Two new paint colors round out the changes.

Mileage Category: M

Body Styles	TMV Pricing			Body Styles	TMV Pricing		
	Trade	Private	Dealer		Trade	Private	Dealer
2 Dr LS 4WD SUV	3160	4123	5301	4 Dr LS SUV	3336	4353	5595
2 Dr LS SUV	2739	3574	4595	4 Dr LT 4WD SUV	3742	4882	6275
2 Dr STD 4WD SUV	2959	3861	4963	4 Dr LT SUV	3482	4543	5839
2 Dr STD SUV	2398	3129	4022	4 Dr STD 4WD SUV	3251	4242	5453
4 Dr LS 4WD SUV	3410	4449	5719	4 Dr STD SUV	2724	3554	4568

Options	Price	Options	Price
Automatic 4-Speed Transmission [Opt on 2 Dr]	+316	Wide Stance Suspension Package	+526
Power Moonroof	+198		

1996

More power, available all-wheel drive and five new colors improve the 1996 Blazer. A five-speed manual transmission is optional on two-door models.

Mileage Category: M

Body Styles	TMV Pricing			Body Styles	TMV Pricing		
	Trade	Private	Dealer		Trade	Private	Dealer
2 Dr LS 4WD SUV	2557	3453	4691	4 Dr LS SUV	2545	3438	4671
2 Dr LS SUV	2231	3013	4093	4 Dr LT 4WD SUV	2965	4004	5439
2 Dr STD 4WD SUV	2192	2960	4021	4 Dr LT SUV	2825	3816	5185
2 Dr STD SUV	1969	2660	3614	4 Dr STD 4WD SUV	2538	3427	4655
4 Dr LS 4WD SUV	2691	3635	4938	4 Dr STD SUV	2136	2885	3919

1995

All-new SUV appears based on revamped S10. S10 nomenclature is dropped, and full-size Blazer becomes Tahoe. Four-wheel-drive models have electronic transfer case as standard equipment. Spare tire on four-door model is mounted beneath cargo bay instead of in it. Five different suspension packages are available. One engine, a 195-horsepower 4.3-liter V6, is available. All-wheel drive is optional. Driver airbag and air conditioning are standard equipment.

Mileage Category: M

Body Styles	TMV Pricing			Body Styles	TMV Pricing		
	Trade	Private	Dealer		Trade	Private	Dealer
2 Dr LS 4WD SUV	1887	2598	3784	4 Dr LS SUV	1869	2570	3737
2 Dr LS SUV	1739	2396	3490	4 Dr LT 4WD SUV	2191	3018	4397
2 Dr STD 4WD SUV	1687	2325	3388	4 Dr LT SUV	2055	2832	4127
2 Dr STD SUV	1543	2125	3096	4 Dr STD 4WD SUV	1858	2560	3729
4 Dr LS 4WD SUV	1994	2747	4002	4 Dr STD SUV	1709	2356	3434

1995 (cont'd)

Options	Price
AM/FM/CD Audio System	+76

C/K 1500 Series

1999

Mileage Category: K

Body Styles	TMV Pricing		
	Trade	Private	Dealer
3 Dr C1500 LS Ext Cab SB	8137	9684	11294

Options	Price
5.7L V8 OHV 16V FI Engine	+261
Aluminum/Alloy Wheels	+127

Body Styles	TMV Pricing		
	Trade	Private	Dealer
3 Dr K1500 LS 4WD Ext Cab SB	9381	11165	13021

Options	Price
Leather Seats	+373

A few new colors are added to Chevrolet's popular pickup in anticipation of the all-new Silverado.

1998

This year's big news is a standard theft-deterrent system, revised color choices and fresh tailgate lettering. The Sport package has been dropped from the option list. Second-generation airbags are standard on models under 8,600 GVWR.

Mileage Category: K

Body Styles	TMV Pricing		
	Trade	Private	Dealer
2 Dr C1500 Cheyenne Ext Cab LB	5629	6841	8208
2 Dr C1500 Cheyenne Ext Cab SB	5309	6452	7741
2 Dr C1500 Cheyenne Std Cab LB	4589	5577	6692
2 Dr C1500 Cheyenne Std Cab SB	4350	5287	6344
2 Dr C1500 Cheyenne Std Cab Step SB	4783	5813	6974
2 Dr C1500 Silverado Ext Cab LB	6369	7740	9287
2 Dr C1500 Silverado Ext Cab SB	6168	7497	8995
2 Dr C1500 Silverado Ext Cab Step SB	6982	8486	10181
2 Dr C1500 Silverado Std Cab LB	5342	6493	7790
2 Dr C1500 Silverado Std Cab SB	5167	6279	7534
2 Dr C1500 Silverado Std Cab Step SB	5404	6568	7880
2 Dr C1500 WT Std Cab LB	4207	5113	6135
2 Dr C1500 WT Std Cab SB	4114	5000	5999
2 Dr K1500 Cheyenne 4WD Ext Cab LB	6935	8428	10112
2 Dr K1500 Cheyenne 4WD Ext Cab SB	6601	8022	9625

Body Styles	TMV Pricing		
	Trade	Private	Dealer
2 Dr K1500 Cheyenne 4WD Std Cab LB	5692	6918	8300
2 Dr K1500 Cheyenne 4WD Std Cab SB	5657	6876	8250
2 Dr K1500 Cheyenne 4WD Std Cab Step SB	5740	6976	8370
2 Dr K1500 Silverado 4WD Ext Cab LB	7412	9008	10808
2 Dr K1500 Silverado 4WD Ext Cab SB	7270	8836	10601
2 Dr K1500 Silverado 4WD Ext Cab Step SB	8526	10362	12432
2 Dr K1500 Silverado 4WD Std Cab LB	6633	8061	9672
2 Dr K1500 Silverado 4WD Std Cab SB	6464	7856	9425
2 Dr K1500 Silverado 4WD Std Cab Step SB	6694	8136	9762
2 Dr K1500 WT 4WD Std Cab LB	5500	6684	8019
2 Dr K1500 WT 4WD Std Cab SB	5370	6526	7830

Options	Price
5.0L V8 OHV 16V FI Engine	+156
5.7L V8 OHV 16V FI Engine	+220
6.5L V8 Turbodiesel OHV 16V Engine	+1064
Air Conditioning [Std on Silverado]	+253

Options	Price
Automatic 4-Speed Transmission	+305
Bucket Seats	+121
Hinged Third Door	+132
Leather Seats	+314

1997

On trucks under 8,600 pounds, the passenger airbag can be deactivated when a rear-facing child safety seat is installed. Low-speed steering effort is reduced this year, and a refined transmission fluid pump results in smoother shifts. An alternative fuel version of the Vortec 5700 is available, but only on a specific model. K1500's get a tighter turning radius, and three new colors debut. The third door option will be more widely available, because it is now a required option on all C/K 1500 short-bed extended cab trucks.

Mileage Category: K

Body Styles	TMV Pricing		
	Trade	Private	Dealer
2 Dr C1500 Cheyenne Ext Cab LB	4637	5780	7176
2 Dr C1500 Cheyenne Ext Cab SB	4314	5377	6677
2 Dr C1500 Cheyenne Ext Cab Step SB	4545	5665	7034
2 Dr C1500 Cheyenne Std Cab LB	3811	4750	5898
2 Dr C1500 Cheyenne Std Cab SB	3663	4566	5669
2 Dr C1500 Cheyenne Std Cab Step SB	3902	4864	6039
2 Dr C1500 Silverado Ext Cab LB	5552	6921	8594
2 Dr C1500 Silverado Ext Cab SB	5050	6295	7816
2 Dr C1500 Silverado Ext Cab Step SB	5279	6580	8170
2 Dr C1500 Silverado Std Cab LB	4363	5438	6751
2 Dr C1500 Silverado Std Cab SB	4223	5264	6536

Body Styles	TMV Pricing		
	Trade	Private	Dealer
2 Dr C1500 Silverado Std Cab Step SB	4493	5600	6953
2 Dr C1500 WT Std Cab LB	3581	4463	5542
2 Dr C1500 WT Std Cab SB	3536	4407	5472
2 Dr K1500 Cheyenne 4WD Ext Cab LB	5863	7308	9074
2 Dr K1500 Cheyenne 4WD Ext Cab SB	5464	6810	8456
2 Dr K1500 Cheyenne 4WD Ext Cab Step SB	5691	7094	8808
2 Dr K1500 Cheyenne 4WD Std Cab LB	4773	5950	7388
2 Dr K1500 Cheyenne 4WD Std Cab SB	4591	5722	7105

Body Styles	TMV Pricing		
	Trade	Private	Dealer
2 Dr K1500 Cheyenne 4WD Std Cab Step SB	4855	6052	7514
2 Dr K1500 Silverado 4WD Ext Cab LB	6195	7722	9589
2 Dr K1500 Silverado 4WD Ext Cab SB	5980	7454	9255
2 Dr K1500 Silverado 4WD Ext Cab Step SB	6177	7699	9559
2 Dr K1500 Silverado 4WD Std Cab LB	5648	7040	8741

Body Styles	TMV Pricing		
	Trade	Private	Dealer
2 Dr K1500 Silverado 4WD Std Cab SB	5508	6866	8525
2 Dr K1500 Silverado 4WD Std Cab Step SB	5737	7151	8880
2 Dr K1500 WT 4WD Std Cab LB	4507	5618	6975
2 Dr K1500 WT 4WD Std Cab SB	4451	5548	6889

Options	Price
5.0L V8 OHV 16V FI Engine	+141
5.7L V8 OHV 16V FI Engine	+199
6.5L V8 Turbodiesel OHV 16V Engine	+961
Air Conditioning [Std on Silverado]	+229

Options	Price
Automatic 4-Speed Transmission	+276
Hinged Third Door	+119
Leather Seats	+284

Mileage Category: K

1996

A new series of engines is introduced, providing more power and torque than last year's offerings. Called Vortec, this family of engines includes a 4.3-liter V6 (the only six-cylinder of the bunch) capable of 200 hp at 4,400 rpm and 255 lb-ft of torque at 2,800 rpm; a 5.0-liter V8, producing 220 hp at 4,600 rpm and 285 lb-ft of torque at 2,800 rpm; and a 5.7-liter V8, rated at 250 hp at 4,600 rpm and 335 lb-ft of torque at 2,800 rpm. (There is also a 7.4-liter Vortec V8, but it's only available on the heavier-duty C/K 3500 trucks.) All of these figures represent increases in output when compared to their respective 1995 predecessors. An optional electronic shift transfer case for the K1500 (i.e. 4WD; C=2WD; K=4WD) rounds out the list of the most significant powertrain updates for the year. Other noteworthy updates include the introduction of an optional passenger-side third door, called the "Easy-Access System," in GM vernacular. This feature is only available on the extended cab body styles. Improved comfort and convenience comes in the way of such new features as illuminated entry, 12-volt power outlets, an electrochromic inside rearview mirror and height-adjustable D-rings for the front three-point safety belts, among others. Daytime running lamps (DRLs) are part of the list of new exterior features. A new level of sophistication in exhaust emissions monitoring is found with the addition of OBD II, the second generation of On-Board Diagnostics.

Body Styles	TMV Pricing		
	Trade	Private	Dealer
2 Dr C1500 Cheyenne Ext Cab LB	3821	4903	6398
2 Dr C1500 Cheyenne Ext Cab SB	3349	4298	5608
2 Dr C1500 Cheyenne Ext Cab Step SB	3526	4525	5904
2 Dr C1500 Cheyenne Std Cab LB	3016	3870	5050
2 Dr C1500 Cheyenne Std Cab SB	3076	3948	5151
2 Dr C1500 Cheyenne Std Cab Step SB	3009	3861	5038
2 Dr C1500 Silverado Ext Cab LB	4381	5622	7336
2 Dr C1500 Silverado Ext Cab SB	3987	5117	6677
2 Dr C1500 Silverado Ext Cab Step SB	4114	5280	6889
2 Dr C1500 Silverado Std Cab LB	3570	4582	5979
2 Dr C1500 Silverado Std Cab SB	3315	4254	5551
2 Dr C1500 Silverado Std Cab Step SB	3564	4574	5968
2 Dr C1500 WT Std Cab LB	2939	3771	4921
2 Dr C1500 WT Std Cab SB	2855	3664	4780
2 Dr K1500 Cheyenne 4WD Ext Cab LB	4577	5873	7663
2 Dr K1500 Cheyenne 4WD Ext Cab SB	4347	5578	7279

Body Styles	TMV Pricing		
	Trade	Private	Dealer
2 Dr K1500 Cheyenne 4WD Ext Cab Step SB	4401	5648	7369
2 Dr K1500 Cheyenne 4WD Std Cab LB	3863	4957	6468
2 Dr K1500 Cheyenne 4WD Std Cab SB	3778	4848	6326
2 Dr K1500 Cheyenne 4WD Std Cab Step SB	3904	5010	6538
2 Dr K1500 Silverado 4WD Ext Cab LB	4995	6410	8364
2 Dr K1500 Silverado 4WD Ext Cab SB	5038	6465	8435
2 Dr K1500 Silverado 4WD Ext Cab Step SB	5245	6731	8784
2 Dr K1500 Silverado 4WD Std Cab LB	4415	5666	7393
2 Dr K1500 Silverado 4WD Std Cab SB	4371	5609	7318
2 Dr K1500 Silverado 4WD Std Cab Step SB	4533	5817	7591
2 Dr K1500 WT 4WD Std Cab LB	3442	4417	5764
2 Dr K1500 WT 4WD Std Cab SB	3399	4362	5693

Options	Price
5.0L V8 OHV 16V FI Engine	+142
5.7L V8 OHV 16V FI Engine	+200
6.5L V8 Turbodiesel OHV 16V Engine	+1019

Options	Price
Air Conditioning [Std on Silverado]	+231
Automatic 4-Speed Transmission	+250
Leather Seats	+258

Mileage Category: K

1995

A revised interior graces these full-size trucks this year. A new driver-side airbag and a shift interlock are added in the interest of safety. The latter requires the brake pedal to be depressed before the automatic transmission's gear selector can be shifted out of "Park," reducing the likelihood that the vehicle will move suddenly and unexpectedly. Power mirrors, revised climate controls and cupholders provide a more user-friendly interior environment. Mechanical enhancements include the addition of standard four-wheel antilock brakes, improvements in the engines and modifications to the heavy-duty automatic gearbox. The four-wheel ABS replaces last year's rear-wheel-only antilock system. Various upgrades to the engines are intended to reduce noise improve durability and/or increase efficiency. The transmission is revised for quicker 1-2 upshifts during full-throttle applications.

Body Styles	TMV Pricing		
	Trade	Private	Dealer
2 Dr C1500 Cheyenne Ext Cab LB	3042	3954	5473
2 Dr C1500 Cheyenne Ext Cab SB	2760	3587	4966
2 Dr C1500 Cheyenne Ext Cab Step SB	2999	3898	5396
2 Dr C1500 Cheyenne Std Cab LB	2471	3227	4488
2 Dr C1500 Cheyenne Std Cab SB	2379	3092	4280
2 Dr C1500 Cheyenne Std Cab Step SB	2517	3271	4528
2 Dr C1500 Silverado Ext Cab LB	3314	4307	5962
2 Dr C1500 Silverado Ext Cab SB	3115	4049	5605

Body Styles	TMV Pricing		
	Trade	Private	Dealer
2 Dr C1500 Silverado Ext Cab Step SB	3268	4247	5879
2 Dr C1500 Silverado Std Cab LB	2958	3845	5322
2 Dr C1500 Silverado Std Cab SB	2830	3678	5092
2 Dr C1500 Silverado Std Cab Step SB	3035	3945	5461
2 Dr C1500 WT Std Cab LB	2367	3076	4258
2 Dr C1500 WT Std Cab SB	2328	3026	4188
2 Dr K1500 Cheyenne 4WD Ext Cab LB	3353	4358	6032

C/K 1500/2500 Series

1995 (cont'd)

Body Styles	TMV Pricing		
	Trade	Private	Dealer
2 Dr K1500 Cheyenne 4WD Ext Cab SB	3233	4202	5817
2 Dr K1500 Cheyenne 4WD Ext Cab Step SB	3310	4302	5954
2 Dr K1500 Cheyenne 4WD Std Cab LB	3033	3942	5456
2 Dr K1500 Cheyenne 4WD Std Cab SB	2997	3895	5392
2 Dr K1500 Cheyenne 4WD Std Cab Step SB	3076	3998	5534
2 Dr K1500 Silverado 4WD Ext Cab LB	4024	5230	7239
2 Dr K1500 Silverado 4WD Ext Cab SB	3824	4970	6881

Options	Price
5.0L V8 OHV 16V FI Engine	+115
5.7L V8 OHV 16V FI Engine	+162
6.5L V8 Diesel OHV 16V Engine	+630
6.5L V8 Turbodiesel OHV 16V Engine	+782

Body Styles	TMV Pricing		
	Trade	Private	Dealer
2 Dr K1500 Silverado 4WD Ext Cab Step SB	3944	5126	7096
2 Dr K1500 Silverado 4WD Std Cab LB	3278	4261	5899
2 Dr K1500 Silverado 4WD Std Cab SB	3157	4102	5678
2 Dr K1500 Silverado 4WD Std Cab Step SB	3314	4307	5962
2 Dr K1500 WT 4WD Std Cab LB	2727	3561	4951
2 Dr K1500 WT 4WD Std Cab SB	2698	3507	4854

Options	Price
7.4L V8 OHV 16V FI Engine	+195
Air Conditioning [Std on Silverado]	+186
Automatic 4-Speed Transmission	+224
Leather Seats	+231

C/K 2500 Series

2000

One new paint color. Last year for "C/K" nomenclature.

Mileage Category: K

Body Styles	TMV Pricing		
	Trade	Private	Dealer
2 Dr C2500 Ext Cab LB HD	8510	9828	11119
2 Dr C2500 LS Ext Cab LB HD	10149	11720	13260
2 Dr C2500 LS Std Cab LB HD	9364	10814	12235
2 Dr C2500 Std Cab LB HD	7995	9233	10446
2 Dr K2500 4WD Ext Cab LB HD	10773	12442	14077
2 Dr K2500 4WD Ext Cab SB HD	10664	12315	13934
2 Dr K2500 4WD Std Cab LB HD	9422	10880	12310
2 Dr K2500 LS 4WD Ext Cab LB HD	11419	13187	14919

Options	Price
6.5L V8 Turbodiesel OHV 16V Engine	+1271
7.4L V8 OHV 16V FI Engine	+281
AM/FM/Cassette/CD Audio System	+136
Air Conditioning	+377

Body Styles	TMV Pricing		
	Trade	Private	Dealer
2 Dr K2500 LS 4WD Ext Cab SB HD	11297	13046	14760
2 Dr K2500 LS 4WD Std Cab LB HD	10839	12517	14162
4 Dr C2500 Crew Cab SB HD	10332	11932	13500
4 Dr C2500 LS Crew Cab SB HD	11591	13386	15145
4 Dr K2500 4WD Crew Cab SB HD	11549	13337	15090
4 Dr K2500 LS 4WD Crew Cab SB HD	13084	15110	17095

Options	Price
Automatic 4-Speed Transmission	+512
Bucket Seats	+126
Leather Seats	+468
Limited Slip Differential	+134

1999

Model consolidation takes place in anticipation of the all-new Silverado. Trim levels have been changed from three to two (Base and LS) and two new Crew Cab Short Box models (C/K2500 and C/K3500 Series) are offered. Additionally, the C/K1500 will be available only as an LS Extended Cab Short Box with the third door. Mechanical upgrades include new internal components and seals for automatic transmissions, improved cooling system and starter motor durability and three new exterior paint colors.

Mileage Category: K

Body Styles	TMV Pricing		
	Trade	Private	Dealer
2 Dr C2500 Ext Cab LB HD	6839	8139	9492
2 Dr C2500 LS Ext Cab LB HD	8385	9979	11638
2 Dr C2500 LS Std Cab LB HD	7254	8633	10068
2 Dr C2500 Std Cab LB HD	6478	7709	8991
2 Dr K2500 4WD Ext Cab LB HD	8729	10389	12116
2 Dr K2500 4WD Ext Cab SB HD	8554	10180	11872
2 Dr K2500 4WD Std Cab LB HD	7823	9311	10859

Options	Price
6.5L V8 Turbodiesel OHV 16V Engine	+1014
7.4L V8 OHV 16V FI Engine	+224
Air Conditioning	+300

Body Styles	TMV Pricing		
	Trade	Private	Dealer
2 Dr K2500 LS 4WD Ext Cab LB HD	9416	11206	13069
2 Dr K2500 LS 4WD Ext Cab SB HD	9245	11003	12832
2 Dr K2500 LS 4WD Std Cab LB HD	8904	10597	12360
4 Dr C2500 Crew Cab SB HD	8439	10043	11713
4 Dr K2500 4WD Crew Cab SB HD	9896	11778	13736
4 Dr K2500 LS 4WD Crew Cab SB HD	11155	13276	15483

Options	Price
Automatic 4-Speed Transmission	+372
Leather Seats	+438

1998

This year's big news is a standard theft-deterrent system, revised color choices and fresh tailgate lettering. The Sport package has been dropped from the option list. Second-generation airbags are standard on models under 8,600 GVWR.

Mileage Category: K

Body Styles	TMV Pricing		
	Trade	Private	Dealer
2 Dr C2500 Cheyenne Ext Cab LB HD	6166	7494	8992

Body Styles	TMV Pricing		
	Trade	Private	Dealer
2 Dr C2500 Cheyenne Ext Cab SB	5882	7150	8579

Body Styles	TMV Pricing		
	Trade	Private	Dealer
2 Dr C2500 Cheyenne Std Cab LB	4740	5761	6913
2 Dr C2500 Cheyenne Std Cab LB HD	5405	6570	7883
2 Dr C2500 Silverado Ext Cab LB HD	7299	8872	10646
2 Dr C2500 Silverado Ext Cab SB	7027	8541	10248
2 Dr C2500 Silverado Std Cab LB	5740	6977	8371
2 Dr C2500 Silverado Std Cab LB HD	6528	7935	9521
2 Dr K2500 Cheyenne 4WD Ext Cab LB HD	7473	9084	10900
2 Dr K2500 Cheyenne 4WD Ext Cab SB HD	7434	9036	10843

Body Styles	TMV Pricing		
	Trade	Private	Dealer
2 Dr K2500 Cheyenne 4WD Std Cab LB HD	6580	7998	9596
2 Dr K2500 Silverado 4WD Ext Cab LB HD	8186	9950	11939
2 Dr K2500 Silverado 4WD Ext Cab SB HD	7828	9515	11417
2 Dr K2500 Silverado 4WD Std Cab LB HD	7719	9383	11259

Options	Price
5.7L V8 OHV 16V FI Engine [Std on HD]	+220
6.5L V8 Turbodiesel OHV 16V Engine	+854
7.4L V8 OHV 16V FI Engine	+189
Air Conditioning [Std on Silverado]	+253

Options	Price
Automatic 4-Speed Transmission	+305
Bucket Seats	+121
Leather Seats	+314

Mileage Category: K

1997

Body Styles	TMV Pricing		
	Trade	Private	Dealer
2 Dr C2500 Cheyenne Ext Cab LB HD	4827	6017	7471
2 Dr C2500 Cheyenne Ext Cab SB	4956	6178	7671
2 Dr C2500 Cheyenne Std Cab LB	4062	5063	6287
2 Dr C2500 Cheyenne Std Cab LB HD	4314	5377	6677
2 Dr C2500 Silverado Ext Cab LB HD	5463	6809	8454
2 Dr C2500 Silverado Ext Cab SB	5691	7094	8808
2 Dr C2500 Silverado Std Cab LB	4637	5780	7176
2 Dr C2500 Silverado Std Cab LB HD	5225	6513	8087
2 Dr K2500 Cheyenne 4WD Ext Cab LB HD	5976	7449	9250

Body Styles	TMV Pricing		
	Trade	Private	Dealer
2 Dr K2500 Cheyenne 4WD Ext Cab LB HD	5882	7332	9105
2 Dr K2500 Cheyenne 4WD Std Cab LB HD	5276	6577	8166
2 Dr K2500 Silverado 4WD Ext Cab LB HD	6590	8214	10199
2 Dr K2500 Silverado 4WD Ext Cab SB HD	6541	8154	10125
2 Dr K2500 Silverado 4WD Std Cab LB HD	6024	7509	9323

On trucks under 8,600 pounds GVWR, the passenger airbag can be deactivated when a rear-facing child safety seat is installed. Low-speed steering effort is reduced this year, and a refined transmission fluid pump results in smoother shifts. An alternative fuel version of the Vortec 5700 is available, but only on a specific model. K1500's get a tighter turning radius, and three new colors debut. The third door option will be more widely available.

Options	Price
5.7L V8 OHV 16V FI Engine [Std on HD]	+199
6.5L V8 Turbodiesel OHV 16V Engine	+772
7.4L V8 OHV 16V FI Engine	+171

Options	Price
Air Conditioning [Std on Silverado]	+229
Automatic 4-Speed Transmission	+283
Leather Seats	+334

Mileage Category: K

1996

A new series of engines is introduced, providing more power and torque than last year's offerings. Called Vortec, this family of engines includes a 4.3-liter V6 (the only six-cylinder of the bunch) capable of 200 hp at 4,400 rpm and 255 lb-ft of torque at 2,800 rpm; a 5.0-liter V8, producing 220 hp at 4,600 rpm and 285 lb-ft of torque at 2,800 rpm; and a 5.7-liter V8, rated at 250 hp at 4,600 rpm and 335 lb-ft of torque at 2,800 rpm. (There is also a 7.4-liter Vortec V8, but it's only available on the heavier-duty C/K 3500 trucks.) All of these figures represent increases in output when compared to their respective 1995 predecessors. An optional electronic shift transfer case for the K1500 (i.e. 4WD; C=2WD; K=4WD) rounds out the list of the most significant powertrain updates for the year. Other noteworthy updates include the introduction of an optional passenger-side third door, called the "Easy-Access System," in GM vernacular. This feature is only available on the extended cab body styles. Improved comfort and convenience comes in the way of such new features as illuminated entry, 12-volt power outlets, an electrochromic inside rearview mirror and height-adjustable D-rings for the shoulder section of the front three-point safety belts, among others. Daytime running lamps (DRLs) are part of the list of new exterior features. A new level of sophistication in exhaust emissions monitoring is found with the addition of OBD II, the second generation of On-Board Diagnostics.

Body Styles	TMV Pricing		
	Trade	Private	Dealer
2 Dr C2500 Cheyenne Ext Cab LB HD	4098	5198	6718
2 Dr C2500 Cheyenne Ext Cab SB	3991	5062	6542
2 Dr C2500 Cheyenne Std Cab LB	3325	4218	5450
2 Dr C2500 Silverado Ext Cab LB HD	4437	5629	7274
2 Dr C2500 Silverado Ext Cab SB	4323	5483	7086
2 Dr C2500 Silverado Std Cab LB	3675	4661	6023
2 Dr K2500 Cheyenne 4WD Ext Cab LB HD	4982	6320	8167
2 Dr K2500 Cheyenne 4WD Ext Cab SB HD	4919	6239	8062

Body Styles	TMV Pricing		
	Trade	Private	Dealer
2 Dr K2500 Cheyenne 4WD Std Cab LB HD	4197	5323	6879
2 Dr K2500 Silverado 4WD Ext Cab LB HD	5644	7159	9250
2 Dr K2500 Silverado 4WD Ext Cab SB HD	5593	7095	9168
2 Dr K2500 Silverado 4WD Std Cab LB HD	5161	6546	8459

Options	Price
5.7L V8 OHV 16V FI Engine [Std on HD]	+180
6.5L V8 Turbodiesel OHV 16V Engine	+700
7.4L V8 OHV 16V FI Engine	+155

Options	Price
Air Conditioning [Std on Silverado]	+207
Automatic 4-Speed Transmission	+278
Leather Seats	+258

Chevrolet
C/K 2500/3500 Series

1995

A revised interior graces these full-size trucks this year. A new driver-side airbag and a shift interlock are added in the interest of safety. The latter requires the brake pedal to be depressed before the automatic transmission's gear selector can be shifted out of "Park," reducing the likelihood that the vehicle will move suddenly and unexpectedly. Power mirrors, revised climate controls and cupholders provide a more user-friendly interior environment. Mechanical enhancements include the addition of standard four-wheel antilock brakes, improvements in the engines and modifications to the heavy-duty automatic gearbox. The four-wheel ABS replaces last year's rear-wheel-only antilock system. Various upgrades to the engines are intended to reduce noise improve durability and/or increase efficiency. The transmission is revised for quicker 1-2 upshifts during full-throttle applications.

Mileage Category: K

Body Styles	TMV Pricing		
	Trade	Private	Dealer
2 Dr C2500 Cheyenne Ext Cab LB	3272	4253	5888
2 Dr C2500 Cheyenne Ext Cab SB	3233	4202	5817
2 Dr C2500 Cheyenne Std Cab LB	2715	3528	4884
2 Dr C2500 Silverado Ext Cab LB	3601	4672	6458
2 Dr C2500 Silverado Ext Cab SB	3565	4633	6413
2 Dr C2500 Silverado Std Cab LB	2812	3655	5059
2 Dr K2500 Cheyenne 4WD Ext Cab LB	3944	5126	7096
2 Dr K2500 Cheyenne 4WD Ext Cab SB	3549	4613	6386

Body Styles	TMV Pricing		
	Trade	Private	Dealer
2 Dr K2500 Cheyenne 4WD Std Cab LB	3196	4153	5749
2 Dr K2500 Silverado 4WD Ext Cab LB	4338	5638	7804
2 Dr K2500 Silverado 4WD Ext Cab SB	4221	5486	7593
2 Dr K2500 Silverado 4WD Std Cab LB	3511	4563	6315

Options	Price
5.0L V8 OHV 16V FI Engine	+162
5.7L V8 OHV 16V FI Engine	+162
6.5L V8 Diesel OHV 16V Engine	+630
6.5L V8 Turbodiesel OHV 16V Engine	+628
7.4L V8 OHV 16V FI Engine	+138

Options	Price
Air Conditioning [Std on Silverado]	+186
Automatic 4-Speed Transmission	+224
Driver Side Airbag Restraint [Opt on Std Cab]	+81
Leather Seats	+231

C/K 3500 Series

2000

One new paint color. Last year for "C/K" nomenclature.

Mileage Category: K

Body Styles	TMV Pricing		
	Trade	Private	Dealer
2 Dr C3500 Ext Cab LB	9620	11109	12569
2 Dr C3500 LS Ext Cab LB	10417	12030	13611
2 Dr C3500 LS Std Cab LB	9082	10488	11866
2 Dr C3500 Std Cab LB	8077	9327	10553
2 Dr K3500 4WD Ext Cab LB	10433	12048	13632
2 Dr K3500 4WD Std Cab LB	9199	10623	12019
2 Dr K3500 LS 4WD Ext Cab LB	12153	14035	15879
2 Dr K3500 LS 4WD Std Cab LB	9807	11326	12814

Body Styles	TMV Pricing		
	Trade	Private	Dealer
4 Dr C3500 Crew Cab LB	9202	10627	12023
4 Dr C3500 Crew Cab SB	9647	11140	12604
4 Dr C3500 LS Crew Cab LB	11124	12846	14534
4 Dr C3500 LS Crew Cab SB	12142	14022	15864
4 Dr K3500 4WD Crew Cab LB	10465	12085	13673
4 Dr K3500 4WD Crew Cab SB	12043	13907	15735
4 Dr K3500 LS 4WD Crew Cab LB	12442	14368	16256
4 Dr K3500 LS 4WD Crew Cab SB	13672	15789	17864

Options	Price
6.5L V8 Turbodiesel OHV 16V Engine	+1271
7.4L V8 OHV 16V FI Engine	+281
AM/FM/Cassette/CD Audio System	+136
Air Conditioning	+377
Automatic 4-Speed Transmission	+465

Options	Price
Bucket Seats	+126
Dual Rear Wheels	+401
Leather Seats	+468
Limited Slip Differential	+134
Locking Differential	+134

1999

Model consolidation takes place in anticipation of the all-new Silverado. Trim levels have been changed from three to two (Base and LS) and two new Crew Cab Short Box models (C/K2500 and C/K3500 Series) are offered. Additionally, the C/K1500 will be available only as an LS Extended Cab Short Box with the third door. Mechanical upgrades include new internal components and seals for automatic transmissions, improved cooling system and starter motor durability and three new exterior paint colors.

Mileage Category: K

Body Styles	TMV Pricing		
	Trade	Private	Dealer
2 Dr C3500 Ext Cab LB	7624	9073	10581
2 Dr C3500 LS Ext Cab LB	8443	10048	11719
2 Dr C3500 LS Std Cab LB	7238	8613	10045
2 Dr C3500 Std Cab LB	6273	7466	8707
2 Dr K3500 4WD Ext Cab LB	8538	10161	11851
2 Dr K3500 4WD Std Cab LB	7430	8842	10312
2 Dr K3500 LS 4WD Ext Cab LB	10083	12000	13995
2 Dr K3500 LS 4WD Std Cab LB	8251	9819	11452

Body Styles	TMV Pricing		
	Trade	Private	Dealer
4 Dr C3500 Crew Cab LB	7572	9012	10511
4 Dr C3500 Crew Cab SB	8054	9586	11180
4 Dr C3500 LS Crew Cab LB	9426	11218	13083
4 Dr C3500 LS Crew Cab SB	9937	11826	13793
4 Dr K3500 4WD Crew Cab LB	8597	10232	11933
4 Dr K3500 4WD Crew Cab SB	9497	11303	13182
4 Dr K3500 LS 4WD Crew Cab LB	10131	12057	14062
4 Dr K3500 LS 4WD Crew Cab SB	10615	12633	14733

Options	Price
6.5L V8 Turbodiesel OHV 16V Engine	+1014
7.4L V8 OHV 16V FI Engine	+224
Air Conditioning	+300

Options	Price
Automatic 4-Speed Transmission	+372
Dual Rear Wheels	+320
Leather Seats	+438

1998

Mileage Category: K

Body Styles	TMV Pricing		
	Trade	Private	Dealer
2 Dr C3500 Cheyenne Ext Cab LB	6343	7710	9251
2 Dr C3500 Cheyenne Std Cab LB	5279	6416	7699
2 Dr C3500 Silverado Ext Cab LB	7178	8724	10468
2 Dr C3500 Silverado Std Cab LB	5988	7278	8733
2 Dr K3500 Cheyenne 4WD Ext Cab LB	7181	8729	10474
2 Dr K3500 Cheyenne 4WD Std Cab LB	6164	7492	8990
2 Dr K3500 Silverado 4WD Ext Cab LB	7982	9702	11642

Body Styles	TMV Pricing		
	Trade	Private	Dealer
2 Dr K3500 Silverado 4WD Std Cab LB	7089	8617	10339
4 Dr C3500 Cheyenne Crew Cab LB	6209	7547	9056
4 Dr C3500 Silverado Crew Cab LB	7621	9263	11115
4 Dr K3500 Cheyenne 4WD Crew Cab LB	7205	8757	10508
4 Dr K3500 Silverado 4WD Crew Cab LB	8605	10459	12549

Options	Price
6.5L V8 Turbodiesel OHV 16V Engine	+854
7.4L V8 OHV 16V FI Engine	+189
Air Conditioning [Std on Silverado]	+253
Automatic 4-Speed Transmission	+305

Options	Price
Bucket Seats	+121
Dual Rear Wheels	+269
Leather Seats	+314

The year 1998 brings subtle refinements to Chevy's one-ton truck. Passlock is added to aid in theft prevention. If someone starts the vehicle without the proper key, the engine will shut off immediately, not allowing the truck to move on its own power for 10 minutes. The 4L60-E (light-duty) and 4L80-E (heavy-duty) electronically controlled four-speed automatic transmissions are updated to increase durability, improve gas mileage, reduce vibration (4L60-E only) and operate more smoothly overall. Some exterior colors are replaced.

1997

Mileage Category: K

Body Styles	TMV Pricing		
	Trade	Private	Dealer
2 Dr C3500 Cheyenne Ext Cab LB	5292	6597	8191
2 Dr C3500 Cheyenne Std Cab LB	4182	5213	6473
2 Dr C3500 Silverado Ext Cab LB	5491	6844	8498
2 Dr C3500 Silverado Std Cab LB	4883	6086	7557
2 Dr K3500 Cheyenne 4WD Ext Cab LB	5787	7213	8956
2 Dr K3500 Cheyenne 4WD Std Cab LB	5237	6527	8104
2 Dr K3500 Silverado 4WD Ext Cab LB	6205	7734	9603

Body Styles	TMV Pricing		
	Trade	Private	Dealer
2 Dr K3500 Silverado 4WD Std Cab LB	5402	6734	8361
4 Dr C3500 Cheyenne Crew Cab LB	5257	6553	8137
4 Dr C3500 Silverado Crew Cab LB	6173	7694	9554
4 Dr K3500 Cheyenne 4WD Crew Cab LB	6153	7669	9522
4 Dr K3500 Silverado 4WD Crew Cab LB	6969	8687	10787

Options	Price
6.5L V8 Turbodiesel OHV 16V Engine	+772
7.4L V8 OHV 16V FI Engine	+171
Air Conditioning [Std on Silverado]	+229

Options	Price
Automatic 4-Speed Transmission	+276
Dual Rear Wheels	+244
Leather Seats	+284

On trucks under 8,600 pounds GVWR, the passenger airbag can be deactivated when a rear-facing child safety seat is installed. Low-speed steering effort is reduced this year, and a refined transmission fluid pump results in smoother shifts. An alternative fuel version of the Vortec 5700 is available, but only on a specific model. K1500s get a tighter turning radius, and three new colors debut. The third door option will be more widely available.

1996

Mileage Category: K

Body Styles	TMV Pricing		
	Trade	Private	Dealer
2 Dr C3500 Cheyenne Ext Cab LB	4308	5528	7213
2 Dr C3500 Cheyenne Std Cab LB	3524	4522	5901
2 Dr C3500 Silverado Ext Cab LB	4585	5884	7677
2 Dr C3500 Silverado Std Cab LB	3993	5124	6686
2 Dr K3500 Cheyenne 4WD Ext Cab LB	4911	6302	8222
2 Dr K3500 Cheyenne 4WD Std Cab LB	4192	5379	7019
2 Dr K3500 Silverado 4WD Ext Cab LB	5066	6501	8482

Body Styles	TMV Pricing		
	Trade	Private	Dealer
2 Dr K3500 Silverado 4WD Std Cab LB	4544	5831	7608
4 Dr C3500 Cheyenne Crew Cab LB	4225	5422	7074
4 Dr C3500 Silverado Crew Cab LB	5014	6434	8395
4 Dr K3500 Cheyenne 4WD Crew Cab LB	4985	6397	8348
4 Dr K3500 Silverado 4WD Crew Cab LB	5758	7389	9641

Options	Price
6.5L V8 Turbodiesel OHV 16V Engine	+700
7.4L V8 OHV 16V FI Engine	+155
Air Conditioning [Std on Silverado]	+207

Options	Price
Automatic 4-Speed Transmission	+250
Dual Rear Wheels	+221
Leather Seats	+258

A new series of engines is introduced, providing more power and torque than last year's offerings. Called Vortec, this family of engines includes a 4.3-liter V6 (the only six-cylinder of the bunch) capable of 200 hp at 4,400 rpm and 255 lb-ft of torque at 2,800 rpm; a 5.0-liter V8, producing 220 hp at 4,600 rpm and 285 lb-ft of torque at 2,800 rpm; and a 5.7-liter V8, rated at 250 hp at 4,600 rpm and 335 lb-ft of torque at 2,800 rpm. (There is also a 7.4-liter Vortec V8, but it's only available on the heavier-duty C/K 3500 trucks.) All of these figures represent increases in output when compared to their respective 1995 predecessors. An optional electronic shift transfer case for the K1500 (i.e. 4WD; C=2WD; K=4WD) rounds out the list of the most significant powertrain updates for the year. Other noteworthy updates include the introduction of an optional passenger-side third door, called the "Easy-Access System," in GM vernacular. This feature is only available on the extended cab body styles. Improved comfort and convenience comes in the way of such new features as illuminated entry, 12-volt power outlets, an electrochromic inside rearview mirror and height-adjustable D-rings for the shoulder section of the front three-point safety belts, among others. Daytime running lamps (DRLs) are part of the list of new exterior features. A new level of sophistication in exhaust emissions monitoring is found with the addition of OBD II, the second generation of On-Board Diagnostics.

C/K 3500 Series/Camaro

1995

A revised interior graces these full-size trucks this year. A new driver-side airbag and a shift interlock are added in the interest of safety. The latter requires the brake pedal to be depressed before the automatic transmission's gear selector can be shifted out of "Park," reducing the likelihood that the vehicle will move suddenly and unexpectedly. Power mirrors, revised climate controls and cupholders provide a more user-friendly interior environment. Mechanical enhancements include the addition of standard four-wheel antilock brakes, improvements in the engines and modifications to the heavy-duty automatic gearbox. The four-wheel ABS replaces last year's rear-wheel-only antilock system. Various upgrades to the engines are intended to reduce noise improve durability and/or increase efficiency. The transmission is revised for quicker 1-2 upshifts during full-throttle applications.

Mileage Category: K

Body Styles	TMV Pricing		
	Trade	Private	Dealer
2 Dr C3500 Cheyenne Ext Cab LB	3374	4385	6071
2 Dr C3500 Cheyenne Std Cab LB	2977	3869	5355
2 Dr C3500 Silverado Ext Cab LB	3884	5048	6988
2 Dr C3500 Silverado Std Cab LB	3302	4291	5940
2 Dr K3500 Cheyenne 4WD Ext Cab LB	3811	4953	6856
2 Dr K3500 Cheyenne 4WD Std Cab LB	3332	4330	5994
2 Dr K3500 Silverado 4WD Ext Cab LB	4170	5420	7503

Body Styles	TMV Pricing		
	Trade	Private	Dealer
2 Dr K3500 Silverado 4WD Std Cab LB	3737	4857	6724
4 Dr C3500 Cheyenne Crew Cab LB	3345	4347	6018
4 Dr C3500 Silverado Crew Cab LB	4101	5330	7378
4 Dr C3500 Cheyenne 4WD Crew Cab LB	3921	5096	7053
4 Dr K3500 Silverado 4WD Crew Cab LB	4755	6180	8554

Options	Price
6.5L V8 Turbodiesel OHV 16V Engine	+628
7.4L V8 OHV 16V FI Engine	+138
Air Conditioning [Std on Silverado]	+186

Options	Price
Automatic 4-Speed Transmission	+224
Dual Rear Wheels	+185
Leather Seats	+231

Camaro

2002

Few changes are made to the Camaro in what is its final year of production. Minor additions include a special 35th anniversary package and Sebring Silver to the color palette.

Mileage Category: E

Body Styles	TMV Pricing		
	Trade	Private	Dealer
2 Dr STD Conv	11140	12325	14301
2 Dr STD Hbk	8088	8949	10383

Body Styles	TMV Pricing		
	Trade	Private	Dealer
2 Dr Z28 Conv	14384	15915	18466
2 Dr Z28 Hbk	11676	12919	14991

Options	Price
17 Inch Wheels	+373
Automatic 4-Speed Transmission [Opt on STD]	+467
Chrome Wheels	+416
Compact Disc Changer	+341
Leather Seats	+287
Limited Slip Differential [Opt on STD]	+158

Options	Price
Monsoon Audio System [Opt on STD Hbk]	+201
Power Driver Seat [Std on Z28 Conv]	+138
Power Windows [Opt on Hbk]	+129
SS Package	+2079
T-Tops - Glass	+571
Traction Control System	+143

2001

More horsepower is on tap for the Z28 and SS models, while styled chrome 16-inch wheels are a new option for base and Z28 models and Sunset Orange Metallic is added to the list of colors.

Mileage Category: E

Body Styles	TMV Pricing		
	Trade	Private	Dealer
2 Dr STD Conv	9266	10893	12394
2 Dr STD Hbk	6065	7130	8114

Body Styles	TMV Pricing		
	Trade	Private	Dealer
2 Dr Z28 Conv	11030	12968	14756
2 Dr Z28 Hbk	9758	11471	13052

Options	Price
5.7L V8 OHV 16V FI w/Ram Air Engine	+2072
Aluminum/Alloy Wheels [Opt on STD]	+144
Automatic 4-Speed Transmission [Opt on STD]	+428
Chrome Wheels	+380
Compact Disc Changer	+312
Leather Seats	+262
Limited Slip Differential [Opt on STD]	+236

Options	Price
Monsoon Audio System	+184
Power Door Locks [Opt on STD,Cpe]	+115
Power Driver Seat [Opt on STD,Cpe]	+142
Power Windows [Opt on STD,Cpe]	+137
T-Tops - Glass	+522
Traction Control System	+131

2000

New interior colors and fabrics, redundant steering-wheel audio controls, new alloy wheels, and a new exterior color debut. V6 and V8 engines meet California's low emission vehicle (LEV) standards.

Mileage Category: E

Body Styles	TMV Pricing		
	Trade	Private	Dealer
2 Dr STD Conv	8053	9687	11288
2 Dr STD Hbk	5035	6056	7057
2 Dr Z28 Conv	9496	11423	13312

Body Styles	TMV Pricing		
	Trade	Private	Dealer
2 Dr Z28 Hbk	8376	10076	11742
2 Dr Z28 SS Conv	10314	12406	14457
2 Dr Z28 SS Hbk	8987	10810	12596

Options	Price
AM/FM/CD Audio System	+147
Aluminum/Alloy Wheels [Opt on STD]	+129
Automatic 4-Speed Transmission [Opt on STD]	+381
Compact Disc Changer	+278
Ground Effects	+630

Options	Price
Leather Seats	+210
Limited Slip Differential [Opt on STD]	+210
Monsoon Audio System	+164
Power Driver Seat [Opt on STD,Cpe]	+126
Power Windows [Opt on STD,Cpe]	+122

Options	Price
T-Tops - Glass	+465

Mileage Category: E

Body Styles	TMV Pricing		
	Trade	Private	Dealer
2 Dr STD Conv	5993	7609	9291
2 Dr STD Hbk	3567	4528	5529
2 Dr Z28 Conv	6914	8778	10718

Options	Price
AM/FM/CD Audio System	+118
Automatic 4-Speed Transmission [Opt on STD]	+304
Chrome Wheels	+187
Compact Disc Changer	+222

Body Styles	TMV Pricing		
	Trade	Private	Dealer
2 Dr Z28 Hbk	6437	8173	9980
2 Dr Z28 SS Conv	7987	10141	12382
2 Dr Z28 SS Hbk	6699	8505	10385

Options	Price
Leather Seats	+205
Limited Slip Differential [Opt on STD]	+168
Performance/Handling Package	+448
T-Tops - Glass	+372

1999

Traction control (Acceleration Slip Regulation in Chevrolet parlance) is available on all models in 1999, and on the Z28 ASR allows for some tire slip before cutting the power to the rear wheels. Electronic throttle control is newly standard on V6 models, a new engine oil-life monitor tracks specific driving conditions to determine when the next change should occur and a Zexel Torsen differential is employed in the limited-slip rear axle.

Body Styles	TMV Pricing		
	Trade	Private	Dealer
2 Dr STD Conv	4946	6402	8043
2 Dr STD Hbk	3064	3965	4980
2 Dr Z28 Conv	5900	7636	9593

Options	Price
AM/FM/Cassette/CD Audio System [Opt on STD Cpe]	+141
Automatic 4-Speed Transmission [Opt on STD]	+256
Chrome Wheels	+157
Compact Disc Changer	+187

Body Styles	TMV Pricing		
	Trade	Private	Dealer
2 Dr Z28 Hbk	5400	6988	8778
2 Dr Z28 SS Conv	7022	9087	11415
2 Dr Z28 SS Hbk	5699	7375	9264

Options	Price
Leather Seats	+173
Limited Slip Differential [Opt on STD]	+141
Performance/Handling Package	+370
T-Tops - Glass	+313

1998

Chevrolet dumps a 305-horsepower version of the Corvette's V8 engine under a new front end, adds standard four-wheel disc brakes on all models, adds a couple of new colors, makes second-generation airbags standard and revises trim levels. The midyear SS package makes 320 horsepower.

1997

Body Styles	TMV Pricing		
	Trade	Private	Dealer
2 Dr RS Conv	3999	5377	7061
2 Dr RS Hbk	3181	4277	5616
2 Dr STD Conv	3760	5056	6639
2 Dr STD Hbk	2516	3383	4443

Options	Price
Automatic 4-Speed Transmission [Opt on STD]	+225
Chrome Wheels	+220
Compact Disc Changer	+169
Leather Seats	+156

Body Styles	TMV Pricing		
	Trade	Private	Dealer
2 Dr Z28 Conv	4695	6312	8289
2 Dr Z28 Hbk	4112	5530	7262
2 Dr Z28 SS Conv	5706	7671	10073
2 Dr Z28 SS Hbk	4468	6007	7889

Options	Price
Limited Slip Differential [Opt on RS,STD]	+128
Performance/Handling Package	+341
T-Tops - Glass [Opt on Hbk]	+283

Chevrolet celebrates the Camaro's 30th Anniversary with a special-edition Z28 that emulates the appearance of the 1969 SS Indy Pace Car with white paint, Hugger Orange stripes, and black-and-white houndstooth seat inserts. Interior revisions to seats, center console and dashboard freshen the look inside for 1997. Two new shades of gray are available for interiors, while exteriors get new green and purple hues. Tricolor taillamps debut, and new five-spoke alloy wheels are optional. On the safety front, daytime running lights are standard and side-impact regulations are met.

Mileage Category: E

1996

A new 200-hp base V6 is available. Z28's 285-hp LT1 V8 (gets 10 more horsepower this year). SLP Engineering provides a 305-horse Z28 SS. The RS trim level returns, and chrome-aluminum wheels are optional.

Body Styles	TMV Pricing		
	Trade	Private	Dealer
2 Dr RS Conv	3088	4280	5925
2 Dr RS Hbk	2603	3606	4992
2 Dr STD Conv	2895	4011	5553
2 Dr STD Hbk	1983	2748	3804

Options	Price
Air Conditioning [Opt on STD,Cpe]	+231
Automatic 4-Speed Transmission	+204
Chrome Wheels	+129
Compact Disc Changer	+154
Delco/Bose Audio System	+156

Body Styles	TMV Pricing		
	Trade	Private	Dealer
2 Dr Z28 Conv	3899	5403	7480
2 Dr Z28 Hbk	2965	4109	5689
2 Dr Z28 SS Conv	4536	6286	8702
2 Dr Z28 SS Hbk	3483	4825	6679

Options	Price
Leather Seats	+142
Limited Slip Differential [Opt on RS,STD]	+116
Performance/Handling Package	+303
T-Tops - Glass	+250

1995

Z28 gets optional traction control. Z28 can now be ordered with body-color roof and side mirrors (standard color is gloss black). Chrome-plated alloys are newly optional.

Mileage Category: E

Body Styles	TMV Pricing			Body Styles	TMV Pricing		
	Trade	Private	Dealer		Trade	Private	Dealer
2 Dr STD Conv	2224	3109	4585	2 Dr Z28 Conv	3274	4579	6753
2 Dr STD Hbk	1680	2349	3464	2 Dr Z28 Hbk	2447	3422	5047

Options	Price	Options	Price
Air Conditioning	+207	Leather Seats	+127
Automatic 4-Speed Transmission	+162	T-Tops - Glass	+224
Delco/Bose Audio System	+140		

Caprice

1996

Body Styles	TMV Pricing			Body Styles	TMV Pricing		
	Trade	Private	Dealer		Trade	Private	Dealer
4 Dr STD Sdn	2334	3187	4365	4 Dr STD Wgn	2743	3745	5128

Mileage Category: G

Options	Price	Options	Price
5.7L V8 OHV 16V FI Engine [Opt on Sdn]	+157	Sport Suspension	+131
Leather Seats	+222		

No changes as Caprice enters final year of production.

1995

Impala SS styling treatment for C-pillar is carried over to more mainstream sedan. New seats and radios debut. Outside mirrors can be folded in, and a new option is a radio with speed-compensated volume control.

Mileage Category: G

Body Styles	TMV Pricing			Body Styles	TMV Pricing		
	Trade	Private	Dealer		Trade	Private	Dealer
4 Dr STD Sdn	1896	2639	3877	4 Dr STD Wgn	2010	2798	4110

Options	Price	Options	Price
5.7L V8 OHV 16V FI Engine [Std on Wgn]	+141	Leather Seats	+180
AM/FM/CD Audio System	+91	Sport Suspension	+117

Cavalier

2004

An upgraded stereo with a CD and MP3 player is now available on the base coupe and sedan. The Sport Appearance package that includes 16-inch wheels, a rear spoiler and sport suspension is also available on the base coupe and sedan.

Mileage Category: B

Body Styles	TMV Pricing			Body Styles	TMV Pricing		
	Trade	Private	Dealer		Trade	Private	Dealer
2 Dr LS Cpe	7520	8268	9515	4 Dr LS Sdn	7721	8527	9869
2 Dr LS Sport Cpe	8431	9104	10226	4 Dr LS Sport Sdn	8594	9416	10786
2 Dr STD Cpe	6930	7603	8725	4 Dr STD Sdn	7021	7694	8815
2 Dr Special Value Cpe	5147	5841	6998				

Options	Price	Options	Price
AM/FM/CD Audio System [Opt on STD]	+185	OnStar Telematics System [Opt on LS]	+695
Antilock Brakes [Opt on STD]	+400	Polished Aluminum/Alloy Wheels [Opt on STD]	+300
Automatic 4-Speed Transmission [Opt on STD, LS, LS Sport]	+650	Power Moonroof [Opt on STD Cpe, LS Cpe, LS Sport Cpe]	+725
Cruise Control [Opt on STD, LS, LS Sport]	+275	Sport Suspension [Opt on STD]	+200
Front Side Airbag Restraints [Opt on STD, LS, LS Sport]	+395	Traction Control System [Opt on STD, LS, LS Sport]	+200
Keyless Entry System [Opt on STD, LS, LS Sport]	+120		

2003

The Cavalier gets a refresh this year that adds new front and rear fascias, revised headlights and taillights, redesigned ground effects, body-colored mirrors and door handles and a new hood. LS Sport models also get integrated foglights and new rocker moldings. The 2.2-liter Ecotec four-cylinder is now the only engine offered, as the Z24 model has been dropped from the lineup. Base model Cavs no longer come with standard ABS brakes, but it remains an available option. Inside, the Cavalier now features a center rear three-point seatbelt, a leather-wrapped steering wheel and shift lever, a rear 60/40-split bench seat, new child-seat anchors and optional side airbags. Finally, you can get XM Satellite Radio on all cars, and LS and LS Sport trims are available with the OnStar communications system.

Mileage Category: B

Body Styles	TMV Pricing			Body Styles	TMV Pricing		
	Trade	Private	Dealer		Trade	Private	Dealer
2 Dr LS Cpe	6076	6802	8014	4 Dr LS Sdn	6246	7055	8403
2 Dr LS Sport Cpe	6665	7468	8807	4 Dr LS Sport Sdn	7263	8176	9698
2 Dr STD Cpe	5517	6231	7421	4 Dr STD Sdn	5522	6237	7427

Options	Price	Options	Price
AM/FM/CD Audio System [Opt on STD]	+192	Automatic 4-Speed Transmission	+520
Antilock Brakes [Opt on STD]	+447	Cruise Control [Opt on STD]	+160

Options	Price
Front Side Airbag Restraints	+223
Keyless Entry System [Opt on STD]	+236
OnStar Telematics System [Opt on LS,LS Sport]	+444

Options	Price
Power Moonroof [Opt on Cpe]	+415
Satellite Radio System	+207

2002

New LS Sport trim level for coupes and sedans that features an all-new 2.2-liter EcoTec engine. A Z24 sedan joins the Z24 coupe at the top end of the lineup, while both the LS and base model Cavalier gain additional standard equipment and an optional Sport appearance package. Both Z24 models get an upgraded stereo and an optional Sport appearance package will be available later in the year. Three new colors have also been added along with an upgraded cloth interior.

Mileage Category: B

Body Styles	TMV Pricing		
	Trade	Private	Dealer
2 Dr LS Cpe	5054	5870	7231
2 Dr LS Sport Cpe	5553	6450	7944
2 Dr STD Cpe	4270	4960	6110
2 Dr Z24 Cpe	5734	6661	8205

Body Styles	TMV Pricing		
	Trade	Private	Dealer
4 Dr LS Sdn	5082	5903	7272
4 Dr LS Sport Sdn	6050	7028	8657
4 Dr STD Sdn	4321	5020	6185
4 Dr Z24 Sdn	6038	7013	8638

Options	Price
16 Inch Wheels [Opt on STD]	+330
2.4L I4 DOHC 16V FI Engine [Opt on LS]	+258
AM/FM/Cassette/CD Audio System [Opt on LS,STD]	+132
Aluminum/Alloy Wheels [Std on Z24]	+169
Automatic 4-Speed Transmission	+447

Options	Price
Cruise Control [Opt on STD]	+135
Flex Fuel Option	+3404
Keyless Entry System [Opt on STD]	+212
Power Moonroof [Opt on Cpe]	+341

2001

Indigo Blue is added to the exterior palette. A CD player is made standard on the LS Sedan and Z24 Coupe. The Z24 Convertible has vanished from the lineup.

Mileage Category: B

Body Styles	TMV Pricing		
	Trade	Private	Dealer
2 Dr STD Cpe	3669	4702	5656
2 Dr Z24 Cpe	4633	5939	7144

Body Styles	TMV Pricing		
	Trade	Private	Dealer
4 Dr LS Sdn	4452	5707	6865
4 Dr STD Sdn	3672	4706	5660

Options	Price
2.4L I4 DOHC 16V FI Engine [Opt on LS]	+236
AM/FM/CD Audio System	+168
Aluminum/Alloy Wheels [Std on Z24]	+155
Automatic 3-Speed Transmission	+367

Options	Price
Automatic 4-Speed Transmission [Std on LS]	+409
Flex Fuel Option	+3113
Power Moonroof	+312
Power Windows [Std on Z24]	+138

2000

Still available as a coupe, sedan or convertible, Chevy's best-selling car gets several subtle changes for 2000. Outside it has new body-colored front and rear facias, new headlamp/taillamp assemblies, new badging and restyled wheel covers/alloy wheels. Inside, the instrument panel now features an electronic odometer and tripmeter, a revamped center console with three front cupholders and an improved storage area. Functionally, it gets a better-shifting five-speed manual transaxle, smoother-operating ABS, Passlock II security system and standard air conditioning.

Mileage Category: B

Body Styles	TMV Pricing		
	Trade	Private	Dealer
2 Dr STD Cpe	3088	4163	5217
2 Dr Z24 Conv	4548	6131	7683
2 Dr Z24 Cpe	3827	5158	6463

Body Styles	TMV Pricing		
	Trade	Private	Dealer
4 Dr LS Sdn	3421	4612	5779
4 Dr STD Sdn	3103	4183	5241

Options	Price
2.4L I4 DOHC 16V FI Engine [Opt on LS]	+210
AM/FM/CD Audio System	+150
Aluminum/Alloy Wheels [Std on Z24]	+138
Automatic 3-Speed Transmission	+281

Options	Price
Automatic 4-Speed Transmission [Std on LS]	+365
Power Moonroof [Opt on Cpe]	+278
Power Windows [Std on Z24]	+123

1999

The 2.4 twin-cam engine benefits from reliability, emissions and fuel economy enhancements, and new front brake linings increase pad life. Minor interior and exterior revisions have been made, and Fern Green Metallic and Sandrift Metallic replace Bright Aqua and Deep Purple on the paint chart.

Body Styles	TMV Pricing		
	Trade	Private	Dealer
2 Dr RS Cpe	2492	3491	4531
2 Dr STD Cpe	2257	3162	4103
2 Dr Z24 Conv	3285	4602	5973

Body Styles	TMV Pricing		
	Trade	Private	Dealer
2 Dr Z24 Cpe	3269	4579	5943
4 Dr LS Sdn	2761	3868	5021
4 Dr STD Sdn	2264	3172	4117

Options	Price
2.4L I4 DOHC 16V FI Engine [Opt on LS]	+168
AM/FM/CD Audio System	+119
Air Conditioning [Std on LS,Z24]	+297

Options	Price
Automatic 3-Speed Transmission	+224
Automatic 4-Speed Transmission [Std on LS]	+291
Power Sunroof	+222

1998

A Z24 convertible is introduced, cruise control is standard on all but base models, power windows and remote keyless entry are no longer available on base cars, and buyers can no longer delete the AM/FM radio. Second-generation airbags debut on all models.

Mileage Category: B

Body Styles	TMV Pricing		
	Trade	Private	Dealer
2 Dr RS Cpe	1730	2548	3470

Body Styles	TMV Pricing		
	Trade	Private	Dealer
2 Dr STD Cpe	1521	2240	3050

1998 (cont'd)

Body Styles	TMV Pricing		
	Trade	Private	Dealer
2 Dr Z24 Conv	2363	3480	4739
2 Dr Z24 Cpe	2049	3017	4108

Options	Price
2.4L I4 DOHC 16V FI Engine [Opt on LS]	+141
Air Conditioning [Opt on RS,STD]	+250
Automatic 3-Speed Transmission	+189

Body Styles	TMV Pricing		
	Trade	Private	Dealer
4 Dr LS Sdn	1889	2781	3787
4 Dr STD Sdn	1548	2279	3104

Options	Price
Automatic 4-Speed Transmission [Std on LS]	+245
Power Sunroof	+187

1997

The Rally Sport (RS) trim is available for 1997 on the coupe and slotted between base and Z24 editions of the Cavalier. RS trim nets buyers the rear spoiler from the Z24, 15-inch tires, AM/FM stereo, tachometer, interior and exterior trim upgrades and a 3D rear-quarter panel decal. Base coupes have new wheel covers and safety belt guide loops. All 1997 Cavaliers meet federal side-impact standards for the first time. One new interior color and three new exterior colors freshen the lineup.

Mileage Category: B

Body Styles	TMV Pricing		
	Trade	Private	Dealer
2 Dr LS Conv	1942	2984	4258
2 Dr RS Cpe	1410	2166	3089
2 Dr STD Cpe	1204	1850	2639

Options	Price
Air Conditioning [Opt on RS,STD]	+226
Automatic 3-Speed Transmission [Std on LS]	+156

Body Styles	TMV Pricing		
	Trade	Private	Dealer
2 Dr Z24 Cpe	1640	2520	3595
4 Dr LS Sdn	1512	2323	3314
4 Dr STD Sdn	1204	1850	2639

Options	Price
Automatic 4-Speed Transmission	+226
Power Sunroof	+191

1996

The 2.3-liter Quad 4 is replaced after just one year by a 2.4-liter twin-cam engine. Four-speed automatic transmission includes traction control. Daytime running lights debut, remote keyless entry is optional on LS and Z24 and base models get new interior fabrics and an Appearance Package.

Mileage Category: B

Body Styles	TMV Pricing		
	Trade	Private	Dealer
2 Dr LS Conv	1513	2448	3738
2 Dr STD Cpe	827	1338	2044
2 Dr Z24 Cpe	1176	1901	2903

Options	Price
2.4L I4 DOHC 16V FI Engine [Opt on LS]	+121
Air Conditioning [Opt on STD]	+205
Automatic 3-Speed Transmission [Std on LS]	+142

Body Styles	TMV Pricing		
	Trade	Private	Dealer
4 Dr LS Sdn	1085	1757	2686
4 Dr STD Sdn	875	1416	2162

Options	Price
Automatic 4-Speed Transmission	+205
Power Sunroof	+173

1995

First redesign since 1982 debut. Sedan, coupe and convertible are available. Wagon is dropped. Sedan comes in base and LS trim. Coupe comes in base and Z24 trim. Convertible is available as LS only. Dual airbags and ABS are standard. Base engine is a 2.2-liter, 120-horsepower four-cylinder engine. Optional on LS sedan and convertible is the Z24's standard power plant; a 2.3-liter, DOHC four-cylinder making 150 horsepower.

Mileage Category: B

Body Styles	TMV Pricing		
	Trade	Private	Dealer
2 Dr LS Conv	1012	1783	3068
2 Dr STD Cpe	581	1024	1761
2 Dr Z24 Cpe	817	1440	2477

Options	Price
2.3L I4 DOHC 16V FI Engine [Opt on LS Conv]	+150
AM/FM/CD Audio System	+91
Air Conditioning [Opt on STD]	+184

Body Styles	TMV Pricing		
	Trade	Private	Dealer
4 Dr LS Sdn	701	1235	2124
4 Dr STD Sdn	586	1033	1778

Options	Price
Automatic 3-Speed Transmission [Std on LS]	+127
Automatic 4-Speed Transmission	+81
Power Sunroof	+138

Classic

2004

Mileage Category: C

Body Styles	TMV Pricing		
	Trade	Private	Dealer
4 Dr STD Sdn	7870	9102	11156

Options	Price
AM/FM/Cassette/CD Audio System	+150
Aluminum/Alloy Wheels	+400
Antilock Brakes	+400

Options	Price
Power Driver Seat	+275
Split Folding Rear Seat	+195

While Chevy is releasing a completely redesigned Malibu for 2004, the 1997-2003 design will remain in production. This previous-generation Malibu will be sold under the name Classic to fleet customers like rental car agencies. Other than the name change and a much slimmer selection of options, the Classic is unchanged from the 2003 Malibu.

Colorado
2004

Mileage Category: J

Body Styles	TMV Pricing			Body Styles	TMV Pricing		
	Trade	Private	Dealer		Trade	Private	Dealer
2 Dr Z71 4WD Std Cab SB	13019	14251	16305	4 Dr Z71 LS Base Crew Cab SB	15854	17094	19160
2 Dr Z71 LS 4WD Std Cab SB	13985	15232	17310	4 Dr Z71 LS Crew Cab SB	16713	17953	20019
2 Dr Z71 LS Std Cab SB	11777	12999	15035	4 Dr Z71 LS Ext Cab SB	13970	15168	17164
2 Dr Z71 Std Cab SB	10970	12097	13976	4 Dr Z85 4WD Ext Cab SB	13583	14804	16839
2 Dr Z85 4WD Std Cab SB	11580	12782	14786	4 Dr Z85 Ext Cab SB	11457	12503	14246
2 Dr Z85 LS 4WD Std Cab SB	12125	13327	15331	4 Dr Z85 LS 4WD Crew Cab SB	16111	17501	19817
2 Dr Z85 LS Std Cab SB	10471	11598	13477	4 Dr Z85 LS 4WD Ext Cab SB	14617	15838	17873
2 Dr Z85 Std Cab SB	9926	11053	12932	4 Dr Z85 LS Base 4WD Crew Cab SB	15362	16752	19068
2 Dr ZQ8 LS Std Cab SB	11680	12882	14886	4 Dr Z85 LS Base Crew Cab SB	13715	14955	17021
2 Dr ZQ8 Std Cab SB	10799	11926	13805	4 Dr Z85 LS Crew Cab SB	14480	15720	17786
4 Dr Z71 4WD Ext Cab SB	14706	15916	17932	4 Dr Z85 LS Ext Cab SB	12968	14058	15874
4 Dr Z71 Ext Cab SB	12978	14068	15884	4 Dr ZQ8 Ext Cab SB	12807	13897	15713
4 Dr Z71 LS 4WD Crew Cab SB	18619	20009	22325	4 Dr ZQ8 LS Base Crew Cab SB	15763	17003	19069
4 Dr Z71 LS 4WD Ext Cab SB	15674	16895	18930	4 Dr ZQ8 LS Crew Cab SB	16531	17771	19837
4 Dr Z71 LS Base 4WD Crew Cab SB	17555	18945	21261	4 Dr ZQ8 LS Ext Cab SB	13872	15037	16978

Options	Price	Options	Price
3.5L I5 DOHC 20V FI Engine [Std on Z71 Crew, ZQ8 Crew]	+1000	OnStar Telematics System [Opt on LS Crew]	+695
AM/FM/CD Changer Audio System [Opt on LS]	+395	Power Driver Seat [Opt on Crew]	+220
Appearance Package [Opt on Z85]	+300	Power Passenger Seat [Opt on Crew]	+220
Automatic 4-Speed Transmission [Std on Z71 Crew, ZQ8 Crew]	+1095	Power Windows [Opt on LS Std, LS Ext, LS Base Crew]	+250
Automatic Dimming Rearview Mirror [Opt on LS Ext, LS Crew]	+175	Satellite Radio System	+325
		Skid Plates [Opt on Z85 4WD]	+120
Cruise Control [Opt on Z85 LS Std, Z85 LS Ext]	+200	Sliding Rear Window	+120
Front and Rear Head Airbag Restraints [Std on Z71 Crew, Z85 Crew, ZQ8 Crew]	+195	Special Factory Paint	+165
Heated Front Seats [Opt on Crew]	+150		
Leather Seats [Opt on Crew]	+530		

The Colorado is an all-new compact pickup from Chevrolet.

Corsica
1996

Mileage Category: C

Body Styles	TMV Pricing		
	Trade	Private	Dealer
4 Dr STD Sdn	856	1455	2282

Options	Price	Options	Price
3.1L V6 OHV 12V FI Engine	+172	Automatic 4-Speed Transmission	+180

Long-life coolant is standard. Last year for Corsica.

1995

Daytime running lights debut. Rear suspension is revised, and larger tires are standard.

Mileage Category: C

Body Styles	TMV Pricing		
	Trade	Private	Dealer
4 Dr STD Sdn	571	1039	1820

Options	Price	Options	Price
3.1L V6 OHV 12V FI Engine	+154	Automatic 4-Speed Transmission	+162
AM/FM/CD Audio System	+91	Power Windows	+79

Corvette

2004

To celebrate the last year of the C5, Chevrolet is offering a Commemorative Edition package on all models, including the Z06. In addition to special Le Mans Blue exterior paint and a Shale interior, Commemorative Edition 'Vettes will have special badging and polished aluminum wheels. The Z06 version will have a carbon-fiber hood, Le Mans stripes and "Z06 only" wheels. Other changes for 2004 include revised shock valving on the Z06.

Mileage Category: F

Body Styles	TMV Pricing		
	Trade	Private	Dealer
2 Dr STD Conv	34160	36008	39089
2 Dr STD Hbk	29333	30998	33774

Options	Price
6-Speed Transmission [Opt on STD]	+915
Automatic On/Off Headlights	+200
Commemorative Edition	+3700
Compact Disc Changer [Opt on STD]	+600
Electronic Suspension Control [Opt on STD]	+1695
Heads-Up Display [Opt on STD]	+280
Magnesium Wheels [Opt on STD]	+995

Body Styles	TMV Pricing		
	Trade	Private	Dealer
2 Dr Z06 Cpe	33821	35781	39047

Options	Price
Performance/Handling Package [Opt on STD]	+395
Polished Aluminum/Alloy Wheels [Opt on STD]	+1295
Power Driver Seat w/Memory	+250
Power Telescopic Steering Wheel [Opt on STD]	+220
Special Factory Paint	+750
Targa Top - Glass [Opt on Cpe]	+750
Targa Top - Solid and Glass [Opt on Cpe]	+1400

2003

Most notable for 2003 is the 50th Anniversary package available on coupe and convertible models. The commemorative package includes Anniversary red exterior paint, a unique shale interior color, champagne-colored wheels and "50th Anniversary" exterior badging with matching embroidery on the headrests and floor mats. Also included in the Anniversary package (or as a stand-alone option on coupes and convertibles) is an all-new Magnetic Ride Control system that provides instantaneous shock adjustment for optimum ride quality and handling. All models also get additional standard equipment that includes sport seats, a power passenger seat, foglamps, dual-zone auto climate control and a parcel net and luggage shade on coupe models.

Mileage Category: F

Body Styles	TMV Pricing		
	Trade	Private	Dealer
2 Dr STD Conv	31734	33624	36776
2 Dr STD Hbk	27464	29041	31671

Options	Price
6-Speed Transmission [Opt on STD]	+584
Compact Disc Changer [Opt on STD]	+383
Electronic Damping Suspension Control [Opt on STD]	+1082
Heads-Up Display [Opt on STD]	+479
Magnesium Wheels [Opt on STD]	+958
Performance/Handling Package [Opt on STD]	+252

Body Styles	TMV Pricing		
	Trade	Private	Dealer
2 Dr Z06 Cpe	30489	32305	35333

Options	Price
Power Driver Seat w/Memory	+131
Power Tilt and Telescopic Steering Wheel	+192
Special Factory Paint	+383
Targa Top - Glass [Opt on Cpe]	+479
Targa Top - Solid and Glass [Opt on Cpe]	+766

2002

The track-ready Z06 model gains more power and performance. Electron Blue replaces Navy Blue metallic on the color palette, while Dark Bowling Green metallic gets dropped.

Mileage Category: F

Body Styles	TMV Pricing		
	Trade	Private	Dealer
2 Dr STD Conv	28310	30171	33271
2 Dr STD Hbk	24315	25912	28573

Options	Price
6-Speed Transmission [Std on Z06]	+525
Automatic Climate Control (2 Zone) - Driver and Passenger [Std on Z06]	+330
Compact Disc Changer	+344
Electronic Damping Suspension Control	+972
Fog Lights [Std on Z06]	+115
Metallic Paint	+344
Performance/Handling Package [Std on Z06]	+227

Body Styles	TMV Pricing		
	Trade	Private	Dealer
2 Dr Z06 Cpe	27228	29017	31998

Options	Price
Power Driver Seat w/Memory	+118
Power Passenger Seat	+138
Power Tilt and Telescopic Steering Wheel	+172
Special Factory Paint	+344
Sport Seats	+258
Targa Top - Solid [Opt on Cpe]	+430
Targa Top - Solid and Glass [Opt on Cpe]	+688

2001

The entire Corvette lineup receives a dose of additional horsepower and torque. The Z06 model joins the lineup, and Active Handling is now standard on all Corvettes.

Mileage Category: F

Body Styles	TMV Pricing		
	Trade	Private	Dealer
2 Dr STD Conv	24723	27354	29782
2 Dr STD Hbk	21884	24212	26361

Options	Price
6-Speed Transmission	+428
Automatic Climate Control (2 Zone) - Driver and Passenger	+302
Compact Disc Changer	+315
Electronic Damping Suspension Control	+889

Body Styles	TMV Pricing		
	Trade	Private	Dealer
2 Dr Z06 Cpe	23342	25826	28119

Options	Price
Heads-Up Display	+197
Magnesium Wheels	+1049
Metallic Paint	+315
Power Passenger Seat [Opt on STD]	+160

Options	Price
Power Tilt and Telescopic Steering Wheel [Opt on STD]	+157
Special Factory Paint	+315

Options	Price
Sport Seats	+236
Targa Top - Solid and Glass	+498

2000

Minor refinements improve the Corvette for 2000. The Z51 performance-handling package has larger front and rear stabilizer bars for improved handling, while new thin-spoke alloy wheels with optional high-polish finish subtly change the outward appearance. Two new colors are available on coupe and convertible: extra-cost Millennium Yellow and no-cost Dark Bowling Green Metallic. A Torch Red interior can be ordered, the stupendous LS1 5.7-liter V8 engine meets LEV regulations in California, the remote keyless-entry system has been upgraded, and the passenger door-lock cylinder has been deleted.

Mileage Category: F

Body Styles	TMV Pricing		
	Trade	Private	Dealer
2 Dr STD Conv	21827	24498	27117
2 Dr STD Cpe	19343	21711	24033

Body Styles	TMV Pricing		
	Trade	Private	Dealer
2 Dr STD Hbk	19497	21885	24225

Options	Price
Automatic Climate Control (2 Zone) - Driver and Passenger	+171
Automatic Stability Control	+234
Bose Audio System [Opt on Cpe]	+384
Compact Disc Changer	+281
Electronic Damping Suspension Control	+793
Heads-Up Display	+175
Magnesium Wheels	+936
Polished Aluminum/Alloy Wheels	+419

Options	Price
Power Driver Seat [Opt on Cpe]	+143
Power Passenger Seat	+143
Power Tilt and Telescopic Steering Wheel	+164
Special Factory Paint	+234
Sport Seats	+327
Targa Top - Glass	+304
Targa Top - Solid and Glass	+515

1999

A hardtop model aimed at enthusiasts is introduced, and its options list is short. Other Corvettes can be equipped with numerous options including a new heads-up display and a power tilt/telescope steering wheel.

Mileage Category: F

Body Styles	TMV Pricing		
	Trade	Private	Dealer
2 Dr STD Conv	18888	21556	24333
2 Dr STD Cpe	16922	19312	21799

Body Styles	TMV Pricing		
	Trade	Private	Dealer
2 Dr STD Hbk	17088	19501	22013

Options	Price
Automatic Climate Control	+136
Automatic Stability Control	+207
Compact Disc Changer	+224
Delco/Bose Audio System [Opt on Cpe]	+306
Electronic Damping Suspension Control	+633
Magnesium Wheels	+1244

Options	Price
Power Passenger Seat [Opt on Conv,Hbk]	+127
Sport Seats	+233
Targa Top - Glass	+355
Targa Top - Solid and Glass	+355
Tilt and Telescopic Steering Wheel [Opt on Conv,Hbk]	+145

1998

Two fresh colors are available, but the available convertible model is the big news. Equipped with a manual-folding top, a hard tonneau that extends along the rear wall of the passenger compartment and a trunk that holds golf bags. Lower-powered airbags are not available on the Corvette.

Mileage Category: F

Body Styles	TMV Pricing		
	Trade	Private	Dealer
2 Dr STD Conv	16366	19027	22028

Body Styles	TMV Pricing		
	Trade	Private	Dealer
2 Dr STD Hbk	15050	17497	20256

Options	Price
Automatic Climate Control	+115
Compact Disc Changer	+189
Electronic Damping Suspension Control	+533
Magnesium Wheels	+1048

Options	Price
Sport Seats	+196
Targa Top - Glass	+205
Targa Top - Solid and Glass	+299

1997

Fifth-generation Corvette debuts 44 years after the original, and is better than ever with world-class build quality and performance at a bargain price.

Mileage Category: F

Body Styles	TMV Pricing		
	Trade	Private	Dealer
2 Dr STD Hbk	13035	15414	18321

Options	Price
Compact Disc Changer	+171
Electronic Damping Suspension Control	+482
Sport Seats	+178

Options	Price
Targa Top - Glass	+185
Targa Top - Solid and Glass	+270

1996

Mileage Category: F

Body Styles	TMV Pricing		
	Trade	Private	Dealer
2 Dr Grand Sport Conv	12911	15372	18770
2 Dr Grand Sport Hbk	11660	13883	16952

Options	Price
Hardtop Roof	+514
Sport Seats [Opt on STD]	+161

Body Styles	TMV Pricing		
	Trade	Private	Dealer
2 Dr STD Conv	11973	14255	17406
2 Dr STD Hbk	10330	12298	15016

Options	Price
Targa Top - Glass	+168
Targa Top - Solid and Glass	+168

New 330-horsepower LT4 engine debuts on all manually shifted Corvettes. Two special editions are available, the Collector Edition and the Grand Sport. Next year, an all-new Corvette debuts. Other additions for 1996 include a Selective Real Time Damping system for the shock absorbers, and a stiffer Z51 suspension setup.

1995

ZR-1's brakes trickle down to base models. Front fenders get revised gills. Only 448 ZR-1s produced in 1995.

Mileage Category: F

Body Styles	TMV Pricing		
	Trade	Private	Dealer
2 Dr STD Conv	10020	12038	15400
2 Dr STD Hbk	8878	10665	13644

Options	Price
AM/FM/Cassette/CD Audio System [Opt on STD]	+138
Automatic Climate Control [Opt on STD]	+84
Delco/Bose Audio System [Opt on STD]	+91
Electronic Suspension Control [Opt on STD]	+382
Hardtop Roof	+461

Body Styles	TMV Pricing		
	Trade	Private	Dealer
2 Dr ZR1 Hbk	17567	21103	26997

Options	Price
Performance/Handling Package	+393
Sport Seats	+145
Targa Top - Glass	+150
Targa Top - Solid and Glass	+150

Impala

2004

The supercharged Impala SS joins the lineup for 2004. Besides offering 240 horsepower, the SS features a tightened suspension to allow it to take corners with a bit more gusto. Base and LS models have redesigned bench and bucket seats, and a sport appearance package is now available on the base sedan.

Mileage Category: G

Body Styles	TMV Pricing		
	Trade	Private	Dealer
4 Dr LS Sdn	12184	13452	15564
4 Dr SS S/C Sdn	14941	16387	18797

Options	Price
3.8L V6 OHV 12V FI Engine [Opt on STD]	+400
AM/FM/CD Audio System	+225
Alarm System [Opt on SS]	+200
Aluminum/Alloy Wheels [Opt on STD]	+700
Antilock Brakes [Opt on STD]	+200
Appearance Package [Opt on LS]	+995
Bucket Seats [Opt on STD]	+250
Cruise Control [Opt on STD]	+450
Driver Side Airbag Restraint	+350
Garage Door Opener [Opt on LS, SS]	+150
Heated Front Seats	+200

Body Styles	TMV Pricing		
	Trade	Private	Dealer
4 Dr STD Sdn	10008	11202	13191

Options	Price
Leather Seats [Std on SS]	+625
OnStar Telematics System	+300
Power Driver Seat [Opt on STD]	+150
Power Sunroof	+900
Rear Spoiler [Opt on STD]	+600
Satellite Radio System	+325
Tire Pressure Monitoring System [Opt on STD]	+150
Touring Suspension [Opt on STD]	+150
Traction Control System [Opt on STD]	+195
Trip Computer [Opt on LS, SS]	+150

2003

There are only minor upgrades in store for the 2003 Impala. New options include a side airbag for the driver and XM Satellite Radio. Remote keyless entry is now standard and four new exterior colors are available. Both base and LS models get new wheel designs.

Mileage Category: G

Body Styles	TMV Pricing		
	Trade	Private	Dealer
4 Dr LS Sdn	10731	11782	13534

Options	Price
3.8L V6 OHV 12V FI Engine [Opt on STD]	+252
AM/FM/CD Audio System	+156
Aluminum/Alloy Wheels [Opt on STD]	+223
Antilock Brakes [Opt on STD]	+447
Cruise Control [Opt on STD]	+118
Front Side Airbag Restraints [Opt on STD]	+223
Heated Front Seats	+176

Body Styles	TMV Pricing		
	Trade	Private	Dealer
4 Dr STD Sdn	8513	9347	10736

Options	Price
Leather Seats	+383
OnStar Telematics System	+444
Power Driver Seat [Opt on STD]	+153
Power Moonroof	+508
Power Passenger Seat	+153
Satellite Radio System	+207
Trip Computer	+188

2002

Now into its third year of production, the Impala soldiers on as Chevrolet's bread-and-butter family sedan. Minor upgrades this year include standard dual-zone air conditioning, an AM/FM stereo and LATCH child seat tether anchors. A leather-accented 60/40 split bench seat will be available later this year on LS models, and two new exterior colors have been added.

Mileage Category: G

Body Styles	TMV Pricing		
	Trade	Private	Dealer
4 Dr LS Sdn	8556	9531	11156

Options	Price
16 Inch Wheels	+172
3.8L V6 OHV 12V FI Engine [Opt on STD]	+227
AM/FM/CD Audio System	+141
AM/FM/Cassette/CD Audio System	+198
Aluminum/Alloy Wheels [Opt on STD]	+201
Antilock Brakes [Opt on STD]	+401
Front Side Airbag Restraints [Opt on STD]	+143
Heated Front Seats	+129

Body Styles	TMV Pricing		
	Trade	Private	Dealer
4 Dr STD Sdn	7019	7819	9151

Options	Price
Leather Seats	+344
OnStar Telematics System [Opt on STD]	+399
Power Driver Seat [Opt on STD]	+138
Power Moonroof	+456
Power Passenger Seat	+138
Split Front Bench Seat [Opt on LS]	+115
Trip Computer	+169

2001

No changes this year.

Mileage Category: G

Body Styles	TMV Pricing		
	Trade	Private	Dealer
4 Dr LS Sdn	6938	8187	9340

Options	Price
3.8L V6 OHV 12V FI Engine [Opt on STD]	+517
AM/FM/Cassette/CD Audio System	+117
Aluminum/Alloy Wheels [Opt on STD]	+157
Antilock Brakes [Opt on STD]	+357
Cruise Control [Opt on STD]	+125
Front Side Airbag Restraints [Opt on STD]	+131
Heated Front Seats	+131

Body Styles	TMV Pricing		
	Trade	Private	Dealer
4 Dr STD Sdn	5508	6499	7415

Options	Price
Leather Seats	+328
OnStar Telematics System [Opt on STD]	+365
Power Driver Seat	+160
Power Moonroof	+417
Power Passenger Seat	+160
Trip Computer	+144

2000

GM has resurrected the Impala nameplate (a staple in Chevy's lineup from 1959 to the early '80s and then briefly from 1994 to '96) and put it on an all-new full-size sedan body that rides on the Lumina front-drive platform. Although the Lumina itself is back for the 2000 model year, Impala will eventually replace it as Chevy's large-car entry to battle the likes of Ford's Crown Victoria, Buick's LeSabre and Chrysler's LH cars.

Mileage Category: G

Body Styles	TMV Pricing		
	Trade	Private	Dealer
4 Dr LS Sdn	5601	6800	7976

Options	Price
3.8L V6 OHV 12V FI Engine [Opt on STD]	+461
AM/FM/CD Audio System	+189
AM/FM/Cassette/CD Audio System	+236
Aluminum/Alloy Wheels [Opt on STD]	+140
Antilock Brakes [Opt on STD]	+318

Body Styles	TMV Pricing		
	Trade	Private	Dealer
4 Dr STD Sdn	4425	5373	6303

Options	Price
Front Side Airbag Restraints [Opt on STD]	+117
Heated Front Seats	+117
Leather Seats	+292
OnStar Telematics System	+419
Power Moonroof	+327

1996

Mileage Category: G

Body Styles	TMV Pricing		
	Trade	Private	Dealer
4 Dr SS Sdn	7050	8494	10487

A tachometer and floor shifter are available. Last year for this generation of Impala.

1995

Dark Cherry and Green Gray paint colors join basic black. New seats and radios debut. Outside mirrors can be folded in, and a new option is a radio with speed-compensated volume control.

Mileage Category: G

Body Styles	TMV Pricing		
	Trade	Private	Dealer
4 Dr SS Sdn	5466	6588	8458

Options	Price
Premium Audio System	+116

Lumina

Lumina

2000

Mileage Category: D

Body Styles	TMV Pricing		
	Trade	Private	Dealer
4 Dr STD Sdn	3778	4814	5829

Options	Price
AM/FM/CD Audio System	+152
Aluminum/Alloy Wheels	+140

Options	Price
Antilock Brakes	+318
Power Driver Seat	+143

Base models receive additional standard equipment, while the standard 3.1-liter V6 gets more power and torque. The sporty LTZ and upscale LS models are dropped. This is the final year for the Lumina.

1999

Chevrolet adds standard equipment to the LTZ and introduces Auburn Nightmist Medium Metallic to the base and LS models.

Mileage Category: D

Body Styles	TMV Pricing		
	Trade	Private	Dealer
4 Dr LS Sdn	3000	3979	4998
4 Dr LTZ Sdn	3112	4127	5184

Options	Price
AM/FM/CD Audio System	+121
Antilock Brakes [Opt on STD]	+282
Leather Seats	+241

Body Styles	TMV Pricing		
	Trade	Private	Dealer
4 Dr STD Sdn	2981	3954	4966

Options	Price
OnStar Telematics System	+371
Power Moonroof	+261

1998

Last year's aborted LTZ sport sedan comes on strong for 1998, with a 200-horsepower 3800 V6 engine and machine-faced aluminum wheels. Four new exterior colors and one new interior color are also available on all Lumina models. To help give Lumina a more upscale image than Malibu, an OnStar Mobile Communications system is a dealer-installed option. Second-generation airbags are standard equipment.

Mileage Category: D

Body Styles	TMV Pricing		
	Trade	Private	Dealer
4 Dr LS Sdn	2463	3391	4437
4 Dr LTZ Sdn	2553	3515	4599

Options	Price
3.8L V6 OHV 12V FI Engine [Opt on LTZ]	+141
Antilock Brakes [Opt on STD]	+238
Leather Seats	+202

Body Styles	TMV Pricing		
	Trade	Private	Dealer
4 Dr STD Sdn	2304	3172	4151

Options	Price
OnStar Telematics System	+313
Power Moonroof	+220

1997

Performance-oriented Lumina LTZ debuts, with a spoiler, special front and rear styling, graphics and alloy wheels. Daytime running lamps are standard on all Luminas, and the power sunroof expected last year finally arrives. New colors and an oil life monitor round out changes to Lumina for 1997.

Mileage Category: D

Body Styles	TMV Pricing		
	Trade	Private	Dealer
4 Dr LS Sdn	1916	2753	3775
4 Dr LTZ Sdn	2163	3107	4261

Options	Price
3.4L V6 DOHC 24V FI Engine	+262
Antilock Brakes [Opt on STD]	+215

Body Styles	TMV Pricing		
	Trade	Private	Dealer
4 Dr STD Sdn	1896	2724	3735

Options	Price
Leather Seats	+183
Power Moonroof	+199

1996

The ultimate family sedan is now available with an integrated child safety seat. Driver and passenger get their own climate controls. LS models offer available leather, and four-wheel disc brakes when equipped with the 3.4-liter V6.

Mileage Category: D

Body Styles	TMV Pricing		
	Trade	Private	Dealer
4 Dr LS Sdn	1518	2267	3302

Options	Price
3.4L V6 DOHC 24V FI Engine	+238
Antilock Brakes [Std on LS]	+195

Body Styles	TMV Pricing		
	Trade	Private	Dealer
4 Dr STD Sdn	1407	2102	3062

Options	Price
Leather Seats	+166

1995

Midsize sedan is redesigned; features dual airbags. Base and LS trim levels are available. ABS is optional on base model; standard on LS. Standard power plant is a 160-horsepower, 3.1-liter V6. Optional on LS is a 210-horsepower, 3.4-liter V6. Air conditioning is standard.

Mileage Category: D

Body Styles	TMV Pricing		
	Trade	Private	Dealer
4 Dr LS Sdn	1035	1673	2735

Options	Price
3.4L V6 DOHC 24V FI Engine	+214
AM/FM/CD Audio System	+75

Body Styles	TMV Pricing		
	Trade	Private	Dealer
4 Dr STD Sdn	912	1473	2408

Options	Price
AM/FM/Cassette/CD Audio System	+117
Antilock Brakes [Std on LS]	+175

Options	Price
Premium Audio System	+116

Lumina Minivan

1996

Mileage Category: P

Body Styles	TMV Pricing		
	Trade	Private	Dealer
3 Dr STD Pass Van	1981	2770	3860

Options	Price
Air Conditioning - Front and Rear	+116

Last year for this van. A 3.4-liter V6 good for 180 horsepower replaces standard and optional V6 engines from last year. Air conditioning, seven-passenger seating and an electronically controlled four-speed automatic transmission are standard.

1995

Transmission gets brake/shift interlock.

Mileage Category: P

Body Styles	TMV Pricing		
	Trade	Private	Dealer
3 Dr STD Pass Van	1443	2069	3112

Options	Price	Options	Price
3.8L V6 OHV 12V FI Engine	+142	Air Conditioning - Front and Rear	+104
7 Passenger Seating	+127	Automatic 4-Speed Transmission	+185
AM/FM/CD Audio System	+91	Power Sliding Door	+81
Air Conditioning	+185	Sunroof	+116

Malibu

2004

Mileage Category: C

Body Styles	TMV Pricing			Body Styles	TMV Pricing		
	Trade	Private	Dealer		Trade	Private	Dealer
4 Dr LS Sdn	11101	12321	14353	4 Dr STD Sdn	10050	11269	13301
4 Dr LT Sdn	12972	14245	16368				

Options	Price	Options	Price
AM/FM/CD Changer Audio System	+300	OnStar Telematics System [Opt on LS, LT]	+695
Antilock Brakes [Opt on STD]	+200	Power Adjustable Foot Pedals [Opt on STD]	+180
Automatic Dimming Rearview Mirror [Opt on LT]	+155	Power Moonroof [Opt on LS, LT]	+600
Cruise Control [Opt on STD]	+150	Rear Spoiler [Opt on LS]	+175
Front and Rear Head Airbag Restraints [Std on LT]	+395	Satellite Radio System [Opt on LS, LT]	+325
Garage Door Opener [Opt on LT]	+150	Traction Control System [Opt on STD]	+200
Keyless Entry System [Opt on STD]	+250		

The midsize Malibu has been totally redesigned for 2004. It now rides on an entirely new vehicle platform and offers a more powerful V6 along with must-have safety features like side curtain airbags and adjustable pedals.

2003

Mileage Category: C

Body Styles	TMV Pricing			Body Styles	TMV Pricing		
	Trade	Private	Dealer		Trade	Private	Dealer
4 Dr LS Sdn	7770	8698	10244	4 Dr STD Sdn	7322	8195	9651

Options	Price	Options	Price
Aluminum/Alloy Wheels [Opt on STD]	+239	Power Driver Seat [Opt on STD]	+153
Antilock Brakes [Opt on STD]	+447	Power Moonroof [Opt on LS]	+431
Cruise Control [Opt on STD]	+118	Power Windows [Opt on STD]	+156
Keyless Entry System [Opt on STD]	+121	Split Folding Rear Seat [Opt on STD]	+124
Leather Seats [Opt on LS]	+380		

The Malibu gets little in the way of upgrades for 2003. There are two new colors to choose from -- Summit White and Medium Gray Metallic -- and a new seat fabric on LS models. ABS brakes are now optional on base models, but remain standard on the LS.

2002

Mileage Category: C

Body Styles	TMV Pricing			Body Styles	TMV Pricing		
	Trade	Private	Dealer		Trade	Private	Dealer
4 Dr LS Sdn	6768	7709	9276	4 Dr STD Sdn	6172	7029	8459

Only minor changes are added to Chevrolet's midsize sedan. Floor mats and an AM/FM CD stereo are now standard on all models. Three new colors have been added along with newly styled 15-inch cast-aluminum wheels.

2002 (cont'd)

Options	Price	Options	Price
Aluminum/Alloy Wheels [Opt on STD]	+215	Power Moonroof	+387
Cruise Control [Opt on STD]	+129	Power Windows [Opt on STD]	+152
Leather Seats [Opt on STD]	+341		

2001

Base models receive black rocker moldings, black molded-in-color outside rearview mirrors and a rear window defogger. LS models get front seat back map pockets. Both models receive auto headlamp on/off, new stereos and new cloth interiors.

Mileage Category: C

Body Styles	TMV Pricing			Body Styles	TMV Pricing		
	Trade	Private	Dealer		Trade	Private	Dealer
4 Dr LS Sdn	4999	6213	7334	4 Dr STD Sdn	4461	5545	6546

Options	Price	Options	Price
Aluminum/Alloy Wheels [Opt on STD]	+163	Power Sunroof	+341
Cruise Control [Opt on STD]	+118	Power Windows [Opt on STD]	+137
Leather Seats	+312		

2000

Revised front styling ties Malibu to Impala, and the 1999's brushed-aluminum wheels have been redesigned. The 3.1-liter V6 engine is standard this year, and has been improved to offer more horsepower while meeting low emission vehicle (LEV) standards. A spoiler and a gold package are available.

Mileage Category: C

Body Styles	TMV Pricing			Body Styles	TMV Pricing		
	Trade	Private	Dealer		Trade	Private	Dealer
4 Dr LS Sdn	3817	4976	6113	4 Dr STD Sdn	3215	4191	5148

Options	Price	Options	Price
AM/FM/CD Audio System	+150	Power Driver Seat [Opt on STD]	+145
AM/FM/Cassette/CD Audio System [Opt on STD]	+197	Power Sunroof	+305
Aluminum/Alloy Wheels [Opt on STD]	+145	Power Windows [Opt on STD]	+122
Leather Seats	+278		

1999

The 1999 Malibu is identical to the 1998 model, except for the addition of Medium Bronzemist Metallic to the paint chart.

Mileage Category: C

Body Styles	TMV Pricing			Body Styles	TMV Pricing		
	Trade	Private	Dealer		Trade	Private	Dealer
4 Dr LS Sdn	2918	3973	5070	4 Dr STD Sdn	2539	3459	4416

Options	Price	Options	Price
3.1L V6 OHV 12V FI Engine [Opt on STD]	+222	Power Driver Seat [Opt on STD]	+116
Aluminum/Alloy Wheels [Opt on STD]	+116	Power Sunroof	+243
Leather Seats	+222		

1998

Leather trim is newly optional on LS models, aluminum wheels are revised, a sunroof can be ordered and Base models can be equipped with Medium Oak colored interior. Second-generation airbags debut.

Mileage Category: C

Body Styles	TMV Pricing			Body Styles	TMV Pricing		
	Trade	Private	Dealer		Trade	Private	Dealer
4 Dr LS Sdn	2392	3416	4571	4 Dr STD Sdn	2038	2911	3896

Options	Price	Options	Price
3.1L V6 OHV 12V FI Engine [Opt on STD]	+156	Power Sunroof	+187
Leather Seats	+173		

1997

First year for new midsize sedan with classic name.

Mileage Category: C

Body Styles	TMV Pricing			Body Styles	TMV Pricing		
	Trade	Private	Dealer		Trade	Private	Dealer
4 Dr LS Sdn	1758	2728	3915	4 Dr STD Sdn	1542	2395	3437

Malibu Maxx

2004

Mileage Category: C

Body Styles	TMV Pricing			Body Styles	TMV Pricing		
	Trade	Private	Dealer		Trade	Private	Dealer
4 Dr LS Hbk	13024	14225	16227	4 Dr LT Hbk	14506	15707	17708

Options	Price	Options	Price
AM/FM/CD Changer Audio System	+300	OnStar Telematics System	+695
DVD Entertainment System	+995	Power Driver Seat [Opt on LS]	+300
Front and Rear Head Airbag Restraints [Opt on LS]	+500	Power Moonroof	+655
Garage Door Opener [Opt on LT]	+150	Rear Audio Controls [Opt on LS]	+125

2004 (cont'd)

Options	Price
Satellite Radio System	+325

Based on the 2004 Chevy Malibu, the Malibu Maxx is an all-new vehicle. A cross between a sedan and a wagon, it's designed to give midsize car buyers a little more space so that they don't have to resort to an SUV.

Metro
2000

Mileage Category: A

Body Styles	TMV Pricing		
	Trade	Private	Dealer
2 Dr LSi Hbk	1918	2801	3666
2 Dr STD Hbk	1711	2499	3272

Options	Price
AM/FM Audio System	+155
AM/FM/CD Audio System	+210
AM/FM/Cassette Audio System	+257
Air Conditioning	+367

Body Styles	TMV Pricing		
	Trade	Private	Dealer
4 Dr LSi Sdn	2020	2950	3862

Options	Price
Antilock Brakes	+318
Automatic 3-Speed Transmission	+278
Power Door Locks	+278
Power Steering	+136

Two new colors help buyers differentiate between 1999 and 2000 Metros.

1999

Mileage Category: A

Body Styles	TMV Pricing		
	Trade	Private	Dealer
2 Dr LSi Hbk	1425	2258	3126
2 Dr STD Hbk	1276	2024	2803

Options	Price
AM/FM Audio System	+124
AM/FM/CD Audio System	+168
AM/FM/Cassette Audio System	+205

Body Styles	TMV Pricing		
	Trade	Private	Dealer
4 Dr LSi Sdn	1570	2488	3444

Options	Price
Air Conditioning	+293
Antilock Brakes	+282
Automatic 3-Speed Transmission	+222

After getting a makeover last year to mark its move from the old Geo nameplate to the Chevrolet model family, the Metro is a carryover product for 1999, save for the addition of two new exterior colors: Dark Green Metallic and Silver Metallic.

1998

Mileage Category: A

Body Styles	TMV Pricing		
	Trade	Private	Dealer
2 Dr LSi Hbk	989	1650	2396
2 Dr STD Hbk	911	1520	2207

Options	Price
AM/FM/CD Audio System	+141
AM/FM/Cassette Audio System	+173
Air Conditioning	+247

Body Styles	TMV Pricing		
	Trade	Private	Dealer
4 Dr LSi Sdn	1123	1872	2716

Options	Price
Antilock Brakes	+238
Automatic 3-Speed Transmission	+187

The Geo badge is replaced with a Chevy bowtie. Styling is updated front and rear. The LSi's four-cylinder engine gets four valves per cylinder for more power and better acceleration. Second-generation airbags are standard equipment. Wheel covers are revised, new radios, new interior fabrics and the addition of California Gold Metallic to the paint palette round out the changes.

Monte Carlo
2004

Mileage Category: D

Body Styles	TMV Pricing		
	Trade	Private	Dealer
2 Dr LS Cpe	12667	13855	15835
2 Dr SS Cpe	14045	15233	17213

Options	Price
AM/FM/CD Audio System	+200
Alarm System [Opt on SS, SS S/C]	+210
Aluminum/Alloy Wheels [Opt on LS]	+590
Antilock Brakes [Opt on LS]	+300
Appearance Package [Opt on LS, SS]	+500
Cruise Control [Opt on LS]	+150
Driver Side Airbag Restraint	+350
Garage Door Opener	+140
Heated Front Seats	+200

Body Styles	TMV Pricing		
	Trade	Private	Dealer
2 Dr SS S/C Cpe	15950	17138	19118

Options	Price
Leather Seats	+625
OnStar Telematics System	+300
Power Driver Seat	+200
Power Moonroof	+900
Power Passenger Seat	+220
Satellite Radio System	+325
Traction Control System [Opt on LS]	+200
Trip Computer	+145

In an attempt to revive Monte Carlo's performance image, Chevrolet adds a supercharged SS version for 2004. The LS gets new 17-inch aluminum wheels, and there are a couple new appearance packages, Sport and Winner's Circle, available on the LS and non-supercharged SS.

Chevrolet
Monte Carlo

2003

The Monte Carlo receives only minor changes for the 2003 model year. The base LS model has been upgraded with standard four-wheel disc brakes, traction control and remote keyless entry. Both the LS and SS models sport newly styled wheels, four new exterior colors and the option of adding XM Satellite Radio.

Mileage Category: D

Body Styles	TMV Pricing		
	Trade	Private	Dealer
2 Dr LS Cpe	9652	10618	12228

Options	Price
AM/FM/CD Audio System	+220
Aluminum/Alloy Wheels [Opt on LS]	+223
Antilock Brakes [Opt on LS]	+447
Cruise Control [Opt on LS]	+153
Front Side Airbag Restraints	+223
Ground Effects [Opt on SS]	+319
Jeff Gordon Signature Edition [Opt on SS]	+1979
Leather Seats	+399

Body Styles	TMV Pricing		
	Trade	Private	Dealer
2 Dr SS Cpe	11947	13142	15134

Options	Price
Leather Steering Wheel [Opt on LS]	+124
OnStar Telematics System	+444
Pace Car Package [Opt on SS]	+1724
Power Driver Seat	+153
Power Moonroof	+508
Power Passenger Seat	+153
Satellite Radio System	+207
Special Factory Paint [Opt on SS]	+255

2002

Chevy's personal-luxury coupe receives only minor changes for 2002. LATCH child safety-seat anchors, dual-zone air conditioning and three-point seatbelts for rear passengers are now standard on all models. Bright Red and Medium Green Pearl replace Torch Red and Dark Jade Green as exterior color options.

Mileage Category: D

Body Styles	TMV Pricing		
	Trade	Private	Dealer
2 Dr LS Cpe	8172	9103	10654

Options	Price
16 Inch Wheels	+143
AM/FM/CD Audio System	+198
AM/FM/Cassette/CD Audio System	+129
Aluminum/Alloy Wheels [Opt on LS]	+172
Cruise Control [Opt on LS]	+137
Front Side Airbag Restraints [Opt on LS]	+143

Body Styles	TMV Pricing		
	Trade	Private	Dealer
2 Dr SS Cpe	10069	11216	13128

Options	Price
Leather Seats	+330
OnStar Telematics System [Opt on LS]	+244
Power Driver Seat	+138
Power Moonroof	+456
Power Passenger Seat	+138
Special Factory Paint	+229

2001

Chevy's personal-luxury coupe receives optional sport appearance packages, a standard driver-side-impact airbag and traction control and OnStar comes with the SS model.

Mileage Category: D

Body Styles	TMV Pricing		
	Trade	Private	Dealer
2 Dr LS Cpe	6727	8038	9249

Options	Price
AM/FM/Cassette/CD Audio System	+117
Aero Kit [Opt on SS]	+393
Aluminum/Alloy Wheels [Opt on LS]	+157
Cruise Control [Opt on LS]	+125
Front Side Airbag Restraints [Opt on LS]	+131
Leather Seats	+328

Body Styles	TMV Pricing		
	Trade	Private	Dealer
2 Dr SS Cpe	8000	9561	11001

Options	Price
OnStar Telematics System [Opt on LS]	+365
Power Driver Seat	+160
Power Passenger Seat	+160
Power Sunroof	+417
Sport Package	+1102
Trip Computer [Opt on LS]	+144

2000

Chevy's personal-luxury coupe is all new for 2000, based on the Impala platform and sporting distinctive, heritage styling cues.

Mileage Category: D

Body Styles	TMV Pricing		
	Trade	Private	Dealer
2 Dr LS Cpe	4859	6191	7496

Options	Price
Aluminum/Alloy Wheels [Opt on LS]	+140
Leather Seats	+302

Body Styles	TMV Pricing		
	Trade	Private	Dealer
2 Dr SS Cpe	5843	7443	9012

Options	Price
OnStar Telematics System	+419
Power Moonroof	+327

1999

Mileage Category: D

Body Styles	TMV Pricing		
	Trade	Private	Dealer
2 Dr LS Cpe	3517	4665	5859

Options	Price
Leather Seats	+241
OnStar Telematics System	+371

Body Styles	TMV Pricing		
	Trade	Private	Dealer
2 Dr Z34 Cpe	3663	4858	6102

Options	Price
Power Moonroof	+261

Deep Purple paint is gone. First year for the optional OnStar communications system, a 24-hour roadside assistance network that is accessed through a dealer-installed cellular phone.

1998

The Z34 model gets a different engine and fresh wheels. Second-generation airbags are added. New paint colors and one new interior hue round out the changes.

Mileage Category: D

Body Styles	TMV Pricing		
	Trade	Private	Dealer
2 Dr LS Cpe	2628	3619	4736

Options	Price
Leather Seats	+202
OnStar Telematics System	+313

Body Styles	TMV Pricing		
	Trade	Private	Dealer
2 Dr Z34 Cpe	3021	4157	5439

Options	Price
Power Moonroof	+220

1997

Z34 gets a new transmission, while all models have daytime running lights. A power sunroof is optional.

Mileage Category: D

Body Styles	TMV Pricing		
	Trade	Private	Dealer
2 Dr LS Cpe	2098	3015	4135

Options	Price
Leather Seats	+183

Body Styles	TMV Pricing		
	Trade	Private	Dealer
2 Dr Z34 Cpe	2431	3492	4789

Options	Price
Power Sunroof	+199

1996

Dual-zone climate controls reduce marital spats. The 3.4-liter V6 makes more power this year, and four-wheel disc brakes, standard on the Z34, are optional on the LS.

Mileage Category: D

Body Styles	TMV Pricing		
	Trade	Private	Dealer
2 Dr LS Cpe	1670	2494	3631

Options	Price
Leather Seats	+166

Body Styles	TMV Pricing		
	Trade	Private	Dealer
2 Dr Z34 Cpe	1897	2832	4123

Options	Price
Power Sunroof	+180

1995

Available in LS or Z34 trim levels. Dual airbags and ABS are standard. LS comes with 160-horsepower, 3.1-liter V6, while Z34 is powered by 3.4-liter, twin-cam V6 good for 210 horsepower. All Monte Carlos have automatic transmissions. Air conditioning is standard.

Body Styles	TMV Pricing		
	Trade	Private	Dealer
2 Dr LS Cpe	1109	1792	2930

Options	Price
Leather Seats	+149

Body Styles	TMV Pricing		
	Trade	Private	Dealer
2 Dr Z34 Cpe	1278	2065	3376

Options	Price
Premium Audio System	+116

Prizm

2002

Mileage Category: B

Body Styles	TMV Pricing		
	Trade	Private	Dealer
4 Dr LSi Sdn	5855	6801	8378

Options	Price
Aluminum/Alloy Wheels	+162
Antilock Brakes	+390
Automatic 3-Speed Transmission	+284
Automatic 4-Speed Transmission	+459

Body Styles	TMV Pricing		
	Trade	Private	Dealer
4 Dr STD Sdn	5137	5967	7349

Options	Price
Front Side Airbag Restraints	+169
Power Door Locks [Opt on STD]	+126
Power Sunroof	+387
Power Windows [Opt on STD]	+172

The Prizm remains unchanged for 2002.

2001

The Prizm remains relatively unchanged for 2001. An emergency trunk release becomes standard issue and Medium Red Metallic is added to the color palette.

Mileage Category: B

Body Styles	TMV Pricing		
	Trade	Private	Dealer
4 Dr LSi Sdn	4553	5836	7021

Options	Price
AM/FM/Cassette Audio System [Opt on STD]	+291
Aluminum/Alloy Wheels	+148
Antilock Brakes	+357
Automatic 3-Speed Transmission	+260
Automatic 4-Speed Transmission	+420

Body Styles	TMV Pricing		
	Trade	Private	Dealer
4 Dr STD Sdn	4061	5206	6262

Options	Price
Front Side Airbag Restraints	+155
Power Door Locks [Opt on STD]	+115
Power Sunroof	+344
Power Windows [Opt on STD]	+157

2000

New standard features improve the Prizm's value quotient, and variable valve timing boosts power and torque. The tweaked engine now meets low emission vehicle status in California, and three new colors freshen the exterior.

Mileage Category: B

Body Styles	TMV Pricing		
	Trade	Private	Dealer
4 Dr LSi Sdn	3415	4604	5770

Body Styles	TMV Pricing		
	Trade	Private	Dealer
4 Dr STD Sdn	3084	4158	5211

2000 (cont'd)

Options	Price
AM/FM/CD Audio System	+306
AM/FM/Cassette Audio System [Opt on STD]	+260
Aluminum/Alloy Wheels	+157
Antilock Brakes	+318
Automatic 3-Speed Transmission	+232

Options	Price
Automatic 4-Speed Transmission	+374
Front Side Airbag Restraints	+138
Power Sunroof	+315
Power Windows [Opt on STD]	+140

1999

After a thorough revision last year, the only changes for 1999 are four new paint colors.

Mileage Category: B

Body Styles	TMV Pricing		
	Trade	Private	Dealer
4 Dr LSi Sdn	2608	3654	4743

Body Styles	TMV Pricing		
	Trade	Private	Dealer
4 Dr STD Sdn	2231	3125	4056

Options	Price
AM/FM/CD Audio System	+244
AM/FM/Cassette Audio System [Opt on STD]	+207
Air Conditioning [Opt on STD]	+293
Aluminum/Alloy Wheels	+125

Options	Price
Antilock Brakes	+282
Automatic 3-Speed Transmission	+185
Automatic 4-Speed Transmission	+298
Power Sunroof	+252

1998

Chevy replaces the Geo badge with its own on the completely redesigned Prizm. Among the improvements are a larger standard engine, optional side airbags, an optional handling package for LSi models and new colors inside and out. Front airbags are of the depowered variety.

Mileage Category: B

Body Styles	TMV Pricing		
	Trade	Private	Dealer
4 Dr LSi Sdn	2134	3141	4277

Body Styles	TMV Pricing		
	Trade	Private	Dealer
4 Dr STD Sdn	1794	2641	3596

Options	Price
AM/FM/CD Audio System	+206
AM/FM/Cassette Audio System	+175
Air Conditioning	+247
Antilock Brakes	+238

Options	Price
Automatic 3-Speed Transmission	+156
Automatic 4-Speed Transmission	+251
Power Sunroof	+212

S-10

2004

The Chevrolet S-10, like its GMC cousin, the Sonoma, is only available as a crew cab 4x4 for the 2004 model year.

Mileage Category: J

Body Styles	TMV Pricing		
	Trade	Private	Dealer
4 Dr LS 4WD Crew Cab SB	14608	16178	18795

Options	Price
AM/FM/CD Changer Audio System	+395
Appearance Package	+1500
Heated Front Seats	+195
Leather Seats	+600
Locking Differential	+270

Options	Price
Power Driver Seat	+350
Power Passenger Seat	+350
Sliding Rear Window	+120
Special Factory Paint	+165
Tonneau Cover	+395

2003

The S-10 gets few changes for what may be the final year of production of the current model. There's new cloth upholstery for the seats and door panels, a new fuel-injection system for the 4.3-liter V6 and a sport package for crew cab models.

Mileage Category: J

Body Styles	TMV Pricing		
	Trade	Private	Dealer
2 Dr LS Std Cab LB	8772	9693	11227
2 Dr LS Std Cab SB	8544	9441	10935
2 Dr LS Xtreme Std Cab SB	10044	11098	12854
2 Dr STD Std Cab LB	8568	9467	10966
2 Dr STD Std Cab SB	7702	8510	9857
3 Dr LS 4WD Ext Cab SB	12350	13646	15806

Body Styles	TMV Pricing		
	Trade	Private	Dealer
3 Dr LS Ext Cab SB	9725	10745	12446
3 Dr LS Xtreme Ext Cab SB	11353	12544	14529
3 Dr LS ZR2 4WD Ext Cab SB	12737	14074	16301
3 Dr STD 4WD Ext Cab SB	11237	12416	14381
3 Dr STD Ext Cab SB	8643	9550	11061
4 Dr LS 4WD Crew Cab SB	13477	14891	17248

Options	Price
4.3L V6 OHV 12V FI Engine [Std on 4WD]	+638
AM/FM/CD Audio System [Opt on STD]	+193
AM/FM/CD Changer Audio System	+252
Automatic 4-Speed Transmission [Std on Crew,Std Cab LB]	+699
Bed Liner [Opt on LS Xtreme]	+134
Bucket Seats	+218

Options	Price
Chrome Bumpers [Opt on LS]	+128
Cruise Control [Opt on STD]	+118
Heated Front Seats [Opt on Crew]	+176
Keyless Entry System [Opt on LS,LS Xtreme,LS ZR2]	+118
Leather Seats [Opt on Crew]	+479
Locking Differential [Std on LS ZR2]	+172
Luggage Rack [Opt on Crew]	+160

2003 (cont'd)

Options	Price
Power Driver Seat [Opt on Crew]	+153
Power Moonroof	+444
Power Passenger Seat [Opt on Crew]	+153

Options	Price
Power Windows [Opt on LS,LS Xtreme,LS ZR2]	+153
Stepside Bed [Opt on LS,LS Xtreme]	+303
ZQ8 Sport Suspension Package [Opt on LS 2WD]	+501

Mileage Category: J

Body Styles	TMV Pricing		
	Trade	Private	Dealer
2 Dr LS Std Cab LB	7639	8557	10087
2 Dr LS Std Cab SB	7354	8251	9745
2 Dr STD Std Cab LB	6666	7479	8833
2 Dr STD Std Cab SB	6197	6952	8211
3 Dr LS 4WD Ext Cab SB	10878	12204	14415

Body Styles	TMV Pricing		
	Trade	Private	Dealer
3 Dr LS Ext Cab SB	8286	9296	10980
3 Dr STD 4WD Ext Cab SB	9156	10272	12133
3 Dr STD Ext Cab SB	6938	7784	9195
4 Dr LS 4WD Crew Cab SB	11334	12716	15018

Options	Price
4.3L V6 OHV 12V FI Engine [Std on 4WD]	+573
AM/FM/CD Audio System [Opt on STD]	+173
AM/FM/CD Changer Audio System [Opt on LS]	+227
Automatic 4-Speed Transmission [Std on LS]	+628
Heated Front Seats [Opt on LS Crew]	+146
LS Xtreme Package [Opt on LS]	+1299
Leather Seats [Opt on LS Crew]	+407
Locking Differential [Std on LS - Crew Cab,Ext 4WD]	+155
Luggage Rack [Opt on LS Crew]	+143

Options	Price
Power Door Locks [Std on LS Crew]	+129
Power Driver Seat [Opt on LS Crew]	+152
Power Passenger Seat [Opt on LS Crew]	+152
Power Windows [Std on LS Crew]	+146
Side Steps [Opt on LS Crew]	+172
Tonneau Cover [Opt on LS Crew]	+155
ZQ8 Sport Suspension Package [Opt on LS]	+444
ZR2 Highrider Suspension Package	+1105

2002

Additional standard features are added to the S-10 for 2002 including a tachometer, air conditioning and a third door for extended-cab models. Vehicles sold in Northern states also get the Cold Weather package as standard equipment.

Mileage Category: J

Body Styles	TMV Pricing		
	Trade	Private	Dealer
2 Dr LS 4WD Ext Cab SB	8116	9686	11135
2 Dr LS Ext Cab SB	6315	7538	8666
2 Dr LS Std Cab LB	5455	6510	7484
2 Dr LS Std Cab SB	5325	6355	7306
2 Dr STD 4WD Ext Cab SB	7822	9335	10732

Body Styles	TMV Pricing		
	Trade	Private	Dealer
2 Dr STD Ext Cab SB	6099	7278	8367
2 Dr STD Std Cab LB	5246	6261	7197
2 Dr STD Std Cab SB	5144	6139	7058
4 Dr LS 4WD Crew Cab SB	10080	12030	13830

Options	Price
4.3L V6 OHV 12V FI Engine [Opt on 2WD]	+679
AM/FM/CD Audio System	+158
AM/FM/Cassette/CD Audio System	+211
Air Conditioning [Opt on STD]	+422
Aluminum/Alloy Wheels [Opt on 2WD Reg Cab LB,LS,STD]	+147
Automatic 4-Speed Transmission	+574
Bucket Seats	+179
LS Xtreme Package	+1149

Options	Price
Locking Differential	+122
Power Door Locks [Std on LS Wide Stance]	+118
Power Heated Mirrors [Std on LS Wide Stance]	+123
Power Windows [Std on LS Wide Stance]	+134
Sport Suspension [Std on LS]	+365
Stepside Bed	+249
Wide Stance Suspension Package	+2122

2001

A new four-door crew cab 4WD version is offered with enough room for five passengers. Chevy's compact truck now offers a national low emission vehicle (NLEV) option.

Mileage Category: J

Body Styles	TMV Pricing		
	Trade	Private	Dealer
2 Dr LS 4WD Ext Cab SB	6684	8109	9505
2 Dr LS 4WD Ext Cab Step SB	7322	8882	10411
2 Dr LS 4WD Std Cab SB	6436	7808	9153
2 Dr LS 4WD Std Cab Step SB	6534	7927	9292
2 Dr LS Ext Cab SB	5102	6189	7255
2 Dr LS Ext Cab Step SB	5551	6734	7894
2 Dr LS Std Cab LB	4577	5552	6508
2 Dr LS Std Cab SB	4325	5247	6150
2 Dr LS Std Cab Step SB	4597	5577	6537
2 Dr LS Xtreme Ext Cab SB	6483	7865	9220

Body Styles	TMV Pricing		
	Trade	Private	Dealer
2 Dr LS Xtreme Ext Cab Step SB	6581	7984	9360
2 Dr LS Xtreme Std Cab SB	5309	6440	7548
2 Dr STD 4WD Ext Cab SB	6633	8046	9432
2 Dr STD 4WD Std Cab SB	5648	6852	8032
2 Dr STD Ext Cab SB	5012	6080	7127
2 Dr STD Std Cab LB	4128	5008	5870
2 Dr STD Std Cab SB	4077	4946	5798
3 Dr LS Wide Stance 4WD Ext Cab SB	9040	10967	12856

2000

Performance and durability enhancements have been made to the engine, exhaust system, manual transmission and antilock braking system, but they don't result in more horsepower. Trucks equipped with the ZR2 package get a new axle ratio designed to improve acceleration. Extended cabs are available in Base trim this year, and LS models have revised exterior moldings.

2000 (cont'd)

Options	Price
4.3L V6 OHV 12V FI Engine [Std on 4WD]	+510
AM/FM/CD Audio System	+141
AM/FM/Cassette/CD Audio System	+188
Air Conditioning [Opt on STD]	+377
Aluminum/Alloy Wheels [Opt on 2WD Reg Cab LB,LS,STD]	+131
Automatic 4-Speed Transmission	+512

Options	Price
Bucket Seats	+136
Hinged Third Door [Std on LS Wide Stance]	+138
Limited Slip Differential [Std on LS Wide Stance]	+126
Locking Differential	+126
Power Windows [Std on LS Wide Stance]	+119
Sport Suspension [Std on LS Xtreme]	+326

1999

An all-new sport package called the Xtreme debuts. All S-10s get automatic transmission enhancements to improve sealing and durability and larger outside mirrors with an optional power-heated mirror. Other changes for '99 include a content theft alarm, headlamp flash-to-pass feature, three new exterior paint choices and the availability of GM's AutoTrac electronic push-button transfer case on select four-wheel-drive models.

Mileage Category: J

Body Styles	TMV Pricing		
	Trade	Private	Dealer
2 Dr LS 4WD Ext Cab SB	5706	7042	8432
2 Dr LS 4WD Ext Cab Step SB	6033	7444	8913
2 Dr LS 4WD Std Cab LB	5603	6914	8279
2 Dr LS 4WD Std Cab SB	5341	6591	7891
2 Dr LS 4WD Std Cab Step SB	5656	6979	8357
2 Dr LS Ext Cab SB	4053	5001	5988
2 Dr LS Ext Cab Step SB	4375	5399	6464
2 Dr LS Std Cab LB	3819	4713	5644
2 Dr LS Std Cab SB	3591	4431	5306
2 Dr LS Std Cab Step SB	3811	4703	5632
2 Dr LS Wide Stance 4WD Std Cab SB	6921	8540	10226

Body Styles	TMV Pricing		
	Trade	Private	Dealer
2 Dr LS Xtreme Ext Cab SB	5279	6514	7800
2 Dr LS Xtreme Ext Cab Step SB	5386	6647	7959
2 Dr LS Xtreme Std Cab SB	4326	5338	6392
2 Dr STD 4WD Std Cab LB	5179	6392	7654
2 Dr STD 4WD Std Cab SB	4834	5965	7143
2 Dr STD Std Cab LB	3546	4376	5239
2 Dr STD Std Cab SB	3457	4265	5106
3 Dr LS Wide Stance 4WD Ext Cab SB	7458	9203	11020

Options	Price
AM/FM/Cassette/CD Audio System	+151
Air Conditioning [Std on ZR2]	+300

Options	Price
Automatic 4-Speed Transmission	+409
Sport Suspension	+259

1998

The S-10 gets a sheet metal makeover and a new interior with dual airbags that incorporate second-generation technology for reduced force deployments. The basic four-cylinder engine benefits from Vortec technology this year, while 4WD models now have four-wheel disc brakes and a more refined transfer case on trucks with an automatic transmission. New radios, automatic headlight control and a standard theft-deterrent system sum up the changes.

Mileage Category: J

Body Styles	TMV Pricing		
	Trade	Private	Dealer
2 Dr LS 4WD Ext Cab SB	4975	6235	7655
2 Dr LS 4WD Ext Cab Step SB	5018	6288	7721
2 Dr LS 4WD Std Cab LB	4573	5731	7036
2 Dr LS 4WD Std Cab SB	4396	5508	6763
2 Dr LS 4WD Std Cab Step SB	4585	5745	7053
2 Dr LS Ext Cab SB	3483	4364	5358
2 Dr LS Ext Cab Step SB	3627	4545	5580
2 Dr LS Std Cab LB	3230	4048	4970

Body Styles	TMV Pricing		
	Trade	Private	Dealer
2 Dr LS Std Cab SB	3164	3964	4867
2 Dr LS Std Cab Step SB	3278	4108	5044
2 Dr STD 4WD Std Cab LB	4109	5149	6322
2 Dr STD 4WD Std Cab SB	3796	4757	5840
2 Dr STD Std Cab LB	3051	3823	4694
2 Dr STD Std Cab SB	2963	3713	4558
2 Dr ZR2 4WD Ext Cab SB	6327	7928	9734
2 Dr ZR2 4WD Std Cab SB	6051	7583	9310

Options	Price
AM/FM/Cassette/CD Audio System	+126
Air Conditioning [Std on ZR2]	+253

Options	Price
Automatic 4-Speed Transmission [Std on ZR2]	+336
Sport Suspension	+218

1997

S-10 frame by using tougher components. Refinements to the automatic transmission result in improved efficiency and smoother shifts. Four-wheel-drive models have lighter-weight plug-in half shafts. Two new colors are available.

Mileage Category: J

Body Styles	TMV Pricing		
	Trade	Private	Dealer
2 Dr LS 4WD Ext Cab SB	4161	5321	6738
2 Dr LS 4WD Ext Cab Step SB	4290	5485	6946
2 Dr LS 4WD Std Cab LB	3888	4972	6296
2 Dr LS 4WD Std Cab SB	3731	4771	6041
2 Dr LS 4WD Std Cab Step SB	3938	5035	6376
2 Dr LS Ext Cab SB	2814	3598	4557
2 Dr LS Ext Cab Step SB	3026	3869	4899

Body Styles	TMV Pricing		
	Trade	Private	Dealer
2 Dr LS Std Cab LB	2685	3433	4348
2 Dr LS Std Cab SB	2637	3372	4271
2 Dr LS Std Cab Step SB	2695	3446	4364
2 Dr STD 4WD Std Cab LB	3396	4342	5498
2 Dr STD 4WD Std Cab SB	3265	4175	5288
2 Dr STD Std Cab LB	2616	3345	4237
2 Dr STD Std Cab SB	2405	3075	3893

Options	Price
Air Conditioning	+229
Automatic 4-Speed Transmission	+304

Options	Price
Wide Stance Suspension Package	+496

Mileage Category: J

1996

Body Styles	TMV Pricing		
	Trade	Private	Dealer
2 Dr LS 4WD Ext Cab SB	3413	4456	5897
2 Dr LS 4WD Ext Cab Step SB	3453	4509	5967
2 Dr LS 4WD Std Cab LB	3360	4387	5806
2 Dr LS 4WD Std Cab SB	3249	4243	5615
2 Dr LS 4WD Std Cab Step SB	3291	4297	5687
2 Dr LS Ext Cab SB	2437	3183	4212
2 Dr LS Ext Cab Step SB	2681	3501	4634

Options	Price
Air Conditioning	+207
Antilock Brakes [Opt on 2WD]	+195

Body Styles	TMV Pricing		
	Trade	Private	Dealer
2 Dr LS Std Cab LB	2152	2810	3719
2 Dr LS Std Cab SB	2111	2757	3648
2 Dr LS Std Cab Step SB	2236	2919	3862
2 Dr STD 4WD Std Cab LB	2833	3699	4895
2 Dr STD 4WD Std Cab SB	2695	3519	4658
2 Dr STD Std Cab LB	1949	2545	3369
2 Dr STD Std Cab SB	1909	2493	3300

Options	Price
Automatic 4-Speed Transmission	+276
Wide Stance Suspension Package	+444

Improved V6 engines make more power and torque this year. A new five-speed manual gives four-cylinder models better acceleration, and four-bangers also get four-wheel antilock brakes. Extended-cab models get third-door access panel on the driver side to make loading cargo and passengers easier. A new sport suspension turns the S-10 into a competent sports truck, and the new Sportside cargo box allows the S-Series to go head to head with the Ford Ranger Splash.

Mileage Category: J

1995

Body Styles	TMV Pricing		
	Trade	Private	Dealer
2 Dr LS 4WD Ext Cab SB	2811	3737	5281
2 Dr LS 4WD Std Cab LB	2718	3614	5107
2 Dr LS 4WD Std Cab SB	2640	3510	4961
2 Dr LS Ext Cab SB	1950	2593	3665
2 Dr LS Std Cab LB	1831	2434	3439

Options	Price
4.3L V6 OHV 12V FI Engine [Opt on 2WD]	+229
4.3L V6 OHV 12V HO FI Engine	+129
AM/FM/CD Audio System	+93
AM/FM/Cassette Audio System	+80
Air Conditioning	+186

Body Styles	TMV Pricing		
	Trade	Private	Dealer
2 Dr LS Std Cab SB	1679	2233	3156
2 Dr STD 4WD Std Cab LB	2354	3131	4425
2 Dr STD 4WD Std Cab SB	2146	2854	4033
2 Dr STD Std Cab LB	1605	2134	3016
2 Dr STD Std Cab SB	1569	2086	2947

Options	Price
Aluminum/Alloy Wheels	+79
Antilock Brakes [Opt on 2WD]	+175
Automatic 4-Speed Transmission	+248
Wide Stance Suspension Package	+399

Driver airbag is added, and daytime running lights are standard. ZR2 off-road package can be ordered on the extended cab. Power window and lock buttons are illuminated at night. Remote keyless entry is a new option. A single key operates both the door locks and the ignition. A manual transmission can now be ordered with the 191-horsepower, 4.3-liter V6.

SSR

2004

Mileage Category: K

Body Styles	TMV Pricing		
	Trade	Private	Dealer
2 Dr LS Conv Std Cab SB	32724	34546	37582

Options	Price	Options	Price
AM/FM/CD Changer Audio System	+300	Garage Door Opener	+130
Automatic Dimming Rearview Mirror	+150	Heated Front Seats	+250
Automatic Dimming Sideview Mirror(s)	+170	Power Driver Seat w/Memory	+350
Bose Audio System	+400	Special Factory Paint	+350
Chrome Wheels	+1500		

Introduced as a late 2003 model, Chevrolet's "Super Sport Roadster" is unchanged for its sophomore year.

2003

Mileage Category: K

Body Styles	TMV Pricing		
	Trade	Private	Dealer
2 Dr LS Conv Std Cab SB	30910	32594	35400

Options	Price	Options	Price
AM/FM/CD Changer Audio System	+239	Heated Front Seats	+271
Bose Audio System	+192	Special Factory Paint	+223

Chevrolet brings to market a sport pickup with a retractable hardtop, retro styling and 300 horsepower.

Silverado 1500

2004

The value-priced Work Truck package is now available on both regular and extended cabs. Base models pick up cruise control, a sound system, chrome rear bumper and chrome wheels. An automatic transmission is now standard on LS models, and the V6 is no longer an option in this trim. Other updates include new polished aluminum wheels and 265/70R16 tires with either black sidewalls or raised white lettering. The Quadrasteer option no longer requires the buyer to order trailering equipment. There's also a new tonneau cover, and inside, you'll find underseat storage. Finally, Chevrolet has deleted the Silverado's passenger-side outside door lock.

Mileage Category: K

Body Styles	TMV Pricing			Body Styles	TMV Pricing		
	Trade	Private	Dealer		Trade	Private	Dealer
2 Dr LS 4WD Std Cab LB	17411	18778	21056	4 Dr LS Ext Cab SB	16896	18198	20368
2 Dr LS 4WD Std Cab SB	17228	18595	20873	4 Dr LT 4WD Crew Cab SB	23159	24480	26681
2 Dr LS Std Cab LB	15561	16979	19343	4 Dr LT 4WD Ext Cab LB	22175	23588	25942
2 Dr LS Std Cab SB	14940	16318	18616	4 Dr LT 4WD Ext Cab SB	22002	23414	25769
2 Dr STD 4WD Std Cab LB	14772	16146	18438	4 Dr LT Crew Cab SB	21119	22568	24983
2 Dr STD 4WD Std Cab SB	14589	15963	18254	4 Dr LT Ext Cab LB	20150	21666	24193
2 Dr STD Std Cab LB	12200	13391	15376	4 Dr LT Ext Cab SB	19968	21381	23735
2 Dr STD Std Cab SB	12025	13216	15201	4 Dr STD 4WD Ext Cab LB	18412	19824	22178
2 Dr Work Truck 4WD Std Cab LB	13309	14610	16779	4 Dr STD 4WD Ext Cab SB	17715	19127	21481
2 Dr Work Truck 4WD Std Cab SB	13250	14552	16720	4 Dr STD Ext Cab LB	16677	17978	20148
2 Dr Work Truck Std Cab LB	11518	12709	14693	4 Dr STD Ext Cab SB	15548	16850	19019
2 Dr Work Truck Std Cab SB	11460	12651	14636	4 Dr Work Truck 4WD Ext Cab LB	17848	19234	21545
2 Dr Z71 4WD Std Cab LB	18217	19571	21829	4 Dr Work Truck 4WD Ext Cab SB	17157	18459	20629
2 Dr Z71 4WD Std Cab SB	18036	19391	21648	4 Dr Work Truck Ext Cab LB	16110	17412	19582
4 Dr LS 4WD Crew Cab SB	20825	22329	24836	4 Dr Work Truck Ext Cab SB	14577	15878	18048
4 Dr LS 4WD Ext Cab LB	19266	20679	23033	4 Dr Z71 4WD Crew Cab SB	21123	22627	25134
4 Dr LS 4WD Ext Cab SB	18946	20386	22788	4 Dr Z71 4WD Ext Cab LB	19937	21349	23703
4 Dr LS Crew Cab SB	18803	20142	22373	4 Dr Z71 4WD Ext Cab SB	19246	20658	23012
4 Dr LS Ext Cab LB	17592	18894	21064				

Options	Price	Options	Price
4 Wheel Steering [Opt on LS Ext SB, LT Ext SB]	+1995	Leather Seats [Opt on Z71 Ext, Z71Crew]	+800
5.3L V8 OHV 16V FI Engine [Opt on Std]	+900	Locking Differential (Center) [Opt on Z71 Ext, Z71Crew]	+200
AM/FM/CD Changer Audio System [Opt on LS Ext, LS Crew]	+795	Power Door Locks [Opt on STD, Work Truck]	+162
Aluminum/Alloy Wheels [Opt on Z71]	+200	Power Driver Seat w/Memory [Opt on Z71 Ext, Z71Crew]	+220
Appearance Package [Opt on LS Ext SB, LT Ext SB]	+1995	Power Passenger Seat [Opt on Z71 Ext, Z71Crew]	+200
Automatic 4-Speed Transmission [Opt on Work Truck]	+1095	Power Retractable Mirrors [Opt on LS, Z71]	+150
Cruise Control [Opt on Work Truck]	+240	Power Windows [Opt on STD, Work Truck]	+738
DVD Entertainment System [Opt on Crew]	+1295	Rear Window Defroster [Opt on STD]	+175
Electronic Damping Suspension Control [Opt on LS, LT non-Crew]	+325	Stepside Bed [Opt on non-Crew SB]	+795
Fog Lights [Opt on LS]	+140	Traction Control System [Opt on STD, LS, LT 2WD]	+225
Heated Front Seats [Opt on Z71 Ext, Z71Crew]	+150	Two-Tone Paint [Opt on LS]	+250

2003

The Silverado gets a makeover this year that includes a new front fascia and revised side moldings and taillights. Top-of-the-line models get power-folding heated mirrors with puddle lamps and turn signal indicators. On the inside, the Silverado is the first full-size pickup to offer a Bose stereo system and XM Satellite Radio. The instrument panel and center console have been redesigned, and Chevrolet has added new seats, a more comprehensive driver information center and a dual-zone climate control system. For increased safety, Silverados now feature a standard front-passenger-sensing system and dual-stage airbags. On the hardware side, all 4.3-liter V6-equipped Silverados and California-emission V8s are now ULEV-certified, while electronic throttle control is now standard on all V8 engines. The Autotrac four-wheel-drive system has been modified for less intrusiveness at low speeds, and the brake system received upgrades that provide better pedal feel and improved overall performance.

Mileage Category: K

Body Styles	TMV Pricing			Body Styles	TMV Pricing		
	Trade	Private	Dealer		Trade	Private	Dealer
2 Dr LS 4WD Std Cab LB	14642	15717	17508	4 Dr LS Ext Cab LB	16153	17339	19316
2 Dr LS 4WD Std Cab SB	14520	15586	17363	4 Dr LS Ext Cab SB	14725	15807	17609
2 Dr LS Std Cab LB	12978	13931	15519	4 Dr LT 4WD Ext Cab LB	20462	21964	24468
2 Dr LS Std Cab SB	12878	13823	15398	4 Dr LT 4WD Ext Cab SB	20123	21600	24062
2 Dr STD 4WD Std Cab LB	12818	13759	15327	4 Dr LT Ext Cab LB	18429	19782	22036
2 Dr STD 4WD Std Cab SB	12386	13295	14811	4 Dr LT Ext Cab SB	18249	19588	21821
2 Dr STD Std Cab LB	10577	11354	12649	4 Dr STD 4WD Ext Cab LB	16583	17801	19830
2 Dr STD Std Cab SB	10418	11182	12457	4 Dr STD 4WD Ext Cab SB	15867	17032	18974
2 Dr Work Truck 4WD Std Cab LB	12580	13504	15043	4 Dr STD Ext Cab LB	14493	15557	17330
2 Dr Work Truck Std Cab LB	10488	11258	12542	4 Dr STD Ext Cab SB	13261	14235	15857
4 Dr LS 4WD Ext Cab LB	17771	19075	21249	4 Dr Work Truck Ext Cab SB	13063	14022	15621
4 Dr LS 4WD Ext Cab SB	17177	18438	20539				

Options	Price	Options	Price
4 Wheel Steering [Opt on Ext Cab SB - LS,LT]	+2870	AM/FM/CD Changer Audio System [Std on LT]	+255
5.3L V8 OHV 16V FI Engine [Std on Ext Cab LB,LT]	+511	Aluminum/Alloy Wheels [Std on LT]	+128
AM/FM/CD Audio System [Opt on STD]	+163	Appearance Package	+322

2003 (cont'd)

Options	Price
Automatic 4-Speed Transmission [Std on Ext Cab LB,LT]	+699
Automatic Climate Control (2 Zone) - Driver and Passenger [Opt on LS]	+124
Bose Audio System [Opt on LS]	+252
Bucket Seats [Opt on Ext Cab - LS,STD]	+271
Cruise Control [Opt on STD,Work]	+153
Electronic Suspension Control [Opt on LS,LT]	+207
Leather Seats [Opt on LS]	+511
Limited Slip Differential [Opt on Ext SB - LS,LT]	+188
Locking Differential	+188
OnStar Telematics System [Opt on LS]	+444

Options	Price
Power Driver Seat [Std on LT]	+153
Power Mirrors [Opt on STD,Work]	+121
Power Retractable Mirrors [Opt on LS]	+117
Power Windows [Opt on STD,Work]	+156
Satellite Radio System [Opt on LS,LT]	+207
Stepside Bed [Opt on SB]	+508
Traction Control System [Opt on 2WD]	+144
Two-Tone Paint [Opt on LS]	+160
Z71 Off-Road Suspension Package [Opt on LS 4WD]	+166

2002

Only minor changes are made to Chevrolet's bread-and-butter Silverado pickup for 2002. Some options packages have been revamped for easier ordering and all extended-cab models now come standard with a four-speed automatic transmission, with the manual no longer available.

Mileage Category: K

Body Styles	Trade	Private	Dealer
2 Dr LS 4WD Std Cab LB	11885	12924	14654
2 Dr LS 4WD Std Cab SB	11694	12716	14418
2 Dr LS Std Cab LB	10632	11560	13108
2 Dr LS Std Cab SB	10561	11484	13021
2 Dr STD 4WD Std Cab LB	10601	11527	13070
2 Dr STD 4WD Std Cab SB	9990	10863	12317
2 Dr STD Std Cab LB	8471	9211	10444
2 Dr STD Std Cab SB	8373	9105	10324
2 Dr Work Truck 4WD Std Cab LB	10256	11151	12644
2 Dr Work Truck Std Cab LB	8435	9172	10400
4 Dr LS 4WD Ext Cab LB	14890	16191	18358

Body Styles	Trade	Private	Dealer
4 Dr LS 4WD Ext Cab SB	14507	15774	17886
4 Dr LS Ext Cab LB	13759	14961	16964
4 Dr LS Ext Cab SB	12237	13306	15088
4 Dr LT 4WD Ext Cab LB	16723	18183	20617
4 Dr LT 4WD Ext Cab SB	16558	18004	20414
4 Dr LT Ext Cab LB	15151	16474	18679
4 Dr LT Ext Cab SB	15001	16311	18495
4 Dr STD 4WD Ext Cab LB	14226	15468	17538
4 Dr STD 4WD Ext Cab SB	13563	14748	16722
4 Dr STD Ext Cab LB	12219	13286	15065
4 Dr STD Ext Cab SB	11065	12031	13642

Options	Price
4 Wheel Steering [Opt on Ext Cab SB - LS,LT]	+3028
5.3L V8 Flex Fuel OHV 16V FI Engine	+459
5.3L V8 OHV 16V FI Engine [Std on LS Ext LB,LT,STD Ext LB]	+459
Automatic 4-Speed Transmission [Std on Ext]	+628
Bucket Seats [Opt on LS]	+244
Chrome Step Bumper [Opt on STD]	+115
Chrome Wheels [Opt on STD]	+186
Cruise Control [Opt on STD,Work Truck]	+138

Options	Price
Electronic Suspension Control [Opt on LS,LT]	+186
Leather Seats [Std on LT]	+459
Locking Differential [Std on LT 4WD]	+163
Power Driver Seat [Opt on LS]	+138
Power Passenger Seat [Opt on LS]	+138
Traction Control System	+129
Two-Tone Paint [Opt on LS]	+143

2001

A 1500HD crew cab makes its debut in 2001 featuring the 6.0-liter Vortec V8. An available PRO TEC composite truck box and optional traction control are also added to the Silverado this year along with new colors and the OnStar vehicle assistance system.

Mileage Category: K

Body Styles	Trade	Private	Dealer
2 Dr LS 4WD Std Cab LB	10007	11458	12797
2 Dr LS 4WD Std Cab SB	9838	11265	12582
2 Dr LS Std Cab LB	8894	10183	11374
2 Dr LS Std Cab SB	8840	10121	11304
2 Dr STD 4WD Std Cab LB	8450	9674	10805
2 Dr STD 4WD Std Cab SB	8035	9200	10275
2 Dr STD Std Cab LB	6670	7636	8528
2 Dr STD Std Cab SB	6651	7616	8506
4 Dr LS 4WD Ext Cab LB	12752	14600	16306
4 Dr LS 4WD Ext Cab SB	12689	14529	16227

Body Styles	Trade	Private	Dealer
4 Dr LS Ext Cab LB	11397	13050	14575
4 Dr LS Ext Cab SB	10396	11903	13294
4 Dr LT 4WD Ext Cab LB	13731	15721	17559
4 Dr LT 4WD Ext Cab SB	13620	15595	17417
4 Dr LT Ext Cab LB	12835	14696	16414
4 Dr LT Ext Cab SB	12814	14672	16387
4 Dr STD 4WD Ext Cab LB	11509	13177	14717
4 Dr STD 4WD Ext Cab SB	11286	12922	14432
4 Dr STD Ext Cab LB	9766	11182	12489
4 Dr STD Ext Cab SB	9117	10439	11659

Options	Price
4.8L V8 OHV 16V FI Engine	+365
5.3L V8 OHV 16V FI Engine [Opt on LS,STD]	+420
Air Conditioning	+433
Automatic 4-Speed Transmission	+574
Cruise Control	+126
Electronic Suspension Control	+170

Options	Price
Leather Seats [Opt on LS]	+671
Locking Differential	+150
Off-Road Suspension Package	+207
Power Driver Seat [Opt on LS]	+126
Power Passenger Seat [Opt on LS]	+126
Stepside Bed [Opt on SB]	+417

2001 (cont'd)

Options	Price
Tonneau Cover	+126
Traction Control System	+118

Options	Price
Trailer Hitch	+150
Two-Tone Paint	+131

2000

After a complete redesign last year, few changes make news for 2000. Most substantial is the addition of an optional fourth access door to extended cab models. The already potent Vortec 4800 and 5300 V8 engines make more power, and programmable door locks can be instructed to unlock automatically when the Silverado is shut off. A Sportside cargo box is available on 1500 LT models, and 1500 4WD trucks can be equipped with wheel flares this year. LS and LT trucks get a standard electrochromic self-dimming rearview mirror with compass and exterior temperature display, and a soft tonneau cover is available from the factory.

Mileage Category: K

Body Styles	TMV Pricing		
	Trade	Private	Dealer
2 Dr LS 4WD Std Cab LB	8932	10314	11669
2 Dr LS 4WD Std Cab SB	8798	10161	11496
2 Dr LS 4WD Std Cab Step SB	10220	11803	13354
2 Dr LS Std Cab LB	7918	9144	10346
2 Dr LS Std Cab SB	7867	9086	10280
2 Dr LS Std Cab Step SB	8508	9826	11117
2 Dr STD 4WD Std Cab LB	7422	8570	9696
2 Dr STD 4WD Std Cab SB	7205	8320	9414
2 Dr STD 4WD Std Cab Step SB	7819	9030	10217
2 Dr STD Std Cab LB	6035	6970	7886
2 Dr STD Std Cab SB	5878	6788	7680
2 Dr STD Std Cab Step SB	6630	7656	8662
3 Dr LS 4WD Ext Cab LB	11061	12774	14452
3 Dr LS 4WD Ext Cab SB	10986	12687	14354
3 Dr LS 4WD Ext Cab Step SB	11197	12930	14630

Body Styles	TMV Pricing		
	Trade	Private	Dealer
3 Dr LS Ext Cab LB	9679	11178	12647
3 Dr LS Ext Cab SB	8758	10114	11444
3 Dr LS Ext Cab Step SB	9626	11116	12576
3 Dr LT 4WD Ext Cab LB	12225	14117	15972
3 Dr LT 4WD Ext Cab SB	12223	14115	15970
3 Dr LT 4WD Ext Cab Step SB	13736	15862	17947
3 Dr LT Ext Cab LB	11412	13178	14910
3 Dr LT Ext Cab SB	11250	12993	14700
3 Dr LT Ext Cab Step SB	12067	13935	15767
3 Dr STD 4WD Ext Cab LB	10238	11823	13377
3 Dr STD 4WD Ext Cab SB	9830	11352	12843
3 Dr STD 4WD Ext Cab Step SB	10659	12310	13927
3 Dr STD Ext Cab LB	8719	10069	11392
3 Dr STD Ext Cab SB	7833	9046	10235
3 Dr STD Ext Cab Step SB	8578	9906	11208

Options	Price
4.8L V8 OHV 16V FI Engine	+326
5.3L V8 OHV 16V FI Engine [Opt on LS,STD]	+374
Air Conditioning	+386
Automatic 4-Speed Transmission	+465
Bucket Seats	+176

Options	Price
Camper/Towing Package	+134
Hinged Fourth Door	+155
Leather Seats [Opt on LS]	+537
Limited Slip Differential	+134
Off-Road Suspension Package [Opt on 4WD]	+185

1999

Chevrolet has redesigned the decade-old C/K pickup and given the truck a new name. Major structural, power, braking and interior enhancements characterize the new Silverado. Styling is evolutionary rather than revolutionary, inside and out.

Mileage Category: K

Body Styles	TMV Pricing		
	Trade	Private	Dealer
2 Dr LS 4WD Std Cab LB	7826	9314	10863
2 Dr LS 4WD Std Cab SB	7622	9071	10579
2 Dr LS 4WD Std Cab Step SB	8329	9913	11561
2 Dr LS Std Cab LB	6904	8217	9583
2 Dr LS Std Cab SB	6643	7906	9220
2 Dr LS Std Cab Step SB	7220	8593	10022
2 Dr STD 4WD Std Cab LB	6327	7529	8781
2 Dr STD 4WD Std Cab SB	6271	7464	8705
2 Dr STD 4WD Std Cab Step SB	6591	7843	9148
2 Dr STD Std Cab LB	5168	6150	7172
2 Dr STD Std Cab SB	5068	6031	7033
2 Dr STD Std Cab Step SB	5376	6398	7462
3 Dr LS 4WD Ext Cab LB	9427	11219	13084
3 Dr LS 4WD Ext Cab SB	9369	11150	13004

Body Styles	TMV Pricing		
	Trade	Private	Dealer
3 Dr LS 4WD Ext Cab Step SB	9684	11526	13442
3 Dr LS Ext Cab LB	8118	9661	11268
3 Dr LS Ext Cab SB	7503	8929	10413
3 Dr LS Ext Cab Step SB	7815	9300	10846
3 Dr LT 4WD Ext Cab LB	10717	12755	14876
3 Dr LT 4WD Ext Cab SB	10602	12617	14714
3 Dr LT Ext Cab LB	9792	11654	13591
3 Dr LT Ext Cab SB	9686	11528	13445
3 Dr STD 4WD Ext Cab LB	8514	10133	11817
3 Dr STD 4WD Ext Cab SB	8382	9975	11634
3 Dr STD 4WD Ext Cab Step SB	8804	10478	12220
3 Dr STD Ext Cab LB	7322	8714	10162
3 Dr STD Ext Cab SB	6747	8030	9365
3 Dr STD Ext Cab Step SB	7276	8658	10098

Options	Price
4.8L V8 OHV 16V FI Engine	+259
5.3L V8 OHV 16V FI Engine	+298
Air Conditioning [Opt on STD]	+308

Options	Price
Automatic 4-Speed Transmission	+372
Bucket Seats	+140
Leather Seats	+429

Silverado 1500 SS

2004

Body Styles	TMV Pricing		
	Trade	Private	Dealer
4 Dr STD AWD Ext Cab SB	25615	27446	30498

Mileage Category: K

Options	Price	Options	Price
AM/FM/CD Changer Audio System	+200	Chrome Wheels	+1195
Automatic Climate Control (2 Zone) - Driver and Passenger	+195	OnStar Telematics System	+695
Camper/Towing Package	+235	Satellite Radio System	+325

The SS was introduced late in 2003; the 2004 version incorporates no major changes.

2003

Introduced late in the model year, the SS version of the Silverado features a 6.0-liter V8 with 345 horsepower, all-wheel drive, 20-inch wheels and a more aggressive front end.

Mileage Category: K

Body Styles	TMV Pricing		
	Trade	Private	Dealer
4 Dr STD AWD Ext Cab SB	23521	24802	26938

Options	Price	Options	Price
AM/FM/CD Changer Audio System	+255	OnStar Telematics System	+444
Automatic Climate Control (2 Zone) - Driver and Passenger	+124	Satellite Radio System	+207
Camper/Towing Package	+137	Tonneau Cover	+179

Silverado 1500HD

2003

Mileage Category: K

Body Styles	TMV Pricing			Body Styles	TMV Pricing		
	Trade	Private	Dealer		Trade	Private	Dealer
4 Dr LS 4WD Crew Cab SB HD	20526	21883	24145	4 Dr LT 4WD Crew Cab SB HD	22952	24470	26999
4 Dr LS Crew Cab SB HD	18236	19442	21451	4 Dr LT Crew Cab SB HD	20757	22130	24417

Options	Price	Options	Price
4 Wheel Steering	+2870	Limited Slip Differential	+188
AM/FM/CD Changer Audio System [Opt on LS]	+255	Locking Differential	+188
Aluminum/Alloy Wheels [Opt on LS]	+128	OnStar Telematics System [Opt on LS]	+444
Automatic Climate Control (2 Zone) - Driver and Passenger [Opt on LS]	+124	Power Driver Seat [Opt on LS]	+153
Bose Audio System [Opt on LS]	+252	Power Retractable Mirrors [Opt on LS]	+117
Bucket Seats [Opt on LS]	+271	Privacy Glass [Opt on LS]	+115
DVD Entertainment System	+827	Satellite Radio System	+207
Electronic Suspension Control	+207	Traction Control System [Opt on 2WD]	+144
Leather Seats [Opt on LS]	+511		

The Silverado gets a makeover this year that includes a new front fascia and revised side moldings and taillights. Up-level LT models get power-folding heated mirrors with puddle lamps and turn signal indicators. On the inside, the Silverado offers new entertainment options, such as a Bose audio system with rear-seat controls, XM Satellite Radio and a DVD-based entertainment system. The instrument panel and center console have been redesigned, and Chevrolet has added new seats, a more comprehensive driver information center and a dual-zone climate control system. For increased safety, Silverados now feature a standard front-passenger-sensing system that deactivates the airbag for children. On the hardware side, the all-new Quadrasteer four-wheel steering system, which increases low-speed maneuverability and towing stability, is now optional. The standard 6.0-liter V8 gets electronic throttle control, as well as the ability to run exclusively on Compressed Natural Gas (CNG) or a mix of CNG and gasoline.

2002

Debuting late last year as an all-new 2001 model, the 1500HD Crew Cab gets few changes for the 2002 model year. A high-capacity air cleaner is now standard, along with extended sunshades for both the driver and passenger.

Mileage Category: K

Body Styles	TMV Pricing			Body Styles	TMV Pricing		
	Trade	Private	Dealer		Trade	Private	Dealer
4 Dr LS 4WD Crew Cab SB HD	17495	18850	21109	4 Dr LT 4WD Crew Cab SB HD	19235	20725	23208
4 Dr LS Crew Cab SB HD	15588	16796	18808	4 Dr LT Crew Cab SB HD	17364	18709	20951

Options	Price	Options	Price
Bucket Seats [Std on LT]	+244	Locking Differential [Opt on 2WD]	+169
Flex Fuel Option	+430	Power Driver Seat [Opt on LS]	+138
Leather Seats [Std on LT]	+459	Power Passenger Seat [Opt on LS]	+138

Chevrolet
Silverado 1500HD/2500

2001

A 1500HD crew cab makes its debut in 2001 featuring the 6.0-liter Vortec V8. An available PRO TEC composite truck box and optional traction control are also added to the Silverado this year along with new colors and the OnStar vehicle assistance system.

Mileage Category: K

Body Styles	TMV Pricing		
	Trade	Private	Dealer
4 Dr LS 4WD Crew Cab SB HD	14878	16738	18454
4 Dr LS Crew Cab SB HD	13234	14888	16414

Options	Price
Leather Seats [Opt on LS]	+708
Locking Differential [Std on LT]	+150
Power Driver Seat [Opt on LS]	+126

Body Styles	TMV Pricing		
	Trade	Private	Dealer
4 Dr LT 4WD Crew Cab SB HD	16364	18409	20297
4 Dr LT Crew Cab SB HD	14754	16598	18301

Options	Price
Power Passenger Seat [Opt on LS]	+126
Tonneau Cover	+126

Silverado 2500

2004

A short bed crew cab version is now available that offers the innovative Quadrasteer four-wheel steering system. The standard features list is plumped up with the addition of cruise control, power door locks, black body side moldings, chrome bumpers, upgraded wheels and an AM/FM radio with CD player. OnStar is now standard on the LT trim level, the Z71 Off-Road package is upgraded to include more luxury items (such as power windows and deep-tinted glass) and six-lug, polished aluminum wheels are now optional.

Mileage Category: K

Body Styles	TMV Pricing		
	Trade	Private	Dealer
2 Dr LS Std Cab LB	16230	17456	19499
2 Dr STD Std Cab LB	15383	16607	18646
2 Dr Work Truck Std Cab LB	14536	15757	17793
4 Dr LS 4WD Crew Cab SB	21895	23533	26262
4 Dr LS 4WD Ext Cab SB	20494	21832	24061
4 Dr LS Crew Cab SB	19773	21336	23940

Options	Price
4 Wheel Steering [Opt on Crew]	+1995
AM/FM/CD Changer Audio System [Opt on LS Ext, LS Crew]	+795
Automatic 4-Speed Transmission [Std on Ext, Crew]	+1095
Automatic Climate Control (2 Zone) - Driver and Passenger [Opt on LS Ext, LS Crew]	+195
Bucket Seats [Opt on LS Ext, LS Crew]	+300
Cruise Control [Opt on Work Truck]	+240
DVD Entertainment System [Opt on Crew]	+1295
Flex Fuel Option	+850
Fog Lights [Opt on LS]	+140
Leather Seats [Opt on LS Ext, LS Crew]	+800

Body Styles	TMV Pricing		
	Trade	Private	Dealer
4 Dr LT 4WD Crew Cab SB	24597	26235	28964
4 Dr LT 4WD Ext Cab SB	23280	24618	26847
4 Dr LT Crew Cab SB	22496	24059	26663
4 Dr STD 4WD Ext Cab SB	19431	20769	22998
4 Dr Work Truck 4WD Ext Cab SB	18831	20169	22398

Options	Price
Locking Differential	+295
OnStar Telematics System [Opt on LS]	+695
Power Door Locks [Opt on STD]	+162
Power Driver Seat [Opt on LS Ext, LS Crew]	+240
Power Retractable Mirrors [Opt on LS]	+213
Rear Audio Controls [Opt on Crew]	+165
Rear Window Defroster [Opt on STD]	+175
Steering Wheel Radio Controls [Opt on LS]	+125
Traction Control System [Opt on STD, LS non-Ext, all Crew]	+225
Two-Tone Paint [Opt on LS]	+250

2003

The Silverado gets a makeover this year that includes a new front fascia and revised side moldings and taillights. Top-of-the-line models also get power-folding heated mirrors with puddle lamps and turn signal indicators. On the inside, the Silverado is the first full-size pickup to offer a Bose stereo system and XM Satellite Radio. The instrument panel and center console have been redesigned, and Chevrolet has added new seats, a more comprehensive driver information center and a dual-zone climate control system. For increased safety, Silverados now feature a standard front-passenger-sensing system and dual-stage airbags. On the hardware side, the standard 6.0-liter V8 gets electronic throttle control as well as the ability to run exclusively on Compressed Natural Gas (CNG) or a mix of CNG and gasoline.

Mileage Category: K

Body Styles	TMV Pricing		
	Trade	Private	Dealer
2 Dr LS Std Cab LB	14999	16128	18010
2 Dr STD Std Cab LB	13797	14836	16567
2 Dr Work Truck Std Cab LB	13727	14761	16483

Options	Price
AM/FM/CD Audio System [Opt on STD,Work]	+163
AM/FM/CD Changer Audio System [Opt on LS]	+255
Aluminum/Alloy Wheels [Opt on LS]	+128
Appearance Package [Opt on LS]	+367
Automatic 4-Speed Transmission [Opt on Std Cab]	+699
Automatic Climate Control (2 Zone) - Driver and Passenger [Opt on LS Ext]	+124
Bose Audio System [Opt on LS Ext]	+252
Bucket Seats [Opt on LS Ext]	+271
Compressed Natural Gas (CNG) Option [Opt on Std Cab]	+5937

Body Styles	TMV Pricing		
	Trade	Private	Dealer
4 Dr LS 4WD Ext Cab SB	18598	19998	22331
4 Dr LT 4WD Ext Cab SB	21067	22653	25295
4 Dr STD 4WD Ext Cab SB	17501	18818	21014

Options	Price
Cruise Control [Opt on STD,Work]	+153
Leather Seats [Opt on LS Ext]	+511
Locking Differential	+188
OnStar Telematics System [Opt on LS Ext]	+444
Power Driver Seat [Opt on LS]	+153
Power Retractable Mirrors [Opt on LS]	+117
Satellite Radio System [Opt on LS,LT]	+207
Traction Control System [Opt on 2WD]	+144
Two-Tone Paint [Opt on LS Ext]	+160

2002

Three-quarter-ton Silverados get few changes for 2002. A high-capacity air cleaner and air conditioning are now standard on all models. All extended cabs get a four-speed automatic transmission standard.

Mileage Category: K

Body Styles	TMV Pricing		
	Trade	Private	Dealer
2 Dr LS Std Cab LB	13037	14127	15944
2 Dr STD Std Cab LB	11896	12891	14548

Body Styles	TMV Pricing		
	Trade	Private	Dealer
4 Dr LS 4WD Ext Cab SB	16632	18022	20339
4 Dr LT 4WD Ext Cab SB	18469	20013	22587

Body Styles	TMV Pricing		
	Trade	Private	Dealer
4 Dr STD 4WD Ext Cab SB	15172	16440	18554

Options	Price	Options	Price
Automatic 4-Speed Transmission [Std on Ext]	+628	Leather Seats [Std on LT]	+459
Bucket Seats [Std on LT]	+244	Locking Differential [Std on LT]	+169
Chrome Step Bumper [Std on LS,LT]	+115	Power Driver Seat [Opt on LS]	+138
Chrome Wheels [Opt on STD]	+186	Power Passenger Seat [Opt on LS]	+138
Cruise Control [Std on LS,LT]	+138	Traction Control System [Opt on LS]	+129
Flex Fuel Option	+430	Two-Tone Paint [Opt on LS]	+143

Mileage Category: K

Body Styles	TMV Pricing			Body Styles	TMV Pricing		
	Trade	Private	Dealer		Trade	Private	Dealer
2 Dr LS Std Cab LB	11156	12670	14068	4 Dr LT 4WD Ext Cab SB	15495	17598	19539
2 Dr STD Std Cab LB	9784	11112	12337	4 Dr STD 4WD Ext Cab SB	12152	13801	15324
4 Dr LS 4WD Ext Cab SB	13644	15496	17205				

Options	Price	Options	Price
Air Conditioning	+433	Power Driver Seat [Opt on LS]	+126
Automatic 4-Speed Transmission	+574	Power Passenger Seat [Opt on LS]	+126
Cruise Control	+126	Tonneau Cover	+126
Leather Seats [Opt on LS]	+671	Two-Tone Paint	+131
Locking Differential	+150		

2001

Both light- and heavy-duty 2500s sport new torsion bar front suspensions. Light-duty models get an 8,600-pound Gross Vehicle Weight Rating in addition to optional traction control and standard child safety-seat tether hooks. Heavy-duty models are completely redesigned for 2001 offering two new engines and transmissions, bigger interiors and numerous other improvements.

Mileage Category: K

Body Styles	TMV Pricing			Body Styles	TMV Pricing		
	Trade	Private	Dealer		Trade	Private	Dealer
2 Dr LS 4WD Std Cab LB HD	10217	11809	13370	3 Dr LS Ext Cab SB	11081	12808	14501
2 Dr LS Std Cab LB	10285	11908	13499	3 Dr LT 4WD Ext Cab LB HD	14770	17072	19328
2 Dr LS Std Cab LB HD	9544	11032	12490	3 Dr LT 4WD Ext Cab SB HD	14556	16824	19048
2 Dr STD 4WD Std Cab LB HD	10260	11859	13426	3 Dr LT Ext Cab LB HD	13346	15426	17465
2 Dr STD Std Cab LB	8617	9960	11277	3 Dr LT Ext Cab SB	12753	14741	16689
2 Dr STD Std Cab LB HD	8221	9503	10759	3 Dr STD 4WD Ext Cab LB HD	11251	13005	14724
3 Dr LS 4WD Ext Cab LB HD	12810	14807	16764	3 Dr STD 4WD Ext Cab SB HD	11006	12722	14404
3 Dr LS 4WD Ext Cab SB HD	12611	14577	16504	3 Dr STD Ext Cab LB HD	9380	10842	12275
3 Dr LS Ext Cab LB HD	10787	12468	14116	3 Dr STD Ext Cab SB	9438	10909	12351

Options	Price	Options	Price
6.0L V8 OHV 16V FI Engine	+166	Hinged Fourth Door	+155
Air Conditioning	+386	Leather Seats [Opt on LS]	+692
Automatic 4-Speed Transmission	+465	Limited Slip Differential	+134
Bucket Seats	+176	Tonneau Cover	+197
Camper/Towing Package	+134	Trailer Hitch	+134

2000

After a complete redesign last year, few changes make news for 2000. Most substantial is the addition of a fourth access door to extended cab models, but it's optional, unlike the standard quad-portal arrangement on the Ford F-150. The already potent Vortec 4800 and 5300 V8 engines make more power, and programmable door locks can be instructed to unlock automatically when the Silverado is shut off. LS and LT get a standard electrochromic self-dimming rearview mirror with compass and exterior temperature display, and a soft tonneau cover is available from the factory.

Mileage Category: K

Body Styles	TMV Pricing			Body Styles	TMV Pricing		
	Trade	Private	Dealer		Trade	Private	Dealer
2 Dr LS 4WD Std Cab LB HD	9484	11136	12854	3 Dr LS Ext Cab SB	8708	10364	12087
2 Dr LS Std Cab LB	7699	9163	10686	3 Dr LT 4WD Ext Cab LB HD	12588	14981	17471
2 Dr LS Std Cab LB HD	8151	9701	11315	3 Dr LT 4WD Ext Cab SB HD	12474	14846	17314
2 Dr STD 4WD Std Cab LB HD	8559	10186	11879	3 Dr LT Ext Cab LB HD	11513	13702	15980
2 Dr STD Std Cab LB	7012	8345	9733	3 Dr LT Ext Cab SB	10346	12312	14359
2 Dr STD Std Cab LB HD	6196	7374	8600	3 Dr STD 4WD Ext Cab LB HD	9609	11436	13337
3 Dr LS 4WD Ext Cab LB HD	10886	12955	15109	3 Dr STD 4WD Ext Cab SB HD	9352	11130	12981
3 Dr LS 4WD Ext Cab SB HD	10645	12668	14774	3 Dr STD Ext Cab LB HD	8200	9759	11381
3 Dr LS Ext Cab LB HD	8765	10431	12165	3 Dr STD Ext Cab SB	7697	9160	10683

Options	Price	Options	Price
6.0L V8 OHV 16V FI Engine	+133	Air Conditioning [Opt on STD]	+308

1999

Chevrolet has redesigned the decade-old C/K pickup and given the truck a new name. Major structural, power, braking and interior enhancements characterize the new Silverado. Styling is evolutionary rather than revolutionary, inside and out.

Silverado 2500/2500HD

1999 (cont'd)

Options	Price		Options	Price
Bucket Seats	+140		Leather Seats	+553

Silverado 2500HD

2004

A trio of new colors -- Sandstone Metallic, Silver Birch and Sport Red Metallic -- are the lone changes for this year.

Mileage Category: K

Body Styles	Trade	Private	Dealer	Body Styles	Trade	Private	Dealer
2 Dr LS 4WD Std Cab LB HD	20150	21596	24005	4 Dr LT Ext Cab LB HD	23516	24848	27068
2 Dr LS Std Cab LB HD	17652	18948	21109	4 Dr LT Ext Cab SB HD	23319	24651	26871
2 Dr STD 4WD Std Cab LB HD	19087	20417	22634	4 Dr STD 4WD Crew Cab LB HD	22614	24209	26866
2 Dr STD Std Cab LB HD	16749	18043	20200	4 Dr STD 4WD Crew Cab SB HD	22417	24012	26669
2 Dr Work Truck 4WD Std Cab LB HD	17717	19013	21174	4 Dr STD 4WD Ext Cab LB HD	20782	22227	24634
				4 Dr STD 4WD Ext Cab SB HD	20491	21929	24326
2 Dr Work Truck Std Cab LB HD	15845	17137	19290	4 Dr STD Crew Cab LB HD	20618	22025	24370
4 Dr LS 4WD Crew Cab LB HD	23616	25211	27868	4 Dr STD Crew Cab SB HD	20421	21828	24173
4 Dr LS 4WD Crew Cab SB HD	23419	25014	27671	4 Dr STD Ext Cab LB HD	18947	20279	22499
4 Dr LS 4WD Ext Cab LB HD	21915	23360	25767	4 Dr STD Ext Cab SB HD	18750	20082	22302
4 Dr LS 4WD Ext Cab SB HD	21718	23163	25570	4 Dr Work Truck 4WD Crew Cab LB HD	21974	23569	26226
4 Dr LS Crew Cab LB HD	21620	23027	25372	4 Dr Work Truck 4WD Crew Cab SB HD	21776	23371	26028
4 Dr LS Crew Cab SB HD	21423	22830	25175				
4 Dr LS Ext Cab LB HD	20042	21487	23894	4 Dr Work Truck 4WD Ext Cab LB HD	20140	21585	23992
4 Dr LS Ext Cab SB HD	19851	21183	23403	4 Dr Work Truck 4WD Ext Cab SB HD	19943	21388	23795
4 Dr LT 4WD Crew Cab LB HD	27345	28940	31597	4 Dr Work Truck Crew Cab LB HD	19978	21385	23730
4 Dr LT 4WD Crew Cab SB HD	27148	28743	31400	4 Dr Work Truck Crew Cab SB HD	19780	21187	23532
4 Dr LT 4WD Ext Cab LB HD	25486	26931	29338	4 Dr Work Truck Ext Cab LB HD	18307	19639	21859
4 Dr LT 4WD Ext Cab SB HD	25289	26734	29141	4 Dr Work Truck Ext Cab SB HD	17566	18858	21011
4 Dr LT Crew Cab LB HD	25244	26651	28996				
4 Dr LT Crew Cab SB HD	25047	26454	28799				

Options	Price		Options	Price
6.6L V8 Turbodiesel OHV 32V Engine	+4100		Fog Lights [Opt on LS]	+140
8.1L V8 OHV 16V FI Engine	+950		Leather Seats [Opt on LS Ext, LS Crew]	+800
AM/FM/CD Changer Audio System [Opt on LS Ext, LS Crew]	+795		Locking Differential	+295
			Locking Differential (Rear)	+200
Automatic 4-Speed Transmission [Std on LT]	+1095		OnStar Telematics System [Opt on LS]	+695
Automatic 5-Speed Transmission	+1500		Power Door Locks [Opt on STD]	+162
Automatic Climate Control (2 Zone) - Driver and Passenger [Opt on LS Ext, LS Crew]	+195		Power Driver Seat [Opt on LS Crew, LT Crew]	+240
			Power Retractable Mirrors [Opt on LS]	+213
Bucket Seats [Opt on LS Ext, LS Crew]	+300		Rear Audio Controls [Opt on LS Crew, LT Crew]	+165
Compressed Natural Gas (CNG) Option	+9300		Rear Window Defroster [Opt on STD]	+175
Cruise Control [Opt on Work Truck]	+240		Steering Wheel Radio Controls [Opt on LS]	+125
DVD Entertainment System [Opt on LS Crew, LT Crew]	+1295			
Flex Fuel Option	+850			

2003

The Silverado 2500HD now sports a new front fascia and revised side moldings and taillights. Top-of-the-line models also get power-folding heated mirrors with puddle lamps and turn signal indicators. On the inside, the Silverado offers numerous entertainment options including a Bose stereo system (with rear-seat controls on crew cab models), XM Satellite Radio and a rear-passenger DVD-based entertainment system (crew cab models only). The instrument panel and center console have been redesigned, and Chevrolet has added new seats, a more comprehensive driver information center and a dual-zone climate control system. On the hardware side, the standard 6.0-liter V8 gets electronic throttle control, as well as the ability to run exclusively on compressed natural gas (CNG) or a mix of CNG and gasoline.

Mileage Category: K

Body Styles	Trade	Private	Dealer	Body Styles	Trade	Private	Dealer
2 Dr LS 4WD Std Cab LB HD	17606	18823	20852	4 Dr LS Ext Cab LB HD	17571	18786	20810
2 Dr LS Std Cab LB HD	15439	16506	18285	4 Dr LS Ext Cab SB HD	17154	18340	20316
2 Dr STD 4WD Std Cab LB HD	16062	17172	19023	4 Dr LT 4WD Crew Cab LB HD	23859	25508	28257
2 Dr STD Std Cab LB HD	14062	15034	16654	4 Dr LT 4WD Crew Cab SB HD	23691	25329	28059
2 Dr Work Truck 4WD Std Cab LB HD	15916	17016	18850	4 Dr LT 4WD Ext Cab LB HD	21766	23271	25779
				4 Dr LT 4WD Ext Cab SB HD	21563	23054	25538
2 Dr Work Truck Std Cab LB HD	13890	14850	16451	4 Dr LT Crew Cab LB HD	21766	23271	25778
4 Dr LS 4WD Crew Cab LB HD	20491	21908	24269	4 Dr LT Crew Cab SB HD	21579	23071	25557
4 Dr LS 4WD Crew Cab SB HD	20368	21776	24123	4 Dr LT Ext Cab LB HD	20400	21810	24160
4 Dr LS 4WD Ext Cab LB HD	18976	20287	22473	4 Dr LT Ext Cab SB HD	20320	21725	24066
4 Dr LS 4WD Ext Cab SB HD	18919	20227	22408	4 Dr STD 4WD Crew Cab LB HD	19053	20370	22565
4 Dr LS Crew Cab LB HD	18558	19841	21979	4 Dr STD 4WD Crew Cab SB HD	18895	20201	22378
4 Dr LS Crew Cab SB HD	18370	19640	21756	4 Dr STD 4WD Ext Cab LB HD	17853	19087	21144

For the latest vehicle information, visit www.edmunds.com

Body Styles	TMV Pricing		
	Trade	Private	Dealer
4 Dr STD 4WD Ext Cab LB HD	17555	18769	20791
4 Dr STD Crew Cab LB HD	17185	18373	20353
4 Dr STD Crew Cab SB HD	16995	18170	20128

Body Styles	TMV Pricing		
	Trade	Private	Dealer
4 Dr STD Ext Cab LB HD	15980	17085	18926
4 Dr STD Ext Cab SB HD	15622	16702	18502

Options	Price
6.6L V8 Turbodiesel OHV 32V Engine	+3198
8.1L V8 OHV 16V FI Engine	+543
AM/FM/CD Audio System [Opt on STD,Work]	+163
AM/FM/CD Changer Audio System [Opt on LS]	+255
Appearance Package [Opt on STD]	+367
Automatic 4-Speed Transmission	+699
Automatic 5-Speed Transmission	+766
Automatic Climate Control (2 Zone) - Driver and Passenger [Opt on LS]	+124
Bose Audio System [Opt on LS]	+252
Bucket Seats [Opt on LS]	+271

Options	Price
Compressed Natural Gas (CNG) Option	+5937
Cruise Control [Opt on STD,Work]	+153
DVD Entertainment System [Opt on Crew - LS,LT]	+827
Leather Seats [Opt on LS]	+511
Locking Differential	+188
OnStar Telematics System [Opt on LS]	+444
Power Driver Seat [Opt on LS]	+153
Power Retractable Mirrors [Opt on LS]	+117
Satellite Radio System [Opt on LS,LT]	+207

2002

After undergoing a full redesign last year, Chevrolet's heavy-duty three-quarter-ton truck gets few changes for 2002. Air conditioning is now standard on all trim levels along with extendable sunshade visors and improved base model radios.

Mileage Category: K

Body Styles	TMV Pricing		
	Trade	Private	Dealer
2 Dr LS 4WD Std Cab LB HD	15243	16517	18641
2 Dr LS Std Cab LB HD	13204	14308	16147
2 Dr STD 4WD Std Cab LB HD	13988	15158	17107
2 Dr STD Std Cab LB HD	11961	12961	14627
4 Dr LS 4WD Crew Cab LB HD	17587	19057	21507
4 Dr LS 4WD Crew Cab SB HD	17547	19014	21458
4 Dr LS 4WD Ext Cab LB HD	16693	18088	20414
4 Dr LS 4WD Ext Cab SB HD	16382	17752	20034
4 Dr LS Crew Cab LB HD	15966	17300	19524
4 Dr LS Crew Cab SB HD	15808	17130	19332
4 Dr LS Ext Cab LB HD	15240	16514	18637
4 Dr LS Ext Cab SB HD	15063	16322	18421
4 Dr LT 4WD Crew Cab LB HD	20146	21830	24637
4 Dr LT 4WD Crew Cab SB HD	20000	21672	24459

Body Styles	TMV Pricing		
	Trade	Private	Dealer
4 Dr LT 4WD Ext Cab LB HD	18987	20574	23220
4 Dr LT 4WD Ext Cab SB HD	18780	20350	22966
4 Dr LT Crew Cab LB HD	18311	19841	22392
4 Dr LT Crew Cab SB HD	18166	19684	22215
4 Dr LT Ext Cab LB HD	17163	18598	20989
4 Dr LT Ext Cab SB HD	16956	18374	20736
4 Dr STD 4WD Crew Cab LB HD	16488	17866	20163
4 Dr STD 4WD Crew Cab SB HD	16367	17735	20016
4 Dr STD 4WD Ext Cab LB HD	15713	17027	19216
4 Dr STD 4WD Ext Cab SB HD	15352	16635	18773
4 Dr STD Crew Cab LB HD	15000	16254	18343
4 Dr STD Crew Cab SB HD	14843	16084	18152
4 Dr STD Ext Cab LB HD	13673	14816	16721
4 Dr STD Ext Cab SB HD	13552	14685	16573

Options	Price
6.6L V8 Turbodiesel OHV 32V Engine	+2758
8.1L V8 OHV 16V FI Engine	+487
Automatic 4-Speed Transmission [Std on LT]	+628
Automatic 5-Speed Transmission	+688
Automatic Dimming Rearview Mirror [Std on LT]	+181
Bucket Seats [Std on LT]	+244

Options	Price
Cruise Control [Opt on STD]	+138
Flex Fuel Option	+430
Leather Seats [Std on LT]	+459
Locking Differential	+169
Power Driver Seat [Opt on LS]	+138
Power Passenger Seat [Opt on LS]	+138

2001

Both light- and heavy-duty 2500s sport new torsion bar front suspensions. Light-duty models get an 8,600-pound Gross Vehicle Weight Rating in addition to optional traction control and standard child safety-seat tether hooks. Heavy-duty models are completely redesigned for 2001 offering two new engines and transmissions, bigger interiors and numerous other improvements.

Mileage Category: K

Body Styles	TMV Pricing		
	Trade	Private	Dealer
2 Dr LS 4WD Std Cab LB HD	13178	14974	16631
2 Dr LS Std Cab LB HD	11422	12978	14415
2 Dr STD 4WD Std Cab LB HD	12146	13801	15329
2 Dr STD Std Cab LB HD	9893	11241	12485
4 Dr LS 4WD Crew Cab LB HD	15472	17580	19526
4 Dr LS 4WD Crew Cab SB HD	15216	17289	19202
4 Dr LS 4WD Ext Cab LB HD	14316	16267	18067
4 Dr LS 4WD Ext Cab SB HD	14265	16208	18002
4 Dr LS Crew Cab LB HD	13653	15513	17229
4 Dr LS Crew Cab SB HD	13517	15359	17059
4 Dr LS Ext Cab LB HD	13056	14834	16476
4 Dr LS Ext Cab SB HD	12659	14384	15976
4 Dr LT 4WD Crew Cab LB HD	17268	19620	21792

Body Styles	TMV Pricing		
	Trade	Private	Dealer
4 Dr LT 4WD Crew Cab SB HD	17144	19479	21635
4 Dr LT 4WD Ext Cab LB HD	16560	18816	20898
4 Dr LT 4WD Ext Cab SB HD	16494	18741	20815
4 Dr LT Crew Cab LB HD	15668	17803	19774
4 Dr LT Crew Cab SB HD	15549	17667	19622
4 Dr LT Ext Cab LB HD	15212	17285	19198
4 Dr LT Ext Cab SB HD	15099	17156	19055
4 Dr STD 4WD Crew Cab LB HD	13704	15571	17294
4 Dr STD 4WD Crew Cab SB HD	13529	15372	17074
4 Dr STD 4WD Ext Cab LB HD	13236	15039	16704
4 Dr STD 4WD Ext Cab SB HD	12911	14670	16293
4 Dr STD Crew Cab LB HD	12423	14115	15677
4 Dr STD Crew Cab SB HD	12290	13964	15510

Chevrolet
Silverado 2500HD/3500

2001 (cont'd)

Body Styles	TMV Pricing		
	Trade	Private	Dealer
4 Dr STD Ext Cab LB HD	11437	12995	14433

Options	Price
6.6L V8 Turbodiesel OHV 32V Engine	+2523
8.1L V8 OHV 16V FI Engine	+446
Air Conditioning [Opt on STD]	+433
Automatic 4-Speed Transmission [Std on LT]	+574
Automatic 5-Speed Transmission	+630
Cruise Control [Opt on STD]	+126

Body Styles	TMV Pricing		
	Trade	Private	Dealer
4 Dr STD Ext Cab SB HD	11335	12879	14304

Options	Price
Leather Seats [Std on LT]	+671
Locking Differential [Std on LT]	+150
Power Driver Seat [Opt on LS]	+126
Power Passenger Seat [Opt on LS]	+126
Tonneau Cover	+126

Silverado 3500

2004

A single-rear-wheel 4WD version is now available in all body styles.

Mileage Category: K

Body Styles	TMV Pricing		
	Trade	Private	Dealer
2 Dr LS 4WD Std Cab LB	20063	21705	24442
2 Dr LS 4WD Std Cab LB DRW	20000	21650	24401
2 Dr STD 4WD Std Cab LB	19098	20748	23499
2 Dr STD 4WD Std Cab LB DRW	18973	20623	23374
2 Dr Work Truck 4WD Std Cab LB	18715	20468	23390
2 Dr Work Truck 4WD Std Cab LB DRW	18552	20202	22953
4 Dr LS 4WD Crew Cab LB	23757	25557	28558
4 Dr LS 4WD Crew Cab LB DRW	23476	25276	28277
4 Dr LS 4WD Ext Cab LB	21395	23083	25896
4 Dr LS 4WD Ext Cab LB DRW	21259	22947	25760
4 Dr LS Crew Cab LB DRW	21499	23056	25650
4 Dr LS Ext Cab LB DRW	18949	20749	23750
4 Dr LT 4WD Crew Cab LB	26457	28257	31258
4 Dr LT 4WD Crew Cab LB DRW	26882	28682	31683
4 Dr LT 4WD Ext Cab LB	23945	25633	28446
4 Dr LT 4WD Ext Cab LB DRW	24511	26199	29012

Body Styles	TMV Pricing		
	Trade	Private	Dealer
4 Dr LT Crew Cab LB DRW	24804	26361	28955
4 Dr LT Ext Cab LB DRW	22099	23899	26900
4 Dr STD 4WD Crew Cab LB	22737	24537	27538
4 Dr STD 4WD Crew Cab LB DRW	22483	24283	27284
4 Dr STD 4WD Ext Cab LB	20249	22012	24950
4 Dr STD 4WD Ext Cab LB DRW	20155	21918	24856
4 Dr STD Crew Cab LB DRW	20495	22295	25296
4 Dr STD Ext Cab LB DRW	18575	20297	23168
4 Dr Work Truck 4WD Crew Cab LB	22354	24154	27155
4 Dr Work Truck 4WD Crew Cab LB DRW	22068	23718	26469
4 Dr Work Truck 4WD Ext Cab LB	20140	22003	25109
4 Dr Work Truck 4WD Ext Cab LB DRW	20123	21816	24637
4 Dr Work Truck Crew Cab LB DRW	20083	21640	24234
4 Dr Work Truck Ext Cab LB DRW	17452	19027	21653

Options	Price
6.6L V8 Turbodiesel OHV 32V Engine	+4100
8.1L V8 OHV 16V FI Engine	+950
AM/FM/CD Changer Audio System [Opt on LS Ext, LS Crew]	+795
Automatic 4-Speed Transmission [Opt on DRW non-LT]	+1095
Automatic 5-Speed Transmission	+1500
Automatic Climate Control (2 Zone) - Driver and Passenger [Opt on LS Ext, LS Crew]	+195
Bucket Seats [Opt on LS Ext, LS Crew]	+300
Cruise Control [Opt on Work Truck]	+240
DVD Entertainment System [Opt on LS Crew, LT Crew]	+1295
Flex Fuel Option	+850

Options	Price
Fog Lights [Opt on LS]	+140
Leather Seats [Opt on LS Ext, LS Crew]	+800
Locking Differential (Rear) [Opt on DRW]	+200
OnStar Telematics System [Opt on LS]	+695
Power Door Locks [Opt on STD]	+162
Power Driver Seat [Opt on LS Ext, LS Crew]	+240
Power Retractable Mirrors [Opt on LS, LT non-DRW]	+213
Rear Audio Controls [Opt on LS Crew, LT Crew]	+165
Rear Window Defroster [Opt on STD]	+175
Steering Wheel Radio Controls [Opt on LS]	+125

2003

The Silverado 3500 now sports the same look as its light-duty siblings, including a new front fascia and revised side moldings and taillights. Top-of-the-line models also get power-folding heated mirrors with puddle lamps and turn signal indicators. On the inside, the 2003 Silverado offers numerous entertainment options, including a Bose stereo system (with rear-seat controls on crew cab models), XM Satellite Radio and a DVD-based entertainment system (crew cab models only). The instrument panel and center console have been redesigned, and Chevrolet has added new seats, a more comprehensive driver information center and a dual-zone climate control system. On the hardware side, the standard 6.0-liter V8 gets electronic throttle control as well as the ability to run exclusively on compressed natural gas (CNG) or a mix of CNG and gasoline.

Mileage Category: K

Body Styles	TMV Pricing		
	Trade	Private	Dealer
2 Dr LS 4WD Std Cab LB DRW	17973	19161	21142
2 Dr STD 4WD Std Cab LB DRW	16851	17965	19822
4 Dr LS 4WD Crew Cab LB DRW	21085	22479	24803
4 Dr LS 4WD Ext Cab LB DRW	19646	20945	23110
4 Dr LS Crew Cab LB DRW	19055	20315	22415
4 Dr LS Ext Cab LB DRW	17606	18770	20709
4 Dr LT 4WD Crew Cab LB DRW	23741	25311	27927

Body Styles	TMV Pricing		
	Trade	Private	Dealer
4 Dr LT 4WD Ext Cab LB DRW	22532	24022	26505
4 Dr LT Crew Cab LB DRW	21927	23377	25793
4 Dr LT Ext Cab LB DRW	20587	21948	24217
4 Dr STD 4WD Crew Cab LB DRW	19698	21000	23171
4 Dr STD 4WD Ext Cab LB DRW	18606	19836	21886
4 Dr STD Crew Cab LB DRW	17646	18813	20757
4 Dr STD Ext Cab LB DRW	16400	17485	19292

2003 (cont'd)

Options	Price
6.6L V8 Turbodiesel OHV 32V Engine	+3198
8.1L V8 OHV 16V FI Engine	+543
AM/FM/CD Audio System [Opt on STD]	+163
AM/FM/CD Changer Audio System [Opt on LS]	+255
Automatic 4-Speed Transmission	+699
Automatic 5-Speed Transmission	+766
Automatic Climate Control (2 Zone) - Driver and Passenger [Opt on LS]	+124
Bose Audio System [Opt on LS]	+252
Bucket Seats [Opt on LS]	+271

Options	Price
Cruise Control [Opt on STD]	+153
DVD Entertainment System [Opt on Crew - LS,LT]	+827
Leather Seats [Opt on LS]	+511
Locking Differential	+188
OnStar Telematics System [Opt on LS]	+444
Power Driver Seat [Opt on LS]	+153
Power Retractable Mirrors [Opt on LS]	+152
Satellite Radio System [Opt on LS,LT]	+207

2002

After undergoing a full redesign last year, Chevrolet's heavy-duty one-ton truck gets few changes for 2002. Air conditioning is now standard on all trim levels along with extendable sunshade visors and improved base model radios.

Mileage Category: K

Body Styles	TMV Pricing		
	Trade	Private	Dealer
2 Dr LS 4WD Std Cab LB	15417	16611	18601
2 Dr STD 4WD Std Cab LB	14413	15529	17390
4 Dr LS 4WD Crew Cab LB	17993	19387	21709
4 Dr LS 4WD Ext Cab LB	16814	18116	20287
4 Dr LS Crew Cab LB	16173	17426	19514
4 Dr LS Ext Cab LB	15186	16362	18323
4 Dr LT 4WD Crew Cab LB	19349	20848	23346

Body Styles	TMV Pricing		
	Trade	Private	Dealer
4 Dr LT 4WD Ext Cab LB	18457	19887	22270
4 Dr LT Crew Cab LB	18114	19517	21855
4 Dr LT Ext Cab LB	17406	18754	21001
4 Dr STD 4WD Crew Cab LB	16702	17996	20152
4 Dr STD 4WD Ext Cab LB	16001	17240	19306
4 Dr STD Crew Cab LB	14905	16060	17984
4 Dr STD Ext Cab LB	13913	14991	16787

Options	Price
6.6L V8 Turbodiesel OHV 32V Engine	+2758
8.1L V8 OHV 16V FI Engine	+487
Automatic 4-Speed Transmission [Std on LT]	+628
Automatic 5-Speed Transmission	+688
Bucket Seats [Std on LT]	+244
Camper/Towing Package	+123

Options	Price
Cruise Control [Opt on STD]	+138
Flex Fuel Option	+430
Leather Seats [Std on LT]	+459
Locking Differential	+169
Power Driver Seat [Opt on LS]	+138
Power Passenger Seat [Opt on LS]	+138

2001

Chevrolet's heavy-duty pickups get a complete redesign for 2001 including two new engines and transmissions, new exterior styling, and numerous other improvements.

Mileage Category: K

Body Styles	TMV Pricing		
	Trade	Private	Dealer
2 Dr LS 4WD Std Cab LB	13083	14782	16350
2 Dr STD 4WD Std Cab LB	11926	13475	14904
4 Dr LS 4WD Crew Cab LB	15273	17257	19088
4 Dr LS 4WD Ext Cab LB	14268	16121	17831
4 Dr LS Crew Cab LB	13700	15479	17121
4 Dr LS Ext Cab LB	12872	14544	16087
4 Dr LT 4WD Crew Cab LB	16356	18480	20440

Body Styles	TMV Pricing		
	Trade	Private	Dealer
4 Dr LT 4WD Ext Cab LB	15616	17644	19516
4 Dr LT Crew Cab LB	15332	17323	19161
4 Dr LT Ext Cab LB	14765	16682	18452
4 Dr STD 4WD Crew Cab LB	13753	15539	17188
4 Dr STD 4WD Ext Cab LB	13344	15077	16677
4 Dr STD Crew Cab LB	12209	13794	15258
4 Dr STD Ext Cab LB	11527	13024	14406

Options	Price
6.6L V8 Turbodiesel OHV 32V Engine	+2523
8.1L V8 OHV 16V FI Engine	+446
Air Conditioning [Opt on STD]	+433
Automatic 4-Speed Transmission [Std on LT]	+574
Automatic 5-Speed Transmission	+630

Options	Price
Cruise Control [Opt on STD]	+126
Leather Seats [Std on LT]	+671
Locking Differential	+150
Power Driver Seat [Opt on LS]	+126
Power Passenger Seat [Opt on LS]	+126

Suburban
2004

Mileage Category: N

Body Styles	TMV Pricing		
	Trade	Private	Dealer
4 Dr 1500 4WD SUV	23374	24788	27144
4 Dr 1500 LS 4WD SUV	24830	26272	28674
4 Dr 1500 LS SUV	22704	24119	26476
4 Dr 1500 LT 4WD SUV	27770	29208	31605
4 Dr 1500 LT SUV	25645	27059	29415
4 Dr 1500 SUV	22192	23606	25962
4 Dr 1500 Z71 4WD SUV	27915	29353	31749

Body Styles	TMV Pricing		
	Trade	Private	Dealer
4 Dr 2500 4WD SUV	24192	25605	27961
4 Dr 2500 LS 4WD SUV	25576	27008	29394
4 Dr 2500 LS SUV	23651	25065	27422
4 Dr 2500 LT 4WD SUV	28776	30213	32608
4 Dr 2500 LT SUV	26591	28005	30362
4 Dr 2500 SUV	22535	23895	26162

2004 (cont'd)

Half-ton models now feature standard Hydroboost brakes, a tire-pressure monitoring system and newly styled 16- and 17-inch aluminum wheels. Two-wheel-drive models with traction control now feature a locking rear differential, and the trailering package includes a 7-to-4 pin brake wiring adapter. For added safety, there is now a front passenger seatbelt reminder. Lastly, Chevrolet has lowered the output figures for the Vortec 8100 -- the engine is now rated at 320 hp and 440 lb-ft of torque.

Options	Price
17 Inch Wheels [Opt on 1500 LS, LT]	+295
4 Wheel Steering [Opt on 2500]	+1995
8.1L V8 OHV 16V FI Engine [Opt on 2500]	+950
AM/FM/CD Changer Audio System [Opt on LS]	+300
Automatic Stability Control [Opt on 1500]	+750
Autoride Suspension Package	+1120
Bose Audio System [Opt on LS]	+250
Brush Guard [Opt on Z71]	+845
Bucket Seats [Opt on LS, Z71]	+350
Camper/Towing Package	+210

Options	Price
DVD Entertainment System	+350
Front Side Airbag Restraints	+300
Leather Seats [Opt on LS]	+370
Limited Slip Differential (Rear) [Opt on 2500]	+295
OnStar Telematics System [Opt on LS]	+250
Power Moonroof	+750
Power Retractable Mirrors [Opt on LS]	+355
Rear Bucket Seats [Opt on LT, Z71]	+490
Satellite Radio System	+325
Traction Control System [Opt on 2500 2WD]	+200

2003

The Suburban gets numerous functional enhancements for 2003. The Quadrasteer four-wheel steering system is now available on 3/4-ton models for increased maneuverability and better stability when towing, while 1/2-ton versions now offer the StabiliTrak stability control system. New power heated mirrors feature puddle lamps, in-glass turn signal indicators and a memory function, and extendable power camper mirrors are optional. The interior gets numerous upgrades that include tri-zone climate control, an enhanced driver-information center, a redesigned center console and options such as second-row captain's chairs and adjustable pedals. A revised lineup of entertainment options includes a Bose audio system as well as XM Satellite Radio and a DVD-based entertainment system. For increased safety, the Suburban now features a standard front-passenger-sensing system and dual-stage airbags.

Mileage Category: N

Body Styles	TMV Pricing		
	Trade	Private	Dealer
4 Dr 1500 LS 4WD SUV	21316	22784	25230
4 Dr 1500 LS SUV	18696	19983	22128
4 Dr 1500 LT 4WD SUV	23126	24719	27373
4 Dr 1500 LT SUV	21693	23187	25677

Body Styles	TMV Pricing		
	Trade	Private	Dealer
4 Dr 2500 LS 4WD SUV	22290	23825	26384
4 Dr 2500 LS SUV	20225	21496	23615
4 Dr 2500 LT 4WD SUV	23867	25511	28250
4 Dr 2500 LT SUV	22485	24033	26613

Options	Price
4 Wheel Steering [Opt on 2500]	+2870
8.1L V8 OHV 16V FI Engine [Opt on 2500]	+447
AM/FM/Cassette/CD Changer Audio System [Opt on LS]	+252
Automatic Stability Control [Opt on 1500]	+479
Autoride Suspension Package	+715
Bose Audio System [Opt on LS]	+223
Captain Chairs (4)	+313
DVD Entertainment System	+827
Front Side Airbag Restraints	+223
Heated Front Seats	+223
Leather Seats [Opt on LS]	+575
Limited Slip Differential [Opt on 2500]	+188

Options	Price
Locking Differential	+188
OnStar Telematics System [Opt on LS]	+524
Power Adjustable Foot Pedals	+176
Power Moonroof	+631
Power Passenger Seat [Opt on LS]	+153
Power Retractable Mirrors [Opt on LS]	+227
Rear Window Wiper	+160
Satellite Radio System	+207
Skid Plates [Opt on 4WD]	+176
Traction Control System [Opt on 2500 2WD]	+144
Z71 Off-Road Suspension Package [Opt on 1500 LS 4WD]	+3299

2002

The base trim level has been dropped. New for this year on LS are standard six-way power driver and front passenger seats, heated outside mirrors, exterior side steps that make getting in and out easier and the HomeLink system that can be programmed to control automatic garage doors or community gates all from one keypad. 5300 V8s can now burn gasoline/ethanol mixed fuels.

Mileage Category: N

Body Styles	TMV Pricing		
	Trade	Private	Dealer
4 Dr 1500 LS 4WD SUV	18460	19973	22495
4 Dr 1500 LS SUV	16973	18364	20682
4 Dr 1500 LT 4WD SUV	19937	21571	24294
4 Dr 1500 LT SUV	18705	20238	22792

Body Styles	TMV Pricing		
	Trade	Private	Dealer
4 Dr 2500 LS 4WD SUV	19323	20906	23545
4 Dr 2500 LS SUV	17887	19353	21795
4 Dr 2500 LT 4WD SUV	20546	22230	25036
4 Dr 2500 LT SUV	19380	20968	23614

Options	Price
8.1L V8 OHV 16V FI Engine	+401
Autoride Suspension Package	+502
Captain Chairs (4)	+281
Leather Seats [Std on LT]	+510
Locking Differential [Opt on 2WD]	+145

Options	Price
OnStar Telematics System [Std on LT]	+399
Power Sunroof	+538
Traction Control System [Opt on 2WD]	+172
Z71 Off-Road Suspension Package [Opt on K1500 LS]	+1302

2001

Though completely redesigned last year, 2001 still sees improvements to the powertrain. Chevy has upped the horsepower rating of the Vortec 6000 to 320, and 360 pound-feet of torque is now made at 4,000 revs. A new 8.1-liter engine cranks out 340 horsepower at 4,200 rpm and 455 lb-ft of torque at 3,200 rpm. The recommended oil change interval goes from 7,500 miles to 10,000 miles.

Mileage Category: N

Body Styles	TMV Pricing		
	Trade	Private	Dealer
4 Dr 1500 4WD SUV	12302	13944	15460
4 Dr 1500 LS 4WD SUV	15381	17434	19330
4 Dr 1500 LS SUV	13264	15035	16670
4 Dr 1500 LT 4WD SUV	17375	19695	21836
4 Dr 1500 LT SUV	16462	18660	20689
4 Dr 1500 SUV	10854	12302	13639

Body Styles	TMV Pricing		
	Trade	Private	Dealer
4 Dr 2500 4WD SUV	13110	14860	16475
4 Dr 2500 LS 4WD SUV	16138	18292	20280
4 Dr 2500 LS SUV	14788	16762	18584
4 Dr 2500 LT 4WD SUV	17597	19946	22114
4 Dr 2500 LT SUV	16681	18909	20965
4 Dr 2500 SUV	11863	13446	14908

2001 (cont'd)

Options	Price
8.1L V8 OHV 16V FI Engine	+367
Air Conditioning [Opt on STD]	+424
Autoride Suspension Package	+367
Leather Seats	+498
Locking Differential [Opt on STD]	+132
Off-Road Suspension Package	+1781
OnStar Telematics System [Std on LT]	+365
Power Driver Seat [Opt on LS]	+126

Options	Price
Power Moonroof	+495
Power Passenger Seat [Opt on LS]	+126
Privacy Glass	+152
Running Boards [Opt on LS]	+207
Split Front Bench Seat [Opt on STD]	+330
Third Seat	+645
Traction Control System	+242

2000

The 2000 Chevrolet Suburban is completely redesigned. It's roomier, safer, more comfortable and a more powerful ride.

Mileage Category: N

Body Styles	TMV Pricing		
	Trade	Private	Dealer
4 Dr 1500 4WD SUV	9918	11478	13008
4 Dr 1500 LS 4WD SUV	12438	14394	16311
4 Dr 1500 LS SUV	11079	12821	14529
4 Dr 1500 LT 4WD SUV	13759	15923	18045
4 Dr 1500 LT SUV	12905	14935	16925
4 Dr 1500 SUV	8604	9957	11283

Body Styles	TMV Pricing		
	Trade	Private	Dealer
4 Dr 2500 4WD SUV	10571	12234	13864
4 Dr 2500 LS 4WD SUV	13091	15150	17169
4 Dr 2500 LS SUV	12416	14369	16284
4 Dr 2500 LT 4WD SUV	14776	17101	19380
4 Dr 2500 LT SUV	13634	15779	17882
4 Dr 2500 SUV	9586	11094	12573

Options	Price
AM/FM/CD Audio System	+134
AM/FM/Cassette/CD Audio System	+179
Air Conditioning - Front and Rear	+620
Autoride Suspension Package [Opt on 4WD]	+327
Bucket Seats	+120
Center and Rear Bench Seat [Std on LS,LT]	+486

Options	Price
Leather Seats	+444
OnStar Telematics System [Opt on LS]	+325
Power Moonroof	+442
Privacy Glass	+136
Side Steps	+145
Traction Control System	+216

1999

A couple of new colors are the only modifications to the Suburban as Chevrolet prepares a redesigned model for 2000.

Mileage Category: N

Body Styles	TMV Pricing		
	Trade	Private	Dealer
4 Dr C1500 SUV	7166	8517	9923
4 Dr C2500 SUV	7876	9362	10909

Body Styles	TMV Pricing		
	Trade	Private	Dealer
4 Dr K1500 4WD SUV	8158	9697	11299
4 Dr K2500 4WD SUV	8253	9810	11431

Options	Price
6.5L V8 Turbodiesel OHV 16V Engine	+1186
7.4L V8 OHV 16V FI Engine	+249
AM/FM/Cassette/CD Audio System	+143
Air Conditioning	+299
Air Conditioning - Front and Rear	+495
Center Bench Seat	+224
Center and Rear Bench Seat	+389

Options	Price
Heated Front Seats	+124
LS Package	+1088
LT Package	+1646
Leather Seats	+394
OnStar Telematics System	+288
Running Boards	+115

1998

New colors, a standard theft-deterrent system, optional heated seats, second-generation airbags and an automatic 4WD system improve the 1998 Suburban.

Mileage Category: N

Body Styles	TMV Pricing		
	Trade	Private	Dealer
4 Dr C1500 SUV	6402	7760	9291
4 Dr C2500 SUV	7146	8662	10371

Body Styles	TMV Pricing		
	Trade	Private	Dealer
4 Dr K1500 4WD SUV	7252	8790	10525
4 Dr K2500 4WD SUV	7450	9030	10812

Options	Price
6.5L V8 Turbodiesel OHV 16V Engine [Opt on 2500]	+999
7.4L V8 OHV 16V FI Engine [Opt on 2500]	+210
Air Conditioning	+253
Air Conditioning - Front and Rear	+417
Center Bench Seat	+189

Options	Price
Center and Rear Bench Seat	+328
LS Package	+1146
LT Package	+1387
Leather Seats	+332
OnStar Telematics System	+243

1997

Dual airbags debut, and a cargo area power lock switch makes locking up the vehicle after unloading cargo more convenient. Variable power steering lightens low-speed steering effort, and automatic transmissions are improved. Two new exterior colors are added to the paint roster.

Mileage Category: N

Body Styles	TMV Pricing		
	Trade	Private	Dealer
4 Dr C1500 SUV	5380	6664	8234
4 Dr C2500 SUV	5822	7212	8910

Body Styles	TMV Pricing		
	Trade	Private	Dealer
4 Dr K1500 4WD SUV	6109	7567	9349
4 Dr K2500 4WD SUV	6269	7765	9593

Chevrolet
Suburban/Tahoe

1997 (cont'd)

Options	Price
6.5L V8 Turbodiesel OHV 16V Engine	+772
7.4L V8 OHV 16V FI Engine	+190
Air Conditioning	+228
Air Conditioning - Front and Rear	+350
Center Bench Seat	+171

Options	Price
LS Package	+1035
LT Package	+1254
Leather Seats	+300
Third Seat	+373

1996

Improved engines generate more horsepower and torque. Four-wheel-drive models get an optional electronic shift transfer case. Daytime running lights, rear-seat heating ducts and two new paint colors summarize the changes.

Mileage Category: N

Body Styles	TMV Pricing		
	Trade	Private	Dealer
4 Dr C1500 SUV	4428	5617	7258
4 Dr C2500 SUV	4696	5956	7697

Body Styles	TMV Pricing		
	Trade	Private	Dealer
4 Dr K1500 4WD SUV	4964	6296	8136
4 Dr K2500 4WD SUV	5043	6397	8266

Options	Price
6.5L V8 Turbodiesel OHV 16V Engine	+809
7.4L V8 OHV 16V FI Engine	+172
Air Conditioning	+207
Air Conditioning - Front and Rear	+317
Center Bench Seat	+155

Options	Price
LS Package	+869
LT Package	+1067
Leather Seats	+245
Third Seat	+338

1995

New interior with driver airbag debuts. New dashboard features modular design with controls that are much easier to read and use. The 1500 models can now be ordered with turbodiesel engine. Brake/transmission shift interlock is added to automatic transmission. Seats and door panels are revised. New console on models with bucket seats features pivoting writing surface, along with rear cupholders and storage drawer. Uplevel radios come with automatic volume controls that raise or lower the volume depending on vehicle speed.

Mileage Category: N

Body Styles	TMV Pricing		
	Trade	Private	Dealer
4 Dr C1500 SUV	3208	4161	5750
4 Dr C2500 SUV	3524	4572	6319

Body Styles	TMV Pricing		
	Trade	Private	Dealer
4 Dr K1500 4WD SUV	3674	4766	6586
4 Dr K2500 4WD SUV	3785	4910	6786

Options	Price
6.5L V8 Turbodiesel OHV 16V Engine	+726
7.4L V8 OHV 16V FI Engine	+154
Air Conditioning	+185
Air Conditioning - Front and Rear	+285

Options	Price
Center Bench Seat	+139
LS Package	+779
LT Package	+957
Leather Seats	+219

Tahoe
2004

Chevrolet offers revised 16- and 17-inch aluminum wheels, and 17-inch all-season tires are now optional on LT models. Other new features include a tire-pressure monitor and Hydroboost brakes that provide more reserve stopping power and decreased pedal effort, according to Chevrolet. A traction assist feature is available on two-wheel-drive Tahoes equipped with a locking rear differential. The trailering package includes a 7-to-4 pin brake wiring adapter. Finally, for added safety, there is now a front-passenger seatbelt reminder.

Mileage Category: N

Body Styles	TMV Pricing		
	Trade	Private	Dealer
4 Dr LS 4WD SUV	24388	25992	28663
4 Dr LS SUV	21957	23514	26109
4 Dr LT 4WD SUV	28619	30225	32902
4 Dr LT SUV	26187	27755	30367

Body Styles	TMV Pricing		
	Trade	Private	Dealer
4 Dr STD 4WD SUV	22129	23845	26706
4 Dr STD SUV	18957	20505	23084
4 Dr Z71 4WD SUV	27470	29055	31697

Options	Price
17 Inch Wheels [Opt on LT]	+295
AM/FM/CD Changer Audio System [Opt on LS]	+300
Automatic Stability Control	+750
Bose Audio System [Opt on LS]	+635
Brush Guard [Opt on Z71]	+845
Bucket Seats [Opt on LS, Z71]	+450
Camper/Towing Package	+305
DVD Entertainment System	+1295
Front Side Airbag Restraints	+300
Leather Seats [Opt on LS]	+470

Options	Price
Locking Differential	+295
OnStar Telematics System [Opt on LS]	+250
Power Driver Seat w/Memory [Opt on Z71]	+150
Power Moonroof	+995
Power Passenger Seat [Opt on LS]	+130
Rear Audio Controls [Opt on LS, Z71]	+150
Rear Bucket Seats [Opt on LT, Z71]	+490
Rear Window Wiper	+250
Third Seat	+360
Traction Control System [Opt on 2WD]	+195

2003

Body Styles	TMV Pricing		
	Trade	Private	Dealer
4 Dr LS 4WD SUV	21848	23352	25858
4 Dr LS SUV	20054	21435	23736

Options	Price
AM/FM/Cassette/CD Changer Audio System [Opt on LS]	+252
Automatic Stability Control	+479
Autoride Suspension Package [Opt on LT]	+715
Bose Audio System [Opt on LS]	+223
Camper/Towing Package	+182
Captain Chairs (4)	+313
DVD Entertainment System	+827
Front Side Airbag Restraints	+223
Leather Seats [Opt on LS]	+479
Locking Differential	+188

Body Styles	TMV Pricing		
	Trade	Private	Dealer
4 Dr LT 4WD SUV	24204	25870	28648
4 Dr LT SUV	22301	23838	26398

Options	Price
OnStar Telematics System [Opt on LS]	+524
Power Adjustable Foot Pedals	+176
Power Moonroof	+631
Power Passenger Seat [Opt on LS]	+153
Rear Window Wiper	+160
Satellite Radio System	+207
Skid Plates [Opt on 4WD]	+176
Third Seat	+319
Z71 Off-Road Suspension Package [Opt on LS 4WD]	+3299

The Tahoe gets a host of upgrades for 2003. On the inside, you'll find tri-zone climate controls, an enhanced driver-information center and a redesigned center console and instrument panel. Second-row bucket seats are now available when leather buckets are specified in front. A revised lineup of entertainment options offers buyers Bose sound, as well as XM Satellite Radio and a DVD-based entertainment system. For increased safety, there are dual-stage airbags, a standard front-passenger-sensing system and three-point belts for all second-row passengers. Like many Ford products, the Tahoe now has adjustable gas and brake pedals. The braking system has also been upgraded for what Chevrolet says is better pedal feel and performance. Two- and four-wheel-drive trucks with the 5.3-liter engine can be ordered with an optional stability control system. Trucks sold in California now earn ULEV certification. No longer standard are third-row floormats, an underhood light, a 7-to-4 pin trailer brake adapter, an auxiliary door lock switch in the cargo area and a lock for the center console.

2002

Body Styles	TMV Pricing		
	Trade	Private	Dealer
4 Dr LS 4WD SUV	17953	19424	21876
4 Dr LS SUV	16533	17887	20145

Options	Price
5.3L V8 Flex Fuel OHV 16V FI Engine [Opt on 1500]	+401
Autoride Suspension Package	+502
Camper/Towing Package	+149
Leather Seats [Opt on LS]	+660
Locking Differential [Opt on 2WD]	+145

Body Styles	TMV Pricing		
	Trade	Private	Dealer
4 Dr LT 4WD SUV	19882	21512	24227
4 Dr LT SUV	18262	19758	22253

Options	Price
OnStar Telematics System [Std on LT]	+399
Power Sunroof	+538
Third Seat	+287
Traction Control System [Opt on 2WD]	+172
Z71 Off-Road Suspension Package [Opt on LS 4WD]	+1793

All models get the previously optional Premium Ride suspension. LS Tahoes get six-way power driver and front passenger seats, along with foglights, heated outside mirrors, side-mounted assist steps and a programmable HomeLink transmitter for opening garage doors or automatic gates. The 5300 V8 is now capable of running gasoline/ethanol fuel blends.

2001

Body Styles	TMV Pricing		
	Trade	Private	Dealer
4 Dr LS 4WD SUV	15236	17269	19146
4 Dr LS SUV	13920	15780	17496
4 Dr LT 4WD SUV	17338	19653	21790

Options	Price
Air Conditioning [Opt on STD]	+424
Autoride Suspension Package	+367
Camper/Towing Package	+142
Leather Seats [Opt on LS]	+656
Locking Differential	+132
Luggage Rack [Opt on STD]	+150
Off-Road Suspension Package	+1781
OnStar Telematics System [Opt on LS]	+365

Body Styles	TMV Pricing		
	Trade	Private	Dealer
4 Dr LT SUV	16005	18143	20116
4 Dr STD 4WD SUV	12868	14585	16170
4 Dr STD SUV	11557	13098	14521

Options	Price
Power Driver Seat [Opt on LS]	+126
Power Moonroof	+498
Power Passenger Seat [Opt on LS,LT]	+126
Privacy Glass [Opt on STD]	+169
Running Boards [Opt on LS]	+207
Third Seat	+374
Traction Control System	+125

Two new exterior colors and OnStar availability are the only changes for 2001.

2000

Body Styles	TMV Pricing		
	Trade	Private	Dealer
4 Dr LS 4WD SUV	13557	15690	17781
4 Dr LS SUV	12369	14315	16222
4 Dr LT 4WD SUV	14716	17031	19301

Options	Price
5.3L V8 OHV 16V FI Engine [Opt on STD]	+311
Air Conditioning [Opt on STD]	+378
Automatic Load Leveling	+163
Bucket Seats [Opt on LS]	+167

Body Styles	TMV Pricing		
	Trade	Private	Dealer
4 Dr LT SUV	13694	15848	17960
4 Dr STD 4WD SUV	11338	13122	14869
4 Dr STD SUV	10102	11692	13250

Options	Price
Camper/Towing Package	+127
Leather Seats [Opt on LS]	+400
Luggage Rack [Opt on STD]	+133
OnStar Telematics System [Opt on LS]	+325

The engineers at Chevy redesigned the Tahoe from top to bottom, making it safer, more powerful and a more pleasurable vehicle to drive.

Chevrolet
Tahoe

2000 (cont'd)

Options	Price
Power Moonroof	+391
Privacy Glass [Opt on STD]	+151

Options	Price
Running Boards [Opt on LS]	+145
Third Seat	+333

1999

The standard cargo net is deleted, and new colors are added as Tahoe enters final model year on this platform.

Mileage Category: N

Body Styles	TMV Pricing		
	Trade	Private	Dealer
2 Dr LS 4WD SUV	8730	10378	12092
2 Dr LS SUV	8458	10053	11713
2 Dr LT 4WD SUV	8863	10535	12274
2 Dr LT SUV	8603	10226	11915
2 Dr STD 4WD SUV	8114	9646	11239

Body Styles	TMV Pricing		
	Trade	Private	Dealer
2 Dr STD SUV	6990	8309	9682
4 Dr LS 4WD SUV	8953	10641	12399
4 Dr LS SUV	8648	10278	11975
4 Dr LT 4WD SUV	9232	10973	12785
4 Dr LT SUV	8751	10402	12120

Options	Price
6.5L V8 Turbodiesel OHV 16V Engine	+1172
Air Conditioning [Opt on STD]	+299
Air Conditioning - Front and Rear	+195

Options	Price
Heated Front Seats	+115
OnStar Telematics System [Opt on LS,LT]	+288
Running Boards	+115

1998

Autotrac is a new optional automatic four-wheel-drive system that switches from 2WD to 4WD automatically as conditions warrant. A new option package includes heated seats and heated exterior mirrors. Second-generation airbags deploy with less force than last year. A theft-deterrent system is standard, and color selections are modified.

Mileage Category: N

Body Styles	TMV Pricing		
	Trade	Private	Dealer
2 Dr LS 4WD SUV	6769	8206	9827
2 Dr LS SUV	6374	7727	9253
2 Dr LT 4WD SUV	7410	8983	10757
2 Dr LT SUV	6422	7785	9322
2 Dr STD 4WD SUV	5857	7100	8501

Body Styles	TMV Pricing		
	Trade	Private	Dealer
2 Dr STD SUV	4907	5949	7124
4 Dr LS 4WD SUV	7542	9142	10947
4 Dr LS SUV	6594	7993	9571
4 Dr LT 4WD SUV	7582	9191	11005
4 Dr LT SUV	6816	8262	9892

Options	Price
6.5L V8 Turbodiesel OHV 16V Engine [Opt on 2 Dr]	+987
Air Conditioning [Opt on STD]	+253
Air Conditioning - Front and Rear	+164

Options	Price
Camper/Towing Package	+132
OnStar Telematics System [Opt on LS,LT]	+243

1997

A passenger-side airbag is added, and the automatic transmission is improved. Variable steering debuts, and cargo areas have a power door lock switch. A new center console comes with high-back bucket seats, and two new paint colors are available.

Mileage Category: N

Body Styles	TMV Pricing		
	Trade	Private	Dealer
2 Dr LS 4WD SUV	5946	7364	9098
2 Dr LS SUV	5390	6676	8249
2 Dr LT 4WD SUV	6682	8276	10225
2 Dr LT SUV	5562	6889	8511
2 Dr STD 4WD SUV	4964	6148	7596

Body Styles	TMV Pricing		
	Trade	Private	Dealer
2 Dr STD SUV	4398	5447	6730
4 Dr LS 4WD SUV	6112	7571	9353
4 Dr LS SUV	5397	6686	8261
4 Dr LT 4WD SUV	6730	8335	10297
4 Dr LT SUV	6010	7444	9197

Options	Price
6.5L V8 Turbodiesel OHV 16V Engine	+892
Air Conditioning [Opt on STD]	+228

Options	Price
Air Conditioning - Front and Rear	+148

1996

For 1996, Tahoe gets 50 additional horsepower and more torque out of a new 5700 V8. Other improvements include rear-seat heating ducts, quieter-riding P-metric tires, improved automatic transmissions and extended interval service schedules. Daytime running lights are new for 1996.

Mileage Category: N

Body Styles	TMV Pricing		
	Trade	Private	Dealer
2 Dr LS 4WD SUV	4564	5789	7482
2 Dr LS SUV	4235	5372	6942
2 Dr LT 4WD SUV	4969	6303	8145
2 Dr LT SUV	4282	5431	7017
2 Dr STD 4WD SUV	4176	5296	6844

Body Styles	TMV Pricing		
	Trade	Private	Dealer
2 Dr STD SUV	3220	4084	5278
4 Dr LS 4WD SUV	4982	6319	8166
4 Dr LS SUV	4312	5469	7067
4 Dr LT 4WD SUV	5411	6863	8868
4 Dr LT SUV	4459	5656	7310

Options	Price
6.5L V8 Turbodiesel OHV 16V Engine	+809

Options	Price
Air Conditioning [Opt on STD]	+207

1995

Full-size SUV gets a new name as S10-based model takes Blazer moniker. New interior with driver airbag debuts. New dashboard features modular design with controls that are much easier to read and use. New five-door model is added midyear, sized between Blazer and Suburban. New model is offered only in LS or LT trim with a 5.7-liter V8 and an automatic transmission in either 2WD or 4WD. Brake/transmission shift interlock is added to automatic transmission. New console on models with bucket seats features pivoting writing surface, along with rear cupholders and storage drawer.

Mileage Category: N

Body Styles	TMV Pricing			Body Styles	TMV Pricing		
	Trade	Private	Dealer		Trade	Private	Dealer
2 Dr LS 4WD SUV	3570	4631	6399	4 Dr LS SUV	3601	4671	6455
2 Dr LT 4WD SUV	3657	4743	6554	4 Dr LT 4WD SUV	3813	4947	6837
2 Dr STD 4WD SUV	3204	4157	5744	4 Dr LT SUV	3695	4793	6625
4 Dr LS 4WD SUV	3697	4796	6629				

Options	Price	Options	Price
6.5L V8 Turbodiesel OHV 16V Engine	+726	Automatic 4-Speed Transmission [Std on 4 Dr]	+229
Air Conditioning [Opt on STD]	+185		

Tahoe Limited/Z71

2000

Mileage Category: N

Body Styles	TMV Pricing			Body Styles	TMV Pricing		
	Trade	Private	Dealer		Trade	Private	Dealer
4 Dr Limited SUV	11923	13799	15637	4 Dr Z71 4WD SUV	13308	15402	17454

Options	Price	Options	Price
Camper/Towing Package	+127	Heated Front Seats	+140

All old-style Tahoes are dropped, except these two four-door special editions. The 4WD Z71 is for off-road use, while the 2WD Limited appeals to on-road customers.

Tracker

2004

Mileage Category: L

Body Styles	TMV Pricing			Body Styles	TMV Pricing		
	Trade	Private	Dealer		Trade	Private	Dealer
4 Dr LT 4WD SUV	11415	12614	14613	4 Dr STD SUV	10008	11208	13207
4 Dr LT SUV	10872	12072	14071	4 Dr ZR2 4WD SUV	11218	12418	14417
4 Dr STD 4WD SUV	10551	11751	13750				

Options	Price	Options	Price
Antilock Brakes	+595	Power Mirrors [Opt on STD]	+200
Cruise Control [Opt on STD]	+190	Power Windows [Opt on STD]	+350
Keyless Entry System [Opt on STD]	+150	Tilt Steering Wheel [Opt on STD]	+200
Leather Seats [Opt on ZR2, LT]	+595		

The two-door body style has been discontinued taking with it the base four-cylinder engine and the five-speed manual transmission.

2003

The aging Tracker gets only minimal changes for 2003. Yellow has been added to the color palette while LT models get monochromatic paint. Tinted windows are now available and base models get a chrome grille.

Body Styles	TMV Pricing			Body Styles	TMV Pricing		
	Trade	Private	Dealer		Trade	Private	Dealer
2 Dr STD 4WD Conv	7693	8514	9883	4 Dr LT SUV	9481	10493	12180
2 Dr STD Conv	7164	7929	9204	4 Dr STD 4WD SUV	8043	8901	10332
2 Dr ZR2 4WD Conv	9164	10143	11774	4 Dr STD SUV	7518	8321	9659
4 Dr LT 4WD SUV	10134	11216	13019	4 Dr ZR2 4WD SUV	9914	10973	12737

Options	Price	Options	Price
2.5L V6 DOHC 24V FI Engine [Opt on 4 Dr STD]	+469	Leather Seats [Opt on LT,ZR2]	+380
Aluminum/Alloy Wheels [Opt on STD]	+128	Power Door Locks [Opt on STD]	+134
Antilock Brakes	+447	Power Windows [Opt on STD]	+153
Automatic 4-Speed Transmission [Opt on 2 Dr - STD,ZR2]	+699		

2002

The Tracker gets only minor changes for 2002. An AM/FM/CD stereo is now standard equipment on all models, while both LT and ZR2 models get new alloy wheel designs. Four new colors have been added to the color palette: Medium Green Pearl Metallic, Medium Red Metallic, Light Bronzemist Metallic and Indigo Blue Metallic.

Mileage Category: L

Body Styles	TMV Pricing			Body Styles	TMV Pricing		
	Trade	Private	Dealer		Trade	Private	Dealer
2 Dr STD 4WD Conv	6121	6904	8208	4 Dr LT SUV	7654	8632	10262
2 Dr STD Conv	5554	6264	7447	4 Dr STD 4WD SUV	6266	7067	8401
2 Dr ZR2 4WD Conv	7460	8414	10003	4 Dr STD SUV	5845	6592	7837
4 Dr LT 4WD SUV	7984	9004	10705	4 Dr ZR2 4WD SUV	7802	8799	10461

2002 (cont'd)

Options	Price
Aluminum/Alloy Wheels [Opt on STD]	+209
Antilock Brakes	+401
Automatic 4-Speed Transmission [Std on LT,ZR2 4 Dr]	+573

Options	Price
Leather Seats	+341
Power Door Locks [Opt on STD]	+120
Power Windows [Opt on STD]	+137

2001

The Tracker gets two new trim packages (LT and ZR2) and a new V6 on four-door models. Air conditioning, AM/FM cassette stereo and child-seat tether anchors are now standard on all models. The base 1.6-liter engine has been dropped in favor of the more powerful 127-horsepower 2.0-liter that is now standard on all two-door and base four-door models.

Mileage Category: L

Body Styles	TMV Pricing		
	Trade	Private	Dealer
2 Dr STD 4WD Conv	4929	5979	6948
2 Dr STD Conv	4476	5429	6309
2 Dr ZR2 4WD Conv	6079	7374	8570
4 Dr LT 4WD SUV	6555	7952	9241

Body Styles	TMV Pricing		
	Trade	Private	Dealer
4 Dr LT SUV	6084	7380	8576
4 Dr STD 4WD SUV	5097	6183	7185
4 Dr STD SUV	4699	5699	6623
4 Dr ZR2 4WD SUV	6333	7681	8926

Options	Price
Aluminum/Alloy Wheels	+191
Antilock Brakes	+357
Automatic 4-Speed Transmission	+525

Options	Price
Leather Seats	+312
Power Windows	+125

2000

After a complete redesign in 1999, new colors sum up the changes for 2000.

Mileage Category: L

Body Styles	TMV Pricing		
	Trade	Private	Dealer
2 Dr STD 4WD Conv	3813	4728	5624
2 Dr STD Conv	3444	4270	5080

Body Styles	TMV Pricing		
	Trade	Private	Dealer
4 Dr STD 4WD SUV	4159	5156	6134
4 Dr STD SUV	3837	4758	5660

Options	Price
2.0L I4 DOHC 16V FI Engine [Std on 4 Dr]	+187
AM/FM/CD Audio System	+150
Air Conditioning	+437

Options	Price
Aluminum/Alloy Wheels	+171
Antilock Brakes	+318
Automatic 4-Speed Transmission	+468

1999

The redesigned-for-1999 Tracker, available in either two-door convertible or four-door hardtop versions and in two- or four-wheel drive, features sporty new looks, more power, improved ride and handling and a roomier, more comfortable interior.

Mileage Category: L

Body Styles	TMV Pricing		
	Trade	Private	Dealer
2 Dr STD 4WD Conv	3156	4055	4990
2 Dr STD Conv	2722	3497	4304

Body Styles	TMV Pricing		
	Trade	Private	Dealer
4 Dr STD 4WD SUV	3389	4354	5359
4 Dr STD SUV	3271	4203	5173

Options	Price
2.0L I4 DOHC 16V FI Engine [Std on 4 Dr]	+149
AM/FM/CD Audio System	+119
Air Conditioning	+349

Options	Price
Aluminum/Alloy Wheels	+136
Antilock Brakes	+282
Automatic 4-Speed Transmission	+373

1998

Mileage Category: L

Body Styles	TMV Pricing		
	Trade	Private	Dealer
2 Dr STD 4WD Conv	2751	3558	4469
2 Dr STD Conv	2442	3158	3966

Body Styles	TMV Pricing		
	Trade	Private	Dealer
4 Dr STD 4WD SUV	2951	3817	4793
4 Dr STD SUV	2805	3628	4557

Options	Price
AM/FM/CD Audio System	+165
AM/FM/Cassette Audio System	+165
Air Conditioning	+294
Aluminum/Alloy Wheels	+115

Options	Price
Antilock Brakes	+238
Automatic 3-Speed Transmission	+196
Automatic 4-Speed Transmission	+314

Geo is gone, so all Trackers are now badged as Chevrolets. The LSi models are dropped, though an LSi equipment package is available on Base models. Two new colors are available. Second-generation airbags are standard.

TrailBlazer

2004

Mileage Category: M

Body Styles	TMV Pricing		
	Trade	Private	Dealer
4 Dr LS 4WD SUV	17179	18635	21062
4 Dr LS SUV	15785	17206	19575

Options	Price
17 Inch Wheels	+150
AM/FM/CD Changer Audio System [Opt on LT]	+245
AM/FM/Cassette/CD Audio System	+150
Alarm System [Opt on LS]	+270
Automatic Climate Control (2 Zone) - Driver and Passenger [Opt on LT]	+225
Cruise Control [Opt on LS]	+180
DVD Entertainment System [Opt on LT]	+1295
Front Side Airbag Restraints	+350
Keyless Entry System [Opt on LS]	+270
Leather Seats [Opt on LT]	+430
Locking Differential	+270
Luggage Rack [Opt on LS]	+200
Metallic Paint [Opt on LT]	+165

Body Styles	TMV Pricing		
	Trade	Private	Dealer
4 Dr LT 4WD SUV	19205	20683	23147
4 Dr LT SUV	17279	18707	21087

Options	Price
Navigation System [Opt on LT]	+1845
OnStar Telematics System	+300
Power Adjustable Foot Pedals [Opt on LT]	+120
Power Driver Seat [Opt on LS]	+300
Power Heated Mirrors [Opt on LS]	+160
Power Moonroof	+800
Power Passenger Seat [Opt on LT]	+120
Rear Window Defroster [Opt on LS]	+200
Satellite Radio System	+325
Side Steps	+375
Skid Plates [Opt on 4WD]	+130
Traction Control System [Opt on LT 2WD]	+195
Two-Tone Paint [Opt on LT]	+150

For 2004, Chevrolet has dropped the high-line LTZ trim level. Power-adjustable pedals, a DVD-based navigation system, automatically locking doors and XM Satellite Radio are new features this year. The instrument panel now sports a freshened monochromatic look. The North Face Edition package gets unique 17-inch wheels, while all models get new 17-inch aluminum wheels.

2003

Mileage Category: M

Body Styles	TMV Pricing		
	Trade	Private	Dealer
4 Dr EXT LS 4WD SUV	16845	18346	20848
4 Dr EXT LS SUV	15692	17090	19421
4 Dr EXT LT 4WD SUV	17798	19384	22028
4 Dr EXT LT SUV	16586	18064	20528
4 Dr LS 4WD SUV	15056	16398	18635

Options	Price
5.3L V8 OHV 16V FI Engine [Opt on EXT]	+958
AM/FM/CD Changer Audio System [Opt on LT,LTZ]	+188
Bose Audio System [Opt on LT,LTZ]	+316
Cruise Control [Opt on LS]	+118
DVD Entertainment System [Opt on LT,LTZ]	+638
Front Side Airbag Restraints	+223
Heated Front Seats [Opt on EXT LT,LTZ]	+160
Leather Seats [Opt on LT]	+511
Locking Differential	+172

Body Styles	TMV Pricing		
	Trade	Private	Dealer
4 Dr LS SUV	13306	14492	16468
4 Dr LT 4WD SUV	16718	18208	20691
4 Dr LT SUV	15523	16906	19212
4 Dr LTZ 4WD SUV	18473	20120	22864
4 Dr LTZ SUV	17255	18793	21356

Options	Price
OnStar Telematics System [Opt on LS,LT]	+444
Power Driver Seat w/Memory [Opt on EXT LT]	+131
Power Moonroof	+351
Power Passenger Seat [Opt on LT]	+144
Running Boards	+239
The Northface Edition [Opt on EXT LT,LTZ]	+974
Tinted Glass [Opt on LS]	+144
Traction Control System [Opt on 2WD]	+124

For 2003, a new trim package, named The North Face Edition, comes with items that Chevy hopes will attract people who like to venture off the beaten path. Starting with a TrailBlazer LTZ or TrailBlazer EXT with the Leather Plus Package, Chevy adds body-color cladding, unique seats, mesh map pockets, rain-sensing wipers, liftgate lighting, an underfloor storage cargo liner, heavy-duty cargo mats, an adjustable cargo shelf (EXT model only) and The North Face duffel bags and blanket. Not for you? Perhaps a V8 will suit your fancy. Chevy's 5.3-liter V8 is available on the TrailBlazer EXT only. Other changes for 2003 include a larger 22-gallon fuel tank (late fall availability) and additional child-seat anchors on EXT models. Chevy has also made some previously standard equipment optional, such as the side airbags, rear cargo shade, interior lighting and auto-dimming driver-side mirror.

2002

Mileage Category: M

Body Styles	TMV Pricing		
	Trade	Private	Dealer
4 Dr EXT LT 4WD SUV	15208	16768	19367
4 Dr EXT LT SUV	14162	15614	18035
4 Dr LS 4WD SUV	12781	14092	16277
4 Dr LS SUV	11763	12969	14980

Options	Price
AM/FM/CD Changer Audio System	+169
Bose Audio System	+284
DVD Entertainment System [Opt on LS,LTZ]	+571
Heated Front Seats	+143
Leather Seats [Opt on LT]	+459
Locking Differential [Opt on 2WD]	+155

Body Styles	TMV Pricing		
	Trade	Private	Dealer
4 Dr LT 4WD SUV	14268	15732	18171
4 Dr LT SUV	13246	14605	16869
4 Dr LTZ 4WD SUV	15723	17336	20024
4 Dr LTZ SUV	14669	16174	18682

Options	Price
OnStar Telematics System [Opt on LS]	+399
Power Driver Seat w/Memory [Opt on LT]	+118
Power Moonroof	+459
Power Passenger Seat [Opt on LT]	+129
Running Boards	+215
Tinted Glass [Opt on LS]	+129

This fully redesigned TrailBlazer now sports a longer, wider and noticeably stiffer chassis, along with an all-new 4.2-liter inline six-cylinder engine and a more refined suspension compared to its predecessor, the Blazer. Unique sheet metal now differentiates the TrailBlazer from its GM cousins, the GMC Envoy and Oldsmobile Bravada, while a restyled interior makes better use of the additional passenger room. An extended wheelbase EXT model offers true seven-passenger seating and class-leading cargo capacity.

TrailBlazer EXT

2004

Power-adjustable pedals, a DVD-based navigation system, automatically locking doors and XM Satellite Radio are new options this year. Additionally, the instrument panel now sports a freshened monochromatic look. The North Face Edition package gets unique 17-inch wheels standard, while LT models get a new optional 17-inch wheel design.

Mileage Category: M

Body Styles	TMV Pricing		
	Trade	Private	Dealer
4 Dr LS 4WD SUV	19756	21203	23614
4 Dr LS SUV	17796	19168	21454

Options	Price
5.3L V8 OHV 16V FI Engine	+1500
AM/FM/CD Changer Audio System [Opt on LT]	+245
AM/FM/Cassette/CD Audio System	+150
Alarm System [Opt on LS]	+200
Automatic Climate Control (2 Zone) - Driver and Passenger [Opt on LT]	+280
Cruise Control [Opt on LS]	+170
DVD Entertainment System [Opt on LT]	+1295
Front Side Airbag Restraints	+350
Keyless Entry System [Opt on LS]	+250
Leather Seats [Opt on LT]	+300
Locking Differential	+270
Luggage Rack [Opt on LS]	+175
Metallic Paint [Opt on LT]	+165

Body Styles	TMV Pricing		
	Trade	Private	Dealer
4 Dr LT 4WD SUV	20923	22370	24781
4 Dr LT SUV	18961	20333	22619

Options	Price
Navigation System [Opt on LT]	+1845
OnStar Telematics System	+350
Power Driver Seat [Opt on LS]	+300
Power Heated Mirrors [Opt on LS]	+150
Power Moonroof	+800
Premium Audio System [Opt on LT]	+495
Satellite Radio System	+325
Side Steps	+375
Skid Plates [Opt on 4WD]	+130
Steering Wheel Radio Controls [Opt on LT]	+120
Traction Control System [Opt on LT 2WD]	+195
Two-Tone Paint [Opt on LT]	+150

Venture

2004

The standard-wheelbase Value van and the Warner Brothers edition are no longer available. An upgraded stereo with MP3 capability is now an option on LS and LT models along with XM Satellite Radio. LT models now offer the sport appearance package as an option and come standard with the DVD entertainment system when equipped with all-wheel drive. The leather seating option now includes a power passenger seat and heated front seats. Captain's chairs are now offered on the LS.

Mileage Category: P

Body Styles	TMV Pricing		
	Trade	Private	Dealer
4 Dr LS AWD Pass Van Ext	13892	15315	17685
4 Dr LS Pass Van	11683	13105	15474
4 Dr LS Pass Van Ext	11978	13370	15691
4 Dr LT Entertainer AWD Pass Van Ext	15368	16789	19158

Options	Price
16 Inch Wheels [Opt on LS FWD]	+140
7 Passenger Seating [Opt on LS FWD]	+335
8 Passenger Seating [Opt on LS,LT]	+330
AM/FM/CD Changer Audio System [Opt on LT]	+395
Antilock Brakes [Opt on Plus Ext]	+950
Automatic Load Leveling [Opt on Plus, LS]	+130
Keyless Entry System [Opt on Plus, Cargo]	+175
Leather Seats [Opt on LT]	+730

Body Styles	TMV Pricing		
	Trade	Private	Dealer
4 Dr LT Entertainer Pass Van Ext	13985	15406	17775
4 Dr Plus Pass Van	9665	11056	13375
4 Dr Plus Pass Van Ext	10443	11835	14155

Options	Price
OnStar Telematics System [Opt on non-Cargo]	+220
Power Sliding Door [Opt on LS, LT]	+210
Rear Audio Controls [Opt on LS]	+215
Rear Window Defroster [Opt on Plus]	+250
Rear Window Wiper [Opt on Plus]	+200
Sport Suspension [Opt on Plus, LS, Cargo]	+150
Traction Control System [Opt on Cargo, LS, Plus Ext]	+195
Trip Computer [Opt on Plus, LS]	+185

2003

The Venture remains relatively unchanged for 2003. Base vans now have additional color options but many previously standard features are now optional to keep prices down.

Mileage Category: P

Body Styles	TMV Pricing		
	Trade	Private	Dealer
4 Dr LS AWD Pass Van Ext	11262	12465	14469
4 Dr LS Pass Van	9470	10480	12164
4 Dr LS Pass Van Ext	9696	10732	12457
4 Dr LT AWD Pass Van Ext	13117	14517	16850
4 Dr LT Entertainer Pass Van Ext	11452	12673	14710
4 Dr LT Pass Van Ext	11131	12319	14299

Options	Price
8 Passenger Seating [Opt on LS]	+185
AM/FM/CD Audio System [Opt on STD]	+236
AM/FM/CD Changer Audio System	+252
Air Conditioning - Front and Rear [Opt on Ext - LS,STD]	+303
Aluminum/Alloy Wheels [Opt on LS,STD]	+188

Body Styles	TMV Pricing		
	Trade	Private	Dealer
4 Dr STD Pass Van	9111	10084	11704
4 Dr STD Pass Van Ext	9386	10388	12057
4 Dr Value Pass Van	7744	8571	9949
4 Dr Warner Brothers AWD Pass Van Ext	13587	15037	17454
4 Dr Warner Brothers Pass Van Ext	12907	14285	16581

Options	Price
Antilock Brakes [Opt on STD,Value]	+606
Automatic Load Leveling [Opt on LS,Warner]	+230
Heated Front Seats [Opt on LT,LT Entertainer]	+124
Leather Seats [Opt on LT,LT Entertainer]	+399
Luggage Rack [Opt on LS,STD]	+144
OnStar Telematics System [Opt on LS,LT]	+271

Options	Price
Park Distance Control (Rear) [Opt on LS,LT,Warner]	+140
Power Driver Seat [Opt on LS]	+166
Power Dual Sliding Doors [Opt on LS,LT,Warner]	+246
Power Sliding Door [Opt on LS]	+370

Options	Price
Privacy Glass [Opt on STD,Value]	+179
Rear Window Defroster [Opt on STD,Value]	+115
Traction Control System [Opt on LS,Warner]	+124
Trip Computer [Opt on LS,STD,Value]	+118

2002

The Venture becomes the first minivan to offer a factory-installed DVD video player; it comes standard on the popular Warner Bros. Edition. The WB and LT models get an all-new AWD option package. Two new colors and LATCH child safety-seat anchors sum up the changes for 2002.

Mileage Category: P

Body Styles	TMV Pricing		
	Trade	Private	Dealer
4 Dr LS AWD Pass Van Ext	9011	10085	11875
4 Dr LS Pass Van	7584	8476	9963
4 Dr LS Pass Van Ext	7879	8819	10386
4 Dr LT AWD Pass Van Ext	10987	12297	14480
4 Dr LT Pass Van Ext	9149	10239	12057
4 Dr Plus Pass Van	7515	8410	9903

Body Styles	TMV Pricing		
	Trade	Private	Dealer
4 Dr Plus Pass Van Ext	7624	8533	10048
4 Dr STD Pass Van	6971	7802	9186
4 Dr Value Pass Van	6254	6999	8241
4 Dr Warner Brothers AWD Pass Van Ext	11348	12700	14954
4 Dr Warner Brothers Pass Van Ext	9575	10702	12580

Options	Price
Air Conditioning - Front and Rear [Std on LT,Warner Brothers]	+272
Aluminum/Alloy Wheels [Opt on Plus,Value]	+169
Automatic Load Leveling [Opt on LS]	+206
Captain Chairs (4) [Opt on LS]	+166
Compact Disc Changer	+169
Leather Seats [Opt on LT]	+358
Luggage Rack [Opt on Plus]	+129

Options	Price
Park Distance Control (Rear) [Opt on LS Ext]	+126
Power Driver Seat [Std on LT,Warner Brothers]	+155
Power Dual Sliding Doors	+201
Power Sliding Door [Opt on Plus]	+201
Tinted Glass [Opt on STD]	+152
Trip Computer [Opt on LS]	+169

2001

A new grille and front fascia give the 2001 Venture an updated look, while a rear parking aid system helps keep extended wheelbase drivers from inadvertently updating the tail. OnStar is now standard on all models except the Value Van; a six-disc CD changer and fold-flat captain's chairs are available options on passenger models.

Mileage Category: P

Body Styles	TMV Pricing		
	Trade	Private	Dealer
4 Dr LS Pass Van	6148	7381	8518
4 Dr LS Pass Van Ext	6429	7717	8906
4 Dr LT Pass Van Ext	7132	8561	9881
4 Dr Plus Pass Van	5966	7162	8266

Body Styles	TMV Pricing		
	Trade	Private	Dealer
4 Dr Plus Pass Van Ext	6166	7402	8542
4 Dr Value Pass Van	5032	6040	6971
4 Dr Warner Brothers Pass Van Ext	7356	8829	10190

Options	Price
8 Passenger Seating	+152
Air Conditioning - Front and Rear [Opt on LS,Plus]	+249
Aluminum/Alloy Wheels [Opt on Plus]	+155
Automatic Load Leveling [Std on LT]	+212
Compact Disc Changer	+207

Options	Price
Leather Seats [Opt on LT]	+328
Luggage Rack [Opt on LS,Plus]	+118
Park Distance Control (Rear) [Std on LT,Warner Bros]	+115
Power Sliding Door [Opt on LS,Plus]	+378
Rear Window Defroster [Opt on Value]	+160

2000

Chevy adds two new models on either end of the price spectrum for 2000. On the low end, a new Value Van includes basic equipment for a low price, while on the high end, a Warner Bros. Edition provides leather and a video entertainment system. New radios include radio data system (RDS) on uplevel versions. Three-door models die this year, while remaining models get new interior fabric patterns and a redesigned gauge cluster with a scratch-resistant lens. Smokey Carmel is a new paint color.

Mileage Category: P

Body Styles	TMV Pricing		
	Trade	Private	Dealer
4 Dr LS Pass Van	4872	6008	7122
4 Dr LS Pass Van Ext	5204	6418	7608
4 Dr LT Pass Van Ext	5568	6867	8139
4 Dr Plus Pass Van	4753	5860	6945

Body Styles	TMV Pricing		
	Trade	Private	Dealer
4 Dr Plus Pass Van Ext	4872	6008	7122
4 Dr STD Pass Van	4449	5487	6504
4 Dr Value Pass Van	3995	4927	5840
4 Dr Warner Brothers Pass Van Ext	5841	7204	8539

Options	Price
8 Passenger Seating	+131
AM/FM/CD Audio System	+173
AM/FM/Cassette/CD Audio System [Opt on LS,Plus,STD]	+219
Air Conditioning - Front and Rear [Opt on LS,Plus]	+222
Aluminum/Alloy Wheels [Opt on Plus]	+138
Captain Chairs (4) [Std on LT]	+131

Options	Price
Leather Seats [Opt on LT]	+419
OnStar Telematics System	+419
Power Driver Seat	+126
Power Sliding Door [Opt on LS,Plus]	+210
Rear Window Defroster [Opt on Value]	+143

Chevrolet
Venture

1999

Venture gets some performance and safety enhancements. Other changes include additional seating choices, four new exterior and two new interior colors, as well as wider standard tires. There's a new LT model that packages an upgraded audio system with a touring suspension, traction control and captain's seats with available leather.

Mileage Category: P

Body Styles	TMV Pricing		
	Trade	Private	Dealer
3 Dr STD Pass Van	3680	4641	5642
4 Dr LS Pass Van	4307	5382	6500
4 Dr LS Pass Van Ext	4528	5711	6943

Options	Price
AM/FM/CD Audio System	+139
AM/FM/Cassette/CD Audio System [Std on LT]	+175
Air Conditioning - Front and Rear [Std on LT]	+178

Body Styles	TMV Pricing		
	Trade	Private	Dealer
4 Dr LT Pass Van Ext	4887	6164	7494
4 Dr STD Pass Van	3962	4945	5968
4 Dr STD Pass Van Ext	4168	5256	6389

Options	Price
Leather Seats	+334
OnStar Telematics System [Opt on LS,LT]	+371
Power Sliding Door [Std on LT]	+168

1998

Venture is the first minivan to get side-impact airbags. Other changes include the availability of a cargo van edition, a wider variety of dual door models, and an optional power sliding door on regular wheelbase vans. Power rear window vents are also added for 1998. Front airbags deploy with less force thanks to second-generation technology.

Mileage Category: P

Body Styles	TMV Pricing		
	Trade	Private	Dealer
3 Dr LS Pass Van	3076	4017	5077
3 Dr LS Pass Van Ext	3246	4237	5354

Options	Price
AM/FM/CD Audio System	+116
AM/FM/Cassette/CD Audio System	+148
Air Conditioning - Front and Rear	+141
Bucket Seats	+141

Body Styles	TMV Pricing		
	Trade	Private	Dealer
3 Dr STD Pass Van	2784	3635	4594
3 Dr STD Pass Van Ext	3048	3979	5029

Options	Price
OnStar Telematics System [Opt on LS]	+313
Power Sliding Door	+137
Sliding Driver Side Door	+121

1997

Complete redesign of Chevy's minivan results in a new name, a left-side sliding door, optional traction control, a powerful standard engine and a fun-to-drive demeanor.

Mileage Category: P

Body Styles	TMV Pricing		
	Trade	Private	Dealer
3 Dr LS Pass Van	2495	3379	4460
3 Dr LS Pass Van Ext	2592	3510	4632

Options	Price
AM/FM/Cassette/CD Audio System	+133
Air Conditioning - Front and Rear	+128

Body Styles	TMV Pricing		
	Trade	Private	Dealer
3 Dr STD Pass Van	2312	3130	4130
3 Dr STD Pass Van Ext	2480	3358	4432

Options	Price
Bucket Seats [Opt on LS]	+128
Power Sliding Door	+128

300M

2004

Mileage Category: H

Body Styles	TMV Pricing				Body Styles	TMV Pricing		
	Trade	Private	Dealer			Trade	Private	Dealer
4 Dr STD Sdn	16698	17871	19827		4 Dr Special Sdn	19251	20464	22485

Options	Price		Options	Price
Power Sunroof	+895		Sport Suspension [Opt on Special]	+260
Satellite Radio System	+520			

For 2004, the 300M's notable upgrades come in the form of a six-disc changer and optional Sirius Satellite Radio. Both the 300M and 300M Special now offer a navigation system that offers voice prompts and comes with a 360-watt premium sound system.

2003

Mileage Category: H

Body Styles	TMV Pricing				Body Styles	TMV Pricing		
	Trade	Private	Dealer			Trade	Private	Dealer
4 Dr STD Sdn	13712	14793	16594		4 Dr Special Sdn	16058	17324	19435

Options	Price		Options	Price
17 Inch Wheels - Chrome [Opt on STD]	+447		Power Moonroof	+534
AM/FM/Cassette/CD Changer Audio System [Opt on STD]	+262		Sport Suspension [Opt on Special]	+334
Front Side Airbag Restraints	+233		Tire Pressure Monitoring System [Opt on STD]	+149
Leather and Wood Steering Wheel [Opt on STD]	+149			

For 2003, Chrysler introduces the option of a factory-installed Sirius Satellite Radio, a first for Chrysler vehicles. Other changes include an updated audio system that features a six-disc CD changer in place of the old four-disc unit.

2002

Mileage Category: H

Body Styles	TMV Pricing				Body Styles	TMV Pricing		
	Trade	Private	Dealer			Trade	Private	Dealer
4 Dr STD Sdn	11527	12688	14624		4 Dr Special Sdn	13025	14337	16524

Options	Price		Options	Price
17 Inch Wheels - Chrome	+390		Power Moonroof	+466
Front Side Airbag Restraints	+203		Sport Suspension	+291

A special 300M debuts this year, called the Special. Designed to appeal to performance enthusiasts, the Special comes with 18-inch wheels wearing 245/45ZR18 Michelin Pilot Sport tires, a firmer suspension, increased-effort steering and an upgraded brake system. All models get a revised grille.

2001

Mileage Category: H

Body Styles	TMV Pricing		
	Trade	Private	Dealer
4 Dr STD Sdn	9888	11509	13005

Options	Price		Options	Price
Chrome Wheels	+336		Power Moonroof	+401
Compact Disc Changer	+231		Sport Package	+251
Front Side Airbag Restraints	+175			

DaimlerChrysler ups the feature content for the 300M by including standard steering wheel controls for the stereo, offering the option of side airbags and adding a luxury group package that includes real wood trim and an overhead console-mounted vehicle information center. The rear end gets a makeover in the form of clear-lens taillamps and chrome dual-exhaust outlets while new 17-inch wheels and anodized aluminum window trim dresses up the 300M's profile. There's now a three-point shoulder/lap belt for the central rear-seat passenger and an internal emergency trunk release. Additional luxury package features include an auto-dimming rearview mirror and exterior mirrors that tilt down automatically when the vehicle is placed in reverse. Two new exterior colors (Black and Deep Sapphire Blue) plus three new interior colors (Sandstone, Dark Slate Grey and Taupe) round out the changes for 2001.

2000

Mileage Category: H

Body Styles	TMV Pricing		
	Trade	Private	Dealer
4 Dr STD Sdn	7491	9100	10677

Options	Price		Options	Price
Chrome Wheels	+254		Power Moonroof	+289
Compact Disc Changer	+187			

There are five new colors, interior upgrades such as rear-seat cupholders and color-keyed switches and a four-disc in-dash CD player. The rear suspension has been improved for less noise, vibration and harshness. The 2000 has the brake-shift interlock safety feature, which won't allow the driver to shift out of "Park" unless his foot is on the brake.

1999

Mileage Category: H

Body Styles	TMV Pricing		
	Trade	Private	Dealer
4 Dr STD Sdn	5494	6983	8532

This all-new car from Chrysler will try to win some international recognition for the marque.

300M/Cirrus

1999 (cont'd)

Options	Price
Chrome Wheels	+202

Options	Price
Power Moonroof	+230

Cirrus

2000

Mileage Category: C

Body Styles	TMV Pricing		
	Trade	Private	Dealer
4 Dr LX Sdn	3794	4838	5861

Options	Price
AM/FM/CD Audio System	+123
Antilock Brakes [Opt on LX]	+247
Automatic 4-Speed Transmission [Opt on LX]	+381
Chrome Wheels	+127

Body Styles	TMV Pricing		
	Trade	Private	Dealer
4 Dr LXi Sdn	4217	5377	6514

Options	Price
Compact Disc Changer	+138
Power Driver Seat [Opt on LX]	+118
Premium Audio System [Opt on LX]	+205

With a redesigned Cirrus successor modeled after the exceptionally attractive Concorde due in showrooms for 2001, the 2000 model is essentially a carryover model. Child-seat tethers have been added behind the backseat, and four new colors debut.

1999

A slightly revised suspension gives the Cirrus a softer ride, and the interior improvements include a new instrument cluster and lower NVH levels. Outside, 15-inch chrome wheel covers are standard, and a winged Chrysler badge now decorates the front grille.

Mileage Category: C

Body Styles		TMV Pricing		
		Trade	Private	Dealer
4 Dr LXi Sdn		3133	4157	5223

Options	Price
Compact Disc Changer	+159
Leather Seats	+289

Options	Price
Power Moonroof	+168

1998

LX model is dropped. A powered driver seat, a 2.5-liter V6 engine, a tilt wheel and power windows, locks, and mirrors are now standard equipment. The LXi also comes in five new colors and as with all other Chrysler products, depowered airbags are standard.

Mileage Category: C

Body Styles		TMV Pricing		
		Trade	Private	Dealer
4 Dr LXi Sdn		2464	3445	4552

Options	Price
Compact Disc Changer	+136
Leather Seats	+247

Options	Price
Power Moonroof	+143

1997

The LXi trim level gets chrome wheels and the LX gets optional aluminum wheels. The Gold Package is also available on the LX. An in-dash CD changer is now available on LX and LXi models, as is a trip computer.

Mileage Category: C

Body Styles	TMV Pricing		
	Trade	Private	Dealer
4 Dr LX Sdn	1729	2503	3448

Options	Price
2.5L V6 SOHC 24V FI Engine	+165

Body Styles	TMV Pricing		
	Trade	Private	Dealer
4 Dr LXi Sdn	1993	2884	3974

1996

Base LX model gets a four-cylinder engine. Uplevel LXi gets a revised torque converter for better V6 response. A power sunroof, chrome-plated aluminum wheels and new colors are available for 1996.

Mileage Category: C

Body Styles	TMV Pricing		
	Trade	Private	Dealer
4 Dr LX Sdn	1317	2021	2993

Options	Price
2.5L V6 SOHC 24V FI Engine [Opt on LX]	+142

Body Styles	TMV Pricing		
	Trade	Private	Dealer
4 Dr LXi Sdn	1574	2416	3579

1995

The Cirrus is replacing the LeBaron sedan. A cab-forward design, a 164-horsepower V6 coupled with an automatic transmission, dual airbags, antilock brakes, air conditioning, power door locks and power windows are just a few of the improvements this car has over the LeBaron.

Mileage Category: C

Body Styles	TMV Pricing		
	Trade	Private	Dealer
4 Dr LX Sdn	1058	1729	2848

Body Styles	TMV Pricing		
	Trade	Private	Dealer
4 Dr LXi Sdn	1154	1886	3107

Concorde

2004

Body Styles	TMV Pricing		
	Trade	Private	Dealer
4 Dr LX Sdn	11207	12193	13835
4 Dr LXi Sdn	13004	14031	15742

Options	Price
17 Inch Wheels [Opt on LXi]	+400
AM/FM/CD Audio System [Opt on LX]	+125
Antilock Brakes [Std on Limited]	+600
Power Moonroof	+895

Body Styles	TMV Pricing		
	Trade	Private	Dealer
4 Dr Limited Sdn	14184	15194	16877

Options	Price
Special Factory Paint	+200
Split Front Bench Seat [Opt on LX, LXi]	+150
Touring Suspension [Opt on LXi]	+300
Traction Control System [Opt on LXi]	+300

The Concorde gets only minor changes to the front fascia design for 2004.

2003

Body Styles	TMV Pricing		
	Trade	Private	Dealer
4 Dr LX Sdn	8906	9715	11063
4 Dr LXi Sdn	10918	11910	13562

Options	Price
17 Inch Wheels - Chrome [Opt on LXi]	+388
AM/FM/CD Audio System [Opt on LX]	+119
AM/FM/Cassette/CD Changer Audio System	+253
Aluminum/Alloy Wheels [Opt on LX]	+209
Antilock Brakes [Std on Limited]	+406

Body Styles	TMV Pricing		
	Trade	Private	Dealer
4 Dr Limited Sdn	12640	13788	15701

Options	Price
Front Side Airbag Restraints	+233
Leather and Wood Steering Wheel [Opt on Limited]	+149
Power Moonroof	+534
Special Factory Paint	+119
Traction Control System [Opt on LXi]	+149

Three new colors -- Deep Lava Red, Brilliant Black Crystal and Deep Graphite -- burst onto the palette. Instead of a four-disc in-dash CD changer, you now get to insert six discs.

2002

Body Styles	TMV Pricing		
	Trade	Private	Dealer
4 Dr LX Sdn	7027	7796	9078
4 Dr LXi Sdn	8450	9374	10915

Options	Price
16 Inch Wheels [Opt on LX]	+182
17 Inch Wheels - Chrome [Opt on LXi]	+338
AM/FM/CD Changer Audio System [Opt on Limited]	+130
AM/FM/Cassette/CD Changer Audio System	+195

Body Styles	TMV Pricing		
	Trade	Private	Dealer
4 Dr Limited Sdn	10702	11874	13826

Options	Price
Antilock Brakes [Std on Limited]	+354
Front Side Airbag Restraints	+203
Power Moonroof	+487
Traction Control System [Opt on LXi]	+130

The Concorde goes uptown by adopting the LHS' (which is dropped this year) front and rear styling. More power is on tap for the LXi. And a new trim level debuts -- the Limited, which essentially replaces the LHS.

2001

Body Styles	TMV Pricing		
	Trade	Private	Dealer
4 Dr LX Sdn	5817	6864	7831

Options	Price
AM/FM/Cassette/CD Changer Audio System [Opt on LXi]	+258
Aluminum/Alloy Wheels [Opt on LX]	+164
Antilock Brakes [Opt on LX]	+305
Chrome Wheels	+269
Front Side Airbag Restraints	+175

Body Styles	TMV Pricing		
	Trade	Private	Dealer
4 Dr LXi Sdn	7035	8301	9469

Options	Price
Leather Seats [Opt on LX]	+336
Power Moonroof	+425
Power Passenger Seat [Opt on LX]	+170
Premium Audio System [Opt on LX]	+258

Supplemental side airbags are a new option for the year, and an internal trunk release and center shoulder belt for the rear seat are standard. A center console power outlet exists for those models equipped with bucket seats, and all models get steering wheel-mounted audio controls. Two new exterior colors and three new interior colors are available this year, and both engines now meet LEV standards for all 50 states.

2000

Body Styles	TMV Pricing		
	Trade	Private	Dealer
4 Dr LX Sdn	4751	5757	6744

Options	Price
AM/FM/Cassette/CD Audio System [Opt on LX]	+134
Aluminum/Alloy Wheels [Opt on LX]	+132
Antilock Brakes [Opt on LX]	+247

Body Styles	TMV Pricing		
	Trade	Private	Dealer
4 Dr LXi Sdn	5430	6580	7708

Options	Price
Chrome Wheels	+218
Compact Disc Changer	+127
Infinity Audio System	+134

All models are given a more refined touring suspension, and variable-assist, speed-proportional steering is standard on LXi. Five new colors come aboard, and the instrument panel has been freshened.

2000 (cont'd)

Options	Price
Leather Seats [Opt on LX]	+361
Power Moonroof	+289

Options	Price
Power Passenger Seat [Opt on LX]	+138

1999

Bigger sway bar links and tubular rear trailing arms will be phased in during the model year, two changes that Chrysler promises will provide more road isolation for a more luxurious ride. Premium carpeting is added to the interior, and the LXi leather is improved.

Mileage Category: G

Body Styles	TMV Pricing		
	Trade	Private	Dealer
4 Dr LX Sdn	3931	4898	5904

Body Styles	TMV Pricing		
	Trade	Private	Dealer
4 Dr LXi Sdn	4269	5320	6414

Options	Price
Antilock Brakes [Opt on LX]	+218
Leather Seats [Opt on LX]	+287

Options	Price
Power Moonroof	+230
Power Passenger Seat [Opt on LX]	+122

1998

The Concorde is all new for 1998. The only thing they didn't change is the name.

Mileage Category: G

Body Styles	TMV Pricing		
	Trade	Private	Dealer
4 Dr LX Sdn	3217	4179	5264

Body Styles	TMV Pricing		
	Trade	Private	Dealer
4 Dr LXi Sdn	3472	4511	5683

Options	Price
Antilock Brakes [Opt on LX]	+186
Leather Seats	+245

Options	Price
Power Moonroof	+196

1997

Mileage Category: G

Body Styles	TMV Pricing		
	Trade	Private	Dealer
4 Dr LX Sdn	2328	3125	4098

Body Styles	TMV Pricing		
	Trade	Private	Dealer
4 Dr LXi Sdn	2935	3939	5165

Options	Price
AM/FM/Cassette/CD Audio System	+124
Antilock Brakes [Std on LXi]	+156

Options	Price
Leather Seats [Opt on LX]	+206
Power Moonroof	+149

The 3.5-liter engine is now standard on the LX trim level. An upgraded stereo debuts along with hood-mounted windshield-washer nozzles. The automatic transmission receives refinements.

1996

Improved headlight illumination, a revised exterior appearance, a quieter interior and new colors bow on all Concorde models. Base cars get standard 16-inch wheels. LXi models get gold-accented wheels and trim.

Mileage Category: G

Body Styles	TMV Pricing		
	Trade	Private	Dealer
4 Dr LX Sdn	1647	2295	3190

Body Styles	TMV Pricing		
	Trade	Private	Dealer
4 Dr LXi Sdn	2047	2854	3969

Options	Price
3.5L V6 SOHC 24V FI Engine	+128
Leather Seats [Opt on LX]	+177

Options	Price
Power Moonroof	+128

1995

No significant changes for the 1995 Concorde.

Mileage Category: G

Body Styles	TMV Pricing		
	Trade	Private	Dealer
4 Dr STD Sdn	1401	2004	3010

Options	Price
3.5L V6 SOHC 24V FI Engine	+106
Leather Seats	+146

Options	Price
Power Moonroof	+106

Crossfire
2004

Body Styles	*Mileage Category: E* TMV Pricing		
	Trade	Private	Dealer
2 Dr STD Hbk	20168	22276	25789

Options	Price
Automatic 5-Speed Transmission	+1075

For 2004, Chrysler introduces an all-new sport coupe called the Crossfire. The first true product of the Mercedes-Chrysler collaborative effort, the Crossfire is designed to lure traditional luxury import buyers away from the likes of Acura, Infiniti and Audi and into a Chrysler showroom instead.

Grand Voyager
2000

Body Styles	*Mileage Category: P* TMV Pricing			Body Styles	TMV Pricing		
	Trade	Private	Dealer		Trade	Private	Dealer
4 Dr SE Pass Van Ext	5917	7165	8388	4 Dr STD Pass Van Ext	5500	6660	7798

Options	Price	Options	Price
Air Conditioning - Front and Rear [Opt on SE]	+218	Camper/Towing Package	+158
Aluminum/Alloy Wheels [Opt on SE]	+151	Captain Chairs (4) [Opt on SE]	+252
Antilock Brakes [Opt on STD]	+247	Infinity Audio System [Opt on SE]	+152

With Plymouth's impending death, the Grand Voyager turns into a Chrysler this year, but it is otherwise unchanged. Four new colors and a new Value-Plus option package that includes a V6 and power features are new this year.

LHS
2001

Body Styles	*Mileage Category: H* TMV Pricing		
	Trade	Private	Dealer
4 Dr STD Sdn	7564	8803	9948

Options	Price	Options	Price
Compact Disc Changer	+231	Power Moonroof	+401
Front Side Airbag Restraints	+175		

An optional luxury package includes automatic adjusting side mirrors, electrochromic driver-side mirror, walnut wood trim and an overhead console-mounted vehicle information display. There's an additional electrical power outlet in the center console, an overhead console with a driver information display, standard steering wheel-mounted stereo controls and three new interior colors. The LHS' 17-inch wheels now come in a Sparkle Silver finish while aluminum replaces the chrome window molding trim and two new exterior colors, Black and Deep Sapphire Blue Pearl Coat, further dress up this upscale sedan. For safety's sake, an internal trunk release and a center shoulder belt for the rear seat come standard while side airbags are now optional for front passengers.

2000

Body Styles	*Mileage Category: H* TMV Pricing		
	Trade	Private	Dealer
4 Dr STD Sdn	6015	7395	8748

Options	Price	Options	Price
Chrome Wheels	+254	Power Moonroof	+289
Compact Disc Changer	+187		

Nothing dramatically changes for 2000. There are interior upgrades, including an in-dash four-disc CD changer, and a modified rear suspension for less noise, vibration and harshness. An automatic transaxle brake-shift interlock is now standard, and there are four more color choices.

1999

Body Styles	*Mileage Category: H* TMV Pricing		
	Trade	Private	Dealer
4 Dr STD Sdn	4597	5985	7429

Options	Price	Options	Price
Chrome Wheels	+202	Power Moonroof	+230

The luxury-tuned LHS has been completely redesigned for 1999.

1997

Mileage Category: H

Body Styles	TMV Pricing		
	Trade	Private	Dealer
4 Dr STD Sdn	2966	4145	5587

Options	Price
Power Moonroof	+165

The automatic transmission receives some fine-tuning.

1996

A quieter interior and new colors entice buyers for 1996. Revised sound systems and a HomeLink Universal transmitter that opens your garage door for you when you pull in the driveway debut.

Mileage Category: H

Body Styles	TMV Pricing		
	Trade	Private	Dealer
4 Dr STD Sdn	1950	2892	4193

Options	Price
Power Moonroof	+141

1995

No changes this year.

Mileage Category: H

Body Styles	TMV Pricing		
	Trade	Private	Dealer
4 Dr STD Sdn	1510	2330	3696

Options	Price
Power Moonroof	+117

Le Baron

1995

Mileage Category: C

Body Styles	TMV Pricing		
	Trade	Private	Dealer
2 Dr GTC Conv	1047	1712	2819

Options	Price	Options	Price
Antilock Brakes	+111	Leather Seats	+110

The last of the K-Cars, the LeBaron convertible rides into the sunset in GTC trim.

New Yorker

1996

Mileage Category: H

Body Styles	TMV Pricing		
	Trade	Private	Dealer
4 Dr STD Sdn	2016	2990	4334

Options	Price	Options	Price
Leather Seats	+192	Power Moonroof	+141

After a short 1996 production run, the New Yorker is cut from the lineup in favor of the more popular LHS.

1995

No changes to the New Yorker this year.

Mileage Category: H

Body Styles	TMV Pricing		
	Trade	Private	Dealer
4 Dr STD Sdn	1344	2075	3292

Options	Price	Options	Price
Infinity Audio System	+96	Power Moonroof	+117
Leather Seats	+159		

Pacifica

2004

Mileage Category: H

Body Styles	TMV Pricing			Body Styles	TMV Pricing		
	Trade	Private	Dealer		Trade	Private	Dealer
4 Dr STD AWD Wgn	18176	19355	21319	4 Dr STD Wgn	15856	17011	18937

Options	Price	Options	Price
17 Inch Wheels - Chrome	+750	Heated Front and Rear Seats	+500
AM/FM/Cassette/CD Audio System	+700	Leather Seats	+890
Automatic On/Off Headlights [Std on AWD]	+200	Navigation System	+1595
Compact Disc Changer	+250	Power Driver Seat w/Memory [Opt on FWD]	+200
DVD Entertainment System	+305	Power Moonroof	+895
Fog Lights [Std on AWD]	+150	Power Rear Liftgate	+400
Front Side Airbag Restraints [Opt on FWD]	+200	Special Factory Paint	+225
Front, Rear and Third Row Head Airbag Restraints [Opt on FWD]	+400	Xenon Headlamps	+500

The Pacifica is an all-new six-passenger vehicle that combines the attributes of a wagon, minivan and SUV.

Prowler

2002

Mileage Category: F

Body Styles	TMV Pricing		
	Trade	Private	Dealer
2 Dr STD Conv	27721	29542	32577

Options	Price
Special Factory Paint	+234

One new color, Inca Gold, is added.

2001

Mileage Category: F

Body Styles	TMV Pricing		
	Trade	Private	Dealer
2 Dr STD Conv	24771	27135	29317

Options	Price
Special Factory Paint	+897

In January, the Plymouth brand was dropped from the Prowler name, and it became a Chrysler. To mark the change, a new "Mulholland Edition" was introduced in a dark blue coupe with white pinstriping. Also new this year, Chrysler is offering two new paint schemes for its Prowler. A two-tone version (the top of the car will be black and the sides will be silver), called the "Black Tie Edition," will appear. It also includes a silver instrument cluster bezel and silver floor mats. And, later in 2001, a new color, Prowler Orange, will also be available. Silver will still be offered, but red, yellow, black and purple are discontinued.

PT Cruiser

2004

Mileage Category: L

Body Styles	TMV Pricing			Body Styles	TMV Pricing		
	Trade	Private	Dealer		Trade	Private	Dealer
4 Dr Dream Cruiser 3 Turbo Wgn	15561	16904	19141	4 Dr Limited Wgn	10882	11856	13478
4 Dr GT Turbo Wgn	13740	14970	17020	4 Dr STD Wgn	8751	9710	11307
4 Dr Limited Edition Platinum Series Wgn	12407	13388	15024	4 Dr Touring Edition Turbo Wgn	10725	11725	13391
4 Dr Limited Edition Turbo Wgn	12124	13134	14816	4 Dr Touring Wgn	9693	10659	12268

Options	Price	Options	Price
AM/FM/CD Changer Audio System [Std on Dream Crsr, Platinum Ser]	+200	Heated Front Seats [Std on Dream Crsr]	+250
Aluminum/Alloy Wheels [Opt on STD]	+570	Keyless Entry System [Opt on STD]	+200
Antilock Brakes [Std on Dream Crsr, GT]	+595	Navigation System [Opt on Touring, Limited, GT]	+1000
Automatic 4-Speed Transmission [Opt on Dream Crsr, GT]	+440	Power Moonroof [Opt on Touring]	+695
Chrome Wheels [Opt on Touring]	+700	Privacy Glass [Opt on STD]	+275
Front Side Airbag Restraints [Opt on STD, Touring]	+390	Rear Spoiler [Std on Dream Crsr, GT]	+150

For 2004, a PT Dream Cruiser Series 3 "True Blue" model is available in limited production. Also, a 180-horsepower turbocharged engine will be available on the Limited and Touring Edition models. Additionally, a Chrome Accent Group is available for the Limited that includes various exterior accents (including a chrome fuel door), as well as metallic-finish pedals and shift knob.

2003

The PT Turbo debuts with a 215-horsepower engine that gives the unique and versatile Cruiser a much needed boost in performance.

Mileage Category: L

Body Styles	TMV Pricing		
	Trade	Private	Dealer
4 Dr Dream Cruiser Series 2 Turbo Wgn	12361	13593	15647
4 Dr GT Turbo Wgn	11489	12634	14543
4 Dr Limited Wgn	9427	10367	11933

Options	Price
17 Inch Wheels - Chrome [Opt on GT]	+358
Antilock Brakes [Opt on Limited,STD,Touring]	+447
Automatic 4-Speed Transmission	+262
Chrome Wheels [Opt on Touring]	+358
Cruise Control [Opt on STD]	+140
Front Side Airbag Restraints [Opt on GT,STD,Touring]	+233
Heated Front Seats [Opt on GT,Limited]	+149

Body Styles	TMV Pricing		
	Trade	Private	Dealer
4 Dr STD Wgn	7766	8540	9830
4 Dr Touring Wgn	8222	9041	10406

Options	Price
Keyless Entry System [Opt on STD]	+119
Power Door Locks [Opt on STD]	+134
Power Moonroof [Opt on GT,Touring]	+415
Privacy Glass [Opt on STD]	+164
Special Factory Paint	+119
Special Graphics	+295

2002

Taking a cue from custom cars of the past, Chrysler offers a flame-accented paint job on its popular retro-styled PT Cruiser. The optional flames, which are actually a decal. Also, two new trim levels debut this year: the Touring Edition (which was previously an option package) and the Dream Cruiser. A Woodie appearance option is also available.

Mileage Category: L

Body Styles	TMV Pricing		
	Trade	Private	Dealer
4 Dr Dream Cruiser Series I Wgn	9933	11095	13031
4 Dr Limited Edition Wgn	8542	9541	11205

Options	Price
Antilock Brakes [Std on Dream Cruiser]	+390
Automatic 4-Speed Transmission	+429
Chrome Wheels [Opt on Touring]	+312
Cruise Control [Std on Dream Cruiser,Limited]	+122
Front Side Airbag Restraints [Std on Dream Cruiser,Limited]	+182

Body Styles	TMV Pricing		
	Trade	Private	Dealer
4 Dr STD Wgn	7053	7867	9224
4 Dr Touring Edition Wgn	7337	8195	9624

Options	Price
Heated Front Seats [Std on Dream Cruiser]	+130
Power Door Locks [Opt on STD]	+117
Power Moonroof [Opt on STD]	+310
Privacy Glass [Opt on STD]	+143
Special Graphics	+258

2001

Classic styling and modern utility were the guiding forces behind Chrysler's all-new PT Cruiser. Based loosely on the Neon platform, this small van offers a flexible interior, head-turning looks and, sadly, only 150 horsepower. But feature content is high and a more powerful engine is reportedly in the works for 2002.

Mileage Category: L

Body Styles	TMV Pricing		
	Trade	Private	Dealer
4 Dr Limited Edition Wgn	7354	8668	9881

Options	Price
Aluminum/Alloy Wheels	+135
Antilock Brakes	+336
Automatic 4-Speed Transmission	+370
Chrome Wheels [Opt on STD]	+179

Body Styles	TMV Pricing		
	Trade	Private	Dealer
4 Dr STD Wgn	5854	6901	7868

Options	Price
Front Side Airbag Restraints [Opt on STD]	+157
Power Moonroof [Opt on STD]	+269
Privacy Glass [Opt on STD]	+123

Sebring

2004

The Sebring's former trim designations have been replaced with base, Touring and Limited while GTC trim carries over unchanged. Sedan and convertible models receive a restyled front fascia and new wheels, while the coupe gets new dash, door and instrument panel trim. Low-speed traction control now comes on all models equipped with antilock brakes.

Mileage Category: D

Body Styles	TMV Pricing		
	Trade	Private	Dealer
2 Dr GTC Conv	11880	13196	15389
2 Dr LX Conv	11353	12656	14829
2 Dr Limited Conv	16598	18080	20551
2 Dr Limited Cpe	10829	12047	14077
2 Dr Limited Platinum Series Cpe	11295	12539	14612
2 Dr STD Conv	11353	12670	14864
2 Dr STD Cpe	9129	10108	11739

Options	Price
17 Inch Wheels - Chrome [Opt on Limited, Limited Plat Cpe]	+750
AM/FM/Cassette/CD Changer Audio System [Opt on Limited Sdn, GTC Conv]	+200
Antilock Brakes [Std on Limited Conv, GTC Conv]	+400
Front Side Airbag Restraints [Opt on Cpe]	+390

Body Styles	TMV Pricing		
	Trade	Private	Dealer
2 Dr Touring Conv	13409	14683	16806
2 Dr Touring Platinum Series Conv	13478	14843	17119
4 Dr LX Sdn	9233	10352	12217
4 Dr Limited Sdn	10965	12193	14240
4 Dr STD Sdn	9410	10529	12394
4 Dr Touring Platinum Series Sdn	9838	10956	12820
4 Dr Touring Sdn	9258	10377	12242

Options	Price
Front and Rear Head Airbag Restraints [Opt on Sdn]	+390
Heated Front Seats [Opt on Limited Conv, Lxi Conv, Touring Conv]	+250
Leather Seats [Opt on Limited Cpe, STD, Touring Sdn]	+800
Power Driver Seat [Opt on STD, GTC Conv, STD, Touring Sdn]	+150

Options	Price
Power Moonroof [Opt on STD, Touring Sdn]	+695
Traction Control System [Opt on non-Limited, Limited Cpe]	+300

Options	Price
Trip Computer [Opt on STD, Touring Sdn]	+200

2003

For 2003, a six-disc in-dash CD changer replaces last year's four-disc in-dash model in the Sebring convertible. The Sebring LX sedan has been dressed with new 15-inch painted 10-spoke wheel covers. And the Sebring coupe gets a complete makeover this year. Its exterior has been freshened with a new hood, front and rear fascias, side sill moldings, deck lid, grille, headlamps, taillamps and foglamps. Within its cabin, the Sebring coupe gets a new instrument panel, gauge cluster, center console, center stack, door trim style and bezel surface appearance.

Mileage Category: D

Body Styles	TMV Pricing		
	Trade	Private	Dealer
2 Dr GTC Conv	10827	11904	13699
2 Dr LX Conv	10229	11290	13059
2 Dr LX Cpe	8519	9250	10468
2 Dr LXi Conv	11877	12939	14710

Body Styles	TMV Pricing		
	Trade	Private	Dealer
2 Dr LXi Cpe	9809	10651	12054
2 Dr Limited Conv	14668	15979	18165
4 Dr LX Sdn	7744	8437	9591
4 Dr LXi Sdn	8310	9053	10291

Options	Price
16 Inch Wheels - Chrome [Opt on LXi Sdn]	+447
17 Inch Wheels - Chrome [Opt on LXi Cpe]	+447
AM/FM/Cassette/CD Changer Audio System [Opt on GTC,Limited,LXi]	+179
Aluminum/Alloy Wheels [Opt on LX]	+233
Antilock Brakes [Std on GTC,Limited]	+429
Compact Disc Changer [Opt on LX Cvt]	+253
Cruise Control [Opt on LX Cvt]	+140
Front Side Airbag Restraints [Opt on LX Cpe,LXi Cpe]	+233
Front and Rear Head Airbag Restraints [Opt on LX Sdn,LXi Sdn]	+268

Options	Price
Heated Front Seats [Opt on Limited Cnv,LXi Cnv,LXi Sdn]	+149
Infinity Audio System [Opt on GTC Cnv,LXi Cnv]	+283
Leather Seats [Opt on LXi Cpe,LXi Sdn]	+304
Power Driver Seat [Std on Limited Cnv,LXi Cnv,LXi Sdn]	+122
Power Moonroof [Opt on LX Cpe,LXi Cpe,LXi Sdn]	+415
Premium Audio System [Opt on LXi Sdn]	+149
Special Factory Paint	+119
Sport Suspension [Opt on LXi Sdn]	+116

2002

Even though it was revamped last year, the Sebring line receives a number of changes. An Enthusiast package for the sedan debuts, as will a sporty GTC convertible later in the model year. And to put the Sebring ragtop in reach of more buyers, a lower-priced LX version with the 2.4-liter inline four becomes available.

Mileage Category: D

Body Styles	TMV Pricing		
	Trade	Private	Dealer
2 Dr GTC Conv	9893	10918	12626
2 Dr LX Conv	9078	10154	11948
2 Dr LX Cpe	7605	8347	9584
2 Dr LXi Conv	10313	11381	13162
2 Dr LXi Cpe	8571	9408	10804

Body Styles	TMV Pricing		
	Trade	Private	Dealer
2 Dr Limited Conv	11763	12982	15013
4 Dr LX Plus Sdn	6618	7304	8446
4 Dr LX Sdn	6519	7168	8249
4 Dr LXi Sdn	7630	8421	9738

Options	Price
17 Inch Wheels - Chrome [Opt on LXi Cpe]	+390
2.7L V6 DOHC 24V FI Engine [Opt on LX,LX Plus]	+442
3.0L V6 SOHC 24V FI Engine [Opt on LX Cpe]	+460
AM/FM/CD Changer Audio System [Opt on LX Cpe]	+174
Aluminum/Alloy Wheels [Opt on LX,LX Plus]	+169
Antilock Brakes [Std on GTC,Limited]	+375
Chrome Wheels [Opt on LXi Sdn]	+312
Compact Disc Changer	+130

Options	Price
Cruise Control [Opt on LX Conv,LX Sdn]	+122
Front and Rear Head Airbag Restraints [Opt on Sdn]	+203
Heated Front Seats [Opt on Conv - Limited,LXi]	+130
Infinity Audio System [Opt on Conv - GTC,LX]	+247
Leather Seats [Opt on LXi]	+338
Power Moonroof	+362
Premium Audio System [Opt on LXi,LX Plus Sdn]	+130
Sport Suspension [Opt on LXi Sdn]	+130

2001

The Sebring sedan debuts for 2001 along with redesigned versions of the coupe and convertible. A new, more powerful V6 joins the enlarged four-cylinder, with a manual five-speed available in the coupe. The Autostick automanual is still an option for those who can't decide where they stand on the shift issue, but only on upscale LXi models with the V6. An Infinity premium sound system with an in-dash CD changer is also new this year.

Mileage Category: D

Body Styles	TMV Pricing		
	Trade	Private	Dealer
2 Dr LX Conv	7661	8960	10159
2 Dr LX Cpe	6342	7415	8405
2 Dr LXi Conv	8533	9980	11315
2 Dr LXi Cpe	7172	8385	9505

Body Styles	TMV Pricing		
	Trade	Private	Dealer
2 Dr Limited Conv	9424	11022	12497
4 Dr LX Sdn	5411	6328	7174
4 Dr LXi Sdn	6668	7799	8843

Options	Price
17 Inch Wheels - Chrome	+336
2.7L V6 DOHC 24V FI Engine [Opt on LX Sdn]	+359
3.0L V6 SOHC 24V FI Engine [Opt on LX Cpe]	+426
Aluminum/Alloy Wheels [Opt on LX]	+146
Antilock Brakes [Std on Limited]	+305
Automatic 4-Speed Transmission [Opt on LXi Cpe]	+370

Options	Price
Chrome Wheels [Opt on LXi Sdn]	+247
Compact Disc Changer	+168
Front and Rear Head Airbag Restraints [Opt on Sdn]	+175
Infinity Audio System [Opt on LX Conv]	+213
Leather Seats [Opt on LXi Cpe]	+381
Power Moonroof	+307

2000

For 2000, the standard-equipment list has increased. Also, Ice Silver is the newest color, and the LX trim fabric has been updated.

Mileage Category: D

Body Styles	TMV Pricing		
	Trade	Private	Dealer
2 Dr JX Conv	5744	7061	8352
2 Dr JXi Conv	6024	7406	8760
2 Dr JXi Limited Conv	6881	8459	10006

Options	Price
Antilock Brakes [Opt on Cpe]	+247
Chrome Wheels [Opt on JXi]	+127
Compact Disc Changer [Opt on Conv]	+181

Body Styles	TMV Pricing		
	Trade	Private	Dealer
2 Dr LX Cpe	5022	6102	7160
2 Dr LXi Cpe	5701	6927	8128

Options	Price
Infinity Audio System [Opt on Cpe]	+118
Power Moonroof [Opt on Cpe]	+249
Traction Control System [Opt on JXi]	+145

1999

Body-colored mirrors lend the Sebring LXi a more elegant style.

Mileage Category: D

Body Styles	TMV Pricing		
	Trade	Private	Dealer
2 Dr JX Conv	4600	5855	7162
2 Dr JXi Conv	4668	5942	7269

Options	Price
2.5L V6 SOHC 24V FI Engine [Opt on JX,LX]	+221
Antilock Brakes [Opt on Cpe]	+218
Automatic 4-Speed Transmission [Opt on LX]	+201
Compact Disc Changer [Opt on Conv]	+144

Body Styles	TMV Pricing		
	Trade	Private	Dealer
2 Dr LX Cpe	3560	4529	5537
2 Dr LXi Cpe	4366	5554	6790

Options	Price
Leather Seats [Opt on LXi]	+217
Power Moonroof	+185
Traction Control System [Opt on JXi]	+115

1998

Evolutionary, mostly aesthetic changes enhance the Sebrings this year. The Sebring Coupe LX and LXi now offer a black and gray interior, and a new exterior color, Caffe Latte.

Mileage Category: D

Body Styles	TMV Pricing		
	Trade	Private	Dealer
2 Dr JX Conv	3046	4033	5145
2 Dr JXi Conv	3700	4898	6248

Options	Price
2.5L V6 SOHC 24V FI Engine [Opt on JX,LX]	+188
Aluminum/Alloy Wheels [Opt on JX,LX]	+121
Antilock Brakes [Opt on JX,LX]	+186
Automatic 4-Speed Transmission [Opt on LX]	+171

Body Styles	TMV Pricing		
	Trade	Private	Dealer
2 Dr LX Cpe	2876	3788	4816
2 Dr LXi Cpe	3657	4816	6123

Options	Price
Compact Disc Changer	+123
Leather Seats [Opt on LXi]	+185
Power Moonroof	+158

1997

After just one year in production, the Sebring Convertible receives several changes. The most significant are a quieter intake manifold for the 2.4-liter engine and the availability of Chrysler's AutoStick transmission. Other changes include the addition of new colors, auto-dimming mirror, trip computer, enhanced vehicle theft system and damage-resistant power antenna to the options list.

Mileage Category: D

Body Styles	TMV Pricing		
	Trade	Private	Dealer
2 Dr JX Conv	2516	3454	4601
2 Dr JXi Conv	3140	4311	5742

Options	Price
2.5L V6 SOHC 24V FI Engine [Opt on JX,LX]	+158
Antilock Brakes [Opt on JX,LX]	+156
Automatic 4-Speed Transmission [Opt on LX]	+144

Body Styles	TMV Pricing		
	Trade	Private	Dealer
2 Dr LX Cpe	2265	3105	4132
2 Dr LXi Cpe	2934	4023	5353

Options	Price
Leather Seats [Opt on LXi]	+155
Power Moonroof	+133

1996

Remote keyless-entry system gets a panic feature, and a HomeLink Universal Transmitter debuts on this suave sport coupe. Three new paint colors are also available. Chrysler dumps its final K-Car variant this year in favor of the Sebring Convertible. Based on the Cirrus platform and drivetrains, this drop top shares only the name of the Sebring Coupe.

Mileage Category: D

Body Styles	TMV Pricing		
	Trade	Private	Dealer
2 Dr JX Conv	2052	2906	4085
2 Dr JXi Conv	2630	3725	5237

Options	Price
24V FI Engine [Opt on JX,LX]	+136
Antilock Brakes [Opt on JX]	+134

Body Styles	TMV Pricing		
	Trade	Private	Dealer
2 Dr LX Cpe	1887	2663	3735
2 Dr LXi Cpe	2325	3283	4606

Options	Price
Automatic 4-Speed Transmission [Opt on LX]	+124
Leather Seats [Opt on LXi]	+133

1995

Chrysler's replacement for the LeBaron coupe is the Sebring. Based on the Dodge Avenger, the Sebring offers more luxury than its corporate cousin. The Sebring is available as a four-cylinder LX or an upscale 2.5-liter V6 LXi; both come standard with an automatic transmission.

Mileage Category: E

Body Styles	TMV Pricing		
	Trade	Private	Dealer
2 Dr LX Cpe	1481	2188	3367

Body Styles	TMV Pricing		
	Trade	Private	Dealer
2 Dr LXi Cpe	1792	2648	4074

Options	Price
2.5L V6 SOHC 24V FI Engine [Opt on LX]	+112
Automatic 4-Speed Transmission [Opt on LX]	+102
Leather Seats	+110

Options	Price
Power Moonroof	+94
Premium Audio System	+124

Town & Country

2004

Mileage Category: P

Body Styles	TMV Pricing		
	Trade	Private	Dealer
4 Dr EX Pass Van Ext	15387	16655	18767
4 Dr LX Pass Van Ext	13759	15028	17142
4 Dr Limited AWD Pass Van Ext	21363	22734	25018
4 Dr Limited Pass Van Ext	19928	21264	23490
4 Dr STD Pass Van	11511	12781	14898

Body Styles	TMV Pricing		
	Trade	Private	Dealer
4 Dr Touring AWD Pass Van Ext	17148	18414	20525
4 Dr Touring Pass Van Ext	15830	17098	19210
4 Dr Touring Platinum Series Pass Van Ext	18208	19474	21584

A limited-edition Platinum Series is offered as a late-year edition that adds 16-inch chrome wheels, two-tone leather seats, the rear-seat DVD entertainment system and special embroidered floor mats to the touring model. All Town and Countrys include a tire-pressure monitoring system and updated audio and entertainment packages. With the discontinuation of the lower-priced Voyager model, a short-wheelbase Town & Country has been added to the lineup.

Options	Price
AM/FM/CD Changer Audio System [Opt on STD, EX, Touring]	+150
Air Conditioning - Front and Rear [Opt on EX, LX, Touring FWD]	+450
Alarm System [Std on Limited]	+220
Antilock Brakes [Opt on STD]	+565
Automatic Climate Control (3 Zone) [Opt on EX, Touring]	+500
Automatic Dimming Rearview Mirror [Opt on EX, Touring]	+250
Automatic Dimming Sideview Mirror(s) [Opt on EX, Touring]	+300
Automatic Load Leveling [Opt on EX, LX, Touring, Limited FWD]	+290
Automatic On/Off Headlights [Opt on EX, Touring]	+250
DVD Entertainment System [Std on Touring Platinum]	+280
Fog Lights [Opt on EX, Touring]	+150

Options	Price
Front Side Airbag Restraints [Std on Limited]	+390
Heated Front Seats [Std on Limited]	+200
Leather Seats [Std on Touring Platinum, Limited]	+900
Luggage Rack [Opt on STD, LX]	+145
Navigation System [Opt on LX, Touring]	+1000
Power Adjustable Foot Pedals [Std on Limited]	+180
Power Driver Seat [Opt on STD, LX]	+370
Power Dual Sliding Doors [Opt on LX]	+800
Power Sliding Door [Opt on STD]	+400
Power Sunroof [Opt on EX, Limited, Touring, Platinum]	+895

2003

Mileage Category: P

Two new options debut -- a one-touch power sunroof (that Chrysler boasts is one of the largest available in a minivan) and a factory-, not dealer-, installed DVD entertainment system that comes with wireless headphones. Audiophiles will appreciate the new six-CD changer, an upgrade over the previous four-disc unit. Note that the LX AWD model has been discontinued, thus requiring buyers who want all-wheel drive to step up to the more expensive LXi and Limited models to get it.

Body Styles	TMV Pricing		
	Trade	Private	Dealer
4 Dr EX Pass Van Ext	14204	15409	17418
4 Dr LX Pass Van Ext	12289	13332	15071
4 Dr LXi AWD Pass Van Ext	15638	16966	19178
4 Dr LXi Pass Van Ext	14281	15494	17516

Body Styles	TMV Pricing		
	Trade	Private	Dealer
4 Dr Limited AWD Pass Van Ext	18556	20131	22757
4 Dr Limited Pass Van Ext	17683	19185	21687
4 Dr STD Pass Van Ext	12327	13374	15119
4 Dr eL Pass Van Ext	12036	13058	14762

Options	Price
16 Inch Wheels [Opt on LX]	+161
3.8L V6 OHV 12V FI Engine [Opt on eL, LX]	+200
Air Conditioning - Front and Rear [Opt on STD]	+119
Alarm System [Opt on LXi]	+116
Automatic Climate Control (3 Zone) [Opt on STD]	+164
Automatic Load Leveling	+173
Camper/Towing Package [Opt on Limited, LXi]	+212
Captain Chairs (4) [Opt on LX]	+444
Compact Disc Changer [Opt on LXi]	+119
DVD Entertainment System [Opt on Limited, LXi]	+537

Options	Price
Front Side Airbag Restraints [Std on Limited]	+233
Heated Front Seats [Opt on LXi]	+149
Luggage Rack [Std on Limited, LXi]	+149
Power Driver Seat [Opt on LX]	+143
Power Moonroof [Opt on Limited, LXi]	+534
Power Rear Liftgate [Opt on LX]	+239
Power Sliding Door [Opt on LX]	+239
Privacy Glass [Opt on STD]	+239
Special Factory Paint	+119

2002

Mileage Category: P

Chrysler makes this already opulent minivan more luxurious with the availability of power-adjustable pedals, rear-seat audio with wireless headsets and a DVD video system for the rear seat that also includes wireless headsets. A value-leader eL model is introduced that lists for around $24,000.

Body Styles	TMV Pricing		
	Trade	Private	Dealer
4 Dr EX Pass Van Ext	11530	12732	14736
4 Dr LX AWD Pass Van Ext	13167	14540	16827
4 Dr LX Pass Van Ext	10739	11859	13725
4 Dr LXi AWD Pass Van Ext	13935	15388	17809

Body Styles	TMV Pricing		
	Trade	Private	Dealer
4 Dr LXi Pass Van Ext	12145	13411	15521
4 Dr Limited AWD Pass Van Ext	16438	18152	21008
4 Dr Limited Pass Van Ext	15676	17310	20034
4 Dr eL Pass Van Ext	10182	11244	13013

2002 (cont'd)

Options	Price
16 Inch Wheels [Opt on EX]	+195
3.8L V6 OHV 12V FI Engine [Opt on LXi 2WD]	+174
AM/FM/Cassette/CD Audio System [Opt on LX 2WD,LXi]	+117
Air Conditioning - Front and Rear [Opt on LX 2WD]	+258
Aluminum/Alloy Wheels [Opt on LX,LXi FWD]	+232
Automatic Load Leveling [Opt on FWD - LX,LXi]	+151
Captain Chairs (4) [Opt on LX 2WD]	+388
DVD Entertainment System	+468
Front Side Airbag Restraints [Std on Limited]	+203
Heated Front Seats	+130

Options	Price
Infinity Audio System [Opt on LX]	+258
Leather Seats [Opt on LXi]	+463
Luggage Rack [Std on EX,Limited]	+130
Power Driver Seat [Opt on LX 2WD]	+192
Power Dual Sliding Doors [Opt on EX]	+208
Power Passenger Seat [Opt on LXi]	+192
Power Rear Liftgate [Std on EX,Limited]	+208
Power Sliding Door [Opt on eL,LX FWD]	+208
Tinted Glass [Opt on LX 2WD]	+122

2001

Chrysler's top-of-the-line minivans are all new for the 2001 model year, with new gewgaws such as a power liftgate and a removable center console with three power outlets.

Mileage Category: P

Body Styles	TMV Pricing		
	Trade	Private	Dealer
4 Dr EX Pass Van Ext	8274	9796	11201
4 Dr LX AWD Pass Van Ext	9083	10754	12296
4 Dr LX Pass Van Ext	7530	8914	10192
4 Dr LXi AWD Pass Van Ext	9537	11291	12911

Body Styles	TMV Pricing		
	Trade	Private	Dealer
4 Dr LXi Pass Van Ext	8296	9822	11230
4 Dr Limited AWD Pass Van Ext	11453	13560	15504
4 Dr Limited Pass Van Ext	10468	12393	14170

Options	Price
3.8L V6 OHV 12V FI Engine [Opt on LXi 2WD]	+206
Air Conditioning - Front and Rear [Opt on LX 2WD]	+247
Aluminum/Alloy Wheels	+186
Automatic Climate Control (3 Zone) [Opt on LX]	+146
Automatic Load Leveling [Std on Limited,AWD]	+130
Front Side Airbag Restraints	+175

Options	Price
Infinity Audio System [Opt on LX]	+222
Leather Seats [Opt on LXi]	+399
Power Driver Seat [Opt on LX 2WD]	+166
Power Rear Liftgate [Opt on LX,LXi]	+179
Power Sliding Door [Opt on LX 2WD]	+173

2000

The model lineup changes this year, and telling the difference between the LX and LXi will be easier to the untrained eye, thanks to distinctive exterior and interior modifications. New colors for 2000 are Shale Green, Bright White, Patriot Blue, Bright Silver and Inferno Red.

Mileage Category: P

Body Styles	TMV Pricing		
	Trade	Private	Dealer
4 Dr LX AWD Pass Van Ext	6815	8253	9662
4 Dr LX Pass Van Ext	5966	7224	8458
4 Dr LXi AWD Pass Van Ext	7599	9202	10774

Body Styles	TMV Pricing		
	Trade	Private	Dealer
4 Dr LXi Pass Van Ext	6790	8222	9626
4 Dr Limited AWD Pass Van Ext	8337	10096	11821
4 Dr Limited Pass Van Ext	8101	9809	11484

Options	Price
3.8L V6 OHV 12V FI Engine [Opt on LXi FWD]	+167
AM/FM/Cassette/CD Audio System [Opt on LX,LXi]	+143
Air Conditioning - Front and Rear [Opt on LX,LXi]	+172
Aluminum/Alloy Wheels	+151

Options	Price
Compact Disc Changer	+199
Infinity Audio System [Opt on LX]	+127
Leather Seats [Opt on LXi]	+323
Power Passenger Seat [Opt on LXi]	+167

1999

The top-of-the-line trim level is now called "Limited," and it offers more standard equipment (hence less options) than any other Chrysler minivan. Leather upgrades, steering wheel-mounted stereo controls and a center armrest in the rear bench are new this year, and the exterior features such details as 16-inch 15-spoke chrome wheels and chrome door handles.

Mileage Category: P

Body Styles	TMV Pricing		
	Trade	Private	Dealer
4 Dr LX AWD Pass Van Ext	5909	7301	8750
4 Dr LX Pass Van Ext	5379	6517	7700
4 Dr LXi AWD Pass Van Ext	6608	8165	9786
4 Dr LXi Pass Van Ext	5959	7363	8825

Body Styles	TMV Pricing		
	Trade	Private	Dealer
4 Dr Limited AWD Pass Van Ext	6878	8498	10185
4 Dr Limited Pass Van Ext	6521	8058	9657
4 Dr SX Pass Van	5473	6763	8106

Options	Price
3.8L V6 OHV 12V FI Engine [Opt on SX,LX FWD]	+132
Air Conditioning - Front and Rear [Opt on LX]	+144
Aluminum/Alloy Wheels [Opt on LX]	+120

Options	Price
Compact Disc Changer	+159
Leather Seats [Opt on LX,SX]	+257

1998

Chrysler's luxury minivans get a few improvements this year, with the addition of a new Chrysler-signature grille, more powerful 3.8-liter V6, high-performance headlights and three fancy new colors.

Mileage Category: P

Body Styles	TMV Pricing		
	Trade	Private	Dealer
4 Dr LX AWD Pass Van Ext	4463	5735	7169
4 Dr LX Pass Van Ext	4133	5312	6641

Body Styles	TMV Pricing		
	Trade	Private	Dealer
4 Dr LXi AWD Pass Van Ext	5111	6568	8212
4 Dr LXi Pass Van Ext	4709	6052	7567

1998 (cont'd)

Body Styles	TMV Pricing		
	Trade	Private	Dealer
4 Dr SX Pass Van	3898	5010	6264

Options	Price	Options	Price
Compact Disc Changer	+136	Leather Seats [Std on LXi]	+219

Mileage Category: P

1997

Chrysler's luxury minivans get a few improvements this year, as AWD extended length models are added to the lineup. Also new this year is a sporty SX model, which replaces last year's LX as the regular length Town & Country. Families with kids will love the standard left-side sliding door on this vehicle.

Body Styles	TMV Pricing			Body Styles	TMV Pricing		
	Trade	Private	Dealer		Trade	Private	Dealer
4 Dr LX AWD Pass Van Ext	3261	4390	5770	4 Dr LXi Pass Van Ext	3663	4932	6483
4 Dr LX Pass Van Ext	3101	4175	5487	4 Dr SX Pass Van	3051	4107	5398
4 Dr LXi AWD Pass Van Ext	3807	5126	6737				

Options	Price
Leather Seats [Std on LXi]	+184

Mileage Category: P

1996

Totally redesigned for 1996, the T&C raises the bar for luxury minivans. In a departure from last year, the TandC is offered in a short wheelbase version, and is available in two trim levels: LX and LXi. New innovations include a driver-side passenger door, dual-zone temperature controls and a one-hand latch system on the integrated child safety seats.

Body Styles	TMV Pricing			Body Styles	TMV Pricing		
	Trade	Private	Dealer		Trade	Private	Dealer
3 Dr LX Pass Van	2471	3457	4818	4 Dr LXi Pass Van Ext	2990	4182	5829
3 Dr STD Pass Van Ext	2535	3546	4943				

Options	Price
Leather Seats [Std on LXi]	+158

Mileage Category: P

1995

Body Styles	TMV Pricing			Body Styles	TMV Pricing		
	Trade	Private	Dealer		Trade	Private	Dealer
3 Dr STD AWD Pass Van Ext	2073	2951	4413	3 Dr STD Pass Van Ext	1860	2648	3960

There are no changes for the 1995 Town & Country.

Voyager

2003

Mileage Category: P

Body Styles	TMV Pricing		
	Trade	Private	Dealer
4 Dr LX Pass Van	10650	11554	13061

Options	Price	Options	Price
3.3L V6 Flex Fuel OHV 12V FI Engine	+579	Luggage Rack	+149
3.3L V6 OHV 12V FI Engine	+579	Power Door Locks	+140
Child Seat (1)	+134	Power Driver Seat	+221
Front Side Airbag Restraints	+233	Power Windows	+158

Chrysler has reorganized the lineup, eliminating all "base" models as well as the four-cylinder-only "eC" model (extra-cheap?). Now there's only one trim level, LX. If you stick with the base Value Package, you'll get the 2.4-liter four-cylinder engine. If you opt for the Popular Equipment Package, you'll get the 3.3-liter V6. Mercifully, Chrysler has done away with the archaic three-speed automatic formerly available on four-cylinder models. New exterior colors include Satin Jade and Butane Blue.

2002

Chrysler brings out the Voyager eC, a value leader that lists for just $17,000. Power-adjustable pedals debut as well.

Mileage Category: P

Body Styles	TMV Pricing			Body Styles	TMV Pricing		
	Trade	Private	Dealer		Trade	Private	Dealer
4 Dr LX Pass Van	9107	10044	11606	4 Dr eC Pass Van	6207	6854	7933
4 Dr STD Pass Van	7337	8102	9377				

Options	Price	Options	Price
3.3L V6 OHV 12V FI Engine [Opt on STD]	+505	Antilock Brakes	+375
AM/FM/Cassette/CD Audio System [Opt on LX]	+117	Automatic 4-Speed Transmission [Opt on STD]	+156

2002 (cont'd)

Options	Price
Captain Chairs (4) [Opt on LX]	+336
Center and Rear Bench Seat	+117
Child Seat (1)	+117
Compact Disc Changer [Opt on LX]	+195
Front Side Airbag Restraints	+203
Infinity Audio System [Opt on LX]	+258
Luggage Rack	+130

Options	Price
Power Door Locks [Std on LX]	+117
Power Driver Seat [Opt on LX]	+192
Power Sliding Door [Opt on LX]	+208
Power Windows [Std on LX]	+137
Temperature Controls - Driver and Passenger [Opt on LX]	+117
Tinted Glass [Std on LX]	+156

2001

Chrysler's low-end minivan receives an available 3.3-liter V6 engine that's been massaged to put forth more power; an improved suspension and drivetrain to increase ride comfort and reduce vibrations; upgraded brakes; standard dual sliding doors; and available side airbags, all under new, sleek sheet metal.

Mileage Category: P

Body Styles	TMV Pricing		
	Trade	Private	Dealer
4 Dr LX Pass Van	6887	8154	9324

Options	Price
3.3L V6 OHV 12V FI Engine [Opt on STD]	+435
Antilock Brakes [Opt on STD]	+305
Automatic Load Leveling	+130
Compact Disc Changer	+312
Front Side Airbag Restraints	+175
Infinity Audio System	+222

Body Styles	TMV Pricing		
	Trade	Private	Dealer
4 Dr STD Pass Van	5193	6148	7029

Options	Price
Power Driver Seat	+166
Power Sliding Door	+173
Power Windows [Opt on STD]	+118
Temperature Controls - Driver and Passenger [Opt on LX]	+123

2000

Mileage Category: P

Body Styles	TMV Pricing		
	Trade	Private	Dealer
3 Dr STD Pass Van	3805	4608	5395

Options	Price
3.0L V6 SOHC 12V FI Engine [Opt on STD]	+291
3.3L V6 Flex Fuel OHV 12V FI Engine [Opt on STD]	+352
7 Passenger Seating [Opt on STD]	+136
Air Conditioning [Opt on STD]	+313
Aluminum/Alloy Wheels	+151

Body Styles	TMV Pricing		
	Trade	Private	Dealer
4 Dr SE Pass Van	5351	6480	7587

Options	Price
Antilock Brakes [Opt on STD]	+247
Camper/Towing Package	+158
Captain Chairs (4)	+252
Infinity Audio System	+152
Sliding Driver Side Door [Opt on STD]	+216

With Plymouth's impending death, the Voyager turns into a Chrysler this year, but it is otherwise unchanged. Four new colors and a new Value-Plus option package that includes a V6 and power features are new this year.

Lanos

2002

Mileage Category: A

Body Styles	TMV Pricing		
	Trade	Private	Dealer
2 Dr S Hbk	1750	2614	4053
2 Dr Sport Hbk	2538	3791	5880

Options	Price
AM/FM/Cassette/CD Audio System [Opt on S]	+207
Air Conditioning [Opt on S]	+311

Body Styles	TMV Pricing		
	Trade	Private	Dealer
4 Dr S Sdn	2058	3074	4767

Options	Price
Automatic 4-Speed Transmission	+332

A new Comfort Package for the S Hatchback and S Sedan includes air conditioning and power steering, while the Convenience Package adds power windows, power locks and a power passenger-side exterior mirror.

2001

Mileage Category: A

Body Styles	TMV Pricing		
	Trade	Private	Dealer
2 Dr S Hbk	1394	2429	3385
2 Dr Sport Hbk	1975	3443	4798

Options	Price
Air Conditioning [Opt on S]	+250
Aluminum/Alloy Wheels [Opt on S]	+134

Body Styles	TMV Pricing		
	Trade	Private	Dealer
4 Dr S Sdn	1658	2890	4027

Options	Price
Automatic 4-Speed Transmission	+267

Daewoo adds the new Sport Hatchback model to the Lanos lineup for 2001, but discontinues the SE Hatchback and SX Sedan. Pacific Blue Mica and Red Rock Mica are added to the palette for the sedan and hatchback, while Super Red and Granada Black Mica are available exclusively on the Sport. The new premium package available on the S models includes power windows, door locks and passenger rearview mirror; tilt steering wheel; AM/FM/cassette/CD stereo; digital clock; and variable intermittent wipers.

2000

Mileage Category: A

Body Styles	TMV Pricing		
	Trade	Private	Dealer
2 Dr S Hbk	1026	1972	2900
2 Dr SE Hbk	1175	2262	3328

Options	Price
Air Conditioning [Opt on S,SE]	+212
Antilock Brakes	+205

Body Styles	TMV Pricing		
	Trade	Private	Dealer
4 Dr S Sdn	1160	2231	3281
4 Dr SX Sdn	1289	2479	3645

Options	Price
Automatic 4-Speed Transmission	+242
Power Moonroof	+151

The three-door SX disappears, as does the SE Sedan. Daewoo picks up the tab for all scheduled maintenance during the warranty period and has added ownership peace of mind with 24-hour roadside assistance for three years or 36,000 miles.

1999

Mileage Category: A

Body Styles	TMV Pricing		
	Trade	Private	Dealer
2 Dr S Hbk	719	1441	2192
2 Dr SE Hbk	809	1620	2464
2 Dr SX Hbk	909	1823	2774

Options	Price
Air Conditioning [Opt on S,SE]	+148
Antilock Brakes	+160

Body Styles	TMV Pricing		
	Trade	Private	Dealer
4 Dr S Sdn	775	1553	2363
4 Dr SE Sdn	825	1652	2512
4 Dr SX Sdn	979	1962	2985

Options	Price
Automatic 4-Speed Transmission	+169

This entry into the subcompact class is Daewoo's attack on the Honda Civic.

Leganza

2002

Mileage Category: C

Body Styles	TMV Pricing		
	Trade	Private	Dealer
4 Dr CDX Sdn	3527	4963	7355

Options	Price
AM/FM/Cassette/CD Audio System [Opt on SE]	+116
Antilock Brakes [Opt on CDX]	+282
Automatic 4-Speed Transmission [Opt on SE]	+415

Body Styles	TMV Pricing		
	Trade	Private	Dealer
4 Dr SE Sdn	2679	3769	5585

Options	Price
Leather Seats [Opt on CDX]	+270
Power Moonroof [Opt on CDX]	+290
Traction Control System [Opt on CDX]	+124

The Leganza is a carryover. The midlevel SX trim has been eliminated, leaving the base SE and the upscale CDX. To help bridge the gap, the CDX has been decontented and its price lowered.

Daewoo
Leganza/Nubira

2001

Scarlet Mica and Harbor Mist Mica are the new exterior colors. Outside rearview mirrors get a blue tint and a new audio head unit is added for improved sound quality. A new option package for the SE includes front and rear power windows, power door locks, AM/FM/cassette/CD stereo with six speakers, dual body-color heated power rearview mirrors, anti-theft alarm with remote keyless entry, tilt steering wheel and front foglamps.

Mileage Category: C

Body Styles	TMV Pricing		
	Trade	Private	Dealer
4 Dr CDX Sdn	2319	4375	6272
4 Dr SE Sdn	1696	3199	4586

Options	Price
Aluminum/Alloy Wheels [Opt on SX]	+167
Automatic 4-Speed Transmission [Opt on SE]	+267

Body Styles	TMV Pricing		
	Trade	Private	Dealer
4 Dr SX Sdn	1708	3223	4621

Options	Price
Compact Disc Changer	+150
Power Moonroof [Opt on SX]	+217

2000

Content is pulled from the base SE model, but all Leganzas have new grilles and larger stereo knobs. New seat fabric on SE models, revised alloy wheels and a more convenient remote keyless-entry design debut, and buyers now get 24-hour roadside assistance and free scheduled maintenance for the duration of the basic warranty period. New colors round out the changes.

Mileage Category: C

Body Styles	TMV Pricing		
	Trade	Private	Dealer
4 Dr CDX Sdn	1774	3608	5406
4 Dr SE Sdn	1263	2569	3850

Options	Price
Automatic 4-Speed Transmission [Opt on SE]	+242
Compact Disc Changer	+157

Body Styles	TMV Pricing		
	Trade	Private	Dealer
4 Dr SX Sdn	1308	2662	3989

Options	Price
Power Moonroof [Opt on SX]	+257

1999

The whole car is new to the United States, as is the motor company that makes it.

Mileage Category: C

Body Styles	TMV Pricing		
	Trade	Private	Dealer
4 Dr CDX Sdn	1500	3098	4762
4 Dr SE Sdn	960	1983	3048

Options	Price
Automatic 4-Speed Transmission [Opt on SE]	+169

Body Styles	TMV Pricing		
	Trade	Private	Dealer
4 Dr SX Sdn	990	2046	3145

Options	Price
Power Moonroof [Opt on SX]	+179

Nubira

2002

Mileage Category: B

Body Styles	TMV Pricing		
	Trade	Private	Dealer
4 Dr CDX Wgn	3235	4558	6762

Options	Price
AM/FM/Cassette/CD Audio System	+118
Air Conditioning [Opt on SE]	+332

Body Styles	TMV Pricing		
	Trade	Private	Dealer
4 Dr SE Sdn	2744	3867	5738

Options	Price
Automatic 4-Speed Transmission	+332

Daewoo trims the Nubira ranks for 2002 -- you can purchase either an SE sedan or a CDX wagon.

2001

You can pick up a Daewoo Nubira with Diamond Blue Metallic paint. The sedan gets a new 14-inch standard wheel cover and the wagon has a fresh rear taillamp design.

Mileage Category: B

Body Styles	TMV Pricing		
	Trade	Private	Dealer
4 Dr CDX Sdn	2041	3455	4760
4 Dr CDX Wgn	2608	4413	6080

Options	Price
Air Conditioning [Opt on SE]	+284
Automatic 4-Speed Transmission	+267

Body Styles	TMV Pricing		
	Trade	Private	Dealer
4 Dr SE Sdn	2005	3394	4676

Options	Price
Leather Seats	+217
Power Moonroof	+167

2000

Nubira, already the most appealing choice from the Daewoo buffet, is restyled inside and out and becomes even more attractive to cash-strapped buyers. Firmer springs and a new rear stabilizer bar tighten handling, and the new SE trim level replaces last year's SX model. The five-door hatchback is dropped, but four new colors debut. Scheduled maintenance for the duration of the basic warranty, and three-year/36,000-mile 24-hour roadside assistance is standard.

Mileage Category: B

Body Styles	TMV Pricing		
	Trade	Private	Dealer
4 Dr CDX Sdn	1588	2868	4122
4 Dr CDX Wgn	2020	3644	5236

Options	Price
Air Conditioning [Opt on SE]	+212
Automatic 4-Speed Transmission	+242

Body Styles	TMV Pricing		
	Trade	Private	Dealer
4 Dr SE Sdn	1479	2670	3838

Options	Price
Leather Seats	+151
Power Moonroof	+151

1999

Mileage Category: B

In an attempt to lure consumers away from the likes of Honda and Toyota, the new Korean upstart fields its loaded-with-features Nubira. Air conditioner, power windows, keyless entry, four-wheel disc brakes, 129 horsepower and a funny name all come as standard equipment.

Body Styles	TMV Pricing		
	Trade	Private	Dealer
4 Dr CDX Hbk	1188	2165	3182
4 Dr CDX Sdn	1170	2133	3136
4 Dr CDX Wgn	1553	2829	4157

Options	Price
Antilock Brakes [Opt on SX]	+160

Body Styles	TMV Pricing		
	Trade	Private	Dealer
4 Dr SX Hbk	1079	1966	2889
4 Dr SX Sdn	1027	1871	2749
4 Dr SX Wgn	1109	2021	2970

Options	Price
Automatic 4-Speed Transmission	+169

Dodge

Avenger

Avenger

2000

Mileage Category: E

Body Styles	TMV Pricing				Body Styles	TMV Pricing		
	Trade	Private	Dealer			Trade	Private	Dealer
2 Dr ES Cpe	5462	6739	7991		2 Dr STD Cpe	4295	5298	6281

Options	Price		Options	Price
AM/FM/Cassette/CD Audio System [Opt on STD]	+197		Infinity Audio System	+147
Alarm System [Opt on STD]	+138		Power Moonroof	+289
Antilock Brakes	+307			

Base Avengers get new standard equipment, including the 2.5-liter V6 and automatic transmission from the uplevel ES, new cloth fabric on the seats and standard 16-inch wheels with luxury wheelcovers. A sport package is optional. A power leather-trimmed driver's seat is included with ES trim for 2000. Two key fobs come with the remote keyless-entry system this year, and two new colors are available. The Avenger will be completely redesigned and take the Stratus nameplate for 2001.

1999

One new color for the exterior: Shark Blue (replaces Silver Mist).

Mileage Category: E

Body Styles	TMV Pricing				Body Styles	TMV Pricing		
	Trade	Private	Dealer			Trade	Private	Dealer
2 Dr ES Cpe	3902	5079	6304		2 Dr STD Cpe	3407	4435	5504

Options	Price		Options	Price
2.5L V6 SOHC 24V FI Engine	+225		Automatic 4-Speed Transmission	+255
AM/FM/Cassette/CD Audio System	+120		Infinity Audio System [Opt on STD]	+120
Air Conditioning [Opt on STD]	+291		Leather Seats	+203
Aluminum/Alloy Wheels [Opt on STD]	+181		Power Moonroof	+236
Antilock Brakes	+278			

1998

Interior fabrics are new, as is a black and gray color scheme. The ES model gets a new Sport package that affects appearance, not performance. Also available for the ES are new 16-inch aluminum wheels and a rear sway bar that improves handling.

Mileage Category: E

Body Styles	TMV Pricing				Body Styles	TMV Pricing		
	Trade	Private	Dealer			Trade	Private	Dealer
2 Dr ES Cpe	3708	4774	5976		2 Dr STD Cpe	3008	3873	4849

Options	Price		Options	Price
2.5L V6 SOHC 24V FI Engine	+199		Automatic 4-Speed Transmission	+227
Air Conditioning [Opt on STD]	+257		Leather Seats	+179
Aluminum/Alloy Wheels [Opt on STD]	+160		Power Moonroof	+209
Antilock Brakes	+246			

1997

Front and rear styling is updated, while ES models lose the standard V6 engine. The V6 is available on base and ES models, and includes 17-inch wheels and tires on the ES. New colors inside and out and two additional speakers with cassette stereos further broaden the appeal of this roomy coupe.

Mileage Category: E

Body Styles	TMV Pricing				Body Styles	TMV Pricing		
	Trade	Private	Dealer			Trade	Private	Dealer
2 Dr ES Cpe	3131	4180	5463		2 Dr STD Cpe	2488	3321	4339

Options	Price		Options	Price
2.5L V6 SOHC 24V FI Engine	+175		Antilock Brakes [Opt on STD]	+217
AM/FM/CD Audio System [Opt on STD]	+125		Automatic 4-Speed Transmission	+196
AM/FM/Cassette/CD Audio System	+125		Compact Disc Changer	+129
Air Conditioning [Opt on STD]	+226		Leather Seats	+158
Aluminum/Alloy Wheels [Opt on STD]	+140		Power Moonroof	+183

1996

Dodge's sporty coupe gets a panic mode for the remote keyless entry system and a HomeLink transmitter that will open your garage door. ES models get new seat fabric, and three new colors are on the roster.

Mileage Category: E

Body Styles	TMV Pricing				Body Styles	TMV Pricing		
	Trade	Private	Dealer			Trade	Private	Dealer
2 Dr ES Cpe	2571	3568	4944		2 Dr STD Cpe	2117	2937	4070

Options	Price		Options	Price
AM/FM/Cassette/CD Audio System	+220		Automatic 4-Speed Transmission [Opt on STD]	+178
Air Conditioning [Opt on STD]	+206		Leather Seats	+144
Aluminum/Alloy Wheels	+121		Power Moonroof	+167
Antilock Brakes [Opt on STD]	+197		Premium Audio System	+143

1995

New coupe is late replacement for Daytona. Based on a Mitsubishi Galant platform, the Avenger is about the size of a Camry coupe. Base and ES models are available. Base cars have a 2.0-liter, 140-horsepower four-cylinder engine underhood. ES gets a Mitsubishi-built 2.5-liter V6 making 155 horsepower. An automatic is the only transmission available on the ES. ABS is optional on base models; standard on ES. All Avengers have dual airbags, height-adjustable driver's seat, split-folding rear seat, rear defroster, and tilt steering wheel.

Mileage Category: E

Body Styles	TMV Pricing		
	Trade	Private	Dealer
2 Dr ES Cpe	1848	2587	3819

Options	Price
AM/FM/CD Audio System	+100
Air Conditioning [Opt on STD]	+181
Antilock Brakes [Opt on STD]	+172
Automatic 4-Speed Transmission [Opt on STD]	+156

Body Styles	TMV Pricing		
	Trade	Private	Dealer
2 Dr Highline Cpe	1556	2178	3215

Options	Price
Leather Seats	+126
Power Moonroof	+146
Premium Audio System	+125

Caravan

2004

New features for 2004 include a tire-pressure monitoring system and an integrated remote/key design. Audio systems have been upgraded as well.

Mileage Category: P

Body Styles	TMV Pricing		
	Trade	Private	Dealer
4 Dr SE Pass Van	10655	11862	13873

Options	Price
AM/FM/CD Changer Audio System [Opt on SXT]	+200
Antilock Brakes [Opt on SXT]	+565
Captain Chairs (4) [Opt on SXT]	+200
Front Side Airbag Restraints	+390
Keyless Entry System [Std on SXT]	+265
Luggage Rack	+200
Power Adjustable Foot Pedals	+185
Power Door Locks [Std on SXT]	+235

Body Styles	TMV Pricing		
	Trade	Private	Dealer
4 Dr SXT Pass Van	12371	13604	15660

Options	Price
Power Driver Seat [Opt on SXT]	+200
Power Sliding Door [Opt on SXT]	+400
Power Windows [Std on SXT]	+265
Rear Window Defroster [Opt on SE]	+195
Special Factory Paint	+200
Split Folding Rear Seat [Opt on SXT]	+300
Tilt Steering Wheel [Std on SXT]	+165

2003

A new trim level dubbed "CV" has been added. The bargain-basement, four-cylinder-only "eC" model (extra-cheap?) has been dropped, but we doubt its passing will be mourned.

Mileage Category: P

Body Styles	TMV Pricing		
	Trade	Private	Dealer
4 Dr SE Pass Van	9714	10642	12189

Options	Price
16 Inch Wheels [Opt on Sport]	+237
3.3L V6 Flex Fuel OHV 12V FI Engine [Opt on SE]	+613
3.3L V6 OHV 12V FI Engine [Opt on SE]	+613
AM/FM/CD Changer Audio System [Opt on Sport]	+126
AM/FM/Cassette/CD Audio System [Opt on Sport]	+142
Antilock Brakes [Opt on SE]	+430
Captain Chairs (4) [Opt on Sport]	+471
Child Seats (2)	+142
Cruise Control [Opt on CV,SE]	+117
Front Side Airbag Restraints	+246
Infinity Audio System [Opt on Sport]	+313

Body Styles	TMV Pricing		
	Trade	Private	Dealer
4 Dr Sport Pass Van	10861	11899	13630

Options	Price
Luggage Rack	+158
Power Adjustable Foot Pedals	+117
Power Door Locks [Opt on CV,SE]	+148
Power Driver Seat	+234
Power Heated Mirrors [Opt on CV,SE]	+123
Power Sliding Door [Opt on Sport]	+253
Power Windows [Opt on CV,SE]	+167
Privacy Glass [Opt on SE]	+174
Special Factory Paint	+126
Split Folding Rear Seat [Opt on Sport]	+126

2002

Dodge brings out the Caravan eC, a value leader that lists for just $17,000. Power adjustable pedals debut as well.

Mileage Category: P

Body Styles	TMV Pricing		
	Trade	Private	Dealer
4 Dr SE Pass Van	7111	7944	9333
4 Dr Sport Pass Van	8202	9164	10767

Options	Price
3.3L V6 OHV 12V FI Engine [Opt on SE]	+527
7 Passenger Seating [Opt on eC]	+245
AM/FM/Cassette/CD Audio System [Opt on Sport]	+122
Antilock Brakes [Opt on SE,Sport]	+370
Automatic 4-Speed Transmission [Opt on SE]	+163
Captain Chairs (4) [Opt on Sport]	+408
Center and Rear Bench Seat [Opt on Sport]	+122
Child Seat (1) [Opt on Sport]	+122
Child Seats (2) [Opt on SE]	+122

Body Styles	TMV Pricing		
	Trade	Private	Dealer
4 Dr eC Pass Van	5917	6611	7767

Options	Price
Compact Disc Changer [Opt on Sport]	+204
Front Side Airbag Restraints	+212
Infinity Audio System [Opt on Sport]	+269
Luggage Rack [Opt on SE,Sport]	+136
Power Door Locks [Std on Sport]	+128
Power Driver Seat [Opt on SE,Sport]	+201
Power Sliding Door [Opt on Sport]	+217
Power Windows [Opt on SE]	+144

Dodge
Caravan

2002 (cont'd)

Options	Price
Temperature Controls - Driver and Passenger [Opt on Sport]	+163

Options	Price
Tinted Glass [Opt on SE]	+163

2001

America's best-selling minivan has been revised for 2001 and boasts new sheet metal, boosted horsepower, a refined suspension, upgraded brakes, improved safety features and plenty of additional gadgets. Third-row seats are now easier to remove and install, but still don't fold flat.

Mileage Category: P

Body Styles	TMV Pricing		
	Trade	Private	Dealer
4 Dr SE Pass Van	5717	6796	7792

Options	Price
Aluminum/Alloy Wheels	+339
Antilock Brakes [Opt on SE]	+339
Automatic Load Leveling	+145
Captain Chairs (4) [Opt on Sport]	+372
Compact Disc Changer	+347
Front Side Airbag Restraints	+195
Infinity Audio System	+247
Luggage Rack	+125

Body Styles	TMV Pricing		
	Trade	Private	Dealer
4 Dr Sport Pass Van	6277	7461	8554

Options	Price
Power Door Locks [Opt on SE]	+157
Power Driver Seat	+185
Power Sliding Door [Opt on Sport]	+200
Power Windows [Opt on SE]	+130
Rear Window Defroster [Opt on SE]	+115
Temperature Controls - Driver and Passenger [Opt on Sport]	+187

2000

New colors and more standard equipment keep Chrysler's best-selling minivans up to date until the redesigned 2001 model arrives.

Mileage Category: P

Body Styles	TMV Pricing		
	Trade	Private	Dealer
3 Dr STD Pass Van	3822	4696	5552

Options	Price
3.0L V6 SOHC 12V FI Engine [Opt on SE,STD]	+361
3.3L V6 Flex Fuel OHV 12V FI Engine	+438
3.3L V6 OHV 12V FI Engine	+438
AM/FM/Cassette/CD Audio System	+140
Air Conditioning [Opt on STD]	+389
Aluminum/Alloy Wheels	+119
Antilock Brakes [Opt on STD]	+307

Body Styles	TMV Pricing		
	Trade	Private	Dealer
4 Dr SE Pass Van	4811	5911	6989

Options	Price
Automatic Load Leveling	+131
Camper/Towing Package	+136
Captain Chairs (4)	+314
Compact Disc Changer	+181
Infinity Audio System	+204
Sunscreen Glass	+159

1999

A revised front fascia is common to all models.

Mileage Category: P

Body Styles	TMV Pricing		
	Trade	Private	Dealer
3 Dr STD Pass Van	3053	3854	4688
4 Dr LE Pass Van	4369	5517	6712

Options	Price
3.0L V6 SOHC 12V FI Engine	+295
3.3L V6 OHV 12V FI Engine	+357
3.8L V6 OHV 12V FI Engine	+138
7 Passenger Seating	+138
AM/FM/CD Audio System [Opt on STD]	+120
AM/FM/Cassette/CD Audio System	+146
Air Conditioning	+317
Antilock Brakes	+278

Body Styles	TMV Pricing		
	Trade	Private	Dealer
4 Dr SE Pass Van	3708	4683	5698

Options	Price
Automatic Load Leveling	+119
Captain Chairs (4)	+219
Infinity Audio System [Opt on SE]	+265
Leather Seats [Opt on LE]	+293
Power Door Locks [Std on LE]	+123
Sliding Driver Side Door [Opt on STD]	+219
Sunscreen Glass [Std on LE]	+166

1998

Available this year is a 3.8-liter V6 that puts out 180 horsepower and 240 foot-pounds of torque. And for convenience, Caravans come with rear-seat mounted grocery bag hooks, and driver's-side easy-entry Quad seating. All Chrysler products are equipped with "Next Generation" depowered airbags.

Mileage Category: P

Body Styles	TMV Pricing		
	Trade	Private	Dealer
3 Dr STD Pass Van	2578	3373	4269
4 Dr LE Pass Van	3684	4821	6104

Options	Price
3.0L V6 SOHC 12V FI Engine [Opt on STD]	+251
3.3L V6 OHV 12V FI Engine [Opt on SE,STD]	+316
3.8L V6 OHV 12V FI Engine [Opt on LE,SE]	+122
AM/FM/Cassette/CD Audio System	+129
Air Conditioning [Std on LE]	+281

Body Styles	TMV Pricing		
	Trade	Private	Dealer
4 Dr SE Pass Van	3125	4090	5178

Options	Price
Antilock Brakes [Opt on STD]	+246
Captain Chairs (4)	+218
Leather Seats	+259
Sliding Driver Side Door [Opt on STD]	+194

1997

Traction control is a new option, so long as you get LE or ES trim, and an enhanced accident response system will automatically unlock the doors and illuminate the interior when an airbag deploys. Appearance and equipment refinements complete the modest changes to this best-in-class minivan.

Mileage Category: P

Body Styles	TMV Pricing		
	Trade	Private	Dealer
3 Dr SE Pass Van	2569	3496	4630
3 Dr STD Pass Van	2114	2877	3810

Options	Price
Air Conditioning [Opt on SE,STD]	+247
Antilock Brakes [Opt on STD]	+217
Captain Chairs (4)	+171

Body Styles	TMV Pricing		
	Trade	Private	Dealer
4 Dr ES Pass Van	3354	4565	6046
4 Dr LE Pass Van	3067	4174	5528

Options	Price
Leather Seats	+228
Sliding Driver Side Door [Opt on STD]	+171
Sunscreen Glass	+129

1996

A complete redesign yields a cavernous interior, best-in-class driveability, and new innovations such as the optional driver's side passenger door. And although the all-wheel drive version is discontinued for now, Caravan dethrones the Ford Windstar and once again reigns as king of the minivans.

Mileage Category: P

Body Styles	TMV Pricing		
	Trade	Private	Dealer
3 Dr ES Pass Van	2512	3531	4938
3 Dr LE Pass Van	2480	3486	4876

Options	Price
3.0L V6 SOHC 12V FI Engine	+201
3.3L V6 Flex Fuel OHV 12V FI Engine	+229
3.3L V6 OHV 12V FI Engine [Opt on SE]	+232
Air Conditioning [Opt on SE,STD]	+225
Air Conditioning - Front and Rear	+232

Body Styles	TMV Pricing		
	Trade	Private	Dealer
3 Dr SE Pass Van	2086	2932	4100
3 Dr STD Pass Van	1593	2239	3132

Options	Price
Antilock Brakes [Opt on SE,STD]	+197
Captain Chairs (4)	+163
Leather Seats	+208
Sliding Driver Side Door	+156
Sunscreen Glass	+117

1995

Newly optional is a 3.3-liter V6 engine designed to operate on compressed natural gas. Sport and SE decor packages are available this year. The five-speed manual transmission, available only with the four-cylinder engine, has been canceled.

Mileage Category: P

Body Styles	TMV Pricing		
	Trade	Private	Dealer
3 Dr ES Pass Van	1693	2479	3788
3 Dr LE Pass Van	1610	2358	3605

Options	Price
3.3L V6 Flex Fuel OHV 12V FI Engine	+200
7 Passenger Seating [Opt on STD]	+80
Air Conditioning [Opt on SE,STD]	+196

Body Styles	TMV Pricing		
	Trade	Private	Dealer
3 Dr SE Pass Van	1457	2135	3264
3 Dr STD Pass Van	1165	1706	2607

Options	Price
Antilock Brakes	+172
Captain Chairs (4)	+136
Infinity Audio System [Opt on ES,SE]	+77

Dakota

2004

A new 210-horsepower, 3.7-liter Magnum V6 replaces the previous 3.9-liter engine, while the R/T model (along with its ancient 5.9-liter V8) is dropped and a Stampede Appearance package debuts.

Mileage Category: J

Body Styles	TMV Pricing		
	Trade	Private	Dealer
2 Dr SLT 4WD Ext Cab SB	12661	13972	16158
2 Dr SLT 4WD Std Cab SB	11651	12831	14798
2 Dr SLT Ext Cab SB	10843	12023	13990
2 Dr SLT Plus 4WD Ext Cab SB	13732	15196	17637
2 Dr SLT Plus 4WD Std Cab SB	12610	13865	15957
2 Dr SLT Plus Ext Cab SB	11815	12883	14662
2 Dr SLT Plus Std Cab SB	10791	11859	13638
2 Dr SLT Std Cab SB	9829	10897	12676
2 Dr STD 4WD Ext Cab SB	12648	13959	16145
2 Dr STD 4WD Std Cab SB	11079	12259	14226
2 Dr STD Ext Cab SB	10845	11913	13692
2 Dr STD Std Cab SB	9358	10426	12205
2 Dr SXT 4WD Ext Cab SB	13270	14568	16732
2 Dr SXT 4WD Std Cab SB	12116	13352	15413
2 Dr SXT Ext Cab SB	11512	12580	14359
2 Dr SXT Std Cab SB	10297	11365	13144
2 Dr Sport 4WD Ext Cab SB	12661	13972	16158

Body Styles	TMV Pricing		
	Trade	Private	Dealer
2 Dr Sport 4WD Std Cab SB	11651	12831	14798
2 Dr Sport Ext Cab SB	10852	11920	13699
2 Dr Sport Plus 4WD Ext Cab SB	13439	14872	17261
2 Dr Sport Plus 4WD Std Cab SB	12411	13722	15908
2 Dr Sport Plus Ext Cab SB	11732	12886	14809
2 Dr Sport Plus Std Cab SB	10591	11734	13638
2 Dr Sport Std Cab SB	9629	10772	12676
4 Dr SLT 4WD Crew Cab SB	15136	16767	19487
4 Dr SLT Crew Cab SB	13410	14893	17365
4 Dr SLT Plus 4WD Crew Cab SB	16586	18239	20995
4 Dr SLT Plus Crew Cab SB	14644	16127	18598
4 Dr SXT 4WD Crew Cab SB	15708	17339	20058
4 Dr SXT Crew Cab SB	13973	15456	17927
4 Dr Sport 4WD Crew Cab SB	15349	17003	19761
4 Dr Sport Crew Cab SB	13410	14893	17365
4 Dr Sport Plus 4WD Crew Cab SB	16586	18239	20995
4 Dr Sport Plus Crew Cab SB	14644	16127	18598

2004 (cont'd)

Options	Price
17 Inch Wheels - Chrome [Opt on SLT]	+700
4.7L V8 SOHC 16V FI Engine [Opt on non-STD, non-SXT]	+785
AM/FM/CD Changer Audio System [Opt on non-STD]	+300
Alarm System [Opt on Sport Plus, SLT Plus]	+225
Antilock Brakes	+495
Automatic 4-Speed Transmission	+1095
Automatic 5-Speed Transmission [Opt on non-STD, non-SXT]	+755
Bed Liner	+245
Bucket Seats [Opt on non-STD, non-SXT]	+210
Fog Lights [Opt on Sport, SLT, SXT Crew]	+120

Options	Price
Keyless Entry System [Opt on Sport , SLT Crew]	+250
Leather Seats [Opt on Sport Plus, SLT Plus Crew]	+580
Limited Slip Differential	+285
Power Driver Seat [Opt on Sport, SLT Ext, Crew]	+320
Power Mirrors [Opt on Sport, SLT Crew]	+200
Power Windows [Opt on Sport, SLT Crew]	+400
Skid Plates [Opt on 4WD]	+130
Tilt Steering Wheel [Opt on STD, Sport, SLT, non-Crew SXT]	+140
Tonneau Cover [Opt on non-Crew]	+290

2003

Finally realizing that a 120-horsepower engine has no business being in a 3,500-pound (or more) pickup, Dodge drops the 2.5-liter inline four from the Dakota's powertrain roster. An optional five-speed automatic transmission for the 4.7-liter V8 debuts, as does a Stampede package that provides the show but not the go of the R/T model. Speaking of the R/T, that model receives four-wheel disc brakes this year.

Mileage Category: J

Body Styles	Trade	Private	Dealer
2 Dr R/T Ext Cab	14446	15676	17725
2 Dr R/T Std Cab SB	12267	13311	15052
2 Dr SLT 4WD Ext Cab SB	11929	12945	14637
2 Dr SLT 4WD Std Cab SB	11013	11951	13513
2 Dr SLT Ext Cab SB	10261	11134	12590
2 Dr SLT Plus 4WD Ext Cab SB	12916	14016	15848
2 Dr SLT Plus 4WD Std Cab SB	11841	12849	14529
2 Dr SLT Plus Ext Cab SB	11098	12043	13617
2 Dr SLT Plus Std Cab SB	9811	10646	12038
2 Dr SLT Std Cab SB	8963	9726	10998
2 Dr STD 4WD Ext Cab SB	11917	12931	14622
2 Dr STD 4WD Std Cab SB	10384	11268	12742
2 Dr STD Ext Cab SB	10218	11088	12537
2 Dr STD Std Cab SB	8524	9250	10460
2 Dr SXT 4WD Ext Cab SB	12267	13311	15051
2 Dr SXT 4WD Std Cab SB	11501	12480	14112
2 Dr SXT Ext Cab SB	10723	11635	13156
2 Dr SXT Std Cab SB	9114	9890	11183

Body Styles	Trade	Private	Dealer
2 Dr Sport 4WD Ext Cab SB	11930	12946	14638
2 Dr Sport 4WD Std Cab SB	10992	11928	13488
2 Dr Sport Ext Cab SB	10225	11096	12547
2 Dr Sport Plus 4WD Ext Cab SB	12637	13713	15506
2 Dr Sport Plus 4WD Std Cab SB	11682	12676	14333
2 Dr Sport Plus Ext Cab SB	11089	12033	13606
2 Dr Sport Plus Std Cab SB	9943	10789	12200
2 Dr Sport Std Cab SB	8650	9386	10613
4 Dr SLT 4WD Crew Cab SB	14328	15547	17578
4 Dr SLT Crew Cab SB	12726	13809	15615
4 Dr SLT Plus 4WD Crew Cab SB	15748	17089	19325
4 Dr SLT Plus Crew Cab SB	13710	14876	16821
4 Dr SXT 4WD Crew Cab SB	14528	15764	17825
4 Dr SXT Crew Cab SB	13208	14332	16207
4 Dr Sport 4WD Crew Cab SB	14445	15674	17722
4 Dr Sport Crew Cab SB	12647	13724	15518
4 Dr Sport Plus 4WD Crew Cab SB	15635	16966	19184
4 Dr Sport Plus Crew Cab SB	13715	14882	16828

Options	Price
5.9L V8 OHV 16V FI Engine [Opt on Sport,SLT]	+404
AM/FM/CD Changer Audio System	+126
Alarm System	+142
Antilock Brakes	+430
Automatic 4-Speed Transmission	+332
Automatic 5-Speed Transmission	+692
Bed Liner	+155
Camper/Towing Package	+174
Cruise Control [Opt on SLT,Sport]	+117

Options	Price
Infinity Audio System	+300
Leather Seats [Opt on R/T,Sport Plus,SLT Plus]	+303
Limited Slip Differential	+180
Power Door Locks [Opt on R/T,SLT,Sport]	+145
Power Driver Seat [Opt on SLT Plus,Sport Plus]	+202
Power Windows [Opt on R/T,SLT,Sport]	+180
Rear Window Defroster [Opt on Crew Cab,EXT Cab]	+145
Tonneau Cover	+183
Two-Tone Paint [Opt on SLT]	+123

2002

A new value-priced Dakota SXT debuts and includes 16-inch alloys, automatic tranny, air conditioning, bucket seats and CD player. An appearance group consisting of graphite-colored bumpers, grille and fender flares is also fitted to the SXT.

Mileage Category: J

Body Styles	Trade	Private	Dealer
2 Dr SLT 4WD Ext Cab SB	9883	10904	12605
2 Dr SLT 4WD Std Cab SB	8923	9844	11380
2 Dr SLT Ext Cab SB	8080	8915	10306
2 Dr SLT Plus 4WD Ext Cab SB	10386	11459	13247
2 Dr SLT Plus 4WD Std Cab SB	9412	10384	12003
2 Dr SLT Plus Ext Cab SB	8921	9842	11378
2 Dr SLT Plus Std Cab SB	7644	8433	9749
2 Dr SLT Std Cab SB	7118	7853	9077
2 Dr STD 4WD Ext Cab SB	9891	10913	12616
2 Dr STD 4WD Std Cab SB	8107	8945	10341

Body Styles	Trade	Private	Dealer
2 Dr STD Ext Cab SB	7598	8383	9690
2 Dr STD Std Cab SB	6196	6836	7902
2 Dr SXT 4WD Ext Cab SB	9674	10673	12339
2 Dr SXT 4WD Std Cab SB	8503	9381	10845
2 Dr SXT Ext Cab SB	7979	8803	10177
2 Dr SXT Std Cab SB	6862	7570	8751
2 Dr Sport 4WD Ext Cab SB	9823	10837	12528
2 Dr Sport 4WD Std Cab SB	8889	9807	11337
2 Dr Sport Ext Cab SB	7711	8508	9836
2 Dr Sport Plus 4WD Ext Cab SB	10318	11383	13159

Body Styles	TMV Pricing		
	Trade	Private	Dealer
2 Dr Sport Plus 4WD Std Cab SB	9525	10509	12148
2 Dr Sport Plus Ext Cab SB	8590	9477	10956
2 Dr Sport Plus Std Cab SB	7894	8710	10069
2 Dr Sport Std Cab SB	6858	7567	8748
4 Dr SLT 4WD Crew Cab SB	11769	12985	15011
4 Dr SLT Crew Cab SB	10385	11457	13245

Body Styles	TMV Pricing		
	Trade	Private	Dealer
4 Dr SLT Plus 4WD Crew Cab SB	13178	14538	16806
4 Dr SLT Plus Crew Cab SB	11148	12298	14215
4 Dr Sport 4WD Crew Cab SB	11981	13218	15280
4 Dr Sport Crew Cab SB	10512	11597	13405
4 Dr Sport Plus 4WD Crew Cab SB	12961	14299	16529
4 Dr Sport Plus Crew Cab SB	11169	12322	14244

Options	Price
16 Inch Wheels [Opt on SLT,SLT Plus]	+253
17 Inch Wheels [Opt on Sport Plus]	+381
3.9L V6 OHV 12V FI Engine [Opt on 2WD - Sport,STD]	+275
4.7L V8 SOHC 16V FI Engine	+321
5.9L V8 OHV 16V FI Engine	+612
Alarm System [Opt on SLT Plus,Sport Plus]	+122
Antilock Brakes	+370
Automatic 4-Speed Transmission	+530
Automatic 5-Speed Transmission	+530
Bed Liner	+133

Options	Price
Camper/Towing Package	+149
Infinity Audio System	+258
Leather Seats [Opt on Crew - SLT Plus,Sport Plus]	+315
Limited Slip Differential	+155
Power Door Locks [Opt on Crew - SLT,Sport]	+125
Power Driver Seat [Opt on SLT Plus,Sport Plus]	+174
Power Windows [Opt on Crew - SLT,Sport]	+141
Rear Window Defroster	+125
Sport Suspension [Opt on Sport Plus 2WD]	+163
Tonneau Cover	+158

Mileage Category: J

2001

The Dakota gets a redesigned interior with upgraded audio components, optional steering wheel controls, larger exterior mirrors and a redesigned front fascia on the Sport models. Four-wheel-drive models get a dash-mounted, electronically controlled transfer case. New 15x7-inch cast aluminum wheels are standard on Sport and SLT models, and a leather interior is now available in Quad Cab models. Quad Cabs also benefit from front seatbelt pre-tensioners, Club Cabs have added rear window defrost as an option, and Sentry Key Engine Immobilizer technology is now part of the optional security alarm system. Finally, the 3.9-liter V6, 4.7-liter V8 and 5.9-liter V8 engines meet low-emission-vehicle standards for 2001.

Body Styles	TMV Pricing		
	Trade	Private	Dealer
2 Dr SLT 4WD Ext Cab SB	8419	9791	11058
2 Dr SLT 4WD Std Cab SB	7782	9050	10221
2 Dr SLT Ext Cab SB	6970	8106	9154
2 Dr SLT Std Cab SB	6208	7220	8154
2 Dr STD 4WD Ext Cab SB	8251	9595	10836
2 Dr STD 4WD Std Cab SB	6822	7934	8960
2 Dr STD Ext Cab SB	6427	7474	8440
2 Dr STD Std Cab SB	5170	6012	6790

Body Styles	TMV Pricing		
	Trade	Private	Dealer
2 Dr Sport 4WD Ext Cab SB	8238	9581	10821
2 Dr Sport 4WD Std Cab SB	7427	8638	9756
2 Dr Sport Ext Cab SB	6772	7876	8895
2 Dr Sport Std Cab SB	5790	6734	7606
4 Dr SLT 4WD Crew Cab SB	10551	12271	13857
4 Dr SLT Crew Cab SB	9215	10716	12102
4 Dr Sport 4WD Crew Cab SB	10276	11951	13498
4 Dr Sport Crew Cab SB	8686	10101	11407

Options	Price
4.7L V8 SOHC 16V FI Engine	+294
5.9L V8 OHV 16V FI Engine	+561
AM/FM/CD Audio System	+239
AM/FM/Cassette/CD Audio System	+329
Air Conditioning	+399
Antilock Brakes	+339
Automatic 4-Speed Transmission	+486

Options	Price
Bed Liner	+122
Camper/Towing Package	+137
Leather Seats [Opt on Crew Cab]	+289
Limited Slip Differential	+142
Power Driver Seat	+160
Rear Window Defroster [Opt on SLT,Sport]	+115
Sport Suspension [Opt on SLT,Sport]	+175

Mileage Category: J

2000

The biggest change this year is design oriented -- the Dakota is now available with four full-size doors, and with that comes a family name: Quad Cab. A 4.7-liter V8 has been added, but the 8-foot bed is gone. You can select from five more colors as well.

Body Styles	TMV Pricing		
	Trade	Private	Dealer
2 Dr R/T Sport Ext Cab SB	8098	9590	11052
2 Dr R/T Sport Std Cab SB	6735	7976	9192
2 Dr SLT 4WD Ext Cab SB	7225	8556	9860
2 Dr SLT 4WD Std Cab SB	6888	8157	9400
2 Dr SLT Ext Cab SB	5825	6898	7949
2 Dr SLT Plus 4WD Ext Cab SB	8310	9841	11342
2 Dr SLT Plus 4WD Std Cab SB	7169	8490	9784
2 Dr SLT Plus Ext Cab SB	6860	8124	9363
2 Dr SLT Plus Std Cab SB	5709	6761	7792
2 Dr SLT Std Cab SB	5120	6063	6988
2 Dr STD 4WD Ext Cab SB	6979	8264	9524
2 Dr STD 4WD Std Cab SB	5700	6750	7779
2 Dr STD Ext Cab SB	5473	6482	7471
2 Dr STD Std Cab SB	4376	5182	5972

Body Styles	TMV Pricing		
	Trade	Private	Dealer
2 Dr Sport 4WD Ext Cab SB	7315	8662	9983
2 Dr Sport 4WD Std Cab SB	6458	7648	8814
2 Dr Sport Ext Cab SB	5839	6914	7968
2 Dr Sport Plus 4WD Ext Cab SB	7789	9224	10631
2 Dr Sport Plus 4WD Std Cab SB	6884	8152	9395
2 Dr Sport Plus Ext Cab SB	6406	7586	8742
2 Dr Sport Plus Std Cab SB	5018	5942	6848
2 Dr Sport Std Cab SB	4824	5712	6583
4 Dr SLT 4WD Crew Cab SB	9411	11146	12846
4 Dr SLT Crew Cab SB	7911	9367	10794
4 Dr SLT Plus 4WD Crew Cab SB	10262	12152	14006
4 Dr SLT Plus Crew Cab SB	8128	9625	11093
4 Dr Sport 4WD Crew Cab SB	9368	11093	12783
4 Dr Sport Plus Crew Cab SB	7944	9408	10843

2000 (cont'd)

Options	Price
3.9L V6 OHV 12V FI Engine [Opt on Std Cab]	+253
4.7L V8 SOHC 16V FI Engine	+239
5.9L V8 OHV 16V FI Engine [Std on R/T Sport]	+508
AM/FM/CD Audio System	+127
AM/FM/Cassette/CD Audio System	+163
Air Conditioning	+361
Antilock Brakes	+307

Options	Price
Automatic 4-Speed Transmission [Std on R/T Sport - Ext Cab,Std Cab]	+441
Compact Disc Changer	+181
Limited Slip Differential [Std on R/T Sport - Ext Cab,Std Cab]	+129
Power Driver Seat	+145

1999

Solar Yellow paint is now available. Other un-pickuplike refinements include an express down feature for the driver window, extra storage space for cassettes or CDs, and remote radio controls on the steering wheel.

Mileage Category: J

Body Styles	TMV Pricing		
	Trade	Private	Dealer
2 Dr R/T Sport Ext Cab SB	6796	8203	9668
2 Dr R/T Sport Std Cab SB	5549	6699	7895
2 Dr SLT 4WD Ext Cab SB	5976	7214	8503
2 Dr SLT 4WD Std Cab SB	5656	6827	8045
2 Dr SLT Ext Cab SB	4886	5898	6951
2 Dr SLT Std Cab LB	4641	5601	6601
2 Dr SLT Std Cab SB	4515	5450	6424
2 Dr STD 4WD Ext Cab SB	5740	6928	8165
2 Dr STD 4WD Std Cab SB	4849	5854	6899

Body Styles	TMV Pricing		
	Trade	Private	Dealer
2 Dr STD Ext Cab SB	4771	5759	6787
2 Dr STD Std Cab LB	4267	5150	6070
2 Dr STD Std Cab SB	3669	4429	5220
2 Dr Sport 4WD Ext Cab SB	5731	6918	8154
2 Dr Sport 4WD Std Cab SB	5115	6174	7276
2 Dr Sport Ext Cab SB	4733	5713	6732
2 Dr Sport Std Cab LB	4492	5423	6391
2 Dr Sport Std Cab SB	4296	5185	6111

Options	Price
5.2L V8 OHV 16V FI Engine	+217
AM/FM/CD Audio System	+177
AM/FM/Cassette/CD Audio System	+243
Air Conditioning [Std on SLT]	+295

Options	Price
Antilock Brakes	+278
Automatic 4-Speed Transmission [Std on R/T Sport]	+399
Compact Disc Changer	+276
Power Driver Seat	+118

1998

The Dakota R/T, featuring a 250-horsepower V8, is available for those seeking a performance pickup. The passenger airbag can now be deactivated in all Dakotas, so a rear-facing child seat can be used. The Dakota is also available in three new colors.

Mileage Category: J

Body Styles	TMV Pricing		
	Trade	Private	Dealer
2 Dr R/T Sport Ext Cab SB	4921	6157	7550
2 Dr R/T Sport Std Cab SB	4180	5230	6414
2 Dr SLT 4WD Ext Cab SB	4960	6205	7608
2 Dr SLT 4WD Std Cab SB	4451	5569	6830
SB	4192	5244	6431
2 Dr SLT Std Cab LB	3715	4648	5700
2 Dr SLT Std Cab SB	3591	4493	5510
2 Dr STD 4WD Ext Cab SB	4758	5953	7301
2 Dr STD 4WD Std Cab SB	4185	5236	6421

Body Styles	TMV Pricing		
	Trade	Private	Dealer
2 Dr STD Ext Cab SB	3800	4755	5832
2 Dr STD Std Cab LB	3343	4182	5128
2 Dr STD Std Cab SB	3019	3777	4632
2 Dr Sport 4WD Ext Cab SB	4987	6240	7653
2 Dr Sport 4WD Std Cab SB	4315	5399	6621
2 Dr Sport Ext Cab SB	4200	5265	6467
2 Dr Sport Std Cab LB	3552	4443	5448
2 Dr Sport Std Cab SB	3406	4261	5225

Options	Price
3.9L V6 OHV 12V FI Engine [Opt on Std Cab RWD - SLT,Sport,STD]	+181
5.2L V8 OHV 16V FI Engine	+214
AM/FM/CD Audio System	+156
AM/FM/Cassette/CD Audio System	+215

Options	Price
Air Conditioning [Std on SLT]	+261
Antilock Brakes	+246
Automatic 4-Speed Transmission [Std on R/T Sport]	+344

1997

Powertrains are carried over, but everything else is new. Distinctions? Tightest turning circle in class, roomiest cabs and dual airbags are standard. Faux pas? No third door option, and the passenger airbag cannot be deactivated, so a rear-facing child seat is out of the question unless you cram it into the rear of the Club Cab.

Mileage Category: J

Body Styles	TMV Pricing		
	Trade	Private	Dealer
2 Dr SLT 4WD Ext Cab SB	4227	5429	6897
2 Dr SLT 4WD Std Cab SB	3914	5027	6387
2 Dr SLT Ext Cab SB	3502	4497	5714
2 Dr SLT Std Cab LB	3157	4054	5151
2 Dr SLT Std Cab SB	2846	3654	4642
2 Dr STD 4WD Ext Cab SB	4126	5299	6733
2 Dr STD 4WD Std Cab SB	3461	4444	5646
2 Dr STD Ext Cab SB	3342	4292	5453

Body Styles	TMV Pricing		
	Trade	Private	Dealer
2 Dr STD Std Cab LB	2737	3515	4465
2 Dr STD Std Cab SB	2599	3338	4242
2 Dr Sport 4WD Ext Cab SB	4192	5384	6840
2 Dr Sport 4WD Std Cab SB	3782	4857	6170
2 Dr Sport Ext Cab SB	3357	4311	5476
2 Dr Sport Std Cab LB	2776	3565	4530
2 Dr Sport Std Cab SB	2755	3538	4495

Options	Price
3.9L V6 OHV 12V FI Engine	+223
5.2L V8 OHV 16V FI Engine	+187
AM/FM/CD Audio System	+138
AM/FM/Cassette/CD Audio System	+189

Options	Price
Air Conditioning [Std on SLT]	+229
Antilock Brakes	+217
Automatic 4-Speed Transmission	+279

1996

Mileage Category: J

Body Styles	TMV Pricing		
	Trade	Private	Dealer
2 Dr SLT 4WD Ext Cab SB	3473	4526	5980
2 Dr SLT 4WD Std Cab LB	3324	4333	5726
2 Dr SLT 4WD Std Cab SB	3185	4151	5485
2 Dr SLT Ext Cab SB	2675	3486	4607
2 Dr SLT Std Cab LB	2562	3339	4413
2 Dr SLT Std Cab SB	2422	3157	4172
2 Dr STD 4WD Ext Cab SB	3351	4368	5772
2 Dr STD 4WD Std Cab LB	3035	3954	5224
2 Dr STD 4WD Std Cab SB	2965	3864	5106
2 Dr STD Ext Cab SB	2617	3411	4507

Body Styles	TMV Pricing		
	Trade	Private	Dealer
2 Dr STD Std Cab LB	2022	2635	3482
2 Dr STD Std Cab SB	2177	2838	3751
2 Dr Sport 4WD Ext Cab SB	3262	4252	5618
2 Dr Sport 4WD Std Cab SB	2929	3818	5045
2 Dr Sport Ext Cab SB	2600	3389	4478
2 Dr Sport Std Cab SB	2069	2697	3564
2 Dr WS 4WD Std Cab LB	2727	3554	4695
2 Dr WS 4WD Std Cab SB	2615	3408	4503
2 Dr WS Std Cab LB	1873	2441	3226
2 Dr WS Std Cab SB	1810	2359	3116

America's first midsized pickup gets a more powerful standard four-cylinder engine, revised sound system, and three new colors.

Options	Price
3.9L V6 OHV 12V FI Engine	+203
5.2L V8 OHV 16V FI Engine	+170
AM/FM/CD Audio System	+125

Options	Price
Air Conditioning [Std on SLT]	+208
Antilock Brakes	+197
Automatic 4-Speed Transmission	+269

1995

A 2WD Club Cab Sport is added to the model mix.

Body Styles	TMV Pricing		
	Trade	Private	Dealer
2 Dr SLT 4WD Ext Cab SB	2605	3495	4979
2 Dr SLT 4WD Std Cab LB	2425	3255	4637
2 Dr SLT 4WD Std Cab SB	2376	3188	4540
2 Dr SLT Ext Cab SB	2068	2775	3954
2 Dr SLT Std Cab LB	1963	2634	3751
2 Dr SLT Std Cab SB	1735	2327	3314
2 Dr STD 4WD Ext Cab SB	2541	3410	4858
2 Dr STD 4WD Std Cab LB	2370	3180	4530
2 Dr STD 4WD Std Cab SB	2317	3109	4430
2 Dr STD Ext Cab SB	2034	2730	3889

Body Styles	TMV Pricing		
	Trade	Private	Dealer
2 Dr STD Std Cab LB	1744	2340	3332
2 Dr STD Std Cab SB	1670	2241	3192
2 Dr Sport 4WD Ext Cab SB	2411	3235	4609
2 Dr Sport 4WD Std Cab SB	2286	3067	4368
2 Dr Sport Ext Cab SB	1926	2585	3682
2 Dr Sport Std Cab SB	1494	2004	2853
2 Dr WS 4WD Std Cab LB	2292	3075	4380
2 Dr WS 4WD Std Cab SB	2034	2729	3888
2 Dr WS Std Cab LB	1592	2136	3043
2 Dr WS Std Cab SB	1463	1963	2796

Options	Price
3.9L V6 OHV 12V FI Engine	+127
5.2L V8 OHV 16V FI Engine	+149
AM/FM/CD Audio System	+110

Options	Price
Air Conditioning [Std on SLT]	+182
Antilock Brakes	+172
Automatic 4-Speed Transmission	+235

Durango

2004

Mileage Category: M

Body Styles	TMV Pricing		
	Trade	Private	Dealer
4 Dr Limited 4WD SUV	21549	23067	25598
4 Dr Limited SUV	19689	21208	23739
4 Dr SLT 4WD SUV	19592	21110	23641

Body Styles	TMV Pricing		
	Trade	Private	Dealer
4 Dr SLT SUV	17337	18661	20867
4 Dr ST 4WD SUV	18164	19682	22213
4 Dr ST SUV	15908	17232	19438

The Durango is reborn and now sports the option of Hemi V8 power.

Options	Price
4.7L V8 SOHC 16V FI Engine [Opt on ST, SLT 2WD]	+400
5.7L V8 OHV 16V FI Engine [Opt on SLT, Limited]	+550
AM/FM/CD Changer Audio System [Opt on ST, SLT]	+300
Alarm System [Opt on SLT]	+200
Aluminum/Alloy Wheels [Opt on SLT, Limited]	+280
Automatic 5-Speed Transmission [Opt on ST 2WD, SLT, Limited]	+385

Options	Price
Chrome Wheels [Opt on Limited]	+700
DVD Entertainment System [Opt on SLT, Limited]	+1200
Front, Rear and Third Row Head Airbag Restraints	+495
Heated Front Seats [Opt on Limited]	+250
Leather Seats [Opt on SLT]	+725
Overhead Console [Opt on SLT]	+200
Power Adjustable Foot Pedals [Opt on SLT]	+120

Dodge
Durango

2004 (cont'd)

Options	Price
Power Heated Mirrors [Opt on ST, SLT]	+145
Running Boards [Opt on SLT, Limited]	+395
Skid Plates [Opt on 4WD]	+170

Options	Price
Special Factory Paint	+150
Traction Control System	+200
Trailer Hitch	+325

2003

Entry-level Sport model gets bigger wheels (16s versus last year's 15s) and all Durangos now have four-wheel disc brakes. Inside, you'll find a six-disc CD changer as a new option. A redesign is due for 2004.

Mileage Category: M

Body Styles	TMV Pricing		
	Trade	Private	Dealer
4 Dr R/T 4WD SUV	19067	20611	23185
4 Dr SLT 4WD SUV	15729	17003	19127
4 Dr SLT Plus 4WD SUV	17296	18697	21033
4 Dr SLT Plus SUV	16348	17672	19879
4 Dr SLT SUV	14068	15208	17107

Body Styles	TMV Pricing		
	Trade	Private	Dealer
4 Dr SXT 4WD SUV	13940	15069	16951
4 Dr SXT SUV	13039	14095	15856
4 Dr Sport 4WD SUV	13527	14623	16449
4 Dr Sport SUV	12765	13799	15522

Options	Price
Air Conditioning - Front and Rear [Opt on SXT]	+385
Antilock Brakes	+430
Camper/Towing Package	+373
Front Head Airbag Restraints	+313
Infinity Audio System [Opt on SLT]	+338

Options	Price
Leather Seats [Opt on SLT]	+502
Limited Slip Differential [Std on R/T]	+180
Running Boards [Opt on SLT]	+250
Third Seat [Opt on SXT]	+423

2002

Like its sibling, the Dakota, the Durango gets a new trim level dubbed SXT that serves as the entry-level Durango. Other improvements this year include side-curtain airbags, a five-speed automatic gearbox and an optional DVD video entertainment system.

Mileage Category: M

Body Styles	TMV Pricing		
	Trade	Private	Dealer
4 Dr R/T 4WD SUV	15413	16888	19345
4 Dr SLT 4WD SUV	12682	13895	15916
4 Dr SLT Plus 4WD SUV	14015	15355	17589
4 Dr SLT Plus SUV	13278	14548	16665
4 Dr SLT SUV	11817	12948	14832

Body Styles	TMV Pricing		
	Trade	Private	Dealer
4 Dr SXT 4WD SUV	11578	12686	14532
4 Dr SXT SUV	10615	11631	13323
4 Dr Sport 4WD SUV	11188	12259	14043
4 Dr Sport SUV	10387	11375	13021

Options	Price
5.9L V8 OHV 16V FI Engine [Opt on SLT,SLT Plus]	+323
Antilock Brakes	+370
Camper/Towing Package	+253
Front and Rear Head Airbag Restraints	+269

Options	Price
Infinity Audio System [Opt on SLT]	+291
Leather Seats [Opt on SLT]	+432
Limited Slip Differential	+155
Running Boards [Opt on SXT,SLT]	+215

2001

Dodge's brute of a midsize 'ute receives numerous improvements for 2001. An electronic transfer case for its four-wheel drive system is now standard on 4WD models. A new instrument panel, center console with cupholders, interior trim and upgraded stereo has been added, and a tilt steering column is now standard on all Durangos. The 5.2-liter V8 engine is dropped, leaving the more efficient 4.7-liter V8 as standard equipment in both 4x2 and 4x4 Durangos. A variable-delay intermittent rear wiper is offered, and auto-dimming, heated outside power mirrors can be had on in SLT trim. A new appearance option group for the SLT includes 16-inch aluminum wheels, along with special body side moldings, running boards and lower panels. New 15-inch Sparkle Silver aluminum wheels are standard across the Durango lineup.

Mileage Category: M

Body Styles	TMV Pricing		
	Trade	Private	Dealer
4 Dr SLT 4WD SUV	10958	12675	14259
4 Dr SLT SUV	9770	11300	12713

Body Styles	TMV Pricing		
	Trade	Private	Dealer
4 Dr Sport 4WD SUV	9962	11523	12964
4 Dr Sport SUV	9174	10611	11938

Options	Price
5.9L V8 OHV 16V FI Engine [Opt on SLT]	+296
AM/FM/Cassette/CD Audio System	+150
Air Conditioning - Front and Rear	+399
Antilock Brakes	+339
Camper/Towing Package	+137

Options	Price
Heated Front Seats [Opt on SLT]	+137
Leather Seats	+299
Limited Slip Differential	+142
Power Passenger Seat [Opt on SLT]	+224
Third Seat	+249

2000

The next-generation 4.7-liter V8 is now available on four-wheel-drive models and is linked to an all-new automatic transmission. Rack-and-pinion steering becomes standard for both two- and four-wheel-drives. A performance-oriented R/T model has been added to the lineup that already includes the SLT and the decked-out SLT Plus.

Mileage Category: M

Body Styles	TMV Pricing		
	Trade	Private	Dealer
4 Dr R/T 4WD SUV	11665	13581	15459
4 Dr SLT 4WD SUV	9110	10606	12073
4 Dr SLT Plus 4WD SUV	11008	12815	14586
4 Dr SLT Plus SUV	9316	10847	12347

Body Styles	TMV Pricing		
	Trade	Private	Dealer
4 Dr SLT SUV	8010	9327	10617
4 Dr Sport 4WD SUV	8414	9797	11152
4 Dr Sport SUV	7972	9281	10564

Options	Price
5.9L V8 OHV 16V FI Engine [Std on R/T 4WD Wgn]	+268
AM/FM/Cassette/CD Audio System [Std on R/T 4WD Wgn]	+136
Air Conditioning - Front and Rear	+194

Options	Price
Antilock Brakes	+307
Camper/Towing Package	+124
Infinity Audio System [Std on R/T 4WD Wgn]	+149

Options	Price
Limited Slip Differential	+129
Running Boards [Opt on SLT]	+178

Options	Price
Third Seat	+249
Trailer Hitch	+124

1999

Two-wheel drive models finally show up for true flatlander use, and all Durangos gain a rear power outlet. Also available are steering wheel-mounted radio controls, heated mirrors, and two new colors: Bright Platinum Metallic and Patriot Blue.

Mileage Category: M

Body Styles	TMV Pricing		
	Trade	Private	Dealer
4 Dr SLT 4WD SUV	7611	9137	10726

Body Styles	TMV Pricing		
	Trade	Private	Dealer
4 Dr SLT SUV	6945	8337	9786

Options	Price
5.9L V8 OHV 16V FI Engine	+219
Air Conditioning - Front and Rear	+176
Antilock Brakes	+278
Infinity Audio System	+122

Options	Price
Leather Seats	+247
Power Driver Seat	+118
Third Seat	+203

1998

As the most recent addition to the Dodge truck lineup, the Durango makes quite an entry. Offering the most cargo space in its class, along with eight-passenger seating and three-and-a-half tons of towing capacity, the Durango is the most versatile sport-utility on the market.

Mileage Category: M

Body Styles	TMV Pricing		
	Trade	Private	Dealer
4 Dr SLT 4WD SUV	7076	8453	10006

Body Styles	TMV Pricing		
	Trade	Private	Dealer
4 Dr STD 4WD SUV	7056	8430	9979

Options	Price
5.9L V8 OHV 16V FI Engine	+129
Air Conditioning - Front and Rear	+140
Antilock Brakes	+246

Options	Price
Leather Seats	+218
Third Seat	+180

Grand Caravan

2004

To celebrate 20 years of building minivans, Dodge will offer an Anniversary Edition package for the Grand Caravan with such features as chrome wheels, two-tone leather upholstery, embroidered floor mats and an in-dash CD/DVD changer paired with a rear entertainment system. Additionally, the company has simplified the trim level structure this year, so that buyers need only choose a base SE, a midlevel EX or a top-of-the-line SXT. The Grand Caravan also gets a tire-pressure monitor, upgraded audio systems and a new integrated key/remote.

Mileage Category: P

Body Styles	TMV Pricing		
	Trade	Private	Dealer
4 Dr SE Pass Van Ext	12053	13248	15240
4 Dr SXT AWD Pass Van Ext	16283	17474	19459
4 Dr SXT Aniversary Edition Pass Van Ext	16990	18181	20165

Body Styles	TMV Pricing		
	Trade	Private	Dealer
4 Dr SXT Pass Van Ext	15004	16196	18182
4 Dr eX Pass Van Ext	14155	15348	17335

Options	Price
AM/FM/CD Changer Audio System [Opt on EX, SXT non-Anniv]	+200
Air Conditioning - Front and Rear [Opt on non-Cargo, Anniv]	+650
Alarm System [Opt on non-SE, Anniv]	+200
DVD Entertainment System [Opt on EX, SXT non-Anniv]	+895
Front Side Airbag Restraints [Opt on non-Cargo, Anniv]	+390
Heated Front Seats [Opt on EX, SXT non-Anniv]	+200
Keyless Entry System [Opt on Cargo, SE]	+265
Leather Seats [Opt on EX, SXT non-Anniv]	+850
Luggage Rack [Opt on Cargo, SE]	+250

Options	Price
Power Adjustable Foot Pedals	+185
Power Door Locks [Opt on Cargo, SE]	+250
Power Heated Mirrors [Opt on Cargo, SE]	+200
Power Retractable Mirrors [Opt on Cargo, SE]	+200
Power Windows [Opt on Cargo, SE]	+300
Privacy Glass [Opt on SE]	+265
Special Factory Paint	+200
Trip Computer [Opt on EX, SXT non-Anniv]	+150

2003

Two new options debut, a power sunroof (that Dodge boasts as one of the largest available in a minivan) and a factory-, not dealer-, installed DVD entertainment system that comes with wireless headphones. Audiophiles will appreciate the CD changer being upgraded from four-disc capacity to six.

Mileage Category: P

Body Styles	TMV Pricing		
	Trade	Private	Dealer
4 Dr ES AWD Pass Van Ext	15240	16642	18978
4 Dr ES Pass Van Ext	15059	16444	18753
4 Dr SE Pass Van Ext	10190	11127	12689
4 Dr Sport AWD Pass Van Ext	13742	15005	17111

Body Styles	TMV Pricing		
	Trade	Private	Dealer
4 Dr Sport Pass Van Ext	12241	13367	15243
4 Dr eL Pass Van Ext	10851	11849	13511
4 Dr eX Pass Van Ext	11932	13030	14859

Options	Price
3.8L V6 OHV 12V FI Engine [Opt on eL,Sport]	+212
AM/FM/Cassette/CD Audio System [Opt on SE,Sport]	+142
Air Conditioning - Front and Rear [Opt on SE]	+174
Alarm System [Opt on CV,ES]	+123

Options	Price
Automatic Climate Control (3 Zone) [Opt on SE]	+237
Automatic Load Leveling [Opt on ES,SE,Sport]	+190
Camper/Towing Package [Opt on ES,Sport]	+224
Center Console [Opt on Sport]	+123

2003 (cont'd)

Options	Price
Compact Disc Changer [Opt on ES,Sport]	+126
Cruise Control [Opt on CV,SE]	+117
DVD Entertainment System [Opt on ES,eX,Sport]	+569
Front Side Airbag Restraints	+246
Heated Front Seats [Opt on ES]	+158
Leather Seats [Opt on ES,EX]	+521
Luggage Rack [Opt on CV,eL,SE,Sport]	+158
Power Adjustable Foot Pedals	+117
Power Door Locks [Opt on CV,SE]	+142

Options	Price
Power Driver Seat [Opt on SE,Sport]	+234
Power Dual Sliding Doors [Opt on eX]	+253
Power Moonroof [Opt on ES]	+565
Power Rear Liftgate [Opt on eL,Sport]	+253
Power Sliding Door [Opt on eL,Sport]	+253
Power Windows [Opt on CV,SE]	+164
Privacy Glass [Opt on SE]	+174
Special Factory Paint	+126
Tinted Glass [Opt on SE]	+221

2002

Dodge brings out the Caravan eL, a value leader that lists for around $24,000. The luxury factor on higher-line trims is boosted with the availability of power adjustable pedals, rear-seat audio with wireless headsets and the coupe de grace: a DVD video system for the rear seat, which also includes wireless headsets.

Mileage Category: P

Body Styles	TMV Pricing		
	Trade	Private	Dealer
4 Dr ES AWD Pass Van Ext	11871	13169	15332
4 Dr ES Pass Van Ext	10545	11698	13619
4 Dr SE Pass Van Ext	7826	8682	10108
4 Dr Sport AWD Pass Van Ext	10663	11829	13771

Body Styles	TMV Pricing		
	Trade	Private	Dealer
4 Dr Sport Pass Van Ext	8744	9700	11293
4 Dr eL Pass Van Ext	8393	9310	10839
4 Dr eX Pass Van Ext	9288	10303	11995

Options	Price
16 Inch Wheels [Opt on Sport 2WD]	+149
17 Inch Wheels - Chrome [Opt on ES FWD]	+299
AM/FM/CD Audio System [Opt on SE]	+122
AM/FM/Cassette/CD Audio System [Opt on Sport]	+122
Air Conditioning - Front and Rear [Opt on SE,Sport FWD]	+353
Automatic Load Leveling [Opt on FWD - ES,Sport]	+163
Captain Chairs (4) [Opt on Sport]	+405
Center and Rear Bench Seat [Opt on Sport 2WD]	+122
Child Seats (2) [Opt on SE,Sport FWD]	+122
Front Side Airbag Restraints	+212
Heated Front Seats [Opt on ES]	+136

Options	Price
Infinity Audio System [Opt on Sport]	+269
Leather Seats [Opt on ES,eX]	+448
Luggage Rack [Std on eX]	+136
Power Door Locks [Opt on SE]	+122
Power Driver Seat [Opt on Sport]	+130
Power Dual Sliding Doors [Opt on eX]	+217
Power Rear Liftgate [Opt on ES,Sport]	+217
Power Sliding Door [Opt on eL,Sport FWD]	+217
Power Windows [Opt on SE]	+141
Temperature Controls - Driver and Passenger [Opt on SE,Sport FWD]	+177

2001

America's best-selling minivan is all new for 2001, with many industry-first features including a power rear tailgate, a power sliding door obstacle detection system, a removable and powered center console and a pop-up rear cargo organizer, all residing under new sheet metal.

Mileage Category: P

Body Styles	TMV Pricing		
	Trade	Private	Dealer
4 Dr ES AWD Pass Van Ext	9859	11690	13380
4 Dr ES Pass Van Ext	8809	10445	11955
4 Dr EX Pass Van Ext	8175	9693	11094

Body Styles	TMV Pricing		
	Trade	Private	Dealer
4 Dr SE Pass Van Ext	6709	7954	9104
4 Dr Sport AWD Pass Van Ext	9557	11331	12968
4 Dr Sport Pass Van Ext	7470	8857	10137

Options	Price
17 Inch Wheels - Chrome [Opt on ES]	+339
3.8L V6 OHV 12V FI Engine [Std on AWD]	+167
Air Conditioning - Front and Rear [Opt on Sport]	+274
Aluminum/Alloy Wheels	+339
Automatic Climate Control (3 Zone) [Opt on Sport]	+200
Automatic Load Leveling	+145
Camper/Towing Package [Opt on ES,Sport]	+304
Front Side Airbag Restraints	+195
Heated Front Seats [Opt on ES]	+125

Options	Price
Infinity Audio System [Opt on Sport]	+247
Leather Seats [Opt on ES]	+623
Luggage Rack	+125
Power Driver Seat [Opt on Sport]	+185
Power Heated Mirrors [Opt on SE]	+125
Power Rear Liftgate [Opt on ES,Sport]	+200
Power Sliding Door [Opt on Sport]	+192
Power Windows [Opt on SE]	+130
Rear Window Defroster [Opt on SE]	+115

2000

Mileage Category: P

Body Styles	TMV Pricing		
	Trade	Private	Dealer
4 Dr ES AWD Pass Van Ext	7197	8842	10455
4 Dr ES Pass Van Ext	6522	8013	9474
4 Dr LE AWD Pass Van Ext	6779	8327	9844
4 Dr LE Pass Van Ext	6349	7799	9221

Body Styles	TMV Pricing		
	Trade	Private	Dealer
4 Dr SE Pass Van Ext	4980	6118	7234
4 Dr STD Pass Van Ext	4696	5769	6820
4 Dr Sport AWD Pass Van Ext	6409	7873	9308

Options	Price
3.3L V6 OHV 12V FI Engine [Opt on FWD - LE,SE,STD]	+438
3.8L V6 OHV 12V FI Engine [Opt on LE FWD]	+230
AM/FM/Cassette/CD Audio System	+140
Air Conditioning - Front and Rear [Opt on ES,SE,Sport]	+271
Aluminum/Alloy Wheels [Opt on LE,SE,Sport]	+119
Antilock Brakes [Opt on STD]	+310
Automatic Load Leveling [Opt on FWD]	+131
Captain Chairs (4)	+270

Options	Price
Infinity Audio System [Opt on SE,Sport]	+326
Leather Seats [Opt on LE,ES]	+359
Power Door Locks [Opt on STD]	+152
Power Driver Seat [Opt on SE,Sport]	+126
Power Passenger Seat [Opt on ES]	+172
Power Windows [Opt on STD]	+117
Sunscreen Glass [Opt on SE,STD]	+204

Mileage Category: P

Body Styles	TMV Pricing		
	Trade	Private	Dealer
4 Dr ES AWD Pass Van Ext	5964	7532	9165
4 Dr ES Pass Van Ext	5443	6874	8364
4 Dr LE AWD Pass Van Ext	5820	7352	8946
4 Dr LE Pass Van Ext	5171	6532	7948

Body Styles	TMV Pricing		
	Trade	Private	Dealer
4 Dr SE AWD Pass Van Ext	5100	6442	7838
4 Dr SE Pass Van Ext	4126	5212	6342
4 Dr STD Pass Van Ext	3906	4933	6002

1999

A revised front fascia is common to all models. The Grand Caravan ES gets an AutoStick transmission, 17-inch wheels and tires, and steering wheel-mounted radio controls.

Options	Price
3.0L V6 SOHC 12V FI Engine	+295
3.3L V6 OHV 12V FI Engine	+357
3.8L V6 OHV 12V FI Engine	+170
AM/FM/CD Audio System [Opt on STD]	+120
AM/FM/Cassette/CD Audio System	+120
Air Conditioning	+184
Air Conditioning - Front and Rear	+255
Aluminum/Alloy Wheels	+153
Antilock Brakes	+281

Options	Price
Automatic Load Leveling [Opt on STD AWD]	+119
Camper/Towing Package	+155
Captain Chairs (4)	+247
Compact Disc Changer	+166
Infinity Audio System [Opt on SE]	+265
Leather Seats	+328
Power Passenger Seat [Opt on ES]	+131
Sunscreen Glass [Opt on SE,STD]	+166

Mileage Category: P

Body Styles	TMV Pricing		
	Trade	Private	Dealer
4 Dr ES AWD Pass Van Ext	4827	6317	7998
4 Dr ES Pass Van Ext	4337	5676	7186
4 Dr LE AWD Pass Van Ext	4818	6306	7985
4 Dr LE Pass Van Ext	4328	5665	7172

Body Styles	TMV Pricing		
	Trade	Private	Dealer
4 Dr SE AWD Pass Van Ext	4314	5646	7149
4 Dr SE Pass Van Ext	3301	4320	5469
4 Dr STD Pass Van Ext	3120	4084	5172

1998

Available this year is a 3.8-liter V6 that puts out 180 horsepower and 240 pound-feet of torque. Caravans come with rear-seat mounted grocery bag hooks, and driver-side easy-entry Quad seating. All Chrysler products are equipped with "Next Generation" depowered airbags.

Options	Price
3.8L V6 OHV 12V FI Engine [Opt on FWD]	+122
AM/FM/Cassette/CD Audio System	+129
Air Conditioning [Opt on STD,SE]	+281
Air Conditioning - Front and Rear	+290

Options	Price
Antilock Brakes [Opt on STD]	+248
Captain Chairs (4) [Opt on ES,LE,SE]	+218
Infinity Audio System [Opt on SE]	+129
Leather Seats [Opt on ES,LE]	+259

Mileage Category: P

Body Styles	TMV Pricing		
	Trade	Private	Dealer
3 Dr SE AWD Pass Van Ext	3151	4289	5679
3 Dr SE Pass Van Ext	2513	3420	4528
3 Dr STD Pass Van Ext	2324	3162	4186
4 Dr ES AWD Pass Van Ext	3817	5195	6879

Body Styles	TMV Pricing		
	Trade	Private	Dealer
4 Dr ES Pass Van Ext	3399	4626	6126
4 Dr LE AWD Pass Van Ext	3805	5179	6858
4 Dr LE Pass Van Ext	3386	4610	6105

1997

After a one year hiatus, all-wheel drive returns to the lineup, available on SE and LE models. Traction control is newly available, and an enhanced accident response system will automatically unlock the doors and illuminate the interior when an airbag deployment is detected. A Sport decor group is newly available on Grand Caravan SE.

Options	Price
Air Conditioning [Opt on SE,STD]	+247
Air Conditioning - Front and Rear [Opt on ES,LE,SE]	+255
Antilock Brakes [Opt on STD]	+219
Captain Chairs (4) [Opt on ES,LE,SE]	+171
Compact Disc Changer [Opt on ES]	+158

Options	Price
Leather Seats [Opt on ES,LE]	+228
Sliding Driver Side Door [Opt on SE,STD]	+171
Sport Package [Opt on SE]	+355
Sunscreen Glass	+129

Dodge
Grand Caravan/Intrepid

1996

A complete redesign yields a cavernous interior, best-in-class driveability and new innovations such as the optional driver-side passenger door. And although the all-wheel-drive version is discontinued for now, Caravan dethrones the Ford Windstar and once again reigns as king of the minivans.

Mileage Category: P

Body Styles	TMV Pricing		
	Trade	Private	Dealer
3 Dr ES Pass Van Ext	2525	3549	4963
3 Dr LE Pass Van Ext	2444	3434	4802

Options	Price
3.0L V6 SOHC 12V FI Engine [Opt on STD]	+201
3.3L V6 OHV 12V FI Engine [Opt on SE]	+232
Air Conditioning [Opt on SE,STD]	+225
Air Conditioning - Front and Rear [Opt on ES,LE,SE]	+232
Antilock Brakes [Opt on STD]	+199

Body Styles	TMV Pricing		
	Trade	Private	Dealer
3 Dr SE Pass Van Ext	2132	2996	4189
3 Dr STD Pass Van Ext	1918	2696	3771

Options	Price
Captain Chairs (4) [Opt on ES,LE,SE]	+163
Leather Seats [Opt on ES,LE]	+208
Sliding Driver Side Door	+156
Sunscreen Glass	+117

1995

Newly optional is a 3.3-liter V6 engine designed to operate on compressed natural gas, and new Sport and SE decor packages are available this year.

Mileage Category: P

Body Styles	TMV Pricing		
	Trade	Private	Dealer
3 Dr ES AWD Pass Van Ext	1709	2504	3829
3 Dr ES Pass Van Ext	1647	2412	3686
3 Dr LE AWD Pass Van Ext	1694	2482	3794
3 Dr LE Pass Van Ext	1569	2297	3511

Options	Price
3.8L V6 OHV 12V FI Engine [Opt on ES,LE]	+85
Air Conditioning [Opt on SE,STD]	+196
Air Conditioning - Front and Rear	+159
Antilock Brakes [Opt on SE,STD]	+174

Body Styles	TMV Pricing		
	Trade	Private	Dealer
3 Dr SE AWD Pass Van Ext	1521	2227	3404
3 Dr SE Pass Van Ext	1440	2109	3225
3 Dr STD Pass Van Ext	1297	1899	2902

Options	Price
Captain Chairs (4) [Opt on ES,LE,SE]	+136
Infinity Audio System [Opt on ES,SE]	+77
Leather Seats [Opt on ES,LE]	+182

Intrepid

2004

No changes for 2004.

Mileage Category: G

Body Styles	TMV Pricing		
	Trade	Private	Dealer
4 Dr ES Sdn	11506	12704	14701
4 Dr SE Sdn	9719	10919	12918

Options	Price
AM/FM/CD Audio System [Opt on SE]	+125
Antilock Brakes	+600
Cruise Control [Opt on SE]	+235
Front Side Airbag Restraints	+990
Keyless Entry System [Opt on SE]	+125

Body Styles	TMV Pricing		
	Trade	Private	Dealer
4 Dr SXT Sdn	12000	13265	15372

Options	Price
Pearlescent Metallic Paint	+200
Power Moonroof	+895
Split Folding Rear Seat [Opt on SE]	+210
Split Front Bench Seat [Opt on SE]	+150

2003

The high-performance R/T model is dropped, although the new SXT offers virtually all of the go-fast goodies, including the 244-horsepower V6 and firmer suspension tuning. Music buffs will appreciate the new six-disc CD changer that replaces the former four-disc unit.

Mileage Category: G

Body Styles	TMV Pricing		
	Trade	Private	Dealer
4 Dr ES Sdn	9332	10422	12239
4 Dr SE Sdn	7216	8060	9465

Options	Price
Aluminum/Alloy Wheels [Opt on ES,SE]	+186
Antilock Brakes	+490
Compact Disc Changer	+268
Cruise Control [Opt on SE]	+117
Front Side Airbag Restraints	+246

Body Styles	TMV Pricing		
	Trade	Private	Dealer
4 Dr SXT Sdn	9722	10858	12752

Options	Price
Power Driver Seat [Opt on SE]	+152
Power Moonroof	+565
Special Factory Paint	+126
Split Folding Rear Seat [Opt on SE]	+133

2002

A few functional upgrades take place. The 3.2-liter V6 is dropped as the 3.5-liter engine becomes an option on the ES model, a new SXT model debuts, sporting the R/T's higher-output engine, and the antilock brakes now have Electronic Brakeforce Distribution.

Mileage Category: G

Body Styles	TMV Pricing		
	Trade	Private	Dealer
4 Dr ES Sdn	7324	8241	9769
4 Dr R/T Sdn	9297	10461	12401

Body Styles	TMV Pricing		
	Trade	Private	Dealer
4 Dr SE Sdn	5987	6736	7985
4 Dr SXT Sdn	8414	9468	11224

Options	Price
16 Inch Wheels [Opt on SE]	+160
AM/FM/Cassette/CD Changer Audio System	+204
Antilock Brakes [Std on R/T]	+421
Chrome Wheels [Opt on ES]	+326

Options	Price
Front Side Airbag Restraints	+212
Leather Seats	+326
Power Driver Seat [Opt on SE]	+130
Power Moonroof	+487

Mileage Category: G

2001

Changes to this family sedan for the 2001 model year include optional side airbags, a shoulder belt for the central rear passenger, an internal trunk release, three new interior colors, two additional exterior colors and an additional power outlet in the center console if you get a model with bucket seats. For those cars equipped with the Infinity sound system, you'll receive steering wheel-mounted controls and a four-disc in-dash CD player. SE is now the base Intrepid designation (previously it was the mid-level model), and it includes higher grade fabric this year. All engine choices meet LEV standards, and all models receive thicker side glass and upgraded windshield moldings for a quieter ride.

Body Styles	TMV Pricing		
	Trade	Private	Dealer
4 Dr ES Sdn	5640	6868	8001
4 Dr R/T Sdn	7270	8853	10314

Body Styles	TMV Pricing		
	Trade	Private	Dealer
4 Dr SE Sdn	4892	5957	6940

Options	Price
3.2L V6 SOHC 24V FI Engine	+249
AM/FM/Cassette/CD Audio System [Std on R/T]	+287
Aluminum/Alloy Wheels [Opt on STD]	+195
Antilock Brakes [Std on R/T]	+387
Compact Disc Changer	+175

Options	Price
Front Side Airbag Restraints	+195
Leather Seats	+436
Power Driver Seat [Std on ES]	+190
Power Moonroof	+446
Power Passenger Seat [Opt on R/T]	+190

Mileage Category: G

2000

A performance R/T model is onboard for 2000. Intrepids get five new colors, new seat fabric in Base models, and added horsepower and torque to ES models powered by the 2.7-liter V6. AutoStick is available with that engine, and ES buyers can order an in-dash CD changer. Tether-ready child-seat anchors have been added behind the rear seat, and cars sold in California meet LEV standards.

Body Styles	TMV Pricing		
	Trade	Private	Dealer
4 Dr ES Sdn	4315	5371	6406
4 Dr R/T Sdn	5667	7052	8410

Body Styles	TMV Pricing		
	Trade	Private	Dealer
4 Dr STD Sdn	3981	4955	5909

Options	Price
3.2L V6 SOHC 24V FI Engine	+226
AM/FM/CD Audio System	+147
AM/FM/Cassette/CD Audio System [Opt on ES,STD]	+260
Antilock Brakes [Opt on ES,STD]	+350
Compact Disc Changer	+159

Options	Price
Infinity Audio System	+260
Leather Seats	+395
Power Moonroof	+359
Power Passenger Seat [Opt on ES]	+172

Mileage Category: G

1999

Minor appearance tweaks such as chrome badging and improved floor carpeting debut for 1999. A new engine immobilizer is available on the ES.

Body Styles	TMV Pricing		
	Trade	Private	Dealer
4 Dr ES Sdn	3727	4742	5798

Body Styles	TMV Pricing		
	Trade	Private	Dealer
4 Dr STD Sdn	3263	4150	5074

Options	Price
AM/FM/CD Audio System	+120
AM/FM/Cassette/CD Audio System	+182
Antilock Brakes [Opt on STD]	+317
Compact Disc Changer	+129

Options	Price
Leather Seats	+323
Power Moonroof	+293
Power Passenger Seat [Opt on ES]	+156

Mileage Category: G

1998

Completely redesigned for 1998, the Intrepid is a sedan that has the graceful styling of a coupe, thanks to a continuation of Chrysler's cab-forward design. Dodge's trademark cross hair grille dominates the front end along with two large, sparkling headlights. And the new Intrepid is powered by your choice of two new V6 engines.

Body Styles	TMV Pricing		
	Trade	Private	Dealer
4 Dr ES Sdn	3051	4069	5217

Body Styles	TMV Pricing		
	Trade	Private	Dealer
4 Dr STD Sdn	2592	3457	4432

Options	Price
AM/FM/Cassette/CD Audio System	+162
Antilock Brakes [Opt on STD]	+281
Leather Seats	+285

Options	Price
Power Moonroof	+259
Power Passenger Seat [Opt on ES]	+138

Dodge
Intrepid/Neon

1997

Mileage Category: G

Body Styles	TMV Pricing		
	Trade	Private	Dealer
4 Dr ES Sdn	2243	3126	4206

Options	Price
3.5L V6 SOHC 24V FI Engine [Std on ES]	+208
AM/FM/Cassette/CD Audio System	+142
Antilock Brakes [Std on ES]	+247
Leather Seats	+251

Body Styles	TMV Pricing		
	Trade	Private	Dealer
4 Dr STD Sdn	1968	2743	3691

Options	Price
Power Moonroof	+228
Power Passenger Seat [Opt on ES]	+121
Premium Audio System	+201

Few changes as first-generation Intrepid enters final year of production. A Sport Group including the 3.5-liter V6 engine is optional on base models, which also get an upgraded cassette stereo standard. Bolt-on wheel covers debut, and a new exterior color is introduced. Automatic transmissions get new software.

1996

ES carries over, but the base model gets several improvements to remain competitive with the new Ford Taurus. ES styling cues and 16-inch wheels come standard on the base Intrepid. New colors and seat fabrics update this full-size sedan, and all Intrepids get noise, vibration and harshness improvements.

Mileage Category: G

Body Styles	TMV Pricing		
	Trade	Private	Dealer
4 Dr ES Sdn	1752	2543	3635

Options	Price
Antilock Brakes [Std on Sport]	+225
Leather Seats	+229

Body Styles	TMV Pricing		
	Trade	Private	Dealer
4 Dr STD Sdn	1548	2246	3210

Options	Price
Power Moonroof	+208

1995

ABS is standard on ES. Traction control is a new ES option.

Mileage Category: G

Body Styles	TMV Pricing		
	Trade	Private	Dealer
4 Dr ES Sdn	1240	1845	2853

Options	Price
3.5L V6 SOHC 24V FI Engine	+165
Antilock Brakes [Opt on STD]	+197
Infinity Audio System	+137

Body Styles	TMV Pricing		
	Trade	Private	Dealer
4 Dr STD Sdn	1193	1775	2746

Options	Price
Leather Seats	+200
Power Moonroof	+182

Neon

2004

Mileage Category: B

Body Styles	TMV Pricing		
	Trade	Private	Dealer
4 Dr R/T Sdn	8306	9274	10886
4 Dr SE Sdn	5904	6900	8559

Options	Price
AM/FM/CD Audio System [Opt on SE]	+175
AM/FM/Cassette/CD Changer Audio System [Opt on SXT]	+350
Antilock Brakes [Opt on SE, SXT]	+595
Automatic 4-Speed Transmission [Opt on SE, SXT]	+825
Chrome Wheels [Opt on SXT]	+700

Body Styles	TMV Pricing		
	Trade	Private	Dealer
4 Dr SXT Sdn	7456	8424	10036

Options	Price
Cruise Control [Opt on SE, SXT]	+250
Fog Lights [Opt on SXT]	+150
Front Side Airbag Restraints	+390
Leather Seats [Opt on R/T]	+715

After last year's facelift, the Neon sees only a couple of new paint colors for 2004.

2003

The fire-breathing Neon SRT-4 debuts, sporting a 215-horsepower turbocharged engine, a tweaked suspension and Viper-inspired sport seats. Zero to 60 is said to take about 6 seconds. All Neons receive a facelift in the form of new front and rear ends as well as interior changes that include a new steering wheel.

Mileage Category: B

Body Styles	TMV Pricing		
	Trade	Private	Dealer
4 Dr R/T Sdn	7195	8126	9677
4 Dr SE Sdn	5261	5942	7077

Options	Price
AM/FM/Cassette/CD Changer Audio System [Opt on SXT]	+190
Air Conditioning [Opt on SE]	+632
Antilock Brakes [Opt on SE, SXT]	+430
Automatic 4-Speed Transmission [Opt on SE, SXT]	+521
Chrome Wheels [Opt on SXT]	+190

Body Styles	TMV Pricing		
	Trade	Private	Dealer
4 Dr SXT Sdn	6311	7128	8490

Options	Price
Cruise Control [Opt on SE, SXT]	+158
Front Side Airbag Restraints [Opt on R/T, SE, SXT]	+246
Leather Seats [Opt on R/T]	+452
Power Moonroof [Opt on R/T, SXT]	+439

2002

A four-speed automatic gearbox replaces the archaic three-speed unit, a new base model is introduced, as is a value-packed SXT. Both SE and ES trims are relegated to fleet-only sales, and all Neons get a new "Dodge-signature" (crosshair-style) front end.

Mileage Category: B

Body Styles	TMV Pricing		
	Trade	Private	Dealer
4 Dr ACR Sdn	4790	5571	6873
4 Dr ES Sdn	4863	5658	6982
4 Dr R/T Sdn	5223	6076	7497

Options	Price
AM/FM/Cassette/CD Changer Audio System	+166
Air Conditioning	+353
Aluminum/Alloy Wheels [Opt on SE]	+193
Antilock Brakes [Std on ACR,R/T]	+370
Automatic 4-Speed Transmission	+448

Body Styles	TMV Pricing		
	Trade	Private	Dealer
4 Dr SE Sdn	4604	5271	6381
4 Dr STD Sdn	3962	4608	5686
4 Dr SXT Sdn	4424	5147	6351

Options	Price
Chrome Wheels [Opt on SE,SXT]	+326
Front Side Airbag Restraints	+160
Leather Seats	+302
Power Moonroof	+321

2001

The Neon R/T and Neon ACR, both models sporting a 2.0-liter 150-horsepower engine, make their much-anticipated return this year. Side-impact airbags and leather seats are available, as is a new interior color and four new exterior colors. An internal trunk release keeps young and old from being trapped in the Neon's cargo hold, and four new option packages, one of which includes a four-disc in-dash CD player, further widen its appeal to buyers seeking an American-made economy car.

Mileage Category: B

Body Styles	TMV Pricing		
	Trade	Private	Dealer
4 Dr Highline ACR Sdn	3994	5121	6161
4 Dr Highline ES Sdn	3798	4869	5856

Options	Price
AM/FM/CD Audio System	+197
Air Conditioning [Opt on ES]	+349
Alarm System [Opt on ACR]	+125
Aluminum/Alloy Wheels	+204
Antilock Brakes	+339
Automatic 3-Speed Transmission	+299

Body Styles	TMV Pricing		
	Trade	Private	Dealer
4 Dr Highline R/T Sdn	4508	5778	6950
4 Dr Highline SE Sdn	3330	4268	5134

Options	Price
Compact Disc Changer	+187
Cruise Control [Std on ES]	+117
Front Side Airbag Restraints	+175
Leather Seats	+329
Power Moonroof	+296
Power Windows [Std on ES]	+127

2000

Everything's new inside and out, as the second-generation Neon grows up, not old. A totally redesigned suspension and steering system, low-speed traction control, and a complete exterior redesign head up the notable changes.

Mileage Category: B

Body Styles	TMV Pricing		
	Trade	Private	Dealer
4 Dr ES Sdn	2651	3573	4477

Options	Price
AM/FM/CD Audio System	+178
Air Conditioning [Opt on ES]	+452
Aluminum/Alloy Wheels	+160
Antilock Brakes	+307

Body Styles	TMV Pricing		
	Trade	Private	Dealer
4 Dr Highline Sdn	2590	3493	4377

Options	Price
Automatic 3-Speed Transmission	+271
Compact Disc Changer	+226
Power Moonroof	+268
Power Windows [Std on ES Sdn]	+115

1999

Mileage Category: B

Body Styles	TMV Pricing		
	Trade	Private	Dealer
2 Dr Competition Cpe	1900	2685	3502
2 Dr Highline Cpe	1961	2771	3614
2 Dr R/T Cpe	2270	3208	4185
2 Dr Sport Cpe	2241	3168	4133

Options	Price
AM/FM/CD Audio System	+146
Air Conditioning [Std on R/T,Sport]	+368
Aluminum/Alloy Wheels [Std on R/T]	+131
Antilock Brakes	+278

Body Styles	TMV Pricing		
	Trade	Private	Dealer
4 Dr Competition Sdn	1945	2750	3588
4 Dr Highline Sdn	1974	2790	3639
4 Dr R/T Sdn	2302	3254	4245
4 Dr Sport Sdn	2211	3126	4078

Options	Price
Automatic 3-Speed Transmission	+246
Compact Disc Changer	+184
Competition Package	+759
Power Moonroof	+219

One new color is available for the Neon Style Package: Inferno Red.

1998

An R/T appearance package debuts. Improved option packages, LEV emissions and next-generation airbags round out the changes.

Mileage Category: B

Body Styles	TMV Pricing		
	Trade	Private	Dealer
2 Dr Competition Cpe	1359	2079	2891
2 Dr Highline Cpe	1407	2151	2991
2 Dr R/T Cpe	1501	2295	3191
2 Dr Sport Cpe	1453	2223	3092

Body Styles	TMV Pricing		
	Trade	Private	Dealer
4 Dr Competition Sdn	1395	2132	2963
4 Dr Highline Sdn	1431	2187	3041
4 Dr R/T Sdn	1530	2339	3252
4 Dr Sport Sdn	1481	2264	3148

1998 (cont'd)

Options	Price
AM/FM/CD Audio System	+121
Air Conditioning [Opt on Competition,Highline]	+326
Aluminum/Alloy Wheels [Opt on Competition,Highline]	+116
Antilock Brakes	+246

Options	Price
Automatic 3-Speed Transmission	+196
Compact Disc Changer	+163
Competition Package	+671
Power Moonroof	+194

1997

Sport trim level disappears in favor of Sport Package for Highline models. Twin-cam engine is optional on Highline models. Federal side-impact standards are met for the first time. More work has been done to quiet the Neon's boisterous demeanor.

Mileage Category: B

Body Styles	TMV Pricing		
	Trade	Private	Dealer
2 Dr Highline Cpe	1054	1731	2558
2 Dr STD Cpe	1002	1646	2433
2 Dr Sport Cpe	1066	1752	2589

Body Styles	TMV Pricing		
	Trade	Private	Dealer
4 Dr Highline Sdn	1066	1751	2588
4 Dr STD Sdn	1029	1690	2498
4 Dr Sport Sdn	1116	1832	2708

Options	Price
Air Conditioning [Opt on STD]	+287
Antilock Brakes	+217
Automatic 3-Speed Transmission	+172

Options	Price
Compact Disc Changer	+143
Competition Package	+591
Power Moonroof	+171

1996

A raft of improvements make the sprightly Neon even more attractive to compact buyers. Base models get more equipment, and the gray bumpers are discontinued. A base coupe is newly available. Interior noise levels are supposedly subdued this year. ABS is available across the board this year.

Mileage Category: B

Body Styles	TMV Pricing		
	Trade	Private	Dealer
2 Dr Highline Cpe	752	1318	2101
2 Dr STD Cpe	734	1287	2052
2 Dr Sport Cpe	866	1519	2421

Body Styles	TMV Pricing		
	Trade	Private	Dealer
4 Dr Highline Sdn	757	1327	2115
4 Dr STD Sdn	741	1302	2077
4 Dr Sport Sdn	848	1486	2367

Options	Price
AM/FM/CD Audio System	+125
Air Conditioning	+261
Antilock Brakes	+197
Automatic 3-Speed Transmission	+174

Options	Price
Compact Disc Changer	+131
Competition Package [Opt on STD]	+473
Power Moonroof	+156

1995

Neon is the new Shadow replacement. Base, Highline and Sport models are available. Coupe and sedan body styles are offered. All except Sport Coupe have a 132-horsepower, 2.0-liter four-cylinder engine. Sport Coupe gets a 150-horsepower twin-cam edition of the base motor. Dual airbags are standard on all models; ABS is standard on Sport and optional on others. Integrated child seats are optional.

Mileage Category: B

Body Styles	TMV Pricing		
	Trade	Private	Dealer
2 Dr Highline Cpe	580	1095	1952
2 Dr Sport Cpe	645	1218	2173
4 Dr Highline Sdn	564	1064	1897

Body Styles	TMV Pricing		
	Trade	Private	Dealer
4 Dr STD Sdn	496	937	1672
4 Dr Sport Sdn	613	1158	2067

Options	Price
AM/FM/CD Audio System	+96
Air Conditioning	+228
Aluminum/Alloy Wheels	+77
Antilock Brakes	+172

Options	Price
Automatic 3-Speed Transmission	+152
Leather Seats [Opt on Sport]	+126
Premium Audio System	+114

Neon SRT-4

2004

Mileage Category: E

Body Styles	TMV Pricing		
	Trade	Private	Dealer
4 Dr Turbo Sdn	14326	15415	17231

Options	Price
Compact Disc Changer	+795
Front Side Airbag Restraints	+390

Options	Price
Power Sunroof	+695

New fuel injectors and a recalibrated engine control module bump the horsepower and torque numbers to 230 and 250. A limited-slip differential is now standard equipment, along with new high-performance BFGoodrich tires and bright pedal pads, while a sunroof is now available as an option. Electric Blue replaces Solar Yellow on the color chart.

2003

The fire-breathing Neon SRT-4 debuts, sporting a 215-horsepower turbocharged engine, a tweaked suspension and Viper-inspired sport seats. Zero to 60 takes only about 6 seconds.

Mileage Category: E

Body Styles	TMV Pricing		
	Trade	Private	Dealer
4 Dr Turbo Sdn	10655	12030	14322

Ram Pickup 1500

Mileage Category: K

Body Styles	TMV Pricing		
	Trade	Private	Dealer
2 Dr Laramie 4WD Std Cab LB	16794	18293	20791
2 Dr Laramie 4WD Std Cab SB	16603	18103	20604
2 Dr Laramie Std Cab LB	14845	16207	18477
2 Dr Laramie Std Cab SB	14685	16048	18320
2 Dr SLT 4WD Std Cab LB	14066	15449	17753
2 Dr SLT 4WD Std Cab SB	13881	15264	17568
2 Dr SLT Std Cab LB	12176	13409	15463
2 Dr SLT Std Cab SB	12018	13251	15305
2 Dr ST 4WD Std Cab LB	12692	14075	16379
2 Dr ST 4WD Std Cab SB	12507	13890	16194
2 Dr ST Std Cab LB	10427	11660	13714
2 Dr ST Std Cab SB	10271	11504	13558

Body Styles	TMV Pricing		
	Trade	Private	Dealer
4 Dr Laramie 4WD Crew Cab LB	21206	22848	25585
4 Dr Laramie 4WD Crew Cab SB	21007	22651	25390
4 Dr Laramie Crew Cab LB	19177	20611	23001
4 Dr Laramie Crew Cab SB	19010	20445	22837
4 Dr SLT 4WD Crew Cab LB	18107	19649	22218
4 Dr SLT 4WD Crew Cab SB	17914	19455	22023
4 Dr SLT Crew Cab LB	16285	17847	20450
4 Dr SLT Crew Cab SB	16121	17682	20285
4 Dr ST 4WD Crew Cab LB	17006	18548	21117
4 Dr ST 4WD Crew Cab SB	16813	18354	20923
4 Dr ST Crew Cab LB	15107	16669	19273
4 Dr ST Crew Cab SB	14486	16048	18651

Options	Price
17 Inch Wheels - Chrome [Opt on ST]	+500
20 Inch Wheels [Opt on Laramie, SLT]	+1025
4.7L V8 SOHC 16V FI Engine [Opt on ST]	+590
5.7L V8 OHV 16V FI Engine	+495
AM/FM/CD Audio System	+125
AM/FM/CD Changer Audio System [Opt on SLT]	+200
Alarm System [Opt on SLT]	+190
Aluminum/Alloy Wheels [Opt on SLT]	+300
Antilock Brakes [Std on Laramie]	+495
Automatic 5-Speed Transmission [Opt on SLT, ST]	+1170
Automatic Climate Control (2 Zone) - Driver and Passenger [Opt on Laramie]	+500
Bed Liner	+245
Camper/Towing Package	+335
Fog Lights	+120

Options	Price
Front Head Airbag Restraints	+390
Garage Door Opener [Opt on Laramie]	+150
Heated Front Seats [Opt on Laramie]	+140
Infinity Audio System [Opt on SLT]	+600
Limited Slip Differential	+285
Limited Slip Differential (Rear)	+300
Navigation System [Opt on SLT, Laramie]	+925
Power Adjustable Foot Pedals [Opt on SLT]	+120
Skid Plates [Opt on 4WD]	+140
Sliding Rear Window	+125
Special Factory Paint	+150
Two-Tone Paint	+225
Velour/Cloth Seats [Opt on ST]	+275

The Laramie edition gains more flash via a new grille, body molding and interior accents. A full-time four-wheel-drive system debuts, as does a hands-free Bluetooth-enabled cell phone and a navigation system.

Mileage Category: K

Body Styles	TMV Pricing		
	Trade	Private	Dealer
2 Dr Laramie 4WD Std Cab LB	15726	16959	19014
2 Dr Laramie 4WD Std Cab SB	15535	16753	18783
2 Dr Laramie Std Cab LB	13990	15087	16916
2 Dr Laramie Std Cab SB	13833	14918	16726
2 Dr SLT 4WD Std Cab LB	13187	14221	15944
2 Dr SLT 4WD Std Cab SB	12988	14007	15705
2 Dr SLT Std Cab LB	11339	12228	13709
2 Dr SLT Std Cab SB	10922	11779	13206
2 Dr ST 4WD Std Cab LB	11940	12876	14437
2 Dr ST 4WD Std Cab SB	11609	12519	14036
2 Dr ST Std Cab LB	9323	10054	11273
2 Dr ST Std Cab SB	9157	9876	11073

Body Styles	TMV Pricing		
	Trade	Private	Dealer
4 Dr Laramie 4WD Crew Cab LB	19701	21246	23821
4 Dr Laramie 4WD Crew Cab SB	19526	21057	23609
4 Dr Laramie Crew Cab LB	17562	18939	21234
4 Dr Laramie Crew Cab SB	17412	18778	21054
4 Dr SLT 4WD Crew Cab LB	16244	17518	19642
4 Dr SLT 4WD Crew Cab SB	16047	17305	19402
4 Dr SLT Crew Cab LB	15434	16644	18662
4 Dr SLT Crew Cab SB	15229	16423	18412
4 Dr ST 4WD Crew Cab LB	15145	16333	18313
4 Dr ST 4WD Crew Cab SB	14945	16117	18070
4 Dr ST Crew Cab LB	14144	15253	17102
4 Dr ST Crew Cab SB	13757	14835	16634

Options	Price
20 Inch Wheels [Opt on Laramie, SLT]	+483
4.7L V8 SOHC 16V FI Engine [Opt on ST]	+373
5.7L V8 OHV 16V FI Engine	+565
AM/FM/CD Changer Audio System [Opt on SLT]	+600
Alarm System [Opt on SLT]	+120
Aluminum/Alloy Wheels [Opt on SLT]	+190
Antilock Brakes [Std on Laramie]	+430
Automatic 5-Speed Transmission [Opt on SLT, ST]	+739

Options	Price
Bed Liner	+155
Camper/Towing Package	+212
Cruise Control [Opt on ST]	+117
Front Head Airbag Restraints [Opt on STD Cab]	+246
Front and Rear Head Airbag Restraints [Opt on Crew Cab]	+310
Infinity Audio System [Opt on SLT]	+190
Limited Slip Differential	+180
Off-Road Suspension Package [Opt on Laramie, SLT]	+550

Two new packages debut, "Off-Road" and "Work Special," and the old Laramie trim level returns to replace the SLT Plus. For better performance, a five-speed automatic transmission is now optional on the 3.7-liter V6 and 4.7-liter V8 engines.

2003 (cont'd)

Options	Price
Tonneau Cover	+183
Two-Tone Paint	+142

Options	Price
Velour/Cloth Seats [Opt on ST]	+174

2002

Just about everything on the truck has undergone a complete redesign with improvements in safety, passenger comfort and handling.

Mileage Category: K

Body Styles	TMV Pricing		
	Trade	Private	Dealer
2 Dr SLT 4WD Std Cab LB	11341	12387	14130
2 Dr SLT 4WD Std Cab SB	11158	12187	13902
2 Dr SLT Plus 4WD Std Cab LB	14171	15478	17657
2 Dr SLT Plus 4WD Std Cab SB	13980	15269	17418
2 Dr SLT Plus Std Cab LB	12321	13457	15351
2 Dr SLT Plus Std Cab SB	12166	13288	15158
2 Dr SLT Std Cab LB	9533	10412	11878
2 Dr SLT Std Cab SB	9177	10023	11434
2 Dr ST 4WD Std Cab LB	10095	11026	12578
2 Dr ST 4WD Std Cab SB	9929	10845	12371
2 Dr ST Std Cab LB	7875	8601	9812
2 Dr ST Std Cab SB	7722	8434	9621

Body Styles	TMV Pricing		
	Trade	Private	Dealer
4 Dr SLT 4WD Crew Cab LB	14102	15403	17571
4 Dr SLT 4WD Crew Cab SB	13900	15182	17319
4 Dr SLT Crew Cab LB	12367	13508	15409
4 Dr SLT Crew Cab SB	12191	13315	15189
4 Dr SLT Plus 4WD Crew Cab LB	17713	19346	22069
4 Dr SLT Plus 4WD Crew Cab SB	17544	19162	21859
4 Dr SLT Plus Crew Cab LB	15729	17180	19597
4 Dr SLT Plus Crew Cab SB	15588	17026	19422
4 Dr ST 4WD Crew Cab LB	13123	14334	16352
4 Dr ST 4WD Crew Cab SB	12947	14141	16131
4 Dr ST Crew Cab LB	11306	12349	14087
4 Dr ST Crew Cab SB	11184	12216	13936

Options	Price
17 Inch Wheels - Chrome [Opt on SLT Plus,ST]	+163
20 Inch Wheels [Opt on SLT, SLT Plus]	+367
4.7L V8 SOHC 16V FI Engine [Opt on ST Std Cab 2WD]	+321
5.9L V8 OHV 16V FI Engine [Std on SLT Plus]	+323
Antilock Brakes [Opt on SLT,ST]	+370
Automatic 4-Speed Transmission [Std on SLT Plus]	+530
Bed Liner	+133
Camper/Towing Package	+182

Options	Price
Front Head Airbag Restraints [Opt on Std Cab]	+212
Front and Rear Head Airbag Restraints [Opt on Crew Cab]	+266
Infinity Audio System [Opt on SLT]	+353
Leather Seats [Opt on SLT Crew]	+476
Limited Slip Differential	+155
Power Driver Seat [Std on SLT Plus]	+196
Tonneau Cover	+158
Two-Tone Paint	+122

2001

Electronic cruise control is offered for the Cummings turbodiesel models with a manual transmission, two new exterior colors debut and child-seat anchors are mounted on the rear of the cab. A high-output Cummings turbodiesel model, with a six-speed transmission, 245 horsepower and 505 foot-pounds of torque, is offered in addition to a slightly improved 235-horsepower/460-ft-lbs version, available with a manual or automatic tranny.

Mileage Category: K

Body Styles	TMV Pricing		
	Trade	Private	Dealer
2 Dr SLT 4WD Ext Cab SB	9996	11555	12994
2 Dr SLT 4WD Std Cab LB	9454	10928	12289
2 Dr SLT 4WD Std Cab SB	9313	10765	12106
2 Dr SLT Ext Cab SB	8783	10153	11417
2 Dr SLT Std Cab LB	7847	9071	10201
2 Dr SLT Std Cab SB	7624	8813	9911
2 Dr ST 4WD Ext Cab SB	9154	10582	11900
2 Dr ST 4WD Std Cab LB	8425	9739	10952
2 Dr ST 4WD Std Cab SB	8283	9575	10768
2 Dr ST Ext Cab SB	7384	8536	9599
2 Dr ST Std Cab LB	6741	7792	8763
2 Dr ST Std Cab SB	6502	7516	8452
2 Dr WS Std Cab LB	6303	7286	8194

Body Styles	TMV Pricing		
	Trade	Private	Dealer
2 Dr WS Std Cab SB	6200	7167	8060
4 Dr SLT 4WD Ext Cab LB	10725	12397	13941
4 Dr SLT 4WD Ext Cab SB	10565	12213	13734
4 Dr SLT Ext Cab LB	9364	10825	12173
4 Dr SLT Ext Cab SB	9223	10662	11990
4 Dr SLT Plus 4WD Ext Cab LB	12365	14294	16074
4 Dr SLT Plus 4WD Ext Cab SB	12233	14141	15902
4 Dr SLT Plus Ext Cab LB	10984	12697	14278
4 Dr SLT Plus Ext Cab SB	10874	12570	14135
4 Dr ST 4WD Ext Cab LB	9778	11303	12710
4 Dr ST 4WD Ext Cab SB	9640	11143	12531
4 Dr ST Ext Cab LB	8354	9657	10860
4 Dr ST Ext Cab SB	8259	9548	10737

Options	Price
5.2L V8 OHV 16V FI Engine [Opt on ST Std Cab 2WD]	+294
5.9L V8 OHV 16V FI Engine [Std on SLT Plus]	+297
AM/FM/CD Audio System [Std on SLT Plus]	+254
AM/FM/Cassette/CD Audio System	+344
Air Conditioning [Std on SLT Plus]	+402
Antilock Brakes	+339
Automatic 4-Speed Transmission [Std on SLT Plus]	+486

Options	Price
Bed Liner	+122
Camper/Towing Package	+137
Infinity Audio System	+254
Leather Seats [Std on SLT Plus]	+324
Limited Slip Differential	+142
Power Driver Seat [Std on SLT Plus]	+180
Side Steps [Opt on ST]	+150

Mileage Category: K

2000

The Ram 1500 Pickup Club Cab models with the 8-foot bed have been discontinued; also eliminated for 2000 are the 2500 Club Cabs. All Ram Pickups receive a new front suspension and steering system to improve ride quality and steering precision, and 2500s and 3500s have a revised rear suspension for a better ride when loaded. An off-road package is now available for the short-wheelbase four-wheel-drive 1500.

Body Styles	TMV Pricing		
	Trade	Private	Dealer
2 Dr SLT 4WD Ext Cab SB	8754	10235	11687
2 Dr SLT 4WD Std Cab LB	8321	9729	11109
2 Dr SLT 4WD Std Cab SB	8166	9547	10901
2 Dr SLT Ext Cab SB	7855	9184	10487
2 Dr SLT Std Cab LB	6607	7725	8821
2 Dr SLT Std Cab SB	6560	7670	8759
2 Dr ST 4WD Ext Cab SB	8166	9547	10901
2 Dr ST 4WD Std Cab LB	7292	8526	9735
2 Dr ST 4WD Std Cab SB	7272	8502	9708
2 Dr ST Ext Cab SB	6682	7812	8920
2 Dr ST Std Cab LB	5956	6963	7951

Body Styles	TMV Pricing		
	Trade	Private	Dealer
2 Dr ST Std Cab SB	5700	6664	7609
2 Dr WS Std Cab LB	5386	6298	7191
2 Dr WS Std Cab SB	5362	6269	7158
4 Dr SLT 4WD Ext Cab LB	9449	11047	12614
4 Dr SLT 4WD Ext Cab SB	9313	10889	12433
4 Dr SLT Ext Cab LB	8240	9634	11000
4 Dr SLT Ext Cab SB	8072	9438	10776
4 Dr ST 4WD Ext Cab LB	8649	10112	11546
4 Dr ST 4WD Ext Cab SB	8467	9899	11303
4 Dr ST Ext Cab LB	7282	8514	9722
4 Dr ST Ext Cab SB	6959	8137	9291

Options	Price
5.2L V8 OHV 16V FI Engine	+267
5.9L V8 OHV 16V FI Engine	+268
AM/FM/CD Audio System	+192
AM/FM/Cassette/CD Audio System	+312
Air Conditioning	+364
Antilock Brakes	+307
Automatic 4-Speed Transmission	+441

Options	Price
Camper/Towing Package	+124
Infinity Audio System [Opt on SLT]	+206
Leather Seats	+565
Limited Slip Differential	+129
Off-Road Suspension Package	+395
Power Driver Seat	+145
Trailer Hitch	+124

Mileage Category: K

1999

The Sport model gets a new front bumper, fascia, grille, headlamps, graphics and Solar Yellow exterior color just to make sure it won't go unnoticed in traffic. All Ram Pickups get an express-down feature for the power windows, a new headlamp switch and four-wheel ABS are standard on vehicles over 10,000 pounds.

Body Styles	TMV Pricing		
	Trade	Private	Dealer
2 Dr Laramie SLT 4WD Ext Cab LB	7698	9185	10732
2 Dr Laramie SLT 4WD Ext Cab SB	7423	8857	10350
2 Dr Laramie SLT 4WD Std Cab LB	7194	8584	10031
2 Dr Laramie SLT 4WD Std Cab SB	7049	8411	9828
2 Dr Laramie SLT Ext Cab LB	6726	8025	9377
2 Dr Laramie SLT Ext Cab SB	6628	7908	9241
2 Dr Laramie SLT Std Cab LB	5686	6785	7928
2 Dr Laramie SLT Std Cab SB	5485	6544	7647
2 Dr ST 4WD Ext Cab LB	7084	8453	9877
2 Dr ST 4WD Ext Cab SB	7063	8428	9848
2 Dr ST 4WD Std Cab SB	6255	7463	8721
2 Dr ST 4WD Std Cab SB	6104	7283	8511
2 Dr ST Ext Cab LB	5888	7026	8210

Body Styles	TMV Pricing		
	Trade	Private	Dealer
2 Dr ST Ext Cab SB	5783	6900	8063
2 Dr ST Std Cab LB	5167	6165	7204
2 Dr ST Std Cab SB	5031	6003	7014
2 Dr WS Std Cab LB	4667	5569	6507
2 Dr WS Std Cab SB	4631	5526	6457
4 Dr Laramie SLT 4WD Ext Cab LB	8292	9894	11561
4 Dr Laramie SLT 4WD Ext Cab SB	8024	9574	11187
4 Dr Laramie SLT Ext Cab LB	7083	8451	9875
4 Dr Laramie SLT Ext Cab SB	6978	8326	9728
4 Dr ST 4WD Ext Cab LB	7325	8740	10212
4 Dr ST 4WD Ext Cab SB	7308	8720	10189
4 Dr ST Ext Cab LB	6131	7316	8549
4 Dr ST Ext Cab SB	5952	7102	8299

Options	Price
5.2L V8 OHV 16V FI Engine [Opt on Std Cab - Laramie SLT,ST]	+217
5.9L V8 OHV 16V FI Engine	+146
AM/FM/CD Audio System	+156
AM/FM/Cassette/CD Audio System	+203
Air Conditioning [Opt on ST,WS]	+297

Options	Price
Antilock Brakes	+278
Automatic 4-Speed Transmission	+359
Infinity Audio System [Opt on Laramie SLT]	+168
Leather Seats	+460
Power Driver Seat	+118

Mileage Category: K

1998

The Ram Quad Cab, as in four doors, becomes the first pickup on the market with two rear access doors. And for convenience, the front seatbelts are now integrated into the front seats, making for obstruction-free rear access. All Ram Pickups get a totally redesigned interior, standard passenger-side airbag with cutoff switch, and all airbags are "depowered" for safety.

Body Styles	TMV Pricing		
	Trade	Private	Dealer
2 Dr Laramie SLT 4WD Ext Cab LB	6788	8241	9879
2 Dr Laramie SLT 4WD Ext Cab SB	6472	7857	9419
2 Dr Laramie SLT 4WD Std Cab LB	6286	7632	9149
2 Dr Laramie SLT 4WD Std Cab SB	6144	7459	8942
2 Dr Laramie SLT Ext Cab LB	5879	7137	8556
2 Dr Laramie SLT Ext Cab SB	5845	7096	8506
2 Dr Laramie SLT Std Cab LB	4944	6002	7195
2 Dr Laramie SLT Std Cab SB	4837	5872	7039
2 Dr SS/T Std Cab SB	5561	6751	8092

Body Styles	TMV Pricing		
	Trade	Private	Dealer
2 Dr ST 4WD Ext Cab LB	6232	7565	9069
2 Dr ST 4WD Ext Cab SB	6114	7422	8898
2 Dr ST 4WD Std Cab LB	5273	6401	7674
2 Dr ST 4WD Std Cab SB	5139	6239	7479
2 Dr ST Ext Cab SB	5035	6112	7327
2 Dr ST Ext Cab SB	4963	6025	7223
2 Dr ST Std Cab LB	4425	5372	6439
2 Dr ST Std Cab SB	4162	5052	6056
2 Dr WS Std Cab LB	3870	4698	5631

1998 (cont'd)

Body Styles	TMV Pricing		
	Trade	Private	Dealer
2 Dr WS Std Cab SB	3812	4627	5547
4 Dr Laramie SLT 4WD Ext Cab LB	6975	8468	10151
4 Dr Laramie SLT 4WD Ext Cab SB	6867	8337	9995
4 Dr Laramie SLT Ext Cab LB	6201	7528	9025
4 Dr Laramie SLT Ext Cab SB	6008	7294	8744

Body Styles	TMV Pricing		
	Trade	Private	Dealer
4 Dr ST 4WD Ext Cab LB	6370	7733	9270
4 Dr ST 4WD Ext Cab SB	6343	7700	9231
4 Dr ST Ext Cab LB	5202	6315	7571
4 Dr ST Ext Cab SB	5111	6205	7438

Options	Price
5.2L V8 OHV 16V FI Engine [Opt on Std Cab - Laramie SLT,ST]	+192
AM/FM/CD Audio System	+138
AM/FM/Cassette/CD Audio System	+180
Air Conditioning [Opt on ST,WS]	+262

Options	Price
Antilock Brakes	+246
Automatic 4-Speed Transmission [Std on SS/T]	+310
Leather Seats	+407

1997
No major changes to this popular truck for 1997. Refinements include available leather seating and woodgrain trim on SLT models, optional remote keyless entry, and standard deep-tinted quarter glass on Club Cab models. Also available is a combination CD/cassette stereo. Items from the 1996 Indy 500 Special Edition are available in a new Sport Package upgrade. Fresh interior and exterior colors sum up the changes this year.

Mileage Category: K

Body Styles	TMV Pricing		
	Trade	Private	Dealer
2 Dr LT 4WD Std Cab LB	4622	5740	7106
2 Dr LT 4WD Std Cab SB	4527	5622	6961
2 Dr LT Std Cab LB	3880	4819	5966
2 Dr LT Std Cab SB	3744	4649	5756
2 Dr Laramie SLT 4WD Ext Cab LB	5969	7413	9177
2 Dr Laramie SLT 4WD Ext Cab SB	5694	7072	8756
2 Dr Laramie SLT 4WD Std Cab LB	5278	6555	8116
2 Dr Laramie SLT 4WD Std Cab SB	4858	6033	7468
2 Dr Laramie SLT Ext Cab LB	4758	5909	7316
2 Dr Laramie SLT Ext Cab SB	4697	5833	7222

Body Styles	TMV Pricing		
	Trade	Private	Dealer
2 Dr Laramie SLT Std Cab LB	4185	5197	6434
2 Dr Laramie SLT Std Cab SB	3892	4834	5985
2 Dr SS/T Std Cab SB	4642	5765	7138
2 Dr ST 4WD Ext Cab LB	5326	6615	8191
2 Dr ST 4WD Ext Cab SB	5184	6438	7970
2 Dr ST Ext Cab LB	4405	5471	6773
2 Dr ST Ext Cab SB	4217	5237	6484
2 Dr WS Std Cab LB	3305	4105	5082
2 Dr WS Std Cab SB	3182	3952	4893

Options	Price
5.2L V8 OHV 16V FI Engine [Opt on Std Cab - Laramie SLT,LT]	+169
AM/FM/CD Audio System	+122
AM/FM/Cassette/CD Audio System	+158
Air Conditioning [Opt on LT,ST,WS]	+231

Options	Price
Antilock Brakes	+217
Automatic 4-Speed Transmission	+272
Leather Seats	+358

1996
The Ram Pickup gets some mild mechanical changes, including electronically governed automatic transmissions and a torque increase for the optional 5.9L turbodiesel V8 to 440 lb-ft. CD controls are added to cassette audio systems and cast alloy wheels are standard with SLT and Sport trims. New color offerings are Light Kiwi Pearl and Spruce Pearl.

Mileage Category: K

Body Styles	TMV Pricing		
	Trade	Private	Dealer
2 Dr LT 4WD Std Cab LB	3758	4785	6204
2 Dr LT 4WD Std Cab SB	3594	4577	5934
2 Dr LT Std Cab LB	3022	3849	4990
2 Dr LT Std Cab SB	2980	3795	4921
2 Dr Laramie SLT 4WD Ext Cab LB	4646	5917	7672
2 Dr Laramie SLT 4WD Ext Cab SB	4186	5331	6913
2 Dr Laramie SLT 4WD Std Cab LB	4138	5270	6833
2 Dr Laramie SLT 4WD Std Cab SB	4101	5222	6771
2 Dr Laramie SLT Ext Cab LB	4015	5114	6631

Body Styles	TMV Pricing		
	Trade	Private	Dealer
2 Dr Laramie SLT Ext Cab SB	3838	4888	6337
2 Dr Laramie SLT Std Cab LB	3387	4314	5593
2 Dr Laramie SLT Std Cab SB	3208	4085	5297
2 Dr ST 4WD Ext Cab LB	3985	5074	6579
2 Dr ST 4WD Ext Cab SB	3957	5039	6533
2 Dr ST Ext Cab LB	3540	4508	5845
2 Dr ST Ext Cab SB	3274	4169	5406
2 Dr WS Std Cab LB	2738	3487	4521
2 Dr WS Std Cab SB	2480	3158	4095

Options	Price
5.2L V8 OHV 16V FI Engine [Opt on Std Cab - Laramie SLT,LT]	+153
Air Conditioning [Std on Laramie SLT]	+208
Antilock Brakes	+197

Options	Price
Automatic 4-Speed Transmission	+242
Compact Disc Changer	+143
Leather Seats	+366

1995
After a complete redesign in 1994, the Ram Pickup offers a club cab body on a 134.7-inch wheelbase. Torque increases to 430 pound-feet with the Cummins 5.9L diesel with manual transmission. Optional equipment includes a natural gas 5.2L V8 and Infinity CD audio system. Foglights are bundled with the Sport Package.

Mileage Category: K

Body Styles	TMV Pricing		
	Trade	Private	Dealer
2 Dr LT 4WD Std Cab LB	3055	3969	5492
2 Dr LT 4WD Std Cab SB	3000	3897	5393
2 Dr LT Std Cab LB	2458	3193	4419
2 Dr LT Std Cab SB	2435	3164	4378

Body Styles	TMV Pricing		
	Trade	Private	Dealer
2 Dr Laramie SLT 4WD Ext Cab LB	3754	4878	6750
2 Dr Laramie SLT 4WD Ext Cab SB	3605	4684	6481
2 Dr Laramie SLT 4WD Std Cab LB	3474	4514	6247
2 Dr Laramie SLT 4WD Std Cab SB	3443	4473	6190

Body Styles	TMV Pricing		
	Trade	Private	Dealer
2 Dr Laramie SLT Ext Cab LB	3206	4165	5764
2 Dr Laramie SLT Ext Cab SB	3116	4048	5602
2 Dr Laramie SLT Std Cab LB	2607	3387	4687
2 Dr Laramie SLT Std Cab SB	2567	3335	4616
2 Dr ST 4WD Ext Cab LB	3451	4483	6204

Options	Price
5.2L V8 OHV 16V FI Engine [Opt on Std Cab - Laramie SLT,LT]	+134
AM/FM/CD Audio System	+97
Air Conditioning [Std on Laramie SLT]	+182
Antilock Brakes	+172

Body Styles	TMV Pricing		
	Trade	Private	Dealer
2 Dr ST 4WD Ext Cab SB	3353	4356	6027
2 Dr ST Ext Cab LB	2864	3721	5148
2 Dr ST Ext Cab SB	2620	3404	4711
2 Dr WS Std Cab LB	2018	2622	3629
2 Dr WS Std Cab SB	2014	2617	3621

Options	Price
Automatic 4-Speed Transmission	+212
Infinity Audio System	+76
Power Driver Seat	+75

Ram Pickup 1500 SRT-10
2004

Mileage Category: K

Body Styles	TMV Pricing		
	Trade	Private	Dealer
2 Dr STD Std Cab SB	35684	37488	40494

Options	Price
AM/FM/CD Audio System	+175
Front Head Airbag Restraints	+390

Options	Price
Navigation System	+600

The SRT-10 is a new high-performance sport truck based on the existing Ram pickup.

Ram Pickup 2500
2004

Mileage Category: K

Body Styles	TMV Pricing		
	Trade	Private	Dealer
2 Dr Laramie 4WD Std Cab LB	18621	20133	22654
2 Dr Laramie Std Cab LB	16616	18035	20399
2 Dr SLT 4WD Std Cab LB	17088	18600	21121
2 Dr SLT Std Cab LB	15161	16580	18944
2 Dr ST 4WD Std Cab LB	16061	17573	20094
2 Dr ST Std Cab LB	14133	15552	17916
4 Dr Laramie 4WD Crew Cab LB	22772	24388	27082
4 Dr Laramie 4WD Crew Cab SB	22650	24266	26961
4 Dr Laramie Crew Cab LB	20078	21709	24428

Body Styles	TMV Pricing		
	Trade	Private	Dealer
4 Dr Laramie Crew Cab SB	19958	21590	24308
4 Dr SLT 4WD Crew Cab LB	20450	22217	25164
4 Dr SLT 4WD Crew Cab SB	20331	22099	25045
4 Dr SLT Crew Cab LB	18504	20135	22855
4 Dr SLT Crew Cab SB	18386	20017	22736
4 Dr ST 4WD Crew Cab LB	19273	21041	23988
4 Dr ST 4WD Crew Cab SB	19155	20923	23869
4 Dr ST Crew Cab LB	17328	18959	21679
4 Dr ST Crew Cab SB	17209	18841	21560

Options	Price
5.9L I6 Turbodiesel OHV 24V HO Engine	+5200
AM/FM/CD Audio System	+125
AM/FM/CD Changer Audio System [Opt on SLT]	+300
Alarm System [Opt on SLT]	+190
Aluminum/Alloy Wheels [Opt on SLT]	+300
Automatic 4-Speed Transmission	+1095
Automatic 5-Speed Transmission	+1170
Automatic 6-Speed Transmission	+660
Automatic Climate Control (2 Zone) - Driver and Passenger [Opt on Laramie]	+400
Bed Liner	+245
Camper/Towing Package	+275
Cruise Control [Opt on ST]	+250
Fog Lights [Opt on SLT]	+140

Options	Price
Front Head Airbag Restraints	+390
Heated Front Seats [Opt on Laramie]	+140
Limited Slip Differential	+285
Limited Slip Differential (Rear)	+300
Navigation System [Opt on SLT, Laramie]	+800
Overhead Console [Opt on Laramie]	+125
Power Adjustable Foot Pedals [Opt on SLT]	+120
Power Passenger Seat [Opt on Laramie Crew]	+200
Skid Plates [Opt on 4WD]	+150
Special Factory Paint	+150
Tonneau Cover	+290
Trip Computer [Opt on Laramie]	+165
Two-Tone Paint	+225

An automatic transmission debuts for the high-output Cummins turbodiesel that was formerly available only with a manual gearbox. The Laramie model gains more flash via a new grille, body molding and interior accents. A hands-free cell phone with Bluetooth technology is now available, as is a new Off-Road package and a navigation system. Lastly, the Magnum V10 engine is dropped from the power plant roster.

2003

Dodge redid its Ram 1500 full-size truck for 2002. For 2003, the heavies -- the 2500 and 3500 -- get their day in the sun. Along with the new Ram styling, these trucks receive more powerful engines, increased towing capacities, improved handling characteristics and additional safety equipment.

Mileage Category: K

Body Styles	TMV Pricing		
	Trade	Private	Dealer
2 Dr Laramie 4WD Std Cab LB	16857	18074	20101
2 Dr Laramie Std Cab LB	15964	17124	19057
2 Dr SLT 4WD Std Cab LB	15928	17078	18994
2 Dr SLT Std Cab LB	13903	14907	16579
2 Dr ST 4WD Std Cab LB	14721	15783	17554
2 Dr ST Std Cab LB	12704	13621	15149
4 Dr Laramie 4WD Crew Cab LB	19024	20397	22686
4 Dr Laramie 4WD Crew Cab SB	18636	19981	22223
4 Dr Laramie Crew Cab LB	18782	20138	22397

Body Styles	TMV Pricing		
	Trade	Private	Dealer
4 Dr Laramie Crew Cab SB	19133	20514	22816
4 Dr SLT 4WD Crew Cab LB	18190	19503	21690
4 Dr SLT 4WD Crew Cab SB	18078	19383	21558
4 Dr SLT Crew Cab LB	16170	17337	19283
4 Dr SLT Crew Cab SB	16045	17203	19133
4 Dr ST 4WD Crew Cab LB	16868	18086	20115
4 Dr ST 4WD Crew Cab SB	16789	18001	20020
4 Dr ST Crew Cab LB	14953	16032	17831
4 Dr ST Crew Cab SB	14715	15777	17547

Options	Price
5.9L I6 Turbodiesel OHV 24V Engine	+2922
5.9L I6 Turbodiesel OHV 24V HO Engine	+3301
6-Speed Transmission	+253
8.0L V10 OHV 20V FI Engine	+379
AM/FM/CD Changer Audio System [Opt on SLT]	+600
Alarm System [Opt on SLT]	+120
Aluminum/Alloy Wheels [Opt on SLT]	+190
Automatic 4-Speed Transmission	+692
Automatic 5-Speed Transmission	+739

Options	Price
Bed Liner	+155
Camper/Towing Package	+174
Cruise Control [Opt on ST]	+117
Front Head Airbag Restraints [Opt on STD Cab]	+246
Front and Rear Head Airbag Restraints [Opt on Crew Cab]	+310
Limited Slip Differential	+180
Tonneau Cover	+183
Two-Tone Paint	+142

2002

Three new colors: Atlantic Blue and Light Almond Pearls and Graphite metallic are added for 2002. Although the Ram 1500 was completely revamped this year, the heavier-duty 2500 Ram pickup must wait one more year for its update.

Mileage Category: K

Body Styles	TMV Pricing		
	Trade	Private	Dealer
2 Dr SLT 4WD Std Cab LB	12781	13966	15941
2 Dr SLT Std Cab LB	11197	12235	13965
2 Dr ST 4WD Std Cab LB	11396	12447	14199
2 Dr ST Std Cab LB	9748	10647	12145
4 Dr SLT 4WD Ext Cab LB	13976	15265	17413
4 Dr SLT 4WD Ext Cab SB	13891	15172	17308
4 Dr SLT Ext Cab LB	12354	13493	15392
4 Dr SLT Ext Cab SB	12236	13364	15245

Body Styles	TMV Pricing		
	Trade	Private	Dealer
4 Dr SLT Plus 4WD Ext Cab LB	15881	17346	19788
4 Dr SLT Plus 4WD Ext Cab SB	15771	17225	19649
4 Dr SLT Plus Ext Cab LB	14233	15546	17734
4 Dr SLT Plus Ext Cab SB	14102	15403	17571
4 Dr ST 4WD Ext Cab LB	12760	13937	15898
4 Dr ST 4WD Ext Cab SB	12642	13808	15751
4 Dr ST Ext Cab LB	11116	12141	13850
4 Dr ST Ext Cab SB	10997	12011	13702

Options	Price
5.9L I6 Turbodiesel OHV 24V Engine	+2514
5.9L I6 Turbodiesel OHV 24V HO Engine	+2840
6-Speed Transmission	+544
8.0L V10 OHV 20V FI Engine	+326
AM/FM/CD Audio System [Opt on SLT]	+277
AM/FM/Cassette/CD Audio System [Opt on SLT]	+375
Air Conditioning	+381
Appearance Package [Opt on SLT,SLT Plus]	+179

Options	Price
Automatic 4-Speed Transmission	+530
Bed Liner	+133
Camper/Towing Package	+149
Leather Seats [Opt on SLT]	+299
Limited Slip Differential	+155
Power Driver Seat [Opt on SLT]	+174
Two-Tone Paint	+122

2001

Electronic cruise control is now offered for the Cummings turbodiesel models with a manual transmission, improved braking systems with standard ABS come on all 2500 and 3500 Rams, two new exterior colors debut and child-seat anchors are mounted on the rear of the cab. A high-output Cummings turbodiesel model, with a six-speed transmission, 245 horsepower and 505 pound-feet of torque, is offered in addition to a slightly improved 235-horsepower/460-lb-ft version, available with a manual or automatic tranny.

Mileage Category: K

Body Styles	TMV Pricing		
	Trade	Private	Dealer
2 Dr SLT 4WD Std Cab LB	10889	12580	14141
2 Dr SLT Std Cab LB	9435	10901	12254
2 Dr ST 4WD Std Cab LB	9693	11205	12600
2 Dr ST Std Cab LB	8215	9496	10679
4 Dr SLT 4WD Ext Cab LB	11844	13692	15397
4 Dr SLT 4WD Ext Cab SB	11775	13611	15306
4 Dr SLT Ext Cab LB	10463	12095	13601
4 Dr SLT Ext Cab SB	10363	11980	13472

Body Styles	TMV Pricing		
	Trade	Private	Dealer
4 Dr SLT Plus 4WD Ext Cab LB	12788	14783	16624
4 Dr SLT Plus 4WD Ext Cab SB	12692	14672	16500
4 Dr SLT Plus Ext Cab LB	11393	13170	14810
4 Dr SLT Plus Ext Cab SB	11283	13043	14667
4 Dr ST 4WD Ext Cab LB	10871	12566	14131
4 Dr ST 4WD Ext Cab SB	10838	12528	14088
4 Dr ST Ext Cab LB	9408	10875	12230
4 Dr ST Ext Cab SB	9309	10761	12101

Options	Price
5.9L I6 Turbodiesel OHV 24V Engine	+2307
5.9L I6 Turbodiesel OHV 24V HO Engine	+2606

Options	Price
6-Speed Transmission	+200
8.0L V10 OHV 20V FI Engine	+234

Options	Price
AM/FM/CD Audio System [Opt on SLT]	+254
AM/FM/Cassette/CD Audio System [Opt on SLT]	+344
Air Conditioning [Opt on ST]	+402
Automatic 4-Speed Transmission	+486
Bed Liner	+122

Options	Price
Camper/Towing Package	+137
Infinity Audio System [Opt on SLT]	+254
Leather Seats [Opt on SLT]	+624
Limited Slip Differential	+142
Power Driver Seat [Opt on SLT]	+160

Mileage Category: K

Body Styles	TMV Pricing		
	Trade	Private	Dealer
2 Dr SLT 4WD Std Cab LB	9588	11245	12870
2 Dr SLT Std Cab LB	8159	9574	10960
2 Dr ST 4WD Std Cab LB	8636	10133	11601
2 Dr ST Std Cab LB	7185	8430	9651
ab LB	10312	12100	13852
4 Dr SLT 4WD Ext Cab SB	10275	12057	13803

Body Styles	TMV Pricing		
	Trade	Private	Dealer
4 Dr SLT Ext Cab LB	9125	10707	12258
4 Dr SLT Ext Cab SB	9044	10612	12149
4 Dr ST 4WD Ext Cab LB	9552	11208	12831
4 Dr ST 4WD Ext Cab SB	9519	11169	12787
4 Dr ST Ext Cab LB	8149	9562	10947
4 Dr ST Ext Cab SB	8033	9425	10790

Options	Price
5.9L I6 Turbodiesel OHV 24V Engine	+2090
8.0L V10 OHV 20V FI Engine	+212
AM/FM/CD Audio System	+192
AM/FM/Cassette/CD Audio System	+312
Air Conditioning	+364
Antilock Brakes	+307
Automatic 4-Speed Transmission	+441

Options	Price
Camper/Towing Package	+124
Chrome Wheels	+147
Leather Seats	+565
Limited Slip Differential	+129
Power Driver Seat	+145
Trailer Hitch	+124

2000

The Ram Pickup 1500 Club Cab models with the 8-foot bed box have been discontinued; also eliminated for 2000 are the 2500 Club Cabs. All Ram Pickups receive a new front suspension and steering system to improve ride quality and steering precision, and 2500s and 3500s have a revised rear suspension for a better ride when loaded. An off-road package is now available for the short-wheelbase four-wheel-drive 1500.

Mileage Category: K

Body Styles	TMV Pricing		
	Trade	Private	Dealer
2 Dr Laramie SLT 4WD Ext Cab LB	9110	10870	12702
2 Dr Laramie SLT 4WD Ext Cab SB	9044	10791	12610
2 Dr Laramie SLT 4WD Std Cab LB	8014	9562	11173
2 Dr Laramie SLT Ext Cab LB	7946	9481	11078
2 Dr Laramie SLT Ext Cab SB	7788	9292	10858
2 Dr Laramie SLT Std Cab LB	7102	8474	9902
2 Dr ST 4WD Ext Cab LB	8097	9670	11306
2 Dr ST 4WD Ext Cab SB	8308	9912	11582
2 Dr ST 4WD Std Cab LB	7465	8907	10408
2 Dr ST Ext Cab LB	6903	8236	9624

Body Styles	TMV Pricing		
	Trade	Private	Dealer
2 Dr ST Ext Cab SB	6810	8126	9495
2 Dr ST Std Cab LB	6219	7420	8670
4 Dr Laramie SLT 4WD Ext Cab LB	9295	11092	12962
4 Dr Laramie SLT 4WD Ext Cab SB	9258	11047	12908
4 Dr Laramie SLT Ext Cab LB	8062	9619	11240
4 Dr Laramie SLT Ext Cab SB	8133	9703	11338
4 Dr ST 4WD Ext Cab LB	8485	10124	11830
4 Dr ST 4WD Ext Cab SB	8444	10075	11773
4 Dr ST Ext Cab LB	7134	8512	9946
4 Dr ST Ext Cab SB	7082	8450	9874

Options	Price
5.9L I6 Turbodiesel OHV 24V Engine	+1894
8.0L V10 OHV 20V FI Engine	+173
AM/FM/CD Audio System	+156
AM/FM/Cassette/CD Audio System	+255
Air Conditioning [Opt on ST]	+297

Options	Price
Antilock Brakes	+278
Automatic 4-Speed Transmission	+359
Chrome Wheels [Opt on ST]	+120
Leather Seats	+460
Power Driver Seat	+118

1999

The Sport model gets a new front bumper, fascia, grille, headlamps, graphics and Solar Yellow exterior color just to make sure it won't go unnoticed in traffic. All Ram Pickups get an express-down feature for the power windows, a new headlamp switch and four-wheel ABS are standard on vehicles over 10,000 pounds.

Mileage Category: K

Body Styles	TMV Pricing		
	Trade	Private	Dealer
2 Dr Laramie SLT 4WD Ext Cab LB	7460	9056	10856
2 Dr Laramie SLT 4WD Ext Cab SB	7317	8884	10650
2 Dr Laramie SLT 4WD Std Cab LB	7151	8681	10407
2 Dr Laramie SLT Ext Cab LB	7025	8529	10224
2 Dr Laramie SLT Ext Cab SB	6946	8433	10109
2 Dr Laramie SLT Std Cab LB	6078	7378	8845
2 Dr ST 4WD Ext Cab LB	7149	8679	10404
2 Dr ST 4WD Ext Cab SB	7095	8613	10325
2 Dr ST 4WD Std Cab LB	6718	8156	9777
2 Dr ST Ext Cab LB	6039	7332	8789

Body Styles	TMV Pricing		
	Trade	Private	Dealer
2 Dr ST Ext Cab SB	6019	7307	8759
2 Dr ST Std Cab LB	5388	6541	7841
4 Dr Laramie SLT 4WD Ext Cab LB	7869	9553	11451
4 Dr Laramie SLT 4WD Ext Cab SB	7839	9516	11408
4 Dr Laramie SLT Ext Cab LB	7095	8613	10325
4 Dr Laramie SLT Ext Cab SB	7045	8553	10253
4 Dr ST 4WD Ext Cab LB	7287	8846	10605
4 Dr ST 4WD Ext Cab SB	7349	8922	10696
4 Dr ST Ext Cab LB	6482	7869	9433
4 Dr ST Ext Cab SB	6429	7805	9357

1998

Available as a sedan! The Ram Quad Cab, as in four doors, becomes the first pickup on the market with two rear access doors. And for convenience, the front seatbelts are now integrated into the front seats, making for obstruction-free rear access. All Ram Pickups get a totally redesigned interior, standard passenger-side airbag with cutoff switch, and all airbags are "depowered" for safety.

1998 (cont'd)

Options	Price
5.9L I6 Turbodiesel OHV 12V Engine	+1376
5.9L I6 Turbodiesel OHV 24V Engine	+1675
8.0L V10 OHV 20V FI Engine	+318
AM/FM/CD Audio System	+138
AM/FM/Cassette/CD Audio System	+225

Options	Price
Air Conditioning [Opt on ST]	+262
Antilock Brakes	+246
Automatic 4-Speed Transmission	+310
Leather Seats	+407

1997

No major changes for 1997. Refinements include available leather seating and woodgrain trim on SLT models, optional remote keyless entry, and standard deep-tinted quarter glass on Club Cab models. Also available is a combination CD/cassette stereo. Fresh interior and exterior colors sum up the changes this year.

Mileage Category: K

Body Styles	TMV Pricing		
	Trade	Private	Dealer
2 Dr LT 4WD Std Cab LB	5314	6600	8171
2 Dr LT Std Cab LB	4342	5393	6677
2 Dr Laramie SLT 4WD Ext Cab LB	6330	7861	9733
2 Dr Laramie SLT 4WD Ext Cab SB	6283	7803	9661
2 Dr Laramie SLT 4WD Std Cab LB	5544	6885	8524
2 Dr Laramie SLT Ext Cab LB	5458	6779	8393
2 Dr Laramie SLT Ext Cab SB	5454	6773	8385

Body Styles	TMV Pricing		
	Trade	Private	Dealer
2 Dr Laramie SLT Std Cab LB	4939	6133	7593
2 Dr ST 4WD Ext Cab LB	5514	6847	8477
2 Dr ST 4WD Ext Cab SB	5474	6798	8416
2 Dr ST 4WD Std Cab LB	5386	6688	8280
2 Dr ST Ext Cab LB	4898	6083	7531
2 Dr ST Ext Cab SB	4853	6027	7461
2 Dr ST Std Cab LB	4402	5466	6767

Options	Price
5.9L I6 Turbodiesel OHV 12V Engine	+1416
8.0L V10 OHV 20V FI Engine	+279
AM/FM/CD Audio System	+122
AM/FM/Cassette/CD Audio System	+198
Air Conditioning [Opt on LT,ST]	+231

Options	Price
Antilock Brakes	+217
Automatic 4-Speed Transmission	+279
Leather Seats	+358
Premium Audio System	+122

1996

The Ram Pickup gets some mild mechanical changes, including electronically governed automatic transmissions and a torque increase for the optional 5.9L turbodiesel V8 to 440 pound-feet. CD controls are added to cassette audio systems and cast alloy wheels are standard with SLT and Sport trims. New color offerings are Light Kiwi Pearl and Spruce Pearl.

Mileage Category: K

Body Styles	TMV Pricing		
	Trade	Private	Dealer
2 Dr LT 4WD Std Cab LB	4016	5115	6632
2 Dr LT Std Cab LB	3405	4337	5623
2 Dr Laramie SLT 4WD Ext Cab LB	5364	6831	8857
2 Dr Laramie SLT 4WD Ext Cab SB	5407	6886	8928
2 Dr Laramie SLT 4WD Std Cab LB	4557	5804	7525
2 Dr Laramie SLT Ext Cab LB	4684	5965	7733
2 Dr Laramie SLT Ext Cab SB	4598	5855	7592

Body Styles	TMV Pricing		
	Trade	Private	Dealer
2 Dr Laramie SLT Std Cab LB	3846	4898	6351
2 Dr ST 4WD Ext Cab LB	4816	6133	7951
2 Dr ST 4WD Ext Cab SB	4744	6041	7832
2 Dr ST 4WD Std Cab LB	4069	5182	6718
2 Dr ST Ext Cab LB	4166	5305	6879
2 Dr ST Ext Cab SB	4140	5272	6836
2 Dr ST Std Cab LB	3493	4449	5768

Options	Price
5.9L I6 Turbodiesel OHV 12V Engine	+1202
8.0L V10 OHV 20V FI Engine	+122
Air Conditioning [Opt on LT,ST]	+208
Antilock Brakes	+197

Options	Price
Automatic 4-Speed Transmission	+242
Compact Disc Changer	+176
Infinity Audio System	+133

1995

After a complete redesign in 1994, the Ram Pickup offers a club cab on a 134.7-inch wheelbase. Torque increases to 430 pound-feet with the Cummins 5.9L diesel with manual transmission and an illuminated overdrive lockout switch is standard. An Infinity CD audio system is optional and foglights are included with the Sport Package.

Mileage Category: K

Body Styles	TMV Pricing		
	Trade	Private	Dealer
2 Dr LT 4WD Std Cab LB	3185	4139	5728
2 Dr LT Std Cab LB	2684	3487	4826
2 Dr Laramie SLT 4WD Ext Cab LB	4340	5639	7805
2 Dr Laramie SLT 4WD Ext Cab SB	4301	5588	7734
2 Dr Laramie SLT 4WD Std Cab LB	3695	4801	6645
2 Dr Laramie SLT Ext Cab LB	3777	4907	6791
2 Dr Laramie SLT Std Cab LB	3226	4191	5800
2 Dr ST 4WD Ext Cab LB	3946	5127	7096

Body Styles	TMV Pricing		
	Trade	Private	Dealer
2 Dr ST 4WD Ext Cab SB	3866	5024	6954
2 Dr ST 4WD Std Cab LB	3276	4257	5891
2 Dr ST Ext Cab LB	3317	4310	5965
2 Dr ST Ext Cab SB	3300	4288	5934
2 Dr ST Std Cab LB	2720	3534	4890
2 Dr Sport 4WD Ext Cab SB	4026	5231	7239
2 Dr Sport Ext Cab SB	3644	4735	6552

Options	Price
5.9L I6 Turbodiesel OHV 12V Engine	+964
8.0L V10 OHV 20V FI Engine	+107
AM/FM/CD Audio System	+97
Air Conditioning [Opt on LT,Sport,ST]	+182

Options	Price
Antilock Brakes	+172
Automatic 4-Speed Transmission	+212
Infinity Audio System	+117

Ram Pickup 3500
2004

Mileage Category: K

Body Styles	TMV Pricing		
	Trade	Private	Dealer
2 Dr Laramie 4WD Std Cab LB DRW	20271	21807	24367
2 Dr Laramie Std Cab LB DRW	18252	19638	21948
2 Dr SLT 4WD Std Cab LB DRW	18665	20201	22761
2 Dr SLT Std Cab LB DRW	16727	18113	20423
2 Dr ST 4WD Std Cab LB DRW	17987	19523	22083
2 Dr ST Std Cab LB DRW	16049	17435	19745
4 Dr Laramie 4WD Crew Cab LB DRW	24419	26211	29198
4 Dr Laramie 4WD Crew Cab SB	27641	29433	32418
4 Dr Laramie Crew Cab LB DRW	22278	23914	26640

Body Styles	TMV Pricing		
	Trade	Private	Dealer
4 Dr Laramie Crew Cab SB	25535	27171	29897
4 Dr SLT 4WD Crew Cab LB DRW	22690	24326	27052
4 Dr SLT 4WD Crew Cab SB	25908	27699	30685
4 Dr SLT Crew Cab LB DRW	20629	22265	24991
4 Dr SLT Crew Cab SB	23887	25522	28248
4 Dr ST 4WD Crew Cab LB DRW	21868	23660	26647
4 Dr ST 4WD Crew Cab SB	25088	26880	29866
4 Dr ST Crew Cab LB DRW	19810	21446	24173
4 Dr ST Crew Cab SB	23067	24703	27429

Options	Price
5.9L I6 Turbodiesel OHV 24V HO Engine	+5200
AM/FM/CD Audio System	+125
AM/FM/CD Changer Audio System [Opt on SLT]	+300
Alarm System [Opt on SLT]	+125
Aluminum/Alloy Wheels [Opt on SLT]	+345
Automatic 4-Speed Transmission	+950
Automatic 5-Speed Transmission	+1170
Automatic 6-Speed Transmission	+660
Automatic Climate Control (2 Zone) - Driver and Passenger [Opt on Laramie]	+400
Bed Liner	+245
Cruise Control [Opt on ST]	+250
Fog Lights [Opt on SLT]	+150
Front Head Airbag Restraints	+390

Options	Price
Garage Door Opener [Opt on Laramie]	+150
Heated Front Seats [Opt on Laramie]	+140
Limited Slip Differential (Rear)	+300
Navigation System [Opt on SLT, Laramie]	+825
Overhead Console [Opt on Laramie]	+125
Power Adjustable Foot Pedals [Opt on SLT]	+120
Power Passenger Seat [Opt on Laramie Crew]	+200
Skid Plates [Opt on 4WD]	+150
Special Factory Paint	+150
Tonneau Cover	+290
Trailer Hitch	+275
Trip Computer [Opt on Laramie]	+165
Two-Tone Paint	+225

The Laramie model gains more flash via a new grille, body molding and interior accents. A hands-free cell phone with Bluetooth technology is now available, as is a new Off-Road package and a navigation system. Lastly, the Magnum V10 engine is dropped from the power plant roster.

2003

Dodge redid its Ram 1500 full-size truck for 2002. For 2003, the heavies -- the 2500 and 3500 -- get their day in the sun. Along with the new Ram styling, these trucks receive more powerful engines, increased towing capacities, improved handling characteristics and additional safety equipment.

Mileage Category: K

Body Styles	TMV Pricing		
	Trade	Private	Dealer
2 Dr Laramie 4WD Std Cab LB DRW	18875	20180	22354
2 Dr Laramie Std Cab LB DRW	16952	18124	20077
2 Dr SLT 4WD Std Cab LB DRW	16743	17900	19829
2 Dr SLT Std Cab LB DRW	14805	15828	17534
2 Dr ST 4WD Std Cab LB DRW	15901	17000	18832
2 Dr ST Std Cab LB DRW	13974	14940	16550
4 Dr Laramie 4WD Crew Cab LB DRW	22414	23963	26546
4 Dr Laramie 4WD Crew Cab SB	23873	25524	28274
4 Dr Laramie Crew Cab LB DRW	20155	21548	23871

Body Styles	TMV Pricing		
	Trade	Private	Dealer
4 Dr Laramie Crew Cab SB	21316	22790	25246
4 Dr SLT 4WD Crew Cab LB DRW	19560	20912	23166
4 Dr SLT 4WD Crew Cab SB	21045	22500	24924
4 Dr SLT Crew Cab LB DRW	17540	18752	20773
4 Dr SLT Crew Cab SB	19599	20954	23212
4 Dr ST 4WD Crew Cab LB DRW	18655	19945	22094
4 Dr ST 4WD Crew Cab SB	20356	21763	24108
4 Dr ST Crew Cab LB DRW	16679	17832	19754
4 Dr ST Crew Cab SB	18700	19993	22148

Options	Price
5.9L I6 Turbodiesel OHV 24V Engine [Std on HD]	+2922
5.9L I6 Turbodiesel OHV 24V HO Engine	+379
6-Speed Transmission	+253
8.0L V10 OHV 20V FI Engine	+379
AM/FM/CD Changer Audio System [Opt on SLT]	+600
Alarm System [Opt on SLT]	+120
Automatic 4-Speed Transmission	+692
Automatic 5-Speed Transmission	+739

Options	Price
Bed Liner	+155
Camper/Towing Package	+174
Cruise Control [Opt on ST]	+117
Front Head Airbag Restraints [Opt on STD Cab]	+246
Front and Rear Head Airbag Restraints [Opt on Crew Cab]	+310
Tonneau Cover	+183
Two-Tone Paint	+142

2002

Three new colors: Atlantic Blue and Light Almond Pearls and Graphite metallic are available for 2002. Although the Ram 1500 was completely revamped this year, the heavy-duty 3500 Ram pickups must wait one more year for their update.

Mileage Category: K

Body Styles	TMV Pricing		
	Trade	Private	Dealer
2 Dr SLT 4WD Std Cab LB	13366	14605	16670
2 Dr SLT Std Cab LB	11577	12645	14425
2 Dr ST 4WD Std Cab LB	12467	13623	15549
2 Dr ST Std Cab LB	10690	11676	13320
4 Dr SLT 4WD Ext Cab LB	14961	16341	18641

Options	Price
5.9L I6 Turbodiesel OHV 24V Engine	+2514
5.9L I6 Turbodiesel OHV 24V HO Engine	+2840
6-Speed Transmission	+544
8.0L V10 OHV 20V FI Engine	+326
AM/FM/CD Audio System [Opt on SLT]	+277
AM/FM/Cassette/CD Audio System [Opt on SLT]	+375
Air Conditioning	+381

Body Styles	TMV Pricing		
	Trade	Private	Dealer
4 Dr SLT Ext Cab LB	13356	14588	16641
4 Dr SLT Plus 4WD Ext Cab LB	16834	18387	20974
4 Dr SLT Plus Ext Cab LB	15223	16627	18967
4 Dr ST 4WD Ext Cab LB	14095	15395	17562
4 Dr ST Ext Cab LB	12439	13586	15498

Options	Price
Appearance Package [Opt on SLT,SLT Plus]	+179
Automatic 4-Speed Transmission	+530
Bed Liner	+133
Camper/Towing Package	+149
Leather Seats [Opt on SLT]	+788
Limited Slip Differential	+155
Power Driver Seat [Opt on SLT]	+174

2001

Electronic cruise control is offered for the Cummings turbodiesel models with a manual transmission, improved braking systems with standard ABS come on all 2500 and 3500 Rams, two new exterior colors debut and child-seat anchors are mounted on the rear of the cab. A high-output Cummings turbodiesel model, with a six-speed transmission, 245 horsepower and 505 foot-pounds of torque, is offered in addition to a slightly improved 235-horsepower/460-ft-lbs version, available with a manual or automatic tranny.

Mileage Category: K

Body Styles	TMV Pricing		
	Trade	Private	Dealer
2 Dr SLT 4WD Std Cab LB	11369	13105	14707
2 Dr SLT Std Cab LB	9777	11276	12660
2 Dr ST 4WD Std Cab LB	10572	12187	13677
2 Dr ST Std Cab LB	9023	10407	11684
4 Dr SLT 4WD Ext Cab LB	12695	14641	16437

Options	Price
5.9L I6 Turbodiesel OHV 24V Engine	+2307
5.9L I6 Turbodiesel OHV 24V HO Engine	+2606
6-Speed Transmission	+200
8.0L V10 OHV 20V FI Engine	+234
AM/FM/CD Audio System [Opt on SLT]	+254
AM/FM/Cassette/CD Audio System [Opt on SLT]	+344
Air Conditioning [Opt on ST]	+402

Body Styles	TMV Pricing		
	Trade	Private	Dealer
4 Dr SLT Ext Cab LB	11301	13034	14633
4 Dr SLT Plus 4WD Ext Cab LB	13604	15690	17615
4 Dr SLT Plus Ext Cab LB	12239	14116	15848
4 Dr ST 4WD Ext Cab LB	11914	13741	15427
4 Dr ST Ext Cab LB	10541	12157	13649

Options	Price
Automatic 4-Speed Transmission	+486
Bed Liner	+122
Camper/Towing Package	+137
Leather Seats [Opt on SLT]	+624
Limited Slip Differential	+142
Power Driver Seat [Opt on SLT]	+160

2000

The 1500 Club Cab models with the 8-foot bed box have been discontinued; also eliminated for 2000 are the 2500 Club Cabs. All Ram Pickups receive a new front suspension and steering system to improve ride quality and steering precision, and 2500s and 3500s have a revised rear suspension for a better ride when loaded. An off-road package is now available for the short-wheelbase four-wheel-drive 1500.

Mileage Category: K

Body Styles	TMV Pricing		
	Trade	Private	Dealer
2 Dr SLT 4WD Std Cab LB	9410	11002	12562
2 Dr SLT Std Cab LB	8461	9892	11295
2 Dr ST 4WD Std Cab LB	9221	10777	12302
2 Dr ST Std Cab LB	7673	8971	10243

Options	Price
5.9L I6 Turbodiesel OHV 24V Engine	+2090
6-Speed Transmission	+181
8.0L V10 OHV 20V FI Engine	+212
AM/FM/CD Audio System	+230
AM/FM/Cassette/CD Audio System	+312
Air Conditioning	+364

Body Styles	TMV Pricing		
	Trade	Private	Dealer
4 Dr SLT 4WD Ext Cab LB	11282	13191	15062
4 Dr SLT Ext Cab LB	9305	10879	12422
4 Dr ST 4WD Ext Cab LB	10132	11846	13526
4 Dr ST Ext Cab LB	9154	10702	12220

Options	Price
Automatic 4-Speed Transmission	+441
Camper/Towing Package	+124
Leather Seats	+565
Limited Slip Differential	+129
Power Driver Seat	+145
Trailer Hitch	+124

1999

The Sport model gets a new front bumper, fascia, grille, headlamps, graphics and Solar Yellow exterior color just to make sure it won't go unnoticed in traffic. All Ram Pickups get an express-down feature for the power windows, a new headlamp switch, and four-wheel ABS is standard on vehicles over 10,000 pounds.

Mileage Category: K

Body Styles	TMV Pricing		
	Trade	Private	Dealer
2 Dr Laramie SLT 4WD Std Cab LB	8318	9905	11556
2 Dr Laramie SLT Std Cab LB	7199	8590	10037
2 Dr ST 4WD Std Cab LB	8103	9649	11257
2 Dr ST Std Cab LB	6635	7916	9249

Body Styles	TMV Pricing		
	Trade	Private	Dealer
4 Dr Laramie SLT 4WD Ext Cab LB	9859	11763	13745
4 Dr Laramie SLT Ext Cab LB	8263	9859	11521
4 Dr ST 4WD Ext Cab LB	8877	10592	12376
4 Dr ST Ext Cab LB	8012	9560	11171

Options	Price
5.9L I6 Turbodiesel OHV 24V Engine	+1894
8.0L V10 OHV 20V FI Engine	+173
AM/FM/CD Audio System	+188
AM/FM/Cassette/CD Audio System	+255

Options	Price
Air Conditioning [Opt on ST]	+297
Automatic 4-Speed Transmission	+359
Leather Seats	+460
Power Driver Seat	+118

Mileage Category: K

1998

All Ram Pickups get a totally redesigned interior, standard passenger-side airbag with cutoff switch, and all airbags are "depowered" for safety.

Body Styles	TMV Pricing		
	Trade	Private	Dealer
2 Dr Laramie SLT 4WD Std Cab LB	7194	8734	10471
2 Dr Laramie SLT Std Cab LB	6201	7529	9026
2 Dr ST 4WD Std Cab LB	6619	8036	9634
2 Dr ST Std Cab LB	5870	7127	8544

Body Styles	TMV Pricing		
	Trade	Private	Dealer
4 Dr Laramie SLT 4WD Ext Cab LB	8705	10569	12671
4 Dr Laramie SLT Ext Cab LB	7384	8965	10748
4 Dr ST 4WD Ext Cab LB	7807	9479	11364
4 Dr ST Ext Cab LB	6847	8313	9966

Options	Price
5.9L I6 Turbodiesel OHV 12V Engine	+1376
5.9L I6 Turbodiesel OHV 24V Engine	+1675
8.0L V10 OHV 20V FI Engine	+318
AM/FM/CD Audio System	+166
AM/FM/Cassette/CD Audio System	+225

Options	Price
Air Conditioning [Opt on ST]	+262
Antilock Brakes	+246
Automatic 4-Speed Transmission	+310
Leather Seats	+407

Mileage Category: K

1997

No major changes for 1997. Refinements include available leather seating and woodgrain trim on SLT models, optional remote keyless entry, and standard deep-tinted quarter glass on Club Cab models. Also available is a combination CD/cassette stereo. Fresh interior and exterior colors sum up the changes this year.

Body Styles	TMV Pricing		
	Trade	Private	Dealer
2 Dr LT 4WD Std Cab LB	5555	6928	8605
2 Dr LT Std Cab LB	5026	6268	7785
2 Dr Laramie SLT 4WD Ext Cab LB	6859	8553	10624
2 Dr Laramie SLT 4WD Std Cab LB	6296	7851	9751
2 Dr Laramie SLT Ext Cab LB	5784	7212	8958

Body Styles	TMV Pricing		
	Trade	Private	Dealer
2 Dr Laramie SLT Std Cab LB	5409	6745	8377
2 Dr ST 4WD Ext Cab LB	6218	7754	9632
2 Dr ST 4WD Std Cab LB	5686	7091	8808
2 Dr ST Ext Cab LB	5170	6447	8008
2 Dr ST Std Cab LB	5137	6406	7956

Options	Price
5.9L I6 Turbodiesel OHV 12V Engine	+1416
8.0L V10 OHV 20V FI Engine	+279
AM/FM/CD Audio System	+146
AM/FM/Cassette/CD Audio System	+198

Options	Price
Air Conditioning [Opt on LT,ST]	+231
Antilock Brakes	+217
Automatic 4-Speed Transmission	+279
Leather Seats	+358

Mileage Category: K

1996

The Ram Pickup gets some mild mechanical changes, including electronically governed automatic transmissions and a torque increase for the optional 5.9L turbodiesel V8 to 440 pound-feet. CD controls are added to cassette audio systems and cast alloy wheels are standard with SLT and Sport trims. New color offerings are Light Kiwi Pearl and Spruce Pearl.

Body Styles	TMV Pricing		
	Trade	Private	Dealer
2 Dr LT 4WD Std Cab LB	4825	6145	7967
2 Dr LT Std Cab LB	4130	5259	6819
2 Dr Laramie SLT 4WD Ext Cab LB	5595	7125	9239
2 Dr Laramie SLT 4WD Std Cab LB	5394	6869	8907
2 Dr Laramie SLT Ext Cab LB	5009	6379	8271

Body Styles	TMV Pricing		
	Trade	Private	Dealer
2 Dr Laramie SLT Std Cab LB	4657	5931	7690
2 Dr ST 4WD Ext Cab LB	5373	6842	8871
2 Dr ST 4WD Std Cab LB	4918	6263	8121
2 Dr ST Ext Cab LB	4450	5667	7348
2 Dr ST Std Cab LB	4151	5286	6854

Options	Price
5.9L I6 Turbodiesel OHV 12V Engine	+1202
8.0L V10 OHV 20V FI Engine	+122
AM/FM/CD Audio System	+133

Options	Price
Air Conditioning [Opt on LT,ST]	+208
Antilock Brakes	+197
Automatic 4-Speed Transmission	+242

Mileage Category: K

1995

After a complete redesign in 1994, the Ram Pickup offers a club cab on a 134.7-inch wheelbase. Torque increases to 430 pound-feet with the Cummins 5.9L diesel with manual transmission, and an illuminated overdrive lockout switch is standard. An Infinity CD audio system, foglights and four-wheel ABS are optional.

Body Styles	TMV Pricing		
	Trade	Private	Dealer
2 Dr LT 4WD Std Cab LB	3947	5128	7095
2 Dr LT Std Cab LB	3216	4178	5781
2 Dr Laramie SLT 4WD Ext Cab LB	4586	5958	8245
2 Dr Laramie SLT 4WD Std Cab LB	4404	5722	7919
2 Dr Laramie SLT Ext Cab LB	4087	5310	7347

Body Styles	TMV Pricing		
	Trade	Private	Dealer
2 Dr Laramie SLT Std Cab LB	3821	4964	6869
2 Dr ST 4WD Std Cab LB	4359	5663	7837
2 Dr ST Ext Cab LB	3566	4633	6411
2 Dr ST Std Cab LB	3401	4418	6113

Options	Price
5.9L I6 Turbodiesel OHV 12V Engine	+964

Options	Price
8.0L V10 OHV 20V FI Engine	+107

1995 (cont'd)

Options	Price
AM/FM/CD Audio System	+117
Air Conditioning [Opt on LT,ST]	+182
Antilock Brakes	+172

Options	Price
Automatic 4-Speed Transmission	+212
Infinity Audio System	+76

Spirit
1995

Mileage Category: C

Body Styles	TMV Pricing		
	Trade	Private	Dealer
4 Dr STD Sdn	699	1194	2020

Options	Price
3.0L V6 SOHC 12V FI Engine	+158

Flexible fuel model and optional four-speed automatic transmission are dropped. A three-speed automatic continues as standard equipment.

Stealth
1996

Mileage Category: F

Body Styles	TMV Pricing		
	Trade	Private	Dealer
2 Dr R/T Hbk	5093	6364	8118
2 Dr R/T Turbo AWD Hbk	6840	8547	10904

Body Styles	TMV Pricing		
	Trade	Private	Dealer
2 Dr STD Hbk	3480	4407	5688

Options	Price
18 Inch Wheels [Opt on R/T AWD]	+265
Antilock Brakes	+208
Automatic 4-Speed Transmission	+230

Options	Price
Compact Disc Changer	+157
Leather Seats	+220
Power Moonroof	+184

Final year for Japanese-built sports car. A new rear spoiler and body-color roof mark the 1996 model. A chrome 18-inch wheel package is available with Pirelli P-Zero tires and base models get an optional Infinity sound system.

1995

Chromed 18-inch aluminum wheels are available on R/T Turbo.

Mileage Category: F

Body Styles	TMV Pricing		
	Trade	Private	Dealer
2 Dr R/T Hbk	3594	4707	6563
2 Dr R/T Turbo AWD Hbk	5031	6590	9188

Body Styles	TMV Pricing		
	Trade	Private	Dealer
2 Dr STD Hbk	2618	3488	4938

Options	Price
18 Inch Wheels [Opt on R/T AWD]	+231
Antilock Brakes [Opt on R/T,STD]	+182
Automatic 4-Speed Transmission	+224
Compact Disc Changer	+137

Options	Price
Infinity Audio System [Opt on R/T,R/T AWD]	+89
Leather Seats	+192
Moonroof	+92

Stratus
2004

Mileage Category: C

Body Styles	TMV Pricing		
	Trade	Private	Dealer
2 Dr R/T Cpe	10937	12378	14779
2 Dr SXT Cpe	9017	10144	12021
4 Dr ES Sdn	9661	10746	12554

Body Styles	TMV Pricing		
	Trade	Private	Dealer
4 Dr R/T Sdn	10562	11728	13670
4 Dr SE Sdn	8681	9767	11578
4 Dr SXT Sdn	8802	9888	11698

2004 (cont'd)

Options	Price
17 Inch Wheels - Chrome [Opt on R/T Cpe]	+750
AM/FM/Cassette/CD Changer Audio System [Opt on ES, R/T Sdn]	+400
Aluminum/Alloy Wheels [Opt on SXT, SE]	+425
Antilock Brakes [Std on R/T Sdn]	+440
Front Side Airbag Restraints [Opt on Cpe]	+390
Front and Rear Head Airbag Restraints [Opt on Sdn]	+390

Options	Price
Leather Seats [Opt on R/T, ES Sdn]	+695
Power Driver Seat [Std on ES]	+200
Power Moonroof	+695
Rear Spoiler [Opt on SXT Cpe]	+120
Traction Control System [Opt on SXT, R/T Cpe, ES]	+300

Chrysler and Dodge have restyled most vehicles this year to bring out similarities and cohesiveness among the Chrysler group cars. To that end, the Stratus sedan receives a new front fascia, and R/T sedans get a monochromatic grille. Sedan interior changes include the addition of steering wheel-mounted audio controls and an auto-dimming rearview mirror, along with new door panels, new seat fabric and three new interior choices. Two new 16-inch wheel options, plus two new exterior colors have been added as well. Also this year, Stratus sedans without optional antilock brakes receive a downgraded braking system with rear drums in place of discs. On the plus side, traction control is now available when combined with antilock brakes. A manual transmission is no longer available. Changes to the coupe are minimal. The interior features a new "Satin Silver" finish on the center stack bezels, and door accents.

2003

Mileage Category: C

Body Styles	TMV Pricing		
	Trade	Private	Dealer
2 Dr R/T Cpe	9865	10987	12857
2 Dr SXT Cpe	7781	8666	10142
4 Dr ES Sdn	8288	9277	10925

Body Styles	TMV Pricing		
	Trade	Private	Dealer
4 Dr R/T Sdn	9237	10339	12176
4 Dr SE Sdn	7038	7878	9278
4 Dr SXT Sdn	6972	7805	9192

Options	Price
17 Inch Wheels - Chrome [Opt on R/T Cpe]	+474
AM/FM/Cassette/CD Changer Audio System [Opt on ES, R/T Sdn]	+190
Aluminum/Alloy Wheels [Opt on SE]	+268
Antilock Brakes	+430
Automatic 4-Speed Transmission [Opt on R/T, SXT Cpe]	+521
Front Side Airbag Restraints [Opt on Cpe]	+246
Front and Rear Head Airbag Restraints [Opt on Sdn]	+246

Options	Price
Leather Seats [Opt on ES, R/T]	+379
Power Door Locks [Opt on SE]	+126
Power Driver Seat	+130
Power Moonroof	+439
Premium Audio System [Opt on ES]	+221
Special Factory Paint	+126

The 2003 Stratus coupe gains revisions to its front and rear styling and an updated instrument panel and center console. The SE coupe is dropped in a sense; it will only be available to fleet buyers, such as rental car agencies. Sedans continue as before except the SE Plus is subtracted and the V6 engine (with the automatic transmission) is now flexible fuel-rated, meaning it can run on ethanol as well as gasoline.

2002

Mileage Category: C

Body Styles	TMV Pricing		
	Trade	Private	Dealer
2 Dr R/T Cpe	7707	8749	10486
2 Dr SE Cpe	6183	7019	8412
2 Dr SXT Cpe	6280	7130	8546
4 Dr ES Sdn	6910	7841	9393

Body Styles	TMV Pricing		
	Trade	Private	Dealer
4 Dr R/T Sdn	7838	8940	10776
4 Dr SE Plus Sdn	6296	7180	8653
4 Dr SE Sdn	5790	6605	7962
4 Dr SXT Sdn	5775	6554	7852

Options	Price
17 Inch Wheels [Opt on R/T]	+204
2.7L V6 DOHC 24V FI Engine [Opt on Sdn - SE, SE Plus]	+462
3.0L V6 SOHC 24V FI Engine [Opt on SE Cpe]	+481
AM/FM/Cassette/CD Changer Audio System [Std on R/T Sdn, SXT]	+136
Aluminum/Alloy Wheels [Opt on SE Cpe]	+198
Antilock Brakes [Std on R/T Sdn]	+370

Options	Price
Chrome Wheels [Opt on ES Sdn]	+326
Cruise Control [Opt on SE Plus Sdn]	+128
Front and Rear Head Airbag Restraints [Opt on Sdn]	+212
Leather Seats [Opt on ES, R/T]	+326
Power Driver Seat [Opt on R/T]	+144
Power Moonroof [Opt on Cpe, Sdn]	+378

A new R/T sedan joins the lineup, complete with a healthy V6 and manual gearbox. Other additions to the family include the SE Plus and SXT sedans and an SXT coupe. All Strati gain a "battery saver" device and new audio features. For coupes, a stereo with a four-CD in-dash changer is available in the Touring Package and is standard on the R/T model. For sedans the new option of a stereo with both CD and cassette players debuts. New color choices include Steel Blue, Onyx Green and Light Almond Pearl now available for sedans, and Dark Titanium and Caffe Latte added to the coupes' color palette.

2001

Mileage Category: C

Body Styles	TMV Pricing		
	Trade	Private	Dealer
2 Dr R/T Cpe	6413	7836	9150
2 Dr SE Cpe	4983	6088	7108

Body Styles	TMV Pricing		
	Trade	Private	Dealer
4 Dr ES Sdn	5114	6267	7331
4 Dr SE Sdn	5023	6156	7202

Options	Price
3.0L V6 SOHC 24V FI Engine [Opt on SE Cpe]	+424
AM/FM/Cassette/CD Audio System	+125
AM/FM/Cassette/CD Changer Audio System [Opt on ES, SE]	+125
Aluminum/Alloy Wheels	+175
Antilock Brakes	+339

Options	Price
Automatic 4-Speed Transmission [Opt on Cpe]	+411
Chrome Wheels [Opt on SE Sdn]	+299
Front and Rear Head Airbag Restraints [Opt on Sdn]	+195
Leather Seats	+289
Power Driver Seat	+189
Power Moonroof	+342

The Avenger nameplate has been dropped from the Dodge lineup, replaced by the all-new Stratus Coupe. The Stratus Sedan continues with a full redesign but retains much of its predecessor's look and feel. A new engine debuts along with additional safety features that make the Stratus a family sedan in the truest sense.

2001 (cont'd)

Options	Price
Premium Audio System	+175

2000

Mileage Category: C

Body Styles	TMV Pricing		
	Trade	Private	Dealer
4 Dr ES Sdn	3503	4545	5567

Options	Price
2.4L I4 DOHC 16V FI Engine [Opt on SE]	+204
AM/FM/Cassette/CD Audio System	+154
Antilock Brakes [Opt on SE]	+307
Automatic 4-Speed Transmission [Opt on SE]	+475

Body Styles	TMV Pricing		
	Trade	Private	Dealer
4 Dr SE Sdn	3004	3899	4776

Options	Price
Compact Disc Changer	+249
Power Driver Seat	+171
Power Sunroof	+314
Power Windows [Opt on SE]	+117

A new entry-level SE replaces last year's Base model and comes with so much standard equipment. The upper-level ES steps up to a 2.5-liter V6, and new colors also debut.

1999

The instrument panel gauges are now white-faced, wheels are better looking, and some work has been done to reduce the interior noise levels.

Mileage Category: C

Body Styles	TMV Pricing		
	Trade	Private	Dealer
4 Dr ES Sdn	2560	3486	4450

Options	Price
2.4L I4 DOHC 16V FI Engine	+166
AM/FM/Cassette/CD Audio System	+203
Antilock Brakes [Opt on STD]	+278
Automatic 4-Speed Transmission [Opt on STD]	+387

Body Styles	TMV Pricing		
	Trade	Private	Dealer
4 Dr STD Sdn	2285	3113	3975

Options	Price
Compact Disc Changer	+203
Leather Seats	+230
Power Driver Seat	+140
Power Sunroof	+214

1998

The 2.4-liter engine with automatic transmission is now standard on the ES. New colors are available this year and numerous refinements are made to reduce noise and vibration.

Mileage Category: C

Body Styles	TMV Pricing		
	Trade	Private	Dealer
4 Dr ES Sdn	1917	2765	3722

Options	Price
2.4L I4 DOHC 16V FI Engine [Opt on STD]	+146
2.5L V6 SOHC 24V FI Engine	+310
AM/FM/Cassette/CD Audio System	+180
Antilock Brakes	+246
Automatic 4-Speed Transmission [Opt on STD]	+342

Body Styles	TMV Pricing		
	Trade	Private	Dealer
4 Dr STD Sdn	1653	2385	3210

Options	Price
Compact Disc Changer	+180
Leather Seats	+203
Power Driver Seat	+124
Power Sunroof	+189

1997

Subtle styling revisions are the most obvious change to the Stratus for 1997. Sound systems have been improved, rear seat heat ducts benefit from improved flow, and the optional 2.4-liter engine runs quieter. New colors and a revised console round out changes.

Mileage Category: C

Body Styles	TMV Pricing		
	Trade	Private	Dealer
4 Dr ES Sdn	1433	2144	3012

Options	Price
2.4L I4 DOHC 16V FI Engine	+129
2.5L V6 SOHC 24V FI Engine	+272
AM/FM/Cassette/CD Audio System	+158
Antilock Brakes [Std on ES]	+217

Body Styles	TMV Pricing		
	Trade	Private	Dealer
4 Dr STD Sdn	1303	1948	2737

Options	Price
Automatic 4-Speed Transmission	+236
Compact Disc Changer	+158
Leather Seats	+179

1996

Excellent midsized sedan gets a more responsive torque converter when equipped with the 2.5-liter V6. New colors and a power sunroof are also new for 1996.

Mileage Category: C

Body Styles	TMV Pricing		
	Trade	Private	Dealer
4 Dr ES Sdn	1061	1677	2527

Options	Price
2.4L I4 DOHC 16V FI Engine	+117
2.5L V6 SOHC 24V FI Engine	+248
AM/FM/CD Audio System	+129
Antilock Brakes [Std on ES]	+197

Body Styles	TMV Pricing		
	Trade	Private	Dealer
4 Dr STD Sdn	1020	1612	2429

Options	Price
Automatic 4-Speed Transmission	+215
Leather Seats	+163
Power Sunroof	+151

1995

Mileage Category: C

Body Styles	TMV Pricing		
	Trade	Private	Dealer
4 Dr ES Sdn	824	1410	2386

Options	Price
2.4L I4 DOHC 16V FI Engine	+102
Antilock Brakes [Opt on STD]	+172
Automatic 4-Speed Transmission [Opt on STD]	+188

Body Styles	TMV Pricing		
	Trade	Private	Dealer
4 Dr STD Sdn	733	1255	2124

Options	Price
Leather Seats	+143
Power Driver Seat	+80
Premium Audio System	+84

Spirit replacement features cutting-edge styling and class-leading accommodations. Dual airbags and ABS are standard. Base and ES models are available. Base model has 2.0-liter, four-cylinder engine making 132 horsepower and a five-speed manual transmission. ES is powered by 155-horsepower, Mitsubishi 2.5-liter V6. A credit option on the ES is the Neon's 2.0-liter four hooked to a five-speed manual transmission.

Viper

2004

Mileage Category: R

Body Styles	TMV Pricing		
	Trade	Private	Dealer
2 Dr SRT-10 Conv	64663	67454	72105

After last year's complete redesign, the Viper sees only detail changes for '04 that include a new color called "Viper White," racy red brake calipers, carpeting for the trunk and a folding tonneau cover.

2003

Mileage Category: R

Body Styles	TMV Pricing		
	Trade	Private	Dealer
2 Dr SRT-10 Conv	61156	63820	68261

Dodge hatches a new snake with a real roadster body, scary output figures (how's 500 horsepower sound?) and improved build quality.

2002

Mileage Category: R

Body Styles	TMV Pricing		
	Trade	Private	Dealer
2 Dr ACR Competition Cpe	57232	60072	64805
2 Dr GTS Cpe	50255	52749	56905

Options	Price
AM/FM/CD Audio System [Opt on ACR]	+245
Alpine Audio System [Opt on ACR]	+217
Special Factory Paint	+1631

Body Styles	TMV Pricing		
	Trade	Private	Dealer
2 Dr RT/10 Conv	49635	52098	56203

Options	Price
Special Leather Seat Trim	+408
Tonneau Cover [Opt on RT/10]	+136

Nothing's new except for an available color scheme on the GTS: Graphite metallic with silver stripes.

2001

Mileage Category: R

Body Styles	TMV Pricing		
	Trade	Private	Dealer
2 Dr ACR Competition Cpe	53187	57255	61010
2 Dr GTS Cpe	45541	49024	52239

Options	Price
AM/FM/CD Audio System [Std on GTS,R/T 10]	+275
Hardtop Roof	+1247

Body Styles	TMV Pricing		
	Trade	Private	Dealer
2 Dr RT/10 Conv	45314	48780	51980

Options	Price
Special Factory Paint [Opt on ACR,GTS]	+1496
Tonneau Cover	+125

Slightly refining the snake's venomous bite are standard four-wheel disc ABS, an ACR option group with air conditioning and a CD player, and an internal trunk. New Race Yellow or Deep Sapphire Blue exterior hues are offered.

2000

Mileage Category: R

Body Styles	TMV Pricing		
	Trade	Private	Dealer
2 Dr ACR Competition Cpe	49160	53252	57263
2 Dr GTS Cpe	40095	43432	46703

Options	Price
AM/FM/CD Audio System [Opt on ACR]	+249
Hardtop Roof	+1130

Body Styles	TMV Pricing		
	Trade	Private	Dealer
2 Dr RT/10 Conv	39728	43034	46275

Options	Price
Special Factory Paint [Opt on GTS]	+1130

The 2000 Viper is available in a new Steel Gray color and the new ACR version offers additional performance.

1999

Goodies for the '99 Viper include power mirrors, Connolly leather for various interior surfaces, a new shift knob, aluminum interior accents, and a remote release for the glass hatch on the GTS. Black is again an exterior color choice, available with or without silver stripes. New 18-inch aluminum wheels with the Viper logo on the caps round out the changes.

Mileage Category: R

Body Styles	TMV Pricing			Body Styles	TMV Pricing		
	Trade	Private	Dealer		Trade	Private	Dealer
2 Dr GTS Cpe	36067	39658	43395	2 Dr RT/10 Conv	35874	39445	43162

Options	Price	Options	Price
Hardtop Roof	+921	Special Factory Paint [Opt on GTS]	+737

1998

Tubular, stainless steel exhaust manifolds help reduce emissions and weight. Silver Metallic paint is a new option and the powerful Dodge gets a passenger airbag cutoff switch and second-generation depowered airbags.

Mileage Category: R

Body Styles	TMV Pricing			Body Styles	TMV Pricing		
	Trade	Private	Dealer		Trade	Private	Dealer
2 Dr GTS Cpe	31300	34592	38304	2 Dr RT/10 Conv	30809	34050	37704

Options	Price	Options	Price
Hardtop Roof	+815	Special Factory Paint [Opt on GTS]	+489

1997

One new color, flame red, with or without white stripes, is available for 1997. Silver, sparkle gold or yellow gold wheels come with red Vipers. The original blue with white stripes paint scheme is available as an option, as are last year's standard polished aluminum wheels. The RT/10 roadster is set to return later this year, with dual airbags, power windows and door locks, and the 450-horsepower V10 from the GTS. Also set to debut on the revamped drop top are the four-wheel independent suspension and adjustable pedals from the GTS.

Mileage Category: R

Body Styles	TMV Pricing			Body Styles	TMV Pricing		
	Trade	Private	Dealer		Trade	Private	Dealer
2 Dr GTS Cpe	28750	31991	35952	2 Dr RT/10 Conv	27282	30358	34117

Options	Price	Options	Price
Hardtop Roof	+717	Special Factory Paint [Opt on GTS]	+344

1996

Final year for Viper in current form. More power is offered from the V10 engine via a low-restriction rear outlet exhaust system, and an optional hardtop with sliding side curtains is available. Five-spoke aluminum wheels and three exterior styling themes replace the trim on the 1995 Viper. GTS coupe begins production when convertibles have completed their run. The GTS arrives with dual airbags and air conditioning.

Mileage Category: R

Body Styles	TMV Pricing			Body Styles	TMV Pricing		
	Trade	Private	Dealer		Trade	Private	Dealer
2 Dr GTS Cpe	26596	29692	33968	2 Dr RT/10 Conv	24143	26953	30834

Options	Price	Options	Price
Air Conditioning [Opt on RT/10]	+348	Hardtop Roof	+653

1995

No changes.

Mileage Category: R

Body Styles	TMV Pricing		
	Trade	Private	Dealer
2 Dr RT/10 Conv	22344	24900	29159

Options	Price	Options	Price
AM/FM/CD Audio System	+125	Air Conditioning	+304

Summit/Talon

Summit

1996

Mileage Category: B

Body Styles	TMV Pricing		
	Trade	Private	Dealer
2 Dr DL Cpe	773	1201	1792
2 Dr ESi Cpe	853	1326	1978
4 Dr DL Wgn	1094	1699	2535
4 Dr ESi Sdn	1042	1618	2414

Options	Price
Air Conditioning	+147
Antilock Brakes	+131

Body Styles	TMV Pricing		
	Trade	Private	Dealer
4 Dr LX Sdn	986	1532	2287
4 Dr LX Wgn	1199	1864	2782
4 Dr STD AWD Wgn	1265	1966	2933

Options	Price
Automatic 4-Speed Transmission	+129

Nothing changes for the Mitsubishi-built Summit except a new choice of paint colors. The Summit wagon, a cross between a sedan and a minivan, gets new colors and seat fabrics.

1995

Mileage Category: B

Body Styles	TMV Pricing		
	Trade	Private	Dealer
2 Dr DL Cpe	582	923	1490
2 Dr ESi Cpe	677	1074	1736
4 Dr DL Wgn	775	1229	1985
4 Dr ESi Sdn	749	1189	1921

Options	Price
Air Conditioning	+123
Antilock Brakes	+109

Body Styles	TMV Pricing		
	Trade	Private	Dealer
4 Dr LX Sdn	727	1153	1862
4 Dr LX Wgn	848	1344	2171
4 Dr STD AWD Wgn	871	1381	2231

Options	Price
Automatic 3-Speed Transmission	+76
Automatic 4-Speed Transmission	+108

Dual airbags for the slow-selling Eagle Summit are the only change for 1995.

Talon

1998

Mileage Category: E

Body Styles	TMV Pricing		
	Trade	Private	Dealer
2 Dr ESi Hbk	3462	4256	5151
2 Dr STD Hbk	3361	4132	5001

Options	Price
AM/FM/CD Audio System	+122
AM/FM/Cassette/CD Audio System	+122
Air Conditioning	+260
Aluminum/Alloy Wheels [Opt on ESi]	+154
Antilock Brakes	+238

Body Styles	TMV Pricing		
	Trade	Private	Dealer
2 Dr TSi Turbo AWD Hbk	4567	5614	6794
2 Dr TSi Turbo Hbk	4216	5182	6272

Options	Price
Automatic 4-Speed Transmission	+225
Infinity Audio System	+240
Leather Seats	+166
Power Sunroof	+220

New silver exterior badging and a new black and gray interior mark the Eagle in its final year of production. A new four-speaker CD/cassette player is now optional on the ESi, and all Talons benefit from Chrysler's next-generation depowered airbags.

1997

New front and rear fascias, bodyside cladding, bright new paint colors and "sparkle" wheels and wheel covers are guaranteed to attract attention to this overshadowed model.

Mileage Category: E

Body Styles	TMV Pricing		
	Trade	Private	Dealer
2 Dr ESi Hbk	2803	3545	4451
2 Dr STD Hbk	2660	3364	4225

Options	Price
AM/FM/Cassette Audio System [Opt on ESi,STD]	+116
Air Conditioning	+199
Aluminum/Alloy Wheels [Opt on ESi]	+117
Antilock Brakes	+182

Body Styles	TMV Pricing		
	Trade	Private	Dealer
2 Dr TSi Turbo AWD Hbk	3733	4722	5931
2 Dr TSi Turbo Hbk	3454	4368	5486

Options	Price
Automatic 4-Speed Transmission	+208
Leather Seats	+127
Power Sunroof	+169
Premium Audio System	+171

1996

Based on Mitsubishi mechanicals, Talon receives minor upgrades for 1996, including revised sound systems, a panic alarm, a HomeLink transmitter and two new colors. ESi trim level gets standard 16-inch wheels.

Mileage Category: E

Body Styles	TMV Pricing		
	Trade	Private	Dealer
2 Dr ESi Hbk	2045	2733	3683
2 Dr STD Hbk	1962	2622	3534

Body Styles	TMV Pricing		
	Trade	Private	Dealer
2 Dr TSi Turbo AWD Hbk	2545	3401	4584
2 Dr TSi Turbo Hbk	2338	3124	4210

1996 (cont'd)

Options	Price
AM/FM/Cassette/CD Audio System	+137
Air Conditioning	+149
Antilock Brakes	+137

Options	Price
Automatic 4-Speed Transmission	+155
Power Sunroof	+127

1995

The Talon is redesigned for 1995. The new model features a new body and more power. Base engine creeps up to 140 horsepower, the turbo to 210 horsepower. Dual airbags replace the antiquated motorized seatbelts on the previous edition, and the Talon now meets 1997 federal side-impact standards.

Mileage Category: E

Body Styles	TMV Pricing		
	Trade	Private	Dealer
2 Dr ESi Hbk	1462	2090	3136
2 Dr TSi Turbo AWD Hbk	1856	2652	3979

Body Styles	TMV Pricing		
	Trade	Private	Dealer
2 Dr TSi Turbo Hbk	1640	2345	3519

Options	Price
Air Conditioning	+124
Antilock Brakes	+114
Automatic 4-Speed Transmission	+108

Options	Price
Leather Seats	+80
Power Sunroof	+106

Vision

1997

The 3.5-liter engine, formerly exclusive to the TSi, is now available on the ESi. Automatic transmission refinements are intended to improve shifting. Eagle Vision ESi gets an improved stereo. A new color, Deep Amethyst Pearl, is now available.

Mileage Category: G

Body Styles	TMV Pricing		
	Trade	Private	Dealer
4 Dr ESi Sdn	2039	2819	3773

Body Styles	TMV Pricing		
	Trade	Private	Dealer
4 Dr TSi Sdn	2366	3271	4378

Options	Price
AM/FM/Cassette/CD Audio System	+139
Antilock Brakes [Opt on ESi]	+182
Compact Disc Changer [Opt on ESi]	+161

Options	Price
Infinity Audio System	+131
Leather Seats	+143
Power Moonroof	+166

1996

An automanual transmission called AutoStick gives the 1996 Vision a feature to distinguish it as Chrysler's premier sport sedan. Interiors have been quieted down, and the ESi gets standard 16-inch wheels. Headlight illumination has been improved, new colors and seat fabrics are on board, and improved sound systems debut.

Mileage Category: G

Body Styles	TMV Pricing		
	Trade	Private	Dealer
4 Dr ESi Sdn	1694	2363	3287

Body Styles	TMV Pricing		
	Trade	Private	Dealer
4 Dr TSi Sdn	1979	2763	3846

Options	Price
Antilock Brakes [Opt on ESi]	+137

Options	Price
Power Moonroof	+125

1995

No changes to the Vision.

Mileage Category: G

Body Styles	TMV Pricing		
	Trade	Private	Dealer
4 Dr ESi Sdn	1305	1857	2776

Body Styles	TMV Pricing		
	Trade	Private	Dealer
4 Dr TSi Sdn	1563	2224	3326

Options	Price
AM/FM/CD Audio System	+76
Antilock Brakes [Opt on ESi]	+114

Options	Price
Leather Seats	+90
Power Moonroof	+104

Aerostar

1997

Body Styles	TMV Pricing		
	Trade	Private	Dealer
3 Dr XLT AWD Pass Van Ext	2209	3064	4110
3 Dr XLT Pass Van	1707	2367	3173

Options	Price
AM/FM/Cassette Audio System	+119
Air Conditioning - Front and Rear	+255

Mileage Category: P

Body Styles	TMV Pricing		
	Trade	Private	Dealer
3 Dr XLT Pass Van Ext	1998	2771	3716

Options	Price
Captain Chairs (4)	+197
Privacy Glass	+122

Ford's aging minivan gets a five-speed automatic transmission this year. The sound systems are upgraded and the seats are restyled as well.

1996

Smoother shifting transmission debuts, along with revised air conditioning controls and a new radio with visible controls. Solar-tinted glass is standard.

Body Styles	TMV Pricing		
	Trade	Private	Dealer
3 Dr XLT AWD Pass Van Ext	1688	2405	3395
3 Dr XLT Pass Van	1337	1904	2687

Options	Price
Air Conditioning - Front and Rear	+227
Captain Chairs (2)	+122

Mileage Category: P

Body Styles	TMV Pricing		
	Trade	Private	Dealer
3 Dr XLT Pass Van Ext	1588	2262	3193

Options	Price
Captain Chairs (4)	+174

1995

The XL and Eddie Bauer trim levels are dropped; only the XLT remains. The AWD system is available only in extended-length versions. Antilock brakes become standard for the Aerostar.

Body Styles	TMV Pricing		
	Trade	Private	Dealer
3 Dr XLT AWD Pass Van Ext	1161	1747	2723
3 Dr XLT Pass Van	960	1445	2252

Options	Price
Air Conditioning - Front and Rear	+196
Aluminum/Alloy Wheels	+82

Mileage Category: P

Body Styles	TMV Pricing		
	Trade	Private	Dealer
3 Dr XLT Pass Van Ext	1072	1612	2513

Options	Price
Captain Chairs (4)	+151
Privacy Glass	+93

Aspire

1997

Body Styles	TMV Pricing		
	Trade	Private	Dealer
2 Dr STD Hbk	705	1216	1841

Options	Price
AM/FM/Cassette Audio System	+151
Air Conditioning	+242

Mileage Category: A

Body Styles	TMV Pricing		
	Trade	Private	Dealer
4 Dr STD Hbk	745	1285	1946

Options	Price
Antilock Brakes	+222
Automatic 3-Speed Transmission	+193

This Kia-built entry-level Ford gets a higher final drive ratio on models equipped with an automatic transmission. New wheel covers, paint choices and interior trim are the only other changes.

1996

The Aspire loses the SE trim level and several items of standard and optional equipment. Four new colors debut.

Body Styles	TMV Pricing		
	Trade	Private	Dealer
2 Dr STD Hbk	492	888	1436

Options	Price
AM/FM/Cassette Audio System	+121
Air Conditioning	+215

Mileage Category: A

Body Styles	TMV Pricing		
	Trade	Private	Dealer
4 Dr STD Hbk	527	954	1544

Options	Price
Antilock Brakes	+197
Automatic 3-Speed Transmission	+172

1995

Available as a two- or four-door hatchback, the Aspire comes with dual airbags and available antilock brakes.

Body Styles	TMV Pricing		
	Trade	Private	Dealer
2 Dr SE Hbk	412	761	1342
2 Dr STD Hbk	386	715	1262

Mileage Category: A

Body Styles	TMV Pricing		
	Trade	Private	Dealer
4 Dr STD Hbk	399	739	1306

1995 (cont'd)

Options	Price
AM/FM/CD Audio System	+79
AM/FM/Cassette Audio System	+105
Air Conditioning	+186

Options	Price
Antilock Brakes	+170
Automatic 3-Speed Transmission	+149

Bronco

1996

Mileage Category: N

Body Styles	TMV Pricing		
	Trade	Private	Dealer
2 Dr Eddie Bauer 4WD SUV	4933	6198	7945
2 Dr XL 4WD SUV	3946	4957	6354

Body Styles	TMV Pricing		
	Trade	Private	Dealer
2 Dr XLT 4WD SUV	4396	5523	7079

Options	Price
Air Conditioning [Opt on XL,XLT]	+205
Automatic 4-Speed Transmission [Opt on XL,XLT]	+268

Options	Price
Leather Seats	+181

Trick new turn signal system is embedded in sideview mirrors. Otherwise, minor trim changes mark the passing of the last Bronco.

1995

An available Sport Package and new exterior styling for the Eddie Bauer model are the sole changes for 1995.

Mileage Category: N

Body Styles	TMV Pricing		
	Trade	Private	Dealer
2 Dr Eddie Bauer 4WD SUV	3811	4941	6823
2 Dr XL 4WD SUV	3065	3974	5488

Body Styles	TMV Pricing		
	Trade	Private	Dealer
2 Dr XLT 4WD SUV	3344	4336	5988

Options	Price
AM/FM/CD Audio System	+98
Air Conditioning [Opt on XL,XLT]	+177
Automatic 4-Speed Transmission [Opt on XL,XLT]	+232

Options	Price
Camper/Towing Package	+81
Chrome Wheels	+90
Leather Seats	+157

Contour

2000

Mileage Category: C

Body Styles	TMV Pricing		
	Trade	Private	Dealer
4 Dr SE Sdn	3041	3872	4687

Body Styles	TMV Pricing		
	Trade	Private	Dealer
4 Dr SE Sport Sdn	3051	3885	4702

Options	Price
2.5L V6 DOHC 24V FI Engine [Opt on SE]	+233
AM/FM/CD Audio System	+130
AM/FM/Cassette/CD Audio System	+130
Aluminum/Alloy Wheels [Opt on SE]	+200

Options	Price
Antilock Brakes	+320
Automatic 4-Speed Transmission	+384
Power Driver Seat	+165
Power Moonroof	+280

The Contour LX is dropped, leaving either the Contour SE Sport or SVT Contour to pick from. New colors are offered and an emergency trunk-release handle is standard.

1999

Base and GL models are both dropped and the LX and SE receive minor suspension tweaks.

Mileage Category: C

Body Styles	TMV Pricing		
	Trade	Private	Dealer
4 Dr LX Sdn	2293	3055	3848

Body Styles	TMV Pricing		
	Trade	Private	Dealer
4 Dr SE Sdn	2336	3113	3921

Options	Price
2.5L V6 DOHC 24V FI Engine [Std on SE]	+193
Aluminum/Alloy Wheels	+165
Antilock Brakes	+293
Automatic 4-Speed Transmission	+317

Options	Price
Leather Seats [Opt on SE]	+348
Power Driver Seat	+136
Power Moonroof	+231
Power Windows [Opt on LX]	+138

1998

A redesigned face gives this Ford more character, but the new taillight treatment is almost identical to the Contour's sibling, the Mercury Mystique. New alloy wheels and a slightly more commodious rear seat debut. Midyear changes included a model consolidation, the addition of depowered airbags, as well as improved handling and new wheels for the SVT.

Mileage Category: C

Body Styles	TMV Pricing		
	Trade	Private	Dealer
4 Dr GL Sdn	1629	2368	3202
4 Dr LX Sdn	1700	2472	3343

Body Styles	TMV Pricing		
	Trade	Private	Dealer
4 Dr SE Sdn	1799	2615	3535
4 Dr STD Sdn	1507	2191	2962

1998 (cont'd)

Options	Price
2.5L V6 DOHC 24V FI Engine	+157
Air Conditioning	+255
Aluminum/Alloy Wheels	+135
Antilock Brakes	+240

Options	Price
Automatic 4-Speed Transmission	+259
Compact Disc Changer	+143
Leather Seats	+284
Power Moonroof	+188

1997

The addition of a Sport Package for the GL and LX models and the inclusion of a standard trunk light are the only changes for the 1997 Contour.

Mileage Category: C

Body Styles	TMV Pricing		
	Trade	Private	Dealer
4 Dr GL Sdn	1081	1784	2644
4 Dr LX Sdn	1120	1849	2740

Body Styles	TMV Pricing		
	Trade	Private	Dealer
4 Dr SE Sdn	1260	2081	3084

Options	Price
2.5L V6 DOHC 24V FI Engine [Std on SE]	+317
Air Conditioning	+233
Aluminum/Alloy Wheels [Std on SE]	+124
Antilock Brakes	+222

Options	Price
Automatic 4-Speed Transmission	+239
Leather Seats	+262
Power Moonroof	+174

1996

Designers sculpt and adjust interior seating to make more leg- and headroom in the backseat. Five new colors are available and improvements to shift effort on manual transmission models make the 1996 Contour more competitive.

Mileage Category: C

Body Styles	TMV Pricing		
	Trade	Private	Dealer
4 Dr GL Sdn	733	1287	2051
4 Dr LX Sdn	769	1349	2151

Body Styles	TMV Pricing		
	Trade	Private	Dealer
4 Dr SE Sdn	875	1536	2449

Options	Price
2.5L V6 DOHC 24V FI Engine [Opt on GL,LX]	+282
Air Conditioning	+204
Antilock Brakes	+197

Options	Price
Automatic 4-Speed Transmission	+213
Leather Seats	+168
Power Moonroof	+155

1995

The Contour replaces the Tempo to compete with European and Japanese compacts. Based on the European Mondeo, the Contour has front-wheel drive and dual airbags. Traction control and antilock brakes are available on all models, as is a V6 engine that produces an impressive 170 horsepower.

Mileage Category: C

Body Styles	TMV Pricing		
	Trade	Private	Dealer
4 Dr GL Sdn	596	1065	1846
4 Dr LX Sdn	615	1096	1898

Body Styles	TMV Pricing		
	Trade	Private	Dealer
4 Dr SE Sdn	694	1239	2146

Options	Price
2.5L V6 DOHC 24V FI Engine [Opt on GL,LX]	+112
AM/FM/CD Audio System	+79
Air Conditioning	+176
Aluminum/Alloy Wheels	+96
Antilock Brakes	+170

Options	Price
Automatic 4-Speed Transmission	+184
Leather Seats	+146
Power Moonroof	+134
Power Windows	+77

Contour SVT

2000

Mileage Category: E

Body Styles	TMV Pricing		
	Trade	Private	Dealer
4 Dr STD Sdn	6494	8170	9813

Options	Price
AM/FM/CD Audio System	+130

Options	Price
Power Moonroof	+280

The 2000 Contour is unchanged from 1999.

1999

After being introduced, and receiving midyear tweaks for 1998, Ford's bargain sport sedan stands pat for its sophomore year.

Mileage Category: E

Body Styles	TMV Pricing		
	Trade	Private	Dealer
4 Dr STD Sdn	5253	6963	8743

Options	Price
Power Moonroof	+231

1998

Ford's SVT gurus turn their attention to the Contour, and the end result is this thoroughly enjoyable, near 200-horsepower sport sedan. As with all Contour models for this year, the SVT has the new face that gives this Ford more character (though the new taillight treatment is almost identical to the Contour's cousin, the Mercury Mystique). Halfway through the model year, the SVT got new wheels and tires, a slightly revised suspension and depowered airbags.

Mileage Category: E

Body Styles	TMV Pricing		
	Trade	Private	Dealer
4 Dr STD Sdn	4271	6115	8195

Options	Price
Power Moonroof	+188

Crown Victoria

2004

The only noticeable changes are the elimination of chrome trim from the door handles and bumpers and the addition of a mini spare as standard equipment. Heated side mirrors are now optional and side windows receive the added safety of laminated glass. LX models lose standard features like a power passenger seat, leather-wrapped steering wheel and auto-dimming rearview mirror -- but they can be readded by ordering the LX Premier Group.

Mileage Category: G

Body Styles	TMV Pricing			Body Styles	TMV Pricing		
	Trade	Private	Dealer		Trade	Private	Dealer
4 Dr LWB Sdn	13082	14404	16606	4 Dr S Sdn	12724	14037	16224
4 Dr LX Sdn	13319	14588	16703	4 Dr STD Sdn	12877	14260	16566

Options	Price	Options	Price
17 Inch Wheels [Opt on LX]	+600	Front Side Airbag Restraints [Opt on LX]	+300
AM/FM/Cassette Audio System [Opt on LX]	+185	Keyless Entry System [Opt on STD]	+255
AM/FM/Cassette/CD Audio System [Opt on STD]	+185	Leather Seats [Opt on LX]	+600
Automatic Climate Control [Opt on LX]	+400	Leather Steering Wheel [Opt on LX]	+125
Automatic Dimming Rearview Mirror [Opt on LX]	+150	Performance/Handling Package [Opt on LX]	+615
Automatic Load Leveling [Opt on LX]	+200	Power Adjustable Foot Pedals	+120
Bucket Seats [Opt on LX]	+150	Power Driver Seat [Opt on LX]	+200
Compact Disc Changer [Opt on LX]	+165	Power Moonroof [Opt on LX, LX Sport]	+1025
Digital Instrument Panel [Opt on LX]	+235	Traction Control System	+175

2003

Ford's big sedan receives a number of updates for 2003. A new full-perimeter frame uses strong, lightweight hydroformed steel sections for the front rails to improve frontal and offset crash performance. Redesigned frame crossmembers and new optional side impact airbags improve side impact crash performance. Additionally, the new frame -- combined with a redesigned independent front suspension and new monotube shock absorbers -- contributes to a smoother, more controlled ride and improved handling. Other changes include a new variable ratio rack and pinion steering system with variable power assist and a new dual-rate brake booster that automatically supplies full braking power in a panic stop. Inside, revised seats offer improved comfort and appearance; the cupholders are new; and a three-point seatbelt has been added for the rear center passenger.

Mileage Category: G

Body Styles	TMV Pricing			Body Styles	TMV Pricing		
	Trade	Private	Dealer		Trade	Private	Dealer
4 Dr LX Sdn	11749	12816	14594	4 Dr STD Sdn	10471	11422	13007

Options	Price	Options	Price
17 Inch Wheels [Opt on LX]	+274	Digital Instrument Panel [Opt on LX]	+152
4.6L V8 CNG SOHC 16V FI Engine [Opt on STD]	+4486	Front Side Airbag Restraints [Opt on LX]	+164
AM/FM/Cassette/CD Audio System [Opt on STD]	+119	Keyless Entry System [Opt on STD]	+155
Automatic Load Leveling [Opt on LX]	+161	Leather Seats [Opt on LX]	+319
Bucket Seats [Opt on LX]	+171	Sport Suspension [Opt on LX]	+129

2002

A new Crown Vic LX Sport model with 235 horsepower, boosted torque, a performance-oriented axle ratio and five-spoke 17-inch wheels debuts. The Sport also comes with leather front bucket seats and a nifty center console. Standard Crown Vics get new included equipment like an auto-dimming rearview mirror, front seat back pockets and wheel covers. Newly optional on Standard models is luxury cloth seating and power-adjustable pedals. Those pedals, floor mats, heated side mirrors, antilock brakes, 12-spoke alloy wheels and steering wheel controls for the stereo and climate controls are now standard on LX models. Electronic gauges have been thoughtfully moved to the LX options list. LX and LX Sport get an optional trunk storage system. All Vics benefit from upgraded cupholders.

Mileage Category: G

Body Styles	TMV Pricing			Body Styles	TMV Pricing		
	Trade	Private	Dealer		Trade	Private	Dealer
4 Dr LX Sdn	9208	10266	12028	4 Dr STD Sdn	8198	9140	10709

Options	Price	Options	Price
16 Inch Wheels [Opt on LX]	+206	Digital Instrument Panel [Opt on LX]	+138
4.6L V8 CNG SOHC 16V FI Engine [Opt on STD]	+3971	Keyless Entry System [Opt on STD]	+141
Antilock Brakes [Opt on STD]	+400	Leather Seats [Opt on LX]	+291
Automatic Load Leveling [Opt on LX]	+147	Sport Suspension [Opt on LX]	+118
Compact Disc Changer [Opt on LX]	+206		

2001

Power from the V8 engine is increased. The interior gets minor improvements and an optional adjustable pedal assembly. Safety has been improved via a crash severity sensor, safety belt pre-tensioners, dual-stage airbags and seat-position sensors.

Mileage Category: G

Body Styles	TMV Pricing			Body Styles	TMV Pricing		
	Trade	Private	Dealer		Trade	Private	Dealer
4 Dr LX Sdn	6983	8282	9480	4 Dr STD Sdn	6563	7784	8911

Options	Price	Options	Price
4.6L V8 CNG SOHC 16V FI Engine	+3248	Keyless Entry System [Opt on STD]	+126
Aluminum/Alloy Wheels	+224	Leather Seats	+387
Antilock Brakes	+358	Power Driver Seat	+190
Automatic Load Leveling	+142	Power Passenger Seat	+184
Compact Disc Changer	+184	Traction Control System	+132

2000

New safety items have been added, including an emergency trunk release, child seat-anchor brackets and the Belt Minder system. The rear-axle ratio for Crown Victorias with the handling package changes from 3.27 to 3.55, for quicker acceleration. Two new shades of green are offered -- Tropical Green and Dark Green Satin.

Mileage Category: G

Body Styles	TMV Pricing		
	Trade	Private	Dealer
4 Dr LX Sdn	5742	7050	8331

Options	Price
Aluminum/Alloy Wheels	+200
Automatic Load Leveling	+127
Compact Disc Changer	+165

Body Styles	TMV Pricing		
	Trade	Private	Dealer
4 Dr STD Sdn	5442	6609	7753

Options	Price
Leather Seats	+346
Power Driver Seat [Opt on STD]	+170
Power Passenger Seat [Opt on LX]	+170

1999

Antilock brakes are now standard on Base and LX models. A stereo with cassette player is also newly standard on the Base model. Deep Wedgewood Blue, Light Blue and Harvest Gold are new exterior colors. Medium Wedgewood Blue, Light Denim Blue and Light Prairie Tan are no longer available.

Mileage Category: G

Body Styles	TMV Pricing		
	Trade	Private	Dealer
4 Dr LX Sdn	4691	5945	7250

Options	Price
Aluminum/Alloy Wheels	+165
Automatic Load Leveling	+117
Compact Disc Changer	+136

Body Styles	TMV Pricing		
	Trade	Private	Dealer
4 Dr STD Sdn	4456	5579	6747

Options	Price
Leather Seats	+286
Power Driver Seat [Opt on STD]	+140
Power Passenger Seat [Opt on LX]	+155

1998

A formal roofline graces this favorite of police officers and taxi drivers. To further add to the Crown Victoria's driving excitement, the power steering and suspension have been improved.

Mileage Category: G

Body Styles	TMV Pricing		
	Trade	Private	Dealer
4 Dr LX Sdn	3504	4617	5873

Options	Price
Aluminum/Alloy Wheels	+135
Antilock Brakes	+240

Body Styles	TMV Pricing		
	Trade	Private	Dealer
4 Dr STD Sdn	3251	4219	5311

Options	Price
Leather Seats	+233
Power Passenger Seat [Opt on LX]	+127

1997

Mileage Category: G

Body Styles	TMV Pricing		
	Trade	Private	Dealer
4 Dr LX Sdn	2723	3620	4716

Options	Price
Aluminum/Alloy Wheels	+124
Antilock Brakes	+222

Body Styles	TMV Pricing		
	Trade	Private	Dealer
4 Dr STD Sdn	2547	3503	4671

Options	Price
Leather Seats	+216
Power Passenger Seat [Opt on LX]	+117

After a mild facelift last year, the Crown Vic soldiers on with a few color changes, improved power steering and the addition of rear air suspension to the handling package.

1996

A new steering wheel and gas cap are standard, and some equipment has been dropped from the roster, including the JBL sound system and trailer towing package.

Mileage Category: G

Body Styles	TMV Pricing		
	Trade	Private	Dealer
4 Dr LX Sdn	1982	2918	4211

Options	Price
Antilock Brakes	+197
Leather Seats	+168

Body Styles	TMV Pricing		
	Trade	Private	Dealer
4 Dr STD Sdn	1935	2686	3723

Options	Price
Performance/Handling Package	+177

1995

New grille, trunk lid, wheels and bumpers freshen the Crown Victoria's styling. Rear window defroster and heated outside mirrors move from the options list to the standard equipment roster. A new interior includes a revised stereo, backlit door switches, restyled instrument panel and a fresh climate control system.

Mileage Category: G

Body Styles	TMV Pricing		
	Trade	Private	Dealer
4 Dr LX Sdn	1381	1994	3016

Options	Price
Aluminum/Alloy Wheels	+96
Antilock Brakes	+170
JBL Audio System	+124
Leather Seats	+146

Body Styles	TMV Pricing		
	Trade	Private	Dealer
4 Dr STD Sdn	1257	1817	2749

Options	Price
Performance/Handling Package	+153
Power Driver Seat [Opt on STD]	+81
Power Passenger Seat [Opt on LX]	+90

Ford
Escape

Escape

2004

The Escape remains largely unchanged for 2004 although the price has been lowered on the plush Limited model and certain appearance packages are now available on lower trim levels which, in effect, reduce the final price. Also, Chrome Yellow is no longer a color choice. To eliminate confusion, trim levels and option packages have been consolidated.

Mileage Category: L

Body Styles	TMV Pricing		
	Trade	Private	Dealer
4 Dr Limited 4WD SUV	16078	17255	19216
4 Dr Limited SUV	14921	16112	18098
4 Dr XLS 4WD SUV	13562	14740	16702

Options	Price
Alarm System [Opt on XLS]	+150
Aluminum/Alloy Wheels [Opt on XLT, XLS]	+375
Antilock Brakes [Opt on XLS]	+575
Camper/Towing Package	+350
Cruise Control [Opt on XLS]	+175
Front Side Airbag Restraints [Opt on XLT, XLS]	+345

Body Styles	TMV Pricing		
	Trade	Private	Dealer
4 Dr XLS SUV	11228	12373	14281
4 Dr XLT 4WD SUV	14915	16092	18054
4 Dr XLT SUV	13733	14894	16829

Options	Price
Heated Front Seats [Opt on Limited]	+200
Leather Seats [Opt on XLT]	+500
Park Distance Control (Rear) [Opt on Limited]	+200
Power Moonroof [Opt on XLT, Limited]	+585
Side Steps [Opt on XLT, XLS]	+400

2003

Need more luxury when you Escape? For 2003, Ford will offer a new Limited edition that includes body-color trim, polished aluminum wheels, a reverse sensing system, a Mach audio system with six-disc CD changer, heated front seats and sideview mirrors, premium leather seats, front side airbags and an autodimming rearview mirror. The XLT can also be upgraded this year with an appearance package that includes special wheels, side step bars and body-color exterior trim. For all Escapes, there are upgraded interior materials and fabrics, an available two-tone cabin color scheme, illuminated power window and lock switches and three new colors. Finally, the XLS 4WD with a four-cylinder engine and a manual transmission is dropped for 2003.

Mileage Category: L

Body Styles	TMV Pricing		
	Trade	Private	Dealer
4 Dr Limited 4WD SUV	15000	16193	18182
4 Dr Limited SUV	14166	15293	17170
4 Dr XLS 4WD SUV	12511	13506	15165

Options	Price
3.0L V6 DOHC 24V FI Engine [Opt on XLS 2WD]	+451
AM/FM/CD/MP3 Audio System [Opt on XLS]	+145
Aluminum/Alloy Wheels [Opt on XLS]	+242
Antilock Brakes [Opt on XLS]	+439
Automatic 4-Speed Transmission [Opt on XLS 2WD]	+451
Camper/Towing Package	+226
Cruise Control [Opt on XLS]	+116

Body Styles	TMV Pricing		
	Trade	Private	Dealer
4 Dr XLS SUV	9892	10679	11990
4 Dr XLT 4WD SUV	13695	14784	16600
4 Dr XLT SUV	12661	13668	15346

Options	Price
Front Side Airbag Restraints [Opt on XLS,XLT]	+223
Leather Seats [Opt on XLT]	+319
MACH Audio System [Opt on XLT]	+326
Power Moonroof [Opt on Limited,XLT]	+377
Privacy Glass [Opt on XLS]	+177
Running Boards [Opt on XLS,XLT]	+177

2002

Additional standard equipment makes Escape an even better value for 2002. XLS models get a dual-media cassette/CD stereo, while XLT adds a V6 engine, privacy glass, power driver seat and an in-dash six-CD changer. New Sport packages also debut. The XLS Sport includes 15-inch alloy wheels with larger tires, side-step bars, Sport-embroidered floor mats and dark tinted privacy glass. The XLT Sport, new for 2002, provides, in addition to XLS Sport equipment, a special No Boundaries roof rack system and unique 16-inch alloy wheels with meatier rubber. Four new colors are also available.

Mileage Category: L

Body Styles	TMV Pricing		
	Trade	Private	Dealer
4 Dr XLS 4WD SUV	10229	11209	12842
4 Dr XLS SUV	8972	9831	11263

Options	Price
3.0L V6 DOHC 24V FI Engine [Opt on XLS]	+412
AM/FM/CD/MP3 Audio System [Opt on XLT]	+174
AM/FM/Cassette/CD/MP3 Audio System [Opt on XLS]	+174
Aluminum/Alloy Wheels [Opt on XLS]	+147
Antilock Brakes [Opt on XLS]	+400
Automatic 4-Speed Transmission [Opt on XLS]	+506

Body Styles	TMV Pricing		
	Trade	Private	Dealer
4 Dr XLT 4WD SUV	11489	12590	14424
4 Dr XLT SUV	10733	11761	13475

Options	Price
Compact Disc Changer [Opt on XLT]	+206
Front Side Airbag Restraints	+147
Leather Seats [Opt on XLT]	+291
Locking Differential [Opt on XLT 4WD]	+118
MACH Audio System [Opt on XLT]	+132
Power Moonroof [Opt on XLT]	+344

2001

The Escape is Ford's new SUV. Smaller in size than the Explorer (and dwarfed by an Excursion), the Escape competes in the same class as the Honda CR-V and Toyota RAV4. Its main calling cards are an optional V6 engine and a large interior.

Mileage Category: L

Body Styles	TMV Pricing		
	Trade	Private	Dealer
4 Dr XLS 4WD SUV	9195	10537	11775
4 Dr XLS SUV	7987	9152	10228

Options	Price
3.0L V6 DOHC 24V FI Engine	+369
Aluminum/Alloy Wheels [Std on XLT]	+198
Antilock Brakes [Std on XLT]	+358
Automatic 4-Speed Transmission	+369
Compact Disc Changer	+308

Body Styles	TMV Pricing		
	Trade	Private	Dealer
4 Dr XLT 4WD SUV	9868	11308	12637
4 Dr XLT SUV	8811	10096	11283

Options	Price
Cruise Control [Std on XLT]	+119
Front Side Airbag Restraints	+182
Leather Seats	+342
Power Driver Seat	+126
Power Moonroof	+308

For the latest vehicle information, visit www.edmunds.com

Options	Price	Options	Price
Privacy Glass	+145	Trailer Hitch	+184
Running Boards	+145		

Escort

2003

Mileage Category: B

Body Styles	TMV Pricing		
	Trade	Private	Dealer
2 Dr ZX2 Cpe	6351	7224	8678

Options	Price	Options	Price
Air Conditioning	+448	Keyless Entry System	+116
Antilock Brakes	+439	Power Door Locks	+132
Automatic 4-Speed Transmission	+526	Power Windows	+158
Cruise Control	+119		

The aged Escort receives a few changes this year. On the outside, there are stylistic changes to its front and rear fascias, including standard foglamps. Inside, new cloth spruces up the seats, and the standard model receives a cassette player. Fifteen-inch wheels are standard on all models, and two new colors make their debut. For 2003, Ford has renamed the options packages "deluxe" and "premium." The deluxe package gets you a CD player, a leather-wrapped steering wheel that tilts, cruise control and map lights as standard equipment. Premium models also get power windows, locks and remote keyless entry. Finally, the in-dash six-disc CD changer is no longer available.

2002

Mileage Category: B

Body Styles	TMV Pricing		
	Trade	Private	Dealer
2 Dr ZX2 Cpe	5161	5938	7232

Options	Price	Options	Price
Air Conditioning	+353	Automatic 4-Speed Transmission	+480
Antilock Brakes	+400		

Other than a couple of new exterior colors, the Escort ZX2 is unchanged for 2002. The Comfort and Power Groups have been replaced by the Deluxe and Premium Groups, which include new items of standard equipment.

2001

Mileage Category: B

Body Styles	TMV Pricing		
	Trade	Private	Dealer
2 Dr ZX2 Cpe	4196	5221	6167

Options	Price	Options	Price
AM/FM/Cassette/CD Changer Audio System	+155	Chrome Wheels	+313
Air Conditioning	+419	Leather Seats	+261
Antilock Brakes	+358	Power Moonroof	+313
Automatic 4-Speed Transmission	+429	Power Windows	+121

Other than a couple of new exterior colors, the Escort ZX2 is unchanged for 2001. The high-performance S/R Package is no longer available.

2000

Body Styles	TMV Pricing			Body Styles	TMV Pricing		
	Trade	Private	Dealer		Trade	Private	Dealer
2 Dr ZX2 Cpe	2981	3990	4980	4 Dr STD Sdn	2985	3996	4987

Options	Price	Options	Price
AM/FM/Cassette/CD Audio System	+139	Chrome Wheels	+280
Air Conditioning	+375	Compact Disc Changer	+139
Aluminum/Alloy Wheels [Std on ZX2]	+125	Leather Seats	+233
Antilock Brakes	+320	Power Moonroof	+280
Automatic 4-Speed Transmission	+384		

The 2000 Escort line has been simplified. The station wagon is discontinued, and there is now only one trim level for the sedan and coupe models.

1999

Mileage Category: B

Body Styles	TMV Pricing			Body Styles	TMV Pricing		
	Trade	Private	Dealer		Trade	Private	Dealer
2 Dr ZX2 Cool Cpe	2113	3061	4048	4 Dr SE Sdn	2361	3421	4525
2 Dr ZX2 Hot Cpe	2420	3506	4637	4 Dr SE Wgn	2523	3655	4834
4 Dr LX Sdn	2095	3035	4014				

Options	Price	Options	Price
Air Conditioning [Std on SE, ZX2 Hot]	+309	Antilock Brakes	+293

Ford's entry-level car gets new colors, new interior fabrics and revised options. An AM/FM stereo with cassette is now standard on the Escort SE. An interior trunk release is now standard on all models. The sedans and wagon get all-door remote keyless entry added to their standard equipment lists. An integrated child seat is no longer available.

1999 (cont'd)

Options	Price
Automatic 4-Speed Transmission	+317
Compact Disc Changer	+115

Options	Price
Power Moonroof	+231

1998

Packages are reshuffled on Ford's entry-level cars. Available this year as sedans, wagons or stylish coupes, the Ford Escort now qualifies as a low emissions vehicle, thanks to the car's split-port induction 2.0-liter four-cylinder engine.

Mileage Category: B

Body Styles	TMV Pricing		
	Trade	Private	Dealer
2 Dr ZX2 Cool Cpe	1517	2351	3291
2 Dr ZX2 Hot Cpe	1675	2596	3635
4 Dr LX Sdn	1441	2234	3129

Body Styles	TMV Pricing		
	Trade	Private	Dealer
4 Dr SE Sdn	1605	2488	3483
4 Dr SE Wgn	1767	2739	3836

Options	Price
AM/FM/CD Audio System [Opt on SE Sdn]	+163
AM/FM/Cassette/CD Audio System [Opt on ZX2]	+163
Air Conditioning	+252

Options	Price
Antilock Brakes	+240
Automatic 4-Speed Transmission	+259
Power Moonroof	+188

1997

The Ford Escort is totally redesigned this year with improvements across the board. The most noticeable improvements are in the powertrain and ride quality. New sheet metal gives the Escort a rounder, more aerodynamic appearance as well. The GT hatchback version is dropped.

Mileage Category: B

Body Styles	TMV Pricing		
	Trade	Private	Dealer
4 Dr LX Sdn	1104	1860	2783
4 Dr LX Wgn	1165	1964	2940

Body Styles	TMV Pricing		
	Trade	Private	Dealer
4 Dr STD Sdn	1055	1778	2661

Options	Price
Air Conditioning	+233
Antilock Brakes	+222

Options	Price
Automatic 4-Speed Transmission	+239

1996

Mileage Category: B

Body Styles	TMV Pricing		
	Trade	Private	Dealer
2 Dr GT Hbk	902	1612	2593
2 Dr LX Hbk	777	1389	2235
2 Dr STD Hbk	727	1299	2089

Body Styles	TMV Pricing		
	Trade	Private	Dealer
4 Dr LX Hbk	791	1414	2275
4 Dr LX Sdn	813	1454	2338
4 Dr LX Wgn	859	1536	2470

Options	Price
AM/FM/Cassette Audio System [Std on LX]	+121
Air Conditioning	+205

Options	Price
Antilock Brakes	+197
Automatic 4-Speed Transmission	+213

Last year for the second-generation Escort. The 1.9-liter engine gets 100,000-mile tune-up interval. Automatic transmissions have lower final drive ratio when coupled with 1.9-liter engine to improve acceleration. Sport/Appearance Group available on four-door models. Ultra Violet decor no longer offered on GT. Integrated child safety seat, added during 1995 model year, continues for 1996 on sedan and wagon.

1995

A passenger airbag is now available. A more powerful, optional air conditioner appears in the revised instrument panel. An integrated child seat is available on sedans and wagons.

Mileage Category: B

Body Styles	TMV Pricing		
	Trade	Private	Dealer
2 Dr GT Hbk	638	1187	2102
2 Dr LX Hbk	547	1019	1805
2 Dr STD Hbk	503	937	1660

Body Styles	TMV Pricing		
	Trade	Private	Dealer
4 Dr LX Hbk	558	1040	1842
4 Dr LX Sdn	579	1077	1908
4 Dr LX Wgn	603	1123	1990

Options	Price
Air Conditioning	+177
Antilock Brakes	+170

Options	Price
Automatic 4-Speed Transmission	+184
Power Moonroof	+96

Excursion

Ford's excellent new 6.0-liter turbodiesel V8 replaces last year's 7.3-liter diesel. Besides offering considerably more horsepower and torque, the new engine has cleaner emissions and gets better gas mileage. Several new options are available; these include wireless headphones for the rear-seat entertainment package and an auto-dimming rearview mirror. Body-side cladding and illuminated running boards are no longer available on XLT models. Also note that the trim level structure has been revised slightly, as base XLS and midlevel XLT trim replace XLT Value and XLT Premium.

Body Styles	TMV Pricing		
	Trade	Private	Dealer
4 Dr Eddie Bauer 4WD SUV	27281	29027	31936
4 Dr Eddie Bauer SUV	25402	27148	30059
4 Dr Limited 4WD SUV	28091	29837	32746
4 Dr Limited SUV	25712	27425	30281

Body Styles	TMV Pricing		
	Trade	Private	Dealer
4 Dr XLS 4WD SUV	24887	26633	29542
4 Dr XLS SUV	22416	24125	26973
4 Dr XLT 4WD SUV	25491	27237	30146
4 Dr XLT SUV	23021	24731	27580

Options	Price
6.0L V8 Turbodiesel OHV 32V Engine	+4755
AM/FM/CD Changer Audio System [Opt on non-Limited]	+300
Captain Chairs (4) [Opt on Eddie Bauer, Limited]	+795
DVD Entertainment System [Opt on XLT, Eddie Bauer, Limited]	+1500
Garage Door Opener [Opt on Eddie Bauer]	+175
Heated Front Seats [Opt on Eddie Bauer]	+200

Options	Price
Leather Seats [Opt on XLT]	+1360
Limited Slip Differential (Rear)	+250
Park Distance Control (Rear) [Opt on XLT]	+245
Power Adjustable Foot Pedals [Opt on XLS, XLT]	+120
Trip Computer [Opt on XLT]	+200

A new Eddie Bauer trim level debuts. It's equipped similarly to last year's Limited trim and also includes Arizona Beige exterior trim, two-tone leather seating and available second-row captain's chairs. Limited models get as standard equipment a six-disc in-dash CD changer, new aluminum wheels, cherrywood interior trim and a reversible cargo mat. In terms of mechanical changes, the new 6.0-liter turbodiesel engine arrives mid-year with more power and efficiency, connected to an all new five-speed TorqShift automatic transmission. Why anyone would use this mammoth rig to go trail busting we have no idea, but Ford will be offering an off-road package shortly after the first of the year. Finally, all Excursions get revised front suspensions for improved ride and handling.

Body Styles	TMV Pricing		
	Trade	Private	Dealer
4 Dr Eddie Bauer 4WD SUV	20317	21846	24393
4 Dr Eddie Bauer SUV	19281	20731	23148
4 Dr Limited 4WD SUV	20548	22094	24671

Body Styles	TMV Pricing		
	Trade	Private	Dealer
4 Dr Limited SUV	19523	20992	23439
4 Dr XLT 4WD SUV	19137	20576	22975
4 Dr XLT SUV	16929	18203	20325

Options	Price
6.0L V8 Turbodiesel OHV 32V Engine	+871
7.3L V8 Turbodiesel OHV 16V Engine	+2667
AM/FM/CD Changer Audio System [Opt on Eddie Bauer, XLT]	+164
Captain Chairs (2) [Opt on XLT]	+164
Captain Chairs (4) [Opt on Eddie Bauer, Limited]	+513
Compact Disc Changer	+164

Options	Price
DVD Entertainment System	+835
Limited Slip Differential [Opt on Eddie Bauer, Limited]	+161
Park Distance Control (Rear) [Opt on XLT]	+158
Power Driver Seat [Opt on XLT]	+155
Power Passenger Seat [Opt on XLT]	+155
Trip Computer [Opt on XLT]	+126

Excursions get crystalline headlamp lenses for 2002, as well as "smart" intermittent front and rear wipers. XLTs gain a new auto-lock feature as well as standard third-row child seat tethers with a BeltMinder system. Excursion Limited receives a chrome side strip, automatic climate control and power-adjustable pedals. New options on XLT include power-adjustable pedals and a power front passenger seat. Limited models can be equipped with memory seats and pedals, second-row captain's chairs and redundant controls for climate and audio on the steering wheel. Both XLT and Limited will get a DVD-based entertainment system for rear-seat passengers later this year. Skid plates are no longer optional.

Body Styles	TMV Pricing		
	Trade	Private	Dealer
4 Dr Limited 4WD SUV	17071	18596	21137
4 Dr Limited SUV	16408	17874	20316

Body Styles	TMV Pricing		
	Trade	Private	Dealer
4 Dr XLT 4WD SUV	15926	17348	19719
4 Dr XLT SUV	13932	15176	17250

Options	Price
7.3L V8 Turbodiesel OHV 16V Engine	+2155
Captain Chairs (2) [Opt on XLT]	+235
Captain Chairs (4) [Opt on Limited]	+468
Compact Disc Changer	+150
Heated Front and Rear Seats [Opt on Limited]	+171

Options	Price
Limited Slip Differential	+147
Park Distance Control (Rear) [Opt on XLT]	+144
Power Driver Seat [Opt on XLT]	+153
Power Passenger Seat [Opt on XLT]	+153
Trip Computer [Opt on XLT]	+121

Performance is beefed up to 250 horsepower on the 7.3-liter Power Stroke turbodiesel V8 and all engines are now LEV compliant. An in-dash six-disc CD player is made available. The Excursion XLT gets platinum cladding and standard chrome steel wheels, and the Limited offers standard power signal aero mirrors, foglamps and an optional rear-seat entertainment system.

Body Styles	TMV Pricing		
	Trade	Private	Dealer
4 Dr Limited 4WD SUV	14353	16373	18237
4 Dr Limited SUV	13299	15170	16898

Body Styles	TMV Pricing		
	Trade	Private	Dealer
4 Dr XLT 4WD SUV	12198	13915	15499
4 Dr XLT SUV	11930	13610	15160

Options	Price
6.8L V10 SOHC 20V FI Engine [Std on 4WD]	+313
7.3L V8 Turbodiesel OHV 16V Engine	+2142
Aluminum/Alloy Wheels [Opt on XLT]	+163
Compact Disc Changer	+134

Options	Price
Heated Front Seats [Opt on Limited]	+153
Leather Seats [Opt on XLT]	+558
Limited Slip Differential	+132
Park Distance Control (Rear) [Opt on XLT]	+129

2001 (cont'd)

Options	Price
Power Driver Seat [Opt on XLT]	+126

Options	Price
VCR Entertainment System [Opt on Limited]	+803

2000

The Excursion is an entirely new SUV based on Ford's F-250 Super Duty truck platform. It is the largest vehicle of its type, outgunning even the Chevy Suburban in terms of overall size and interior space.

Mileage Category: N

Body Styles	TMV Pricing		
	Trade	Private	Dealer
4 Dr Limited 4WD SUV	11983	13985	15948
4 Dr Limited SUV	11097	12951	14769

Body Styles	TMV Pricing		
	Trade	Private	Dealer
4 Dr XLT 4WD SUV	10395	12133	13836
4 Dr XLT SUV	9752	11382	12980

Options	Price
6.8L V10 SOHC 20V FI Engine [Std on 4WD]	+280
7.3L V8 Turbodiesel OHV 16V Engine	+2060
Chrome Wheels	+147
Compact Disc Changer	+233

Options	Price
Heated Front Seats	+137
Leather Seats [Opt on XLT]	+518
Limited Slip Differential	+118
Park Distance Control (Rear) [Opt on XLT]	+115

Expedition

2004

Redesigned last year, the Expedition offers few changes for 2004. Option packages and trim levels have been slightly revised, and in some cases, renamed. The XLS replaces last year's XLT Value trim level, while a new NBX trim level replaces the FX4 off-road package. And there is now an XLT Sport trim level. A tire-pressure monitoring system is now standard on XLT, XLT Sport and Eddie Bauer, while the previously standard limited-slip rear axle is now an option.

Mileage Category: N

Body Styles	TMV Pricing		
	Trade	Private	Dealer
4 Dr Eddie Bauer 4WD SUV	23744	25502	28432
4 Dr Eddie Bauer SUV	21369	23095	25971
4 Dr XLS 4WD SUV	19952	21716	24657
4 Dr XLS SUV	18111	19837	22713

Body Styles	TMV Pricing		
	Trade	Private	Dealer
4 Dr XLT 4WD SUV	21053	22816	25753
4 Dr XLT NBX 4WD SUV	21953	23714	26649
4 Dr XLT SUV	19110	20836	23712

Options	Price
5.4L V8 SOHC 16V FI Engine [Opt on XLT, Eddie Bauer 2WD]	+395
AM/FM/CD Changer Audio System [Opt on Eddie Bauer, XLT]	+255
Automatic Load Leveling	+815
Captain Chairs (2) [Opt on XLT]	+385
Captain Chairs (4) [Opt on Eddie Bauer]	+530
DVD Entertainment System	+1500
Leather Seats [Opt on XLT]	+1200

Options	Price
Navigation System [Opt on Eddie Bauer]	+1995
Park Distance Control (Rear) [Opt on XLT]	+255
Power Driver Seat [Opt on XLT]	+240
Power Moonroof [Opt on Eddie Bauer]	+860
Power Third Seat [Opt on Eddie Bauer]	+495
Ventilated Seats (Front) [Opt on Eddie Bauer]	+750

2003

Ford's full-size SUV sports changes inside and out. Outside, the Expedition looks bigger and bolder. Some of its new styling cues, such as the egg-crate grille and raised hood, are from its little brother, the Explorer. Inside you'll find fold-flat second- and third-row seats, with a power-folding option for the third row. The second row is split-40/20/40 enabling the middle section to slide forward. The Eddie Bauer package has an in-dash six-disc changer (optional on the XLT) and steering wheel-mounted stereo and climate controls, as well as an optional DVD player, navigation system and heated-cooled seats. But the big changes are the ones you can't readily see. Underneath the skin a double-wishbone independent rear suspension system and a rack and pinion steering configuration improve road handling. AdvanceTrac stability control, along with ControlTrac four-wheel-drive system and an increased width of 1.7 inches should help keep the rubber down and the shiny side up.

Mileage Category: N

Body Styles	TMV Pricing		
	Trade	Private	Dealer
4 Dr Eddie Bauer 4WD SUV	22080	23741	26509
4 Dr Eddie Bauer SUV	19053	20486	22875

Body Styles	TMV Pricing		
	Trade	Private	Dealer
4 Dr XLT 4WD SUV	17376	18683	20862
4 Dr XLT SUV	15785	16972	18951

Options	Price
5.4L V8 SOHC 16V FI Engine [Opt on XLT, Eddie Bauer 2WD]	+332
AM/FM/CD Changer Audio System [Opt on Eddie Bauer, XLT]	+164
Air Conditioning - Front and Rear [Opt on XLT]	+387
Aluminum/Alloy Wheels [Opt on XLT]	+161
Automatic Load Leveling	+316
Automatic Stability Control [Opt on Eddie Bauer]	+319
Captain Chairs (2) [Opt on XLT]	+248
Captain Chairs (4) [Opt on Eddie Bauer]	+513
DVD Entertainment System	+967
FX4 Off-Road Suspension Package [Opt on XLT 4WD]	+2432
Front and Rear Head Airbag Restraints	+419

Options	Price
Leather Seats [Opt on XLT]	+580
Limited Slip Differential [Opt on XLT]	+164
Navigation System [Opt on Eddie Bauer]	+1287
Park Distance Control (Rear) [Opt on XLT]	+164
Power Driver Seat [Opt on XLT]	+155
Power Moonroof [Opt on Eddie Bauer]	+555
Power Third Seat [Opt on Eddie Bauer]	+319
Running Boards [Opt on XLT]	+210
Traction Control System [Opt on Eddie Bauer]	+193
Ventilated Seats (Front) [Opt on Eddie Bauer]	+484

2002

Body Styles	TMV Pricing		
	Trade	Private	Dealer
4 Dr Eddie Bauer 4WD SUV	17394	18948	21537
4 Dr Eddie Bauer SUV	15771	17179	19526

Options	Price
17 Inch Wheels	+235
5.4L V8 SOHC 16V FI Engine [Opt on 2WD,XLT 4WD]	+409
Air Conditioning - Front and Rear [Std on Eddie Bauer]	+353
Automatic Load Leveling	+288
Camper/Towing Package	+230
Captain Chairs (2) [Opt on XLT]	+227
Captain Chairs (4) [Opt on Eddie Bauer]	+265
Compact Disc Changer [Opt on XLT]	+291
DVD Entertainment System	+792

Body Styles	TMV Pricing		
	Trade	Private	Dealer
4 Dr XLT 4WD SUV	14384	15669	17810
4 Dr XLT SUV	12992	14153	16087

Options	Price
Front Side Airbag Restraints	+233
Heated Front Seats [Opt on Eddie Bauer]	+174
Leather Seats [Opt on XLT]	+530
Limited Slip Differential	+150
Park Distance Control (Rear)	+118
Power Driver Seat [Opt on XLT]	+141
Power Moonroof	+471
Running Boards [Opt on XLT]	+191

For 2002, the Expedition gets Ford's BeltMinder audible warning system to remind buyers to buckle up. The XLT can be equipped with a rear video entertainment system for the first time. Eddie Bauer models can be done up in Premier Group packaging, which includes monochromatic exterior paint, second-row captain's chairs, moonroof, 17-inch alloy wheels, foglights and illuminated running boards.

2001

Body Styles	TMV Pricing		
	Trade	Private	Dealer
4 Dr Eddie Bauer 4WD SUV	14590	16643	18539
4 Dr Eddie Bauer SUV	13404	15291	17032

Options	Price
5.4L V8 SOHC 16V FI Engine [Opt on XLT,2WD]	+366
Air Conditioning - Front and Rear [Opt on XLT]	+398
Automatic Load Leveling	+258
Camper/Towing Package	+205
Front Side Airbag Restraints	+208
Heated Front Seats	+155
Leather Seats [Opt on XLT]	+558

Body Styles	TMV Pricing		
	Trade	Private	Dealer
4 Dr XLT 4WD SUV	12180	13894	15477
4 Dr XLT SUV	10967	12511	13936

Options	Price
Limited Slip Differential	+134
Power Driver Seat [Opt on XLT]	+126
Power Moonroof	+421
Premium Audio System [Opt on XLT]	+261
Running Boards [Opt on XLT]	+229
VCR Entertainment System [Opt on Eddie Bauer]	+709

Ford's second-largest SUV changes little for 2001. XLT models get privacy glass as standard equipment, while the upscale Eddie Bauer trim level now comes with HomeLink and a class IV trailer towing package (4x4 models only). Eddie Bauers also get second-row leather captain's chairs and a rear-seat entertainment system as optional equipment. A new "No Boundaries" option package includes a monochromatic black exterior, side body cladding, 17-inch wheels, illuminated running boards and special front seats.

2000

The Expedition receives power-adjustable foot pedals, a rear sonar system for when the vehicle is backing up, optional side airbags, a revised center console and restyled wheels.

Body Styles	TMV Pricing		
	Trade	Private	Dealer
4 Dr Eddie Bauer 4WD SUV	11172	13039	14870
4 Dr Eddie Bauer SUV	10512	12269	13991

Options	Price
5.4L V8 SOHC 16V FI Engine [Opt on XLT,2WD]	+328
AM/FM/Cassette/CD Audio System	+167
Air Conditioning - Front and Rear [Opt on XLT]	+332
Aluminum/Alloy Wheels	+147
Automatic Load Leveling	+231
Camper/Towing Package	+414
Captain Chairs (2) [Opt on XLT]	+132
Captain Chairs (4)	+375

Body Styles	TMV Pricing		
	Trade	Private	Dealer
4 Dr XLT 4WD SUV	9616	11223	12798
4 Dr XLT SUV	8531	9958	11356

Options	Price
Compact Disc Changer [Opt on XLT]	+224
Front Side Airbag Restraints	+186
Heated Front Seats	+137
Leather Seats [Opt on XLT]	+471
Limited Slip Differential	+120
Park Distance Control (Rear)	+115
Power Moonroof	+377
Running Boards [Opt on XLT]	+205

1999

Power output is improved for both Triton V8 engines on Ford's full-size sport-ute. Package content is added for both XLT and Eddie Bauer trim levels. Power-adjustable accelerator and brake pedals have been added. An updated Command Trac four-wheel-drive system allows automatic four-wheel-drive operation when required. Spruce Green, Harvest Gold, Tropic Green and Deep Wedgewood Blue replace Light Prairie Tan, Vermont Green, Light Denim Blue and Pacific Green on the color chart.

Body Styles	TMV Pricing		
	Trade	Private	Dealer
4 Dr Eddie Bauer 4WD SUV	9273	11165	13134
4 Dr Eddie Bauer SUV	8212	9889	11634

Options	Price
5.4L V8 SOHC 16V FI Engine [Opt on XLT,2WD]	+258
AM/FM/Cassette/CD Audio System	+138
Air Conditioning - Front and Rear [Opt on XLT]	+274
Automatic Load Leveling	+352
Camper/Towing Package	+151

Body Styles	TMV Pricing		
	Trade	Private	Dealer
4 Dr XLT 4WD SUV	7862	9466	11136
4 Dr XLT SUV	6565	7905	9299

Options	Price
Compact Disc Changer	+185
Leather Seats [Opt on XLT]	+388
Power Moonroof	+311
Running Boards [Opt on XLT]	+169
Third Seat [Opt on XLT]	+249

Ford
Expedition/Explorer

1998
No changes.

Mileage Category: N

Body Styles	TMV Pricing		
	Trade	Private	Dealer
4 Dr Eddie Bauer 4WD SUV	6916	8515	10319
4 Dr Eddie Bauer SUV	6370	7843	9504

Options	Price
5.4L V8 SOHC 16V FI Engine	+211
Air Conditioning - Front and Rear	+224
Automatic Load Leveling	+173
Camper/Towing Package	+159
Compact Disc Changer	+151

Body Styles	TMV Pricing		
	Trade	Private	Dealer
4 Dr XLT 4WD SUV	6323	7786	9435
4 Dr XLT SUV	5809	7153	8669

Options	Price
Leather Seats [Opt on XLT]	+317
Power Moonroof	+254
Running Boards	+138
Third Seat	+190

1997
Ford's replacement for the aging Bronco is the all-new Expedition. Based on the 1997 F-150 platform, this full-size sport-utility vehicle is poised to do battle with the Chevrolet Tahoe and GMC Yukon.

Mileage Category: N

Body Styles	TMV Pricing		
	Trade	Private	Dealer
4 Dr Eddie Bauer 4WD SUV	5796	7348	9245
4 Dr Eddie Bauer SUV	5538	7022	8836

Options	Price
5.4L V8 SOHC 16V FI Engine	+166
Air Conditioning - Front and Rear	+207
Automatic Load Leveling	+160
Camper/Towing Package	+161
Compact Disc Changer	+139

Body Styles	TMV Pricing		
	Trade	Private	Dealer
4 Dr XLT 4WD SUV	5430	6885	8663
4 Dr XLT SUV	4917	6234	7843

Options	Price
Leather Seats [Opt on XLT]	+293
Power Moonroof	+228
Running Boards	+128
Third Seat	+176

Explorer

2004

Ford's AdvanceTrac electronic stability control that was previously available on V8 models only is now available on all models, except the XLS and XLS Sport and all AWD models. The NBX version now comes standard with the off-road package and "NBX" tailgate badging, and can be ordered with a moonroof. Limited and Eddie Bauer models get a quad bucket seating option when equipped with the third-row bench, which adds second-row buckets and a floor console. Family buyers should note that the optional rear air conditioner no longer requires the purchase of the third-row seat. Finally, a tire-pressure monitoring system is now standard on XLS Sport and higher trim levels, and a rear cargo shade is optional on XLT, Eddie Bauer and Limited models.

Mileage Category: M

Body Styles	TMV Pricing		
	Trade	Private	Dealer
4 Dr Eddie Bauer 4WD SUV	19310	20699	23015
4 Dr Eddie Bauer AWD SUV	19310	20699	23015
4 Dr Eddie Bauer SUV	18127	19517	21832
4 Dr Limited 4WD SUV	19774	21163	23479
4 Dr Limited AWD SUV	19774	21163	23479
4 Dr Limited SUV	18591	19981	22296
4 Dr NBX 4WD SUV	17768	19158	21473

Options	Price
4.6L V8 SOHC 16V FI Engine [Opt on non-XLS, XLS Sport]	+800
AM/FM/CD Changer Audio System [Opt on XLT, XLT Sport, NBX]	+510
Air Conditioning - Front and Rear [Opt on non-XLS, XLS Sport]	+650
Automatic Stability Control [Opt on non-XLS, XLS Sport]	+795
DVD Entertainment System [Opt on non-XLS, XLS Sport, NBX]	+1295
Front and Rear Head Airbag Restraints	+560
Leather Seats [Opt on XLT, XLT Sport]	+695

Body Styles	TMV Pricing		
	Trade	Private	Dealer
4 Dr XLS 4WD SUV	15689	17078	19393
4 Dr XLS AWD SUV	15689	17078	19393
4 Dr XLS SUV	14378	15768	18083
4 Dr XLT 4WD SUV	17143	18533	20848
4 Dr XLT AWD SUV	17143	18533	20848
4 Dr XLT SUV	15962	17351	19666

Options	Price
Limited Slip Differential (Rear) [Opt on non-XLS, XLS Sport, XLT 2WD]	+290
Park Distance Control (Rear) [Opt on non-XLS, XLS Sport, NBX]	+255
Power Adjustable Foot Pedals [Opt on XLT, XLT Sport, NBX]	+120
Power Moonroof [Opt on non-XLS, XLS Sport]	+850
Running Boards [Opt on XLT, Limited]	+450
Third Seat [Opt on non-XLS, XLS Sport]	+745

2003

Mileage Category: M

Body Styles	TMV Pricing		
	Trade	Private	Dealer
4 Dr Eddie Bauer 4WD SUV	16357	17703	19948
4 Dr Eddie Bauer AWD SUV	15698	16991	19146
4 Dr Eddie Bauer SUV	15156	16404	18484
4 Dr Limited 4WD SUV	16520	17881	20148
4 Dr Limited AWD SUV	16082	17406	19613
4 Dr Limited SUV	15389	16657	18768
4 Dr NBX 4WD SUV	14436	15624	17605

Body Styles	TMV Pricing		
	Trade	Private	Dealer
4 Dr NBX SUV	13466	14574	16422
4 Dr XLS 4WD SUV	12388	13408	15109
4 Dr XLS AWD SUV	12726	13774	15520
4 Dr XLS SUV	10786	11675	13155
4 Dr XLT 4WD SUV	13643	14767	16639
4 Dr XLT AWD SUV	13920	15066	16977
4 Dr XLT SUV	13152	14235	16040

Options	Price
TJ	+319
4.6L V8 SOHC 16V FI Engine	+516
AM/FM/CD Changer Audio System [Opt on NBX,XLT]	+329
Air Conditioning - Front and Rear	+393
Aluminum/Alloy Wheels [Opt on XLS]	+290
Camper/Towing Package	+255
DVD Entertainment System	+835
Front and Rear Head Airbag Restraints	+361
Leather Seats [Opt on XLT]	+422

Options	Price
Limited Slip Differential [Opt on XLS]	+187
Park Distance Control (Rear) [Opt on Eddie Bauer,Limited,XLT]	+164
Power Moonroof [Opt on Eddie Bauer,Limited,XLT]	+516
Running Boards [Opt on XLT]	+255
Side Steps [Opt on XLS,XLT]	+177
Special Factory Paint [Opt on Limited]	+129
Special Leather Seat Trim [Opt on Limited]	+577
Third Seat	+432

Sport versions of the XLS and XLT debut, along with a new trim level called NBX (No Boundaries Experience). The NBX includes special exterior trim, unique 17-inch alloy wheels, all-terrain tires, a Yakima roof rack, rubber floormats and a cargo area liner. All-wheel drive is newly available on all but the NBX model. XLS models come standard with an automatic transmission and a CD player for 2003, while XLT models get a chrome grille and metallic interior accents. Eddie Bauer models get upgrades such as chromed exterior trim, chrome wheels, a leather-upholstered center console cover and new woodgrain interior trim. A tire-pressure monitoring system is available on Limited models. An Off-Road Package including underbody skid plates, suspension upgrades, front tow hooks and unique wheels debuts. Finally, a rear seat DVD-based entertainment system will be available later in the year.

2002

Mileage Category: M

Body Styles	TMV Pricing		
	Trade	Private	Dealer
4 Dr Eddie Bauer 4WD SUV	13620	14968	17216
4 Dr Eddie Bauer SUV	12577	13822	15897
4 Dr Limited 4WD SUV	13708	15065	17327
4 Dr Limited SUV	12736	13997	16099

Body Styles	TMV Pricing		
	Trade	Private	Dealer
4 Dr XLS 4WD SUV	10649	11704	13461
4 Dr XLS SUV	8655	9512	10940
4 Dr XLT 4WD SUV	11118	12219	14054
4 Dr XLT SUV	10871	11948	13742

Options	Price
17 Inch Wheels [Opt on XLT]	+294
4.6L V8 SOHC 16V FI Engine	+471
AM/FM/CD Changer Audio System [Opt on XLT]	+171
Air Conditioning - Front and Rear	+359
Aluminum/Alloy Wheels [Opt on XLS]	+162
Automatic 5-Speed Transmission [Opt on XLS]	+645
Camper/Towing Package	+233
Chrome Wheels	+144
Front and Rear Head Airbag Restraints	+147

Options	Price
Leather Seats [Opt on XLT]	+309
Park Distance Control (Rear)	+150
Pearlescent Metallic Paint [Opt on Limited]	+118
Power Moonroof	+471
Power Passenger Seat [Opt on XLT]	+191
Rollover Protection System	+147
Running Boards [Opt on XLT]	+233
Sport Seats [Opt on XLT]	+159
Third Seat	+394

Ford has overhauled its Explorer for model-year 2002 in an attempt to make it more carlike than ever before. Among the improvements are a 2.5-inch-wider stance and 2-inch-longer wheelbase for improved handling and roominess, a new independent rear suspension that improves ride and handling, while at the same time accommodating an optional third row of seats, larger door openings with a lower step-in height, an optional side curtain airbag system and an optional Reverse Sensing System.

2001

Mileage Category: M

Body Styles	TMV Pricing		
	Trade	Private	Dealer
4 Dr Eddie Bauer 4WD SUV	10779	12514	14116
4 Dr Eddie Bauer AWD SUV	11135	12929	14585
4 Dr Eddie Bauer SUV	9924	11522	12998
4 Dr Limited 4WD SUV	10846	12592	14204
4 Dr Limited AWD SUV	11144	12938	14595
4 Dr Limited SUV	10214	11859	13378

Body Styles	TMV Pricing		
	Trade	Private	Dealer
4 Dr XLS 4WD SUV	8615	10003	11284
4 Dr XLS SUV	7708	8950	10097
4 Dr XLT 4WD SUV	8972	10417	11751
4 Dr XLT AWD SUV	8981	10427	11762
4 Dr XLT SUV	8714	10117	11412

Options	Price
5.0L V8 OHV 16V FI Engine	+222
Automatic Load Leveling	+184
Camper/Towing Package	+187
Compact Disc Changer	+208
Front Side Airbag Restraints	+208
Heated Front Seats [Opt on Eddie Bauer]	+134
Leather Seats [Opt on Sport,XLT]	+500

Options	Price
Park Distance Control (Rear) [Opt on Eddie Bauer,Limited,XLT]	+134
Power Moonroof	+421
Power Passenger Seat [Opt on XLT]	+171
Running Boards [Opt on XLS,XLT]	+208
Sport Seats	+148

A complete redesign is planned for 2002, so the Explorer changes little in 2001. The SOHC V6 is standard on all models, and the 4.0-liter OHV V6 and manual transmission are no longer available. Additional child safety-seat tether anchors have been added to the second-row seats.

Ford
Explorer

2000

A color-keyed, two-spoke leather-wrapped steering wheel (with auxiliary audio, climate and speed control) is now standard on Eddie Bauer models. XLT Sport/Eddie Bauer/Limited models with 5.0-liter V8s receive a trailer-towing package as standard equipment. The XL is available only for fleet sales, and the XLS replaces the XL Appearance as the base retail model.

Mileage Category: M

Body Styles	TMV Pricing		
	Trade	Private	Dealer
2 Dr Sport 4WD SUV	5611	6751	7868
2 Dr Sport SUV	4852	5837	6803
4 Dr Eddie Bauer 4WD SUV	7727	9297	10837
4 Dr Eddie Bauer AWD SUV	7851	9446	11010
4 Dr Eddie Bauer SUV	7275	8755	10204
4 Dr Limited 4WD SUV	7808	9395	10952
4 Dr Limited AWD SUV	7902	9508	11082
4 Dr Limited SUV	7352	8847	10312

Body Styles	TMV Pricing		
	Trade	Private	Dealer
4 Dr XL 4WD SUV	5913	7115	8293
4 Dr XL SUV	5041	6065	7069
4 Dr XLS 4WD SUV	6064	7296	8505
4 Dr XLS SUV	5684	6840	7973
4 Dr XLT 4WD SUV	6671	8026	9355
4 Dr XLT AWD SUV	6777	8154	9504
4 Dr XLT SUV	6292	7570	8823

Options	Price
4.0L V6 SOHC 12V FI Engine [Opt on Sport,XL,XLS,XLT]	+254
5.0L V8 OHV 16V FI Engine	+198
Automatic 5-Speed Transmission [Opt on Sport,XL,XLS]	+516
Automatic Load Leveling	+165
Bucket Seats [Opt on XLT]	+132
Camper/Towing Package	+167
Captain Chairs (2) [Opt on XL]	+132
Compact Disc Changer	+175
Front Side Airbag Restraints	+184
Heated Front Seats [Opt on Eddie Bauer]	+115

Options	Price
Leather Seats [Opt on Sport,XLT]	+448
Limited Slip Differential	+147
Park Distance Control (Rear)	+120
Power Driver Seat [Opt on Sport]	+123
Power Moonroof	+377
Power Passenger Seat [Opt on Sport,XLT]	+123
Running Boards [Opt on XL,XLS,XLT]	+186
Side Steps	+139
Split Front Bench Seat [Opt on XL,XLS]	+137

1999

The Explorer gets exterior revisions including new foglamps, rocker panel moldings, wheel moldings, running boards and wheels. Harvest Gold, Chestnut, Deep Wedgewood, Spruce Green and Tropic Green replace Light Prairie Tan, Desert Violet, Light Denim Blue, Pacific Green and Evergreen Frost on the color chart. New options include a reverse sensing system and rear load leveling. Side-impact airbags are also newly available.

Mileage Category: M

Body Styles	TMV Pricing		
	Trade	Private	Dealer
2 Dr Sport 4WD SUV	4340	5373	6449
2 Dr Sport SUV	3765	4663	5597
4 Dr Eddie Bauer 4WD SUV	5870	7269	8724
4 Dr Eddie Bauer AWD SUV	5923	7334	8803
4 Dr Eddie Bauer SUV	5552	6874	8251
4 Dr Limited 4WD SUV	6012	7443	8934
4 Dr Limited AWD SUV	6048	7489	8989
4 Dr Limited SUV	5840	7231	8679

Body Styles	TMV Pricing		
	Trade	Private	Dealer
4 Dr XL 4WD SUV	4501	5572	6687
4 Dr XL SUV	3893	4821	5786
4 Dr XLS 4WD SUV	4627	5730	6877
4 Dr XLS SUV	4603	5699	6840
4 Dr XLT 4WD SUV	5105	6321	7587
4 Dr XLT AWD SUV	5140	6364	7638
4 Dr XLT SUV	4692	5808	6971

Options	Price
4.0L V6 SOHC 12V FI Engine [Opt on Sport,XL,XLS,XLT]	+210
5.0L V8 OHV 16V FI Engine	+167
AM/FM/Cassette/CD Audio System [Opt on Sport,XL,XLS,XLT]	+124
Automatic 4-Speed Transmission	+367
Automatic 5-Speed Transmission [Opt on Sport,XL,XLS]	+413
Automatic Load Leveling	+151
Camper/Towing Package	+138
Compact Disc Changer	+144

Options	Price
Front Side Airbag Restraints	+168
Leather Seats [Std on Eddie Bauer,Limited]	+369
Limited Slip Differential	+120
Power Moonroof	+311
Power Passenger Seat [Opt on Sport,XLT]	+119
Running Boards [Std on Eddie Bauer,Limited]	+154
Side Steps [Opt on Sport]	+115

1998

The Ford Explorer gets a restyled tailgate for 1998.

Mileage Category: M

Body Styles	TMV Pricing		
	Trade	Private	Dealer
2 Dr Sport 4WD SUV	3437	4362	5405
2 Dr Sport SUV	3200	4062	5034
4 Dr Eddie Bauer 4WD SUV	4659	5914	7329
4 Dr Eddie Bauer AWD SUV	4423	5613	6956
4 Dr Eddie Bauer SUV	4331	5499	6815
4 Dr Limited 4WD SUV	5078	6446	7989
4 Dr Limited AWD SUV	4899	6219	7706

Body Styles	TMV Pricing		
	Trade	Private	Dealer
4 Dr Limited SUV	4748	6028	7470
4 Dr XL 4WD SUV	3644	4626	5733
4 Dr XL SUV	3346	4247	5264
4 Dr XLT 4WD SUV	3999	5078	6295
4 Dr XLT AWD SUV	3852	4890	6061
4 Dr XLT SUV	3674	4664	5780

1998 (cont'd)

Options	Price
4.0L V6 SOHC 12V FI Engine [Opt on Sport,XLT]	+190
5.0L V8 OHV 16V FI Engine	+152
Automatic 4-Speed Transmission	+299
Automatic 5-Speed Transmission [Opt on Sport,XL,XLT]	+338
Center Console [Opt on Eddie Bauer,Sport]	+124

Options	Price
Compact Disc Changer	+117
Leather Seats [Opt on Eddie Bauer,Sport,XLT]	+208
Power Moonroof	+254
Running Boards [Opt on Eddie Bauer,XL,XLT]	+125

Mileage Category: M

1997

Ford's best-selling Explorer receives a few appreciated improvements this year. A new SOHC V6 engine is now available, providing nearly as much power as the 5.0-liter V8. Also new is a five-speed automatic transmission, the first ever offered by an American auto manufacturer, which is standard on V6 models equipped with automatic.

Body Styles	TMV Pricing		
	Trade	Private	Dealer
2 Dr Sport 4WD SUV	3035	3949	5066
2 Dr Sport SUV	2759	3590	4605
2 Dr XL 4WD SUV	3016	3924	5033
2 Dr XL SUV	2734	3557	4562
4 Dr Eddie Bauer 4WD SUV	4076	5304	6804
4 Dr Eddie Bauer AWD SUV	3871	5036	6460
4 Dr Eddie Bauer SUV	3777	4915	6305
4 Dr Limited 4WD SUV	4345	5652	7251

Body Styles	TMV Pricing		
	Trade	Private	Dealer
4 Dr Limited AWD SUV	4314	5613	7200
4 Dr Limited SUV	4077	5304	6804
4 Dr XL 4WD SUV	3065	3988	5116
4 Dr XL SUV	2775	3610	4631
4 Dr XLT 4WD SUV	3423	4453	5712
4 Dr XLT AWD SUV	3338	4343	5570
4 Dr XLT SUV	3125	4065	5215

Options	Price
4.0L V6 SOHC 12V FI Engine [Opt on Sport,XL,XLT]	+124
5.0L V8 OHV 16V FI Engine	+232
Automatic 4-Speed Transmission	+277
Automatic 5-Speed Transmission [Opt on Sport,XL,XLT]	+312

Options	Price
JBL Audio System [Std on Limited]	+161
Leather Seats [Std on Limited]	+192
Power Moonroof	+235
Running Boards [Std on Limited]	+116

Mileage Category: M

1996

The long-awaited V8 AWD Explorers are available in XLT, Eddie Bauer or Limited Edition flavors. An integrated child safety seat is optional, and the Expedition model has been replaced by a Premium trim package for the Sport.

Body Styles	TMV Pricing		
	Trade	Private	Dealer
2 Dr Sport 4WD SUV	2502	3338	4492
2 Dr Sport SUV	2323	3099	4171
2 Dr XL 4WD SUV	2381	3176	4274
2 Dr XL SUV	2200	2935	3949
4 Dr Eddie Bauer 4WD SUV	3365	4489	6042
4 Dr Eddie Bauer AWD SUV	3406	4544	6116
4 Dr Eddie Bauer SUV	3127	4171	5614
4 Dr Limited 4WD SUV	3590	4789	6444

Body Styles	TMV Pricing		
	Trade	Private	Dealer
4 Dr Limited AWD SUV	3518	4693	6315
4 Dr Limited SUV	3494	4661	6273
4 Dr XL 4WD SUV	2559	3415	4597
4 Dr XL SUV	2338	3119	4198
4 Dr XLT 4WD SUV	2860	3815	5135
4 Dr XLT AWD SUV	2916	3890	5234
4 Dr XLT SUV	2633	3512	4728

Options	Price
5.0L V8 OHV 16V FI Engine	+251
Automatic 4-Speed Transmission [Opt on Sport,XL,XLT]	+246
JBL Audio System [Std on Limited]	+144

Options	Price
Leather Seats [Std on Limited]	+163
Power Moonroof	+209

Mileage Category: M

1995

Dual airbags top the changes for the redesigned Explorer. Integrated child safety seats are optional on four-door models. Exterior changes include new sheet metal, headlights, grille, taillights and side moldings. The Control-Trac four-wheel-drive system automatically sends power to front wheels if it senses rear-wheel slippage. This feature can be locked in for full-time four-wheeling.

Body Styles	TMV Pricing		
	Trade	Private	Dealer
2 Dr Expedition 4WD SUV	2415	3327	4847
2 Dr Sport 4WD SUV	1992	2745	4000
2 Dr Sport SUV	1820	2507	3653
2 Dr XL 4WD SUV	1962	2704	3941
2 Dr XL SUV	1598	2203	3210
4 Dr Eddie Bauer 4WD SUV	2751	3791	5523
4 Dr Eddie Bauer SUV	2551	3516	5124

Body Styles	TMV Pricing		
	Trade	Private	Dealer
4 Dr Limited 4WD SUV	2907	4005	5836
4 Dr Limited SUV	2802	3860	5624
4 Dr XL 4WD SUV	2077	2862	4170
4 Dr XL SUV	1829	2520	3672
4 Dr XLT 4WD SUV	2329	3210	4678
4 Dr XLT SUV	2104	2899	4225

Options	Price
Automatic 4-Speed Transmission [Opt on Sport,XL,XLT]	+213
Camper/Towing Package	+77
Compact Disc Changer	+83
JBL Audio System [Std on Limited]	+124

Options	Price
Leather Seats [Std on Limited]	+141
Power Moonroof	+180
Running Boards [Std on Limited]	+89

Explorer Sport

2003

Mileage Category: M

Body Styles	TMV Pricing		
	Trade	Private	Dealer
2 Dr XLS 4WD SUV	10867	11912	13654
2 Dr XLS SUV	9302	10196	11687

Options	Price
AM/FM/CD Changer Audio System [Opt on XLT]	+193
Limited Slip Differential	+229
Pioneer Audio System [Opt on XLT]	+135

Body Styles	TMV Pricing		
	Trade	Private	Dealer
2 Dr XLT 4WD SUV	11741	12870	14751
2 Dr XLT SUV	10430	11432	13103

Options	Price
Power Driver Seat [Opt on XLT]	+168
Side Steps [Opt on XLT]	+135

Very few changes are in store for this two-door SUV. Trim levels equipped with the Comfort Group now includes power lumbar support. This, along with heated seats, will also be included if you opt for the leather trim. Two coat hooks and a power point make an appearance in the cargo area, and Red Fire Clearcoat Metallic replaces Toreador Red Clearcoat Metallic.

2002

Sixteen-inch aluminum wheels are made standard, along with an AM/FM/CD/cassette stereo. You now have a choice between an automatic or manual transmission with the base model.

Mileage Category: M

Body Styles	TMV Pricing		
	Trade	Private	Dealer
2 Dr STD 4WD SUV	8839	9849	11531

Options	Price
AM/FM/CD Changer Audio System	+177
Automatic 5-Speed Transmission	+615
Front Side Airbag Restraints	+233
Leather Seats	+386
Limited Slip Differential	+209

Body Styles	TMV Pricing		
	Trade	Private	Dealer
2 Dr STD SUV	7812	8704	10191

Options	Price
Pioneer Audio System	+124
Power Driver Seat	+153
Power Moonroof	+471
Running Boards	+118

2001

The 2001 Ford Explorer Sport receives a few styling changes as well as minor mechanical and interior improvements.

Mileage Category: M

Body Styles	TMV Pricing		
	Trade	Private	Dealer
2 Dr STD 4WD SUV	7708	9037	10263

Options	Price
AM/FM/CD Changer Audio System	+163
Automatic 5-Speed Transmission	+577
Bucket Seats	+148
Front Side Airbag Restraints	+205
Leather Seats	+500

Body Styles	TMV Pricing		
	Trade	Private	Dealer
2 Dr STD SUV	6615	7755	808

Options	Price
Limited Slip Differential	+187
Power Driver Seat	+137
Power Moonroof	+421
Running Boards	+208

Explorer Sport Trac

2004

The interior gets a minor refresh that includes a revised instrument cluster. XLT models now come with additional standard features, while the high-line XLT Premium gets a new monochrome exterior look. The Adrenalin model now features an even more powerful premium audio system. All models get a flexible fuel feature that allows them to run on ethanol-blended fuel, as well as traditional gasoline. Finally, there is no longer a manual transmission option on XLS models.

Mileage Category: J

Body Styles	TMV Pricing		
	Trade	Private	Dealer
4 Dr Adrenalin 4WD Crew Cab SB	19352	20730	23027
4 Dr Adrenalin Crew Cab SB	17616	18919	21091
4 Dr XLS 4WD Crew Cab SB	16583	17961	20258

Options	Price
AM/FM/CD Changer Audio System [Opt on XLT]	+255
AM/FM/Cassette/CD Audio System [Opt on XLT, XLT Prem]	+150
Automatic Dimming Rearview Mirror	+150
Automatic On/Off Headlights	+200
Fog Lights	+150
Front and Rear Head Airbag Restraints	+560
Leather Seats [Opt on XLT Prem, Adrenalin]	+1000
Limited Slip Differential	+355

Body Styles	TMV Pricing		
	Trade	Private	Dealer
4 Dr XLS Crew Cab SB	14890	16118	18165
4 Dr XLT 4WD Crew Cab SB	17383	18761	21058
4 Dr XLT Crew Cab SB	15653	16881	18928

Options	Price
Overhead Console [Opt on XLT, Adrenalin]	+200
Pioneer Audio System [Opt on XLT]	+255
Polished Aluminum/Alloy Wheels [Opt on XLT]	+600
Power Driver Seat [Opt on XLT]	+200
Power Moonroof [Opt on XLT Prem, Adrenalin]	+800
Power Passenger Seat [Opt on XLT Prem, Adrenalin]	+200
Side Steps [Opt on XLT]	+300
Tonneau Cover	+590

2003

Ford updates the Sport Trac's interior with new low-back bucket seats, revised door trim and updated colors. When leather upholstery is ordered, the front seats are six-way power adjustable and can be heated and equipped with power lumbar support. To improve safety, Ford's Safety Canopy side airbag system with rollover sensors is newly available, as are standard rear disc brakes. Lastly, an Adrenaline Edition debuts mid-year with a 485-watt Pioneer sound system and new colors.

Mileage Category: J

Body Styles	TMV Pricing		
	Trade	Private	Dealer
4 Dr XLS 4WD Crew Cab SB	13791	15009	17040
4 Dr XLS Crew Cab SB	12198	13275	15071

Options	Price
AM/FM/CD Changer Audio System [Opt on XLT]	+193
Front and Rear Head Airbag Restraints	+361
Limited Slip Differential	+229
Pioneer Audio System [Opt on XLT]	+135

Body Styles	TMV Pricing		
	Trade	Private	Dealer
4 Dr XLT 4WD Crew Cab SB	14799	16106	18284
4 Dr XLT Crew Cab SB	13305	14480	16437

Options	Price
Power Driver Seat [Opt on XLT]	+168
Side Steps [Opt on XLT]	+135
Tonneau Cover	+381

2002

The Explorer Sport Trac enters 2002 with slightly more power and torque from its 4.0-liter V6 engine, some new exterior colors and a simplified options list. You can now also get an automatic transmission with the value package.

Mileage Category: J

Body Styles	TMV Pricing		
	Trade	Private	Dealer
4 Dr STD 4WD Crew Cab SB	12595	13875	16009

Options	Price
AM/FM/CD Changer Audio System	+182
Automatic 5-Speed Transmission	+615
Bed Extender	+115
Leather Seats	+386
Limited Slip Differential	+209

Body Styles	TMV Pricing		
	Trade	Private	Dealer
4 Dr STD Crew Cab SB	11199	12338	14236

Options	Price
Pioneer Audio System	+118
Power Driver Seat	+153
Power Moonroof	+471
Side Steps	+127
Tonneau Cover	+347

2001

The Sport Trac is a combination of a pickup and an SUV. Basically, Ford has grafted a small cargo bed to the back of an updated Ford Explorer.

Mileage Category: J

Body Styles	TMV Pricing		
	Trade	Private	Dealer
4 Dr STD 4WD Crew Cab SB	10825	12557	14156

Options	Price
AM/FM/CD Changer Audio System	+163
Automatic 5-Speed Transmission	+577
Leather Seats	+500
Limited Slip Differential	+187

Body Styles	TMV Pricing		
	Trade	Private	Dealer
4 Dr STD Crew Cab SB	9642	11185	12609

Options	Price
Power Driver Seat	+137
Power Moonroof	+421
Running Boards	+208
Tonneau Cover	+311

F-150

2004

The F-150 is fully redesigned for 2004. It's bigger, more powerful and offers a greater variety of features and body styles than ever before.

Mileage Category: K

Body Styles	TMV Pricing		
	Trade	Private	Dealer
2 Dr FX4 4WD Std Cab 6.5 ft. SB	17432	18691	20791
2 Dr FX4 4WD Std Cab Step 6.5 ft. SB	17928	19128	21128
2 Dr STX 4WD Std Cab 6.5 ft. SB	14808	16008	18009
2 Dr STX 4WD Std Cab Step 6.5 ft. SB	15303	16503	18503
2 Dr STX Std Cab 6.5 ft. SB	12587	13719	15605
2 Dr STX Std Cab Step 6.5 ft. SB	13081	14213	16100
2 Dr XL 4WD Std Cab 6.5 ft. SB	14337	15617	17752
2 Dr XL 4WD Std Cab 8 ft. LB	14512	15713	17713
2 Dr XL Std Cab 6.5 ft. SB	12100	13232	15119
2 Dr XL Std Cab 8 ft. LB	12276	13408	15295
2 Dr XLT 4WD Std Cab 6.5 ft. SB	16202	17453	19538
2 Dr XLT 4WD Std Cab 8 ft. LB	16378	17646	19760
2 Dr XLT 4WD Std Cab Step 6.5 ft. SB	16698	17898	19898
2 Dr XLT Std Cab 6.5 ft. SB	13938	15070	16957
2 Dr XLT Std Cab 8 ft. LB	14379	15531	17453
2 Dr XLT Std Cab Step 6.5 ft. SB	14566	15783	17811
4 Dr FX4 4WD Crew Cab 5.5 ft. SB	20237	21676	24073
4 Dr FX4 4WD Ext Cab 5.5 ft. SB	18626	19928	22099
4 Dr FX4 4WD Ext Cab 6.5 ft. SB	18801	20103	22273

Body Styles	TMV Pricing		
	Trade	Private	Dealer
4 Dr FX4 4WD Ext Cab Step 6.5 ft. SB	19295	20597	22768
4 Dr Lariat 4WD Crew Cab 5.5 ft. SB	21492	23016	25556
4 Dr Lariat 4WD Ext Cab 5.5 ft. SB	19129	20431	22602
4 Dr Lariat 4WD Ext Cab 6.5 ft. SB	19304	20606	22776
4 Dr Lariat Crew Cab 5.5 ft. SB	19023	20514	22998
4 Dr Lariat Ext Cab 5.5 ft. SB	17200	18503	20674
4 Dr Lariat Ext Cab 6.5 ft. SB	17487	18798	20982
4 Dr STX 4WD Ext Cab 5.5 ft. SB	15960	17263	19434
4 Dr STX 4WD Ext Cab 6.5 ft. SB	16225	17535	19718
4 Dr STX 4WD Ext Cab Step 6.5 ft. SB	16809	18125	20319
4 Dr STX Ext Cab 5.5 ft. SB	14137	15440	17612
4 Dr STX Ext Cab 6.5 ft. SB	14461	15777	17972
4 Dr STX Ext Cab Step 6.5 ft. SB	14845	16152	18329
4 Dr XL 4WD Ext Cab 6.5 ft. SB	15755	17057	19229
4 Dr XL 4WD Ext Cab 8 ft. LB	17156	18459	20629
4 Dr XL Ext Cab 6.5 ft. SB	13836	14979	16884
4 Dr XL Ext Cab 8 ft. LB	15333	16636	18808
4 Dr XLT 4WD Crew Cab 5.5 ft. SB	19095	20535	22934
4 Dr XLT 4WD Ext Cab 5.5 ft. SB	17521	18833	21019
4 Dr XLT 4WD Ext Cab 6.5 ft. SB	17572	18874	21045

2004 (cont'd)

Body Styles	TMV Pricing		
	Trade	Private	Dealer
4 Dr XLT 4WD Ext Cab 8 ft. LB	18973	20276	22446
4 Dr XLT 4WD Ext Cab Step 6.5 ft. SB	18066	19368	21539
4 Dr XLT Crew Cab 5.5 ft. SB	17214	18653	21051
4 Dr XLT Ext Cab 5.5 ft. SB	15603	16905	19076

Body Styles	TMV Pricing		
	Trade	Private	Dealer
4 Dr XLT Ext Cab 6.5 ft. SB	15778	17080	19251
4 Dr XLT Ext Cab 8 ft. LB	17180	18483	20653
4 Dr XLT Ext Cab Step 6.5 ft. SB	16272	17575	19746

Options	Price
18 Inch Wheels [Opt on FX4]	+320
AM/FM/CD Changer Audio System [Opt on non-XL]	+225
Bed Extender [Opt on 5.5ft SB]	+195
Camper/Towing Package	+350
Captain Chairs (2) [Opt on Ext, Crew XLT, FX4, Lariat]	+200
Cruise Control [Opt on XL, XTS]	+225
DVD Entertainment System [Opt on Crew]	+1295
Fog Lights [Opt on XL, XTS, 2WD XLT]	+140
Heavy Duty Suspension [Opt on XL, XLT LB]	+900
Leather Seats [Opt on Ext, Crew FX4, Lariat]	+555
Park Distance Control (Rear) [Opt on XLT, FX4, Lariat]	+245

Options	Price
Power Adjustable Foot Pedals [Opt on non-Lariat]	+120
Power Moonroof [Opt on Ext, Crew XLT, FX4, Lariat]	+810
Power Rear Window [Opt on Ext, Crew XLT, FX4, Lariat]	+245
Rear Window Defroster [Opt on non-Lariat]	+150
Running Boards	+250
Side Steps	+350
Skid Plates [Opt on 4WD non-FX4, STX]	+160
Sliding Rear Window	+125
Two-Tone Paint [Opt on XLT, FX4 non-Step, Lariat]	+225

2003

Arriving in 2003 for the XLT supercab styleside configuration is the Heritage Edition, which includes 17-inch wheels, a chrome cab step and various stylistic flairs such as a black bedliner, a lower valance, paint striping and a paint scheme with a raised cut-line. Also new is an STX edition for the XL- and XLT-trimmed regular and supercabs that includes an MP3 player combined with a monochromatic color scheme and clear lights, among others. Upgrades for the fancy King Ranch flavor consist of fake wood for the interior, lighted step bars and an in-dash six-disc CD changer. For the Lariat, expect a standard rear window defroster and a Pioneer CD and cassette system (the latter is also newly available on the XL and XLT). Harley-Davidson models have the option of getting a two-tone black-and-silver paint. Finally, a new LATCH system helps you tie down the kiddie seats properly.

Mileage Category: K

Body Styles	TMV Pricing		
	Trade	Private	Dealer
2 Dr XL 4WD Std Cab LB	11927	12825	14321
2 Dr XL 4WD Std Cab SB	11766	12651	14127
2 Dr XL 4WD Std Cab Step SB	12276	13200	14740
2 Dr XL Std Cab LB	10053	10810	12071
2 Dr XL Std Cab SB	9889	10634	11875
2 Dr XL Std Cab Step SB	10417	11201	12509
2 Dr XLT 4WD Std Cab LB	13387	14395	16075
2 Dr XLT 4WD Std Cab SB	13183	14175	15829
2 Dr XLT 4WD Std Cab Step SB	13696	14728	16446
2 Dr XLT Std Cab LB	11564	12435	13887
2 Dr XLT Std Cab SB	11376	12233	13660
2 Dr XLT Std Cab Step SB	11909	12806	14300
4 Dr Harley-Davidson S/C Crew Cab SB	23423	25186	28125
4 Dr King Ranch 4WD Crew Cab SB	19614	21090	23551
4 Dr King Ranch 4WD Ext Cab Step SB	19098	20536	22931
4 Dr King Ranch Crew Cab SB	17601	18925	21133
4 Dr King Ranch Ext Cab Step SB	16888	18160	20279
4 Dr Lariat 4WD Crew Cab SB	18967	20394	22773
4 Dr Lariat 4WD Ext Cab LB	16856	18124	20238
4 Dr Lariat 4WD Ext Cab SB	16668	17922	20013

Body Styles	TMV Pricing		
	Trade	Private	Dealer
4 Dr Lariat 4WD Ext Cab Step SB	17210	18505	20664
4 Dr Lariat Crew Cab SB	16128	17342	19365
4 Dr Lariat Ext Cab LB	15088	16224	18117
4 Dr Lariat Ext Cab SB	14815	15930	17788
4 Dr Lariat Ext Cab Step SB	15334	16489	18413
4 Dr XL 4WD Ext Cab LB	13693	14724	16442
4 Dr XL 4WD Ext Cab SB	13542	14561	16259
4 Dr XL 4WD Ext Cab Step SB	14046	15103	16866
4 Dr XL Ext Cab LB	11550	12419	13868
4 Dr XL Ext Cab SB	11364	12220	13647
4 Dr XL Ext Cab Step SB	11893	12789	14282
4 Dr XLT 4WD Crew Cab SB	16812	18078	20188
4 Dr XLT 4WD Ext Cab LB	15160	16301	18203
4 Dr XLT 4WD Ext Cab SB	14994	16123	18004
4 Dr XLT 4WD Ext Cab Step SB	15499	16666	18611
4 Dr XLT Crew Cab SB	15017	16148	18033
4 Dr XLT Ext Cab LB	13014	13993	15625
4 Dr XLT Ext Cab SB	12869	13837	15452
4 Dr XLT Ext Cab Step SB	13380	14388	16067

Options	Price
17 Inch Wheels [Opt on XLT]	+322
4.6L V8 SOHC 16V FI Engine [Opt on XL,XLT]	+484
5.4L V8 CNG SOHC 16V FI Engine [Opt on XL,XLT]	+5054
5.4L V8 Propane SOHC 16V FI Engine [Opt on XL,XLT]	+5054
5.4L V8 SOHC 16V FI Engine	+516
AM/FM/CD Audio System [Opt on XL]	+123
Aluminum/Alloy Wheels [Opt on XL]	+161
Automatic 4-Speed Transmission [Opt on XL,XLT]	+706
Bed Extender	+126
Bed Liner	+148
Camper/Towing Package	+226
Captain Chairs (2) [Opt on Lariat,XLT]	+316
Compact Disc Changer [Opt on Lariat,XLT]	+145

Options	Price
Cruise Control [Opt on XL]	+116
FX4 Off-Road Suspension Package [Opt on Lariat,XLT]	+555
Heated Front and Rear Seats	+158
Heritage Edition [Opt on XLT]	+774
Limited Slip Differential	+184
Polished Aluminum/Alloy Wheels [Opt on XL]	+129
Power Driver Seat [Opt on XLT]	+187
Power Moonroof	+522
Power Rear Window	+158
Running Boards	+158
STX Edition [Opt on XL,XLT]	+642
Split Front Bench Seat [Opt on XL]	+126
Two-Tone Paint [Opt on Lariat,XLT]	+145

Options	Price
VCR Entertainment System	+835

Mileage Category: K

Body Styles	TMV Pricing		
	Trade	Private	Dealer
2 Dr XL 4WD Std Cab LB	10307	11218	12736
2 Dr XL 4WD Std Cab SB	10152	11049	12545
2 Dr XL 4WD Std Cab Step SB	10656	11598	13168
2 Dr XL Std Cab LB	8725	9497	10782
2 Dr XL Std Cab SB	8596	9355	10621
2 Dr XL Std Cab Step SB	9090	9894	11233
2 Dr XLT 4WD Std Cab LB	11351	12354	14027
2 Dr XLT 4WD Std Cab SB	11227	12220	13875
2 Dr XLT 4WD Std Cab Step SB	11693	12726	14449
2 Dr XLT Std Cab LB	9764	10627	12066
2 Dr XLT Std Cab SB	9606	10455	11871
2 Dr XLT Std Cab Step SB	10102	10996	12485
4 Dr Harley-Davidson S/C Crew Cab SB	20228	22017	24998
4 Dr King Ranch 4WD Crew Cab SB	17820	19396	22022
4 Dr King Ranch 4WD Ext Cab SB	17049	18556	21068
4 Dr King Ranch Crew Cab SB	15724	17114	19431
4 Dr King Ranch Ext Cab SB	13816	15038	17075
4 Dr Lariat 4WD Crew Cab SB	17454	18997	21569
4 Dr Lariat 4WD Ext Cab LB	14213	15469	17563
4 Dr Lariat 4WD Ext Cab SB	14026	15266	17334

Body Styles	TMV Pricing		
	Trade	Private	Dealer
4 Dr Lariat 4WD Ext Cab Step SB	14556	15844	17989
4 Dr Lariat Crew Cab SB	13559	14758	16755
4 Dr Lariat Ext Cab LB	12624	13740	15600
4 Dr Lariat Ext Cab SB	12480	13583	15422
4 Dr Lariat Ext Cab Step SB	12951	14097	16005
4 Dr XL 4WD Ext Cab LB	11770	12810	14545
4 Dr XL 4WD Ext Cab SB	11653	12684	14401
4 Dr XL 4WD Ext Cab Step SB	12122	13194	14980
4 Dr XL Ext Cab LB	9982	10865	12330
4 Dr XL Ext Cab SB	9829	10699	12148
4 Dr XL Ext Cab Step SB	10314	11227	12747
4 Dr XLT 4WD Crew Cab SB	14274	15536	17640
4 Dr XLT 4WD Ext Cab LB	12874	14012	15909
4 Dr XLT 4WD Ext Cab SB	12723	13848	15722
4 Dr XLT 4WD Ext Cab Step SB	13194	14361	16305
4 Dr XLT Crew Cab SB	12753	13880	15760
4 Dr XLT Ext Cab LB	11087	12068	13702
4 Dr XLT Ext Cab SB	10947	11915	13528
4 Dr XLT Ext Cab Step SB	11442	12454	14140

Options	Price
17 Inch Wheels [Opt on XLT]	+294
4.6L V8 SOHC 16V FI Engine [Std on Crew,Lariat,Ext LB]	+442
5.4L V8 CNG SOHC 16V FI Engine	+4612
5.4L V8 Flex Fuel SOHC 16V FI Engine	+921
5.4L V8 Propane SOHC 16V FI Engine	+4630
5.4L V8 SOHC 16V FI Engine	+471
AM/FM/Cassette/CD Changer Audio System [Std on King Ranch]	+174
Automatic 4-Speed Transmission [Std on Crew,Lariat]	+645
Bed Extender [Opt on Crew Cab]	+115
Bed Liner	+191
Camper/Towing Package	+206
Captain Chairs (2) [Opt on Lariat,XLT]	+288
Compact Disc Changer [Opt on Harley]	+174

Options	Price
Flex Fuel Option	+3709
Heated Front Seats	+144
Limited Slip Differential	+168
Power Driver Seat [Std on Harley,King Ranch,Lariat]	+165
Power Moonroof	+477
Power Rear Window	+144
Running Boards [Std on Harley,King Ranch]	+144
Side Steps	+235
Split Front Bench Seat [Opt on XL]	+235
Tonneau Cover	+141
Two-Tone Paint	+132
VCR Entertainment System	+762

2002

A new King Ranch SuperCab arrives for 2002, joining the SuperCrew version near the top of the F-150 food chain. All King Ranch trucks get lighted visor mirrors with a HomeLink universal transmitter and a Travel Note recording device, while KR SuperCrews have automatic climate control and an available second-row bench seat that replaces the standard rear captain's chairs. Get the Harley-Davidson edition for a supercharged 5.4-liter Triton V-8 engine that adds 80 horsepower and new styling cues in the form of flame pin striping and chrome accessories, a new upper chrome billet grille, clear-lens headlamps and clear-lens parking lamps embossed with the label and rivets surrounding the center cap of the 20-inch wheels. The lower-line F-150 XL gets standard air conditioning, and its 4.2-liter V6 receives a ULEV rating. An FX4 off-road equipment package can be added to XLT or Lariat 4WD models and includes upgrades like Rancho shocks, skid plates, special wheels and unique trim. Carryover improvements from late 2001 include seat-mounted seatbelts on SuperCabs, child seat-tether anchors and rear head restraints on SuperCrew models. Also added late in 2001 were optional heated front seats (XLT and Lariat), a power sunroof (XLT and Lariat SuperCab and Crew) and a rear-seat entertainment system (XLT and Lariat SuperCrew).

Mileage Category: K

Body Styles	TMV Pricing		
	Trade	Private	Dealer
2 Dr XL 4WD Std Cab LB	8559	9836	11014
2 Dr XL 4WD Std Cab SB	8430	9687	10847
2 Dr XL 4WD Std Cab Step SB	8860	10181	11401
2 Dr XL Std Cab LB	7201	8275	9266
2 Dr XL Std Cab SB	7090	8146	9122
2 Dr XL Std Cab Step SB	7517	8638	9673
2 Dr XLT 4WD Std Cab LB	9780	11238	12584
2 Dr XLT 4WD Std Cab SB	9675	11118	12449
2 Dr XLT 4WD Std Cab Step SB	10073	11575	12961
2 Dr XLT Std Cab LB	8419	9675	10833
2 Dr XLT Std Cab SB	8289	9524	10665
2 Dr XLT Std Cab Step SB	8706	10005	11203

Body Styles	TMV Pricing		
	Trade	Private	Dealer
4 Dr Harley-Davidson Crew Cab SB	14910	17133	19186
4 Dr King Ranch 4WD Crew Cab SB	16163	18573	20798
4 Dr King Ranch Crew Cab SB	12412	14263	15972
4 Dr Lariat 4WD Crew Cab SB	12976	14912	16698
4 Dr Lariat 4WD Ext Cab LB	12349	14191	15890
4 Dr Lariat 4WD Ext Cab SB	12236	14061	15745
4 Dr Lariat 4WD Ext Cab Step SB	12640	14525	16265
4 Dr Lariat Crew Cab SB	11585	13313	14907
4 Dr Lariat Ext Cab LB	11030	12675	14193
4 Dr Lariat Ext Cab SB	10905	12530	14031
4 Dr Lariat Ext Cab Step SB	11312	12998	14555
4 Dr XL 4WD Ext Cab LB	9820	11284	12636

2001

Besides the introduction of the four-door SuperCrew and limited-edition Harley-Davidson and King Ranch models, America's most popular truck receives only minor changes in 2001. Power-adjustable accelerator and brake pedals are now standard on all F-150 Lariat models and optional on XL and XLT trucks. The Work Series model is no longer available, but there is a new Work Truck option group that deletes certain equipment from the XL model. Child safety-seat anchors and four-wheel ABS are now standard equipment on all trucks. XL and XLT trucks have upgraded standard-equipment radios.

2001 (cont'd)

Body Styles	TMV Pricing		
	Trade	Private	Dealer
4 Dr XL 4WD Ext Cab SB	9720	11169	12506
4 Dr XL 4WD Ext Cab Step SB	10119	11628	13021
4 Dr XL Ext Cab LB	8281	9516	10656
4 Dr XL Ext Cab SB	8154	9370	10492
4 Dr XL Ext Cab Step SB	8571	9849	11028
4 Dr XLT 4WD Crew Cab SB	12267	14097	15786
4 Dr XLT 4WD Ext Cab LB	11091	12744	14270

Body Styles	TMV Pricing		
	Trade	Private	Dealer
4 Dr XLT 4WD Ext Cab SB	10992	12631	14144
4 Dr XLT 4WD Ext Cab Step SB	11364	13059	14624
4 Dr XLT Crew Cab SB	10960	12595	14104
4 Dr XLT Ext Cab LB	9550	10974	12288
4 Dr XLT Ext Cab SB	9436	10842	12140
4 Dr XLT Ext Cab Step SB	9859	11329	12687

Options	Price
4.6L V8 SOHC 16V FI Engine	+395
5.4L V8 CNG SOHC 16V FI Engine	+3485
5.4L V8 Propane SOHC 16V FI Engine	+3561
5.4L V8 SOHC 16V FI Engine	+421
AM/FM/Cassette/CD Changer Audio System [Opt on Harley,Lariat,XLT]	+155
Air Conditioning	+424
Automatic 4-Speed Transmission	+577
Bed Liner	+171
Camper/Towing Package	+156
Captain Chairs (2)	+258

Options	Price
Heated Front Seats [Opt on Harley,Lariat,XLT]	+129
Limited Slip Differential	+150
Off-Road Suspension Package	+237
Power Driver Seat [Opt on XLT]	+190
Power Moonroof	+427
Running Boards	+132
Split Front Bench Seat [Opt on XL]	+211
Two-Tone Paint [Opt on Lariat,XLT]	+119
VCR Entertainment System [Opt on Crew]	+682

2000

The F-150 SuperCrew, a crew-cab truck with full-size doors and a larger rear-passenger compartment, will bow in the first quarter of 2000 as a 2001 model. A limited-edition Harley-Davidson F-150 is available for 2000. The under-8,500-pound GVW F-250 has been discontinued and replaced by the F-150 7700 Payload Group. A new overhead console and left- and right-side visor vanity mirrors are optional on XL models and standard on XLT and Lariat F-150 pickups. A driver-side keypad entry system is available on Lariat models. Chromed steel wheels and 17-inch tires are now available on 4x2 models. A comfort-enhancing flip-up 40/60 rear seat has been added to the F-150 SuperCab.

Mileage Category: K

Body Styles	TMV Pricing		
	Trade	Private	Dealer
2 Dr Work 4WD Std Cab LB	6939	8125	9288
2 Dr Work 4WD Std Cab SB	6899	8079	9236
2 Dr Work Std Cab LB	5860	6863	7846
2 Dr Work Std Cab SB	5760	6745	7711
2 Dr XL 4WD Std Cab LB	7337	8592	9823
2 Dr XL 4WD Std Cab SB	7228	8464	9676
2 Dr XL 4WD Std Cab Step SB	7612	8914	10191
2 Dr XL Std Cab LB	6117	7164	8190
2 Dr XL Std Cab SB	6087	7129	8150
2 Dr XL Std Cab Step SB	6372	7462	8531
2 Dr XLT 4WD Std Cab LB	8442	9886	11301
2 Dr XLT 4WD Std Cab SB	8271	9686	11073
2 Dr XLT 4WD Std Cab Step SB	8705	10195	11655
2 Dr XLT Std Cab LB	7203	8435	9642
2 Dr XLT Std Cab SB	7052	8259	9441
2 Dr XLT Std Cab Step SB	7372	8633	9869
4 Dr Harley-Davidson Ext Cab Step SB	12492	14629	16724
4 Dr Lariat 4WD Ext Cab LB	10528	12329	14094
4 Dr Lariat 4WD Ext Cab SB	10475	12266	14022
4 Dr Lariat 4WD Ext Cab Step SB	10633	12452	14235

Body Styles	TMV Pricing		
	Trade	Private	Dealer
4 Dr Lariat Ext Cab LB	9531	11161	12760
4 Dr Lariat Ext Cab SB	9305	10897	12458
4 Dr Lariat Ext Cab Step SB	9807	11485	13129
4 Dr Work 4WD Ext Cab LB	8185	9584	10956
4 Dr Work 4WD Ext Cab SB	8173	9572	10942
4 Dr Work Ext Cab LB	6838	8008	9155
4 Dr Work Ext Cab SB	6732	7885	9015
4 Dr XL 4WD Ext Cab LB	8443	9887	11302
4 Dr XL 4WD Ext Cab SB	8406	9844	11253
4 Dr XL 4WD Ext Cab Step SB	8718	10209	11671
4 Dr XL Ext Cab LB	7099	8314	9504
4 Dr XL Ext Cab SB	6985	8179	9350
4 Dr XL Ext Cab Step SB	7342	8598	9828
4 Dr XLT 4WD Ext Cab LB	9542	11174	12774
4 Dr XLT 4WD Ext Cab SB	9376	10980	12552
4 Dr XLT 4WD Ext Cab Step SB	9826	11506	13152
4 Dr XLT Ext Cab LB	8196	9597	10971
4 Dr XLT Ext Cab SB	8241	9650	11032
4 Dr XLT Ext Cab Step SB	8442	9886	11301

Options	Price
4.6L V8 SOHC 16V FI Engine	+353
5.4L V8 CNG SOHC 16V FI Engine	+3479
5.4L V8 Propane SOHC 16V FI Engine	+3186
5.4L V8 SOHC 16V FI Engine	+377
AM/FM/CD Audio System [Opt on XL,XLT]	+151
Air Conditioning	+379
Aluminum/Alloy Wheels	+151
Antilock Brakes	+320
Automatic 4-Speed Transmission	+516
Bed Liner	+153

Options	Price
Camper/Towing Package	+140
Captain Chairs (2)	+231
Compact Disc Changer	+189
Limited Slip Differential	+127
Off-Road Suspension Package	+292
Power Driver Seat [Opt on XLT]	+170
Running Boards	+118
Side Steps	+139
Split Front Bench Seat [Opt on XL]	+123
Velour/Cloth Seats [Opt on Work]	+118

Mileage Category: K

1999

Body Styles	TMV Pricing		
	Trade	Private	Dealer
2 Dr Lariat 4WD Std Cab LB	7888	9530	11239
2 Dr Lariat 4WD Std Cab SB	7716	9322	10993
2 Dr Lariat 4WD Std Cab Step SB	8218	9927	11706
2 Dr Lariat Std Cab LB	6722	8121	9577
2 Dr Lariat Std Cab SB	6667	8055	9499
2 Dr Lariat Std Cab Step SB	6882	8314	9805
2 Dr Work 4WD Std Cab LB	5584	6746	7955
2 Dr Work 4WD Std Cab SB	5578	6738	7946
2 Dr Work Std Cab LB	4569	5520	6509
2 Dr Work Std Cab SB	4480	5413	6383
2 Dr XL 4WD Std Cab LB	5850	7067	8334
2 Dr XL 4WD Std Cab SB	5751	6949	8195
2 Dr XL 4WD Std Cab Step SB	5945	7182	8470
2 Dr XL Std Cab LB	4748	5737	6766
2 Dr XL Std Cab SB	4653	5621	6629
2 Dr XL Std Cab Step SB	4970	6004	7081
2 Dr XLT 4WD Std Cab LB	6751	8156	9618
2 Dr XLT 4WD Std Cab SB	6703	8098	9550
2 Dr XLT 4WD Std Cab Step SB	7053	8521	10049
2 Dr XLT Std Cab LB	5723	6913	8152
2 Dr XLT Std Cab SB	5601	6766	7978
2 Dr XLT Std Cab Step SB	5922	7155	8438

Body Styles	TMV Pricing		
	Trade	Private	Dealer
4 Dr Lariat 4WD Ext Cab LB	8405	10154	11975
4 Dr Lariat 4WD Ext Cab SB	8364	10105	11917
4 Dr Lariat 4WD Ext Cab Step SB	8477	10242	12078
4 Dr Lariat Ext Cab LB	7322	8846	10432
4 Dr Lariat Ext Cab SB	7248	8757	10327
4 Dr Lariat Ext Cab Step SB	7820	9448	11142
4 Dr Work 4WD Ext Cab LB	6540	7900	9316
4 Dr Work 4WD Ext Cab SB	6371	7696	9076
4 Dr Work Ext Cab LB	5360	6476	7637
4 Dr Work Ext Cab SB	5272	6370	7513
4 Dr XL 4WD Ext Cab LB	6815	8233	9710
4 Dr XL 4WD Ext Cab SB	6744	8148	9608
4 Dr XL 4WD Ext Cab Step SB	7102	8580	10118
4 Dr XL Ext Cab LB	5683	6866	8096
4 Dr XL Ext Cab SB	5588	6751	7962
4 Dr XL Ext Cab Step SB	5877	7101	8374
4 Dr XLT 4WD Ext Cab LB	7766	9382	11064
4 Dr XLT 4WD Ext Cab SB	7469	9023	10642
4 Dr XLT 4WD Ext Cab Step SB	7929	9579	11297
4 Dr XLT Ext Cab LB	6593	7965	9393
4 Dr XLT Ext Cab SB	6376	7703	9083
4 Dr XLT Ext Cab Step SB	6753	8158	9620

Options	Price
4.6L V8 SOHC 16V FI Engine [Std on Lariat]	+291
5.4L V8 Flex Fuel SOHC 16V FI Engine	+352
5.4L V8 Propane SOHC 16V FI Engine	+2488
5.4L V8 SOHC 16V FI Engine	+287
AM/FM/CD Audio System [Opt on XL,XLT]	+124
Air Conditioning [Opt on XL,Work]	+312
Aluminum/Alloy Wheels [Opt on XL]	+124
Antilock Brakes [Opt on XL,Work]	+293

Options	Price
Automatic 4-Speed Transmission [Std on Lariat]	+387
Bed Liner	+126
Camper/Towing Package	+115
Captain Chairs (2) [Opt on XLT]	+190
Compact Disc Changer	+155
Power Driver Seat [Opt on XLT]	+140
Side Steps	+115

The Standard trim level is replaced by the Work trim level. XLT and Lariat models get standard four-wheel antilock brakes, and the XLT gets standard air conditioning. All SuperCab models get a fourth door and horsepower is improved for engines across the board. Option content is shuffled and simplified as Ford reduces the number of optional features.

Mileage Category: K

1998

Body Styles	TMV Pricing		
	Trade	Private	Dealer
2 Dr Lariat 4WD Std Cab LB	6441	7899	9544
2 Dr Lariat 4WD Std Cab SB	6374	7818	9446
2 Dr Lariat 4WD Std Cab Step SB	6516	7991	9654
2 Dr Lariat Std Cab LB	5544	6800	8216
2 Dr Lariat Std Cab SB	5469	6708	8106
2 Dr Lariat Std Cab Step SB	5724	7021	8483
2 Dr STD 4WD Std Cab LB	4635	5685	6869
2 Dr STD 4WD Std Cab SB	4596	5636	6810
td Cab LB	3924	4813	5815
2 Dr STD Std Cab SB	3624	4445	5371
2 Dr XL 4WD Std Cab LB	5047	6190	7479
2 Dr XL 4WD Std Cab SB	4907	6018	7271
2 Dr XL 4WD Std Cab Step SB	5095	6248	7549
2 Dr XL Std Cab LB	4079	5003	6044
2 Dr XL Std Cab SB	3995	4899	5919
2 Dr XL Std Cab Step SB	4258	5222	6309
2 Dr XLT 4WD Std Cab LB	5731	7029	8493
2 Dr XLT 4WD Std Cab SB	5656	6938	8383
2 Dr XLT 4WD Std Cab Step SB	5893	7228	8732
2 Dr XLT Std Cab LB	4783	5866	7087
2 Dr XLT Std Cab SB	4701	5766	6967

Body Styles	TMV Pricing		
	Trade	Private	Dealer
2 Dr XLT Std Cab Step SB	5004	6137	7415
3 Dr Lariat 4WD Ext Cab LB	6968	8545	10325
3 Dr Lariat 4WD Ext Cab SB	6912	8477	10242
3 Dr Lariat 4WD Ext Cab Step SB	7017	8606	10397
3 Dr Lariat Ext Cab LB	6231	7642	9233
3 Dr Lariat Ext Cab SB	6171	7568	9143
3 Dr Lariat Ext Cab Step SB	6461	7925	9575
3 Dr STD 4WD Ext Cab LB	5507	6753	8159
3 Dr STD 4WD Ext Cab SB	5434	6664	8051
3 Dr STD Ext Cab LB	4514	5537	6690
3 Dr STD Ext Cab SB	4334	5316	6422
3 Dr XL 4WD Ext Cab LB	5955	7303	8824
3 Dr XL 4WD Ext Cab SB	5781	7090	8566
3 Dr XL 4WD Ext Cab Step SB	6122	7508	9071
3 Dr XL Ext Cab LB	4777	5859	7079
3 Dr XL Ext Cab SB	4693	5756	6955
3 Dr XL Ext Cab Step SB	4896	6005	7255
3 Dr XLT 4WD Ext Cab LB	6655	8161	9860
3 Dr XLT 4WD Ext Cab SB	6559	8044	9719
3 Dr XLT 4WD Ext Cab Step SB	6790	8328	10062
3 Dr XLT Ext Cab LB	5625	6899	8336

The 1998 F-150 gets a 50th Anniversary decal affixed to the lower left corner of the windshield. Other changes include making the locking tailgate standard on XLT and Lariat trims, optional on XL and Standard models. Foglights become optional this year on all four-wheel-drive models except for the Lariat, which gets them standard. An STX package featuring 17-inch tires, aluminum wheels and color-keyed grille debuts as an option for the XLT 2WD. The Lariat receives a color-keyed steering column, leather-wrapped steering wheel and outside power signal mirrors. Silver Metallic paint replaces Silver Frost paint, and Light Denim Blue replaces Portofino Blue.

1998 (cont'd)

Body Styles	TMV Pricing		
	Trade	Private	Dealer
3 Dr XLT Ext Cab SB	5550	6807	8225

Options	Price
4.6L V8 SOHC 16V FI Engine	+202
5.4L V8 SOHC 16V FI Engine	+211
Air Conditioning	+255
Antilock Brakes	+240

Body Styles	TMV Pricing		
	Trade	Private	Dealer
3 Dr XLT Ext Cab Step SB	5742	7043	8509

Options	Price
Automatic 4-Speed Transmission	+308
Captain Chairs (2) [Opt on XLT]	+155
Compact Disc Changer	+127
Rear Bench Seat [Opt on XL Ext Cab]	+132

1997

New engines, new sheet metal and a new suspension compliment dual airbags and class-leading side-impact protection in this user-friendly heavy hauler. All SuperCab models get a third door for easy access to the rear compartment. Grille styling is slightly different depending on what drive system is selected.

Mileage Category: K

Body Styles	TMV Pricing		
	Trade	Private	Dealer
2 Dr Lariat 4WD Std Cab LB	5359	6716	8375
2 Dr Lariat 4WD Std Cab SB	5338	6690	8343
2 Dr Lariat 4WD Std Cab Step SB	5413	6785	8461
2 Dr Lariat Std Cab LB	4790	6004	7487
2 Dr Lariat Std Cab SB	4732	5931	7397
2 Dr Lariat Std Cab Step SB	5058	6339	7905
2 Dr STD 4WD Std Cab LB	4189	5231	6505
2 Dr STD 4WD Std Cab SB	4085	5119	6384
2 Dr STD Std Cab LB	3351	4200	5238
2 Dr STD Std Cab SB	2982	3737	4660
2 Dr XL 4WD Std Cab LB	4390	5503	6862
2 Dr XL 4WD Std Cab SB	4361	5466	6816
2 Dr XL 4WD Std Cab Step SB	4508	5650	7045
2 Dr XL Std Cab LB	3444	4317	5384
2 Dr XL Std Cab SB	3395	4255	5307
2 Dr XL Std Cab Step SB	3640	4563	5690
2 Dr XLT 4WD Std Cab LB	4986	6250	7795
2 Dr XLT 4WD Std Cab SB	4916	6162	7684
2 Dr XLT 4WD Std Cab Step SB	5076	6362	7934
2 Dr XLT Std Cab LB	4197	5260	6560
2 Dr XLT Std Cab SB	4102	5142	6413
2 Dr XLT Std Cab Step SB	4452	5580	6959

Body Styles	TMV Pricing		
	Trade	Private	Dealer
3 Dr Lariat 4WD Ext Cab LB	5781	7245	9035
3 Dr Lariat 4WD Ext Cab SB	5722	7170	8941
3 Dr Lariat 4WD Ext Cab Step SB	5835	7313	9120
3 Dr Lariat Ext Cab LB	5303	6647	8289
3 Dr Lariat Ext Cab SB	5263	6596	8226
3 Dr Lariat Ext Cab Step SB	5371	6732	8395
3 Dr STD 4WD Ext Cab LB	4761	5967	7442
3 Dr STD 4WD Ext Cab SB	4672	5857	7304
3 Dr STD Ext Cab LB	3861	4840	6036
3 Dr STD Ext Cab SB	3815	4782	5965
3 Dr XL 4WD Ext Cab LB	5143	6446	8039
3 Dr XL 4WD Ext Cab SB	5124	6424	8011
3 Dr XL 4WD Ext Cab Step SB	5248	6578	8204
3 Dr XL Ext Cab LB	4135	5182	6462
3 Dr XL Ext Cab SB	4075	5107	6368
3 Dr XL Ext Cab Step SB	4230	5301	6611
3 Dr XLT 4WD Ext Cab LB	5588	7004	8734
3 Dr XLT 4WD Ext Cab SB	5474	6861	8557
3 Dr XLT 4WD Ext Cab Step SB	5687	7127	8888
3 Dr XLT Ext Cab LB	4800	6016	7501
3 Dr XLT Ext Cab SB	4767	5975	7452
3 Dr XLT Ext Cab Step SB	5023	6295	7851

Options	Price
4.6L V8 SOHC 16V FI Engine	+187
5.4L V8 SOHC 16V FI Engine	+166
Air Conditioning	+236
Antilock Brakes	+222
Automatic 4-Speed Transmission	+285

Options	Price
Captain Chairs (2)	+144
Compact Disc Changer	+118
Off-Road Suspension Package	+202
Rear Bench Seat	+122

1996

Flareside styles and the Lightning model are dropped in 1996, and the silver instrument panel trim is replaced by a new black finish for all but Eddie Bauer styles which instead get wood grain trim on instrument and door panels. Improvements are made to the hub-locking systems and transfer case on 4WD styles, and XLT exteriors receive the slotted style front bumper. Interior upgrades include a new seat design with integrated headrest and Automatic Locking Restraint/Emergency Locking Restraint safety belts for all outboard seating positions.

Mileage Category: K

Body Styles	TMV Pricing		
	Trade	Private	Dealer
2 Dr Eddie Bauer 4WD Ext Cab LB	4764	6147	8058
2 Dr Eddie Bauer 4WD Ext Cab SB	4913	6341	8314
2 Dr Eddie Bauer 4WD Ext Cab Step SB	4959	6400	8389
2 Dr Eddie Bauer 4WD Std Cab LB	4335	5594	7333
2 Dr Eddie Bauer 4WD Std Cab SB	4228	5455	7150
2 Dr Eddie Bauer 4WD Std Cab Step SB	4572	5901	7736
2 Dr Eddie Bauer Ext Cab LB	4259	5496	7204
2 Dr Eddie Bauer Ext Cab SB	4117	5314	6966
2 Dr Eddie Bauer Ext Cab Step SB	4358	5625	7374
2 Dr Eddie Bauer Std Cab LB	3625	4678	6132
2 Dr Eddie Bauer Std Cab SB	3547	4578	6001
2 Dr Eddie Bauer Std Cab Step SB	3805	4910	6436
2 Dr Special 4WD Std Cab LB	3392	4377	5738

Body Styles	TMV Pricing		
	Trade	Private	Dealer
2 Dr Special 4WD Std Cab SB	3362	4338	5686
2 Dr Special Ext Cab LB	3096	3996	5239
2 Dr Special Ext Cab SB	3036	3917	5134
2 Dr Special Std Cab LB	2721	3511	4603
2 Dr Special Std Cab SB	2699	3482	4564
2 Dr XL 4WD Ext Cab LB	3904	5039	6606
2 Dr XL 4WD Ext Cab SB	3890	5020	6580
2 Dr XL 4WD Ext Cab Step SB	4056	5235	6863
2 Dr XL 4WD Std Cab LB	3461	4467	5856
2 Dr XL 4WD Std Cab SB	3398	4385	5747
2 Dr XL 4WD Std Cab Step SB	3558	4592	6019
2 Dr XL Ext Cab LB	3375	4356	5709
2 Dr XL Ext Cab SB	3284	4238	5554
2 Dr XL Ext Cab Step SB	3418	4410	5781
2 Dr XL Std Cab LB	2843	3668	4808

Body Styles	Trade	Private	Dealer
2 Dr XL Std Cab SB	2828	3650	4785
2 Dr XL Std Cab Step SB	3115	4020	5269
2 Dr XLT 4WD Ext Cab LB	4592	5926	7768
2 Dr XLT 4WD Ext Cab SB	4339	5601	7343
2 Dr XLT 4WD Ext Cab Step SB	4602	5939	7785
2 Dr XLT 4WD Std Cab LB	3775	4871	6386
2 Dr XLT 4WD Std Cab SB	4098	5289	6934

Options	Price
5.0L V8 OHV 16V FI Engine	+166
5.8L V8 OHV 16V FI Engine	+286
Air Conditioning [Opt on Special,XL]	+210

Body Styles	Trade	Private	Dealer
2 Dr XLT 4WD Std Cab Step SB	3853	4973	6519
2 Dr XLT Ext Cab LB	3833	4947	6484
2 Dr XLT Ext Cab SB	3780	4878	6394
2 Dr XLT Ext Cab Step SB	3989	5147	6747
2 Dr XLT Std Cab LB	3369	4348	5700
2 Dr XLT Std Cab SB	3268	4217	5528
2 Dr XLT Std Cab Step SB	3494	4509	5909

Options	Price
Automatic 4-Speed Transmission	+253
Captain Chairs (2)	+127

Mileage Category: K

1995

Body Styles	Trade	Private	Dealer
2 Dr Eddie Bauer 4WD Ext Cab LB	3688	4837	6751
2 Dr Eddie Bauer 4WD Ext Cab SB	3666	4808	6710
2 Dr Eddie Bauer 4WD Ext Cab Step SB	3781	4958	6920
2 Dr Eddie Bauer 4WD Std Cab LB	3344	4385	6120
2 Dr Eddie Bauer 4WD Std Cab SB	3285	4308	6013
2 Dr Eddie Bauer 4WD Std Cab Step SB	3422	4488	6264
2 Dr Eddie Bauer Ext Cab LB	3333	4371	6100
2 Dr Eddie Bauer Ext Cab SB	3292	4318	6027
2 Dr Eddie Bauer Ext Cab Step SB	3406	4467	6236
2 Dr Eddie Bauer Std Cab LB	2933	3846	5368
2 Dr Eddie Bauer Std Cab SB	2896	3798	5301
2 Dr Eddie Bauer Std Cab Step SB	3039	3985	5562
2 Dr Special 4WD Std Cab LB	2769	3631	5067
2 Dr Special 4WD Std Cab SB	2714	3559	4968
2 Dr Special Ext Cab LB	2561	3359	4689
2 Dr Special Ext Cab SB	2525	3311	4621
2 Dr Special Std Cab LB	2292	3006	4196
2 Dr Special Std Cab SB	2251	2952	4119
2 Dr XL 4WD Ext Cab LB	3130	4105	5730
2 Dr XL 4WD Ext Cab SB	3109	4077	5690
2 Dr XL 4WD Ext Cab Step SB	3221	4225	5897

Options	Price
5.0L V8 OHV 16V FI Engine	+144
5.8L V8 OHV 16V FI Engine	+247
Air Conditioning [Opt on Special,XL]	+182

Body Styles	Trade	Private	Dealer
2 Dr XL 4WD Std Cab LB	2862	3754	5240
2 Dr XL 4WD Std Cab SB	2817	3694	5155
2 Dr XL 4WD Std Cab Step SB	2954	3874	5406
2 Dr XL Ext Cab LB	2774	3638	5078
2 Dr XL Ext Cab SB	2708	3551	4957
2 Dr XL Ext Cab Step SB	2851	3739	5218
2 Dr XL Std Cab LB	2440	3200	4467
2 Dr XL Std Cab SB	2404	3153	4401
2 Dr XL Std Cab Step SB	2546	3339	4661
2 Dr XLT 4WD Ext Cab LB	3418	4482	6256
2 Dr XLT 4WD Ext Cab SB	3394	4452	6214
2 Dr XLT 4WD Ext Cab Step SB	3510	4603	6424
2 Dr XLT 4WD Std Cab LB	3171	4158	5804
2 Dr XLT 4WD Std Cab SB	3145	4125	5758
2 Dr XLT 4WD Std Cab Step SB	3283	4305	6009
2 Dr XLT Ext Cab LB	3092	4054	5658
2 Dr XLT Ext Cab SB	3050	4000	5584
2 Dr XLT Ext Cab Step SB	3193	4187	5844
2 Dr XLT Std Cab LB	2709	3553	4959
2 Dr XLT Std Cab SB	2712	3557	4964
2 Dr XLT Std Cab Step SB	2855	3744	5225

Options	Price
Automatic 4-Speed Transmission	+219
Captain Chairs (2)	+110

Ford introduces the premium Eddie Bauer model. Adorned with two-toned paint, air conditioning, a full array of power features, deep-dish aluminum wheels and signature badging, it's fair to say that this truck paves the way for the ultraluxury truck segment to come. Other changes include optional privacy glass for side and rear windows (including manual-sliding rear window, when equipped) and cab steps for regular and SuperCab Styleside trims.

F-150 Heritage
2004

Mileage Category: K

Body Styles	Trade	Private	Dealer
2 Dr XL 4WD Std Cab LB	11964	13145	15113
2 Dr XL 4WD Std Cab SB	11814	12959	14867
2 Dr XL 4WD Std Cab Step SB	12234	13415	15382
2 Dr XL Std Cab LB	10287	11306	13004
2 Dr XL Std Cab SB	10138	11157	12855
2 Dr XL Std Cab Step SB	10575	11594	13291
2 Dr XLT 4WD Std Cab LB	13328	14508	16475
2 Dr XLT 4WD Std Cab SB	13179	14359	16326
2 Dr XLT 4WD Std Cab Step SB	14162	15486	17693

Body Styles	Trade	Private	Dealer
2 Dr XLT Std Cab LB	11631	12650	14347
2 Dr XLT Std Cab SB	11482	12501	14198
2 Dr XLT Std Cab Step SB	11901	13028	14905
4 Dr XL 4WD Ext Cab LB	14012	15354	17591
4 Dr XL 4WD Ext Cab SB	13862	15205	17442
4 Dr XL Ext Cab LB	11621	12639	14336
4 Dr XL Ext Cab SB	11472	12482	14164
4 Dr XLT 4WD Ext Cab LB	15409	16751	18987
4 Dr XLT 4WD Ext Cab SB	15261	16603	18839

2004 (cont'd)

The F-150 Heritage is a carryover of last year's model and therefore presents no new changes. Intended primarily as an affordable work truck, the F-150 Heritage is offered as a standard or extended cab in XL and XLT trim with limited features lists. Notably, the Heritage models are the only F-150s that can still be equipped with a V6 engine and a manual transmission.

Body Styles	TMV Pricing		
	Trade	Private	Dealer
4 Dr XLT Ext Cab LB	13138	14303	16245

Options	Price
4.6L V8 SOHC 16V FI Engine	+750
5.4L V8 CNG SOHC 16V FI Engine [Opt on 2WD XL Std LB]	+8445
5.4L V8 Flex Fuel SOHC 16V FI Engine [Opt on non-Ext LB, Crew SB]	+1565
AM/FM/CD Changer Audio System [Opt on XLT]	+295
AM/FM/Cassette/CD Audio System	+125
Automatic 4-Speed Transmission	+1095
Automatic On/Off Headlights [Opt on XLT]	+160
Captain Chairs (2) [Opt on XLT]	+360
Cruise Control [Opt on XL]	+150
Fog Lights [Opt on XL, 2WD XLT]	+140

Body Styles	TMV Pricing		
	Trade	Private	Dealer
4 Dr XLT Ext Cab SB	12896	14052	15979

Options	Price
Heavy Duty Suspension [Opt on Std LB, Ext SB]	+900
Limited Slip Differential	+285
Power Adjustable Foot Pedals	+120
Power Driver Seat [Opt on XLT]	+200
Running Boards	+250
Sliding Rear Window	+125
Split Front Bench Seat [Opt on XL]	+250
Trailer Hitch	+350
Two-Tone Paint [Opt on XLT]	+225

F-150 SVT Lightning

2004

Mileage Category: K

Body Styles		TMV Pricing		
		Trade	Private	Dealer
2 Dr S/C Std Cab Step SB		23898	25513	28205

Options	Price		Options	Price
Bed Liner	+295		Tonneau Cover	+240

No major changes for the 2004 model year.

2003

In the face of new competition from Dodge and General Motors, Ford updates the SVT F-150 Lightning to remain competitive in the sport-truck class. The steering is upgraded and retuned for better on-center feel, while suspension tweaks raise payload capacity from 800 to 1,400 pounds. The standard 18-inch alloy wheels are redesigned, and the interior gets door handles finished in a brushed aluminum appearance and upgraded carpet. A six-disc in-dash CD changer is standard this year, and new colors include Dark Shadow Gray and Sonic Blue.

Mileage Category: K

Body Styles	TMV Pricing		
	Trade	Private	Dealer
2 Dr S/C Std Cab Step SB	22027	23328	25496

Options	Price
Bed Liner	+190

2002

Ford's bad-boy pickup receives minimal changes in 2002. True Blue Clearcoat Metallic is a new color option and locking lug nuts and keyless entry keypad are added as standard equipment.

Mileage Category: K

Body Styles	TMV Pricing		
	Trade	Private	Dealer
2 Dr S/C Std Cab Step SB	20002	21240	23304

2001

Ford's bad-boy pickup receives a few changes in 2001. Acceleration times should be even faster thanks to an increase in power and a shorter final drive ratio. The front turn signals and taillights have unique clear lenses. Styling of the 18-by-9.5-inch wheels is new. A six-disc CD changer is now standard.

Mileage Category: K

Body Styles	TMV Pricing		
	Trade	Private	Dealer
2 Dr S/C Std Cab Step SB	16817	18758	20550

2000

Completely new in 1999, the 2000 Lightning is the same, except for a new Silver Clearcoat exterior color.

Mileage Category: K

Body Styles	TMV Pricing		
	Trade	Private	Dealer
2 Dr S/C Std Cab Step SB	14371	16264	18119

1999

Ford has revived its F-150-based performance truck with all-new features like an Eaton supercharger, performance suspension and Z-rated Goodyear tires.

Mileage Category: K

Body Styles	TMV Pricing		
	Trade	Private	Dealer
2 Dr S/C Std Cab Step SB	12392	14198	16077

Options	Price
Side Steps	+115

Mileage Category: K

Body Styles	TMV Pricing		
	Trade	Private	Dealer
2 Dr STD Std Cab SB	3722	4882	6814

Options	Price
Premium Audio System	+124

The somewhat rare and aptly named Lightning, with its tire-smoking 240 horsepower, 5.8-liter V8, continues unchanged for this year.

Mileage Category: K

Body Styles	TMV Pricing		
	Trade	Private	Dealer
2 Dr Lariat 4WD Std Cab LB	9002	10875	12825
2 Dr Lariat Std Cab LB	7913	9559	11273
2 Dr Work 4WD Std Cab LB	6764	8172	9637
2 Dr Work Std Cab LB	5901	7129	8407
2 Dr XL 4WD Std Cab LB	7028	8491	10013
2 Dr XL Std Cab LB	5911	7141	8422
2 Dr XLT 4WD Std Cab LB	8037	9709	11450
2 Dr XLT Std Cab LB	6977	8429	9940

Body Styles	TMV Pricing		
	Trade	Private	Dealer
4 Dr Lariat 4WD Ext Cab SB	9644	11651	13740
4 Dr Lariat Ext Cab SB	8611	10403	12268
4 Dr Work 4WD Ext Cab SB	7912	9558	11272
4 Dr Work Ext Cab SB	6751	8156	9618
4 Dr XL 4WD Ext Cab SB	8022	9691	11428
4 Dr XL Ext Cab SB	6940	8384	9887
4 Dr XLT 4WD Ext Cab SB	9094	10986	12956
4 Dr XLT Ext Cab SB	7976	9636	11363

Options	Price
5.4L V8 SOHC 16V FI Engine	+258
AM/FM/CD Audio System [Opt on XL]	+117
Air Conditioning [Opt on XL,Work]	+312
Antilock Brakes [Opt on XL,Work]	+293
Automatic 4-Speed Transmission [Opt on XL,XLT,Work]	+387

Options	Price
Automatic Load Leveling	+190
Camper/Towing Package	+115
Captain Chairs (2) [Opt on XLT]	+190
Power Driver Seat [Opt on XLT]	+140
Side Steps	+115

The Standard trim level is replaced by the Work trim level. XLT and Lariat models get standard four-wheel antilock brakes, and the XLT gets standard air conditioning. All SuperCab models get a fourth door and horsepower is improved for engines across the board. Option content is shuffled and simplified as Ford reduces the number of optional features to a mere 78.

The 1998 F-150 gets a 50th Anniversary decal affixed to the lower left corner of the windshield. Other changes include making the locking tailgate standard on XLT and Lariat trims, optional on XL and Standard models. Foglights become optional this year on all four-wheel-drive models except for the Lariat, which gets them standard. An STX package featuring 17-inch tires, aluminum wheels and color-keyed grille debuts as an option for the XLT 2WD. The Lariat receives a color-keyed steering column, leather-wrapped steering wheel and outside power signal mirrors. Silver Metallic paint replaces Silver Frost paint, and Light Denim Blue replaces Portofino Blue.

Body Styles	TMV Pricing		
	Trade	Private	Dealer
2 Dr Lariat 4WD Std Cab LB	7537	9244	11169
2 Dr Lariat Std Cab LB	6386	7832	9462
2 Dr STD 4WD Std Cab LB	5664	6947	8393
2 Dr STD Std Cab LB	4831	5925	7159
2 Dr XL 4WD Std Cab LB	6045	7493	9125
2 Dr XL Std Cab LB	4919	6032	7288
2 Dr XLT 4WD Std Cab LB	6819	8363	10105
2 Dr XLT Std Cab LB	5956	7305	8826

Body Styles	TMV Pricing		
	Trade	Private	Dealer
3 Dr Lariat 4WD Ext Cab SB	7796	9561	11552
3 Dr Lariat Ext Cab SB	6958	8533	10310
3 Dr STD 4WD Ext Cab SB	6175	7573	9150
3 Dr STD Ext Cab SB	5650	6929	8372
3 Dr XL 4WD Ext Cab SB	6765	8297	10025
3 Dr XL Ext Cab SB	5792	7104	8583
3 Dr XLT 4WD Ext Cab SB	7627	9354	11302
3 Dr XLT Ext Cab SB	6540	8021	9690

Options	Price
5.4L V8 SOHC 16V FI Engine	+211
Air Conditioning	+255
Antilock Brakes	+240
Automatic 4-Speed Transmission	+308
Automatic Load Leveling	+155

Options	Price
Camper/Towing Package	+143
Captain Chairs (2)	+155
Compact Disc Changer	+127
Rear Bench Seat [Opt on STD Ext Cab]	+132

Ford's F-250 joins the F-150 this year in a dramatic redesign. The new model has swoopy styling, a greatly improved interior, a much more rigid chassis, and carlike handling.

Mileage Category: K

Body Styles	TMV Pricing		
	Trade	Private	Dealer
2 Dr Lariat 4WD Std Cab LB	6486	8129	10137
2 Dr Lariat Std Cab LB	5653	7085	8836
2 Dr STD 4WD Std Cab LB	4975	6235	7776

Body Styles	TMV Pricing		
	Trade	Private	Dealer
2 Dr STD Std Cab LB	4034	5056	6305
2 Dr XL 4WD Ext Cab LB HD	5902	7398	9226
2 Dr XL 4WD Ext Cab SB HD	5949	7456	9298

1997 (cont'd)

Body Styles	TMV Pricing		
	Trade	Private	Dealer
2 Dr XL 4WD Std Cab LB	5415	6846	8594
2 Dr XL 4WD Std Cab LB HD	5411	6781	8456
2 Dr XL Ext Cab LB HD	4882	6119	7631
2 Dr XL Ext Cab SB HD	5196	6513	8122
2 Dr XL Std Cab LB	4152	5204	6490
2 Dr XL Std Cab LB HD	4664	5845	7289
2 Dr XLT 4WD Ext Cab LB HD	6496	8142	10153
2 Dr XLT 4WD Ext Cab SB HD	6546	8205	10232
2 Dr XLT 4WD Std Cab LB	5969	7481	9330
2 Dr XLT 4WD Std Cab LB HD	6028	7556	9423
2 Dr XLT Ext Cab LB HD	5729	7181	8955
2 Dr XLT Ext Cab SB HD	5774	7237	9025
2 Dr XLT Std Cab LB	5239	6566	8188

Body Styles	TMV Pricing		
	Trade	Private	Dealer
2 Dr XLT Std Cab LB HD	5280	6618	8253
3 Dr Lariat 4WD Ext Cab SB	6593	8264	10306
3 Dr Lariat Ext Cab SB	6050	7584	9458
3 Dr STD 4WD Ext Cab SB	5470	6903	8654
3 Dr STD Ext Cab SB	4749	5952	7423
3 Dr XL 4WD Ext Cab SB	5974	7487	9337
3 Dr XL Ext Cab SB	4894	6134	7650
3 Dr XLT 4WD Ext Cab SB	6587	8256	10296
3 Dr XLT Ext Cab SB	5819	7292	9092
4 Dr XL 4WD Crew Cab SB HD	6178	7743	9656
4 Dr XL Crew Cab SB HD	5597	7015	8748
4 Dr XLT 4WD Crew Cab SB HD	6616	8292	10341
4 Dr XLT Crew Cab SB HD	6104	7650	9540

Options	Price
5.4L V8 SOHC 16V FI Engine [Std on HD]	+166
7.3L V8 Turbodiesel OHV 16V Engine	+1115
Air Conditioning	+262
Antilock Brakes [Std on Lariat]	+222
Automatic 4-Speed Transmission	+285

Options	Price
Automatic Load Leveling	+144
Captain Chairs (2) [Opt on XLT]	+182
Compact Disc Changer	+118
Rear Bench Seat	+122

1996

Short wheelbase Crew Cab and Superab styles are now offered with a 6.75-foot box in 2- and 4WD configurations, and an improved hub-locking system and transfer case equip all 4WD models. The 7.5L V8 receives a standard integral oil cooler, and a throttle-control module for power takeoffs with the 7.3L diesel is now optional. Interior improvements include black finish on instrument panels, a revised seat design with integrated headrest and Automatic Locking Restraint/Emergency Locking Restraint safety belts for all outboard seating positions. A standard slotted style front bumper and trailer tow wiring harness (except chassis cab) complete the changes.

Mileage Category: K

Body Styles	TMV Pricing		
	Trade	Private	Dealer
2 Dr XL 4WD Ext Cab LB HD	4821	6221	8155
2 Dr XL 4WD Ext Cab SB HD	4907	6332	8301
2 Dr XL 4WD Std Cab LB HD	4304	5554	7281
2 Dr XL Ext Cab LB HD	3896	5028	6591
2 Dr XL Ext Cab SB HD	3922	5061	6635
2 Dr XL Std Cab LB	3165	4084	5354
2 Dr XL Std Cab LB HD	3343	4314	5655
2 Dr XLT 4WD Ext Cab LB HD	5389	6954	9116
2 Dr XLT 4WD Ext Cab SB HD	5503	7101	9308

Body Styles	TMV Pricing		
	Trade	Private	Dealer
2 Dr XLT 4WD Std Cab LB HD	5025	6485	8501
2 Dr XLT Ext Cab LB HD	4346	5609	7353
2 Dr XLT Ext Cab SB HD	4435	5723	7502
2 Dr XLT Std Cab LB	3810	4917	6445
2 Dr XLT Std Cab LB HD	4248	5482	7186
4 Dr XL 4WD Crew Cab LB HD	5353	6908	9056
4 Dr XL Crew Cab LB HD	4338	5598	7339
4 Dr XLT 4WD Crew Cab LB HD	5827	7519	9856
4 Dr XLT Crew Cab LB HD	5286	6822	8943

Options	Price
5.0L V8 OHV 16V FI Engine [Opt on 2WD Std Cab - XL,XLT]	+166
5.8L V8 OHV 16V FI Engine [Opt on 2WD Std Cab - XL,XLT]	+286
7.3L V8 Turbodiesel OHV 16V Engine	+884
Air Conditioning [Opt on XL]	+210

Options	Price
Automatic 3-Speed Transmission	+194
Automatic 4-Speed Transmission	+258
Captain Chairs (2)	+127
Split Front Bench Seat [Opt on XLT]	+137

1995

The F-Super Duty's Stripped Commercial Chassis is deleted, optional privacy glass now includes manual-sliding rear windows (when equipped), forged aluminum wheels are offered and cab steps on regular and SuperCab Styleside trims are available.

Mileage Category: K

Body Styles	TMV Pricing		
	Trade	Private	Dealer
2 Dr Special Ext Cab LB	3180	4169	5817
2 Dr XL 4WD Ext Cab LB	3887	5096	7110
2 Dr XL 4WD Std Cab LB	3523	4619	6445
2 Dr XL Ext Cab LB	3310	4339	6055
2 Dr XL Std Cab LB	2672	3503	4888

Body Styles	TMV Pricing		
	Trade	Private	Dealer
2 Dr XLT 4WD Ext Cab LB	4195	5499	7672
2 Dr XLT 4WD Std Cab LB	4080	5349	7464
2 Dr XLT Ext Cab LB	3593	4711	6573
2 Dr XLT Std Cab LB	3231	4236	5910

Options	Price
5.0L V8 OHV 16V FI Engine [Opt on 2WD Std Cab - XL,XLT]	+144
5.8L V8 OHV 16V FI Engine [Opt on 2WD Std Cab - XL,XLT]	+247
7.3L V8 Turbodiesel OHV 16V Engine	+856
7.5L V8 OHV 16V FI Engine	+87
Air Conditioning [Opt on Special,XL]	+182

Options	Price
Aluminum/Alloy Wheels [Opt on XL]	+86
Automatic 3-Speed Transmission	+167
Automatic 4-Speed Transmission [Opt on XL,XLT]	+219
Captain Chairs (2)	+110

F-250 Super Duty
2004

Mileage Category: K

Body Styles	Trade	Private	Dealer
2 Dr XL 4WD Std Cab LB	15360	16709	18957
2 Dr XL Std Cab LB	12746	14015	16129
2 Dr XLT 4WD Std Cab LB	17496	18873	21167
2 Dr XLT Std Cab LB	15434	16783	19031
4 Dr Lariat 4WD Crew Cab LB	22468	23852	26159
4 Dr Lariat 4WD Crew Cab SB	22349	23734	26041
4 Dr Lariat 4WD Ext Cab LB	20601	21967	24244
4 Dr Lariat 4WD Ext Cab SB	20482	21848	24125
4 Dr Lariat Crew Cab LB	20627	22143	24670
4 Dr Lariat Crew Cab SB	20508	22024	24551
4 Dr Lariat Ext Cab LB	18775	20141	22418
4 Dr Lariat Ext Cab SB	18657	20023	22300
4 Dr XL 4WD Crew Cab LB	18101	19617	22144
4 Dr XL 4WD Crew Cab SB	17978	19494	22021

Body Styles	Trade	Private	Dealer
4 Dr XL 4WD Ext Cab LB	16977	18343	20620
4 Dr XL 4WD Ext Cab SB	16858	18224	20501
4 Dr XL Crew Cab LB	15982	17348	19625
4 Dr XL Crew Cab SB	15862	17228	19505
4 Dr XL Ext Cab LB	15143	16509	18786
4 Dr XL Ext Cab SB	15024	16390	18667
4 Dr XLT 4WD Crew Cab LB	21030	22546	25073
4 Dr XLT 4WD Crew Cab SB	20911	22427	24954
4 Dr XLT 4WD Ext Cab LB	19352	20718	22995
4 Dr XLT 4WD Ext Cab SB	19233	20599	22876
4 Dr XLT Crew Cab LB	18871	20237	22514
4 Dr XLT Crew Cab SB	18752	20118	22395
4 Dr XLT Ext Cab LB	17485	18851	21128
4 Dr XLT Ext Cab SB	17366	18732	21009

Options	Price
18 Inch Wheels [Opt on Lariat Crew 4WD]	+780
6.0L V8 Turbodiesel OHV 32V Engine	+5085
6.8L V10 SOHC 20V FI Engine	+600
[Opt on Lariat, XLT]	+210
Air Conditioning [Opt on XL]	+850
Aluminum/Alloy Wheels [Opt on XLT]	+185
Automatic 4-Speed Transmission	+1095
Automatic 5-Speed Transmission	+1480
Automatic On/Off Headlights	+125
Bucket Seats [Opt on XL]	+230
Camper Mirrors	+125
Chrome Bumpers [Opt on XL]	+175
Cruise Control [Opt on XL]	+200
Fog Lights [Opt on XLT]	+140
Harley Davidson Package [Opt on Lariat 4WD]	+4345
Heated Drivers Seat [Opt on Lariat]	+220
King Ranch Package [Opt on Lariat]	+2995

Options	Price
Leather Seats [Opt on Lariat]	+415
Leather Steering Wheel	+125
Limited Slip Differential	+300
Park Distance Control (Rear) [Opt on Lariat, XLT]	+245
Power Adjustable Foot Pedals	+120
Power Driver Seat [Opt on XLT]	+290
Power Moonroof [Opt on Lariat, XLT]	+810
Power Passenger Seat [Opt on XLT]	+290
Power Rear Window [Opt on Lariat]	+125
Side Steps [Opt on XLT]	+300
Sliding Rear Window	+125
Split Front Bench Seat [Opt on XL]	+400
Tilt Steering Wheel [Opt on XL]	+185
Trailer Hitch	+175
Two-Tone Paint [Opt on Lariat, XLT]	+225
Velour/Cloth Seats [Opt on XL]	+160

A Harley-Davidson package can now be had on the F-250. Other changes worth noting are a new keypad mounted above the driver door handle when equipped with the Advanced Security Group and the availability of foglights on 4x2 XLT models. The full bench front seat is now offered with a recline feature. Trucks sold in California now have a standard 3.73 rear axle, and trucks sold in New York or Vermont require California emissions. Diesel emissions have been lowered as well.

2003

Mileage Category: K

Body Styles	Trade	Private	Dealer
2 Dr XL 4WD Std Cab LB	13860	14929	16711
2 Dr XL Std Cab LB	11877	12794	14321
2 Dr XLT 4WD Std Cab LB	16286	17527	19596
2 Dr XLT Std Cab LB	13887	14958	16744
4 Dr Lariat 4WD Crew Cab LB	19733	21256	23793
4 Dr Lariat 4WD Crew Cab SB	19606	21119	23640
4 Dr Lariat 4WD Ext Cab LB	18441	19864	22235
4 Dr Lariat 4WD Ext Cab SB	18264	19673	22021
4 Dr Lariat Crew Cab LB	18871	20327	22754
4 Dr Lariat Crew Cab SB	18758	20206	22618
4 Dr Lariat Ext Cab LB	17544	18898	21154
4 Dr Lariat Ext Cab SB	17419	18763	21003
4 Dr XL 4WD Crew Cab LB	16713	18003	20152
4 Dr XL 4WD Crew Cab SB	16607	17888	20024

Body Styles	Trade	Private	Dealer
4 Dr XL 4WD Ext Cab LB	15843	17066	19103
4 Dr XL 4WD Ext Cab SB	15721	16934	18955
4 Dr XL Crew Cab LB	14822	15966	17872
4 Dr XL Crew Cab SB	14706	15841	17732
4 Dr XL Ext Cab LB	13814	14880	16656
4 Dr XL Ext Cab SB	13711	14769	16532
4 Dr XLT 4WD Crew Cab LB	19312	20802	23286
4 Dr XLT 4WD Crew Cab SB	19199	20680	23149
4 Dr XLT 4WD Ext Cab LB	17989	19377	21690
4 Dr XLT 4WD Ext Cab SB	17869	19248	21545
4 Dr XLT Crew Cab LB	17384	18725	20961
4 Dr XLT Crew Cab SB	17261	18593	20813
4 Dr XLT Ext Cab LB	16241	17494	19583
4 Dr XLT Ext Cab SB	16122	17366	19439

Options	Price
6.0L V8 Turbodiesel OHV 32V Engine	+3280
6.8L V10 SOHC 20V FI Engine	+387

Options	Price
7.3L V8 Turbodiesel OHV 16V Engine	+3122

The 2003 model year sees a new FX4 Off-Road Package with skid plates, Rancho front and rear shocks, a steering damper and decals. The regular off-road package is no longer available, but a skid plate package can still be had on all 4WD trucks. All XLs can be had with a vinyl 40/20/40 reclining split bench that has a fold down armrest with a console and cupholders. Ford has also upgraded seat material quality, and installed a tailgate lock on this trim level. If you order a SuperCab or Crew Cab in XLT trim with the Sport Package, you can also order a reverse sensing system and a power driver seat. Late-availability additions include an optional power moonroof for Crew Cabs and optional heated telescoping trailer tow mirrors with integrated turn signals. A King Ranch version of the Crew Cab will also appear later in the year. Finally, the torque rating for the 7.3-liter turbodiesel V8 has been boosted to 525 pound feet. By mid-year, expect an even more-powerful 6.0-liter diesel to appear.

2003 (cont'd)

Options	Price
AM/FM/CD Changer Audio System [Opt on Lariat,XLT]	+135
Air Conditioning [Opt on XL]	+519
Aluminum/Alloy Wheels [Opt on XLT]	+119
Automatic 4-Speed Transmission	+706
Automatic 5-Speed Transmission	+955
Captain Chairs (4) [Opt on Lariat]	+400
Cruise Control [Opt on XL]	+119
FX4 Off-Road Suspension Package	+145
Heated Front and Rear Seats [Opt on Lariat]	+142
King Ranch Package [Opt on Lariat]	+1932
Limited Slip Differential	+193

Options	Price
Park Distance Control (Rear) [Opt on Lariat,XLT]	+158
Power Driver Seat [Opt on XLT]	+187
Power Moonroof [Opt on Lariat,XLT]	+522
Power Passenger Seat [Opt on XLT]	+187
Power Retractable Mirrors [Opt on Lariat,XLT]	+142
Side Steps [Opt on XLT]	+177
Special Leather Seat Trim [Opt on Lariat]	+242
Split Front Bench Seat [Opt on XL]	+258
Tilt Steering Wheel [Opt on XL]	+116
Two-Tone Paint [Opt on Lariat,XLT]	+145

2002

A six-speed manual transmission is now standard with the 5.4- and 6.8-liter V8 gas engines, and the 6.8-liter has been enhanced to provide better performance. If you order an automatic transmission, a gauge that measures transmission oil temperature replaces the battery gauge, and you can opt to add adjustable pedals to your Super Duty XLT or Lariat truck. Trucks with the Power Stroke diesel get an air filter service indicator. All F-250s get roof ride handles standard for 2002, and the available telescoping trailer mirrors can now be folded forward. SuperCabs have new rear door panel map pockets with molded-in cupholders. XL gets upgraded visors, while XLT and Lariat get new seats with increased width, bolstering and lumbar support; jewellike headlamp lenses and an available Advanced Security Group that includes remote keyless entry, automatic door locks and automatic headlamps. Optional on the XLT Crew Cab and standard on the Lariat Crew Cab is a power front passenger seat. The Lariat also gets a larger standard overhead console with improved storage.

Mileage Category: K

Body Styles	Trade	Private	Dealer
2 Dr XL 4WD Std Cab LB	12706	13821	15680
2 Dr XL Std Cab LB	10883	11845	13449
2 Dr XLT 4WD Std Cab LB	13982	15218	17279
2 Dr XLT Std Cab LB	12340	13431	15249
4 Dr Lariat 4WD Crew Cab LB	17604	19161	21755
4 Dr Lariat 4WD Crew Cab SB	17503	19051	21630
4 Dr Lariat 4WD Ext Cab LB	16510	17970	20402
4 Dr Lariat 4WD Ext Cab SB	16411	17862	20281
4 Dr Lariat Crew Cab LB	16029	17447	19809
4 Dr Lariat Crew Cab SB	15932	17341	19689
4 Dr Lariat Ext Cab LB	14936	16257	18458
4 Dr Lariat Ext Cab SB	14823	16134	18318
4 Dr XL 4WD Crew Cab LB	14418	15693	17817
4 Dr XL 4WD Crew Cab SB	14327	15594	17705

Body Styles	Trade	Private	Dealer
4 Dr XL 4WD Ext Cab LB	13681	14891	16907
4 Dr XL 4WD Ext Cab SB	13584	14785	16787
4 Dr XL Crew Cab LB	12957	14103	16013
4 Dr XL Crew Cab SB	12883	14022	15920
4 Dr XL Ext Cab LB	12120	13191	14977
4 Dr XL Ext Cab SB	12013	13075	14846
4 Dr XLT 4WD Crew Cab LB	16385	17834	20249
4 Dr XLT 4WD Crew Cab SB	16289	17729	20130
4 Dr XLT 4WD Ext Cab LB	15457	16824	19101
4 Dr XLT 4WD Ext Cab SB	15354	16712	18974
4 Dr XLT Crew Cab LB	14774	16081	18258
4 Dr XLT Crew Cab SB	14651	15947	18106
4 Dr XLT Ext Cab LB	13844	15068	17108
4 Dr XLT Ext Cab SB	13724	14938	16960

Options	Price
6.8L V10 SOHC 20V FI Engine	+353
7.3L V8 Turbodiesel OHV 16V Engine	+2849
AM/FM/CD Changer Audio System	+124
Air Conditioning [Opt on XL]	+474
Automatic 4-Speed Transmission	+645
Bucket Seats [Opt on XL]	+118
Heated Front and Rear Seats [Opt on Lariat]	+130

Options	Price
Leather Seats [Opt on XLT]	+291
Limited Slip Differential	+168
Park Distance Control (Rear) [Opt on Lariat,XLT]	+144
Power Driver Seat [Std on Lariat]	+171
Power Passenger Seat [Std on Lariat]	+341
Tinted Glass [Opt on XLT]	+118
Two-Tone Paint	+132

2001

A trailer tow package is standard on all models, as is four-wheel ABS. XLT and Lariat models can be equipped with an ultrasonic reverse vehicle-aid sensor, an in-dash six-disc CD changer and chrome tubular cab steps. Heated seats are available on Lariat models. Rounding out the 2001 changes are minor interior updates and a horsepower upgrade for the 7.3-liter Power Stroke turbodiesel engine.

Mileage Category: K

Body Styles	Trade	Private	Dealer
2 Dr XL 4WD Std Cab LB	10779	12386	13870
2 Dr XL Std Cab LB	9451	10860	12161
2 Dr XLT 4WD Std Cab LB	12066	13865	15526
2 Dr XLT Std Cab LB	10666	12257	13725
4 Dr Lariat 4WD Crew Cab LB	14716	16910	18936
4 Dr Lariat 4WD Crew Cab SB	14417	16567	18551
4 Dr Lariat 4WD Ext Cab LB	13958	16039	17960
4 Dr Lariat 4WD Ext Cab SB	13870	15939	17848
4 Dr Lariat Crew Cab LB	13382	15378	17220
4 Dr Lariat Crew Cab SB	13303	15287	17118
4 Dr Lariat Ext Cab LB	12621	14503	16240
4 Dr Lariat Ext Cab SB	12525	14393	16117
4 Dr XL 4WD Crew Cab LB	12400	14249	15956
4 Dr XL 4WD Crew Cab SB	12322	14160	15856

Body Styles	Trade	Private	Dealer
4 Dr XL 4WD Ext Cab LB	11815	13577	15203
4 Dr XL 4WD Ext Cab SB	11743	13494	15110
4 Dr XL Crew Cab LB	11044	12691	14211
4 Dr XL Crew Cab SB	10963	12598	14107
4 Dr XL Ext Cab LB	10493	12058	13502
4 Dr XL Ext Cab SB	10406	11958	13390
4 Dr XLT 4WD Crew Cab LB	13850	15915	17822
4 Dr XLT 4WD Crew Cab SB	13769	15822	17717
4 Dr XLT 4WD Ext Cab LB	13104	15058	16861
4 Dr XLT 4WD Ext Cab SB	13017	14958	16750
4 Dr XLT Crew Cab LB	12479	14340	16058
4 Dr XLT Crew Cab SB	12374	14219	15922
4 Dr XLT Ext Cab LB	11736	13486	15101
4 Dr XLT Ext Cab SB	11634	13369	14970

Options	Price
6.8L V10 SOHC 20V FI Engine	+316
7.3L V8 Turbodiesel OHV 16V Engine	+2487
Air Conditioning [Opt on XL]	+424
Automatic 4-Speed Transmission	+577
Heated Front Seats [Opt on Lariat]	+116

Options	Price
Limited Slip Differential	+150
Park Distance Control (Rear) [Opt on Lariat,XLT]	+129
Power Driver Seat [Opt on XLT]	+153
Two-Tone Paint	+119

2000

Four-wheel antilock brakes are now standard on F-250 and F-350 trucks with Lariat trim levels. XL trim level trucks now have optional bucket seats. Clean fuel (LEV) gasoline engines are standard on all Super Duty trucks. Power windows and locks are now standard on XLT trim levels. The trailer/tow mirrors now telescope manually. Rear bumpers are standard on all F-250 and F-350 pickups. All Super Duty trucks get new interior and exterior colors.

Mileage Category: K

Body Styles	TMV Pricing		
	Trade	Private	Dealer
2 Dr Lariat 4WD Std Cab LB	11407	13322	15199
2 Dr Lariat Std Cab LB	9709	11339	12937
2 Dr XL 4WD Std Cab LB	9203	10748	12262
2 Dr XL Std Cab LB	8001	9344	10661
2 Dr XLT 4WD Std Cab LB	10283	12009	13701
2 Dr XLT Std Cab LB	9043	10561	12049
4 Dr Lariat 4WD Crew Cab LB	12881	15043	17163
4 Dr Lariat 4WD Crew Cab SB	12704	14837	16927
4 Dr Lariat 4WD Ext Cab LB	12054	14078	16061
4 Dr Lariat 4WD Ext Cab SB	11812	13795	15738
4 Dr Lariat Crew Cab LB	11731	13700	15630
4 Dr Lariat Crew Cab SB	11638	13592	15507
4 Dr Lariat Ext Cab LB	10609	12390	14135
4 Dr Lariat Ext Cab SB	10495	12256	13983
4 Dr XL 4WD Crew Cab LB	10733	12534	14300

Body Styles	TMV Pricing		
	Trade	Private	Dealer
4 Dr XL 4WD Crew Cab SB	10683	12476	14234
4 Dr XL 4WD Ext Cab LB	10157	11862	13533
4 Dr XL 4WD Ext Cab SB	10113	11811	13475
4 Dr XL Crew Cab LB	9447	11033	12588
4 Dr XL Crew Cab SB	9363	10935	12476
4 Dr XL Ext Cab LB	8953	10456	11929
4 Dr XL Ext Cab SB	8865	10353	11812
4 Dr XLT 4WD Crew Cab LB	12120	14155	16149
4 Dr XLT 4WD Crew Cab SB	12006	14021	15997
4 Dr XLT 4WD Ext Cab LB	11501	13432	15324
4 Dr XLT 4WD Ext Cab SB	11431	13350	15231
4 Dr XLT Crew Cab LB	10639	12425	14175
4 Dr XLT Crew Cab SB	10562	12335	14073
4 Dr XLT Ext Cab LB	9831	11481	13099
4 Dr XLT Ext Cab SB	9786	11429	13039

Options	Price
6.8L V10 SOHC 20V FI Engine	+283
7.3L V8 Turbodiesel OHV 16V Engine	+2060
Air Conditioning	+379
Aluminum/Alloy Wheels	+179
Antilock Brakes	+320
Automatic 4-Speed Transmission	+516

Options	Price
Camper/Towing Package	+189
Captain Chairs (2)	+231
Limited Slip Differential	+134
Power Driver Seat [Opt on XLT]	+170
Side Steps [Opt on XL,XLT]	+139

1999

The all-new Super Duty F-Series is a full-size truck developed and built on a separate platform from the under-8,500lb GVWR F150 and F250. For '99 the Super Duty is available in Regular Cab, four-door Super Cab or Crew Cab models, as well as in a class A Motor Home Chassis model.

Mileage Category: K

Body Styles	TMV Pricing		
	Trade	Private	Dealer
2 Dr Lariat 4WD Std Cab LB	9139	10978	12893
2 Dr Lariat Std Cab LB	8041	9659	11344
2 Dr XL 4WD Std Cab LB	7919	9513	11173
2 Dr XL Std Cab LB	6822	8195	9625
2 Dr XLT 4WD Std Cab LB	8408	10100	11862
2 Dr XLT Std Cab LB	7310	8781	10313
4 Dr Lariat 4WD Crew Cab LB	10442	12544	14731
4 Dr Lariat 4WD Crew Cab SB	10371	12458	14631
4 Dr Lariat 4WD Ext Cab LB	9755	11719	13763
4 Dr Lariat 4WD Ext Cab SB	9759	11724	13769
4 Dr Lariat Crew Cab LB	9343	11224	13181
4 Dr Lariat Crew Cab SB	9274	11140	13083
4 Dr Lariat Ext Cab LB	8659	10401	12215
4 Dr Lariat Ext Cab SB	8588	10316	12115
4 Dr XL 4WD Crew Cab LB	9222	11079	13011

Body Styles	TMV Pricing		
	Trade	Private	Dealer
4 Dr XL 4WD Crew Cab SB	9154	10996	12914
4 Dr XL 4WD Ext Cab LB	8613	10347	12151
4 Dr XL 4WD Ext Cab SB	8772	10538	12377
4 Dr XL Crew Cab LB	8126	9762	11464
4 Dr XL Crew Cab SB	8055	9676	11364
Ext Cab LB	7515	9028	10602
4 Dr XL Ext Cab SB	7444	8942	10501
4 Dr XLT 4WD Crew Cab LB	9714	11669	13703
4 Dr XLT 4WD Crew Cab SB	9641	11582	13602
4 Dr XLT 4WD Ext Cab LB	9100	10932	12839
4 Dr XLT 4WD Ext Cab SB	9032	10849	12741
4 Dr XLT Crew Cab LB	8615	10349	12153
4 Dr XLT Crew Cab SB	8544	10263	12052
4 Dr XLT Ext Cab LB	8004	9615	11292
4 Dr XLT Ext Cab SB	7932	9529	11191

Options	Price
6.8L V10 SOHC 20V FI Engine	+136
7.3L V8 Turbodiesel OHV 16V Engine	+1679
AM/FM/Cassette/CD Audio System	+126
Air Conditioning	+312
Aluminum/Alloy Wheels	+124
Antilock Brakes	+293
Automatic 4-Speed Transmission	+387

Options	Price
Camper/Towing Package	+115
Leather Seats	+214
Limited Slip Differential	+124
Rear Bench Seat [Opt on XL Ext Cab]	+161
Side Steps [Opt on XL,XLT]	+115
Skid Plates	+115

F-350

1997

While its younger siblings receive complete redesigns, the elder 350 remains virtually unchanged. The 7.3L diesel receives minor improvements and the three-speed automatic transmission is eliminated.

Mileage Category: K

Body Styles	Trade	Private	Dealer
2 Dr XL 4WD Std Cab LB	5716	7163	8932
2 Dr XL Ext Cab LB	5681	7120	8878
2 Dr XL Std Cab LB	4793	6007	7490
2 Dr XLT 4WD Std Cab LB	6241	7821	9753
2 Dr XLT Ext Cab LB	6035	7564	9432

Options	Price
7.3L V8 Turbodiesel OHV 16V Engine	+1115
Air Conditioning [Opt on XL]	+236

Body Styles	Trade	Private	Dealer
2 Dr XLT Std Cab LB	5498	6891	8594
4 Dr XL 4WD Crew Cab LB	6587	8255	10294
4 Dr XL Crew Cab LB	5842	7322	9130
4 Dr XLT 4WD Crew Cab LB	7356	9219	11497
4 Dr XLT Crew Cab LB	6404	8026	10008

Options	Price
Automatic 4-Speed Transmission	+285
Dual Rear Wheels	+230

1996

Minimal changes include an improved hub-locking system and transfer case for all 4WD models. The 7.5L V8 receives a standard integral oil cooler, and a throttle-control module for power takeoffs with the 7.3L diesel is now optional. Interior improvements include black finish on instrument panels, a revised seat design with integrated headrest and Automatic Locking Restraint/Emergency Locking Restraint safety belts for all outboard seating positions. A standard slotted-style front bumper and trailer tow wiring harness (except chassis cab) complete the changes.

Mileage Category: K

Body Styles	Trade	Private	Dealer
2 Dr XL 4WD Std Cab LB	4634	5980	7839
2 Dr XL Ext Cab LB	4653	6005	7871
2 Dr XL Std Cab LB	3996	5156	6759
2 Dr XLT 4WD Std Cab LB	5164	6664	8736
2 Dr XLT Ext Cab LB	4990	6439	8441

Options	Price
7.3L V8 Turbodiesel OHV 16V Engine	+1025
Air Conditioning [Opt on XL]	+210
Automatic 3-Speed Transmission	+194

Body Styles	Trade	Private	Dealer
2 Dr XLT Std Cab LB	4425	5710	7485
4 Dr XL 4WD Crew Cab LB	5393	6960	9123
4 Dr XL Crew Cab LB	4750	6130	8035
4 Dr XLT 4WD Crew Cab LB	5944	7671	10056
4 Dr XLT Crew Cab LB	5237	6758	8859

Options	Price
Automatic 4-Speed Transmission	+260
Dual Rear Wheels	+151
Split Front Bench Seat [Opt on XLT]	+137

1995

Mirroring that of its smaller F-250 sibling, the F-Super Duty's Stripped Commercial Chassis is deleted, optional privacy glass now includes manual-sliding rear windows (when equipped), forged aluminum wheels are offered and cab steps on regular and SuperCab Styleside trims are available.

Mileage Category: K

Body Styles	Trade	Private	Dealer
2 Dr XL 4WD Std Cab LB	3713	4868	6792
2 Dr XL Ext Cab LB	3825	5015	6998
2 Dr XL Std Cab LB	3346	4387	6122
2 Dr XLT 4WD Std Cab LB	4178	5478	7645
2 Dr XLT Ext Cab LB	4052	5313	7415

Options	Price
7.3L V8 Turbodiesel OHV 16V Engine	+856
7.5L V8 OHV 16V FI Engine	+87
Air Conditioning [Opt on XL]	+180
Automatic 3-Speed Transmission	+167

Body Styles	Trade	Private	Dealer
2 Dr XLT Std Cab LB	3736	4899	6836
4 Dr XL 4WD Crew Cab LB	4333	5681	7928
4 Dr XL Crew Cab LB	3776	4950	6906
4 Dr XLT 4WD Crew Cab LB	4821	6321	8822
4 Dr XLT Crew Cab LB	4188	5491	7663

Options	Price
Automatic 4-Speed Transmission	+219
Dual Rear Wheels	+131
Power Sunroof	+180

F-350 Super Duty

2004

Mileage Category: K

Body Styles	Trade	Private	Dealer
2 Dr XL 4WD Std Cab LB	16628	17763	19655
2 Dr XL Std Cab LB	14596	15722	17599
2 Dr XLT 4WD Std Cab LB	19504	20910	23252
2 Dr XLT Std Cab LB	16946	18082	19976
4 Dr Lariat 4WD Crew Cab LB	25060	26599	29165
4 Dr Lariat 4WD Crew Cab SB	24929	26468	29034
4 Dr Lariat 4WD Ext Cab LB	23377	24841	27282
4 Dr Lariat 4WD Ext Cab SB	23244	24708	27149
4 Dr Lariat Crew Cab LB	23190	24654	27095
4 Dr Lariat Crew Cab SB	23058	24522	26963

Body Styles	Trade	Private	Dealer
4 Dr Lariat Ext Cab LB	21052	22441	24757
4 Dr Lariat Ext Cab SB	20920	22309	24625
4 Dr XL 4WD Crew Cab LB	20242	21781	24347
4 Dr XL 4WD Crew Cab SB	20109	21648	24214
4 Dr XL 4WD Ext Cab LB	19201	20665	23106
4 Dr XL 4WD Ext Cab SB	19070	20534	22975
4 Dr XL Crew Cab LB	18011	19475	21916
4 Dr XL Crew Cab SB	17879	19343	21784
4 Dr XL Ext Cab LB	16492	17619	19497
4 Dr XL Ext Cab SB	16382	17522	19423

2004 (cont'd)

The F-350 incorporates minor changes for 2004, including a reclining front bench seat, 60/40-split rear seat in crew-cab models, newly available foglights on the XLT 4x2 and a two-tone paint scheme on the Lariat and Harley-Davidson packages. All F-350s sold in California now have a 3.73 rear axle as standard equipment. An AM/FM stereo with single CD player is now standard on the XLT, while a cassette stereo is optional. Finally, a power-sliding rear window is available (late in the model year) on SuperCab and Super Crew models.

Body Styles	Trade	Private	Dealer
4 Dr XLT 4WD Crew Cab LB	23573	25112	27678
4 Dr XLT 4WD Crew Cab SB	23441	24980	27546
4 Dr XLT 4WD Ext Cab LB	22284	23673	25989
4 Dr XLT 4WD Ext Cab SB	22152	23541	25857

Body Styles	Trade	Private	Dealer
4 Dr XLT Crew Cab LB	21456	22920	25361
4 Dr XLT Crew Cab SB	21324	22788	25229
4 Dr XLT Ext Cab LB	19713	21102	23418
4 Dr XLT Ext Cab SB	19581	20970	23286

Options	Price
18 Inch Wheels [Opt on Lariat Crew 4WD SRW]	+780
6.0L V8 Turbodiesel OHV 32V Engine	+5085
6.8L V10 SOHC 20V FI Engine	+600
AM/FM/CD Changer Audio System [Opt on Lariat, XLT]	+300
Air Conditioning [Opt on XL]	+850
Aluminum/Alloy Wheels [Opt on XLT]	+185
Automatic 4-Speed Transmission	+1095
Automatic 5-Speed Transmission	+1480
Automatic On/Off Headlights	+125
Bucket Seats [Opt on XL]	+130
Chrome Bumpers [Opt on XL]	+175
Cruise Control [Opt on XL]	+200
Dual Rear Wheels	+605
Fog Lights	+140
Harley Davidson Package [Opt on Lariat Crew 4WD SRW]	+4345
Heated Drivers Seat [Opt on Lariat]	+220
Keyless Entry System	+150
King Ranch Package [Opt on Lariat]	+2995

Options	Price
Leather Seats [Opt on XLT]	+415
Leather Steering Wheel [Opt on XLT]	+125
Limited Slip Differential	+300
Park Distance Control (Rear)	+245
Power Adjustable Foot Pedals	+120
Power Driver Seat [Opt on XLT]	+290
Power Moonroof [Opt on Lariat, XLT]	+810
Power Passenger Seat [Opt on XLT]	+290
Power Rear Window [Opt on Lariat]	+125
Power Retractable Mirrors [Opt on Lariat, XLT]	+220
Running Boards [Opt on XL, XLT]	+320
Side Steps [Opt on XL, XLT, Lariat]	+300
Sliding Rear Window	+125
Split Front Bench Seat [Opt on XL, XLT Ext, Crew]	+400
Tilt Steering Wheel [Opt on XL]	+185
Trailer Hitch	+175
Two-Tone Paint [Opt on Lariat, XLT]	+225

2003

Mileage Category: K

The 2003 model year sees a new FX4 Off-Road Package with skid plates, Rancho front and rear shocks, a steering damper and decals. The regular off-road package is no longer available, but a skid plate package can still be had on all 4WD trucks. All XLs can be had with a vinyl 40/20/40 reclining split bench that has a fold-down armrest with a console and cupholders. Ford has also upgraded seat material quality and installed a tailgate lock on this trim level. If you order a SuperCab or Crew Cab in XLT trim with the Sport Package, you can also order a reverse sensing system and a power driver seat. Late-availability additions include an optional power moonroof for Crew Cabs and optional heated telescoping trailer tow mirrors with integrated turn signals. A King Ranch version of the Crew Cab will also appear later in the year. Finally, the torque rating for the 7.3-liter turbodiesel V8 has been boosted to 525 pound-feet. By mid-year, expect an even more powerful 6.0-liter diesel to appear.

Body Styles	Trade	Private	Dealer
2 Dr XL 4WD Std Cab LB	14677	15810	17697
2 Dr XL Std Cab LB	12787	13774	15418
2 Dr XLT 4WD Std Cab LB	16840	18139	20304
2 Dr XLT Std Cab LB	14895	16044	17960
4 Dr Lariat 4WD Crew Cab LB	21228	22866	25596
4 Dr Lariat 4WD Crew Cab SB	21096	22724	25437
4 Dr Lariat 4WD Ext Cab LB	20053	21600	24179
4 Dr Lariat 4WD Ext Cab SB	19933	21471	24034
4 Dr Lariat Crew Cab LB	19524	21031	23542
4 Dr Lariat Crew Cab SB	19430	20929	23428
4 Dr Lariat Ext Cab LB	18173	19575	21912
4 Dr Lariat Ext Cab SB	18059	19453	21775
4 Dr XL 4WD Crew Cab LB	17120	18441	20642
4 Dr XL 4WD Crew Cab SB	17027	18341	20530

Body Styles	Trade	Private	Dealer
4 Dr XL 4WD Ext Cab LB	16350	17612	19714
4 Dr XL 4WD Ext Cab SB	16214	17465	19550
4 Dr XL Crew Cab LB	15249	16425	18386
4 Dr XL Crew Cab SB	15056	16218	18154
4 Dr XL Ext Cab LB	14438	15552	17409
4 Dr XL Ext Cab SB	14315	15419	17260
4 Dr XLT 4WD Crew Cab LB	19821	21350	23899
4 Dr XLT 4WD Crew Cab SB	19702	21222	23756
4 Dr XLT 4WD Ext Cab LB	18955	20419	22860
4 Dr XLT 4WD Ext Cab SB	18762	20210	22623
4 Dr XLT Crew Cab LB	18071	19466	21790
4 Dr XLT Crew Cab SB	17921	19304	21608
4 Dr XLT Ext Cab LB	17057	18373	20566
4 Dr XLT Ext Cab SB	16845	18145	20311

Options	Price
6.0L V8 Turbodiesel OHV 32V Engine	+3280
7.3L V8 Turbodiesel OHV 16V Engine	+3122
AM/FM/CD Changer Audio System [Opt on Lariat, XLT]	+135
Air Conditioning [Opt on XL]	+519
Aluminum/Alloy Wheels [Opt on XLT]	+119
Automatic 4-Speed Transmission	+706
Automatic 5-Speed Transmission	+955
Captain Chairs (4) [Opt on Lariat]	+226
Cruise Control [Opt on XL]	+119
Dual Rear Wheels	+648
FX4 Off-Road Suspension Package	+145

Options	Price
Heated Drivers Seat [Opt on Lariat]	+142
King Ranch Package [Opt on Lariat]	+1932
Leather Seats [Opt on XLT]	+319
Limited Slip Differential	+193
Park Distance Control (Rear) [Opt on Lariat, XLT]	+158
Power Driver Seat [Opt on XLT]	+187
Power Moonroof [Opt on Lariat, XLT]	+522
Power Passenger Seat [Opt on XLT]	+187
Power Retractable Mirrors [Opt on Lariat, XLT]	+142
Running Boards [Opt on XL, XLT]	+126
Special Leather Seat Trim [Opt on Lariat]	+577

F-350 Super Duty

2003 (cont'd)

Options	Price
Tilt Steering Wheel [Opt on XL]	+116
Tinted Glass [Opt on XLT]	+129

Options	Price
Two-Tone Paint [Opt on Lariat,XLT]	+145

2002

A six-speed manual transmission is now standard with the 5.4- and 6.8-liter V8 gas engines, and the 6.8-liter has been enhanced to provide better performance and shift feel than before. If you order an automatic transmission, a gauge that measures transmission oil temperature replaces the battery gauge, and you can opt to add adjustable pedals to your Super Duty XLT or Lariat truck. Trucks with the Power Stroke diesel get an air filter service indicator. All F-350s get roof ride handles standard for 2002, and the available telescoping trailer mirrors can now be folded forward. SuperCabs have new rear door panel map pockets with molded-in cupholders. XL gets upgraded visors, while XLT and Lariat get new seats with increased width, bolstering and lumbar support; jewellike headlamp lenses and an available Advanced Security Group that includes remote keyless entry, automatic door locks and automatic headlamps. Optional on the XLT Crew Cab and standard on the Lariat Crew Cab is a power front passenger seat. The Lariat also gets a larger standard overhead console with improved storage.

Mileage Category: K

Body Styles	TMV Pricing		
	Trade	Private	Dealer
2 Dr XL 4WD Std Cab LB	12697	13820	15691
2 Dr XL Std Cab LB	11107	12089	13726
2 Dr XLT 4WD Std Cab LB	14396	15669	17790
2 Dr XLT Std Cab LB	12759	13887	15768
4 Dr Lariat 4WD Crew Cab LB	18064	19661	22323
4 Dr Lariat 4WD Crew Cab SB	17957	19544	22190
4 Dr Lariat 4WD Ext Cab LB	17029	18535	21044
4 Dr Lariat 4WD Ext Cab SB	16930	18427	20922
4 Dr Lariat Crew Cab LB	16528	17989	20425
4 Dr Lariat Crew Cab SB	16433	17886	20308
4 Dr Lariat Ext Cab LB	15461	16828	19107
4 Dr Lariat Ext Cab SB	15364	16722	18986
4 Dr XL 4WD Crew Cab LB	14747	16051	18224
4 Dr XL 4WD Crew Cab SB	14694	15993	18159

Body Styles	TMV Pricing		
	Trade	Private	Dealer
4 Dr XL 4WD Ext Cab LB	14125	15374	17455
4 Dr XL 4WD Ext Cab SB	13989	15226	17288
4 Dr XL Crew Cab LB	13175	14340	16281
4 Dr XL Crew Cab SB	13062	14217	16142
4 Dr XL Ext Cab LB	12492	13596	15437
4 Dr XL Ext Cab SB	12394	13490	15317
4 Dr XLT 4WD Crew Cab LB	16814	18301	20779
4 Dr XLT 4WD Crew Cab SB	16709	18186	20648
4 Dr XLT 4WD Ext Cab LB	16039	17457	19821
4 Dr XLT 4WD Ext Cab SB	15952	17362	19713
4 Dr XLT Crew Cab LB	15294	16646	18900
4 Dr XLT Crew Cab SB	15236	16583	18829
4 Dr XLT Ext Cab LB	14443	15720	17848
4 Dr XLT Ext Cab SB	14345	15613	17727

Options	Price
6.8L V10 SOHC 20V FI Engine	+353
7.3L V8 Turbodiesel OHV 16V Engine	+2849
AM/FM/CD Changer Audio System [Opt on Lariat]	+206
Air Conditioning [Opt on XL]	+474
Automatic 4-Speed Transmission	+645
Bucket Seats [Opt on XL]	+118
Dual Rear Wheels	+353
Heated Front Seats [Opt on Lariat]	+130

Options	Price
Leather Seats [Opt on XLT]	+291
Limited Slip Differential	+168
Park Distance Control (Rear) [Opt on Lariat,XLT]	+144
Power Driver Seat [Std on Lariat]	+171
Power Passenger Seat [Std on Lariat]	+341
Premium Audio System	+124
Side Steps [Opt on XLT]	+118
Two-Tone Paint	+132

2001

The Trailer Tow package is standard on all models, as is four-wheel ABS. XLT and Lariat models can be equipped with an ultrasonic reverse vehicle-aid sensor, an in-dash six-disc CD changer and chrome tubular cab steps. Heated seats are available on Lariat models. Rounding out the 2001 changes are minor interior updates and a horsepower upgrade to the 7.3-liter diesel engine.

Mileage Category: K

Body Styles	TMV Pricing		
	Trade	Private	Dealer
2 Dr XL 4WD Std Cab LB	10990	12629	14142
2 Dr XL Std Cab LB	9638	11075	12401
2 Dr XLT 4WD Std Cab LB	12416	14268	15977
2 Dr XLT Std Cab LB	11029	12674	14192
4 Dr Lariat 4WD Crew Cab LB	15008	17246	19311
4 Dr Lariat 4WD Crew Cab SB	14916	17141	19194
4 Dr Lariat 4WD Ext Cab LB	14396	16543	18524
4 Dr Lariat 4WD Ext Cab SB	14313	16448	18418
4 Dr Lariat Crew Cab LB	13741	15790	17682
4 Dr Lariat Crew Cab SB	13660	15697	17577
4 Dr Lariat Ext Cab LB	13055	15001	16798
4 Dr Lariat Ext Cab SB	12967	14901	16686
4 Dr XL 4WD Crew Cab LB	12680	14571	16316
4 Dr XL 4WD Crew Cab SB	12609	14489	16224

Body Styles	TMV Pricing		
	Trade	Private	Dealer
4 Dr XL 4WD Ext Cab LB	12174	13989	15665
4 Dr XL 4WD Ext Cab SB	12080	13881	15544
4 Dr XL Crew Cab LB	11340	13031	14592
4 Dr XL Crew Cab SB	11244	12920	14468
4 Dr XL Ext Cab LB	10808	12419	13907
4 Dr XL Ext Cab SB	10725	12325	13801
4 Dr XLT 4WD Crew Cab LB	14186	16301	18254
4 Dr XLT 4WD Crew Cab SB	14111	16215	18158
4 Dr XLT 4WD Ext Cab LB	13600	15628	17500
4 Dr XLT 4WD Ext Cab SB	13527	15544	17406
4 Dr XLT Crew Cab LB	12922	14849	16628
4 Dr XLT Crew Cab SB	12834	14748	16515
4 Dr XLT Ext Cab LB	12241	14067	15752
4 Dr XLT Ext Cab SB	12163	13977	15651

Options	Price
6.8L V10 SOHC 20V FI Engine	+316
7.3L V8 Turbodiesel OHV 16V Engine	+2302
Air Conditioning [Opt on XL]	+424
Automatic 4-Speed Transmission	+577
Dual Rear Wheels	+448

Options	Price
Heated Front Seats [Opt on Lariat]	+116
Limited Slip Differential	+150
Park Distance Control (Rear) [Opt on Lariat,XLT]	+129
Power Driver Seat [Opt on XLT]	+153
Two-Tone Paint	+119

2000

Four-wheel antilock brakes are now standard on F-250 and F-350 trucks with Lariat trim levels. XL trim level trucks now have optional bucket seats. Clean fuel (LEV) gasoline engines are standard on all Super Duty trucks. Power windows and locks are now standard on XLT trim levels. The trailer/tow mirrors now telescope manually. Rear bumpers are standard on all F-250 and F-350 pickups. All Super Duty trucks get new interior and exterior colors.

Body Styles	TMV Pricing		
	Trade	Private	Dealer
2 Dr Lariat 4WD Std Cab LB	11416	13319	15185
2 Dr Lariat Std Cab LB	10349	12076	13768
2 Dr XL 4WD Std Cab LB	9461	11039	12586
2 Dr XL Std Cab LB	8222	9593	10937
2 Dr XLT 4WD Std Cab LB	10711	12497	14248
2 Dr XLT Std Cab LB	9388	10954	12489
4 Dr Lariat 4WD Crew Cab LB	13327	15550	17729
4 Dr Lariat 4WD Crew Cab SB	12687	14803	16877
4 Dr Lariat 4WD Ext Cab LB	12393	14460	16486
4 Dr Lariat 4WD Ext Cab SB	12262	14307	16311
4 Dr Lariat Crew Cab LB	11741	13699	15618
4 Dr Lariat Crew Cab SB	11631	13571	15473
4 Dr Lariat Ext Cab LB	11093	12943	14757
4 Dr Lariat Ext Cab SB	11035	12875	14679
4 Dr XL 4WD Crew Cab LB	11031	12871	14674

Body Styles	TMV Pricing		
	Trade	Private	Dealer
4 Dr XL 4WD Crew Cab SB	10890	12706	14486
4 Dr XL 4WD Ext Cab LB	10626	12398	14135
4 Dr XL 4WD Ext Cab SB	10575	12338	14067
4 Dr XL Crew Cab LB	9739	11363	12955
4 Dr XL Crew Cab SB	9645	11253	12830
4 Dr XL Ext Cab LB	9267	10813	12328
4 Dr XL Ext Cab SB	9183	10715	12216
4 Dr XLT 4WD Crew Cab LB	12116	14137	16117
4 Dr XLT 4WD Crew Cab SB	12057	14068	16039
4 Dr XLT 4WD Ext Cab LB	11561	13489	15379
4 Dr XLT 4WD Ext Cab SB	11484	13400	15278
4 Dr XLT Crew Cab LB	11046	12888	14694
4 Dr XLT Crew Cab SB	10925	12747	14533
4 Dr XLT Ext Cab LB	10435	12176	13882
4 Dr XLT Ext Cab SB	10398	12132	13832

Options	Price
6.8L V10 SOHC 20V FI Engine	+283
7.3L V8 Turbodiesel OHV 16V Engine	+2060
Air Conditioning	+379
Antilock Brakes	+320
Automatic 4-Speed Transmission	+516

Options	Price
Camper/Towing Package	+162
Dual Rear Wheels	+274
Limited Slip Differential	+134
Power Driver Seat	+137
Side Steps [Opt on XL,XLT]	+139

1999

The all-new Super Duty F-Series is a full-size truck developed and built on a separate platform from the under-8,500-pound GVWR F150 and F250. For '99 the Super Duty is available in Regular Cab, four-door SuperCab or Crew Cab models.

Body Styles	TMV Pricing		
	Trade	Private	Dealer
2 Dr Lariat 4WD Std Cab LB	8942	10803	12740
2 Dr Lariat Std Cab LB	7786	9406	11093
2 Dr XL 4WD Std Cab LB	7674	9271	10934
2 Dr XL Std Cab LB	6396	7727	9112
2 Dr XLT 4WD Std Cab LB	8071	9751	11500
2 Dr XLT Std Cab LB	7207	8706	10267
4 Dr Lariat 4WD Crew Cab LB	10492	12675	14948
4 Dr Lariat 4WD Crew Cab SB	10055	12148	14326
4 Dr Lariat 4WD Ext Cab LB	9531	11515	13579
4 Dr Lariat 4WD Ext Cab SB	9504	11482	13540
4 Dr Lariat Crew Cab LB	9123	11021	12997
4 Dr Lariat Crew Cab SB	9030	10910	12866
4 Dr Lariat Ext Cab LB	8541	10319	12169
4 Dr Lariat Ext Cab SB	8486	10252	12090
4 Dr XL 4WD Crew Cab LB	8978	10847	12792

Body Styles	TMV Pricing		
	Trade	Private	Dealer
4 Dr XL 4WD Crew Cab SB	8930	10788	12722
4 Dr XL 4WD Ext Cab LB	8328	10061	11865
4 Dr XL 4WD Ext Cab SB	8251	9968	11756
4 Dr XL Crew Cab LB	7935	9586	11305
4 Dr XL Crew Cab SB	7868	9505	11209
4 Dr XL Ext Cab LB	7321	8845	10431
4 Dr XL Ext Cab SB	7306	8826	10409
4 Dr XLT 4WD Crew Cab LB	9374	11325	13355
4 Dr XLT 4WD Crew Cab SB	9321	11261	13280
4 Dr XLT 4WD Ext Cab LB	9006	10881	12832
4 Dr XLT 4WD Ext Cab SB	8950	10812	12751
4 Dr XLT Crew Cab LB	8413	10164	11986
4 Dr XLT Crew Cab SB	8383	10128	11944
4 Dr XLT Ext Cab LB	7990	9653	11384
4 Dr XLT Ext Cab SB	7901	9545	11257

Options	Price
6.8L V10 SOHC 20V FI Engine	+136
7.3L V8 Turbodiesel OHV 16V Engine	+1679
AM/FM/Cassette/CD Audio System	+126
Air Conditioning	+312
Antilock Brakes	+293

Options	Price
Automatic 4-Speed Transmission	+387
Camper/Towing Package	+115
Dual Rear Wheels	+225
Leather Seats	+214
Side Steps	+115

Focus

2004

The emissions-friendly 2.3-liter PZEV engine released in limited states in 2003 is now available as an option in all states (it comes standard in California, Massachusetts, New York, Vermont and Maine). The only other notable changes are newly optional leather seating for ZX3 models, and a slightly revised suspension offers improved handling.

Mileage Category: B

Body Styles	TMV Pricing		
	Trade	Private	Dealer
2 Dr ZX3 Hbk	7370	8202	9589
4 Dr LX Sdn	7497	8327	9709
4 Dr SE Sdn	8131	8931	10264
4 Dr SE Wgn	9636	10466	11848

Options	Price
16 Inch Wheels [Opt on ZTS, ZTW]	+130
AM/FM/CD Changer Audio System [Opt on non LX, SE]	+280
Air Conditioning [Opt on ZX3, LX]	+500
Antilock Brakes	+400
Automatic 4-Speed Transmission [Std on Wgn]	+815
Cruise Control [Opt on LX, SE]	+150

Body Styles	TMV Pricing		
	Trade	Private	Dealer
4 Dr ZTS Sdn	8759	9720	11321
4 Dr ZTW Wgn	9953	10970	12665
4 Dr ZX5 Hbk	8483	9500	11195

Options	Price
Front Side Airbag Restraints	+350
Keyless Entry System [Opt on Sdn]	+200
Leather Seats [Opt on ZX3, ZX5, ZTS, ZTW]	+695
Power Moonroof [Opt on ZX3, ZX5, ZTS, ZTW]	+525
Rear Spoiler [Opt on ZTS]	+120

2003

Minor changes are in store for the Focus. Two new trim levels increase the breadth of prices for Ford's economy car; a base trim for the three door hatchback renders air conditioning optional and only comes with a manual transmission. For the five door hatchback, a tilt and telescoping steering wheel, cruise control, front reading lights and a center console are available when you step up to the comfort trim level from the base level. Heated front seats are a new option, as is a traction control and ABS package. New colors for the exterior brighten up the color palette, and the interior is freshened with two new fabric trims. Finally, a CD/MP3 player is now standard on the ZX3 and ZX5. A SVT version of the ZX5 is also scheduled to appear later in the year.

Mileage Category: B

Body Styles	TMV Pricing		
	Trade	Private	Dealer
2 Dr ZX3 Hbk	6004	6757	8013
4 Dr LX Sdn	6118	6885	8164
4 Dr SE Sdn	6549	7371	8741
4 Dr SE Wgn	7995	8998	10669

Options	Price
2.0L I4 DOHC 16V FI Engine [Opt on SE]	+164
AM/FM/CD Changer Audio System	+181
Air Conditioning [Opt on LX, ZX3]	+513
Antilock Brakes	+439
Automatic 4-Speed Transmission [Opt on SE, ZTS, ZX5]	+526
Automatic Stability Control [Opt on ZTS, ZTW]	+371
Cruise Control	+119

Body Styles	TMV Pricing		
	Trade	Private	Dealer
4 Dr ZTS Sdn	7703	8670	10282
4 Dr ZTW Wgn	8777	9879	11716
4 Dr ZX5 Hbk	7371	8297	9839

Options	Price
Front Side Airbag Restraints	+226
Heated Front Seats [Opt on ZTS, ZTW]	+177
Leather Seats [Opt on ZTS, ZTW, ZX5]	+448
Power Moonroof [Opt on ZTS, ZTW, ZX5]	+371
Power Windows [Opt on LX, ZX3]	+142
Special Leather Seat Trim [Opt on ZTS]	+513
Tilt and Telescopic Steering Wheel [Std on ZTS, ZTW]	+129

2002

Four new Focus models debut for 2002: the ZX5 five-door hatchback, the well-equipped ZTW wagon, the sport-tuned SVT hatchback and the Mach Audio ZTS. No matter what Focus you pick in 2002, a power moonroof can now be ordered. The high-end ZTS Sedan loses its standard ABS and crummy fake wood dash trim while gaining a rear spoiler. An in-dash six-disc CD changer is standard on ZX5, ZTS and ZTW but optional on all other Foci except the LX Sedan.

Mileage Category: B

Body Styles	TMV Pricing		
	Trade	Private	Dealer
2 Dr ZX3 Hbk	4600	5270	6387
4 Dr LX Sdn	4633	5331	6494
4 Dr SE Sdn	4901	5638	6867
4 Dr SE Wgn	6060	6972	8493

Options	Price
2.0L I4 DOHC 16V FI Engine [Opt on SE Sdn]	+165
AM/FM/CD Changer Audio System [Opt on ZTS, ZX3]	+165
Air Conditioning [Opt on LX, ZX3]	+468
Antilock Brakes	+400
Automatic 4-Speed Transmission [Std on Wgn]	+480
Automatic Stability Control	+338
Front Side Airbag Restraints	+206

Body Styles	TMV Pricing		
	Trade	Private	Dealer
4 Dr ZTS Sdn	5550	6386	7779
4 Dr ZTW Wgn	6892	7896	9569
4 Dr ZX5 Hbk	6043	6924	8391

Options	Price
Leather Seats [Opt on ZTS, ZX5]	+409
MACH Audio System [Opt on ZTS]	+306
Power Moonroof	+350
Power Windows [Opt on ZX3]	+130
Traction Control System	+147
Xenon Headlamps [Opt on ZTS]	+235

2001

Raising the bar for compact vehicles, Ford is offering its stability system -- called AdvanceTrac -- on ZTS Sedans and ZX3 Hatchbacks. Ford has also made previously optional features standard equipment. Highlights include a driver armrest on every model except LX and power windows on SE Sedans and Wagons. SE Wagons also get the Zetec engine as standard and can be ordered with a manual transmission. A new manual moonroof is offered on the ZX3 and new 16-inch wheels are standard on ZTS Sedans and optional on ZX3 Coupes.

Mileage Category: B

Body Styles	TMV Pricing		
	Trade	Private	Dealer
2 Dr ZX3 Hbk	3611	4492	5306
4 Dr LX Sdn	3757	4676	5524
4 Dr SE Sdn	4041	5027	5937
4 Dr SE Wgn	5069	6307	7450

Options	Price
2.0L I4 DOHC 16V FI Engine [Opt on SE]	+148
Air Conditioning [Opt on LX,SE]	+419
Antilock Brakes [Std on ZTS]	+358
Automatic 4-Speed Transmission [Std on Wgn]	+429
Automatic Stability Control [Opt on Street,ZTS,ZX3]	+303
Compact Disc Changer	+184

Body Styles	TMV Pricing		
	Trade	Private	Dealer
4 Dr Street Sdn	4140	5151	6085
4 Dr Street Wgn	5328	6630	7831
4 Dr ZTS Sdn	4578	5695	6726

Options	Price
Front Side Airbag Restraints	+184
Leather Seats	+366
Moonroof	+261
Power Windows [Std on ZTS]	+118
Traction Control System	+132

2000

This is Ford's all-new "world car" that will be sold initially concurrently with the Escort. Everything from interior room to performance has been addressed to make this European-engineered compact a winner in the small-car segment.

Mileage Category: B

Body Styles	TMV Pricing		
	Trade	Private	Dealer
2 Dr ZX3 Hbk	2744	3673	4584
4 Dr LX Sdn	2874	3847	4801
4 Dr SE Sdn	3320	4445	5547

Options	Price
2.0L I4 DOHC 16V FI Engine [Opt on SE]	+132
Air Conditioning [Opt on LX,SE]	+375
Aluminum/Alloy Wheels [Opt on LX]	+170
Antilock Brakes [Std on ZTS]	+320

Body Styles	TMV Pricing		
	Trade	Private	Dealer
4 Dr SE Wgn	3995	5348	6675
4 Dr Sony Limited Sdn	3704	4959	6189
4 Dr ZTS Sdn	3748	5017	6261

Options	Price
Automatic 4-Speed Transmission [Std on Wgn]	+384
Front Side Airbag Restraints	+165
Kona Mountain Bike Package	+705
Leather Seats	+328

Focus SVT

2004

Mileage Category: B

Body Styles	TMV Pricing		
	Trade	Private	Dealer
2 Dr STD Hbk	12486	13584	15413

Options	Price
Compact Disc Changer	+200
Heated Front Seats	+150
Power Moonroof	+900

Body Styles	TMV Pricing		
	Trade	Private	Dealer
4 Dr STD Hbk	12791	13889	15718

Options	Price
Traction Control System	+245
Xenon Headlamps	+300

The European Appearance package is now available on four-door models, while both two- and four-door models receive new 17-inch six-spoke Euro-flange wheels. Sonic Blue is added as a color choice, coupled with blue seat inserts to tie in the interior. The 100,000-mile powertrain extended service plan is now standard.

2003

A four-door version of the hot-rod Focus hatchback debuts later in the year, making for a more practical choice for those with family obligations.

Mileage Category: B

Body Styles	TMV Pricing		
	Trade	Private	Dealer
2 Dr STD Hbk	10184	11135	12719

Options	Price
AM/FM/CD Changer Audio System	+181
Heated Front Seats	+129
Leather Seats	+448
Power Moonroof	+384

Body Styles	TMV Pricing		
	Trade	Private	Dealer
4 Dr STD Hbk	10646	11690	13430

Options	Price
Premium Audio System	+129
Traction Control System	+126
Xenon Headlamps	+290

2002

Ford's in-house tuning team, known as SVT, works its magic on the Focus ZX3 hatchback. The result is a well-balanced, 170-horsepower canyon carver.

Mileage Category: B

Body Styles	TMV Pricing		
	Trade	Private	Dealer
2 Dr STD Hbk	8587	9525	11089

Options	Price	Options	Price
AM/FM/CD Changer Audio System	+280	Power Moonroof	+350
Heated Front Seats	+118	Premium Audio System	+306

2002 (cont'd)

Options	Price
Traction Control System	+115

Freestar

2004

The Freestar is an all-new minivan that replaces Ford's aged Windstar. Recognizing the increased competition in this segment, the company has incorporated must-haves like a fold-flat third-row seat, rear DVD entertainment system and a power liftgate, while adding new items like side curtain airbags that cover all three rows of seating and an available large-displacement V6 for hauling heavy loads.

Mileage Category: P

Body Styles	TMV Pricing		
	Trade	Private	Dealer
4 Dr Limited Pass Van	17577	18921	21160
4 Dr S Pass Van	11642	12868	14911
4 Dr SE Pass Van	12884	14116	16168

Options	Price
AM/FM/CD Changer Audio System [Opt on SEL, Limited]	+150
Automatic Climate Control (3 Zone) [Opt on S, SE]	+675
Automatic On/Off Headlights [Opt on S, SE, SES]	+140
Captain Chairs (4) [Opt on SE, SES]	+795
Center Console [Opt on non-S, Cargo]	+150
DVD Entertainment System [Opt on non-S, Cargo]	+1395
Front Side Airbag Restraints	+300
Front, Rear and Third Row Head Airbag Restraints	+395
Leather Seats [Opt on SEL]	+890

Body Styles	TMV Pricing		
	Trade	Private	Dealer
4 Dr SEL Pass Van	14424	15661	17722
4 Dr SES Pass Van	13798	15033	17090

Options	Price
Park Distance Control (Rear) [Opt on non-S, Cargo]	+250
Power Adjustable Foot Pedals [Opt on non-S, Cargo]	+145
Power Driver Seat [Opt on SE]	+325
Power Driver Seat w/Memory [Opt on Limited]	+305
Power Heated Mirrors [Opt on SEL]	+130
Power Passenger Seat [Opt on SEL, Limited]	+305
Power Rear Liftgate [Opt on SEL, Limited]	+400
Privacy Glass [Opt on S, Cargo]	+415
Traction Control System [Opt on non-SEL. Limited]	+725

Mustang

2004

With an all-new model scheduled for 2005, there are few changes for '04. All models wear commemorative 40th anniversary exterior badging, while V6 and GT models can be ordered with a full 40th anniversary package that includes additional exterior and interior enhancements.

Mileage Category: E

Body Styles	TMV Pricing		
	Trade	Private	Dealer
2 Dr GT Conv	17303	18588	20728
2 Dr GT Cpe	14081	15309	17355
2 Dr Mach 1 Cpe	18521	19951	22334

Options	Price
AM/FM/CD Changer Audio System [Opt on GT, STD]	+250
Antilock Brakes [Opt on STD]	+400
Automatic 4-Speed Transmission	+815
Cruise Control [Opt on STD]	+250
Leather Seats [Opt on GT, STD]	+595

Body Styles	TMV Pricing		
	Trade	Private	Dealer
2 Dr STD Conv	12514	13695	15663
2 Dr STD Cpe	9996	11187	13172

Options	Price
MACH Audio System [Opt on GT, STD]	+300
Polished Aluminum/Alloy Wheels [Opt on STD]	+520
Power Driver Seat [Opt on STD]	+225
Rear Spoiler [Opt on STD]	+200
Traction Control System [Opt on STD]	+330

2003

Heavily updated is the 2003 SVT Mustang Cobra, which makes 390 horsepower and 390 pound-feet of torque thanks to the addition of an Eaton supercharger. A new six-speed manual transmission drives the rear wheels through a 3.55 rear axle ratio. Larger wheels and tires come standard, along with stiffer springs and a tubular cross brace. Cobra convertibles have a cloth top, while both cars get new seats with upgraded leather and suede upholstery. A limited-production Mach 1 model arrives later in the year with a massaged 4.6-liter V8 engine making at least 300 horsepower and 300 pound-feet of torque, a functional shaker hood with ram-air scoop, black striping, unique leather seating and retro-design Magnum 500 alloy wheels, and, of course, a Mach 460 audio system. Mach 1 can be ordered in a variety of colors with either a manual or automatic transmission. Like the Mustang Bullitt before it, the Mach 1 comes with a lowered, retuned suspension and additional frame rail connectors for a stiffer body. Large 13-inch Brembo front rotors and upgraded calipers are standard. Standard V6 and V8 GT models change little for 2003. A V6 Pony Package includes 16-inch polished alloy wheels and the GT's scooped hood. All V6 models get a new hood design, and four new colors debut.

Mileage Category: E

Body Styles	TMV Pricing		
	Trade	Private	Dealer
2 Dr GT Conv	14932	15930	17594
2 Dr GT Cpe	12656	13502	14912
2 Dr Mach 1 Cpe	16824	17948	19822

Options	Price
AM/FM/CD Changer Audio System [Opt on GT,STD]	+210
Aluminum/Alloy Interior Trim [Opt on GT,STD,MACH 1]	+223
Antilock Brakes [Opt on STD]	+439
Automatic 4-Speed Transmission [Opt on GT,STD,MACH 1]	+526
Cruise Control [Opt on STD]	+119
Leather Seats [Opt on GT,STD]	+384

Body Styles	TMV Pricing		
	Trade	Private	Dealer
2 Dr STD Conv	10848	11861	13548
2 Dr STD Cpe	8489	9308	10672

Options	Price
MACH Audio System [Opt on GT,STD]	+190
Power Driver Seat [Opt on STD]	+158
Rear Spoiler [Opt on STD]	+139
Special Graphics [Opt on STD]	+158
Traction Control System [Opt on STD]	+135

2002

Lower-line V6 models get standard 16-inch alloy wheels and a new hood while losing the fake side scoops. Premium models can be equipped with a Mach 1000 audio system. Both this system and the Mach 460 get speed-sensitive volume. Later this year, an MP3 player will be available. Performance Red paint is replaced with Torch Red.

Mileage Category: E

Body Styles	TMV Pricing		
	Trade	Private	Dealer
2 Dr GT Conv	12774	13991	16020
2 Dr GT Cpe	10590	11599	13280

Options	Price
16 Inch Wheels [Opt on STD]	+191
AM/FM/CD Changer Audio System	+191
Antilock Brakes [Opt on STD]	+400
Automatic 4-Speed Transmission	+383

Body Styles	TMV Pricing		
	Trade	Private	Dealer
2 Dr STD Conv	9160	10033	11488
2 Dr STD Cpe	7299	7994	9153

Options	Price
Leather Seats	+309
MACH Audio System	+174
Power Driver Seat [Opt on STD Cpe]	+147
Traction Control System [Opt on STD]	+135

2001

GT models get unique hood and side scoops. They also receive standard 17-inch wheels, and V6 Convertibles get 16-inch wheels as standard. All cars have a revised center console and blacked-out headlights and spoilers. The Mach 460 stereo system comes with an in-dash six-disc CD changer. A new "premium" trim line is created for both V6 and V8 models.

Mileage Category: E

Body Styles	TMV Pricing		
	Trade	Private	Dealer
2 Dr GT Bullitt Cpe	11217	12920	14492
2 Dr GT Conv	11078	12760	14313
2 Dr GT Cpe	8789	10124	11356

Options	Price
AM/FM/Cassette/CD Changer Audio System	+184
Antilock Brakes [Opt on STD]	+358
Automatic 4-Speed Transmission	+429

Body Styles	TMV Pricing		
	Trade	Private	Dealer
2 Dr STD Conv	7999	9214	10335
2 Dr STD Cpe	6116	7045	7902

Options	Price
Leather Seats	+248
Sport Seats [Opt on STD Conv]	+132
Traction Control System	+132

2000

The Mustang has three updated colors: Performance Red, Amazon Green and Sunburst Gold. A child safety-seat anchoring system is standard on both the coupe and convertible. New 16-inch wheels and tires are offered as an option on appearance package-equipped V6 Mustangs. The 2000 Mustang also features a tri-color bar emblem on the sides of the front fenders.

Mileage Category: E

Body Styles	TMV Pricing		
	Trade	Private	Dealer
2 Dr GT Conv	8995	10573	12120
2 Dr GT Cpe	7128	8380	9606

Options	Price
Antilock Brakes [Opt on STD]	+320
Automatic 4-Speed Transmission	+384

Body Styles	TMV Pricing		
	Trade	Private	Dealer
2 Dr STD Conv	6965	8187	9384
2 Dr STD Cpe	5040	5925	6792

Options	Price
Leather Seats	+236
MACH Audio System	+186

1999

Ford gives its sports car fresh styling and more motor. The 3.8-liter V6 engine makes 190 horsepower and 220 pound-feet of torque. The SOHC V8 found in GT models gets an 16-percent increase in horsepower. Improvements to the V6 and GT suspension and steering gear, as well as a styling update.

Body Styles	TMV Pricing		
	Trade	Private	Dealer
2 Dr GT Conv	7240	8852	10530
2 Dr GT Cpe	5950	7275	8654

Options	Price
AM/FM/Cassette Audio System	+154
Antilock Brakes [Opt on STD]	+293
Automatic 4-Speed Transmission	+317
Bucket Seats	+194

Body Styles	TMV Pricing		
	Trade	Private	Dealer
2 Dr STD Conv	5613	6864	8166
2 Dr STD Cpe	4284	5238	6231

Options	Price
Compact Disc Changer [Opt on STD]	+174
Leather Seats	+214
Spoke Wheels	+194

1998

Mileage Category: E

Body Styles	TMV Pricing		
	Trade	Private	Dealer
2 Dr GT Conv	5628	7095	8750
2 Dr GT Cpe	4352	5486	6765

Options	Price
AM/FM/Cassette Audio System	+125
Antilock Brakes	+240

Body Styles	TMV Pricing		
	Trade	Private	Dealer
2 Dr STD Conv	4167	5253	6477
2 Dr STD Cpe	3388	4270	5266

Options	Price
Automatic 4-Speed Transmission	+259
Leather Seats	+159

The Mustang gains standard equipment, such as power windows and door locks, air conditioning, and premium sound. Options are shuffled as well, making it easier to choose the car you want. GT models get a slight boost in power.

1997

GT models and base convertibles get new interior color options, and cars equipped with an automatic transmission get a thicker shift lever. New 17-inch aluminum wheels are optional on the GT. The Passive Anti-Theft System has been introduced to all Mustangs.

Mileage Category: E

Body Styles	TMV Pricing		
	Trade	Private	Dealer
2 Dr GT Conv	4780	6127	7773

Body Styles	TMV Pricing		
	Trade	Private	Dealer
2 Dr GT Cpe	3448	4420	5608

Mustang/SVT Cobra

1997 (cont'd)

Body Styles	TMV Pricing		
	Trade	Private	Dealer
2 Dr STD Conv	3712	4758	6036

Options	Price
AM/FM/Cassette/CD Audio System	+116
Air Conditioning	+262
Antilock Brakes	+222
Automatic 4-Speed Transmission	+239

Body Styles	TMV Pricing		
	Trade	Private	Dealer
2 Dr STD Cpe	2871	3680	4669

Options	Price
Bucket Seats	+147
Leather Seats	+147
Premium Audio System [Opt on Conv]	+116

1996

Ford plugs a 4.6-liter modular V8 into its pony car. Base cars also get engine improvements, and all Mustangs get minor styling revisions. The GTS model, a midyear 1995 V8 base Mustang, has been dropped.

Mileage Category: E

Body Styles	TMV Pricing		
	Trade	Private	Dealer
2 Dr GT Conv	4253	5547	7334
2 Dr GT Cpe	3032	3954	5226

Options	Price
17 Inch Wheels [Opt on GT]	+116
Air Conditioning	+234
Antilock Brakes	+197

Body Styles	TMV Pricing		
	Trade	Private	Dealer
2 Dr STD Conv	3049	3976	5257
2 Dr STD Cpe	2226	2903	3838

Options	Price
Automatic 4-Speed Transmission	+213
Leather Seats	+130

1995

A power driver seat moves from the standard equipment list to the options list. A powerful new stereo with a CD changer also debuts on the options list.

Mileage Category: E

Body Styles	TMV Pricing		
	Trade	Private	Dealer
2 Dr GT Conv	3451	4540	6356
2 Dr GT Cpe	2785	3599	4956
2 Dr GTS Cpe	2279	2999	4198

Options	Price
AM/FM/Cassette/CD Audio System	+89
Air Conditioning	+202
Antilock Brakes	+170

Body Styles	TMV Pricing		
	Trade	Private	Dealer
2 Dr STD Conv	2675	3520	4928
2 Dr STD Cpe	1879	2472	3461

Options	Price
Automatic 4-Speed Transmission	+184
Compact Disc Changer	+101
Leather Seats [Opt on GT]	+135

Mustang SVT Cobra

2004

Mileage Category: E

Body Styles	TMV Pricing		
	Trade	Private	Dealer
2 Dr S/C Conv	27145	28787	31523

Options	Price
17 Inch Wheels - Chrome	+695
Chrome Wheels	+400

Body Styles	TMV Pricing		
	Trade	Private	Dealer
2 Dr S/C Cpe	23182	24825	27564

Options	Price
Special Factory Paint	+2500
Special Leather Seat Trim	+625

Changes to the Cobra are minimal for 2004. Screaming Yellow and Competition Orange are new exterior colors, and dark seat inserts are available this year. The Cobra can also be equipped with a limited-edition Mystichrome Appearance Package that provides a "color-shifting" exterior paint job and interior leather.

2003

Heavily updated is the 2003 SVT Mustang Cobra, which makes 390 horsepower and 390 pound-feet of torque thanks to the addition of an Eaton supercharger. A new six-speed manual transmission drives the rear wheels through a 3.55 rear axle ratio. Larger wheels and tires come standard, along with stiffer springs and a tubular strut tower brace. Cobra convertibles have a cloth top, while both cars get new seats with upgraded leather and suede upholstery.

Mileage Category: E

Body Styles	TMV Pricing		
	Trade	Private	Dealer
2 Dr 10th Anniv S/C Conv	26127	27873	30783
2 Dr 10th Anniv S/C Cpe	23281	24837	27431

Options	Price
17 Inch Wheels - Chrome	+448

Body Styles	TMV Pricing		
	Trade	Private	Dealer
2 Dr S/C Conv	23978	25581	28252
2 Dr S/C Cpe	21221	22639	25001

2001

After a one-year hiatus, the Ford SVT Mustang Cobra returns to the Mustang stable.

Mileage Category: E

Body Styles	TMV Pricing		
	Trade	Private	Dealer
2 Dr STD Conv	15361	17694	19847

Body Styles	TMV Pricing		
	Trade	Private	Dealer
2 Dr STD Cpe	13512	15563	17457

1999

A new SVT Cobra debuts, boasting 320 ponies, an independent rear suspension and the fresh but controversial styling that all Mustangs received this year.

Mileage Category: E

Body Styles	TMV Pricing			Body Styles	TMV Pricing		
	Trade	Private	Dealer		Trade	Private	Dealer
2 Dr STD Conv	9884	12086	14377	2 Dr STD Cpe	8498	10390	12360

Options	Price
Leather Seats	+220

1998

Mileage Category: E

Body Styles	TMV Pricing			Body Styles	TMV Pricing		
	Trade	Private	Dealer		Trade	Private	Dealer
2 Dr STD Conv	7670	9669	11923	2 Dr STD Cpe	6650	8383	10338

Options	Price	Options	Price
AM/FM/Cassette Audio System	+125	Leather Seats	+180

The Cobra sees virtually no changes as a heavily revamped version is due next year.

1997

After last year's significant underhood upgrade, the SVT folks saw no reason to make changes to the Cobra for this year.

Mileage Category: E

Body Styles	TMV Pricing			Body Styles	TMV Pricing		
	Trade	Private	Dealer		Trade	Private	Dealer
2 Dr STD Conv	6586	8443	10712	2 Dr STD Cpe	5655	7249	9198

Options	Price	Options	Price
AM/FM/Cassette/CD Audio System	+116	Leather Seats	+147

1996

Ford's most potent pony gets a 32-valve, 305-horsepower version of the Mustang's new 4.6-liter V8. The Cobra also receives the subtle styling tweaks, such as the vertically themed taillights, that its stablemates received this year.

Mileage Category: E

Body Styles	TMV Pricing			Body Styles	TMV Pricing		
	Trade	Private	Dealer		Trade	Private	Dealer
2 Dr STD Conv	5480	7147	9448	2 Dr STD Cpe	4935	6436	8508

Options	Price	Options	Price
Leather Seats	+148	Special Factory Paint	+420

1995

No changes for this year.

Mileage Category: E

Body Styles	TMV Pricing			Body Styles	TMV Pricing		
	Trade	Private	Dealer		Trade	Private	Dealer
2 Dr R Cpe	5387	7088	9923	2 Dr STD Cpe	3767	4957	6939
2 Dr STD Conv	4456	5863	8209				

Options	Price	Options	Price
AM/FM/Cassette/CD Audio System	+89	Automatic 4-Speed Transmission	+184
Air Conditioning	+202	Leather Seats	+135

Probe

1997

Mileage Category: E

Body Styles	TMV Pricing			Body Styles	TMV Pricing		
	Trade	Private	Dealer		Trade	Private	Dealer
2 Dr GT Hbk	2377	3203	4212	2 Dr STD Hbk	2002	2698	3548

Options	Price	Options	Price
AM/FM/CD Audio System	+126	Automatic 4-Speed Transmission	+262
Air Conditioning	+262	Leather Seats	+147
Aluminum/Alloy Wheels [Opt on STD]	+138	Power Sunroof	+181
Antilock Brakes	+222		

Ford adds a GTS Sport Appearance Package to the GT's option sheet. The package includes a rear spoiler, racing stripes and 16-inch chrome wheels.

Ford
Probe/Ranger

1996

Ford concentrates on the SE and GT trim levels this year, revising and simplifying options lists and making minor cosmetic and trim revisions.

Mileage Category: E

Body Styles	TMV Pricing		
	Trade	Private	Dealer
2 Dr GT Hbk	1794	2412	3266
2 Dr SE Hbk	1553	2088	2826

Options	Price
Air Conditioning	+234
Aluminum/Alloy Wheels	+139
Antilock Brakes	+197

Body Styles	TMV Pricing		
	Trade	Private	Dealer
2 Dr STD Hbk	1458	1961	2655

Options	Price
Automatic 4-Speed Transmission	+213
Leather Seats	+130
Power Sunroof	+161

1995

Base and GT models receive new taillights. GTs receive 16-inch directional wheels. The rear-window wiper washer, four-way seat-height adjuster and graphic equalizer have been deleted from the options list.

Mileage Category: E

Body Styles	TMV Pricing		
	Trade	Private	Dealer
2 Dr GT Hbk	1290	1786	2613
2 Dr SE Hbk	1295	1789	2612

Options	Price
AM/FM/CD Audio System	+97
AM/FM/Cassette/CD Audio System	+124
Air Conditioning [Std on SE]	+202
Aluminum/Alloy Wheels	+106
Antilock Brakes	+170

Body Styles	TMV Pricing		
	Trade	Private	Dealer
2 Dr STD Hbk	1127	1556	2272

Options	Price
Automatic 4-Speed Transmission	+184
Chrome Wheels	+88
Leather Seats	+113
Power Sunroof	+139

Ranger

2004

All Rangers get a more aggressive raised hood and a partitioned grille that more closely matches that of other Ford trucks. Inside, seats have been revised to improve comfort, and leather upholstery is a new option. A new leather-wrapped, four-spoke steering wheel is available on some models, as is a floor console. New white-faced gauges are standard on all models, except the base XL. The Tremor model's 510-watt stereo now has MP3 capability, and other models are eligible for a 290-watt Pioneer Sound package with an in-dash CD/MP3 player. Additionally, the Tremor is available with four-wheel drive this year, and the off-road-ready FX4 gets an electronic shift-on-the-fly transfer case. Sixteen-inch aluminum wheels are optional on two-wheel-drive Edge models, and an engine block heater is standard in select states.

Mileage Category: J

Body Styles	TMV Pricing		
	Trade	Private	Dealer
2 Dr Edge 4WD Std Cab SB	11276	12412	14305
2 Dr Edge Ext Cab SB	10127	11300	13256
2 Dr Edge Std Cab SB	8753	9814	11582
2 Dr Tremor Ext Cab SB	11311	12484	14440
2 Dr XL 4WD Ext Cab SB	14077	15540	17980
2 Dr XL 4WD Std Cab LB	11534	12705	14657
2 Dr XL Ext Cab SB	9808	10981	12937
2 Dr XL Std Cab LB	8347	9408	11176
2 Dr XL Std Cab SB	7675	8736	10504
2 Dr XLT 4WD Ext Cab SB	12380	13628	15709
2 Dr XLT Ext Cab SB	9898	11071	13027

Options	Price
4.0L V6 SOHC 12V FI Engine [Opt on XLT, Edge, Tremor]	+720
AM/FM/CD Changer/MP3 Audio System [Opt on 4WD non-Std Tremor, 2WD Ext Edge, XLT]	+295
Aluminum/Alloy Wheels [Opt on Edge 2WD]	+205
Bed Liner	+235
Chrome Bumpers [Opt on 2WD XLT]	+200

Body Styles	TMV Pricing		
	Trade	Private	Dealer
2 Dr XLT Std Cab LB	9986	11132	13043
2 Dr XLT Std Cab SB	8543	9604	11372
4 Dr Edge 4WD Ext Cab SB	12847	14095	16176
4 Dr Edge Ext Cab SB	12015	13188	15144
4 Dr Tremor 4WD Ext Cab SB	13916	15164	17245
4 Dr Tremor Ext Cab SB	12440	13688	15769
4 Dr XL 4WD Ext Cab SB	13085	14435	16685
4 Dr XL Ext Cab SB	11006	12217	14236
4 Dr XLT 4WD Ext Cab SB	13333	14688	16946
4 Dr XLT Ext Cab SB	11644	12817	14773
4 Dr XLT FX4 4WD Ext Cab SB	13998	15246	17327

Options	Price
Jump Seat(s) [Opt on Ext 2 Dr non-Tremor]	+225
Leather Seats [Opt on Ext non-Tremor]	+165
Power Windows [Opt on 2WD Edge, Tremor, non-FX4 4WD]	+150
Sliding Rear Window [Opt on 2WD non-XLT, 4WD Tremor 2 Dr]	+125
Velour/Cloth Seats [Opt on XL non-Ext]	+200

2003

Ford's popular compact pickup receives a number of minor changes for 2003. The 2002 Tremor package, with its ear-splitting 485-watt sound system, returns for 2003 as a trim level, joining XL, Edge and XLT in the lineup. A chrome appearance package for select XLT models is available, and last year's FX4 package for four-wheel-drive Rangers is offered in two guises: Off Road and Level II. New Sonic Blue paint is unique to FX4 Level II Rangers. Other changes include covered visor vanity mirrors for XLT models, standard step bars on XLT 4WD SuperCab and Edge 4WD models and minor interior trim and fabric revisions on some models. Finally, crew cab rear seats get LATCH anchors, and some new colors are available.

Mileage Category: J

Body Styles	TMV Pricing		
	Trade	Private	Dealer
2 Dr Edge Ext Cab SB	9630	10641	12325
2 Dr Edge Plus 4WD Std Cab SB	10556	11665	13512
2 Dr Edge Std Cab SB	8259	9125	10569
2 Dr Tremor Ext Cab SB	10484	11584	13417
2 Dr XL 4WD Ext Cab SB	11036	12191	14117
2 Dr XL 4WD Std Cab LB	10939	12087	13999
2 Dr XL Ext Cab SB	9323	10301	11932
2 Dr XL Std Cab LB	7868	8693	10069
2 Dr XL Std Cab SB	7260	8022	9292

Body Styles	TMV Pricing		
	Trade	Private	Dealer
2 Dr XLT 4WD Ext Cab SB	11349	12540	14524
2 Dr XLT Ext Cab SB	9436	10427	12078
2 Dr XLT Std Cab LB	9385	10370	12012
2 Dr XLT Std Cab SB	7978	8815	10210
4 Dr Edge 4WD Ext Cab SB	11762	12996	15052
4 Dr Edge Plus Ext Cab SB	11102	12267	14208
4 Dr Tremor Plus Ext Cab SB	11527	12737	14753
4 Dr XL 4WD Ext Cab SB	11994	13252	15349
4 Dr XL Ext Cab SB	9991	11039	12785

Body Styles	TMV Pricing		
	Trade	Private	Dealer
4 Dr XLT 4WD Ext Cab SB	12208	13489	15624
4 Dr XLT Ext Cab SB	11074	12236	14173

Options	Price
3.0L V6 Flex Fuel OHV 12V FI Engine [Opt on XLT]	+252
3.0L V6 OHV 12V FI Engine [Opt on XL,XLT]	+252
4.0L V6 SOHC 12V FI Engine [Opt on EDGE,XL,XLT]	+116
AM/FM/CD Audio System [Opt on XL]	+177
AM/FM/CD Changer Audio System [Opt on EDGE]	+210
Air Conditioning	+419
Aluminum/Alloy Wheels [Opt on EDGE]	+145
Automatic 5-Speed Transmission [Std on Tremor]	+645
Bed Extender	+126
Bed Liner	+177
Bucket Seats [Opt on XLT FX4]	+161

Body Styles	TMV Pricing		
	Trade	Private	Dealer
4 Dr XLT FX4 4WD Ext Cab SB	13048	14342	16498

Options	Price
Chrome Wheels [Opt on XLT]	+148
Compact Disc Changer [Opt on XLT]	+190
Cruise Control	+119
Limited Slip Differential	+190
Power Windows	+139
Side Steps	+190
Sport Seats [Opt on EDGE,XLT]	+129
Stepside Bed	+319
Tonneau Cover	+258
Trailer Hitch	+139

Mileage Category: J

2002

A new FX4 model debuts, designed to appeal to Ranger XLT Extended Cab buyers who need to do some serious off-roading. Among the hardware goodies are a limited-slip differential, 31-inch BFGoodrich all-terrain tires, special 15-inch alloy wheels, tow hooks, skid plates, Bilstein shocks, special exterior trim and sport seats. All Rangers get a SecuriLock antitheft system, while XLT and Edge 4WD models have a new 16-inch wheel design. An MP3 player is newly optional, and models equipped with a 3.0-liter V6 get improved fuel economy.

Body Styles	TMV Pricing		
	Trade	Private	Dealer
2 Dr Edge Ext Cab SB	8171	9107	10668
2 Dr Edge Plus 4WD Std Cab SB	9109	10153	11893
2 Dr Edge Std Cab SB	7044	7852	9198
2 Dr Tremor Ext Cab SB	8929	9952	11658
2 Dr XL 4WD Ext Cab SB	9248	10309	12076
2 Dr XL 4WD Std Cab LB	9089	10131	11868
2 Dr XL Ext Cab SB	7699	8581	10052
2 Dr XL Std Cab LB	6783	7560	8856
2 Dr XL Std Cab SB	6233	6948	8140

Options	Price
3.0L V6 OHV 12V FI Engine [Opt on 2WD - XL,XLT]	+230
AM/FM/CD Audio System [Opt on XL]	+162
AM/FM/CD Changer Audio System [Opt on Edge,XLT]	+174
Air Conditioning	+383
Aluminum/Alloy Wheels [Opt on Edge 2WD]	+132
Appearance Package [Opt on XLT Ext Cab]	+356
Automatic 5-Speed Transmission [Opt on Edge,Edge Plus,XL,XLT]	+589
Bed Extender	+115
Bed Liner	+162
Chrome Wheels [Opt on XLT]	+191

Body Styles	TMV Pricing		
	Trade	Private	Dealer
2 Dr XLT 4WD Ext Cab SB	9764	10883	12749
2 Dr XLT Ext Cab SB	7970	8884	10408
2 Dr XLT Std Cab LB	8053	8964	10481
2 Dr XLT Std Cab SB	6890	7680	8996
4 Dr Edge 4WD Ext Cab SB	10011	11158	13070
4 Dr Edge Plus 4WD Ext Cab SB	11235	12523	14669
4 Dr Edge Plus Ext Cab SB	9321	10389	12169
4 Dr XLT FX4 4WD Ext Cab SB	11924	13291	15570

Options	Price
Hinged Fourth Door [Opt on 2 Dr Ext Cab]	+391
Limited Slip Differential [Std on FX4]	+174
Off-Road Suspension Package [Opt on XLT]	+983
Power Windows [Std on Edge,Edge Plus,Tremor,XLT]	+115
Running Boards	+174
Sport Seats [Opt on Edge,Edge Plus,XLT Ext Cab]	+118
Stepside Bed	+291
Tonneau Cover	+235
Trailer Hitch	+127

Mileage Category: J

2001

Most notable for the '01 Ranger is the availability of the Explorer's 207-horsepower, 4.0-liter SOHC V6. In other engine news, the flexible-fuel feature on the 3.0-liter V6 has been dropped and there is a new base 2.3-liter four-cylinder. ABS is now standard on all models. A new Edge trim level has a monochromatic appearance, which includes color-keyed bumpers and wheel lip moldings. Exterior changes are numerous. All models get a new grille, bumpers and headlamps, while the XLT 4x4 and Edge get a new hood and wheel lip moldings. Four colors are new as well as an optional in-dash six-disc CD changer.

Body Styles	TMV Pricing		
	Trade	Private	Dealer
2 Dr Edge Ext Cab SB	6580	7847	9017
2 Dr Edge Plus 4WD Std Cab SB	7604	9069	10421
2 Dr Edge Plus 4WD Std Cab Step SB	7882	9401	10803
2 Dr Edge Plus Ext Cab SB	7075	8665	10132
2 Dr Edge Plus Ext Cab Step SB	7425	8855	10175
2 Dr Edge Plus Std Cab Step SB	6160	7346	8441
2 Dr Edge Std Cab SB	5679	6774	7785
2 Dr XL Ext Cab SB	6250	7454	8566
2 Dr XL Std Cab LB	5033	6002	6897
2 Dr XL Std Cab SB	4670	5570	6401

Body Styles	TMV Pricing		
	Trade	Private	Dealer
2 Dr XLT Ext Cab SB	6404	7638	8777
2 Dr XLT Ext Cab Step SB	7985	9524	10944
2 Dr XLT Std Cab LB	6297	7511	8631
2 Dr XLT Std Cab SB	5394	6433	7393
2 Dr XLT Std Cab Step SB	5575	6649	7640
4 Dr Edge 4WD Ext Cab SB	7865	9380	10779
4 Dr Edge Plus 4WD Ext Cab SB	9013	10749	12351
4 Dr Edge Plus 4WD Ext Cab Step SB	9173	10940	12571
4 Dr XLT 4WD Ext Cab SB	8327	9931	11412
4 Dr XLT 4WD Ext Cab Step SB	8589	10244	11771

2001 (cont'd)

Options	Price
4.0L V6 SOHC 12V FI Engine	+290
AM/FM/CD Audio System [Opt on XL]	+126
Air Conditioning	+342
Appearance Package [Opt on XLT]	+171
Automatic 4-Speed Transmission	+527
Automatic 5-Speed Transmission	+527
Bed Liner	+158

Options	Price
Hinged Fourth Door	+350
Limited Slip Differential	+155
Off-Road Suspension Package [Opt on XLT]	+387
Power Door Locks	+126
Power Windows	+145
Running Boards [Opt on Edge,Edge Plus]	+155
Tonneau Cover	+211

2000

For 2000, the 2WD can be had with a "Trailhead" off-road style suspension package complete with larger tires and wheels, giving it the tough look of its 4WD cousin. All Ranger models have new wheel designs, and the XLT 4WD Off-Road Group receives a stainless-steel front-suspension skid plate.

Mileage Category: J

Body Styles	TMV Pricing		
	Trade	Private	Dealer
2 Dr XL 4WD Ext Cab SB	5446	6703	7936
2 Dr XL 4WD Std Cab LB	5105	6284	7440
2 Dr XL 4WD Std Cab SB	4981	6130	7257
2 Dr XL Ext Cab SB	4682	5764	6824
2 Dr XL Ext Cab Step SB	4680	5760	6819
2 Dr XL Std Cab LB	3743	4608	5456
2 Dr XL Std Cab SB	3617	4452	5271
2 Dr XL Std Cab Step SB	3709	4565	5404
2 Dr XLT 4WD Ext Cab SB	6170	7595	8991

Body Styles	TMV Pricing		
	Trade	Private	Dealer
2 Dr XLT 4WD Ext Cab Step SB	6126	7541	8928
2 Dr XLT 4WD Std Cab LB	5796	7134	8445
2 Dr XLT 4WD Std Cab SB	5659	6966	8247
2 Dr XLT 4WD Std Cab Step SB	5779	7114	8422
2 Dr XLT Ext Cab SB	4941	6083	7202
2 Dr XLT Ext Cab Step SB	4934	6074	7191
2 Dr XLT Std Cab LB	4426	5448	6450
2 Dr XLT Std Cab SB	4255	5237	6200
2 Dr XLT Std Cab Step SB	4381	5393	6385

Options	Price
3.0L V6 Flex Fuel OHV 12V FI Engine [Opt on XL,XLT]	+186
4.0L V6 OHV 12V FI Engine	+328
AM/FM/Cassette/CD Audio System	+137
Air Conditioning	+379
Aluminum/Alloy Wheels	+118
Antilock Brakes	+320
Automatic 4-Speed Transmission	+516

Options	Price
Automatic 5-Speed Transmission	+540
Bucket Seats	+170
Compact Disc Changer	+236
Hinged Fourth Door	+271
Limited Slip Differential	+162
Power Windows	+130
Split Front Bench Seat [Opt on XL]	+137

1999

This year's changes include standard 15-inch silver styled wheels, a class III frame-mounted hitch receiver for V6 applications, and a spare tire access lock. All models get dual front cupholders and Dark Graphite has been added to the interior colors options list while Willow Green and Denim Blue have been removed as interior choices. The "Splash" model has been discontinued. A 3.0-liter V6 flexible fuel engine is available that is designed specifically for ethanol/gasoline fuel blends.

Mileage Category: J

Body Styles	TMV Pricing		
	Trade	Private	Dealer
2 Dr XL 4WD Ext Cab SB	4544	5708	6920
2 Dr XL 4WD Ext Cab Step SB	4660	5855	7098
2 Dr XL 4WD Std Cab LB	4162	5228	6338
2 Dr XL 4WD Std Cab SB	4002	5027	6094
2 Dr XL 4WD Std Cab Step SB	4114	5168	6265
2 Dr XL Ext Cab SB	3894	4892	5930
2 Dr XL Ext Cab Step SB	4015	5044	6114
2 Dr XL Std Cab LB	3123	3923	4755
2 Dr XL Std Cab SB	2971	3732	4525
2 Dr XL Std Cab Step SB	3117	3916	4748

Body Styles	TMV Pricing		
	Trade	Private	Dealer
2 Dr XLT 4WD Ext Cab SB	5078	6380	7736
2 Dr XLT 4WD Ext Cab Step SB	5199	6532	7919
2 Dr XLT 4WD Std Cab LB	4795	6023	7301
2 Dr XLT 4WD Std Cab SB	4646	5837	7076
2 Dr XLT 4WD Std Cab Step SB	4762	5983	7254
2 Dr XLT Ext Cab SB	4072	5116	6203
2 Dr XLT Ext Cab Step SB	4234	5318	6447
2 Dr XLT Std Cab LB	3690	4635	5619
2 Dr XLT Std Cab SB	3554	4465	5413
2 Dr XLT Std Cab Step SB	3697	4645	5632

Options	Price
3.0L V6 OHV 12V FI Engine [Std on 4WD]	+202
4.0L V6 OHV 12V FI Engine	+262
Air Conditioning	+312
Antilock Brakes [Std on XLT 4WD]	+293
Automatic 4-Speed Transmission	+426

Options	Price
Automatic 5-Speed Transmission	+439
Bucket Seats	+140
Compact Disc Changer	+194
Hinged Fourth Door [Opt on XLT]	+300

1998

The Ranger gets new sheet metal, a new grille and revised headlamps. The wheelbase on regular cab models has been stretched to provide more cabin room and the displacement of the base engine has been increased. A short- and long-arm (SLA) suspension replaces the Twin-I-Beam suspension found on last year's models. A four-door Ranger join the lineup midyear.

Mileage Category: J

Body Styles	TMV Pricing		
	Trade	Private	Dealer
2 Dr Splash 4WD Ext Cab Step SB	4600	5920	7409
2 Dr Splash 4WD Std Cab Step SB	4249	5468	6842
2 Dr Splash Ext Cab Step SB	3903	5022	6284
2 Dr Splash Std Cab Step SB	3450	4440	5557
2 Dr XL 4WD Ext Cab SB	4055	5217	6528
2 Dr XL 4WD Ext Cab Step SB	4157	5349	6693

Body Styles	TMV Pricing		
	Trade	Private	Dealer
2 Dr XL 4WD Std Cab LB	3674	4727	5915
2 Dr XL 4WD Std Cab SB	3563	4586	5739
2 Dr XL 4WD Std Cab Step SB	3664	4716	5902
2 Dr XL Ext Cab SB	3388	4359	5455
2 Dr XL Ext Cab Step SB	3459	4451	5570
2 Dr XL Std Cab LB	2709	3486	4363

Body Styles	TMV Pricing		
	Trade	Private	Dealer
2 Dr XL Std Cab SB	2414	3106	3887
2 Dr XL Std Cab Step SB	2698	3472	4345
2 Dr XLT 4WD Ext Cab SB	4257	5478	6855
2 Dr XLT 4WD Ext Cab Step SB	4379	5635	7052
2 Dr XLT 4WD Std Cab LB	4198	5403	6761
2 Dr XLT 4WD Std Cab SB	4072	5240	6557

Options	Price
3.0L V6 OHV 12V FI Engine [Std on 4WD,Splash 2WD Ext Cab]	+143
4.0L V6 OHV 12V FI Engine	+214
Air Conditioning	+255
Antilock Brakes	+240

Body Styles	TMV Pricing		
	Trade	Private	Dealer
2 Dr XLT 4WD Std Cab Step SB	4173	5370	6720
2 Dr XLT Ext Cab SB	3478	4476	5601
2 Dr XLT Ext Cab Step SB	3618	4655	5825
2 Dr XLT Std Cab LB	3112	4005	5012
2 Dr XLT Std Cab SB	2965	3816	4775
2 Dr XLT Std Cab Step SB	3091	3978	4978

Options	Price
Automatic 4-Speed Transmission	+347
Automatic 5-Speed Transmission	+351
Compact Disc Changer	+159

Mileage Category: J

1997

Body Styles	TMV Pricing		
	Trade	Private	Dealer
2 Dr STX 4WD Ext Cab SB	3785	4966	6409
2 Dr STX 4WD Std Cab LB	3675	4823	6225
2 Dr STX 4WD Std Cab SB	3561	4673	6031
2 Dr Splash 4WD Ext Cab Step SB	3979	5221	6739
2 Dr Splash 4WD Std Cab Step SB	3796	4981	6429
2 Dr Splash Ext Cab Step SB	3192	4189	5407
2 Dr Splash Std Cab Step SB	2889	3791	4894
2 Dr XL 4WD Ext Cab SB	3528	4630	5976
2 Dr XL 4WD Ext Cab Step SB	3620	4750	6130
2 Dr XL 4WD Std Cab LB	3260	4278	5522
2 Dr XL 4WD Std Cab SB	3177	4169	5382
2 Dr XL 4WD Std Cab Step SB	3260	4278	5522
2 Dr XL Ext Cab SB	2790	3661	4725
2 Dr XL Ext Cab Step SB	2903	3808	4915

Options	Price
3.0L V6 OHV 12V FI Engine	+197
Air Conditioning	+236
Antilock Brakes	+222
Automatic 4-Speed Transmission	+314

Body Styles	TMV Pricing		
	Trade	Private	Dealer
2 Dr XL Std Cab LB	2200	2887	3727
2 Dr XL Std Cab SB	1988	2609	3367
2 Dr XL Std Cab Step SB	2240	2939	3793
2 Dr XLT 4WD Ext Cab SB	3800	4986	6435
2 Dr XLT 4WD Ext Cab Step SB	3887	5100	6583
2 Dr XLT 4WD Std Cab LB	3628	4760	6144
2 Dr XLT 4WD Std Cab SB	3514	4611	5952
2 Dr XLT 4WD Std Cab Step SB	3602	4726	6100
2 Dr XLT Ext Cab SB	2904	3810	4917
2 Dr XLT Ext Cab Step SB	2990	3923	5063
2 Dr XLT Std Cab LB	2558	3356	4332
2 Dr XLT Std Cab SB	2459	3227	4165
2 Dr XLT Std Cab Step SB	2545	3339	4309

Options	Price
Automatic 5-Speed Transmission	+345
Compact Disc Changer	+132
Dual Front Airbag Restraints	+118

Ford introduces its brand-new five-speed automatic transmission to the Ranger lineup. Available with the V6 engines, the five-speed automatic is designed to improve the Ranger's acceleration, towing and hill-climbing ability.

1996

An optional passenger-side airbag is available, and it comes with a switch that will disable the system if a child seat is installed in the truck. Super Cab models get standard privacy glass, Splash models lose that putrid green tape stripe, and the Flareside box from the Splash is now available on two-wheel-drive, four-cylinder XL and XLT models.

Body Styles	TMV Pricing		
	Trade	Private	Dealer
2 Dr STX 4WD Ext Cab SB	3211	4256	5700
2 Dr STX 4WD Std Cab LB	3110	4123	5521
2 Dr STX 4WD Std Cab SB	3012	3993	5348
2 Dr Splash 4WD Ext Cab Step SB	3384	4485	6006
2 Dr Splash 4WD Std Cab Step SB	3214	4261	5707
2 Dr Splash Ext Cab Step SB	2614	3465	4640
2 Dr Splash Std Cab Step SB	2346	3110	4164
2 Dr XL 4WD Ext Cab SB	2994	3968	5314
2 Dr XL 4WD Ext Cab Step SB	3072	4071	5451
2 Dr XL 4WD Std Cab LB	2761	3660	4902
2 Dr XL 4WD Std Cab SB	2647	3508	4698
2 Dr XL 4WD Std Cab Step SB	2758	3655	4894
2 Dr XL Ext Cab SB	2269	3007	4027
2 Dr XL Ext Cab Step SB	2365	3135	4198

Options	Price
3.0L V6 OHV 12V FI Engine	+174
Air Conditioning	+210

Mileage Category: J

Body Styles	TMV Pricing		
	Trade	Private	Dealer
2 Dr XL Std Cab LB	1773	2351	3149
2 Dr XL Std Cab SB	1678	2224	2979
2 Dr XL Std Cab Step SB	1825	2419	3239
2 Dr XLT 4WD Ext Cab SB	3237	4291	5746
2 Dr XLT 4WD Ext Cab Step SB	3295	4368	5849
2 Dr XLT 4WD Std Cab LB	3032	4019	5382
2 Dr XLT 4WD Std Cab SB	2937	3892	5211
2 Dr XLT 4WD Std Cab Step SB	3004	3981	5330
2 Dr XLT Ext Cab SB	2347	3111	4166
2 Dr XLT Ext Cab Step SB	2421	3209	4296
2 Dr XLT Std Cab LB	2079	2755	3688
2 Dr XLT Std Cab SB	1976	2619	3508
2 Dr XLT Std Cab Step SB	2043	2708	3627

Options	Price
Antilock Brakes [Opt on 2WD]	+197
Automatic 4-Speed Transmission	+272

1996 (cont'd)

Options	Price
Compact Disc Changer	+117

1995

A driver airbag and optional four-wheel antilock brakes are two of the features added to the safety equipment roster of the capable Ford Ranger. SuperCab models can now be had with a power driver seat.

Mileage Category: J

Body Styles	TMV Pricing		
	Trade	Private	Dealer
2 Dr STX 4WD Ext Cab SB	2695	3612	5139
2 Dr STX 4WD Std Cab LB	2663	3569	5078
2 Dr STX 4WD Std Cab SB	2564	3436	4889
2 Dr Splash 4WD Ext Cab Step SB	2861	3833	5454
2 Dr Splash 4WD Std Cab Step SB	2728	3655	5199
2 Dr Splash Ext Cab Step SB	2170	2908	4137
2 Dr Splash Std Cab Step SB	1910	2559	3641
2 Dr XL 4WD Ext Cab SB	2512	3366	4788
2 Dr XL 4WD Std Cab LB	2333	3127	4449
2 Dr XL 4WD Std Cab SB	2203	2952	4200

Body Styles	TMV Pricing		
	Trade	Private	Dealer
2 Dr XL Ext Cab SB	1808	2423	3447
2 Dr XL Std Cab LB	1536	2059	2930
2 Dr XL Std Cab SB	1462	1959	2788
2 Dr XLT 4WD Ext Cab SB	2729	3657	5204
2 Dr XLT 4WD Std Cab LB	2597	3480	4951
2 Dr XLT 4WD Std Cab SB	2486	3331	4740
2 Dr XLT Ext Cab SB	1903	2550	3629
2 Dr XLT Std Cab LB	1774	2377	3383
2 Dr XLT Std Cab SB	1679	2249	3199
2 Dr XLT Std Cab Step SB	1742	2335	3322

Options	Price
3.0L V6 OHV 12V FI Engine	+101
Air Conditioning	+182
Antilock Brakes [Opt on XL,XLT]	+170
Automatic 4-Speed Transmission	+236

Options	Price
Bucket Seats	+81
Compact Disc Changer	+101
Sport Seats	+81

Taurus

2004

New front and rear fascias give the Taurus a slightly updated look. Minor interior enhancements include a revised instrument cluster, new steering wheel design and a passenger seat weight sensor for determining airbag deployment.

Mileage Category: D

Body Styles	TMV Pricing		
	Trade	Private	Dealer
4 Dr LX Sdn	8909	9965	11726
4 Dr SE Sdn	9078	10135	11896
4 Dr SE Wgn	9854	10927	12714

Body Styles	TMV Pricing		
	Trade	Private	Dealer
4 Dr SEL Sdn	11193	12329	14223
4 Dr SEL Wgn	10707	11788	13589
4 Dr SES Sdn	10376	11513	13407

Options	Price
3.0L V6 DOHC 24V FI Engine [Opt on SEL Wgn]	+685
AM/FM/CD Audio System [Opt on SE Wgn]	+140
Antilock Brakes [Opt on LX, SE]	+600
Automatic Dimming Rearview Mirror [Opt on SES, SEL]	+120
Cruise Control [Opt on LX Sdn]	+220
Front Side Airbag Restraints	+390
Leather Seats [Opt on SEL]	+895
Leather and Wood Steering Wheel [Opt on SEL]	+190
Power Adjustable Foot Pedals [Opt on SE Sdn, SES, SEL]	+120

Options	Price
Power Driver Seat [Opt on SE]	+250
Power Moonroof [Opt on SES, SEL Sdn]	+895
Power Passenger Seat [Opt on SEL Sdn]	+350
Rear Spoiler [Opt on SE, SES, SEL Sdn]	+230
Split Folding Rear Seat [Opt on SE, SES Sdn]	+140
Sport Package [Opt on SES Sdn]	+290
Third Seat [Opt on SE, SEL Wgn]	+215
Traction Control System	+175

2003

New for 2003, the SEL trim level offers a unique instrument cluster with a satin-finish background, as well as Imola leather trimmed seats and dark wood trim. You can now get a real wood- and leather-trimmed steering wheel, and you'll want to note that power windows and locks, as well as tilt steering and floor mats, are standard on all models.

Mileage Category: D

Body Styles	TMV Pricing		
	Trade	Private	Dealer
4 Dr LX Sdn	7346	8219	9674
4 Dr SE Sdn	7589	8492	9996
4 Dr SE Wgn	7903	8842	10408

Body Styles	TMV Pricing		
	Trade	Private	Dealer
4 Dr SEL Sdn	9776	10938	12875
4 Dr SEL Wgn	9511	10642	12526
4 Dr SES Sdn	8238	9217	10849

Options	Price
3.0L V6 DOHC 24V FI Engine [Opt on SE,SEL,SES]	+306
AM/FM/CD Changer Audio System [Opt on SE]	+168
AM/FM/Cassette Audio System [Opt on LX]	+119
Antilock Brakes [Opt on LX,SE]	+439
Compact Disc Changer [Opt on SEL,SES]	+119
Cruise Control [Opt on LX]	+119
Front Side Airbag Restraints [Opt on SE,SEL,SES]	+252
Leather Seats [Opt on SES,SEL]	+577

Options	Price
Leather and Wood Steering Wheel [Opt on SEL]	+123
MACH Audio System [Opt on SES,SEL]	+171
Power Driver Seat [Opt on LX,SE]	+155
Power Moonroof [Opt on SES,SEL]	+577
Premium Audio System [Opt on SES,SEL]	+223
Rear Spoiler [Opt on SE,SEL,SES]	+148
Special Leather Seat Trim [Opt on SEL]	+610

2002

Mileage Category: D

Body Styles	TMV Pricing		
	Trade	Private	Dealer
4 Dr LX Sdn	5797	6580	7884
4 Dr SE Sdn	6224	7065	8465
4 Dr SE Wgn	6377	7238	8674

Options	Price
3.0L V6 DOHC 24V FI Engine [Opt on SE Wgn,SES]	+409
Antilock Brakes [Opt on LX,SE Sdn]	+400
Compact Disc Changer [Opt on SEL Wgn]	+124
Front Side Airbag Restraints	+147
Leather Seats [Std on SEL Wgn]	+265

Body Styles	TMV Pricing		
	Trade	Private	Dealer
4 Dr SEL Sdn	8510	9659	11574
4 Dr SEL Wgn	8250	9365	11222
4 Dr SES Sdn	6508	7350	8752

Options	Price
MACH Audio System [Opt on SEL Wgn]	+188
Power Driver Seat [Opt on SE Sdn]	+141
Power Moonroof [Opt on Sdn - SE,SEL]	+412
Power Passenger Seat [Opt on SEL Sdn]	+141

Floor mats become standard on all Taurus models, and the base V6 benefits from improved fuel economy. All but the base LX get security approach lamps, while LX and SE come standard with six-passenger seating. A slew of no-charge options are available on various Taurus models for 2002: SE gets a free power driver seat and CD player; SES comes with free leather or a moonroof (regionally available); SEL adds leather or moonroof, or both (regionally available). SEL also has standard adjustable pedals for 2002. A new SEL Wagon debuts. A new SEL premium package includes a Mach audio system, side airbags and traction control. Optional on SES and SEL is a new Luxury and Convenience group, which provides an auto-dimming rearview mirror with compass and heated side mirrors. Four new colors round out the list of changes.

2001

Mileage Category: D

Body Styles	TMV Pricing		
	Trade	Private	Dealer
4 Dr LX Sdn	4806	5925	6958
4 Dr SE Sdn	4848	5978	7021
4 Dr SE Wgn	5036	6210	7293

Options	Price
Antilock Brakes [Opt on LX,SE]	+358
Front Side Airbag Restraints	+205
Leather Seats [Opt on LX]	+472
Power Driver Seat [Opt on LX,SE]	+184

Body Styles	TMV Pricing		
	Trade	Private	Dealer
4 Dr SEL Sdn	5623	6934	8145
4 Dr SES Sdn	5268	6495	7629

Options	Price
Power Moonroof	+469
Power Passenger Seat	+184
Premium Audio System	+169
Rear Spoiler	+121

After the 2000 redesign, updates are minor. A Lower Anchor and Tether for Children (LATCH) is now standard on all models. LATCH is an anchoring system for child safety seats. Also new is Spruce Green Clearcoat Metallic, an increase in fuel tank capacity to 18 gallons, a six-disc CD changer is standard on SES models, power locks are standard on LX and an optional rear spoiler can give your Taurus that extra bit of attitude.

2000

Mileage Category: D

Body Styles	TMV Pricing		
	Trade	Private	Dealer
4 Dr LX Sdn	3612	4604	5576
4 Dr SE Sdn	3866	4928	5970
4 Dr SE Wgn	3903	4975	6026

Options	Price
3.0L V6 DOHC 24V FI Engine	+328
3.0L V6 Flex Fuel OHV 12V FI Engine	+549
Aluminum/Alloy Wheels [Opt on LX]	+148
Antilock Brakes [Opt on LX,SE]	+320
Compact Disc Changer	+165
Front Side Airbag Restraints	+184

Body Styles	TMV Pricing		
	Trade	Private	Dealer
4 Dr SEL Sdn	4312	5497	6659
4 Dr SES Sdn	3841	4897	5932

Options	Price
Leather Seats [Opt on LX]	+422
Power Door Locks [Opt on LX]	+125
Power Driver Seat [Opt on LX,SE]	+165
Power Moonroof	+349
Power Passenger Seat [Opt on SEL]	+165
Rear Spoiler	+118

Many changes are in store for the 2000 Taurus. Styling is the most obvious, with a new look for both the front and rear. Improved safety comes from a new airbag-deployment system, adjustable pedals, seatbelt pre-tensioners and child safety-seat anchors. The ride has been made more comfortable and the powertrain has been updated for more power and less noise. The V8-powered SHO has been dropped from the lineup.

1999

Mileage Category: D

Body Styles	TMV Pricing		
	Trade	Private	Dealer
4 Dr LX Sdn	2818	3688	4594
4 Dr SE Sdn	2853	3733	4650

Options	Price
3.0L V6 DOHC 24V FI Engine	+193
3.0L V6 Flex Fuel OHV 12V FI Engine	+452
Aluminum/Alloy Wheels	+123
Antilock Brakes [Opt on LX,SE]	+293
Chrome Wheels [Opt on SE]	+193
Compact Disc Changer [Opt on SE]	+136

Body Styles	TMV Pricing		
	Trade	Private	Dealer
4 Dr SE Wgn	2830	3704	4614
4 Dr SHO Sdn	4561	5969	7434

Options	Price
Leather Seats [Opt on SE]	+348
Power Driver Seat	+170
Power Moonroof [Opt on SE]	+288
Power Passenger Seat [Opt on SE]	+170
Spoke Wheels	+225

The light group and speed control are now optional on LX level cars. Chrome wheels on the SE models have been replaced with five-spoke aluminum wheels.

1998

A mild facelift, revised trim levels and fewer options are the only changes to Ford's midsize sedan.

Body Styles	TMV Pricing		
	Trade	Private	Dealer
Dr LX Sdn	2160	2957	3856
4 Dr SE Sdn	2186	2992	3901

Body Styles	TMV Pricing		
	Trade	Private	Dealer
4 Dr SE Wgn	2315	3169	4132
4 Dr SHO Sdn	3511	4806	6267

1998 (cont'd)

Options	Price
3.0L V6 DOHC 24V FI Engine [Opt on LX,SE]	+157
3.0L V6 Flex Fuel OHV 12V FI Engine	+369
Antilock Brakes [Std on SHO]	+240
Chrome Wheels [Opt on SE]	+157
Leather Seats	+180

Options	Price
Power Driver Seat	+123
Power Moonroof [Opt on SE]	+235
Power Passenger Seat [Opt on SE]	+123
Premium Audio System [Opt on SE]	+127

1997

A few new exterior color choices are added and there are minor changes to a couple of optional equipment packages.

Mileage Category: D

Body Styles	TMV Pricing		
	Trade	Private	Dealer
4 Dr G Sdn	1432	2044	2792
4 Dr GL Sdn	1524	2176	2973
4 Dr GL Wgn	1644	2347	3206

Body Styles	TMV Pricing		
	Trade	Private	Dealer
4 Dr LX Sdn	1669	2382	3254
4 Dr LX Wgn	1832	2615	3572
4 Dr SHO Sdn	2721	3885	5308

Options	Price
3.0L V6 Flex Fuel OHV 12V FI Engine	+342
Antilock Brakes	+222
Chrome Wheels	+145

Options	Price
Compact Disc Changer	+174
Leather Seats	+291
Power Moonroof	+217

1996

All-new Taurus debuts in sedan and wagon format, available in GL, LX and SHO trim levels. New or substantially revised engines and suspensions improve the performance of the Taurus, while several functional innovations make the car easier and more enjoyable to drive.

Mileage Category: D

Body Styles	TMV Pricing		
	Trade	Private	Dealer
4 Dr GL Sdn	1177	1759	2562
4 Dr GL Wgn	1267	1893	2758
4 Dr LX Sdn	1331	1990	2899

Body Styles	TMV Pricing		
	Trade	Private	Dealer
4 Dr LX Wgn	1426	2131	3105
4 Dr SHO Sdn	2193	3278	4777

Options	Price
3.0L V6 Flex Fuel OHV 12V FI Engine	+304
Antilock Brakes [Std on SHO]	+197
Chrome Wheels	+129
Compact Disc Changer	+155

Options	Price
JBL Audio System	+130
Leather Seats [Opt on LX]	+258
Power Moonroof	+193

1995

Sport-edition model is introduced as an SE. The SE includes aluminum wheels, sport bucket seats, air conditioning and a rear defroster. The base engine has been revised to decrease engine noise.

Mileage Category: D

Body Styles	TMV Pricing		
	Trade	Private	Dealer
4 Dr GL Sdn	727	1200	1989
4 Dr GL Wgn	762	1257	2082
4 Dr LX Sdn	770	1272	2109

Body Styles	TMV Pricing		
	Trade	Private	Dealer
4 Dr LX Wgn	840	1386	2296
4 Dr SE Sdn	755	1247	2068
4 Dr SHO Sdn	1060	1752	2904

Options	Price
3.0L V6 Flex Fuel OHV 12V FI Engine	+256
3.8L V6 OHV 12V FI Engine	+125
AM/FM/Cassette/CD Audio System	+94
Antilock Brakes [Std on SHO]	+170
Automatic 4-Speed Transmission [Opt on SHO]	+198

Options	Price
JBL Audio System	+113
Leather Seats	+124
Power Driver Seat [Opt on GL]	+77
Power Moonroof	+167

Thunderbird

2004

Mileage Category: H

Body Styles	TMV Pricing		
	Trade	Private	Dealer
2 Dr STD Conv	25540	27069	29616

Options	Price
Chrome Wheels	+145

Options	Price
Hardtop Roof	+800

For 2004, the Thunderbird gets revised seat trim, an Audiophile stereo, Homelink and newly styled aluminum accents. Exterior changes include new V8 badging, redesigned 17-inch wheels and a Light Sand Appearance package, which includes cream-colored gauges, a sand-colored top and bronze interior accents. Merlot, Platinum Silver and Vintage Mint Green are new exterior paint choices this year.

2003

Mileage Category: H

Body Styles	TMV Pricing		
	Trade	Private	Dealer
2 Dr STD Conv	22627	24121	26612

Options	Price	Options	Price
17 Inch Wheels - Chrome	+451	Heated Front Seats	+223
Hardtop Roof	+1609		

Now in its second year, the Thunderbird gains 28 more horsepower and 25 more pound-feet of torque, bringing the totals to 280 and 286, respectively. The bump in power is due to new electronic throttle control and variable cam timing. All-speed traction control comes standard, and heated seats are now available as options. The instrument cluster has been revised, and new exterior and colors brighten up the palette. Finally, a new saddle interior package makes its debut with full saddle-style leather for the seats, steering wheel and shift knob.

2002

Mileage Category: H

Body Styles	TMV Pricing		
	Trade	Private	Dealer
2 Dr Neiman Marcus Edition Conv	27385	28906	31441

Options	Price
17 Inch Wheels - Chrome [Opt on STD]	+412
Hardtop Roof [Opt on STD]	+1472

Body Styles	TMV Pricing		
	Trade	Private	Dealer
2 Dr STD Conv	20189	21310	23179

Options	Price
Traction Control System [Opt on STD]	+177

Following a four-year absence, the Thunderbird nameplate returns on an all-new two-seat roadster platform designed to recall the first-generation '55-'57 T-Birds.

1997

Mileage Category: D

Body Styles	TMV Pricing		
	Trade	Private	Dealer
2 Dr LX Cpe	1889	2698	3687

Options	Price	Options	Price
4.6L V8 SOHC 16V FI Engine	+332	Leather Seats	+161
Antilock Brakes	+222	Power Moonroof	+217
Chrome Wheels	+170	Premium Audio System	+126

The Thunderbird receives few updates this year. A revised center console, a few new colors, and standard four-wheel disc brakes are the big news for 1997.

1996

Mileage Category: D

Body Styles	TMV Pricing		
	Trade	Private	Dealer
2 Dr LX Cpe	1366	2043	2977

Options	Price	Options	Price
4.6L V8 SOHC 16V FI Engine	+327	Leather Seats	+143
Antilock Brakes	+197	Power Moonroof	+193
Chrome Wheels	+151		

Revised styling greatly improves the look of the Thunderbird for 1996. The Super Coupe is deleted, replaced by a Sport Package for the V8 model. Base V6 engines have been upgraded, and go 100,000 miles between tune-ups. Equipment rosters have been shuffled.

1995

Body Styles	TMV Pricing		
	Trade	Private	Dealer
2 Dr LX Cpe	1023	1493	2275

Options	Price
4.6L V8 SOHC 16V FI Engine	+255
AM/FM/CD Audio System	+97
Antilock Brakes [Opt on LX]	+170
Automatic 4-Speed Transmission [Opt on SC]	+147

Body Styles	TMV Pricing		
	Trade	Private	Dealer
2 Dr SC S/C Cpe	2270	3293	4998

Options	Price
Leather Seats [Opt on LX]	+124
Power Moonroof	+167
Premium Audio System	+97

The trunk-mounted CD changer is deleted in favor of an in-dash CD-player. Variable-assist power steering is lost from the standard equipment list.

Ford
Windstar

Windstar

2003

AdvanceTrac stability control system was supposed to be available for 2002, but it was postponed. It makes its appearance for the 2003 model year. The LX base trim level is rechristened to Windstar.

Mileage Category: P

Body Styles	TMV Pricing		
	Trade	Private	Dealer
4 Dr LX Pass Van	10314	11544	13594
4 Dr Limited Pass Van	14790	16553	19492
4 Dr SE Pass Van	11422	12784	15054

Options	Price
16 Inch Wheels [Opt on LX]	+190
Air Conditioning - Front and Rear [Opt on STD]	+306
Alarm System [Opt on SE,SEL]	+161
Camper/Towing Package [Opt on SEL]	+287
Captain Chairs (4) [Opt on LX]	+481
Front Side Airbag Restraints [Std on Limited]	+252
Park Distance Control (Rear) [Opt on SE,SEL]	+193

Body Styles	TMV Pricing		
	Trade	Private	Dealer
4 Dr SEL Pass Van	13441	15043	17714
4 Dr STD Pass Van	9805	10974	12923

Options	Price
Power Adjustable Foot Pedals [Opt on LX]	+161
Power Driver Seat [Opt on LX]	+171
Power Dual Sliding Doors [Opt on SE]	+580
Tinted Glass [Opt on STD]	+184
Traction Control System [Opt on SE,SEL]	+226
VCR Entertainment System	+642

2002

The biggest news is the availability of the AdvanceTrac stability control system. All Windstars have sliding doors on both sides for 2002. Entry-level LX models get upgraded appearance items, and buyers of this trim can opt for the Autovision entertainment system and 16-inch alloy wheels for the first time. The short-lived SE Sport model is dropped, and SE buyers can no longer have leather seats. Four new colors freshen the outside of the Windstar.

Mileage Category: P

Body Styles	TMV Pricing		
	Trade	Private	Dealer
4 Dr LX Pass Van	8624	9679	11437
4 Dr Limited Pass Van	12682	14214	16766

Options	Price
Air Conditioning - Front and Rear [Opt on LX]	+471
Aluminum/Alloy Wheels [Opt on LX]	+206
Camper/Towing Package [Opt on SEL]	+262
Front Side Airbag Restraints [Std on Limited]	+230
Park Distance Control (Rear) [Opt on SE,SEL]	+177

Body Styles	TMV Pricing		
	Trade	Private	Dealer
4 Dr SE Pass Van	10437	11697	13797
4 Dr SEL Pass Van	11484	12889	15231

Options	Price
Power Dual Sliding Doors [Opt on SE]	+530
Tilt Steering Wheel [Opt on LX]	+118
Tinted Glass [Opt on LX]	+168
Traction Control System [Std on Limited]	+206
VCR Entertainment System	+586

2001

There are several model/series changes for Windstar this year, as well as updates to the exterior, interior and powertrain. Ford says a new transmission has improved shift quality and the 3.8-liter V6 is standard on all Windstars. The base model is now called the Windstar LX three-door. The SE Sport is a new trim level and it includes driving lights, painted bumpers and body-side molding, a rear liftgate spoiler, second-row bucket/console seats, a roof rack with brushed aluminum crossbars, black rocker cladding and different wheels and tires.

Mileage Category: P

Body Styles	TMV Pricing		
	Trade	Private	Dealer
3 Dr LX Pass Van	6636	8028	9313
4 Dr LX Pass Van	7389	8940	10372
4 Dr Limited Pass Van	9492	11484	13323

Options	Price
AM/FM/Cassette/CD Audio System [Opt on LX,SE]	+132
Air Conditioning - Front and Rear	+263
Aluminum/Alloy Wheels [Opt on LX]	+219
Camper/Towing Package [Std on Limited]	+234
Front Side Airbag Restraints [Std on Limited]	+205
Leather Seats [Opt on SE]	+456
Luggage Rack [Opt on LX]	+129

Body Styles	TMV Pricing		
	Trade	Private	Dealer
4 Dr SE Pass Van	8304	10047	11656
4 Dr SE Sport Pass Van	7768	9399	10904
4 Dr SEL Pass Van	8489	10271	11916

Options	Price
Power Driver Seat [Opt on LX]	+171
Power Dual Sliding Doors [Opt on SE]	+474
Power Sliding Door [Opt on LX,SE]	+474
Privacy Glass [Opt on LX,STD]	+219
Traction Control System [Std on Limited]	+208
VCR Entertainment System	+524

2000

The Windstar now has standard power-adjustable pedals and an optional rear-seat video entertainment center. There's also a new trim level called the Limited. Available midyear 2000, it will contain more standard features than the previously top-line SEL.

Mileage Category: P

Body Styles	TMV Pricing		
	Trade	Private	Dealer
3 Dr LX Pass Van	4908	6132	7331
3 Dr STD Pass Van	4599	5745	6869
4 Dr Limited Pass Van	7016	8763	10475

Options	Price
3.8L V6 OHV 12V FI Engine [Opt on STD]	+323
AM/FM/Cassette/CD Audio System [Opt on LX,SE]	+141
Air Conditioning - Front and Rear [Opt on LX]	+224
Aluminum/Alloy Wheels [Opt on LX]	+196
Camper/Towing Package [Opt on LX,SE,SEL]	+205
Captain Chairs (4) [Opt on Limited,LX]	+337

Body Styles	TMV Pricing		
	Trade	Private	Dealer
4 Dr SE Pass Van	5424	6775	8100
4 Dr SEL Pass Van	6406	8003	9568

Options	Price
Compact Disc Changer [Opt on LX]	+189
Front Side Airbag Restraints [Std on Limited]	+184
Leather Seats [Opt on SE]	+408
Luggage Rack [Opt on LX]	+115
Power Driver Seat [Opt on LX]	+153
Power Dual Sliding Doors [Opt on SE]	+424

For the latest vehicle information, visit www.edmunds.com

Options	Price
Power Sliding Door [Opt on LX,SE]	+236
Privacy Glass [Opt on LX,STD]	+196
Sliding Driver Side Door [Opt on LX,STD]	+165

Options	Price
Traction Control System [Opt on LX,SE,SEL]	+186
VCR Entertainment System [Opt on LX,SE,SEL]	+611

Mileage Category: P

Body Styles	TMV Pricing		
	Trade	Private	Dealer
3 Dr LX Pass Van	4111	5300	6537
3 Dr STD Pass Van	3640	4692	5786

Options	Price
AM/FM/Cassette/CD Audio System [Std on SEL]	+117
Air Conditioning [Opt on STD]	+332
Air Conditioning - Front and Rear [Opt on LX]	+185
Aluminum/Alloy Wheels [Opt on LX]	+161
Bucket Seats	+190
Camper/Towing Package	+169
Captain Chairs (4) [Opt on LX]	+278
Compact Disc Changer	+155

Body Styles	TMV Pricing		
	Trade	Private	Dealer
4 Dr SE Pass Van	4577	5901	7279
4 Dr SEL Pass Van	5014	6465	7976

Options	Price
Front Side Airbag Restraints	+151
Leather Seats [Opt on SE]	+336
Power Driver Seat [Opt on LX,SE]	+126
Power Dual Sliding Doors [Opt on SE]	+311
Power Sliding Door	+194
Privacy Glass [Opt on LX,STD]	+161
Sliding Driver Side Door [Opt on LX,STD]	+136
Traction Control System	+154

1999

This year the Windstar has been totally redesigned. The biggest news for '99, in addition to the completely new exterior and interior styling, is a left-hand sliding door. The second- and third-row seats are now on rollers for easier removal/interchangeability and the instrument panel has been redesigned for improved ergonomics. There's also a more powerful and cleaner-burning 3.8-liter V6 plus upgraded suspension, transmission, brakes and air conditioning components. New options include side airbags and a trick reverse sensing system.

Body Styles	TMV Pricing		
	Trade	Private	Dealer
3 Dr GL Pass Van	2777	3727	4799
3 Dr LX Pass Van	2896	3888	5006

Options	Price
3.8L V6 OHV 12V FI Engine [Opt on GL]	+217
Air Conditioning [Std on LX]	+272
Air Conditioning - Front and Rear [Opt on GL,LX]	+151
Aluminum/Alloy Wheels [Opt on GL]	+132
Camper/Towing Package	+130

Body Styles	TMV Pricing		
	Trade	Private	Dealer
3 Dr Limited Pass Van	3516	4720	6077
3 Dr STD Pass Van	2428	3258	4195

Options	Price
Captain Chairs (4) [Opt on GL]	+227
JBL Audio System	+162
Leather Seats [Opt on LX]	+274
Privacy Glass	+132
Traction Control System	+125

1998

Ford widens the driver door as a stop-gap measure until the 1999 Windstar arrives with a fourth door. Subtle styling revisions and a new Limited model round out the changes for 1998.

Mileage Category: P

Body Styles	TMV Pricing		
	Trade	Private	Dealer
3 Dr GL Pass Van	2123	2946	3951

Options	Price
3.8L V6 OHV 12V FI Engine [Opt on GL]	+201
Air Conditioning	+251
Air Conditioning - Front and Rear	+139
Aluminum/Alloy Wheels	+122

Body Styles	TMV Pricing		
	Trade	Private	Dealer
3 Dr LX Pass Van	2279	3162	4242

Options	Price
Captain Chairs (4)	+204
JBL Audio System	+149
Leather Seats	+254
Privacy Glass	+122

1997

Nothing is new for the 1997 Ford Windsar.

Mileage Category: P

Body Styles	TMV Pricing		
	Trade	Private	Dealer
3 Dr GL Pass Van	1588	2262	3193

Options	Price
3.8L V6 OHV 12V FI Engine [Std on LX]	+178
Air Conditioning [Std on LX]	+223
Air Conditioning - Front and Rear	+124

Body Styles	TMV Pricing		
	Trade	Private	Dealer
3 Dr LX Pass Van	1891	2694	3803

Options	Price
Captain Chairs (4)	+156
JBL Audio System	+133
Leather Seats [Opt on LX]	+225

1996

Ford boosted output on the 3.8-liter V6 from 155 to 200 horsepower. Trim and equipment have been revised, and four-wheel disc brakes come with traction control or the tow package. A new integrated child safety seat has been added to the options list. Tune-ups happen every 100,000 miles. Traction control is now optional.

Mileage Category: P

Body Styles	TMV Pricing		
	Trade	Private	Dealer
3 Dr GL Pass Van	1231	1853	2889
3 Dr GL Pass Van (1995.5)	1297	1952	3044

Body Styles	TMV Pricing		
	Trade	Private	Dealer
3 Dr LX Pass Van	1410	2121	3305
3 Dr LX Pass Van (1995.5)	1541	2319	3615

1995

This year, Ford introduces its version of the front-wheel drive minivan. Designed to replace the Aerostar, the Windstar offers an extensive standard equipment list. Dual airbags, antilock brakes, a four-speed automatic transmission and V6 power are just a few of the things Windstar owners will find included on their vehicle. The Windstar has seating for seven that includes a unique integrated child seat.

1995 (cont'd)

Options	Price
Air Conditioning [Std on LX]	+193
Air Conditioning - Front and Rear	+107
Aluminum/Alloy Wheels [Opt on GL]	+94
Bucket Seats [Opt on LX]	+110
Camper/Towing Package [Std on LX]	+79
Captain Chairs (4)	+135

Options	Price
Compact Disc Changer	+90
JBL Audio System	+115
Leather Seats	+195
Premium Audio System	+124
Privacy Glass	+94

Metro

1997

Mileage Category: A

Body Styles	TMV Pricing			Body Styles	TMV Pricing		
	Trade	Private	Dealer		Trade	Private	Dealer
2 Dr LSi Hbk	629	1143	1772	4 Dr LSi Sdn	670	1218	1888
2 Dr STD Hbk	585	1065	1652				

Options	Price	Options	Price
Air Conditioning	+149	Antilock Brakes	+144

Geo drops the base sedan variant of the Metro for 1997. A new convenience package is available on LSi models, and the LSi hatchback comes with the larger 1.3-liter engine standard. Two new colors debut.

1996

Mileage Category: A

Body Styles	TMV Pricing			Body Styles	TMV Pricing		
	Trade	Private	Dealer		Trade	Private	Dealer
2 Dr LSi Hbk	431	839	1402	4 Dr LSi Sdn	500	973	1627
2 Dr STD Hbk	422	821	1371	4 Dr STD Sdn	465	903	1509

Options		Price
Antilock Brakes		+124

A zoned rear window defroster clears the center of the Metro's tiny rear backlight first, base coupes get dual exterior mirrors and LSi coupes get hubcaps and body-color bumpers.

1995

Mileage Category: A

Body Styles	TMV Pricing			Body Styles	TMV Pricing		
	Trade	Private	Dealer		Trade	Private	Dealer
2 Dr LSi Hbk	333	659	1201	4 Dr LSi Sdn	374	739	1348
2 Dr STD Hbk	316	624	1136	4 Dr STD Sdn	346	685	1249

Options	Price	Options	Price
AM/FM/Cassette/CD Audio System	+81	Antilock Brakes	+107
Air Conditioning	+85		

All-new car is larger than previous model, and comes as a two-door hatchback or four-door sedan in base or LSi trim. Dual airbags are standard. ABS is optional on all models. Hatchbacks get the carryover 1.0-liter three-cylinder motor. Optional on LSi hatchback and standard on sedans is a 70-horsepower, 1.3-liter four-cylinder engine. Daytime running lights are standard.

Prizm

1997

Mileage Category: B

Body Styles	TMV Pricing			Body Styles	TMV Pricing		
	Trade	Private	Dealer		Trade	Private	Dealer
4 Dr LSi Sdn	1278	2120	3149	4 Dr STD Sdn	1208	2004	2977

Options	Price	Options	Price
Air Conditioning	+152	Automatic 4-Speed Transmission	+152
Antilock Brakes	+144	Power Sunroof	+129

The Prizm is essentially carried over for 1997, sporting new door trim panels, standard power steering, new exterior colors, and strengthened side-impact protection.

1996

Mileage Category: B

Body Styles	TMV Pricing			Body Styles	TMV Pricing		
	Trade	Private	Dealer		Trade	Private	Dealer
4 Dr LSi Sdn	903	1635	2646	4 Dr STD Sdn	843	1526	2470

Options	Price	Options	Price
Air Conditioning	+130	Automatic 4-Speed Transmission	+131
Antilock Brakes	+124		

An integrated child safety seat is optional on the LSi, and daytime running lights debut. Three new exterior colors and added equipment to the base model round out the changes to this excellent compact.

1995

Mileage Category: B

Body Styles	TMV Pricing			Body Styles	TMV Pricing		
	Trade	Private	Dealer		Trade	Private	Dealer
4 Dr LSi Sdn	572	1132	2066	4 Dr STD Sdn	522	1034	1888

Options	Price	Options	Price
Air Conditioning	+112	Automatic 4-Speed Transmission	+113
Antilock Brakes	+107	Leather Seats	+84

Base 1.6-liter engine loses horsepower. All models get new wheel covers, and leather is newly optional on LSi.

1995 (cont'd)

Options	Price
Power Sunroof	+95

Tracker

1997

Mileage Category: L

Body Styles	TMV Pricing			Body Styles	TMV Pricing		
	Trade	Private	Dealer		Trade	Private	Dealer
2 Dr STD 4WD Conv	1606	2290	3125	4 Dr LSi SUV	1696	2418	3300
2 Dr STD Conv	1496	2131	2908	4 Dr STD 4WD SUV	1699	2422	3305
4 Dr LSi 4WD SUV	1782	2541	3468	4 Dr STD SUV	1649	2350	3207

Options	Price	Options	Price
Air Conditioning	+159	Automatic 3-Speed Transmission	+119
Antilock Brakes	+144	Automatic 4-Speed Transmission	+181

After a heavy makeover for 1996, changes for 1997 are limited. Convertibles get a standard fold-and-stow rear bench seat along with an enhanced evaporative emissions system. All Trackers can be painted Sunset Red Metallic or Azurite Blue Metallic for the first time.

1996

A new four-door model joins the lineup, and dual airbags are standard on all Trackers. Four-wheel antilock brakes are optional. Revised styling freshens the new exterior, and daytime running lights make the Tracker more conspicuous to motorists. Cruise control is a new convenience option.

Mileage Category: L

Body Styles	TMV Pricing			Body Styles	TMV Pricing		
	Trade	Private	Dealer		Trade	Private	Dealer
2 Dr LSi 4WD Conv	1410	2028	2881	4 Dr LSi 4WD SUV	1522	2188	3107
2 Dr LSi Conv	1276	1835	2606	4 Dr LSi SUV	1423	2045	2905
2 Dr STD 4WD Conv	1324	1903	2702	4 Dr STD 4WD SUV	1444	2076	2948
2 Dr STD Conv	1171	1683	2391	4 Dr STD SUV	1363	1960	2784

Options	Price	Options	Price
Air Conditioning	+122	Automatic 4-Speed Transmission	+131
Antilock Brakes	+124		

1995

All 4WD models and Massachusetts-bound Trackers get 95-horsepower engine. Convertible top has been redesigned for easier operation. Expressions Packages offer color-coordinated tops and wheels.

Mileage Category: L

Body Styles	TMV Pricing			Body Styles	TMV Pricing		
	Trade	Private	Dealer		Trade	Private	Dealer
2 Dr LSi 4WD Conv	1128	1640	2494	2 Dr STD 4WD SUV	1001	1455	2212
2 Dr LSi 4WD SUV	1172	1703	2588	2 Dr STD Conv	879	1278	1943
2 Dr STD 4WD Conv	1027	1493	2269				

Options	Price	Options	Price
AM/FM/Cassette/CD Audio System	+81	Automatic 3-Speed Transmission	+84
Air Conditioning	+105	Hardtop Roof	+106

Canyon

2004

Mileage Category: J

Body Styles	Trade	Private	Dealer
2 Dr Z71 SL 4WD Regular Cab SB	11317	12569	14655
2 Dr Z71 SL Regular Cab SB	9573	10825	12911
2 Dr Z71 SLE 4WD Regular Cab SB	12153	13405	15491
2 Dr Z71 SLE Regular Cab SB	10504	11792	13938
2 Dr Z85 SL 4WD Regular Cab SB	10358	11610	13696
2 Dr Z85 SL Regular Cab SB	8654	9906	11992
2 Dr Z85 SLE 4WD Regular Cab SB	10873	12125	14211
2 Dr Z85 SLE Regular Cab SB	9169	10421	12507
4 Dr Z71 SL 4WD Ext Cab SB	12828	14122	16279
4 Dr Z71 SL Ext Cab SB	11136	12388	14474
4 Dr Z71 SL 4WD Crew Cab SB	16391	17923	20475
4 Dr Z71 SLE 4WD Ext Cab SB	13831	15102	17219
4 Dr Z71 SLE Base 4WD Crew Cab SB	16036	17569	20125

Body Styles	Trade	Private	Dealer
4 Dr Z71 SLE Base Crew Cab SB	14359	15904	18480
4 Dr Z71 SLE Crew Cab SB	14434	15967	18523
4 Dr Z71 SLE Ext Cab SB	11924	13176	15262
4 Dr Z85 SL 4WD Ext Cab SB	11871	13142	15259
4 Dr Z85 SL Ext Cab SB	10216	11468	13554
4 Dr Z85 SLE 4WD Crew Cab SB	14376	15921	18496
4 Dr Z85 SLE 4WD Ext Cab SB	12794	14065	16182
4 Dr Z85 SLE Base 4WD Crew Cab SB	13812	15362	17945
4 Dr Z85 SLE Base Crew Cab SB	12108	13634	16177
4 Dr Z85 SLE Crew Cab SB	12685	14207	16744
4 Dr Z85 SLE Ext Cab SB	11138	12390	14476

The Canyon is an all-new compact pickup from GMC.

Options	Price
3.5L I5 DOHC 20V FI Engine [Std on Z71 Crew]	+1000
AM/FM/CD Changer Audio System [Opt on SLE, SLE Base Crew]	+395
Automatic 4-Speed Transmission [Std on Z71 Crew]	+1095
Automatic Dimming Rearview Mirror [Opt on SLE, SLE Base Crew]	+175
Front and Rear Head Airbag Restraints	+195
Heated Front Seats [Opt on Crew]	+195
Leather Seats [Opt on Crew]	+800
Locking Differential [Opt on Z85 non-SLE Crew]	+270
OnStar Telematics System [Opt on SLE, SLE Base Crew]	+695

Options	Price
Power Driver Seat [Opt on Crew]	+250
Power Mirrors [Opt on SLE, SLE Base Crew]	+150
Power Passenger Seat [Opt on Crew]	+250
Power Windows [Opt on SLE, SLE Base Crew]	+250
Satellite Radio System	+325
Skid Plates [Opt on Z85 SLE 4WD, SLE Base Crew 4WD]	+120
Sliding Rear Window	+120
Special Factory Paint	+165

Envoy

2004

Mileage Category: O

Body Styles	Trade	Private	Dealer
4 Dr SLE 4WD SUV	17944	19419	21878
4 Dr SLE SUV	17002	18430	20809

Body Styles	Trade	Private	Dealer
4 Dr SLT 4WD SUV	21368	22872	25380
4 Dr SLT SUV	20068	21495	23874

Options	Price
AM/FM/CD Changer Audio System	+245
AM/FM/Cassette/CD Audio System	+150
Automatic Load Leveling	+375
Bose Audio System	+225
DVD Entertainment System	+1295
Front Side Airbag Restraints	+350
Garage Door Opener [Opt on SLE]	+120
Headlight Washers [Opt on SLT]	+150
Heated Front Seats [Opt on SLT]	+250
Locking Differential	+270
Metallic Paint	+165
Navigation System [Opt on SLT]	+1800
OnStar Telematics System [Opt on SLE]	+220

Options	Price
Overhead Console [Opt on SLE]	+125
Polished Aluminum/Alloy Wheels	+495
Power Adjustable Foot Pedals	+150
Power Driver Seat [Opt on SLE]	+275
Power Heated Mirrors	+133
Power Moonroof	+800
Power Passenger Seat [Opt on SLE]	+275
Rain Sensing Windshield Wipers [Opt on SLT]	+220
Rear Window Defroster [Opt on SLE]	+177
Satellite Radio System	+325
Side Steps	+375
Skid Plates	+200
Traction Control System	+175

For 2004, the Envoy adds several items to the options list, including XM Satellite Radio (and a new stereo to accommodate it), a DVD-based navigation system and adjustable pedals. There are also a few minor equipment changes this year. In SLE models, the door trim is now vinyl instead of cloth, and lumbar adjustment for the front seats is two-way manual rather than the previous four-way feature. Additionally, there is no longer a power outlet in the cargo area, and SLE badging will no longer grace the B-pillars. SLT models also get a revised steering wheel. Lastly, when playing a DVD in Envoys with the optional entertainment system, you can now hear it through the audio system in addition to the wireless headphones.

GMC
Envoy

2003

For 2003, Envoy buyers are able to order certain options individually, rather than as part of an equipment package, adding potential savings and increased flexibility. The sport-ute's already powerful Vortec 4.2-liter inline six also gets a slight bump in horsepower, up from 270 to 275, and Envoys now boast a new four-position headlamp switch that permits drivers to turn off the vehicle's daytime running lamps and automatic headlamps when necessary. Additionally, the Envoy gets a larger fuel tank that holds 22 gallons. Previously standard side airbags are now optional, while autodimming side mirrors and the rear seat overhead compartment have been deleted.

Mileage Category: O

Body Styles	TMV Pricing		
	Trade	Private	Dealer
4 Dr SLE 4WD SUV	16283	17404	19271
4 Dr SLE SUV	14170	15146	16772

Options	Price
AM/FM/CD Changer Audio System	+158
Automatic Load Leveling	+241
Bose Audio System [Opt on SLT]	+319
DVD Entertainment System	+644
Front Side Airbag Restraints	+225
Heated Front Seats [Opt on SLT]	+161
Locking Differential	+174

Body Styles	TMV Pricing		
	Trade	Private	Dealer
4 Dr SLT 4WD SUV	17780	19004	21044
4 Dr SLT SUV	16673	17821	19734

Options	Price
OnStar Telematics System [Opt on SLE]	+447
Power Driver Seat [Opt on SLE]	+177
Power Moonroof	+515
Power Passenger Seat [Opt on SLE]	+177
Rain Sensing Windshield Wipers [Opt on SLT]	+119
Running Boards	+241
Skid Plates	+129

2002

Long overdue for a redesign, GMC's all-new Envoy finally gets the goods to compete in the highly competitive midsize SUV segment. An all-aluminum inline six-cylinder engine replaces the aging 4.3-liter V6, and a revised suspension dramatically improves the ride. Unlike the 2000 Envoy that was virtually indistinguishable from its Chevrolet and Oldsmobile siblings, the 2002 model now sports a new look that is unique to the GMC brand.

Mileage Category: O

Body Styles	TMV Pricing		
	Trade	Private	Dealer
4 Dr SLE 4WD SUV	13936	15056	16922
4 Dr SLE SUV	12812	13841	15555

Options	Price
17 Inch Wheels	+237
AM/FM/CD Changer Audio System	+147
Automatic Load Leveling	+150
Bose Audio System [Opt on SLT]	+180
Compact Disc Changer [Opt on SLE]	+299
DVD Entertainment System	+539

Body Styles	TMV Pricing		
	Trade	Private	Dealer
4 Dr SLT 4WD SUV	15554	16804	18887
4 Dr SLT SUV	14514	15679	17622

Options	Price
Heated Front Seats [Opt on SLT]	+150
Locking Differential [Opt on 2WD]	+162
Power Moonroof	+479
Power Passenger Seat [Opt on SLE]	+135
Running Boards	+195

2000

Mileage Category: O

Body Styles	TMV Pricing		
	Trade	Private	Dealer
4 Dr STD 4WD SUV	8941	10479	11987

Options	Price	Options	Price
Limited Slip Differential	+134	Power Moonroof	+373
OnStar Telematics System	+445		

Upgraded seats and V6 engine improvements headline changes to GM's high-end compact SUV. There's also a new metallic paint color, and a heavy-duty battery is now standard.

1999

After its debut as General Motors' high-end compact SUV last year, the GMC Envoy gets equipment upgrades for '99. A new mini-module for the driver airbag allows for steering wheel radio controls, and the turn signal stalk now incorporates a flash-to-pass headlamp feature. Heated, eight-way power front seating is improved, thanks to available two-position memory for the driver and power recliners. A liftgate ajar telltale resides in the instrument cluster, and the outside rearview mirrors have been redesigned, featuring electrochromic dimming and power-folding capability. GM's advanced AutoTrac active transfer case is now standard, while a new shift lever-mounted button selects a tow/haul mode to optimize transmission shift points. There are three new metallic exterior paint colors: Topaz Gold, Meadow Green and Indigo Blue.

Mileage Category: O

Body Styles	TMV Pricing		
	Trade	Private	Dealer
4 Dr STD 4WD SUV	7537	9000	10524

Options	Price	Options	Price
OnStar Telematics System	+401	Power Moonroof	+302

1998

GMC introduces its finest luxury compact SUV to date: the Envoy.

Mileage Category: O

Body Styles	TMV Pricing		
	Trade	Private	Dealer
4 Dr STD 4WD SUV	6564	7949	9510

Options	Price
Power Moonroof	+260

Envoy XL

2004

Mileage Category: M

Body Styles	TMV Pricing		
	Trade	Private	Dealer
4 Dr SLE 4WD SUV	19067	20575	23089
4 Dr SLE SUV	17813	19245	21632

Options	Price
5.3L V8 OHV 16V FI Engine	+1500
AM/FM/CD Changer Audio System	+245
AM/FM/Cassette/CD Audio System	+150
Automatic Load Leveling	+375
Bose Audio System [Opt on SLT]	+225
DVD Entertainment System	+1295
Front Side Airbag Restraints	+350
Headlight Washers [Opt on SLT]	+150
Heated Front Seats [Opt on SLT]	+250
Locking Differential	+270
Metallic Paint	+165
Navigation System [Opt on SLT]	+1800
OnStar Telematics System [Opt on SLE]	+235

Body Styles	TMV Pricing		
	Trade	Private	Dealer
4 Dr SLT 4WD SUV	22303	23811	26324
4 Dr SLT SUV	21051	22445	24766

Options	Price
Polished Aluminum/Alloy Wheels	+495
Power Adjustable Foot Pedals	+150
Power Driver Seat [Opt on SLE]	+250
Power Heated Mirrors [Opt on SLE]	+120
Power Moonroof	+800
Power Passenger Seat [Opt on SLE]	+275
Premium Audio System	+495
Rain Sensing Windshield Wipers [Opt on SLT]	+220
Satellite Radio System	+325
Side Steps	+375
Skid Plates	+200
Traction Control System	+175

For 2004, the Envoy XL adds several items to the options list, including XM Satellite Radio (and a new stereo to accommodate it), a DVD-based navigation system and adjustable pedals. There are a few minor equipment changes this year. In SLE models, the door trim is now vinyl instead of cloth, and lumbar adjustment for the front seats is two-way manual rather than the previous four-way feature. Additionally, there is no longer a power outlet in the cargo area. The SLT gets a slightly revised steering wheel, and vehicles equipped with the DVD entertainment system can now hear it through the vehicle's audio system in addition to the wireless headphones.

2003

Mileage Category: M

Body Styles	TMV Pricing		
	Trade	Private	Dealer
4 Dr SLE 4WD SUV	17681	19265	21904
4 Dr SLE SUV	16222	17675	20096

Options	Price
5.3L V8 OHV 16V FI Engine	+966
AM/FM/CD Changer Audio System	+158
Automatic Load Leveling	+241
Bose Audio System [Opt on SLT]	+319
DVD Entertainment System	+644
Front Side Airbag Restraints	+225
Heated Front Seats [Opt on SLT]	+161
Locking Differential	+174

Body Styles	TMV Pricing		
	Trade	Private	Dealer
4 Dr SLT 4WD SUV	19476	21220	24127
4 Dr SLT SUV	18285	19923	22652

Options	Price
OnStar Telematics System [Opt on SLE]	+447
Power Driver Seat [Opt on SLE]	+177
Power Moonroof	+515
Power Passenger Seat [Opt on SLE]	+177
Rain Sensing Windshield Wipers [Opt on SLT]	+119
Running Boards	+241
Skid Plates	+129

For 2003, Envoy XL buyers are able to order options individually, rather than as part of an equipment package, adding potential savings and increased flexibility. The sport-ute's already powerful 4.2-liter inline six engine also gets a slight bump in horsepower, up from 270 to 275; XL buyers seeking increased low-end torque, greater cargo-hauling and trailering capability and speedier acceleration may step up to the newly offered 5.3-liter V8, which spews 290 horsepower and 325 pound-feet of torque. Additionally, Envoy XLs now boast a new four-position headlamp switch that permits drivers to turn off the vehicle's daytime running lamps and automatic headlamps when necessary.

2002

Mileage Category: M

Debuting as a midyear addition to the Envoy lineup, the Envoy XL is an extended-wheelbase seven-passenger version of the standard Envoy.

Body Styles	TMV Pricing		
	Trade	Private	Dealer
4 Dr SLE 4WD SUV	15410	16904	19395
4 Dr SLE SUV	14347	15738	18056

Options	Price
17 Inch Wheels	+269
AM/FM/CD Changer Audio System	+147
Automatic Load Leveling	+150
Bose Audio System [Opt on SLT]	+150
DVD Entertainment System	+539

Body Styles	TMV Pricing		
	Trade	Private	Dealer
4 Dr SLT 4WD SUV	16716	18336	21036
4 Dr SLT SUV	15643	17160	19688

Options	Price
Heated Front Seats [Opt on SLT]	+150
Locking Differential [Opt on 2WD]	+135
Power Passenger Seat [Opt on SLE]	+135
Power Sunroof	+479

Envoy XUV

2004

The Envoy XUV is an all-new model based on the Envoy XL sport-utility model with the third-row seating area turned into a reconfigurable cargo hold a la Chevy Avalanche. But the XUV goes one better by offering a power-sliding rear roof section in addition to its fold-down midgate and all-weather cargo area.

Mileage Category: O

Body Styles	TMV Pricing		
	Trade	Private	Dealer
4 Dr SLE 4WD SUV	18703	20172	22620
4 Dr SLE SUV	17623	19017	21340

Options	Price
5.3L V8 OHV 16V FI Engine	+1500
AM/FM/CD Changer Audio System	+245
AM/FM/Cassette/CD Audio System	+150
Automatic Dimming Rearview Mirror [Opt on SLE]	+120
Automatic Load Leveling	+375
Bose Audio System [Opt on SLT]	+220
Front Side Airbag Restraints	+350
Headlight Washers [Opt on SLT]	+150
Locking Differential	+270
Metallic Paint	+165
Navigation System [Opt on SLT]	+1845

Body Styles	TMV Pricing		
	Trade	Private	Dealer
4 Dr SLT 4WD SUV	21322	22791	25239
4 Dr SLT SUV	20241	21635	23958

Options	Price
OnStar Telematics System [Opt on SLT]	+225
Polished Aluminum/Alloy Wheels	+395
Power Adjustable Foot Pedals	+150
Power Driver Seat [Opt on SLE]	+250
Power Moonroof	+800
Power Passenger Seat [Opt on SLE]	+275
Rain Sensing Windshield Wipers [Opt on SLT]	+220
Satellite Radio System	+325
Side Steps	+375
Skid Plates [Opt on 4WD]	+200
Traction Control System [Opt on 2WD]	+175

Jimmy

2001

The Vortec 4300 V6 enjoys another round of improvements, plus the Jimmy adds programmable door locks and a new cargo management system to its long list of features for 2001. A floor-shift option is now available on two-door models with automatic transmission, and the four-wheel-drive SLE version touts restyled alloy wheels. The tarted-up Envoy has been redesigned for 2002, but the glitzy Diamond Edition, introduced last year to mark the 30th anniversary of the Jimmy nameplate, is back -- packing more pizzazz.

Mileage Category: M

Body Styles	TMV Pricing		
	Trade	Private	Dealer
2 Dr SLS 4WD SUV	6477	7674	8778
2 Dr SLS Convenience 4WD SUV	7328	8682	9931
2 Dr SLS Convenience SUV	6435	7623	8719
2 Dr SLS SUV	5541	6564	7509
4 Dr Diamond Edition 4WD SUV	9697	11487	13139
4 Dr Diamond Edition SUV	9070	10745	12291

Options	Price
Automatic 4-Speed Transmission [Opt on SLS]	+546
Bose Audio System	+270
Brush Guard	+300
Camper/Towing Package	+115
Compact Disc Changer	+216
Heated Front Seats	+137
Locking Differential	+147
OnStar Telematics System	+380

Body Styles	TMV Pricing		
	Trade	Private	Dealer
4 Dr Diamond Edition Special 4WD SUV	10901	12914	14772
4 Dr SLE 4WD SUV	8534	10110	11564
4 Dr SLE SUV	7862	9314	10655
4 Dr SLT 4WD SUV	9113	10796	12349
4 Dr SLT SUV	8177	9687	11081

Options	Price
Power Door Locks [Opt on SLS]	+123
Power Driver Seat	+131
Power Passenger Seat	+131
Power Sunroof	+437
Power Windows [Opt on SLS]	+131
Trailer Hitch	+115
Two-Tone Paint	+123

2000

For 2000, GMC is celebrating the 30th anniversary of its Jimmy nameplate with a Diamond Edition model. Other changes center on new equipment and suspension packaging. A heavy-duty battery is now standard, and Jimmy's V6 has been upgraded with a roller timing chain, sprocket and rocker arms for improved durability and reduced noise. There are also two new exterior colors, while the SLE gets a revised cloth interior.

Mileage Category: M

Body Styles	TMV Pricing		
	Trade	Private	Dealer
2 Dr SLS 4WD SUV	5267	6449	7607
2 Dr SLS Convenience 4WD SUV	5893	7216	8512
2 Dr SLS Convenience SUV	5069	6206	7321
2 Dr SLS SUV	4427	5420	6394
4 Dr Diamond Edition 4WD SUV	7221	8842	10430

Options	Price
AM/FM/Cassette/CD Audio System	+170
Automatic 4-Speed Transmission [Opt on SLS]	+497
Automatic Load Leveling	+125
Compact Disc Changer	+197
Delco/Bose Audio System	+246
Heated Front Seats	+125

Body Styles	TMV Pricing		
	Trade	Private	Dealer
4 Dr Diamond Edition SUV	6700	8203	9677
4 Dr SLE 4WD SUV	6603	8085	9537
4 Dr SLE SUV	5942	7275	8581
4 Dr SLT 4WD SUV	6740	8252	9734
4 Dr SLT SUV	6479	7933	9358

Options	Price
Limited Slip Differential [Std on SLS,STD 2WD 2 Dr]	+134
Power Driver Seat [Opt on SLE,SLS,SLS Convenience]	+119
Power Moonroof	+373
Power Passenger Seat	+119
Power Windows [Opt on SLS]	+125

1999

There are three new colors and revised outside mirrors, but most changes to the '99 Jimmy are inside. You'll find new power-seating features, redundant radio controls and a mini-module depowered airbag in the steering wheel, as well as a new Bose premium sound system and six-disc CD changer. A vehicle content theft alarm, flash-to-pass headlamp feature and liftgate ajar warning lamp have also been added. Four-wheel-drive versions get the new AutoTrac active transfer case and four-door models gain a tow/haul mode for the transmission. Finally, the optional Z85 Euro-Ride suspension has been retuned.

Mileage Category: M

Body Styles	Trade	Private	Dealer
2 Dr SL 4WD SUV	4530	5646	6807
2 Dr SL SUV	3775	4705	5672
2 Dr SLS Sport 4WD SUV	4632	5773	6960
2 Dr SLS Sport SUV	3854	4803	5791
4 Dr SL 4WD SUV	5007	6241	7525

Options	Price
AM/FM/Cassette/CD Audio System	+137
Automatic 4-Speed Transmission [Std on SLE,SLS Sport,SLT,Wgn]	+403
Compact Disc Changer	+159

Body Styles	Trade	Private	Dealer
4 Dr SL SUV	4595	5727	6905
4 Dr SLE 4WD SUV	5765	7186	8664
4 Dr SLE SUV	5034	6274	7565
4 Dr SLT 4WD SUV	6115	7621	9189
4 Dr SLT SUV	5739	7153	8624

Options	Price
Delco/Bose Audio System	+200
Power Moonroof	+302

1998

A revised interior contains dual second-generation airbags, improved climate controls and available premium sound systems. Outside, the front bumper, grille and headlights are new. Side cladding is restyled and SLT models have new alloy wheels. Fresh colors inside and out sum up the changes.

Mileage Category: M

Body Styles	Trade	Private	Dealer
2 Dr SL 4WD SUV	3884	4949	6150
2 Dr SL SUV	3272	4170	5182
2 Dr SLS Sport 4WD SUV	4143	5280	6562
2 Dr SLS Sport SUV	3398	4331	5383
4 Dr SL 4WD SUV	4182	5329	6622
4 Dr SL SUV	3921	4996	6209

Options	Price
AM/FM/Cassette/CD Audio System	+118
Compact Disc Changer	+137

Body Styles	Trade	Private	Dealer
4 Dr SLE 4WD SUV	4691	5977	7427
4 Dr SLE SUV	4240	5403	6715
4 Dr SLS Sport 4WD SUV	4506	5742	7136
4 Dr SLS Sport SUV	4067	5182	6440
4 Dr SLT 4WD SUV	4982	6348	7889
4 Dr SLT SUV	4542	5788	7193

Options	Price
Power Moonroof	+260

1997

Highrider off-road package deleted as GMC realigns Jimmy as luxury sport-ute. Instead, buyers can opt for a Gold Edition in one of four colors. New options include a power sunroof and HomeLink universal transmitter. Radar Purple and Bright Teal paint colors are replaced by Fairway Green and Smoky Caramel.

Mileage Category: M

Body Styles	Trade	Private	Dealer
2 Dr SL 4WD SUV	2977	3891	5009
2 Dr SL SUV	2703	3533	4547
2 Dr SLS Sport 4WD SUV	3019	3947	5082
2 Dr SLS Sport SUV	3016	3943	5076
4 Dr SL 4WD SUV	3059	3999	5147
4 Dr SL SUV	2741	3583	4613

Body Styles	Trade	Private	Dealer
4 Dr SLE 4WD SUV	3620	4732	6092
4 Dr SLE SUV	3198	4181	5382
4 Dr SLS Sport 4WD SUV	3374	4411	5678
4 Dr SLS Sport SUV	3091	4041	5203
4 Dr SLT 4WD SUV	3725	4870	6269
4 Dr SLT SUV	3409	4456	5736

Options	Price
Power Moonroof	+218

1996

GMC's popular compact sport-utility gets an optional off-road package called Highrider, as well as an available five-speed transmission. Either of these are available on two-door models only. All Jimmys receive glow-in-the-day headlights and long-life engine coolant. Spark plugs last 100,000 miles. All-wheel drive, which became optional in mid-1995, continues. Conspicuously absent is a passenger airbag.

Mileage Category: M

Body Styles	Trade	Private	Dealer
2 Dr SL 4WD SUV	2462	3268	4382
2 Dr SL SUV	2327	3089	4141
2 Dr SLS 4WD SUV	2606	3459	4636
2 Dr SLS SUV	2393	3177	4259
2 Dr STD 4WD SUV	2338	3104	4161
2 Dr STD SUV	2047	2717	3642
4 Dr SL 4WD SUV	2696	3578	4797
4 Dr SL SUV	2450	3253	4361

Body Styles	Trade	Private	Dealer
4 Dr SLE 4WD SUV	2891	3837	5144
4 Dr SLE SUV	2663	3535	4738
4 Dr SLS 4WD SUV	2824	3749	5026
4 Dr SLS SUV	2597	3447	4621
4 Dr SLT 4WD SUV	3116	4136	5545
4 Dr SLT SUV	2856	3791	5083
4 Dr STD 4WD SUV	2535	3365	4510
4 Dr STD SUV	2272	3017	4045

1995

All-new SUV appears based on revamped Sonoma. Four-wheel-drive models have electronic transfer case as standard equipment. Spare tire on four-door model is mounted beneath cargo bay instead of in it. Five different suspension packages are available. One engine, a 195-horsepower 4.3-liter V6, is available. All-wheel drive is optional. Driver airbag and air conditioning are standard equipment.

Mileage Category: M

Body Styles	Trade	Private	Dealer
2 Dr SL 4WD SUV	1839	2528	3675
2 Dr SL SUV	1635	2247	3267
2 Dr SLS 4WD SUV	2143	2946	4283
2 Dr SLS SUV	1812	2491	3623

Body Styles	Trade	Private	Dealer
2 Dr STD 4WD SUV	1799	2473	3596
2 Dr STD SUV	1609	2212	3216
4 Dr SLE 4WD SUV	2230	3066	4458
4 Dr SLE SUV	2133	2932	4264

Jimmy/Sierra 1500

1995 (cont'd)

Body Styles	TMV Pricing		
	Trade	Private	Dealer
4 Dr SLS 4WD SUV	2384	3278	4767
4 Dr SLS SUV	2168	2980	4333
4 Dr SLT 4WD SUV	2573	3536	5141

Options	Price
AM/FM/CD Audio System	+85

Body Styles	TMV Pricing		
	Trade	Private	Dealer
4 Dr SLT SUV	2384	3278	4767
4 Dr STD 4WD SUV	2107	2896	4212
4 Dr STD SUV	1783	2451	3565

Options	Price
AM/FM/Cassette/CD Audio System [Opt on SLS]	+88

Sierra 1500

2004

The big news for 2004 is the addition of an all-new light-duty 1500 Crew cab model with a five-and-a-half-foot bed that replaces last year's 1500HD model. The Work truck package is now available on all Sierras, while base models get standard cruise control along with a chrome grille, wheels and bumper. Other changes include newly designed 17-inch wheels on 4WD models, the deletion of the Professional package and a Quadrasteer package that is now available without additional trailering equipment.

Mileage Category: K

Body Styles	TMV Pricing		
	Trade	Private	Dealer
2 Dr SLE 4WD Std Cab LB	16388	17627	19692
2 Dr SLE 4WD Std Cab SB	16213	17451	19515
2 Dr SLE Std Cab LB	14214	15420	17429
2 Dr SLE Std Cab SB	14038	15243	17250
2 Dr STD 4WD Std Cab LB	14847	16079	18132
2 Dr STD 4WD Std Cab SB	14673	15904	17956
2 Dr STD Std Cab LB	11582	12766	14739
2 Dr STD Std Cab SB	11408	12590	14561
2 Dr Work Truck 4WD Std Cab LB	13784	15010	17054
2 Dr Work Truck 4WD Std Cab SB	13727	14953	16996
2 Dr Work Truck Std Cab LB	10520	11693	13647
2 Dr Work Truck Std Cab SB	10463	11635	13587
4 Dr Denali AWD Ext Cab SB	25173	26732	29329
4 Dr SLE 4WD Crew Cab SB	20819	22319	24818
4 Dr SLE 4WD Ext Cab LB	19361	20673	22860
4 Dr SLE 4WD Ext Cab SB	18667	19979	22166
4 Dr SLE Crew Cab SB	18789	20289	22788

Body Styles	TMV Pricing		
	Trade	Private	Dealer
4 Dr SLE Ext Cab LB	17273	18563	20714
4 Dr SLE Ext Cab SB	16578	17868	20017
4 Dr SLT 4WD Crew Cab SB	23058	24558	27057
4 Dr SLT 4WD Ext Cab LB	21789	23101	25288
4 Dr SLT 4WD Ext Cab SB	21614	22926	25113
4 Dr SLT Crew Cab SB	21027	22527	25026
4 Dr SLT Ext Cab LB	19528	20821	22976
4 Dr SLT Ext Cab SB	19393	20710	22905
4 Dr STD 4WD Ext Cab LB	18339	19651	21838
4 Dr STD 4WD Ext Cab SB	17645	18957	21144
4 Dr STD Ext Cab LB	16309	17598	19747
4 Dr STD Ext Cab SB	15731	17019	19166
4 Dr Work Truck 4WD Ext Cab LB	16370	17609	19674
4 Dr Work Truck 4WD Ext Cab SB	16449	17746	19907
4 Dr Work Truck Ext Cab LB	14631	15862	17913
4 Dr Work Truck Ext Cab SB	13646	14872	16914

Options	Price
4 Wheel Steering [Opt on SLE, SLT Ext SB]	+1995
5.3L V8 Flex Fuel OHV 16V FI Engine [Opt on non-Denali, Crew]	+1050
5.3L V8 OHV 16V FI Engine [Opt on STD, SLE, Work Truck]	+800
AM/FM/CD Changer Audio System [Opt on SLE non-Std]	+795
Aluminum/Alloy Wheels [Opt on SLE, SLT]	+400
Automatic Climate Control (2 Zone) - Driver and Passenger [Opt on SLE non-Std]	+195
Cruise Control [Opt on Work Truck]	+240
DVD Entertainment System [Opt on Crew]	+1295
Leather Seats [Opt on SLE non-Std]	+800
Locking Differential [Opt on non-Denali, 4WD SLT]	+295
OnStar Telematics System [Opt on SLE Ext]	+695

Options	Price
Power Door Locks [Opt on STD, Work Truck]	+162
Power Retractable Mirrors [Opt on SLE, SLT]	+213
Power Windows [Opt on STD, Work Truck]	+738
Rear Audio Controls [Opt on Crew]	+165
Rear Window Defroster [Opt on STD]	+175
Steering Wheel Radio Controls [Opt on SLE]	+125
Stepside Bed [Opt on STD, SLE, SLT non-Crew SB]	+795
Traction Control System [Opt on 2WD STD, SLE, SLT]	+225
Two-Tone Paint [Opt on SLE, SLT Ext SB]	+250
Z71 Off-Road Suspension Package [Opt on 4WD SLE, SLT]	+150

2003

The Sierra gets a revised look this year that includes a new front fascia, revised side moldings and an additional wheel design. Top-of-the-line models get power-folding heated mirrors with puddle lamps and turn signal indicators. Inside, the Sierra now offers a Bose stereo system and XM Satellite Radio. The instrument panel and center console have been redesigned, and GMC has added new seats, a more comprehensive driver information center, optional satellite steering wheel controls and a dual-zone climate control system. For increased safety, Sierras now feature a standard front-passenger-sensing system and dual-stage airbags. All 4.3-liter V6-equipped Sierras and California-emission V8s are now ULEV certified, while electronic throttle control is now standard on all V8 engines. Finally, the Autotrac four-wheel-drive system has been modified for less intrusiveness at low speeds, and the brake system received upgrades that provide better pedal feel and improved overall performance.

Mileage Category: K

Body Styles	TMV Pricing		
	Trade	Private	Dealer
2 Dr SLE 4WD Std Cab LB	15220	16363	18269
2 Dr SLE 4WD Std Cab SB	15064	16196	18082
2 Dr SLE Std Cab LB	12953	13926	15547
2 Dr SLE Std Cab SB	12776	13736	15335
2 Dr STD 4WD Std Cab LB	13221	14214	15869
2 Dr STD 4WD Std Cab SB	13063	14044	15680
2 Dr STD Std Cab LB	10672	11473	12809
2 Dr STD Std Cab SB	10514	11304	12620
2 Dr Work Truck 4WD Std Cab LB	12848	13813	15422
2 Dr Work Truck Std Cab LB	9458	10168	11352

Body Styles	TMV Pricing		
	Trade	Private	Dealer
4 Dr Denali AWD Ext Cab SB	23215	24959	27865
4 Dr SLE 4WD Ext Cab LB	16972	18247	20372
4 Dr SLE 4WD Ext Cab SB	16398	17630	19684
4 Dr SLE Ext Cab LB	15355	16509	18431
4 Dr SLE Ext Cab SB	14778	15888	17739
4 Dr SLT 4WD Ext Cab LB	17933	19280	21525
4 Dr SLT 4WD Ext Cab SB	17356	18660	20834
4 Dr SLT Ext Cab LB	16313	17539	19581
4 Dr SLT Ext Cab SB	15740	16922	18893
4 Dr STD 4WD Ext Cab LB	15540	16707	18653

Body Styles	TMV Pricing		
	Trade	Private	Dealer
4 Dr STD 4WD Ext Cab SB	14968	16092	17966
4 Dr STD Ext Cab LB	13976	15026	16775

Options	Price
4 Wheel Steering [Opt on SLE,SLT]	+2894
5.3L V8 Flex Fuel OHV 16V FI Engine	+515
5.3L V8 OHV 16V FI Engine	+515
AM/FM/CD Audio System [Std on SLE,SLT]	+164
AM/FM/CD Changer Audio System [Opt on SLE,SLT]	+383
Aluminum/Alloy Wheels [Opt on SLE,SLT]	+129
Automatic 4-Speed Transmission [Opt on STD,Work]	+705
Automatic Climate Control (2 Zone) - Driver and Passenger [Opt on SLE]	+126
Bed Liner	+161
Bose Audio System [Opt on SLE,SLT]	+129
Bucket Seats [Opt on SLE,SLT]	+274
Chrome Wheels [Opt on STD,Work]	+200
Cruise Control [Opt on STD,Work]	+155
Electronic Suspension Control [Opt on SLE,SLT]	+209

Body Styles	TMV Pricing		
	Trade	Private	Dealer
4 Dr STD Ext Cab SB	13404	14411	16088
4 Dr Work Truck Ext Cab SB	12359	13288	14835

Options	Price
Flex Fuel Option	+207
Limited Slip Differential	+190
Locking Differential	+190
OnStar Telematics System [Opt on SLE]	+447
Power Driver Seat [Opt on SLE]	+155
Power Passenger Seat [Opt on SLT]	+158
Power Retractable Mirrors [Opt on SLE,SLT]	+118
Power Windows [Opt on STD,Work]	+171
Satellite Radio System [Opt on Denali,SLE,SLT]	+209
Stepside Bed [Opt on STD,SLE,SLT]	+512
Traction Control System [Opt on STD,SLE,SLT]	+145
Two-Tone Paint [Opt on SLE,SLT]	+161
Z71 Off-Road Suspension Package [Opt on SLE,SLT]	+177

2002

The Sierra C3 gets a name change to Sierra Denali in addition to a trick new four-wheel steering system. On standard Sierras, the previously optional Z85 firm-ride suspension is now standard on all 1500 models for improved handling and towing capacity. Base SL models now include air conditioning while uplevel SLE and SLT models add deep-tinted glass to the standard feature list.

Mileage Category: K

Body Styles	TMV Pricing		
	Trade	Private	Dealer
2 Dr HT 4WD Std Cab SB	12970	14056	15865
2 Dr HT Std Cab SB	11249	12191	13760
2 Dr SL 4WD Std Cab LB	12267	13294	15005
2 Dr SL 4WD Std Cab SB	12211	13233	14936
2 Dr SL Std Cab LB	9706	10519	11873
2 Dr SL Std Cab SB	9565	10366	11700
2 Dr SLE 4WD Std Cab LB	13403	14525	16395
2 Dr SLE 4WD Std Cab SB	13250	14360	16209
2 Dr SLE Std Cab LB	11813	12802	14450
2 Dr SLE Std Cab SB	11683	12661	14291
2 Dr STD 4WD Std Cab LB	11334	12283	13864
2 Dr STD 4WD Std Cab SB	11239	12180	13748
2 Dr STD Std Cab LB	8982	9734	10988
2 Dr STD Std Cab SB	8898	9643	10885
2 Dr Work Truck 4WD Std Cab LB	11227	12167	13733
2 Dr Work Truck Std Cab LB	8566	9271	10446
4 Dr Denali AWD Ext Cab SB	21490	23289	26287

Body Styles	TMV Pricing		
	Trade	Private	Dealer
4 Dr SL 4WD Ext Cab LB	13999	15171	17125
4 Dr SL 4WD Ext Cab SB	13859	15019	16953
4 Dr SL Ext Cab LB	12549	13599	15350
4 Dr SL Ext Cab SB	12395	13433	15163
4 Dr SLE 4WD Ext Cab LB	14786	16024	18087
4 Dr SLE 4WD Ext Cab SB	14627	15851	17892
4 Dr SLE Ext Cab LB	13273	14384	16235
4 Dr SLE Ext Cab SB	13096	14192	16019
4 Dr SLT 4WD Ext Cab LB	15661	16972	19158
4 Dr SLT 4WD Ext Cab SB	15510	16808	18972
4 Dr SLT Ext Cab LB	14119	15301	17271
4 Dr SLT Ext Cab SB	13953	15121	17068
4 Dr STD 4WD Ext Cab LB	13474	14602	16482
4 Dr STD 4WD Ext Cab SB	13332	14448	16308
4 Dr STD Ext Cab LB	12299	13329	15045
4 Dr STD Ext Cab SB	12246	13271	14980

Options	Price
4 Wheel Steering [Opt on Ext Cab - SLE,SLT]	+3105
4.8L V8 OHV 16V FI Engine [Opt on Std Cab 2WD - SL,STD,Work]	+416
5.3L V8 OHV 16V FI Engine	+479
AM/FM/CD Audio System [Opt on Ext Cab - SLE,SLT]	+117
Air Conditioning [Opt on Std Cab - STD,Work]	+494
Automatic 4-Speed Transmission [Opt on Std Cab 2WD - SL,STD,Work]	+656
Bed Liner [Opt on Ext Cab - SLE,SLT]	+150
Bucket Seats [Opt on SLE,SLT]	+153
Cruise Control [Std on SLE,SLT]	+144

Options	Price
Electronic Suspension Control [Opt on SLE,SLT]	+195
Locking Differential [Std on Denali,SLT 4WD]	+171
Off-Road Suspension Package [Opt on 4WD - SLE,SLT]	+180
Power Driver Seat [Opt on SLE]	+147
Power Passenger Seat [Opt on SLE]	+147
Running Boards [Opt on Ext Cab SB - Denali,SLE,SLT]	+150
Traction Control System [Opt on 2WD]	+135
Two-Tone Paint [Opt on Ext Cab SB - SLE,SLT]	+150

Sierra 1500

2001

Reliability improvements for all Vortec V6 and V8 engines top the list of changes this year. Consequently, oil-change intervals have been extended to 7,500 miles. A traction assist feature is now available on two-wheel-drive V8 automatics, thanks to a new electronic throttle control system. Factory-installed OnStar, GM's mobile communications and security system, has been made standard with the SLT trim level. New this year is a 325-horse, all-wheel-drive performance version called the C3.

Mileage Category: K

Body Styles	TMV Pricing			Body Styles	TMV Pricing		
	Trade	Private	Dealer		Trade	Private	Dealer
2 Dr SL 4WD Std Cab LB	10341	11710	12974	4 Dr SL Ext Cab LB	10732	12153	13464
2 Dr SL 4WD Std Cab SB	10288	11650	12907	4 Dr SL Ext Cab SB	10587	11988	13282
2 Dr SL Std Cab LB	7643	8654	9588	4 Dr SLE 4WD Ext Cab LB	13249	15003	16622
2 Dr SL Std Cab SB	7531	8528	9448	4 Dr SLE 4WD Ext Cab SB	13102	14836	16437
2 Dr SLE 4WD Std Cab LB	11850	13418	14866	4 Dr SLE Ext Cab LB	11878	13450	14902
2 Dr SLE 4WD Std Cab SB	11711	13261	14692	4 Dr SLE Ext Cab SB	11723	13275	14707
2 Dr SLE Std Cab LB	10424	11804	13077	4 Dr SLT 4WD Ext Cab LB	14208	16089	17825
2 Dr SLE Std Cab SB	10389	11764	13033	4 Dr SLT 4WD Ext Cab SB	13472	15256	16902
4 Dr SL 4WD Ext Cab LB	12138	13744	15227	4 Dr SLT Ext Cab LB	12671	14348	15896
4 Dr SL 4WD Ext Cab SB	12009	13599	15066	4 Dr SLT Ext Cab SB	12569	14233	15769

Options	Price	Options	Price
4.8L V8 OHV 16V FI Engine [Opt on SL Std Cab 2WD]	+380	Off-Road Suspension Package	+216
5.3L V8 OHV 16V FI Engine	+437	Power Driver Seat [Opt on SLE]	+131
Air Conditioning [Opt on SL]	+440	Power Passenger Seat [Opt on SLE]	+131
Automatic 4-Speed Transmission [Opt on SL]	+598	Stepside Bed [Opt on SB]	+434
Bucket Seats	+137	Tonneau Cover	+131
Chrome Wheels [Opt on SL]	+169	Traction Control System [Opt on 2WD]	+123
Electronic Suspension Control	+177	Trailer Hitch	+156
Heated Front Seats	+137	Two-Tone Paint	+137
Locking Differential	+156		

2000

After a complete redesign last year, GMC's Silverado-based pickup finally gets a fourth door on the extended cab. There's also more power on tap from the 4.8- and 5.3-liter engines, increased trailer ratings and standard programmable automatic door locks. New factory appearance items, such as wheel-lip flares and a soft tonneau cover, are now available on some models.

Mileage Category: K

Body Styles	TMV Pricing			Body Styles	TMV Pricing		
	Trade	Private	Dealer		Trade	Private	Dealer
2 Dr SL 4WD Std Cab LB	7698	8852	9984	3 Dr SL Ext Cab LB	8794	10112	11403
2 Dr SL 4WD Std Cab SB	7587	8724	9839	3 Dr SL Ext Cab SB	8677	9978	11253
2 Dr SL 4WD Std Cab Step SB	7926	9114	10278	3 Dr SL Ext Cab Step SB	9015	10366	11691
2 Dr SL Std Cab LB	6535	7515	8475	3 Dr SLE 4WD Ext Cab LB	10857	12484	14078
2 Dr SL Std Cab SB	6421	7384	8327	3 Dr SLE 4WD Ext Cab SB	10741	12350	13928
2 Dr SL Std Cab Step SB	6759	7773	8766	3 Dr SLE 4WD Ext Cab Step SB	11044	12699	14321
2 Dr SLE 4WD Std Cab LB	9099	10464	11801	3 Dr SLE Ext Cab LB	9696	11149	12573
2 Dr SLE 4WD Std Cab SB	8986	10333	11653	3 Dr SLE Ext Cab SB	9582	11018	12426
2 Dr SLE 4WD Std Cab Step SB	9288	10680	12045	3 Dr SLE Ext Cab Step SB	9883	11365	12817
2 Dr SLE Std Cab LB	7941	9132	10299	3 Dr SLT 4WD Ext Cab LB	11657	13405	15118
2 Dr SLE Std Cab SB	7827	9001	10152	3 Dr SLT 4WD Ext Cab SB	11544	13275	14972
2 Dr SLE Std Cab Step SB	8129	9348	10542	3 Dr SLT 4WD Ext Cab Step SB	11848	13624	15364
3 Dr SL 4WD Ext Cab LB	9950	11441	12903	3 Dr SLT Ext Cab LB	10359	11911	13433
3 Dr SL 4WD Ext Cab SB	9835	11310	12755	3 Dr SLT Ext Cab SB	10244	11779	13284
3 Dr SL 4WD Ext Cab Step SB	10175	11700	13195	3 Dr SLT Ext Cab Step SB	10546	12127	13677

Options	Price	Options	Price
4.8L V8 OHV 16V FI Engine [Opt on SL,SLE]	+346	Heated Front Seats	+125
5.3L V8 OHV 16V FI Engine [Opt on SLE,SLT]	+399	Hinged Fourth Door	+164
AM/FM/Cassette/CD Audio System	+144	Limited Slip Differential	+134
Air Conditioning [Opt on SL]	+401	Power Driver Seat [Opt on SLE]	+119
Aluminum/Alloy Wheels	+154	Power Passenger Seat [Opt on SLE]	+119
Automatic 4-Speed Transmission [Opt on SL,SLE]	+545	Tonneau Cover	+119
Bucket Seats	+125	Trailer Hitch	+142
Chrome Wheels [Opt on SLE]	+154		

1999

Finally, the decade-old, full-size GMC pickup based on the C/K gets a complete redesign from the ground-up. Major structural, power, braking and interior enhancements characterize the all-new Sierra. Styling is evolutionary rather than revolutionary, both inside and out.

Mileage Category: K

Body Styles	TMV Pricing			Body Styles	TMV Pricing		
	Trade	Private	Dealer		Trade	Private	Dealer
2 Dr SL 4WD Std Cab LB	6601	7704	8853	2 Dr SL Std Cab LB	5586	6519	7490
2 Dr SL 4WD Std Cab SB	6501	7588	8719	2 Dr SL Std Cab SB	5484	6401	7356
2 Dr SL 4WD Std Cab Step SB	6730	7855	9026	2 Dr SL Std Cab Step SB	5713	6669	7663

For the latest vehicle information, visit www.edmunds.com

Body Styles	TMV Pricing		
	Trade	Private	Dealer
2 Dr SLE 4WD Std Cab LB	7837	9147	10511
2 Dr SLE 4WD Std Cab SB	7739	9033	10379
2 Dr SLE 4WD Std Cab Step SB	7936	9262	10643
2 Dr SLE Std Cab LB	6825	7966	9154
2 Dr SLE Std Cab SB	6727	7852	9022
2 Dr SLE Std Cab Step SB	6924	8081	9286
3 Dr SL 4WD Ext Cab LB	8567	9999	11490
3 Dr SL 4WD Ext Cab SB	8467	9883	11357
3 Dr SL 4WD Ext Cab Step SB	8944	10439	11995
3 Dr SL Ext Cab LB	7556	8819	10133
3 Dr SL Ext Cab SB	7456	8703	10000
3 Dr SL Ext Cab Step SB	7687	8972	10309

Body Styles	TMV Pricing		
	Trade	Private	Dealer
3 Dr SLE 4WD Ext Cab LB	9575	11175	12841
3 Dr SLE 4WD Ext Cab SB	9470	11053	12701
3 Dr SLE 4WD Ext Cab Step SB	9668	11284	12965
3 Dr SLE Ext Cab LB	8290	9677	11120
3 Dr SLE Ext Cab SB	8192	9562	10987
3 Dr SLE Ext Cab Step SB	8389	9791	11251
3 Dr SLT 4WD Ext Cab LB	10310	12033	13827
3 Dr SLT 4WD Ext Cab SB	10207	11913	13689
3 Dr SLT 4WD Ext Cab Step SB	10506	12262	14089
3 Dr SLT Ext Cab LB	9141	10669	12260
3 Dr SLT Ext Cab SB	9040	10551	12124
3 Dr SLT Ext Cab Step SB	9241	10786	12394

Options	Price
4.8L V8 OHV 16V FI Engine [Std on SLT]	+239
5.3L V8 OHV 16V FI Engine	+282
AM/FM/Cassette/CD Audio System	+117
Air Conditioning [Opt on SL]	+324

Options	Price
Aluminum/Alloy Wheels [Std on SLT]	+125
Automatic 4-Speed Transmission [Std on SLT]	+401
Chrome Wheels [Opt on SL]	+125

1998

Mileage Category: K

Body Styles	TMV Pricing		
	Trade	Private	Dealer
2 Dr C1500 SL Ext Cab LB	5633	6748	8005
2 Dr C1500 SL Ext Cab SB	5408	6479	7686
2 Dr C1500 SL Std Cab LB	4927	5902	7002
2 Dr C1500 SL Std Cab SB	4842	5801	6882
2 Dr C1500 SL Std Cab Step SB	5006	5997	7115
2 Dr C1500 SLE Ext Cab LB	6138	7353	8723
2 Dr C1500 SLE Ext Cab SB	5912	7083	8403
2 Dr C1500 SLE Ext Cab Step SB	6748	8084	9590
2 Dr C1500 SLE Std Cab LB	5432	6507	7720
2 Dr C1500 SLE Std Cab SB	5345	6404	7598
2 Dr C1500 SLE Std Cab Step SB	5511	6602	7832
2 Dr C1500 SLT Ext Cab LB	6792	8136	9652
2 Dr C1500 SLT Ext Cab SB	6565	7866	9333
2 Dr C1500 SLT Ext Cab Step SB	7260	8698	10320
2 Dr C1500 SLT Std Cab LB	6068	7269	8624
2 Dr C1500 SLT Std Cab SB	5983	7167	8503
2 Dr C1500 SLT Std Cab Step SB	6147	7364	8736
2 Dr C1500 Special Std Cab LB	4531	5428	6440
2 Dr C1500 Special Std Cab SB	4440	5319	6311
2 Dr C1500 SL 4WD Ext Cab LB	6481	7764	9210
2 Dr K1500 SL 4WD Ext Cab SB	6254	7492	8889

Body Styles	TMV Pricing		
	Trade	Private	Dealer
2 Dr K1500 SL 4WD Std Cab LB	5775	6919	8208
2 Dr K1500 SL 4WD Std Cab SB	5690	6817	8088
2 Dr K1500 SL 4WD Std Cab Step SB	5853	7012	8319
2 Dr K1500 SLE 4WD Ext Cab LB	6982	8365	9925
2 Dr K1500 SLE 4WD Ext Cab SB	6758	8097	9606
2 Dr K1500 SLE 4WD Ext Cab Step SB	7597	9101	10796
2 Dr K1500 SLE 4WD Std Cab LB	6280	7523	8925
2 Dr K1500 SLE 4WD Std Cab SB	6195	7422	8805
2 Dr K1500 SLE 4WD Std Cab Step SB	6357	7616	9036
2 Dr K1500 SLT 4WD Ext Cab LB	7639	9151	10856
2 Dr K1500 SLT 4WD Ext Cab SB	7413	8881	10536
2 Dr K1500 SLT 4WD Ext Cab Step SB	8109	9714	11524
2 Dr K1500 SLT 4WD Std Cab LB	6915	8285	9829
2 Dr K1500 SLT 4WD Std Cab SB	6832	8185	9710
2 Dr K1500 SLT 4WD Std Cab Step SB	6992	8377	9938
2 Dr K1500 Special 4WD Std Cab LB	5575	6679	7924
2 Dr K1500 Special 4WD Std Cab SB	5485	6571	7796

Options	Price
5.0L V8 OHV 16V FI Engine	+172
5.7L V8 OHV 16V FI Engine	+243
6.5L V8 Turbodiesel OHV 16V Engine	+1173
Air Conditioning [Opt on SL,Special]	+279

Options	Price
Aluminum/Alloy Wheels	+118
Automatic 4-Speed Transmission	+337
Hinged Third Door	+146

With an all-new Sierra just one year away, changes are minimal. Diesel engines make more power and torque, extended cab models get rear heater ducts, a PassLock theft-deterrent system is standard, 1500-Series trucks get reduced rolling resistance tires and three new colors debut. Second-generation airbags are standard.

1997

Mileage Category: K

Body Styles	TMV Pricing		
	Trade	Private	Dealer
2 Dr C1500 GT Std Cab SB	4855	5874	7120
2 Dr C1500 SL Ext Cab LB	4991	6038	7317
2 Dr C1500 SL Ext Cab SB	4739	5733	6948
2 Dr C1500 SL Ext Cab Step SB	4885	5910	7162
2 Dr C1500 SL Std Cab LB	4287	5187	6286
2 Dr C1500 SL Std Cab SB	4211	5095	6176

Body Styles	TMV Pricing		
	Trade	Private	Dealer
2 Dr C1500 SL Std Cab Step SB	4358	5272	6390
2 Dr C1500 SLE Ext Cab LB	5474	6623	8027
2 Dr C1500 SLE Ext Cab SB	5225	6321	7660
2 Dr C1500 SLE Ext Cab Step SB	5495	6648	8057
2 Dr C1500 SLE Std Cab LB	4773	5774	6998
2 Dr C1500 SLE Std Cab SB	4697	5683	6887

A passenger airbag is added to models with a GVWR under 8,600 pounds, and all models get speed-sensitive steering that reduces low-speed effort. K1500 models have a tighter turning radius for better maneuverability. Automatic transmissions are refined to provide smoother shifts and improved efficiency. Three new paint colors debut.

1997 (cont'd)

Body Styles	TMV Pricing		
	Trade	Private	Dealer
2 Dr C1500 SLE Std Cab Step SB	4842	5858	7099
2 Dr C1500 SLT Ext Cab LB	5911	7151	8666
2 Dr C1500 SLT Ext Cab SB	5659	6846	8297
2 Dr C1500 SLT Ext Cab Step SB	5930	7175	8696
2 Dr C1500 SLT Std Cab LB	5191	6280	7612
2 Dr C1500 SLT Std Cab SB	5115	6188	7500
2 Dr C1500 SLT Std Cab Step SB	5260	6364	7713
2 Dr C1500 Special Std Cab LB	3962	4793	5809
2 Dr C1500 Special Std Cab SB	3855	4664	5653
2 Dr K1500 SL 4WD Ext Cab LB	5699	6895	8356
2 Dr K1500 SL 4WD Ext Cab SB	5449	6592	7989
2 Dr K1500 SL 4WD Ext Cab Step SB	5594	6768	8203
2 Dr K1500 SL 4WD Std Cab LB	5046	6105	7400
2 Dr K1500 SL 4WD Std Cab SB	4971	6014	7289
2 Dr K1500 SL 4WD Std Cab Step SB	5117	6191	7503
2 Dr K1500 SLE 4WD Ext Cab LB	6183	7481	9067

Body Styles	TMV Pricing		
	Trade	Private	Dealer
2 Dr K1500 SLE 4WD Ext Cab SB	5934	7179	8700
2 Dr K1500 SLE 4WD Ext Cab Step SB	6204	7506	9097
2 Dr K1500 SLE 4WD Std Cab LB	5532	6693	8112
2 Dr K1500 SLE 4WD Std Cab SB	5456	6601	8000
2 Dr K1500 SLE 4WD Std Cab Step SB	5601	6776	8213
2 Dr K1500 SLT 4WD Ext Cab LB	6549	7924	9604
2 Dr K1500 SLT 4WD Ext Cab SB	6367	7704	9337
2 Dr K1500 SLT 4WD Ext Cab Step SB	6514	7881	9551
2 Dr K1500 SLT 4WD Std Cab LB	5951	7199	8725
2 Dr K1500 SLT 4WD Std Cab SB	5875	7108	8615
2 Dr K1500 SLT 4WD Std Cab Step SB	6021	7284	8828
2 Dr K1500 Special 4WD Std Cab LB	4872	5894	7144
2 Dr K1500 Special 4WD Std Cab SB	4793	5798	7027

Options	Price
5.0L V8 OHV 16V FI Engine	+156
5.7L V8 OHV 16V FI Engine	+220
6.5L V8 Turbodiesel OHV 16V Engine	+1062

Options	Price
Air Conditioning [Opt on SL,Special]	+253
Automatic 4-Speed Transmission	+305
Hinged Third Door	+132

1996

A new series of engines is introduced, providing more power and torque than last year's offerings. Called Vortec, this family of engines includes a 4.3-liter V6 (the only six-cylinder of the bunch) capable of 200 hp @ 4,400 rpm and 255 lb-ft of torque @ 2,800 rpm; a 5.0-liter V8, producing 220 hp @ 4,600 rpm and 285 lb-ft of torque @ 2,800 rpm; and a 5.7-liter V8, rated at 250 hp @ 4,600 rpm and 335 lb-ft of torque @ 2,800 rpm. (There is also a 7.4-liter Vortec V8, but it's only available on the heavier duty C/K 3500 trucks.) All of these figures represent increases in output when compared to their respective 1995 predecessors. An optional electronic shift transfer case for the K1500 (i.e. 4WD; C= 2WD; K= 4WD) rounds out the list of the most significant powertrain updates for this year.

Other noteworthy updates include the introduction of an optional passenger-side third door, called the "Easy-Access System," in GM vernacular. This feature is only available on the extended cab body styles.

Improved comfort and convenience comes in the way of such new features as illuminated entry, 12-volt power outlets, an electrochromic inside rearview mirror and height-adjustable D-rings for the shoulder section of the front three-point safety belts, among others. Daytime Running Lamps (DRLs) are part the list of new exterior features.

A new level of sophistication in exhaust emissions monitoring is found with the addition of OBD II, the second generation of On-Board Diagnostics.

Mileage Category: K

Body Styles	TMV Pricing		
	Trade	Private	Dealer
2 Dr C1500 SL Ext Cab LB	4180	5109	6391
2 Dr C1500 SL Ext Cab SB	3973	4856	6075
2 Dr C1500 SL Ext Cab Step SB	4065	4968	6214
2 Dr C1500 SL Std Cab LB	3586	4382	5481
2 Dr C1500 SL Std Cab SB	3590	4387	5487
2 Dr C1500 SL Std Cab Step SB	3523	4305	5386
2 Dr C1500 SLE Ext Cab LB	4710	5755	7199
2 Dr C1500 SLE Ext Cab SB	4502	5502	6883
2 Dr C1500 SLE Ext Cab Step SB	4614	5639	7054
2 Dr C1500 SLE Std Cab LB	4114	5027	6288
2 Dr C1500 SLE Std Cab SB	4053	4953	6195
2 Dr C1500 SLE Std Cab Step SB	4230	5169	6466
2 Dr C1500 SLT Ext Cab LB	5082	6211	7769
2 Dr C1500 SLT Ext Cab SB	4877	5959	7454
2 Dr C1500 SLT Ext Cab Step SB	4987	6095	7624
2 Dr C1500 SLT Std Cab LB	4471	5464	6835
2 Dr C1500 SLT Std Cab SB	4411	5390	6743
2 Dr C1500 SLT Std Cab Step SB	4588	5607	7014
2 Dr C1500 Special Std Cab LB	3303	4037	5050
2 Dr C1500 Special Std Cab SB	3215	3929	4915
2 Dr K1500 SL 4WD Ext Cab LB	4742	5795	7249
2 Dr K1500 SL 4WD Ext Cab SB	4572	5587	6989

Body Styles	TMV Pricing		
	Trade	Private	Dealer
2 Dr K1500 SL 4WD Ext Cab Step SB	4661	5697	7127
2 Dr K1500 SL 4WD Std Cab LB	4225	5163	6458
2 Dr K1500 SL 4WD Std Cab SB	4162	5085	6360
2 Dr K1500 SL 4WD Std Cab Step SB	4282	5233	6546
2 Dr K1500 SLE 4WD Ext Cab LB	5269	6440	8056
2 Dr K1500 SLE 4WD Ext Cab LB	5101	6234	7798
2 Dr K1500 SLE 4WD Ext Cab Step SB	5211	6369	7967
2 Dr K1500 SLE 4WD Std Cab LB	4752	5807	7265
2 Dr K1500 SLE 4WD Std Cab SB	4687	5728	7165
2 Dr K1500 SLE 4WD Std Cab Step SB	4811	5879	7354
2 Dr K1500 SLT 4WD Ext Cab LB	5642	6895	8626
2 Dr K1500 SLT 4WD Ext Cab SB	5474	6689	8368
2 Dr K1500 SLT 4WD Ext Cab Step SB	5563	6799	8505
2 Dr K1500 SLT 4WD Std Cab LB	5110	6245	7813
2 Dr K1500 SLT 4WD Std Cab SB	5046	6167	7714
2 Dr K1500 SLT 4WD Std Cab Step SB	5167	6315	7900
2 Dr K1500 Special 4WD Std Cab LB	4050	4949	6190
2 Dr K1500 Special 4WD Std Cab SB	4004	4893	6121

Options	Price
5.0L V8 OHV 16V FI Engine	+138
5.7L V8 OHV 16V FI Engine	+194
6.5L V8 Turbodiesel OHV 16V Engine	+939

Options	Price
Air Conditioning [Opt on SL,Special]	+223
Automatic 4-Speed Transmission	+269
Hinged Third Door	+116

1995

Mileage Category: K

Body Styles	TMV Pricing		
	Trade	Private	Dealer
2 Dr C1500 SL Ext Cab LB	3618	4435	5796
2 Dr C1500 SL Ext Cab SB	3456	4236	5535
2 Dr C1500 SL Ext Cab Step SB	3557	4360	5697
2 Dr C1500 SL Std Cab LB	3095	3794	4958
2 Dr C1500 SL Std Cab SB	3040	3726	4870
2 Dr C1500 SL Std Cab Step SB	3113	3816	4987
2 Dr C1500 SLE Ext Cab LB	4027	4936	6450
2 Dr C1500 SLE Ext Cab SB	3841	4708	6152
2 Dr C1500 SLE Ext Cab Step SB	3941	4831	6313
2 Dr C1500 SLE Std Cab LB	3463	4244	5546
2 Dr C1500 SLE Std Cab SB	3406	4175	5456
2 Dr C1500 SLE Std Cab Step SB	3566	4371	5713
2 Dr C1500 SLT Ext Cab LB	4404	5398	7055
2 Dr C1500 SLT Ext Cab SB	4218	5171	6758
2 Dr C1500 SLT Ext Cab Step SB	4321	5296	6921
2 Dr C1500 Special Std Cab LB	2843	3484	4553
2 Dr C1500 Special Std Cab SB	2764	3388	4428
2 Dr K1500 SL 4WD Ext Cab LB	4064	4981	6508
2 Dr K1500 SL 4WD Ext Cab SB	3933	4820	6298
2 Dr K1500 SL 4WD Ext Cab Step SB	4012	4918	6427

Body Styles	TMV Pricing		
	Trade	Private	Dealer
2 Dr K1500 SL 4WD Std Cab LB	3609	4424	5781
2 Dr K1500 SL 4WD Std Cab SB	3550	4351	5687
2 Dr K1500 SL 4WD Std Cab Step SB	3709	4546	5942
2 Dr K1500 SLE 4WD Ext Cab LB	4528	5550	7253
2 Dr K1500 SLE 4WD Ext Cab SB	4318	5293	6917
2 Dr K1500 SLE 4WD Ext Cab Step SB	4397	5390	7045
2 Dr K1500 SLE 4WD Std Cab LB	3974	4871	6367
2 Dr K1500 SLE 4WD Std Cab SB	3916	4800	6273
2 Dr K1500 SLE 4WD Std Cab Step SB	4077	4997	6530
2 Dr K1500 SLS 4WD Ext Cab SB	3932	4819	6298
2 Dr K1500 SLS 4WD Ext Cab Step SB	4012	4918	6427
2 Dr K1500 SLT 4WD Ext Cab LB	4846	5940	7764
2 Dr K1500 SLT 4WD Ext Cab SB	4698	5758	7524
2 Dr K1500 SLT 4WD Ext Cab Step SB	4777	5855	7652
2 Dr K1500 Special 4WD Std Cab LB	3460	4241	5542
2 Dr K1500 Special 4WD Std Cab SB	3419	4191	5478

Options	Price
5.0L V8 OHV 16V FI Engine	+128
5.7L V8 OHV 16V FI Engine	+180
6.5L V8 Turbodiesel OHV 16V Engine	+873
AM/FM/Cassette/CD Audio System	+75

Options	Price
Air Conditioning [Opt on SL,SLS,Special]	+207
Automatic 4-Speed Transmission	+250
Compact Disc Changer	+142

A revised interior graces these full-size trucks this year. A new driver-side airbag and a shift interlock are added in the interest of safety. The latter requires the brake pedal to be depressed before the automatic transmission's gear selector can be shifted out of "park." This reduces the likelihood that the vehicle will move suddenly and unexpectedly when the transmission is taken out of "park." Power mirrors, revised climate controls and cupholders provide a more user-friendly interior environment. Mechanical enhancements include the addition of standard 4-wheel antilock brakes, improvements in the engines and modifications to the heavy-duty 4L80-E. The four-wheel ABS replaces last year's rear-wheel-only antilock system. Various upgrades to the engines are intended to reduce noise, improve durability and/or increase efficiency. The transmission is revised for quicker 1-2 upshifts during full-throttle applications.

Sierra 1500HD
2003

Mileage Category: K

Body Styles	TMV Pricing		
	Trade	Private	Dealer
4 Dr SLE 4WD Crew Cab SB HD	19217	20485	22599
4 Dr SLE Crew Cab SB HD	17381	18528	20439

Body Styles	TMV Pricing		
	Trade	Private	Dealer
4 Dr SLT 4WD Crew Cab SB HD	20400	21746	23990
4 Dr SLT Crew Cab SB HD	18480	19700	21732

Options	Price
4 Wheel Steering	+2894
AM/FM/CD Changer Audio System	+383
Aluminum/Alloy Wheels	+129
Automatic Climate Control (2 Zone) - Driver and Passenger [Opt on SLE]	+126
Bose Audio System	+129
Bucket Seats	+274
DVD Entertainment System	+834
Electronic Suspension Control	+209

Options	Price
Limited Slip Differential	+190
Locking Differential	+190
OnStar Telematics System [Opt on SLE]	+447
Power Driver Seat [Opt on SLE]	+155
Power Passenger Seat [Opt on SLT]	+158
Power Retractable Mirrors	+118
Satellite Radio System	+209
Traction Control System	+145

The Sierra gets a new look this year that includes a new front fascia and revised side moldings. On the inside, the Sierra offers new entertainment options, such as a Bose audio system with rear seat controls, XM Satellite Radio and a rear-passenger DVD entertainment system. The instrument panel and center console have been redesigned, and GMC has added new seats, a more comprehensive driver information center and a dual-zone climate control system. For increased safety, Sierras now feature a standard front-passenger-sensing system that deactivates the airbag for children. On the hardware side, the all-new Quadrasteer four-wheel steering system, which increases low-speed maneuverability and towing stability, is now optional. The standard 6.0-liter V8 gets electronic throttle control, as well as the ability to run exclusively on Compressed Natural Gas (CNG) or a mix of CNG and gasoline.

2002

Mileage Category: K

Body Styles	TMV Pricing		
	Trade	Private	Dealer
4 Dr SLE 4WD Crew Cab SB HD	17649	18989	21222
4 Dr SLE Crew Cab SB HD	15821	17042	19078

Options	Price
Bucket Seats	+254
Flex Fuel Option	+449

Body Styles	TMV Pricing		
	Trade	Private	Dealer
4 Dr SLT 4WD Crew Cab SB HD	18612	20049	22443
4 Dr SLT Crew Cab SB HD	16743	18036	20190

Options	Price
Locking Differential [Opt on 2WD]	+177

Debuting late last year as an all-new 2001 model, the 1500HD Crew Cab gets few changes for the 2002 model year. Deep-tinted glass is now standard, and a Cold Weather option package with heated exterior mirrors and a rear window defogger have been added.

2001

A crew cab version debuts, called Sierra 1500HD. Oil-change intervals have been extended to 10,000 miles. A traction control system is now available on two-wheel-drive V8 automatics, thanks to a new electronic throttle control system. OnStar, GM's mobile communications and security system, has been made standard with the SLT trim level.

Mileage Category: K

Body Styles	TMV Pricing		
	Trade	Private	Dealer
4 Dr SLE 4WD Crew Cab SB HD	15045	16892	18596
4 Dr SLE Crew Cab SB HD	13452	15103	16627

Options	Price
Bucket Seats [Opt on SLE]	+137
Heated Front Seats	+137
Leather Seats [Opt on SLE]	+699
Locking Differential	+156

Body Styles	TMV Pricing		
	Trade	Private	Dealer
4 Dr SLT 4WD Crew Cab SB HD	15893	17844	19645
4 Dr SLT Crew Cab SB HD	14263	16014	17630

Options	Price
Power Driver Seat [Opt on SLE]	+131
Power Passenger Seat [Opt on SLE]	+131
Tonneau Cover	+131

Sierra 2500

2004

A short-bed crew cab model debuts and the base truck's standard features list is plumped up with the addition of cruise control, chrome bumpers and chrome wheels. The Work Truck package is available on all models. Midlevel SLE models get standard foglamps and optional leather seating.

Mileage Category: K

Body Styles	TMV Pricing		
	Trade	Private	Dealer
2 Dr SLE Std Cab LB	15755	17136	19438
2 Dr STD Std Cab LB	15080	16459	18758
2 Dr Work Truck Std Cab LB	13853	15229	17521
4 Dr SLE 4WD Crew Cab SB	21773	23459	26269
4 Dr SLE 4WD Ext Cab SB	20319	21743	24115
4 Dr SLE Crew Cab SB	19381	20805	23177

Body Styles	TMV Pricing		
	Trade	Private	Dealer
4 Dr SLT 4WD Crew Cab SB	24181	25867	28677
4 Dr SLT 4WD Ext Cab SB	22629	24053	26425
4 Dr SLT Crew Cab SB	22077	23666	26313
4 Dr STD 4WD Ext Cab SB	19181	20605	22977
4 Dr Work Truck 4WD Ext Cab SB	18158	19582	21954

Options	Price
4 Wheel Steering [Opt on Crew]	+1995
AM/FM/CD Changer Audio System [Opt on SLE non-Std]	+795
Automatic 4-Speed Transmission [Opt on STD, SLE, Work Truck Std]	+1095
Automatic Climate Control (2 Zone) - Driver and Passenger [Opt on SLE non-Std]	+195
Bucket Seats [Opt on SLE non-Std]	+350
Cruise Control [Opt on Work Truck]	+240
DVD Entertainment System [Opt on Crew]	+1295
Forged Alloy Wheels [Opt on SLE, Crew]	+200
Leather Seats [Opt on SLE]	+800
Locking Differential	+295

Options	Price
OnStar Telematics System [Opt on SLE]	+695
Power Door Locks [Opt on STD]	+162
Power Driver Seat [Opt on SLE]	+240
Power Retractable Mirrors [Opt on SLE, SLT]	+213
Rear Audio Controls [Opt on SLE Crew]	+165
Rear Window Defroster [Opt on STD]	+175
Steering Wheel Radio Controls [Opt on SLE]	+125
Traction Control System [Opt on 2WD STD, SLE Ext, Crew]	+225
Two-Tone Paint [Opt on SLE, SLT Ext]	+250

2003

The Sierra gets a revised look this year that includes a new front fascia, revised side moldings and an additional wheel design. Top-of-the-line models get power-folding heated mirrors with puddle lamps and turn signal indicators. On the inside, the Sierra now offers a Bose stereo system and XM Satellite Radio. The instrument panel and center console have been redesigned, and GMC has added new seats, a more comprehensive driver information center, optional satellite steering wheel controls and a dual-zone climate control system. For increased safety, Sierras now feature a standard front-passenger-sensing system and dual-stage airbags. On the hardware side, the standard 6.0-liter V8 gets electronic throttle control, as well as the ability to run exclusively on compressed natural gas (CNG) or a mix of CNG and gasoline. The Autotrac four-wheel-drive system has been modified for less intrusiveness at low speeds, and the brake system received upgrades that provide better pedal feel and improved overall performance.

Mileage Category: K

Body Styles	TMV Pricing		
	Trade	Private	Dealer
2 Dr SLE Std Cab LB	14575	15625	17375
2 Dr STD Std Cab LB	13428	14395	16007
2 Dr Work Truck Std Cab LB	12910	13840	15389

Options	Price
AM/FM/CD Audio System [Opt on STD,Work]	+164
AM/FM/CD Changer Audio System [Opt on SLE,SLT]	+383
Automatic 4-Speed Transmission [Opt on SLE,STD,Work]	+705
Automatic Climate Control (2 Zone) - Driver and Passenger [Opt on SLE]	+126
Bose Audio System [Opt on SLE,SLT]	+129
Bucket Seats [Opt on SLE,SLT]	+274
Chrome Wheels [Opt on STD]	+200
Compressed Natural Gas (CNG) Option [Opt on SLE,STD,Work]	+5988
Cruise Control [Opt on STD,Work]	+155

Body Styles	TMV Pricing		
	Trade	Private	Dealer
4 Dr SLE 4WD Ext Cab SB	19065	20438	22727
4 Dr SLT 4WD Ext Cab SB	20096	21544	23957
4 Dr STD 4WD Ext Cab SB	17437	18693	20787

Options	Price
Locking Differential	+190
OnStar Telematics System [Opt on SLE]	+447
Power Driver Seat [Opt on SLE]	+155
Power Passenger Seat [Opt on SLT]	+158
Power Retractable Mirrors [Opt on SLE,SLT]	+118
Satellite Radio System [Opt on SLE,SLT]	+209
Traction Control System [Opt on SLE,STD]	+145
Two-Tone Paint [Opt on SLE,SLT]	+161

2002

GMC's light-duty 2500s get only minor changes for 2002. Base model SLs now come standard with air conditioning, while uplevel SLE and SLT models get standard deep-tinted glass. All Sierras get redesigned badging and extendable sun visors.

Mileage Category: K

Body Styles	TMV Pricing		
	Trade	Private	Dealer
2 Dr SL Std Cab LB	12657	13685	15398
2 Dr SLE Std Cab LB	13220	14294	16083
2 Dr STD Std Cab LB	11532	12468	14029
4 Dr SL 4WD Ext Cab SB	16023	17324	19493

Options	Price
AM/FM/CD Audio System [Opt on STD]	+117
Air Conditioning [Opt on STD Std Cab]	+494
Automatic 4-Speed Transmission [Opt on Std Cab]	+656
Bucket Seats [Opt on SLE,SLT]	+254
Cruise Control [Opt on SL,STD]	+144
Flex Fuel Option	+449

Body Styles	TMV Pricing		
	Trade	Private	Dealer
4 Dr SLE 4WD Ext Cab SB	17028	18411	20716
4 Dr SLT 4WD Ext Cab SB	17955	19413	21843
4 Dr STD 4WD Ext Cab SB	15296	16538	18609

Options	Price
Locking Differential [Opt on 2WD]	+177
Power Driver Seat [Opt on SLE]	+147
Power Passenger Seat [Opt on SLE]	+147
Traction Control System [Opt on 2WD]	+135
Trailer Hitch	+129
Two-Tone Paint [Opt on Ext Cab SB - SLE,SLT]	+150

2001

Both light- and heavy-duty 2500s sport new torsion bar front suspensions. Light-duty models now offer optional traction control and standard child safety-seat tethers. Heavy-duty Sierras are completely redesigned for 2001 offering two new engines and transmissions, bigger interiors and numerous other improvements aimed at buyers looking for a "professional grade" truck from GM.

Mileage Category: K

Body Styles	TMV Pricing		
	Trade	Private	Dealer
2 Dr SL Std Cab LB	10229	11544	12757
2 Dr SLE Std Cab LB	11338	12795	14139
4 Dr SL 4WD Ext Cab SB	13211	14909	16476

Options	Price
Air Conditioning [Opt on SL]	+440
Automatic 4-Speed Transmission [Opt on SL,SLE]	+598
Bucket Seats	+137
Heated Front Seats	+137
Locking Differential	+156

Body Styles	TMV Pricing		
	Trade	Private	Dealer
4 Dr SLE 4WD Ext Cab SB	14356	16200	17903
4 Dr SLT 4WD Ext Cab SB	15389	17366	19191

Options	Price
Power Driver Seat [Opt on SLE]	+131
Power Passenger Seat [Opt on SLE]	+131
Tonneau Cover	+131
Traction Control System [Opt on Std Cab]	+123
Two-Tone Paint	+137

2000

After a complete redesign last year, GMC's Silverado-based pickup finally gets a fourth door on the extended cab. There's also more power on tap in the 4.8- and 5.3-liter engines, increased trailer ratings and standard programmable automatic door locks. New factory appearance items, such as wheel-lip flares and a soft tonneau cover, are now available on some models.

Mileage Category: K

Body Styles	TMV Pricing		
	Trade	Private	Dealer
2 Dr SL 4WD Std Cab LB HD	10014	11504	12965
2 Dr SL Std Cab LB	8899	10224	11522
2 Dr SL Std Cab LB HD	8689	9982	11250
2 Dr SLE 4WD Std Cab LB HD	10992	12628	14232
2 Dr SLE Std Cab LB	9844	11310	12746
2 Dr SLE Std Cab LB HD	9455	10862	12241
3 Dr SL 4WD Ext Cab LB HD	11507	13220	14899
3 Dr SL 4WD Ext Cab SB HD	11394	13090	14753

Body Styles	TMV Pricing		
	Trade	Private	Dealer
3 Dr SL Ext Cab LB HD	10244	11769	13263
3 Dr SL Ext Cab SB	9557	10979	12373
3 Dr SLE 4WD Ext Cab LB HD	12487	14345	16167
3 Dr SLE 4WD Ext Cab SB HD	12374	14216	16021
3 Dr SLE Ext Cab LB HD	11091	12742	14360
3 Dr SLE Ext Cab SB	10818	12428	14007
3 Dr SLT 4WD Ext Cab LB HD	13805	15859	17873
3 Dr SLT 4WD Ext Cab SB HD	13682	15719	17715

2000 (cont'd)

Body Styles	TMV Pricing		
	Trade	Private	Dealer
3 Dr SLT Ext Cab LB HD	11678	13416	15120

Options	Price
6.0L V8 OHV 16V FI Engine	+177
AM/FM/Cassette/CD Audio System	+144
Air Conditioning [Opt on SL]	+401
Automatic 4-Speed Transmission [Opt on SL,SLE]	+545
Bucket Seats	+125
Heated Front Seats	+125

Body Styles	TMV Pricing		
	Trade	Private	Dealer
3 Dr SLT Ext Cab SB	11558	13279	14965

Options	Price
Hinged Fourth Door	+164
Limited Slip Differential	+134
Power Driver Seat [Opt on SLE]	+119
Power Passenger Seat [Opt on SLE]	+119
Tonneau Cover	+119
Trailer Hitch	+162

1999

Finally, the decade-old, full-size GMC pickup based on the C/K gets a complete redesign from the ground up. Major structural, power, braking and interior enhancements characterize the all-new Sierra. Styling is evolutionary rather than revolutionary, both inside and out.

Mileage Category: K

Body Styles	TMV Pricing		
	Trade	Private	Dealer
2 Dr SL 4WD Std Cab LB HD	8822	10297	11832
2 Dr SL Std Cab LB	7847	9159	10524
2 Dr SL Std Cab LB HD	7331	8556	9832
2 Dr SLE 4WD Std Cab LB HD	9594	11198	12867
2 Dr SLE Std Cab LB	8421	9829	11294
2 Dr SLE Std Cab LB HD	8303	9691	11135
3 Dr SL 4WD Ext Cab LB HD	10242	11955	13737
3 Dr SL 4WD Ext Cab SB HD	10135	11829	13593
3 Dr SL Ext Cab LB HD	8831	10307	11843

Options	Price
6.0L V8 OHV 16V FI Engine [Std on SLT]	+201
AM/FM/Cassette/CD Audio System	+117

Body Styles	TMV Pricing		
	Trade	Private	Dealer
3 Dr SL Ext Cab SB	8452	9865	11335
3 Dr SLE 4WD Ext Cab LB HD	11031	12875	14794
3 Dr SLE 4WD Ext Cab SB HD	11014	12855	14772
3 Dr SLE Ext Cab LB HD	9769	11402	13101
3 Dr SLE Ext Cab SB	9402	10974	12610
3 Dr SLT 4WD Ext Cab LB HD	12367	14435	16587
3 Dr SLT 4WD Ext Cab SB HD	12198	14237	16360
3 Dr SLT Ext Cab LB HD	10410	12150	13962
3 Dr SLT Ext Cab SB	10212	11919	13696

Options	Price
Air Conditioning [Opt on SL]	+324
Automatic 4-Speed Transmission [Std on SLT]	+401

1998

With an all-new Sierra just one year away, changes are minimal. Diesel engines make more power and torque, extended cab models get rear heater ducts, a PassLock theft-deterrent system is standard, 1500-Series trucks get reduced rolling resistance tires and three new colors debut. Second-generation airbags are standard.

Mileage Category: K

Body Styles	TMV Pricing		
	Trade	Private	Dealer
2 Dr C2500 SL Ext Cab LB HD	6542	7837	9298
2 Dr C2500 SL Ext Cab SB	6493	7779	9229
2 Dr C2500 SL Std Cab LB	5644	6762	8022
2 Dr C2500 SL Std Cab LB HD	6003	7192	8532
2 Dr C2500 SLE Ext Cab LB HD	7282	8724	10350
2 Dr C2500 SLE Ext Cab SB	7243	8677	10294
2 Dr C2500 SLE Std Cab LB	6395	7661	9089
2 Dr C2500 SLE Std Cab LB HD	6601	7908	9381
2 Dr C2500 SLT Ext Cab LB HD	7732	9263	10989
2 Dr C2500 SLT Ext Cab SB	7724	9253	10978
2 Dr C2500 SLT Std Cab LB	6840	8194	9721

Options	Price
5.7L V8 OHV 16V FI Engine [Std on HD]	+243
6.5L V8 Turbodiesel OHV 16V Engine	+942
7.4L V8 OHV 16V FI Engine	+208

Body Styles	TMV Pricing		
	Trade	Private	Dealer
2 Dr C2500 SLT Std Cab LB HD	7221	8651	10263
2 Dr K2500 SL 4WD Ext Cab LB HD	7345	8799	10438
2 Dr K2500 SL 4WD Ext Cab SB HD	7332	8783	10420
2 Dr K2500 SL 4WD Std Cab LB HD	6861	8220	9752
2 Dr K2500 SLE 4WD Ext Cab LB HD	8261	9897	11741
2 Dr K2500 SLE 4WD Ext Cab SB HD	8200	9823	11654
2 Dr K2500 SLE 4WD Std Cab LB HD	7571	9070	10760
2 Dr K2500 SLT 4WD Ext Cab LB HD	8442	10113	11998
2 Dr K2500 SLT 4WD Ext Cab SB HD	8395	10057	11932
2 Dr K2500 SLT 4WD Std Cab LB HD	8168	9785	11609

Options	Price
Air Conditioning [Opt on SL]	+279
Automatic 4-Speed Transmission	+337
Hinged Third Door	+146

1997

A passenger airbag is added to models with a GVWR under 8,600 pounds, and all models get speed-sensitive steering that reduces low-speed effort. K1500 models have a tighter turning radius for better maneuverability. Automatic transmissions are refined to provide smoother shifts and improved efficiency. Three new paint colors debut.

Mileage Category: K

Body Styles	TMV Pricing		
	Trade	Private	Dealer
2 Dr C2500 SL Ext Cab LB HD	5648	6834	8283
2 Dr C2500 SL Ext Cab SB	5677	6869	8325
2 Dr C2500 SL Std Cab LB	4907	5937	7195
2 Dr C2500 SL Std Cab LB HD	5165	6249	7573
2 Dr C2500 SLE Ext Cab LB HD	6331	7660	9284
2 Dr C2500 SLE Ext Cab SB	6356	7690	9320
2 Dr C2500 SLE Std Cab LB	5601	6776	8213
2 Dr C2500 SLE Std Cab LB HD	5734	6938	8409
2 Dr C2500 SLT Ext Cab LB HD	6703	8109	9828

Body Styles	TMV Pricing		
	Trade	Private	Dealer
2 Dr C2500 SLT Ext Cab SB	6819	8250	9998
2 Dr C2500 SLT Std Cab LB	6039	7306	8855
2 Dr C2500 SLT Std Cab LB HD	6283	7602	9213
2 Dr K2500 SL 4WD Ext Cab LB HD	6379	7717	9353
2 Dr K2500 SL 4WD Ext Cab SB HD	6359	7694	9325
2 Dr K2500 SL 4WD Std Cab LB HD	5871	7103	8609
2 Dr K2500 SLE 4WD Ext Cab LB HD	7085	8571	10388
2 Dr K2500 SLE 4WD Ext Cab SB HD	7085	8571	10388
2 Dr K2500 SLE 4WD Std Cab LB HD	6629	8020	9720

Body Styles	TMV Pricing		
	Trade	Private	Dealer
2 Dr K2500 SLT 4WD Ext Cab LB HD	7249	8770	10630
2 Dr K2500 SLT 4WD Ext Cab SB HD	7093	8582	10401

Body Styles	TMV Pricing		
	Trade	Private	Dealer
2 Dr K2500 SLT 4WD Std Cab LB HD	6984	8449	10240

Options	Price
5.7L V8 OHV 16V FI Engine [Std on HD]	+220
6.5L V8 Turbodiesel OHV 16V Engine	+1062
7.4L V8 OHV 16V FI Engine	+188

Options	Price
Air Conditioning [Opt on SL]	+253
Automatic 4-Speed Transmission	+305
Hinged Third Door	+132

Mileage Category: K

1996

Vortec, a new family of engines, is introduced, providing more power and torque than last year's offerings. The Vortec engines available on the C/K 2500 pickups include a 5.0-liter V8, producing 220 hp @ 4,600 rpm and 285 lb-ft of torque @ 2,800 rpm and a 5.7-liter V8, rated at 250 hp @ 4,600 rpm and 335 lb-ft of torque @ 2,800 rpm. All of these figures represent increases in output when compared to their respective 1995 predecessors. Noteworthy comfort and convenience additions include illuminated entry, additional 12-volt power outlets, an electrochromic inside rearview mirror and height-adjustable front safety belts. Daytime Running Lamps (DRLs) are added this year as well.

Body Styles	TMV Pricing		
	Trade	Private	Dealer
2 Dr C2500 SL Ext Cab LB HD	4701	5745	7186
2 Dr C2500 SL Ext Cab SB	4667	5703	7133
2 Dr C2500 SL Std Cab LB	4075	4979	6228
2 Dr C2500 SLE Ext Cab LB HD	5607	6851	8569
2 Dr C2500 SLE Ext Cab SB	5273	6443	8059
2 Dr C2500 SLE Std Cab LB	4643	5673	7096
2 Dr C2500 SLT Ext Cab SB	5749	7025	8787
2 Dr C2500 SLT Std Cab LB	4988	6095	7624

Body Styles	TMV Pricing		
	Trade	Private	Dealer
2 Dr K2500 SL 4WD Ext Cab LB HD	5558	6792	8496
2 Dr K2500 SL 4WD Ext Cab SB HD	5558	6792	8496
2 Dr K2500 SL 4WD Std Cab LB HD	5082	6210	7768
2 Dr K2500 SLE 4WD Ext Cab LB HD	6175	7545	9438
2 Dr K2500 SLE 4WD Ext Cab SB HD	6128	7488	9366
2 Dr K2500 SLE 4WD Std Cab LB HD	5653	6908	8641
2 Dr K2500 SLT 4WD Ext Cab LB HD	6590	8052	10072
2 Dr K2500 SLT 4WD Std Cab LB HD	6034	7373	9223

Options	Price
5.7L V8 OHV 16V FI Engine [Std on HD]	+194
6.5L V8 Turbodiesel OHV 16V Engine	+755
7.4L V8 OHV 16V FI Engine	+166

Options	Price
Air Conditioning [Opt on SL]	+223
Automatic 4-Speed Transmission	+269
Hinged Third Door	+116

Mileage Category: K

1995

A revised interior graces these full-size trucks this year. A new driver-side airbag and a shift interlock are added in the interest of safety. The latter requires the brake pedal to be depressed before the automatic transmission's gear selector can be shifted out of "park." This reduces the likelihood that the vehicle will move suddenly and unexpectedly when the transmission is taken out of "park." Power mirrors, revised climate controls and cupholders provide a more user-friendly interior environment. Mechanical enhancements include the addition of standard 4-wheel antilock brakes, improvements in the engines and modifications to the heavy-duty 4L80-E. The four-wheel ABS replaces last year's rear-wheel-only antilock system. Various upgrades to the engines are intended to reduce noise, improve durability and/or increase efficiency. The transmission is revised for quicker 1-2 upshifts during full-throttle applications.

Body Styles	TMV Pricing		
	Trade	Private	Dealer
2 Dr C2500 SL Ext Cab LB HD	4047	4960	6482
2 Dr C2500 SL Ext Cab SB	3941	4831	6314
2 Dr C2500 SL Std Cab LB	3388	4153	5427
2 Dr C2500 SLE Ext Cab LB HD	4727	5794	7572
2 Dr C2500 SLE Ext Cab SB	4579	5613	7336
2 Dr C2500 SLE Std Cab LB	3822	4685	6122
2 Dr C2500 SLT Ext Cab LB HD	4918	6028	7877
2 Dr C2500 SLT Ext Cab SB	4865	5963	7794

Body Styles	TMV Pricing		
	Trade	Private	Dealer
2 Dr K2500 SL 4WD Ext Cab LB HD	4770	5847	7641
2 Dr K2500 SL 4WD Ext Cab SB	4573	5606	7327
2 Dr K2500 SL 4WD Std Cab LB	3910	4792	6263
2 Dr K2500 SLE 4WD Ext Cab LB HD	5260	6447	8425
2 Dr K2500 SLE 4WD Ext Cab SB	5137	6296	8228
2 Dr K2500 SLE 4WD Std Cab LB	4548	5574	7284
2 Dr K2500 SLT 4WD Ext Cab LB HD	5731	7025	9181
2 Dr K2500 SLT 4WD Ext Cab SB	5474	6709	8768

Options	Price
5.0L V8 OHV 16V FI Engine [Opt on Std Cab - SL,SLE 2WD/4WD]	+148
5.7L V8 OHV 16V FI Engine	+180
6.5L V8 Turbodiesel OHV 16V Engine	+701
7.4L V8 OHV 16V FI Engine	+154

Options	Price
AM/FM/Cassette/CD Audio System	+75
Air Conditioning [Opt on SL]	+207
Automatic 4-Speed Transmission	+250

Sierra 2500HD
2004

Mileage Category: K

Body Styles	TMV Pricing		
	Trade	Private	Dealer
2 Dr SLE 4WD Std Cab LB HD	18546	19839	21993
2 Dr SLE Std Cab LB HD	16689	17978	20126
2 Dr STD 4WD Std Cab LB HD	18005	19317	21504
2 Dr STD Std Cab LB HD	15990	17277	19423
2 Dr Work Truck 4WD Std Cab LB HD	16468	17757	19904
2 Dr Work Truck Std Cab LB HD	14720	16004	18145
4 Dr SLE 4WD Crew Cab LB HD	23172	24761	27409
4 Dr SLE 4WD Crew Cab SB HD	22987	24576	27224
4 Dr SLE 4WD Ext Cab LB HD	21730	23074	25315
4 Dr SLE 4WD Ext Cab SB HD	21643	22994	25245

Body Styles	TMV Pricing		
	Trade	Private	Dealer
4 Dr SLE Crew Cab LB HD	21329	22871	25441
4 Dr SLE Crew Cab SB HD	21145	22687	25257
4 Dr SLE Ext Cab LB HD	19713	21039	23250
4 Dr SLE Ext Cab SB HD	19530	20856	23067
4 Dr SLT 4WD Crew Cab LB HD	25783	27372	30020
4 Dr SLT 4WD Crew Cab SB HD	25599	27188	29836
4 Dr SLT 4WD Ext Cab LB HD	23820	25259	27657
4 Dr SLT 4WD Ext Cab SB HD	23632	25127	27619
4 Dr SLT Crew Cab LB HD	23431	25001	27618
4 Dr SLT Crew Cab SB HD	23241	24849	27528

2004 (cont'd)

Base trucks get upgraded via newly standard cruise control, chrome wheels, chrome rear bumper and chrome grille surround. The SLE trim adds foglamps to its generous list of features. The Work Truck Package (with unique grille treatment) is now available on all models. Lastly, a trio of new colors, Sand Beige Metallic, Silver Birch and Sport Red Metallic debut.

Body Styles	TMV Pricing		
	Trade	Private	Dealer
4 Dr SLT Ext Cab LB HD	22105	23431	25642
4 Dr SLT Ext Cab SB HD	21922	23248	25459
4 Dr STD 4WD Crew Cab LB HD	22304	23893	26541
4 Dr STD 4WD Crew Cab SB HD	22120	23709	26357
4 Dr STD 4WD Ext Cab LB HD	20492	21818	24029
4 Dr STD 4WD Ext Cab SB HD	20308	21634	23845
4 Dr STD Crew Cab LB HD	20072	21586	24109
4 Dr STD Crew Cab SB HD	19887	21401	23924
4 Dr STD Ext Cab LB HD	18798	20124	22335
4 Dr STD Ext Cab SB HD	18614	19940	22151

Body Styles	TMV Pricing		
	Trade	Private	Dealer
4 Dr Work Truck 4WD Crew Cab LB HD	21244	22833	25481
4 Dr Work Truck 4WD Crew Cab SB HD	21058	22647	25295
4 Dr Work Truck 4WD Ext Cab LB HD	19431	20757	22968
4 Dr Work Truck 4WD Ext Cab SB HD	19248	20574	22785
4 Dr Work Truck Crew Cab LB HD	18990	20504	23027
4 Dr Work Truck Crew Cab SB HD	18804	20318	22841
Dr Work Truck Ext Cab LB HD	17715	19041	21252
4 Dr Work Truck Ext Cab SB HD	17531	18857	21068

Options	Price
6.6L V8 Turbodiesel OHV 32V Engine	+5310
8.1L V8 OHV 16V FI Engine	+850
AM/FM/CD Changer Audio System [Opt on SLE non-Std]	+795
Automatic 5-Speed Transmission	+1200
Automatic Climate Control (2 Zone) - Driver and Passenger [Opt on SLE non-Std]	+195
Bucket Seats [Opt on SLE non-Std]	+350
Compressed Natural Gas (CNG) Option [Opt on Std, Ext non-SLT LB]	+9300
Cruise Control [Opt on Work Truck]	+240
DVD Entertainment System [Opt on SLE, SLT Crew]	+1295
Forged Alloy Wheels [Opt on SLE]	+200

Options	Price
Leather Seats [Opt on SLE non-Std]	+800
Locking Differential	+295
OnStar Telematics System [Opt on SLE]	+695
Power Door Locks [Opt on STD]	+162
Power Driver Seat [Opt on SLE]	+240
Power Retractable Mirrors [Opt on SLE]	+213
Rear Audio Controls [Opt on SLE, SLT Crew]	+165
Rear Window Defroster [Opt on STD]	+175
Steering Wheel Radio Controls [Opt on SLE]	+125

2003

The Sierra gets a revised look this year that includes a new front fascia, revised side moldings and optional multifunction, fold-away mirrors. On the inside, GMC has added new seats, a more comprehensive driver information center, a redesigned instrument panel and optional dual-zone climate control and satellite steering wheel controls. On the hardware side, the standard 6.0-liter V8 gets electronic throttle control as well as the ability to run exclusively on Compressed Natural Gas (CNG) or a mix of CNG and gasoline. Other upgrades include an improved Insta-Trac part-time four-wheel drive system for reduced service costs, a more efficient starter for the 8.1-liter V8 and a revised headlight switch that allows drivers to turn off the daytime running lamps.

Mileage Category: K

Body Styles	TMV Pricing		
	Trade	Private	Dealer
2 Dr SLE 4WD Std Cab LB HD	17158	18342	20314
2 Dr SLE Std Cab LB HD	15443	16508	18284
2 Dr STD 4WD Std Cab LB HD	15835	16927	18748
2 Dr STD Std Cab LB HD	14249	15232	16870
2 Dr Work Truck 4WD Std Cab LB HD	15322	16379	18141
2 Dr Work Truck Std Cab LB HD	13710	14656	16233
4 Dr SLE 4WD Crew Cab LB HD	20681	22108	24486
4 Dr SLE 4WD Crew Cab SB HD	20510	21925	24283
4 Dr SLE 4WD Ext Cab LB HD	19347	20682	22907
4 Dr SLE 4WD Ext Cab SB HD	19178	20501	22707
4 Dr SLE Crew Cab LB HD	18846	20146	22313
4 Dr SLE Crew Cab SB HD	18675	19964	22111
4 Dr SLE Ext Cab LB HD	17760	18985	21027
4 Dr SLE Ext Cab SB HD	17589	18803	20825
4 Dr SLT 4WD Crew Cab LB HD	21729	23228	25726

Body Styles	TMV Pricing		
	Trade	Private	Dealer
4 Dr SLT 4WD Crew Cab SB HD	21557	23044	25523
4 Dr SLT 4WD Ext Cab LB HD	20520	21936	24295
4 Dr SLT 4WD Ext Cab SB HD	20350	21754	24093
4 Dr SLT Crew Cab LB HD	20015	21396	23697
4 Dr SLT Crew Cab SB HD	19844	21213	23494
4 Dr SLT Ext Cab LB HD	18800	20097	22258
4 Dr SLT Ext Cab SB HD	18629	19914	22056
4 Dr STD 4WD Crew Cab LB HD	19193	20517	22724
4 Dr STD 4WD Crew Cab SB HD	19025	20338	22525
4 Dr STD 4WD Ext Cab LB HD	17920	19156	21217
4 Dr STD 4WD Ext Cab SB HD	17753	18978	21019
4 Dr STD Crew Cab LB HD	17491	18698	20709
4 Dr STD Crew Cab SB HD	17320	18515	20507
4 Dr STD Ext Cab LB HD	16360	17488	19369
4 Dr STD Ext Cab SB HD	16191	17308	19169

Options	Price
6.6L V8 Turbodiesel OHV 32V Engine	+3226
8.1L V8 OHV 16V FI Engine	+547
AM/FM/CD Audio System [Opt on STD, Work]	+164
AM/FM/CD Changer Audio System [Opt on SLE, SLT]	+258
Automatic 4-Speed Transmission	+705
Automatic 5-Speed Transmission	+773
Automatic Climate Control (2 Zone) - Driver and Passenger [Opt on SLE, SLT]	+126
Bed Liner	+161
Bose Audio System [Opt on SLE, SLT]	+254
Bucket Seats [Opt on SLE, SLT]	+274

Options	Price
Chrome Wheels [Opt on STD]	+200
Compressed Natural Gas (CNG) Option [Opt on SLE, STD, Work]	+5988
Cruise Control [Opt on STD, Work]	+155
DVD Entertainment System	+834
Locking Differential	+190
OnStar Telematics System [Opt on SLE]	+447
Power Driver Seat [Opt on SLE]	+155
Power Passenger Seat [Opt on SLT]	+158
Power Retractable Mirrors [Opt on SLE, SLT]	+118
Satellite Radio System [Opt on SLE, SLT]	+209

Fully redesigned last year, the Sierra 2500HD gets only minor updates for 2002. Air conditioning is now standard on all trim levels along with extendable sunshade visors and redesigned exterior badging.

2002

Mileage Category: K

Body Styles	TMV Pricing		
	Trade	Private	Dealer
2 Dr SL 4WD Std Cab LB HD	14293	15454	17388
2 Dr SL Std Cab LB HD	12762	13799	15526
2 Dr SLE 4WD Std Cab LB HD	14992	16210	18239
2 Dr SLE Std Cab LB HD	13360	14445	16254
2 Dr STD 4WD Std Cab LB HD	13522	14620	16451
2 Dr STD Std Cab LB HD	11729	12682	14269
4 Dr SL 4WD Crew Cab LB HD	17440	18856	21217
4 Dr SL 4WD Crew Cab SB HD	17281	18685	21024
4 Dr SL 4WD Ext Cab LB HD	16359	17688	19902
4 Dr SL 4WD Ext Cab SB HD	16204	17520	19714
4 Dr SL Crew Cab LB HD	15820	17105	19246
4 Dr SL Crew Cab SB HD	15559	16823	18929
4 Dr SL Ext Cab LB HD	14833	16038	18046
4 Dr SL Ext Cab SB HD	14642	15831	17813
4 Dr SLE 4WD Crew Cab LB HD	18202	19680	22144
4 Dr SLE 4WD Crew Cab SB HD	18052	19518	21961
4 Dr SLE 4WD Ext Cab LB HD	17169	18563	20887
4 Dr SLE 4WD Ext Cab SB HD	17148	18540	20861
4 Dr SLE Crew Cab LB HD	16556	17900	20141

Body Styles	TMV Pricing		
	Trade	Private	Dealer
4 Dr SLE Crew Cab SB HD	16421	17755	19978
4 Dr SLE Ext Cab LB HD	15499	16758	18856
4 Dr SLE Ext Cab SB HD	15489	16747	18843
4 Dr SLT 4WD Crew Cab LB HD	19159	20715	23308
4 Dr SLT 4WD Crew Cab SB HD	18972	20513	23081
4 Dr SLT 4WD Ext Cab LB HD	18100	19570	22020
4 Dr SLT 4WD Ext Cab SB HD	17918	19373	21798
4 Dr SLT Crew Cab LB HD	17510	18932	21302
4 Dr SLT Crew Cab SB HD	17335	18743	21089
4 Dr SLT Ext Cab LB HD	16590	17937	20183
4 Dr SLT Ext Cab SB HD	16523	17865	20101
4 Dr STD 4WD Crew Cab LB HD	16593	17941	20187
4 Dr STD 4WD Crew Cab SB HD	16479	17818	20049
4 Dr STD 4WD Ext Cab LB HD	15848	17135	19280
4 Dr STD 4WD Ext Cab SB HD	15725	17002	19131
4 Dr STD Crew Cab LB HD	14906	16117	18135
4 Dr STD Crew Cab SB HD	14662	15853	17837
4 Dr STD Ext Cab LB HD	14348	15513	17455
4 Dr STD Ext Cab SB HD	14086	15230	17137

Options	Price
6.6L V8 Turbodiesel OHV 32V Engine	+2880
8.1L V8 OHV 16V FI Engine	+509
AM/FM/CD Audio System [Opt on STD]	+117
Air Conditioning [Opt on STD]	+494
Automatic 4-Speed Transmission [Opt on Std Cab]	+656
Automatic 5-Speed Transmission	+719
Bed Liner [Opt on Ext Cab SB - SLE,SLT]	+150

Options	Price
Bucket Seats [Opt on SLE,SLT]	+153
Cruise Control [Opt on STD]	+144
Flex Fuel Option	+449
Locking Differential	+177
Power Driver Seat [Opt on SLE]	+147
Power Passenger Seat [Opt on SLE]	+147
Running Boards [Opt on Ext Cab SB - SLE,SLT]	+150

2001

Both light- and heavy-duty 2500s sport new torsion bar front suspensions. Light-duty models now offer optional traction control and standard child safety-seat tethers. Heavy-duty Sierras are completely redesigned for 2001 offering two new engines and transmissions, bigger interiors and numerous other improvements aimed at buyers looking for a "professional grade" truck from GM.

Mileage Category: K

Body Styles	TMV Pricing		
	Trade	Private	Dealer
2 Dr SL 4WD Std Cab LB HD	11763	13275	14670
2 Dr SL Std Cab LB HD	10429	11769	13006
2 Dr SLE 4WD Std Cab LB HD	12826	14474	15996
2 Dr SLE Std Cab LB HD	11504	12982	14346
4 Dr SL 4WD Crew Cab LB HD	14374	16221	17926
4 Dr SL 4WD Crew Cab SB HD	14244	16074	17764
4 Dr SL 4WD Ext Cab LB HD	13831	15608	17248
4 Dr SL 4WD Ext Cab SB HD	13612	15361	16975
4 Dr SL Crew Cab LB HD	12961	14626	16163
4 Dr SL Crew Cab SB HD	12534	14145	15632
4 Dr SL Ext Cab LB HD	12277	13855	15311
4 Dr SL Ext Cab SB HD	12101	13656	15091
4 Dr SLE 4WD Crew Cab LB HD	15535	17531	19374
4 Dr SLE 4WD Crew Cab SB HD	15017	16947	18728

Body Styles	TMV Pricing		
	Trade	Private	Dealer
4 Dr SLE 4WD Ext Cab LB HD	14693	16581	18323
4 Dr SLE 4WD Ext Cab SB HD	14541	16409	18134
4 Dr SLE Crew Cab LB HD	14096	15907	17579
4 Dr SLE Crew Cab SB HD	13844	15623	17266
4 Dr SLE Ext Cab LB HD	13360	15077	16661
4 Dr SLE Ext Cab SB HD	13212	14909	16476
4 Dr SLT 4WD Crew Cab LB HD	16793	18950	20942
4 Dr SLT 4WD Crew Cab SB HD	16747	18899	20886
4 Dr SLT 4WD Ext Cab LB HD	15602	17607	19458
4 Dr SLT 4WD Ext Cab SB HD	15440	17424	19256
4 Dr SLT Crew Cab LB HD	14938	16857	18629
4 Dr SLT Crew Cab SB HD	14847	16755	18516
4 Dr SLT Ext Cab LB HD	14200	16025	17709
4 Dr SLT Ext Cab SB HD	14056	15862	17529

Options	Price
6.6L V8 Turbodiesel OHV 32V Engine	+2627
8.1L V8 OHV 16V FI Engine	+464
Air Conditioning [Opt on SL]	+451
Automatic 5-Speed Transmission	+655
Bucket Seats [Opt on SLE]	+137
Chrome Wheels [Opt on SL]	+169

Options	Price
Cruise Control [Opt on SL]	+131
Heated Front Seats	+137
Locking Differential	+156
Power Driver Seat [Opt on SLE]	+131
Power Passenger Seat [Opt on SLE]	+131
Tonneau Cover	+131

Sierra 3500

2004

For 2004, a single-rear-wheel 4WD version is available in all body styles. Additionally, GMC has slotted in a value-priced Work Truck trim level below the base model. Base models pick up a chrome grille and bumpers, along with cruise control, while SLE models get foglights and can be equipped with leather upholstery. New accessories include a lockable storage area under the rear seat, and a choice between a soft tonneau bed cover and a hard locking cover.

Mileage Category: K

Body Styles	TMV Pricing		
	Trade	Private	Dealer
2 Dr SLE 4WD Std Cab LB	19610	21028	23391
2 Dr SLE 4WD Std Cab LB DRW	19574	20978	23319
2 Dr STD 4WD Std Cab LB	18846	20320	22777
2 Dr STD 4WD Std Cab LB DRW	18772	20189	22551
2 Dr Work Truck 4WD Std Cab LB	17923	19324	21660
2 Dr Work Truck 4WD Std Cab LB DRW	17766	19167	21502
4 Dr SLE 4WD Crew Cab LB	23454	25155	27991
4 Dr SLE 4WD Crew Cab LB DRW	23863	25564	28400
4 Dr SLE 4WD Ext Cab LB	21994	23564	26181
4 Dr SLE 4WD Ext Cab LB DRW	22353	23792	26190
4 Dr SLE Crew Cab LB DRW	21887	23546	26312
4 Dr SLE Ext Cab LB DRW	20448	21887	24285
4 Dr SLT 4WD Crew Cab LB	25850	27551	30387
4 Dr SLT 4WD Crew Cab LB DRW	26258	27959	30795
4 Dr SLT 4WD Ext Cab LB	23982	25421	27819
4 Dr SLT 4WD Ext Cab LB DRW	24647	26086	28484

Body Styles	TMV Pricing		
	Trade	Private	Dealer
4 Dr SLT Crew Cab LB DRW	23968	25557	28205
4 Dr SLT Ext Cab LB DRW	22620	24059	26457
4 Dr STD 4WD Crew Cab LB	22543	24244	27080
4 Dr STD 4WD Crew Cab LB DRW	22975	24676	27512
4 Dr STD 4WD Ext Cab LB	20807	22396	25044
4 Dr STD 4WD Ext Cab LB DRW	21430	22869	25267
4 Dr STD Crew Cab LB DRW	20804	22393	25041
4 Dr STD Ext Cab LB DRW	19517	20956	23354
4 Dr Work Truck 4WD Crew Cab LB	21708	23409	26245
4 Dr Work Truck 4WD Crew Cab LB DRW	22104	23805	26641
4 Dr Work Truck 4WD Ext Cab LB	19453	20849	23175
4 Dr Work Truck 4WD Ext Cab LB DRW	20534	21973	24371
4 Dr Work Truck Crew Cab LB DRW	19935	21524	24172
4 Dr Work Truck Ext Cab LB DRW	18649	20088	22486

Options	Price
6.6L V8 Turbodiesel OHV 32V Engine	+5310
8.1L V8 OHV 16V FI Engine	+950
AM/FM/CD Changer Audio System [Opt on SLE non-Std]	+795
Automatic 5-Speed Transmission	+1200
Automatic Climate Control (2 Zone) - Driver and Passenger [Opt on SLE non-Std]	+195
Bucket Seats [Opt on SLE non-Std]	+350
Cruise Control [Opt on Work Truck]	+240
DVD Entertainment System [Opt on SLE, SLT Crew]	+1295
Leather Seats [Opt on SLE non-Std]	+800

Options	Price
Locking Differential [Opt on DRW]	+295
OnStar Telematics System [Opt on SLE]	+695
Power Door Locks [Opt on STD]	+162
Power Driver Seat [Opt on SLE]	+240
Power Retractable Mirrors [Opt on SLE, SLT SRW]	+213
Rear Audio Controls [Opt on SLE, SLT Crew]	+165
Rear Window Defroster [Opt on STD]	+175
Steering Wheel Radio Controls [Opt on SLE]	+125

2003

The Sierra gets a revised look this year that includes a new front fascia, revised side moldings and optional multifunction, fold-away mirrors. On the inside, GMC has added new seats, a more comprehensive driver information center, a redesigned instrument panel and optional dual-zone climate control and satellite steering wheel controls. On the hardware side, the standard 6.0-liter V8 gets electronic throttle control as well as the ability to run exclusively on compressed natural gas (CNG) or a mix of CNG and gasoline. Other upgrades include an improved Insta-Trac part-time four-wheel-drive system for reduced service costs, a more efficient starter for the 8.1-liter V8 and a revised headlight switch that allows drivers to turn off the daytime running lamps.

Mileage Category: K

Body Styles	TMV Pricing		
	Trade	Private	Dealer
2 Dr SLE 4WD Std Cab LB	17705	18926	20961
2 Dr STD 4WD Std Cab LB	16136	17249	19105
4 Dr SLE 4WD Crew Cab LB	21471	22952	25421
4 Dr SLE 4WD Ext Cab LB	20376	21782	24124
4 Dr SLE Crew Cab LB	19689	21047	23311
4 Dr SLE Ext Cab LB	18487	19762	21888
Dr SLT 4WD Crew Cab LB	22571	24128	26723

Body Styles	TMV Pricing		
	Trade	Private	Dealer
4 Dr SLT 4WD Ext Cab LB	21437	22916	25381
4 Dr SLT Crew Cab LB	20659	22084	24460
4 Dr SLT Ext Cab LB	19612	20965	23220
4 Dr STD 4WD Crew Cab LB	19845	21214	23496
4 Dr STD 4WD Ext Cab LB	18990	20300	22483
4 Dr STD Crew Cab LB	17935	19172	21234
4 Dr STD Ext Cab LB	17066	18244	20206

Options	Price
6.6L V8 Turbodiesel OHV 32V Engine	+3226
8.1L V8 OHV 16V FI Engine	+547
AM/FM/CD Audio System [Opt on STD]	+164
AM/FM/CD Changer Audio System [Opt on SLE,SLT]	+258
Automatic 4-Speed Transmission	+705
Automatic 5-Speed Transmission	+773
Automatic Climate Control (2 Zone) - Driver and Passenger [Opt on SLE]	+126
Bose Audio System [Opt on SLE,SLT]	+254
Bucket Seats [Opt on SLE,SLT]	+274

Options	Price
Cruise Control [Opt on STD,Work]	+155
DVD Entertainment System	+834
Flex Fuel Option	+483
Locking Differential	+190
OnStar Telematics System [Opt on SLE]	+447
Power Driver Seat [Opt on SLE]	+155
Power Passenger Seat [Opt on SLT]	+158
Power Retractable Mirrors [Opt on SLE,SLT]	+153
Satellite Radio System [Opt on SLE]	+209

Mileage Category: K

Body Styles	TMV Pricing		
	Trade	Private	Dealer
2 Dr SL 4WD Std Cab LB	14924	16124	18125
2 Dr SLE 4WD Std Cab LB	15635	16871	18932
2 Dr STD 4WD Std Cab LB	14045	15175	17057
4 Dr SL 4WD Crew Cab LB	18016	19465	21880
4 Dr SL 4WD Ext Cab LB	17021	18390	20672
4 Dr SL Crew Cab LB	16367	17683	19877
4 Dr SL Ext Cab LB	15398	16637	18701
4 Dr SLE 4WD Crew Cab LB	18753	20261	22775
4 Dr SLE 4WD Ext Cab LB	17808	19241	21628
4 Dr SLE Crew Cab LB	17112	18488	20782

Body Styles	TMV Pricing		
	Trade	Private	Dealer
4 Dr SLE Ext Cab LB	16172	17473	19641
4 Dr SLT 4WD Crew Cab LB	19702	21287	23928
4 Dr SLT 4WD Ext Cab LB	18757	20266	22781
4 Dr SLT Crew Cab LB	18038	19489	21907
4 Dr SLT Ext Cab LB	17151	18530	20829
4 Dr STD 4WD Crew Cab LB	17290	18681	20998
4 Dr STD 4WD Ext Cab LB	16547	17878	20096
4 Dr STD Crew Cab LB	15734	16999	19108
4 Dr STD Ext Cab LB	14927	16127	18128

After undergoing a full redesign last year, the Sierra 3500 gets only minor changes for 2002. Air conditioning is now standard on all trim levels, and a Cold Weather package is now available that includes heated exterior mirrors and a rear window defogger.

Options	Price
6.6L V8 Turbodiesel OHV 32V Engine	+2880
8.1L V8 OHV 16V FI Engine	+509
AM/FM/CD Audio System [Opt on STD]	+117
Air Conditioning [Opt on STD]	+494
Automatic 4-Speed Transmission [Opt on Std Cab]	+656
Automatic 5-Speed Transmission	+719

Options	Price
Bucket Seats [Opt on SLE,SLT]	+254
Cruise Control [Opt on STD]	+144
Flex Fuel Option	+449
Locking Differential	+177
Power Driver Seat [Opt on SLE]	+147
Power Passenger Seat [Opt on SLE]	+147

Mileage Category: K

The General's brand-new HD truck lineup debuts with stronger frames; beefed-up suspensions, axles, brakes and cooling systems; new sheet metal; bigger interiors; and a trio of powerful new V8s -- a 6.6-liter Duramax turbodiesel and two gas engines, a hefty 8.1-liter and an improved 6.0-liter. One of the four transmissions, a new Allison five-speed automatic, is designed especially for towing and hauling with GM's helpful tow/haul mode and a new "grade-braking" feature.

Body Styles	TMV Pricing		
	Trade	Private	Dealer
2 Dr SL 4WD Std Cab LB	12804	14375	15826
2 Dr SL Std Cab LB	11883	13342	14688
2 Dr SLE 4WD Std Cab LB	13349	14988	16500
2 Dr SLE Std Cab LB	12081	13564	14933
4 Dr SL 4WD Crew Cab LB	15520	17425	19184
4 Dr SL 4WD Ext Cab LB	14352	16114	17740
4 Dr SL Crew Cab LB	13760	15449	17009
4 Dr SL Ext Cab LB	12931	14519	15984

Body Styles	TMV Pricing		
	Trade	Private	Dealer
4 Dr SLE 4WD Crew Cab LB	16034	18002	19819
4 Dr SLE 4WD Ext Cab LB	15659	17581	19355
4 Dr SLE Crew Cab LB	14599	16391	18045
4 Dr SLE Ext Cab LB	13835	15533	17101
4 Dr SLT 4WD Crew Cab LB	16961	19043	20965
4 Dr SLT 4WD Ext Cab LB	16161	18145	19976
4 Dr SLT Crew Cab LB	15677	17602	19378
4 Dr SLT Ext Cab LB	14890	16718	18405

Options	Price
6.6L V8 Turbodiesel OHV 32V Engine	+2627
8.1L V8 OHV 16V FI Engine	+464
Air Conditioning [Opt on SL]	+451
Automatic 4-Speed Transmission	+598
Automatic 5-Speed Transmission	+655
Bucket Seats [Opt on SLE]	+137
Chrome Wheels [Opt on SL]	+169

Options	Price
Cruise Control [Opt on SL]	+131
Heated Front Seats	+137
Locking Differential	+156
Power Driver Seat [Opt on SLE]	+131
Power Passenger Seat [Opt on SLE]	+131
Tonneau Cover	+131

Mileage Category: K

Diesel engines make more power and torque, extended cab models get rear heater ducts, a PassLock theft-deterrent system is standard and three new colors debut. Second-generation airbags are standard.

Body Styles	TMV Pricing		
	Trade	Private	Dealer
2 Dr C3500 SL Ext Cab LB	7593	9011	10611
2 Dr C3500 SL Std Cab LB	6443	7647	9004
2 Dr C3500 SLE Ext Cab LB	8275	9821	11565
2 Dr C3500 SLE Std Cab LB	7262	8618	10148
2 Dr C3500 SLT Ext Cab LB	9105	10806	12724
2 Dr C3500 SLT Std Cab LB	7770	9222	10859
2 Dr K3500 SL 4WD Ext Cab LB	8395	9963	11732
2 Dr K3500 SL 4WD Std Cab LB	7357	8732	10282
2 Dr K3500 SLE 4WD Ext Cab LB	9192	10909	12845

Body Styles	TMV Pricing		
	Trade	Private	Dealer
2 Dr K3500 SLE 4WD Std Cab LB	8230	9767	11500
2 Dr K3500 SLT 4WD Ext Cab LB	9531	11311	13319
2 Dr K3500 SLT 4WD Std Cab LB	8846	10499	12362
4 Dr C3500 SL Crew Cab LB	7500	8901	10481
4 Dr C3500 SLE Crew Cab LB	9074	10769	12681
4 Dr C3500 SLT Crew Cab LB	9178	10892	12825
4 Dr K3500 SL 4WD Crew Cab LB	8742	10375	12216
4 Dr K3500 SLE 4WD Crew Cab LB	9350	11097	13067
4 Dr K3500 SLT 4WD Crew Cab LB	10124	12015	14148

Options	Price
6.5L V8 Turbodiesel OHV 16V Engine	+942
7.4L V8 OHV 16V FI Engine	+208
Air Conditioning [Opt on SL]	+279

Options	Price
Automatic 4-Speed Transmission	+337
Dual Rear Wheels	+297

Sierra 3500

1997

A passenger airbag is added to models with a GVWR under 8,600 pounds, and all models get speed-sensitive steering that reduces low-speed effort. Automatic transmissions are refined to provide smoother shifts and improved efficiency. Three new paint colors debut.

Mileage Category: K

Body Styles	TMV Pricing			Body Styles	TMV Pricing		
	Trade	Private	Dealer		Trade	Private	Dealer
2 Dr C3500 SL Ext Cab LB	6752	8095	9736	2 Dr K3500 SLE 4WD Std Cab LB	7102	8514	10240
2 Dr C3500 SL Std Cab LB	5720	6858	8248	2 Dr K3500 SLT 4WD Ext Cab LB	8314	9967	11988
2 Dr C3500 SLE Ext Cab LB	7126	8543	10274	2 Dr K3500 SLT 4WD Std Cab LB	7947	9527	11458
2 Dr C3500 SLE Std Cab LB	6275	7523	9049	4 Dr C3500 SL Crew Cab LB	6718	8054	9686
2 Dr C3500 SLT Ext Cab LB	7985	9574	11515	4 Dr C3500 SLE Crew Cab LB	7956	9538	11472
2 Dr C3500 SLT Std Cab LB	6984	8373	10071	4 Dr C3500 SLT Crew Cab LB	8071	9676	11637
2 Dr K3500 SL 4WD Ext Cab LB	7576	9083	10924	4 Dr K3500 SL 4WD Crew Cab LB	7635	9153	11009
2 Dr K3500 SL 4WD Std Cab LB	6540	7841	9430	4 Dr K3500 SLE 4WD Crew Cab LB	8267	9911	11920
2 Dr K3500 SLE 4WD Ext Cab LB	8100	9711	11680	4 Dr K3500 SLT 4WD Crew Cab LB	8814	10567	12709

Options	Price	Options	Price
6.5L V8 Turbodiesel OHV 16V Engine	+853	Automatic 4-Speed Transmission	+305
7.4L V8 OHV 16V FI Engine	+188	Dual Rear Wheels	+269
Air Conditioning [Opt on SL]	+253		

1996

Vortec, a new family of engines, is introduced, providing more power and torque than last year's offerings. The Vortec engines available on the Sierra 3500 pickups include a 5.7-liter V8, rated at 250 hp at 4,600 rpm and 355 lb-ft of torque at 2,800 rpm and a 7.4-liter V8, capable of 290 hp at 4,200 rpm and 410 lb-ft of torque at 3,200 rpm. Noteworthy comfort and convenience additions include illuminated entry, additional 12-volt power outlets, an electrochromic inside rearview mirror and height-adjustable front safety belts. Also the crew cab body styles get rear-seat heating ducts. Daytime Running Lamps (DRLs) are added this year as well.

Mileage Category: K

Body Styles	TMV Pricing			Body Styles	TMV Pricing		
	Trade	Private	Dealer		Trade	Private	Dealer
2 Dr C3500 SL Ext Cab LB	5688	6888	8546	2 Dr K3500 SLT 4WD Ext Cab LB	7104	8603	10674
2 Dr C3500 SL Std Cab LB	4888	5920	7344	2 Dr K3500 SLT 4WD Std Cab LB	6559	7943	9854
2 Dr C3500 SLE Ext Cab LB	5997	7262	9010	4 Dr C3500 SL Crew Cab LB	5608	6792	8426
2 Dr C3500 SLT Ext Cab LB	6739	8161	10124	4 Dr C3500 SLE Crew Cab LB	6724	8142	10101
2 Dr C3500 SLT Std Cab LB	5877	7117	8829	4 Dr C3500 SLT Crew Cab LB	6768	8196	10169
2 Dr K3500 SL 4WD Ext Cab LB	6390	7738	9600	4 Dr K3500 SL 4WD Crew Cab LB	6447	7807	9685
2 Dr K3500 SL 4WD Std Cab LB	5556	6729	8348	4 Dr K3500 SLE 4WD Crew Cab LB	7024	8507	10554
2 Dr K3500 SLE 4WD Ext Cab LB	6764	8191	10162	4 Dr K3500 SLT 4WD Crew Cab LB	7508	9092	11280
2 Dr K3500 SLE 4WD Std Cab LB	6372	7717	9574				

Options	Price	Options	Price
6.5L V8 Turbodiesel OHV 16V Engine	+755	Automatic 4-Speed Transmission	+269
7.4L V8 OHV 16V FI Engine	+166	Dual Rear Wheels	+238
Air Conditioning [Opt on SL]	+223		

1995

A revised interior graces these full-size trucks this year. A shift interlock is added, requiring the brake pedal to be depressed before the automatic transmission's gear selector can be shifted out of "park." This reduces the likelihood that the vehicle will move suddenly and unexpectedly when the transmission is taken out of "park." Power mirrors, revised climate controls and cupholders provide a more user-friendly interior environment. Mechanical enhancements include the addition of standard 4-wheel antilock brakes, improvements in the engines and modifications to the heavy-duty 4L80-E. The four-wheel ABS replaces last year's rear-wheel-only antilock system. Various upgrade to the engines are intended to reduce noise, improve durability and/or increase efficiency. The transmission is revised for quicker 1-2 upshifts during full-power applications.

Mileage Category: K

Body Styles	TMV Pricing			Body Styles	TMV Pricing		
	Trade	Private	Dealer		Trade	Private	Dealer
2 Dr C3500 SL Ext Cab LB	4727	5794	7571	2 Dr K3500 SLE 4WD Ext Cab LB	5624	6893	9008
2 Dr C3500 SL Std Cab LB	3951	4843	6329	2 Dr K3500 SLE 4WD Std Cab LB	4894	5998	7839
2 Dr C3500 SLE Ext Cab LB	4950	6068	7930	2 Dr K3500 SLT 4WD Ext Cab LB	5923	7260	9488
2 Dr C3500 SLE Std Cab LB	4471	5480	7161	4 Dr C3500 SL Crew Cab LB	4584	5619	7343
2 Dr C3500 SLT Ext Cab LB	5503	6745	8816	4 Dr C3500 SLE Crew Cab LB	5414	6635	8671
2 Dr K3500 SL 4WD Ext Cab LB	5225	6404	8370	4 Dr K3500 SL 4WD Crew Cab LB	5277	6468	8453
2 Dr K3500 SL 4WD Std Cab LB	4514	5533	7230	4 Dr K3500 SLE 4WD Crew Cab LB	5798	7106	9287

Options	Price	Options	Price
6.5L V8 Turbodiesel OHV 16V Engine	+701	Air Conditioning [Opt on SL]	+207
7.4L V8 OHV 16V FI Engine	+154	Automatic 4-Speed Transmission	+250
AM/FM/Cassette/CD Audio System	+75	Dual Rear Wheels	+221

Sierra C3
2001

Mileage Category: K

Body Styles	TMV Pricing		
	Trade	Private	Dealer
4 Dr STD AWD Ext Cab SB	16992	18919	20697

The extended-cab C3 is a new truck based on the Sierra 1500 half-ton full-size pickup. It's powered by a specially tuned version of the 6.0-liter Vortec V8. It also gets full-time all-wheel drive, 3/4-ton brakes and a standard heavy-duty suspension. With styling cues and feature content similar to GMC's SUVs, think of the C3 as the Denali version of the Sierra.

Sierra Classic 1500
1999

Mileage Category: K

Body Styles	TMV Pricing			Body Styles	TMV Pricing		
	Trade	Private	Dealer		Trade	Private	Dealer
3 Dr C1500 SLE Ext Cab SB	9321	10899	12542	3 Dr K1500 SLE 4WD Ext Cab SB	10582	12373	14238
3 Dr C1500 SLT Ext Cab SB	9573	11314	13126	3 Dr K1500 SLT 4WD Ext Cab SB	10701	12618	14613

Options	Price	Options	Price
5.7L V8 OHV 16V FI Engine	+282	Bucket Seats	+121
AM/FM/Cassette/CD Audio System	+117	Chrome Wheels	+125
Aluminum/Alloy Wheels	+125		

With an all-new Sierra 1500 just months away, changes are limited to a few new colors.

Sierra Classic 2500
1999

Mileage Category: K

Body Styles	TMV Pricing			Body Styles	TMV Pricing		
	Trade	Private	Dealer		Trade	Private	Dealer
2 Dr C2500 SL Ext Cab LB HD	7778	9169	10616	2 Dr K2500 SLT 4WD Ext Cab LB HD	10899	12848	14876
2 Dr C2500 SL Std Cab LB HD	6868	8096	9374	2 Dr K2500 SLT 4WD Ext Cab SB HD	10715	12630	14624
2 Dr C2500 SLE Ext Cab LB HD	8915	10508	12167	2 Dr K2500 SLT 4WD Std Cab LB HD	9863	11627	13462
2 Dr C2500 SLE Std Cab LB HD	8092	9539	11045	4 Dr C2500 SL Crew Cab SB HD	8988	10595	12268
2 Dr C2500 SLT Ext Cab LB HD	9800	11552	13375	4 Dr C2500 SLE Crew Cab SB HD	9741	11482	13294
2 Dr C2500 SLT Std Cab LB HD	8835	10415	12059	4 Dr C2500 SLT Crew Cab SB HD	10687	12598	14587
2 Dr K2500 SL 4WD Ext Cab LB HD	9126	10758	12457	4 Dr K2500 SL 4WD Crew Cab SB HD	10176	11995	13889
2 Dr K2500 SL 4WD Ext Cab SB HD	9049	10666	12350	4 Dr K2500 SLE 4WD Crew Cab SB HD	10795	12725	14734
2 Dr K2500 SL 4WD Std Cab LB HD	8229	9700	11232	4 Dr K2500 SLT 4WD Crew Cab SB HD	11882	14006	16217
2 Dr K2500 SLE 4WD Ext Cab LB HD	10097	11902	13781				
2 Dr K2500 SLE 4WD Ext Cab SB HD	10046	11842	13712				
2 Dr K2500 SLE 4WD Std Cab LB HD	9417	11101	12854				

Options	Price	Options	Price
6.5L V8 Turbodiesel OHV 16V Engine	+1094	Automatic 4-Speed Transmission	+401
7.4L V8 OHV 16V FI Engine	+242	Bucket Seats	+121
AM/FM/Cassette/CD Audio System [Opt on SLE,SLT]	+117	Locking Differential	+115
Air Conditioning [Opt on SL]	+324		

Mechanical upgrades include new internal components and seals for automatic transmissions, improved cooling system and starter motor durability, and three new exterior paint colors. With an all-new Sierra 2500 just months away, changes are limited to a few new colors.

Sierra Classic 3500

1999

Mechanical upgrades include new internal components and seals for automatic transmissions, improved cooling system and starter motor durability, and three new exterior paint colors. With an all-new Sierra just months away, changes are limited to a few new colors.

Mileage Category: K

Body Styles	TMV Pricing			Body Styles	TMV Pricing		
	Trade	Private	Dealer		Trade	Private	Dealer
2 Dr C3500 SL Ext Cab LB	8745	10207	11728	4 Dr C3500 SL Crew Cab LB	8684	10135	11646
2 Dr C3500 SL Std Cab LB	7772	9071	10423	4 Dr C3500 SL Crew Cab SB	9432	11009	12650
2 Dr C3500 SLE Ext Cab LB	9865	11514	13230	4 Dr C3500 SLE Crew Cab LB	10743	12539	14408
2 Dr C3500 SLE Std Cab LB	8440	9851	11319	4 Dr C3500 SLE Crew Cab SB	11161	13026	14968
2 Dr C3500 SLT Ext Cab LB	10896	12717	14613	4 Dr C3500 SLT Crew Cab LB	11304	13193	15160
2 Dr C3500 SLT Std Cab LB	9354	10918	12545	4 Dr C3500 SLT Crew Cab SB	11532	13460	15466
2 Dr K3500 SL 4WD Ext Cab LB	10010	11683	13425	4 Dr K3500 SL 4WD Crew Cab LB	10184	11886	13658
2 Dr K3500 SL 4WD Std Cab LB	8551	9980	11468	4 Dr K3500 SL 4WD Crew Cab SB	11039	12884	14805
2 Dr K3500 SLE 4WD Ext Cab LB	11331	13225	15197	4 Dr K3500 SLE 4WD Crew Cab LB	11570	13504	15517
2 Dr K3500 SLE 4WD Std Cab LB	9795	11433	13137	4 Dr K3500 SLE 4WD Crew Cab SB	12001	14007	16094
2 Dr K3500 SLT 4WD Ext Cab LB	11574	13509	15523	4 Dr K3500 SLT 4WD Crew Cab LB	12089	14110	16214
2 Dr K3500 SLT 4WD Std Cab LB	10560	12325	14162	4 Dr K3500 SLT 4WD Crew Cab SB	12822	14966	17197

Options	Price	Options	Price
6.5L V8 Turbodiesel OHV 16V Engine	+1094	Air Conditioning [Opt on SL]	+324
7.4L V8 OHV 16V FI Engine	+242	Automatic 4-Speed Transmission	+401
AM/FM/Cassette/CD Audio System	+117	Dual Rear Wheels	+345

Sonoma

2004

The Sonoma is offered only as a 4x4 Crew Cab for 2004.

Mileage Category: J

Body Styles	TMV Pricing		
	Trade	Private	Dealer
4 Dr SLS 4WD Crew Cab SB	15134	16451	18645

Options	Price	Options	Price
AM/FM/CD Changer Audio System	+395	Power Driver Seat	+240
AM/FM/Cassette/CD Audio System	+250	Power Passenger Seat	+240
Fog Lights	+150	Side Steps	+300
Leather Seats	+600	Sliding Rear Window	+130
Locking Differential	+270	Special Factory Paint	+165
Locking Differential (Rear)	+300	Tonneau Cover	+395
Luggage Rack	+300		

2003

The Sonoma gets a few changes for what will be the final year of production of the current model. There's a new split-folding bench seat on all two-wheel-drive models, new seat materials, an optional six-disc CD changer and a sport package for crew-cab models.

Mileage Category: J

Body Styles	TMV Pricing			Body Styles	TMV Pricing		
	Trade	Private	Dealer		Trade	Private	Dealer
2 Dr SL Std Cab LB	7844	8650	9992	3 Dr SL Ext Cab SB	8850	9759	11274
2 Dr SL Std Cab SB	7055	7780	8988	3 Dr SLS 4WD Ext Cab SB	11700	12902	14905
2 Dr SLS Std Cab LB	10154	11197	12936	3 Dr SLS Ext Cab SB	10334	11396	13165
2 Dr SLS Std Cab SB	8075	8905	10287	3 Dr SLS ZR2 4WD Ext Cab SB	12530	13817	15961
3 Dr SL 4WD Ext Cab SB	10825	11937	13791	4 Dr SLS 4WD Crew Cab SB	13861	15285	17658

Options	Price	Options	Price
4.3L V6 OHV 12V FI Engine [Std on 4WD]	+644	Luggage Rack	+161
AM/FM/CD Audio System [Opt on SL]	+194	Power Door Locks [Opt on SLS]	+138
AM/FM/CD Changer Audio System [Opt on SLS]	+254	Power Driver Seat [Opt on SLS]	+155
Automatic 4-Speed Transmission	+705	Power Moonroof [Opt on SLS]	+447
Bucket Seats	+220	Power Passenger Seat [Opt on SLS]	+155
Cruise Control [Opt on SL]	+119	Power Windows [Opt on SLS]	+158
Heated Front Seats [Opt on SLS]	+177	Side Steps	+161
Keyless Entry System [Opt on SLS]	+119	Stepside Bed [Opt on SLS]	+306
Leather Seats [Opt on SLS]	+483	Tonneau Cover	+254
Locking Differential	+174	ZQ8 Sport Suspension Package [Opt on SLS]	+505

Mileage Category: J

2002

In what is likely the last year of production before a full redesign, the Sonoma gets a host of minor equipment upgrades. All extended cabs get a standard third door, while all models get a bed extender and upgraded stereos. The top-of-the-line SLE trim level has been discontinued along with the regular cab, long-bed model. Graphite leather trim is now available on crew cab models and Sandalwood has been added to the color palette.

Body Styles	TMV Pricing		
	Trade	Private	Dealer
2 Dr SL Std Cab LB	6358	7090	8310
2 Dr SL Std Cab SB	6104	6807	7979
2 Dr SLS Std Cab LB	9074	10119	11861
2 Dr SLS Std Cab SB	7587	8398	9750
3 Dr SL 4WD Ext Cab SB	9898	11038	12939

Body Styles	TMV Pricing		
	Trade	Private	Dealer
3 Dr SL Ext Cab SB	7428	8283	9709
3 Dr SLS 4WD Ext Cab SB	10696	11897	13898
3 Dr SLS Ext Cab SB	9079	10125	11867
4 Dr SLS 4WD Crew Cab SB	12236	13646	15995

Options	Price
4.3L V6 OHV 12V FI Engine [Opt on 2WD]	+599
AM/FM/CD Audio System [Opt on SL]	+181
AM/FM/CD Changer Audio System [Opt on SLS]	+177
Automatic 4-Speed Transmission [Opt on SL SB]	+656
Bucket Seats [Opt on SLS]	+159
Cruise Control [Opt on SL]	+117
Leather Seats [Opt on Crew Cab]	+928
Locking Differential	+162
Luggage Rack [Opt on Crew Cab]	+150
Power Door Locks [Opt on SLS]	+129

Options	Price
Power Driver Seat [Opt on Crew Cab]	+144
Power Passenger Seat [Opt on Crew Cab]	+144
Power Windows [Opt on SLS]	+147
Side Steps [Opt on Crew Cab]	+150
Tilt Steering Wheel [Opt on SL]	+117
Tonneau Cover [Opt on Crew Cab]	+341
ZQ8 Sport Suspension Package [Opt on SLS 2WD]	+464
ZR2 Highrider Suspension Package [Opt on SLS 4WD Ext Cab]	+1154

Mileage Category: J

2001

An all-new model has been added to the Sonoma lineup for 2001, a four-door Crew Cab, complete with Vortec 4300 V6, automatic transmission, InstaTrac four-wheel-drive system and SLS trim. Powertrain improvements incorporate an advanced control module for the V6 and flex-fuel capability for the four-cylinder. There are also new aluminum wheels with the sport suspension, and programmable automatic power door locks.

Body Styles	TMV Pricing		
	Trade	Private	Dealer
2 Dr SL 4WD Ext Cab SB	7892	9441	10870
2 Dr SL Ext Cab SB	6379	7631	8786
2 Dr SL Std Cab LB	5233	6260	7208
2 Dr SL Std Cab SB	4941	5911	6806
2 Dr SLS Sport 4WD Ext Cab SB	8722	10433	12013

Body Styles	TMV Pricing		
	Trade	Private	Dealer
2 Dr SLS Sport Ext Cab SB	6651	7956	9160
2 Dr SLS Sport Std Cab LB	6051	7238	8334
2 Dr SLS Sport Std Cab SB	5666	6778	7804
4 Dr SLS 4WD Crew Cab SB	10247	12258	14114

Options	Price
4.3L V6 OHV 12V FI Engine [Std on 4WD]	+707
AM/FM/CD Audio System	+165
Air Conditioning	+440
Aluminum/Alloy Wheels	+153
Automatic 4-Speed Transmission	+598

Options	Price
Locking Differential	+147
Power Windows	+131
Sport Suspension	+402
Tonneau Cover	+224
ZR2 Highrider Suspension Package	+1035

Mileage Category: J

2000

Four-wheel-drive Sonomas get a higher-output V6 and a handling/trailering suspension standard. GMC drops the 4WD long-bed and High-Rider regular-cab models and adds a new, lower-priced base-trim extended-cab model. All versions get a boost in trailer ratings and a new paint color.

Body Styles	TMV Pricing		
	Trade	Private	Dealer
2 Dr SL 4WD Ext Cab SB	6505	7876	9220
2 Dr SL 4WD Std Cab SB	6205	7513	8795
2 Dr SL Ext Cab SB	5260	6369	7457
2 Dr SL Std Cab LB	4421	5353	6266
2 Dr SL Std Cab SB	4195	5080	5947
2 Dr SLE 4WD Ext Cab SB	7349	8898	10417
2 Dr SLE 4WD Std Cab SB	6554	7935	9289
2 Dr SLE Ext Cab SB	6157	7455	8727
2 Dr SLE Std Cab SB	4866	5892	6897
2 Dr SLS Sport 4WD Ext Cab SB	6951	8416	9852

Body Styles	TMV Pricing		
	Trade	Private	Dealer
2 Dr SLS Sport 4WD Ext Cab Step SB	7150	8657	10134
2 Dr SLS Sport 4WD Std Cab SB	6406	7756	9080
2 Dr SLS Sport 4WD Std Cab Step SB	6453	7813	9147
2 Dr SLS Sport Ext Cab SB	5510	6672	7811
2 Dr SLS Sport Ext Cab Step SB	5710	6913	8093
2 Dr SLS Sport Std Cab LB	4806	5819	6812
2 Dr SLS Sport Std Cab SB	4766	5770	6755
2 Dr SLS Sport Std Cab Step SB	4828	5846	6843

Options	Price
4.3L V6 OHV 12V FI Engine	+645
AM/FM/CD Audio System	+150
AM/FM/Cassette/CD Audio System	+200
Air Conditioning	+401
Aluminum/Alloy Wheels	+139
Automatic 4-Speed Transmission	+545

Options	Price
Bucket Seats	+145
Hinged Third Door	+147
Limited Slip Differential	+134
Power Windows	+119
Sport Suspension	+366
ZR2 Highrider Suspension Package	+893

GMC
Sonoma

1999

The '99 Sonoma touts four new exterior colors, a new steering wheel with mini-module depowered airbag and larger, more robust outside rearview mirrors, with the uplevel power mirror gaining a heated feature. AutoTrac, GM's electronic push-button two-speed transfer case, is now standard on four-wheel-drive models, and all Sonomas get a content theft alarm with remote keyless entry as well as a flash-to-pass headlamp feature for the smart stalk. Serious four-wheelers can now order composite skid plates.

Mileage Category: J

Body Styles	TMV Pricing		
	Trade	Private	Dealer
2 Dr SL 4WD Std Cab LB	5193	6384	7624
2 Dr SL 4WD Std Cab SB	5045	6202	7407
2 Dr SL Std Cab LB	3838	4719	5636
2 Dr SL Std Cab SB	3652	4490	5363
2 Dr SLE 4WD Ext Cab SB	6396	7864	9392
2 Dr SLE 4WD Std Cab SB	5809	7142	8529
2 Dr SLE Ext Cab SB	4981	6123	7312
2 Dr SLE Std Cab SB	4306	5295	6324
2 Dr SLS Sport 4WD Ext Cab SB	6089	7486	8941
2 Dr SLS Sport 4WD Ext Cab Step SB	6364	7824	9344

Body Styles	TMV Pricing		
	Trade	Private	Dealer
2 Dr SLS Sport 4WD Std Cab LB	5673	6975	8330
2 Dr SLS Sport 4WD Std Cab SB	5339	6564	7839
2 Dr SLS Sport 4WD Std Cab Step SB	5761	7083	8459
2 Dr SLS Sport Ext Cab SB	4588	5641	6737
2 Dr SLS Sport Ext Cab Step SB	4917	6045	7220
2 Dr SLS Sport Std Cab LB	4074	5008	5981
2 Dr SLS Sport Std Cab SB	4026	4950	5912
2 Dr SLS Sport Std Cab Step SB	4260	5238	6256

Options	Price
AM/FM/CD Audio System	+122
AM/FM/Cassette/CD Audio System	+162
Air Conditioning	+324
Automatic 4-Speed Transmission	+431

Options	Price
Bucket Seats	+117
Hinged Third Door	+119
Sport Suspension	+296
ZR2 Highrider Suspension Package	+723

1998

Styling is retuned inside and out, resulting in a sleeker look and better interior ergonomics. Dual second-generation airbags are standard, and seats are upgraded for improved comfort and appearance. Four-wheel disc brakes are standard on 4WD models and uplevel stereos are new for 1998. New colors inside and out round out the changes.

Mileage Category: J

Body Styles	TMV Pricing		
	Trade	Private	Dealer
2 Dr SL 4WD Std Cab LB	4240	5317	6531
2 Dr SL 4WD Std Cab SB	4117	5162	6341
2 Dr SL Std Cab LB	3131	3926	4823
2 Dr SL Std Cab SB	3096	3882	4769
2 Dr SLE 4WD Ext Cab SB	5271	6609	8118
2 Dr SLE 4WD Std Cab SB	4929	6181	7592
2 Dr SLE Ext Cab SB	4032	5056	6210
2 Dr SLE Std Cab SB	3602	4517	5549
2 Dr SLS Sport 4WD Ext Cab SB	5104	6401	7863
2 Dr SLS Sport 4WD Ext Cab Step SB	5425	6803	8357

Body Styles	TMV Pricing		
	Trade	Private	Dealer
2 Dr SLS Sport 4WD Std Cab LB	4751	5957	7317
2 Dr SLS Sport 4WD Std Cab SB	4607	5777	7096
2 Dr SLS Sport 4WD Std Cab Step SB	4879	6118	7515
2 Dr SLS Sport Ext Cab SB	3903	4894	6012
2 Dr SLS Sport Ext Cab Step SB	3987	5000	6142
2 Dr SLS Sport Std Cab LB	3358	4211	5172
2 Dr SLS Sport Std Cab SB	3243	4066	4995
2 Dr SLS Sport Std Cab Step SB	3559	4463	5482

Options	Price
AM/FM/Cassette/CD Audio System	+118
Air Conditioning	+279
Automatic 4-Speed Transmission	+371

Options	Price
Hinged Third Door	+130
Sport Suspension	+158
ZR2 Highrider Suspension Package	+623

1997

Changes are limited to new colors, availability of the Sport Suspension on extended cab models, engine and transmission improvements, lighter-weight plug-in half shafts for 4WD Sonomas and console-mounted shifter for trucks equipped with a center console and bucket seats.

Mileage Category: J

Body Styles	TMV Pricing		
	Trade	Private	Dealer
2 Dr SL 4WD Std Cab LB	3693	4718	5970
2 Dr SL 4WD Std Cab SB	3482	4449	5630
2 Dr SL Std Cab LB	2585	3302	4179
2 Dr SL Std Cab SB	2550	3257	4122
2 Dr SLE 4WD Ext Cab SB	4595	5870	7429
2 Dr SLE 4WD Ext Cab Step SB	5027	6422	8126
2 Dr SLE 4WD Std Cab SB	4172	5329	6743
2 Dr SLE 4WD Std Cab Step SB	4309	5505	6966
2 Dr SLE Ext Cab SB	3461	4421	5594
2 Dr SLE Ext Cab Step SB	3475	4439	5618
2 Dr SLE Std Cab SB	3042	3886	4918
2 Dr SLE Std Cab Step SB	3167	4046	5120

Body Styles	TMV Pricing		
	Trade	Private	Dealer
2 Dr SLS Sport 4WD Ext Cab SB	4419	5646	7145
2 Dr SLS Sport 4WD Ext Cab Step SB	4508	5759	7288
2 Dr SLS Sport 4WD Std Cab LB	4054	5179	6555
2 Dr SLS Sport 4WD Std Cab SB	3955	5052	6393
2 Dr SLS Sport 4WD Std Cab Step SB	4098	5235	6624
2 Dr SLS Sport Ext Cab SB	3295	4209	5327
2 Dr SLS Sport Ext Cab Step SB	3419	4368	5528
2 Dr SLS Sport Std Cab LB	2874	3671	4646
2 Dr SLS Sport Std Cab SB	2607	3330	4214
2 Dr SLS Sport Std Cab Step SB	3002	3835	4853

Options	Price
AM/FM/CD Audio System	+127
Air Conditioning	+253
Automatic 4-Speed Transmission	+336

Options	Price
Hinged Third Door	+118
Sport Suspension	+221
ZR2 Highrider Suspension Package	+419

For the latest vehicle information, visit www.edmunds.com

1996

Mileage Category: J

Body Styles	TMV Pricing			Body Styles	TMV Pricing		
	Trade	Private	Dealer		Trade	Private	Dealer
2 Dr SL 4WD Std Cab LB	2985	3885	5129	2 Dr SLS Sport 4WD Ext Cab Step SB	3527	4592	6062
2 Dr SL 4WD Std Cab SB	2892	3764	4968	2 Dr SLS Sport 4WD Std Cab LB	3212	4181	5519
2 Dr SL Std Cab LB	2057	2677	3533	2 Dr SLS Sport 4WD Std Cab SB	3116	4056	5355
2 Dr SL Std Cab SB	1993	2594	3423	2 Dr SLS Sport 4WD Std Cab Step SB	3156	4107	5420
2 Dr SLE 4WD Ext Cab SB	3832	4987	6582	2 Dr SLS Sport Ext Cab SB	2531	3295	4349
2 Dr SLE 4WD Ext Cab Step SB	3930	5115	6752	2 Dr SLS Sport Ext Cab Step SB	2797	3640	4805
2 Dr SLE 4WD Std Cab SB	3042	3960	5227	2 Dr SLS Sport Std Cab LB	2402	3127	4127
2 Dr SLE Ext Cab SB	2836	3691	4871	2 Dr SLS Sport Std Cab SB	2227	2899	3826
2 Dr SLE Ext Cab Step SB	2873	3739	4936	2 Dr SLS Sport Std Cab Step SB	2441	3177	4194
2 Dr SLE Std Cab SB	2215	2883	3805				
2 Dr SLS Sport 4WD Ext Cab SB	3454	4496	5934				

Options	Price	Options	Price
Air Conditioning	+223	ZR2 Highrider Suspension Package	+479
Automatic 4-Speed Transmission	+297		

Extended-cab models get an optional driver-side rear access panel. All Sonomas are now equipped with four-wheel ABS. A new sport suspension provides sporty handling, and a snazzy Sportside box ends Ford's reign as lord of compact stepsides. A new five-speed transmission improves shifter location and operation when equipped with the base four-cylinder. Still missing is the availability of a passenger airbag.

1995

Mileage Category: J

Body Styles	TMV Pricing			Body Styles	TMV Pricing		
	Trade	Private	Dealer		Trade	Private	Dealer
2 Dr SL 4WD Std Cab LB	2449	3157	4336	2 Dr SLE Std Cab SB	1990	2565	3523
2 Dr SL 4WD Std Cab SB	2368	3054	4196	2 Dr SLS 4WD Ext Cab SB	3128	4032	5539
2 Dr SL Std Cab LB	1684	2170	2981	2 Dr SLS 4WD Std Cab LB	2677	3451	4740
2 Dr SL Std Cab SB	1646	2122	2914	2 Dr SLS 4WD Std Cab SB	2601	3353	4606
2 Dr SLE 4WD Ext Cab SB	3426	4416	6066	2 Dr SLS Ext Cab SB	2257	2910	3997
2 Dr SLE 4WD Std Cab SB	2601	3353	4606	2 Dr SLS Std Cab LB	2105	2713	3727
2 Dr SLE Ext Cab SB	2296	2960	4066	2 Dr SLS Std Cab SB	1874	2416	3319

Options	Price	Options	Price
4.3L V6 OHV 12V FI Engine	+255	Automatic 4-Speed Transmission	+276
4.3L V6 OHV 12V HO FI Engine	+144	Sport Suspension	+117
Air Conditioning	+207	ZR2 Highrider Suspension Package	+400
Antilock Brakes [Opt on 2WD]	+195		

Driver airbag is added, and daytime running lights are standard. Highrider off-road package can be ordered on the Club Coupe. Power window and lock buttons are illuminated at night. Remote keyless entry is a new option. A single key operates both the door locks and the ignition. A manual transmission can now be ordered with the 191-horsepower, 4.3-liter V6.

Suburban

1999

Mileage Category: N

Body Styles	TMV Pricing			Body Styles	TMV Pricing		
	Trade	Private	Dealer		Trade	Private	Dealer
4 Dr C1500 SUV	7770	9158	10602	4 Dr K1500 4WD SUV	8564	10094	11686
4 Dr C2500 SUV	8167	9626	11145	4 Dr K2500 4WD SUV	8612	10150	11751

Options	Price	Options	Price
6.5L V8 Turbodiesel OHV 16V Engine [Opt on 2500]	+1094	Heated Front Seats	+134
7.4L V8 OHV 16V FI Engine [Opt on 2500]	+230	Leather Seats	+478
Air Conditioning	+323	OnStar Telematics System	+311
Air Conditioning - Front and Rear	+534	Privacy Glass	+116
Aluminum/Alloy Wheels	+119	Running Boards	+124
Center Bench Seat	+242	SLE Package	+1467
Center and Rear Bench Seat	+419	SLT Package	+1777

A couple of new colors are the only modifications to the Suburban.

1998

Mileage Category: N

Body Styles	TMV Pricing			Body Styles	TMV Pricing		
	Trade	Private	Dealer		Trade	Private	Dealer
4 Dr C1500 SUV	6673	8014	9527	4 Dr K1500 4WD SUV	7348	8826	10492
4 Dr C2500 SUV	7062	8482	10083	4 Dr K2500 4WD SUV	7727	9280	11031

Options	Price	Options	Price
6.5L V8 Turbodiesel OHV 16V Engine [Opt on 2500]	+942	Air Conditioning	+279
7.4L V8 OHV 16V FI Engine [Opt on 2500]	+198	Air Conditioning - Front and Rear	+460

Depowered second-generation airbags protect front-seat occupants for 1998. Carpeted floor mats become standard. Standard equipment also includes PassLock theft-deterrent system, electrochromic rearview mirror and automatic four-wheel drive on K-series models.

1998 (cont'd)

Options	Price
Center Bench Seat	+209
Center and Rear Bench Seat	+361
Heated Front Seats	+115
Leather Seats	+412

Options	Price
OnStar Telematics System	+268
SLE Package	+1264
SLT Package	+1530

1997

GMC has added a passenger-side airbag and a power lock switch in the cargo compartment. SLE and SLT trim now includes rear heat and air conditioning, as well as remote keyless entry. Uplevel SLT trim also includes a combination CD and cassette player stereo system. All Suburbans receive speed-sensitive power steering, and 4WD models have a tighter turning circle. Two new colors freshen the dated exterior design this year.

Mileage Category: N

Body Styles	TMV Pricing		
	Trade	Private	Dealer
4 Dr C1500 SUV	5363	6592	8094
4 Dr C2500 SUV	5691	6996	8591

Body Styles	TMV Pricing		
	Trade	Private	Dealer
4 Dr K1500 4WD SUV	5964	7331	9002
4 Dr K2500 4WD SUV	6267	7704	9460

Options	Price
6.5L V8 Turbodiesel OHV 16V Engine	+853
7.4L V8 OHV 16V FI Engine	+179
Air Conditioning	+252
Air Conditioning - Front and Rear	+416
Center Bench Seat	+189

Options	Price
Leather Seats	+335
SLE Package	+1144
SLT Package	+1385
Third Seat	+412

1996

Giant SUV gets daytime running lights to make it more visible to other drivers. New V8s, quieter tires and long-life spark plugs and coolant make the Suburban less costly to maintain. Rear passengers get warmer faster, thanks to new rear-seat heat ducting. Illuminated entry is newly standard, and electronic 4WD controls are a new option.

Mileage Category: N

Body Styles	TMV Pricing		
	Trade	Private	Dealer
4 Dr C1500 SUV	4658	5746	7248
4 Dr C2500 SUV	4936	6088	7680

Body Styles	TMV Pricing		
	Trade	Private	Dealer
4 Dr K1500 4WD SUV	5131	6329	7984
4 Dr K2500 4WD SUV	5389	6647	8385

Options	Price
6.5L V8 Turbodiesel OHV 16V Engine	+755
7.4L V8 OHV 16V FI Engine	+158
Air Conditioning	+223
Air Conditioning - Front and Rear	+342
Center Bench Seat	+167

Options	Price
Compact Disc Changer	+158
Leather Seats	+296
SLE Package	+936
SLT Package	+1149
Third Seat	+365

1995

New interior with driver airbag debuts. New dashboard features modular design with controls that are much easier to read and use. The 1500 models can now be ordered with turbodiesel engine. Brake/transmission shift interlock is added to automatic transmission. Seats and door panels are revised. New console on models with bucket seats features pivoting writing surface, along with rear cupholders and storage drawer. Uplevel radios come with automatic volume controls that raise or lower the volume depending on vehicle speed.

Mileage Category: N

Body Styles	TMV Pricing		
	Trade	Private	Dealer
4 Dr C1500 SUV	3542	4385	5789
4 Dr C2500 SUV	3837	4749	6269

Body Styles	TMV Pricing		
	Trade	Private	Dealer
4 Dr K1500 4WD SUV	3956	4897	6465
4 Dr K2500 4WD SUV	4235	5242	6920

Options	Price
6.5L V8 Turbodiesel OHV 16V Engine	+701
7.4L V8 OHV 16V FI Engine	+147
Air Conditioning	+207
Air Conditioning - Front and Rear	+318
Compact Disc Changer	+147

Options	Price
Leather Seats	+275
Privacy Glass	+75
SLE Package	+869
SLT Package	+1068

Yukon

2004

Mileage Category: N

Body Styles	TMV Pricing		
	Trade	Private	Dealer
4 Dr Denali AWD SUV	32066	33878	36899
4 Dr SLE 4WD SUV	24057	25599	28170
4 Dr SLE SUV	21906	23416	25934
4 Dr SLT 4WD SUV	25893	27452	30051

Body Styles	TMV Pricing		
	Trade	Private	Dealer
4 Dr SLT SUV	23743	25272	27822
4 Dr STD 4WD SUV	25135	26663	29211
4 Dr STD SUV	23062	24591	27138

Options	Price
17 Inch Wheels [Opt on SLT]	+295
5.3L V8 OHV 16V FI Engine [Std on SLT]	+495
AM/FM/CD Changer Audio System [Opt on SLT]	+200
Aluminum/Alloy Wheels [Opt on STD]	+320
Automatic Dimming Sideview Mirror(s) [Opt on SLT]	+120
Automatic Stability Control [Opt on SLE, SLT]	+555

Options	Price
Bucket Seats [Opt on SLE]	+450
Camper/Towing Package	+330
DVD Entertainment System	+1295
Electronic Suspension Control [Opt on SLT]	+720
Front Side Airbag Restraints [Opt on SLE, SLT]	+350
Heated Front Seats [Opt on SLT]	+120

2004 (cont'd)

Options	Price
Navigation System [Opt on Denali]	+1995
OnStar Telematics System [Opt on SLE, SLT]	+820
Power Adjustable Foot Pedals	+120
Power Driver Seat w/Memory [Opt on SLT]	+220
Power Moonroof	+995
Power Passenger Seat [Opt on SLE, SLT]	+200
Power Retractable Mirrors [Opt on SLT]	+120

Options	Price
Rear Bucket Seats [Opt on SLT]	+490
Satellite Radio System [Opt on SLE, SLT]	+200
Side Steps [Opt on SLE]	+390
Third Seat [Opt on SLE, SLT]	+200
Traction Control System [Opt on STD 2WD]	+225
Z71 Off-Road Suspension Package [Opt on 4WD SLT]	+639

For 2004, the Yukon features the addition of a tire-pressure monitoring system and newly styled optional 17-inch wheels. A chrome exhaust tip is now standard and the trailering package includes a seven-to-four-pin adapter and electric brake wiring harness. For added safety, the Yukon now features Hydroboost brakes, and there is a front passenger seatbelt reminder. The antenna for the optional XM Satellite Radio is smaller this year, and the rear-seat entertainment system can now be combined with a sunroof. Lastly, the passenger-side exterior door lock has been eliminated.

2003

Mileage Category: N

Body Styles	TMV Pricing		
	Trade	Private	Dealer
4 Dr Denali AWD SUV	28818	30892	34349
4 Dr SLE 4WD SUV	21380	22913	25467
4 Dr SLE SUV	19850	21273	23644

Body Styles	TMV Pricing		
	Trade	Private	Dealer
4 Dr SLT 4WD SUV	22621	24244	26948
4 Dr SLT SUV	21068	22578	25095

Options	Price
AM/FM/Cassette/CD Changer Audio System [Opt on SLE,SLT]	+161
Automatic Stability Control [Opt on SLE,SLT]	+195
Autoride Suspension Package [Opt on SLT]	+721
Bose Audio System [Opt on SLE]	+254
Bucket Seats [Opt on SLE]	+274
Camper/Towing Package	+200
Captain Chairs (4)	+315
DVD Entertainment System	+834
Front Side Airbag Restraints [Opt on SLE,SLT]	+161

Options	Price
Navigation System [Opt on Denali]	+1285
Off-Road Suspension Package [Opt on SLT]	+411
OnStar Telematics System [Opt on SLE,SLT]	+447
Power Driver Seat w/Memory [Opt on SLT]	+132
Power Moonroof	+644
Power Passenger Seat [Opt on SLE,SLT]	+155
Running Boards [Opt on SLE]	+254
Satellite Radio System [Opt on SLE,SLT]	+225
Third Seat [Opt on SLE,SLT]	+232

Despite numerous 2003 upgrades, there's not much different on the outside other than optional multifunction mirrors and new machined aluminum wheels for SLT models. Inside, you'll find tri-zone climate controls, an enhanced driver-information center and a redesigned center console and instrument panel. Satellite steering wheel controls are now optional (standard on Denali models) as are second-row captain's chairs. New entertainment options include a Bose audio system, as well as XM Satellite Radio and a DVD-based entertainment system. For increased safety, there is a standard front-passenger sensing system, three-point belts for all second-row passengers, adjustable pedals and an available StabiliTrak stability control system. GMC also upgraded the braking system for better pedal feel and performance and retuned the Autotrac four-wheel-drive system for better efficiency and less binding at low speeds. Finally, Yukons sold in California are fitted with a new catalytic converter that earns the truck ULEV certification.

2002

Mileage Category: N

Body Styles	TMV Pricing		
	Trade	Private	Dealer
4 Dr Denali AWD SUV	23005	24860	27953
4 Dr SLE 4WD SUV	18154	19577	21950
4 Dr SLE SUV	16787	18103	20297

Body Styles	TMV Pricing		
	Trade	Private	Dealer
4 Dr SLT 4WD SUV	19194	20699	23207
4 Dr SLT SUV	17814	19210	21538

Options	Price
5.3L V8 Flex Fuel OHV 16V FI Engine	+419
5.3L V8 OHV 16V FI Engine	+419
Autoride Suspension Package	+509
Bucket Seats [Opt on SLE]	+225
Cast Alloy Wheels [Opt on SLT]	+120
Off-Road Suspension Package [Opt on 4WD]	+371

Options	Price
OnStar Telematics System [Opt on SLT]	+416
Power Driver Seat w/Memory [Opt on SLT]	+123
Power Moonroof	+562
Running Boards	+237
Third Seat	+216

GMC's strong-selling Yukon heads into 2002 with few changes. The 5300 V8 is now ultralow emission certified (ULEV) for California. For states with less restrictive emission requirements, the Yukon offers flexible fuel capability with the use of cleaner burning gasoline blends. A more efficient starter, more durable steering gear housing and LATCH child seat attachments anchors round out the Yukon's upgrades for 2002.

2001

Mileage Category: N

Body Styles	TMV Pricing		
	Trade	Private	Dealer
4 Dr Denali AWD SUV	19926	22430	24741
4 Dr SLE 4WD SUV	15483	17524	19409
4 Dr SLE SUV	14207	16080	17809

Body Styles	TMV Pricing		
	Trade	Private	Dealer
4 Dr SLT 4WD SUV	16113	18237	20197
4 Dr SLT SUV	14836	16791	18596

Options	Price
5.3L V8 OHV 16V FI Engine	+382
Autoride Suspension Package	+382
Bucket Seats	+205
Camper/Towing Package	+116
Locking Differential [Opt on 2WD]	+138

Options	Price
OnStar Telematics System	+380
Power Sunroof	+512
Running Boards	+216
Third Seat	+355

The recently redesigned Yukon is virtually unchanged from last year. The high-level Yukon Denali is now based on the revamped Yukon. The Denali gets a 6.0-liter V8 engine along with standard all-wheel drive and a host of other new features designed to elevate the top-of-the-line GMC above and beyond its more basic Yukon cousin.

2000

Completely redesigned, Yukon is based on the new Sierra pickup platform with zippy V8 engines and a stouter chassis for a better, more isolated ride.

Mileage Category: N

Body Styles	TMV Pricing		
	Trade	Private	Dealer
4 Dr SLE 4WD SUV	13067	15065	17023
4 Dr SLE SUV	12388	14282	16138

Options	Price
5.3L V8 OHV 16V FI Engine	+348
Bucket Seats	+118
Compact Disc Changer	+274
Heated Front Seats	+174
Limited Slip Differential	+125

Body Styles	TMV Pricing		
	Trade	Private	Dealer
4 Dr SLT 4WD SUV	13923	16051	18138
4 Dr SLT SUV	12895	14867	16799

Options	Price
OnStar Telematics System [Opt on SLT]	+346
Power Moonroof	+372
Running Boards	+162
Third Seat	+475

1999

An upscale version of the Yukon dubbed the Yukon Denali joins the lineup featuring distinct exterior colors, chrome wheels and a fully optioned interior.

Mileage Category: N

Body Styles	TMV Pricing		
	Trade	Private	Dealer
4 Dr Denali 4WD SUV	11455	13529	15687
4 Dr SLE 4WD SUV	8477	10054	11694
4 Dr SLE SUV	7865	9328	10851

Options	Price
Air Conditioning - Front and Rear	+222
Compact Disc Changer	+222
Heated Front Seats	+141

Body Styles	TMV Pricing		
	Trade	Private	Dealer
4 Dr SLT 4WD SUV	8830	10472	12181
4 Dr SLT SUV	8151	9667	11244

Options	Price
OnStar Telematics System [Opt on SLE,SLT]	+311
Running Boards	+131

1998

The two-door model gets the ax this year. Rear-seat passengers are cooled by a newly optional rear air conditioning system. A host of new standard features has been added, including carpeted floor mats. Three new colors spruce up the outside a bit, and second-generation airbags are standard inside.

Mileage Category: N

Body Styles	TMV Pricing		
	Trade	Private	Dealer
4 Dr SLE 4WD SUV	7427	8919	10602
4 Dr SLE SUV	6794	8160	9701

Options	Price
Air Conditioning - Front and Rear [Opt on SLE]	+190
Bucket Seats	+135
Compact Disc Changer	+190

Body Styles	TMV Pricing		
	Trade	Private	Dealer
4 Dr SLT 4WD SUV	7827	9400	11174
4 Dr SLT SUV	7241	8698	10340

Options	Price
Heated Front Seats	+121
OnStar Telematics System	+268

1997

Dual airbags, speed-sensitive steering and a tighter turning circle for 4WD models. A power lock switch is added to the cargo compartment, and SLT models have a standard CD/cassette combo stereo. Remote keyless entry is standard on four-door models, and on SLE and SLT two-door models. Optional on four-door models is a rear air conditioning unit.

Mileage Category: N

Body Styles	TMV Pricing		
	Trade	Private	Dealer
2 Dr SL 4WD SUV	4892	6014	7384
2 Dr SL SUV	4443	5462	6708
2 Dr SLE 4WD SUV	5423	6666	8185
2 Dr SLE SUV	5219	6416	7878
2 Dr SLT 4WD SUV	5585	6865	8430

Options	Price
6.5L V8 Turbodiesel OHV 16V Engine	+986
Air Conditioning [Opt on SL]	+265

Body Styles	TMV Pricing		
	Trade	Private	Dealer
2 Dr SLT SUV	5331	6554	8048
4 Dr SLE 4WD SUV	5452	6702	8229
4 Dr SLE SUV	5262	6469	7945
4 Dr SLT 4WD SUV	5663	6961	8547
4 Dr SLT SUV	5427	6671	8192

Options	Price
Air Conditioning - Front and Rear	+265

1996

A two-wheel-drive two-door Yukon becomes available. A new 5700 Vortec V8 gets long-life coolant and spark plugs, as well as a hefty bump in power and torque. Passenger car tires on less stout Yukons result in a softer, quieter ride. Rear heat ducts, illuminated entry, and height-adjustable seatbelts debut. Four-wheel-drive models get an optional electronic shift mechanism.

Mileage Category: N

Body Styles	TMV Pricing		
	Trade	Private	Dealer
2 Dr SL 4WD SUV	4095	5093	6470
2 Dr SL SUV	3740	4651	5909
2 Dr SLE 4WD SUV	4515	5615	7134
2 Dr SLE SUV	4415	5490	6975
2 Dr SLT 4WD SUV	4728	5880	7470

Options	Price
6.5L V8 Turbodiesel OHV 16V Engine	+871

Body Styles	TMV Pricing		
	Trade	Private	Dealer
2 Dr SLT SUV	4509	5607	7124
4 Dr SLE 4WD SUV	4588	5706	7249
4 Dr SLE SUV	4444	5526	7021
4 Dr SLT 4WD SUV	4801	5970	7585
4 Dr SLT SUV	4536	5641	7166

Options	Price
Air Conditioning [Opt on SL]	+234

1995

New interior with driver airbag debuts. New dashboard features modular design with controls that are much easier to read and use. New four-door model is added midyear, nicely sized between Jimmy and Suburban. New model is offered only in SLE or SLT trim with a 5.7-liter V8 and an automatic transmission in either 2WD or 4WD. Brake/transmission shift interlock is added to automatic transmission. New console on models with bucket seats features pivoting writing surface, along with rear cupholders and storage drawer.

Mileage Category: N

Body Styles	TMV Pricing		
	Trade	Private	Dealer
2 Dr SLE 4WD SUV	3598	4454	5881
2 Dr SLT 4WD SUV	3800	4704	6210
2 Dr STD 4WD SUV	3405	4215	5565
4 Dr SLE 4WD SUV	3896	4823	6367

Options	Price
6.5L V8 Turbodiesel OHV 16V Engine	+810
Air Conditioning [Opt on STD]	+217

Body Styles	TMV Pricing		
	Trade	Private	Dealer
4 Dr SLE SUV	3703	4583	6051
4 Dr SLT 4WD SUV	4107	5084	6712
4 Dr SLT SUV	3843	4757	6281

Options	Price
Aluminum/Alloy Wheels	+80
Automatic 4-Speed Transmission [Std on Wgn]	+255

Yukon Denali

2000

Mileage Category: O

Body Styles	TMV Pricing		
	Trade	Private	Dealer
4 Dr Denali 4WD SUV	15708	18296	20832

For the 2000 model year, GMC's Yukon Denali gets a new exterior color and adds GM's OnStar communications system.

Yukon XL

2004

Mileage Category: N

Body Styles	TMV Pricing		
	Trade	Private	Dealer
4 Dr 1500 4WD SUV	25609	27168	29766
4 Dr 1500 SLE 4WD SUV	23999	25659	28425
4 Dr 1500 SLE SUV	22181	23821	26553
4 Dr 1500 SLT 4WD SUV	26168	27846	30642
4 Dr 1500 SLT SUV	24350	26011	28778
4 Dr 1500 SUV	23443	25002	27601
4 Dr 2500 4WD SUV	25953	27547	30203

Body Styles	TMV Pricing		
	Trade	Private	Dealer
4 Dr 2500 SLE 4WD SUV	25094	26770	29562
4 Dr 2500 SLE SUV	23076	24719	27457
4 Dr 2500 SLT 4WD SUV	27062	28742	31541
4 Dr 2500 SLT SUV	25246	26909	29680
4 Dr 2500 SUV	24938	26497	29095
4 Dr Denali AWD SUV	32036	34065	37447

Half-ton models now feature standard Hydroboost brakes, a tire-pressure monitoring system and newly styled optional 17-inch aluminum wheels. The trailering package now includes a 7-to-4-pin brake wiring adapter. For added safety, there is now a front passenger seatbelt reminder. Also, a sunroof and rear-seat entertainment system can be ordered together for the first time. Lastly, GMC has lowered the output figures for the Vortec 8100 -- the engine is now rated at 320 horsepower and 440 pound-feet of torque.

Options	Price
17 Inch Wheels [Opt on 1500 SLT]	+295
4 Wheel Steering [Opt on SLE, SLT]	+1995
8.1L V8 OHV 16V FI Engine [Opt on 2500 SLE, SLT]	+950
AM/FM/CD Changer Audio System [Opt on SLE, SLT]	+200
Automatic Dimming Sideview Mirror(s) [Opt on SLE, SLT]	+120
Automatic Stability Control [Opt on SLE, SLT]	+555
Autoride Suspension Package [Opt on SLT]	+1120
Bucket Seats [Opt on SLE]	+450
Camper/Towing Package	+235
DVD Entertainment System	+1295
Front Side Airbag Restraints [Opt on SLE, SLT]	+350

Options	Price
Heated Front Seats [Opt on SLT]	+120
Navigation System [Opt on Denali]	+1995
OnStar Telematics System [Opt on SLE, SLT]	+820
Power Adjustable Foot Pedals	+120
Power Driver Seat w/Memory [Opt on SLT]	+220
Power Moonroof	+900
Power Passenger Seat [Opt on SLE, SLT]	+200
Power Retractable Mirrors [Opt on SLT]	+120
Rear Bucket Seats [Opt on SLT, Denali]	+490
Satellite Radio System [Opt on SLE, SLT]	+350
Side Steps [Opt on SLE]	+390

2003

Mileage Category: N

Body Styles	TMV Pricing		
	Trade	Private	Dealer
4 Dr 1500 SLE 4WD SUV	21769	23330	25931
4 Dr 1500 SLE SUV	19955	21385	23769
4 Dr 1500 SLT 4WD SUV	22715	24343	27056
4 Dr 1500 SLT SUV	21962	23536	26159
4 Dr 2500 SLE 4WD SUV	22421	24028	26706

Body Styles	TMV Pricing		
	Trade	Private	Dealer
4 Dr 2500 SLE SUV	20941	22443	24945
4 Dr 2500 SLT 4WD SUV	23702	25402	28234
4 Dr 2500 SLT SUV	22511	24125	26814
4 Dr Denali AWD SUV	28322	30360	33756

Yukon XL

2003 (cont'd)

The Yukon XL gains numerous functional enhancements for 2003. The Quadrasteer four-wheel steering system is now available on 3/4-ton models for increased maneuverability and better stability when towing, while 1/2-ton versions now offer the Stabilitrak stability control system. Also this year, buyers get a choice of two new optional exterior mirrors: a multifunction power fold-away version with puddle lamps and integrated turn signal lights or extended camper mirrors that are also power foldable. The interior gets numerous upgrades that include tri-zone climate control, an enhanced driver-information center and a redesigned center console and instrument panel. Steering wheel-mounted audio controls are now optional, as are second-row captain's chairs and power adjustable pedals. A revised lineup of entertainment options offers buyers a Bose audio system as well as XM Satellite Radio and a DVD-based entertainment system. Finally, for increased safety, the Yukon XL now features a standard front-passenger-sensing system, dual-stage airbags and three point seatbelts for all positions in the first and second rows.

Options	Price
4 Wheel Steering [Opt on SLE,SLT]	+2894
8.1L V8 OHV 16V FI Engine [Opt on SLE,SLT]	+451
AM/FM/Cassette/CD Changer Audio System [Opt on SLT]	+161
Automatic Stability Control [Opt on SLE,SLT]	+195
Autoride Suspension Package [Opt on SLT]	+721
Bucket Seats [Opt on SLE]	+274
Camper/Towing Package	+138
Captain Chairs (4)	+315

Options	Price
DVD Entertainment System	+834
Front Side Airbag Restraints [Opt on SLE,SLT]	+161
Limited Slip Differential [Opt on SLE,SLT]	+190
Navigation System [Opt on Denali]	+1285
OnStar Telematics System [Opt on SLE,SLT]	+447
Power Moonroof	+644
Power Passenger Seat [Opt on SLE,SLT]	+155
Running Boards [Opt on SLE]	+254
Satellite Radio System [Opt on SLE,SLT]	+225

2002

Three-quarter-ton models equipped with the 8100 V8 get the new 4L85 heavy-duty transmission, while the previous 4L80 version also gets upgraded with more durable internal parts. A more efficient starter and a stronger steering gear housing have also been added to all gas engines along with flexible fuel capability for the 5300 V8.

Mileage Category: N

Body Styles	TMV Pricing		
	Trade	Private	Dealer
4 Dr 1500 SLE 4WD SUV	19292	20805	23326
4 Dr 1500 SLE SUV	17533	18907	21198
4 Dr 1500 SLT 4WD SUV	19970	21535	24144
4 Dr 1500 SLT SUV	19009	20499	22982
4 Dr 2500 SLE 4WD SUV	19853	21410	24004

Body Styles	TMV Pricing		
	Trade	Private	Dealer
4 Dr 2500 SLE SUV	18485	19934	22349
4 Dr 2500 SLE 4WD SUV	20922	22562	25296
4 Dr 2500 SLT SUV	19651	21192	23759
4 Dr Denali AWD SUV	22897	24722	27763

Options	Price
8.1L V8 OHV 16V FI Engine [Opt on 2500]	+841
Autoride Suspension Package	+509
Bucket Seats [Opt on SLE]	+225
Captain Chairs (4) [Opt on Denali,SLT]	+293

Options	Price
Cast Alloy Wheels [Opt on SLT]	+120
OnStar Telematics System [Opt on SLT]	+416
Power Sunroof	+562
Running Boards [Opt on SLE,SLT]	+237

2001

The Yukon XL gets a new top-of-the-line engine in addition to more horsepower for the 6.0-liter V8. Debuting this year is the Yukon Denali XL featuring standard all-wheel drive and a host of other new features designed to elevate the top-of-the-line GMC above and beyond its more basic Yukon XL stablemate.

Mileage Category: N

Body Styles	TMV Pricing		
	Trade	Private	Dealer
4 Dr 1500 SLE 4WD SUV	15975	18056	19977
4 Dr 1500 SLE SUV	14637	16545	18306
4 Dr 1500 SLT 4WD SUV	16980	19193	21235
4 Dr 1500 SLT SUV	15824	17886	19789
4 Dr 2500 SLE 4WD SUV	16612	18777	20776

Body Styles	TMV Pricing		
	Trade	Private	Dealer
4 Dr 2500 SLE SUV	15491	17509	19372
4 Dr 2500 SLT 4WD SUV	17555	19843	21955
4 Dr 2500 SLT SUV	16376	18510	20480
4 Dr Denali AWD SUV	20629	23193	25559

Options	Price
8.1L V8 OHV 16V FI Engine	+631
Autoride Suspension Package	+329
Bucket Seats	+205
Heated Front Seats	+137

Options	Price
OnStar Telematics System	+380
Power Sunroof	+546
Running Boards	+216

2000

The 2000 GMC Yukon XL is a complete redesign of last year's Suburban model, adding mechanical and comfort upgrades.

Mileage Category: N

Body Styles	TMV Pricing		
	Trade	Private	Dealer
4 Dr C1500 SLE SUV	12581	14505	16390
4 Dr C1500 SLT SUV	13687	15779	17830
4 Dr C2500 SLE SUV	13505	15569	17593
4 Dr C2500 SLT SUV	14240	16418	18552

Body Styles	TMV Pricing		
	Trade	Private	Dealer
4 Dr K1500 SLE 4WD SUV	13774	15879	17943
4 Dr K1500 SLT 4WD SUV	14901	17179	19412
4 Dr K2500 SLE 4WD SUV	14700	16948	19151
4 Dr K2500 SLT 4WD SUV	16022	18471	20872

Options	Price
Autoride Suspension Package	+300
Bucket Seats	+187
Camper/Towing Package	+129
Heated Front Seats	+125
Limited Slip Differential	+125

Options	Price
OnStar Telematics System [Opt on SLT]	+346
Power Moonroof	+495
Running Boards	+162
Trailer Hitch	+129

Accord

Mileage Category: D

Body Styles	TMV Pricing		
	Trade	Private	Dealer
2 Dr EX Cpe	16130	17275	19183
2 Dr EX V6 Cpe	19495	20990	23481
2 Dr LX Cpe	14243	15379	17271
2 Dr LX V6 Cpe	17407	18517	20366
4 Dr DX Sdn	11492	12473	14109

Body Styles	TMV Pricing		
	Trade	Private	Dealer
4 Dr EX Sdn	15596	16798	18802
4 Dr EX V6 Sdn	19240	20344	22183
4 Dr LX Sdn	13843	14820	16449
4 Dr LX V6 Sdn	17350	18468	20331

Options	Price
Front Side Airbag Restraints [Opt on LX]	+250
Front and Rear Head Airbag Restraints [Opt on EX]	+300

Options	Price
Leather Seats [Opt on EX]	+1800
Navigation System [Opt on EX]	+2000

As the Accord was fully redesigned for the 2003 model year, there are only a few changes on '04 models. Availability of side curtain airbags has been expanded this year to four-cylinder EX models -- standard on those with leather, optional on cars with a cloth interior. All four- and six-cylinder EX models equipped with a leather interior now have XM Satellite Radio with three months of free service as standard equipment. And as with all Honda cars this year, a new seatbelt reminder system is standard. Accord models meeting California's stringent Partial Zero Emissions Vehicle (PZEV) standards -- all four-cylinder sedans equipped with automatic transmission -- will also be sold in the states of New York, Maine, Vermont and Massachusetts.

Mileage Category: D

Body Styles	TMV Pricing		
	Trade	Private	Dealer
2 Dr EX Cpe	14712	15940	17986
2 Dr EX V6 Cpe	17878	19370	21856
2 Dr LX Cpe	12976	14059	15864
2 Dr LX V6 Cpe	15090	16400	18582
4 Dr DX Sdn	10569	11451	12920

Body Styles	TMV Pricing		
	Trade	Private	Dealer
4 Dr EX Sdn	14171	15354	17325
4 Dr EX V6 Sdn	16697	18090	20411
4 Dr LX Sdn	12680	13739	15503
4 Dr LX V6 Sdn	15041	16296	18388

Options	Price
Automatic 5-Speed Transmission [Opt on DX,EX,EX V6,LX]	+624
Front Side Airbag Restraints [Opt on LX]	+195

Options	Price
Leather Seats [Opt on EX]	+1014
Navigation System [Opt on EX]	+1560

The Honda Accord -- one of America's favorite vehicles -- has been substantially changed for 2003. Continuing as a sedan and a coupe, the '03 Accord features more powerful and fuel-efficient engines, increased safety and higher levels of interior comfort. A voice-activated GPS navigation system is optional, and a sporty EX coupe debuts in early 2003.

Mileage Category: D

Body Styles	TMV Pricing		
	Trade	Private	Dealer
2 Dr EX Cpe	11754	12923	14870
2 Dr EX V6 Cpe	14077	15477	17809
2 Dr LX Cpe	10904	11989	13796
2 Dr LX V6 Cpe	12435	13671	15732
2 Dr SE Cpe	11509	12654	14563
4 Dr DX Sdn	9009	9905	11398

Body Styles	TMV Pricing		
	Trade	Private	Dealer
4 Dr EX Sdn	11963	13154	15138
4 Dr EX V6 Sdn	13604	14957	17213
4 Dr LX Sdn	10488	11532	13271
4 Dr LX V6 Sdn	12240	13458	15487
4 Dr SE Sdn	11485	12628	14532
4 Dr Value Sdn	9827	10805	12434

Options	Price
Antilock Brakes [Opt on LX]	+671
Automatic 4-Speed Transmission [Std on V6]	+537

Options	Price
Front Side Airbag Restraints [Std on EX,EX V6]	+168
Leather Seats [Std on EX V6]	+772

Honda has added a new trim level for 2002, the SE. The Accord SE is based on the LX four-cylinder coupe or sedan trim level with an automatic transmission. Features setting the SE apart from LX models include an upgraded audio system, a driver seat power height adjustment, interior wood grain trim, antilock brakes, remote keyless entry and 15-inch alloy wheels.

Mileage Category: D

Body Styles	TMV Pricing		
	Trade	Private	Dealer
2 Dr EX Cpe	10061	11626	13071
2 Dr EX V6 Cpe	12293	14205	15970
2 Dr LX Cpe	8820	10192	11458
2 Dr LX V6 Cpe	10165	11746	13206
4 Dr DX Sdn	7105	8211	9232

Body Styles	TMV Pricing		
	Trade	Private	Dealer
4 Dr EX Sdn	10061	11627	13073
4 Dr EX V6 Sdn	11772	13603	15293
4 Dr LX Sdn	8772	10136	11395
4 Dr LX V6 Sdn	10169	11750	13210
4 Dr Value Sdn	7879	9104	10234

Options	Price
Antilock Brakes [Opt on LX]	+408
Automatic 4-Speed Transmission [Std on V6]	+480

Options	Price
Front Side Airbag Restraints [Opt on EX]	+150
Leather Seats [Opt on EX]	+570

Freshened exterior styling debuts for 2001, with a more aggressive-looking front fascia and hood and a new taillight design. Honda also ups the safety features list, making dual-stage, dual-threshold front airbags standard and side airbags available on all models. All Accords now either meet or exceed California's low-emission vehicle (LEV) standards (some Accords meet ULEV standards, and one model sold in California is rated SULEV). Improvements aimed at reducing road and wind noise have been made, while EX models get a standard in-dash six-disc CD changer, and all V6 models come with traction control. Midyear, a DX four-banger equipped with a special value package debuted, adding an automatic transmission, air conditioning, a CD player, floor mats, fake wood interior accents and special exterior trim.

2001 (cont'd)

Options	Price
Power Driver Seat [Opt on EX]	+132

2000

The four-cylinder engines now have a 100,000-mile no-tune-up service life. Side airbags are standard for all V6 models and EX four-cylinders with the leather interior. The feature-laden Accord SE Sedan makes its debut this year. In the paint department, Nighthawk Black replaces Starlight Black, and Naples Gold Metallic replaces Heather Mist Metallic; Raisin and Currant have been dropped.

Mileage Category: D

Body Styles	TMV Pricing		
	Trade	Private	Dealer
2 Dr EX Cpe	8215	9664	11085
2 Dr EX V6 Cpe	9945	11699	13419
2 Dr LX Cpe	7001	8236	9447
2 Dr LX V6 Cpe	8383	9862	11311
4 Dr DX Sdn	5737	6750	7742

Body Styles	TMV Pricing		
	Trade	Private	Dealer
4 Dr EX Sdn	8227	9679	11101
4 Dr EX V6 Sdn	8903	10473	12012
4 Dr LX Sdn	7081	8330	9555
4 Dr LX V6 Sdn	7756	9125	10466
4 Dr SE Sdn	7565	8901	10210

Options	Price
AM/FM/Cassette/CD Audio System	+152
Air Conditioning [Opt on DX]	+276
Antilock Brakes [Opt on LX]	+375
Automatic 4-Speed Transmission [Std on V6]	+442
Compact Disc Changer	+249

Options	Price
Front Side Airbag Restraints [Opt on EX]	+138
Leather Seats [Opt on EX]	+510
Power Driver Seat [Opt on EX]	+121
Rear Spoiler	+193

1999

The coupes remain unchanged after their recent overhaul, but the sedans receive new seat fabric, and the LX and EX sedans now feature fold-away side mirrors.

Mileage Category: D

Body Styles	TMV Pricing		
	Trade	Private	Dealer
2 Dr EX Cpe	6743	8107	9527
2 Dr EX V6 Cpe	8203	9862	11589
2 Dr LX Cpe	5903	7097	8339
2 Dr LX V6 Cpe	6935	8338	9798
4 Dr DX Sdn	4638	5576	6553

Body Styles	TMV Pricing		
	Trade	Private	Dealer
4 Dr EX Sdn	6483	7795	9160
4 Dr EX V6 Sdn	7504	9022	10601
4 Dr LX Sdn	5945	7147	8398
4 Dr LX V6 Sdn	6216	7473	8781

Options	Price
AM/FM/Cassette/CD Audio System	+147
Air Conditioning [Opt on DX]	+319
Aluminum/Alloy Wheels [Opt on LX, LX V6]	+123

Options	Price
Antilock Brakes [Opt on LX]	+333
Automatic 4-Speed Transmission [Std on V6]	+392
Leather Seats [Std on EX V6]	+417

1998

Honda redesigns its best-seller for 1998. A 3.0-liter V6 engine makes its debut in LX V6 and EX V6 models, marking the first six-cylinder VTEC in the Honda lineup. The standard 2.3-liter four-cylinder is also re-engineered, as is the chassis. The new Accord is also larger, and the interior boasts more room inside.

Mileage Category: D

Body Styles	TMV Pricing		
	Trade	Private	Dealer
2 Dr EX Cpe	5530	6764	8155
2 Dr EX V6 Cpe	7150	8746	10546
2 Dr LX Cpe	4908	6004	7240
2 Dr LX V6 Cpe	6017	7360	8874
4 Dr DX Sdn	3764	4605	5553

Body Styles	TMV Pricing		
	Trade	Private	Dealer
4 Dr EX Sdn	5492	6717	8099
4 Dr EX V6 Sdn	6477	7923	9554
4 Dr LX Sdn	4927	6026	7266
4 Dr LX V6 Sdn	5649	6909	8330

Options	Price
Air Conditioning [Opt on DX]	+189
Antilock Brakes [Std on EX, V6]	+285
Automatic 4-Speed Transmission [Std on EX V6, LX V6]	+302

Options	Price
Leather Seats [Std on EX V6]	+349
Rear Spoiler [Opt on Sdn]	+132

1997

Changes to the ever-popular Accord include the deletion of antilock brakes on the LX five-speed models and the discontinuation of the EX Coupes with leather. No other changes for the 1997 Accord.

Mileage Category: D

Body Styles	TMV Pricing		
	Trade	Private	Dealer
2 Dr EX Cpe	4524	5625	6971
2 Dr LX Cpe	3972	4939	6120
2 Dr Special Edition Cpe	4481	5571	6903
4 Dr DX Sdn	2932	3645	4517
4 Dr EX Sdn	4575	5688	7048
4 Dr EX V6 Sdn	5441	6765	8383

Body Styles	TMV Pricing		
	Trade	Private	Dealer
4 Dr EX Wgn	5387	6697	8299
4 Dr LX Sdn	3972	4939	6120
4 Dr LX V6 Sdn	4619	5743	7116
4 Dr LX Wgn	4454	5538	6862
4 Dr Special Edition Sdn	4499	5593	6931
4 Dr Value Sdn	3641	4527	5610

Options	Price
Air Conditioning [Opt on DX]	+168
Antilock Brakes [Opt on LX]	+285
Automatic 4-Speed Transmission [Opt on DX, EX, LX]	+269

Options	Price
Compact Disc Changer	+152
Leather Seats [Opt on EX]	+311
Rear Spoiler	+117

1996

All Accords get revised styling, featuring new taillights and bumper covers. Wagons have a new roof rack, while sedans boast a new pass-through ski sack.

Mileage Category: D

Body Styles	TMV Pricing		
	Trade	Private	Dealer
2 Dr EX Cpe	3925	4931	6321
2 Dr LX Cpe	3611	4536	5813
4 Dr 25th Anniv Sdn	3539	4445	5697
4 Dr DX Sdn	2633	3306	4236
4 Dr EX Sdn	4071	5114	6555

Options	Price
Air Conditioning [Opt on DX]	+151
Antilock Brakes [Opt on LX]	+288
Automatic 4-Speed Transmission [Opt on DX,EX,LX]	+243

Body Styles	TMV Pricing		
	Trade	Private	Dealer
4 Dr EX V6 Sdn	4929	6192	7936
4 Dr EX Wgn	4341	5453	6988
4 Dr LX Sdn	3615	4542	5823
4 Dr LX V6 Sdn	4283	5329	6775
4 Dr LX Wgn	3906	4907	6289

Options	Price
Compact Disc Changer	+137
Leather Seats [Opt on EX]	+280

1995

A V6 is offered in this midsize Honda. Unfortunately, it fails to improve performance figures because of the mandatory automatic transmission. V6 Accords gain different front styling as a result of the increased size of the engine bay. All V6 Accords come with standard antilock brakes.

Mileage Category: D

Body Styles	TMV Pricing		
	Trade	Private	Dealer
2 Dr EX Cpe	3428	4357	5905
2 Dr LX Cpe	2854	3628	4918
4 Dr DX Sdn	2379	2967	3948
4 Dr EX Sdn	3486	4431	6005
4 Dr EX V6 Sdn	4200	5337	7233

Options	Price
Air Conditioning [Opt on DX]	+134
Antilock Brakes [Opt on LX]	+203
Automatic 4-Speed Transmission [Opt on DX,EX,LX]	+215

Body Styles	TMV Pricing		
	Trade	Private	Dealer
4 Dr EX Wgn	3617	4653	6379
4 Dr LX Sdn	2884	3665	4967
4 Dr LX V6 Sdn	3716	4659	6230
4 Dr LX Wgn	3415	4342	5886

Options	Price
Compact Disc Changer	+120
Leather Seats [Std on EX V6]	+248

CR-V

2004

Mileage Category: L

Body Styles	TMV Pricing		
	Trade	Private	Dealer
4 Dr EX AWD SUV	17270	18309	20040
4 Dr LX AWD SUV	15628	16611	18248

Options	Price
Automatic 4-Speed Transmission [Std on 2WD]	+800

Other than a new seatbelt reminder there are no significant changes for 2004.

Body Styles	TMV Pricing		
	Trade	Private	Dealer
4 Dr LX SUV	15370	16221	17640

Options	Price
Front Side Airbag Restraints [Std on EX]	+250

2003

Fully revamped last year, the CR-V receives no significant changes for 2003.

Mileage Category: L

Body Styles	TMV Pricing		
	Trade	Private	Dealer
4 Dr EX AWD SUV	15972	17102	18985
4 Dr LX AWD SUV	14534	15562	17275

Options	Price
Automatic 4-Speed Transmission [Std on 2WD]	+624

Body Styles	TMV Pricing		
	Trade	Private	Dealer
4 Dr LX SUV	13688	14656	16270

Options	Price
Front Side Airbag Restraints [Std on EX]	+195

2002

Redesigned for 2002, Honda's CR-V boasts a number of improvements and refinements. Major changes include more power, more interior room and increased passenger protection.

Mileage Category: L

Body Styles	TMV Pricing		
	Trade	Private	Dealer
4 Dr EX AWD SUV	14080	15158	16954
4 Dr LX AWD SUV	12803	13784	15418

Options	Price
Automatic 4-Speed Transmission [Opt on AWD]	+537

Body Styles	TMV Pricing		
	Trade	Private	Dealer
4 Dr LX SUV	12517	13476	15073

Options	Price
Front Side Airbag Restraints [Std on EX]	+168

2001

Mileage Category: L

Body Styles	TMV Pricing		
	Trade	Private	Dealer
4 Dr EX AWD SUV	12184	13634	14973
4 Dr LX AWD SUV	11024	12336	13547

Body Styles	TMV Pricing		
	Trade	Private	Dealer
4 Dr LX SUV	10909	12207	13405
4 Dr SE AWD SUV	12728	14243	15642

Options	Price
Automatic 4-Speed Transmission [Opt on EX,LX AWD]	+480

A darker shade of silver debuts, and child seat-tether anchors are standard. EX and SE models have standard floor mats.

2000

The 2000 Honda CR-V gets a new SE (Special Edition) package that features a leather-lined cabin.

Mileage Category: L

Body Styles	TMV Pricing		
	Trade	Private	Dealer
4 Dr EX AWD SUV	10232	11694	13128
4 Dr LX AWD SUV	9269	10594	11892

Body Styles	TMV Pricing		
	Trade	Private	Dealer
4 Dr LX SUV	9132	10437	11717
4 Dr SE AWD SUV	10743	12279	13784

Options	Price
AM/FM/CD Audio System [Std on EX]	+152

Options	Price
Automatic 4-Speed Transmission [Opt on EX,LX AWD]	+442

1999

The CR-V gains 20 horsepower, bringing the total output to 146. Automatic transmission models have a revised column shifter with an overdrive switch. The power window buttons are illuminated, the spare tire cover has been upgraded and the front passenger seat is equipped with an armrest.

Mileage Category: L

Body Styles	TMV Pricing		
	Trade	Private	Dealer
4 Dr EX AWD SUV	8195	9645	11154
4 Dr LX AWD SUV	7773	9147	10578

Body Styles	TMV Pricing		
	Trade	Private	Dealer
4 Dr LX SUV	7363	8667	10024

Options	Price
AM/FM/CD Audio System	+122

Options	Price
Automatic 4-Speed Transmission [Std on 2WD]	+353

1998

A manual transmission debuts. Also available is a front-wheel-drive LX model, and the EX trim level now includes a CD player, antilock brakes and remote keyless entry.

Mileage Category: L

Body Styles	TMV Pricing		
	Trade	Private	Dealer
4 Dr EX AWD SUV	6768	8126	9657
4 Dr LX AWD SUV	6412	7699	9150

Body Styles	TMV Pricing		
	Trade	Private	Dealer
4 Dr LX SUV	6076	7294	8668

Options	Price
Automatic 4-Speed Transmission [Std on 2WD]	+302

1997

Priced competitively with mini-utes, the new CR-V offers more passenger room and cargo capacity than its peers. The CR-V is available with antilock brakes.

Mileage Category: L

Body Styles	TMV Pricing		
	Trade	Private	Dealer
4 Dr STD AWD SUV	5875	7054	8496

Options	Price
Antilock Brakes	+254

Civic

2004

Mileage Category: B

Body Styles	TMV Pricing		
	Trade	Private	Dealer
2 Dr EX Cpe	12793	13451	14548
2 Dr HX Cpe	10346	11004	12101
2 Dr LX Cpe	11472	12130	13227
2 Dr Si Hbk	14357	15128	16412
2 Dr Value Cpe	10113	10771	11868
4 Dr DX Sdn	9610	10249	11315

Body Styles	TMV Pricing		
	Trade	Private	Dealer
4 Dr EX Sdn	13104	13762	14859
4 Dr GX Sdn	15538	16757	18788
4 Dr Hybrid Sdn	16037	17201	19142
4 Dr LX Sdn	11627	12285	13382
4 Dr Value Sdn	10889	11547	12644

2004 (cont'd)

changes this year in order to keep it fresh. For the coupe and sedan, there's new exterior styling, including restyling for the front and rear bumpers, hood, headlights and grille. Inside, the audio speakers have been upgraded, extra sound deadening material has been added and floor mats are now standard in the LX and EX. The LX trim has slightly bigger wheels this year (15 inches) and standard keyless entry. A new value package contains air conditioning, a CD player and a new center console. For the Si hatchback, there are new headlight and taillight designs, larger 16-inch wheels and flashier interior trim. Like the regular sedan, the Civic Hybrid has updated styling, standard floor mats and improved speakers. It also has a new interior console with an armrest, adjustable rear headrests and a manual driver-seat height adjuster. Finally, all Civic sedans and coupes have a new seatbelt reminder system.

Options	Price
Automatic 4-Speed Transmission [Opt on EX, LX]	+250
Continuously Variable Transmission [Opt on HX, Hybrid]	+1000

Options	Price
Front Side Airbag Restraints	+250

2003

A host of minor changes bring the Civic into 2003. On the inside, all models gain improved seat fabrics, rear adjustable outboard headrests and new four-spoke steering wheels. On HX, LX and EX Civics, you'll find improved gauge illumination. There's a new center console for LX and EX, and a CD player is standard for HX and LX. On the outside, the Civic has freshened taillamps and new wheel designs. Also, there is a Hybrid Civic available for the 2003 model year.

Mileage Category: B

Body Styles	TMV Pricing		
	Trade	Private	Dealer
2 Dr DX Cpe	8443	9247	10587
2 Dr EX Cpe	10796	11824	13537
2 Dr HX Cpe	9056	9919	11356
2 Dr LX Cpe	9772	10702	12253
2 Dr Si Hbk	11377	12495	14358

Body Styles	TMV Pricing		
	Trade	Private	Dealer
4 Dr DX Sdn	8475	9282	10628
4 Dr EX Sdn	11107	12165	13927
4 Dr GX Sdn	13970	15299	17515
4 Dr Hybrid Sedan	14055	15393	17624
4 Dr LX Sdn	9925	10870	12444

Options	Price
Automatic 4-Speed Transmission	+624
Continuously Variable Transmission [Opt on Hybrid]	+780

Options	Price
Front Side Airbag Restraints [Std on Hybrid]	+195

2002

The big news this year is the return of the Civic Si. Featuring an exclusive two-door hatchback body style, the new Si has a 160-horsepower engine. All Civic sedans and coupes feature a revised steering box for improved driving feel, added sound insulation and slightly tweaked suspension tuning. There are also some smattering of interior storage and comfort upgrades this year.

Mileage Category: B

Body Styles	TMV Pricing		
	Trade	Private	Dealer
2 Dr DX Cpe	7184	7946	9216
2 Dr EX Cpe	9428	10428	12094
2 Dr HX Cpe	7732	8552	9919
2 Dr LX Cpe	8458	9355	10850
2 Dr Si Hbk	10010	11141	13025

Body Styles	TMV Pricing		
	Trade	Private	Dealer
4 Dr DX Sdn	7195	7958	9229
4 Dr EX Sdn	9764	10800	12526
4 Dr GX Sdn	12394	13684	15834
4 Dr LX Sdn	8568	9478	10994

Options	Price
Antilock Brakes [Opt on GX]	+671
Automatic 4-Speed Transmission	+537

Options	Price
Continuously Variable Transmission	+671
Front Side Airbag Restraints	+168

2001

Honda redesigns its cars and trucks every four to five years, whether they need it or not. For 2001, it's the Civic's turn. Larger inside and out, with more powerful engines but a less sophisticated suspension, coupes and sedans return in familiar DX, LX and EX trims, while HX models come with two doors only. The GX Sedan is powered by natural gas. Unfortunately, the hatchback dies just when Americans are once again figuring out how useful they can be, and the sporty Si goes on hiatus for a year or two.

Mileage Category: B

Body Styles	TMV Pricing		
	Trade	Private	Dealer
2 Dr DX Cpe	6270	7377	8398
2 Dr EX Cpe	8295	9759	11110
2 Dr HX Cpe	6676	7854	8942
2 Dr LX Cpe	7356	8654	9852

Body Styles	TMV Pricing		
	Trade	Private	Dealer
4 Dr DX Sdn	6401	7531	8574
4 Dr EX Sdn	8582	10096	11494
4 Dr LX Sdn	7444	8758	9970

Options	Price
Automatic 4-Speed Transmission [Std on VP]	+480
Continuously Variable Transmission [Opt on HX]	+600

Options	Price
Front Side Airbag Restraints	+150

2000

Mileage Category: B

Body Styles	TMV Pricing		
	Trade	Private	Dealer
2 Dr CX Hbk	5262	6266	7251
2 Dr DX Cpe	5440	6479	7498
2 Dr DX Hbk	5328	6346	7343
2 Dr EX Cpe	6939	8265	9565
2 Dr HX Cpe	6012	7160	8285

Body Styles	TMV Pricing		
	Trade	Private	Dealer
2 Dr Si Cpe	9461	11374	13250
4 Dr DX Sdn	5675	6759	7822
4 Dr EX Sdn	7574	9021	10440
4 Dr LX Sdn	6655	7927	9174
4 Dr VP Sdn	6537	7786	9011

2000 (cont'd)

No styling, content or trim changes for this year. The performance-oriented Si continues for 2000, and there have been paint comings and goings: Taffeta White has been added to the CX and DX Hatchback, and Dark Amethyst has been dropped; Titanium Metallic comes to the DX, LX and EX Sedan, and Vogue Silver is gone. Vintage Plum is now available to the LX and EX Sedan, and Inza Red has been eliminated.

Options	Price
AM/FM/CD Audio System [Opt on DX,LX]	+138
AM/FM/Cassette/CD Audio System	+160
Air Conditioning [Opt on CX,DX,HX]	+469
Antilock Brakes [Std on Sdn]	+375
Automatic 4-Speed Transmission [Std on VP]	+442

Options	Price
Compact Disc Changer	+273
Continuously Variable Transmission [Opt on HX]	+553
Power Steering [Opt on CX]	+138
Rear Spoiler [Std on CX,Hbk]	+152

1999

The Civic gets new front and rear styling as well as an improved instrument panel. The DX trim gets a rear wiper and washer, a cargo cover and a low-fuel warning light. A hot-rod Si model is introduced midyear with a 160-hp VTEC engine.

Mileage Category: B

Body Styles	TMV Pricing		
	Trade	Private	Dealer
2 Dr CX Hbk	4001	4943	5924
2 Dr DX Cpe	4281	5289	6338
2 Dr DX Hbk	4196	5184	6213
2 Dr EX Cpe	5260	6498	7787
2 Dr HX Cpe	4504	5565	6669

Body Styles	TMV Pricing		
	Trade	Private	Dealer
2 Dr Si Cpe	7426	9224	11096
4 Dr DX Sdn	4349	5373	6438
4 Dr EX Sdn	5602	6922	8296
4 Dr LX Sdn	5043	6231	7467
4 Dr VP Sdn	5030	6215	7448

Options	Price
AM/FM/Cassette/CD Audio System [Opt on DX,LX]	+128
Air Conditioning [Opt on CX,DX,HX]	+375
Antilock Brakes [Std on SI,Sdn]	+333
Automatic 4-Speed Transmission [Std on VP]	+353

Options	Price
Continuously Variable Transmission [Opt on HX]	+451
Leather Seats	+221
Rear Spoiler [Std on CX,Hbk]	+122

1998

Select models get new wheel covers, a rear hatch handle and map lights.

Mileage Category: B

Body Styles	TMV Pricing		
	Trade	Private	Dealer
2 Dr CX Hbk	3287	4204	5237
2 Dr DX Cpe	3542	4529	5642
2 Dr DX Hbk	3516	4496	5602
2 Dr EX Cpe	4367	5584	6956

Body Styles	TMV Pricing		
	Trade	Private	Dealer
2 Dr HX Cpe	3714	4748	5915
4 Dr DX Sdn	3592	4593	5721
4 Dr EX Sdn	4526	5788	7211
4 Dr LX Sdn	4017	5137	6399

Options	Price
Air Conditioning [Std on EX,LX]	+321
Antilock Brakes [Opt on Cpe]	+285
Automatic 4-Speed Transmission	+302

Options	Price
Compact Disc Changer	+225
Continuously Variable Transmission [Opt on HX]	+378

1997

Honda deletes the Civic EX Coupe five-speed with ABS model. DX models receive new wheel covers, all Civics get 14-inch wheels, and the LX Sedan gets air conditioning.

Mileage Category: B

Body Styles	TMV Pricing		
	Trade	Private	Dealer
2 Dr CX Hbk	2807	3602	4574
2 Dr DX Cpe	3097	3975	5048
2 Dr DX Hbk	2964	3804	4830
2 Dr EX Cpe	3895	4999	6348

Body Styles	TMV Pricing		
	Trade	Private	Dealer
2 Dr HX Cpe	3121	4005	5085
4 Dr DX Sdn	3104	3984	5059
4 Dr EX Sdn	4041	5186	6585
4 Dr LX Sdn	3484	4472	5679

Options	Price
Air Conditioning [Std on EX,LX]	+285
Antilock Brakes [Opt on Cpe]	+254
Automatic 4-Speed Transmission	+269

Options	Price
Compact Disc Changer	+200
Continuously Variable Transmission [Opt on HX]	+336
Leather Seats	+168

1996

Honda engineers have created a more powerful and more contemporary Civic for 1996.

Mileage Category: B

Body Styles	TMV Pricing		
	Trade	Private	Dealer
2 Dr CX Hbk	2228	2929	3896
2 Dr DX Cpe	2510	3299	4388
2 Dr DX Hbk	2345	3082	4100
2 Dr EX Cpe	3107	4084	5433

Body Styles	TMV Pricing		
	Trade	Private	Dealer
2 Dr HX Cpe	2603	3421	4550
4 Dr DX Sdn	2590	3404	4528
4 Dr EX Sdn	3399	4467	5943
4 Dr LX Sdn	2775	3648	4854

Options	Price
Air Conditioning [Std on EX]	+257
Antilock Brakes [Opt on LX,Cpe]	+229
Automatic 4-Speed Transmission	+243

Options	Price
Compact Disc Changer	+181
Continuously Variable Transmission [Opt on HX]	+303

Civic/del Sol/Element

1995

Mileage Category: B

Body Styles	TMV Pricing		
	Trade	Private	Dealer
2 Dr CX Hbk	1657	2217	3149
2 Dr DX Cpe	1720	2300	3266
2 Dr DX Hbk	1711	2288	3250
2 Dr EX Cpe	2215	2962	4208
2 Dr Si Hbk	2182	2918	4144

Body Styles	TMV Pricing		
	Trade	Private	Dealer
2 Dr VX Hbk	2003	2679	3805
4 Dr DX Sdn	2021	2702	3838
4 Dr EX Sdn	2374	3175	4510
4 Dr LX Sdn	2135	2855	4054

Options	Price
Air Conditioning [Std on EX Sdn]	+228
Antilock Brakes [Opt on LX,Cpe]	+203

Options	Price
Automatic 4-Speed Transmission	+215
Leather Seats	+134

No changes for the last year of the current Civic.

Civic del Sol

1997

Mileage Category: E

Body Styles	TMV Pricing		
	Trade	Private	Dealer
2 Dr S Cpe	4124	5126	6350
2 Dr Si Cpe	4765	5923	7338

Body Styles	TMV Pricing		
	Trade	Private	Dealer
2 Dr VTEC Cpe	5065	6296	7800

Options	Price
Air Conditioning	+285

Options	Price
Automatic 4-Speed Transmission	+336

No changes to Honda's two-seater.

1996

Mileage Category: E

Body Styles	TMV Pricing		
	Trade	Private	Dealer
2 Dr S Cpe	3523	4432	5687
2 Dr Si Cpe	4013	5048	6478

Body Styles	TMV Pricing		
	Trade	Private	Dealer
2 Dr VTEC Cpe	4377	5507	7067

Options	Price
Air Conditioning	+257

Options	Price
Automatic 4-Speed Transmission	+303

The base S model gets more power by swapping its 1.5-liter four for a 1.6-liter unit, gaining four horsepower. The front fascia is freshened and the Si gets the suspension upgrades of the VTEC.

1995

Mileage Category: E

Body Styles	TMV Pricing		
	Trade	Private	Dealer
2 Dr S Cpe	3165	3975	5326
2 Dr Si Cpe	3336	4190	5614

Body Styles	TMV Pricing		
	Trade	Private	Dealer
2 Dr VTEC Cpe	3795	4767	6386

Options	Price
AM/FM/Cassette/CD Audio System	+94
Air Conditioning	+228

Options	Price
Automatic 4-Speed Transmission	+268

Antilock brakes are now standard on VTEC models. Power door locks are also new to the standard equipment lists of Si and VTEC models. All del Sols get a remote trunk release.

Element

2004

Mileage Category: L

Body Styles	TMV Pricing		
	Trade	Private	Dealer
4 Dr DX AWD SUV	13920	14644	15850
4 Dr DX SUV	12831	13555	14761
4 Dr EX AWD SUV	16284	17064	18364

Body Styles	TMV Pricing		
	Trade	Private	Dealer
4 Dr EX SUV	15195	15975	17275
4 Dr LX AWD SUV	14697	15421	16627
4 Dr LX SUV	13608	14332	15538

Options	Price
Automatic 4-Speed Transmission	+250

Options	Price
Front Side Airbag Restraints [Opt on EX]	+250

Honda adds an LX model to slot between the existing DX and EX models. New equipment on EX models includes keyless entry, a passenger-seat armrest as standard, and bungee-cord fasteners on the driver-side front and rear seat backs.

2003

Mileage Category: L

Body Styles	TMV Pricing		
	Trade	Private	Dealer
4 Dr DX AWD SUV	11901	12689	14002

Body Styles	TMV Pricing		
	Trade	Private	Dealer
4 Dr DX SUV	10977	11692	12883

The Element is a completely new vehicle for Honda. It's also the most adventurous Honda vehicle in quite a long time. Its blend of features, such as barn-style doors and waterproof seats, make it a good choice for those with active lifestyles.

2003 (cont'd)

Body Styles	TMV Pricing		
	Trade	Private	Dealer
4 Dr EX AWD SUV	13590	14511	16045

Options	Price
Automatic 4-Speed Transmission	+624

Body Styles	TMV Pricing		
	Trade	Private	Dealer
4 Dr EX SUV	12664	13512	14925

Options	Price
Front Side Airbag Restraints [Opt on EX]	+195

Insight

2004

Mileage Category: B

Body Styles	TMV Pricing		
	Trade	Private	Dealer
2 Dr STD Hbk	13605	14773	16720

Options	Price
Air Conditioning	+2300

Options	Price
Continuously Variable Transmission	+1300

The CD-equipped audio system with four speakers is now standard equipment, and the fuel consumption gauge's illumination color changes from green to red. All Honda cars gain a new seatbelt reminder system this year.

2003

No changes are in store for Honda's clever gas/electric hybrid vehicle.

Mileage Category: B

Body Styles	TMV Pricing		
	Trade	Private	Dealer
2 Dr STD Hbk	12252	13379	15256

Options	Price
Air Conditioning	+780
Compact Disc Changer	+394

Options	Price
Continuously Variable Transmission	+780

2002

No changes are in store for Honda's clever gas-electric hybrid vehicle.

Mileage Category: B

Body Styles	TMV Pricing		
	Trade	Private	Dealer
2 Dr STD Hbk	9602	10693	12512

Options	Price
Air Conditioning	+671
Compact Disc Changer	+339

Options	Price
Continuously Variable Transmission [Opt on HX]	+671

2001

A continuously variable transmission (CVT) is available for 2001, and Monte Carlo Blue Pearl replaces Citrus Yellow on the color chart.

Mileage Category: B

Body Styles	TMV Pricing		
	Trade	Private	Dealer
2 Dr STD Hbk	8340	9970	11474

Options	Price
Air Conditioning	+600
Compact Disc Changer	+303

Options	Price
Continuously Variable Transmission	+600

2000

Honda brings North America the first gasoline-electric hybrid for 2000.

Mileage Category: B

Body Styles	TMV Pricing		
	Trade	Private	Dealer
2 Dr STD Hbk	7203	8774	10314

Options	Price
Air Conditioning	+552

Options	Price
Compact Disc Changer	+279

Odyssey

Odyssey

2004

Body Styles	TMV Pricing		
	Trade	Private	Dealer
4 Dr EX Pass Van	19931	20895	22502

Options	Price
DVD Entertainment System [Opt on EX]	+750
Leather Seats [Opt on EX]	+1500

Body Styles	TMV Pricing		
	Trade	Private	Dealer
4 Dr LX Pass Van	17890	18854	20461

Options	Price
Navigation System [Opt on EX]	+2000

Other than an improved database for the navigation system and a seatbelt reminder system, there are no significant changes for the '04 Odyssey.

2003

Body Styles	TMV Pricing		
	Trade	Private	Dealer
4 Dr EX Pass Van	17593	18718	20594

Options	Price
DVD Entertainment System	+1170
Leather Seats [Opt on EX]	+1170

Body Styles	TMV Pricing		
	Trade	Private	Dealer
4 Dr LX Pass Van	16022	17013	18664

Options	Price
Navigation System [Opt on EX]	+1560

The Odyssey gains an intermittent rear window wiper this year, as well as an auto up-and-down driver-side window.

2002

Body Styles	TMV Pricing		
	Trade	Private	Dealer
4 Dr EX Pass Van	14940	16181	18248

Options	Price
DVD Entertainment System [Opt on EX]	+1006
Leather Seats	+1006

Body Styles	TMV Pricing		
	Trade	Private	Dealer
4 Dr LX Pass Van	13326	14414	16228

Options	Price
Navigation System	+1342

The Odyssey gains a number of improvements this year. Included with the Odyssey 2.1 upgrade is more power, a new five-speed transmission, standard rear disc brakes and side airbags, optional leather seating and DVD entertainment, two new exterior colors and minor interior storage refinements.

2001

Body Styles	TMV Pricing		
	Trade	Private	Dealer
4 Dr EX Pass Van	12550	14210	15743

Body Styles	TMV Pricing		
	Trade	Private	Dealer
4 Dr LX Pass Van	11112	12559	13895

Options	Price
Navigation System	+1199

Second- and third-row seats get new child seat-tether anchors, stereo speakers are upgraded, an intermittent feature for the rear window wiper is added and floor mats are made standard. LX models get a driver seat height adjuster and traction control, while EX models benefit from a new alarm feature for the remote control. A brighter Starlight Silver paint color replaces Canyon Stone Silver.

2000

Body Styles	TMV Pricing		
	Trade	Private	Dealer
4 Dr EX Pass Van	10457	12058	13627

Options	Price
AM/FM/Cassette/CD Audio System	+193
Aluminum/Alloy Wheels [Std on EX]	+152
Compact Disc Changer	+304

Body Styles	TMV Pricing		
	Trade	Private	Dealer
4 Dr LX Pass Van	9682	11146	12581

Options	Price
Leather Seats	+442
Navigation System	+1104

The only new feature is an optional navigation system on the EX.

1999

Body Styles	TMV Pricing		
	Trade	Private	Dealer
4 Dr EX Pass Van	9482	11063	12708

Options	Price
Leather Seats	+353

Body Styles	TMV Pricing		
	Trade	Private	Dealer
4 Dr LX Pass Van	8163	9491	10873

Honda's latest minivan, the totally redesigned Odyssey, features the most powerful V6 in the minivan segment.

Honda
Odyssey/Passport

1998

Mileage Category: P

Body Styles	TMV Pricing			Body Styles	TMV Pricing		
	Trade	Private	Dealer		Trade	Private	Dealer
4 Dr EX Pass Van	6290	7753	9402	4 Dr LX Pass Van	5886	7256	8800

Options	Price	Options	Price
6 Passenger Seating [Opt on LX]	+137	Compact Disc Changer	+226

The engine is upgraded to a more sophisticated 2.3-liter, good for an extra 10 horsepower and seven pound-feet of torque. New looks up front come from a revised bumper and grille, and the interior gets dressed in new fabric.

1997

No changes for the 1997 Honda Odyssey.

Mileage Category: P

Body Styles	TMV Pricing			Body Styles	TMV Pricing		
	Trade	Private	Dealer		Trade	Private	Dealer
4 Dr EX Pass Van	5013	6427	8155	4 Dr LX Pass Van	4593	5888	7471

1996

Minivan-wagon hybrid carries into 1996 sans changes.

Mileage Category: P

Body Styles	TMV Pricing			Body Styles	TMV Pricing		
	Trade	Private	Dealer		Trade	Private	Dealer
4 Dr EX Pass Van	4364	5669	7470	4 Dr LX Pass Van	3825	4968	6546

1995

Honda gets its minivan in the form of the Odyssey. Unique to the Odyssey is a five-door design that includes four passenger carlike swing-out doors. LX and EX models come standard with antilock brakes and dual airbags.

Mileage Category: P

Body Styles	TMV Pricing			Body Styles	TMV Pricing		
	Trade	Private	Dealer		Trade	Private	Dealer
4 Dr EX Pass Van	3940	5058	6921	4 Dr LX Pass Van	3436	4410	6033

Passport

2002

Mileage Category: M

Body Styles	TMV Pricing			Body Styles	TMV Pricing		
	Trade	Private	Dealer		Trade	Private	Dealer
4 Dr EX 4WD SUV	14004	15128	17001	4 Dr LX 4WD SUV	12430	13428	15091
4 Dr EX SUV	12741	13764	15468	4 Dr LX SUV	10929	11806	13267

Options	Price	Options	Price
AM/FM/Cassette/CD Changer Audio System	+265	Leather Seats	+436
Automatic 4-Speed Transmission [Opt on LX]	+772	Power Driver Seat	+161

There are no significant changes to the Passport this year.

2001

Honda adds a LATCH child seat-tether anchor system to the Passport, and all models get a new eight-speaker audio system.

Mileage Category: M

Body Styles	TMV Pricing			Body Styles	TMV Pricing		
	Trade	Private	Dealer		Trade	Private	Dealer
4 Dr EX 4WD SUV	11220	12688	14044	4 Dr LX 4WD SUV	10043	11358	12571
4 Dr EX SUV	10287	11634	12877	4 Dr LX SUV	8849	10007	11076

Options	Price	Options	Price
Automatic 4-Speed Transmission [Std on EX]	+690	Leather Seats	+420
Compact Disc Changer	+240		

2000

The Passport receives new front and rear fascias, a modified grille, redesigned front combination lamps and a host of fresh features for a new top-of-the-line EX-L trim level.

Mileage Category: M

Body Styles	TMV Pricing			Body Styles	TMV Pricing		
	Trade	Private	Dealer		Trade	Private	Dealer
4 Dr EX 4WD SUV	9376	10820	12236	4 Dr LX 4WD SUV	8390	9683	10950
4 Dr EX SUV	8594	9918	11216	4 Dr LX SUV	7395	8534	9651

Options	Price	Options	Price
AM/FM/Cassette/CD Audio System	+221	Compact Disc Changer	+304
Automatic 4-Speed Transmission [Std on EX]	+635	Leather Seats	+553

1999

Last year, the Passport and the identical Isuzu Rodeo were completely redesigned, so there are no new changes this year.

Mileage Category: M

Body Styles	TMV Pricing		
	Trade	Private	Dealer
4 Dr EX 4WD SUV	8451	9907	11423
4 Dr EX SUV	7726	9057	10443

Options	Price
AM/FM/Cassette/CD Audio System	+177
Automatic 4-Speed Transmission [Std on VP]	+507

Body Styles	TMV Pricing		
	Trade	Private	Dealer
4 Dr LX 4WD SUV	7416	8694	10024
4 Dr LX SUV	6513	7636	8804

Options	Price
Leather Seats	+441

1998

Like its Isuzu Rodeo counterpart, the Passport has been completely revised from top to bottom. The Passport gets modernized styling, a user-friendly interior, more powerful V6 and added room for passengers and cargo.

Mileage Category: M

Body Styles	TMV Pricing		
	Trade	Private	Dealer
4 Dr EX 4WD SUV	6207	7686	9354
4 Dr EX SUV	5689	7045	8574

Options	Price
AM/FM/Cassette/CD Audio System	+151
Automatic 4-Speed Transmission [Opt on LX]	+434

Body Styles	TMV Pricing		
	Trade	Private	Dealer
4 Dr LX 4WD SUV	5467	6770	8239
4 Dr LX SUV	4931	6106	7431

Options	Price
Leather Seats	+377

1997

Mileage Category: M

Body Styles	TMV Pricing		
	Trade	Private	Dealer
4 Dr EX 4WD SUV	4605	5868	7412
4 Dr EX SUV	4560	5811	7340

Options	Price
AM/FM/Cassette/CD Audio System	+134
Air Conditioning [Std on EX,4WD]	+201
Automatic 4-Speed Transmission [Opt on LX,4WD]	+326

Body Styles	TMV Pricing		
	Trade	Private	Dealer
4 Dr LX 4WD SUV	3964	5051	6379
4 Dr LX SUV	3576	4557	5755

Options	Price
Compact Disc Changer	+185
Leather Seats	+336
Premium Audio System [Opt on EX]	+134

Honda drops the slow-selling DX four-cylinder Passport.

1996

New wheels, dual airbags, available ABS and a stronger V6 engine are the changes for the 1996.

Mileage Category: M

Body Styles	TMV Pricing		
	Trade	Private	Dealer
4 Dr DX SUV	2736	3539	4648
4 Dr EX 4WD SUV	4032	5214	6847
4 Dr EX SUV	3932	5086	6679

Options	Price
Air Conditioning [Std on EX,4WD]	+182

Body Styles	TMV Pricing		
	Trade	Private	Dealer
4 Dr LX 4WD SUV	3490	4514	5929
4 Dr LX SUV	3199	4138	5434

Options	Price
Automatic 4-Speed Transmission [Opt on LX,4WD]	+243

1995

Midyear change gives the Passport driver and passenger airbags in a redesigned dashboard.

Mileage Category: M

Body Styles	TMV Pricing		
	Trade	Private	Dealer
4 Dr DX SUV	2206	2878	3998
4 Dr DX Wgn (1995.5)	2484	3240	4500
4 Dr EX 4WD SUV	3300	4304	5978
4 Dr EX 4WD Wgn (1995.5)	3718	4849	6735
4 Dr EX Wgn (1995.5)	3369	4395	6104

Options	Price
Air Conditioning [Opt on DX,LX]	+161
Automatic 4-Speed Transmission	+215

Body Styles	TMV Pricing		
	Trade	Private	Dealer
4 Dr LX 4WD SUV	2897	3779	5248
4 Dr LX 4WD Wgn (1995.5)	3286	4287	5954
4 Dr LX SUV	2659	3469	4818
4 Dr LX Wgn (1995.5)	2825	3686	5120

Options	Price
Leather Seats	+268

Pilot

2004

Mileage Category: M

Body Styles	TMV Pricing		
	Trade	Private	Dealer
4 Dr EX AWD SUV	24093	25287	27276

Options	Price
DVD Entertainment System	+1500
Leather Seats [Opt on EX]	+1400

Body Styles	TMV Pricing		
	Trade	Private	Dealer
4 Dr LX AWD SUV	22142	23336	25325

Options	Price
Navigation System [Opt on EX]	+2000

Leather-equipped EX models get heated seats and side mirrors as standard equipment. Honda has improved the navigation system this year with a larger database, and all models have improved walk-in accessibility to the third-row seat. All Hondas have a seatbelt reminder system added for 2004.

2003

The Pilot is an all-new crossover SUV from Honda. It features eight-passenger seating, standard four-wheel drive, a 240-horsepower V6 and optional DVD-based navigation and entertainment systems.

Mileage Category: M

Body Styles	TMV Pricing		
	Trade	Private	Dealer
4 Dr EX AWD SUV	21590	22975	25283

Options	Price
DVD Entertainment System	+1170
Leather Seats [Opt on EX]	+1170

Body Styles	TMV Pricing		
	Trade	Private	Dealer
4 Dr LX AWD SUV	19867	21141	23265

Options	Price
Navigation System [Opt on EX]	+1560

Prelude

2001

Mileage Category: E

Body Styles	TMV Pricing		
	Trade	Private	Dealer
2 Dr STD Cpe	11089	12436	13679

Body Styles	TMV Pricing		
	Trade	Private	Dealer
2 Dr Type SH Cpe	12668	14207	15627

Options	Price
Automatic 4-Speed Transmission	+690

Floor mats, rear child seat-tether anchors and an emergency trunk opener are added to the '01 Prelude. Two new colors, Electron Blue and Satin Silver, are also available.

2000

The 2000 Prelude is a carryover from 1999 and remains unchanged.

Mileage Category: E

Body Styles	TMV Pricing		
	Trade	Private	Dealer
2 Dr STD Cpe	9602	10936	12244

Options	Price
AM/FM/Cassette Audio System	+124
Automatic 4-Speed Transmission	+553

Body Styles	TMV Pricing		
	Trade	Private	Dealer
2 Dr Type SH Cpe	11287	12855	14391

Options	Price
Compact Disc Changer	+276
Rear Spoiler [Opt on STD]	+193

1999

Prelude gets another five horsepower, bringing it up to 200 horsepower with the manual transmission and 195 horsepower with the automatic. A remote keyless entry system is added, as is an air filtration system, mesh-style grille and new interior color choices.

Mileage Category: E

Body Styles	TMV Pricing		
	Trade	Private	Dealer
2 Dr STD Cpe	8678	9999	11373

Options	Price
Automatic 4-Speed Transmission	+441
Compact Disc Changer	+221

Body Styles	TMV Pricing		
	Trade	Private	Dealer
2 Dr Type SH Cpe	10039	11567	13157

Options	Price
Rear Spoiler [Opt on STD]	+154

1998

The Prelude doesn't change for 1998.

Mileage Category: E

Body Styles	TMV Pricing		
	Trade	Private	Dealer
2 Dr STD Cpe	6616	7936	9425

Options	Price
Automatic 4-Speed Transmission	+377
Compact Disc Changer	+189

Body Styles	TMV Pricing		
	Trade	Private	Dealer
2 Dr Type SH Cpe	7464	8953	10633

Options	Price
Rear Spoiler [Opt on STD]	+132

1997

The Prelude is totally redesigned for 1997. A base model is available with a five-speed manual or four-speed automatic gearbox, but the top-of-the-line Type SH model, featuring Honda's new Active Torque Transfer System, can only be had as a manual. Both the base and Type SH Preludes feature last year's VTEC engine which produces 195 horsepower for 1997.

Mileage Category: E

Body Styles	TMV Pricing		
	Trade	Private	Dealer
2 Dr STD Cpe	5678	6939	8481

Options	Price
Automatic 4-Speed Transmission	+336
Compact Disc Changer	+168

Body Styles	TMV Pricing		
	Trade	Private	Dealer
2 Dr Type SH Cpe	6331	7738	9457

Options	Price
Leather Seats	+218
Rear Spoiler	+117

1996

Mileage Category: E

Body Styles	TMV Pricing		
	Trade	Private	Dealer
2 Dr S Cpe	4044	5087	6528
2 Dr Si Cpe	4578	5759	7391

Body Styles	TMV Pricing		
	Trade	Private	Dealer
2 Dr VTEC Cpe	5148	6476	8310

Options	Price
Automatic 4-Speed Transmission	+243

This is the last year for the current-generation Prelude.

1995

The Si 4WS is dropped from the Prelude lineup. The fourth-generation Prelude is nearing the end of its life. Few changes for 1995, except the addition of air conditioning to the standard equipment list of S models.

Mileage Category: E

Body Styles	TMV Pricing		
	Trade	Private	Dealer
2 Dr S Cpe	3608	4532	6073
2 Dr SE Cpe	4189	5262	7049

Body Styles	TMV Pricing		
	Trade	Private	Dealer
2 Dr Si Cpe	4047	5084	6811
2 Dr VTEC Cpe	4531	5692	7626

Options	Price
Automatic 4-Speed Transmission	+215

Options	Price
Leather Seats	+174

S2000

2004

Honda has made a number of enhancements to the 2004 S2000. Most importantly, a larger 2.2-liter engine has been fitted. This, along with revised transmission gearing, is meant to improve power delivery. Other changes include updated suspension tuning, 17-inch wheels (16s were the previous standard), upgraded brakes, larger tailpipes and restyled front and rear bumpers with new headlights and taillights. Inside, there's a new center console (with two cupholders and a storage tray) and a bit more shoulder, elbow and hiproom for the driver and passenger. All Honda cars have a new seatbelt reminder system this year.

Mileage Category: F

Body Styles	TMV Pricing		
	Trade	Private	Dealer
2 Dr STD Conv	23530	25063	27619

2003

There are no changes this year for Honda's high-performance roadster.

Mileage Category: F

Body Styles	TMV Pricing		
	Trade	Private	Dealer
2 Dr STD Conv	21683	23065	25368

2002

For 2002, Honda has added a glass rear window with a defroster, an improved transmission and a more powerful audio system. There are also a handful of minor changes that only '00-'01 S2000 owners would notice, such as chrome-bezel taillights, an upgraded center console, door panel net storage pockets, a new shifter knob, an aluminum-accented foot rest and silver trim interior accents. There's also a new color for 2002: Suzuka Blue.

Mileage Category: F

Body Styles	TMV Pricing		
	Trade	Private	Dealer
2 Dr STD Conv	19052	20470	22832

2001

Indy Yellow is a new color for 2001. Floor mats, a rear wind deflector, a clock and an emergency trunk release are also new standard items. Midyear, a removable aluminum hardtop became available and can be retrofitted to all S2000s.

Mileage Category: F

Body Styles	TMV Pricing		
	Trade	Private	Dealer
2 Dr STD Conv	16856	18736	20471

Honda
S2000

2000

Honda brings out the high-revving, high-horsepower S2000 for 2000. The S2000's naturally aspirated inline four makes an amazing 240 horsepower, sending it to the rear wheels through a six-speed manual gearbox.

Mileage Category: F

Body Styles	TMV Pricing		
	Trade	Private	Dealer
2 Dr STD Conv	14948	16701	18420

H2

Mileage Category: O

Body Styles	TMV Pricing		
	Trade	Private	Dealer
4 Dr Adventure Series 4WD SUV	39762	41417	44174
4 Dr Lux Series 4WD SUV	40406	42060	44816

Options	Price
AM/FM/CD Changer Audio System [Opt on STD]	+425
Automatic Load Leveling [Opt on STD, LUX]	+1175
Brush Guard [Opt on STD, LUX]	+525
Chrome Trim [Opt on STD, Adventure]	+500
Chrome Wheels [Opt on Lux]	+1500
Heated Front and Rear Seats [Opt on Adventure, STD]	+500

Body Styles	TMV Pricing		
	Trade	Private	Dealer
4 Dr STD 4WD SUV	37843	39501	42263

Options	Price
Leather Seats [Opt on Adventure, STD]	+900
Navigation System	+1570
Power Moonroof	+1395
Side Steps [Opt on Lux]	+400
Third Seat	+500

New rubber floor mats and an optional integrated CD player/navigation system are the only changes this year.

Mileage Category: O

Macho for the masses. The H2 is an all-new vehicle in the Hummer lineup. Though possessing styling similar to the original, this all-new Hummer is more manageable and more affordable.

Body Styles	TMV Pricing		
	Trade	Private	Dealer
4 Dr Adventure Series 4WD SUV	34278	36425	40003
4 Dr Lux Series 4WD SUV	34517	36678	40280

Options	Price
AM/FM/CD Changer Audio System [Opt on STD]	+340
Automatic Load Leveling [Opt on STD, LUX]	+940
Brush Guard [Opt on STD, LUX]	+420
Heated Front and Rear Seats [Opt on Adventure, STD]	+316

Body Styles	TMV Pricing		
	Trade	Private	Dealer
4 Dr STD 4WD SUV	32660	34706	38116

Options	Price
Leather Seats [Opt on Adventure, STD]	+800
Power Moonroof	+1115
Third Seat	+400

Accent

2004

Mileage Category: A

Body Styles	TMV Pricing			Body Styles	TMV Pricing		
	Trade	Private	Dealer		Trade	Private	Dealer
2 Dr GL Hbk	6257	6910	7999	2 Dr STD Hbk	6044	6727	7864
2 Dr GT Hbk	6817	7500	8637	4 Dr GL Sdn	6467	7225	8487

Options	Price	Options	Price
AM/FM/Cassette/CD Audio System [Opt on GL, GT]	+150	Compact Disc Changer [Opt on GL, GT]	+750
Air Conditioning [Opt on STD]	+750	Power Door Locks [Opt on GL, GT]	+120
Automatic 4-Speed Transmission [Opt on GL, GT]	+800	Power Windows [Opt on GL, GT]	+150

Side-impact airbags are now standard equipment on all models. A GT version of the hatchback is now available that adds performance features like a sport-tuned suspension and larger wheels and tires.

2003

For 2003, the base single overhead cam 1.5-liter engine is dropped from the L hatchback; all Accents now come with the dual-overhead cam 1.6-liter inline four-cylinder. The 1.6 is rated at 104 horsepower – a drop of only one horsepower following Hyundai's September 2002 announcement that it had misstated engine outputs across the board. Note that the engine itself is unchanged. In other news, all Accents get a facelift this year. In front, you'll see a new bumper, grille, hood and headlight assemblies, and in the back, the bumper, rear quarter panels and taillight units are new.

Mileage Category: A

Body Styles	TMV Pricing			Body Styles	TMV Pricing		
	Trade	Private	Dealer		Trade	Private	Dealer
2 Dr GL Hbk	4427	5301	6758	4 Dr GL Sdn	4815	5766	7351
2 Dr STD Hbk	4048	4847	6179				

Options	Price	Options	Price
AM/FM/CD Audio System [Opt on GL]	+134	Power Windows [Opt on GL]	+134
Air Conditioning [Opt on STD]	+502	Rear Spoiler [Opt on GL]	+117
Automatic 4-Speed Transmission [Opt on GL]	+435	Sport Suspension [Opt on GL]	+124

2002

Air conditioning becomes standard equipment on GS and GL models. Otherwise, Hyundai's bargain-basement car soldiers on to 2002 with no changes in store. In September 2002, Hyundai announced that it had misstated the horsepower ratings for all of the models in its lineup – the Accent's 1.5-liter four-cylinder engine is now rated for 89 hp and the 1.6-liter is rated for 103. To compensate, the company is offering owners (of 2000 models and newer) three options: 10 years of roadside assistance, 6-year/72,000-mile basic warranty coverage or 12-year/120,000-mile powertrain coverage.

Mileage Category: A

Body Styles	TMV Pricing			Body Styles	TMV Pricing		
	Trade	Private	Dealer		Trade	Private	Dealer
2 Dr GS Hbk	3271	4063	5383	4 Dr GL Sdn	3552	4414	5851
2 Dr L Hbk	2951	3666	4858				

Options	Price	Options	Price
AM/FM/CD Audio System	+117	Power Windows	+117
Air Conditioning [Opt on L]	+440	Rear Spoiler	+232
Automatic 4-Speed Transmission	+352		

2001

For 2001, Accent GL and GS get a more powerful and fuel-efficient 1.6-liter, DOHC inline four-cylinder engine.

Mileage Category: A

Body Styles	TMV Pricing			Body Styles	TMV Pricing		
	Trade	Private	Dealer		Trade	Private	Dealer
2 Dr GS Hbk	2719	3787	4773	4 Dr GL Sdn	2968	4135	5212
2 Dr L Hbk	2459	3425	4316				

Options	Price	Options	Price
AM/FM/CD Audio System	+181	Power Windows	+126
Air Conditioning	+386	Rear Spoiler	+203
Automatic 4-Speed Transmission	+309		

2000

The Accent has been completely redesigned for the 2000 model year.

Mileage Category: A

Body Styles	TMV Pricing			Body Styles	TMV Pricing		
	Trade	Private	Dealer		Trade	Private	Dealer
2 Dr GS Hbk	2149	3199	4229	4 Dr GL Sdn	2312	3443	4552
2 Dr L Hbk	1995	2968	3922				

Options	Price	Options	Price
AM/FM/CD Audio System	+150	Automatic 4-Speed Transmission	+341
Air Conditioning	+424	Rear Spoiler	+168

1999

Mileage Category: A

Body Styles	TMV Pricing		
	Trade	Private	Dealer
2 Dr GS Hbk	1676	2733	3834
2 Dr L Hbk	1448	2362	3313

Options	Price
AM/FM/CD Audio System	+119
Air Conditioning	+340
Automatic 4-Speed Transmission	+273

Body Styles	TMV Pricing		
	Trade	Private	Dealer
4 Dr GL Sdn	1711	2791	3915

Options	Price
Rear Spoiler	+135
Sunroof	+151

The L model has power steering standard, the GS and GL models have standard alloy wheels and a couple of new paint options are available. Hyundai's new industry-leading buyer assurance program is also worth taking note of.

1998

Mileage Category: A

Body Styles	TMV Pricing		
	Trade	Private	Dealer
2 Dr GS Hbk	1183	2092	3117
2 Dr GSi Hbk	1313	2322	3459

Options	Price
Air Conditioning	+259
Antilock Brakes	+199

Body Styles	TMV Pricing		
	Trade	Private	Dealer
2 Dr L Hbk	898	1587	2365
4 Dr GL Sdn	1234	2182	3250

Options	Price
Automatic 4-Speed Transmission	+199
Sunroof	+117

The Accent GSi replaces the Accent GT this year. New front and rear fascias, and new engine mounts, which reduce engine vibration and harshness, are the only other changes to Hyundai's smallest car.

1997

Mileage Category: A

Body Styles	TMV Pricing		
	Trade	Private	Dealer
2 Dr GS Hbk	595	1171	1875
2 Dr GT Hbk	673	1324	2119

Options	Price
Air Conditioning	+204
Antilock Brakes	+156

Body Styles	TMV Pricing		
	Trade	Private	Dealer
2 Dr L Hbk	548	1078	1725
4 Dr GL Sdn	619	1218	1951

Options	Price
Automatic 4-Speed Transmission	+156

In the absence of truly ground-breaking improvement, Hyundai revises trim levels, adding GS hatchback and GL sedan midrange models.

1996

Mileage Category: A

Body Styles	TMV Pricing		
	Trade	Private	Dealer
2 Dr GT Hbk	414	954	1700
2 Dr L Hbk	329	757	1349

Options	Price
Air Conditioning	+131

Body Styles	TMV Pricing		
	Trade	Private	Dealer
2 Dr STD Hbk	347	800	1426
4 Dr STD Sdn	366	844	1504

Hyundai is painting the Accent in some new colors this year, and height-adjustable seatbelt anchors are standard. Front and rear center consoles with cupholders debut, and optional air conditioning is now CFC-free. A new 105-horsepower GT hatch debuted midyear.

1995

Mileage Category: A

Body Styles	TMV Pricing		
	Trade	Private	Dealer
2 Dr L Hbk	200	541	1109
2 Dr STD Hbk	210	571	1173

Options	Price
Air Conditioning	+109
Antilock Brakes	+91

Body Styles	TMV Pricing		
	Trade	Private	Dealer
4 Dr STD Sdn	224	604	1238

Options	Price
Automatic 4-Speed Transmission	+90

Dramatically improved Accent replaces Excel in lineup. Dual airbags are standard, and ABS is optional. Power comes from the 1.5-liter Alpha engine which debuted in 1993 Scoupe.

Hyundai
Elantra

Elantra

2004

Mileage Category: B

Body Styles	TMV Pricing		
	Trade	Private	Dealer
4 Dr GLS Sdn	7369	8191	9561
4 Dr GT Hbk	8519	9372	10794

Options	Price
AM/FM/CD Changer Audio System [Opt on GLS]	+300
Antilock Brakes	+300
Automatic 4-Speed Transmission	+800
Compact Disc Changer [Opt on GLS]	+200
Cruise Control [Opt on GLS]	+300

Body Styles	TMV Pricing		
	Trade	Private	Dealer
4 Dr GT Sdn	8519	9372	10794

Options	Price
Power Moonroof	+700
Rear Spoiler [Opt on GLS]	+395
Traction Control System	+225
Wood Interior Trim	+225

The Elantra received a slight refresh for this year in the form of a new hood, deck lid, front and rear bumpers, grille, headlamps and taillights. Interior revisions include a redesigned instrument cluster, vents, center console and climate controls. The engine has been fitted with continuously variable valve timing, and it is now sold in SULEV or ULEV configurations (depending on the state in which it's purchased) which offer horsepower ratings of 138 and 132, respectively. The base GLS model now offers remote keyless entry as standard equipment, while GT models now have a Kenwood CD/MP3 audio system as standard.

2003

Hyundai has added a GT sedan to the lineup. It has the same price and equipment as the GT hatchback, save for a rear wiper, and it gets a body-color rear spoiler. The hatchback will wear a black rear lip spoiler, and both GTs will come with floor mats. Meanwhile, the value-packed GLS sedan remains unchanged, except ABS will be slightly more affordable, as it has been added to the Accessory Group 3 options package, which costs $925. Finally, Hyundai announced that it had misstated the horsepower ratings for all of the models in its lineup -- the Elantra is now rated at 135 hp, rather than 140, though the engine itself is unchanged.

Mileage Category: B

Body Styles	TMV Pricing		
	Trade	Private	Dealer
4 Dr GLS Sdn	5969	6953	8594
4 Dr GT Hbk	6767	7884	9745

Options	Price
AM/FM/CD Audio System [Opt on GLS]	+211
AM/FM/CD/MP3 Audio System [Opt on GLS]	+295
Antilock Brakes	+455
Automatic 4-Speed Transmission	+536

Body Styles	TMV Pricing		
	Trade	Private	Dealer
4 Dr GT Sdn	6758	7873	9732

Options	Price
Cruise Control [Opt on GLS]	+124
Power Moonroof	+469
Rear Spoiler [Opt on GLS]	+265
Traction Control System	+167

2002

Hyundai's Elantra sedan was redesigned last year, but the big news for 2002 is the release of the GT version, an all-new five-door hatchback that boasts such upscale standard equipment as a leather-trimmed interior, European suspension tuning, four-wheel disc brakes, 15-inch wheels, foglamps and a CD player. In September 2002, Hyundai announced that it had misstated the horsepower ratings for all of the models in its lineup -- the Elantra is now rated at 135 hp, rather than 140. To compensate, the company is offering owners (of 2000 models and newer) three options: 10 years of roadside assistance, 6-year/72,000-mile basic warranty coverage or 12-year/120,000-mile powertrain coverage.

Mileage Category: B

Body Styles	TMV Pricing		
	Trade	Private	Dealer
4 Dr GLS Sdn	4859	5874	7565

Options	Price
AM/FM/CD Audio System	+185
Antilock Brakes	+399
Automatic 4-Speed Transmission	+352

Body Styles	TMV Pricing		
	Trade	Private	Dealer
4 Dr GT Hbk	5469	6611	8515

Options	Price
Power Moonroof	+381
Traction Control System	+117

2001

Bigger inside and out, the redesigned 2001 Elantra boasts stylish sheet metal, a refined 140-horsepower engine and improved noise, vibration and harshness characteristics. Poised to tackle the best in the class, the Elantra comes well equipped for less than $13,000. Though the useful station wagon model has been stricken from the lineup, a five-door hatchback is set to debut next year.

Mileage Category: B

Body Styles	TMV Pricing		
	Trade	Private	Dealer
4 Dr GLS Sdn	3838	5222	6499

Options	Price
AM/FM/CD Audio System	+167
Antilock Brakes	+443
Automatic 4-Speed Transmission	+309

Body Styles	TMV Pricing		
	Trade	Private	Dealer
4 Dr GT Hbk	4288	5833	7259

Options	Price
Cruise Control	+129
Power Moonroof	+386

2000

Mileage Category: B

Body Styles	TMV Pricing		
	Trade	Private	Dealer
4 Dr GLS Sdn	3020	4467	5886

Body Styles	TMV Pricing		
	Trade	Private	Dealer
4 Dr GLS Wgn	3340	4938	6505

2000 (cont'd)

Options	Price
AM/FM/CD Audio System	+139
Antilock Brakes	+367
Automatic 4-Speed Transmission	+341

Options	Price
Power Moonroof	+320
Rear Spoiler	+168

In an effort to mold its image into that of a serious first-rate automobile manufacturer, Hyundai has recently added standard equipment and enhanced the performance of several of its cars. The redesigned Accent and new Sonata are proving that this South Korean automaker has finally learned how to build a good car. The current Elantra provides even more proof, and the company offers an industry-leading warranty program to back it up.

1999

The 1999 Elantra boasts a more powerful engine, styling changes and the best buyer assurance program of any car in this class.

Mileage Category: B

Body Styles	TMV Pricing		
	Trade	Private	Dealer
4 Dr GL Sdn	2270	3653	5093
4 Dr GL Wgn	2299	3702	5162

Body Styles	TMV Pricing		
	Trade	Private	Dealer
4 Dr GLS Sdn	2334	3757	5239
4 Dr GLS Wgn	2407	3875	5403

Options	Price
Antilock Brakes	+294
Automatic 4-Speed Transmission [Std on GLS Wgn]	+273

Options	Price
Power Moonroof	+256
Rear Spoiler	+135

1998

No changes to the Elantra for 1998.

Mileage Category: B

Body Styles	TMV Pricing		
	Trade	Private	Dealer
4 Dr GLS Sdn	1469	2637	3954
4 Dr GLS Wgn	1506	2703	4053

Body Styles	TMV Pricing		
	Trade	Private	Dealer
4 Dr STD Sdn	1364	2450	3674
4 Dr STD Wgn	1401	2516	3773

Options	Price
Air Conditioning	+262
Antilock Brakes	+227

Options	Price
Automatic 4-Speed Transmission [Std on GLS Wgn]	+210
Power Moonroof	+197

1997

Elantra rolls into 1997 with zero changes, save for a slight price increase.

Mileage Category: B

Body Styles	TMV Pricing		
	Trade	Private	Dealer
4 Dr GLS Sdn	1061	2101	3373
4 Dr GLS Wgn	1124	2229	3579

Body Styles	TMV Pricing		
	Trade	Private	Dealer
4 Dr STD Sdn	898	1780	2858
4 Dr STD Wgn	953	1889	3032

Options	Price
Air Conditioning	+187
Antilock Brakes	+156

Options	Price
Automatic 4-Speed Transmission [Opt on STD]	+166
Power Moonroof	+155

1996

All-new Elantra is a slickly styled sedan or wagon featuring dual airbags, side-impact protection and a more powerful engine. Pricing is up as well, pushing this Hyundai squarely into Dodge Neon and Honda Civic territory.

Body Styles	TMV Pricing		
	Trade	Private	Dealer
4 Dr GLS Sdn	542	1236	2194
4 Dr GLS Wgn	548	1251	2221

Body Styles	TMV Pricing		
	Trade	Private	Dealer
4 Dr STD Sdn	482	1096	1945
4 Dr STD Wgn	519	1183	2099

Options	Price
Air Conditioning	+131

Options	Price
Automatic 4-Speed Transmission [Opt on STD,Sdn]	+116

1995

Body Styles	TMV Pricing		
	Trade	Private	Dealer
4 Dr GLS Sdn	273	767	1589
4 Dr SE Sdn	244	686	1423

Body Styles	TMV Pricing		
	Trade	Private	Dealer
4 Dr STD Sdn	241	677	1403

Options	Price
1.8L I4 DOHC 16V FI Engine [Opt on SE,STD]	+119
Air Conditioning	+109
Antilock Brakes	+91

Options	Price
Automatic 4-Speed Transmission	+97
Power Moonroof	+91

No changes.

Hyundai
Santa Fe

Santa Fe

2004

The 3.5-liter V6 is now standard on all LX models and optional for the GLS.

Body Styles	TMV Pricing		
	Trade	Private	Dealer
4 Dr GLS AWD SUV	14240	15316	17110
4 Dr GLS SUV	12368	13370	15038
4 Dr LX AWD SUV	16068	17142	18932

Body Styles	TMV Pricing		
	Trade	Private	Dealer
4 Dr LX SUV	14552	15585	17305
4 Dr STD SUV	10645	11647	13317

Options	Price
3.5L V6 DOHC 24V FI Engine [Opt on GLS]	+800
AM/FM/CD Changer Audio System [Opt on GLS]	+195
Alarm System [Opt on STD]	+150
Antilock Brakes [Opt on STD, GLS]	+300
Automatic 4-Speed Transmission [Opt on STD]	+800
Automatic 5-Speed Transmission [Opt on GLS]	+200
Cruise Control [Opt on STD]	+200

Options	Price
Keyless Entry System [Opt on STD]	+200
Power Moonroof [Opt on GLS]	+590
Running Boards	+495
Traction Control System [Opt on GLS]	+300
Trailer Hitch [Opt on GLS, LX]	+350
Wood Interior Trim	+225

2003

For 2003, side airbags become standard equipment for every Santa Fe. New this year is Homelink and a Monsoon sound system with a six-CD changer -- these are standard items on the LX, and the audio upgrades are optional for the GLS. There is a newly available 3.5-liter V6 which will be offered in addition to the 2.4-liter inline four and the 2.7-liter V6. The 3.5-liter engine replaces the 2.7-liter unit and is now standard on the LX as is a new five-speed automatic transmission.

Body Styles	TMV Pricing		
	Trade	Private	Dealer
4 Dr GLS AWD SUV	12682	13926	15999
4 Dr GLS SUV	11373	12379	14054
4 Dr LX AWD SUV	14421	15835	18192

Body Styles	TMV Pricing		
	Trade	Private	Dealer
4 Dr LX SUV	12835	14093	16191
4 Dr STD SUV	9754	10711	12305

Options	Price
3.5L V6 DOHC 24V FI Engine [Opt on GLS,LX]	+389
AM/FM/CD Changer Audio System [Opt on GLS]	+134
Alarm System [Opt on STD]	+127
Antilock Brakes [Opt on GLS,STD]	+455
Automatic 4-Speed Transmission [Opt on STD]	+536

Options	Price
Cruise Control [Opt on STD]	+134
Monsoon Audio System [Opt on GLS]	+131
Power Moonroof [Opt on GLS,LX]	+399
Traction Control System [Opt on GLS]	+134
Trailer Hitch [Opt on GLS,LX]	+234

2002

Entering its second year of production, the Santa Fe gets four-wheel disc brakes as standard equipment as well as an optional upgraded stereo system. In May 2002, Hyundai responds to customer requests and makes a power sunroof optional for GLS and LX models. Besides that, all models benefit from midyear interior upgrades, among these larger air conditioning vents; a center stack-mounted clock; illumination for the power window buttons and glovebox; chrome accents; ISOFIX child-seat anchors for the outboard rear seating positions and an improved rear-seat recliner and folding mechanism. In September 2002, Hyundai announced that it had misstated the horsepower ratings for all of the models in its lineup -- the Santa Fe's 2.4-liter four-cylinder is now rated for 138 hp and its V6 is now at 173 hp. To compensate, the company is offering Hyundai owners (of 2000 models and newer) three options: 10 years of roadside assistance, 6-year/72,000-mile basic warranty coverage or 12-year/120,000-mile powertrain coverage.

Body Styles	TMV Pricing		
	Trade	Private	Dealer
4 Dr GLS AWD SUV	11078	12322	14394
4 Dr GLS SUV	9806	10907	12742
4 Dr LX AWD SUV	12237	13611	15899

Body Styles	TMV Pricing		
	Trade	Private	Dealer
4 Dr LX SUV	11132	12381	14463
4 Dr STD SUV	8619	9587	11200

Options	Price
Antilock Brakes [Opt on GLS,STD]	+399
Automatic 4-Speed Transmission [Opt on STD]	+469
Cruise Control [Opt on STD]	+117

Options	Price
Power Moonroof	+349
Traction Control System [Opt on GLS,STD]	+117

2001

For 2001, Hyundai brings to market its very own sport-utility. The Santa Fe is based on a modified Sonata midsize car platform and is available with either front-wheel drive or full-time four-wheel drive with either a four-cylinder or V6 engine.

Body Styles	TMV Pricing		
	Trade	Private	Dealer
4 Dr GL AWD SUV	8795	10253	11600
4 Dr GL SUV	7057	8227	9307
4 Dr GLS AWD SUV	9214	10741	12151

Body Styles	TMV Pricing		
	Trade	Private	Dealer
4 Dr GLS SUV	8169	9524	10774
4 Dr LX AWD SUV	9711	11322	12808
4 Dr LX SUV	8927	10408	11776

Options	Price
2.7L V6 DOHC 24V FI Engine [Opt on GL]	+618
Antilock Brakes	+350
Automatic 4-Speed Transmission [Opt on GL]	+309

Options	Price
Heated Front Seats	+134
Limited Slip Differential [Opt on GL,GLS]	+129

Scoupe
1995

Body Styles	TMV Pricing		
	Trade	Private	Dealer
2 Dr LS Cpe	306	799	1621
2 Dr STD Cpe	267	699	1420

Options	Price
Air Conditioning	+97

No changes.

Mileage Category: E

Body Styles	TMV Pricing		
	Trade	Private	Dealer
2 Dr Turbo Cpe	337	882	1789

Options	Price
Automatic 4-Speed Transmission	+78

Sonata
2004

Body Styles	TMV Pricing		
	Trade	Private	Dealer
4 Dr GLS Sdn	10734	11872	13768
4 Dr LX Sdn	11299	12437	14333

Options	Price
Antilock Brakes [Opt on GLS, LX]	+350
Automatic 4-Speed Transmission [Opt on LX, STD]	+800
Compact Disc Changer [Opt on GLS, LX]	+550

There are no significant changes for 2004.

Mileage Category: C

Body Styles	TMV Pricing		
	Trade	Private	Dealer
4 Dr STD Sdn	9153	10291	12187
4 Dr V6 Sdn	10086	11224	13120

Options	Price
Power Moonroof [Opt on GLS, LX]	+595
Traction Control System [Opt on GLS, LX]	+150

2003

After receiving significant upgrades last year, the Sonata receives only minor changes this year. Among these are a battery-saver feature (in the event that any of lights are left on); illuminated window switches; a 12-volt power point in the trunk; and electronic, rather than cable-operated, releases for the trunk lid and fuel door. Additionally, Hyundai announced that it had misstated the horsepower ratings for all of the models in its lineup in previous years, so the Sonata's four-cylinder is now rated at 138 horsepower (down from 149) and its V6 is rated at 170 (down from 181), though the engines themselves are unchanged.

Body Styles	TMV Pricing		
	Trade	Private	Dealer
4 Dr GLS Sdn	9214	10341	12218
4 Dr LX Sdn	9297	10434	12328

Options	Price
2.7L V6 DOHC 24V FI Engine [Opt on STD]	+569
Antilock Brakes [Opt on STD]	+455

Mileage Category: C

Body Styles	TMV Pricing		
	Trade	Private	Dealer
4 Dr STD Sdn	8002	8980	10611

Options	Price
Automatic 4-Speed Transmission	+335

2002

The 2002 Sonata receives a new look, a refined suspension and an available automanual transmission. The standard features list is lengthened to include such niceties as remote keyless entry and, on GLS and new-for-2002 LX models, 16-inch wheels. In September 2002, Hyundai announced that it had misstated the horsepower ratings for all of the models in its lineup -- the Sonata's 2.4-liter four-cylinder is now rated for 138 hp, while the V6 is now at 170, the previously advertised 2002 power upgrade (11 horsepower) apparently notwithstanding. To compensate, the company is offering owners (of 2000 models and newer) three options: 10 years of roadside assistance, 6-year/72,000-mile basic warranty coverage or 12-year/120,000-mile powertrain coverage.

Body Styles	TMV Pricing		
	Trade	Private	Dealer
4 Dr GLS Sdn	6271	7408	9302
4 Dr LX Sdn	6766	7992	10036

Options	Price
2.7L V6 DOHC 24V FI Engine [Opt on STD]	+293
Antilock Brakes	+399
Automatic 4-Speed Transmission	+293

Mileage Category: C

Body Styles	TMV Pricing		
	Trade	Private	Dealer
4 Dr STD Sdn	5804	6856	8608

Options	Price
Power Moonroof	+323
Traction Control System	+147

2001

The Sonata gets only minor trim changes for 2001, such as a new grille design and some tweaks to the rear deck lid. Additional features are ladled onto the standard equipment list.

Body Styles	TMV Pricing		
	Trade	Private	Dealer
4 Dr GLS Sdn	4779	6345	7790

Options	Price
AM/FM/CD Audio System [Opt on STD]	+155
Antilock Brakes [Opt on GLS]	+350
Automatic 4-Speed Transmission	+258
Leather Seats	+682

Mileage Category: C

Body Styles	TMV Pricing		
	Trade	Private	Dealer
4 Dr STD Sdn	4178	5547	6811

Options	Price
Power Moonroof	+335
Rear Spoiler	+227
Traction Control System [Opt on GLS]	+129

Hyundai
Sonata

2000

With new standard 15-inch alloy wheels, standard side airbags and some option changes, Hyundai's 2000 Sonata maintains the same base MSRP as last year.

Mileage Category: C

Body Styles	TMV Pricing		
	Trade	Private	Dealer
4 Dr GLS Sdn	3870	5383	6866

Options	Price
AM/FM/CD Audio System [Opt on STD]	+128
AM/FM/Cassette/CD Audio System	+192
Antilock Brakes	+290
Automatic 4-Speed Transmission	+213

Body Styles	TMV Pricing		
	Trade	Private	Dealer
4 Dr STD Sdn	3292	4579	5841

Options	Price
Leather Seats	+341
Power Moonroof	+277
Rear Spoiler	+177

1999

Hyundai's Sonata is completely new and much improved for 1999.

Mileage Category: C

Body Styles	TMV Pricing		
	Trade	Private	Dealer
4 Dr GLS Sdn	3014	4464	5974

Options	Price
AM/FM/Cassette/CD Audio System	+153
Antilock Brakes	+258
Automatic 4-Speed Transmission	+303

Body Styles	TMV Pricing		
	Trade	Private	Dealer
4 Dr STD Sdn	2604	3857	5162

Options	Price
Leather Seats [Opt on GLS]	+273
Power Moonroof	+222
Rear Spoiler	+142

1998

Mileage Category: C

Body Styles	TMV Pricing		
	Trade	Private	Dealer
4 Dr GL Sdn	1483	2503	3653
4 Dr GL V6 Sdn	1570	2651	3869

Options	Price
AM/FM/Cassette/CD Audio System	+118
Antilock Brakes	+199
Automatic 4-Speed Transmission [Opt on STD]	+234

Body Styles	TMV Pricing		
	Trade	Private	Dealer
4 Dr GLS Sdn	1816	3066	4475
4 Dr STD Sdn	1452	2452	3579

Options	Price
Leather Seats	+210
Power Moonroof	+175

No changes to the Sonata for 1998.

1997

Sheet metal is all new, and gives Sonata a more substantial look despite somewhat controversial retro-style front fascia and grille. Flush-fitting doors and restyled exterior mirrors help quiet the ride, while horn activation switches from spoke button to center steering wheel pad.

Mileage Category: C

Body Styles	TMV Pricing		
	Trade	Private	Dealer
4 Dr GL Sdn	935	1839	2943
4 Dr GLS Sdn	1122	2209	3537

Options	Price
3.0L V6 SOHC 12V FI Engine [Opt on GL]	+230
Antilock Brakes	+156
Automatic 4-Speed Transmission [Opt on STD]	+184

Body Styles	TMV Pricing		
	Trade	Private	Dealer
4 Dr STD Sdn	898	1766	2827

Options	Price
Leather Seats	+166
Power Moonroof	+145

1996

Noise, vibration and harshness are quelled with the addition of insulation to the floor and cowl, and liquid-filled V6 engine mounts. ABS is available as a stand-alone option on the GLS, and Steel Gray joins the color chart. Upgraded seat fabric comes in the base and GL models, while all Sonatas get CFC-free A/C.

Mileage Category: C

Body Styles	TMV Pricing		
	Trade	Private	Dealer
4 Dr GL Sdn	561	1260	2225
4 Dr GL V6 Sdn	599	1342	2367

Options	Price
Automatic 4-Speed Transmission [Opt on STD]	+121

Body Styles	TMV Pricing		
	Trade	Private	Dealer
4 Dr GLS Sdn	658	1473	2598
4 Dr STD Sdn	560	1254	2213

Options	Price
Leather Seats	+116

1995

Brand-new Sonata debuted in mid-1994. Dual airbags are standard. A 137-horsepower engine powers base and GL models while a 142-horsepower V6 is optional on midlevel GL and standard on GLS. Both engines are Mitsubishi-based designs. New car meets 1997 side-impact standards. Air conditioning and cassette stereo are standard on all models.

Mileage Category: C

Body Styles	TMV Pricing		
	Trade	Private	Dealer
4 Dr GL Sdn	407	971	1910
4 Dr GL V6 Sdn	433	1033	2034

Options	Price
Antilock Brakes	+91
Automatic 4-Speed Transmission [Opt on STD]	+101

Body Styles	TMV Pricing		
	Trade	Private	Dealer
4 Dr GLS Sdn	473	1128	2219
4 Dr STD Sdn	367	874	1720

Options	Price
Leather Seats	+97
Power Moonroof	+78

Tiburon

2004

Body Styles	TMV Pricing		
	Trade	Private	Dealer
2 Dr GT V6 Hbk	11388	12402	14093
2 Dr GT V6 Special Edition Hbk	12801	13815	15506

Options	Price
6-Speed Transmission [Opt on GT]	+950
AM/FM/Cassette/CD Audio System [Opt on STD]	+195
Antilock Brakes [Opt on GT]	+300
Compact Disc Changer	+649

Body Styles	TMV Pricing		
	Trade	Private	Dealer
2 Dr STD Hbk	10649	11663	13354

Options	Price
Infinity Audio System	+318
Leather Seats [Opt on GT]	+400
Power Moonroof [Opt on GT]	+835

The Tiburon's base 2.0-liter inline four has been fitted with continuously variable valve timing. As a result, horsepower creeps up slightly to 138; torque also rises to 136 pound-feet. The base Tiburon now features a standard rear spoiler. The Tiburon GT V6 Special Edition is a late 2004 introduction, and comes loaded with most of the GT's options as standard equipment, as well as unique trim and badging.

2003

Body Styles	TMV Pricing		
	Trade	Private	Dealer
2 Dr GT V6 Hbk	8594	9792	11789

Options	Price
AM/FM/Cassette/CD Audio System [Opt on STD]	+134
Antilock Brakes	+455
Automatic 4-Speed Transmission	+603
Infinity Audio System [Opt on STD]	+251

Body Styles	TMV Pricing		
	Trade	Private	Dealer
2 Dr STD Hbk	7538	8589	10341

Options	Price
Leather Seats [Opt on STD]	+335
Power Moonroof	+435
Rear Spoiler [Opt on STD]	+131

Completely redesigned for 2003, the Tiburon has progressed from a sporty economy hatchback to a legitimate sport coupe. And it's the sleekest Hyundai we've ever laid eyes on -- more than a few journalists have compared it to the Ferrari 456GT. The previous generation's 134-horsepower inline four will still power the base coupe, but Hyundai predicts that the volume leader will be the 170-hp Tiburon GT V6. Of course, this Tiburon will cost more than its predecessor, but you can still get into a GT V6 for less than 20 grand. Available features include a six-speed manual transmission, 17-inch wheels and a seven-speaker Infinity sound system. Note that the engines were originally rated for 140 hp and 181 hp, respectively; Hyundai downgraded the output for both in September 2002 (along with all of the other models in its lineup). To compensate, the company is offering owners (of 2000 models and newer) three options: 10 years of roadside assistance, 6-year/72,000-mile basic warranty coverage or 12-year/120,000-mile powertrain coverage.

2001

Body Styles	TMV Pricing		
	Trade	Private	Dealer
2 Dr STD Hbk	4475	5839	7098

Options	Price
AM/FM/Cassette/CD Audio System	+207
Antilock Brakes	+386
Automatic 4-Speed Transmission	+412

Options	Price
Leather Seats	+386
Power Sunroof	+361

Following last year's freshening, the Tiburon sees only minor trim changes for 2001, such as redesigned wheels and the addition of a rear spoiler as standard equipment.

2000

Body Styles	TMV Pricing		
	Trade	Private	Dealer
2 Dr STD Hbk	3597	4920	6217

Options	Price
AM/FM/Cassette/CD Audio System	+171
Alarm System	+122
Antilock Brakes	+320
Automatic 4-Speed Transmission	+341

Options	Price
Leather Seats	+320
Power Moonroof	+299
Rear Spoiler	+213

Hyundai's Tiburon is now offered in just one trim level. It receives new interior and exterior styling as well as alloy wheels, a power package and four-wheel disc brakes standard.

1999

Body Styles	TMV Pricing		
	Trade	Private	Dealer
2 Dr FX Hbk	3108	4587	6126

Options	Price
AM/FM/CD Audio System	+119
AM/FM/Cassette/CD Audio System	+136

Body Styles	TMV Pricing		
	Trade	Private	Dealer
2 Dr STD Hbk	2831	4179	5582

Options	Price
Air Conditioning	+307
Aluminum/Alloy Wheels [Opt on STD]	+171

Nothing changes on the Tiburon for 1999.

1999 (cont'd)

Options	Price
Antilock Brakes	+258
Automatic 4-Speed Transmission	+273
Leather Seats	+256

Options	Price
Power Sunroof	+239
Rear Spoiler [Opt on STD]	+171

1998

Base Tiburons get the 2.0-liter 140-horsepower engine as standard equipment.

Mileage Category: E

Body Styles	TMV Pricing		
	Trade	Private	Dealer
2 Dr FX Hbk	2123	3539	5135

Body Styles	TMV Pricing		
	Trade	Private	Dealer
2 Dr STD Hbk	1887	3145	4564

Options	Price
Air Conditioning	+237
Aluminum/Alloy Wheels [Opt on STD]	+131
Antilock Brakes	+199
Automatic 4-Speed Transmission	+210

Options	Price
Leather Seats	+197
Power Sunroof	+185
Rear Spoiler [Opt on STD]	+118

1997

Loosely based on the 1993 HCD-II concept car, the Tiburon (Spanish for shark) debuts as a budget sport coupe that promises to gobble competitors such as the Toyota Paseo like so much chum.

Mileage Category: E

Body Styles	TMV Pricing		
	Trade	Private	Dealer
2 Dr FX Hbk	1252	2553	4142

Body Styles	TMV Pricing		
	Trade	Private	Dealer
2 Dr STD Hbk	1128	2301	3734

Options	Price
Air Conditioning	+182
Antilock Brakes	+156
Automatic 4-Speed Transmission	+166

Options	Price
Leather Seats	+155
Power Sunroof	+145

XG300

2001

Mileage Category: D

Body Styles	TMV Pricing		
	Trade	Private	Dealer
4 Dr L Sdn	7115	8612	9994

Body Styles	TMV Pricing		
	Trade	Private	Dealer
4 Dr STD Sdn	6696	8105	9405

Options	Price
Compact Disc Changer	+258

Options	Price
Power Moonroof [Opt on STD]	+386

Hyundai goes after the Honda Accord V6 and Toyota Camry V6 by offering more for less. Fully loaded with equipment, the new XG300 undercuts both competitors on price. But, as we all know, there's more to the value equation than an attractive MSRP, especially in the meat of the sedan marketplace.

XG350

2004

Mileage Category: D

Body Styles	TMV Pricing		
	Trade	Private	Dealer
4 Dr L Sdn	15012	16181	18130

Body Styles	TMV Pricing		
	Trade	Private	Dealer
4 Dr STD Sdn	14448	15580	17466

Options	Price
Compact Disc Changer	+500

Other than a few cosmetic enhancements, the XG350 remains largely unchanged for 2004. The front end was slightly reworked and projector-type foglights were added. The rear of the car looks slightly different as well -- the license plate is now housed in the rear deck lid rather than the bumper. Inside, the XG350 offers lighter tone wood grain trim, a new Infinity sound system and recessed child seat tethers. The only mechanical changes to the XG are larger front brake rotors and a trunk lid that is lifted by gas-charged struts rather than torsion bars. All XG350s now come with a full-size spare.

2003

For 2003, Hyundai's flagship sedan gets a new instrument panel and trip computer. Otherwise, the XG350 is unchanged.

Mileage Category: D

Body Styles	TMV Pricing		
	Trade	Private	Dealer
4 Dr L Sdn	12055	13488	15875

Body Styles	TMV Pricing		
	Trade	Private	Dealer
4 Dr STD Sdn	11704	13095	15412

Options	Price
Compact Disc Changer	+335

2002

The XG300 becomes the XG350, as engine displacement is bumped up 0.5 liters to 3.5. Although horsepower is only increased by 2 to 194, 39 more pound-feet is on tap for a grand total of 217, which should provide quicker acceleration.

Mileage Category: D

Body Styles	TMV Pricing		
	Trade	Private	Dealer
4 Dr L Sdn	9260	10574	12764

Body Styles	TMV Pricing		
	Trade	Private	Dealer
4 Dr STD Sdn	8680	9912	11964

Options	Price
Compact Disc Changer	+293

Infiniti
FX35/FX45

FX35

2004

All models receive minor suspension revisions, an air filtration system and an eight-way power front passenger seat. New options include chrome plating for the 20-inch wheels and a snow mode for added traction in slippery conditions.

Mileage Category: O

Body Styles	Trade	Private	Dealer
4 Dr STD AWD SUV	27555	29328	32284

Options	Price
20 Inch Wheels	+750
Bose Audio System	+500
Chrome Wheels	+1600
DVD Entertainment System	+1600
Heated Front Seats	+250
Leather Seats	+400
Luggage Rack	+150
Navigation System	+1800

Body Styles	Trade	Private	Dealer
4 Dr STD SUV	26905	28487	31123

Options	Price
Power Driver Seat w/Memory	+220
Power Moonroof	+875
Power Tilt and Telescopic Steering Wheel	+250
Rear View Camera	+500
Satellite Radio System	+400
Sport Suspension	+530
Tire Pressure Monitoring System	+500
Trailer Hitch	+600

2003

The FX35 is an all-new crossover SUV from Infiniti. It is performance-oriented, and boasts a powerful V6, sharp handling and available all-wheel drive. It's also a less expensive alternative to the V8-powered FX45.

Mileage Category: O

Body Styles	Trade	Private	Dealer
4 Dr STD AWD SUV	25855	27471	30164

Options	Price
20 Inch Wheels	+573
Adaptive Cruise Control	+611
Bose Audio System	+382
DVD Entertainment System	+993
Heated Front Seats	+267
Keyless Ignition System	+531
Leather Seats	+649
Luggage Rack	+168

Body Styles	Trade	Private	Dealer
4 Dr STD SUV	24747	26294	28871

Options	Price
Navigation System	+1375
Power Driver Seat w/Memory	+191
Power Moonroof	+687
Rear View Camera	+382
Satellite Radio System	+305
Sport Suspension	+191
Tire Pressure Monitoring System	+191
Trailer Hitch	+382

FX45

2004

Minor suspension revisions, an air filtration system and an eight-way power front passenger seat are now standard. New options include chrome plating for the 20-inch wheels and a snow mode for added traction in slippery conditions.

Mileage Category: O

Body Styles		Trade	Private	Dealer
4 Dr STD AWD SUV		32942	34706	37646

Options	Price
Automatic On/Off Headlights	+300
Bose Audio System	+700
Chrome Wheels	+1600
DVD Entertainment System	+1600
Garage Door Opener	+150
Navigation System	+1800

Options	Price
Power Moonroof	+1000
Rear View Camera	+500
Satellite Radio System	+400
Steering Wheel Radio Controls	+150
Tire Pressure Monitoring System	+500
Trailer Hitch	+600

2003

The FX45 is an all-new crossover SUV from Infiniti. It is performance-oriented, and therefore boasts V8 power, sharp handling and standard all-wheel drive.

Mileage Category: O

Body Styles		Trade	Private	Dealer
4 Dr STD AWD SUV		30656	32209	34797

Options	Price
Adaptive Cruise Control	+611
Bose Audio System	+382
DVD Entertainment System	+993
Keyless Ignition System	+531
Luggage Rack	+168
Navigation System	+1375

Options	Price
Power Moonroof	+687
Rear View Camera	+382
Satellite Radio System	+305
Sport Suspension	+191
Tire Pressure Monitoring System	+191
Trailer Hitch	+382

For the latest vehicle information, visit www.edmunds.com

G20
2002

Mileage Category: H

Body Styles	TMV Pricing		
	Trade	Private	Dealer
4 Dr STD Sdn	10203	11251	12997

Options	Price	Options	Price
16 Inch Wheels	+213	Leather Seats	+426
Automatic 4-Speed Transmission	+487	Power Driver Seat	+143
Heated Front Seats	+173	Power Moonroof	+456

A Sport package featuring a body-color grille, dark tint headlight trim and 16-inch aluminum-alloy wheels debuts this year, as do two new exterior colors -- Silver Crystal and Maui Blue. The G20t, as Infiniti dubs the Touring package-equipped model, disappears this year.

2001

G20t comes with standard leather and a power sunroof this year. Luxury models can be equipped with leather and a manual transmission simultaneously. And hold on to your hat -- the side marker lights switch from amber lenses to clear.

Mileage Category: H

Body Styles	TMV Pricing			Body Styles	TMV Pricing		
	Trade	Private	Dealer		Trade	Private	Dealer
4 Dr STD Sdn	8508	9859	11106	4 Dr Touring Sdn	9955	11536	12995

Options	Price	Options	Price
Automatic 4-Speed Transmission	+409	Leather Seats	+434
Compact Disc Changer	+235	Power Heated Mirrors	+115
Heated Front Seats	+128	Power Moonroof	+485
Infiniti Communicator	+817		

2000

The G20 entry-level compact receives numerous mechanical improvements, exterior and interior enhancements and safety additions for 2000, including more horsepower, revised transmissions and a new muffler.

Mileage Category: H

Body Styles	TMV Pricing			Body Styles	TMV Pricing		
	Trade	Private	Dealer		Trade	Private	Dealer
4 Dr STD Sdn	7003	8327	9625	4 Dr Touring Sdn	7455	8865	10247

Options	Price	Options	Price
Automatic 4-Speed Transmission	+359	Leather Seats	+381
Compact Disc Changer	+322	Power Driver Seat	+123
Infiniti Communicator	+359	Power Moonroof	+426

1999

The G20 returns to the Infiniti lineup after a two-year hiatus. This entry-level compact is based on the European- and Japanese- market Primera, which has garnered a great deal of acclaim from the foreign automotive press.

Mileage Category: H

Body Styles	TMV Pricing			Body Styles	TMV Pricing		
	Trade	Private	Dealer		Trade	Private	Dealer
4 Dr STD Sdn	5297	6457	7665	4 Dr Touring Sdn	6260	7632	9059

Options	Price	Options	Price
Automatic 4-Speed Transmission	+273	Power Moonroof	+325
Leather Seats	+291		

1996

Mileage Category: H

Body Styles	TMV Pricing			Body Styles	TMV Pricing		
	Trade	Private	Dealer		Trade	Private	Dealer
4 Dr STD Sdn	2500	3378	4591	4 Dr Touring Sdn	2712	3664	4979

Options	Price	Options	Price
Automatic 4-Speed Transmission	+186	Power Moonroof [Opt on STD]	+186
Leather Seats [Opt on STD]	+158		

Emergency locking front and rear seatbelts have been installed, and fake wood is applied on models equipped with the Leather Appointment Package. This is the last year for the entry-level Infiniti.

1995

All-season tires are added to the G20. No other changes are made to the entry-level Infiniti.

Mileage Category: H

Body Styles	TMV Pricing			Body Styles	TMV Pricing		
	Trade	Private	Dealer		Trade	Private	Dealer
4 Dr STD Sdn	2045	2814	4096	4 Dr Touring Sdn	2192	3017	4392

1995 (cont'd)

Options	Price
Automatic 4-Speed Transmission	+117
Leather Seats [Opt on STD]	+125

Options	Price
Power Moonroof [Opt on STD]	+139

G35

2004

Mileage Category: H

Body Styles	TMV Pricing		
	Trade	Private	Dealer
2 Dr STD Cpe	25743	27029	29172
4 Dr STD AWD Sdn	23127	24504	26800

Body Styles	TMV Pricing		
	Trade	Private	Dealer
4 Dr STD Sdn	21667	23044	25340

Options	Price
17 Inch Wheels - Chrome [Opt on Sdn]	+1320
AM/FM/Cassette/CD Changer Audio System	+200
Aero Kit	+550
Automatic Climate Control (2 Zone) - Driver and Passenger	+300
Automatic Dimming Rearview Mirror	+150
Automatic On/Off Headlights	+120
Bose Audio System	+500

Options	Price
Garage Door Opener	+125
Navigation System	+1800
Power Driver Seat w/Memory	+250
Power Moonroof	+850
Satellite Radio System	+400
Trip Computer	+200

Sedans get standard heated outside mirrors, heated front seats and, on leather-equipped six-speed models only, a four-way power passenger seat and a limited-slip differential. Other changes include a standard tire-pressure monitoring system, Low Emissions Vehicle status and a revised front console with an additional cupholder on leather-equipped six-speed coupes. 2004 also sees the addition of an all-wheel-drive sport sedan to the G35 lineup.

2003

The G35 is Infiniti's new entry-level luxury sport sedan and coupe. Aimed at buyers who would otherwise choose an Audi A4, BMW 3 Series or Lexus IS 300, the G35 offers impressive performance and comfort for a price that's less than most of the competition's.

Mileage Category: H

Body Styles	TMV Pricing		
	Trade	Private	Dealer
2 Dr STD Cpe	23501	24856	27114

Body Styles	TMV Pricing		
	Trade	Private	Dealer
4 Dr STD Sdn	19589	20822	22878

Options	Price
Aero Kit	+420
Automatic Climate Control (2 Zone) - Driver and Passenger	+210
Bose Audio System	+420
Heated Front Seats [Opt on Sdn]	+267
Navigation System	+1527

Options	Price
Power Driver Seat w/Memory	+191
Power Moonroof	+687
Power Passenger Seat	+210
Satellite Radio System	+305
Trip Computer	+115

I30

2001

Mileage Category: H

Body Styles	TMV Pricing		
	Trade	Private	Dealer
4 Dr STD Sdn	11617	13069	14410

Body Styles	TMV Pricing		
	Trade	Private	Dealer
4 Dr Touring Sdn	12242	13772	15184

Options	Price
Compact Disc Changer	+307
Heated Front Seats	+192
Infiniti Communicator	+817
Navigation System	+1022

Options	Price
Rear Spoiler	+128
Traction Control System	+153
Xenon Headlamps	+256

This year, two new colors are added along with steering wheel-mounted controls, an antiglare rearview mirror with integrated compass and an emergency inside trunk release. The brilliant blue xenon headlights previously available only on Touring models can now be ordered on base trim cars, as well.

2000

The year 2000 marks the introduction of the all-new Infiniti I30.

Mileage Category: H

Body Styles	TMV Pricing		
	Trade	Private	Dealer
4 Dr STD Sdn	9816	11272	12700

Body Styles	TMV Pricing		
	Trade	Private	Dealer
4 Dr Touring Sdn	10366	11904	13412

Options	Price
Compact Disc Changer	+269
Heated Front Seats	+168

Options	Price
Infiniti Communicator	+363

1999

Mileage Category: H

Body Styles	TMV Pricing		
	Trade	Private	Dealer
4 Dr STD Sdn	7117	8428	9792

Options	Price
Automatic 4-Speed Transmission [Opt on Touring]	+341
Compact Disc Changer	+228
Heated Front Seats	+142

Body Styles	TMV Pricing		
	Trade	Private	Dealer
4 Dr Touring Sdn	7804	9240	10735

Options	Price
Infiniti Communicator	+307
Leather Seats [Opt on STD]	+342
Power Moonroof [Opt on STD]	+325

Traction control is available as an option, the audio faceplate has been updated and an ignition immobilizer is offered on the I30.

1998

Side-impact airbags make their way into the Infiniti I30, as do new headlamps, taillamps, center console and wheels.

Body Styles	TMV Pricing		
	Trade	Private	Dealer
4 Dr STD Sdn	5566	6808	8209

Options	Price
Automatic 4-Speed Transmission [Opt on Touring]	+281
Compact Disc Changer	+187
Heated Front Seats [Opt on STD]	+117

Body Styles	TMV Pricing		
	Trade	Private	Dealer
4 Dr Touring Sdn	6152	7524	9072

Options	Price
Infiniti Communicator	+253
Leather Seats [Opt on STD]	+281
Power Moonroof [Opt on STD]	+267

1997

A few new paint colors are the only changes to the 1997 I30.

Body Styles	TMV Pricing		
	Trade	Private	Dealer
4 Dr STD Sdn	4351	5544	7001

Options	Price
Automatic 4-Speed Transmission	+231
Leather Seats [Opt on STD]	+231

Body Styles	TMV Pricing		
	Trade	Private	Dealer
4 Dr Touring Sdn	4880	6217	7851

Options	Price
Power Moonroof [Opt on STD]	+220

1996

New luxo-sport sedan based on the Nissan Maxima arrived during 1995. Slotted between the G20 and the J30, the I30 competes with the Lexus ES 300, BMW 3 Series and the new Acura TL-Series. If you like big chrome grilles, this is the car to buy.

Body Styles	TMV Pricing		
	Trade	Private	Dealer
4 Dr STD Sdn	3626	4713	6214

Options	Price
Automatic 4-Speed Transmission	+186
Leather Seats [Opt on STD]	+185

Body Styles	TMV Pricing		
	Trade	Private	Dealer
4 Dr Touring Sdn	4051	5266	6943

Options	Price
Power Moonroof [Opt on STD]	+176

I35

2004

Mileage Category: H

Body Styles	TMV Pricing		
	Trade	Private	Dealer
4 Dr STD Sdn	18976	20266	22415

Options	Price
Compact Disc Changer	+200
Heated Front and Rear Seats	+380
Heated Steering Wheel	+150
Navigation System	+1800

Options	Price
Power Heated Mirrors	+170
Rear Spoiler	+520
Satellite Radio System	+400

All models get a sunroof, power rear sunshade and body side sills as standard equipment.

2003

There aren't that many changes for the I35 this year. It gains the option of having an integrated satellite radio, and on the inside the use of wood-tone trim is expanded on the center console.

Mileage Category: H

Body Styles	TMV Pricing		
	Trade	Private	Dealer
4 Dr STD Sdn	17162	18295	20184

Options	Price
17 Inch Wheels - Chrome	+573
Automatic Stability Control	+267
Compact Disc Changer	+225
Heated Front and Rear Seats	+229

Options	Price
Navigation System	+1527
Power Heated Mirrors	+130
Power Moonroof	+706
Power Rear Window Sunshade	+286

2003 (cont'd)

Options	Price
Satellite Radio System	+305

Options	Price
Sport Suspension	+218

2002

The I35 is an evolution of the second-generation I30 entry-level luxury sedan. It features a more powerful engine, updated exterior styling, standard 17-inch wheels, an upgraded braking system, stability control and more luxurious interior appointments.

Mileage Category: H

Body Styles	TMV Pricing		
	Trade	Private	Dealer
4 Dr STD Sdn	14605	15743	17639

Options	Price
17 Inch Wheels	+347
Automatic Stability Control	+213
Chrome Wheels	+974
Compact Disc Changer	+335
Heated Front and Rear Seats	+183

Options	Price
Navigation System	+1096
Power Moonroof	+548
Power Rear Window Sunshade	+213
Rear Spoiler	+304
Sport Suspension	+173

J30

1997

Mileage Category: H

Body Styles	TMV Pricing		
	Trade	Private	Dealer
4 Dr STD Sdn	5081	6483	8196
4 Dr STD Sdn (1997.5)	5081	6483	8196

Last year for the J30.

Body Styles	TMV Pricing		
	Trade	Private	Dealer
4 Dr Touring Sdn	4781	6100	7713
4 Dr Touring Sdn (1997.5)	4781	6100	7713

1996

Three new colors join the paint palette.

Mileage Category: H

Body Styles	TMV Pricing		
	Trade	Private	Dealer
4 Dr STD Sdn	4136	5377	7090

Body Styles	TMV Pricing		
	Trade	Private	Dealer
4 Dr Touring Sdn	4244	5518	7277

1995

Redesigned taillights, power lumbar support for the driver seat and an antiglare mirror mark the changes for the 1995 J30.

Mileage Category: H

Body Styles	TMV Pricing		
	Trade	Private	Dealer
4 Dr STD Sdn	3006	4079	5868

Options	Price
Forged Alloy Wheels	+82

Options	Price
Touring Suspension	+114

M45

2004

Mileage Category: H

Body Styles	TMV Pricing		
	Trade	Private	Dealer
4 Dr STD Sdn	29851	31453	34123

Options	Price
Chrome Wheels	+1000
Climate Controlled Seats (Front)	+800
Navigation System	+2500

Options	Price
Power Moonroof	+1200
Rear Spoiler	+540
Satellite Radio System	+400

Infiniti has moved the CD changer from the glovebox to the dash. Several of last year's options are standard for 2004, including heated outside mirrors, an auto-dimming rearview mirror with Homelink and compass, two-position memory for the driver seat, a tire-pressure monitoring system and a full-size spare tire. The navigation system (with voice recognition technology) is now available as a stand-alone option.

2003

The M45 performance sport sedan comes standard with class-leading V8 performance and a long list of world-class amenities.

Mileage Category: H

Body Styles	TMV Pricing		
	Trade	Private	Dealer
4 Dr STD Sdn	27973	29565	32218

Options	Price
18 Inch Wheels - Chrome	+764

Options	Price
Adaptive Cruise Control	+535

Options	Price
Automatic Dimming Sideview Mirror(s)	+134
Navigation System	+1375
Power Moonroof	+916
Rear Spoiler	+412
Satellite Radio System	+305

Options	Price
Tire Pressure Monitoring System	+115
Trip Computer	+153
Ventilated Seats (Front)	+573
Voice Recognition System	+496

Q45

2004

Mileage Category: I

Body Styles	TMV Pricing		
	Trade	Private	Dealer
4 Dr STD Sdn	37114	38995	42130

Options	Price
18 Inch Wheels	+2000
Electronic Suspension Control	+1700
Navigation System	+2000
Power Rear Window Sunshade	+700
Rear Air Conditioning Controls	+400

Options	Price
Rear Audio Controls	+300
Runflat Tire System	+400
Satellite Radio System	+400
Ventilated Seats (Front)	+500

The Q's five-speed automatic transmission gets a revised manual-shift mode, and the rearview backup camera now comes standard.

2003

The Q45 enters into 2003 with a few changes. Refinements include a higher numerical final drive ratio for better acceleration, slightly revised front and rear styling, new exterior colors, the addition of standard heated seats and a full-size spare tire. An optional satellite radio is now being offered along with some new optional equipment packages.

Mileage Category: I

Body Styles	TMV Pricing		
	Trade	Private	Dealer
4 Dr STD Sdn	31322	33155	36211

Options	Price
18 Inch Wheels	+496
Adaptive Cruise Control	+611
Air Conditioning - Front and Rear	+191
Electronic Damping Suspension Control	+649
Heated Front and Rear Seats	+382

Options	Price
Navigation System	+1527
Power Rear Window Sunshade	+382
Runflat Tire System	+191
Satellite Radio System	+305
Ventilated Seats (Front)	+496

2002

Infiniti takes aim at the BMW 5 Series, Lexus GS and the Mercedes-Benz E-Class with the all-new Q45 sedan. Unlike the forgettable previous version, the new Q has power and panache, just what it takes to woo the mid-luxury crowd.

Mileage Category: I

Body Styles	TMV Pricing		
	Trade	Private	Dealer
4 Dr STD Sdn	23075	24926	28012

Options	Price
18 Inch Wheels	+396
Adaptive Cruise Control	+487
Electronic Damping Suspension Control	+517
Heated Front Seats	+274

Options	Price
Navigation System	+1217
Power Rear Seat	+487
Power Rear Window Sunshade	+304

2001

Mileage Category: I

Body Styles	TMV Pricing		
	Trade	Private	Dealer
4 Dr STD Sdn	17610	20037	22278

Body Styles	TMV Pricing		
	Trade	Private	Dealer
4 Dr Touring Sdn	17823	20281	22549

Options	Price
Compact Disc Changer	+307
Heated Front Seats	+215
Infiniti Communicator	+817

Options	Price
Navigation System	+1022
Rear Spoiler	+271
Two-Tone Paint	+256

Few changes accompany the current Q45 as it gasps a few final breaths before a welcome, and long overdue, redesign debuts in spring of 2001. A new Luxury model replaces last year's Anniversary Edition. All Qs get body-colored door handles and license plate surrounds, revised taillights, real bird's eye maple wood interior trim and a leather-wrapped steering wheel rim trimmed in ersatz timber. The Touring model has standard bright-finish 17-inch wheels.

2000

For 2000 the Q45 celebrates a decade of production with a special 10th Anniversary model. All Qs receive a new 100,000-mile tune-up interval and special child seat tethers.

Mileage Category: I

Body Styles	TMV Pricing		
	Trade	Private	Dealer
4 Dr Anniv Sdn	14716	17028	19295

Body Styles	TMV Pricing		
	Trade	Private	Dealer
4 Dr STD Sdn	13949	16142	18292

2000 (cont'd)

Body Styles	TMV Pricing		
	Trade	Private	Dealer
4 Dr Touring Sdn	14324	16575	18781

Options	Price		Options	Price
Compact Disc Changer	+269		Infiniti Communicator	+363
Heated Front Seats	+157		Rear Spoiler	+157

1999

Several small exterior and interior enhancements have been added to the Q for 1999, including a new sunroof, revised front styling and the return of the analog clock.

Mileage Category: I

Body Styles	TMV Pricing				Body Styles	TMV Pricing		
	Trade	Private	Dealer			Trade	Private	Dealer
4 Dr STD Sdn	10916	12879	14922		4 Dr Touring Sdn	11065	13055	15125

Options	Price		Options	Price
Compact Disc Changer	+228		Infiniti Communicator	+307
Heated Front Seats	+133		Rear Spoiler	+133

1998

The Q45 gets front seatbelt pre-tensioners. No other changes for Infiniti's flagship.

Mileage Category: I

Body Styles	TMV Pricing				Body Styles	TMV Pricing		
	Trade	Private	Dealer			Trade	Private	Dealer
4 Dr STD Sdn	9162	11024	13125		4 Dr Touring Sdn	9232	11109	13225

Options	Price		Options	Price
Compact Disc Changer [Opt on STD]	+187		Infiniti Communicator	+253

1997

This totally redesigned car has almost nothing in common with its predecessor. Power now comes via a 4.1-liter V8 engine and is still delivered through the rear wheels. The Q45 no longer has aspirations to be a sport sedan, its prime duties now are interstate cruising.

Mileage Category: I

Body Styles	TMV Pricing				Body Styles	TMV Pricing		
	Trade	Private	Dealer			Trade	Private	Dealer
4 Dr STD Sdn	7458	9073	11048		4 Dr Touring Sdn	7570	9210	11215
4 Dr STD Sdn (1997.5)	7527	9158	11152		4 Dr Touring Sdn (1997.5)	7712	9383	11425

1996

Mileage Category: I

Body Styles	TMV Pricing				Body Styles	TMV Pricing		
	Trade	Private	Dealer			Trade	Private	Dealer
4 Dr STD Sdn	5727	7160	9140		4 Dr Touring Sdn	5981	7476	9541

Options	Price
Traction Control System	+124

Active suspension model is canceled, but two new exterior colors are available.

1995

Alloy wheels for the base model are about the only changes for the Q45.

Mileage Category: I

Body Styles	TMV Pricing				Body Styles	TMV Pricing		
	Trade	Private	Dealer			Trade	Private	Dealer
4 Dr A Sdn	4811	6071	8170		4 Dr STD Sdn	4648	5866	7896

Options	Price		Options	Price
4 Wheel Steering	+269		Forged Alloy Wheels [Opt on STD]	+82
Compact Disc Changer [Opt on STD]	+98		Limited Slip Differential [Opt on STD]	+90
Electronic Suspension Control [Opt on STD]	+240		Traction Control System [Opt on STD]	+98

QX4

2003

Mileage Category: O

Body Styles	TMV Pricing		
	Trade	Private	Dealer
4 Dr STD 4WD SUV	20418	21820	24156

Options	Price
Adaptive Cruise Control	+611
Camper/Towing Package	+321
Chrome Wheels	+1222
DVD Entertainment System	+1222
Heated Front and Rear Seats	+382

Body Styles	TMV Pricing		
	Trade	Private	Dealer
4 Dr STD SUV	18966	20268	22438

Options	Price
Navigation System	+1527
Power Moonroof	+764
Two-Tone Paint	+382
VCR Entertainment System	+993

For 2003, QX4 receives packaging enhancements, including the addition of previously optional Premium Package as standard equipment. This includes 17-inch wheels and tires, a leather and genuine wood steering wheel, driver seat memory and steering wheel-mounted audio control switches.

2002

Mileage Category: O

Body Styles	TMV Pricing		
	Trade	Private	Dealer
4 Dr STD 4WD SUV	17544	19035	21521

Options	Price
17 Inch Wheels	+274
Adaptive Cruise Control	+487
Camper/Towing Package	+256
Chrome Wheels	+974
DVD Entertainment System	+974
Heated Front and Rear Seats	+304

Body Styles	TMV Pricing		
	Trade	Private	Dealer
4 Dr STD SUV	16503	17906	20244

Options	Price
Limited Slip Differential	+183
Navigation System	+1217
Power Driver Seat w/Memory	+134
Power Sunroof	+609
Two-Tone Paint	+304
VCR Entertainment System	+791

For 2002, the QX4 receives a few interior enhancements including a refined audio system, a faster functioning in-dash CD changer and a newly optional wood-trim steering wheel with audio controls. It also gets an available Intelligent Cruise Control system, the same system found on the Q45. Rounding out the updates are optional chrome-plated 17-inch wheels and seven new exterior colors.

2001

Body Styles	TMV Pricing		
	Trade	Private	Dealer
4 Dr STD 4WD SUV	15890	17931	19815

Options	Price
Camper/Towing Package	+166
DVD Entertainment System	+818
Heated Front and Rear Seats	+230
Limited Slip Differential	+153

Body Styles	TMV Pricing		
	Trade	Private	Dealer
4 Dr STD SUV	14661	16544	18282

Options	Price
Navigation System	+1022
Power Moonroof	+486
Two-Tone Paint	+256
VCR Entertainment System	+664

For 2001, the QX4 gets a substantial power boost from a brand-new V6 engine. Cosmetic updates include the addition of standard xenon high-intensity headlights, revised exterior styling, new alloy wheels and a more upscale interior. A navigation system is available, as is an onboard entertainment system. A less costly 2WD model is offered for the first time, and Infiniti's signature analog clock has been added to the dash, along with electrofluorescent gauge illumination.

2000

Mileage Category: O

Body Styles	TMV Pricing		
	Trade	Private	Dealer
4 Dr STD 4WD SUV	12617	14331	16011

Options	Price
Camper/Towing Package	+146
Compact Disc Changer	+269
Heated Front Seats	+157
Infiniti Communicator	+363

Options	Price
Limited Slip Differential	+135
Power Moonroof	+426
Trailer Hitch	+123

Infiniti's luxury SUV gets minor improvements to its emissions system but is otherwise a carryover from the 1999 model year. A more powerful QX4 will be available soon as a 2001 model.

1999

Mileage Category: O

Body Styles	TMV Pricing		
	Trade	Private	Dealer
4 Dr STD 4WD SUV	9845	11506	13235

Options	Price
Camper/Towing Package	+123
Compact Disc Changer	+228
Heated Front Seats	+133

Options	Price
Infiniti Communicator	+307
Power Moonroof	+325
Running Boards	+123

Infiniti's luxury sport-ute enters its third year with no major changes.

Infiniti
QX4/QX56

1998
No changes to the QX4.

Mileage Category: 0

Body Styles			TMV Pricing		
			Trade	Private	Dealer
4 Dr STD 4WD SUV			8302	9936	11779

Options	Price	Options	Price
Compact Disc Changer	+187	Power Moonroof	+267

1997
A version of Nissan's wonderful four-wheeler is introduced by Infiniti, aiming to compete with the Mercury Mountaineer, Acura SLX and Land Rover Discovery. Differences between the QX4 and the Pathfinder include the Q's full-time four-wheel-drive system, a more luxurious interior and some different sheet metal.

Mileage Category: 0

Body Styles			TMV Pricing		
			Trade	Private	Dealer
4 Dr STD 4WD SUV			6818	8284	10075

Options	Price
Power Moonroof	+220

QX56

2004

Mileage Category: 0

Body Styles		TMV Pricing			Body Styles		TMV Pricing		
		Trade	Private	Dealer			Trade	Private	Dealer
4 Dr STD 4WD SUV		39055	41198	44769	4 Dr STD SUV		36750	38893	42465

Options	Price	Options	Price
DVD Entertainment System	+1600	Rear View Camera	+500
Power Moonroof	+1200	Satellite Radio System	+400

The QX56 is an all-new full-size luxury SUV from Infiniti designed to compete against the likes of Cadillac's Escalade and the Lincoln Navigator.

Amigo

2000

Mileage Category: L

Body Styles	TMV Pricing		
	Trade	Private	Dealer
2 Dr S Conv	3995	5007	5999
2 Dr S SUV	4132	5179	6206
2 Dr S V6 4WD Conv	5028	6302	7550

Options	Price
AM/FM/CD Audio System	+137
Air Conditioning	+372
Aluminum/Alloy Wheels	+157
Automatic 4-Speed Transmission [Opt on V6 4WD Conv]	+313

Body Styles	TMV Pricing		
	Trade	Private	Dealer
2 Dr S V6 4WD SUV	5234	6560	7859
2 Dr S V6 Conv	4750	5953	7132
2 Dr S V6 SUV	4637	5812	6963

Options	Price
Compact Disc Changer	+196
Ironman Package	+377
Side Steps	+139

Redesigned front styling and several new colors are available for the new year. The Ironman package offers the Rodeo's Intelligent Suspension Control system.

1999

Two body styles are available, hardtop or soft top, and an automatic transmission is now offered with the V6 engine.

Mileage Category: L

Body Styles	TMV Pricing		
	Trade	Private	Dealer
2 Dr S 4WD Conv	3770	4974	6227
2 Dr S Conv	3360	4433	5549
2 Dr S SUV	3422	4514	5651
2 Dr S V6 4WD Conv	3794	5005	6265

Options	Price
AM/FM/CD Audio System	+152
Air Conditioning	+288
Aluminum/Alloy Wheels	+182

Body Styles	TMV Pricing		
	Trade	Private	Dealer
2 Dr S V6 4WD SUV	3817	5036	6304
2 Dr S V6 Conv	3697	4877	6105
2 Dr S V6 SUV	3829	5052	6324

Options	Price
Automatic 4-Speed Transmission	+237
Compact Disc Changer	+197

1998

Isuzu reintroduces its convertible sport-utility after a three-year hiatus. This model comes with a modest four-cylinder engine, but the powerful V6 from the Rodeo is available and turns this 4WD droptop into a screamer.

Mileage Category: L

Body Styles	TMV Pricing		
	Trade	Private	Dealer
2 Dr S 4WD Conv	3000	4060	5256
2 Dr S Conv	2486	3363	4353

Options	Price
AM/FM/CD Audio System	+133
Air Conditioning	+253

Body Styles	TMV Pricing		
	Trade	Private	Dealer
2 Dr S V6 4WD Conv	3286	4447	5756

Options	Price
Aluminum/Alloy Wheels	+133
Compact Disc Changer	+173

Ascender

2004

Mileage Category: M

Body Styles	TMV Pricing		
	Trade	Private	Dealer
4 Dr LS 5 Pass 4WD SUV	17867	19494	22205
4 Dr LS 5 Pass SUV	16427	18023	20683
4 Dr LS 7 Pass 4WD SUV	19908	21532	24238
4 Dr LS 7 Pass SUV	17980	19587	22265
4 Dr Limited 7 Pass 4WD SUV	22110	23731	26432
4 Dr Limited 7 Pass SUV	20063	21659	24319

Options	Price
5.3L V8 OHV 16V FI Engine [Opt on LS 7 Psgr]	+1499
Alarm System [Opt on S]	+200
Cruise Control [Opt on S 5 Psgr]	+200
Front Side Airbag Restraints [Opt on S]	+350
Keyless Entry System [Opt on S]	+150
Leather Seats [Opt on LS]	+1000

Body Styles	TMV Pricing		
	Trade	Private	Dealer
4 Dr Luxury 5 Pass 4WD SUV	19374	20999	23706
4 Dr Luxury 5 Pass SUV	18021	19617	22277
4 Dr S 5 Pass 4WD SUV	15837	17468	20186
4 Dr S 5 Pass SUV	14397	15993	18653
4 Dr S 7 Pass 4WD SUV	17763	19390	22102
4 Dr S 7 Pass SUV	15954	17580	20289

Options	Price
Overhead Console [Opt on S 5 Psgr]	+150
Power Driver Seat [Opt on S]	+299
Power Passenger Seat [Opt on LS]	+299
Privacy Glass [Opt on S 5 Psgr]	+141
Skid Plates [Opt on Limited 7 Psgr]	+199

A smaller, five-passenger version joins the lineup. The bigger Ascender is pretty much the same as last year, though Isuzu has added a bit of content and fiddled with the option packages. On base 2WD S models, the formerly standard keyless entry and side airbags are now optional. LS models now have a leather-wrapped steering wheel as standard and leather seating, formerly exclusive to the Limited trim, can be ordered as an option. For the Limited, driver-adjustable pedals are new this year.

Isuzu
Ascender/Axiom/Hombre

2003

With its product lineup getting stale, Isuzu has called up the Ascender from the bull pen. Essentially a rebadged GMC Envoy XL, the Ascender offers seating for seven and V8 power.

Mileage Category: M

Body Styles	TMV Pricing		
	Trade	Private	Dealer
4 Dr LS 4WD SUV	18180	19557	21853
4 Dr LS SUV	16877	18155	20286
4 Dr Limited 4WD SUV	20020	21536	24063

Options	Price
5.3L V8 OHV 16V FI Engine [Opt on LS]	+960
Power Driver Seat [Opt on S]	+196

Body Styles	TMV Pricing		
	Trade	Private	Dealer
4 Dr Limited SUV	18314	19702	22014
4 Dr S 4WD SUV	16341	17579	19641
4 Dr S SUV	14961	16094	17983

Options	Price
Power Heated Mirrors [Opt on S]	+126

Axiom

2004

Mileage Category: M

Body Styles	TMV Pricing		
	Trade	Private	Dealer
4 Dr S 4WD SUV	16128	17410	19547
4 Dr S SUV	14294	15549	17641

Options	Price
Compact Disc Changer [Opt on S 2WD]	+350
Leather Steering Wheel	+120
Power Heated Mirrors [Opt on S 2WD]	+180

Body Styles	TMV Pricing		
	Trade	Private	Dealer
4 Dr XS 4WD SUV	17820	19100	21232
4 Dr XS SUV	16352	17607	19699

Options	Price
Power Moonroof [Opt on S]	+1000
Rear Spoiler [Opt on S]	+250

More power is the word for 2004. The Axiom's 3.5-liter V6 engine features new gasoline "direct injection" technology to improve both horsepower and torque. Of a less exciting nature, the audio system doesn't include a tape player anymore and the speaker count drops by two for a total of six. Outside, there's a new chrome finish for the front grille and for the XS model's optional alloy wheels.

2003

There are no major changes for the Axiom this year.

Mileage Category: M

Body Styles	TMV Pricing		
	Trade	Private	Dealer
4 Dr S 4WD SUV	14531	15826	17985
4 Dr S SUV	13093	14260	16206

Options	Price
AM/FM/Cassette/CD Changer Audio System [Opt on S]	+190
Chrome Wheels [Opt on XS]	+254
Luggage Rack	+193

Body Styles	TMV Pricing		
	Trade	Private	Dealer
4 Dr XS 4WD SUV	15571	16959	19272
4 Dr XS SUV	14818	16138	18339

Options	Price
Power Moonroof [Opt on S]	+644
Trailer Hitch	+155

2002

Debuting this year as Isuzu's fifth sport-ute model, the Axiom attempts to blend the rugged nature of a sport-utility with the style and driving dynamics of a sedan. It features a retuned version of the Trooper's 3.5-liter V6, Isuzu's Torque On Demand (TOD) four-wheel-drive system, an Integrated Monitor System (IMS) that controls both the climate control and audio systems and a trick trip computer synchronized with the U.S. Atomic clock.

Mileage Category: M

Body Styles	TMV Pricing		
	Trade	Private	Dealer
4 Dr STD 4WD SUV	11732	13094	15364
4 Dr STD SUV	10707	11950	14022

Options	Price
Leather Seats [Std on XS]	+426

Body Styles	TMV Pricing		
	Trade	Private	Dealer
4 Dr XS 4WD SUV	12639	14107	16553
4 Dr XS SUV	11630	12980	15231

Options	Price
Power Moonroof [Std on XS]	+428

Hombre

2000

Mileage Category: J

Body Styles	TMV Pricing		
	Trade	Private	Dealer
2 Dr S 4WD Std Cab SB	5617	7025	8405
2 Dr S Ext Cab SB	4306	5385	6443
2 Dr S Std Cab SB	3969	4964	5939
2 Dr S V6 4WD Ext Cab SB	5879	7353	8797
2 Dr S V6 Ext Cab SB	5268	6589	7883

Options	Price
AM/FM/CD Audio System	+215
AM/FM/Cassette Audio System [Opt on S,S V6,Std Cab]	+149

Body Styles	TMV Pricing		
	Trade	Private	Dealer
2 Dr XS 4WD Ext Cab SB	6706	8387	10034
2 Dr XS Ext Cab SB	5165	6459	7728
2 Dr XS Std Cab SB	4196	5247	6278
2 Dr XS V6 Ext Cab SB	5579	6978	8349

Options	Price
Air Conditioning [Opt on S,S V6]	+373
Aluminum/Alloy Wheels [Opt on 2WD,XS V6]	+196
Automatic 4-Speed Transmission [Opt on S,XS]	+419

Hombres receive an upgraded standard suspension package and V6 engines get a horsepower boost. The three-door Spacecab gets a bare-bones S trim model.

2000 (cont'd)

Options	Price
Hinged Third Door	+147

1999

Hombres receive additional exterior colors and a new bumper fascia. A three-door spacecab model is now available.

Mileage Category: J

Body Styles	TMV Pricing		
	Trade	Private	Dealer
2 Dr S 4WD Std Cab SB	4190	5352	6561
2 Dr S Std Cab SB	3050	3896	4776
2 Dr XS 4WD Ext Cab SB	5416	6917	8480

Options	Price
AM/FM/CD Audio System	+167
AM/FM/Cassette Audio System	+115
Air Conditioning	+288

Body Styles	TMV Pricing		
	Trade	Private	Dealer
2 Dr XS Ext Cab SB	4182	5342	6549
2 Dr XS Std Cab SB	3344	4271	5236
2 Dr XS V6 Ext Cab SB	4717	6025	7386

Options	Price
Aluminum/Alloy Wheels [Std on 4WD]	+152
Automatic 4-Speed Transmission [Std on XS V6]	+324

1998

Four-wheel drive arrives, finally. Also new are a theft-deterrent system and dual airbags housed in a revised instrument panel, with a passenger-side airbag cutoff switch so the kiddies can ride up front.

Mileage Category: J

Body Styles	TMV Pricing		
	Trade	Private	Dealer
2 Dr S 4WD Std Cab SB	3609	4685	5898
2 Dr S Std Cab SB	2644	3432	4321
2 Dr XS 4WD Ext Cab SB	4636	6017	7575

Options	Price
Air Conditioning	+222

Body Styles	TMV Pricing		
	Trade	Private	Dealer
2 Dr XS Ext Cab SB	3469	4503	5668
2 Dr XS Std Cab SB	2721	3532	4446
2 Dr XS V6 Ext Cab SB	3832	4974	6262

Options	Price
Automatic 4-Speed Transmission [Std on XS V6]	+285

1997

A Spacecab model debuts, with seating for five passengers and your choice of four-cylinder or V6 power. Other news includes two fresh paint colors and revised graphics.

Mileage Category: J

Body Styles	TMV Pricing		
	Trade	Private	Dealer
2 Dr S Std Cab SB	2252	2981	3871
2 Dr XS Ext Cab SB	2873	3803	4939

Options	Price
Air Conditioning	+187

Body Styles	TMV Pricing		
	Trade	Private	Dealer
2 Dr XS Std Cab SB	2295	3038	3945
2 Dr XS V6 Ext Cab SB	3119	4129	5363

Options	Price
Automatic 4-Speed Transmission [Opt on S,XS]	+219

1996

Isuzu clones a Chevy S-10 and dumps its Japanese-built compact truck. Sheet metal is unique to Isuzu, but everything else is pure General Motors.

Mileage Category: J

Body Styles	TMV Pricing		
	Trade	Private	Dealer
2 Dr S Std Cab SB	1864	2521	3428

Options	Price
Air Conditioning	+159

Body Styles	TMV Pricing		
	Trade	Private	Dealer
2 Dr XS Std Cab SB	2028	2742	3728

Oasis

1999

Mileage Category: P

Body Styles	TMV Pricing		
	Trade	Private	Dealer
4 Dr S Pass Van	4784	6140	7551

Options	Price
6 Passenger Seating	+582
AM/FM/CD Audio System	+142

Options	Price
Compact Disc Changer	+171
Power Sunroof	+288

Only one trim level is available for 1999. Oasis has a new seating arrangement, interior and exterior refinements and a couple of new colors.

1998

The engine is upgraded to a more sophisticated 2.3-liter, good for an extra 10 horsepower and 7 pound-feet of torque, and the transmission is revised. A tachometer is now standard, so you can better measure all that extra power.

Body Styles	TMV Pricing		
	Trade	Private	Dealer
4 Dr LS Pass Van	4032	5290	6709

Options	Price
AM/FM/CD Audio System	+125

Body Styles	TMV Pricing		
	Trade	Private	Dealer
4 Dr S Pass Van	3833	5028	6375

Options	Price
Compact Disc Changer	+150

Isuzu
Oasis/Pickup/Rodeo

1997

Cruise control is added to the S model's standard equipment list, and four new colors are available.

Mileage Category: P

Body Styles	TMV Pricing		
	Trade	Private	Dealer
4 Dr LS Pass Van	3614	4830	6316

Body Styles	TMV Pricing		
	Trade	Private	Dealer
4 Dr S Pass Van	3323	4441	5807

1996

New Isuzu minivan is a clone of the Honda Odyssey, except for the grille, badging and wheels. The Isuzu offers a better warranty, too.

Mileage Category: P

Body Styles	TMV Pricing		
	Trade	Private	Dealer
4 Dr LS Pass Van	3282	4341	5803

Body Styles	TMV Pricing		
	Trade	Private	Dealer
4 Dr S Pass Van	2898	3833	5123

Pickup
1995

Mileage Category: J

Body Styles	TMV Pricing		
	Trade	Private	Dealer
2 Dr S 4WD Std Cab SB	1968	2682	3872
2 Dr S Std Cab LB	1415	1928	2783

Body Styles	TMV Pricing		
	Trade	Private	Dealer
2 Dr S Std Cab SB	1305	1778	2566

Options	Price
Air Conditioning	+139

Spacecab, V6 power and automatic transmission are canceled for 1995. All that's left are four-cylinder regular-cab trucks in 2WD or 4WD. California didn't get any 1995 Pickups, thanks to strict emissions regulations.

Rodeo
2004

Mileage Category: M

Body Styles	TMV Pricing		
	Trade	Private	Dealer
4 Dr S 4WD SUV	10575	11770	13761

Body Styles	TMV Pricing		
	Trade	Private	Dealer
4 Dr S SUV	9200	10395	12386

Options	Price
3.5L V6 DOHC 24V FI Engine	+2870
Air Conditioning	+500
Aluminum/Alloy Wheels	+400
Automatic 4-Speed Transmission [Std on 4WD]	+1150

Options	Price
Luggage Rack	+220
Power Door Locks	+200
Power Windows	+280

Isuzu has made a few changes this year to make the Rodeo more appealing to SUV shoppers. First off, there's a new range-topping 3.5-liter V6 that makes 250 horsepower. Last year's 3.2-liter V6 has a new home in the base model; the four-cylinder engine has been dropped. Other alterations this year include a new Sound Package, a new Color Package and a new tire-pressure monitoring system.

2003

Rodeo receives no major changes for the 2003 model year.

Mileage Category: M

Body Styles	TMV Pricing		
	Trade	Private	Dealer
4 Dr S SUV	7020	7798	9094
4 Dr S V6 4WD SUV	9813	10900	12712

Body Styles	TMV Pricing		
	Trade	Private	Dealer
4 Dr S V6 SUV	8561	9510	11090

Options	Price
AM/FM/CD Changer Audio System [Opt on V6]	+225
AM/FM/Cassette/CD Changer Audio System [Opt on V6]	+271
Air Conditioning	+531
Aluminum/Alloy Wheels [Opt on V6]	+258
Automatic 4-Speed Transmission [Opt on S,V6 4WD]	+644
Leather Seats [Opt on V6]	+512
Luggage Rack [Opt on V6]	+126

Options	Price
Power Door Locks [Opt on V6]	+138
Power Driver Seat [Opt on V6]	+196
Power Moonroof [Opt on V6]	+451
Power Windows [Opt on V6]	+177
Running Boards	+213
Side Steps	+206
Trailer Hitch	+155

2002

For 2002, Isuzu has fiddled with the Rodeo's option packages and improved the available Intelligent Suspension Control (ISC) system.

Mileage Category: M

Body Styles	TMV Pricing		
	Trade	Private	Dealer
4 Dr LS 4WD SUV	9899	11048	12964
4 Dr LS SUV	8887	9919	11639
4 Dr LSE 4WD SUV	10091	11263	13215
4 Dr LSE SUV	9950	11105	13031

Body Styles	TMV Pricing		
	Trade	Private	Dealer
4 Dr S SUV	5658	6315	7410
4 Dr S V6 4WD SUV	8010	8940	10491
4 Dr S V6 SUV	7944	8867	10404

2002 (cont'd)

Options	Price
18 Inch Wheels - Chrome [Opt on LS 4WD]	+392
Air Conditioning [Opt on S,S V6]	+452
Aluminum/Alloy Wheels [Opt on LS]	+190
Automatic 4-Speed Transmission [Opt on S,S V6]	+475
Electronic Suspension Control [Opt on LS 4WD]	+357

Options	Price
Power Moonroof [Opt on LS]	+333
Power Windows [Opt on S V6]	+131
Running Boards	+157
Side Steps	+119

2001

An Anniversary Edition trim package that includes two-tone paint, leather seating and special chrome wheels is the only addition to 2001 Rodeos.

Mileage Category: M

Body Styles	TMV Pricing		
	Trade	Private	Dealer
4 Dr LS 4WD SUV	7130	8463	9693
4 Dr LS SUV	6414	7613	8719
4 Dr LSE 4WD SUV	8604	10212	11696
4 Dr LSE SUV	7296	8660	9919

Body Styles	TMV Pricing		
	Trade	Private	Dealer
4 Dr S SUV	4810	5709	6538
4 Dr S V6 4WD SUV	6540	7763	8891
4 Dr S V6 SUV	6248	7415	8493

Options	Price
AM/FM/Cassette/CD Changer Audio System [Opt on LS]	+142
Air Conditioning [Std on LS,LSE]	+382
Aluminum/Alloy Wheels [Std on LS,LSE]	+161
Automatic 4-Speed Transmission [Std on LSE]	+402
Leather Seats [Opt on LS]	+402

Options	Price
Nakamichi Audio System [Opt on LS]	+362
Power Moonroof [Opt on LS]	+281
t on S]	+121
Running Boards	+145
Two-Tone Paint [Opt on LS]	+121

2000

The Rodeo marches into the 2000 model year with an aggressive exterior restyle, a collection of ergonomic and quality improvements and interior upgrades.

Mileage Category: M

Body Styles	TMV Pricing		
	Trade	Private	Dealer
4 Dr LS 4WD SUV	5966	7359	8725
4 Dr LS SUV	5364	6616	7844
4 Dr LSE 4WD SUV	7120	8782	10412
4 Dr LSE SUV	6076	7495	8886

Body Styles	TMV Pricing		
	Trade	Private	Dealer
4 Dr S SUV	4037	4980	5904
4 Dr S V6 4WD SUV	5405	6667	7904
4 Dr S V6 SUV	4686	5780	6853

Options	Price
AM/FM/CD Audio System	+145
AM/FM/Cassette/CD Audio System	+167
Air Conditioning [Std on LS,LSE]	+373
Automatic 4-Speed Transmission [Std on LSE]	+392
Brush Guard	+117

Options	Price
Compact Disc Changer [Std on LSE]	+254
Ironman Package	+412
Power Moonroof [Opt on LS]	+274
Running Boards	+141
Side Steps	+139

1999

Isuzu juggles minor standard and optional equipment for 1999, making items from last year's S V6 preferred equipment package standard on the LS, and last year's LS equipment standard on a new trim level called LSE.

Mileage Category: M

Body Styles	TMV Pricing		
	Trade	Private	Dealer
4 Dr LS 4WD SUV	4819	6164	7564
4 Dr LS SUV	4292	5490	6737
4 Dr LSE 4WD SUV	5562	7114	8730
4 Dr LSE SUV	5044	6451	7916

Body Styles	TMV Pricing		
	Trade	Private	Dealer
4 Dr S SUV	3260	4170	5118
4 Dr S V6 4WD SUV	4383	5606	6878
4 Dr S V6 SUV	3791	4849	5950

Options	Price
AM/FM/Cassette/CD Audio System	+129
Air Conditioning [Std on LS,LSE]	+288
Automatic 4-Speed Transmission [Std on LSE 4WD]	+303

Options	Price
Compact Disc Changer	+197
Power Moonroof [Opt on LS]	+212

1998

Though it may not look like it, Isuzu has completely revised the Rodeo from top to bottom, giving it more modern styling, a user-friendly interior, more V6 power and added room for passengers and cargo.

Mileage Category: M

Body Styles	TMV Pricing		
	Trade	Private	Dealer
4 Dr LS 4WD SUV	4108	5426	6913
4 Dr LS SUV	3604	4760	6064
4 Dr S SUV	2445	3229	4114

Body Styles	TMV Pricing		
	Trade	Private	Dealer
4 Dr S V6 4WD SUV	3149	4160	5299
4 Dr S V6 SUV	2841	3752	4780

Options	Price
Air Conditioning [Std on LS]	+253
Automatic 4-Speed Transmission [Std on LS]	+266
Compact Disc Changer	+173

Options	Price
Leather Seats	+265
Power Moonroof	+186

1997

Mileage Category: M

Body Styles	TMV Pricing		
	Trade	Private	Dealer
4 Dr LS 4WD SUV	2919	3903	5105
4 Dr LS SUV	2775	3709	4850
4 Dr S SUV	1907	2550	3335

Options	Price
Air Conditioning [Std on LS]	+213
Antilock Brakes	+179
Automatic 4-Speed Transmission [Opt on 4WD,S V6]	+217

Body Styles	TMV Pricing		
	Trade	Private	Dealer
4 Dr S V6 4WD SUV	2488	3326	4350
4 Dr S V6 SUV	2265	3028	3961

Options	Price
Compact Disc Changer	+145
Leather Seats	+267

All 4WD models get a standard shift-on-the-fly transfer case, and improvements have been made to reduce noise, vibration and harshness.

1996

Finally, Isuzu's Rodeo can be equipped with four-wheel antilock brakes, and 4WD models get a standard shift-on-the-fly system. New style wheels debut, and the engine now makes 190 horsepower. Increased wheel track improves ride quality, and spare tire covers are redesigned.

Mileage Category: M

Body Styles	TMV Pricing		
	Trade	Private	Dealer
4 Dr LS 4WD SUV	2564	3439	4648
4 Dr LS SUV	2493	3344	4518
4 Dr S SUV	1719	2306	3116

Options	Price
Air Conditioning [Std on LS]	+180
Aluminum/Alloy Wheels [Std on LS]	+152
Antilock Brakes	+152

Body Styles	TMV Pricing		
	Trade	Private	Dealer
4 Dr S V6 4WD SUV	2223	2982	4029
4 Dr S V6 SUV	2028	2719	3674

Options	Price
Automatic 4-Speed Transmission [Opt on 4WD,S V6]	+184
Compact Disc Changer	+124
Leather Seats	+227

1995

Midyear change gives the Rodeo driver and passenger airbags in a redesigned dashboard. S V6 models can be equipped with a Bright Package that includes lots of chrome trim and aluminum wheels.

Mileage Category: M

Body Styles	TMV Pricing		
	Trade	Private	Dealer
4 Dr LS 4WD SUV	2039	2796	4057
4 Dr LS SUV	1897	2601	3774
4 Dr S 4WD SUV	1720	2358	3421

Options	Price
Air Conditioning [Std on LS]	+165
Antilock Brakes	+139
Automatic 4-Speed Transmission [Opt on 4WD,S,S V6]	+168

Body Styles	TMV Pricing		
	Trade	Private	Dealer
4 Dr S SUV	1346	1846	2678
4 Dr S V6 SUV	1613	2212	3210

Options	Price
Compact Disc Changer	+113

Rodeo Sport

2003

Isuzu's two-door Rodeo Sport SUV is unchanged for 2003.

Mileage Category: L

Body Styles	TMV Pricing		
	Trade	Private	Dealer
2 Dr S Conv	7477	8387	9903
2 Dr S SUV	7906	8868	10471

Options	Price
Air Conditioning	+644
Aluminum/Alloy Wheels [Opt on V6]	+290
Limited Slip Differential [Opt on V6 4WD]	+161
Power Door Locks [Opt on V6]	+138

Body Styles	TMV Pricing		
	Trade	Private	Dealer
2 Dr S V6 4WD SUV	9190	10308	12171
2 Dr S V6 SUV	8442	9469	11180

Options	Price
Power Windows [Opt on V6]	+158
Side Steps	+206
Trailer Hitch	+145

2002

Other than new 16-inch wheels, Isuzu's two-door Rodeo Sport SUV is unchanged for 2002.

Mileage Category: L

Body Styles	TMV Pricing		
	Trade	Private	Dealer
2 Dr S Conv	6088	6948	8380
2 Dr S SUV	6011	6860	8276
2 Dr S V6 4WD Conv	8683	9909	11953

Options	Price
AM/FM/CD Changer Audio System [Opt on S V6]	+178
AM/FM/Cassette/CD Changer Audio System [Opt on S V6]	+178

Body Styles	TMV Pricing		
	Trade	Private	Dealer
2 Dr S V6 4WD SUV	7417	8465	10211
2 Dr S V6 Conv	6865	7835	9451
2 Dr S V6 SUV	6818	7781	9386

Options	Price
Air Conditioning	+378
Aluminum/Alloy Wheels	+214
Automatic 4-Speed Transmission [Opt on S 2 Dr]	+475

2002 (cont'd)

Options	Price
Side Steps	+152

2001

Formerly the Amigo, Isuzu's two-door sport-ute gets a name change and two new colors. A wheezing four-cylinder automatic with either a hard- or soft top is also new for 2001.

Mileage Category: L

Body Styles	TMV Pricing		
	Trade	Private	Dealer
2 Dr STD Conv	4752	5897	6954
2 Dr STD SUV	4576	5678	6696
2 Dr V6 4WD Conv	5989	7431	8763

Options	Price
AM/FM/Cassette/CD Changer Audio System [Opt on V6]	+142
Air Conditioning	+382
Aluminum/Alloy Wheels	+161

Body Styles	TMV Pricing		
	Trade	Private	Dealer
2 Dr V6 4WD SUV	5990	7432	8764
2 Dr V6 Conv	5428	6736	7944
2 Dr V6 SUV	5352	6642	7832

Options	Price
Automatic 4-Speed Transmission [Std on V6]	+402
Power Windows	+121
Running Boards	+143

Trooper

2002

Mileage Category: M

Body Styles	TMV Pricing		
	Trade	Private	Dealer
4 Dr LS 4WD SUV	10896	12161	14269
4 Dr LS SUV	10569	11796	13842
4 Dr Limited 4WD SUV	12924	14425	16926

Options	Price
Automatic 4-Speed Transmission [Opt on S 4WD]	+404
Rear Spoiler [Opt on Limited]	+159
Running Boards [Opt on LS,S]	+152

Body Styles	TMV Pricing		
	Trade	Private	Dealer
4 Dr Limited SUV	12535	13990	16416
4 Dr S 4WD SUV	9428	10523	12347
4 Dr S SUV	8558	9552	11208

Options	Price
Side Steps [Opt on LS,S]	+152
Special Factory Paint [Opt on Limited]	+250

The flagship of the Isuzu line, the Trooper, receives minor changes for 2002. Privacy glass and solar green UV-cut glass are now standard for S models, and Trooper's famous extra-large power moonroof is now standard for the LS. Manual climate control and map lamps are now standard on S models, while LS models feature a new standard digital clock with outside temperature read-out, stop watch, average speed and service reminder. The Limited model now offers a Nakamichi premium audio system.

2001

An Anniversary package commemorating Isuzu's 85th year is the only new option for 2001 Troopers.

Mileage Category: M

Body Styles	TMV Pricing		
	Trade	Private	Dealer
4 Dr LS 4WD SUV	8558	10158	11634
4 Dr LS SUV	8130	9649	11052
4 Dr Limited 4WD SUV	9602	11396	13052

Options	Price
Automatic 4-Speed Transmission [Opt on S]	+623
Leather Seats [Opt on LS]	+493
Nakamichi Audio System [Opt on LS]	+362

Body Styles	TMV Pricing		
	Trade	Private	Dealer
4 Dr Limited SUV	9017	10702	12257
4 Dr S 4WD SUV	7618	9042	10356
4 Dr S SUV	7422	8809	10089

Options	Price
Pearlescent Metallic Paint	+181
Power Moonroof [Opt on LS]	+442
Running Boards	+136

2000

A two-wheel-drive model is available in the S trim, as well as the new midlevel LS and top-level Limited guises; all receive slight exterior restyling. The 10-year/120,000-mile powertrain warranty, the longest in America, ensures longevity.

Body Styles	TMV Pricing		
	Trade	Private	Dealer
4 Dr LS 4WD SUV	6885	8493	10069
4 Dr LS SUV	6381	7871	9332
4 Dr Limited 4WD SUV	7691	9487	11248

Options	Price
AM/FM/CD Audio System	+215
AM/FM/Cassette/CD Audio System	+245
Automatic 4-Speed Transmission [Opt on S]	+588
Brush Guard	+154

Body Styles	TMV Pricing		
	Trade	Private	Dealer
4 Dr Limited SUV	7461	9203	10911
4 Dr S 4WD SUV	6086	7508	8901
4 Dr S SUV	6016	7420	8797

Options	Price
Compact Disc Changer [Opt on S]	+254
Power Moonroof [Opt on LS]	+431
Running Boards	+133
Side Steps	+133

1999

A gold trim package is added to the Trooper's option list and Torque on Demand is now standard with the automatic transmission.

Mileage Category: M

Body Styles	TMV Pricing		
	Trade	Private	Dealer
4 Dr S 4WD SUV	4716	6032	7402

Trooper

1999 (cont'd)

Options	Price
AM/FM/CD Audio System	+167
AM/FM/Cassette/CD Audio System	+190
Automatic 4-Speed Transmission	+424

Options	Price
Compact Disc Changer	+197
Leather Seats	+379
Power Moonroof	+333

1998

A bigger and lighter engine provides huge improvements in horsepower and torque (up 13 and 22 percent, respectively). And the new Torque On Demand (TOD) drive system replaces conventional four-high mode for better performance on paved or slippery roads.

Mileage Category: M

Body Styles	TMV Pricing		
	Trade	Private	Dealer
4 Dr Luxury 4WD SUV	4859	6419	8178

Body Styles	TMV Pricing		
	Trade	Private	Dealer
4 Dr S 4WD SUV	4062	5366	6836

Options	Price
AM/FM/CD Audio System	+147
AM/FM/Cassette/CD Audio System	+166
Automatic 4-Speed Transmission [Opt on S]	+370
Compact Disc Changer [Opt on S]	+173

Options	Price
Leather Seats [Opt on S]	+318
Performance/Handling Package	+296
Power Moonroof [Opt on S]	+325

1997

Antilock brakes are now standard on all models, and dealers get a wider profit margin to help increase sales. Despite delirious requests by a certain consumer group, Isuzu will not equip the Trooper with training wheels for 1997.

Mileage Category: M

Body Styles	TMV Pricing		
	Trade	Private	Dealer
4 Dr LS 4WD SUV	3873	5178	6773
4 Dr Limited 4WD SUV	4154	5554	7265

Body Styles	TMV Pricing		
	Trade	Private	Dealer
4 Dr S 4WD SUV	3554	4751	6215

Options	Price
AM/FM/CD Audio System	+123
Air Conditioning [Opt on S]	+179
Automatic 4-Speed Transmission [Opt on S]	+280

Options	Price
Compact Disc Changer [Opt on S]	+145
Leather Seats [Opt on LS]	+280
Power Moonroof [Opt on LS]	+246

1996

More standard equipment, a horsepower boost for the SOHC V6 engine, and standard shift-on-the-fly debut for 1996.

Mileage Category: M

Body Styles	TMV Pricing		
	Trade	Private	Dealer
4 Dr LS 4WD SUV	3165	4245	5736
4 Dr Limited 4WD SUV	3801	5098	6889

Body Styles	TMV Pricing		
	Trade	Private	Dealer
4 Dr S 4WD SUV	2828	3793	5126
4 Dr SE 4WD SUV	3940	5284	7140

Options	Price
Air Conditioning [Opt on S]	+152
Antilock Brakes [Opt on LS,S]	+228
Automatic 4-Speed Transmission [Opt on S]	+237

Options	Price
Compact Disc Changer [Opt on LS,S]	+124
Leather Seats [Opt on LS]	+237
Power Moonroof [Opt on LS]	+209

1995

Dual airbags are standard. Styling is revised. A new top-of-the-line trim level debuts. The Limited has a power sunroof, leather upholstery, heated seats and wood grain trim. Suspensions have been reworked to provide a better ride.

Mileage Category: M

Body Styles	TMV Pricing		
	Trade	Private	Dealer
2 Dr RS 4WD SUV	2483	3406	4943
4 Dr LS 4WD SUV	2498	3425	4971
4 Dr Limited 4WD SUV	2984	4092	5939

Body Styles	TMV Pricing		
	Trade	Private	Dealer
4 Dr S 4WD SUV	2296	3148	4568
4 Dr SE 4WD SUV	2956	4053	5882

Options	Price
AM/FM/CD Audio System	+95
Air Conditioning [Opt on S]	+139
Aluminum/Alloy Wheels [Opt on S]	+80
Antilock Brakes [Opt on S]	+208

Options	Price
Automatic 4-Speed Transmission [Opt on LS,S,RS]	+217
Compact Disc Changer [Opt on S,SE]	+113
Premium Audio System [Opt on S]	+78

VehiCROSS

2001

Body Styles	TMV Pricing		
	Trade	Private	Dealer
2 Dr STD 4WD SUV	9848	11688	13387

Options	Price
Luggage Rack	+117

Mileage Category: M

Rear child seat-tether anchors are the only new additions for 2001.

2000

Body Styles	TMV Pricing		
	Trade	Private	Dealer
2 Dr STD 4WD SUV	7507	9260	10979

Options	Price
Ironman Package	+390

Mileage Category: M

Fat 18-inch wheels replace the previous 16-inchers. The new year also brings standard A/C, new exterior colors and a 10-year/120,000-mile powertrain warranty, the longest in America.

1999

Body Styles	TMV Pricing		
	Trade	Private	Dealer
2 Dr STD 4WD SUV	6043	7730	9485

Options	Price
Ironman Package	+302

Mileage Category: M

Isuzu imports its unique-looking SUV to the U.S. in 1999.

Jaguar
S-Type

S-Type

2004

Jaguar adds adaptive cruise control to the options list, and a six-speed automatic transmission is now standard on the V6 version -- the five-speed manual remains a no-cost option.

Mileage Category: I

Body Styles	TMV Pricing		
	Trade	Private	Dealer
4 Dr 3.0 Sdn	25370	26941	29557

Options	Price
Adaptive Cruise Control	+2200
Automatic Dimming Rearview Mirror [Opt on 3.0]	+200
Automatic Dimming Sideview Mirror(s) [Opt on 3.0]	+220
Garage Door Opener [Opt on 3.0]	+150
Heated Front and Rear Seats	+500
Navigation System	+2300
Power Adjustable Foot Pedals [Opt on 3.0]	+250

Body Styles	TMV Pricing		
	Trade	Private	Dealer
4 Dr 4.2 Sdn	28580	30150	32766

Options	Price
Power Driver Seat w/Memory [Opt on 3.0]	+375
Power Moonroof [Opt on 3.0]	+1100
Premium Audio System	+1600
Rain Sensing Windshield Wipers [Opt on 3.0]	+300
Special Interior Trim	+1000
Sport Package	+1200
Xenon Headlamps	+675

2003

For the 2003 S-Type, Jaguar has redesigned the interior, upgraded its hardware and added models to the range. The model lineup includes the S-Type 3.0 SE and 3.0 Sport, 4.2 V8 and the supercharged R. The S-Type R is the most powerful Jaguar sedan ever created, making about 400 horsepower and moving from rest to 60 mph in 5.3 seconds. A new five-speed manual transmission is attached to the 3.0-liter V6 this year, while a new six-speed automatic transmission puts V8 power to the rear wheels. The suspension is also new in front and heavily revised in the rear. New standard safety features include stability control, panic assist brakes, anti-whiplash front seats, dual-stage front airbags, side curtain airbags for front and rear occupants and power adjustable pedals with a memory feature. Jaguar has also stiffened the body structure, made slight revisions to the exterior styling and added xenon headlights as an option (standard on the R). Audiophiles can opt for the 320-watt Alpine sound system, and technology buffs will appreciate the new touchscreen telematics system with improved voice recognition.

Mileage Category: I

Body Styles	TMV Pricing		
	Trade	Private	Dealer
4 Dr 3.0 Sdn	21544	22880	25105

Options	Price
Alpine Audio System	+1202
Automatic 6-Speed Transmission [Opt on 3.0]	+922
Automatic Dimming Rearview Mirror [Opt on 3.0]	+120
Automatic Dimming Sideview Mirror(s) [Opt on 3.0]	+134
Heated Front and Rear Seats	+334
Navigation System	+1469
Power Adjustable Foot Pedals [Opt on 3.0]	+167

Body Styles	TMV Pricing		
	Trade	Private	Dealer
4 Dr 4.2 Sdn	25583	27168	29811

Options	Price
Power Driver Seat w/Memory [Opt on 3.0]	+167
Power Moonroof [Opt on 3.0]	+735
Rain Sensing Windshield Wipers [Opt on 3.0]	+134
Sport Package	+1336
Voice Recognition System	+1503
Xenon Headlamps	+451

2002

Jaguar's standard S-Type model comes tinted in three new hues for 2002: Aspen Green, Quartz and Zircon. The car also features a nifty new enhancement with regard to its cupholders: rear cupholders now deploy from the rear-seat cushion, putting them in a more easily accessed position for passengers. The manufacturer tosses performance hounds a tasty new bone with the addition of an S-Type Sport trim level, which comes with a choice of either a 3.0-liter V6 or 4.0-liter V8 engine. Its suspension reflects its performance aspirations; Computer Active Technology Suspension (CATS) ramps up handling with shock-absorber settings that automatically adjust to reflect road conditions. Additionally, a brand-new shade -- Pacific Blue -- is available only in Sport.

Mileage Category: I

Body Styles	TMV Pricing		
	Trade	Private	Dealer
4 Dr 3.0 Sdn	17509	18951	21355

Options	Price
17 Inch Wheels	+444
Automatic Stability Control	+296
Electronic Suspension Control	+266
Heated Front Seats	+169
Navigation System	+1125

Body Styles	TMV Pricing		
	Trade	Private	Dealer
4 Dr 4.0 Sdn	19340	20932	23587

Options	Price
Power Driver Seat w/Memory [Opt on 3.0]	+130
Power Moonroof [Opt on 3.0]	+562
Premium Audio System [Opt on 3.0]	+888
Rain Sensing Windshield Wipers	+118
Telematics System	+414

2001

The S-Type gets new 10-spoke alloy wheels for 2001, along with exterior color options Onyx White and Roman Bronze. The folks at Jaguar have decided to move the six-disc CD changer from the glovebox to the trunk. ISOFIX is added to the rear for securing child seats and Reverse Park Control now comes standard. An electronically controlled, speed-proportional power steering system is new this year and the software for the Voice Activation Control system has been upgraded. A Deluxe Communications Package featuring a Motorola Timeport digital phone system is a new option.

Mileage Category: I

Body Styles	TMV Pricing		
	Trade	Private	Dealer
4 Dr 3.0 Sdn	14821	16660	18357

Options	Price
17 Inch Wheels	+256
Automatic Stability Control [Opt on 3.0]	+256
Compact Disc Changer	+409
Electronic Suspension Control	+230
Heated Front Seats	+146

Body Styles	TMV Pricing		
	Trade	Private	Dealer
4 Dr 4.0 Sdn	15928	17904	19729

Options	Price
Navigation System	+972
Power Moonroof [Opt on 3.0]	+486
Premium Audio System [Opt on 3.0]	+767
Sport Package	+563

2000

From the ground up, this is a completely new sport sedan based on the new Ford midsize platform. Lincoln worked with Jaguar to develop this platform, which is also used for Lincoln's LS sedan.

Mileage Category: I

Body Styles	TMV Pricing		
	Trade	Private	Dealer
4 Dr 3.0 Sdn	12479	14341	16167

Body Styles	TMV Pricing		
	Trade	Private	Dealer
4 Dr 4.0 Sdn	12752	14655	16520

Options	Price
Automatic Stability Control	+213
Compact Disc Changer	+341
Heated Front Seats	+121
Navigation System	+809
Park Distance Control (Rear)	+170

Options	Price
Power Driver Seat w/Memory [Opt on 3.0]	+128
Power Moonroof [Opt on 3.0]	+405
Power Passenger Seat w/Memory [Opt on 3.0]	+128
Premium Audio System	+298
Sport Package	+445

S-Type R

2004

Mileage Category: I

Body Styles	TMV Pricing		
	Trade	Private	Dealer
4 Dr S/C Sdn	40467	42571	46077

Options	Price
Navigation System	+2300

Options	Price
Special Interior Trim	+1000

No major changes for 2004.

2003

Mileage Category: I

Body Styles	TMV Pricing		
	Trade	Private	Dealer
4 Dr S/C Sdn	33719	35808	39291

Options	Price
Navigation System	+1469

Options	Price
Voice Recognition System	+1503

The muscle-bound S-Type R debuts. The S-Type R is the most powerful Jaguar sedan ever created, making about 400 horsepower and moving from rest to 60 mph in 5.3 seconds. A new six-speed automatic transmission puts the considerable power to the rear wheels. This super cat also benefits from the upgrades that all S-Types received this year, namely a revamped cabin, revised suspension and more safety features. Technology buffs will appreciate the new touchscreen telematics system with improved voice recognition.

X-Type

2004

Mileage Category: H

Body Styles	TMV Pricing		
	Trade	Private	Dealer
4 Dr 2.5 AWD Sdn	17040	18212	20165

Body Styles	TMV Pricing		
	Trade	Private	Dealer
4 Dr 3.0 AWD Sdn	21034	22144	23995

Options	Price
18 Inch Wheels	+3000
AM/FM/CD Changer Audio System [Opt on 3.0]	+600
Automatic 5-Speed Transmission [Opt on 2.5]	+1650
Garage Door Opener [Opt on 3.0]	+150
Heated Front Seats	+500
Metallic Paint	+595
Navigation System	+2300

Options	Price
Park Distance Control (Rear)	+325
Power Moonroof	+1000
Power Passenger Seat	+325
Rain Sensing Windshield Wipers	+200
Split Folding Rear Seat	+750
Trip Computer	+200
Xenon Headlamps	+675

For 2004, Jaguar has reduced the base price of the X-Type 3.0 by almost $3,000. In other news, the Sport Package now includes 18-inch wheels and a 320-watt sound system. All X-Types get redesigned alloy wheels, as well as a revised front bumper and new foglights. The trunk lid has been reshaped and the push-button release for the trunk is now easier to operate.

2003

Mileage Category: H

Body Styles	TMV Pricing		
	Trade	Private	Dealer
4 Dr 2.5 AWD Sdn	15519	16775	18868

Body Styles	TMV Pricing		
	Trade	Private	Dealer
4 Dr 3.0 AWD Sdn	18258	19735	22197

Options	Price
17 Inch Wheels [Opt on 2.5]	+301
18 Inch Wheels	+2004
AM/FM/CD Audio System [Opt on 2.5]	+134
Alpine Audio System	+367
Automatic Stability Control	+267
Compact Disc Changer	+401
Heated Front Seats	+200
Leather and Wood Steering Wheel	+167
Navigation System	+1469
Park Distance Control (Rear)	+200

Options	Price
Power Moonroof	+601
Power Passenger Seat	+217
Rain Sensing Windshield Wipers	+134
Rear Spoiler	+150
Special Factory Paint	+384
Split Folding Rear Seat	+184
Sport Seats	+177
Sport Suspension	+184
Telematics System	+1102
Trip Computer	+134

Jaguar introduced its youth-oriented X-Type last year, so 2003 holds little changes for the baby Jag. There's a slight reduction in the price of the base model, and electrochromic mirrors are standard on all trim levels. Cars equipped with the 3.0-liter mill now get 17-inch wheels and a CD player as standard equipment.

Jaguar
X-Type/XJ-Series

2003 (cont'd)

Options	Price
Xenon Headlamps	+451

2002

Jaguar beefs up its presence in the luxury category with the X-Type, a brand-new model that brings the company's range to four. The X-Type is a fresh breed of cat for the manufacturer: it's Jaguar's first-ever all-wheel-drive vehicle, and it's priced to tap the entry-luxury segment.

Mileage Category: H

Body Styles	TMV Pricing			Body Styles	TMV Pricing		
	Trade	Private	Dealer		Trade	Private	Dealer
4 Dr 2.5 AWD Sdn	13596	14835	16901	4 Dr 3.0 AWD Sdn	15571	16990	19356

Options	Price	Options	Price
17 Inch Wheels	+266	Power Moonroof	+533
AM/FM/CD Audio System	+118	Power Passenger Seat	+192
Alpine Audio System	+326	Rain Sensing Windshield Wipers	+118
Automatic 5-Speed Transmission [Opt on 2.5]	+755	Rear Spoiler	+133
Automatic Stability Control	+237	Split Folding Rear Seat	+163
Compact Disc Changer	+355	Sport Seats	+157
Heated Front Seats	+192	Sport Suspension	+163
Metallic Paint	+326	Telematics System	+888
Navigation System	+1302	Trip Computer	+118
Park Distance Control (Rear)	+237	Xenon Headlamps	+400

XJ-Series

2004

Although the exterior styling may look familiar, Jaguar's historic sales leader, the XJ, has been completely redesigned for 2004.

Mileage Category: I

Body Styles	TMV Pricing			Body Styles	TMV Pricing		
	Trade	Private	Dealer		Trade	Private	Dealer
4 Dr Vanden Plas Sdn	41441	43008	45619	4 Dr XJ8 Sdn	35806	37374	39986

Options	Price	Options	Price
18 Inch Wheels [Opt on XJ8]	+800	Navigation System	+2300
Alpine Audio System [Opt on XJ8]	+1000	Park Distance Control (Front and Rear)	+250
Automatic Climate Control (4 Zone)	+1000	Power Rear Seat [Opt on Vanden Plas]	+1750
DVD Entertainment System [Opt on Vanden Plas]	+2000	Power Rear Window Sunshade [Opt on XJ8]	+450
Headlight Washers	+200	Rear Audio Controls [Opt on Vanden Plas]	+650
Heated Front and Rear Seats [Opt on XJ8]	+950	Special Interior Trim	+1000
Heated Steering Wheel	+200	Xenon Headlamps [Opt on XJ8]	+675

2003

Mileage Category: I

Body Styles	TMV Pricing			Body Styles	TMV Pricing		
	Trade	Private	Dealer		Trade	Private	Dealer
4 Dr Super V8 S/C Sdn	42523	45028	49202	4 Dr XJ Sport Sdn	28703	30362	33128
4 Dr Vanden Plas Sdn	33147	35063	38256	4 Dr XJ8 Sdn	25461	26932	29385

Options	Price	Options	Price
Alpine Audio System [Opt on XJ,XJ8]	+217	Leather and Wood Steering Wheel [Opt on XJ8]	+167
Heated Front and Rear Seats [Opt on XJ,XJ8]	+334	Navigation System [Opt on Vanden Plas]	+1135

In its final year of production, the current-generation XJ receives two new packages. XJ8s have the option of the Sovereign Package, offered with an Alpine premium sound system and six-disc changer, heated front and rear seats, wood and leather steering wheel and gearshift knob, boxwood-inlaid walnut trim, chrome grille and splitter, chrome mirror caps and door handles and special wheels. Meanwhile the XJR can be optioned with the R1 Performance Package, which includes Brembo brakes and 18-inch modular wheels.

2002

A new XJ Sport trim debuts, which melds elements of the XJ8 and XJR. Additionally, the Vanden Plas Supercharged model -- previously available only on special order -- is now a regular-production sedan, called Super V8. The long-wheelbase XJ8L is discontinued.

Mileage Category: I

Body Styles	TMV Pricing			Body Styles	TMV Pricing		
	Trade	Private	Dealer		Trade	Private	Dealer
4 Dr Super V8 S/C Sdn	38685	41004	44868	4 Dr XJ Sport Sdn	25375	26919	29491
4 Dr Vanden Plas Sdn	27230	28908	31704	4 Dr XJ8 Sdn	21364	22664	24829

Options	Price	Options	Price
Heated Front and Rear Seats [Opt on XJ8,XJ Sport]	+296	Premium Audio System [Opt on XJ8,XJ Sport]	+592
Navigation System	+1006		

2001

Jaguar's premium sedan receives only minor content changes for 2001. The XJ8 and XJ8 L both receive a six-disc CD changer as standard equipment. The Vanden Plas gets a premium sound system with the CD changer as standard, as well as heated front and rear seats. The navigation system is standard on the Vanden Plas Supercharged. For all models, Jaguar has added a new reverse parking control system and strengthened the chassis with new crush tubes, doors, hinges and steering columns. There are also new exterior colors, a new style of wheel for Vanden Plas models and an optional dealer-installed Motorola Timeport digital phone. Topping things off is a new no-cost scheduled maintenance program that covers four regular service visits under the four-year/50,000-mile limited warranty.

Mileage Category: I

Body Styles	TMV Pricing		
	Trade	Private	Dealer
4 Dr Vanden Plas S/C Sdn	32413	35632	38603
4 Dr Vanden Plas Sdn	21620	23802	25817

Options	Price
Alpine Audio System [Opt on XJ8,XJL]	+512

Body Styles	TMV Pricing		
	Trade	Private	Dealer
4 Dr XJ8 Sdn	17699	19485	21135
4 Dr XJ8L Sdn	20222	22264	24148

Options	Price
Navigation System	+870

2000

A fifth model -- the supercharged Vanden Plas -- has been added. All XJ8 Sedans gain all-speed traction control, improved ABS, rain-sensing windshield wipers, and child seat-anchor brackets as standard equipment. A new navigation system is being offered as optional equipment, as is an upgraded 320-watt Alpine system. The anti-theft system now has an encrypted key transponder. There are two new exterior colors and one new interior color. The XJR gains all-speed traction control, improved ABS, rain-sensing windshield wipers, child seat-anchor brackets and an upgraded 320-watt Alpine system as standard equipment. A new navigation system is being offered as optional equipment. The anti-theft system now has an encrypted key transponder. The XJR also gets new 18-inch wheels and a different new style for the seats.

Mileage Category: I

Body Styles	TMV Pricing		
	Trade	Private	Dealer
4 Dr Vanden Plas S/C Sdn	23400	26040	28627
4 Dr Vanden Plas Sdn	14665	16448	18196

Options	Price
Compact Disc Changer [Opt on Vanden Plas,XJ8,XJ8L]	+213
Harman Kardon Audio System [Opt on Vanden Plas,XJ8,XJ8L]	+490

Body Styles	TMV Pricing		
	Trade	Private	Dealer
4 Dr XJ8 Sdn	13570	15220	16838
4 Dr XJ8L Sdn	13727	15397	17033

Options	Price
Heated Front and Rear Seats [Opt on Vanden Plas,XJ8,XJ8L]	+172
Navigation System	+607

1999

Jaguar's venerable XJ sedans enter '99 largely unchanged after a major workover in '98.

Mileage Category: I

Body Styles	TMV Pricing		
	Trade	Private	Dealer
4 Dr Vanden Plas Sdn	12556	14472	16467
4 Dr XJ8 Sdn	11488	13241	15067

Options	Price
Chrome Wheels	+302
Compact Disc Changer [Opt on Vanden Plas,XJ8,XJ8L]	+184
Harman Kardon Audio System [Opt on Vanden Plas,XJ8,XJ8L]	+422

Body Styles	TMV Pricing		
	Trade	Private	Dealer
4 Dr XJ8L Sdn	11976	13805	15709

Options	Price
Heated Front and Rear Seats [Opt on Vanden Plas,XJ8,XJ8L]	+133
Traction Control System [Opt on Vanden Plas,XJ8,XJ8L]	+184

1998

A new V8 engine, taken from the XK8 Coupe and Convertible, makes its way into the engine bay. A revised instrument panel greatly improves interior ergonomics. Cruise and satellite stereo controls are located on the steering wheel.

Mileage Category: I

Body Styles	TMV Pricing		
	Trade	Private	Dealer
4 Dr Vanden Plas Sdn	9968	11822	13913
4 Dr XJ8 Sdn	9445	11202	13183

Options	Price
Chrome Wheels	+259
Compact Disc Changer	+158

Body Styles	TMV Pricing		
	Trade	Private	Dealer
4 Dr XJ8L Sdn	9794	11617	13672

Options	Price
Harman Kardon Audio System	+362
Traction Control System	+158

1997

The 1997 XJ-Series loses the V12 model that has been a mainstay of the Jaguar lineup for so many years. A long-wheelbase model becomes available this year, filling a niche between the XJ6 and the Vanden Plas. All models receive a contoured bench seat and three-point seatbelts for rear occupants. The XJ6 replaces last year's chrome-vane grille with a black-vane grille, and the convenience group becomes optional on this model.

Mileage Category: I

Body Styles	TMV Pricing		
	Trade	Private	Dealer
4 Dr Vanden Plas Sdn	8076	9758	11813
4 Dr XJ6 Sdn	7698	9300	11259

Options	Price
Chrome Wheels	+203
Compact Disc Changer	+178
Harman Kardon Audio System	+279

Body Styles	TMV Pricing		
	Trade	Private	Dealer
4 Dr XJ6L Sdn	8014	9683	11723

Options	Price
Special Factory Paint	+127
Traction Control System	+127

Jaguar
XJ-Series/XJR

1996

On the XJ6, thicker side window glass insulates passengers from annoying wind noise and outside distractions. After a 20-year reign, the XJS coupe is put out to pasture. The only model offered for 1996 is the six-cylinder convertible; the most popular XJS in its unremarkable history. The changes for 1996 include new wheels, new bucket seats, additional chrome exterior trim and an adjustable wood-trimmed steering wheel.

Mileage Category: I

Body Styles	TMV Pricing		
	Trade	Private	Dealer
2 Dr XJS Conv	9559	11659	14560
4 Dr Vanden Plas Sdn	6027	7430	9368

Options	Price
Chrome Wheels	+155

Body Styles	TMV Pricing		
	Trade	Private	Dealer
4 Dr XJ12 Sdn	7079	8728	11004
4 Dr XJ6 Sdn	6248	7703	9711

Options	Price
Harman Kardon Audio System [Opt on Vanden Plas,XJ6]	+213

1995

Horsepower is upped for naturally aspirated 4.0-liter engine, and inline-six and V12 engines. New sheet metal showcases a more traditional Jaguar; ironic considering the amount of input Ford had into the creation of this car. XJS V12 models get new wheels and a plethora of standard equipment such as heated seats and a multidisc CD changer.

Mileage Category: F

Body Styles	TMV Pricing		
	Trade	Private	Dealer
2 Dr XJS Conv	7115	8869	11793
2 Dr XJS Cpe	5588	6966	9263
2 Dr XJS V12 Conv	7613	9490	12619
2 Dr XJS V12 Cpe	6612	8242	10959

Options	Price
Chrome Wheels	+138
Compact Disc Changer	+138
Harman Kardon Audio System [Opt on Vanden Plas,XJ6]	+173

Body Styles	TMV Pricing		
	Trade	Private	Dealer
4 Dr XJ12 Sdn	5759	7186	9563
4 Dr XJ6 Sdn	5385	6720	8944
4 Dr XJ6 Vanden Plas Sdn	5372	6703	8921

Options	Price
Power Sunroof	+156
Special Factory Paint	+86
Traction Control System	+86

XJR

2004

Mileage Category: F

Body Styles			TMV Pricing		
			Trade	Private	Dealer
4 Dr S/C Sdn			49219	51227	54573

Options	Price
20 Inch Wheels	+4500
DVD Entertainment System	+2000
Headlight Washers	+200
Navigation System	+2300

Options	Price
Park Distance Control (Front and Rear)	+250
Power Rear Seat	+1750
Rear Audio Controls	+650
Special Interior Trim	+1000

Although the exterior styling may look familiar, Jaguar's beefed-up version of its historic sales leader, the XJ, is an all-new car for 2004. The high-performance XJR's supercharged V8 engine now displaces 4.2 liters and puts out 390 horsepower, while an aluminum monocoque frame with all-aluminum body panels help keep curb weight down.

2003

Mileage Category: F

Body Styles			TMV Pricing		
			Trade	Private	Dealer
4 Dr S/C Sdn			36184	38315	41867

Options	Price
Performance/Handling Package	+1002

In its final year of this generation, the XJR nonetheless gets a new option, the R1 Performance Package, which includes Brembo brakes and 18-inch modular wheels.

2002

The XJR sees no changes as it nears the end of this generation's lifecycle.

Mileage Category: F

Body Styles	TMV Pricing		
	Trade	Private	Dealer
4 Dr 100 S/C Sdn	41739	44240	48409

Body Styles	TMV Pricing		
	Trade	Private	Dealer
4 Dr S/C Sdn	33769	35751	39055

2001

Jaguar's high-performance sedan receives only minor changes for 2001. Jaguar has added a new reverse parking control system and strengthened the chassis with new crush tubes, doors, hinges and steering columns. A heated rear seat and a premium audio system are now standard equipment, and there's a new optional dealer-installed Motorola Timeport digital phone. Topping things off is a no-cost scheduled maintenance program that covers four regular service visits under the four-year/50,000-mile limited warranty.

Mileage Category: F

Body Styles			TMV Pricing		
			Trade	Private	Dealer
4 Dr S/C Sdn			30087	33075	35834

Options	Price
Navigation System	+870

2000

The XJR gains all-speed traction control, improved ABS, rain-sensing windshield wipers, child seat-anchor brackets and an upgraded 320-watt Alpine system as standard equipment. A new navigation system is being offered as optional equipment. The anti-theft system now has an encrypted key transponder. The XJR also gets new 18-inch wheels and newly styled seats.

Mileage Category: F

Body Styles	TMV Pricing		
	Trade	Private	Dealer
4 Dr S/C Sdn	23042	25641	28189

Options	Price
Navigation System	+660

1999

Jaguar's potent XJR sedan enters '99 largely unchanged after a major workover in '98.

Mileage Category: F

Body Styles	TMV Pricing		
	Trade	Private	Dealer
4 Dr S/C Sdn	18477	21087	23803

Options	Price
Chrome Wheels	+294

1998

A new V8 engine, taken from the XK8 Coupe and Convertible, makes its way into the engine bay. A revised instrument panel greatly improves interior ergonomics. Cruise and satellite stereo controls are located on the steering wheel.

Mileage Category: F

Body Styles	TMV Pricing		
	Trade	Private	Dealer
4 Dr S/C Sdn	14508	17008	19828

Options	Price
Chrome Wheels	+252

1997

Apart from gaining a contoured bench seat and three-point seatbelts for rear occupants (as with the rest of the XJ sedans) and losing the heater ducts for the same, the XJR cruises into this year unchanged.

Mileage Category: F

Body Styles	TMV Pricing		
	Trade	Private	Dealer
4 Dr S/C Sdn	10272	12274	14720

Options	Price
Special Factory Paint	+127

1996

After last year's rebirth, changes to the XJ sedans, including the XJR are limited to thicker side window glass that better insulates passengers from annoying wind noise and outside distractions.

Mileage Category: F

Body Styles	TMV Pricing		
	Trade	Private	Dealer
4 Dr S/C Sdn	8810	10746	13420

1995

Along with a new body that is more evocative of the classic XJ series comes this new model, the performance-oriented, supercharged XJR that boasts 322 horsepower under its bonnet.

Mileage Category: F

Body Styles	TMV Pricing		
	Trade	Private	Dealer
4 Dr S/C Sdn	7360	9175	12199

XK-Series

2004

Mileage Category: F

Body Styles	TMV Pricing		
	Trade	Private	Dealer
2 Dr XK8 Conv	47722	49797	53255

Options	Price
19 Inch Wheels	+1200
Adaptive Cruise Control	+2200
Navigation System	+2400

Body Styles	TMV Pricing		
	Trade	Private	Dealer
2 Dr XK8 Cpe	46773	48952	52585

Options	Price
Special Interior Trim	+1000
Xenon Headlamps	+375

After extensive updates last year, revised color options are the only changes for 2004.

Jaguar
XK-Series

2003

Trying hard to keep up with blossoming competition, Jaguar makes significant modifications to its sports car. Changes to the exterior are limited to different wheels, slightly different badging, available (standard on the R) xenon headlamps and some new colors, including a lovely Jaguar Racing Green. The most important alterations lie under the hood, with two new engines managed by a six-speed automatic transmission. Standard safety equipment now includes a stability control system and BrakeAssist. In all, there are 900 changes to Jaguar's beautiful XK.

Mileage Category: F

Body Styles	TMV Pricing		
	Trade	Private	Dealer
2 Dr XK8 Conv	40302	42436	45992

Options	Price
19 Inch Wheels [Opt on XK8]	+668
Navigation System [Opt on XK8]	+1603

Body Styles	TMV Pricing		
	Trade	Private	Dealer
2 Dr XK8 Cpe	38149	40169	43535

Options	Price
Xenon Headlamps [Opt on XK8]	+334

2002

No major changes.

Mileage Category: F

Body Styles	TMV Pricing		
	Trade	Private	Dealer
2 Dr XK8 Conv	34148	35987	39052

Options	Price
18 Inch Wheels	+355

Body Styles	TMV Pricing		
	Trade	Private	Dealer
2 Dr XK8 Cpe	31609	33311	36148

Options	Price
Navigation System	+1421

2001

For 2001, there are standard child seat-anchor points for the rear seats and a reverse parking-control system. The premium audio system with a six-disc CD changer and the GPS navigation system are now standard equipment on XK8s. Topping things off are minor exterior styling changes and a new no-cost scheduled maintenance program that covers four regular service visits under the four-year/50,000-mile limited warranty.

Mileage Category: F

Body Styles	TMV Pricing		
	Trade	Private	Dealer
2 Dr XK8 Conv	30515	33170	35620

Options	Price
18 Inch Wheels	+256

Body Styles	TMV Pricing		
	Trade	Private	Dealer
2 Dr XK8 Cpe	28242	30700	32968

Options	Price
Navigation System	+1228

2000

No major changes.

Mileage Category: F

Body Styles	TMV Pricing		
	Trade	Private	Dealer
2 Dr XK8 Conv	24729	27323	29866

Options	Price
Compact Disc Changer	+256
Harman Kardon Audio System	+532

Body Styles	TMV Pricing		
	Trade	Private	Dealer
2 Dr XK8 Cpe	24402	26963	29474

Options	Price
Heated Front Seats	+164
Navigation System	+607

1999

The stunning XK returns for '99 with no significant changes.

Mileage Category: F

Body Styles	TMV Pricing		
	Trade	Private	Dealer
2 Dr XK8 Conv	20512	23301	26205

Options	Price
Chrome Wheels	+314
Compact Disc Changer	+220
Harman Kardon Audio System	+459

Body Styles	TMV Pricing		
	Trade	Private	Dealer
2 Dr XK8 Cpe	20385	23157	26043

Options	Price
Heated Front Seats	+141
Traction Control System	+220

1998

The 1998 XK8 gets automatic on/off headlamps, an engine immobilizer feature as part of the security system and a cellular phone keypad integrated into the stereo controls. Other changes include the addition of two new exterior colors.

Mileage Category: F

Body Styles	TMV Pricing		
	Trade	Private	Dealer
2 Dr XK8 Conv	17095	19906	23076

Options	Price
Chrome Wheels	+269
Compact Disc Changer	+189
Harman Kardon Audio System	+394

Body Styles	TMV Pricing		
	Trade	Private	Dealer
2 Dr XK8 Cpe	15034	17505	20292

Options	Price
Heated Front Seats	+121
Traction Control System	+189

1997

An all-new Jaguar debuts this year, replacing the stodgy XJ-S. This new sports car boasts the first V8 engine ever found in a Jag, as well as an all-new five-speed manual transmission that features normal and sport modes. The XK-Series is available in coupe and convertible forms, but Jaguar insiders expect a full 70 percent of sales to be of the convertible.

Mileage Category: F

Body Styles	TMV Pricing		
	Trade	Private	Dealer
2 Dr XK8 Conv	14728	17436	20745

Options	Price
Chrome Wheels	+217
Compact Disc Changer	+152

Body Styles	TMV Pricing		
	Trade	Private	Dealer
2 Dr XK8 Cpe	12792	15143	18017

Options	Price
Harman Kardon Audio System	+305
Special Factory Paint	+127

Options	Price
Traction Control System	+152

Mileage Category: F

Body Styles	TMV Pricing			Body Styles	TMV Pricing		
	Trade	Private	Dealer		Trade	Private	Dealer
2 Dr S/C Conv	57971	60724	65312	2 Dr S/C Cpe	54596	57349	61937

Options	Price	Options	Price
20 Inch Wheels	+6000	Leather Steering Wheel	+200
Adaptive Cruise Control	+2200	Painted Brake Calipers	+250
BBS Wheels	+4000	Recaro Seats	+1000
Brembo Brakes	+1000	Special Interior Trim	+1000

After extensive updates last year, revised color options are the only changes for 2004.

2003

Mileage Category: F

Body Styles	TMV Pricing			Body Styles	TMV Pricing		
	Trade	Private	Dealer		Trade	Private	Dealer
2 Dr S/C Conv	51939	54689	59273	2 Dr S/C Cpe	47862	50396	54619

Options	Price	Options	Price
20 Inch Wheels	+4007	Performance/Handling Package	+6011
Adaptive Cruise Control	+1202	Recaro Seats	+1336

Trying hard to keep up with blossoming competition; Jaguar makes significant modifications to its top-shelf sports car. Changes to the exterior are limited to different wheels, slightly different badging, standard xenon headlamps and some new colors, including a lovely Jaguar Racing Green. The most important alterations lie under the hood, with a new engine managed by a six-speed automatic transmission. In all, there are 900 changes to Jaguar's beautiful XKR.

2002

Mileage Category: F

Body Styles	TMV Pricing			Body Styles	TMV Pricing		
	Trade	Private	Dealer		Trade	Private	Dealer
2 Dr 100 S/C Conv	53763	56658	61482	2 Dr S/C Conv	43344	45678	49567
2 Dr 100 S/C Cpe	51915	54709	59367	2 Dr S/C Cpe	40059	42217	45813

XKR models get a burst of new color for 2002, with Aspen Green, Quartz and Zircon added to the palette. This year also ushers in a new trim level for the XKR; the limited-edition XKR 100 (created to honor the centenary of Jaguar's founder) offers unique features like special Anthracite paint and top-of-the-line Connolly leather seats.

2001

Mileage Category: F

Body Styles	TMV Pricing			Body Styles	TMV Pricing		
	Trade	Private	Dealer		Trade	Private	Dealer
2 Dr S/C Conv	38100	41414	44474	2 Dr Silverstone S/C Conv	47572	51711	55531
2 Dr S/C Cpe	35132	38189	41011	2 Dr Silverstone S/C Cpe	46294	50322	54040

For 2001, a limited-edition XKR "Silverstone" model will be offered, equipped with 20-inch BBS wheels, Brembo brakes and unique interior treatments. The Silverstone, as well as the regular XKR Coupe and Convertible, have additional safety equipment in the form of seat-mounted side airbags and an Adaptive Restraint Technology System (ARTS) that ultrasonically detects occupants. There are also standard child seat-anchor points for the rear seats and a reverse parking control system. Topping things off are minor exterior styling changes and a new no-cost scheduled maintenance program that covers four regular service visits under the four-year/50,000-mile limited warranty.

2000

Mileage Category: F

Body Styles	TMV Pricing			Body Styles	TMV Pricing		
	Trade	Private	Dealer		Trade	Private	Dealer
2 Dr S/C Conv	31658	34980	38236	2 Dr S/C Cpe	28705	31717	34669

Options	Price
Navigation System	+607

The performance-minded, supercharged, V8-powered XKR joins the lineup this year. It benefits from upgrades made to the rest of the XK8 family that include all-speed traction control, improved ABS and rain-sensing windshield wipers, while a new navigation system is being offered as optional equipment.

Cherokee

2001

The 4.0-liter PowerTech inline-six engine, which now meets LEV requirements in all 50 states, is standard equipment in all 2001 Cherokees. The 2.5-liter inline four, along with the SE trim, is dropped. The previous Limited trim is also dropped, with the former Classic trim now labeled Limited. All 2001 Cherokees offer child seat-tether anchors as standard equipment, and Steel Blue replaces Desert Sand as an exterior color choice. This is the last year for the Cherokee.

Mileage Category: M

Body Styles	TMV Pricing			Body Styles	TMV Pricing		
	Trade	Private	Dealer		Trade	Private	Dealer
2 Dr SE 4WD SUV	6738	7942	9054	4 Dr Limited 4WD SUV	8081	9525	10858
2 Dr SE SUV	6231	7344	8372	4 Dr Limited SUV	7718	9098	10372
2 Dr Sport 4WD SUV	7162	8442	9623	4 Dr SE 4WD SUV	7098	8367	9539
2 Dr Sport SUV	6699	7897	9002	4 Dr SE SUV	6580	7757	8843
4 Dr Classic 4WD SUV	7955	9377	10690	4 Dr Sport 4WD SUV	7898	9310	10614
4 Dr Classic SUV	7466	8800	10032	4 Dr Sport SUV	6999	8250	9404

Options	Price	Options	Price
AM/FM/Cassette/CD Audio System	+200	Infinity Audio System	+171
Air Conditioning [Std on Limited]	+415	Leather Seats [Opt on Limited]	+342
Aluminum/Alloy Wheels [Opt on SE,Sport]	+120	Locking Differential	+139
Antilock Brakes	+332	Off-Road Suspension Package	+354
Automatic 4-Speed Transmission [Opt on SE,Sport]	+461	Power Driver Seat [Opt on Classic,Limited]	+146
Camper/Towing Package	+120	Power Passenger Seat [Opt on Limited]	+146
Cruise Control	+122	Privacy Glass	+132
Heated Front Seats	+269		

2000

The 2000 Cherokee scores the '99 Grand Cherokee's redesigned 4.0-liter PowerTech inline six in addition to a new five-speed manual transmission. The Limited model sports bright chrome accents, including the front grille, the headlamp surrounds, the side graphics, the rear license-plate brow and the 16-inch wheels.

Mileage Category: M

Body Styles	TMV Pricing			Body Styles	TMV Pricing		
	Trade	Private	Dealer		Trade	Private	Dealer
2 Dr SE 4WD SUV	4891	5918	6924	4 Dr Limited 4WD SUV	6576	7957	9310
2 Dr SE SUV	4560	5517	6456	4 Dr Limited SUV	6291	7611	8905
2 Dr Sport 4WD SUV	5539	6703	7843	4 Dr SE 4WD SUV	5243	6343	7422
2 Dr Sport SUV	5199	6290	7360	4 Dr SE SUV	4827	5841	6834
4 Dr Classic 4WD SUV	6253	7565	8852	4 Dr Sport 4WD SUV	5892	7129	8341
4 Dr Classic SUV	5872	7105	8313	4 Dr Sport SUV	5411	6548	7662

Options	Price	Options	Price
4.0L I6 OHV 12V FI Engine [Opt on SE]	+428	Heated Front Seats	+237
AM/FM/Cassette/CD Audio System	+205	Infinity Audio System	+151
Air Conditioning [Std on Limited]	+366	Limited Slip Differential	+123
Antilock Brakes	+293	Power Driver Seat [Opt on Classic 4 Dr]	+129
Automatic 3-Speed Transmission	+269	Privacy Glass [Std on Limited]	+116
Automatic 4-Speed Transmission [Opt on SE,Sport]	+407		

1999

The Cherokee Sport gets a revised front fascia including body-colored grille and bumpers. New exterior colors include Forest Green and Desert Sand, to match the most common Cherokee surroundings.

Mileage Category: M

Body Styles	TMV Pricing			Body Styles	TMV Pricing		
	Trade	Private	Dealer		Trade	Private	Dealer
2 Dr SE 4WD SUV	4140	5090	6078	4 Dr Limited 4WD SUV	5367	6598	7879
2 Dr SE SUV	3743	4601	5494	4 Dr Limited SUV	5129	6305	7530
2 Dr Sport 4WD SUV	4697	5774	6895	4 Dr SE 4WD SUV	4330	5323	6357
2 Dr Sport SUV	4349	5347	6386	4 Dr SE SUV	3902	4797	5729
4 Dr Classic 4WD SUV	5055	6215	7422	4 Dr Sport 4WD SUV	4898	6021	7190
4 Dr Classic SUV	4857	5971	7131	4 Dr Sport SUV	4499	5531	6605

Options	Price	Options	Price
4.0L I6 OHV 12V FI Engine [Opt on SE]	+343	Automatic 4-Speed Transmission [Opt on SE,Sport]	+324
AM/FM/Cassette/CD Audio System	+164	Automatic Locking Hubs (4WD) [Opt on Utility]	+136
Air Conditioning [Std on Limited]	+293	Heated Front Seats	+190
Antilock Brakes	+260	Infinity Audio System	+121
Automatic 3-Speed Transmission	+214		

1998

Cherokee Classic and Limited replace the Cherokee Country. A new 2.5-liter four-cylinder engine is now the base engine for the SE, available with an optional three-speed automatic. New colors include Chili Pepper Red, Emerald Green and Deep Amethyst.

Mileage Category: M

Body Styles	TMV Pricing			Body Styles	TMV Pricing		
	Trade	Private	Dealer		Trade	Private	Dealer
2 Dr SE 4WD SUV	3451	4302	5262	2 Dr SE SUV	3084	3844	4702

Body Styles	TMV Pricing		
	Trade	Private	Dealer
2 Dr Sport 4WD SUV	3805	4744	5802
2 Dr Sport SUV	3602	4491	5493
4 Dr Classic 4WD SUV	4296	5356	6551
4 Dr Classic SUV	4002	4989	6102
4 Dr Limited 4WD SUV	4738	5906	7224

Options	Price
4.0L I6 OHV 12V FI Engine [Opt on SE]	+294
AM/FM/Cassette/CD Audio System	+140
Air Conditioning [Std on Limited]	+250
Antilock Brakes	+223

Body Styles	TMV Pricing		
	Trade	Private	Dealer
4 Dr Limited SUV	4407	5494	6720
4 Dr SE 4WD SUV	3596	4483	5483
4 Dr SE SUV	3231	4028	4927
4 Dr Sport 4WD SUV	4112	5126	6270
4 Dr Sport SUV	3759	4686	5732

Options	Price
Automatic 3-Speed Transmission	+196
Automatic 4-Speed Transmission [Opt on SE,Sport]	+278
Automatic Locking Hubs (4WD) [Opt on Utility]	+116

1997

A new interior sporting modern instrumentation debuts. Front and rear styling is refined, and the rear liftgate is now stamped from steel. Multiplex wiring is designed to improve reliability of the electrical system, while a new paint process aims to polish the finish of all Cherokees.

Mileage Category: M

Body Styles	TMV Pricing		
	Trade	Private	Dealer
2 Dr SE 4WD SUV	2850	3627	4577
2 Dr SE SUV	2389	3040	3835
2 Dr Sport 4WD SUV	3136	3991	5036
2 Dr Sport SUV	2994	3810	4808
4 Dr Country 4WD SUV	3770	4797	6053

Options	Price
4.0L I6 OHV 12V FI Engine [Opt on SE]	+263
AM/FM/Cassette/CD Audio System	+126
Air Conditioning	+225

Body Styles	TMV Pricing		
	Trade	Private	Dealer
4 Dr Country SUV	3558	4528	5713
4 Dr SE 4WD SUV	2959	3765	4750
4 Dr SE SUV	2747	3494	4408
4 Dr Sport 4WD SUV	3279	4173	5265
4 Dr Sport SUV	3098	3942	4974

Options	Price
Antilock Brakes	+200
Automatic 4-Speed Transmission [Std on Country]	+250
Leather Seats	+221

1996

Cherokee rolls into 1996 with improved engines, new colors, upgraded Selec-Trac four-wheel-drive system, more standard equipment and the same sheet metal that it wore on introduction day in 1983.

Mileage Category: M

Body Styles	TMV Pricing		
	Trade	Private	Dealer
2 Dr SE 4WD SUV	1845	2396	3156
2 Dr SE SUV	1708	2217	2921
2 Dr Sport 4WD SUV	2184	2836	3737
2 Dr Sport SUV	2010	2609	3437
4 Dr Country 4WD SUV	2938	3815	5027

Options	Price
4.0L I6 OHV 12V FI Engine [Opt on SE]	+159
Air Conditioning	+163
Antilock Brakes	+147

Body Styles	TMV Pricing		
	Trade	Private	Dealer
4 Dr Country SUV	2479	3219	4240
4 Dr SE 4WD SUV	2020	2623	3455
4 Dr SE SUV	1808	2348	3094
4 Dr Sport 4WD SUV	2287	2970	3912
4 Dr Sport SUV	2150	2792	3678

Options	Price
Automatic 4-Speed Transmission	+175
Leather Seats	+162
Off-Road Suspension Package	+204

1995

Driver airbag is added on all models. SE model gets reclining bucket seats.

Mileage Category: M

Body Styles	TMV Pricing		
	Trade	Private	Dealer
2 Dr SE 4WD SUV	1572	2054	2857
2 Dr SE SUV	1386	1811	2519
2 Dr Sport 4WD SUV	1755	2293	3190
2 Dr Sport SUV	1629	2129	2961
4 Dr Country 4WD SUV	2093	2735	3805

Options	Price
4.0L I6 OHV 12V FI Engine [Opt on SE]	+168
Air Conditioning	+173
Antilock Brakes	+156

Body Styles	TMV Pricing		
	Trade	Private	Dealer
4 Dr Country SUV	1960	2561	3562
4 Dr SE 4WD SUV	1572	2054	2857
4 Dr SE SUV	1459	1906	2652
4 Dr Sport 4WD SUV	1842	2407	3349
4 Dr Sport SUV	1735	2267	3154

Options	Price
Automatic 4-Speed Transmission	+186
Leather Seats	+172
Off-Road Suspension Package	+217

Jeep
Grand Cherokee

Grand Cherokee

2004

For 2004, the Grand Cherokee gets a factory-installed DVD navigation system integrated into the radio. Columbia, Freedom and Special Edition trims are also new for 2004. All of these models incorporate subtle cosmetic touches and equipment upgrades. Additionally, each Columbia Edition Jeep comes with a complimentary Columbia parka.

Mileage Category: M

Body Styles	TMV Pricing		
	Trade	Private	Dealer
4 Dr Columbia Edition 4WD SUV	16866	18072	20083
4 Dr Columbia Edition SUV	15679	16874	18865
4 Dr Freedom Edition 4WD SUV	16479	17684	19693
4 Dr Freedom Edition SUV	15494	16704	18721
4 Dr Laredo 4WD SUV	16116	17344	19390
4 Dr Laredo SUV	14623	15814	17800

Options	Price
17 Inch Wheels - Chrome [Opt on Limited]	+870
4.7L V8 SOHC 16V FI Engine [Opt on Limited, Laredo, Special]	+1070
4.7L V8 SOHC 16V FI HO Engine [Opt on Limited, Laredo, Columbia, Freedom]	+3175
AM/FM/CD Changer Audio System [Opt on Limited]	+200
Alarm System [Opt on Laredo, Freedom, 2WD Special]	+150
DVD Entertainment System [Opt on Columbia, Special, Limited, Overland]	+695
Fog Lights [Opt on Freedom]	+120
Front and Rear Head Airbag Restraints [Std on Overland]	+490

Body Styles	TMV Pricing		
	Trade	Private	Dealer
4 Dr Limited 4WD SUV	20213	21711	24206
4 Dr Limited SUV	18758	20055	22217
4 Dr Overland 4WD SUV	22679	24062	26367
4 Dr Overland SUV	20809	22172	24444
4 Dr Special Edition 4WD SUV	19002	20283	22419
4 Dr Special Edition SUV	15331	16548	18577

Options	Price
Heated Front Seats [Opt on Laredo, Limited, 4WD Special]	+250
Leather Seats [Opt on Laredo, Special]	+850
Navigation System [Opt on Columbia, Limited, Overland, 4WD Special]	+700
Power Adjustable Foot Pedals [Opt on Columbia, Limited, Overland, 4WD Special]	+120
Skid Plates [Opt on Special, Limited 4WD]	+200
Special Factory Paint	+150
Trailer Hitch	+255

2003

For 2003, the Jeep Grand Cherokee has received refinements that improve its ride and handling. The suspension features reduced pressure shocks and the brake master cylinder output has been increased to improve brake pedal feel. There are also new brake calipers and a revised steering gear torsion bar. Available trims have been narrowed from five to three; the Sport and Special Edition trims have been discontinued. Standard on 2003 Laredo models is a new high-back cloth seat. Finally, in all Jeep Grand Cherokee interiors, a new cubby bin for holding sunglasses or cellular phones has been added to the instrument panel, replacing the ashtray.

Mileage Category: M

Body Styles	TMV Pricing		
	Trade	Private	Dealer
4 Dr Laredo 4WD SUV	14532	15794	17898
4 Dr Laredo SUV	13488	14659	16612
4 Dr Limited 4WD SUV	17162	18653	21137

Options	Price
17 Inch Wheels - Chrome [Opt on Limited]	+593
4.7L V8 SOHC 16V FI Engine [Opt on Laredo,Limited]	+303
4.7L V8 SOHC 16V FI HO Engine [Opt on Limited]	+1364
Compact Disc Changer [Opt on Laredo,Limited]	+256
Front and Rear Head Airbag Restraints [Opt on Laredo,Limited]	+334
Heated Front Seats [Opt on Laredo,Limited]	+171
Infinity Audio System [Opt on Laredo]	+153
Leather Seats [Opt on Laredo]	+580

Body Styles	TMV Pricing		
	Trade	Private	Dealer
4 Dr Limited SUV	15642	17000	19264
4 Dr Overland 4WD SUV	19788	21507	24371

Options	Price
Off-Road Suspension Package [Opt on Laredo,Limited]	+198
Power Moonroof [Opt on Laredo,Limited]	+546
Power Passenger Seat [Opt on Laredo]	+191
Quadra-Drive Transfer Case [Opt on Limited]	+375
Quadra-Trac Transfer Case [Opt on Laredo]	+303
Skid Plates	+136
Special Factory Paint	+136

2002

More power for the 4.7-liter V8 and three new trim levels (SE, Sport and Overland) are on tap for this year. Also, several important safety and convenience options such as side curtain airbags, power-adjustable pedals, a tire-pressure monitoring system and automatic windshield wipers debut this year.

Mileage Category: M

Body Styles	TMV Pricing		
	Trade	Private	Dealer
4 Dr Laredo 4WD SUV	12312	13628	15820
4 Dr Laredo SUV	11424	12645	14680
4 Dr Limited 4WD SUV	14354	15888	18445
4 Dr Limited SUV	13298	14720	17088
4 Dr Overland 4WD SUV	17210	19049	22114

Options	Price
17 Inch Wheels - Chrome [Opt on Limited,Overland]	+523
4.7L V8 SOHC 16V FI Engine	+267
4.7L V8 SOHC 16V FI HO Engine [Opt on Limited]	+1202
AM/FM/Cassette/CD Changer Audio System [Opt on Limited]	+180
Compact Disc Changer [Std on Overland,Special Edition]	+225

Body Styles	TMV Pricing		
	Trade	Private	Dealer
4 Dr Special Edition 4WD SUV	13608	15062	17486
4 Dr Special Edition SUV	12538	13878	16111
4 Dr Sport 4WD SUV	12260	13571	15755
4 Dr Sport SUV	11394	12611	14640

Options	Price
Front and Rear Head Airbag Restraints [Std on Overland]	+295
Heated Front Seats [Std on Overland]	+150
Infinity Audio System [Opt on Laredo]	+135
Leather Seats [Opt on Laredo,Special Edition]	+394
Off-Road Suspension Package [Opt on 4WD - Laredo,Limited]	+174
Power Moonroof [Std on Overland]	+481

For the latest vehicle information, visit www.edmunds.com

2002 (cont'd)

Options	Price
Power Passenger Seat [Opt on Laredo]	+147
Quadra-Drive Transfer Case [Opt on Limited 4WD]	+331
Quadra-Trac Transfer Case [Opt on Laredo 4WD]	+267

Options	Price
Skid Plates [Std on Overland]	+120
Special Factory Paint	+120

2001

Mileage Category: M

Body Styles	TMV Pricing		
	Trade	Private	Dealer
4 Dr Laredo 4WD SUV	10158	11973	13649
4 Dr Laredo SUV	9654	11379	12973

Options	Price
4.7L V8 SOHC 16V FI Engine	+522
AM/FM/Cassette/CD Audio System [Opt on Laredo]	+171
AM/FM/Cassette/CD Changer Audio System	+146
Automatic 5-Speed Transmission	+293
Camper/Towing Package	+120
Compact Disc Changer	+146
Heated Leather Seats	+122

Body Styles	TMV Pricing		
	Trade	Private	Dealer
4 Dr Limited 4WD SUV	12426	14648	16698
4 Dr Limited SUV	11453	13501	15390

Options	Price
Leather Seats [Opt on Laredo]	+283
Locking Differential [Opt on 2WD]	+139
Off-Road Suspension Package	+281
Power Driver Seat [Opt on Laredo]	+146
Power Passenger Seat [Opt on Laredo]	+146
Power Sunroof	+391
Quadra-Trac Transfer Case [Opt on Laredo 4WD]	+217

A new five-speed automatic tranny provides a second overdrive ratio, resulting in greater fuel economy and reduced noise, vibration and harshness in models equipped with the 4.7-liter V8. Chrome front tow hooks are now included if you get the skid plate group on the Limited model, while the Laredo model offers a Special Appearance Group package with 17-inch five-spoke aluminum wheels, colored metallic front fascia and body cladding, body-color license brow and liftgate handle, foglamps, body side stripe and leather seats. A hydraulically driven engine-cooling fan improves fuel economy on the 4.7-liter V8 and a quarter-turn fuel cap improves efficiency at the gas station. Limiteds get an AM/FM stereo with cassette and CD player as standard equipment, along with optional new "Euro-style" gathered leather seats. The Trailer Tow Group now includes an underdash connector to make plugging in aftermarket trailer wiring harnesses a snap. Finally, child seat-tether anchors improve the Grand Cherokee's family-friendly nature while a LEV-compliant 4.7-liter V8 makes this Jeep more earth-friendly.

2000

Mileage Category: M

Body Styles	TMV Pricing		
	Trade	Private	Dealer
4 Dr Laredo 4WD SUV	8149	9860	11537
4 Dr Laredo SUV	7649	9255	10829

Options	Price
4.7L V8 SOHC 16V FI Engine	+461
AM/FM/Cassette/CD Audio System [Opt on Laredo]	+151
Compact Disc Changer	+129
Infinity Audio System [Opt on Laredo]	+219
Leather Seats [Opt on Laredo]	+250
Limited Slip Differential	+123

Body Styles	TMV Pricing		
	Trade	Private	Dealer
4 Dr Limited 4WD SUV	10104	12226	14305
4 Dr Limited SUV	9330	11290	13211

Options	Price
Power Driver Seat [Opt on Laredo]	+129
Power Passenger Seat [Opt on Laredo]	+129
Power Sunroof	+345
Quadra-Drive Transfer Case [Opt on Laredo]	+237
Quadra-Trac Transfer Case [Opt on Laredo]	+192

New exterior cladding has been slapped onto the Laredo, and both models have received interior touch-ups. Two-wheel drive is available with the 4.7-liter V8. Shale Green and Silverstone are the new skin tones.

1999

Body Styles	TMV Pricing		
	Trade	Private	Dealer
4 Dr Laredo 4WD SUV	6969	8568	10231
4 Dr Laredo SUV	6476	7962	9508

Options	Price
4.7L V8 SOHC 16V FI Engine	+330
AM/FM/Cassette/CD Audio System [Opt on Laredo]	+121
Infinity Audio System [Opt on Laredo]	+176
Leather Seats [Opt on Laredo]	+199
Power Driver Seat [Opt on Laredo]	+115

Body Styles	TMV Pricing		
	Trade	Private	Dealer
4 Dr Limited 4WD SUV	8568	10533	12578
4 Dr Limited SUV	7448	9156	10934

Options	Price
Power Passenger Seat [Opt on Laredo]	+115
Power Sunroof	+275
Quadra-Drive Transfer Case [Opt on 4WD]	+210
Quadra-Trac Transfer Case [Opt on Laredo 4WD]	+170

The new-for-'99 Grand Cherokee contains only 127 carryover parts from the previous model, and gets a new powertrain, rear suspension, braking and steering systems, 4WD system, interior and exterior styling.

1998

Mileage Category: M

Body Styles	TMV Pricing		
	Trade	Private	Dealer
4 Dr 5.9 Limited 4WD SUV	7334	9142	11181
4 Dr Laredo 4WD SUV	5056	6303	7709
4 Dr Laredo SUV	4766	5942	7268
4 Dr Limited 4WD SUV	6496	8099	9906

Options	Price
5.2L V8 OHV FI Engine	+259
Infinity Audio System	+150
Leather Seats [Opt on Laredo]	+171

Body Styles	TMV Pricing		
	Trade	Private	Dealer
4 Dr Limited SUV	5672	7071	8649
4 Dr TSi 4WD SUV	5493	6849	8377
4 Dr TSi SUV	5126	6390	7815

Options	Price
Power Sunroof [Std on Limited 5.9]	+224
Quadra-Trac Transfer Case [Opt on 4WD - Laredo, TSi]	+146

A 5.9-liter V8 making 245 horsepower and 345 pound-feet torque powers the Grand Cherokee 5.9 Limited, making it the mightiest of all Jeeps. With the addition of the 5.9, the putrid Orvis model dies. Two new colors and "next-generation" airbags round out the changes.

Jeep
Grand Cherokee/Liberty

1997

Last year's integrated child safety seat has mysteriously disappeared from press kit and dealer order sheet radar. Other big news is the availability of the optional 5.2-liter V8 engine in 2WD models, and a six-cylinder that qualifies the JGC as a transitional low emission vehicle (TLEV) in California. Refinements have been made to the ABS system, entry-level cassette stereo and floor carpet fit. In January, a sporty TSi model debuted with monotone paint, special aluminum wheels and other goodies.

Mileage Category: M

Body Styles	TMV Pricing		
	Trade	Private	Dealer
4 Dr Laredo 4WD SUV	4379	5572	7030
4 Dr Laredo SUV	3832	4876	6153
4 Dr Limited 4WD SUV	5498	6996	8827

Options	Price
5.2L V8 OHV 16V FI Engine	+221
Infinity Audio System [Std on Limited]	+135
Leather Seats [Std on Limited]	+153

Body Styles	TMV Pricing		
	Trade	Private	Dealer
4 Dr Limited SUV	4995	6356	8020
4 Dr TSi 4WD SUV	4855	6179	7796
4 Dr TSi SUV	4456	5670	7155

Options	Price
Power Sunroof	+201
Quadra-Trac Transfer Case [Opt on Limited,TSi]	+131

1996

Jeep turns its flagship into an Explorer killer with dual airbags, revised styling, a better V6 engine, improved front suspension and an upgraded Selec-Trac four-wheel-drive system. Interiors have been restyled, featuring new luxury doodads and an optional integrated child safety seat. Trim levels are two: Laredo and Limited.

Mileage Category: M

Body Styles	TMV Pricing		
	Trade	Private	Dealer
4 Dr Laredo 4WD SUV	3521	4572	6023
4 Dr Laredo SUV	3183	4133	5445

Options	Price
5.2L V8 OHV 16V FI Engine	+169

Body Styles	TMV Pricing		
	Trade	Private	Dealer
4 Dr Limited 4WD SUV	4528	5879	7746
4 Dr Limited SUV	3779	4907	6465

Options	Price
Power Sunroof	+148

1995

Rear disc brakes are added to all models. An Orvis trim package is added to the Limited 4WD. New options are an integrated child safety seat and a flip-up liftgate window. Optional V8 engine gets a torque increase. A 2WD Limited model is newly available. A power sunroof is added to the options list.

Mileage Category: M

Body Styles	TMV Pricing		
	Trade	Private	Dealer
4 Dr Laredo 4WD SUV	3029	3957	5505
4 Dr Laredo SUV	2683	3505	4875
4 Dr Limited 4WD SUV	3729	4872	6776

Options	Price
5.2L V8 OHV 16V FI Engine	+179
Infinity Audio System [Std on Limited]	+106
Leather Seats [Std on Limited]	+119

Body Styles	TMV Pricing		
	Trade	Private	Dealer
4 Dr Limited SUV	3168	4139	5758
4 Dr SE 4WD SUV	2770	3620	5036
4 Dr SE SUV	2369	3095	4304

Options	Price
Off-Road Suspension Package [Opt on SE 4WD]	+155
Power Sunroof	+157
Quadra-Trac Transfer Case [Opt on 4WD - Laredo,SE]	+102

Liberty
2004

All Libertys now feature a passenger-side grab handle and a power accessory delay feature, while Renegade models get additional rock rail protection and black accent body side moldings. New options include UConnect, Chrysler's hands-free in-vehicle communication system, a tire-pressure monitoring system and a cargo organizer. Safety is enhanced thanks to a system that unlocks doors, illuminates interior courtesy lights and shuts off the fuel pump after airbag deployment. A new trim -- the Jeep Liberty Columbia Edition -- has been introduced, offering 16-inch graphite-painted aluminum wheels; graphite-painted fascias and body moldings; body-colored fender flares; a sun roof; fog lamps; and Columbia badging.

Mileage Category: M

Body Styles	TMV Pricing		
	Trade	Private	Dealer
4 Dr Columbia Edition 4WD SUV	14069	15415	17659
4 Dr Columbia Edition SUV	13180	14488	16669
4 Dr Limited 4WD SUV	14832	16178	18421
4 Dr Limited SUV	13942	15288	17532
4 Dr Renegade 4WD SUV	14985	16331	18574

Options	Price
17 Inch Wheels - Chrome [Opt on Limited]	+895
3.7L V6 SOHC 12V FI Engine [Opt on Sport]	+850
AM/FM/CD Changer Audio System	+200
Alarm System	+175
Aluminum/Alloy Wheels [Opt on Sport]	+310
Antilock Brakes	+600
Automatic 4-Speed Transmission [Std on Limited]	+825
Cruise Control [Opt on Sport]	+300
Fog Lights [Opt on Sport]	+120
Front and Rear Head Airbag Restraints	+490

Body Styles	TMV Pricing		
	Trade	Private	Dealer
4 Dr Renegade SUV	13981	15322	17556
4 Dr Rocky Mountain 4WD SUV	14110	15456	17699
4 Dr Rocky Mountain SUV	13220	14528	16709
4 Dr Sport 4WD SUV	12069	13416	15661
4 Dr Sport SUV	11179	12489	14671

Options	Price
Heated Front Seats [Opt on Limited]	+250
Keyless Entry System [Opt on Sport]	+200
Limited Slip Differential [Opt on Sport, Limited, Rocky Mtn 4WD]	+285
Power Driver Seat [Opt on Sport, Renegade, Limited]	+300
Power Heated Mirrors [Opt on Renegade, Limited]	+120
Power Mirrors [Opt on Sport]	+150
Privacy Glass [Opt on Sport, Limited]	+270
Skid Plates [Opt on Sport, Limited, Rocky Mtn 4WD]	+155
Trailer Hitch	+245

2003

For 2003, a new overhead console, based on that of the Grand Cherokee, includes a unique interface that allows passengers to program the operation of nine convenience and safety items to their own preference. Liberty owners can now personalize several features, including which doors unlock with the first press of the remote keyless entry unlock button, the miles driven between service intervals and the amount of time the headlamps remain on when exiting the vehicle. Finally, an available six-disc in-dash CD player replaces the cargo area mounted unit. Standard four-wheel disc brakes endow the Jeep with improved brake feel on-road, decreased stopping distances and reduced brake fade. Available electrochromic interior and driver-side rearview mirrors help reduce headlight glare from traffic at night, and standard sliding sun visors have been added, which serve to keep the sun out of your eyes by providing added windshield and side glass coverage.

Mileage Category: M

Body Styles	TMV Pricing		
	Trade	Private	Dealer
4 Dr Freedom Edition 4WD SUV	13969	15277	17457
4 Dr Freedom Edition SUV	13430	14687	16783
4 Dr Limited 4WD SUV	13892	15193	17361
4 Dr Limited SUV	12744	13937	15926

Options	Price
17 Inch Wheels - Chrome [Opt on Limited]	+610
3.7L V6 SOHC 12V FI Engine [Opt on Sport]	+580
Air Conditioning [Opt on Sport]	+477
Alarm System	+119
Aluminum/Alloy Wheels [Opt on Sport]	+211
Antilock Brakes [Opt on Freedom,Limited,Renegade]	+464
Automatic 4-Speed Transmission [Std on Limited]	+563
Camper/Towing Package [Opt on Freedom,Limited,Renegade]	+167
Cruise Control [Opt on Sport]	+205
Front and Rear Head Airbag Restraints	+334
Heated Front Seats [Opt on Limited]	+171

Body Styles	TMV Pricing		
	Trade	Private	Dealer
4 Dr Renegade 4WD SUV	13980	15289	17471
4 Dr Renegade SUV	13231	14470	16534
4 Dr Sport 4WD SUV	10962	11988	13699
4 Dr Sport SUV	10030	10969	12534

Options	Price
Keyless Entry System	+116
Leather Seats [Opt on Limited]	+512
Limited Slip Differential	+194
Luggage Rack [Opt on Sport]	+136
Power Door Locks [Opt on Sport]	+123
Power Driver Seat [Opt on Limited,Renegade]	+160
Power Moonroof	+477
Power Passenger Seat [Opt on Limited,Renegade]	+160
Power Windows [Opt on Sport]	+167
Privacy Glass [Opt on Limited,Sport]	+184
Trip Computer [Opt on Renegade]	+171

2002

Finally replacing the boxy Cherokee that has been in production since 1984, the handsome all-new 2002 Liberty serves as the affordable SUV in Jeep's lineup. Borrowing styling cues from the 1997 Jeep Dakar and 1998 Jeepster concept vehicles, the Liberty is available in three trim levels with your choice of two- or four-wheel drive, a four- or six-cylinder engine and a manual or automatic transmission.

Mileage Category: M

Body Styles	TMV Pricing		
	Trade	Private	Dealer
4 Dr Limited 4WD SUV	11698	12948	15031
4 Dr Limited SUV	10791	11944	13865
4 Dr Renegade 4WD SUV	11861	13129	15241

Options	Price
16 Inch Wheels [Opt on Sport]	+165
3.7L V6 SOHC 12V FI Engine [Opt on Sport]	+511
Air Conditioning [Std on Limited]	+511
Aluminum/Alloy Wheels [Opt on Sport]	+186
Antilock Brakes	+409
Automatic 4-Speed Transmission [Std on Limited]	+496
Camper/Towing Package [Opt on Limited]	+147
Compact Disc Changer	+249
Cruise Control [Opt on Sport]	+180
Front and Rear Head Airbag Restraints	+295

Body Styles	TMV Pricing		
	Trade	Private	Dealer
4 Dr Renegade SUV	11445	12668	14706
4 Dr Sport 4WD SUV	9173	10153	11787
4 Dr Sport SUV	8311	9199	10679

Options	Price
Heated Front Seats [Opt on Limited]	+150
Leather Seats [Opt on Limited]	+451
Limited Slip Differential	+171
Luggage Rack [Opt on Sport]	+120
Power Driver Seat	+141
Power Passenger Seat	+141
Power Sunroof	+421
Power Windows [Opt on Sport]	+147
Privacy Glass	+162

Wrangler

2004

Mileage Category: L

Body Styles	TMV Pricing		
	Trade	Private	Dealer
2 Dr Rubicon 4WD Conv	19126	20289	22227
2 Dr SE 4WD Conv	12100	13147	14890
2 Dr Sahara 4WD Conv	18202	19248	20992

Options	Price
AM/FM/CD Audio System [Opt on SE]	+125
Aluminum/Alloy Wheels [Opt on Sport, SE, X]	+425
Antilock Brakes [Opt on Sport, X, Sahara]	+600
Automatic 4-Speed Transmission [Opt on non-Unlimited]	+515
Automatic Dimming Rearview Mirror [Opt on Sport, Rubicon, Unlimited]	+220
Hardtop Roof	+740
Leather Steering Wheel [Opt on non-Sahara]	+300

Body Styles	TMV Pricing		
	Trade	Private	Dealer
2 Dr Sport 4WD Conv	15667	16713	18457
2 Dr Unlimited 4WD Conv	17574	18620	20364
2 Dr X 4WD Conv	14266	15312	17056

Options	Price
Limited Slip Differential [Opt on Sport, X, Sahara]	+285
Privacy Glass [Opt on Sport, X, Rubicon]	+125
Rear Window Wiper	+150
Running Boards [Opt on Sport, Unlimited]	+150
Soft Top [Opt on Sport, Sahara, Rubicon]	+340
Split Folding Rear Seat [Opt on SE]	+635

An AM/FM/CD stereo and a tilt steering wheel are now standard on all models. A new aluminum wheel design is standard on Sahara models and optional on Sport models. Right-hand-drive versions are also available for fleet utility service. A Columbia Edition option package is also new for 2004, as is a longer-wheelbase "unlimited" version of the Wrangler.

2003

For 2003, the Wrangler gets a new trim level: the Rubicon. All trims have been bestowed with an all-new 42RLE four-speed automatic transmission which is supposed to provide smoother-shifting, better highway fuel efficiency and quieter engine operation at highway speeds compared to the previous three-speed automatic transmission. The SE trim gets a new NV1500 five-speed heavy-duty tranny, which promises to improve shift quality in cold weather, along with a new, more potent 2.4-liter Power Tech inline-four. Available four-wheel disc brakes debut this year, along with a new fold-and-tumble rear seat that can be more easily removed. Finally, the Wrangler's interior has been refurbished for 2003; it gets new front and rear seats, a new electrochromatic rearview mirror with map lights, temperature and compass display (standard on Sahara, optional on Sport and Rubicon trims), and a new four-spoke steering wheel.

Mileage Category: L

Body Styles	TMV Pricing		
	Trade	Private	Dealer
2 Dr Rubicon 4WD Conv	16238	17674	20068
2 Dr SE 4WD Conv	10442	11365	12904
2 Dr Sahara 4WD Conv	16139	17567	19946

Options	Price
Air Conditioning [Opt on Rubicon,SE,Sport,X]	+477
Aluminum/Alloy Wheels [Opt on SE,Sport,X]	+290
Antilock Brakes [Opt on Sahara,Sport,X,X Freedom]	+464
Automatic 4-Speed Transmission	+358
Automatic Dimming Rearview Mirror [Opt on Rubicon,Sport]	+150
Color Match Dual Roofs [Opt on Rubicon,Sahara,Sport]	+979

Body Styles	TMV Pricing		
	Trade	Private	Dealer
2 Dr Sport 4WD Conv	13582	14784	16786
2 Dr X 4WD Conv	12567	13679	15532
2 Dr X Freedom Edition 4WD Conv	13927	15158	17210

Options	Price
Cruise Control [Std on Sahara]	+171
Hardtop Roof	+542
Limited Slip Differential [Opt on Sahara,Sport,X,X Freedom]	+194
Premium Audio System [Opt on Rubicon,Sport,X Freedom]	+201
Split Folding Rear Seat [Opt on SE]	+307

2002

A new "X" model is introduced, combining the potent 4.0-liter inline six with affordability. Sahara and Sport models receive upgrades, including hard doors with roll-up windows. New optional wheels, increased output from the climate control system and an improved premium sound system round out the changes to the tough and ready Wrangler.

Mileage Category: L

Body Styles	TMV Pricing		
	Trade	Private	Dealer
2 Dr SE 4WD Conv	8548	9448	10948
2 Dr Sahara 4WD Conv	13478	14897	17262

Options	Price
AM/FM/Cassette Audio System [Opt on SE]	+192
Air Conditioning	+421
Antilock Brakes [Opt on Sport,X]	+409
Automatic 3-Speed Transmission	+189
Chrome Wheels [Opt on X]	+331
Cruise Control [Std on Sahara]	+150

Body Styles	TMV Pricing		
	Trade	Private	Dealer
2 Dr Sport 4WD Conv	11439	12643	14651
2 Dr X 4WD Conv	10494	11599	13440

Options	Price
Hardtop Roof	+478
Limited Slip Differential	+171
Off-Road Suspension Package [Opt on Sport,X]	+478
Premium Audio System [Opt on Sport]	+177
Split Folding Rear Seat [Opt on SE]	+270

2001

The Wrangler gets a number of improvements for 2001. All models benefit from a new four-ply soft top that reduces wind and road noise at speed. Deep tint windows are now standard on the Sahara hardtop and optional on Sport and SE models with the solid-shell roof. Two new center console designs are available on all models, as is a premium subwoofer. The add-a-trunk feature and removable side steps have been redesigned to improve functionality, and a new instrument cluster, low-pivot steering column, rearview mirror, airbag cutoff switch, child seat-tether anchors and multifunction headlight/wiper stalk are standard across the entire model line. The ABS system is upgraded; intermittent windshield wipers are now standard, and the 4.0-liter inline six now meets LEV requirements in all 50 states. Sienna Pearl Coat, Amber Fire and Steel Blue exterior colors have been added, while Medium Fern Green and Desert Sand have been dropped.

Mileage Category: L

Body Styles	TMV Pricing		
	Trade	Private	Dealer
2 Dr SE 4WD Conv	7298	8541	9688
2 Dr Sahara 4WD Conv	11083	12972	14716

Options	Price
AM/FM/Cassette Audio System [Opt on SE]	+156
Air Conditioning	+437
Aluminum/Alloy Wheels [Std on Sahara]	+242
Antilock Brakes	+332

Body Styles	TMV Pricing		
	Trade	Private	Dealer
2 Dr Sport 4WD Conv	9601	11237	12746

Options	Price
Automatic 3-Speed Transmission	+305
Cruise Control	+122
Hardtop Roof	+369
Locking Differential	+139

2000

A reengineered 4.0-liter PowerTech inline six-cylinder that is more refined and quiet, with reduced emissions, is standard for Sport and Sahara for 2000. Shift quality kicks up a notch, thanks to an all-new five-speed manual transmission. A radio/cassette combo with four speakers is now standard for the Sport, and the Sahara gains a radio/CD. Solar Yellow, Patriot Blue and Silverstone are additional exterior colors.

Mileage Category: L

Body Styles	TMV Pricing		
	Trade	Private	Dealer
2 Dr SE 4WD Conv	6696	7933	9145
2 Dr Sahara 4WD Conv	9977	11820	13626

Options	Price
AM/FM/CD Audio System [Std on Sahara]	+362
AM/FM/Cassette Audio System [Opt on SE]	+138
Air Conditioning	+386
Aluminum/Alloy Wheels [Std on Sahara]	+214
Antilock Brakes	+293
Automatic 3-Speed Transmission	+269

Body Styles	TMV Pricing		
	Trade	Private	Dealer
2 Dr Sport 4WD Conv	8824	10455	12053

Options	Price
Color Match Dual Roofs	+601
Hardtop Roof	+326
Limited Slip Differential	+123
Locking Differential	+123
Privacy Glass	+175

1999

The Wrangler's interior finally enters the '90s with rotary HVAC controls, replacing the old slider control system. The hard- or soft top is available in Dark Tan, and new colors decorate both the exterior and the interior.

Mileage Category: L

Body Styles	TMV Pricing		
	Trade	Private	Dealer
2 Dr SE 4WD Conv	5974	7158	8390

Body Styles	TMV Pricing		
	Trade	Private	Dealer
2 Dr Sahara 4WD Conv	8421	10090	11826

Body Styles	TMV Pricing		
	Trade	Private	Dealer
2 Dr Sport 4WD Conv	7727	9259	10853

Options	Price	Options	Price
Air Conditioning	+308	Color Match Dual Roofs	+480
Antilock Brakes	+260	Hardtop Roof	+260
Automatic 3-Speed Transmission	+214	Privacy Glass	+139

1998

Jeep has improved off-road capability by increasing the axle ratio offered with the 4.0-liter engine and revising the torsion bar for better steering. Optional this year are a tilting driver seat, automatic speed control, a combination CD/cassette stereo, a new Smart Key Immobilizer theft-deterrent system and two new colors.

Mileage Category: L

Body Styles	TMV Pricing		
	Trade	Private	Dealer
2 Dr SE 4WD Conv	5198	6383	7720
2 Dr Sahara 4WD Conv	7264	8921	10789

Body Styles	TMV Pricing		
	Trade	Private	Dealer
2 Dr Sport 4WD Conv	6626	8137	9840

Options	Price	Options	Price
Air Conditioning	+264	Color Match Dual Roofs	+411
Antilock Brakes	+223	Hardtop Roof	+223
Automatic 3-Speed Transmission	+184	Privacy Glass	+119

1997

Jeep has totally redesigned this American icon. A Quadra-coil suspension improves on- and off-road manners; while dual airbags and optional antilock brakes increase the Wrangler's ability to keep occupants safe. Round, retro-style headlights add a nostalgic touch to this venerable ground-pounder. Fortunately, none of these refinements soften the Wrangler's tough exterior. A restyled interior includes integrated air vents, a glovebox and carlike stereo controls and accessory switches.

Mileage Category: L

Body Styles	TMV Pricing		
	Trade	Private	Dealer
2 Dr SE 4WD Conv	4316	5413	6754
2 Dr Sahara 4WD Conv	6237	7824	9763

Body Styles	TMV Pricing		
	Trade	Private	Dealer
2 Dr Sport 4WD Conv	5017	6293	7853

Options	Price	Options	Price
Air Conditioning	+237	Automatic 3-Speed Transmission	+165
Antilock Brakes	+200	Hardtop Roof	+200

Mileage Category: L

1995

Body Styles	TMV Pricing		
	Trade	Private	Dealer
2 Dr Rio Grande 4WD Conv	3334	4241	5752
2 Dr S 4WD Conv	3032	3856	5229

Body Styles	TMV Pricing		
	Trade	Private	Dealer
2 Dr SE 4WD Conv	3416	4345	5893
2 Dr Sahara 4WD Conv	4113	5232	7096

Options	Price	Options	Price
Air Conditioning	+186	Hardtop Roof	+156
Antilock Brakes	+156	Rear Heater	+78
Automatic 3-Speed Transmission	+129		

S model can be equipped with new Rio Grande package. Renegade is dropped from lineup. An optional dome light can be attached to the optional sound bar.

Amanti

2004

Mileage Category: D

Body Styles	TMV Pricing		
	Trade	Private	Dealer
4 Dr STD Sdn	15451	16461	18143

Options	Price	Options	Price
AM/FM/CD Changer Audio System	+200	Leather Seats	+700
Heated Front Seats	+200	Power Driver Seat w/Memory	+250
Infinity Audio System	+400	Power Moonroof	+545

The Amanti is an all-new full-size sedan from Kia geared to compete head-on with the likes of Toyota's Avalon and the Buick LeSabre.

Optima

2004

Mileage Category: C

Body Styles	TMV Pricing			Body Styles	TMV Pricing		
	Trade	Private	Dealer		Trade	Private	Dealer
4 Dr EX Sdn	9226	10184	11781	4 Dr LX Sdn	8121	9108	10753
4 Dr EX V6 Sdn	9850	10801	12386	4 Dr LX V6 Sdn	8940	9878	11443

Options	Price	Options	Price
AM/FM/Cassette/CD Audio System [Opt on LX]	+595	Leather Seats [Opt on EX]	+725
Antilock Brakes [Opt on V6]	+795	Leather and Wood Steering Wheel [Opt on EX]	+120
Automatic 4-Speed Transmission [Opt on LX]	+1020	Power Passenger Seat [Opt on EX]	+250
Compact Disc Changer	+375	Rear Spoiler	+220

The Kia Optima receives only minor revisions for the 2004 model year. The grille has been revised, 16-inch wheels are now standard on V6 models and the alloy wheels on the EX (last year's SE) have been redesigned. Finally, an in-glass antenna replaces the old power mast style unit from last year, but only on the EX and the LX with the optional cassette/CD audio system.

2003

The Optima gets several revisions for its third year on the market. Most obvious is its new front-end styling, which replaces the Optima's reserved countenance with a more upscale European look -- double light clusters call to mind the Mercedes-Benz E-Class. Other changes include new wheel designs, and inside, a new center stack, new door panels and fresh seat fabric. A manual transmission will no longer be available on the four-cylinder SE model; all automatic four-cylinder models will offer Sportmatic manual-shift capability. The LX model now comes with cruise control and a CD player (at the expense of the cassette deck). The SE will include automatic climate control, an auto-dimming rearview mirror, Homelink and Infinity speakers; a wood- and leather-trimmed steering wheel is now part of the Leather Package. Lastly, engine horsepower ratings have been lowered following parent-company Hyundai's announcement that it had misstated outputs (the Optima is a corporate twin of the Sonata), but the engines themselves are unchanged.

Mileage Category: C

Body Styles	TMV Pricing			Body Styles	TMV Pricing		
	Trade	Private	Dealer		Trade	Private	Dealer
4 Dr LX Sdn	6526	7378	8797	4 Dr SE Sdn	7053	7973	9507
4 Dr LX V6 Sdn	6941	7847	9358	4 Dr SE V6 Sdn	7486	8463	10092

Options	Price	Options	Price
AM/FM/Cassette/CD Audio System [Opt on LX,LX V6]	+354	Compact Disc Changer	+223
Antilock Brakes [Opt on LX V6,SE V6]	+473	Leather Seats [Opt on SE,SE V6]	+446
Automatic 4-Speed Transmission [Opt on LX]	+547	Power Passenger Seat [Opt on SE,SE V6]	+149

2002

Now in its second year, Kia's midsize sedan gets an upgraded V6 engine. Four-cylinder LX models trade their 14-inch wheels for standard 15s, while SE models get auto on/off headlights and two keyless remotes. The optional Leather Package for the SE now includes a four-way power passenger seat.

Mileage Category: C

Body Styles	TMV Pricing			Body Styles	TMV Pricing		
	Trade	Private	Dealer		Trade	Private	Dealer
4 Dr LX Sdn	4382	5157	6447	4 Dr SE Sdn	4810	5660	7077
4 Dr LX V6 Sdn	5019	5906	7384	4 Dr SE V6 Sdn	5425	6384	7982

Options	Price	Options	Price
AM/FM/Cassette/CD Audio System [Opt on LX,LX V6]	+289	Cruise Control [Opt on LX]	+121
Antilock Brakes [Opt on V6]	+386	Leather Seats [Opt on SE,SE V6]	+483
Automatic 4-Speed Transmission [Opt on LX,SE]	+413		

2001

Kia joins the high-stakes poker game that is the midsize sedan market with the all-new Optima. Available in four- and six-cylinder models and two trim levels, the Optima offers a loaded deck of standard features, including air conditioning, side airbags, four-wheel independent suspension and power windows, locks and mirrors.

Mileage Category: C

Body Styles	TMV Pricing			Body Styles	TMV Pricing		
	Trade	Private	Dealer		Trade	Private	Dealer
4 Dr LX Sdn	3642	4614	5512	4 Dr SE Sdn	3879	4914	5870
4 Dr LX V6 Sdn	4031	5106	6099	4 Dr SE V6 Sdn	4359	5522	6596

Options	Price
AM/FM/Cassette/CD Audio System [Opt on LX,LX V6]	+241
Antilock Brakes [Opt on V6]	+322

Options	Price
Automatic 4-Speed Transmission [Opt on LX,SE]	+345
Leather Seats [Opt on SE,SE V6]	+403

Rio

2004

Mileage Category: A

Body Styles	TMV Pricing		
	Trade	Private	Dealer
4 Dr Cinco Wgn	6114	6846	8065

Options	Price
AM/FM/CD Audio System [Opt on STD Sdn]	+425
Air Conditioning	+750
Antilock Brakes	+400
Automatic 4-Speed Transmission	+875

Body Styles	TMV Pricing		
	Trade	Private	Dealer
4 Dr STD Sdn	4948	5623	6749

Options	Price
Power Door Locks	+135
Power Steering [Opt on STD Sdn]	+160
Power Windows	+200

Alloy wheels are now standard on the Cinco wagon. Lumbar support has been added to the driver seat in all models, and the center console armrest gets extra padding.

2003

Mileage Category: A

Body Styles	TMV Pricing		
	Trade	Private	Dealer
4 Dr Cinco Wgn	4458	5338	6804

Options	Price
AM/FM/CD Audio System [Opt on STD Sdn]	+253
Air Conditioning	+446
Aluminum/Alloy Wheels	+164

Body Styles	TMV Pricing		
	Trade	Private	Dealer
4 Dr STD Sdn	4198	4911	6100

Options	Price
Antilock Brakes	+405
Automatic 4-Speed Transmission	+399

For 2003, Kia gives the Rio a number of upgrades. Among these are a new 104-horsepower 1.6-liter four-cylinder engine; various suspension tweaks to improve ride and handling; larger disc brakes; new engine mounts and exhaust tuning for a quieter cabin; and reinforcements to the steering wheel and column to minimize vibration. Inside, look for revisions to the instrument cluster, center console and door panels -- the latter will include storage bins and bottle holders -- as well as new seat fabric. New standard features include child-seat anchors, rear heater ducts, auto-off headlights, variable intermittent wipers and, on the wagon only, a CD player. In addition, Kia has added dual map lights and a sunglasses case to the sedan's Upgrade Package, and will offer the Power Package, which provides power windows and locks. Finally, both Rios get fresh front fascias and wheel covers; the sedan gets a sharper-looking tail and the wagon gets an optional body-color spoiler.

2002

Mileage Category: A

Body Styles	TMV Pricing		
	Trade	Private	Dealer
4 Dr Cinco Wgn	3271	4090	5455

Options	Price
AM/FM/Cassette Audio System [Opt on STD]	+155
Air Conditioning	+364
Aluminum/Alloy Wheels	+134

Body Styles	TMV Pricing		
	Trade	Private	Dealer
4 Dr STD Sdn	2904	3632	4845

Options	Price
Antilock Brakes	+330
Automatic 4-Speed Transmission	+425

One of America's least expensive cars now comes in sedan or wagon flavor. Dubbed the Rio Cinco, the five-door Rio provides 44.3 cubic feet of storage space with the rear seat down.

2001

Mileage Category: A

Body Styles	TMV Pricing		
	Trade	Private	Dealer
4 Dr STD Sdn	2299	3162	3958

Options	Price
AM/FM/CD Audio System	+160
AM/FM/Cassette Audio System	+130
Air Conditioning	+304

Options	Price
Aluminum/Alloy Wheels	+128
Antilock Brakes	+276
Automatic 4-Speed Transmission	+355

With a base MSRP that makes it the least expensive car in America, the roomy little Rio is a peppy 96-horsepower entry-level sedan. While the design and materials used on this car are nothing to write home about, build quality is impressively tight. And Kia's new Long Haul Warranty Program offers the added security of a 10-year/100,000-mile limited powertrain warranty, along with impressive levels of bumper-to-bumper and roadside assistance coverage.

Kia
Sedona/Sephia

Sedona

2004

Mileage Category: P

Body Styles	TMV Pricing		
	Trade	Private	Dealer
4 Dr EX Pass Van	12204	13152	14732

Options	Price
Antilock Brakes	+595
DVD Entertainment System	+1100
Leather Seats [Opt on EX]	+850
Luggage Rack [Opt on LX]	+200

Body Styles	TMV Pricing		
	Trade	Private	Dealer
4 Dr LX Pass Van	11064	12012	13593

Options	Price
Power Moonroof [Opt on EX]	+700
Rear Spoiler	+200
Trailer Hitch	+350

For 2004, the Sedona has a revised grille with a larger logo. The EX model has a new alloy wheel design, while the LX has redesigned plastic wheel covers. A center tray table with cupholders is now standard on both EX and LX.

2003

Minor upgrades are in store for the Sedona in its second year on the market. On the outside, buyers will find new taillights, and in the cabin, you'll note a new audio faceplate and a remote fuel-door release. The LX model gets a CD player, while the EX now comes with two keyless remotes, as well as additional leather on the armrests and lower portions of the seats. A trailer hitch is now available for all Sedonas.

Mileage Category: P

Body Styles	TMV Pricing		
	Trade	Private	Dealer
4 Dr EX Pass Van	10092	11352	13454

Options	Price
Antilock Brakes	+405
Leather Seats [Opt on EX]	+506

Body Styles	TMV Pricing		
	Trade	Private	Dealer
4 Dr LX Pass Van	9165	10310	12219

Options	Price
Power Moonroof [Opt on EX]	+342
Trailer Hitch	+208

2002

Kia joins the minivan rumble with the introduction of the Sedona, the lowest-priced minivan in America. Standard on the Sedona are such niceties as air conditioning, power windows, cruise control and auto on/off headlights. Upscale EX models get a CD player, interior wood trim and power front seats. All Sedonas benefit from Kia's impressive Long Haul Warranty with drivetrain protection for 10 years or 100,000 miles.

Mileage Category: P

Body Styles	TMV Pricing		
	Trade	Private	Dealer
4 Dr EX Pass Van	8253	9431	11395

Options	Price
Antilock Brakes	+330
Leather Seats [Opt on EX]	+413

Body Styles	TMV Pricing		
	Trade	Private	Dealer
4 Dr LX Pass Van	7478	8546	10324

Options	Price
Power Moonroof [Opt on EX]	+279

Sephia

2001

Mileage Category: B

Body Styles	TMV Pricing		
	Trade	Private	Dealer
4 Dr LS Sdn	2776	3947	5027

Options	Price
AM/FM/CD Audio System	+120
Air Conditioning	+365
Aluminum/Alloy Wheels	+138

Body Styles	TMV Pricing		
	Trade	Private	Dealer
4 Dr STD Sdn	2431	3455	4400

Options	Price
Automatic 4-Speed Transmission	+395
Compact Disc Changer	+136

The 2001 Sephia features new safety items such as child seat anchors, front seatbelt pre-tensioners and an emergency internal trunk release. Changes for the 2001 model year also include dual visor vanity mirrors, a coin tray and a gas-cap tether.

2000

The Sephia has improved seat fabric, a new audio system and two new colors for 2000.

Mileage Category: B

Body Styles	TMV Pricing		
	Trade	Private	Dealer
4 Dr LS Sdn	1779	2712	3627

Options	Price
AM/FM/CD Audio System	+166
Air Conditioning	+315
Aluminum/Alloy Wheels	+119

Body Styles	TMV Pricing		
	Trade	Private	Dealer
4 Dr STD Sdn	1617	2464	3295

Options	Price
Antilock Brakes	+280
Automatic 4-Speed Transmission	+340
Power Windows	+122

1999

The Sephia was entirely redesigned in '98 and enters '99 essentially unchanged.

Mileage Category: B

Body Styles	TMV Pricing		
	Trade	Private	Dealer
4 Dr LS Sdn	1200	1997	2826

Body Styles	TMV Pricing		
	Trade	Private	Dealer
4 Dr STD Sdn	1071	1781	2520

Options	Price
AM/FM/CD Audio System	+136
Air Conditioning	+258
Antilock Brakes	+229

Options	Price
Automatic 4-Speed Transmission	+279
Leather Seats	+157

1998

The Sephia is totally redesigned for 1998.

Body Styles	TMV Pricing		
	Trade	Private	Dealer
4 Dr LS Sdn	760	1496	2327

Options	Price
Air Conditioning	+216
Antilock Brakes	+192

Mileage Category: B

Body Styles	TMV Pricing		
	Trade	Private	Dealer
4 Dr STD Sdn	662	1302	2024

Options	Price
Automatic 4-Speed Transmission	+234

1997

Body Styles	TMV Pricing		
	Trade	Private	Dealer
4 Dr GS Sdn	428	1013	1729
4 Dr LS Sdn	392	926	1579

Options	Price
Air Conditioning	+171
Antilock Brakes	+175

Mileage Category: B

Body Styles	TMV Pricing		
	Trade	Private	Dealer
4 Dr RS Sdn	356	839	1430

Options	Price
Automatic 4-Speed Transmission	+172

RS models get body-color bumpers this year, and a tan interior is newly available with black exterior paint.

1996

Body Styles	TMV Pricing		
	Trade	Private	Dealer
4 Dr GS Sdn	302	848	1602
4 Dr LS Sdn	262	739	1398

Options	Price
Air Conditioning	+152
Antilock Brakes [Opt on GS]	+140

Mileage Category: B

Body Styles	TMV Pricing		
	Trade	Private	Dealer
4 Dr RS Sdn	249	700	1323

Options	Price
Automatic 4-Speed Transmission	+175

Styling and suspension tweaks, dual airbags and new twin-cam motors appeared with the introduction of the 1995.5 Sephia. These improvements, along with interior revisions and improved equipment levels, make the Kia more competitive in the compact sedan marketplace. Sephia now meets 1997 side-impact standards, and GS models can be equipped with antilock brakes. Sephia comes with five-year/60,000-mile powertrain coverage.

1995

Body Styles	TMV Pricing		
	Trade	Private	Dealer
4 Dr GS Sdn	183	589	1266
4 Dr GS Sdn (1995.5)	187	601	1290
4 Dr LS Sdn	167	538	1157

Options	Price
Air Conditioning	+115
Automatic 4-Speed Transmission	+116

Body Styles	TMV Pricing		
	Trade	Private	Dealer
4 Dr LS Sdn (1995.5)	171	551	1183
4 Dr RS Sdn	150	484	1040
4 Dr RS Sdn (1995.5)	157	507	1091

Options	Price
Dual Front Airbag Restraints	+79

Oh no, another Korean manufacturer trying to break into the American market. But wait, this one is actually worth considering; a lot of help from Mazda and Ford mean that this little upstart is actually making fairly reliable little cars. The Sephia has plenty of Mazda parts and Kia has a long history of building durable, cheap cars.

Sorento
2004

Body Styles	TMV Pricing		
	Trade	Private	Dealer
4 Dr EX 4WD SUV	16275	17665	19981
4 Dr EX SUV	15079	16440	18708

Options	Price
AM/FM/CD Changer Audio System [Opt on EX]	+200
Antilock Brakes	+595
Automatic Climate Control [Opt on EX]	+300
Automatic Load Leveling [Opt on EX]	+510
Automatic On/Off Headlights [Opt on EX]	+205
Heated Front Seats [Opt on EX]	+180

Mileage Category: L

Body Styles	TMV Pricing		
	Trade	Private	Dealer
4 Dr LX 4WD SUV	14716	16099	18404
4 Dr LX SUV	13301	14587	16731

Options	Price
Leather Seats [Opt on EX]	+780
Leather and Wood Steering Wheel [Opt on EX]	+120
Rear Spoiler [Opt on EX]	+200
Running Boards	+345
Trailer Hitch	+340

The LX model is now available with a sport package that includes a new five-speed manual transmission, side step bars, Michelin tires, alloy wheels, roof rack, leather-wrapped steering wheel and keyless entry. A two-tone gray interior color scheme is also new, and metallic interior accents replace last year's wood grain accents.

Kia
Sorento/Spectra

2003

The Sorento is an all-new SUV from Kia. Larger and more powerful than the pint-size Sportage (which is expected to return for 2004 after a 2003 hiatus, by the way), the Sorento straddles the emerging middle ground between small SUVs and midsize SUVs. And it does so while offering interested buyers true off-road ability. Key competitors are the Ford Escape, the Honda CR-V, the Jeep Liberty, the Nissan Xterra and the Toyota Highlander.

Mileage Category: L

Body Styles	TMV Pricing		
	Trade	Private	Dealer
4 Dr EX 4WD SUV	14204	15811	18488
4 Dr EX SUV	13196	14689	17176

Options	Price
AM/FM/CD Changer Audio System [Opt on EX]	+193
Aluminum/Alloy Wheels [Opt on LX]	+268
Antilock Brakes	+405

Body Styles	TMV Pricing		
	Trade	Private	Dealer
4 Dr LX 4WD SUV	12608	14035	16412
4 Dr LX SUV	11540	12846	15023

Options	Price
Automatic Load Leveling [Opt on EX]	+303
Heated Front Seats [Opt on EX]	+176
Leather Seats [Opt on EX]	+446

Spectra

2004

Kia introduces a completely redesigned and much improved Spectra as a midyear 2004 model. However, both the old and new versions are available this year.

Mileage Category: B

Body Styles	TMV Pricing		
	Trade	Private	Dealer
4 Dr EX Sdn (2004.5)	6911	7825	9349
4 Dr GS Hbk	6616	7497	8966
4 Dr GSX Hbk	7138	8019	9488

Options	Price
Air Conditioning [Opt on STD, LX]	+960
Aluminum/Alloy Wheels [Opt on LS, EX]	+360
Antilock Brakes [Opt on LS, EX, GSX]	+400
Automatic 4-Speed Transmission	+975

Body Styles	TMV Pricing		
	Trade	Private	Dealer
4 Dr LS Sdn	6621	7502	8971
4 Dr LX Sdn (2004.5)	6408	7289	8758
4 Dr STD Sdn	6011	6892	8361

Options	Price
Cruise Control [Opt on LS, EX, GSX]	+200
Power Moonroof [Opt on EX]	+700
Rear Spoiler [Opt on STD, LS, LX, EX]	+250

2003

Mileage Category: B

Body Styles	TMV Pricing		
	Trade	Private	Dealer
4 Dr GS Hbk	4531	5472	7041
4 Dr GSX Hbk	5314	6418	8258

Options	Price
Air Conditioning [Opt on GS, STD]	+571
Aluminum/Alloy Wheels [Opt on LS]	+214
Antilock Brakes [Opt on GSX, LS]	+476
Automatic 4-Speed Transmission	+580

Body Styles	TMV Pricing		
	Trade	Private	Dealer
4 Dr LS Sdn	4961	5992	7709
4 Dr STD Sdn	4361	5267	6777

Options	Price
Compact Disc Changer	+199
Keyless Entry System [Opt on GSX, LS]	+125
Rear Spoiler [Opt on LS, STD]	+119

For 2003, all Spectras will come with a CD player and body-color side moldings. Kia has attempted to make the cabin environment more hospitable via additional sound insulation in the roof and floor, an illuminated ignition and revised climate controls. Also, all hatchbacks get a standard rear wiper with an intermittent feature. Finally, note that engine specs have been revised this year -- the Spectra is now rated at 124 horsepower and 119 pound-feet of torque compared with 126 hp and 108 lb-ft for 2002. The four-cylinder engine itself is unchanged.

2002

The Kia Sephia has officially been renamed the Spectra sedan. Got that? So now, there's the Spectra hatchback and the sedan; they've always shared mechanicals, so no big change there. The sedan will now sport some exterior styling cues borrowed from the five-door version.

Mileage Category: B

Body Styles	TMV Pricing		
	Trade	Private	Dealer
4 Dr GS Hbk	3561	4401	5801
4 Dr GSX Hbk	4261	5266	6942

Options	Price
AM/FM/CD Audio System	+143
Air Conditioning [Opt on GS, STD]	+466
Aluminum/Alloy Wheels [Opt on LS]	+175

Body Styles	TMV Pricing		
	Trade	Private	Dealer
4 Dr LS Sdn	3973	4910	6472
4 Dr STD Sdn	3450	4264	5620

Options	Price
Antilock Brakes [Opt on GSX, LS]	+389
Automatic 4-Speed Transmission	+474
Compact Disc Changer [Opt on GSX, LS]	+163

2001

2001 sees few changes to Kia's sporty five-door hatchback, which was introduced last year to attract younger customers to the brand. The top-rung GSX trim level gets a gas-cap tether, coin holder and dual visor vanity mirrors. Kia's Long Haul Warranty Program has also been introduced for this model year.

Mileage Category: B

Body Styles	TMV Pricing		
	Trade	Private	Dealer
4 Dr GS Hbk	2672	3798	4838

Options	Price
AM/FM/CD Audio System	+120
Air Conditioning [Opt on GS]	+365
Antilock Brakes	+324

Body Styles	TMV Pricing		
	Trade	Private	Dealer
4 Dr GSX Hbk	3197	4544	5788

Options	Price
Automatic 4-Speed Transmission	+395
Compact Disc Changer	+136

2000

The Spectra is new for 2000. Similar in size to the Sephia, Kia hopes the Spectra will attract younger buyers due to the versatile four-door hatchback design and sportier styling.

Mileage Category: B

Body Styles	TMV Pricing		
	Trade	Private	Dealer
4 Dr GS Sdn	1933	2946	3939

Options	Price
Air Conditioning [Opt on GS]	+315
Antilock Brakes	+280

Body Styles	TMV Pricing		
	Trade	Private	Dealer
4 Dr GSX Sdn	2142	3267	4369

Options	Price
Automatic 4-Speed Transmission	+347
Compact Disc Changer	+138

Sportage

2002

Body Styles	TMV Pricing		
	Trade	Private	Dealer
2 Dr STD 4WD Conv	5631	6536	8043
2 Dr STD Conv	5436	6309	7764

Options	Price
AM/FM/Cassette Audio System [Opt on Conv]	+170
Air Conditioning [Opt on Conv]	+449
Aluminum/Alloy Wheels [Opt on Conv]	+182
Antilock Brakes [Opt on Wgn]	+330

Body Styles	TMV Pricing		
	Trade	Private	Dealer
4 Dr STD 4WD SUV	6648	7716	9495
4 Dr STD SUV	6352	7372	9073

Options	Price
Automatic 4-Speed Transmission [Opt on Wgn]	+486
Compact Disc Changer	+163
Cruise Control	+121

The Sportage is now in its eighth model year, so to help move its aged sport-ute along, Kia will offer the four-doors in just one trim level (eliminating the EX and Limited trim models) with more standard feature content than before, though you can no longer get leather upholstery. All Sportages are equipped with body-color door handles and an exterior latch on the rear hatch to ease loading cargo. A Two-Tone Package is available for hardtops; this option group contains two-tone cladding, bumpers and fenders and a cladding-color roof rack and hard-face spare tire cover. In addition, Kia has expanded the standard list of safety features to include seatbelt pre-tensioners and force limiters for the airbags. Finally, interested buyers should note that the Sportage will be going on hiatus for the 2003 model year (to make room for production of the new midsize '03 Sorento); a completely redesigned version (likely with unibody construction) is expected to return in the fall of 2003 as an '04 model.

2001

Kia's Long Haul warranty, introduced late in model-year 2000, provides powertrain coverage for 10 years or 100,000 miles, while a new Limited trim level includes lots of standard goodies over the already well-equipped Base and EX versions.

Mileage Category: L

Body Styles	TMV Pricing		
	Trade	Private	Dealer
2 Dr STD 4WD Conv	4398	5670	6845
2 Dr STD Conv	4210	5428	6553
4 Dr EX 4WD SUV	5181	6680	8063

Options	Price
AM/FM/CD Audio System [Opt on STD]	+193
AM/FM/Cassette Audio System	+130
Air Conditioning [Opt on STD]	+365
Aluminum/Alloy Wheels [Opt on STD]	+138

Body Styles	TMV Pricing		
	Trade	Private	Dealer
4 Dr EX SUV	4867	6275	7574
4 Dr STD 4WD SUV	4749	6123	7391
4 Dr STD SUV	4468	5760	6953

Options	Price
Antilock Brakes	+276
Automatic 4-Speed Transmission [Opt on 4 Dr]	+405
Compact Disc Changer	+136
Leather Seats	+345

2000

Kia ushers in the 2000 Sportage with a new sound system, dual airbags, new colors and some additional equipment, but keeps last year's MSRP.

Mileage Category: L

Body Styles	TMV Pricing		
	Trade	Private	Dealer
2 Dr STD 4WD Conv	3430	4576	5699
2 Dr STD Conv	3252	4338	5402
4 Dr EX 4WD SUV	3933	5247	6534

Options	Price
AM/FM/CD Audio System [Opt on STD]	+166
AM/FM/Cassette/CD Audio System	+166
Air Conditioning [Opt on STD]	+315
Aluminum/Alloy Wheels [Opt on STD]	+119

Body Styles	TMV Pricing		
	Trade	Private	Dealer
4 Dr EX SUV	3665	4889	6088
4 Dr STD 4WD SUV	3635	4849	6039
4 Dr STD SUV	3502	4672	5818

Options	Price
Antilock Brakes	+238
Automatic 4-Speed Transmission [Opt on 4 Dr]	+349
Compact Disc Changer	+138
Leather Seats	+297

1999

A new two-door convertible model joins the four-door Sportage in 1999. The convertible comes in either a 4x2 layout with automatic transmission or a 4x4 layout with five-speed manual transmission. It also boasts dual front airbags and a driver-side front knee bag.

Mileage Category: L

Body Styles	TMV Pricing		
	Trade	Private	Dealer
2 Dr STD 4WD Conv	2930	4021	5157
2 Dr STD Conv	2733	3750	4809
4 Dr EX 4WD SUV	3256	4468	5729

Body Styles	TMV Pricing		
	Trade	Private	Dealer
4 Dr EX SUV	3079	4226	5419
4 Dr STD 4WD SUV	3016	4139	5307
4 Dr STD SUV	2970	4075	5226

1999 (cont'd)

Options	Price		Options	Price
AM/FM/CD Audio System [Opt on STD]	+136		Automatic 4-Speed Transmission	+286
Air Conditioning [Opt on STD]	+258		Leather Seats	+244
Antilock Brakes	+216			

1998

There are lots of improvements this year for the Sportage, including a new grille, new alloy wheels, tilt steering wheel, passenger-side airbag, better brakes, improved air conditioning and four-wheel ABS that replaces last year's rear-wheel ABS.

Mileage Category: L

Body Styles	TMV Pricing			Body Styles	TMV Pricing		
	Trade	Private	Dealer		Trade	Private	Dealer
4 Dr EX 4WD SUV	2665	3776	5029	4 Dr STD 4WD SUV	2501	3545	4723
4 Dr EX SUV	2664	3775	5027	4 Dr STD SUV	2424	3435	4576

Options	Price		Options	Price
Air Conditioning	+216		Automatic 4-Speed Transmission	+240
Antilock Brakes	+181		Leather Seats	+216

1997

An automatic transmission is offered on 2WD models, and the EX trim level is available in 2WD for the first time. Power door locks, a theft-deterrent system and a spare tire carrier are all standard on all Sportages for 1997. A new option is a CD player. Sportage gets a new grille. A tan interior can be combined with black paint for the first time. Base 2WD models lose their standard alloy wheels.

Mileage Category: L

Body Styles	TMV Pricing			Body Styles	TMV Pricing		
	Trade	Private	Dealer		Trade	Private	Dealer
4 Dr EX 4WD SUV	2081	3076	4292	4 Dr STD 4WD SUV	2061	3046	4250
4 Dr EX SUV	2032	3002	4188	4 Dr STD SUV	1914	2829	3948

Options	Price		Options	Price
Air Conditioning	+177		Leather Seats	+196
Automatic 4-Speed Transmission	+196			

1996

The world's first knee airbag arrives in conjunction with a driver airbag, and a two-wheel-drive edition is available this year. A spirited twin-cam engine arrived late in 1995, and cured Sportage's power ills.

Mileage Category: L

Body Styles	TMV Pricing			Body Styles	TMV Pricing		
	Trade	Private	Dealer		Trade	Private	Dealer
4 Dr EX 4WD SUV	1665	2591	3869	4 Dr STD 4WD SUV	1548	2409	3598
4 Dr EX SUV	1716	2670	3988	4 Dr STD SUV	1400	2179	3255

Options	Price		Options	Price
Air Conditioning	+158		Leather Seats	+175
Automatic 4-Speed Transmission	+175			

1995

Another mini-SUV is introduced, competing with everything from the Jeep Cherokee to the Geo Tracker. The Sportage offers comfortable seating for four, ample storage space and available four-wheel drive. Designed with Ford and Mazda, with suspension tuning by Lotus, the Sportage should provide a good deal of fun and durability.

Mileage Category: L

Body Styles	TMV Pricing			Body Styles	TMV Pricing		
	Trade	Private	Dealer		Trade	Private	Dealer
4 Dr EX 4WD SUV	1319	2037	3233	4 Dr STD SUV	1039	1606	2551
4 Dr STD 4WD SUV	1148	1774	2818				

Options	Price		Options	Price
2.0L I4 DOHC 16V FI Engine	+79		Automatic 4-Speed Transmission	+132
Air Conditioning	+119		Leather Seats	+112

Defender

1997

Mileage Category: O

Body Styles	TMV Pricing			Body Styles	TMV Pricing		
	Trade	Private	Dealer		Trade	Private	Dealer
2 Dr 90 4WD Conv	17474	20515	24231	2 Dr 90 4WD SUV	19046	22361	26411

Options	Price
Air Conditioning	+409

After a one-year hiatus, Defender returns in convertible and hardtop body styles. A 4.0-liter V8 engine is standard, mated to a ZF four-speed automatic transmission. A redesigned center console includes cupholders, and hardtops have new interior trim. Convertibles get improved top sealing, while all Defender 90s are treated to fresh paint colors.

1995

Mileage Category: O

Body Styles	TMV Pricing		
	Trade	Private	Dealer
2 Dr 90 4WD SUV	11354	14127	18749

Options	Price	Options	Price
Air Conditioning	+303	Special Factory Paint	+88
Aluminum/Alloy Wheels	+391		

Later in the model year, a new five-speed manual transmission (the only gearbox fitted to the Defender) debuts and features full syncromesh for reverse gear, decreasing the likelihood of embarrassing grinding noises when one attempts to back up. Land Rover claims the overall shift action is lighter and more precise, and that the new clutch requires less pressure to operate.

Discovery

2004

Mileage Category: O

Body Styles	TMV Pricing			Body Styles	TMV Pricing		
	Trade	Private	Dealer		Trade	Private	Dealer
4 Dr HSE 4WD SUV	24005	25250	27324	4 Dr SE 4WD SUV	22844	24089	26163
4 Dr S 4WD SUV	20316	21562	23638				

Options	Price	Options	Price
AM/FM/CD Audio System [Opt on SE]	+200	Navigation System [Opt on SE]	+800
Automatic Load Leveling [Opt on SE]	+750	Park Distance Control (Rear) [Opt on S, SE]	+300
DVD Entertainment System [Opt on SE, HSE]	+2000	Rear Air Conditioning Controls	+750
Dual Sunroofs [Opt on S]	+1500	Special Factory Paint	+300
Heated Front Seats	+250	Third Seat	+1000
Heated Windshield	+350		

For 2004, the Discovery gets new tubular roof rails, and a manually lockable center differential is now standard. The S trim gets an in-dash CD player as standard equipment, and the HSE's cabin is enhanced with burled wood trim on the center console. A new interior color scheme -- called Tundra, featuring light earth tones in leather -- has been added. Finally, Land Rover is offering a limited-edition G4 model this year: It's painted an eye-catching orange, and boasts a cabin with unique trim and upholstery.

2003

Mileage Category: O

Body Styles	TMV Pricing			Body Styles	TMV Pricing		
	Trade	Private	Dealer		Trade	Private	Dealer
4 Dr HSE AWD SUV	21588	22934	25177	4 Dr SE AWD SUV	20040	21290	23372
4 Dr S AWD SUV	17664	18765	20601				

Options	Price	Options	Price
Air Conditioning - Front and Rear	+464	Heated Front Seats	+214
Automatic Load Leveling [Opt on SE]	+535	Special Factory Paint	+214
Automatic Stability Control [Opt on HSE,SE]	+1213	Third Seat	+714
Dual Sunroofs [Opt on S]	+1070		

Land Rover has made a number of updates to its 2003 Discovery. In terms of mechanical components, the company has installed a more powerful 4.6-liter V8 engine and has improved the steering, brakes and suspension. Styling is revised front and rear, including headlamps that mimic its bigger brother's, the Range Rover. New interior treatments grace the cabin, and a rear park distance control is now an option. Finally, Land Rover has dropped the "Series II" nomenclature, and it's now simply called "Discovery."

1999

Mileage Category: O

Body Styles	TMV Pricing			Body Styles	TMV Pricing		
	Trade	Private	Dealer		Trade	Private	Dealer
4 Dr SD AWD SUV	8750	10192	11692	4 Dr Series II AWD SUV	9095	10593	12152

Options	Price	Options	Price
Air Conditioning - Front and Rear	+246	Dual Power Moonroofs	+493
Automatic Load Leveling [Opt on Series II]	+201	Heated Front Seats	+164
Compact Disc Changer	+205	Jump Seat(s)	+212

The release of the 1999 Discovery Series II sees the first engineering redesign since the vehicle's European introduction 11 years ago. Traction Control, Active Cornering Enhancement and Hill Descent Control are new standard features.

Land Rover
Discovery/Series II

1999 (cont'd)

Options	Price
Leather Seats [Opt on Series II]	+320
Performance/Handling Package	+904

Options	Price
Power Driver Seat [Opt on Series II]	+119
Power Passenger Seat [Opt on Series II]	+119

1998

Mileage Category: O

Body Styles	TMV Pricing		
	Trade	Private	Dealer
4 Dr 50th Anniv AWD SUV	7617	8990	10538
4 Dr LE AWD SUV	6973	8231	9649

Body Styles	TMV Pricing		
	Trade	Private	Dealer
4 Dr LSE AWD SUV	7249	8556	10029

Options	Price
Air Conditioning - Front and Rear	+207
Compact Disc Changer [Opt on LE]	+172

Options	Price
Jump Seat(s)	+345

Changes to the Discovery include interior trim enhancements for the LE and LSE. The rearview mirror also features map lights for the first time.

1997

A diversity antenna is added, and all interiors are trimmed with polished burled walnut. The sunroof has darker tinting, the airbag system benefits from simplified operation and engine management is improved. Three new exterior colors debut: Oxford Blue, Rioja Red and Charleston Green.

Mileage Category: O

Body Styles	TMV Pricing		
	Trade	Private	Dealer
4 Dr LSE AWD SUV	5666	6859	8318
4 Dr SD AWD SUV	5269	6378	7734
4 Dr SE AWD SUV	5470	6622	8030

Body Styles	TMV Pricing		
	Trade	Private	Dealer
4 Dr SE7 AWD SUV	6003	7267	8812
4 Dr XD AWD SUV	5304	6421	7787

Options	Price
Compact Disc Changer	+213
Jump Seat(s) [Std on SE7]	+401
Leather Seats [Opt on SD]	+333

Options	Price
Power Driver Seat [Opt on SD]	+116
Power Passenger Seat [Opt on SD]	+116

1996

Three new trim levels, a revised engine that gets better around-town fuel economy, new colors, increased seat travel and new power seats sum up the changes for 1996.

Mileage Category: O

Body Styles	TMV Pricing		
	Trade	Private	Dealer
4 Dr SD AWD SUV	4142	5112	6451
4 Dr SE AWD SUV	4381	5407	6824

Body Styles	TMV Pricing		
	Trade	Private	Dealer
4 Dr SE7 AWD SUV	4458	5503	6946

Options	Price
Automatic 4-Speed Transmission [Std on SE]	+232
Compact Disc Changer	+126

Options	Price
Leather Seats [Opt on SD]	+197
Third Seat [Std on SE7]	+121

1995

Introduced as a late-1994 model-year vehicle, the Discovery continues into its second year unchanged.

Mileage Category: O

Body Styles	TMV Pricing		
	Trade	Private	Dealer
4 Dr STD AWD SUV	3530	4393	5830

Options	Price
AM/FM/CD Audio System	+126
Air Conditioning - Front and Rear	+189
Automatic 4-Speed Transmission	+227
Dual Power Moonroofs	+378

Options	Price
Leather Jump Seat(s)	+126
Leather Seats	+246
Special Factory Paint	+76

Discovery Series II

2002

Mileage Category: O

Body Styles	TMV Pricing		
	Trade	Private	Dealer
4 Dr SD AWD SUV	14937	16052	17910

Body Styles	TMV Pricing		
	Trade	Private	Dealer
4 Dr SE AWD SUV	16540	17775	19833

Options	Price
Air Conditioning - Front and Rear	+464
Automatic Load Leveling [Opt on SE]	+774
Dual Power Sunroofs [Opt on SD]	+928

Options	Price
Heated Front Seats	+278
Special Factory Paint	+186
Third Seat	+619

Discovery gets new alloy wheels, along with a standard 300-watt Harman Kardon sound system and an available factory-installed navigation system.

For the latest vehicle information, visit www.edmunds.com

2001

Land Rover introduces three new trim levels to the Discovery Series II lineup -- SD, LE and SE. New paint options are Oslo Blue and Bonatti Gray.

Mileage Category: O

Body Styles	TMV Pricing		
	Trade	Private	Dealer
4 Dr LE AWD SUV	13269	14835	16280
4 Dr SD AWD SUV	13105	14651	16079

Body Styles	TMV Pricing		
	Trade	Private	Dealer
4 Dr SE AWD SUV	14069	15729	17262

Options	Price
Air Conditioning - Front and Rear	+386
Automatic Load Leveling	+386
Dual Power Moonroofs [Opt on LE,SD]	+772

Options	Price
Heated Front Seats	+257
Special Factory Paint	+154
Third Seat	+617

2000

The Discovery was completely redesigned last year and sees only minor interior trim revisions for the 2000 model year.

Mileage Category: O

Body Styles	TMV Pricing		
	Trade	Private	Dealer
4 Dr STD AWD SUV	10554	12140	13694

Options	Price
Air Conditioning - Front and Rear	+300
Automatic Load Leveling	+220
Automatic Stability Control	+260
Compact Disc Changer	+250
Dual Power Moonroofs	+600
Heated Front Seats	+200
Jump Seat(s)	+232

Options	Price
Leather Seats	+390
Performance/Handling Package	+1101
Power Driver Seat	+140
Power Passenger Seat	+140
Special Factory Paint	+120
Split Folding Rear Seat	+160

Freelander

2004

Mileage Category: O

Body Styles	TMV Pricing		
	Trade	Private	Dealer
2 Dr SE3 AWD SUV	18960	20097	21991
4 Dr HSE AWD SUV	20372	21509	23403

Body Styles	TMV Pricing		
	Trade	Private	Dealer
4 Dr SE AWD SUV	18255	19392	21286

Options	Price
18 Inch Wheels	+750
AM/FM/CD Changer Audio System [Opt on SE]	+200
Fog Lights [Opt on SE, HSE]	+150
Heated Front Seats	+200

Options	Price
Leather Seats [Opt on SE, HSE]	+1000
Park Distance Control (Rear) [Opt on SE3, HSE]	+250
Special Factory Paint	+250
Steering Wheel Radio Controls [Opt on SE]	+150

For 2004, the Freelander's exterior has been revamped with a redesigned front bumper and grille; also added are new clear lens headlamps similar to those on the Range Rover. Front and rear bumpers are now body-colored, and in back, the taillamps assume a higher position. In the cabin, the Freelander gets a revised dash, along with new instrumentation, switchgear, door trim panels and front seats. The sport-ute's list of standard equipment grows to include roof rails, tinted windows and an in-dash six-disc CD changer, while the number of available four-door trims shrinks from three to two: SE and HSE. The Freelander's five-speed automatic transmission has also been recalibrated for smoother shifting.

2003

Engineering changes for Land Rover's mini-ute include a larger fuel tank and an improvement in the climate control system for quieter operation and more efficiency. Body side moldings have been added to protect the Freelander against scrapes. The 2003 model year sees the introduction of the three-door SE3 version, with removable top and rear panels for topless fun like a Jeep Wrangler.

Mileage Category: O

Body Styles	TMV Pricing		
	Trade	Private	Dealer
2 Dr SE3 AWD SUV	14672	15865	17854
4 Dr HSE AWD SUV	17496	18919	21290

Body Styles	TMV Pricing		
	Trade	Private	Dealer
4 Dr S AWD SUV	13916	15048	16934
4 Dr SE AWD SUV	15437	16693	18785

Options	Price
Compact Disc Changer [Opt on S,SE,SE3]	+285
Harman Kardon Audio System [Opt on S,SE]	+535
Heated Front Seats	+214

Options	Price
Power Moonroof [Opt on SE]	+624
Special Factory Paint	+143

2002

The first new Land Rover to come to America since 1995, the compact Freelander is expected to boost U.S. sales by 50 percent by offering the go-anywhere cachet of the LR brand name and the daily drivability of a small SUV in a package priced under $30,000.

Mileage Category: O

Body Styles	TMV Pricing		
	Trade	Private	Dealer
4 Dr HSE AWD SUV	15021	16384	18655
4 Dr S AWD SUV	11895	12974	14773

Body Styles	TMV Pricing		
	Trade	Private	Dealer
4 Dr SE AWD SUV	13241	14443	16445

2002 (cont'd)

Options	Price
Harman Kardon Audio System [Opt on S,SE]	+464
Heated Front Seats	+186

Options	Price
Power Moonroof [Opt on S,SE]	+541

Range Rover

2004

Mileage Category: O

Body Styles	TMV Pricing		
	Trade	Private	Dealer
4 Dr HSE 4WD SUV	57483	59832	63747

Options	Price
Heated Front and Rear Seats	+920
Heated Steering Wheel	+200

Options	Price
Leather Interior Trim	+1230
Ski Sack	+180

For 2004, the Range Rover gets an even more luxurious leather interior; buyers also now have the option of outfitting the vehicle with Contour 14-way electrically adjustable seats. A new limited-edition trim -- the Westminster Edition -- has been added; only 300 of these vehicles are slated for production. Each Westminster Edition Range Rover features pearlescent paint, 20-inch alloy wheels, leather-covered dash and center console areas, rain-sensing windshield wipers, leather Contour seats and an abundance of polished hardwood. This trim level comes in Java Black and Bonatti Grey exteriors.

2003

As this is just the third new Range Rover in 31 years, one might hope that the 2003 Range Rover hosts some significant improvements. Indeed it does. Land Rover has focused on improving drivability and livability. As such, this updated flagship SUV features unit body construction, a four-wheel independent suspension and a BMW-engineered V8 mated to a five-speed automatic transmission. It also boasts more interior space, greater ground clearance and a beautifully revised interior.

Mileage Category: O

Body Styles	TMV Pricing		
	Trade	Private	Dealer
4 Dr HSE AWD SUV	48209	50927	55457

Options	Price
Heated Front and Rear Seats	+464
Heated Steering Wheel	+196

Options	Price
Ski Sack	+178
Special Leather Interior Trim	+1284

2002

Mileage Category: O

Body Styles	TMV Pricing		
	Trade	Private	Dealer
4 Dr 4.6 HSE AWD SUV	30512	32790	36587

With an all-new Range Rover set to debut for 2003, the only change to the existing model for 2002 is the addition of a Westminster special edition.

2001

Land Rover's venerable Range Rover will now come standard with a 4.6-liter V8 engine. A navigation system is now standard on the 4.6 HSE model and optional on the 4.6 SE, as is a new premium audio system. New exterior colors are Oslo Blue and Bonatti Grey.

Mileage Category: O

Body Styles	TMV Pricing		
	Trade	Private	Dealer
4 Dr 4.6 HSE AWD SUV	23136	25864	28383

Body Styles	TMV Pricing		
	Trade	Private	Dealer
4 Dr 4.6 SE AWD SUV	19268	21540	23637

Options	Price
Navigation System	+1541

Options	Price
Special Factory Paint	+154

2000

The 2000 Range Rover now qualifies as a low-emissions vehicle. Interior and exterior upgrades improve the vehicle's look and feel, and new trim levels allow buyers to further dress up their Range Rover's appearance

Mileage Category: O

Body Styles	TMV Pricing		
	Trade	Private	Dealer
4 Dr 4.0 SE AWD SUV	14837	16935	18991
4 Dr 4.6 HSE AWD SUV	17591	20078	22516

Body Styles	TMV Pricing		
	Trade	Private	Dealer
4 Dr 4.6 Vitesse AWD SUV	17591	20078	22516
4 Dr County AWD SUV	14549	16606	18622

Options	Price
Navigation System	+1137

Options	Price
Special Factory Paint	+120

1999

Engine upgrades, new color schemes, traction control and standard side-mounted airbags are some of the additions to the 1999 Range Rovers, which will be introduced later in the year. For now, interim Range Rover models called the 4.0 and 4.0S are available.

Mileage Category: O

Body Styles	TMV Pricing		
	Trade	Private	Dealer
4 Dr 4.0 AWD SUV	12359	14395	16514
4 Dr 4.0 S AWD SUV	12516	14578	16725

Body Styles	TMV Pricing		
	Trade	Private	Dealer
4 Dr 4.0 SE AWD SUV	12380	14419	16541
4 Dr 4.6 HSE AWD SUV	14470	16854	19335

Options	Price
Navigation System	+747

Mileage Category: O

Body Styles	TMV Pricing			Body Styles	TMV Pricing		
	Trade	Private	Dealer		Trade	Private	Dealer
4 Dr 4.0 SE AWD SUV	9522	11239	13175	4 Dr 50th Anniv AWD SUV	11004	12989	15227
4 Dr 4.6 HSE AWD SUV	12230	14436	16923				

1998

Range Rover models get a new Harmon Kardon audio system this year. Other changes include a new upholstery stitch pattern and a leather-wrapped gearshift knob.

Mileage Category: O

Body Styles	TMV Pricing			Body Styles	TMV Pricing		
	Trade	Private	Dealer		Trade	Private	Dealer
4 Dr 4.0 SE AWD SUV	8183	9793	11761	4 Dr 4.6 HSE AWD SUV	9682	11587	13916

Options	Price
Vitesse Package	+239

1997

The 4.0 SE gets three new exterior colors (Oxford Blue, Rioja Red and White Gold, all matched to Saddle leather interior), a HomeLink transmitter and jeweled wheel center caps. The 4.6 HSE gets three new exterior colors (British Racing Green, Monza Red and AA Yellow), one new interior color (Lightstone with contrasting piping) and a leather shift handle.

Mileage Category: O

Body Styles	TMV Pricing			Body Styles	TMV Pricing		
	Trade	Private	Dealer		Trade	Private	Dealer
4 Dr 4.0 SE AWD SUV	6457	7851	9776	4 Dr 4.6 HSE AWD SUV	7588	9226	11489

1996

Base 4.0 SE model is unchanged for 1996. A new, more powerful 4.6 HSE model debuts, giving buyers extra horsepower, fat wheels and tires, mud flaps and chrome exhaust for a $7,000 premium over the 4.0 SE.

Mileage Category: O

Body Styles	TMV Pricing			Body Styles	TMV Pricing		
	Trade	Private	Dealer		Trade	Private	Dealer
4 Dr 4.0 SE AWD SUV	5059	6295	8355	4 Dr County LWB AWD SUV	4493	5591	7420
4 Dr County Classic AWD SUV	3924	4883	6481				

Options	Price	Options	Price
Special Factory Paint	+76	Special Interior Trim [Opt on LWB]	+203

1995

The new 4.0 SE is introduced as a late '95 model. Styling is an evolution of the classic Range Rover look. A new chassis sports an electronic air suspension and a 4.0-liter V8 that produces 190 horsepower. This top-of-the-line SUV also includes luxuries such as the obligatory leather and wood-trimmed cabin and a premium stereo with a six-disc CD changer.

Lexus
ES 300

ES 300

2003

Completely redesigned last year, the 2003 ES 300's only change is the addition of power-adjustable pedals.

Mileage Category: H

Body Styles	TMV Pricing		
	Trade	Private	Dealer
4 Dr STD Sdn	21723	23131	25478

Options	Price	Options	Price
AM/FM/CD Changer Audio System	+421	Mark Levinson Audio System	+440
Chrome Wheels	+1300	Navigation System	+1529
Compact Disc Changer	+421	Power Driver Seat w/Memory	+229
Electronic Suspension Control	+474	Power Rear Window Sunshade	+161
Heated Front Seats	+336	Traction Control System	+497
Leather Seats	+765	Xenon Headlamps	+489
Leather and Wood Steering Wheel	+252		

2002

Lexus has introduced a completely redesigned ES 300 for 2002. The new car is roomier and quieter than the previous car, and in many ways has become more closely aligned with the LS 430 flagship model. Safety and feature quotients have been increased, and the car is wrapped in a svelte new body.

Mileage Category: H

Body Styles	TMV Pricing		
	Trade	Private	Dealer
4 Dr STD Sdn	19520	20949	23331

Options	Price	Options	Price
AM/FM/Cassette/CD Changer Audio System	+268	Mark Levinson Audio System	+411
Automatic Stability Control	+286	Navigation System	+1431
Chrome Wheels	+1216	Power Driver Seat w/Memory	+215
Compact Disc Changer	+393	Power Moonroof	+644
Electronic Suspension Control	+443	Power Rear Window Sunshade	+150
Heated Front Seats	+315	Traction Control System	+179
Leather Seats	+715	Xenon Headlamps	+458

2001

A glow-in-the-dark emergency trunk release handle is now located in the cargo compartment, while child seat-tether anchors have been added inside.

Mileage Category: H

Body Styles	TMV Pricing		
	Trade	Private	Dealer
4 Dr STD Sdn	14207	15840	17347

Options	Price	Options	Price
Automatic Stability Control	+349	Leather Seats	+635
Chrome Wheels	+1104	Nakamichi Audio System	+1034
Compact Disc Changer	+685	Power Driver Seat w/Memory	+190
Electronic Suspension Control	+393	Power Moonroof	+543
Heated Front Seats	+279	Xenon Headlamps	+327

2000

The Lexus ES 300 sports new front-end styling and taillights. The rearview and driver-side mirrors are now electrochromatic for improved nighttime performance. The interior gets new colors and additional wood trim on the audio/heater panel. The mirrors are added to the memory seat function. High-intensity discharge headlights are optional, as are 16-inch wheels. BrakeAssist is included in the Vehicle Skid Control option. A particle-and-odor air filter is a new option. The ES 300 also receives child seat-anchor brackets and three new colors.

Mileage Category: H

Body Styles	TMV Pricing		
	Trade	Private	Dealer
4 Dr STD Sdn	12606	14385	16128

Options	Price	Options	Price
AM/FM/Cassette/CD Audio System	+292	Leather Seats	+531
Automatic Stability Control	+292	Nakamichi Audio System	+637
Compact Disc Changer	+319	Power Driver Seat w/Memory	+159
Heated Front Seats	+186	Power Moonroof	+454

1999

A new 3.0-liter V6 engine with VVT-i (Variable Valve Timing with intelligence) gives the 1999 ES 300 more horsepower, lower emissions and improved fuel economy. Optional Vehicle Skid Control (VSC) is available on the new ES as are one-touch open and close front windows and a one-touch operated moonroof.

Mileage Category: H

Body Styles	TMV Pricing		
	Trade	Private	Dealer
4 Dr STD Sdn	10144	11758	13437

1999 (cont'd)

Options	Price	Options	Price
AM/FM/Cassette/CD Audio System	+238	Leather Seats	+481
Chrome Wheels	+385	Nakamichi Audio System	+577
Compact Disc Changer	+289	Power Driver Seat w/Memory	+144
Heated Front Seats	+168	Power Moonroof	+411

1998

Side-impact airbags debut on Lexus's entry-level car, as does an engine immobilizer anti-theft system and an optional Nakamichi audio system. Reduced force front airbags are also new on all 1998 Lexus models.

Mileage Category: H

Body Styles	TMV Pricing		
	Trade	Private	Dealer
4 Dr STD Sdn	8036	9468	11082

Options	Price	Options	Price
AM/FM/Cassette/CD Audio System	+196	Leather Seats	+396
Chrome Wheels	+317	Nakamichi Audio System	+475
Compact Disc Changer	+238	Power Driver Seat w/Memory	+119
Heated Front Seats	+139	Power Moonroof	+339

1997

The entry-level Lexus has been totally redesigned this year, growing in nearly every dimension. Lexus manages to eke out more power from the ES 300's 3.0-liter V6 engine. No longer just a dressed-up Camry, the ES 300 has finally come into its own.

Mileage Category: H

Body Styles	TMV Pricing		
	Trade	Private	Dealer
4 Dr STD Sdn	6910	8288	9972

Options	Price	Options	Price
AM/FM/Cassette/CD Audio System	+160	Leather Seats	+324
Chrome Wheels	+259	Power Moonroof	+277
Compact Disc Changer	+194		

1996

Mileage Category: H

Body Styles	TMV Pricing		
	Trade	Private	Dealer
4 Dr STD Sdn	5530	6742	8416

Options	Price	Options	Price
AM/FM/Cassette/CD Audio System	+130	Leather Seats	+263
Chrome Wheels	+211	Power Moonroof	+225
Compact Disc Changer	+158		

Two new colors are available.

1995

Styling is freshened, and chrome wheels are available. Trunk-mounted CD changer is a new option.

Mileage Category: H

Body Styles	TMV Pricing		
	Trade	Private	Dealer
4 Dr STD Sdn	4802	5888	7698

Options	Price	Options	Price
Chrome Wheels	+189	Leather Seats	+236
Compact Disc Changer	+142	Power Moonroof	+202
Heated Front Seats	+83		

ES 330
2004

Mileage Category: H

Body Styles	TMV Pricing		
	Trade	Private	Dealer
4 Dr STD Sdn	23819	25193	27482

Options	Price	Options	Price
AM/FM/CD Changer Audio System	+400	Mark Levinson Audio System	+1100
Chrome Wheels	+1700	Navigation System	+1620
Compact Disc Changer	+500	Power Adjustable Foot Pedals	+140
Electronic Suspension Control	+620	Power Rear Window Sunshade	+210
Heated Front Seats	+440	Rain Sensing Windshield Wipers	+190
Leather and Wood Steering Wheel	+330	Traction Control System	+650

Lexus
ES 330/GS 300

2004 (cont'd)

A new engine has been fitted -- a 3.3-liter V6 -- and, consequently, the car formerly known as the ES 300 is now badged the ES 330. Besides the newfound power, Lexus' entry-level luxury sedan gains additional content upgrades for 2004, including a memory function for the adjustable pedals, improved navigation system features, power lumbar adjustment for the front-passenger seat, larger side airbags and a maintenance indicator light.

Options	Price
Xenon Headlamps	+450

GS 300

2004

Nothing changes on the GS 300 this year.

Mileage Category: I

Body Styles	Trade	Private	Dealer
TMV Pricing			
4 Dr STD Sdn	27422	29013	31664

Options	Price
AM/FM/Cassette/CD Changer Audio System	+390
Chrome Wheels	+1700
Heated Front Seats	+440
Leather Seats	+1250
Mark Levinson Audio System	+1100

Options	Price
Navigation System	+1620
Power Driver Seat w/Memory	+300
Rear Spoiler	+440
Xenon Headlamps	+515

2003

The only changes of note for the GS 300 this year are a now standard moonroof, an in-dash CD changer and wider tires (going from a 215mm tread to a 225mm tread).

Mileage Category: I

Body Styles	Trade	Private	Dealer
TMV Pricing			
4 Dr STD Sdn	25138	26714	29341

Options	Price
Aluminum/Alloy Interior Trim	+249
Chrome Wheels	+1300
Compact Disc Changer	+497
Heated Front Seats	+336
Leather Seats	+956
Leather and Wood Steering Wheel	+306

Options	Price
Mark Levinson Audio System	+459
Navigation System	+1529
Power Driver Seat w/Memory	+229
Rear Spoiler	+336
Sport Suspension	+344
Xenon Headlamps	+382

2002

After a number of upgrades last year, the GS 300 enters 2002 unchanged.

Mileage Category: I

Body Styles	Trade	Private	Dealer
TMV Pricing			
4 Dr STD Sdn	21467	23022	25613

Options	Price
Aluminum/Alloy Interior Trim	+232
Chrome Wheels	+1216
Compact Disc Changer	+536
Heated Front Seats	+315
Leather Seats	+894
Mark Levinson Audio System	+429

Options	Price
Navigation System	+1431
Power Driver Seat w/Memory	+215
Power Moonroof	+715
Sport Suspension	+322
Xenon Headlamps	+358

2001

Mileage Category: I

Body Styles	TMV Pricing		
	Trade	Private	Dealer
4 Dr STD Sdn	18394	20668	22768

Options	Price	Options	Price
Automatic Dimming Sideview Mirror(s)	+127	Mark Levinson Audio System	+787
Chrome Wheels	+1079	Navigation System	+1269
Compact Disc Changer	+685	Power Driver Seat w/Memory	+190
Heated Front Seats	+279	Power Moonroof	+647
Leather Seats	+762	Xenon Headlamps	+327

GS 430 gets a new ULEV-certified, 4.3-liter V8 good for 300 horsepower and 325 ft-lbs. of torque, resulting in sub-6-second acceleration times to 60 mph. GS 300 has new E-shift buttons on the steering wheel for manual control of the automatic transmission's shift points. On the safety front, standard side curtain airbags debut on both models, and a new sensor detects if the front passenger seat is unoccupied, deactivating the front passenger airbag if nobody is sitting in that seat. Additionally, a new child seat-tether restraint has been added, along with impact-detecting door locks and an emergency trunk release handle that glows in the dark inside the cargo area. Exterior changes include water-repellent front door glass, a new grille with a bigger "L" badge, revised taillights, larger exhaust pipes with stainless-steel tips and new six-spoke alloy wheels. HID headlights are optional on GS 300 but standard on GS 430. Inside, steering wheel controls for the audio system come standard, a compass has been added and a new DVD-based navigation system is optional. Bummer that it's bundled with trip computer, audio and climate control systems. Mark Levinson audio is newly optional, replacing Nakamichi as the premium sound supplier. GS 300 gets more wood trim inside the cabin, while GS 430 dashboards have new metallic-gray trim. A wood and leather steering wheel is optional on the 430. Four new colors round out this long list of updates for 2001.

2000

Mileage Category: I

Body Styles	TMV Pricing		
	Trade	Private	Dealer
4 Dr STD Sdn	16166	18339	20469

Options	Price	Options	Price
Chrome Wheels	+425	Navigation System	+1062
Compact Disc Changer	+319	Platinum Series	+2411
Heated Front Seats	+186	Power Driver Seat w/Memory	+159
Leather Seats	+637	Power Moonroof	+505
Nakamichi Audio System	+691		

The GS 300 gets a new BrakeAssist system and child seat-anchor brackets. The GS 300 is certified as a low-emission vehicle. Crystal White and Millennium Silver Metallic replace Diamond White Pearl and Alpine Silver Metallic.

1999

Mileage Category: I

Body Styles	TMV Pricing		
	Trade	Private	Dealer
4 Dr STD Sdn	13903	15963	18107

Options	Price	Options	Price
Chrome Wheels	+385	Nakamichi Audio System	+626
Compact Disc Changer	+289	Navigation System	+770
Heated Front Seats	+168	Power Driver Seat w/Memory	+144
Leather Seats	+577	Power Moonroof	+457

The GS 300 was totally redesigned last year with improvements in performance and a completely new look. As a result, the 1999 model goes unchanged except for the addition of daytime running lights and standard floor mats.

1998

Mileage Category: I

Body Styles	TMV Pricing		
	Trade	Private	Dealer
4 Dr STD Sdn	12493	14422	16597

Options	Price	Options	Price
Chrome Wheels	+317	Nakamichi Audio System	+515
Compact Disc Changer	+238	Navigation System	+634
Heated Front Seats	+139	Power Driver Seat w/Memory	+119
Leather Seats	+475	Power Moonroof	+376

A totally redesigned GS 300 appears for 1998. Featuring the familiar inline-six engine of the previous model in the GS 300, or an overhead cam V8 with continuously variable valve timing in the GS 400, the new cars lives up to the promise of providing serious fun in an elegant package.

Lexus
GS 300/400

1997

Mileage Category: I

Body Styles			
			TMV Pricing
	Trade	Private	Dealer
4 Dr STD Sdn	10139	11940	14141

Options	Price	Options	Price
Chrome Wheels	+259	Nakamichi Audio System	+421
Compact Disc Changer	+194	Power Moonroof	+307
Leather Seats	+388	Traction Control System	+162

No changes during final year before a redesign.

1996

A five-speed automatic transmission makes the GS 300 feel more sporty, while rear styling revisions and five new exterior colors update the suave exterior. Side-impact standards for 1997 are met this year, and the power moonroof features one-touch operation.

Mileage Category: I

Body Styles			
			TMV Pricing
	Trade	Private	Dealer
4 Dr STD Sdn	8828	10501	12811

Options	Price	Options	Price
Chrome Wheels	+211	Nakamichi Audio System	+343
Compact Disc Changer	+158	Power Moonroof	+250
Leather Seats	+316	Traction Control System	+132

1995

No changes.

Mileage Category: I

Body Styles			
			TMV Pricing
	Trade	Private	Dealer
4 Dr STD Sdn	7436	8905	11353

Options	Price	Options	Price
Compact Disc Changer	+236	Nakamichi Audio System	+260
Heated Front Seats	+118	Power Moonroof	+212
Leather Seats	+283	Traction Control System	+177

GS 400

2000

Mileage Category: I

Body Styles			
			TMV Pricing
	Trade	Private	Dealer
4 Dr STD Sdn	17038	19329	21574

Options	Price	Options	Price
Chrome Wheels	+425	Navigation System	+1062
Compact Disc Changer	+319	Platinum Series	+2544
Heated Front Seats	+186	Power Moonroof	+505
Nakamichi Audio System	+691	Rear Spoiler	+186

The GS 400 gets a new BrakeAssist system and child seat-anchor brackets. Crystal White and Millennium Silver Metallic replace Diamond White Pearl and Alpine Silver Metallic.

1999

The GS 400 was totally redesigned last year with improvements in performance and a completely new look. As a result, the 1999 model goes unchanged except for the addition of daytime running lights and standard floor mats.

Mileage Category: I

Body Styles			
			TMV Pricing
	Trade	Private	Dealer
4 Dr STD Sdn	14933	17145	19447

Options	Price	Options	Price
Chrome Wheels	+385	Navigation System	+770
Compact Disc Changer	+289	Power Moonroof	+457
Heated Front Seats	+168	Rear Spoiler	+168
Nakamichi Audio System	+626		

1998

A totally redesigned GS 400 appears for 1998. Featuring a V8 with continuously variable valve timing, the new car lives up to the promise of providing serious fun in an elegant package.

Mileage Category: I

Body Styles			
			TMV Pricing
	Trade	Private	Dealer
4 Dr STD Sdn	12818	14797	17028

For the latest vehicle information, visit www.edmunds.com

Options	Price	Options	Price
Chrome Wheels	+317	Navigation System	+634
Compact Disc Changer	+238	Power Moonroof	+376
Heated Front Seats	+139	Rear Spoiler	+139
Nakamichi Audio System	+515		

GS 430

2004

Mileage Category: I

Body Styles	TMV Pricing		
	Trade	Private	Dealer
4 Dr STD Sdn	33600	35814	39503

Options	Price	Options	Price
17 Inch Wheels	+215	Mark Levinson Audio System	+1250
17 Inch Wheels - Chrome	+1915	Navigation System	+1500
Chrome Wheels	+1700	Rear Spoiler	+440
Leather and Wood Steering Wheel	+300		

There are no changes for the GS 430 this year.

2003

For the 2003 GS 430, Lexus has made the heated front seats, moonroof, CD changer and leather upholstery standard equipment.

Mileage Category: I

Body Styles	TMV Pricing		
	Trade	Private	Dealer
4 Dr STD Sdn	31190	32958	35905

Options	Price	Options	Price
AM/FM/Cassette/CD Changer Audio System	+497	Mark Levinson Audio System	+459
Chrome Wheels	+1300	Navigation System	+1529
Leather and Wood Steering Wheel	+229	Rear Spoiler	+336

2002

After a number of upgrades last year, the GS 430 enters 2002 unchanged.

Mileage Category: I

Body Styles	TMV Pricing		
	Trade	Private	Dealer
4 Dr STD Sdn	26349	28085	30979

Options	Price	Options	Price
17 Inch Wheels - Chrome	+536	Mark Levinson Audio System	+429
AM/FM/Cassette/CD Changer Audio System	+536	Navigation System	+1431
Chrome Wheels	+1216	Power Moonroof	+715
Heated Front Seats	+322	Rear Spoiler	+315

2001

On the safety front, standard side curtain airbags debut, and a new sensor detects if the front passenger seat is unoccupied, deactivating the front passenger airbag if nobody is sitting in that seat. Additionally, a new child seat-tether restraint has been added, along with impact-detecting door locks and an emergency trunk release handle that glows in the dark inside the cargo area. Exterior changes include water-repellent front door glass, a new grille with a bigger "L" badge, revised taillights, larger exhaust pipes with stainless-steel tips and new six-spoke alloy wheels. HID headlights are standard. Inside, steering wheel controls for the audio system come standard, a compass has been added and a new DVD-based navigation system is optional. Bummer that it's bundled with trip computer, audio and climate control systems. Mark Levinson audio is newly optional, replacing Nakamichi as the premium sound supplier. Dashboards have new metallic-gray trim, and a wood and leather steering wheel is optional. Four new colors round out this long list of updates for 2001.

Mileage Category: I

Body Styles	TMV Pricing		
	Trade	Private	Dealer
4 Dr STD Sdn	21214	23530	25667

Options	Price	Options	Price
AM/FM/Cassette/CD Changer Audio System	+476	Mark Levinson Audio System	+381
Chrome Wheels	+1079	Navigation System	+1269
Heated Front Seats	+279	Power Moonroof	+647
Leather Seats	+762	Rear Spoiler	+279

Lexus
GX 470/IS 300

GX 470

2004

Mileage Category: O

Body Styles	TMV Pricing		
	Trade	Private	Dealer
4 Dr STD 4WD SUV	37173	39302	42850

Options	Price	Options	Price
DVD Entertainment System	+1560	Telematics System	+1215
Mark Levinson Audio System	+1100	Third Seat	+2030
Navigation System	+1650		

The GX has a number of safety upgrades this year that include a roll-sensing feature for the side-curtain airbags, a tire-pressure monitoring system and an optional rear backup camera system (for those vehicles with the navigation system installed). An optional Kinetic Dynamic Suspension System will be available as a late-year addition.

2003
The Lexus GX 470 is a new midsize luxury SUV. It features standard V8 power, excellent off-road performance and the latest luxury and safety features.

Mileage Category: O

Body Styles	TMV Pricing		
	Trade	Private	Dealer
4 Dr STD 4WD SUV	34423	36329	39506

Options	Price	Options	Price
Compact Disc Changer	+268	Rear Spoiler	+394
DVD Entertainment System	+1193	Telematics System	+929
Mark Levinson Audio System	+421	Third Seat	+1552
Navigation System	+1376	Trailer Hitch	+329

IS 300

2004

Mileage Category: H

Body Styles	TMV Pricing			Body Styles	TMV Pricing		
	Trade	Private	Dealer		Trade	Private	Dealer
4 Dr STD Sdn	20713	22046	24268	4 Dr SportCross Wgn	21186	22490	24662

Options	Price	Options	Price
Automatic 5-Speed Transmission [Opt on STD]	+1370	Polished Aluminum/Alloy Wheels	+400
Heated Front Seats	+440	Power Driver Seat w/Memory [Opt on STD]	+350
Leather Seats	+500	Power Moonroof	+415
Limited Slip Differential	+390	Power Passenger Seat	+300
Navigation System	+2000	Rear Spoiler [Opt on STD]	+440

On the outside, look for a new wheel design and smoked surrounding trim for the headlights and taillights. Inside, Lexus has added a memory function for the driver seat, a maintenance indicator light, a new storage compartment on the dash (for cars without the navigation system) and new trim highlights.

2003
Other than having some new wheel designs, the IS 300 is unchanged this year.

Mileage Category: H

Body Styles	TMV Pricing			Body Styles	TMV Pricing		
	Trade	Private	Dealer		Trade	Private	Dealer
4 Dr STD Sdn	19308	20618	22802	4 Dr SportCross Wgn	19559	20886	23098

Options	Price	Options	Price
Automatic 5-Speed Transmission [Opt on STD]	+1048	Power Driver Seat	+161
Automatic Stability Control [Opt on SportCross]	+268	Power Moonroof	+382
Heated Front Seats	+336	Power Passenger Seat	+161
Leather Seats	+765	Rear Spoiler [Opt on STD]	+336
Limited Slip Differential	+298	Sport Package [Opt on STD]	+1036
Navigation System [Opt on STD]	+1529		

2002

Mileage Category: H

Body Styles	TMV Pricing		
	Trade	Private	Dealer
4 Dr STD Sdn	16985	18306	20508

Options	Price
17 Inch Wheels	+286
Automatic 5-Speed Transmission [Opt on Sdn]	+980
Automatic Stability Control	+250
Heated Front Seats	+315
Leather Seats	+715
Limited Slip Differential	+279

Body Styles	TMV Pricing		
	Trade	Private	Dealer
4 Dr SportCross Wgn	17139	18472	20694

Options	Price
Navigation System	+1431
Power Driver Seat	+186
Power Moonroof	+358
Power Passenger Seat	+186
Rear Spoiler [Opt on Sdn]	+315

Once a goal is set, Lexus is not a company to dillydally. Witness the 2002 IS 300. After just one year on the fiercely contested entry-level luxury sport sedan battlefield, Lexus has quickly moved to address the IS 300's short list of faults. A five-speed manual transmission is available, and it comes packaged with a sportier suspension than what is offered on the "regular" IS 300. The luxury side of the equation has also been upped. A navigation system and an all-leather interior are optional this year, and the rearview and driver-side mirrors are auto-dimming. Safety is also enhanced with the addition of head-protecting side curtain airbags (in addition to the regular side airbags), a BrakeAssist function and a stability control system. And for all of those golden retrievers out there tired of riding around in numbing RX 300s, take notice that Lexus has expanded the IS 300's lineup with a wagon version.

2001

Mileage Category: H

Body Styles		TMV Pricing		
		Trade	Private	Dealer
4 Dr STD Sdn		15331	17202	18930

Options	Price	Options	Price
Heated Front Seats	+279	Power Driver Seat	+133
Leather Seats	+635	Power Moonroof	+635
Limited Slip Differential	+247	Power Passenger Seat	+133

Lexus continues to change gears, moving away from single-minded relentless pursuits of perfection to chase performance. The new IS 300, complete with rear-wheel drive and a 215-horse inline six, chases the BMW 3 Series in the entry luxury sport marketplace, and will continue to do so until a proper manual transmission is available next year.

LS 400

2000

Mileage Category: I

Body Styles		TMV Pricing		
		Trade	Private	Dealer
4 Dr STD Sdn		19176	21754	24281

Options	Price	Options	Price
Automatic Load Leveling	+372	Nakamichi Audio System	+637
Chrome Wheels	+425	Navigation System	+1062
Compact Disc Changer	+319	Power Moonroof	+507
Heated Front Seats	+186		

Only minor changes are scheduled for 2000 LS 400s. BrakeAssist has been added to the Vehicle Skid Control system. A new onboard refueling vapor recovery system allows the LS 400 to meet transitional low emission vehicle status. Child seat anchor-brackets are standard.

1999

Body Styles		TMV Pricing		
		Trade	Private	Dealer
4 Dr STD Sdn		16558	19011	21565

Options	Price	Options	Price
Automatic Load Leveling	+337	Nakamichi Audio System	+577
Chrome Wheels	+385	Navigation System	+770
Compact Disc Changer	+289	Power Moonroof	+460
Heated Front Seats	+168		

After a number of improvements to the LS 400 last year, the 1999 model sees only minor upgrades to interior trim levels. Daytime running lights are now standard equipment and Mystic Gold Metallic replaces Cashmere Beige.

1998

Mileage Category: I

Body Styles		TMV Pricing		
		Trade	Private	Dealer
4 Dr STD Sdn		14075	16247	18697

Options	Price	Options	Price
Automatic Load Leveling	+277	Nakamichi Audio System	+475
Chrome Wheels	+317	Navigation System	+634
Compact Disc Changer	+238	Power Moonroof	+378
Heated Front Seats	+139		

Lexus further refines its flagship by introducing a new four-cam V8 engine that features continuously variable valve timing. Also new this year is a five-speed automatic transmission, Vehicle Skid Control (VSC) and a host of interior improvements.

Lexus

LS 400/430

1997
Side-impact airbags are standard.

Mileage Category: I

Body Styles	TMV Pricing		
	Trade	Private	Dealer
4 Dr Coach Sdn	12705	14964	17725

Options	Price
AM/FM/Cassette/CD Audio System	+194
Automatic Load Leveling	+226
Chrome Wheels	+259
Compact Disc Changer	+194

Body Styles	TMV Pricing		
	Trade	Private	Dealer
4 Dr STD Sdn	10607	12493	14798

Options	Price
Nakamichi Audio System	+388
Power Driver Seat w/Memory	+129
Power Moonroof	+306
Traction Control System	+194

1996
Deep Jewel Green Pearl is newly available on the paint palette.

Mileage Category: I

Body Styles		TMV Pricing		
		Trade	Private	Dealer
4 Dr STD Sdn		8460	10063	12277

Options	Price
Automatic Load Leveling	+184
Chrome Wheels	+211
Compact Disc Changer	+158

Options	Price
Nakamichi Audio System	+316
Power Moonroof	+252
Traction Control System	+158

1995
All-new car looks pretty much the same as it has for half a decade. The interior and trunk are larger, the engine more powerful, and the car is quicker than before. Six-disc CD changer is dash-mounted.

Mileage Category: I

Body Styles		TMV Pricing		
		Trade	Private	Dealer
4 Dr STD Sdn		7162	8577	10934

Options	Price
Automatic Load Leveling	+236
Chrome Wheels	+260
Compact Disc Changer	+236
Heated Front Seats	+118

Options	Price
Nakamichi Audio System	+260
Power Driver Seat w/Memory	+106
Power Moonroof	+236
Traction Control System	+177

LS 430

2004

Mileage Category: I

Body Styles		TMV Pricing		
		Trade	Private	Dealer
4 Dr STD Sdn		42562	45304	49875

Options	Price
17 Inch Wheels - Chrome	+1700
AM/FM/Cassette Audio System	+300
AM/FM/Cassette/CD Changer Audio System	+550
Automatic Climate Control (4 Zone)	+700
Automatic Load Leveling	+750
Chrome Wheels	+1700
Climate Controlled Seats (Front)	+420
Electronic Suspension Control	+950
Headlight Washers	+300

Options	Price
Heated Front and Rear Seats	+350
Mark Levinson Audio System	+1300
Navigation System	+2200
Park Distance Control (Front and Rear)	+450
Rear Audio Controls	+400
Rear View Camera	+500
Refrigerator	+1300
Special Leather Seat Trim	+1460
Sport Package	+220

Lexus gives the LS 430 a midcycle freshening for 2004. Along with mild exterior revisions, the LS gets a number of new standard features, including a six-speed automatic transmission (with a manual-shift gate), adaptive headlights that swivel during turning maneuvers, knee airbags for the driver and front passenger and a moonroof. New options include the Pre-Collision system, which uses radar to detect an avoidable collision, and prepares for impact by tightening up the seatbelts, switching to sport mode on air suspension-equipped vehicles and activating maximum braking pressure. Among the other highlights are SmartAccess, which allows the driver to start up the LS without inserting a key; 18-inch wheels as part of the Sport Package; and a rear backup camera, expanded voice recognition functionality and Bluetooth hands-free phone compatibility on vehicles with the navigation system. An upgraded Mark Levinson stereo now offers seating position-optimized sound, and satellite radio is a new dealer-installed option.

2003
For 2003, 17-inch wheels are standard, replacing the 16-inchers. The climate control front seats and park-assist feature, formerly included only with the Ultra Luxury or Custom Luxury packages, are now available as stand-alone options. Finally, base cars ordered with the climate control front seats now feature perforated leather trim throughout.

Mileage Category: I

Body Styles		TMV Pricing		
		Trade	Private	Dealer
4 Dr STD Sdn		37941	40320	44286

2003 (cont'd)

Options	Price
17 Inch Wheels - Chrome	+1300
Adaptive Cruise Control	+956
Air Conditioning - Front and Rear	+765
Automatic Load Leveling	+535
Heated Front and Rear Seats	+593
Mark Levinson Audio System	+948
Nappa Leather Seat Trim	+1116
Navigation System	+1529

Options	Price
Park Distance Control (Rear)	+382
Power Moonroof	+841
Power Rear Seat	+574
Power Rear Window Sunshade	+344
Special Leather Seat Trim	+1606
Telematics System	+929
Ventilated Seats (Front)	+681

2002

Lexus' flagship was completely redesigned last year. The only addition for 2002 is a new Platinum Blue Metallic exterior paint.

Mileage Category: I

Body Styles	TMV Pricing		
	Trade	Private	Dealer
4 Dr STD Sdn	32417	34621	38295

Options	Price
17 Inch Wheels - Chrome	+572
Adaptive Cruise Control	+1252
Air Conditioning - Front and Rear	+715
Automatic Load Leveling	+501
Heated Front and Rear Seats	+554
Mark Levinson Audio System	+887
Navigation System	+1431

Options	Price
Park Distance Control (Rear)	+429
Power Moonroof	+787
Power Rear Seat	+536
Power Rear Window Sunshade	+322
Telematics System	+869
Ventilated Seats (Front)	+715

2001

The completely redesigned third-generation Lexus flagship features a larger 4.3-liter engine that meets ULEV standards, a freshened aerodynamic shape that allows for a more spacious interior and a new suspension that offers greater stability and a smoother ride. A richer, more stylish interior with advanced safety and luxury features also debuts.

Mileage Category: I

Body Styles	TMV Pricing		
	Trade	Private	Dealer
4 Dr STD Sdn	28359	31455	34312

Options	Price
17 Inch Wheels - Chrome	+508
Adaptive Cruise Control	+1111
Air Conditioning - Front and Rear	+635
Automatic Load Leveling	+444
Heated Front and Rear Seats	+558
Mark Levinson Audio System	+787
Navigation System	+1269

Options	Price
Park Distance Control (Rear)	+381
Power Moonroof	+711
Power Rear Seat	+888
Power Rear Window Sunshade	+286
Telematics System	+771
Ventilated Seats (Front)	+635

LX 450
1997

Mileage Category: O

Body Styles	TMV Pricing		
	Trade	Private	Dealer
4 Dr STD 4WD SUV	12468	14543	17079

Options	Price
Compact Disc Changer	+194
Locking Differential	+262

Options	Price
Power Moonroof	+364

There are no changes to the 1997 LX 450.

1996

Lexus clones a Toyota Land Cruiser, puts some fancy wheels on it and slathers leather and wood all over the interior to capitalize on the booming sport-ute market.

Mileage Category: O

Body Styles	TMV Pricing		
	Trade	Private	Dealer
4 Dr STD 4WD SUV	10667	12389	14768

Options	Price
Compact Disc Changer	+158
Locking Differential	+213

Options	Price
Power Moonroof	+296

LX 470

2004

Mileage Category: O

Body Styles			TMV Pricing		
			Trade	Private	Dealer
4 Dr STD 4WD SUV			48625	51091	55200

Options	Price	Options	Price
Luggage Rack	+220	Rear Spoiler	+280
Mark Levinson Audio System	+1280	Telematics System	+1215
Night Vision	+2200		

The LX 470 is enhanced for 2004 with the addition of a rear backup camera system and new Bluetooth wireless technology that allows for hands-free cell phone use.

2003

In a move almost certainly meant to distance the LX 470 from the all-new GX 470, Lexus has made a number of enhancements for 2003. On the outside, the LX has received subtle changes to the headlights, taillights and front grille and bumper. Eighteen-inch wheels are now standard. Inside, there's a redesigned center stack, standard side and side-curtain airbags, additional audio controls for rear passengers, steering wheel-mounted audio controls and a new optional entertainment system (dealer-installed). Mechanically, Lexus has bumped horsepower output by five, added a new five-speed automatic transmission and improved the steering rack. There are also rain-sensing wipers and two new features -- a "Night View" night vision system and the Lexus Link emergency communications service.

Mileage Category: O

Body Styles			TMV Pricing		
			Trade	Private	Dealer
4 Dr STD 4WD SUV			44328	46708	50675

Options	Price	Options	Price
Luggage Rack	+168	Rear Spoiler	+214
Mark Levinson Audio System	+979	Telematics System	+929
Night Vision	+1682		

2002

The LX 470 was updated last year. As such, the only change for 2002 is that the navigation system is now standard equipment.

Mileage Category: O

Body Styles			TMV Pricing		
			Trade	Private	Dealer
4 Dr STD AWD SUV			36588	38834	42577

Options	Price	Options	Price
Chrome Wheels	+930	Mark Levinson Audio System	+916

2001

The LX 470 finally adds the all-important optional DVD-based navigation system (and if you turn down the nav, you get a compass on the rearview mirror). The optional Nakamichi audio system is gone in favor of an optional nine-speaker Mark Levinson system. The standard audio system is enhanced with an Automatic Sound Levelizer (ASL). Last year's optional wood and leather trim on the steering wheel and shift knob is now a standard feature. New security features include a key card immobilizer and a free-wheel key cylinder that prevents people from opening the door with anything other than the LX 470 key. Second-row passengers will benefit from child seat anchors and improved cupholders in the rear of the center console. The standard alloy wheels have a new surface treatment, and chrome wheels are optional. The fuel cap now has a tether to appease the absent-minded. Two new exterior colors will be offered -- Mystic Sea Opalescent and Blue Vapor Metallic.

Mileage Category: O

Body Styles			TMV Pricing		
			Trade	Private	Dealer
4 Dr STD AWD SUV			30433	33619	36559

Options	Price	Options	Price
Chrome Wheels	+825	Mark Levinson Audio System	+812
Compact Disc Changer	+685	Navigation System	+1269

2000

A Vehicle Stability Control system and a BrakeAssist system are now standard, as are last year's optional moonroof and illuminated running boards. The LX 470 also gets an optional wood and leather steering wheel and shift knob.

Mileage Category: O

Body Styles			TMV Pricing		
			Trade	Private	Dealer
4 Dr STD AWD SUV			23942	27003	30004

Options	Price	Options	Price
Luggage Rack	+159	Rear Wind Deflector	+159
Nakamichi Audio System	+637	Trailer Hitch	+120

1999

For 1999 the LX 470 gets a redesigned roof rack, standard floor mats and an optional Nakamichi audio system featuring a dash-mounted, single-feed six-disc CD changer.

Mileage Category: O

Body Styles			TMV Pricing		
			Trade	Private	Dealer
4 Dr STD AWD SUV			20261	23019	25889

Options	Price
Luggage Rack	+144
Nakamichi Audio System	+520

Options	Price
Power Moonroof	+550
Rear Wind Deflector	+144

Mileage Category: O

Body Styles	TMV Pricing		
	Trade	Private	Dealer
4 Dr STD AWD SUV	16755	19329	22232

Options	Price
Power Moonroof	+453

1998

Lexus' new LX 470 luxury SUV replaces the LX 450, offering a completely new body design, a more powerful engine, a roomier interior and more standard perks.

RX 300
2003

Mileage Category: O

Body Styles	TMV Pricing		
	Trade	Private	Dealer
4 Dr STD AWD SUV	24764	26285	28821

Options	Price
Changer Audio System	+363
Automatic Dimming Rearview Mirror	+138
Automatic Dimming Sideview Mirror(s)	+153
Camper/Towing Package	+122
Chrome Wheels	+1300
Compact Disc Changer	+826
Heated Front Seats	+336

Body Styles	TMV Pricing		
	Trade	Private	Dealer
4 Dr STD SUV	23190	24614	26988

Options	Price
Leather Seats	+765
Leather and Wood Steering Wheel	+191
Navigation System	+1529
Power Driver Seat w/Memory	+229
Rear Spoiler	+214
Trailer Hitch	+237
Xenon Headlamps	+363

Nothing has changed for the RX 300 during its move from 2002 to 2003. Prospective buyers should note that it will get a complete redesign for 2004.

2002

Other than the Nakamichi audio system value package no longer being available, there are no changes for the RX 300 this year.

Mileage Category: O

Body Styles	TMV Pricing		
	Trade	Private	Dealer
4 Dr STD AWD SUV	21803	23321	25852

Options	Price
Automatic Dimming Rearview Mirror	+129
Automatic Dimming Sideview Mirror(s)	+143
Chrome Wheels	+1216
Compact Disc Changer	+536
Heated Front Seats	+315
Leather Seats	+715

Body Styles	TMV Pricing		
	Trade	Private	Dealer
4 Dr STD SUV	21087	22557	25006

Options	Price
Navigation System	+1431
Power Driver Seat w/Memory	+215
Power Moonroof	+644
Rear Spoiler	+200
Trailer Hitch	+222
Xenon Headlamps	+368

2001

Vehicle Skid Control (VSC), traction control and BrakeAssist safety technologies are now standard, as is water-repellant front door and sideview mirror glass. Lights front and rear are revised, and the grille has been changed to a simpler design with chrome accents and a larger Lexus badge. HID headlights and chrome-plated wheels are optional for 2001, the full-size spare is newly mounted to a matching alloy wheel and a larger 19.8-gallon fuel tank increases driving range. Inside, new cloth upholstery debuts and an all-black leather option is available. Chrome door handles and scuff plates emblazoned with the Lexus logo class up the joint, while an additional cupholder is available to rear-seat occupants. Optional for 2001 are a wood-trimmed steering wheel and wood trimmed shift knob. Two-level seat heaters are also available. A DVD-based navigation system is optional, with the contiguous U.S. mapped onto a single disc. Child seat-tether anchors and ISO-FIX bars have been added this year. Models with 4WD get prewiring for towing and a standard rear bumper protector. Four new colors round out the list of changes for 2001.

Body Styles	TMV Pricing		
	Trade	Private	Dealer
4 Dr STD AWD SUV	20130	22351	24400

Options	Price
AM/FM/Cassette/CD Changer Audio System	+254
Aluminum/Alloy Interior Trim	+254
Automatic Dimming Sideview Mirror(s)	+127
Camper/Towing Package	+197
Chrome Wheels	+1079
Compact Disc Changer	+685
Heated Front Seats	+279
Leather Seats	+730

Body Styles	TMV Pricing		
	Trade	Private	Dealer
4 Dr STD SUV	19434	21578	23558

Options	Price
Nakamichi Audio System	+1034
Navigation System	+1269
Power Driver Seat w/Memory	+190
Power Moonroof	+635
Rear Spoiler	+178
Trailer Hitch	+197
Xenon Headlamps	+327

2000

The RX 300 remains mechanically unchanged. A Mineral Green Opalescent paint replaces Desert Bronze Metallic on the order sheet.

Mileage Category: O

Body Styles	TMV Pricing		
	Trade	Private	Dealer
4 Dr STD AWD SUV	17164	19359	21510

Body Styles	TMV Pricing		
	Trade	Private	Dealer
4 Dr STD SUV	16404	18502	20557

Lexus
RX 300/330/SC 300

2000 (cont'd)

Options	Price
AM/FM/Cassette/CD Audio System	+305
Compact Disc Changer	+319
Heated Front Seats	+186
Leather Seats	+611
Limited Slip Differential	+186
Luggage Rack	+117

Options	Price
Nakamichi Audio System	+691
Power Driver Seat w/Memory	+159
Power Moonroof	+531
Rear Spoiler	+133
Traction Control System	+159
Trailer Hitch	+120

1999

The RX 300 is an all-new car-based SUV from Lexus designed to compete in the luxury SUV segment.

Mileage Category: O

Body Styles	Trade	Private	Dealer
4 Dr STD AWD SUV	14718	16721	18807

Body Styles	Trade	Private	Dealer
4 Dr STD SUV	14250	16189	18208

Options	Price
AM/FM/CD Audio System	+152
Compact Disc Changer	+289
Heated Front Seats	+168
Leather Seats	+553
Limited Slip Differential	+168

Options	Price
Nakamichi Audio System	+409
Power Driver Seat w/Memory	+144
Power Moonroof	+481
Rear Wind Deflector	+120
Traction Control System	+144

RX 330

2004

The RX 330 is a fully redesigned replacement for the top-selling RX 300.

Mileage Category: O

Body Styles	Trade	Private	Dealer
4 Dr STD AWD SUV	30119	31644	34185

Body Styles	Trade	Private	Dealer
4 Dr STD SUV	28987	30512	33053

Options	Price
18 Inch Wheels	+900
AM/FM/Cassette/CD Changer Audio System	+350
Adaptive Cruise Control	+600
Automatic Load Leveling	+600
DVD Entertainment System	+1840
Heated Front Seats	+540
Heated Front and Rear Seats	+400
Leather Seats	+1200
Leather and Wood Steering Wheel	+250
Luggage Rack	+200

Options	Price
Mark Levinson Audio System	+1100
Navigation System	+1300
Power Moonroof	+800
Power Rear Liftgate	+500
Rain Sensing Windshield Wipers	+250
Rear View Camera	+350
Telematics System	+1215
Tilt and Telescopic Steering Wheel	+200
Trailer Hitch	+160
Xenon Headlamps	+300

SC 300

2000

Mileage Category: I

Body Styles			TMV Pricing		
			Trade	Private	Dealer
2 Dr STD Cpe			15575	17686	19755

Options	Price
Chrome Wheels	+425
Heated Front Seats	+186
Leather Seats	+637
Nakamichi Audio System	+637

Options	Price
Power Driver Seat w/Memory	+159
Power Moonroof	+531
Rear Spoiler	+186
Traction Control System	+319

The 2000 Lexus SC 300 is unchanged except for paint selection; Cinnabar Pearl replaces Baroque Red Metallic.

1999

The SC 300 gets minor enhancements this year including new perforated leather inserts, larger brakes, daytime running lights and a new three-spoke steering wheel similar to the GS sport sedans.

Mileage Category: I

Body Styles			TMV Pricing		
			Trade	Private	Dealer
2 Dr STD Cpe			13100	15041	17061

Options	Price
Chrome Wheels	+385
Heated Front Seats	+168
Leather Seats	+577
Nakamichi Audio System	+520

Options	Price
Power Driver Seat w/Memory	+144
Power Moonroof	+481
Rear Spoiler	+168
Traction Control System	+289

1998

An engine immobilizer, depowered airbags and a sophisticated five-speed automatic transmission are standard this year as well. The SC 300 loses its five-speed manual transmission.

Mileage Category: I

Body Styles	TMV Pricing		
	Trade	Private	Dealer
2 Dr STD Cpe	10995	12693	14607

Options	Price	Options	Price
Chrome Wheels	+317	Power Driver Seat w/Memory	+119
Compact Disc Changer	+238	Power Moonroof	+396
Heated Front Seats	+139	Rear Spoiler	+139
Leather Seats	+475	Traction Control System	+238
Nakamichi Audio System	+428		

1997

Minor interior and exterior enhancements update the look of the SC 300.

Mileage Category: I

Body Styles	TMV Pricing		
	Trade	Private	Dealer
2 Dr STD Cpe	8335	9817	11629

Options	Price	Options	Price
Automatic 4-Speed Transmission	+223	Nakamichi Audio System	+350
Chrome Wheels	+259	Power Moonroof	+324
Compact Disc Changer	+194	Traction Control System	+194
Leather Seats	+388		

1996

SC 300 boasts a larger options roster with the addition of a one-touch operation moonroof and electrochromatic rearview mirrors, and chrome wheels are available. Auto-dimming electrochromic inside and outside rearview mirrors are now standard, a new remote keyless entry system debuts and the optional moonroof now features one-touch operation.

Mileage Category: I

Body Styles	TMV Pricing		
	Trade	Private	Dealer
2 Dr STD Cpe	7255	8629	10527

Options	Price	Options	Price
Automatic 4-Speed Transmission	+181	Nakamichi Audio System	+285
Chrome Wheels	+211	Power Moonroof	+263
Compact Disc Changer	+158	Traction Control System	+158
Leather Seats	+316		

1995

Revised styling and new wheels spruce up the look of the SC 300. Side-impact standards for 1997 are met this year. A cupholder is added inside.

Mileage Category: I

Body Styles	TMV Pricing		
	Trade	Private	Dealer
2 Dr STD Cpe	5892	7056	8997

Options	Price	Options	Price
Automatic 4-Speed Transmission	+212	Nakamichi Audio System	+255
Compact Disc Changer	+236	Power Driver Seat w/Memory	+106
Heated Front Seats	+94	Power Moonroof	+212
Leather Seats	+293	Traction Control System	+118

SC 400

2000

Mileage Category: I

Body Styles	TMV Pricing		
	Trade	Private	Dealer
2 Dr STD Cpe	17441	19786	22084

Options	Price	Options	Price
Chrome Wheels	+425	Power Moonroof	+531
Heated Front Seats	+186	Rear Spoiler	+186
Nakamichi Audio System	+637	Traction Control System	+425

The 2000 Lexus SC 400 is unchanged except for paint selection; Cinnabar Pearl replaces Baroque Red Metallic.

1999

The SC 400 gets minor enhancements this year including new perforated leather inserts, daytime running lights and a new three-spoke steering wheel similar to the GS series sport sedans.

Mileage Category: I

Body Styles	TMV Pricing		
	Trade	Private	Dealer
2 Dr STD Cpe	14766	16954	19231

1999 (cont'd)

Options	Price
Chrome Wheels	+385
Heated Front Seats	+168
Nakamichi Audio System	+520

Options	Price
Power Moonroof	+481
Rear Spoiler	+168
Traction Control System	+289

1998

An engine immobilizer, depowered airbags and a sophisticated five-speed automatic transmission are standard this year as well.

Mileage Category: I

Body Styles	TMV Pricing		
	Trade	Private	Dealer
2 Dr STD Cpe	12709	14671	16884

Options	Price
Chrome Wheels	+317
Compact Disc Changer	+238
Heated Front Seats	+139
Nakamichi Audio System	+428

Options	Price
Power Moonroof	+396
Rear Spoiler	+139
Traction Control System	+238

1997

Minor interior and exterior enhancements update the look of the SC 400.

Mileage Category: I

Body Styles	TMV Pricing		
	Trade	Private	Dealer
2 Dr STD Cpe	9412	11085	13130

Options	Price
Chrome Wheels	+259
Compact Disc Changer	+194
Nakamichi Audio System	+350

Options	Price
Power Moonroof	+324
Traction Control System	+194

1996

The buttery V8 from the LS 400 is installed in the SC 400, and chrome wheels are available. Auto-dimming electrochromic inside and outside rearview mirrors are now standard, a new remote keyless entry system debuts and the optional moonroof now features one-touch operation.

Mileage Category: I

Body Styles	TMV Pricing		
	Trade	Private	Dealer
2 Dr STD Cpe	7844	9330	11382

Options	Price
Chrome Wheels	+211
Compact Disc Changer	+158
Nakamichi Audio System	+285

Options	Price
Power Moonroof	+263
Traction Control System	+158

1995

Revised styling and new wheels spruce up the look of the SC 400. Side-impact standards for 1997 are met this year. A cupholder is added inside.

Mileage Category: I

Body Styles	TMV Pricing		
	Trade	Private	Dealer
2 Dr STD Cpe	6324	7639	9830

Options	Price
Compact Disc Changer	+236
Heated Front Seats	+118
Nakamichi Audio System	+260

Options	Price
Power Moonroof	+212
Rear Spoiler	+94
Traction Control System	+177

SC 430

2004

Mileage Category: F

Body Styles	TMV Pricing		
	Trade	Private	Dealer
2 Dr STD Conv	50420	52600	56233

Options	Price
Rear Spoiler	+440

Options	Price
Telematics System	+1215

There are no significant changes to the SC 430 this year, though Lexus will offer a Pebble Beach Edition package, which includes Azure Pearl exterior paint, black bird's eye maple interior trim, run-flat tires, a rear spoiler and a black leather golf bag.

Mileage Category: F

Body Styles	TMV Pricing		
	Trade	Private	Dealer
2 Dr STD Conv	43813	45614	48616

Options	Price	Options	Price
Rear Spoiler	+336	Telematics System	+929
Runflat Tire System	+306		

2003

Other than the Lexus Link emergency and concierge service becoming available, there are no changes for the SC 430.

Mileage Category: F

Body Styles	TMV Pricing		
	Trade	Private	Dealer
2 Dr STD Conv	37358	39036	41833

Options	Price	Options	Price
Rear Spoiler	+315	Runflat Tire System	+286

2002

After nearly a decade out of the sport coupe spotlight, Lexus returns with a compelling entry. Since its debut of the SC coupe in 1992, Lexus has largely been overlooked by shoppers who wanted avant-garde styling, sports car performance and luxurious appointments. And it has never before offered a convertible roof. They need look no further. The new SC 430 delivers all that in spades.

Lincoln
Aviator/Blackwood/Continental

Aviator

2004

Mileage Category: O

Body Styles	TMV Pricing		
	Trade	Private	Dealer
4 Dr STD AWD SUV	29272	31088	34114

Options	Price
AM/FM/CD Changer Audio System	+895
Camper/Towing Package	+295
Chrome Wheels	+695
Climate Comfort Seats	+500

Body Styles	TMV Pricing		
	Trade	Private	Dealer
4 Dr STD SUV	27155	28915	31847

Options	Price
DVD Entertainment System	+1415
Power Moonroof	+1595
Special Factory Paint	+395
Xenon Headlamps	+375

Lincoln changes the name of the Aviator's high-line trim level from Premium to Ultimate. More substantive improvements include the addition of Roll Stability Control to the optional AdvanceTrac stability system to ward off rollover incidents during panic maneuvers. The previously optional tire-pressure monitoring system is now standard. Additionally, dealer-installed Sirius Satellite Radio is available on Ultimate and Luxury models equipped with the optional Audiophile stereo.

2003

With the Aviator, Lincoln has thrown its hat into the midsize luxury sport-ute ring. It looks like a three-quarter scale Navigator, seats seven and is powered by a strong V8.

Mileage Category: O

Body Styles	TMV Pricing		
	Trade	Private	Dealer
4 Dr STD AWD SUV	24421	26133	28985

Options	Price
17 Inch Wheels - Chrome	+436
AM/FM/CD Changer Audio System	+561
Automatic Stability Control [Opt on AWD]	+314
Camper/Towing Package	+185
Climate Comfort Seats	+596
DVD Entertainment System	+812

Body Styles	TMV Pricing		
	Trade	Private	Dealer
4 Dr STD SUV	21939	23477	26039

Options	Price
Limited Slip Differential [Opt on 2WD]	+310
Navigation System	+1565
Power Moonroof	+1000
Special Factory Paint	+248
Traction Control System [Opt on AWD]	+185
Xenon Headlamps	+345

Blackwood

2002

Mileage Category: O

Body Styles	TMV Pricing		
	Trade	Private	Dealer
4 Dr STD Crew Cab SB	21504	23204	26038

Options	Price
Navigation System	+991

For 2002, Lincoln introduces this cross between a luxury SUV and a pickup truck. Essentially a dolled-up Ford F-150 SuperCrew, the Blackwood offers a truckload of creature comforts and safety features but not a lot of utility.

Continental

2002

Mileage Category: I

Body Styles	TMV Pricing		
	Trade	Private	Dealer
4 Dr STD Sdn	13557	15046	17528

Options	Price
Alpine Audio System	+286
Chrome Wheels	+397
Compact Disc Changer	+248
Electronic Suspension Control	+201
Heated Front and Rear Seats	+199

Options	Price
Metallic Paint	+186
Power Moonroof	+745
Premium Audio System	+137
Runflat Tire System	+489
Telematics System	+293

The Continental remains relatively unchanged for 2002, its last year on the market. One new exterior color debuts, and an optional Vehicle Communication System (with portable analog-digital phone) is now offered. Available at no charge are a power moonroof, a six-disc changer and an Alpine audio system.

2001

The Continental remains relatively unchanged for 2001. A universal garage door opener is standard, and the individual bucket seat option (five-passenger) now requires the Driver's Select System. Two new exterior colors have been added. Like all Lincoln products, the Continental now has complimentary maintenance at no additional charge for the first three years/36,000 miles in service.

Mileage Category: I

Body Styles	TMV Pricing		
	Trade	Private	Dealer
4 Dr STD Sdn	10802	12769	14584

Options	Price	Options	Price
Alpine Audio System	+242	Heated Front Seats	+168
Chrome Wheels	+359	Power Moonroof	+641
Compact Disc Changer	+254	Runflat Tire System	+269

2000

The Continental receives additional safety features, including side airbags, an emergency trunk release, child seat-anchor brackets and Lincoln's Belt Minder system.

Mileage Category: I

Body Styles	TMV Pricing		
	Trade	Private	Dealer
4 Dr STD Sdn	7683	9369	11021

Options	Price	Options	Price
Alpine Audio System	+204	Power Moonroof	+548
Chrome Wheels	+305	Telematics System	+253
Compact Disc Changer	+216		

1999

Lincoln's luxury liner gets added safety in 1999 with the addition of standard side airbags for the driver and front passenger. There's also five new exterior colors, upgraded interior trim options, two new wheel designs and an improved audio system. Otherwise the Lincoln remains unchanged after its major rework in 1998.

Mileage Category: I

Body Styles	TMV Pricing		
	Trade	Private	Dealer
4 Dr STD Sdn	6301	7829	9419

Options	Price	Options	Price
Alpine Audio System	+167	Power Moonroof	+447
Chrome Wheels	+250	Telematics System	+295
Compact Disc Changer	+176		

1998

Lincoln's front-wheel-drive luxo-barge gets a bigger grille (just what it needs) and rounded corners. It also gets an interior freshening that replaces the digital clock with an analog timepiece.

Mileage Category: I

Body Styles	TMV Pricing		
	Trade	Private	Dealer
4 Dr STD Sdn	5119	6525	8111

Options	Price	Options	Price
Chrome Wheels	+219	Power Moonroof	+436
Compact Disc Changer	+171	Telematics System	+259
JBL Audio System	+163		

1997

The changes to the 1997 Continental are minor this year. The first is the addition of a single-key locking system that locks the doors, glovebox and trunk with a turn of the wrist. The second is the addition of all-speed traction control.

Mileage Category: I

Body Styles	TMV Pricing		
	Trade	Private	Dealer
4 Dr STD Sdn	3802	4968	6393

Options	Price	Options	Price
Chrome Wheels	+164	Power Moonroof	+294
JBL Audio System	+115	Telematics System	+194

1996

The big news for Continental is an optional gee-whiz rescue unit that uses a Global Positioning Satellite to pinpoint your location for roadside assistance, medical and law enforcement personnel in the event of an emergency -- likely the greatest safety advance since airbags and antilock brakes. Also new are run-flat Michelin tires, a 75th Diamond Anniversary Edition and a standard anti-theft system. It's getting there.

Mileage Category: I

Body Styles	TMV Pricing		
	Trade	Private	Dealer
4 Dr STD Sdn	2743	3700	5022

Options	Price	Options	Price
Chrome Wheels	+125	Power Moonroof	+224

1995

An all-new Continental is released with a DOHC V8. A new suspension system that adjusts the shock absorbers to the prevailing driving conditions debuts, as does a memory seat system that will retain the seating preferences for two people. The new Continental has swoopier styling which is geared toward attracting a more youthful audience.

Mileage Category: I

Body Styles	TMV Pricing		
	Trade	Private	Dealer
4 Dr STD Sdn	2039	2851	4205

1995 (cont'd)

Options	Price
Chrome Wheels	+108
Compact Disc Changer	+104

Options	Price
Power Moonroof	+194

LS

2004

The V8 Premium Sport is now called the V8 Ultimate. Minor suspension and transmission upgrades provide less noise and smoother shifts. Sirius Satellite Radio is now a dealer-installed option.

Mileage Category: H

Body Styles	TMV Pricing		
	Trade	Private	Dealer
4 Dr V6 Sdn	19222	20653	23037

Options	Price
Appearance Package	+3395
Automatic Stability Control	+775
Chrome Wheels [Opt on V8]	+695
Climate Comfort Seats [Opt on V8]	+595
Front and Rear Head Airbag Restraints	+600
Heated Front and Rear Seats [Opt on V8]	+405
Navigation System [Opt on V8]	+2995

Body Styles	TMV Pricing		
	Trade	Private	Dealer
4 Dr V8 Sdn	23687	25117	27501

Options	Price
Painted Wheels [Opt on V6]	+500
Park Distance Control (Rear)	+245
Power Moonroof [Opt on V8]	+1275
Special Factory Paint	+295
Wood Interior Trim	+130
Xenon Headlamps [Opt on V8]	+595

2003

Lincoln's sport sedan goes into 2003 with more than 500 changes. The V8 sports 28 more horsepower, while the V6 benefits from a 12-horsepower increase. Both engines are controlled by drive-by-wire throttle, and drink slightly less fuel than their 2002 counterparts. Unfortunately, Lincoln decided to kill the five-speed manual that was available with the V6. Meanwhile, the rack and pinion steering has been improved, and Lincoln says it has softened the ride without degrading the car's handling abilities. In terms of safety, Lincoln has added a BrakeAssist function, side curtain airbags (late availability) and power-adjustable pedals. As on the 2003 Jaguar S-Type, a new electronically activated parking brake improves the stowage capability of the center console. Also on the inside, you'll find vastly improved interior materials for the seat and dash, along with little touches like one-touch up and down front windows and a host of new options. Outside you'll find slightly altered fascias front and rear and a host of new wheel choices.

Mileage Category: H

Body Styles	TMV Pricing		
	Trade	Private	Dealer
4 Dr V6 Sdn	17086	18359	20480

Options	Price
17 Inch Wheels - Chrome [Opt on V8]	+314
AM/FM/CD Changer Audio System [Opt on V6]	+185
Aluminum/Alloy Wheels [Opt on V6]	+254
Automatic Dimming Rearview Mirror [Opt on V6]	+125
Automatic Dimming Sideview Mirror(s)	+157
Automatic Stability Control	+367
Front Head Airbag Restraints	+248
Heated Front Seats [Opt on V8]	+219
Heated Front and Rear Seats [Opt on V8]	+251

Body Styles	TMV Pricing		
	Trade	Private	Dealer
4 Dr V8 Sdn	20076	21570	24061

Options	Price
Leather and Wood Steering Wheel	+282
Navigation System [Opt on V8]	+1878
Park Distance Control (Rear)	+185
Power Driver Seat w/Memory [Opt on V6]	+157
Power Moonroof	+630
Premium Audio System [Opt on V6]	+361
Special Factory Paint	+185
Spoke Wheels [Opt on V6]	+345
Xenon Headlamps [Opt on V8]	+373

2002

The LS' already handsome appearance can be further enhanced with the LSE appearance package that includes 17-inch two-tone Blade Grey wheels, a unique front fascia, round foglights, modified Blade Grey grille with color-keyed upper trim piece, side rocker panels and rear valance, low profile spoiler, dual stainless-steel exhaust tips and LSE floor mats. Lincoln makes an in-dash CD changer standard for 2002 (with Alpine Audiophile components on Sport models) and restyles the 16-inch alloy wheels on non-Sport V6 and V8 versions. A Vehicle Communication System, which provides a voice-activated Motorola Timeport mobile phone, is optional and includes safety and security services, route guidance and access to weather reports, stock quotes and sports scores. Three new colors replace three old ones.

Mileage Category: H

Body Styles	TMV Pricing		
	Trade	Private	Dealer
4 Dr V6 Sdn	14008	15575	18187

Options	Price
17 Inch Wheels - Chrome	+248
Alpine Audio System	+286
Automatic Stability Control	+291
Heated Front Seats	+174

Body Styles	TMV Pricing		
	Trade	Private	Dealer
4 Dr V8 Sdn	15239	16944	19785

Options	Price
Metallic Paint	+147
Power Moonroof	+499
Rear Spoiler	+124
Telematics System	+293

2001

V6 models now come with standard traction control and optional AdvanceTrac. All models receive a glow-in-the-dark manual trunk release and child safety-seat anchor points. The sport package has a new 17-inch chrome wheel design and a mini spare tire and wheel instead of the previous 16-inch nonmatching aluminum wheel (both late availability). Inside, there is an additional power point, a revised cupholder design, an optional in-dash six-disc CD changer and an optional mirror-mounted compass. The height-adjustable rear-seat head restraints have been deleted from V8 automatics. Four new exterior colors are offered. Lincoln now offers complimentary maintenance at no additional charge for the first three years/36,000 miles in service.

Mileage Category: H

Body Styles	TMV Pricing		
	Trade	Private	Dealer
4 Dr V6 Sdn	10757	12670	14436

Options	Price
17 Inch Wheels - Chrome	+355
Alpine Audio System	+242
Automatic 5-Speed Transmission [Opt on V6]	+611
Automatic Stability Control	+309
Chrome Wheels	+355

Body Styles	TMV Pricing		
	Trade	Private	Dealer
4 Dr V8 Sdn	11108	13084	14907

Options	Price
Compact Disc Changer	+254
Heated Front Seats	+168
Power Moonroof	+422
Sport Suspension	+126

2000

From the ground up, this is a completely new sport sedan based on an all-new midsize platform. Lincoln worked with Jaguar to develop this platform, which is also being used for Jaguar's S-Type sedan. It is the first Lincoln in over two decades not classified as a full-size vehicle, and should appeal to buyers looking for something sportier and smaller than the Town Car or Continental.

Mileage Category: H

Body Styles	TMV Pricing		
	Trade	Private	Dealer
4 Dr V6 Sdn	8750	10602	12419

Options	Price
5-Speed Transmission [Opt on V6]	+290
Alpine Audio System	+208
Automatic Stability Control	+266
Compact Disc Changer	+219
Heated Front Seats	+145

Body Styles	TMV Pricing		
	Trade	Private	Dealer
4 Dr V8 Sdn	9333	11311	13249

Options	Price
Power Moonroof	+364
Special Factory Paint	+136
Sport Package	+257
Telematics System [Opt on V8]	+394

Mark VIII

1998

Mileage Category: I

Body Styles	TMV Pricing		
	Trade	Private	Dealer
2 Dr LSC Cpe	6124	7806	9703

Options	Price
Chrome Wheels [Opt on STD]	+219
Compact Disc Changer	+174

Body Styles	TMV Pricing		
	Trade	Private	Dealer
2 Dr STD Cpe	5921	7548	9382

Options	Price
Power Moonroof	+393

No changes to Lincoln's muscle car for its last year.

1997

Lincoln thoroughly updates this personal coupe, lighting the darn thing up like a Christmas tree in the process. The Mark now has high-intensity discharge front headlamps, cornering lamps, a neon rear applique and puddle lamps. Wow, you'll see this thing from miles away. The hood, grille and interior have also been slightly redesigned.

Mileage Category: I

Body Styles	TMV Pricing		
	Trade	Private	Dealer
2 Dr LSC Cpe	5112	6679	8595

Options	Price
Chrome Wheels [Opt on STD]	+164
Compact Disc Changer	+130

Body Styles	TMV Pricing		
	Trade	Private	Dealer
2 Dr STD Cpe	4887	6385	8215

Options	Price
Power Moonroof	+294

1996

Mileage Category: I

Body Styles	TMV Pricing		
	Trade	Private	Dealer
2 Dr LSC Cpe	3675	4957	6728

Options	Price
Chrome Wheels [Opt on STD]	+125
Compact Disc Changer	+121

Body Styles	TMV Pricing		
	Trade	Private	Dealer
2 Dr STD Cpe	3529	4760	6459

Options	Price
Power Moonroof	+224

Last year's limited-edition LSC model goes full-time for 1996. Eight new colors are available, and borderless floor mats debut. A Touring Package and 75th Diamond Anniversary model are offered.

1995

Lincoln's premium touring coupe receives significant changes across the board. A new instrument panel houses a new stereo with larger buttons. A feature called retained accessory power makes an appearance on the Mark VIII, allowing passengers 10 seconds to close the window after the car is turned off.

Mileage Category: I

Body Styles	TMV Pricing		
	Trade	Private	Dealer
2 Dr LSC Cpe	2407	3365	4961

Options	Price
Chrome Wheels	+108
Compact Disc Changer	+104

Body Styles	TMV Pricing		
	Trade	Private	Dealer
2 Dr STD Cpe	2280	3188	4701

Options	Price
Power Moonroof	+194

Navigator

2004

Mileage Category: O

Body Styles	TMV Pricing		
	Trade	Private	Dealer
4 Dr STD 4WD SUV	30779	32537	35466

Options	Price
Appearance Package	+2810
Automatic Stability Control	+855
Chrome Wheels	+695
Climate Comfort Seats	+300
Climate Controlled Seats (Front)	+895

Body Styles	TMV Pricing		
	Trade	Private	Dealer
4 Dr STD SUV	28725	30483	33413

Options	Price
DVD Entertainment System	+1415
Power Moonroof	+1595
Power Rear Liftgate	+300
Power Third Seat	+375
Xenon Headlamps	+200

The Navigator is now available in just two trim levels -- Luxury and Ultimate. Vehicles equipped with the Audiophile stereo now include separate tweeters for better sound quality. New safety features include a tire-pressure monitoring system as standard equipment and a Roll Stability Control feature (to help prevent rollover incidents) for the Advance Trac system. Sirius Satellite Radio is a new dealer-installed option.

2003

The 2003 Navigator may look like the previous year's, but significant changes underneath the sheet metal, such as a new suspension system and sophisticated new technologies, allow the Lincoln to continue to be a popular and respected choice in the luxury SUV market.

Mileage Category: O

Body Styles	TMV Pricing		
	Trade	Private	Dealer
4 Dr STD 4WD SUV	27588	29434	32510

Options	Price
Automatic Stability Control	+314
DVD Entertainment System	+887
Power Rear Liftgate	+282
Power Third Seat	+408

Body Styles	TMV Pricing		
	Trade	Private	Dealer
4 Dr STD SUV	24467	26104	28831

Options	Price
Tire Pressure Monitoring System	+185
Traction Control System	+185
Ventilated Seats (Front)	+373

2002

Mileage Category: O

Body Styles	TMV Pricing		
	Trade	Private	Dealer
4 Dr STD 4WD SUV	21114	22868	25790

Options	Price
17 Inch Wheels	+149
Alpine Audio System	+288
Chrome Wheels	+296
Navigation System	+991

Body Styles	TMV Pricing		
	Trade	Private	Dealer
4 Dr STD SUV	18968	20544	23170

Options	Price
Park Distance Control (Rear)	+127
Power Moonroof	+743
VCR Entertainment System	+636
Ventilated Seats (Front)	+296

A new Limited Edition package is designed to drum up interest in the aging Navigator for 2002. It includes monochromatic black paint, special 17-inch machined aluminum wheels and a reverse sensing system.

2001

Auxiliary climate control is standard on both two- and four-wheel-drive models. Both the second- and third-row seats get lower child safety-seat anchors. Lincoln now offers complimentary maintenance at no additional charge for the first three years/36,000 miles in service.

Mileage Category: O

Body Styles	TMV Pricing		
	Trade	Private	Dealer
4 Dr STD 4WD SUV	17544	19773	21830

Options	Price
17 Inch Wheels - Chrome	+250
Alpine Audio System	+244
Compact Disc Changer	+250
Navigation System	+838

Body Styles	TMV Pricing		
	Trade	Private	Dealer
4 Dr STD SUV	16264	18330	20237

Options	Price
Power Moonroof	+628
VCR Entertainment System	+538
Ventilated Seats (Front)	+250

2000

The 2000 Navigator is now available with a fully integrated satellite navigation system, as well as a reverse-sensing system. Side airbags are standard, while new climate-controlled seats for the driver and front passenger are optional. The 2000 Navigator also features several exterior and interior styling changes.

Mileage Category: O

Body Styles	TMV Pricing		
	Trade	Private	Dealer
4 Dr STD 4WD SUV	14382	16453	18482

Options	Price
Air Conditioning - Front and Rear	+259
Alpine Audio System	+206
Chrome Wheels	+127

Body Styles	TMV Pricing		
	Trade	Private	Dealer
4 Dr STD SUV	13765	15747	17690

Options	Price
Compact Disc Changer	+216
Navigation System	+722
Power Moonroof	+599

Mileage Category: 0

Body Styles	TMV Pricing		
	Trade	Private	Dealer
4 Dr STD 4WD SUV	12286	14196	16184

Options	Price
Air Conditioning - Front and Rear	+208
Alpine Audio System	+168

Body Styles	TMV Pricing		
	Trade	Private	Dealer
4 Dr STD SUV	11601	13405	15282

Options	Price
Compact Disc Changer	+176
Power Moonroof	+488

1999

Into its second year, Lincoln's Navigator enters 1999 with more power, adjustable pedals, speed-sensitive stereo volume and a hands-free cellular phone. Also, the optional third-row seat is mounted on rollers this year for easy installation and removal.

Mileage Category: 0

Body Styles	TMV Pricing		
	Trade	Private	Dealer
4 Dr STD 4WD SUV	10857	12597	14558

Options	Price
Air Conditioning - Front and Rear	+183
Chrome Wheels	+206

Body Styles	TMV Pricing		
	Trade	Private	Dealer
4 Dr STD SUV	9825	11398	13171

Options	Price
Compact Disc Changer	+155
Power Moonroof	+389

1998

This all-new entrant into the luxury SUV market is the first truck ever sold by Lincoln. Based on the highly acclaimed Ford Expedition, the Navigator is powered by a 5.4-liter, SOHC V8 engine and has standard goodies that include illuminated running boards and a load-leveling air suspension. This truck also features one of the largest grilles this side of a Kenworth.

Town Car

Mileage Category: I

Body Styles	TMV Pricing		
	Trade	Private	Dealer
4 Dr Executive L Sdn	25204	26726	29263
4 Dr Executive Sdn	23227	24639	26993
4 Dr Signature Sdn	23253	24677	27051

Options	Price
17 Inch Wheels - Chrome [Opt on Ultimate, Ultimate L]	+895
Navigation System [Opt on Ultimate, Ultimate L]	+2495
Power Moonroof [Opt on Ultimate]	+1595

Body Styles	TMV Pricing		
	Trade	Private	Dealer
4 Dr Ultimate L Sdn	28144	29697	32285
4 Dr Ultimate Sdn	25028	26580	29168

Options	Price
Two-Tone Paint [Opt on Signature, Ultimate]	+295
Xenon Headlamps [Opt on Ultimate, Ultimate L]	+495

2004

Having been freshened with a host of changes last year, the Town Car is largely unchanged for 2004. Last year's Executive model is now the Signature, and the Cartier becomes the Ultimate (available in both regular- and long-wheelbase versions). Sirius Satellite Radio is now a dealer-installed option.

Mileage Category: I

Body Styles	TMV Pricing		
	Trade	Private	Dealer
4 Dr Cartier L Sdn	23957	25442	27916
4 Dr Cartier Sdn	22741	24150	26499

Options	Price
Compact Disc Changer [Opt on Cartier,Signature]	+379
Fog Lights [Opt on Signature]	+157
Navigation System [Opt on Cartier,Cartier L,Signature]	+1565
Park Distance Control (Rear) [Opt on Executive]	+157

Body Styles	TMV Pricing		
	Trade	Private	Dealer
4 Dr Executive Sdn	19212	20403	22387
4 Dr Signature Sdn	20461	21729	23843

Options	Price
Power Moonroof [Opt on Cartier,Signature]	+956
Special Leather Seat Trim [Opt on Signature]	+314
Two-Tone Paint [Opt on Signature]	+185
Xenon Headlamps [Opt on Cartier,Signature]	+282

2003

Lincoln's full-size luxury car receives an extensive reengineering for 2003 designed to make it safer, quieter and more luxurious than before. Major hardware revisions include a redesigned frame and modifications to the suspension, steering and braking systems. The standard V8 engine is also more powerful. Visually, the Town Car is more formal in appearance, and the old-fashioned Lincoln "star" hood ornament is back by popular demand. Creature comforts are addressed by the addition of newly standard equipment, increased storage space, additional safety features and improved interior materials.

Mileage Category: I

Body Styles	TMV Pricing		
	Trade	Private	Dealer
4 Dr Cartier L Sdn	18893	20385	22870
4 Dr Cartier Sdn	17236	18596	20863

Options	Price
Alpine Audio System [Opt on Signature]	+174
Chrome Wheels [Opt on Signature]	+224
Compact Disc Changer	+300
Heated Front Seats [Opt on Signature]	+199

Body Styles	TMV Pricing		
	Trade	Private	Dealer
4 Dr Executive Sdn	14050	15159	17007
4 Dr Signature Sdn	14979	16161	18133

Options	Price
Power Moonroof [Opt on Signature]	+472
Telematics System	+293
Touring Suspension [Opt on Signature]	+286
Two-Tone Paint [Opt on Signature]	+129

2002

A new Vehicle Communication System (VCS) is optional. VCS includes a portable hands-free, voice-activated Motorola Timeport analog-digital phone; SOS safety and security services; access to news, stock quotes and weather; and route guidance assistance.

Lincoln
Town Car

2001

Horsepower has been increased throughout the model lineup. Inside, the Town Car gains adjustable pedals, seat-belt pre-tensioners, upgraded map pockets and leather grab handles. Signature models have a wood-trimmed steering wheel as standard and the front seats in Executive models now have power lumbar adjustment. Lincoln now offers complimentary maintenance at no additional charge for the first three years/36,000 miles in service.

Mileage Category: I

Body Styles	TMV Pricing		
	Trade	Private	Dealer
4 Dr Cartier L Sdn	14823	16663	18360
4 Dr Cartier Sdn	14325	16103	17744
4 Dr Executive L Sdn	13577	15262	16818

Options	Price
Chrome Wheels [Opt on Signature]	+292
Compact Disc Changer	+250

Body Styles	TMV Pricing		
	Trade	Private	Dealer
4 Dr Executive Sdn	11613	13054	14385
4 Dr Signature Sdn	12412	13952	15374

Options	Price
Heated Front Seats [Opt on Signature]	+168
Power Moonroof	+636

2000

The Town Car receives additional safety features, including an emergency trunk release, child seat-anchor brackets and Lincoln's Belt Minder system. A new storage armrest has been placed on the front-passenger door-trim panel. One new exterior color has been added: Autumn Red Clearcoat Metallic.

Mileage Category: I

Body Styles	TMV Pricing		
	Trade	Private	Dealer
4 Dr Cartier L Sdn	11403	13043	14649
4 Dr Cartier Sdn	10874	12437	13969
4 Dr Executive L Sdn	10336	11822	13278

Options	Price
Chrome Wheels [Opt on Signature]	+252
Compact Disc Changer	+208

Body Styles	TMV Pricing		
	Trade	Private	Dealer
4 Dr Executive Sdn	8552	9782	10987
4 Dr Signature Sdn	9236	10565	11867

Options	Price
Power Moonroof	+548
Two-Tone Paint	+136

1999

Standard side airbags improve the Town Car's ability to protect occupants and a new JBL audio system makes getting there even more fun.

Mileage Category: I

Body Styles	TMV Pricing		
	Trade	Private	Dealer
4 Dr Cartier Sdn	9307	10717	12184
4 Dr Executive Sdn	7610	8763	9962

Options	Price
Chrome Wheels [Opt on Signature]	+205
Compact Disc Changer	+176

Body Styles	TMV Pricing		
	Trade	Private	Dealer
4 Dr Signature Sdn	8134	9366	10648

Options	Price
Power Moonroof	+447

1998

Lincoln redesigns its Town Car this year, making it lower, stiffer and faster. The interior is nicely improved as well, with softer seats and better positioned controls.

Mileage Category: I

Body Styles	TMV Pricing		
	Trade	Private	Dealer
4 Dr Cartier Sdn	8044	9407	10943
4 Dr Executive Sdn	6388	7469	8689

Options	Price
Chrome Wheels	+181
Compact Disc Changer	+155
JBL Audio System [Opt on Signature]	+147

Body Styles	TMV Pricing		
	Trade	Private	Dealer
4 Dr Signature Sdn	6819	7974	9276

Options	Price
Leather Seats [Opt on Executive, Signature]	+148
Power Moonroof	+393

1997

Mileage Category: I

Body Styles	TMV Pricing		
	Trade	Private	Dealer
4 Dr Cartier Sdn	6125	7293	8721
4 Dr Executive Sdn	4934	5874	7024

Options	Price
Chrome Wheels	+134
Compact Disc Changer	+115

The Town Car's power steering has been improved.

Body Styles	TMV Pricing		
	Trade	Private	Dealer
4 Dr Signature Sdn	5188	6178	7387

Options	Price
JBL Audio System [Opt on Signature]	+158
Power Moonroof	+294

1996

Engine upgrades, new automatic climate controls and real wood on the dashboard in Cartier models sum up the changes to the Town Car.

Mileage Category: I

Body Styles	TMV Pricing		
	Trade	Private	Dealer
4 Dr Cartier Sdn	4720	5670	6981
4 Dr Executive Sdn	3787	4549	5601

Options	Price
Power Moonroof	+224

Body Styles	TMV Pricing		
	Trade	Private	Dealer
4 Dr Signature Sdn	3998	4802	5912

1995

Mileage Category: I

Body Styles	TMV Pricing		
	Trade	Private	Dealer
4 Dr Cartier Sdn	3358	4114	5375
4 Dr Executive Sdn	2613	3201	4182

Options	Price
Compact Disc Changer	+104

Body Styles	TMV Pricing		
	Trade	Private	Dealer
4 Dr Signature Sdn	2825	3461	4522

Options	Price
Power Moonroof	+194

Exterior changes on the Town Car include new headlights, grille, taillights, bumpers and bodyside molding. The outside mirrors have been moved forward slightly to increase visibility. An electronic steering switch selector allows the driver to select the type of steering effort he or she wants. The instrument panel includes a redesigned two-spoke steering wheel, illuminated switches and improved stereos with larger controls. Signature and Cartier models get steering wheel-mounted stereo and climate controls. A gate access unit integrated into the driver-side visor allows up to three frequencies to be programmed into its memory.

626

2002

This year, to get any options on the LX four-cylinder or the ES-V6 model, you must order an automatic transmission. So much for that whole "zoom-zoom" philosophy. The former budget sport sedan, the LX-V6, can't be equipped with any options at all, save a slushbox. And the ES (in V6 format only for the new year) loses standard equipment; the moonroof, cassette player and Bose speakers are part of an optional ES Premium package.

Mileage Category: D

Body Styles	Trade	Private	Dealer
4 Dr ES V6 Sdn	7724	8729	10403
4 Dr LX Sdn	6620	7481	8916

Options	Price
AM/FM/Cassette/CD Audio System [Opt on ES V6]	+167
Alarm System [Std on ES V6]	+139
Aluminum/Alloy Wheels [Std on ES V6]	+250
Antilock Brakes	+379
Automatic 4-Speed Transmission	+445
Compact Disc Changer	+125

Body Styles	Trade	Private	Dealer
4 Dr LX V6 Sdn	6962	7867	9376

Options	Price
Fog Lights	+139
Front Side Airbag Restraints	+195
Power Driver Seat [Std on ES V6]	+139
Power Moonroof	+445
Rear Spoiler	+220
Traction Control System [Opt on ES V6]	+153

2001

The 626's interior gains a new modular audio system, a new rear deck with child safety-seat anchors and an internal emergency trunk release. Mazda has also made EZ-Kool glass standard on all models and side airbags a stand-alone option on models with a V6 and automatic transmissions. All 626s are now 50-state emission compliant.

Mileage Category: D

Body Styles	Trade	Private	Dealer
4 Dr ES Sdn	6495	7822	9046
4 Dr ES V6 Sdn	6647	8006	9260

Options	Price
AM/FM/Cassette/CD Audio System [Std on ES V6]	+170
Alarm System [Std on ES V6]	+122
Aluminum/Alloy Wheels [Std on ES,ES V6]	+219
Antilock Brakes	+331
Automatic 4-Speed Transmission [Std on ES]	+389
Bose Audio System [Std on ES V6]	+170

Body Styles	Trade	Private	Dealer
4 Dr LX Sdn	5661	6817	7884
4 Dr LX V6 Sdn	5790	6972	8064

Options	Price
Fog Lights	+122
Front Side Airbag Restraints	+122
Power Driver Seat [Std on ES V6]	+122
Power Moonroof [Std on ES V6]	+438
Rear Spoiler	+192
Traction Control System	+122

2000

Improvements in styling, handling, steering, interior content and options are the highlights of the 2000 626.

Mileage Category: D

Body Styles	Trade	Private	Dealer
4 Dr ES Sdn	4893	6086	7256
4 Dr ES V6 Sdn	5357	6664	7946

Options	Price
AM/FM/Cassette/CD Audio System [Std on ES V6]	+138
Aluminum/Alloy Wheels [Std on ES,ES V6]	+197
Antilock Brakes	+268
Automatic 4-Speed Transmission [Std on ES]	+315

Body Styles	Trade	Private	Dealer
4 Dr LX Sdn	4263	5303	6323
4 Dr LX V6 Sdn	4472	5563	6633

Options	Price
Bose Audio System [Std on ES V6]	+138
Power Moonroof [Std on ES V6]	+355
Rear Spoiler	+156

1999

After a major makeover in '98, the 626 slides into '99 with only one major change: a new height-adjustable seat for the driver.

Mileage Category: D

Body Styles	Trade	Private	Dealer
4 Dr ES Sdn	3993	5071	6192
4 Dr ES V6 Sdn	4255	5403	6597

Options	Price
Aluminum/Alloy Wheels [Std on ES V6]	+155
Antilock Brakes	+235

Body Styles	Trade	Private	Dealer
4 Dr LX Sdn	3318	4214	5146
4 Dr LX V6 Sdn	3665	4654	5684

Options	Price
Automatic 4-Speed Transmission [Std on ES]	+249
Power Moonroof [Std on ES V6]	+280

1998

Mazda redesigns the 626, giving it more upscale styling, more powerful engines, a tighter body and increased cargo and people space while retaining the sedan's distinctive sporting nature.

Mileage Category: D

Body Styles	Trade	Private	Dealer
4 Dr DX Sdn	2819	3657	4602
4 Dr ES Sdn	3444	4468	5623

Body Styles	Trade	Private	Dealer
4 Dr LX Sdn	3003	3895	4900
4 Dr LX V6 Sdn	3281	4256	5355

1998 (cont'd)

Options	Price
Air Conditioning [Opt on DX]	+260
Aluminum/Alloy Wheels [Std on ES]	+132
Antilock Brakes [Opt on LX]	+200

Options	Price
Automatic 4-Speed Transmission	+211
Leather Seats [Opt on LX]	+184
Power Moonroof [Std on ES]	+238

1997

Mileage Category: D

Body Styles	TMV Pricing		
	Trade	Private	Dealer
4 Dr DX Sdn	2299	3058	3986
4 Dr ES V6 Sdn	2977	3959	5159

Body Styles	TMV Pricing		
	Trade	Private	Dealer
4 Dr LX Sdn	2469	3284	4280
4 Dr LX V6 Sdn	2657	3535	4607

Options	Price
Air Conditioning [Opt on DX]	+232
Aluminum/Alloy Wheels [Opt on LX]	+118
Antilock Brakes [Std on ES]	+189

Options	Price
Automatic 4-Speed Transmission	+189
Leather Seats [Std on ES]	+164
Power Moonroof	+207

LX V6 and ES models gain power and torque, while the four-cylinder LX gets a Lexus-like trim package that includes two-tone paint, chrome wheel covers, leather interior, and other creature comforts. Audio systems are revised and two new colors debut.

1996

Mileage Category: D

Body Styles	TMV Pricing		
	Trade	Private	Dealer
4 Dr DX Sdn	1698	2323	3187
4 Dr ES V6 Sdn	2400	3285	4507

Body Styles	TMV Pricing		
	Trade	Private	Dealer
4 Dr LX Sdn	1868	2556	3507
4 Dr LX V6 Sdn	2087	2856	3918

Options	Price
Air Conditioning [Opt on DX]	+202
Antilock Brakes [Std on ES]	+167
Automatic 4-Speed Transmission	+167

Options	Price
Leather Seats	+146
Power Moonroof [Std on ES]	+183

Chrome is tacked on front and rear, and the hood is raised a bit to give the 626 a more substantial look. ABS is available as a stand alone option on LX and LX-V6 models for the first time (formerly, you had to buy an option package), and side-impact protection meets 1997 standards.

1995

Mileage Category: D

Body Styles	TMV Pricing		
	Trade	Private	Dealer
4 Dr DX Sdn	1135	1593	2357
4 Dr ES V6 Sdn	1660	2329	3445

Body Styles	TMV Pricing		
	Trade	Private	Dealer
4 Dr LX Sdn	1330	1867	2762
4 Dr LX V6 Sdn	1482	2080	3076

Options	Price
Air Conditioning [Opt on DX]	+181
Aluminum/Alloy Wheels [Opt on LX]	+94
Antilock Brakes [Std on ES]	+142

Options	Price
Automatic 4-Speed Transmission	+151
Power Moonroof [Std on ES]	+165

ES gets remote keyless entry, which is available on LX and LX-V6 models. New wheels and wheel covers are added across the board.

929
1995

Mileage Category: H

Body Styles	TMV Pricing		
	Trade	Private	Dealer
4 Dr STD Sdn	1766	2487	3688

Leather seats, wood trim and remote keyless entry are standard. Final year for sleek executive sedan.

B-Series
2004

Mileage Category: J

Body Styles	TMV Pricing		
	Trade	Private	Dealer
2 Dr B2300 SE Ext Cab SB	10709	11544	12935
2 Dr B2300 Std Cab SB	8620	9455	10846
2 Dr B3000 Dual Sport Ext Cab SB	10843	11809	13419
2 Dr B3000 Dual Sport Std Cab SB	9964	10930	12540

Body Styles	TMV Pricing		
	Trade	Private	Dealer
2 Dr B4000 4WD Ext Cab SB	11983	13022	14754
2 Dr B4000 SE 4WD Ext Cab SB	12810	13849	15581
4 Dr B3000 SE Ext Cab SB	11337	12380	14117
4 Dr B4000 Dual Sport Ext Cab SB	12575	13614	15346

The interior gets a slight refresh in the form of a new steering wheel and airbag design, new cloth upholstery and a redesigned center stack.

2004 (cont'd)

Body Styles	TMV Pricing		
	Trade	Private	Dealer
4 Dr B4000 SE 4WD Ext Cab SB	13766	14805	16537

Options	Price
AM/FM/CD Changer/MP3 Audio System [Opt on B4000 SE]	+200
Air Conditioning [Opt on B2300 Std]	+300
Bed Extender	+295
Bed Liner	+235
Cruise Control	+130
Jump Seat(s) [Opt on 2 Dr Ext]	+280

Options	Price
Power Windows	+180
Side Steps	+250
Tilt Steering Wheel	+150
Tonneau Cover	+330
Trailer Hitch [Opt on B3000, non-4 Dr B4000]	+215

2003

Two new extended cab models debut: a B2300 SE and a B3000 SE, and they include cosmetic changes like chrome bumpers and grille and alloy wheels. However, you can no longer order a four-wheel-drive B3000 Truck; 4WD is available on B4000 models only. Otherwise, only minor changes have been made to the rapidly aging Truck, such as the addition of A-pillar grab handles for the interior, thicker brake rotors for 4WD models, and the fact that the Power Package is no longer free when ordered with the Convenience Package.

Mileage Category: J

Body Styles	TMV Pricing		
	Trade	Private	Dealer
2 Dr B2300 SE Ext Cab SB	9588	10585	12246
2 Dr B2300 Std Cab SB	7030	7761	8979
2 Dr B3000 Dual Sport Ext Cab SB	9709	10719	12402
2 Dr B3000 Dual Sport Std Cab SB	8558	9448	10931
2 Dr B4000 4WD Ext Cab SB	10704	11817	13671

Body Styles	TMV Pricing		
	Trade	Private	Dealer
2 Dr B4000 SE 4WD Ext Cab SB	11311	12487	14448
4 Dr B3000 SE Ext Cab SB	10186	11245	13010
4 Dr B4000 Dual Sport Ext Cab SB	11171	12332	14268
4 Dr B4000 SE 4WD Ext Cab SB	12207	13476	15591

Options	Price
AM/FM/CD Audio System [Opt on B2300]	+183
Air Conditioning [Opt on B2300]	+433
Automatic 4-Speed Transmission	+667
Bed Extender	+197
Bed Liner	+157
Cruise Control	+123
Jump Seat(s)	+150
Off-Road Suspension Package [Opt on B4000 SE]	+900

Options	Price
Power Windows	+133
Side Steps	+247
Styled Steel Wheels [Opt on B2300]	+167
Tilt Steering Wheel	+117
Tonneau Cover	+220
Trailer Hitch	+143
Velour/Cloth Seats [Opt on B2300]	+267

2002

The B-Series name gets dropped this year for the far more creative moniker "Truck." To celebrate, Mazda trims the lineup to just six models, all of which include a standard sliding rear window and none of which include SE or SX stickers on the beds because those trims have been killed. New packages include the SE-5 package for B2300s and an Off Road Package for B4000 four-bys. The Convenience package includes a bed liner this year. Color changes round out the updates for 2002.

Mileage Category: J

Body Styles	TMV Pricing		
	Trade	Private	Dealer
2 Dr B2300 Std Cab SB	5809	6557	7803
2 Dr B3000 4WD Ext Cab SB	9280	10474	12465
2 Dr B3000 Dual Sport Ext Cab SB	7728	8709	10345

Body Styles	TMV Pricing		
	Trade	Private	Dealer
2 Dr B3000 Dual Sport Std Cab SB	7077	7988	9506
4 Dr B4000 4WD Ext Cab SB	9821	10972	12889
4 Dr B4000 SE Ext Cab SB	9001	10159	12090

Options	Price
AM/FM/CD Audio System [Opt on B2300]	+153
Air Conditioning [Opt on B2300]	+362
Automatic 4-Speed Transmission	+557
Bed Extender	+164
Bed Liner	+131

Options	Price
Off-Road Suspension Package	+751
Running Boards	+206
Styled Steel Wheels [Opt on B2300]	+139
Tonneau Cover	+184
Trailer Hitch	+120

2001

More power is the big news for Mazda's '01 B-Series Pickups. The B4000 boasts a new 4.0-liter SOHC V6, while the B2300 has a new 2.3-liter, four-cylinder engine. The flexible-fuel feature on the 3.0-liter V6 has been dropped. Mazda has also made ABS standard on all models. A new 4x2 Dual Sport trim level gives a two-wheeler the raised-suspension look of a four-by. While they were at it, Mazda product planners also modified the exterior and interior styling. To the chagrin of Troy Lee but probably nobody else, the B-Series Troy Lee edition has been dropped.

Mileage Category: J

Body Styles	TMV Pricing		
	Trade	Private	Dealer
2 Dr B2300 SE Std Cab SB	5685	6833	7892
2 Dr B2300 SX Std Cab SB	5002	6011	6943
2 Dr B2500 SE Std Cab SB	5125	6159	7113
2 Dr B2500 SX Std Cab SB	4388	5274	6091
2 Dr B3000 DS Ext Cab SB	6529	7847	9063
2 Dr B3000 DS Std Cab SB	5788	6956	8035
2 Dr B3000 SE 4WD Ext Cab SB	7649	9193	10618

Body Styles	TMV Pricing		
	Trade	Private	Dealer
2 Dr B3000 SE 4WD Std Cab SB	6789	8159	9424
2 Dr B3000 SE Ext Cab SB	6315	7590	8766
2 Dr B3000 SE Std Cab SB	5767	6931	8006
4 Dr B3000 SE Ext Cab SB	6972	8380	9679
4 Dr B4000 DS Ext Cab SB	7045	8467	9779
4 Dr B4000 SE 4WD Ext Cab SB	8118	9756	11268

Options	Price
Air Conditioning [Opt on SX - B2500, B3000]	+391
Automatic 4-Speed Transmission	+486
Power Windows [Std on B4000 - SE, TL]	+117

Options	Price
Running Boards	+180
Tonneau Cover	+160

2000

Two B3000 regular-cab models are added: SX and SE. The B2500 Troy Lee edition has been discontinued. Foglights are standard on all 4x4 models. A CD-equipped audio system is standard on all B4000 models. P225/70R15 tires are standard on SX models, and air conditioning is standard on SE and Troy Lee edition models. A 6,000-pound trailer hitch is standard on B4000 4x4s and optional on B4000 4x2 models. Troy Lee editions get standard leather-wrapped steering wheels.

Mileage Category: J

Body Styles	TMV Pricing		
	Trade	Private	Dealer
2 Dr B2500 SE Ext Cab SB	4594	5673	6731
2 Dr B2500 SE Std Cab SB	3710	4582	5436
2 Dr B2500 SX Std Cab SB	3048	3764	4466
2 Dr B3000 SE 4WD Std Cab SB	5033	6215	7374
2 Dr B3000 SE Ext Cab SB	4769	5889	6987
2 Dr B3000 SE Std Cab SB	3844	4746	5631
2 Dr B3000 SX Std Cab SB	3180	3927	4659

Body Styles	TMV Pricing		
	Trade	Private	Dealer
4 Dr B3000 SE 4WD Ext Cab SB	5830	7199	8541
4 Dr B3000 SE Ext Cab SB	4948	6110	7249
4 Dr B3000 TL Ext Cab SB	5388	6654	7894
4 Dr B4000 SE 4WD Ext Cab SB	6539	8074	9579
4 Dr B4000 SE Ext Cab SB	6272	7745	9189
4 Dr B4000 TL 4WD Ext Cab SB	6845	8452	10028

Options	Price
Air Conditioning [Opt on SX - B2500,B3000]	+317
Antilock Brakes	+268
Automatic 4-Speed Transmission	+431

Options	Price
Automatic 5-Speed Transmission [Opt on B4000 4WD]	+451

1999

The B-Series Pickup now comes with a four-door option called the Cab Plus 4. Option packages have been consolidated and simplified this year to reduce buyer confusion. A class III frame-mounted hitch receiver is available with V6 applications.

Mileage Category: J

Body Styles	TMV Pricing		
	Trade	Private	Dealer
2 Dr B2500 SE Ext Cab SB	3842	4819	5836
2 Dr B2500 SE Std Cab SB	3160	3963	4799
2 Dr B2500 SX Std Cab SB	2518	3158	3825
2 Dr B2500 TL Std Cab SB	3373	4231	5123
2 Dr B3000 SE 4WD Ext Cab SB	4792	6011	7279
2 Dr B3000 SE 4WD Std Cab SB	4329	5430	6575
2 Dr B3000 SE Ext Cab SB	3963	4971	6020
2 Dr B4000 SE 4WD Ext Cab SB	5464	6854	8300
2 Dr B4000 SE Ext Cab SB	4806	6028	7300

Body Styles	TMV Pricing		
	Trade	Private	Dealer
2 Dr B4000 SE Std Cab SB	4010	5030	6091
4 Dr B2500 SE Ext Cab SB	3974	4984	6036
4 Dr B3000 SE 4WD Ext Cab SB	4769	5981	7243
4 Dr B3000 SE Ext Cab SB	4185	5249	6356
4 Dr B3000 TL Ext Cab SB	4567	5728	6937
4 Dr B4000 SE 4WD Ext Cab SB	5527	6932	8395
4 Dr B4000 SE Ext Cab SB	4824	6050	7327
4 Dr B4000 TL 4WD Ext Cab SB	5889	7387	8946

Options	Price
Air Conditioning [Opt on B2500 SX]	+251
Antilock Brakes	+235
Automatic 4-Speed Transmission	+341

Options	Price
Automatic 5-Speed Transmission [Std on B4000 SE 2WD Ext Cab]	+341

1998

Fresh styling, a revised front suspension, a larger regular cab, a more powerful 2.5-liter four-cylinder engine, a stiffer frame and a new 4WD system ensure that Mazda's compact truck will remain competitive through the end of the century.

Mileage Category: J

Body Styles	TMV Pricing		
	Trade	Private	Dealer
2 Dr B2500 SE Ext Cab SB	3281	4166	5163
2 Dr B2500 SE Std Cab SB	2713	3444	4269
2 Dr B2500 SX Std Cab SB	2277	2890	3582
2 Dr B3000 SE 4WD Ext Cab SB	4071	5168	6405
2 Dr B3000 SE 4WD Std Cab SB	3848	4885	6054

Body Styles	TMV Pricing		
	Trade	Private	Dealer
2 Dr B3000 SE Ext Cab SB	3459	4391	5442
2 Dr B3000 SX 4WD Std Cab SB	3365	4272	5294
2 Dr B4000 SE 4WD Ext Cab SB	4691	5955	7380
2 Dr B4000 SE Ext Cab SB	3810	4836	5994
4 Dr B2500 SE Ext Cab SB	3379	4289	5315

Options	Price
Air Conditioning	+213
Antilock Brakes	+200

Options	Price
Automatic 4-Speed Transmission	+290
Automatic 5-Speed Transmission [Opt on B4000]	+299

1997

The lineup is trimmed, leaving just B2300 and B4000 models available. SE-5 designation returns to bolster marketing efforts. B4000 pickups can be equipped with a new five-speed automatic transmission.

Mileage Category: J

Body Styles	TMV Pricing		
	Trade	Private	Dealer
2 Dr B2300 SE Ext Cab SB	2634	3411	4361
2 Dr B2300 SE Std Cab SB	2168	2807	3589
2 Dr B2300 Std Cab SB	1827	2366	3024
2 Dr B4000 4WD Ext Cab SB	3678	4763	6090

Body Styles	TMV Pricing		
	Trade	Private	Dealer
2 Dr B4000 4WD Std Cab SB	2955	3826	4891
2 Dr B4000 SE 4WD Ext Cab SB	4031	5220	6674
2 Dr B4000 SE Ext Cab SB	2915	3775	4826

Options	Price
Air Conditioning	+189
Antilock Brakes	+178

Options	Price
Automatic 4-Speed Transmission	+252
Automatic 5-Speed Transmission	+260

1996

A passenger-side airbag comes with SE Plus and LE trim levels, and it can be deactivated in the event that a rear facing child safety seat is installed. SE models also get new chrome bumpers.

Mileage Category: J

Body Styles	TMV Pricing		
	Trade	Private	Dealer
2 Dr B2300 4WD Std Cab SB	2445	3188	4213
2 Dr B2300 Ext Cab SB	2100	2738	3619
2 Dr B2300 SE Ext Cab SB	2198	2866	3788
2 Dr B2300 SE Std Cab SB	1878	2448	3236
2 Dr B2300 Std Cab LB	1718	2240	2961
2 Dr B2300 Std Cab SB	1556	2029	2681

Options	Price
Air Conditioning [Std on B4000 LE]	+169
Antilock Brakes	+158

Body Styles	TMV Pricing		
	Trade	Private	Dealer
2 Dr B3000 4WD Ext Cab SB	2884	3759	4968
2 Dr B3000 SE Ext Cab SB	2406	3136	4145
2 Dr B4000 LE 4WD Ext Cab SB	4239	5526	7304
2 Dr B4000 LE Ext Cab SB	2785	3631	4800
2 Dr B4000 SE 4WD Ext Cab SB	3552	4631	6121
2 Dr B4000 SE 4WD Std Cab SB	2940	3833	5067

Options	Price
Automatic 4-Speed Transmission	+219

1995

Redesigned dashboard with driver airbag debuts. Four-wheel ABS is standard on 4WD and 2WD B4000 models.

Mileage Category: J

Body Styles	TMV Pricing		
	Trade	Private	Dealer
2 Dr B2300 4WD Std Cab SB	2146	2778	3830
2 Dr B2300 Ext Cab SB	1845	2388	3294
2 Dr B2300 SE Ext Cab SB	1961	2538	3500
2 Dr B2300 SE Std Cab SB	1667	2158	2975
2 Dr B2300 Std Cab LB	1517	1963	2707
2 Dr B2300 Std Cab SB	1381	1787	2464
2 Dr B3000 SE 4WD Ext Cab SB	2401	3108	4287

Options	Price
Air Conditioning [Std on B4000 LE]	+152
Automatic 4-Speed Transmission	+197

Body Styles	TMV Pricing		
	Trade	Private	Dealer
2 Dr B3000 SE Ext Cab SB	1997	2585	3564
2 Dr B3000 SE Std Cab SB	1819	2354	3245
2 Dr B4000 LE 4WD Ext Cab SB	3739	4839	6671
2 Dr B4000 LE Ext Cab SB	2370	3067	4228
2 Dr B4000 SE 4WD Ext Cab SB	3146	4071	5613
2 Dr B4000 SE 4WD Std Cab SB	2554	3305	4557
2 Dr B4000 SE Ext Cab SB	2037	2636	3633

Options	Price
Compact Disc Changer	+84

MAZDA3

2004

The Mazda 3 is an all-new economy sedan and hatchback that replaces the Protege in Mazda's lineup.

Mileage Category: B

Body Styles	TMV Pricing		
	Trade	Private	Dealer
4 Dr i Sdn	10275	11462	13441
4 Dr s Hbk	13058	14341	16478

Options	Price
17 Inch Wheels [Opt on s Sdn]	+490
AM/FM/Cassette Audio System	+200
Aero Kit [Opt on i, s Hbk]	+920
Air Conditioning [Opt on i]	+850
Aluminum/Alloy Wheels [Opt on i]	+400
Antilock Brakes	+400
Automatic 4-Speed Transmission	+900
Automatic Dimming Rearview Mirror	+200
Compact Disc Changer	+200

Body Styles	TMV Pricing		
	Trade	Private	Dealer
4 Dr s Sdn	12411	13597	15574

Options	Price
Fog Lights [Opt on i]	+150
Front Side Airbag Restraints	+200
Front and Rear Head Airbag Restraints	+200
Leather Seats [Opt on s]	+590
Navigation System [Opt on s]	+1750
Power Moonroof	+690
Rear Spoiler [Opt on s]	+300
Tire Pressure Monitoring System [Opt on s]	+300
Xenon Headlamps [Opt on s]	+400

MAZDA6

2004

Mileage Category: D

Body Styles	TMV Pricing		
	Trade	Private	Dealer
4 Dr i Hbk	13986	15237	17322
4 Dr i Sdn	12386	13615	15662
4 Dr s Hbk	15348	16599	18684

Options	Price
AM/FM/CD Changer Audio System	+200
AM/FM/Cassette Audio System	+200
Alarm System [Opt on i]	+150
Aluminum/Alloy Wheels [Opt on i Sdn]	+400

Body Styles	TMV Pricing		
	Trade	Private	Dealer
4 Dr s Sdn	14177	15403	17447
4 Dr s Wgn	14913	16164	18249

Options	Price
Antilock Brakes [Opt on i]	+250
Automatic 4-Speed Transmission [Opt on i]	+850
Automatic 5-Speed Transmission [Opt on i Sdn, s]	+900
Automatic Dimming Rearview Mirror	+150

2004 (cont'd)

Options	Price
Bose Audio System	+435
Compact Disc Changer	+500
Fog Lights [Opt on non-Hbk]	+250
Front Side Airbag Restraints	+200
Front and Rear Head Airbag Restraints	+200
Garage Door Opener	+150
Heated Front Seats	+250

Options	Price
Leather Seats	+900
Luggage Rack [Opt on S Sport Wgn]	+300
Power Driver Seat	+190
Power Moonroof	+700
Sport Package [Opt on non-Hbk]	+710
Traction Control System [Opt on i]	+150

New hatchback and wagon body styles are scheduled as midyear additions. Minor adjustments to the 6's optional equipment packages are the only other changes for 2004.

2003

Mileage Category: D

Body Styles	TMV Pricing		
	Trade	Private	Dealer
4 Dr i Sdn	10593	11650	13411

Body Styles	TMV Pricing		
	Trade	Private	Dealer
4 Dr s V6 Sdn	12783	14058	16184

Mazda introduces the successor to its 626 and Millenia midsize sedans, known as the 6. Touted for its sporty characteristics, the 6 hopes to make a splash in the congested family sedan marketplace.

Options	Price
17 Inch Wheels	+250
AM/FM/CD Changer Audio System	+267
AM/FM/Cassette Audio System	+133
Air Dam	+167
Aluminum/Alloy Wheels [Opt on i]	+267
Antilock Brakes [Opt on i]	+453
Automatic 4-Speed Transmission [Opt on i]	+567
Automatic 5-Speed Transmission [Opt on s]	+600
Bose Audio System	+167
Compact Disc Changer	+333

Options	Price
Fog Lights	+167
Front Side Airbag Restraints	+133
Front and Rear Head Airbag Restraints	+167
Ground Effects	+167
Heated Front Seats	+150
Leather Seats	+573
Power Driver Seat [Opt on i]	+167
Power Moonroof	+467
Rear Spoiler	+130
Traction Control System [Opt on i]	+167

Millenia

2002

Mileage Category: H

Body Styles	TMV Pricing		
	Trade	Private	Dealer
4 Dr Premium Sdn	11165	12318	14240
4 Dr Premium Special Edition Sdn	11597	12795	14791

Body Styles	TMV Pricing		
	Trade	Private	Dealer
4 Dr S S/C Sdn	12791	14112	16314
4 Dr S Special Edition S/C Sdn	14071	15524	17946

Options	Price
17 Inch Wheels - Chrome [Opt on S]	+334
Bose Audio System [Opt on Premium]	+445
Compact Disc Changer	+278
Heated Front Seats	+167

Options	Price
Special Factory Paint	+212
Traction Control System [Std on S]	+139
Two-Tone Paint	+212

Now that the brilliant 6 sport sedan has been approved for production, the Millenia's days are numbered. Understandably, changes for 2002 barely register on the Richter scale. Are you ready for this? An auto-dimming mirror with compass is standard, and Snow White Pearl paint is changed to Snow Flake White Pearl paint. You can also get a Special Edition with a chrome-finished front grille, a black exterior and a black-and-ivory interior with titanium trim.

2001

Mileage Category: H

Body Styles	TMV Pricing		
	Trade	Private	Dealer
4 Dr Premium Sdn	9090	10698	12182

Body Styles	TMV Pricing		
	Trade	Private	Dealer
4 Dr S S/C Sdn	9398	11060	12595

Mazda has strengthened the Millenia's body structure to improve torsional rigidity by 30 percent. Combined with a new rear stabilizer bar and a larger front stabilizer bar, improved handling is the result. Visually, the car should be more appealing thanks to new front and rear styling. The interior has been updated significantly, as well. Hardware changes include larger disc brakes, a revised ABS system and standard side airbags for both models.

Options	Price
17 Inch Wheels - Chrome	+292
Bose Audio System [Opt on STD]	+389
Compact Disc Changer	+243
Heated Front Seats	+146

Options	Price
Pearlescent Metallic Paint	+185
Traction Control System [Opt on STD]	+146
Two-Tone Paint	+185

2000

Mileage Category: H

Body Styles	TMV Pricing		
	Trade	Private	Dealer
4 Dr Millennium S/C Sdn	7598	9083	10538
4 Dr S S/C Sdn	7503	8970	10408

Body Styles	TMV Pricing		
	Trade	Private	Dealer
4 Dr STD Sdn	6391	7640	8864

Millenia models receive considerable price reductions to make them more competitive in the market. Mazda is also offering a special 2000 Millennium edition of the Millenia. This version comes with 17-inch chrome wheels, an in-dash six-disc CD changer, suede seat and door trim and a choice of either Highlight Silver Mica or Millennium Red Mica paint.

Mazda
Millenia

2000 (cont'd)

Options	Price
Bose Audio System [Opt on STD]	+276
Chrome Wheels [Opt on S]	+197
Heated Front Seats	+118
Leather Seats [Opt on STD]	+433

Options	Price
Power Moonroof [Opt on STD]	+364
Power Passenger Seat [Opt on STD]	+138
Special Factory Paint	+150
Traction Control System [Opt on STD]	+118

1999

Revised front- and rear-end styling, plus an optional two-tone color scheme, separate the '99 Millenia from past models.

Mileage Category: H

Body Styles	TMV Pricing		
	Trade	Private	Dealer
4 Dr S S/C Sdn	6388	7726	9119

Body Styles	TMV Pricing		
	Trade	Private	Dealer
4 Dr STD Sdn	5672	6860	8097

Options	Price
Bose Audio System [Std on S]	+218
Chrome Wheels	+155
Leather Seats [Std on S]	+342

Options	Price
Power Moonroof [Std on S]	+288
Special Factory Paint	+118

1998

Millenia carries over into 1998 with no changes.

Mileage Category: H

Body Styles	TMV Pricing		
	Trade	Private	Dealer
4 Dr S S/C Sdn	4673	5857	7192

Body Styles	TMV Pricing		
	Trade	Private	Dealer
4 Dr STD Sdn	4243	5318	6530

Options	Price
16 Inch Wheels [Opt on STD]	+147
Bose Audio System [Opt on STD]	+185
Compact Disc Changer [Opt on STD]	+145

Options	Price
Leather Seats [Opt on STD]	+291
Power Moonroof [Opt on STD]	+265

1997

Models equipped with leather are upgraded this year with an eight-way power passenger seat, 16-inch alloy wheels, and revised final drive ratio for better low-end response. S models also get the power passenger seat. All Millenias have a new rear-window-mounted diversity antenna, a new sound system with in-dash CD player, revised center console design and Michelin tires.

Mileage Category: H

Body Styles	TMV Pricing		
	Trade	Private	Dealer
4 Dr L Sdn	3692	4754	6051
4 Dr S S/C Sdn	4042	5204	6624

Body Styles	TMV Pricing		
	Trade	Private	Dealer
4 Dr STD Sdn	3632	4676	5952

Options	Price
Bose Audio System	+165

1996

The Millenia S gets revised bright-finish alloy wheels.

Mileage Category: H

Body Styles	TMV Pricing		
	Trade	Private	Dealer
4 Dr L Sdn	2644	3644	5025
4 Dr S S/C Sdn	2879	3968	5472

Body Styles	TMV Pricing		
	Trade	Private	Dealer
4 Dr STD Sdn	2510	3460	4771

Options	Price
Bose Audio System	+251

Options	Price
Compact Disc Changer	+115

1995

Luxury-oriented model that was to be in Mazda's aborted upscale Amati luxury division. Positioned to do battle with entry-level Lexus, Infiniti and BMW models. S models have 2.3-liter V6 with Miller-cycle technology and 210 horsepower. Dual airbags and ABS are standard on all models. The Millenia S adds traction control.

Mileage Category: H

Body Styles	TMV Pricing		
	Trade	Private	Dealer
4 Dr S S/C Sdn	2117	2981	4422

Body Styles	TMV Pricing		
	Trade	Private	Dealer
4 Dr STD Sdn	1830	2577	3821

Options	Price
Bose Audio System	+132
Compact Disc Changer	+103

Options	Price
Leather Seats [Std on S]	+207
Power Moonroof [Std on S]	+174

MPV

MPV

Mileage Category: P

2004

The MPV gets a facelift for 2004 that includes a new hood, headlamps, front fenders, grille, side skirts and alloy wheels. A rear air conditioner and four-wheel disc brakes are now standard.

Body Styles	TMV Pricing		
	Trade	Private	Dealer
4 Dr ES Pass Van	16856	18133	20260

Options	Price
17 Inch Wheels [Opt on LX]	+200
AM/FM/CD Changer Audio System [Opt on LX]	+150
AM/FM/Cassette Audio System	+200
Automatic Dimming Rearview Mirror	+230
DVD Entertainment System	+1200
Fog Lights [Opt on LX]	+250
Front Side Airbag Restraints [Opt on LX]	+200

Body Styles	TMV Pricing		
	Trade	Private	Dealer
4 Dr LX Pass Van	13934	15211	17339

Options	Price
Luggage Rack	+250
Power Dual Sliding Doors [Opt on LX]	+800
Power Moonroof	+900
Privacy Glass [Opt on LX]	+300
Special Factory Paint	+200
Traction Control System [Opt on LX]	+200
Trailer Hitch	+450

2003

For 2003, power sliding doors are an option for both the LX and ES trim levels. A towing package and a cargo organizer are two other new options. Also, an alarm and engine immobilizer are now part of a security package, and a cassette player is available on the ES trim level. The LX trim now rides on 16-inch wheels. Inside, floor and cargo mats are now standard on both trim levels, while outside, you'll see a new exhaust tip.

Body Styles	TMV Pricing		
	Trade	Private	Dealer
4 Dr ES Pass Van	13905	15259	17515
4 Dr LX Pass Van	11679	12816	14710

Options	Price
17 Inch Wheels [Opt on LX]	+150
AM/FM/CD Changer Audio System [Opt on LX]	+300
AM/FM/Cassette Audio System	+133
Air Conditioning - Front and Rear [Opt on LX]	+397
Alarm System [Opt on ES]	+167
Automatic Dimming Rearview Mirror	+130
Compact Disc Changer [Opt on ES,LX]	+300
DVD Entertainment System	+800

Body Styles	TMV Pricing		
	Trade	Private	Dealer
4 Dr LX-SV Pass Van	11221	12313	14134

Options	Price
Fog Lights	+133
Front Side Airbag Restraints [Opt on LX]	+183
Luggage Rack	+133
Power Dual Sliding Doors [Opt on ES,LX]	+533
Power Moonroof [Opt on ES,LX]	+467
Rear Heater [Opt on ES,LX]	+130
Rear Spoiler	+127
Trailer Hitch	+233

2002

Mazda adds power to the MPV in the form of a 200-horsepower V6 engine governed by a five-speed automatic transmission, which is just what the doctor ordered for this previously underpowered minivan. The MPV also gains power-sliding doors, available 17-inch alloy wheels, traction control, an improved braking system and revised suspension tuning.

Body Styles	TMV Pricing		
	Trade	Private	Dealer
4 Dr ES Pass Van	11550	12851	15019

Options	Price
16 Inch Wheels [Std on ES]	+209
Air Conditioning - Front and Rear [Std on ES]	+331
Automatic Dimming Rearview Mirror	+128
Compact Disc Changer	+250
Fog Lights [Std on ES]	+139

Body Styles	TMV Pricing		
	Trade	Private	Dealer
4 Dr LX Pass Van	9517	10588	12374

Options	Price
Front Side Airbag Restraints [Std on ES]	+153
Power Driver Seat [Std on ES]	+148
Power Moonroof	+390
Traction Control System [Std on ES]	+142

2001

Not much changes on Mazda's minivan. Keyless entry is standard on MPV LX, and the AM/FM/CD/cassette audio system is standard on LX and ES models. Child safety-seat anchors have been added to all MPV models, as have new exterior color choices. The 2.5-liter V6 engine now complies with NLEV emissions standards.

Body Styles	TMV Pricing		
	Trade	Private	Dealer
4 Dr DX Pass Van	7430	8890	10238
4 Dr ES Pass Van	9074	10857	12503

Options	Price
Air Conditioning - Front and Rear [Std on ES]	+289
Aluminum/Alloy Wheels [Std on ES]	+122
Compact Disc Changer [Std on ES]	+219
Fog Lights	+122

Body Styles	TMV Pricing		
	Trade	Private	Dealer
4 Dr LX Pass Van	8048	9630	11089

Options	Price
Front Side Airbag Restraints [Std on ES]	+129
Power Moonroof	+340
Power Windows [Opt on DX]	+124
VCR Entertainment System	+776

2000

The MPV has been completely redesigned from top to bottom. Several unique features, like hinged rear doors and all-wheel drive, have disappeared. At the same time, items like roll-down windows in the sliding doors and tailgate seating in the third-row seats certify the MPV as a standout vehicle.

Body Styles	TMV Pricing		
	Trade	Private	Dealer
4 Dr DX Pass Van	6163	7629	9067
4 Dr ES Pass Van	7549	9347	11109

Body Styles	TMV Pricing		
	Trade	Private	Dealer
4 Dr LX Pass Van	6648	8230	9781

2000 (cont'd)

Options	Price
AM/FM/CD Changer Audio System [Opt on ES,LX]	+236
Air Conditioning - Front and Rear [Std on ES]	+234

Options	Price
Power Moonroof	+276

1998

A CD player is now standard.

Mileage Category: P

Body Styles	Trade	Private	Dealer
4 Dr ES 4WD Pass Van	5270	6766	8452
4 Dr ES Pass Van	4706	6041	7546

Options	Price
Air Conditioning	+159
Air Conditioning - Front and Rear	+318
Aluminum/Alloy Wheels [Std on ES 4WD]	+131
Automatic Load Leveling [Opt on LX]	+131

Body Styles	Trade	Private	Dealer
4 Dr LX 4WD Pass Van	4836	6208	7756
4 Dr LX Pass Van	4064	5217	6517

Options	Price
Captain Chairs (4) [Opt on LX 4WD]	+118
Leather Seats [Opt on LX]	+291
Power Moonroof	+318

1997

Four-wheel ABS is standard across the board, and all but the LX 2WD model are dressed in goofy All-Sport exterior trim.

Mileage Category: P

Body Styles	Trade	Private	Dealer
4 Dr ES 4WD Pass Van	4302	5659	7317
4 Dr ES Pass Van	3836	5046	6525

Options	Price
Air Conditioning	+141
Air Conditioning - Front and Rear	+259
Aluminum/Alloy Wheels [Std on ES,4WD]	+117

Body Styles	Trade	Private	Dealer
4 Dr LX 4WD Pass Van	3999	5260	6802
4 Dr LX Pass Van	3274	4307	5569

Options	Price
Automatic Load Leveling [Opt on LX]	+117
Power Moonroof	+283

1996

New styling up front, a fourth door on the driver side, and a revised instrument panel with dual airbags sum up the changes to Mazda's attempt at a minivan.

Mileage Category: P

Body Styles	Trade	Private	Dealer
4 Dr DX Pass Van	2288	3053	4109
4 Dr ES 4WD Pass Van	3135	4182	5628
4 Dr ES Pass Van	2683	3579	4817

Options	Price
Air Conditioning	+189
Air Conditioning - Front and Rear	+231

Body Styles	Trade	Private	Dealer
4 Dr LX 4WD Pass Van	2854	3807	5123
4 Dr LX Pass Van	2404	3207	4317

Options	Price
Power Moonroof	+251

1995

New lineup includes L, LX and LXE trim levels. All come with seven-passenger seating. Four-cylinder engine has been dropped.

Mileage Category: P

Body Styles	Trade	Private	Dealer
3 Dr L Pass Van	1837	2504	3616
3 Dr LX 4WD Pass Van	2306	3144	4541
3 Dr LX Pass Van	1901	2591	3742

Options	Price
Air Conditioning	+113
Air Conditioning - Front and Rear	+207
Aluminum/Alloy Wheels	+93

Body Styles	Trade	Private	Dealer
3 Dr LXE 4WD Pass Van	2510	3421	4940
3 Dr LXE Pass Van	2186	2979	4301

Options	Price
Automatic Load Leveling [Opt on LX]	+93
Power Moonroof	+226

MX-3

1995

Mileage Category: E

Body Styles	Trade	Private	Dealer
2 Dr STD Hbk	1407	1932	2806

Options	Price
Air Conditioning	+141
Antilock Brakes	+151

Options	Price
Automatic 4-Speed Transmission	+151
Power Sunroof	+132

GS model, and its cool 1.8-liter V6, vanishes. ABS is available only with manual transmission.

2004

Mileage Category: E

Body Styles	TMV Pricing		
	Trade	Private	Dealer
2 Dr LS Conv	14556	15637	17438

Options	Price
6-Speed Transmission [Opt on LS]	+650
AM/FM/Cassette Audio System	+200
Alarm System	+220
Antilock Brakes [Opt on LS]	+550
Automatic 4-Speed Transmission	+800
Automatic Dimming Rearview Mirror	+230
Compact Disc Changer	+500

Body Styles	TMV Pricing		
	Trade	Private	Dealer
2 Dr STD Conv	12944	14026	15828

Options	Price
Cruise Control [Opt on STD]	+150
Hardtop Roof	+1500
Keyless Entry System [Opt on STD]	+200
Limited Slip Differential (Rear) [Opt on STD]	+395
Rear Spoiler	+295
Special Interior Trim [Opt on STD]	+330
Special Leather Seat Trim [Opt on STD]	+1230

A Mazdaspeed version of the Miata makes its debut for 2004. New 16-inch alloy wheels are available and Black Cherry Mica is a new exterior color choice.

2003

Mileage Category: E

Body Styles	TMV Pricing		
	Trade	Private	Dealer
2 Dr LS Conv	13036	14082	15826
2 Dr SE Conv	15324	16554	18604

Options	Price
6-Speed Transmission [Opt on LS]	+433
AM/FM/Cassette Audio System	+133
Air Dam	+300
Alarm System	+147
Antilock Brakes [Opt on LS,SE]	+453
Automatic 4-Speed Transmission	+533

Body Styles	TMV Pricing		
	Trade	Private	Dealer
2 Dr STD Conv	11619	12551	14105
2 Dr Shinsen Conv	12882	13916	15639

Options	Price
Automatic Dimming Rearview Mirror	+153
Cruise Control [Opt on STD]	+130
Keyless Entry System [Opt on STD]	+123
Limited Slip Differential [Opt on STD]	+263
Power Door Locks [Opt on STD]	+137
Sport Suspension [Opt on LS,STD]	+263

Only minor changes are in store for the Miata this year. Base models receive standard 16-inch alloy wheels, a strut-tower brace, larger brakes and a child seat anchoring system. Cloth replaces vinyl on the top of the LS model, and tan leather gives way to a lighter parchment-colored hide. Also, the LS receives aluminum-colored interior trim and, for the first time, black leather is available as an option. New options include a cargo net, an auto-dimming mirror with an integrated compass and outside temperature display and special bezels for the headlights and taillights.

2002

Mileage Category: E

Body Styles	TMV Pricing		
	Trade	Private	Dealer
2 Dr LS Conv	10785	11943	13872
2 Dr SE Conv	11028	12211	14183

Options	Price
16 Inch Wheels [Opt on STD]	+306
6-Speed Transmission [Opt on LS]	+362
Air Dam	+250
Antilock Brakes	+379
Automatic 4-Speed Transmission	+445

Body Styles	TMV Pricing		
	Trade	Private	Dealer
2 Dr STD Conv	9936	11002	12778

Options	Price
Compact Disc Changer [Std on SE]	+278
Hardtop Roof	+835
Limited Slip Differential [Opt on STD]	+139
Rear Spoiler	+164
Sport Suspension	+220

The addition of an optional in-dash six-CD changer, a perimeter theft alarm (on models with remote keyless entry) and a standard trunk light. LS versions get a revised stereo and speed-sensitive volume control. Later in the year, a new Special Edition trim debuts.

2001

Mileage Category: E

Body Styles	TMV Pricing		
	Trade	Private	Dealer
2 Dr LS Conv	9678	11292	12782
2 Dr STD Conv	8142	9500	10754

Options	Price
6-Speed Transmission	+316
Antilock Brakes	+331
Automatic 4-Speed Transmission	+438

Body Styles	TMV Pricing		
	Trade	Private	Dealer
2 Dr Special Edition Conv	10124	11812	13370

Options	Price
Hardtop Roof	+729
Limited Slip Differential [Opt on STD]	+122
Rear Spoiler	+143

For 2001, the Miata receives a host of minor changes. Horsepower has been increased, and a six-speed manual transmission is now optional on the Miata LS. Both the exterior and interior have been updated and there are four new exterior colors. Regular Miatas now have 15-inch wheels as standard equipment, while both the Miata LS and cars equipped with the optional suspension package get 16-inch wheels. Safety and security are improved via seatbelt pre-tensioners, improved ABS, an engine immobilizer, an internal trunk release and optional keyless remote (standard on Miata LS).

2000

Mileage Category: E

Body Styles	TMV Pricing		
	Trade	Private	Dealer
2 Dr LS Conv	7726	9145	10536
2 Dr STD Conv	6456	7641	8803

Body Styles	TMV Pricing		
	Trade	Private	Dealer
2 Dr Special Edition Conv	9074	10739	12372

The Miata's option packages have been simplified. There are now two models -- Miata and Miata LS -- and three option packages. A six-speed Miata Special Edition will also be available by spring 2000.

2000 (cont'd)

Options	Price
Air Conditioning [Opt on LS,STD]	+355
Antilock Brakes	+268
Automatic 4-Speed Transmission	+335

Options	Price
Hardtop Roof	+473
Rear Spoiler	+118

1999

Mazda cautiously redesigns the MX-5 Miata, improving the car in every way without bumping up the price or diluting the car's personality.

Mileage Category: E

Body Styles	TMV Pricing		
	Trade	Private	Dealer
2 Dr 10th Anniv Conv	6995	8593	10257

Body Styles	TMV Pricing		
	Trade	Private	Dealer
2 Dr STD Conv	4913	6036	7205

Options	Price
Air Conditioning	+280
Antilock Brakes	+235
Automatic 4-Speed Transmission	+265

Options	Price
Bose Audio System [Opt on STD]	+171
Hardtop Roof	+415
Leather Seats [Opt on STD]	+279

1997

Mileage Category: E

Body Styles	TMV Pricing		
	Trade	Private	Dealer
2 Dr M-Edition Conv	4581	5836	7370
2 Dr STD Conv	3696	4709	5946

Body Styles	TMV Pricing		
	Trade	Private	Dealer
2 Dr STO Conv	4456	5676	7168

Options	Price
Air Conditioning [Opt on STD]	+212
Antilock Brakes	+212
Automatic 4-Speed Transmission	+201

Options	Price
Hardtop Roof	+314
Leather Seats [Opt on STD]	+211

Mazda adds a Touring Package to the options list, consisting of alloy wheels, power steering, leather-wrapped steering wheel, power mirrors, power windows and door map pockets. Midyear a new M-Edition debuts, sporting Marina Green paint and chromed alloy wheels. Summertime brings the limited-production STO-Edition, of which 1,500 were produced.

1996

Side-impact standards for 1997 are met a year early, and to offset the added weight, Mazda boosts power and torque.

Mileage Category: E

Body Styles	TMV Pricing		
	Trade	Private	Dealer
2 Dr M-Edition Conv	3573	4741	6355

Body Styles	TMV Pricing		
	Trade	Private	Dealer
2 Dr STD Conv	2712	3599	4825

Options	Price
Air Conditioning [Opt on STD]	+189
Antilock Brakes [Opt on STD]	+189
Automatic 4-Speed Transmission	+178

Options	Price
Hardtop Roof	+279
Leather Seats [Opt on STD]	+188
Sensory Audio System [Opt on STD]	+183

1995

Option packages are revised, and a gorgeous M-Edition with Merlot Mica paint, tan top, tan leather interior and 15-inch BBS rims is available.

Mileage Category: E

Body Styles	TMV Pricing		
	Trade	Private	Dealer
2 Dr M-Edition Conv	2821	3873	5626

Body Styles	TMV Pricing		
	Trade	Private	Dealer
2 Dr STD Conv	2160	2964	4305

Options	Price
Air Conditioning [Opt on STD]	+169
Antilock Brakes [Opt on STD]	+142
Automatic 4-Speed Transmission	+160

Options	Price
Hardtop Roof	+251
Leather Seats [Opt on STD]	+169
Sensory Audio System	+165

MAZDASPEED MX-5 Miata

2004

Mileage Category: E

Body Styles	TMV Pricing		
	Trade	Private	Dealer
2 Dr Turbo Conv	19191	20467	22594

Options	Price
AM/FM/Cassette Audio System	+200
Alarm System	+220

Options	Price
Special Leather Seat Trim	+800

The Miata gets the Mazdaspeed makeover, with a 178-horsepower turbocharged engine, high-performance suspension and distinctive styling enhancements.

MX-6

1997

Mileage Category: E

Body Styles	TMV Pricing		
	Trade	Private	Dealer
2 Dr LS Cpe	3426	4366	5514

Options	Price
Air Conditioning [Std on LS]	+212
Antilock Brakes	+189
Automatic 4-Speed Transmission	+189

All LS models get a rear spoiler.

Body Styles	TMV Pricing		
	Trade	Private	Dealer
2 Dr STD Cpe	2874	3662	4624

Options	Price
Leather Seats	+164
Power Sunroof [Std on LS]	+177

1996

No changes for 1996.

Mileage Category: E

Body Styles	TMV Pricing		
	Trade	Private	Dealer
2 Dr LS Cpe	2697	3481	4564
2 Dr M-Edition Cpe	3244	4187	5489

Options	Price
Air Conditioning [Std on STD]	+189
Antilock Brakes [Opt on LS,STD]	+167
Automatic 4-Speed Transmission	+167

Body Styles	TMV Pricing		
	Trade	Private	Dealer
2 Dr STD Cpe	2272	2933	3846

Options	Price
Leather Seats [Opt on LS]	+146
Power Sunroof [Opt on STD]	+157

1995

No changes for 1995.

Mileage Category: E

Body Styles	TMV Pricing		
	Trade	Private	Dealer
2 Dr LS Cpe	1831	2514	3653

Options	Price
Air Conditioning [Std on LS]	+169
Antilock Brakes	+151
Automatic 4-Speed Transmission	+151

Body Styles	TMV Pricing		
	Trade	Private	Dealer
2 Dr STD Cpe	1557	2138	3106

Options	Price
Leather Seats	+131
Power Sunroof [Std on LS]	+141

Protege

2003

Mileage Category: B

Body Styles	TMV Pricing		
	Trade	Private	Dealer
4 Dr DX Sdn	7653	8565	10085
4 Dr ES Sdn	8870	9926	11686

Options	Price
AM/FM/CD Changer Audio System [Opt on ES,LX]	+250
AM/FM/Cassette Audio System	+133
Air Conditioning [Opt on DX]	+567
Alarm System [Opt on ES,LX]	+147
Antilock Brakes [Opt on ES,LX]	+453
Automatic 4-Speed Transmission	+533

Body Styles	TMV Pricing		
	Trade	Private	Dealer
4 Dr LX Sdn	8493	9505	11191

Options	Price
Automatic Dimming Rearview Mirror	+153
Compact Disc Changer	+333
Front Side Airbag Restraints [Opt on ES,LX]	+197
Power Moonroof [Opt on ES,LX]	+333
Rear Spoiler [Opt on DX,LX]	+220

Minor changes limited to feature content are in store for Mazda's economy sedan. The DX trim gets a CD player as standard equipment, while air conditioning is offered as a stand-alone option. The LX trim receives 15-inch wheels as standard. Last year's premium packages for the LX and ES have been discontinued, but you can still get the sunroof, side airbags and antilock brakes as options.

2002

The enthusiast-oriented MP3 goes on hiatus as Mazda tries to extract more power from the engine. In other news, the base 1.6-liter engine is dropped, making the 130-horse 2.0-liter standard on all trim levels. Each model gets added equipment: larger tires and full wheel covers come on DX; air conditioning, body-colored mirrors and remote keyless entry are standard on LX; new carbon-fiber appearance decor and silver trim debut on the dash and doors of the ES. All models get a sporty three-spoke steering wheel and a 14.5-gallon fuel tank. Foglights and an auto-dimming mirror are available on any Protege for 2002.

Mileage Category: B

Body Styles	TMV Pricing		
	Trade	Private	Dealer
4 Dr DX Sdn	6043	6902	8333
4 Dr ES Sdn	7211	8236	9944

Options	Price
Air Conditioning [Opt on DX]	+445
Alarm System	+122
Antilock Brakes	+379

Body Styles	TMV Pricing		
	Trade	Private	Dealer
4 Dr LX Sdn	6791	7756	9364

Options	Price
Automatic 4-Speed Transmission	+445
Automatic Dimming Rearview Mirror	+128
Compact Disc Changer	+278

Mazda
Protege

2002 (cont'd)

Options	Price
Fog Lights [Std on ES]	+139
Front Side Airbag Restraints [Opt on ES,LX]	+181

Options	Price
Power Moonroof	+167
Rear Spoiler [Std on ES]	+184

2001

Already one of the best-looking economy sedans on the market, the Protege receives freshened exterior styling for 2001. ES models now have standard 16-inch wheels, and 15-inch wheels are optional on LX models. A larger 2.0-liter engine replaces the previous 1.8-liter engine. All Proteges get a revised interior and improvements to ride comfort, braking effort and steering feel. Front seatbelt pre-tensioners are standard.

Mileage Category: B

Body Styles	TMV Pricing		
	Trade	Private	Dealer
4 Dr DX Sdn	4589	5647	6623
4 Dr ES Sdn	5596	6884	8073

Body Styles	TMV Pricing		
	Trade	Private	Dealer
4 Dr LX Sdn	4854	5970	7000
4 Dr MP3 Sdn	6619	8143	9549

Options	Price
2.0L I4 DOHC 16V FI Engine [Opt on LX]	+195
Air Conditioning [Std on ES]	+389
Antilock Brakes	+331
Automatic 4-Speed Transmission	+389

Options	Price
Compact Disc Changer	+243
Front Side Airbag Restraints	+122
Power Moonroof	+340
Rear Spoiler	+160

2000

Front-seat side airbags and an improved ABS system are new to the LX premium and ES premium packages. The LX and ES also get illuminated power window switches. Chrome plating has been added to the inner door handles, and a Mazda symbol now appears on the steering wheel, the parking brake button and the automatic transmission shift-lever button. The Twilight Blue Mica exterior color has been discontinued and replaced with Midnight Blue Mica.

Mileage Category: B

Body Styles	TMV Pricing		
	Trade	Private	Dealer
4 Dr DX Sdn	3467	4465	5444
4 Dr ES Sdn	4576	5894	7185

Body Styles	TMV Pricing		
	Trade	Private	Dealer
4 Dr LX Sdn	4013	5169	6303

Options	Price
AM/FM/CD Audio System [Opt on DX]	+197
AM/FM/Cassette/CD Audio System	+138
Air Conditioning [Std on ES]	+433

Options	Price
Antilock Brakes	+315
Automatic 4-Speed Transmission	+315
Power Moonroof	+315

1999

The Protege gets an extensive makeover for '99 that includes new exterior and interior styling, a more powerful engine lineup, additional luxury options and five new colors.

Mileage Category: B

Body Styles	TMV Pricing		
	Trade	Private	Dealer
4 Dr DX Sdn	2556	3387	4251
4 Dr ES Sdn	3612	4785	6006

Body Styles	TMV Pricing		
	Trade	Private	Dealer
4 Dr LX Sdn	2924	3875	4864

Options	Price
AM/FM/CD Audio System [Opt on DX]	+155
Air Conditioning [Std on ES]	+342
Aluminum/Alloy Wheels	+125

Options	Price
Antilock Brakes	+249
Automatic 4-Speed Transmission	+249
Power Moonroof	+249

1998

Mileage Category: B

Body Styles	TMV Pricing		
	Trade	Private	Dealer
4 Dr DX Sdn	1853	2524	3281
4 Dr ES Sdn	2452	3341	4344

Body Styles	TMV Pricing		
	Trade	Private	Dealer
4 Dr LX Sdn	2083	2838	3690

Options	Price
AM/FM/CD Audio System [Opt on DX]	+132
Air Conditioning [Std on ES]	+265
Antilock Brakes	+211

Options	Price
Automatic 4-Speed Transmission	+211
Compact Disc Changer	+145
Power Moonroof	+185

A CD player is standard on ES and LX. It also comes on DX models equipped with an option package.

1997

Styling revisions inside and out update this roomy compact sedan.

Mileage Category: B

Body Styles	TMV Pricing		
	Trade	Private	Dealer
4 Dr DX Sdn	1564	2230	3044
4 Dr ES Sdn	1979	2820	3847

Body Styles	TMV Pricing		
	Trade	Private	Dealer
4 Dr LX Sdn	1695	2416	3297

Options	Price
Air Conditioning [Std on ES]	+236
Antilock Brakes	+189

Options	Price
Automatic 4-Speed Transmission	+189
Power Moonroof	+165

1996

No changes for 1996.

Body Styles	TMV Pricing		
	Trade	Private	Dealer
4 Dr DX Sdn	1174	1770	2593
4 Dr ES Sdn	1542	2324	3403

Options	Price
Air Conditioning [Std on ES]	+210
Antilock Brakes	+167

Mileage Category: B

Body Styles	TMV Pricing		
	Trade	Private	Dealer
4 Dr LX Sdn	1285	1936	2835

Options	Price
Automatic 4-Speed Transmission	+167
Power Moonroof	+147

1995

Totally redesigned, the Protege grows substantially in interior volume and offers 10 more cubic feet inside than the Honda Civic. Dual airbags are finally added. ABS is standard on ES trim level; optional on LX.

Body Styles	TMV Pricing		
	Trade	Private	Dealer
4 Dr DX Sdn	947	1481	2371
4 Dr ES Sdn	1146	1793	2870

Options	Price
Air Conditioning [Std on ES]	+188
Aluminum/Alloy Wheels	+75
Antilock Brakes [Opt on LX]	+151

Mileage Category: B

Body Styles	TMV Pricing		
	Trade	Private	Dealer
4 Dr LX Sdn	996	1558	2495

Options	Price
Automatic 4-Speed Transmission	+151
Power Moonroof	+132

MAZDASPEED Protege

2003

Mazda introduces a new sport-tuned version of its Protege, dubbed Mazdaspeed.

Body Styles	TMV Pricing		
	Trade	Private	Dealer
4 Dr Turbo Sdn	14579	15749	17698

Mileage Category: E

Body Styles	TMV Pricing		
	Trade	Private	Dealer
4 Dr Turbo Sdn (2003.5)	15041	16248	18260

Protege5

2003

Mileage Category: B

Body Styles	TMV Pricing		
	Trade	Private	Dealer
4 Dr STD Wgn	9940	11050	12900

Options	Price	Options	Price
AM/FM/CD Changer Audio System	+250	Automatic Dimming Rearview Mirror	+153
AM/FM/Cassette Audio System	+133	Compact Disc Changer	+333
Alarm System	+147	Front Side Airbag Restraints	+197
Aluminum/Alloy Wheels	+333	Leather Seats	+327
Antilock Brakes	+453	Luggage Rack	+167
Automatic 4-Speed Transmission	+600	Power Moonroof	+333

The Protege5 now has carpeted floor mats as standard equipment, and the moonroof can now only be had with an in-dash six-disc CD changer. There's also a new color this year: Laser Blue Mica.

2002

The Protege is now available as a slick little sport wagon, adding another body style to the Protege lineup.

Mileage Category: B

Body Styles	TMV Pricing		
	Trade	Private	Dealer
4 Dr STD Wgn	8220	9321	11157

Options	Price	Options	Price
Alarm System	+122	Compact Disc Changer	+278
Antilock Brakes	+379	Front Side Airbag Restraints	+181
Automatic 4-Speed Transmission	+445	Leather Seats	+273
Automatic Dimming Rearview Mirror	+128	Power Moonroof	+390

Mazda
RX-7/RX-8/Tribute

RX-7

1995

Mileage Category: F

Body Styles		TMV Pricing	
	Trade	Private	Dealer
2 Dr Turbo Hbk	10710	11991	14127

Options	Price	Options	Price
Automatic 4-Speed Transmission	+141	Power Moonroof	+132
Bose Audio System	+150	Sport Suspension	+141
Leather Seats	+151		

CFC-free refrigerant is added to air conditioner. Touring package ousted. Red leather option dumped. Last year for RX-7.

RX-8

2004

Mileage Category: F

Body Styles		TMV Pricing		Body Styles		TMV Pricing	
	Trade	Private	Dealer		Trade	Private	Dealer
4 Dr STD Cpe	18793	20110	22305	4 Dr STD Cpe	19115	20504	22820

Options	Price	Options	Price
18 Inch Wheels	+400	Navigation System	+2000
AM/FM/Cassette Audio System	+200	Power Driver Seat	+250
Automatic Stability Control	+350	Power Heated Mirrors	+120
Bose Audio System	+650	Power Moonroof	+800
Compact Disc Changer	+500	Rear Spoiler	+355
Fog Lights	+150	Sport Suspension	+200
Leather Seats	+600	Traction Control System	+250
Limited Slip Differential (Rear)	+300	Xenon Headlamps	+300

The RX-8 is an all-new car for 2004. Its arrival marks the return of Mazda's rotary engine to the U.S. market. Priced less than Nissan's 350Z, the RX-8 also offers four doors and a usable backseat.

Tribute

2004

Mileage Category: L

Body Styles		TMV Pricing		Body Styles		TMV Pricing	
	Trade	Private	Dealer		Trade	Private	Dealer
4 Dr DX 4WD SUV	13245	14291	16034	4 Dr ES V6 SUV	16361	17479	19341
4 Dr DX SUV	12120	13162	14898	4 Dr LX V6 4WD SUV	16216	17387	19338
4 Dr ES V6 4WD SUV	17317	18488	20439	4 Dr LX V6 SUV	14989	16085	17911

Options	Price	Options	Price
AM/FM/Cassette Audio System	+200	Heated Front Seats [Opt on ES]	+180
AM/FM/Cassette/CD Changer Audio System [Opt on ES, LX]	+250	Overhead Console [Opt on LX, ES]	+120
Antilock Brakes [Opt on LX]	+300	Power Driver Seat [Opt on LX]	+250
Automatic Dimming Rearview Mirror	+200	Power Moonroof [Opt on ES, LX]	+720
Compact Disc Changer	+500	Rear Spoiler	+250
DVD Entertainment System	+1200	Side Steps	+350
Front Side Airbag Restraints [Opt on LX]	+250	Trailer Hitch [Opt on LX, ES]	+355

New body-colored door edge guards are available as an option, as is Homelink and an auto-dimming rearview mirror with a built-in compass.

2003

DX, LX and ES trims carryover, but the V6 is newly limited to LX and ES. If you want to see what's new on the 2003 Tribute, you'll need to look inside. This year, the dashboard is two-tone, and the insert trim is either brushed aluminum (DX and LX) or fake black wood (ES). ES models are equipped with upgraded leather and a cold package that includes heated seats and exterior mirrors. New options include an auto-dimming rearview mirror with compass and a DVD entertainment system. Four new colors round out the changes.

Mileage Category: L

Body Styles		TMV Pricing		Body Styles		TMV Pricing	
	Trade	Private	Dealer		Trade	Private	Dealer
4 Dr DX 4WD SUV	12151	13226	15017	4 Dr ES V6 SUV	13887	15116	17163
4 Dr DX SUV	11146	12132	13776	4 Dr LX V6 4WD SUV	13824	15047	17085
4 Dr ES V6 4WD SUV	14592	15883	18034	4 Dr LX V6 SUV	13564	14764	16764

Options	Price	Options	Price
AM/FM/Cassette Audio System	+133	Camper/Towing Package [Opt on ES,LX]	+237
AM/FM/Cassette/CD Changer Audio System [Opt on ES,LX]	+337	Compact Disc Changer	+333
Antilock Brakes [Opt on LX]	+453	DVD Entertainment System	+800
Automatic Dimming Rearview Mirror	+153	Front Side Airbag Restraints [Opt on LX]	+167
		Heated Front Seats [Opt on ES]	+150

For the latest vehicle information, visit www.edmunds.com

Options	Price
Power Driver Seat [Opt on LX]	+167
Power Moonroof [Opt on ES,LX]	+400

Options	Price
Rear Spoiler	+167
Side Steps	+233

Mileage Category: L

Body Styles	TMV Pricing		
	Trade	Private	Dealer
4 Dr DX 4WD SUV	10232	11303	13089
4 Dr DX SUV	9335	10312	11941
4 Dr DX V6 4WD SUV	11398	12591	14580
4 Dr DX V6 SUV	10639	11753	13609

Body Styles	TMV Pricing		
	Trade	Private	Dealer
4 Dr ES V6 4WD SUV	12374	13669	15827
4 Dr ES V6 SUV	11744	12974	15023
4 Dr LX V6 4WD SUV	11730	12958	15005
4 Dr LX V6 SUV	11093	12254	14190

Options	Price
AM/FM/Cassette/CD Changer Audio System	+281
Antilock Brakes [Opt on LX V6]	+379
Automatic Dimming Rearview Mirror	+128
Camper/Towing Package	+198
Compact Disc Changer	+278

Options	Price
Front Side Airbag Restraints	+139
Power Driver Seat [Opt on LX V6]	+139
Power Moonroof	+334
Rear Spoiler	+139
Side Steps	+195

2002

After an extremely successful introductory year, Mazda's Tribute SUV receives only minor modifications for 2002. DX models get additional standard equipment in the form of alloy wheels, dark-tinted glass and remote keyless entry. After a short production run, however, the DX-V6 model will be discontinued. Midgrade LX models can be ordered with ABS as a stand-alone option (last year it was bundled with side airbags) and with a six-way power driver seat. Both LX and ES models get a new driver lumbar support feature. Side step tubes are a new option on all Tribs, and four new colors debut for 2002.

Mileage Category: L

Body Styles	TMV Pricing		
	Trade	Private	Dealer
4 Dr DX 4WD SUV	8808	10194	11474
4 Dr DX SUV	7833	9066	10204
4 Dr DX V6 4WD SUV	9768	11306	12726
4 Dr DX V6 SUV	9100	10533	11855

Body Styles	TMV Pricing		
	Trade	Private	Dealer
4 Dr ES V6 4WD SUV	10778	12475	14041
4 Dr ES V6 SUV	10281	11899	13393
4 Dr LX V6 4WD SUV	10345	11973	13476
4 Dr LX V6 SUV	9843	11392	12822

Options	Price
AM/FM/Cassette/CD Changer Audio System [Opt on ES,LX]	+246
Aluminum/Alloy Wheels [Opt on DX]	+182
Antilock Brakes	+331
Camper/Towing Package	+170

Options	Price
Front Side Airbag Restraints	+122
Power Moonroof	+292
Premium Audio System	+246

2001

Mazda's first sport-utility vehicle since the departure of the Navajo half a decade ago, the Tribute combines carlike ride and handling with the ability to go in the snow and tote up to five passengers and a healthy amount of their luggage. With the most powerful V6 in its class, in addition to handsome looks and a spacious cabin, the Tribute should find huge success despite an increasingly crowded small-SUV marketplace.

Mercedes-Benz
C-Class

C-Class

2004

Sport coupes get standard 17-inch wheels and tires, three-spoke sport steering wheel, leather-wrapped gearshift, aluminum pedals and large chrome exhaust outlet. Sport sedans get similar upgrades, as well as new front brakes featuring four-piston calipers and drilled rotors, sport shift manual transmission, lowered sport suspension, a free-flow exhaust and new five-spoke alloy wheels.

Mileage Category: H

Body Styles	TMV Pricing		
	Trade	Private	Dealer
2 Dr C230 Kompressor S/C Hbk	17097	18406	20587
2 Dr C320 Hbk	18646	19954	22134
4 Dr C230 Kompressor S/C Sdn	19292	20600	22780
4 Dr C240 4MATIC AWD Sdn	22262	23569	25748
4 Dr C240 4MATIC AWD Wgn	22211	23460	25542
4 Dr C240 Sdn	21486	22794	24972

Body Styles	TMV Pricing		
	Trade	Private	Dealer
4 Dr C240 Wgn	21454	22703	24784
4 Dr C320 4MATIC AWD Sdn	25395	26813	29176
4 Dr C320 4MATIC AWD Wgn	25551	26804	28891
4 Dr C320 Sdn	24620	26038	28402
4 Dr C320 Wgn	24531	25770	27834

Options	Price
Automatic 5-Speed Transmission [Opt on C230 Kompressor, C320 Hbk, Sdn]	+1360
Automatic Dimming Rearview Mirror	+120
Automatic Dimming Sideview Mirror(s)	+150
COMAND System	+2170
Compact Disc Changer	+410
Garage Door Opener [Opt on Hbk]	+170
Headlight Washers	+250
Heated Front Seats	+670
Leather Door Panels [Opt on Hbk]	+310
Leather Seats [Opt on Hbk]	+1000
Metallic Paint	+670

Options	Price
Power Driver Seat w/Memory [Opt on C230, C240]	+450
Power Panorama Roof	+770
Power Passenger Seat w/Memory [Opt on C230, C240]	+450
Power Rear Window Sunshade [Opt on Sdn]	+400
Rain Sensing Windshield Wipers	+200
Split Folding Rear Seat [Opt on Sdn]	+350
Sport Package [Opt on C320 Sdn]	+760
Telematics System	+800
Wood Interior Trim [Opt on Hbk]	+360
Xenon Headlamps	+520

2003

Changes are light this year. Mercedes' "4Matic" all-wheel-drive system is now available for sedan and wagon models (the C32 sport sedan being the lone exception) and the C230 Sport Coupe's supercharged engine has been revised for greater efficiency and lower emissions. A six-speed manual gearbox is available for the C320 models, and a supercharged C230 Sport Sedan is now available as well.

Mileage Category: H

Body Styles	TMV Pricing		
	Trade	Private	Dealer
2 Dr C230 S/C Hbk	15361	16356	18015
2 Dr C320 Hbk	15967	17002	18726
4 Dr C230 S/C Sdn	17744	18894	20811
4 Dr C240 4MATIC AWD Sdn	19659	20933	23056
4 Dr C240 4MATIC AWD Wgn	20310	21626	23819
4 Dr C240 Sdn	19490	20753	22858

Body Styles	TMV Pricing		
	Trade	Private	Dealer
4 Dr C240 Wgn	18508	19707	21706
4 Dr C320 4MATIC AWD Sdn	22745	24218	26674
4 Dr C320 4MATIC AWD Wgn	22108	23541	25928
4 Dr C320 Sdn	22311	23757	26167
4 Dr C320 Wgn	20805	22153	24400

Options	Price
17 Inch Wheels [Opt on C230, C320]	+411
Automatic 5-Speed Transmission [Opt on C230, C240, C320]	+1037
Bose Audio System [Opt on C230, C240, C320]	+352
COMAND System	+1664
Compact Disc Changer	+313
Designo Charcoal Cinnamora Edition [Opt on Hbk]	+274
Heated Front Seats	+509
Leather Seats [Opt on Hbk]	+705
Metallic Paint	+513
Power Driver Seat w/Memory [Opt on C230, C240, C320]	+254
Power Moonroof [Opt on C230, C240, C320]	+705
Power Panorama Roof [Opt on Hbk]	+783

Options	Price
Power Passenger Seat w/Memory [Opt on C230, C240, C320]	+254
Power Rear Window Sunshade [Opt on C230, C240, C320]	+388
Power Tilt and Telescopic Steering Wheel [Opt on C230, C240, C320]	+196
Rain Sensing Windshield Wipers [Opt on C230, C240, C320]	+157
Ski Sack	+157
Special Leather Seat Trim [Opt on C230, C240, C320]	+1127
Split Folding Rear Seat [Opt on C230, C240, C320]	+196
Sport Suspension [Opt on C320]	+196
Telematics System [Opt on C230, C240, C320]	+607
Xenon Headlamps	+431

2002

Two new models debut: the C230 Kompressor Sport Coupe and the C320 wagon.

Mileage Category: H

Body Styles	TMV Pricing		
	Trade	Private	Dealer
2 Dr C230 S/C Hbk	13091	14124	15847
4 Dr C240 Sdn	16367	17659	19814

Body Styles	TMV Pricing		
	Trade	Private	Dealer
4 Dr C320 Sdn	18272	19699	22078
4 Dr C320 Wgn	17488	18854	21130

Options	Price
17 Inch Wheels [Opt on C230]	+523
Automatic 5-Speed Transmission [Opt on C230, C240]	+907

Options	Price
Bose Audio System [Opt on C230, C240]	+314
Compact Disc Changer	+398

Options	Price
Heated Front Seats	+314
Leather Seats [Opt on C230]	+984
Metallic Paint	+447
Navigation System	+1451
Power Driver Seat w/Memory [Opt on C240]	+227
Power Moonroof	+628
Power Panorama Roof [Opt on C230]	+1047
Power Passenger Seat w/Memory [Opt on C240]	+227
Power Rear Window Sunshade	+345

Options	Price
Power Tilt and Telescopic Steering Wheel [Opt on C240]	+174
Rain Sensing Windshield Wipers	+140
Ski Sack	+140
Special Leather Seat Trim	+984
Split Folding Rear Seat [Opt on C240,C320 Sdn]	+174
Sport Package	+2100
Telematics System [Opt on C230]	+523
Xenon Headlamps	+607

2001

Ever expanding and improving its brood of stately vehicles, Mercedes gives the C-Class a complete overhaul for 2001. A choice of two new engines, increased safety features and sleeker sheet metal tempt those who seek to gain a foothold into the exalted realm of Mercedes ownership.

Mileage Category: H

Body Styles	TMV Pricing		
	Trade	Private	Dealer
4 Dr C240 Sdn	14355	16041	17597

Options	Price
Aluminum/Alloy Interior Trim	+247
Automatic 5-Speed Transmission [Opt on C240]	+804
Bose Audio System [Opt on C240]	+368
Compact Disc Changer	+352
Heated Front Seats	+278
Metallic Paint	+386
Navigation System	+1258
Power Driver Seat w/Memory [Opt on C240]	+201
Power Moonroof	+587
Power Passenger Seat w/Memory [Opt on C240]	+201

Body Styles	TMV Pricing		
	Trade	Private	Dealer
4 Dr C320 Sdn	17041	19042	20889

Options	Price
Power Rear Window Sunshade	+306
Power Tilt and Telescopic Steering Wheel [Opt on C240]	+155
Rain Sensing Windshield Wipers	+124
Ski Sack	+124
Split Folding Rear Seat	+155
Sport Package	+1824
Sport Seats	+247
Xenon Headlamps	+526

2000

TeleAid, which can assist in summoning help if you're ill or involved in a crash, is a brilliant new standard feature. A Touch Shift automanual transmission is added to all C-Class models, and stability control is standard this year. C-Class now comes with free scheduled service for the duration of the warranty period.

Mileage Category: H

Body Styles	TMV Pricing		
	Trade	Private	Dealer
4 Dr C230 S/C Sdn	11209	12867	14492

Options	Price
Bose Audio System [Opt on C230]	+301
Compact Disc Changer	+286
Heated Front Seats	+223
Leather Seats [Opt on C230]	+612
Metallic Paint	+317
Power Moonroof	+529

Body Styles	TMV Pricing		
	Trade	Private	Dealer
4 Dr C280 Sdn	12244	14055	15830

Options	Price
Power Passenger Seat [Opt on C230]	+239
Special Leather Seat Trim	+749
Split Folding Rear Seat	+132
Sport Seats	+370
Sport Suspension	+470
Xenon Headlamps	+334

1999

The SLK's 2.3-liter supercharged engine gets dropped into the C-Class, replacing the normally aspirated engine of the last C230. Performance has been turned up a notch. In addition, leather seating surfaces are now standard across the C-Class line.

Mileage Category: H

Body Styles	TMV Pricing		
	Trade	Private	Dealer
4 Dr C230 S/C Sdn	9507	11126	12811

Options	Price
Automatic Stability Control [Opt on C280]	+272
Bose Audio System [Opt on C230]	+222
Compact Disc Changer	+233
Heated Front Seats	+182
Leather Seats [Opt on C230]	+500
Metallic Paint	+233
Power Moonroof	+431

Body Styles	TMV Pricing		
	Trade	Private	Dealer
4 Dr C280 Sdn	10962	12829	14773

Options	Price
Power Passenger Seat [Opt on C230]	+195
Special Leather Seat Trim	+611
Sport Seats	+272
Sport Suspension	+346
Traction Control System	+182
Xenon Headlamps	+272

1998

The C280 is the lucky recipient of Mercedes' new V-type engine technology, receiving a 2.8-liter unit for the engine bay. BabySmart car seats, BrakeAssist and side airbags also debut on the C-Class this year.

Mileage Category: H

Body Styles	TMV Pricing		
	Trade	Private	Dealer
4 Dr C230 Sdn	7805	9365	11124

Body Styles	TMV Pricing		
	Trade	Private	Dealer
4 Dr C280 Sdn	9465	11356	13488

C-Class/C32 AMG

1998 (cont'd)

Options	Price
Bose Audio System [Opt on C230]	+184
Compact Disc Changer	+194
Heated Front Seats	+151
Leather Seats	+412
Metallic Paint	+194
Power Moonroof	+358

Options	Price
Power Passenger Seat [Opt on C230]	+162
Sport Seats	+226
Sport Suspension	+287
Traction Control System	+226
Xenon Headlamps	+226

1997

The C220 is replaced by a more powerful C230. All C-Class models have redesigned headlamps.

Mileage Category: H

Body Styles	TMV Pricing		
	Trade	Private	Dealer
4 Dr C230 Sdn	6470	7870	9580

Body Styles	TMV Pricing		
	Trade	Private	Dealer
4 Dr C280 Sdn	7326	8912	10851

Options	Price
Bose Audio System [Opt on C230]	+158
Compact Disc Changer	+157
Heated Front Seats	+123
Leather Seats	+313
Metallic Paint	+158

Options	Price
Power Moonroof	+291
Power Passenger Seat [Opt on C230]	+132
Sport Suspension	+233
Traction Control System	+184

1996

An infrared remote security system, dual cupholders in the console, a delayed headlamp dousing system and reconfigured option packages mark the changes to the baby Benz.

Mileage Category: H

Body Styles	TMV Pricing		
	Trade	Private	Dealer
4 Dr C220 Sdn	5320	6544	8235

Body Styles	TMV Pricing		
	Trade	Private	Dealer
4 Dr C280 Sdn	5806	7142	8987

Options	Price
Bose Audio System [Opt on C220]	+130
Compact Disc Changer	+134
Leather Seats	+282
Metallic Paint	+140

Options	Price
Power Moonroof	+249
Sport Suspension	+210
Traction Control System	+157

1995

No major changes.

Mileage Category: H

Body Styles	TMV Pricing		
	Trade	Private	Dealer
4 Dr C220 Sdn	4644	5732	7546

Body Styles	TMV Pricing		
	Trade	Private	Dealer
4 Dr C280 Sdn	5214	6436	8472

Options	Price
Alarm System	+82
Bose Audio System [Opt on C220]	+116
Chrome Wheels [Opt on C280]	+84
Compact Disc Changer [Opt on C220]	+120
Heated Front Seats	+93
Heated Front and Rear Seats	+93

Options	Price
Leather Seats	+251
Metallic Paint	+125
Power Moonroof	+222
Power Passenger Seat [Opt on C220]	+92
Traction Control System	+140

C32 AMG

2004

Mileage Category: F

Body Styles	TMV Pricing		
	Trade	Private	Dealer
4 Dr S/C Sdn	34945	37018	40472

Options	Price
COMAND System	+2170
Compact Disc Changer	+410
Headlight Washers	+520
Metallic Paint	+670

Options	Price
Power Rear Window Sunshade	+460
Ski Sack	+220
Xenon Headlamps	+250

Mercedes' road-burning sport sedan sees no changes this year.

2003

Mercedes' road-burning sport sedan sees no changes this year.

Mileage Category: F

Body Styles	TMV Pricing		
	Trade	Private	Dealer
4 Dr S/C Sdn	32751	34862	38381

Options	Price	Options	Price
COMAND System	+1664	Power Rear Window Sunshade	+352
Compact Disc Changer	+313	Rain Sensing Windshield Wipers	+160
Headlight Washers	+157	Ski Sack	+164
Metallic Paint	+513	Xenon Headlamps	+431

2002

Mercedes' in-house tuners, AMG, lay their hands on the little C-Class and the result is the stunning, 349-horsepower C32.

Mileage Category: F

Body Styles	TMV Pricing		
	Trade	Private	Dealer
4 Dr S/C Sdn	30089	31820	34706

Options	Price	Options	Price
Compact Disc Changer	+398	Rain Sensing Windshield Wipers	+140
Metallic Paint	+447	Ski Sack	+143
Navigation System	+1451	Xenon Headlamps	+607
Power Rear Window Sunshade	+345		

C43 AMG
2000

Mileage Category: F

Body Styles	TMV Pricing		
	Trade	Private	Dealer
4 Dr STD Sdn	26298	29134	31914

Options	Price	Options	Price
Compact Disc Changer	+317	Xenon Headlamps	+334
Metallic Paint	+317		

TeleAid, which can assist in summoning help if you're ill or involved in a crash, is a new standard feature. A Touch Shift automanual transmission is added to simulate the thrill of shifting gears manually. Free scheduled service for the duration of the warranty period has been added to the lengthy standard equipment list.

1999

Mileage Category: F

Body Styles	TMV Pricing		
	Trade	Private	Dealer
4 Dr STD Sdn	17866	20069	22361

Options	Price	Options	Price
Compact Disc Changer	+233	Xenon Headlamps	+272
Metallic Paint	+233		

No major changes for this sizzling sedan.

1998

Mileage Category: F

Body Styles	TMV Pricing		
	Trade	Private	Dealer
4 Dr STD Sdn	15564	17585	19863

Options	Price	Options	Price
Compact Disc Changer	+194	Xenon Headlamps	+226
Metallic Paint	+194		

The C43 AMG bows as a successor to the late C36. Featuring an AMG-modified 4.3-liter V8 with 302 hp, the new C43 promises a high-performance thrill ride.

C36 AMG
1997

Mileage Category: F

Body Styles	TMV Pricing		
	Trade	Private	Dealer
4 Dr STD Sdn	13603	15403	17604

Options	Price	Options	Price
Compact Disc Changer	+157	Metallic Paint	+158
Heated Front Seats	+123	Traction Control System	+184

For its last year in production, the C36 receives a slight boost in horsepower, which now stands at 276 ponies.

Mercedes-Benz
C36 AMG/CL-Class

1996
No changes to the hot-rod baby Benz for this year.

Mileage Category: F

Body Styles	TMV Pricing		
	Trade	Private	Dealer
4 Dr STD Sdn	12305	13922	16156

Options	Price	Options	Price
Compact Disc Changer	+134	Metallic Paint	+140

1995
After years of watching the tuning firm known as AMG modify its cars, Mercedes decides to bring it in-house. If the first effort of this union, the 268-horsepower C36, is any indication, it looks like this should be a happy marriage.

Mileage Category: F

Body Styles	TMV Pricing		
	Trade	Private	Dealer
4 Dr STD Sdn	10368	11723	13980

Options	Price	Options	Price
Alarm System	+82	Metallic Paint	+125
Heated Front Seats	+93	Power Moonroof	+222

CL-Class

2004

Mileage Category: I

Body Styles	TMV Pricing			Body Styles	TMV Pricing		
	Trade	Private	Dealer		Trade	Private	Dealer
2 Dr CL500 Cpe	67075	70026	74944	2 Dr CL600 Turbo Cpe	93754	97342	103323

Options	Price	Options	Price
18 Inch Wheels	+1500	Designo Espresso Edition	+10900
Adaptive Cruise Control	+3010	Designo Silver Edition [Opt on CL500, CL600]	+10900
Aero Kit	+3710	Keyless Ignition System	+1040
Comfort Seats [Opt on CL500]	+1560	Park Distance Control (Front and Rear)	+1060
Designo Cashmere Edition	+11700		

A new seven-speed automatic transmission is now standard on the CL500. The navigation system is now DVD-based, the Keyless Go system no longer requires a separate plastic card and newly styled 18-inch wheels have been added to the options list.

2003
There is more power for the CL55 and CL600 models, both of which now put out nearly 500 horsepower. All CLs see a number of other subtle changes, such as new head- and taillight lenses, a Pre-Safe safety feature, revised switchgear and a larger COMAND screen.

Mileage Category: I

Body Styles	TMV Pricing			Body Styles	TMV Pricing		
	Trade	Private	Dealer		Trade	Private	Dealer
2 Dr CL500 Cpe	62325	65132	69810	2 Dr CL600 Turbo Cpe	80507	84133	90177

Options	Price	Options	Price
Adaptive Cruise Control	+2309	Park Distance Control (Front and Rear)	+810
Designo Cashmere Edition	+9003	Power Trunk Closer	+368
Designo Espresso Edition	+8377	Sport Package [Opt on CL500, CL600]	+3993
Designo Silver Edition [Opt on CL500, CL600]	+8377	Tire Pressure Monitoring System	+493
Keyless Ignition System	+795	Ventilated Seats (Front) [Opt on CL500]	+920

2002
The TeleAid system is enhanced. Now reservations for travel as well as tickets for sporting and theater events can all be acquired from the considerable comfort of the CL's cabin.

Mileage Category: I

Body Styles	TMV Pricing			Body Styles	TMV Pricing		
	Trade	Private	Dealer		Trade	Private	Dealer
2 Dr CL500 Cpe	52046	55042	60034	2 Dr CL600 Cpe	64757	68484	74696

Options	Price	Options	Price
Designo Espresso Edition	+6490	Power Trunk Closer	+321
Designo Silver Edition	+6490	Sport Package [Opt on CL500, CL600]	+3482
Dual Multi-Contour Seats [Opt on CL500]	+1047	Tire Pressure Monitoring System	+429
Keyless Ignition System	+694	Ventilated Seats (Front) [Opt on CL500]	+820
Park Distance Control (Front and Rear)	+708		

2001
The CL600 makes its debut with a 362-horsepower V12. Distronic cruise control, a high-tech system using radar, braking and acceleration to maintain a specified distance from other vehicles, is standard on the CL600 and optional on other CL models. Web-based services, such as e-mail and stock quotes, will also be on board for the 2001 model year.

Mileage Category: I

Body Styles	TMV Pricing			Body Styles	TMV Pricing		
	Trade	Private	Dealer		Trade	Private	Dealer
2 Dr CL500 Cpe	46944	51260	55244	2 Dr CL600 Cpe	59075	64506	69520

2001 (cont'd)

Options	Price	Options	Price
Designo Espresso Edition	+5132	Park Distance Control (Front and Rear)	+615
Designo Silver Edition	+5132	Sport Package	+3030
Keyless Ignition System	+615	Ventilated Seats (Front) [Opt on CL500]	+727

2000

2000 marks the introduction of an all-new CL500 that is lighter, less expensive, and more advanced than the previous version.

Mileage Category: I

Body Styles	TMV Pricing		
	Trade	Private	Dealer
2 Dr CL500 Cpe	38504	42790	46991

Options	Price	Options	Price
Climate Comfort Seats	+668	Park Distance Control (Front and Rear)	+543
Dual Multi-Contour Seats	+585	Power Rear Window Sunshade	+276

1999

Mileage Category: I

Body Styles	TMV Pricing			Body Styles	TMV Pricing		
	Trade	Private	Dealer		Trade	Private	Dealer
2 Dr CL500 Cpe	25971	29605	33388	2 Dr CL600 Cpe	26146	29805	33614

Options	Price	Options	Price
Automatic Stability Control [Opt on CL500]	+272	Power Rear Window Sunshade [Opt on CL500]	+225
Electronic Damping Suspension Control [Opt on CL500]	+590	Traction Control System [Opt on CL500]	+182
Metallic Paint	+233		

The CL coupes are carryover models for 1999 with no changes.

1998

In keeping with Mercedes' somewhat odd habit of changing its cars' names just as people are getting the hang of them, the former S-Class coupes are now dubbed the CL-Class. Other than that confusing switch, the only changes to these big coupes are the addition of BabySmart airbag technology and BrakeAssist to the standard equipment lists.

Mileage Category: I

Body Styles	TMV Pricing			Body Styles	TMV Pricing		
	Trade	Private	Dealer		Trade	Private	Dealer
2 Dr CL500 Cpe	20788	24162	27966	2 Dr CL600 Cpe	21736	25263	29241

Options	Price	Options	Price
Electronic Damping Suspension Control [Opt on CL500]	+491	Power Rear Window Sunshade [Opt on CL500]	+187
Metallic Paint	+194	Traction Control System [Opt on CL500]	+226

CL55 AMG

2003

Mileage Category: I

Body Styles	TMV Pricing		
	Trade	Private	Dealer
2 Dr S/C Cpe	81612	85288	91415

Options	Price	Options	Price
Adaptive Cruise Control	+2309	Park Distance Control (Front and Rear)	+810
Designo Cashmere Edition	+8377	Power Trunk Closer	+368
Designo Espresso Edition	+7750	Tire Pressure Monitoring System	+493
Keyless Ignition System	+795		

There is more power for the CL55 this year, thanks to the installation of a supercharger. Output is staggering at nearly 500 horsepower. Other changes include new head- and taillight lenses, a Pre-Safe safety feature, revised switchgear and a larger COMAND screen.

2002

The CL55 AMG receives no major changes for this year.

Mileage Category: I

Body Styles	TMV Pricing		
	Trade	Private	Dealer
2 Dr STD Cpe	63641	67304	73409

Options	Price	Options	Price
Designo Espresso Edition	+6978	Park Distance Control (Front and Rear)	+708
Designo Silver Edition	+6978	Power Trunk Closer	+321

2001

AMG works its magic and creates the CL55 AMG with a 354-horsepower V8.

Mileage Category: I

Body Styles	TMV Pricing		
	Trade	Private	Dealer
2 Dr STD Cpe	56312	61490	66269

CL55 AMG/CLK-Class

2001 (cont'd)

Options	Price
Park Distance Control (Front and Rear)	+615

CLK-Class

2004

After last year's revamping of the CLK coupe, the convertible (Cabriolet) follows suit this year, sporting the same sleeker body style, along with a soft top that boasts greater outward visibility than before as well as key fob-operated usability.

Mileage Category: F

Body Styles	TMV Pricing		
	Trade	Private	Dealer
2 Dr CLK320 Conv	39842	41616	44572
2 Dr CLK320 Cpe	32946	34649	37487

Options	Price
17 Inch Wheels [Opt on CLK320 Cpe]	+800
Adaptive Cruise Control	+3010
COMAND System	+2170
Comfort Seats [Opt on Cpe]	+1200
Compact Disc Changer	+410
Designo Bronze Edition [Opt on Cpe]	+6200
Designo Espresso Edition [Opt on CLK430]	+6200
Headlight Washers	+350
Heated Front Seats	+670

Body Styles	TMV Pricing		
	Trade	Private	Dealer
2 Dr CLK500 Conv	46381	48512	52063
2 Dr CLK500 Cpe	40394	42346	45601

Options	Price
Keyless Ignition System	+1040
Metallic Paint	+670
Park Distance Control (Front and Rear)	+1060
Power Moonroof [Opt on CLK320, CLK500]	+1000
Power Rear Window Sunshade [Opt on CLK320, CLK500]	+410
Ski Sack	+220
Ventilated Seats (Front) [Opt on Cpe]	+910
Xenon Headlamps	+625

2003

The CLK coupe is revamped this year and its sleeker body sports a grille that echoes the bigger (and much more expensive) CL coupe's. Other news include the CLK430 becoming the CLK500 via a larger, more powerful V8 engine. The convertible ("Cabriolet") models are unchanged.

Mileage Category: F

Body Styles	TMV Pricing		
	Trade	Private	Dealer
2 Dr CLK320 Conv	33126	34778	37532
2 Dr CLK320 Cpe	29433	30900	33345

Options	Price
Adaptive Cruise Control [Opt on CLK320,CLK500]	+2309
Appearance Package [Opt on CLK320]	+822
COMAND System	+1664
Cellular Telephone	+943
Compact Disc Changer	+313
Designo Cashmere Edition [Opt on CLK430]	+5637
Designo Espresso Edition [Opt on CLK430]	+4952
Heated Front Seats [Opt on CLK320,CLK430,CLK500]	+485
Keyless Ignition System [Opt on CLK320,CLK500]	+795
Metallic Paint	+513

Body Styles	TMV Pricing		
	Trade	Private	Dealer
2 Dr CLK430 Conv	39579	41552	44841
2 Dr CLK500 Cpe	34103	35803	38637

Options	Price
Park Distance Control (Front and Rear) [Opt on CLK320,CLK500]	+810
Power Moonroof [Opt on CLK320,CLK500]	+783
Power Rear Window Sunshade [Opt on CLK320,CLK500]	+294
Rain Sensing Windshield Wipers [Opt on CLK320,CLK430]	+157
Ski Sack	+164
Sport Package [Opt on CLK320]	+3679
Xenon Headlamps	+470

2002

No changes this year.

Mileage Category: F

Body Styles	TMV Pricing		
	Trade	Private	Dealer
2 Dr CLK320 Conv	28373	30020	32767
2 Dr CLK320 Cpe	23262	24638	26933

Options	Price
Compact Disc Changer	+398
Designo Cashmere Edition	+4885
Designo Espresso Edition	+4327
Dual Multi-Contour Seats	+516
Heated Front Seats	+433
Metallic Paint	+447
Navigation System	+1451

Body Styles	TMV Pricing		
	Trade	Private	Dealer
2 Dr CLK430 Conv	34141	36125	39431
2 Dr CLK430 Cpe	25831	27360	29908

Options	Price
Power Moonroof	+750
Power Rear Window Sunshade	+345
Rain Sensing Windshield Wipers	+140
Ski Sack	+143
Sport Package [Opt on CLK320]	+3210
Xenon Headlamps	+419

2001

TeleAid comes standard on every CLK model this year, and the front windows lower slightly when you open the doors and seal (foop!) tight when you close them.

Mileage Category: F

Body Styles	TMV Pricing		
	Trade	Private	Dealer
2 Dr CLK320 Conv	26176	28689	31009
2 Dr CLK320 Cpe	20341	22294	24097

Body Styles	TMV Pricing		
	Trade	Private	Dealer
2 Dr CLK430 Conv	30884	33847	36583
2 Dr CLK430 Cpe	23917	26213	28332

2001 (cont'd)

Options	Price
Compact Disc Changer	+352
Designo Espresso Edition	+3741
Designo Slate Blue Edition	+4236
Dual Multi-Contour Seats	+448
Heated Front Seats	+383
Metallic Paint	+386

Options	Price
Navigation System	+1258
Power Moonroof	+652
Power Rear Window Sunshade [Opt on Cpe]	+306
Rain Sensing Windshield Wipers	+124
Ski Sack	+124
Xenon Headlamps	+371

2000

The CLK430 Convertible debuts, reminding us, for a premium price, what a drop-top muscle car from the '70s was like. Turn-signal indicators have been added to exterior mirrors, stability control is standard on all models, automatics get TouchShift manual gear selection and TeleAid emergency cellular service is standard. A new instrument cluster and multifunction steering wheel are added, and buyers can opt for the confusing COMAND navigation/phone/trip computer/sound system. CLK320s benefit from exterior cosmetic changes including new wheels, while 430s are enhanced inside with new black bird's eye maple wood trim. Free maintenance for the duration of the warranty is now included.

Mileage Category: F

Body Styles	TMV Pricing		
	Trade	Private	Dealer
2 Dr CLK320 Conv	23256	25764	28222
2 Dr CLK320 Cpe	17754	19668	21545

Options	Price
AM/FM/CD Audio System	+145
Compact Disc Changer	+317
Heated Front Seats	+139
Metallic Paint	+317

Body Styles	TMV Pricing		
	Trade	Private	Dealer
2 Dr CLK430 Conv	26948	29854	32703
2 Dr CLK430 Cpe	20776	23018	25215

Options	Price
Navigation System	+1055
Power Moonroof	+587
Power Rear Window Sunshade [Opt on Cpe]	+276
Xenon Headlamps	+334

1999

These guys are still on a roll. Last year, Mercedes introduced an all-new sport coupe that is an amalgamation of C- and SLK-Class technologies, available this year with a larger engine in the CLK 430 model, and now they're rolling out the CLK 320 Cabriolet, a convertible version of the fabulous little car.

Mileage Category: F

Body Styles	TMV Pricing		
	Trade	Private	Dealer
2 Dr CLK320 Conv	20475	22999	25625
2 Dr CLK320 Cpe	15989	17960	20011

Options	Price
Automatic Stability Control [Opt on CLK320]	+272
Compact Disc Changer	+233
Metallic Paint	+233

Body Styles	TMV Pricing		
	Trade	Private	Dealer
2 Dr CLK430 Cpe	18129	20364	22690

Options	Price
Power Moonroof	+431
Traction Control System [Opt on CLK320]	+182
Xenon Headlamps	+272

1998

Mercedes rolls out an all-new sport coupe that is an amalgamation of C- and SLK-Class technologies, with E-Class style up front. The CLK-Class is infused with the same 3.2-liter V6 that has made its way into the ML320 and E320.

Mileage Category: F

Body Styles	TMV Pricing		
	Trade	Private	Dealer
2 Dr CLK320 Cpe	13847	15644	17670

Options	Price
Compact Disc Changer	+194
Heated Front Seats	+192

Options	Price
Metallic Paint	+194
Power Moonroof	+358

CLK55 AMG

2004

Mileage Category: F

Body Styles	TMV Pricing		
	Trade	Private	Dealer
2 Dr STD Conv	62778	65642	70415

Options	Price
Adaptive Cruise Control	+3010
COMAND System	+2170
Compact Disc Changer	+410
Designo Bronze Edition	+6200
Designo Espresso Edition	+6900
Keyless Ignition System	+1040

Body Styles	TMV Pricing		
	Trade	Private	Dealer
2 Dr STD Cpe	54106	56745	61143

Options	Price
Park Distance Control (Front and Rear)	+1060
Power Rear Window Sunshade [Opt on Cpe]	+450
Ski Sack	+220
Ventilated Seats (Front)	+675
Wood Interior Trim	+260
Xenon Headlamps	+625

After its late arrival last year, the CLK55 enters the '04 model year unchanged.

2003

A redesigned CLK55 coupe belatedly joins the rest of the revamped CLK family; the ragtop version takes a year off. The sleeker body sports a grille that echoes the bigger (and much more costly) Mercedes' CL coupe's and chassis improvements result in even better driving dynamics.

Mileage Category: F

Body Styles	TMV Pricing		
	Trade	Private	Dealer
2 Dr STD Cpe	50300	52808	56987

Options	Price
Adaptive Cruise Control	+2309

Options	Price
COMAND System	+1664

CLK55 AMG/E-Class

2003 (cont'd)

Options	Price
Cellular Telephone	+943
Compact Disc Changer	+313
Headlight Washers	+137
Keyless Ignition System	+795
Metallic Paint	+513

Options	Price
Park Distance Control (Front and Rear)	+810
Power Rear Window Sunshade	+344
Ski Sack	+164
Xenon Headlamps	+470

2002

Mileage Category: F

Body Styles	TMV Pricing		
	Trade	Private	Dealer
2 Dr STD Conv	49522	52371	57119

Body Styles	TMV Pricing		
	Trade	Private	Dealer
2 Dr STD Cpe	42090	44511	48546

Options	Price
Compact Disc Changer	+398
Designo Cashmere Edition	+4327

Options	Price
Designo Espresso Edition	+3768
Navigation System	+1451

A convertible version of this hot coupe debuts, adding the joy of open-air motoring to its scintillating performance.

2001

The high-performance CLK55 AMG debuts this year. With 342 horsepower at its disposal, this muscle-bound CLK can sprint to 60 mph in just five seconds.

Mileage Category: F

Body Styles			TMV Pricing		
			Trade	Private	Dealer
2 Dr STD Cpe			35224	38430	41390

Options	Price
Compact Disc Changer	+352
Designo Espresso Edition	+3741
Designo Slate Blue Edition	+4236

Options	Price
Navigation System	+1258
Ski Sack	+124

E-Class

2004

For 2004, the E-Class wagon benefits from the same full redesign the sedan received last year. A V8-powered version of the wagon is available this year and the 4Matic all-wheel-drive system is optional on both sedans and wagons. Finally, the DVD-based navigation system, which was delayed for 2003, is on the options list this year.

Mileage Category: I

Body Styles	TMV Pricing		
	Trade	Private	Dealer
4 Dr E320 4MATIC AWD Sdn	35867	37492	40199
4 Dr E320 4MATIC AWD Wgn	37037	38637	41303
4 Dr E320 Sdn	35473	37162	39978
4 Dr E320 Wgn	35279	36878	39542

Body Styles	TMV Pricing		
	Trade	Private	Dealer
4 Dr E500 4MATIC AWD Sdn	43543	45438	48595
4 Dr E500 4MATIC AWD Wgn	43771	45583	48603
4 Dr E500 Sdn	42971	44855	47996

Options	Price
17 Inch Wheels	+800
Adaptive Cruise Control	+3010
Aero Kit [Opt on non-AWD]	+1680
Automatic Climate Control (4 Zone) [Opt on E320]	+560
Automatic Load Leveling [Opt on E320]	+600
Comfort Seats	+1520
Compact Disc Changer	+350
Designo Espresso Edition	+6200
Designo Graphite Edition	+6200
Designo Silver Edition	+6200
Dual Multi-Contour Seats	+780
Harman Kardon Audio System	+550
Headlight Washers	+300
Heated Front Seats	+650

Options	Price
Heated Steering Wheel	+250
Keyless Ignition System	+1040
Navigation System	+900
Park Distance Control (Front and Rear) [Opt on Sdn]	+1060
Power Moonroof	+1050
Power Panorama Roof [Opt on Sdn]	+1530
Power Rear Liftgate [Opt on Wgn]	+500
Premium Audio System	+710
Ski Sack [Opt on Sdn]	+130
Split Folding Rear Seat [Opt on Sdn]	+400
Tire Pressure Monitoring System	+390
Ventilated Seats (Front)	+1230
Xenon Headlamps	+500

2003

The E-Class sedan is completely redesigned this year. A more elegant body, along with more power for the V8 model and more luxury (including four-zone climate control and an optional massaging driver seat), bring the latest midsize Benz up to date. Last year's E-Class station wagon, however, carries over into 2003 virtually unchanged.

Mileage Category: I

Body Styles	TMV Pricing		
	Trade	Private	Dealer
4 Dr E320 4MATIC AWD Wgn	32789	34266	36727
4 Dr E320 Sdn	32536	34002	36444

Body Styles	TMV Pricing		
	Trade	Private	Dealer
4 Dr E320 Wgn	32058	33502	35908
4 Dr E500 Sdn	39694	41482	44462

For the latest vehicle information, visit www.edmunds.com

Options	Price
Adaptive Cruise Control [Opt on E320,E500]	+2309
Automatic Climate Control (4 Zone) [Opt on E320]	+431
Compact Disc Changer	+313
Drive Dynamic Seats [Opt on E320,E500]	+900
Dual Multi-Contour Seats [Opt on E320,E500]	+591
Harman Kardon Audio System [Opt on E320,E500]	+431
Heated Front Seats [Opt on E320,E500]	+497
Heated Steering Wheel [Opt on E320,E500]	+188
Keyless Ignition System [Opt on E320,E500]	+795
Navigation System [Opt on E320]	+1664

Options	Price
Park Distance Control (Front and Rear)	+810
Power Moonroof [Opt on E320,E500]	+826
Power Panorama Roof [Opt on E320,E500]	+1174
Power Rear Window Sunshade [Opt on E320,E500]	+344
Rain Sensing Windshield Wipers [Opt on E320]	+157
Special Factory Paint [Opt on E320,E500]	+513
Sport Package [Opt on E320,E500]	+1076
Tire Pressure Monitoring System [Opt on E320,E500]	+493
Ventilated Seats (Front)	+939
Xenon Headlamps	+548

Mileage Category: I

2002

Body Styles	TMV Pricing		
	Trade	Private	Dealer
4 Dr E320 4MATIC AWD Sdn	21671	22919	24998
4 Dr E320 4MATIC AWD Wgn	19483	20605	22475
4 Dr E320 Sdn	20765	21960	23951

Body Styles	TMV Pricing		
	Trade	Private	Dealer
4 Dr E320 Wgn	19399	20515	22375
4 Dr E430 4MATIC AWD Sdn	22613	23914	26084
4 Dr E430 Sdn	22904	24222	26420

Options	Price
Bose Audio System [Opt on E320]	+283
Compact Disc Changer	+398
Designo Espresso Edition	+4327
Designo Silver Edition	+4327
Heated Front Seats	+443
Metallic Paint [Opt on E320]	+447
Navigation System	+1451

Options	Price
Power Moonroof	+736
Power Rear Window Sunshade	+345
Rain Sensing Windshield Wipers	+140
Sport Package [Opt on Sdn - E320,E430]	+2913
Ventilated Seats (Front)	+820
Xenon Headlamps	+419

The 2002 E-Class soldiers on unchanged, awaiting a redesign that will take place next year.

2001

Though it might not look different, the E55 AMG receives the same substantial freshening for 2000 that other E-Class models get, which includes an entirely new front end and a revised interior. A multifunction steering wheel debuts, and TeleAid, a cellular emergency service, comes with the package for 2000.

Body Styles	TMV Pricing		
	Trade	Private	Dealer
4 Dr E320 4MATIC AWD Sdn	19051	21007	22813
4 Dr E320 4MATIC AWD Wgn	17987	19613	21114
4 Dr E320 Sdn	17970	19815	21517

Body Styles	TMV Pricing		
	Trade	Private	Dealer
4 Dr E320 Wgn	16783	18507	20098
4 Dr E430 4MATIC AWD Sdn	20445	22544	24481
4 Dr E430 Sdn	19809	21843	23720

Options	Price
Bose Audio System [Std on E430]	+265
Compact Disc Changer	+352
Designo Espresso Edition	+3741
Designo Silver Edition	+3741
Dual Multi-Contour Seats	+448
Heated Front Seats	+383
Leather Seats [Opt on E320 Wgn]	+850

Options	Price
Navigation System	+1258
Power Moonroof	+652
Power Rear Window Sunshade [Opt on E320,E430]	+306
Rain Sensing Windshield Wipers	+124
Sport Package [Opt on Sdn]	+2529
Ventilated Seats (Front)	+711
Xenon Headlamps	+371

Mileage Category: I

2000

Though it might not look different, the E-Class receives a substantial freshening for 2000, with an entirely new front end and a revised interior. Stability control, a Touch Shift automanual transmission, and side airbags for all outboard seating positions are now standard. A multifunction steering wheel debuts, and E430 models can be equipped with 4matic all-wheel drive. TeleAid, a cellular emergency service, is standard and the confounding COMAND system is optional. For 2000, free maintenance is provided for the duration of the warranty period. The E300 turbodiesel model has been dropped. Other changes are limited to minor cosmetic and functional upgrades.

Body Styles	TMV Pricing		
	Trade	Private	Dealer
4 Dr E320 4MATIC AWD Sdn	16832	18892	20911
4 Dr E320 4MATIC AWD Wgn	15578	17484	19351
4 Dr E320 Sdn	15298	17170	19006

Body Styles	TMV Pricing		
	Trade	Private	Dealer
4 Dr E320 Wgn	14703	16502	18265
4 Dr E430 4MATIC AWD Sdn	17223	19331	21396
4 Dr E430 Sdn	17122	19216	21270

Options	Price
Bose Audio System [Std on E430]	+238
Compact Disc Changer	+317
Heated Front Seats	+223
Metallic Paint	+317
Nappa Leather Seat Trim	+899
Navigation System	+1055
Park Distance Control (Front and Rear) [Opt on E320,E430]	+543

Options	Price
Power Moonroof	+587
Power Rear Window Sunshade [Opt on Sdn]	+276
Rear Spoiler	+212
Special Leather Seat Trim	+605
Spoke Wheels	+238
Sport Package	+2199
Xenon Headlamps	+334

1999

More airbags find room in the E-Class, which now features a full curtain side airbag protection system. The E300 Turbodiesel and E320 wagon are enhanced with leather seat inserts, and all E-Class cars get fiber-optic technology in their sound system/optional telephone unit.

Mileage Category: I

Body Styles	TMV Pricing		
	Trade	Private	Dealer
4 Dr E300DT Turbodsl Sdn	14252	16184	18196
4 Dr E320 4MATIC AWD Sdn	14081	15991	17978
4 Dr E320 4MATIC AWD Wgn	12796	14532	16339

Options	Price
Automatic Stability Control	+272
Bose Audio System [Std on E430]	+175
Compact Disc Changer	+233
Heated Front Seats	+182
Leather Seats [Opt on E300DT,Wgn]	+515
Metallic Paint	+233
Power Moonroof	+431

Body Styles	TMV Pricing		
	Trade	Private	Dealer
4 Dr E320 Sdn	13399	15216	17106
4 Dr E320 Wgn	12489	14183	15947
4 Dr E430 Sdn	14488	16453	18498

Options	Price
Power Rear Window Sunshade [Opt on Sdn]	+225
Rear Spoiler	+155
Spoke Wheels	+175
Sport Package	+1794
Traction Control System [Opt on E300DT,Wgn]	+182
Xenon Headlamps	+272

1998

All-wheel drive comes to the Mercedes' E-Class lineup via the E320 sedan and all-new E320 wagon. Like the rest of Mercedes' model lineup, E-Class cars formerly powered by an inline-six engine now receive a more fuel-efficient V6 unit that is also supposed to improve the cars' low-end response. The 1998 E-Class cars receive the benefit of BabySmart airbags which are able to detect the presence of a Mercedes' car seat in the front passenger seat and disable the front passenger airbag. BrakeAssist is also a new feature, which aids drivers' stopping distance in a panic-stop situation.

Mileage Category: I

Body Styles	TMV Pricing		
	Trade	Private	Dealer
4 Dr E300DT Turbodsl Sdn	12267	14145	16263
4 Dr E320 4MATIC AWD Sdn	12168	14031	16132
4 Dr E320 4MATIC AWD Wgn	11164	12873	14801

Options	Price
Automatic Stability Control [Opt on Sdn]	+302
Bose Audio System [Std on E430]	+184
Compact Disc Changer	+194
Heated Front Seats	+151
Leather Seats [Opt on E300DT,Wgn]	+427
Park Distance Control (Front and Rear)	+368
Power Moonroof	+358

Body Styles	TMV Pricing		
	Trade	Private	Dealer
4 Dr E320 Sdn	10813	12468	14335
4 Dr E320 Wgn	9923	11442	13155
4 Dr E430 Sdn	12567	14491	16661

Options	Price
Power Rear Window Sunshade [Opt on Sdn]	+187
Rear Spoiler	+129
Spoke Wheels	+145
Sport Package	+1490
Traction Control System	+323
Xenon Headlamps	+226

1997

The Mercedes-Benz E300D and E320 receive the driver-adaptable five-speed automatic transmission. The E-Class also has a smart sensor to determine if anyone is sitting in the passenger seat and to determine whether or not to deploy the airbag. The E420 can be had with a Sport Package.

Mileage Category: I

Body Styles	TMV Pricing		
	Trade	Private	Dealer
4 Dr E300D Dsl Sdn	10038	11683	13694
4 Dr E320 Sdn	9743	11338	13289

Options	Price
AM/FM/Cassette/CD Audio System	+230
Bose Audio System [Std on E420]	+147
Chrome Wheels	+144
Compact Disc Changer	+157
Dual Multi-Contour Seats [Std on S600]	+233
Heated Front Seats	+123

Body Styles	TMV Pricing		
	Trade	Private	Dealer
4 Dr E420 Sdn	10311	12000	14065

Options	Price
Leather Seats [Opt on E300D]	+347
Limited Slip Differential [Opt on E320]	+131
Power Moonroof	+286
Power Rear Window Sunshade	+152
Sport Package	+568
Xenon Headlamps	+184

1996

All new and sporting a face anybody's mother could love, the E-Class comes in three flavors: E300 Diesel, E320 and E420. A new front suspension and larger wheels and tires provide better handling, while optional gas-discharge headlamps mark new technology. Side-impact airbags are included in the doors of all E-Class models. E420's can be had with ESP, which is a new safety system that makes sure the E420 is under control at all times. The E420 also gets a new five-speed transmission.

Mileage Category: I

Body Styles	TMV Pricing		
	Trade	Private	Dealer
4 Dr E300D Dsl Sdn	8477	9867	11786

Options	Price
Bose Audio System	+130
Compact Disc Changer	+134
Leather Seats [Std on E320]	+312
Limited Slip Differential	+118

Body Styles	TMV Pricing		
	Trade	Private	Dealer
4 Dr E320 Sdn	8108	9438	11274

Options	Price
Metallic Paint	+162
Power Moonroof	+252
Xenon Headlamps [Opt on E300D]	+157

Mileage Category: I

Body Styles	TMV Pricing		
	Trade	Private	Dealer
2 Dr E320 Conv	12182	13977	16970
2 Dr E320 Cpe	7473	8575	10411
4 Dr E300D Dsl Sdn	6839	7848	9530

Options	Price
AM/FM/CD Audio System	+128
Compact Disc Changer	+120
Heated Front Seats [Std on E420,Conv]	+93
Leather Seats [Opt on E300D,Wgn]	+279
Limited Slip Differential	+105
Power Driver Seat w/Memory [Std on E420,Cpe,Conv]	+82

Body Styles	TMV Pricing		
	Trade	Private	Dealer
4 Dr E320 Sdn	6954	7979	9688
4 Dr E320 Wgn	6174	7084	8601
4 Dr E420 Sdn	7305	8382	10177

Options	Price
Power Rear Window Sunshade [Opt on Cpe,Sdn]	+96
Premium Audio System	+95
Sport Package	+255
Traction Control System [Opt on E320 Sdn]	+210

No changes for the last year of this rendition of the E-Class.

E55 AMG

Mileage Category: F

Body Styles	TMV Pricing		
	Trade	Private	Dealer
4 Dr S/C Sdn	68884	71984	77151

Options	Price
Adaptive Cruise Control	+3010
Comfort Seats	+1050
Compact Disc Changer	+410
Designo Espresso Edition	+5400
Designo Graphite Edition	+5400
Drive Dynamic Seats	+1170

Options	Price
Keyless Ignition System	+1040
Navigation System	+1200
Park Distance Control (Front and Rear)	+1060
Power Panorama Roof	+1530
Power Rear Window Sunshade	+450
Ventilated Seats (Front)	+650

Introduced late last year, the newest-generation E55 continues into 2004 without change.

A redesigned E55 AMG, sporting nearly 500 horsepower, belatedly joins the rest of the revamped E-Class family.

Mileage Category: F

Body Styles	TMV Pricing		
	Trade	Private	Dealer
4 Dr S/C Sdn	55066	57505	61569

Options	Price
Adaptive Cruise Control	+2309
Compact Disc Changer	+313
Headlight Washers	+235
Keyless Ignition System	+795
Park Distance Control (Front and Rear)	+810
Power Panorama Roof	+1174

Options	Price
Power Rear Window Sunshade	+344
Power Trunk Closer	+372
Tire Pressure Monitoring System	+493
Ventilated Seats (Front)	+509
Xenon Headlamps	+548

Mileage Category: F

Body Styles	TMV Pricing		
	Trade	Private	Dealer
4 Dr STD Sdn	41152	43519	47465

Options	Price
Compact Disc Changer	+398
Designo Espresso Edition	+3768
Designo Silver Edition	+3768

Options	Price
Navigation System	+1451
Ventilated Seats (Front)	+820

Patiently waiting for a redesign, the E55 AMG continues with no changes.

No major changes for this AMG-massaged rocket.

Mileage Category: F

Body Styles	TMV Pricing		
	Trade	Private	Dealer
4 Dr STD Sdn	35194	38397	41354

E55 AMG/G-Class

2001 (cont'd)

Options	Price
Compact Disc Changer	+352
Designo Espresso Edition	+3277
Designo Silver Edition	+3277

Options	Price
Navigation System	+1258
Ventilated Seats (Front)	+711

2000

Though it might not look different, the E55 AMG receives the same substantial freshening for 2000 that other E-Class models get, which includes an entirely new front end and a revised interior. A multifunction steering wheel debuts, and TeleAid, a cellular emergency service, comes with the package for 2000.

Mileage Category: F

Body Styles	TMV Pricing		
	Trade	Private	Dealer
4 Dr STD Sdn	29549	32736	35860

Options	Price
AM/FM/Cassette/CD Audio System	+223
Compact Disc Changer	+317

Options	Price
Metallic Paint	+317
Navigation System	+1111

1999

The performance-oriented E55 AMG debuts, featuring a fire-breathing V8 that can rocket this sedate sedan to 60 mph in well under six seconds.

Mileage Category: F

Body Styles	TMV Pricing		
	Trade	Private	Dealer
4 Dr STD Sdn	24893	27963	31158

Options	Price
AM/FM/Cassette/CD Audio System	+425
Compact Disc Changer	+233

Options	Price
Metallic Paint	+233
Power Rear Window Sunshade	+225

G-Class

2004

Mileage Category: O

Body Styles	TMV Pricing		
	Trade	Private	Dealer
4 Dr G500 4WD SUV	54577	57164	61475

Options	Price
Designo Espresso Edition	+6450

Options	Price
Designo Silver Edition	+6450

A trio of premium features becomes standard: multicontour front seats, a Harman-Kardon audio system and rear parking sensors.

2003

In-house tuner AMG lays its magic hands on the G-Class, this year, empowering the SUV with a 5.4-liter V8 that generates 349 horsepower and a 0-to-60-mph time of 7.2 seconds.

Mileage Category: O

Body Styles	TMV Pricing		
	Trade	Private	Dealer
4 Dr G500 4WD SUV	48058	50626	54907

Options	Price
Designo Espresso Edition	+4971
Designo Silver Edition	+4971

Options	Price
Harman Kardon Audio System	+626
Park Distance Control (Rear)	+431

2002

This vehicle is officially new to the U.S. market, though its basic design dates back over 20 years.

Mileage Category: O

Body Styles	TMV Pricing		
	Trade	Private	Dealer
4 Dr G500 4WD SUV	41425	44115	48597

Options	Price
Designo Espresso Edition	+4327

Options	Price
Designo Silver Edition	+4327

G55 AMG

2004

Mileage Category: O

Body Styles	TMV Pricing		
	Trade	Private	Dealer
4 Dr STD 4WD SUV	61737	65058	70593

Options	Price	Options	Price
Designo Espresso Edition	+5100	Designo Silver Edition	+5100

A trio of premium features becomes standard: multicontour front seats, an upgraded Harman Kardon audio system and rear parking sensors.

2003

Mileage Category: O

Body Styles	TMV Pricing		
	Trade	Private	Dealer
4 Dr STD 4WD SUV	57523	60598	65722

Options	Price	Options	Price
Designo Espresso Edition	+4971	Harman Kardon Audio System	+626
Designo Silver Edition	+4971	Park Distance Control (Rear)	+431

In-house tuner AMG lays its magic hands on the G-Class, this year, empowering the SUV with a 5.4-liter V8 that generates 349 horsepower and a 0-to-60-mph time of 7.2 seconds.

M-Class

2004

Mileage Category: O

Body Styles	TMV Pricing			Body Styles	TMV Pricing		
	Trade	Private	Dealer		Trade	Private	Dealer
4 Dr ML350 AWD SUV	26422	28027	30702	4 Dr ML500 AWD SUV	31114	32664	35247

Options	Price	Options	Price
Automatic Dimming Sideview Mirror(s) [Opt on ML350]	+180	Park Distance Control (Front and Rear)	+1015
Bose Audio System	+700	Power Driver Seat [Opt on ML350]	+250
Compact Disc Changer	+550	Power Driver Seat w/Memory	+300
Designo Ash Edition	+3500	Power Moonroof	+1350
Designo Borneo Edition	+3500	Power Passenger Seat [Opt on ML350]	+350
Designo Charcoal Edition	+3500	Power Retractable Mirrors	+150
Designo Java Edition	+3500	Privacy Glass [Opt on ML350]	+295
Headlight Washers	+225	Rain Sensing Windshield Wipers	+230
Heated Front Seats [Opt on ML350]	+650	Sport Seats	+900
Leather Door Panels [Opt on ML350]	+200	Third Seat	+1200
Leather Seats [Opt on ML350]	+1200	Trip Computer [Opt on ML350]	+150
Metallic Paint	+500	Xenon Headlamps	+650
Navigation System [Opt on ML350]	+995		

Late in 2003, the ML350 replaced the ML320, meaning a larger (3.7-liter) V6 with 232 horsepower supplanted the 215-horse, 3.2-liter V6 used previously. The AMG-tuned ML55 has been discontinued, while a DVD-based navigation system is now optional for the ML350.

2003

Mileage Category: O

Body Styles	TMV Pricing			Body Styles	TMV Pricing		
	Trade	Private	Dealer		Trade	Private	Dealer
4 Dr ML320 AWD SUV	22685	24032	26276	4 Dr ML500 AWD SUV	28052	29717	32491
4 Dr ML350 AWD SUV	23026	24393	26670				

Options	Price	Options	Price
Automatic Dimming Rearview Mirror	+133	Designo Sable Edition [Opt on ML320,ML500]	+2740
Automatic Dimming Sideview Mirror(s) [Opt on ML350]	+137	Designo Savanna Edition [Opt on ML320,ML350,ML500]	+3053
Bose Audio System [Opt on ML320,ML350,ML500]	+431	Heated Front Seats [Opt on ML320,ML350]	+509
Compact Disc Changer [Opt on ML320,ML350,ML500]	+489	Leather Seats [Opt on ML320,ML350]	+920
nac Edition	+3288	Metallic Paint [Opt on ML320,ML350,ML500]	+395
Designo Mystic Green Edition [Opt on ML320,ML350,ML500]	+3288	Nappa Leather Seat Trim [Opt on ML320,ML350,ML500]	+1315
Designo Pearl Edition [Opt on ML320,ML350,ML500]	+2740	Park Distance Control (Front and Rear)	+795

The M-Class' navigation system enters the 21st century by ditching the old CD-ROM-based design for a much more efficient DVD-based setup. This is the lone change as the MLs received numerous updates last year.

2003 (cont'd)

Options	Price
Power Driver Seat w/Memory [Opt on ML320,ML350,ML500]	+196
Power Moonroof [Opt on ML320,ML350,ML500]	+1057
Power Passenger Seat w/Memory [Opt on ML320,ML350,ML500]	+196
Power Retractable Mirrors [Opt on ML350,ML500]	+196
Rain Sensing Windshield Wipers [Opt on ML320,ML350,ML500]	+157

Options	Price
Sport Package [Opt on ML320,ML350,ML500]	+2623
Third Seat [Opt on ML320,ML350,ML500]	+587
Tinted Glass [Opt on ML320,ML350]	+137
Trip Computer [Opt on ML320,ML350]	+117
Xenon Headlamps [Opt on ML320,ML350,ML500]	+509

2002

The ML430 is replaced by the ML500, which has a 5.0-liter V8 packing 288 horsepower. Over 1,100 parts of the truck have been modified, but the ML's exterior remains largely the same. New bumpers, clear-lens headlights and revised side mirrors are the most noticeable exterior changes. Inside, the center console sports a new look, and wood grain trim becomes standard on all models. A new automatic climate control system is now standard, and rear-seat passengers get dual cupholders and separate ventilation controls.

Mileage Category: O

Body Styles	TMV Pricing		
	Trade	Private	Dealer
4 Dr ML320 AWD SUV	20432	21890	24320

Body Styles	TMV Pricing		
	Trade	Private	Dealer
4 Dr ML500 AWD SUV	25087	26848	29782

Options	Price
Automatic Dimming Rearview Mirror [Opt on ML320]	+119
Automatic Dimming Sideview Mirror(s) [Opt on ML320]	+122
Bose Audio System	+366
Compact Disc Changer	+419
Designo Cognac Edition	+2861
Designo Mystic Green Edition	+2861
Designo Pearl Edition	+2373
Designo Sable Edition	+2373
Designo Savanna Edition	+2652
Heated Front Seats	+443
Leather Seats [Opt on ML320]	+820

Options	Price
Metallic Paint	+345
Park Distance Control (Front and Rear)	+708
Power Driver Seat w/Memory	+174
Power Moonroof	+904
Power Passenger Seat w/Memory	+174
Power Retractable Mirrors	+174
Rain Sensing Windshield Wipers	+140
Sport Package	+2338
Third Seat	+680
Tinted Glass [Opt on ML320]	+122
Xenon Headlamps	+454

2001

The TeleAid emergency calling system is now standard on every M-Class model, and smart dual-stage front airbags know when to deploy with partial force or full force. All models also feature expanded off-road capabilities with new downhill traction control and a new crawling mode for very slow and steep off-roading. Finally, a new M-Class sport package debuts this year.

Mileage Category: O

Body Styles	TMV Pricing		
	Trade	Private	Dealer
4 Dr ML320 AWD SUV	16314	18238	20014

Body Styles	TMV Pricing		
	Trade	Private	Dealer
4 Dr ML430 AWD SUV	20461	22874	25102

Options	Price
Automatic Dimming Sideview Mirror(s) [Opt on ML320]	+124
Bose Audio System	+309
Compact Disc Changer	+356
Designo Cognac Edition	+2473
Designo Mystic Green Edition	+2473
Heated Front Seats [Opt on ML320]	+383
Leather Seats [Opt on ML320]	+911
Metallic Paint	+300
Power Driver Seat w/Memory	+155

Options	Price
Power Panorama Roof	+1515
Power Passenger Seat w/Memory	+155
Power Sunroof	+677
Privacy Glass [Opt on ML320]	+147
Rain Sensing Windshield Wipers	+124
Sport Package	+2041
Third Seat	+835
Xenon Headlamps	+526

2000

All M-Class models get an interior facelift available in one of three new colors, optional third-row seating and a Touch Shift automanual transmission. ML320 buyers get body-color bumpers and trim, real walnut inside, leather-wrapped steering wheel and gearshift knob, revised interior fabric, seatback map pockets and footwell lamps. In addition to these items, a standard navigation system, high-grade leather, and heated seats come on all ML430s.

Mileage Category: O

Body Styles	TMV Pricing		
	Trade	Private	Dealer
4 Dr ML320 AWD SUV	13190	15151	17074

Body Styles	TMV Pricing		
	Trade	Private	Dealer
4 Dr ML430 AWD SUV	16825	19327	21779

Options	Price
Bose Audio System	+214
Compact Disc Changer	+286
Exterior Spare Tire Carrier	+119
Heated Front Seats [Opt on ML320]	+251
Leather Seats [Opt on ML320]	+554
Metallic Paint	+286
Power Driver Seat w/Memory	+153

Options	Price
Power Moonroof	+522
Power Panorama Roof	+946
Power Passenger Seat w/Memory	+153
Privacy Glass [Opt on ML320]	+132
Running Boards	+159
Third Seat	+752

M-Class/ML55 AMG

1999

Mercedes expands its M-Class with the addition of the more powerful and luxurious ML430 and gives the 320 more standard equipment.

Mileage Category: O

Body Styles	TMV Pricing		
	Trade	Private	Dealer
4 Dr ML320 AWD SUV	11738	13631	15602

Options	Price
Bose Audio System	+175
Compact Disc Changer	+233
Heated Front Seats	+184
Leather Seats [Opt on ML320]	+602
Metallic Paint	+233
Power Driver Seat [Opt on ML320]	+195

Body Styles	TMV Pricing		
	Trade	Private	Dealer
4 Dr ML430 AWD SUV	14310	16618	19020

Options	Price
Power Moonroof	+425
Power Panorama Roof	+772
Power Passenger Seat [Opt on ML320]	+195
Running Boards	+159
Third Seat	+118

1998

Mercedes enters the sport-ute fray with the introduction of the ML320. Designed from a clean sheet of paper, the ML320 offers the best of the car and truck worlds.

Mileage Category: O

Body Styles	TMV Pricing		
	Trade	Private	Dealer
4 Dr ML320 AWD SUV	10425	12106	14002

Options	Price
Bose Audio System	+339
Compact Disc Changer	+194
Exterior Spare Tire Carrier	+142
Heated Front Seats	+153
Leather Seats	+500

Options	Price
Metallic Paint	+153
Power Driver Seat	+162
Power Moonroof	+354
Power Passenger Seat	+162
Running Boards	+189

ML55 AMG

2003

Mileage Category: O

Body Styles	TMV Pricing		
	Trade	Private	Dealer
4 Dr STD AWD SUV	41544	44009	48118

Options	Price
Designo Cognac Edition	+3288

Options	Price
Park Distance Control (Front and Rear)	+795

The hot-rod ML55 benefits from the upgrades made to every M-Class for this year. Over 1,100 parts of the truck have been modified, but the ML's exterior remains largely the same. New bumpers, clear-lens headlights and revised side mirrors are the most noticeable exterior changes. Inside, the center console sports a new look, and wood grain trim becomes standard on all models. A new automatic climate control system is now standard, and rear-seat passengers get dual cupholders and separate ventilation controls.

2002

Extensive interior and exterior refinements enhance this fast SUV, though most changes will go unnoticed by the casual observer.

Mileage Category: O

Body Styles	TMV Pricing		
	Trade	Private	Dealer
4 Dr STD AWD SUV	33788	36171	40143

Options	Price
Designo Cognac Edition	+2861

Options	Price
Park Distance Control (Front and Rear)	+708

2001

AMG merges high-performance with SUV practicality with the new ML55 AMG.

Mileage Category: O

Body Styles	TMV Pricing		
	Trade	Private	Dealer
4 Dr STD AWD SUV	27431	30729	33774

Options	Price
Designo Cognac Edition	+2473

2000

Mercedes goes overboard on power and performance with the new ML55 AMG. Correct us if we're wrong, but weren't SUVs originally designed for rugged off-road travel?

Mileage Category: O

Body Styles	TMV Pricing		
	Trade	Private	Dealer
4 Dr STD AWD SUV	22754	26139	29457

Options	Price
Metallic Paint	+251

S-Class

2004

An industry-first seven-speed automatic transmission is now standard. The navigation system is now DVD-based, and the Keyless Go system is now built into the SmartKey. Newly styled 18-inch wheels are optional.

Mileage Category: I

Body Styles	TMV Pricing		
	Trade	Private	Dealer
4 Dr S430 4MATIC AWD Sdn	49329	51486	55081
4 Dr S430 Sdn	47782	49801	53165
4 Dr S500 4MATIC AWD Sdn	54888	57045	60639

Options	Price
18 Inch Wheels	+1500
Adaptive Cruise Control	+3010
Aero Kit	+3710
Automatic Climate Control (4 Zone) [Opt on S430, S500]	+750
Comfort Seats [Opt on non-S600]	+2060
Compact Disc Changer [Opt on S430, S500]	+410
Designo Espresso Edition [Opt on S430, S500]	+11400
Designo Graphite Edition	+9100
Designo Silver Edition [Opt on S430, S500]	+11400
Drive Dynamic Seats [Opt on S430, S500, S600]	+1180
Headlight Washers [Opt on S430]	+350
Heated Front Seats [Opt on S430]	+450

Body Styles	TMV Pricing		
	Trade	Private	Dealer
4 Dr S500 Sdn	53341	55359	58723
4 Dr S600 Turbo Sdn	91168	94795	100839

Options	Price
Heated Front and Rear Seats [Opt on S430, S500]	+650
Heated Steering Wheel [Opt on S430]	+450
Keyless Ignition System	+1040
Leather and Wood Gearshift Knob [Opt on non-S600]	+250
Leather and Wood Steering Wheel [Opt on S430, S500]	+610
Nappa Leather Seat Trim [Opt on S430]	+840
Park Distance Control (Front and Rear) [Opt on S430, S500]	+1060
Ventilated Seats (Front and Rear)	+970
Xenon Headlamps [Opt on S430]	+860

2003

For 2003, there is more power for the S55 and S600 models, both of which now put out nearly 500 horsepower. Also Pre-Safe, a system that detects an imminent impact and quickly adjusts seating positions as well as seatbelt tension to better safeguard the occupants, debuts. Mercedes' 4Matic all-wheel-drive system becomes available on the S430 and S500 and a minor freshening inside and out are meant to keep these big Benzes near the top of luxury car buyer's shopping lists.

Mileage Category: I

Body Styles	TMV Pricing		
	Trade	Private	Dealer
4 Dr S430 4MATIC AWD Sdn	46096	48303	51980
4 Dr S430 Sdn	43754	45848	49338
4 Dr S500 4MATIC AWD Sdn	51177	53627	57710

Options	Price
Adaptive Cruise Control	+2309
Armor Rear Protection [Opt on S500]	+25652
Automatic Climate Control (4 Zone) [Opt on S430, S500]	+1503
Compact Disc Changer [Opt on S430, S500]	+313
Designo Espresso Edition [Opt on S430, S500]	+6967
Designo Graphite Edition [Opt on S430, S500]	+6967
Designo Silver Edition [Opt on S430, S500]	+6967
Drive Dynamic Seats [Opt on S430, S500, S600]	+712
Dual Multi-Contour Seats [Opt on S430, S500]	+744
Four Place Seating [Opt on S500, S600]	+4607
Heated Front Seats [Opt on S430]	+352
Heated Front and Rear Seats [Opt on S430, S500]	+509

Body Styles	TMV Pricing		
	Trade	Private	Dealer
4 Dr S500 Sdn	49077	51426	55342
4 Dr S600 Turbo Sdn	83744	87752	94433

Options	Price
Keyless Ignition System	+795
Leather and Wood Steering Wheel [Opt on S430, S500]	+407
Nappa Leather Seat Trim [Opt on S430]	+658
Park Distance Control (Front and Rear) [Opt on S430, S500]	+810
Power Rear Seat [Opt on S430, S500]	+1460
Power Trunk Closer	+368
Sport Package [Opt on S430, S500, S600]	+3993
Tire Pressure Monitoring System	+493
Ventilated Seats (Front and Rear)	+744
Ventilated Seats (Front) [Opt on S430, S500]	+509
Xenon Headlamps [Opt on S430]	+470

2002

The TeleAid system is enhanced. Now reservations for travel as well as tickets for sporting and theater events can all be acquired from the considerable comfort of the S-Class' cabin.

Mileage Category: I

Body Styles	TMV Pricing		
	Trade	Private	Dealer
4 Dr S430 Sdn	33611	35545	38769
4 Dr S500 Sdn	36920	39045	42586

Options	Price
Adaptive Cruise Control	+2006
Automatic Climate Control (4 Zone) [Std on S600]	+698
Automatic Load Leveling [Opt on S430, S500]	+879
Compact Disc Changer [Opt on S430, S500]	+398
Designo Espresso Edition	+5338
Designo Silver Edition	+6106
Electronic Suspension Control [Opt on S430, S500]	+1186
Four Place Seating [Opt on S500, S600]	+2756

Body Styles	TMV Pricing		
	Trade	Private	Dealer
4 Dr S600 Sdn	57677	60997	66530

Options	Price
Heated Front Seats [Opt on S430]	+314
Heated Front and Rear Seats [Std on S600]	+443
Keyless Ignition System	+694
Park Distance Control (Front and Rear) [Std on S600]	+708
Power Rear Seat	+1274
Power Trunk Closer	+321
Sport Package	+3472
Tire Pressure Monitoring System	+429

Options	Price
Ventilated Seats (Front and Rear)	+649

Options	Price
Xenon Headlamps [Opt on S430]	+419

2001

One new model debuts this year with the S600. The S600 gets a powerful 12-cylinder engine along with standard Active Body Control and Internet access to keep up with life in the techno-savvy 21st century.

Mileage Category: I

Body Styles	TMV Pricing		
	Trade	Private	Dealer
4 Dr S430 Sdn	27260	29891	32320
4 Dr S500 Sdn	31648	34703	37522

Body Styles	TMV Pricing		
	Trade	Private	Dealer
4 Dr S600 Sdn	49345	54106	58501

Options	Price
Adaptive Cruise Control	+1731
Automatic Climate Control (4 Zone) [Std on S600]	+618
Compact Disc Changer	+352
Designo Espresso Edition	+4638
Designo Silver Edition	+5287
Four Place Seating	+2393
Heated Front and Rear Seats	+383

Options	Price
Keyless Ignition System	+615
Park Distance Control (Front and Rear) [Std on S600]	+615
Power Rear Seat	+1104
Sport Package	+3030
Ventilated Seats (Front and Rear)	+563
Ventilated Seats (Front) [Std on S600]	+711
Xenon Headlamps	+360

2000

An all-new S-Class debuts for the millennium with enhanced performance and a snazzy COMAND system.

Mileage Category: I

Body Styles	TMV Pricing		
	Trade	Private	Dealer
4 Dr S430 Sdn	23520	26398	29219

Body Styles	TMV Pricing		
	Trade	Private	Dealer
4 Dr S500 Sdn	25618	28752	31825

Options	Price
Adaptive Cruise Control	+1113
Air Conditioning - Front and Rear	+1002
Automatic Load Leveling [Opt on S430]	+515
Climate Comfort Seats	+668
Compact Disc Changer	+308
Dual Multi-Contour Seats	+529
Four Place Seating	+3084

Options	Price
Heated Front and Rear Seats	+305
Park Distance Control (Front and Rear)	+543
Power Rear Seat	+529
Power Rear Window Sunshade	+276
Special Factory Paint	+243
Xenon Headlamps	+324

1999

A limited-production Grand Edition S500 debuts.

Mileage Category: I

Body Styles	TMV Pricing		
	Trade	Private	Dealer
4 Dr S320 LWB Sdn	15987	18224	20552
4 Dr S320 SWB Sdn	15839	18055	20362
4 Dr S420 Sdn	16447	18749	21145

Body Styles	TMV Pricing		
	Trade	Private	Dealer
4 Dr S500 Sdn	19196	21882	24677
4 Dr S600 Sdn	25141	28659	32321

Options	Price
Air Conditioning - Front and Rear [Opt on S500]	+913
Automatic Load Leveling [Std on S500,S600]	+420
Automatic Stability Control [Std on S600]	+450
Compact Disc Changer [Std on S600]	+226
Electronic Damping Suspension Control [Std on S600]	+573
Four Place Seating	+2516

Options	Price
Heated Front Seats [Std on S500,S600]	+225
Park Distance Control (Front and Rear)	+443
Power Rear Seat	+431
Power Rear Window Sunshade [Std on S600]	+225
Xenon Headlamps [Std on S500,S600]	+264

1998

The uber-Mercedes are not changed much in anticipation of the cars' imminent replacement. BrakeAssist and BabySmart appear in the lineup, but the S320s don't receive the V6 engine that now powers the E320, instead, continuing with the inline six.

Mileage Category: I

Body Styles	TMV Pricing		
	Trade	Private	Dealer
4 Dr S320 LWB Sdn	13076	15057	17292
4 Dr S320 SWB Sdn	12515	14412	16550
4 Dr S420 Sdn	13252	15259	17524

Body Styles	TMV Pricing		
	Trade	Private	Dealer
4 Dr S500 Sdn	16070	18505	21250
4 Dr S600 Sdn	20257	23326	26787

Options	Price
Air Conditioning - Front and Rear [Std on S600]	+758
Automatic Load Leveling [Std on S500,S600]	+349
Automatic Stability Control [Std on S600]	+374
Compact Disc Changer [Std on S600]	+188
Electronic Damping Suspension Control [Std on S600]	+476

Options	Price
Four Place Seating	+2090
Heated Front Seats [Std on S500,S600]	+186
Park Distance Control (Front and Rear)	+368
Power Rear Seat [Opt on S500]	+358
Power Rear Window Sunshade [Std on S600]	+187
Xenon Headlamps [Std on S500,S600]	+220

S-Class/S55 AMG

1997

Side-impact airbags debut in all S-Class cars this year. S-Class coupes get new front bumpers. All cars get new alloy wheels. A Parktronic system is available for those who aren't comfortable parking their $100,000 car in a smaller space. Mercedes' outstanding Automatic Slip Reduction (ASR) traction control system is finally available on the S320s. Lastly, a rain sensor system is now standard on all models. (It adjusts the speed of the wipers to the intensity of the rain.)

Mileage Category: I

Body Styles	TMV Pricing		
	Trade	Private	Dealer
2 Dr S500 Cpe	13643	15840	18525
2 Dr S600 Cpe	18025	20927	24474
4 Dr S320 LWB Sdn	11009	12781	14947
4 Dr S320 SWB Sdn	10923	12682	14831

Options	Price
Air Conditioning - Front and Rear [Std on S600]	+357
Automatic Load Leveling [Opt on S320,S420]	+284
Automatic Stability Control [Std on S600]	+396
Electronic Damping Suspension Control	+685
Four Place Seating	+1675
Heated Front Seats [Opt on S320,S420]	+152

Body Styles	TMV Pricing		
	Trade	Private	Dealer
4 Dr S420 Sdn	11310	13131	15356
4 Dr S500 Sdn	12904	14981	17520
4 Dr S600 Sdn	15977	18549	21693

Options	Price
Park Distance Control (Front and Rear)	+299
Power Rear Seat	+529
Power Rear Window Sunshade [Std on S600]	+152
Traction Control System [Opt on S420,S500]	+179
Xenon Headlamps [Std on S500,S600]	+179

1996

No cosmetic improvements to the S-Class this year; everything new is under the skin. ESP is standard on the S600 and optional on V8 models. ESP is a stability control system designed to help the driver keep the S-Class under control at all times. V8 and V12 versions get a new five-speed automatic, and all models get a standard power glass sunroof and smog-sensing climate control system. The S350 Turbodiesel is history.

Mileage Category: I

Body Styles	TMV Pricing		
	Trade	Private	Dealer
2 Dr S500 Cpe	11813	13750	16426
2 Dr S600 Cpe	15008	17469	20867
4 Dr S320 LWB Sdn	9689	11278	13472
4 Dr S320 SWB Sdn	9396	10936	13062

Options	Price
Air Conditioning - Front and Rear [Std on S600]	+305
Automatic Load Leveling [Std on S500,S600]	+232
Automatic Stability Control [Opt on S420]	+157
Compact Disc Changer	+137
Electronic Damping Suspension Control	+330

Body Styles	TMV Pricing		
	Trade	Private	Dealer
4 Dr S420 Sdn	9824	11434	13658
4 Dr S500 Sdn	10770	12537	14976
4 Dr S600 Sdn	13020	15321	18498

Options	Price
Four Place Seating	+1430
Heated Front Seats [Opt on S320,S420]	+136
Power Rear Seat [Opt on S500]	+445
Power Rear Window Sunshade [Std on S600]	+130

1995

Minuscule exterior changes and a drop in price are about the only changes to the S-Class.

Mileage Category: I

Body Styles	TMV Pricing		
	Trade	Private	Dealer
2 Dr S500 Cpe	10671	12408	15301
2 Dr S600 Cpe	13169	15311	18882
4 Dr S320 LWB Sdn	8674	10086	12439
4 Dr S320 SWB Sdn	8524	9911	12222

Options	Price
Air Conditioning - Front and Rear [Std on S600]	+443
Automatic Load Leveling [Std on S500,S600]	+207
Compact Disc Changer	+122
Electronic Damping Suspension Control	+295

Body Styles	TMV Pricing		
	Trade	Private	Dealer
4 Dr S350D Turbodsl Sdn	10120	11766	14509
4 Dr S420 Sdn	8850	10290	12690
4 Dr S500 Sdn	9687	11263	13890
4 Dr S600 Sdn	12119	14091	17378

Options	Price
Four Place Seating	+958
Heated Front Seats [Std on S500,S600]	+121
Power Moonroof	+245
Power Rear Window Sunshade [Std on S600]	+116

S55 AMG

2003

Mileage Category: I

Body Styles	TMV Pricing		
	Trade	Private	Dealer
4 Dr S/C Sdn	75174	78773	84770

Options	Price
Adaptive Cruise Control	+2309
Automatic Climate Control (4 Zone)	+1503
Designo Espresso Edition	+8377
Designo Graphite Edition	+8377
Heated Front and Rear Seats	+509
Keyless Ignition System	+795

Options	Price
Park Distance Control (Front and Rear)	+810
Power Rear Seat	+1460
Power Trunk Closer	+368
Tire Pressure Monitoring System	+493
Ventilated Seats (Front and Rear)	+1253

There is more power for the S55 this year, thanks to the installation of a supercharger. Output is staggering at nearly 500 horsepower. Also Pre-Safe, a system that detects an imminent impact and quickly adjusts seating positions as well as seatbelt tension to better safeguard the occupants, debuts. As with other S-Class Benzes, the S55 receives a minor freshening inside and out.

2002

No changes for this thrilling luxury sedan.

Mileage Category: I

Body Styles	TMV Pricing		
	Trade	Private	Dealer
4 Dr STD Sdn	55785	58781	63775

Options	Price	Options	Price
Adaptive Cruise Control	+2006	Heated Front and Rear Seats	+443
Automatic Climate Control (4 Zone)	+698	Park Distance Control (Front and Rear)	+708
Designo Espresso Edition	+6211	Power Rear Seat	+1274
Designo Silver Edition	+6943	Ventilated Seats (Front and Rear)	+1092

2001

The S55 AMG debuts this year, boasting a powerful V8, 18-inch wheels and suspension upgrades for improved handling.

Mileage Category: I

Body Styles	TMV Pricing		
	Trade	Private	Dealer
4 Dr STD Sdn	46296	50552	54481

Options	Price	Options	Price
Adaptive Cruise Control	+1731	Heated Front and Rear Seats	+383
Automatic Climate Control (4 Zone)	+618	Park Distance Control (Front and Rear)	+615
Designo Espresso Edition	+5380	Power Rear Seat	+1104
Designo Silver Edition	+6029	Ventilated Seats (Front and Rear)	+946

SL-Class

2004

Mileage Category: F

Body Styles	TMV Pricing			Body Styles	TMV Pricing		
	Trade	Private	Dealer		Trade	Private	Dealer
2 Dr SL500 Conv	73047	75752	80261	2 Dr SL600 Turbo Conv	105036	108866	115250

Options	Price	Options	Price
Adaptive Cruise Control	+3010	Leather and Wood Gearshift Knob [Opt on SL500]	+250
Comfort Seats [Opt on SL500]	+1550	Leather and Wood Steering Wheel [Opt on SL500]	+610
Designo Espresso Edition	+7650	Panorama Removable Hardtop	+1840
Designo Graphite Edition	+6850	Park Distance Control (Front and Rear)	+1060
Designo Silver Edition	+7650	Tire Pressure Monitoring System	+650
Keyless Ignition System	+1040		

The V12 SL600 is added to the lineup, while the SL500 gets an industry-first seven-speed automatic transmission and an integrated "Keyless Go" keyfob.

2003

Everything. A new SL debuts to replace the previous version, which dated back to 1990.

Mileage Category: F

Body Styles	TMV Pricing		
	Trade	Private	Dealer
2 Dr SL500 Conv	62689	65465	70092

Options	Price	Options	Price
Adaptive Cruise Control	+2309	Leather and Wood Steering Wheel [Opt on SL500]	+407
Cellular Telephone	+943	Panorama Removable Hardtop	+1409
Designo Espresso Edition	+5871	Park Distance Control (Front and Rear)	+810
Designo Graphite Edition	+5871	Sport Package [Opt on SL500]	+3993
Dual Multi-Contour Seats [Opt on SL500]	+579	Tire Pressure Monitoring System	+493
Keyless Ignition System	+795	Ventilated Seats (Front) [Opt on SL500]	+391

2002

Mileage Category: F

Body Styles	TMV Pricing			Body Styles	TMV Pricing		
	Trade	Private	Dealer		Trade	Private	Dealer
2 Dr SL500 Conv	42526	45199	49655	2 Dr SL600 Conv	65282	69386	76227

Options	Price	Options	Price
Compact Disc Changer [Opt on SL500]	+471	Heated Front Seats [Opt on SL500]	+415
Dual Multi-Contour Seats	+516	Panorama Removable Hardtop	+2812
Electronic Damping Suspension Control [Opt on SL500]	+2826	Xenon Headlamps [Opt on SL500]	+345

To make the last year of this generation SL special, Mercedes creates the Silver Arrow edition, a -- you guessed it -- silver-colored SL (available with either the V8 or the V12 engine) garnished both inside and out with polished aluminum trim.

Mercedes-Benz
SL-Class

2001
The SL line gets some minor aerodynamic enhancements for 2001.

Mileage Category: F

Body Styles	TMV Pricing		
	Trade	Private	Dealer
2 Dr SL500 Conv	37566	41337	44817

Options	Price
Compact Disc Changer [Opt on SL500]	+402
Designo Black Diamond Edition	+3092
Designo Slate Blue Edition	+3617
Dual Multi-Contour Seats	+448

Body Styles	TMV Pricing		
	Trade	Private	Dealer
2 Dr SL600 Conv	53329	58682	63623

Options	Price
Heated Front Seats [Opt on SL500]	+383
Panorama Removable Hardtop	+2442
Xenon Headlamps [Opt on SL500]	+371

2000
Designo editions debut in Slate Blue and Black Diamond with special color-coordinated interior trim. Non-designo versions can be painted in Desert Silver. TeleAid is standard, as is a StarTAC digital phone with voice-recognition technology on the SL600. Free maintenance now covers you during the warranty period.

Mileage Category: F

Body Styles	TMV Pricing		
	Trade	Private	Dealer
2 Dr SL500 Conv	32184	36035	39809

Options	Price
Compact Disc Changer [Opt on SL500]	+362
Electronic Damping Suspension Control [Opt on SL500]	+946
Heated Front Seats [Opt on SL500]	+315

Body Styles	TMV Pricing		
	Trade	Private	Dealer
2 Dr SL600 Conv	42646	47749	52750

Options	Price
Panorama Removable Hardtop	+1582
Sport Package	+1827
Xenon Headlamps [Opt on SL500]	+334

1999
The SL500 gets a brand-spankin'-new 5.0-liter V8 that delivers better performance than ever before. Both SL models get sideview mirrors from the SLK, body-colored door handles and new side molding, new taillights, new exterior colors, a new instrument panel, new shifter and shift gate and a new four-spoke steering wheel.

Mileage Category: F

Body Styles	TMV Pricing		
	Trade	Private	Dealer
2 Dr SL500 Conv	27254	30682	34250

Options	Price
Compact Disc Changer [Opt on SL500]	+295
Panorama Removable Hardtop	+1291

Body Styles	TMV Pricing		
	Trade	Private	Dealer
2 Dr SL600 Conv	32940	37083	41395

Options	Price
Sport Package	+1490
Xenon Headlamps [Opt on SL500]	+272

1998
The bargain basement SL320 was discontinued this year.

Mileage Category: F

Body Styles	TMV Pricing		
	Trade	Private	Dealer
2 Dr SL500 Conv	24881	28082	31692
2 Dr SL500 SL1 Sport Conv	26408	29807	33639

Options	Price
AM/FM/CD Audio System [Opt on SL500]	+162
Automatic Load Leveling [Opt on SL500]	+283
Automatic Stability Control [Opt on SL500]	+374
Compact Disc Changer	+245
Electronic Damping Suspension Control [Opt on SL500]	+641

Body Styles	TMV Pricing		
	Trade	Private	Dealer
2 Dr SL600 Conv	28270	31908	36011
2 Dr SL600 SL1 Sport Conv	28988	32719	36926

Options	Price
Heated Front Seats [Opt on SL500]	+192
Panorama Removable Hardtop	+1072
Traction Control System	+226
Xenon Headlamps [Opt on SL500]	+226

1997
A Panorama hardtop is now available, and it helps improve top-up visibility. ASR traction control is now standard on the SL320. A rain sensor is now standard on all models as well.

Mileage Category: F

Body Styles	TMV Pricing		
	Trade	Private	Dealer
2 Dr SL320 Conv	21169	23971	27395
2 Dr SL500 Conv	23039	26088	29815

Options	Price
Automatic Load Leveling [Opt on SL320,SL500]	+230
Automatic Stability Control [Opt on SL320,SL500]	+304
Compact Disc Changer	+199
Electronic Damping Suspension Control	+521
Heated Front Seats [Opt on SL320,SL500]	+156

Body Styles	TMV Pricing		
	Trade	Private	Dealer
2 Dr SL500 SL1 Sport Conv	24496	27739	31702
2 Dr SL600 Conv	25705	29107	33265

Options	Price
Panorama Removable Hardtop	+872
Rear Spoiler	+131
Sport Package	+1007
Xenon Headlamps [Opt on SL320,SL500]	+184

1996

Tweaked styling and new alloys freshen the exterior of the SL roadster. Underneath, ESP keeps drivers on track in lousy driving conditions. It comes standard on the SL600, and can be ordered for the SL320 and SL500. Side airbags are standard across the board. A five-speed automatic is included with SL500 and SL600. Cool gas-discharge headlamps are not available on the SL320.

Mileage Category: F

Body Styles	TMV Pricing		
	Trade	Private	Dealer
2 Dr SL320 Conv	17915	20271	23525
2 Dr SL500 Conv	20328	23002	26695

Options	Price
Automatic Load Leveling [Opt on SL320,SL500]	+196
Automatic Stability Control [Opt on SL320,SL500]	+490
Electronic Damping Suspension Control	+445

Body Styles	TMV Pricing		
	Trade	Private	Dealer
2 Dr SL600 Conv	21863	24739	28710

Options	Price
Hardtop Roof	+727
Heated Front Seats	+140
Xenon Headlamps	+157

1995

Traction control is now standard on the SL320. Price cuts are the only other change for the Mercedes roadster.

Mileage Category: F

Body Styles	TMV Pricing		
	Trade	Private	Dealer
2 Dr SL320 Conv	16496	18651	22243
2 Dr SL500 Conv	18288	20678	24661

Options	Price
Automatic Load Leveling [Opt on SL320,SL500]	+175
Automatic Stability Control [Opt on SL320]	+231
Electronic Damping Suspension Control [Opt on SL320,SL500]	+397

Body Styles	TMV Pricing		
	Trade	Private	Dealer
2 Dr SL600 Conv	19465	22008	26246

Options	Price
Hardtop Roof	+649
Heated Front Seats [Opt on SL320,SL500]	+125

SL55 AMG
2003

Mileage Category: F

Body Styles	TMV Pricing		
	Trade	Private	Dealer
2 Dr S/C Conv	87408	91278	97728

Options	Price	Options	Price
Adaptive Cruise Control	+2309	Keyless Ignition System	+795
Cellular Telephone	+943	Panorama Removable Hardtop	+1409
Designo Espresso Edition	+5245	Park Distance Control (Front and Rear)	+810
Designo Graphite Edition	+5245	Tire Pressure Monitoring System	+493

An all-new SL debuts this year, and along with it comes this near-500-horsepower AMG version that promises exotic car performance along with grand touring car comfort.

SLK-Class
2004

To stoke interest in this aging drop top, Mercedes brings out a Special Edition that includes unique 17-inch wheels, napa leather trim for the sport seats and roll bar, chrome accents around the windows and a color-keyed front grille and rear spoiler.

Mileage Category: F

Body Styles	TMV Pricing		
	Trade	Private	Dealer
2 Dr SLK230 Kompressor S/C Conv	28180	29710	32260

Options	Price
17 Inch Wheels	+500
Aero Kit	+2640
Automatic 5-Speed Transmission	+1360
Compact Disc Changer	+120
Designo Silver Edition	+5000
Designo Terra Cotta Edition	+5000
Headlight Washers	+350
Heated Front Seats	+550

Body Styles	TMV Pricing		
	Trade	Private	Dealer
2 Dr SLK320 Conv	33142	34803	37572

Options	Price
Nappa Leather Seat Trim	+350
Power Driver Seat [Opt on SLK230]	+350
Power Passenger Seat [Opt on SLK230]	+350
Rear Spoiler	+250
Special Factory Paint	+670
Sport Seats	+300
Telescopic Steering Wheel [Opt on SLK230]	+200
Xenon Headlamps	+750

2003

There are no changes for this year. A revamped SLK is set to debut for 2004.

Mileage Category: F

Body Styles	TMV Pricing		
	Trade	Private	Dealer
2 Dr SLK230 S/C Conv	26615	27972	30234

Options	Price
Automatic 5-Speed Transmission [Opt on SLK230,SLK320]	+1037
Cellular Telephone	+943

Body Styles	TMV Pricing		
	Trade	Private	Dealer
2 Dr SLK320 Conv	29326	30821	33313

Options	Price
Compact Disc Changer	+313
Designo Silver Edition	+3836

2003 (cont'd)

Options	Price
Designo Terra Cotta Edition	+3836
Heated Front Seats [Opt on SLK230,SLK320]	+431
Metallic Paint	+513
Power Driver Seat [Opt on SLK230]	+235

Options	Price
Power Passenger Seat [Opt on SLK230]	+235
Sport Package [Opt on SLK230,SLK320]	+3362
Telescopic Steering Wheel [Opt on SLK230]	+157
Xenon Headlamps	+470

2002
No major changes.

Mileage Category: F

Body Styles	TMV Pricing		
	Trade	Private	Dealer
2 Dr SLK230 S/C Conv	21452	22964	25483

Body Styles	TMV Pricing		
	Trade	Private	Dealer
2 Dr SLK320 Conv	23934	25621	28432

Options	Price
Automatic 5-Speed Transmission [Opt on SLK230]	+907
Compact Disc Changer	+398
Designo Silver Edition	+3350
Designo Terra Cotta Edition	+3350
Heated Front Seats	+384
Metallic Paint	+447

Options	Price
Power Driver Seat [Opt on SLK230]	+209
Power Passenger Seat [Opt on SLK230]	+209
Sport Package	+2945
Telescopic Steering Wheel [Opt on SLK230]	+140
Xenon Headlamps	+419

2001
A new V6-powered SLK320 joins the lineup while the SLK230 gets more power and a $2,100 price reduction. Both versions get a new six-speed manual tranny in addition to the five-speed automatic that's been available since the car's introduction, and all models benefit from a revised interior and exterior.

Mileage Category: F

Body Styles	TMV Pricing		
	Trade	Private	Dealer
2 Dr SLK230 S/C Conv	19986	21992	23844

Body Styles	TMV Pricing		
	Trade	Private	Dealer
2 Dr SLK320 Conv	22438	24690	26769

Options	Price
Automatic 5-Speed Transmission	+587
Compact Disc Changer	+352
Designo Copper Edition	+2968
Designo Goldenrod Edition	+2690
Heated Front Seats	+383
Metallic Paint	+386

Options	Price
Power Driver Seat [Opt on SLK230]	+192
Power Passenger Seat [Opt on SLK230]	+192
Sport Package	+2557
Telescopic Steering Wheel [Opt on SLK230]	+186
Xenon Headlamps	+371

2000
Designo editions debut and include special paint and trim in either Copper or Electric Green hues.

Mileage Category: F

Body Styles	TMV Pricing		
	Trade	Private	Dealer
2 Dr SLK230 S/C Conv	17391	19389	21348

Options	Price
tic 5-Speed Transmission	+501
Compact Disc Changer	+334
Designo Copper Edition	+2361

Options	Price
Electric Green Edition	+2135
Heated Front Seats	+337
Metallic Paint	+340

1999
This year, Mercedes gives the SLK-Class a standard five-speed manual transmission, optional Sport Package, a new-generation stereo with cassette that uses fiber-optic technology and integrated controls for a cellular phone.

Mileage Category: F

Body Styles	TMV Pricing		
	Trade	Private	Dealer
2 Dr SLK230 S/C Conv	14788	16611	18509

Body Styles	TMV Pricing		
	Trade	Private	Dealer
2 Dr SLK230 Sport S/C Conv	16857	18935	21098

Options	Price
AM/FM/CD Audio System	+159
Automatic 5-Speed Transmission	+349
Compact Disc Changer	+272

Options	Price
Heated Front Seats	+232
Metallic Paint	+233

1998
Mercedes-Benz releases an all-new retractable-hardtop roadster. Powered by a supercharged 2.3-liter engine, which is hooked to a five-speed automatic transmission, the SLK-Class races to 60 mph in just over seven seconds.

Mileage Category: F

Body Styles	TMV Pricing		
	Trade	Private	Dealer
2 Dr SLK230 S/C Conv	13559	15319	17304

Options	Price
Compact Disc Changer	+226
Heated Front Seats	+192

Options	Price
Metallic Paint	+194

SLK32 AMG

2004

Mileage Category: F

Body Styles	TMV Pricing		
	Trade	Private	Dealer
2 Dr S/C Conv	38320	40753	44808

Options	Price	Options	Price
Compact Disc Changer	+400	Special Factory Paint	+670
Designo Silver Edition	+5000	Xenon Headlamps	+850
Designo Terra Cotta Edition	+5000		

The SLK32 rolls into 2004 with no changes.

2003

Mileage Category: F

Body Styles	TMV Pricing		
	Trade	Private	Dealer
2 Dr S/C Conv	36047	37886	40950

Options	Price	Options	Price
Cellular Telephone	+943	Headlight Washers	+157
Compact Disc Changer	+313	Metallic Paint	+513
Designo Silver Edition	+3836	Xenon Headlamps	+470
Designo Terra Cotta Edition	+3836		

The SLK32 rolls into 2003 with no changes.

2002

Mileage Category: F

Body Styles	TMV Pricing		
	Trade	Private	Dealer
2 Dr S/C Conv	33447	35371	38577

Options	Price	Options	Price
Compact Disc Changer	+398	Metallic Paint	+447
Designo Silver Edition	+3350	Xenon Headlamps	+419
Designo Terra Cotta Edition	+3350		

Mercedes-Benz gives BMW and Porsche something to think about by introducing an AMG version of its small, retractable-hardtop roadster. The SLK32 AMG brings a ripping 349 horsepower to the party by way of a supercharged 3.2-liter V6.

Cougar

2002

Mileage Category: E

Body Styles	TMV Pricing			Body Styles	TMV Pricing		
	Trade	Private	Dealer		Trade	Private	Dealer
2 Dr I4 Hbk	6218	7111	8599	2 Dr V6 Hbk	7577	8666	10480

Options	Price	Options	Price
17 Inch Wheels [Opt on V6]	+148	Leather Seats [Opt on V6]	+433
Antilock Brakes	+329	Power Driver Seat	+116
Automatic 4-Speed Transmission	+481	Power Moonroof	+363
Front Side Airbag Restraints [Opt on V6]	+157		

New colors spruce up the outside, and all Cougars get the formerly optional Convenience Group (cruise, remote keyless illuminated entry and rear wiper/washer) as standard equipment. Evidently, the Zn (Zinc Yellow) feature car from 2001 failed to get buyers' pulses up, so Mercury tries again for 2002 with the XR package, which includes special red or black paint, a rear spoiler, a fake hood scoop and special logos. The Cougar C2 feature vehicle makes a return engagement for 2002. Sadly, the shelved Cougar S never materialized.

2001

Exterior and interior changes are extensive for the Cougar. At first glance outside, you'll notice new front and rear fascias, new headlights with a projector and reflector system, a new grille, a new spoiler, new foglights and 16-inch painted or 17-inch machined aluminum wheels. New clearcoat metallic colors include Dark Shadow Grey, Tropic Green, French Blue and Sunburst Gold. Later in the year, two special editions -- the Cougar Zn and C2 -- will be offered.

Mileage Category: E

Body Styles	TMV Pricing			Body Styles	TMV Pricing		
	Trade	Private	Dealer		Trade	Private	Dealer
2 Dr I4 Hbk	5175	6352	7438	2 Dr V6 Hbk	6223	7638	8945

Options	Price	Options	Price
Antilock Brakes	+280	Front Side Airbag Restraints	+161
Automatic 4-Speed Transmission [Opt on V6]	+336	Leather Seats	+247
Compact Disc Changer	+144	Power Sunroof	+254

2000

All Cougars receive an emergency trunk release as standard equipment, as well as a redesigned floor console. Citrus Gold, Light Blue and Light Sapphire are the three new clearcoat metallic paints available.

Mileage Category: E

Body Styles	TMV Pricing			Body Styles	TMV Pricing		
	Trade	Private	Dealer		Trade	Private	Dealer
2 Dr I4 Hbk	4525	5646	6744	2 Dr V6 Hbk	5440	6787	8107

Options	Price	Options	Price
Antilock Brakes	+244	Front Side Airbag Restraints	+135
Automatic 4-Speed Transmission	+292	Leather Seats	+321
Compact Disc Changer	+126	Power Sunroof	+221

1999

Mercury reintroduces the Cougar this year after a one-year hiatus that saw the departure of most of Ford Motor Co.'s personal coupes. The new model is built on the Mondeo global platform that is also the basis for the Ford Contour and Mercury Mystique. This new coupe is powered by the same engine choices as the Contour/Mystique, which means that buyers can choose between a zippy Zetec four-cylinder and a high-revving Duratec V6.

Mileage Category: E

Body Styles	TMV Pricing			Body Styles	TMV Pricing		
	Trade	Private	Dealer		Trade	Private	Dealer
2 Dr I4 Hbk	3407	4430	5495	2 Dr V6 Hbk	4347	5651	7009

Options	Price	Options	Price
Antilock Brakes	+211	Power Sunroof	+172
Automatic 4-Speed Transmission	+227	Premium Audio System [Opt on V6]	+146
Leather Seats	+250		

1997

Mileage Category: D

Body Styles	TMV Pricing		
	Trade	Private	Dealer
2 Dr XR7 Cpe	2087	2990	4093

Options	Price	Options	Price
4.6L V8 SOHC 16V FI Engine	+233	Power Moonroof	+152
Antilock Brakes	+155		

Mercury gives you the chance to buy a special anniversary edition replete with plenty of badges, a special interior and a few luxury doo-dads.

1996

New styling and powertrain improvements highlight the 1996 Cougar. Some formerly standard equipment is now optional. New options include a revamped cruise control system and a Total Anti-Theft System. Four new colors debut.

Mileage Category: D

Body Styles	TMV Pricing		
	Trade	Private	Dealer
2 Dr XR7 Cpe	1533	2314	3393

Options	Price
4.6L V8 SOHC 16V FI Engine	+196
Antilock Brakes	+131

Options	Price
Power Moonroof	+129

1995

A Sport Appearance Package is offered to spruce up the Cougar with BBS wheels and a luggage rack. Unfortunately, the trunk-mounted CD changer is deleted from the option list. Antilock brakes and a traction-lock axle are available as separate options for the first time this year.

Mileage Category: D

Body Styles	TMV Pricing		
	Trade	Private	Dealer
2 Dr XR7 Cpe	993	1627	2684

Options	Price
4.6L V8 SOHC 16V FI Engine	+165
Antilock Brakes	+110

Options	Price
Leather Seats	+80
Power Moonroof	+108

Grand Marquis
2004

Mileage Category: G

Body Styles	TMV Pricing		
	Trade	Private	Dealer
4 Dr GS Sdn	12391	13525	15414

Options	Price
AM/FM/Cassette/CD Changer Audio System [Opt on LS]	+895
Automatic Load Leveling [Opt on LS]	+600
Front Side Airbag Restraints [Opt on LS]	+395
Heated Front Seats [Opt on LS]	+295
Keyless Entry System [Opt on GS]	+400

Body Styles	TMV Pricing		
	Trade	Private	Dealer
4 Dr LS Sdn	14548	15832	17971

Options	Price
Leather Seats	+495
Power Adjustable Foot Pedals [Opt on GS]	+200
Steering Wheel Radio Controls [Opt on GS]	+150
Traction Control System [Opt on GS]	+550

For 2004, the Grand Marquis is available with laminated side glass to reduce wind and road noise, as well as provide greater protection in the event of an accident. A CD player is now standard on all models. Side airbags, a moonroof and heated front seats are now optional.

2003

Mileage Category: G

Body Styles	TMV Pricing		
	Trade	Private	Dealer
4 Dr GS Sdn	10931	11847	13374

Options	Price
AM/FM/Cassette/CD Audio System [Opt on GS]	+176
Automatic Load Leveling [Opt on LS]	+162
Compact Disc Changer [Opt on LS]	+213
Front Side Airbag Restraints [Opt on LS]	+213
Heated Front Seats [Opt on LS]	+159

Body Styles	TMV Pricing		
	Trade	Private	Dealer
4 Dr LS Sdn	12894	13976	15778

Options	Price
Leather Seats [Opt on LS]	+267
Leather and Wood Steering Wheel [Opt on LS]	+189
Power Adjustable Foot Pedals [Opt on GS]	+146
Special Leather Seat Trim [Opt on LS]	+430
Sport Suspension [Opt on LS]	+170

The 2003 Grand Mark receives a number of updates. The most important ones are hidden. A new full-perimeter frame uses strong, lightweight hydroformed steel sections for the front rails to improve frontal and offset crash performance. Redesigned frame crossmembers and new optional side impact airbags improve side impact crash performance. Additionally, the new frame -- combined with a redesigned independent front suspension and new monotube shock absorbers at all four wheels -- contributes to a smoother, more controlled ride and improved handling. Other changes include a new variable ratio rack-and-pinion steering system with variable power assist and a new dual-rate brake booster that automatically supplies full braking power in a panic stop. On the inside, the seats have been changed to improve comfort and appearance, the cupholders are new, a three-point seatbelt has been added for the center rear passenger and the door trim has been redesigned for a cleaner appearance and better ergonomics. To spot a 2003 Marquis, look for the brighter headlights and subtle new styling applied to the front and rear of the vehicle.

2002

Mileage Category: G

Body Styles	TMV Pricing		
	Trade	Private	Dealer
4 Dr GS Sdn	9115	10055	11622

Options	Price
Automatic Load Leveling	+218
Compact Disc Changer	+169

Body Styles	TMV Pricing		
	Trade	Private	Dealer
4 Dr LS Sdn	10374	11444	13228

Options	Price
Leather Seats	+481
Sport Suspension	+363

Antilock brakes and traction control now come standard on all Grand Marks, while revised cupholders and a new front seat storage pouch improve the cabin. No-charge leather is available on LS Ultimate models. LS Ultimate and LSE models get standard steering wheel controls for the stereo and climate system, and a new trunk organizer is optional across the board. Three new colors are added this year.

2001

Mileage Category: G

Body Styles	TMV Pricing		
	Trade	Private	Dealer
4 Dr GS Sdn	7316	8599	9784

Options	Price
AM/FM/Cassette Audio System [Opt on LS]	+148
Aluminum/Alloy Wheels	+132

Body Styles	TMV Pricing		
	Trade	Private	Dealer
4 Dr LS Sdn	8099	9521	10833

Options	Price
Antilock Brakes	+280
Automatic Load Leveling	+165

Power from the V8 engine is improved. The interior gets minor improvements and an optional adjustable pedal assembly. Safety has been improved via a crash severity sensor, safety belt pre-tensioners, dual-stage airbags and seat position sensors.

2001 (cont'd)

Options	Price
Compact Disc Changer	+144
Digital Instrument Panel [Opt on LS]	+175

Options	Price
Leather Seats	+303
Power Passenger Seat [Opt on LS]	+144

2000

The Marquis receives additional safety features, including an emergency trunk release, child seat-anchor brackets and Mercury's Belt Minder system. The interior gets a new trim color, Dark Charcoal. One new exterior color will be offered, Tropic Green. The handling package's rear-axle ratio changes from 3.27 to 3.55. The Grand Marquis Limited will be offered later in the 2000 model year.

Mileage Category: G

Body Styles	TMV Pricing		
	Trade	Private	Dealer
4 Dr GS Sdn	5970	7187	8380

Options	Price
Aluminum/Alloy Wheels	+115
Antilock Brakes	+244
Compact Disc Changer	+126

Body Styles	TMV Pricing		
	Trade	Private	Dealer
4 Dr LS Sdn	6527	7857	9161

Options	Price
Digital Instrument Panel [Opt on LS]	+152
Leather Seats	+264
Power Passenger Seat [Opt on LS]	+129

1999

This traditional American sedan got a revised rear suspension and exterior styling last year. This year all it gets are some new color options.

Mileage Category: G

Body Styles	TMV Pricing		
	Trade	Private	Dealer
4 Dr GS Sdn	4942	6068	7239

Options	Price
Antilock Brakes	+211
Digital Instrument Panel [Opt on LS]	+118

Body Styles	TMV Pricing		
	Trade	Private	Dealer
4 Dr LS Sdn	5389	6616	7893

Options	Price
Leather Seats [Opt on LS]	+205

1998

The last of the American rear-drive sedans gets substantial improvements this year, including a new instrument panel, new steering gear and an improved ride, thanks to a Watt's linkage suspension. All-speed traction control debuts this year as well.

Mileage Category: G

Body Styles	TMV Pricing		
	Trade	Private	Dealer
4 Dr GS Sdn	4170	5207	6376

Options	Price
Antilock Brakes	+184

Body Styles	TMV Pricing		
	Trade	Private	Dealer
4 Dr LS Sdn	4524	5649	6918

Options	Price
Leather Seats	+174

1997

After a mild facelift last year, the Grand Marquis soldiers on with a few color changes, improved power steering and the addition of rear air suspension to the handling package.

Mileage Category: G

Body Styles	TMV Pricing		
	Trade	Private	Dealer
4 Dr GS Sdn	3246	4235	5443

Options	Price
Antilock Brakes	+155

Body Styles	TMV Pricing		
	Trade	Private	Dealer
4 Dr LS Sdn	3596	4692	6031

Options	Price
Leather Seats	+151

1996

This distant descendant of the Turnpike Cruiser gets engine and transmission upgrades, a new steering wheel and a new gas cap design. Passenger power lumbar support has been deleted.

Mileage Category: G

Body Styles	TMV Pricing		
	Trade	Private	Dealer
4 Dr GS Sdn	2431	3318	4543

Options	Price
Antilock Brakes	+131

Body Styles	TMV Pricing		
	Trade	Private	Dealer
4 Dr LS Sdn	2739	3739	5121

Options	Price
Camper/Towing Package	+156

1995

Updated styling and an increased number of convenience features improve upon last year's model. A battery saver shuts off power to accessories or lights 10 minutes after the ignition is switched off. The mast antenna has been replaced by an integrated rear window antenna. Interior updates include a 12-volt outlet in a redesigned dashboard. Enlarged stereo controls improve ease of operation and bigger gauges improve the instrument panel.

Mileage Category: G

Body Styles	TMV Pricing		
	Trade	Private	Dealer
4 Dr GS Sdn	1645	2304	3402

Options	Price
Antilock Brakes	+110
Camper/Towing Package	+131

Body Styles	TMV Pricing		
	Trade	Private	Dealer
4 Dr LS Sdn	1890	2648	3911

Options	Price
Leather Seats	+94
Power Sunroof	+102

Marauder

2004

Body Styles	TMV Pricing		
	Trade	Private	Dealer
4 Dr STD Sdn	19445	20712	22824

Mileage Category: G

Options	Price	Options	Price
Compact Disc Changer	+395	Power Moonroof	+1025
Heated Front Seats	+295		

A new heavy-duty four-speed automatic comes standard for quicker shifts along with traction control and an upgraded audio system. Dark Red and Silver are newly available exterior colors. The 4.6-liter V8 now comes with dual knock sensors for improved engine response at low speeds.

2003

Mileage Category: G

Body Styles	TMV Pricing		
	Trade	Private	Dealer
4 Dr STD Sdn	16862	18163	20330

Options	Price	Options	Price
Compact Disc Changer	+213	Heated Front Seats	+159

In an effort to generate interest in what seems to be a dying brand, Mercury takes a page out of a decade-old Chevrolet playbook and paints a Grand Marquis Amish-black, bolts on 18-inch wheels and stuffs a 300-horse V8 under the hood. The result is surprisingly appealing.

Monterey

2004

Mileage Category: P

Body Styles	TMV Pricing		
	Trade	Private	Dealer
4 Dr STD Pass Van	13474	14537	16308

Options	Price	Options	Price
AM/FM/CD Changer Audio System	+200	Leather Seats	+800
Alarm System	+200	Luggage Rack	+200
Automatic Climate Control (2 Zone) - Front and Rear	+400	Power Adjustable Foot Pedals	+175
Automatic On/Off Headlights	+175	Power Driver Seat w/Memory	+175
Automatic Stability Control	+730	Power Dual Sliding Doors	+300
Center Console	+150	Power Heated Mirrors	+150
Climate Comfort Seats	+300	Power Passenger Seat	+150
Front Side Airbag Restraints	+300	Rear Audio Controls	+125
Front, Rear and Third Row Head Airbag Restraints	+395	Steering Wheel Radio Controls	+125
Garage Door Opener	+150	Tilt Steering Wheel	+120
Heated Front Seats	+175		

The Monterey is an all-new minivan that replaces the Mercury Villager.

Mountaineer

2004

Body Styles	TMV Pricing			Body Styles	TMV Pricing		
	Trade	Private	Dealer		Trade	Private	Dealer
4 Dr STD AWD SUV	18370	19701	21920	4 Dr STD SUV	16946	18277	20496

Mileage Category: M

Options	Price	Options	Price
17 Inch Wheels	+500	Park Distance Control (Rear)	+145
4.6L V8 SOHC 16V FI Engine	+830	Power Adjustable Foot Pedals	+120
AM/FM/CD Changer Audio System	+510	Power Driver Seat w/Memory	+175
Air Conditioning - Front and Rear	+500	Power Moonroof	+800
Automatic Climate Control (2 Zone) - Driver and Passenger	+650	Power Passenger Seat	+150
Camper/Towing Package	+400	Rear Air Conditioning Controls	+150
Front and Rear Head Airbag Restraints	+395	Running Boards	+450
Garage Door Opener	+150	Side Steps	+450
Heated Front Seats	+300	Steering Wheel Radio Controls	+150
Leather Seats	+695	Trip Computer	+200

Second-row bucket seats are available on Luxury and Premier models; a tire-pressure monitoring system is now standard on these models. The Advance Trac stability control system is a late-availability option on two-wheel-drive Mountaineers. The upgraded Audiophile sound system with in-dash CD changer is optional on Luxury models, while Convenience models no longer offer a cassette player. Finally, power-adjustable pedals are a new option on the Convenience model.

2003

The Mountaineer comes in three different versions for 2003: Convenience, Luxury and Premier. Mercury has added standard equipment this year, including security approach lamps, automatic headlamps, dual illuminated visor vanity mirrors, heated exterior mirrors and power-adjustable pedals. Luxury models receive color-keyed running boards and an Audiophile sound system as standard, and Premier adds to that a power sunroof and a Security Group that includes a Safety Canopy system of head airbags and rollover protection sensors bundled with a reverse-sensing system. Inside, Mountaineers get new trim for the doors and dash, a three-point seatbelt for the center of the second-row bench and an easy entry/exit system for the third-row seat. Luxury and Premier models can be outfitted with a new DVD entertainment system for the rear seats and a tire pressure monitoring system. A leather-upholstered center console cover is added and leather is a no-charge option for Luxury and Premier models.

Mileage Category: M

Body Styles	TMV Pricing		
	Trade	Private	Dealer
4 Dr STD AWD SUV	15554	16783	18831

Options	Price
17 Inch Wheels	+311
4.6L V8 SOHC 16V FI Engine	+449
AM/FM/CD Changer Audio System	+216
Air Conditioning - Front and Rear	+330
Automatic Climate Control (2 Zone) - Driver and Passenger	+189
Camper/Towing Package	+216
Front and Rear Head Airbag Restraints	+135
Heated Front Seats	+135

Body Styles	TMV Pricing		
	Trade	Private	Dealer
4 Dr STD SUV	14623	15779	17705

Options	Price
Leather Seats	+376
Park Distance Control (Rear)	+138
Power Moonroof	+432
Power Passenger Seat	+130
Premium Audio System	+157
Rollover Protection System	+135
Running Boards	+213

2002

Mercury has overhauled its Mountaineer for model-year 2002 in an attempt to make it more carlike than ever before. Among the changes are a 2.5-inch wider stance for better handling and roominess, a new independent rear suspension that improves ride and handling, while at the same time accommodating a standard third row of seats, larger door openings with a lower step-in height, standard six-way power-adjustable driver seat and optional power-adjustable pedals. With this year's redesign, Mercury is trying to further differentiate the Mountaineer from its look-alike cousin the Ford Explorer.

Mileage Category: M

Body Styles	TMV Pricing		
	Trade	Private	Dealer
4 Dr STD AWD SUV	12906	14145	16211

Options	Price
17 Inch Wheels	+278
4.6L V8 SOHC 16V FI Engine	+336
AM/FM/CD Changer Audio System	+193
Air Conditioning - Front and Rear	+295
Automatic Climate Control (2 Zone) - Driver and Passenger	+169
Camper/Towing Package	+191
Front and Rear Head Airbag Restraints	+121
Heated Front Seats	+121

Body Styles	TMV Pricing		
	Trade	Private	Dealer
4 Dr STD SUV	12044	13200	15129

Options	Price
Leather Seats	+317
Park Distance Control (Rear)	+123
Power Moonroof	+387
Power Passenger Seat	+116
Premium Audio System	+140
Rollover Protection System	+121
Running Boards	+191

2001

Not much changes for 2001, as Mercury's Explorer clone has a new child safety-seat tether anchor system. The rest of the vehicle is all carryover.

Mileage Category: M

Body Styles	TMV Pricing		
	Trade	Private	Dealer
4 Dr STD 4WD SUV	8915	10325	11627
4 Dr STD AWD SUV	9042	10472	11792

Options	Price
5.0L V8 OHV 16V FI Engine [Opt on 2WD]	+192
AM/FM/Cassette/CD Audio System	+181
AM/FM/Cassette/CD Changer Audio System	+163
Automatic Load Leveling	+163
Chrome Wheels	+204
Front Side Airbag Restraints	+163

Body Styles	TMV Pricing		
	Trade	Private	Dealer
4 Dr STD SUV	8360	9683	10904

Options	Price
Leather Seats	+330
Limited Slip Differential [Std on AWD]	+146
Power Driver Seat	+126
Power Moonroof	+330
Power Passenger Seat	+126
Premium Audio System	+181

2000

Mountaineer is uprated with new Premier and Monterey trim packages, which include tan leather upholstery, special paint, upgraded alloy wheels and wood grain dash trim.

Mileage Category: M

Body Styles	TMV Pricing		
	Trade	Private	Dealer
4 Dr STD 4WD SUV	6631	7989	9319
4 Dr STD AWD SUV	6771	8158	9517

Options	Price
5.0L V8 OHV 16V FI Engine [Opt on 2WD]	+166
AM/FM/Cassette/CD Audio System	+158
Automatic Load Leveling	+142
Chrome Wheels	+177
Compact Disc Changer	+133

Body Styles	TMV Pricing		
	Trade	Private	Dealer
4 Dr STD SUV	6076	7321	8541

Options	Price
Front Side Airbag Restraints	+140
Leather Seats	+341
Limited Slip Differential [Std on AWD]	+127
Power Moonroof	+287
Sport Seats	+215

1999

For '99 the Mountaineer gets optional rear load leveling and a reverse parking aid. It also receives a new seat design.

Mileage Category: M

Body Styles	TMV Pricing		
	Trade	Private	Dealer
4 Dr STD 4WD SUV	5242	6459	7726
4 Dr STD AWD SUV	5577	6871	8219

Options	Price
5.0L V8 OHV 16V FI Engine [Opt on 2WD]	+129
AM/FM/Cassette/CD Audio System	+123
Chrome Wheels	+138

Body Styles	TMV Pricing		
	Trade	Private	Dealer
4 Dr STD SUV	4956	6107	7306

Options	Price
Leather Seats	+265
Power Moonroof	+223
Sport Seats	+167

1998

The Mountaineer gets minor front and rear styling tweaks as it enters its second year of production. In addition, a new model, with full-time four-wheel drive, receives the SOHC V6 and five-speed automatic transmission that became available on the Explorer last year.

Mileage Category: M

Body Styles	TMV Pricing		
	Trade	Private	Dealer
4 Dr STD 4WD SUV	4472	5588	6848
4 Dr STD AWD SUV	4568	5707	6992

Options	Price
Bucket Seats	+131
Chrome Wheels	+118

Body Styles	TMV Pricing		
	Trade	Private	Dealer
4 Dr STD SUV	4192	5238	6417

Options	Price
Leather Seats	+156
Power Moonroof	+190

1997

The all-new Mercury Mountaineer is yet another entrant into the booming luxury sport-utility market. Based on the wildly successful Ford Explorer, the Mountaineer is intended to appeal to outdoor sophisticates rather than true roughnecks. Distinguishing characteristics of the Mountaineer include four-wheel antilock brakes, a pushrod V8 engine and optional all-wheel drive.

Mileage Category: M

Body Styles	TMV Pricing		
	Trade	Private	Dealer
4 Dr STD AWD SUV	4089	5109	6357

Options	Price
JBL Audio System	+171
Leather Seats	+135

Body Styles	TMV Pricing		
	Trade	Private	Dealer
4 Dr STD SUV	3805	4755	5917

Options	Price
Power Moonroof	+164

Mystique

2000

Mileage Category: C

Body Styles	TMV Pricing		
	Trade	Private	Dealer
4 Dr GS Sdn	3510	4614	5696

Options	Price
Aluminum/Alloy Wheels [Opt on GS]	+152
Antilock Brakes	+244
Automatic 4-Speed Transmission	+292

Body Styles	TMV Pricing		
	Trade	Private	Dealer
4 Dr LS Sdn	3900	5127	6329

Options	Price
Power Driver Seat [Opt on GS]	+126
Power Moonroof	+213

The Mystique comes standard with an emergency glow-in-the-dark trunk release, designed to allow a child or adult trapped in the trunk to open it from the inside. Two new exterior colors debut.

1999

The Mystique gets a revised instrument panel and redesigned front seats this year. A six-way power-adjustable seat is now standard on the LS model and all Mystiques benefit from a revised suspension and larger fuel tank. Medium Steel Blue replaces Light Denim Blue as an exterior color. A final note to family-oriented shoppers: the optional integrated child safety seat is no longer available.

Mileage Category: C

Body Styles	TMV Pricing		
	Trade	Private	Dealer
4 Dr GS Sdn	2742	3823	4949

Options	Price
Aluminum/Alloy Wheels [Opt on GS]	+118
Antilock Brakes	+211

Body Styles	TMV Pricing		
	Trade	Private	Dealer
4 Dr LS Sdn	3024	4217	5458

Options	Price
Automatic 4-Speed Transmission	+227
Power Moonroof	+166

1998

The 1998 Mystique receives a freshened interior and exterior that includes new wheels and a new front end. Mechanical enhancements include 100,000-mile maintenance intervals for the 2.0-liter Zetec engine, improved manual transmission shifter feel, improved NVH and improved air conditioning performance. New interior pieces are intended to distinguish the Mystique from its otherwise-identical twin, the Ford Contour.

Mileage Category: C

Body Styles	TMV Pricing		
	Trade	Private	Dealer
4 Dr GS Sdn	1975	2978	4110

Options	Price
Antilock Brakes	+179
Automatic 4-Speed Transmission	+194

Body Styles	TMV Pricing		
	Trade	Private	Dealer
4 Dr LS Sdn	2217	3343	4612

Options	Price
Leather Seats	+213
Power Moonroof	+141

1997

The addition of a Spree Package for the GS model and the inclusion of a tilt steering wheel and standard trunk light are the only changes for the 1997 Mystique.

Mileage Category: C

Body Styles	TMV Pricing			Body Styles	TMV Pricing		
	Trade	Private	Dealer		Trade	Private	Dealer
4 Dr GS Sdn	1335	2244	3355	4 Dr STD Sdn	1328	2232	3337
4 Dr LS Sdn	1497	2516	3762				

Options	Price	Options	Price
2.5L V6 DOHC 24V FI Engine	+204	Automatic 4-Speed Transmission	+168
Air Conditioning	+163	Leather Seats	+184
Antilock Brakes	+155	Power Moonroof	+122

1996

More rear seat room is the big story for Mystique in 1996. Gearshift effort has been improved on manual transmissions, a new Sport Appearance Package is available and five new colors are on the palette. Alloy wheels have been restyled on LS models.

Mileage Category: C

Body Styles	TMV Pricing			Body Styles	TMV Pricing		
	Trade	Private	Dealer		Trade	Private	Dealer
4 Dr GS Sdn	870	1632	2684	4 Dr LS Sdn	953	1789	2943

Options	Price	Options	Price
2.5L V6 DOHC 24V FI Engine	+172	Antilock Brakes	+131
Air Conditioning	+135	Automatic 4-Speed Transmission	+142

1995

Introduced to replace the aging Topaz, the Mystique is a virtual twin to the Ford Contour. Euro-styling combined with German engineering results in a $20,000 American car that can compete with import sedans that cost nearly twice as much. You may choose between two trim levels, the base GS or the more luxurious LS. A 170-horsepower V6 engine is optional.

Mileage Category: C

Body Styles	TMV Pricing			Body Styles	TMV Pricing		
	Trade	Private	Dealer		Trade	Private	Dealer
4 Dr GS Sdn	646	1248	2252	4 Dr LS Sdn	708	1368	2467

Options	Price	Options	Price
2.5L V6 DOHC 24V FI Engine	+144	Automatic 4-Speed Transmission	+119
Air Conditioning	+114	Leather Seats	+87
Antilock Brakes	+110	Power Moonroof	+87

Sable

2004

Minor changes include a new front-end treatment with new foglights on the LS Premium, six-spoke alloy wheels as standard equipment on the LS Premium, new taillights on the sedan and new exterior badging. Inside, there's a new steering wheel with lighted cruise control buttons (LS Premium model only), and a 60/40-split rear seat is now standard on all Sables.

Mileage Category: D

Body Styles	TMV Pricing			Body Styles	TMV Pricing		
	Trade	Private	Dealer		Trade	Private	Dealer
4 Dr GS Sdn	9006	9862	11288	4 Dr LS Sdn	10717	11824	13669
4 Dr GS Wgn	9442	10300	11729	4 Dr LS Wgn	11251	12358	14203

Options	Price	Options	Price
AM/FM/Cassette/CD Changer Audio System [Opt on LS]	+695	Power Moonroof [Opt on LS]	+995
Aluminum/Alloy Wheels [Opt on GS]	+495	Power Passenger Seat [Opt on LS]	+395
Chrome Wheels [Opt on LS]	+395	Rear Spoiler [Opt on LS Sdn]	+285
Front Side Airbag Restraints	+250	Third Seat [Opt on Wgn]	+300
Leather and Wood Steering Wheel [Opt on LS]	+195	Traction Control System	+345
Power Driver Seat [Opt on GS]	+395		

2003

Not much has changed for Mercury's 2003 Sable. All cars feature a new cupholder design, and the LS Premium trim level offers a no-charge leather trim. Mercury claims that "customers who appreciate understated sophistication will want to know more about the Platinum Edition," which includes aluminum wheels with a center cap ornament and interior trim pieces, perforated leather and a fender badge. Power windows, locks, tilt steering and floor mats are standard across the board, and two new colors brighten up the Sable.

Mileage Category: D

Body Styles	TMV Pricing			Body Styles	TMV Pricing		
	Trade	Private	Dealer		Trade	Private	Dealer
4 Dr GS Sdn	7590	8493	9997	4 Dr LS Sdn	8610	9634	11340
4 Dr GS Wgn	8157	9126	10742	4 Dr LS Wgn	9002	10072	11856

Options	Price	Options	Price
AM/FM/CD Audio System [Opt on GS]	+143	Power Adjustable Foot Pedals [Opt on GS]	+189
Antilock Brakes	+367	Power Driver Seat [Opt on GS]	+135
Chrome Wheels [Opt on LS]	+213	Power Moonroof [Opt on LS]	+538
Compact Disc Changer [Opt on LS]	+216	Power Passenger Seat [Opt on LS]	+213
Front Side Airbag Restraints	+135	Special Leather Seat Trim [Opt on LS]	+213
Leather Seats [Opt on LS]	+276	Spoke Wheels [Opt on GS]	+267
MACH Audio System [Opt on LS]	+159	Traction Control System	+138

2002

Four new colors are added to the paint chart, while approach lighting and an auto-dimming rearview mirror with compass become standard equipment.

Mileage Category: D

Body Styles	TMV Pricing		
	Trade	Private	Dealer
4 Dr GS Sdn	6077	6917	8317
4 Dr GS Wgn	6448	7340	8825

Options	Price
AM/FM/CD Audio System [Opt on GS]	+128
AM/FM/Cassette/CD Changer Audio System	+169
Antilock Brakes	+329
Chrome Wheels	+143
Front Side Airbag Restraints	+133
Leather Seats	+247

Body Styles	TMV Pricing		
	Trade	Private	Dealer
4 Dr LS Premium Sdn	6949	7910	9512
4 Dr LS Premium Wgn	7135	8122	9765

Options	Price
MACH Audio System	+131
Power Driver Seat [Opt on GS]	+121
Power Moonroof	+431
Power Passenger Seat	+169
Spoke Wheels [Opt on GS]	+191

2001

A new child safety-seat restraint system is in place as well as a larger 18-gallon fuel tank. There's also a clearcoat metallic paint swap, trading Tropic Green for Spruce Green. Otherwise, no changes for the recently freshened Sable.

Mileage Category: D

Body Styles	TMV Pricing		
	Trade	Private	Dealer
4 Dr GS Sdn	5135	6279	7336
4 Dr GS Wgn	5435	6646	7764
4 Dr LS Premium Sdn	5680	6947	8117

Options	Price
3.0L V6 DOHC 24V FI Engine [Opt on LS]	+287
Aluminum/Alloy Wheels [Opt on GS Sdn]	+163
Antilock Brakes	+280
Chrome Wheels	+122
Compact Disc Changer	+144

Body Styles	TMV Pricing		
	Trade	Private	Dealer
4 Dr LS Premium Wgn	5936	7259	8481
4 Dr LS Sdn	5235	6403	7481

Options	Price
Front Side Airbag Restraints	+161
Power Driver Seat [Opt on GS]	+163
Power Moonroof	+367
Power Passenger Seat [Opt on LS Premium]	+144
Premium Audio System	+276

2000

The 2000 Mercury Sable gains new sheet metal and additional refinements. The freshened styling includes a raised hood and deck lid, a larger grille, improved headlamps and taillights and new mirrors. The instrument panel has been updated, and the new integrated control panel provides better functionality. The Sable also gains significant improvements to its safety and powertrain components.

Mileage Category: D

Body Styles	TMV Pricing		
	Trade	Private	Dealer
4 Dr GS Sdn	3886	4916	5926
4 Dr GS Wgn	4235	5357	6457
4 Dr LS Premium Sdn	4410	5578	6723

Options	Price
3.0L V6 DOHC 24V FI Engine [Opt on LS,Wgn]	+249
Aluminum/Alloy Wheels [Opt on GS Sdn]	+142
Antilock Brakes	+244
Chrome Wheels	+208
Compact Disc Changer	+126

Body Styles	TMV Pricing		
	Trade	Private	Dealer
4 Dr LS Premium Wgn	4584	5799	6990
4 Dr LS Sdn	4170	5275	6359

Options	Price
Front Side Airbag Restraints	+140
Power Driver Seat [Opt on GS]	+142
Power Moonroof	+265
Power Passenger Seat [Opt on LS Premium]	+126

1999

Body Styles	TMV Pricing		
	Trade	Private	Dealer
4 Dr GS Sdn	2864	3726	4623
4 Dr LS Sdn	3035	3949	4900

Options	Price
3.0L V6 DOHC 24V FI Engine	+155
Antilock Brakes	+211
Chrome Wheels	+161

Body Styles	TMV Pricing		
	Trade	Private	Dealer
4 Dr LS Wgn	3231	4203	5215

Options	Price
Leather Seats	+250
Power Moonroof	+207

Still smarting from that 1996 "redesign" that had many longtime Sable fans running to the competition, Mercury performed some minor cosmetic surgery in '98 to help soften the Sable's front end. This year's changes are limited to new wheel designs, a revised gauge cluster and interior console, as well as suspension alterations designed to improve overall ride quality. The particulate filtration system has been deleted from this year's models.

1998

A mild facelift and fewer options are the only change to Mercury's midsize sedan.

Mileage Category: D

Body Styles	TMV Pricing		
	Trade	Private	Dealer
4 Dr GS Sdn	2375	3235	4205
4 Dr LS Sdn	2494	3398	4418

Body Styles	TMV Pricing		
	Trade	Private	Dealer
4 Dr LS Wgn	2720	3707	4819

1998 (cont'd)

Options	Price
3.0L V6 DOHC 24V FI Engine	+118
Antilock Brakes	+179
Chrome Wheels	+138

Options	Price
Leather Seats	+213
Power Moonroof	+176

1997

The 1997 Sable LS can now be had with Ford's outstanding Mach audio system. Other changes, occurring at the end of the 1996 model year, include the addition of a mass airflow sensor to the Vulcan V6, and improvements to the Duratec V6 to improve responsiveness.

Mileage Category: D

Body Styles	TMV Pricing		
	Trade	Private	Dealer
4 Dr GS Sdn	1889	2707	3706
4 Dr GS Wgn	1936	2774	3798

Body Styles	TMV Pricing		
	Trade	Private	Dealer
4 Dr LS Sdn	2101	3010	4121
4 Dr LS Wgn	2101	3010	4121

Options	Price
Antilock Brakes	+155
Chrome Wheels	+120
Compact Disc Changer	+122

Options	Price
Leather Seats [Opt on GS]	+204
Power Moonroof	+152

1996

Fresh off the drawing boards for 1996, and it seems the drawing boards were poorly lit. Styling is heavy-handed and homely, but definitely not dull. Otherwise, the new Sable is an excellent car, powered by new engines, suspended by new components and innovative in nearly every way. Longer and wider sedan and wagon bodystyles are offered in GS and LS trim.

Mileage Category: D

Body Styles	TMV Pricing		
	Trade	Private	Dealer
4 Dr G Sdn	1400	2114	3099
4 Dr GS Sdn	1467	2214	3245
4 Dr GS Wgn	1584	2390	3505

Body Styles	TMV Pricing		
	Trade	Private	Dealer
4 Dr LS Sdn	1618	2442	3579
4 Dr LS Wgn	1753	2647	3881

Options	Price
Antilock Brakes	+131
Leather Seats	+172

Options	Price
Power Moonroof	+129

1995

Mileage Category: D

Body Styles	TMV Pricing		
	Trade	Private	Dealer
4 Dr GS Sdn	905	1481	2442
4 Dr GS Wgn	960	1573	2595

Body Styles	TMV Pricing		
	Trade	Private	Dealer
4 Dr LS Sdn	999	1635	2696
4 Dr LS Wgn	1090	1785	2943

Options	Price
3.8L V6 OHV 12V FI Engine	+77
Antilock Brakes [Opt on GS]	+110
Chrome Wheels	+85

Options	Price
Leather Seats	+131
Power Moonroof	+108

Last year for the Sable in its current form. New cylinder heads and crankshafts are intended to decrease engine noise by reducing vibration. Solar control window glass makes a brief appearance on the sedan and wagon.

Tracer

1999

Mileage Category: B

Body Styles	TMV Pricing		
	Trade	Private	Dealer
4 Dr GS Sdn	2106	3033	3998
4 Dr LS Sdn	2252	3243	4275

Body Styles	TMV Pricing		
	Trade	Private	Dealer
4 Dr LS Wgn	2456	3537	4662

Options	Price
Air Conditioning [Opt on GS]	+222
Antilock Brakes	+211

Options	Price
Automatic 4-Speed Transmission	+227
Leather Seats	+153

The Tracer gets a new sport wagon model to help extend its appeal to young buyers. The LS Sport Wagon model comes standard with leather seating surfaces and 15-inch wheels. Other changes include a standard interior trunk release on all sedans. A remote keyless entry and AM/FM cassette player is standard on LS models.

1998

No changes to Mercury's recently redesigned entry-level car.

Mileage Category: B

Body Styles	TMV Pricing		
	Trade	Private	Dealer
4 Dr GS Sdn	1597	2476	3467
4 Dr LS Sdn	1698	2631	3684

Body Styles	TMV Pricing		
	Trade	Private	Dealer
4 Dr LS Wgn	1798	2786	3901

Options	Price
Air Conditioning [Opt on GS]	+189
Antilock Brakes	+179

Options	Price
Automatic 4-Speed Transmission	+194
Compact Disc Changer	+122

1997

The Mercury Tracer is totally redesigned this year with enhancements across the board. The most noticeable improvements are in the powertrain and in the ride quality. New sheet metal gives the Tracer a rounder, more aerodynamic appearance as well. The speedy LTS sedan is discontinued.

Mileage Category: B

Body Styles	TMV Pricing		
	Trade	Private	Dealer
4 Dr GS Sdn	1200	1947	2861
4 Dr LS Sdn	1249	2026	2976

Options	Price
Air Conditioning	+163
Antilock Brakes	+155

Body Styles	TMV Pricing		
	Trade	Private	Dealer
4 Dr LS Wgn	1297	2103	3089

Options	Price
Automatic 4-Speed Transmission	+168

1996

Automatic transmission modifications make base Tracers more responsive, and the standard 1.9-liter engine now goes 100,000 miles between tune-ups. Last year's integrated child seat continues, and Trio models are now available in all colors, including a new one called Toreador Red.

Body Styles	TMV Pricing		
	Trade	Private	Dealer
4 Dr LTS Sdn	1014	1716	2686
4 Dr STD Sdn	883	1493	2336

Options	Price
Air Conditioning	+136
Antilock Brakes	+131

Body Styles	TMV Pricing		
	Trade	Private	Dealer
4 Dr STD Wgn	926	1567	2451

Options	Price
Automatic 4-Speed Transmission	+142

1995

A passenger airbag is finally available for the Tracer. Unfortunately, some engineering genius decided to retain the annoying motorized shoulder belts. An integrated child seat is introduced as an optional safety feature. The Trio package is introduced, designed to give budget shoppers the option of purchasing some of the more popular LTS features such as the spoiler, aluminum wheels and leather-wrapped steering wheel.

Mileage Category: B

Body Styles	TMV Pricing		
	Trade	Private	Dealer
4 Dr LTS Sdn	724	1270	2180
4 Dr STD Sdn	659	1155	1982

Options	Price
Air Conditioning	+114
Antilock Brakes	+110

Body Styles	TMV Pricing		
	Trade	Private	Dealer
4 Dr STD Wgn	673	1180	2026

Options	Price
Automatic 4-Speed Transmission	+119
Power Moonroof	+76

Villager

2002

Mileage Category: P

Body Styles	TMV Pricing		
	Trade	Private	Dealer
4 Dr Estate Pass Van	10916	12190	14314
4 Dr STD Pass Van	8113	9060	10637

Options	Price
AM/FM/Cassette/CD Changer Audio System	+418
Air Conditioning - Front and Rear [Opt on STD]	+387
Antilock Brakes [Opt on Sport,STD]	+329
Automatic Climate Control	+119
Compact Disc Changer	+179

Body Styles	TMV Pricing		
	Trade	Private	Dealer
4 Dr Sport Pass Van	10236	11431	13422

Options	Price
Digital Instrument Panel	+143
Power Driver Seat [Opt on STD]	+121
Power Moonroof	+375
VCR Entertainment System	+626

After 2002, it's outta here. As such, it comes as no surprise that there are virtually no significant changes to the Villager this year.

2001

Numerous exterior and interior revisions are on tap for 2001. Also new are optional 16-inch wheels and tires, drivetrain changes for better engine smoothness, new seatbelt pre-tensioners to improve safety, and the addition of an anchorage point for attaching a child seat.

Mileage Category: P

Body Styles	TMV Pricing		
	Trade	Private	Dealer
4 Dr Estate Pass Van	8629	10312	11865
4 Dr STD Pass Van	6820	8150	9377

Options	Price
AM/FM/Cassette/CD Audio System	+357
AM/FM/Cassette/CD Changer Audio System	+153
Air Conditioning - Front and Rear [Opt on Sport]	+144
Antilock Brakes	+280
Digital Instrument Panel [Opt on Estate]	+122
Leather Seats [Opt on Sport]	+328

Body Styles	TMV Pricing		
	Trade	Private	Dealer
4 Dr Sport Pass Van	8366	9998	11504

Options	Price
Power Driver Seat [Opt on STD]	+126
Power Moonroof	+320
Premium Audio System [Opt on STD]	+128
Two-Tone Paint	+122
VCR Entertainment System	+534

2000

The convenience, comfort and luxury option packages have been simplified. All 2000 Villagers meet federal low emission vehicle status and come standard with a child seat-anchor system. A new rear-seat video entertainment system is now optional.

Mileage Category: P

Body Styles	TMV Pricing		
	Trade	Private	Dealer
4 Dr Estate Pass Van	6992	8609	10194
4 Dr STD Pass Van	5658	6967	8251

Options	Price
AM/FM/Cassette/CD Audio System	+246
Air Conditioning - Front and Rear [Opt on STD]	+166
Antilock Brakes	+244
Compact Disc Changer	+133
Leather Seats [Opt on Sport]	+224

Body Styles	TMV Pricing		
	Trade	Private	Dealer
4 Dr Sport Pass Van	6474	7972	9440

Options	Price
Power Moonroof	+278
Premium Audio System [Opt on STD]	+253
Privacy Glass	+149
VCR Entertainment System	+251

1999

The Mercury Villager is completely redesigned for '99. Improvements range from a more powerful engine to a larger interior to a second sliding door on the driver side. New styling features include larger headlights and a distinctive front grille. Inside, ergonomics have been addressed with easier to reach controls and an innovative storage shelf located behind the third seat.

Mileage Category: P

Body Styles	TMV Pricing		
	Trade	Private	Dealer
4 Dr Estate Pass Van	5098	6490	7938
4 Dr STD Pass Van	4397	5597	6846

Options	Price
AM/FM/Cassette/CD Audio System	+191
Air Conditioning - Front and Rear	+129
Antilock Brakes	+211
Leather Seats	+174

Body Styles	TMV Pricing		
	Trade	Private	Dealer
4 Dr Sport Pass Van	4944	6292	7696

Options	Price
Power Moonroof	+217
Premium Audio System [Opt on STD]	+196
Privacy Glass	+116

1998

No changes to the 1998 Villager as Mercury readies a replacement.

Mileage Category: P

Body Styles	TMV Pricing		
	Trade	Private	Dealer
3 Dr GS Pass Van	3413	4481	5685
3 Dr LS Pass Van	4014	5270	6686

Options	Price
AM/FM/Cassette/CD Audio System	+163
Air Conditioning [Opt on GS]	+203
Air Conditioning - Front and Rear	+203
Antilock Brakes	+179

Body Styles	TMV Pricing		
	Trade	Private	Dealer
3 Dr Nautica Pass Van	4107	5392	6841

Options	Price
Compact Disc Changer	+161
Leather Seats [Opt on LS]	+148
Power Moonroof	+184
Premium Audio System [Opt on GS]	+167

1997

For 1997, the Villager offers a few more luxury items to distinguish it from the Nissan Quest. Quad captain's chairs are a nice alternative to the middle-row bench, and the addition of rear radio controls and rear air conditioning should also make rear-seat passengers happy.

Mileage Category: P

Body Styles	TMV Pricing		
	Trade	Private	Dealer
3 Dr GS Pass Van	2765	3760	4976
3 Dr LS Pass Van	3252	4421	5850

Options	Price
AM/FM/Cassette/CD Audio System	+141
Air Conditioning [Opt on GS]	+176
Air Conditioning - Front and Rear	+176
Antilock Brakes [Opt on GS]	+155

Body Styles	TMV Pricing		
	Trade	Private	Dealer
3 Dr Nautica Pass Van	3281	4462	5905

Options	Price
Captain Chairs (4) [Opt on LS]	+128
Leather Seats [Opt on LS]	+128
Power Moonroof	+160
Premium Audio System [Opt on GS]	+145

1996

A passenger-side airbag is installed in a redesigned dashboard for 1996, and fresh front and rear styling updates this versatile van. Villager also gets an optional integrated child seat, automatic climate control system and remote keyless entry system. Substantial trim and functional changes make Villager competitive once again.

Mileage Category: P

Body Styles	TMV Pricing		
	Trade	Private	Dealer
3 Dr GS Pass Van	2231	3143	4403
3 Dr LS Pass Van	2513	3540	4959

Options	Price
AM/FM/Cassette/CD Audio System	+119
Air Conditioning [Opt on GS]	+148
Air Conditioning - Front and Rear	+148

Body Styles	TMV Pricing		
	Trade	Private	Dealer
3 Dr Nautica Pass Van	2625	3698	5180

Options	Price
Power Moonroof	+134
Premium Audio System [Opt on GS]	+122

1995

Mileage Category: P

No changes for the Villager.

Body Styles	TMV Pricing		
	Trade	Private	Dealer
3 Dr GS Pass Van	1556	2241	3383
3 Dr LS Pass Van	1864	2684	4050

Options	Price
AM/FM/Cassette/CD Audio System	+100
Air Conditioning	+125
Captain Chairs (4) [Opt on LS]	+89

Body Styles	TMV Pricing		
	Trade	Private	Dealer
3 Dr Nautica Pass Van	2015	2902	4381

Options	Price
Leather Seats [Opt on LS]	+91
Power Moonroof	+113
Premium Audio System	+103

Cooper

2004

Both trims offer a new three-spoke leather sport steering wheel. A rear power socket returns as a standard item, and beige leather sport seats are now available. A digital speedometer readout has been added to the electronic display, and an instantaneous fuel-consumption function has been added to its on-board computer.

Mileage Category: E

Body Styles	TMV Pricing		
	Trade	Private	Dealer
2 Dr S S/C Hbk	17134	18223	20037

Options	Price
16 Inch Wheels [Opt on STD]	+500
17 Inch Wheels [Opt on S]	+525
Automatic Climate Control	+300
Automatic Stability Control	+170
Commemorative Edition [Opt on S]	+7000
Continuously Variable Transmission [Opt on STD]	+1300
Cruise Control	+200
Fog Lights	+140
Harman Kardon Audio System	+550
Headlight Washers [Opt on S]	+175
Heated Front Seats	+150
Heated Front and Rear Seats	+270
Leather Seats	+1300

Body Styles	TMV Pricing		
	Trade	Private	Dealer
2 Dr STD Hbk	14679	15461	16763

Options	Price
Leather Steering Wheel [Opt on STD]	+150
Metallic Paint	+400
Navigation System	+1700
Park Distance Control (Rear)	+350
Power Heated Mirrors	+150
Power Panorama Roof	+500
Rain Sensing Windshield Wipers	+150
Sport Seats	+225
Sport Suspension [Opt on STD]	+500
Traction Control System [Opt on STD]	+165
Trip Computer	+150
Xenon Headlamps	+290

2003

For their second season in the U.S. market, the Cooper and the Cooper S will now come with a second remote key and pre-wiring for a dealer-installed alarm system. Anthracite (smoke gray, that is) interior trim is available as a no-cost option for both cars, and the Cooper S is eligible for the high-gloss silver interior treatment found in the base Cooper. Sound systems will be satellite radio-ready this year, and the rear cargo area now has a power point.

Mileage Category: E

Body Styles	TMV Pricing		
	Trade	Private	Dealer
2 Dr S S/C Hbk	16309	17348	19079

Options	Price
16 Inch Wheels [Opt on STD]	+474
17 Inch Wheels [Opt on S]	+497
Automatic Climate Control	+284
Automatic Stability Control	+450
Continuously Variable Transmission [Opt on STD]	+1184
Fog Lights	+133
Harman Kardon Audio System	+521
Heated Front Seats	+256
Heated Front and Rear Seats	+256
Leather Seats	+1184
Leather Steering Wheel [Opt on STD]	+142
Metallic Paint	+379

Body Styles	TMV Pricing		
	Trade	Private	Dealer
2 Dr STD Hbk	13432	14361	15910

Options	Price
Navigation System	+1515
Park Distance Control (Rear)	+284
Power Heated Mirrors	+142
Power Panorama Roof	+758
Rain Sensing Windshield Wipers	+133
Runflat Tire System [Opt on STD]	+284
Sport Seats	+213
Sport Suspension [Opt on STD]	+474
Steering Wheel Radio Controls	+166
Traction Control System [Opt on STD]	+260
Trip Computer	+142
Xenon Headlamps	+331

2002

BMW subsidiary, Mini, resurrects an unforgettable old favorite with the release of the Cooper. Available with either a 115-horsepower four-cylinder or a supercharged version of that engine worthy of 163 hp, the pint-sized but glamorous three-door hatchback features BMW-engineered suspension and steering and a base MSRP under 17 grand. Whether you're a 40-something hoping to relive earlier days, an autocross enthusiast or just the mild-mannered next-door neighbor, we expect that you'll run to the nearest BMW dealership in search of this coveted bundle of joy.

Mileage Category: E

Body Styles	TMV Pricing		
	Trade	Private	Dealer
2 Dr S S/C Hbk	15140	16347	18358

Options	Price
16 Inch Wheels [Opt on STD]	+343
17 Inch Wheels	+455
Automatic Climate Control	+260
Automatic Dimming Rearview Mirror	+117
Automatic Stability Control	+412
Continuously Variable Transmission	+1084
Fog Lights	+121
Harman Kardon Audio System	+477
Heated Front Seats	+234
Leather Seats	+1084
Metallic Paint	+347
Navigation System	+2038

Body Styles	TMV Pricing		
	Trade	Private	Dealer
2 Dr STD Hbk	12368	13427	15191

Options	Price
Park Distance Control (Rear)	+260
Power Heated Mirrors	+130
Power Panorama Roof	+694
Rain Sensing Windshield Wipers	+121
Runflat Tire System [Opt on STD]	+260
Sport Seats	+195
Sport Suspension [Opt on STD]	+434
Steering Wheel Radio Controls	+152
Traction Control System [Opt on STD]	+238
Trip Computer	+130
Xenon Headlamps	+304

3000GT

1999

Mileage Category: F

Body Styles	TMV Pricing		
	Trade	Private	Dealer
2 Dr SL Hbk	11945	13827	15785
2 Dr STD Hbk	8616	9973	11385

Options	Price
AM/FM/CD Audio System	+122
AM/FM/Cassette/CD Audio System [Opt on STD]	+223
Automatic 4-Speed Transmission [Opt on SL,STD]	+273

Body Styles	TMV Pricing		
	Trade	Private	Dealer
2 Dr VR-4 Turbo AWD Hbk	16626	19246	21972

Options	Price
Compact Disc Changer	+184
Leather Seats [Opt on STD]	+253

The 1999 3000GT sees some styling changes and a few choice pieces of standard equipment, including antilock brakes and a power sunroof for the SL. Last year for this once proud supercar.

1998

Mileage Category: F

SL and VR-4 models get a standard power sunroof this year.

Body Styles	TMV Pricing		
	Trade	Private	Dealer
2 Dr SL Hbk	9882	11546	13423
2 Dr STD Hbk	7203	8417	9785

Options	Price
AM/FM/Cassette/CD Audio System [Opt on STD]	+192
Antilock Brakes [Opt on SL]	+226
Automatic 4-Speed Transmission [Opt on SL,STD]	+236

Body Styles	TMV Pricing		
	Trade	Private	Dealer
2 Dr VR-4 Turbo AWD Hbk	14377	16798	19529

Options	Price
Compact Disc Changer	+159
Leather Seats [Opt on STD]	+218

1997

A value-leader base model is introduced. It has less than stellar performance and we think that it's embarrassing that this car is in the same lineup as the earth-scorching VR-4.

Body Styles	TMV Pricing		
	Trade	Private	Dealer
2 Dr SL Hbk	7829	9248	10983
2 Dr STD Hbk	6084	7187	8534

Options	Price
AM/FM/Cassette/CD Audio System [Opt on STD]	+174
Antilock Brakes [Opt on SL]	+205
Automatic 4-Speed Transmission [Opt on SL,STD]	+210

Body Styles	TMV Pricing		
	Trade	Private	Dealer
2 Dr VR-4 Turbo AWD Hbk	12257	14479	17194

Options	Price
Compact Disc Changer	+144
Leather Seats [Opt on STD]	+199
Power Sunroof	+211

1996

Base model gets new cloth interior, while upper trim levels receive a choice of black or tan leather. Remote keyless entry gets panic feature, and several new colors are available.

Body Styles	TMV Pricing		
	Trade	Private	Dealer
2 Dr SL Hbk	6494	7626	9189
2 Dr STD Hbk	5198	6104	7354
2 Dr Spyder SL Conv	11321	13294	16018

Options	Price
Automatic 4-Speed Transmission [Opt on SL,STD]	+191
Chrome Wheels [Opt on SL]	+120

Body Styles	TMV Pricing		
	Trade	Private	Dealer
2 Dr Spyder VR-4 Turbo AWD Conv	13089	15370	18521
2 Dr VR-4 Turbo AWD Hbk	9011	10582	12751

Options	Price
Compact Disc Changer	+123
Power Sunroof	+180

1995

The VR-4 gains chrome-plated alloy wheels as standard equipment. A hardtop drop top joins the 3000GT family this year.

Body Styles	TMV Pricing		
	Trade	Private	Dealer
2 Dr SL Hbk	4938	5902	7508
2 Dr STD Hbk	4179	4995	6354
2 Dr Spyder SL Conv	9330	11152	14188

Options	Price
AM/FM/Cassette/CD Audio System	+120
Automatic 4-Speed Transmission [Opt on SL,STD]	+144
Chrome Wheels [Opt on SL]	+110

Body Styles	TMV Pricing		
	Trade	Private	Dealer
2 Dr Spyder VR-4 Turbo AWD Conv	11069	13230	16831
2 Dr VR-4 Turbo AWD Hbk	6751	8070	10267

Options	Price
Compact Disc Changer	+99
Power Sunroof	+145

Mitsubishi
Diamante

Diamante

2004

Mileage Category: H

Body Styles	TMV Pricing		
	Trade	Private	Dealer
4 Dr ES Sdn	12796	13966	15917
4 Dr LS Sdn	14042	15206	17146

Options	Price
Heated Front Seats [Opt on LS]	+250
Leather Seats [Opt on VR-X]	+450
Power Driver Seat w/Memory [Opt on VR-X]	+140

Body Styles	TMV Pricing		
	Trade	Private	Dealer
4 Dr VR-X Sdn	13955	15146	17130

Options	Price
Power Heated Mirrors [Opt on LS]	+175
Sport Seats [Opt on VR-X]	+150
Traction Control System [Opt on LS]	+295

The Diamante receives a few minor styling changes that include a revised front fascia and a new front grille on the outside and a redesigned center console and dash on the inside. A Sportronic automatic transmission, projector beam foglights and a 270-watt Infinity stereo are now standard on the LS and VR-X. Additionally, all VR-X models get new sport taillamps and a rear spoiler, while the base ES gets upgraded interior fabric.

2003

After introducing the sporty VR-X trim level halfway through 2002, the Diamante continues into 2003 with no changes.

Mileage Category: H

Body Styles	TMV Pricing		
	Trade	Private	Dealer
4 Dr ES Sdn	11028	12085	13847
4 Dr LS Sdn	12054	13210	15138

Options	Price
Heated Front Seats [Opt on LS]	+150
Infinity Audio System [Opt on VR-X]	+209
Leather Seats [Opt on VR-X]	+503

Body Styles	TMV Pricing		
	Trade	Private	Dealer
4 Dr VR-X Sdn	11951	13097	15007

Options	Price
Rear Spoiler [Opt on VR-X]	+147
Traction Control System [Opt on LS]	+165

2002

A sporty new trim level, the VR-X, debuts in an attempt to put some life into the Diamante's sales charts. Otherwise, only minor changes are in store for the Diamante this year. Slight styling tweaks have been applied to the front and rear, and the interior features redesigned audio controls and an emergency inside-trunk release. One mechanical change has been made this year -- Electronic Brakeforce Distribution (EBD) has been added to all trim levels.

Mileage Category: H

Body Styles	TMV Pricing		
	Trade	Private	Dealer
4 Dr ES Sdn	8185	9135	10719
4 Dr LS Sdn	9101	10158	11918

Options	Price
Heated Front Seats	+120
Infinity Audio System [Opt on VR-X]	+168

Body Styles	TMV Pricing		
	Trade	Private	Dealer
4 Dr VR-X Sdn	8610	9610	11276

Options	Price
Power Moonroof [Opt on VR-X]	+409
Traction Control System [Opt on LS]	+132

2001

This Mitsubishi model doesn't change much from last year, but product planners add tether anchors for child seats, foglights on the LS and new seat fabric and wheel cover for the ES. Greenies can rest easy knowing that it meets LEV standards for all states.

Mileage Category: H

Body Styles	TMV Pricing		
	Trade	Private	Dealer
4 Dr ES Sdn	6954	8292	9527

Options	Price
Traction Control System	+116

Body Styles	TMV Pricing		
	Trade	Private	Dealer
4 Dr LS Sdn	7778	9275	10656

2000

Other than bringing back the ES and LS trim levels, this Mitsubishi model doesn't change much from last year. Product planners add a couple of standard features, replace four colors and offer a new all-weather package for the LS buyer.

Mileage Category: H

Body Styles	TMV Pricing		
	Trade	Private	Dealer
4 Dr ES Sdn	5644	6952	8234

Options	Price
AM/FM/Cassette/CD Audio System	+143
Aluminum/Alloy Wheels [Opt on ES]	+301

Body Styles	TMV Pricing		
	Trade	Private	Dealer
4 Dr LS Sdn	6283	7738	9165

Options	Price
Compact Disc Changer	+215

1999

Only one Diamante model is available, replacing the ES and LS models. Mitsubishi also adds some new standard features, options and exterior colors to this top-level model.

Mileage Category: H

Body Styles	TMV Pricing		
	Trade	Private	Dealer
4 Dr STD Sdn	4808	6091	7427

Options	Price
AM/FM/CD Audio System	+122
AM/FM/Cassette/CD Audio System	+122

Options	Price
Aluminum/Alloy Wheels	+258
Chrome Wheels	+258

Options	Price
Compact Disc Changer	+184
Leather Seats	+276

Options	Price
Power Moonroof	+295

1998

All Diamantes get standard ABS and remote keyless entry for 1998.

Mileage Category: H

Body Styles	TMV Pricing		
	Trade	Private	Dealer
4 Dr ES Sdn	3680	4771	6002

Body Styles	TMV Pricing		
	Trade	Private	Dealer
4 Dr LS Sdn	4619	5990	7536

Options	Price
Aluminum/Alloy Wheels [Opt on ES]	+222
Chrome Wheels	+222
Compact Disc Changer	+159

Options	Price
Leather Seats [Opt on ES]	+238
Power Moonroof [Opt on ES]	+255
Power Passenger Seat [Opt on LS]	+139

1997

After a one-year hiatus, the Diamante returns to the Mitsubishi lineup sporting clean and crisp styling, a full-load of luxury features and a lower price. The old car barely registered on near-luxury car buyers' radar; this new one deserves consideration and a close inspection.

Mileage Category: H

Body Styles	TMV Pricing		
	Trade	Private	Dealer
4 Dr ES Sdn	3040	4053	5290

Body Styles	TMV Pricing		
	Trade	Private	Dealer
4 Dr LS Sdn	3674	4898	6394

Options	Price
Aluminum/Alloy Wheels [Opt on ES]	+202
Antilock Brakes	+182
Compact Disc Changer	+144

Options	Price
Leather Seats [Opt on ES]	+217
Power Moonroof	+232

1996

The only Diamantes sold this year were for fleet sales. So unless you see one at a rental car auction, chances are not good that you'll find a used 1996 model.

Mileage Category: H

Body Styles	TMV Pricing		
	Trade	Private	Dealer
4 Dr ES Sdn	2653	3621	4958

1995

Mileage Category: H

Body Styles	TMV Pricing		
	Trade	Private	Dealer
4 Dr ES Sdn	1769	2538	3821
4 Dr LS Sdn	2265	3252	4896

Body Styles	TMV Pricing		
	Trade	Private	Dealer
4 Dr STD Wgn	1814	2604	3921

Options	Price
Antilock Brakes [Opt on STD]	+171
Compact Disc Changer	+136
Leather Seats [Opt on STD]	+181

Options	Price
Power Moonroof	+175
Power Passenger Seat w/Memory [Opt on LS]	+90
Traction Control System	+132

The base Diamante sedan is sent out to pasture, available only to fleet purchasers such as rental car agencies. No other changes for the Mitsubishi flagship.

Eclipse
2004

Mileage Category: E

Body Styles	TMV Pricing		
	Trade	Private	Dealer
2 Dr GS Hbk	11172	12394	14431
2 Dr GT Hbk	12859	14125	16235

Body Styles	TMV Pricing		
	Trade	Private	Dealer
2 Dr GTS Cpe	14530	15789	17886
2 Dr RS Hbk	10402	11604	13608

Options	Price
Automatic 4-Speed Transmission	+800
Infinity Audio System [Opt on GS, GT]	+270

Options	Price
Leather Seats [Opt on GT]	+610
Power Moonroof [Opt on GS, GT]	+800

The base RS now has power mirrors, and the audio system has been upgraded to a six-speaker setup. All Eclipse models get a seatbelt reminder light on the instrument panel.

2003

Mileage Category: E

Body Styles	TMV Pricing		
	Trade	Private	Dealer
2 Dr GS Hbk	9194	10045	11462
2 Dr GT Hbk	10579	11558	13188

Body Styles	TMV Pricing		
	Trade	Private	Dealer
2 Dr GTS Cpe	11913	13014	14849
2 Dr RS Hbk	8930	9755	11131

A new higher-performance Eclipse joins the lineup. Dubbed the GTS, its 3.0-liter V6 has 10 more horses than the same engine found under the hood of the GT, and a number of luxury features justify its standing as the top Eclipse. A new front fascia along with revised front and rear light clusters round out the changes.

2003 (cont'd)

Options	Price
Automatic 4-Speed Transmission	+479
Infinity Audio System [Opt on GS,GT]	+162

Options	Price
Leather Seats [Opt on GT]	+365
Power Moonroof [Opt on GS,GT]	+479

2002

Only trivial changes are in store for Mitsubishi's Eclipse this year. Two new exterior colors (Titanium and Flash Blue) are added, as well as a Mitsubishi triple-diamond chrome badge. GS and GT models get illuminated vanity mirrors and a glovebox lamp as standard equipment.

Mileage Category: E

Body Styles	TMV Pricing		
	Trade	Private	Dealer
2 Dr GS Hbk	7603	8480	9942
2 Dr GT Hbk	8679	9680	11349

Body Styles	TMV Pricing		
	Trade	Private	Dealer
2 Dr RS Hbk	7243	8079	9472

Options	Price
17 Inch Wheels	+192
AM/FM/Cassette/CD Changer Audio System	+168
Antilock Brakes	+327
Automatic 4-Speed Transmission	+385
Front Side Airbag Restraints	+120

Options	Price
Infinity Audio System	+130
Leather Seats	+277
Power Driver Seat	+120
Power Moonroof	+349

2001

The new year for the Eclipse sees a standard spoiler, tether anchors for child seats and engines that meet LEV emissions standards.

Mileage Category: E

Body Styles	TMV Pricing		
	Trade	Private	Dealer
2 Dr GS Hbk	6395	7617	8744
2 Dr GT Hbk	7261	8647	9928

Body Styles	TMV Pricing		
	Trade	Private	Dealer
2 Dr RS Hbk	6100	7266	8342

Options	Price
AM/FM/Cassette/CD Changer Audio System [Opt on GT]	+148
Antilock Brakes	+303
Automatic 4-Speed Transmission	+339

Options	Price
Infinity Audio System	+127
Leather Seats	+193
Power Moonroof [Std on GS]	+310

2000

Mitsubishi's 2000 Eclipse is redesigned inside and out and based on the Galant sedan platform, embodying a youthful image and providing a sporty drive. V6 power is now available, but the spunky turbocharged engine is gone as is the all-wheel-drive model.

Mileage Category: E

Body Styles	TMV Pricing		
	Trade	Private	Dealer
2 Dr GS Hbk	5646	6787	7906
2 Dr GT Hbk	6125	7363	8577

Body Styles	TMV Pricing		
	Trade	Private	Dealer
2 Dr RS Hbk	5220	6275	7309

Options	Price
AM/FM/Cassette/CD Audio System	+143
Antilock Brakes	+257
Automatic 4-Speed Transmission	+287
Compact Disc Changer	+215

Options	Price
Leather Seats	+164
Power Moonroof [Std on GS]	+262
Rear Spoiler [Std on GT]	+115

1999

For 1999, the Eclipse gets a host of new standard equipment, and there is a new Sports Value Option Package for buyers of the GS.

Mileage Category: E

Body Styles	TMV Pricing		
	Trade	Private	Dealer
2 Dr GS Hbk	4856	6017	7225
2 Dr GS-T Turbo Hbk	5523	6803	8135

Body Styles	TMV Pricing		
	Trade	Private	Dealer
2 Dr GSX Turbo AWD Hbk	7362	9122	10955
2 Dr RS Hbk	4307	5338	6410

Options	Price
AM/FM/CD Audio System [Opt on GS,RS]	+122
AM/FM/Cassette/CD Audio System [Opt on GS]	+122
Air Conditioning [Opt on GS,RS]	+264
Antilock Brakes [Std on GSX]	+232

Options	Price
Automatic 4-Speed Transmission	+224
Compact Disc Changer	+184
Leather Seats [Std on GSX]	+169
Power Moonroof [Opt on GS,RS]	+224

1998

The GSX gets a standard sunroof, power driver seat and remote keyless entry.

Mileage Category: E

Body Styles	TMV Pricing		
	Trade	Private	Dealer
2 Dr GS Hbk	3875	4931	6123
2 Dr GS-T Turbo Hbk	4461	5678	7050

Body Styles	TMV Pricing		
	Trade	Private	Dealer
2 Dr GSX Turbo AWD Hbk	5473	6965	8648
2 Dr RS Hbk	3377	4298	5336

Options	Price
Air Conditioning [Opt on GS,RS]	+228

Options	Price
Antilock Brakes	+200

1998 (cont'd)

Options	Price
Automatic 4-Speed Transmission	+183
Compact Disc Changer	+159

Options	Price
Leather Seats [Std on GSX]	+146
Power Moonroof [Std on GSX]	+194

1997

Revised styling makes the attractive Eclipse drop-dead gorgeous. New interior fabrics and paint colors debut as well. Antilock brakes are now available on the GS model, and a CD player joins its standard equipment list. Two new exterior colors, new seat fabrics and a new interior color combination round out the changes.

Mileage Category: E

Body Styles	TMV Pricing		
	Trade	Private	Dealer
2 Dr GS Hbk	3252	4274	5523
2 Dr GS-T Turbo Hbk	3784	4973	6427
2 Dr GSX Turbo AWD Hbk	4313	5669	7326

Body Styles	TMV Pricing		
	Trade	Private	Dealer
2 Dr RS Hbk	2820	3705	4788
2 Dr STD Hbk	2589	3402	4395

Options	Price
Air Conditioning [Opt on GS,RS,STD]	+207
Antilock Brakes	+182
Automatic 4-Speed Transmission	+166

Options	Price
Compact Disc Changer	+144
Leather Seats	+132
Power Moonroof	+176

1996

Three new colors debut. Audio systems are revised, and RS models can be ordered with a rear spoiler. Remote keyless entry systems get a new panic feature.

Mileage Category: E

Body Styles	TMV Pricing		
	Trade	Private	Dealer
2 Dr GS Hbk	2566	3456	4686
2 Dr GS-T Turbo Hbk	2991	4029	5464
2 Dr GSX Turbo AWD Hbk	3143	4235	5742

Body Styles	TMV Pricing		
	Trade	Private	Dealer
2 Dr RS Hbk	2023	2724	3694
2 Dr STD Hbk	1827	2460	3335

Options	Price
Air Conditioning [Opt on GS-T,GSX]	+177
Antilock Brakes	+155
Automatic 4-Speed Transmission	+144

Options	Price
Compact Disc Changer	+123
Power Sunroof	+150

1995

Radically redesigned, the new Eclipse sports bulging shoulders and no-nonsense looks, particularly in GSX guise. Engine ratings are improved for all models, while the turbocharged GS-T and GSX produce a mighty 210 horsepower at 6,000 rpm. Antilock brakes are optional on all models. Dual airbags are finally standard on the Eclipse.

Mileage Category: E

Body Styles	TMV Pricing		
	Trade	Private	Dealer
2 Dr GS Hbk	1615	2314	3479
2 Dr GS-T Turbo Hbk	1929	2763	4155

Body Styles	TMV Pricing		
	Trade	Private	Dealer
2 Dr GSX Turbo AWD Hbk	2373	3400	5113
2 Dr RS Hbk	1396	2002	3012

Options	Price
Air Conditioning [Opt on GS,RS]	+142
Antilock Brakes	+125
Automatic 4-Speed Transmission	+114

Options	Price
Compact Disc Changer	+99
Leather Seats [Opt on GS,RS]	+91
Power Sunroof	+121

Eclipse Spyder

2004

Revised exterior paint and top colors and a seatbelt reminder are the only changes for this year.

Mileage Category: E

Body Styles	TMV Pricing		
	Trade	Private	Dealer
2 Dr GS Conv	12482	13572	15389
2 Dr GT Conv	13718	14819	16654

Body Styles	TMV Pricing		
	Trade	Private	Dealer
2 Dr GTS Conv	15078	16187	18035

Options	Price
Automatic 4-Speed Transmission	+1000

Options	Price
Leather Seats [Opt on GS, GT]	+600

2003

A new, higher-performance Eclipse joins the lineup. Dubbed the GTS, its 3.0-liter V6 boasts 210 horses and a number of luxury features justify its standing as the top Eclipse. Unlike the 200-horse GT coupe, the Spyder GT gets the more powerful GTS engine. A new front fascia along with revised front and rear light clusters round out the changes.

Mileage Category: E

Body Styles	TMV Pricing		
	Trade	Private	Dealer
2 Dr GS Conv	11481	12391	13909
2 Dr GT Conv	12436	13422	15066

Body Styles	TMV Pricing		
	Trade	Private	Dealer
2 Dr GTS Conv	13498	14568	16353

Options	Price
Automatic 4-Speed Transmission	+598

Options	Price
Leather Seats [Opt on GS,GT]	+359

2002

Only trivial changes are in store for the Eclipse drop-top this year. Two new exterior colors (Titanium and Flash Blue) are added, and as well as a Mitsubishi triple-diamond chrome badge. The interior is upgraded slightly with illuminated vanity mirrors and a glovebox lamp.

Mileage Category: E

Body Styles	TMV Pricing		
	Trade	Private	Dealer
2 Dr GS Conv	9388	10250	11687

Options	Price
AM/FM/Cassette/CD Changer Audio System	+168
Antilock Brakes	+327
Automatic 4-Speed Transmission	+476

Body Styles	TMV Pricing		
	Trade	Private	Dealer
2 Dr GT Conv	10230	11169	12733

Options	Price
Front Side Airbag Restraints	+120
Leather Seats	+289
Power Driver Seat	+120

2001

Mitsubishi's 2001 Eclipse Spyder is all new inside and out and based on the recently redesigned Eclipse Coupe, embodying a youthful image and providing a sporty drive. But the turbocharged engine is no longer on the menu.

Mileage Category: E

Body Styles	TMV Pricing		
	Trade	Private	Dealer
2 Dr GS Conv	8005	9195	10293

Options	Price
AM/FM/Cassette/CD Changer Audio System [Opt on GT]	+148
Antilock Brakes	+303

Body Styles	TMV Pricing		
	Trade	Private	Dealer
2 Dr GT Conv	8721	10019	11217

Options	Price
Automatic 4-Speed Transmission	+423
Leather Seats	+254

1999

Mileage Category: E

Body Styles	TMV Pricing		
	Trade	Private	Dealer
2 Dr GS Conv	5628	6867	8157

Options	Price
Antilock Brakes	+232
Automatic 4-Speed Transmission	+224
Compact Disc Changer	+184

Body Styles	TMV Pricing		
	Trade	Private	Dealer
2 Dr GS-T Turbo Conv	7340	8956	10637

Options	Price
Infinity Audio System [Opt on GS]	+134
Leather Seats [Opt on GS]	+174

Sundance Plum Pearl exterior paint replaces Magenta Gray Pearl, black leather interior replaces the gray, and the GS-T model gets white-faced instrumentation.

1998

Eclipse Spyder GS gets air conditioning, AM/FM stereo with CD player and wheel locks. The Spyder GS-T is now flashier than ever before thanks to standard 16-inch chrome-plated alloy wheels. All models have a fresh black interior appearance with gray cloth.

Mileage Category: E

Body Styles	TMV Pricing		
	Trade	Private	Dealer
2 Dr GS Conv	4371	5478	6727

Options	Price
Antilock Brakes	+200
Automatic 4-Speed Transmission	+212
Compact Disc Changer	+159

Body Styles	TMV Pricing		
	Trade	Private	Dealer
2 Dr GS-T Turbo Conv	5817	7292	8955

Options	Price
Infinity Audio System [Opt on GS]	+116
Leather Seats [Opt on GS]	+150

1997

The 1997 Spyder gets revised front and rear styling. Antilock brakes are now available on the GS model. Two new exterior colors, new seat fabrics and a new interior color combination round out the changes.

Mileage Category: E

Body Styles	TMV Pricing		
	Trade	Private	Dealer
2 Dr GS Conv	3192	4195	5421

Options	Price
Air Conditioning [Opt on GS]	+215
Antilock Brakes	+182
Automatic 4-Speed Transmission	+205

Body Styles	TMV Pricing		
	Trade	Private	Dealer
2 Dr GS-T Turbo Conv	4466	5870	7586

Options	Price
Compact Disc Changer	+144
Leather Seats [Opt on GS]	+132

1996

Sleek and eye-catching, the Spyder makes its debut this year. This convertible is based on the popular Eclipse.

Mileage Category: E

Body Styles	TMV Pricing		
	Trade	Private	Dealer
2 Dr GS Conv	2623	3532	4789

Options	Price
Air Conditioning [Opt on GS,RS,STD]	+177
Antilock Brakes	+155

Body Styles	TMV Pricing		
	Trade	Private	Dealer
2 Dr GS-T Turbo Conv	3676	4951	6712

Options	Price
Automatic 4-Speed Transmission	+144
Compact Disc Changer	+123

Endeavor
2004

Mileage Category: M

Body Styles	TMV Pricing		
	Trade	Private	Dealer
4 Dr LS AWD SUV	13769	14991	17028
4 Dr LS AWD SUV (2004.5)	13629	14851	16889
4 Dr LS SUV	12827	14053	16096
4 Dr LS SUV (2004.5)	12545	13772	15818
4 Dr Limited AWD SUV	16406	17620	19642
4 Dr Limited AWD SUV (2004.5)	16219	17433	19457

Body Styles	TMV Pricing		
	Trade	Private	Dealer
4 Dr Limited SUV	15700	16915	18941
4 Dr Limited SUV (2004.5)	15512	16728	18755
4 Dr XLS AWD SUV	14852	16070	18101
4 Dr XLS AWD SUV (2004.5)	14853	16071	18101
4 Dr XLS SUV	13910	15132	17167
4 Dr XLS SUV (2004.5)	14146	15367	17402

Options	Price
Antilock Brakes [Opt on XLS 2WD, 2004.5 LS]	+350
Front Side Airbag Restraints [Opt on XLS]	+300
Heated Front Seats [Opt on XLS]	+150
Leather Seats [Opt on XLS]	+730

Options	Price
Leather Steering Wheel [Opt on XLS]	+120
Power Heated Mirrors [Opt on XLS]	+150
Power Moonroof [Opt on XLS, Limited]	+800

Although the Endeavor is an all-new vehicle for 2004, an upgraded 2004.5 model was released midway through the year to address some initial shortcomings. The list of upgrades includes more horsepower (225), daytime running lamps, advanced dual-stage front airbags and a tire-pressure monitor as standard. An improved ABS system (with Electronic Brakeforce Distribution and traction control) is now available on LS 2WD models and standard on XLS 2WD and Limited 2WD. A full-size spare with alloy wheel and a towing prep package is now standard on LS AWD (optional LS 2WD) and XLS. Standard side-impact airbags for front-seat passengers have been added to the Endeavor XLS. Rounding out the 2004.5 changes are a handful of new options, including a rear-seat DVD entertainment system for XLS and Limited, and traction and stability control for the Limited AWD.

Expo
1995

Mileage Category: B

Body Styles	TMV Pricing		
	Trade	Private	Dealer
4 Dr STD 4WD Hbk	1003	1704	2873

Body Styles	TMV Pricing		
	Trade	Private	Dealer
4 Dr STD Hbk	925	1573	2652

Options	Price
Air Conditioning	+116

Options	Price
Antilock Brakes	+125

This is the last year for the Expo.

Galant
2004

Mileage Category: D

Body Styles	TMV Pricing		
	Trade	Private	Dealer
4 Dr DE Sdn	10137	11227	13044
4 Dr ES Sdn	10684	11774	13590

Body Styles	TMV Pricing		
	Trade	Private	Dealer
4 Dr GTS Sdn	14913	16056	17961
4 Dr LS Sdn	12000	13089	14904

Options	Price
AM/FM/CD Changer Audio System [Opt on ES, LS]	+350
Aluminum/Alloy Wheels [Opt on ES, LS]	+400
Antilock Brakes [Opt on ES]	+500
Front Side Airbag Restraints [Opt on ES, LS]	+350
Heated Front Seats [Opt on non-DE]	+150

Options	Price
Leather Seats [Opt on ES, LS]	+650
Leather Steering Wheel [Opt on ES, LS]	+150
Power Driver Seat [Opt on ES, LS]	+150
Power Moonroof [Opt on ES, LS]	+730

The Mitsubishi Galant has been completely redesigned this year to better suit the North American market. In other words, it's larger, has more power and additional features to better compete against the likes of the Honda Accord, Nissan Altima and Toyota Camry.

Mitsubishi
Galant

2003

The ES Galant now offers a "Sun and Sound" option that provides a 210-watt Infinity audio system along with a power sunroof and 16-inch alloy wheels. LS models come equipped with traction control.

Mileage Category: D

Body Styles	TMV Pricing		
	Trade	Private	Dealer
4 Dr DE Sdn	7459	8289	9671
4 Dr ES Sdn	7700	8556	9983
4 Dr ES V6 Sdn	8399	9332	10888

Options	Price
Antilock Brakes [Opt on ES,ES V6]	+407
Infinity Audio System [Opt on ES,ES V6]	+162
Leather Seats [Opt on LS,LS V6]	+479

Body Styles	TMV Pricing		
	Trade	Private	Dealer
4 Dr GTZ Sdn	10319	11466	13377
4 Dr LS Sdn	9105	10118	11805
4 Dr LS V6 Sdn	9521	10580	12344

Options	Price
Power Driver Seat [Opt on LS,LS V6]	+168
Power Moonroof [Opt on ES,ES V6]	+509
Traction Control System [Opt on ES]	+132

2002

The 2002 Galant features new exterior and interior design changes and other improvements to enhance safety and functionality. A new LS model with the four-cylinder engine offers a standard sunroof and upgraded sound system plus the option of leather trim. Mechanically, changes include larger front ventilated disc brakes (four-cylinder models), an additional remote keyless-entry trunk-opening function, an emergency inside-trunk lid release and available ABS on ES models. The exterior features updated front and rear styling, new 16-inch wheels (GTZ and LS V6) and two new colors. Inside, Mitsubishi has spruced things up with a new audio system faceplate, a rear dome light with the optional sunroof and a redesigned gauge cluster. New titanium- and bronze-finish (ES and LS) or carbon fiber-finish (GTZ) trim panels have also been added.

Mileage Category: D

Body Styles	TMV Pricing		
	Trade	Private	Dealer
4 Dr DE Sdn	5807	6609	7946
4 Dr ES Sdn	6203	7061	8490
4 Dr ES V6 Sdn	6810	7752	9321

Options	Price
Antilock Brakes [Opt on ES]	+327
Leather Seats [Opt on LS,LS V6]	+385

Body Styles	TMV Pricing		
	Trade	Private	Dealer
4 Dr GTZ Sdn	7916	9011	10835
4 Dr LS Sdn	7440	8468	10182
4 Dr LS V6 Sdn	7733	8803	10585

Options	Price
Power Driver Seat [Opt on LS,LS V6]	+135
Power Moonroof [Opt on ES,ES V6]	+409

2001

Mitsubishi's fourth-generation Galant features some new standard and optional equipment, like a LATCH system for child seats and traction control and heated mirrors for cold-weather dwellers who purchase the all-weather package. It now meets LEV standards.

Mileage Category: D

Body Styles	TMV Pricing		
	Trade	Private	Dealer
4 Dr DE Sdn	4692	5709	6648
4 Dr ES Sdn	4913	5977	6960
4 Dr ES V6 Sdn	5603	6817	7937

Options	Price
Antilock Brakes [Opt on ES]	+408
Front Side Airbag Restraints [Opt on ES,ES V6]	+127

Body Styles	TMV Pricing		
	Trade	Private	Dealer
4 Dr GTZ Sdn	6680	8128	9465
4 Dr LS V6 Sdn	6401	7788	9069

Options	Price
Power Moonroof [Opt on ES,ES V6]	+360

2000

After a '99 redesign, Mitsubishi's fourth-generation Galant features some new standard and optional equipment, like cruise-control memory function, an in-dash CD player, larger tires and four new colors.

Mileage Category: D

Body Styles	TMV Pricing		
	Trade	Private	Dealer
4 Dr DE Sdn	3704	4626	5529
4 Dr ES Sdn	3842	4798	5735
4 Dr ES V6 Sdn	4501	5622	6720

Options	Price
Antilock Brakes [Opt on ES]	+346
Compact Disc Changer	+242

Body Styles	TMV Pricing		
	Trade	Private	Dealer
4 Dr GTZ Sdn	5552	6934	8289
4 Dr LS V6 Sdn	4974	6212	7425

Options	Price
Leather Seats [Opt on ES,ES V6]	+305
Power Moonroof [Opt on ES,ES V6]	+305

1999

The all-new '99 Galant lineup features BMW-like styling, a new V6 engine option, more standard equipment and a GTZ model with a sport-tuned suspension.

Mileage Category: D

Body Styles	TMV Pricing		
	Trade	Private	Dealer
4 Dr DE Sdn	2931	3759	4621
4 Dr ES Sdn	3290	4220	5188
4 Dr ES V6 Sdn	3746	4805	5907

Options	Price
AM/FM/CD Audio System	+122
Antilock Brakes [Opt on ES]	+296
Compact Disc Changer	+207

Body Styles	TMV Pricing		
	Trade	Private	Dealer
4 Dr GTZ Sdn	4721	6055	7444
4 Dr LS V6 Sdn	4318	5538	6808

Options	Price
Leather Seats [Opt on ES,ES V6]	+261
Power Moonroof [Opt on ES,ES V6]	+261

1998

Mileage Category: D

Body Styles	TMV Pricing		
	Trade	Private	Dealer
4 Dr DE Sdn	2248	3036	3924
4 Dr ES Sdn	2619	3538	4574

Body Styles	TMV Pricing		
	Trade	Private	Dealer
4 Dr LS Sdn	3144	4247	5491

Options	Price
Air Conditioning [Opt on DE]	+239
Antilock Brakes [Opt on ES]	+255
Automatic 4-Speed Transmission [Std on LS]	+207

Options	Price
Compact Disc Changer	+179
Leather Seats [Opt on ES]	+226
Power Moonroof [Opt on ES]	+226

Solar-tinted glass makes it harder to tan in the new Galant. The ES gets a standard manual transmission, and the ES and LS have a new black grille with chrome accents. The LS also benefits from standard antilock brakes. All models have a new heavy-duty starter and battery.

1997

Mileage Category: D

Body Styles	TMV Pricing		
	Trade	Private	Dealer
4 Dr DE Sdn	1625	2314	3156
4 Dr ES Sdn	2007	2858	3898

Body Styles	TMV Pricing		
	Trade	Private	Dealer
4 Dr LS Sdn	2432	3463	4723

Options	Price
Air Conditioning [Opt on DE]	+217
Antilock Brakes	+232
Automatic 4-Speed Transmission [Opt on DE]	+210

Options	Price
Compact Disc Changer	+159
Leather Seats [Opt on ES]	+205
Power Moonroof [Opt on ES]	+192

Mitsubishi shuffles the Galant lineup, replacing the S sedan with a base model called the DE. Front and rear fascias have been redesigned, and the interiors of all models have been upgraded by the addition of more ergonomically correct center armrests, upgraded upholstery, additional sound deadening material and a new steering wheel.

1996

Mileage Category: D

Body Styles	TMV Pricing		
	Trade	Private	Dealer
4 Dr ES Sdn	1711	2529	3659
4 Dr LS Sdn	1942	2871	4155

Body Styles	TMV Pricing		
	Trade	Private	Dealer
4 Dr S Sdn	1318	1949	2820

Options	Price
Air Conditioning [Opt on S]	+185
Antilock Brakes	+198
Automatic 4-Speed Transmission [Opt on S]	+183

Options	Price
Compact Disc Changer	+136
Power Moonroof [Opt on ES]	+164

A Homelink transmitter is available, and a panic feature debuts on keyless entry systems. New two-tone interiors debut, and four fresh exterior colors join the palette. Other changes include new wheel covers, expanded availability of alloy wheels, and a heavy-duty defroster with timer. LS models have standard leather seating and antilock brakes are available across the line.

1995

Mileage Category: D

Body Styles	TMV Pricing		
	Trade	Private	Dealer
4 Dr ES Sdn	1141	1807	2918
4 Dr LS Sdn	1164	1842	2973

Body Styles	TMV Pricing		
	Trade	Private	Dealer
4 Dr S Sdn	866	1372	2214

Options	Price
Air Conditioning [Opt on S]	+149
Antilock Brakes	+159

Options	Price
Automatic 4-Speed Transmission [Opt on S]	+120
Leather Seats	+141

The much anticipated V6 engine never transpired in the 1995 Galant due to the increased costs and complexity involved in making the model. The 1995 Galants are available in three trim levels, all with the 141-horsepower four-cylinder.

Lancer

2004

Mileage Category: B

Body Styles	TMV Pricing		
	Trade	Private	Dealer
4 Dr ES Sdn	7573	8552	10184
4 Dr LS Sdn	8546	9629	11435

Body Styles	TMV Pricing		
	Trade	Private	Dealer
4 Dr O-Z Rally Sdn	9431	10627	12619
4 Dr Ralliart Sdn	10201	11354	13275

Options	Price
Aluminum/Alloy Wheels [Opt on LS]	+560
Antilock Brakes [Opt on LS]	+250
Automatic 4-Speed Transmission [Std on LS]	+800

Options	Price
Keyless Entry System [Opt on ES]	+175
Power Moonroof [Opt on OZ, Ralliart]	+750
Split Folding Rear Seat [Opt on ES]	+375

The Lancer Sportback wagon joins the lineup, along with performance-oriented Ralliart versions of both the sedan and wagon. All Sportback wagons as well as the Ralliart sedans get a new 2.4-liter, four-cylinder engine rated at 160 horsepower (162 hp in Ralliart form). The entire Lancer line gets a redesigned front fascia with Mitsubishi's corporate grille design, plus new integrated bumpers, halogen headlamps and a relocated rear license plate.

Mitsubishi
Lancer/Evolution/Sportback

2003

Midway through the year, Mitsubishi will unleash its Lancer Evolution, a rally racing-inspired road burner that sends 271 horsepower through all four of its 17-inch wheels.

Mileage Category: B

Body Styles	TMV Pricing		
	Trade	Private	Dealer
4 Dr ES Sdn	6732	7714	9350
4 Dr LS Sdn	7609	8719	10569

Options	Price
Antilock Brakes [Opt on LS]	+407
Automatic 4-Speed Transmission [Opt on ES,O-Z]	+479
Front Side Airbag Restraints [Opt on LS]	+150

Body Styles	TMV Pricing		
	Trade	Private	Dealer
4 Dr O-Z Rally Sdn	7536	8635	10467

Options	Price
Power Moonroof [Opt on LS,O-Z]	+449
Rear Spoiler [Opt on O-Z]	+215
Split Folding Rear Seat [Opt on ES]	+150

2002

The '02 Lancer is Mitsubishi's replacement for its Mirage economy car, though the Mirage continues this year in coupe format only. The chief reason for the new name (for the U.S., as the car has always been called the Lancer elsewhere) is Mitsubishi's desire to emphasize that the Lancer is more upscale, larger and better-engineered than the old Mirage.

Mileage Category: B

Body Styles	TMV Pricing		
	Trade	Private	Dealer
4 Dr ES Sdn	5571	6503	8055
4 Dr LS Sdn	6426	7500	9291

Options	Price
Antilock Brakes [Opt on LS]	+327
Automatic 4-Speed Transmission [Opt on ES,O-Z]	+385
Front Side Airbag Restraints [Opt on LS]	+120

Body Styles	TMV Pricing		
	Trade	Private	Dealer
4 Dr O-Z Rally Sdn	6245	7289	9030

Options	Price
Rear Spoiler	+173
Split Folding Rear Seat [Opt on ES]	+120

Lancer Evolution

2004

Mileage Category: E

Body Styles	TMV Pricing		
	Trade	Private	Dealer
4 Dr RS Turbo AWD Sdn	20503	22032	24581

Options	Price
Infinity Audio System	+400
Leather Seats	+800

Body Styles	TMV Pricing		
	Trade	Private	Dealer
4 Dr VIII Turbo AWD Sdn	22910	24438	26985

Options	Price
Power Moonroof	+800
Recaro Seats	+350

Leather seating is now an option as is an upgraded 315-watt Infinity sound system. A new, decontented RS model has been added this year for those who want maximum performance and nothing else. The Evo RS deletes ABS, air conditioning, the rear spoiler and power features such as locks and windows. Additionally, the RS boasts a helical limited-slip differential, added structural reinforcement in the trunk and less sound-deadening material.

2003

The Lancer Evolution is not necessarily a new car; it's been around in Japan and Europe since 1989. However, this year marks the first time Mitsubishi is offering the Evo to American customers.

Mileage Category: E

Body Styles	TMV Pricing		
	Trade	Private	Dealer
4 Dr Turbo AWD Sdn	20684	22129	24538

Options	Price
AM/FM/CD Changer Audio System	+269

Options	Price
Power Moonroof	+449

Lancer Sportback

2004

Mileage Category: B

Body Styles	TMV Pricing		
	Trade	Private	Dealer
4 Dr LS Wgn	9221	10280	12046

Options	Price
Aluminum/Alloy Wheels	+640
Cruise Control	+200

Body Styles	TMV Pricing		
	Trade	Private	Dealer
4 Dr Ralliart Wgn	10542	11660	13522

Options	Price
Luggage Rack	+150

The Lancer Sportback wagon joins the lineup, along with performance-oriented Ralliart versions of both the sedan and wagon. All Sportback wagons as well as the Ralliart sedans get a new 2.4-liter, four-cylinder engine rated at 160 horsepower (162 hp in Ralliart form). The entire Lancer line gets a redesigned front fascia with Mitsubishi's corporate grille design, plus new integrated bumpers, halogen headlamps and a relocated rear license plate.

For the latest vehicle information, visit www.edmunds.com

Mighty Max Pickup

1996

Mileage Category: J

Body Styles	TMV Pricing		
	Trade	Private	Dealer
2 Dr STD Std Cab SB	1527	2160	3033

Options	Price	Options	Price
AM/FM/CD Audio System	+118	Automatic 4-Speed Transmission	+265
Air Conditioning	+156		

No changes this year, the Mighty Max's last.

1995

Mileage Category: J

Body Styles	TMV Pricing		
	Trade	Private	Dealer
2 Dr STD Std Cab SB	1277	1810	2698

Options	Price	Options	Price
AM/FM/CD Audio System	+95	Air Conditioning	+125
AM/FM/Cassette Audio System	+81	Automatic 4-Speed Transmission	+213

The Mighty Max line is drastically reduced. Remaining is a four-cylinder two-wheel-drive regular-cab model.

Mirage

2002

Mileage Category: B

Body Styles	TMV Pricing			Body Styles	TMV Pricing		
	Trade	Private	Dealer		Trade	Private	Dealer
2 Dr DE Cpe	4323	5137	6495	2 Dr LS Cpe	5317	6320	7991

Options	Price	Options	Price
AM/FM/CD Audio System [Opt on DE]	+132	Automatic 4-Speed Transmission	+385
Air Conditioning [Opt on DE]	+382	Power Moonroof [Opt on LS]	+385
Aluminum/Alloy Wheels [Opt on LS]	+168	Power Windows [Opt on DE]	+125

Though the Mirage sedan has been discontinued to make room for the all-new Lancer sedan, Mitsubishi will continue to offer the Mirage coupe. Only a few minor changes -- a new audio faceplate, an emergency inside-trunk release and a new chrome badge -- are in store this year.

2001

Mileage Category: B

Body Styles	TMV Pricing			Body Styles	TMV Pricing		
	Trade	Private	Dealer		Trade	Private	Dealer
2 Dr DE Cpe	3416	4620	5730	4 Dr ES Sdn	3801	5139	6374
2 Dr LS Cpe	3897	5269	6535	4 Dr LS Sdn	3852	5209	6462

Options	Price	Options	Price
AM/FM/CD Audio System [Opt on DE]	+169	Automatic 4-Speed Transmission	+339
Air Conditioning [Opt on DE]	+373	Power Moonroof [Opt on LS]	+339
Aluminum/Alloy Wheels [Opt on LS]	+170		

All 2001 Mirages now have tether anchors for child seats and meet LEV standards. A power sunroof is now available with the coupe's sport package. Sedan buyers can choose from the LS or the new base ES trim model that replaces the DE model. Nothing else has changed but the designation -- John Mellencamp? John Cougar? John Cougar Mellencamp?

2000

Mileage Category: B

Body Styles	TMV Pricing			Body Styles	TMV Pricing		
	Trade	Private	Dealer		Trade	Private	Dealer
2 Dr DE Cpe	2305	3276	4228	4 Dr DE Sdn	2573	3660	4724
2 Dr LS Cpe	2686	3819	4929	4 Dr LS Sdn	3100	4406	5687

Options	Price	Options	Price
AM/FM/CD Audio System [Opt on DE Cpe]	+143	Aluminum/Alloy Wheels [Opt on DE Sdn,LS]	+144
AM/FM/Cassette Audio System	+126	Automatic 4-Speed Transmission [Opt on DE,LS]	+273
Air Conditioning [Opt on DE Cpe]	+316		

The DE Sedan now comes with the more powerful 1.8-liter engine in place of last year's base 1.5-liter power plant. All DE models (sedans and coupes) get a host of luxury items and larger brakes as standard equipment. The LS Sedan also gets a few more standard goodies for 2000.

1999

Mileage Category: B

Body Styles	TMV Pricing			Body Styles	TMV Pricing		
	Trade	Private	Dealer		Trade	Private	Dealer
2 Dr DE Cpe	1581	2337	3124	2 Dr LS Cpe	2060	3045	4070

A new rear deck lid and taillamps, new seat fabric and some different exterior colors premier on the Mirage. The LS trim level also gets a few interior enhancements.

1999 (cont'd)

Body Styles	TMV Pricing		
	Trade	Private	Dealer
4 Dr DE Sdn	1748	2585	3455

Options	Price
AM/FM/CD Audio System [Std on LS Cpe]	+122
Air Conditioning [Std on LS Cpe]	+270
Aluminum/Alloy Wheels [Std on Cpe]	+123

Body Styles	TMV Pricing		
	Trade	Private	Dealer
4 Dr LS Sdn	1917	2834	3788

Options	Price
Antilock Brakes	+232
Automatic 4-Speed Transmission	+233
Power Moonroof	+243

1998
Some new colors to choose from and a new heavy-duty starter and battery make the Mirage more reliable.

Mileage Category: B

Body Styles	TMV Pricing		
	Trade	Private	Dealer
2 Dr DE Cpe	1121	1763	2486
2 Dr LS Cpe	1478	2322	3275

Options	Price
Air Conditioning [Opt on DE,Sdn]	+233
Antilock Brakes	+200

Body Styles	TMV Pricing		
	Trade	Private	Dealer
4 Dr DE Sdn	1279	2010	2835
4 Dr LS Sdn	1417	2228	3141

Options	Price
Automatic 4-Speed Transmission	+180
Power Moonroof	+210

1997
The Mirage is totally redesigned for 1997, sharing little with the model it replaces. Mitsubishi claims that interior size has been increased and that NVH have been reduced.

Mileage Category: B

Body Styles	TMV Pricing		
	Trade	Private	Dealer
2 Dr DE Cpe	854	1421	2115
2 Dr LS Cpe	1111	1849	2750

Options	Price
Air Conditioning	+212
Antilock Brakes	+182

Body Styles	TMV Pricing		
	Trade	Private	Dealer
4 Dr DE Sdn	998	1662	2474
4 Dr LS Sdn	1093	1819	2708

Options	Price
Automatic 4-Speed Transmission	+171
Power Moonroof	+176

1996

Mileage Category: B

Body Styles	TMV Pricing		
	Trade	Private	Dealer
2 Dr LS Cpe	975	1628	2530
2 Dr S Cpe	735	1227	1907

Options	Price
Air Conditioning	+181

Body Styles	TMV Pricing		
	Trade	Private	Dealer
4 Dr S Sdn	847	1414	2197

Options	Price
Automatic 4-Speed Transmission	+136

Four colors debut, and the Preferred Equipment Packages are revised a bit.

1995
The often changing Mitsubishi Mirage is once again revised, this time with dual airbags. LS versions get bigger alloy wheels.

Mileage Category: B

Body Styles	TMV Pricing		
	Trade	Private	Dealer
2 Dr ES Cpe	690	1172	1976
2 Dr LS Cpe	706	1201	2025
2 Dr S Cpe	584	992	1671

Options	Price
Air Conditioning	+145
Automatic 3-Speed Transmission [Opt on Cpe]	+89

Body Styles	TMV Pricing		
	Trade	Private	Dealer
4 Dr ES Sdn	759	1291	2177
4 Dr S Sdn	704	1198	2021

Options	Price
Automatic 4-Speed Transmission	+109

Montero

2004

Mileage Category: M

Body Styles	TMV Pricing		
	Trade	Private	Dealer
4 Dr Limited 4WD SUV	20609	21974	24247

Options	Price
DVD Entertainment System	+1500

The Montero gets a standard tire-pressure monitoring system and a revised gauge cluster. The base XLS model is history, leaving the Limited as the sole trim level for 2004. Rear air conditioning, automatic climate control and dual power seats are now standard.

2003

Mileage Category: M

Body Styles	TMV Pricing			Body Styles	TMV Pricing		
	Trade	Private	Dealer		Trade	Private	Dealer
4 Dr Limited 4WD SUV	17429	18772	21010	4 Dr XLS 4WD SUV	15194	16364	18315

Options	Price	Options	Price
Air Conditioning - Front and Rear	+344	Leather Seats [Opt on XLS]	+479
Automatic Climate Control [Opt on Limited]	+138	Power Moonroof [Opt on XLS]	+476
Infinity Audio System [Opt on XLS]	+150	Power Passenger Seat [Opt on Limited]	+162

A new grille, front fascia and headlights, designed to provide a "greater sense of luxury," as well as smoother body cladding and dechromed taillights update the Montero. A bigger (3.8 liter) V6 adds some much-needed power to this 4,700-pound SUV.

2002

Mileage Category: M

Body Styles	TMV Pricing			Body Styles	TMV Pricing		
	Trade	Private	Dealer		Trade	Private	Dealer
4 Dr Limited 4WD SUV	13920	15247	17460	4 Dr XLS 4WD SUV	12239	13406	15351

Options	Price	Options	Price
Air Conditioning - Front and Rear	+361	Limited Slip Differential [Opt on XLS]	+120
Infinity Audio System [Opt on XLS]	+120	Power Moonroof [Opt on XLS]	+382
Leather Seats [Opt on XLS]	+385	Power Passenger Seat [Opt on Limited]	+130

For 2002, Montero has several new features and refinements to greater enhance its market position. Montero Limited has new color-keyed exterior features, and both Limited and XLS now have a spare tire cover that matches the body color (except with Munich Silver).

2001

Mileage Category: M

Body Styles	TMV Pricing			Body Styles	TMV Pricing		
	Trade	Private	Dealer		Trade	Private	Dealer
4 Dr Limited 4WD SUV	12091	13985	15733	4 Dr XLS 4WD SUV	10639	12306	13844

Options	Price	Options	Price
Air Conditioning - Front and Rear	+275	Power Moonroof	+402

The Montero is redesigned for 2001 and features a sculpted body, stiffer frame, improved suspension and more interior room.

2000

Mileage Category: M

Body Styles	TMV Pricing		
	Trade	Private	Dealer
4 Dr STD 4WD SUV	8521	10168	11783

Options	Price	Options	Price
Compact Disc Changer	+242	Power Moonroof	+341
Leather Seats	+431		

The Montero's list of standard features has been lengthened, and a new Endeavor package adds even more luxury items to Mitsubishi's largest SUV.

1999

Mileage Category: M

Body Styles	TMV Pricing		
	Trade	Private	Dealer
4 Dr STD 4WD SUV	6944	8431	9978

Options	Price	Options	Price
AM/FM/CD Audio System	+122	Leather Seats	+368
Chrome Wheels	+284	Power Moonroof	+291
Compact Disc Changer	+207		

Nothing changes on the Montero this year, but one less paint color is available.

Mitsubishi
Montero/Sport

1998

A revised front bumper and grille, new fenders and new rear quarter panels mark the exterior changes. Inside is a new steering wheel, while the standard equipment list now includes ABS, air conditioning, third-row seats and alloy wheels.

Mileage Category: M

Body Styles	TMV Pricing		
	Trade	Private	Dealer
4 Dr STD 4WD SUV	6028	7471	9098

Options	Price	Options	Price
Chrome Wheels	+162	Leather Seats	+318
Compact Disc Changer	+179	Power Moonroof	+252

1997

The Montero is unchanged for this year.

Mileage Category: M

Body Styles	TMV Pricing			Body Styles	TMV Pricing		
	Trade	Private	Dealer		Trade	Private	Dealer
4 Dr LS 4WD SUV	4253	5412	6829	4 Dr SR 4WD SUV	5520	7026	8865

Options	Price	Options	Price
Air Conditioning [Opt on LS]	+217	Compact Disc Changer	+163
Antilock Brakes	+182	Leather Seats [Opt on LS]	+289
Chrome Wheels	+223	Power Moonroof [Opt on LS]	+229

1996

Refinements result in a better SUV this year. A passenger airbag has been installed, optional side steps make it easier to clamber aboard and split-fold second-row seats increase versatility. New colors, new seat fabrics and better audio systems round out the package.

Mileage Category: M

Body Styles	TMV Pricing			Body Styles	TMV Pricing		
	Trade	Private	Dealer		Trade	Private	Dealer
4 Dr LS 4WD SUV	3150	4103	5420	4 Dr SR 4WD SUV	4481	5837	7710

Options	Price	Options	Price
Air Conditioning [Opt on LS]	+185	Compact Disc Changer	+178
Antilock Brakes [Opt on LS]	+238	Leather Seats	+308
Automatic 4-Speed Transmission [Opt on LS]	+183	Power Moonroof	+180
Chrome Wheels	+191		

1995

The Montero LS gets a more powerful V6 that offers a 26-horsepower boost over last year's marginal 151-horsepower rating. Towing capacity increases to 5,000 pounds for all models. Tricky electronic shock absorbers return to the Montero SR's standard equipment list, letting drivers choose between soft, medium or hard setting depending on their preferences.

Mileage Category: M

Body Styles	TMV Pricing			Body Styles	TMV Pricing		
	Trade	Private	Dealer		Trade	Private	Dealer
4 Dr LS 4WD SUV	2382	3233	4651	4 Dr SR 4WD SUV	2991	4058	5837

Options	Price	Options	Price
AM/FM/Cassette/CD Audio System	+91	Compact Disc Changer	+111
Antilock Brakes [Opt on LS]	+125	Leather Seats	+248
Automatic 4-Speed Transmission [Opt on LS]	+147	Power Sunroof [Opt on LS]	+145
Chrome Wheels	+153		

Montero Sport

2004

Mileage Category: M

Body Styles	TMV Pricing			Body Styles	TMV Pricing		
	Trade	Private	Dealer		Trade	Private	Dealer
4 Dr LS 4WD SUV	13541	14713	16666	4 Dr XLS 4WD SUV	14626	15798	17751
4 Dr LS SUV	12553	13725	15679	4 Dr XLS SUV	13640	14812	16765

Options	Price	Options	Price
Automatic Dimming Rearview Mirror [Opt on XLS]	+135	Limited Slip Differential (Rear) [Opt on XLS]	+300
Cruise Control [Opt on LS]	+240	Power Moonroof [Opt on XLS]	+900
Keyless Entry System [Opt on LS]	+150	Privacy Glass [Opt on LS]	+200
Leather Seats [Opt on XLS]	+1100	Side Steps [Opt on LS]	+360

The base- and top-level trims, ES and Limited, have been dropped, but their features have been added to the remaining LS and XLS trims. As a result, both the LS and XLS now feature the more powerful 3.5-liter V6 engine, as well as standard 16-inch alloy wheels, new roof rails and new interior fabrics.

2003

Mitsubishi raises the Montero Sport's roof to provide more headroom and ups the wattage (from 100 to 140 watts) on the audio system.

Mileage Category: M

Body Styles	TMV Pricing			Body Styles	TMV Pricing		
	Trade	Private	Dealer		Trade	Private	Dealer
4 Dr ES 4WD SUV	10948	11849	13350	4 Dr LS 4WD SUV	11946	12930	14569
4 Dr ES SUV	10423	11282	12713	4 Dr LS SUV	11032	11940	13453

Body Styles	TMV Pricing		
	Trade	Private	Dealer
4 Dr Limited 4WD SUV	14184	15352	17299
4 Dr Limited SUV	13528	14642	16498

Options	Price
Aluminum/Alloy Wheels [Opt on ES]	+162
Infinity Audio System [Opt on XLS]	+165
Keyless Entry System [Opt on ES]	+120
Leather Seats [Opt on XLS]	+553

Body Styles	TMV Pricing		
	Trade	Private	Dealer
4 Dr XLS 4WD SUV	12766	13818	15570
4 Dr XLS SUV	11873	12850	14479

Options	Price
Limited Slip Differential [Opt on XLS]	+150
Power Moonroof [Opt on XLS]	+509
Side Steps [Opt on ES]	+165
Tinted Glass [Opt on ES]	+120

Mileage Category: M

2002

The 2002 Montero Sport receives a few changes and upgrades this year. Four-wheel-drive Montero Sports have a new mode called ALL4 four-wheel drive. This full-time all-wheel-drive mode automatically provides the appropriate traction for most on-road and light off-road situations -- without the driver having to activate anything. Engine choices remain the same, though the 197-horsepower, 3.5-liter V6 is now standard on XLS. In terms of features, there's a new appearance package for Montero Sport ES, and packages for XLS have been revised. Mitsubishi has also changed the seat fabrics and included metallic-faced gauges on LS, XLS and Limited. In case you are wondering, last year's XS "special edition" apparently wasn't special enough and has been discontinued.

Body Styles	TMV Pricing		
	Trade	Private	Dealer
4 Dr ES 4WD SUV	9093	10028	11585
4 Dr ES SUV	8069	8898	10280
4 Dr LS 4WD SUV	9901	10918	12613
4 Dr LS SUV	9143	10082	11647

Options	Price
Aluminum/Alloy Wheels [Opt on ES]	+130
Infinity Audio System [Opt on XLS]	+132
Leather Seats [Opt on XLS]	+45
Limited Slip Differential [Opt on XLS]	+120

Body Styles	TMV Pricing		
	Trade	Private	Dealer
4 Dr Limited 4WD SUV	11779	12988	15005
4 Dr Limited SUV	11237	12391	14315
4 Dr XLS 4WD SUV	10593	11681	13494
4 Dr XLS SUV	9841	10852	12537

Options	Price
Luggage Rack [Opt on ES]	+120
Power Moonroof [Opt on XLS]	+409
Side Steps [Opt on ES]	+132

Mileage Category: M

2001

Because the Montero Sport underwent an update last year, this midsize SUV pretty much remains static for 2001. You can now get the base level ES trim in a 4WD configuration, and the XS trim level debuts with the 3.5-liter V6 from the pricey Limited model. A Lower Anchor Tether Child (LATCH) restraint system comes standard, and the light trucks meet LEV standards.

Body Styles	TMV Pricing		
	Trade	Private	Dealer
4 Dr 3.5XS 4WD SUV	9117	10657	12079
4 Dr 3.5XS SUV	8355	9766	11068
4 Dr ES 4WD SUV	7815	9135	10353
4 Dr ES SUV	6937	8110	9192
4 Dr LS 4WD SUV	8469	9900	11220

Options	Price
Infinity Audio System [Opt on XLS]	+149
Leather Seats	+423

Body Styles	TMV Pricing		
	Trade	Private	Dealer
4 Dr LS SUV	7875	9206	10434
4 Dr Limited 4WD SUV	10072	11774	13344
4 Dr Limited SUV	9669	11301	12808
4 Dr XLS 4WD SUV	9170	10719	12149
4 Dr XLS SUV	8396	9814	11123

Options	Price
Power Moonroof [Opt on XLS]	+360

Mileage Category: M

2000

The 2000 Montero Sport receives significant interior and exterior styling updates like a new grille, revised headlights, body-colored bumpers and new center console design, as well as several technical improvements, including a limited-slip differential on XLS and Limited models, and 16-inch alloy wheels.

Body Styles	TMV Pricing		
	Trade	Private	Dealer
4 Dr ES SUV	5450	6542	7613
4 Dr LS 4WD SUV	6524	7832	9114
4 Dr LS SUV	6063	7279	8471
4 Dr Limited 4WD SUV	8444	10137	11796

Options	Price
Compact Disc Changer	+215
Infinity Audio System [Opt on XLS]	+126

Body Styles	TMV Pricing		
	Trade	Private	Dealer
4 Dr Limited SUV	7368	8845	10293
4 Dr XLS 4WD SUV	7174	8612	10022
4 Dr XLS SUV	6679	8017	9330

Options	Price
Leather Seats	+359
Power Moonroof [Opt on XLS]	+305

Mileage Category: M

1999

A new Limited model joins the Montero Sport lineup and with it comes a powerful new V6 engine.

Body Styles	TMV Pricing		
	Trade	Private	Dealer
4 Dr ES SUV	4207	5089	6006
4 Dr LS 4WD SUV	5619	6796	8021
4 Dr LS SUV	5356	6477	7644
4 Dr Limited 4WD SUV	7490	9059	10691

Options	Price
AM/FM/CD Audio System [Opt on LS,XLS]	+122
Air Conditioning [Opt on ES]	+281
Automatic 4-Speed Transmission [Opt on LS]	+264

Body Styles	TMV Pricing		
	Trade	Private	Dealer
4 Dr Limited SUV	6650	8043	9492
4 Dr XLS 4WD SUV	6609	7993	9433
4 Dr XLS SUV	6061	7331	8652

Options	Price
Compact Disc Changer	+184
Power Moonroof [Std on Limited]	+261

Mitsubishi
Montero Sport/Outlander

1998

Montero Sports get lots of features added to their option packages, and 4WD models now come with standard ABS.

Mileage Category: M

Body Styles	TMV Pricing		
	Trade	Private	Dealer
4 Dr ES SUV	3524	4416	5422
4 Dr LS 4WD SUV	4644	5820	7145
4 Dr LS SUV	4264	5343	6559

Options	Price
Air Conditioning [Std on XLS]	+243
Appearance Package [Opt on LS]	+200
Automatic 4-Speed Transmission [Opt on LS 4WD]	+228

Body Styles	TMV Pricing		
	Trade	Private	Dealer
4 Dr XLS 4WD SUV	5733	7183	8818
4 Dr XLS SUV	5121	6416	7877

Options	Price
Compact Disc Changer	+179
Power Moonroof [Opt on LS]	+226

1997

This all-new entry from Mitsubishi is poised to steal sales in the ever-growing midsize sport-utility segment. Based on the same floorpan as the full-size Montero, the Montero Sport is shorter in length, lighter in weight and generally more nimble than its big brother.

Mileage Category: M

Body Styles	TMV Pricing		
	Trade	Private	Dealer
4 Dr ES SUV	2818	3610	4578
4 Dr LS 4WD SUV	3935	5041	6393

Options	Price
Air Conditioning [Std on XLS]	+220
Antilock Brakes	+182
Automatic 4-Speed Transmission [Std on 2WD,XLS]	+193

Body Styles	TMV Pricing		
	Trade	Private	Dealer
4 Dr LS SUV	3652	4679	5934
4 Dr XLS 4WD SUV	5108	6544	8299

Options	Price
Compact Disc Changer	+163
Leather Seats [Opt on LS]	+265
Power Moonroof [Opt on LS]	+191

Outlander

2004

The Outlander's 2.4-liter engine receives a much needed boost in power -- it now makes 160 horsepower.

Mileage Category: L

Body Styles	TMV Pricing		
	Trade	Private	Dealer
4 Dr LS AWD SUV	12391	13531	15432
4 Dr LS SUV	11460	12614	14538

Options	Price
Aluminum/Alloy Wheels [Opt on LS]	+275
Antilock Brakes [Opt on XLS]	+545
Automatic Dimming Rearview Mirror [Opt on XLS]	+120
Front Side Airbag Restraints [Opt on XLS]	+295
Heated Front Seats [Opt on XLS]	+150
Infinity Audio System [Opt on XLS]	+250

Body Styles	TMV Pricing		
	Trade	Private	Dealer
4 Dr XLS AWD SUV	13401	14522	16389
4 Dr XLS SUV	12220	13361	15263

Options	Price
Keyless Entry System [Opt on LS]	+200
Leather Seats [Opt on XLS]	+700
Luggage Rack [Opt on LS]	+250
Power Heated Mirrors [Opt on XLS]	+185
Power Moonroof [Opt on XLS]	+800
Privacy Glass [Opt on LS]	+225

2003

Mitsubishi jumps into the mini-SUV battle with the Outlander, which offers different styling but little else to separate it from the likes of the Subaru Forester or Honda CR-V.

Mileage Category: L

Body Styles	TMV Pricing		
	Trade	Private	Dealer
4 Dr LS AWD SUV	10694	11686	13338
4 Dr LS SUV	9994	10921	12466

Options	Price
Aluminum/Alloy Wheels [Opt on LS]	+165
Antilock Brakes [Opt on XLS]	+407
Front Side Airbag Restraints [Opt on XLS]	+177
Heated Front Seats [Opt on XLS]	+165
Infinity Audio System [Opt on XLS]	+209

Body Styles	TMV Pricing		
	Trade	Private	Dealer
4 Dr XLS AWD SUV	11496	12563	14340
4 Dr XLS SUV	10794	11796	13465

Options	Price
Leather Seats [Opt on XLS]	+464
Luggage Rack [Opt on LS]	+120
Power Moonroof [Opt on XLS]	+479
Privacy Glass [Opt on LS]	+135

200SX

1998

Mileage Category: E

Body Styles	TMV Pricing		
	Trade	Private	Dealer
2 Dr SE Cpe	3392	4220	5153
2 Dr SE-R Cpe	3905	4857	5931

Options	Price
AM/FM/CD Audio System	+139
Air Conditioning [Opt on STD]	+297
Antilock Brakes	+224

Body Styles	TMV Pricing		
	Trade	Private	Dealer
2 Dr STD Cpe	2798	3480	4250

Options	Price
Automatic 4-Speed Transmission	+238
Power Moonroof	+148

Exterior enhancements include new headlights, taillights, front and rear bumpers and revised grille. Three new colors are available for 1998.

1997

A spoiler is now standard on all models. An additional exterior color is the only other change for 1997.

Mileage Category: E

Body Styles	TMV Pricing		
	Trade	Private	Dealer
2 Dr SE Cpe	2402	3082	3914
2 Dr SE-R Cpe	3002	3853	4892

Options	Price
AM/FM/CD Audio System	+123
AM/FM/Cassette Audio System [Opt on STD]	+118
Air Conditioning [Opt on STD]	+262
Antilock Brakes	+198

Body Styles	TMV Pricing		
	Trade	Private	Dealer
2 Dr STD Cpe	2319	2976	3780

Options	Price
Automatic 4-Speed Transmission	+210
Compact Disc Changer	+175
Power Moonroof	+118

1996

Body-color door handles and outside mirrors are newly standard on SE and SE-R models.

Mileage Category: E

Body Styles	TMV Pricing		
	Trade	Private	Dealer
2 Dr SE Cpe	1776	2377	3206
2 Dr SE-R Cpe	2274	3043	4106

Options	Price
Air Conditioning [Opt on STD]	+233
Antilock Brakes	+232

Body Styles	TMV Pricing		
	Trade	Private	Dealer
2 Dr STD Cpe	1689	2261	3050

Options	Price
Automatic 4-Speed Transmission	+186

1995

A Sentra-derived 200SX is introduced to the sporting public. Basically a two-door version of the redesigned Sentra, the 200SX comes equipped with dual airbags. The 200SX has two available power plants, a 1.6-liter four-cylinder that produces 115 horsepower or a 2.0-liter four that is good for 140 ponies.

Mileage Category: E

Body Styles	TMV Pricing		
	Trade	Private	Dealer
2 Dr SE Cpe	1391	1907	2767
2 Dr SE-R Cpe	1662	2279	3307

Options	Price
AM/FM/Cassette Audio System [Opt on STD]	+94
Air Conditioning [Opt on STD]	+210
Antilock Brakes	+159

Body Styles	TMV Pricing		
	Trade	Private	Dealer
2 Dr STD Cpe	1352	1854	2691

Options	Price
Automatic 4-Speed Transmission	+168
Power Moonroof	+94

240SX

1998

Mileage Category: E

Body Styles	TMV Pricing		
	Trade	Private	Dealer
2 Dr LE Cpe	5110	6357	7763
2 Dr SE Cpe	4657	5793	7074

Options	Price
AM/FM/CD Audio System	+139
Air Conditioning [Opt on STD]	+297
Aluminum/Alloy Wheels [Opt on STD]	+116
Antilock Brakes	+231

Body Styles	TMV Pricing		
	Trade	Private	Dealer
2 Dr STD Cpe	3899	4851	5924

Options	Price
Automatic 4-Speed Transmission	+264
Compact Disc Changer	+166
Power Moonroof [Std on LE]	+267

No changes to Nissan's sporty coupe.

Nissan
240SX/300ZX

1997

Extensive exterior changes update the look of the 240SX. A luxury model is introduced midyear.

Mileage Category: E

Body Styles	TMV Pricing		
	Trade	Private	Dealer
2 Dr LE Cpe	3744	4805	6102
2 Dr SE Cpe	3417	4385	5569

Options	Price
AM/FM/CD Audio System	+123
Air Conditioning [Opt on STD]	+262
Antilock Brakes	+203
Automatic 4-Speed Transmission	+233

Body Styles	TMV Pricing		
	Trade	Private	Dealer
2 Dr STD Cpe	3004	3855	4895

Options	Price
Compact Disc Changer	+175
Leather Seats [Opt on SE]	+196
Power Moonroof [Std on LE]	+235

1996

Sporty new fabrics and a new grille are the only changes to the attractive 240SX.

Mileage Category: E

Body Styles	TMV Pricing		
	Trade	Private	Dealer
2 Dr SE Cpe	2545	3406	4596

Options	Price
Air Conditioning [Std on SE]	+232
Antilock Brakes	+258
Automatic 4-Speed Transmission	+207

Body Styles	TMV Pricing		
	Trade	Private	Dealer
2 Dr STD Cpe	2481	3321	4480

Options	Price
Leather Seats	+175
Power Sunroof	+209

1995

Totally redesigned, the 240SX loses its hatchback and convertible body styles. Available as a base or SE model, the 240 uses the same engine as the previous-generation model. Dual airbags are standard on the new 240SX as are side door beams that help the car meet federal side-impact standards.

Mileage Category: E

Body Styles	TMV Pricing		
	Trade	Private	Dealer
2 Dr SE Cpe	2091	2868	4163

Options	Price
AM/FM/CD Audio System	+99
Air Conditioning [Std on SE]	+210
Aluminum/Alloy Wheels [Std on SE]	+82
Antilock Brakes	+233
Automatic 4-Speed Transmission	+187

Body Styles	TMV Pricing		
	Trade	Private	Dealer
2 Dr STD Cpe	1969	2701	3922

Options	Price
Leather Seats	+158
Power Moonroof	+189
Power Sunroof	+189
Special Factory Paint	+84

300ZX

1996

Mileage Category: F

Body Styles	TMV Pricing		
	Trade	Private	Dealer
2 Dr 2+2 Hbk	8051	9584	11700
2 Dr STD Conv	9582	11406	13924

Options	Price
Automatic 4-Speed Transmission	+209
Leather Seats [Std on Conv]	+256

Body Styles	TMV Pricing		
	Trade	Private	Dealer
2 Dr STD Hbk	7779	9260	11305
2 Dr Turbo Hbk	8955	10660	13014

Options	Price
T-Tops - Glass [Std on 2+2,Turbo]	+335

It's the end of the world as we know it. The final Z-car is produced for 1996.

1995

No changes for the 300ZX.

Mileage Category: F

Body Styles	TMV Pricing		
	Trade	Private	Dealer
2 Dr 2+2 Hbk	6599	7901	10070
2 Dr STD Conv	7732	9258	11801

Options	Price
Automatic 4-Speed Transmission	+189
Leather Seats [Std on Conv]	+231

Body Styles	TMV Pricing		
	Trade	Private	Dealer
2 Dr STD Hbk	6363	7619	9711
2 Dr Turbo Hbk	7280	8717	11111

Options	Price
Special Factory Paint	+84
T-Tops - Glass [Std on 2+2,Turbo]	+303

350Z
2004

Mileage Category: F

Body Styles	TMV Pricing		
	Trade	Private	Dealer
2 Dr Enthusiast Conv	27032	28667	31391
2 Dr Enthusiast Hbk	22063	23657	26314
2 Dr Performance Hbk	23630	25217	27861
2 Dr STD Hbk	20640	22242	24911

Options	Price
18 Inch Wheels [Opt on Conv]	+1200
18 Inch Wheels - Chrome [Opt on Performance, Touring Cpe]	+1660
Aero Kit [Opt on non-Track Cpe]	+520
Front Head Airbag Restraints [Opt on Cpe]	+310

Body Styles	TMV Pricing		
	Trade	Private	Dealer
2 Dr Touring Conv	28735	30361	33070
2 Dr Touring Hbk	24660	26181	28716
2 Dr Track Hbk	25307	26827	29360

Options	Price
Front Side Airbag Restraints [Opt on Cpe, Enthusiast Conv]	+250
Navigation System [Opt on Performance, Touring, Track Cpe]	+2000

Nissan adds a roadster to the 350Z lineup. Available in Enthusiast and Touring variants, the roadster offers the same performance and handling as the Z coupe but with the added fun of top-down driving. In other news, satellite radio (either XM or Sirius) is a new option this year for the Touring version of the coupe.

2003

Mileage Category: F

Body Styles	TMV Pricing		
	Trade	Private	Dealer
2 Dr Enthusiast Hbk	20798	22138	24372
2 Dr Performance Hbk	22365	23807	26209
2 Dr STD Hbk	19000	20224	22264

Options	Price
18 Inch Wheels - Chrome	+1145
Aero Kit [Opt on Enthusiast, Performance, STD, Touring]	+358
Automatic 5-Speed Transmission [Opt on Enthusiast, Touring]	+670

Body Styles	TMV Pricing		
	Trade	Private	Dealer
2 Dr Touring Hbk	22590	24046	26473
2 Dr Track Hbk	23192	24687	27178

Options	Price
Front Head Airbag Restraints	+242
Front Side Airbag Restraints	+152
Navigation System [Opt on Performance, Touring, Track]	+1380

Nissan's premier sports car has been resurrected after a six-year absence. Possessing excellent handling and power, the 350Z comes with a price tag that is thousands less than the competition's.

Altima
2004

Mileage Category: D

Body Styles	TMV Pricing		
	Trade	Private	Dealer
4 Dr 2.5 S Sdn	12768	13729	15331
4 Dr 2.5 SL Sdn	15757	16890	18778

Options	Price
17 Inch Wheels - Chrome [Opt on 3.5 SE]	+1350
AM/FM/CD Changer Audio System [Opt on S, SE]	+250
Alarm System [Opt on S]	+180
Aluminum/Alloy Wheels [Opt on S]	+480
Antilock Brakes [Opt on S, SL, SE]	+500
Automatic 4-Speed Transmission [Opt on S, SE, STD]	+500
Automatic Climate Control [Opt on 3.5 SE]	+300
Automatic Dimming Rearview Mirror	+150
Automatic On/Off Headlights	+120
Bose Audio System [Opt on S, SE]	+300

Body Styles	TMV Pricing		
	Trade	Private	Dealer
4 Dr 2.5 Sdn	11533	12583	14333
4 Dr 3.5 SE Sdn	15841	17061	19095

Options	Price
Fog Lights [Opt on S, SL, STD]	+280
Front Side Airbag Restraints [Opt on S, SL, SE]	+300
Garage Door Opener [Opt on 3.5 SE]	+120
Heated Front Seats [Opt on SE]	+250
Leather Seats [Opt on SE]	+850
Power Driver Seat [Opt on S]	+255
Power Heated Mirrors	+135
Power Moonroof [Opt on S, SL, SE]	+800
Rear Spoiler [Opt on SE]	+350
Xenon Headlamps [Opt on SE]	+500

The Altima's winning formula continues with few changes. Smoke is a new exterior color choice, and four-cylinder models meet stricter federal emissions standards. Models with California emissions are now classified as Partial Zero Emissions Vehicles (PZEV).

2003

After last year's debut to critical acclaim, Nissan's midsize sedan receives minor changes for 2003. Two new exterior colors, Sonoma Sunset and Crystal Blue add pizzazz to the wardrobe. There's a new charcoal seat fabric, padded cloth front center armrest cover (genuine leather on leather-equipped vehicles) and bright titanium interior accent colors for all models to spruce up the interior. The 2.5 SL receives a standard automatic transmission, heated front seats, heated outside mirrors and simulated wood trim. For the 3.5 SE, there is a Sport Package, which includes a sunroof and spoiler, and a Sport Package Plus, which includes sunroof, spoiler, Bose audio system and HID headlights. The 3.5 SE Leather Package now includes a Bose audio system, sunroof and heated seats, while the Leather Sport Package adds a spoiler and xenon headlights. Finally, a new 3.5 SE Premium Leather Package sports all of the above plus throws in fake wood to boot. How can you go wrong?

Mileage Category: D

Body Styles	TMV Pricing		
	Trade	Private	Dealer
4 Dr 2.5 S Sdn	11642	12607	14215
4 Dr 2.5 SL Sdn	14557	15661	17501

Options	Price
AM/FM/CD Changer Audio System [Opt on S,SE]	+380
Alarm System [Opt on S]	+117
Aluminum/Alloy Wheels [Opt on S]	+242
Antilock Brakes [Opt on S,SL,SE]	+469
Automatic 4-Speed Transmission [Opt on S,SE,STD]	+345
Automatic Climate Control [Opt on 3.5 SE]	+173
Bose Audio System [Opt on S,SE]	+207
Fog Lights [Opt on S,SL,STD]	+193
Front Side Airbag Restraints [Opt on S,SL,SE]	+173

Body Styles	TMV Pricing		
	Trade	Private	Dealer
4 Dr 2.5 Sdn	10585	11462	12923
4 Dr 3.5 SE Sdn	14571	15779	17791

Options	Price
Front and Rear Head Airbag Restraints [Opt on S,SL,SE]	+173
Heated Front Seats [Opt on SE]	+190
Leather Seats [Opt on SE]	+587
Power Driver Seat [Opt on S]	+176
Power Moonroof [Opt on S,SL,SE]	+586
Rear Spoiler [Opt on SE]	+275
Xenon Headlamps [Opt on SE]	+344

2002

The all-new third-generation 2002 Altima represents a total revision and rethinking of Nissan's midsize sedan -- it brings a level of design and performance that currently does not exist in its class. With a choice of a 240-horsepower, 3.5-liter V6 or 175-horsepower, 2.5-liter four-cylinder and an all-new four-wheel independent suspension, the Altima offers spirit with state-of-the-art technology. An aggressive new exterior design with increases in all major dimensions and a driver-oriented interior with myriad convenience and luxury features set the Altima apart in the highly competitive sedan marketplace.

Mileage Category: D

Body Styles	TMV Pricing		
	Trade	Private	Dealer
4 Dr 2.5 S Sdn	9903	10837	12394
4 Dr 2.5 SL Sdn	11867	12987	14852

Options	Price
16 Inch Wheels [Opt on 2.5 S]	+210
AM/FM/CD Changer Audio System	+330
Antilock Brakes [Opt on 2.5]	+408
Automatic 4-Speed Transmission	+480
Automatic Climate Control	+150
Bose Audio System	+180
Fog Lights [Std on 3.5 SE]	+156
Front Side Airbag Restraints	+150

Body Styles	TMV Pricing		
	Trade	Private	Dealer
4 Dr 2.5 Sdn	9535	10434	11933
4 Dr 3.5 SE Sdn	12810	14019	16033

Options	Price
Front and Rear Head Airbag Restraints [Opt on 3.5 SE,S,SL]	+150
Heated Front Seats	+165
Leather Seats	+510
Power Driver Seat [Opt on 2.5 S]	+153
Power Moonroof	+510
Rear Spoiler	+240
Xenon Headlamps	+300

2001

GXE is available with a new Limited Edition package, which includes goodies like an eight-way power driver seat, remote keyless entry, floor mats, special badging and a security system.

Mileage Category: C

Body Styles	TMV Pricing		
	Trade	Private	Dealer
4 Dr GLE Sdn	7696	8982	10168
4 Dr GXE Sdn	6311	7366	8339

Options	Price
AM/FM/CD Audio System	+141
AM/FM/Cassette/CD Audio System [Opt on GXE]	+212
AM/FM/Cassette/CD Changer Audio System [Opt on GLE]	+212
Air Conditioning [Opt on GXE,XE]	+266
Antilock Brakes	+362
Automatic 4-Speed Transmission [Std on GLE]	+425
Compact Disc Changer	+233

Body Styles	TMV Pricing		
	Trade	Private	Dealer
4 Dr SE Sdn	7081	8265	9357
4 Dr XE Sdn	5867	6848	7753

Options	Price
Cruise Control [Std on GLE,SE]	+132
Front Side Airbag Restraints [Std on GLE]	+132
Leather Seats [Opt on SE]	+691
Power Driver Seat [Opt on SE]	+141
Power Moonroof	+452
Rear Spoiler [Std on SE]	+180

2000

For 2000 Altimas receive fresh front and rear styling tweaks, comfort and convenience enhancements, engine refinements and a revised suspension.

Mileage Category: C

Body Styles	TMV Pricing		
	Trade	Private	Dealer
4 Dr GLE Sdn	5999	7186	8350
4 Dr GXE Sdn	4949	5929	6890

Options	Price
AM/FM/CD Audio System	+126
AM/FM/Cassette/CD Audio System [Opt on GXE]	+131
Air Conditioning [Std on GLE,SE]	+238
Aluminum/Alloy Wheels [Opt on GXE]	+284
Antilock Brakes	+323

Body Styles	TMV Pricing		
	Trade	Private	Dealer
4 Dr SE Sdn	5536	6632	7706
4 Dr XE Sdn	4488	5377	6248

Options	Price
Automatic 4-Speed Transmission [Std on GLE]	+380
Cruise Control [Std on GLE,SE]	+118
Front Side Airbag Restraints [Std on GLE]	+119
Leather Seats [Opt on SE]	+473
Power Driver Seat [Opt on SE]	+126

Altima

Options	Price		Options	Price
Power Moonroof	+404		Rear Spoiler [Std on SE]	+195

1999

All 1999 models get two new exterior colors, improved speakers and a new head unit for the three-in-one stereo combo. The GLE trim level gets alloy wheels added to its standard equipment list, and all alloy wheels now have a bright finish instead of a painted finish. All SE trim levels are now called SE Limited (SE-L) models and come with additional equipment.

Mileage Category: C

Body Styles	TMV Pricing			Body Styles	TMV Pricing		
	Trade	Private	Dealer		Trade	Private	Dealer
4 Dr GLE Sdn	4588	5729	6916	4 Dr SE Sdn	4266	5326	6430
4 Dr GXE Sdn	3844	4799	5793	4 Dr XE Sdn	3393	4236	5114
4 Dr SE Limited Sdn	4531	5656	6828				

Options	Price		Options	Price
Air Conditioning [Opt on GXE]	+179		Leather Seats [Std on GLE]	+358
Aluminum/Alloy Wheels [Opt on GXE]	+215		Power Moonroof	+305
Antilock Brakes	+271		Rear Spoiler	+146
Automatic 4-Speed Transmission [Std on GLE]	+287			

1998

The Altima is totally redesigned for 1998. The Altima's new look is more wedge-shaped, with a trunk that looks like it has met the business end of a band saw. Standard equipment is up, including a CD player on every model except the XE.

Mileage Category: C

Body Styles	TMV Pricing			Body Styles	TMV Pricing		
	Trade	Private	Dealer		Trade	Private	Dealer
4 Dr GLE Sdn	3857	4965	6215	4 Dr SE Sdn	3370	4338	5430
4 Dr GXE Sdn	3062	3941	4933	4 Dr XE Sdn	2868	3692	4621

Options	Price		Options	Price
Air Conditioning [Opt on XE]	+149		Leather Seats [Opt on SE]	+296
Antilock Brakes	+224		Power Moonroof	+252
Automatic 4-Speed Transmission [Std on GLE]	+238		Rear Spoiler [Std on SE]	+121

1997

The 1997 models are virtually identical to 1996 models, except for the addition of new emissions equipment.

Mileage Category: C

Body Styles	TMV Pricing			Body Styles	TMV Pricing		
	Trade	Private	Dealer		Trade	Private	Dealer
4 Dr GLE Sdn	3105	4239	5625	4 Dr SE Sdn	2700	3687	4893
4 Dr GLE Sdn (1997.5)	2997	4092	5430	4 Dr SE Sdn (1997.5)	2726	3722	4940
4 Dr GXE Sdn	2377	3244	4304	4 Dr XE Sdn	2160	2949	3913
(1997.5)	2428	3316	4401	4 Dr XE Sdn (1997.5)	2241	3060	4060

Options	Price		Options	Price
AM/FM/CD Audio System	+123		Compact Disc Changer	+175
Air Conditioning [Opt on GXE,XE]	+131		Leather Seats [Std on GLE]	+261
Antilock Brakes	+198		Power Moonroof [Std on GLE]	+222
Automatic 4-Speed Transmission [Std on GLE]	+210			

1996

New wheel covers, power lock logic and fresh GXE upholstery update this hot-selling sedan.

Body Styles	TMV Pricing			Body Styles	TMV Pricing		
	Trade	Private	Dealer		Trade	Private	Dealer
4 Dr GLE Sdn	1950	2834	4055	4 Dr SE Sdn	1818	2642	3779
4 Dr GXE Sdn	1619	2352	3365	4 Dr XE Sdn	1507	2190	3134

Options	Price		Options	Price
Air Conditioning [Opt on GXE,XE]	+116		Leather Seats	+232
Antilock Brakes	+176		Power Moonroof	+198
Automatic 4-Speed Transmission [Std on GLE]	+193		Power Sunroof [Std on SE]	+198

1995

Minor exterior tweaks to the grille, taillights and wheels are the only changes for this attractive compact from Tennessee.

Mileage Category: C

Body Styles	TMV Pricing			Body Styles	TMV Pricing		
	Trade	Private	Dealer		Trade	Private	Dealer
4 Dr GLE Sdn	1550	2357	3703	4 Dr SE Sdn	1472	2237	3513
4 Dr GXE Sdn	1269	1929	3030	4 Dr XE Sdn	1108	1685	2647

Options	Price		Options	Price
AM/FM/CD Audio System	+99		Automatic 4-Speed Transmission [Std on GLE]	+168
Air Conditioning [Opt on GXE,XE]	+105		Compact Disc Changer	+141
Antilock Brakes	+159		Leather Seats	+210

1995 (cont'd)

Options	Price
Power Moonroof [Opt on GXE]	+179

Armada

2004

The Pathfinder Armada is an all-new full-size sport-utility vehicle from Nissan. Based on the Titan pickup, it features a standard V8 engine, seating for eight and numerous family-friendly features.

Mileage Category: N

Body Styles	TMV Pricing		
	Trade	Private	Dealer
4 Dr LE 4WD SUV	27988	29473	31948
4 Dr LE SUV	26187	27561	29850
4 Dr SE 4WD SUV	25080	26565	29040

Body Styles	TMV Pricing		
	Trade	Private	Dealer
4 Dr SE Off-Road 4WD SUV	27114	28599	31074
4 Dr SE Off-Road SUV	25309	26760	29179
4 Dr SE SUV	23279	24662	26968

Options	Price
Automatic Climate Control (2 Zone) - Driver and Passenger [Opt on LE]	+850
Automatic Load Leveling [Opt on SE]	+400
DVD Entertainment System	+1600
Leather Seats [Opt on SE]	+1100
Navigation System [Opt on LE]	+1300
Power Moonroof	+900

Options	Price
Power Passenger Seat [Opt on LE, SE]	+250
Power Rear Liftgate [Opt on LE]	+350
Rear Air Conditioning Controls [Opt on LE]	+150
Satellite Radio System	+400
Trailer Hitch [Opt on SE]	+250

Frontier

2004

The SE now sports 17-inch five-spoke alloy wheels and tires.

Mileage Category: J

Body Styles	TMV Pricing		
	Trade	Private	Dealer
2 Dr SC S/C 4WD Ext Cab SB	16200	17294	19116
2 Dr STD Ext Cab SB	8831	9925	11747
2 Dr SVE S/C 4WD Ext Cab SB	14195	15409	17433
2 Dr XE 4WD Ext Cab SB	12532	13626	15448
2 Dr XE Desert Runner Ext Cab SB	10888	11982	13804
2 Dr XE Ext Cab SB	9496	10590	12412
4 Dr LE Crew Cab LB	15501	16616	18473
4 Dr LE Crew Cab SB	15153	16268	18126
4 Dr SC S/C 4WD Crew Cab LB	17801	18895	20717

Body Styles	TMV Pricing		
	Trade	Private	Dealer
4 Dr SC S/C 4WD Crew Cab SB	17452	18546	20368
4 Dr SC S/C Crew Cab LB	16157	17251	19073
4 Dr SC S/C Crew Cab SB	15808	16902	18724
4 Dr SVE S/C 4WD Crew Cab LB	16555	17649	19471
4 Dr SVE S/C 4WD Crew Cab SB	16207	17301	19123
4 Dr XE 4WD Crew Cab LB	14354	15523	17470
4 Dr XE 4WD Crew Cab SB	14006	15100	16922
4 Dr XE Crew Cab LB	12709	13803	15625
4 Dr XE Crew Cab SB	12362	13456	15278

Options	Price
AM/FM/CD Changer Audio System [Opt on XE, Crew SC]	+350
Air Conditioning [Opt on XE]	+350
Alarm System [Opt on SC Crew]	+200
Aluminum/Alloy Wheels [Opt on XE Ext]	+450
Automatic 4-Speed Transmission [Opt on XE, Ext SVE]	+1150
Bed Extender	+240
Bed Liner	+360
Cruise Control [Opt on XE]	+200
Intermittent Wipers [Opt on XE Ext]	+130

Options	Price
Keyless Entry System [Opt on XE]	+150
Leather Seats [Opt on SC, SVE Crew]	+550
Limited Slip Differential (Center) [Opt on XE Crew]	+170
Luggage Rack [Opt on XE Crew]	+245
Power Door Locks [Opt on XE]	+120
Power Windows [Opt on XE]	+200
Running Boards [Opt on XE]	+285
Tilt Steering Wheel [Opt on XE]	+120

2003

Nissan's compact pickup rolls into 2003 with many new enhancements. Most interesting is a power-operated retractable top. The "Open Sky" top -- essentially a giant sunroof -- is optional on Crew Cab models. For safety, Nissan has added standard dual-stage front airbags for Crew Cabs, standard LATCH child seat anchors on King Cabs and Crew cabs, an optional stability control system and an optional tire pressure monitoring system. Other changes for 2003 include 10 more horsepower for normally aspirated V6 models, a driver seat-height adjuster and standard Electronic Brakeforce Distribution (EBD). King Cabs now have standard ABS, a new storage bin and a new first aid kit (V6 only).

Mileage Category: J

Body Styles	TMV Pricing		
	Trade	Private	Dealer
2 Dr SC S/C 4WD Ext Cab SB	13794	15022	17068
2 Dr SC S/C Ext Cab SB	11574	12605	14322
2 Dr SE 4WD Ext Cab SB	12960	14114	16037
2 Dr SE Desert Runner Ext Cab SB	11412	12428	14121
2 Dr STD Ext Cab SB	7405	8064	9163
2 Dr SVE S/C 4WD Ext Cab SB	12461	13570	15419
2 Dr XE 4WD Ext Cab SB	10937	11911	13534
2 Dr XE Desert Runner Ext Cab SB	9440	10280	11681
2 Dr XE Ext Cab SB	8919	9713	11036
4 Dr SC S/C 4WD Crew Cab LB	15076	16418	18655

Body Styles	TMV Pricing		
	Trade	Private	Dealer
4 Dr SC S/C 4WD Crew Cab SB	15015	16352	18580
4 Dr SC S/C Crew Cab LB	13686	14904	16935
4 Dr SC S/C Crew Cab SB	13374	14565	16549
4 Dr SE 4WD Crew Cab LB	14256	15525	17640
4 Dr SE 4WD Crew Cab SB	14159	15419	17520
4 Dr SE Crew Cab LB	12816	13957	15859
4 Dr SE Crew Cab SB	12601	13723	15593
4 Dr SVE S/C 4WD Crew Cab LB	14092	15347	17438
4 Dr SVE S/C 4WD Crew Cab SB	13747	14971	17010
4 Dr XE 4WD Crew Cab LB	12515	13629	15486

2003 (cont'd)

Body Styles	TMV Pricing		
	Trade	Private	Dealer
4 Dr XE 4WD Crew Cab SB	12010	13079	14861
4 Dr XE Crew Cab LB	11013	11993	13627

Options	Price
AM/FM/CD Audio System [Opt on STD,XE]	+169
AM/FM/CD Changer Audio System [Opt on XE]	+207
Air Conditioning [Opt on STD,XE]	+449
Aluminum/Alloy Wheels [Opt on XE]	+173
Automatic 4-Speed Transmission [Opt on SC,SVE,XE]	+725
Automatic Stability Control [Opt on SE]	+293
Bed Extender	+165
Bed Liner	+248
Leather Seats [Opt on SC,SE]	+552
Luggage Rack [Opt on XE]	+169

Body Styles	TMV Pricing		
	Trade	Private	Dealer
4 Dr XE Crew Cab SB	10851	11817	13427

Options	Price
Power Door Locks [Opt on XE]	+131
Power Windows [Opt on XE]	+173
Rockford Fosgate Audio System [Opt on SC]	+345
Side Steps [Opt on XE]	+179
Skid Plates	+275
Tilt Steering Wheel [Opt on XE]	+128
Tinted Glass [Opt on XE]	+121
Tire Pressure Monitoring System [Opt on SE]	+121
Trailer Hitch [Opt on SE]	+234

Mileage Category: J

2002

Nissan continues to enhance its compact pickup line with the introduction of the 2002 Frontier Crew Cab Long Bed, the first compact crew cab pickup to offer a full-size bed. Other improvements for the Frontier lineup include a redesigned instrument panel and console and an available Rockford Fosgate-powered audio system.

Body Styles	TMV Pricing		
	Trade	Private	Dealer
2 Dr SC S/C 4WD Ext Cab SB	10892	12051	13983
2 Dr SC S/C Ext Cab SB	9718	10752	12476
2 Dr SE 4WD Ext Cab SB	10392	11498	13342
2 Dr SE Desert Runner Ext Cab SB	9575	10594	12292
2 Dr STD Ext Cab SB	6300	6971	8088
2 Dr SVE S/C 4WD Ext Cab SB	10531	11652	13519
2 Dr XE 4WD Ext Cab SB	9275	10262	11907
2 Dr XE Desert Runner Ext Cab SB	8025	8879	10303
2 Dr XE Ext Cab SB	6888	7621	8843
4 Dr SC S/C 4WD Crew Cab LB	12616	13959	16196
4 Dr SC S/C 4WD Crew Cab SB	12603	13944	16179
4 Dr SC S/C Crew Cab LB	11462	12682	14715

Options	Price
AM/FM/CD Audio System [Opt on Ext - STD,XE]	+147
AM/FM/CD Changer Audio System [Opt on Crew Cab,Ext Cab]	+210
Air Conditioning [Opt on Ext - STD,XE]	+390
Aluminum/Alloy Wheels [Opt on XE Ext]	+150
Automatic 4-Speed Transmission [Opt on SC Ext Cab,STD,XE]	+630
Bed Extender [Opt on Crew Cab,Ext Cab]	+144
Bed Liner	+216
Compact Disc Changer [Opt on Crew Cab]	+300

Body Styles	TMV Pricing		
	Trade	Private	Dealer
4 Dr SC S/C Crew Cab SB	11205	12398	14385
4 Dr SE 4WD Crew Cab LB	11876	13140	15247
4 Dr SE 4WD Crew Cab SB	11597	12831	14888
4 Dr SE Crew Cab LB	10743	11886	13792
4 Dr SE Crew Cab SB	10477	11592	13450
4 Dr SVE S/C 4WD Crew Cab LB	11803	13059	15152
4 Dr SVE S/C 4WD Crew Cab SB	11513	12738	14780
4 Dr XE 4WD Crew Cab LB	10279	11373	13196
4 Dr XE 4WD Crew Cab SB	10125	11202	12998
4 Dr XE Crew Cab LB	9313	10304	11955
4 Dr XE Crew Cab SB	9203	10183	11815

Options	Price
Leather Seats	+420
Limited Slip Differential [Opt on XE - Crew Cab,Ext Cab]	+120
Luggage Rack [Opt on XE Crew Cab]	+117
Moonroof [Opt on SC,SE Ext Cab]	+168
Power Windows [Opt on SE Ext Cab,XE]	+150
Rockford Fosgate Audio System [Opt on Crew Cab]	+150
Tonneau Cover [Opt on Crew Cab,Ext Cab]	+666
Trailer Hitch [Opt on Crew Cab,Ext Cab]	+204

Mileage Category: J

2001

Fresh new styling with a decidedly industrial theme injects some much needed personality into the Frontier for 2001. A supercharged V6, making 210 horsepower and 246 pound-feet of torque (231 lb-ft with a manual tranny), is available on special Desert Runner, King Cab and Crew Cab models, which get black-chrome headlight surrounds. Supercharged Frontiers come standard with 17-inch wheels and a limited-slip differential and can be equipped with leather upholstery, bundled in a package that includes a premium audio system with in-dash CD changer and steering wheel controls, plus a security system. Interiors get new fabrics, gauges and dash trimmings, as well as a new steering wheel. Tailgate locks are standard across the board, and a number of new colors, with names straight out of a J.Crew catalog, are available, like Khaki, Salsa and Denim.

Body Styles	TMV Pricing		
	Trade	Private	Dealer
2 Dr SC S/C 4WD Ext Cab SB	9050	10577	11987
2 Dr SC S/C Ext Cab SB	8090	9455	10715
2 Dr SE 4WD Ext Cab SB	8888	10388	11772
2 Dr SE Desert Runner Ext Cab SB	7840	9163	10385
2 Dr XE 4WD Ext Cab SB	7984	9331	10575
2 Dr XE Desert Runner Ext Cab SB	6930	8099	9178
2 Dr XE Ext Cab SB	5937	6939	7864

Options	Price
AM/FM/CD Audio System	+249
AM/FM/Cassette/CD Audio System	+160
Air Conditioning [Std on Desert Runner SE,SE,Crew Cab]	+455

Body Styles	TMV Pricing		
	Trade	Private	Dealer
2 Dr XE Std Cab SB	5169	6042	6847
4 Dr SC S/C 4WD Crew Cab SB	9855	11518	13054
4 Dr SC S/C Crew Cab SB	9000	10519	11921
4 Dr SE 4WD Crew Cab SB	9778	11428	12952
4 Dr SE Crew Cab SB	8708	10178	11534
4 Dr XE 4WD Crew Cab SB	8875	10373	11755
4 Dr XE Crew Cab SB	7819	9139	10357

Options	Price
Aluminum/Alloy Wheels [Std on Desert Runner SE,SE]	+132
Automatic 4-Speed Transmission	+558
Bed Extender	+122
Bed Liner	+164

2001 (cont'd)

Options	Price
Compact Disc Changer	+297
Leather Seats	+532
Moonroof	+160
Power Windows	+133

Options	Price
Running Boards [Std on SE]	+175
Tonneau Cover	+590
Trailer Hitch	+175

2000

Nissan's pickup line expands to 11 models, including the new Desert Runner and a four-door Frontier Crew Cab.

Mileage Category: J

Body Styles	TMV Pricing		
	Trade	Private	Dealer
2 Dr SE 4WD Ext Cab SB	7387	8841	10267
2 Dr SE Desert Runner Ext Cab SB	6402	7662	8898
2 Dr XE 4WD Ext Cab SB	6197	7417	8613
2 Dr XE Desert Runner Ext Cab SB	5662	6777	7869
2 Dr XE Ext Cab SB	4866	5823	6762
2 Dr XE Std Cab SB	4244	5079	5898

Body Styles	TMV Pricing		
	Trade	Private	Dealer
2 Dr XE V6 4WD Ext Cab SB	6610	7912	9188
4 Dr SE 4WD Crew Cab SB	7961	9529	11065
4 Dr SE Crew Cab SB	6656	7966	9251
4 Dr XE 4WD Crew Cab SB	7074	8467	9833
4 Dr XE Crew Cab SB	6189	7407	8601

Options	Price
AM/FM/CD Audio System	+223
AM/FM/Cassette/CD Audio System	+143
Air Conditioning [Std on Desert Runner SE,SE,Crew Cab]	+407
Aluminum/Alloy Wheels [Std on Desert Runner SE,SE]	+118
Automatic 4-Speed Transmission	+499
Bed Extender	+142

Options	Price
Bed Liner	+142
Camper/Towing Package	+119
Compact Disc Changer	+265
Power Windows	+119
Running Boards [Std on SE]	+119
Sunroof	+119

1999

Two new King Cab models debut with a powerful V6 engine under the hood, and new standard and optional equipment is available.

Mileage Category: J

Body Styles	TMV Pricing		
	Trade	Private	Dealer
2 Dr SE 4WD Ext Cab SB	6198	7567	8991
2 Dr SE Ext Cab SB	4660	5689	6760
2 Dr XE 4WD Ext Cab SB	5292	6460	7675
2 Dr XE 4WD Std Cab SB	4835	5903	7014

Body Styles	TMV Pricing		
	Trade	Private	Dealer
2 Dr XE Ext Cab SB	4008	4893	5814
2 Dr XE Std Cab SB	3600	4395	5223
2 Dr XE V6 4WD Ext Cab SB	5581	6813	8095

Options	Price
AM/FM/CD Audio System	+168
Air Conditioning [Std on SE]	+341

Options	Price
Automatic 4-Speed Transmission	+377
Compact Disc Changer	+201

1998

Nissan introduces an all-new truck for 1998. This model, named the Frontier, is larger than the model it replaces, and has improved interior ergonomics.

Mileage Category: J

Body Styles	TMV Pricing		
	Trade	Private	Dealer
2 Dr SE 4WD Ext Cab SB	5164	6396	7785
2 Dr SE Ext Cab SB	4231	5239	6376
2 Dr STD Std Cab SB	3009	3726	4535
2 Dr XE 4WD Ext Cab SB	4625	5728	6971

Body Styles	TMV Pricing		
	Trade	Private	Dealer
2 Dr XE 4WD Std Cab SB	3991	4943	6017
2 Dr XE Ext Cab SB	3611	4471	5441
2 Dr XE Std Cab SB	3167	3922	4773

Options	Price
AM/FM/CD Audio System [Opt on XE]	+139
Automatic 4-Speed Transmission [Opt on 2WD]	+277

Options	Price
Compact Disc Changer	+166

King Cab

1997

Mileage Category: J

Body Styles	TMV Pricing		
	Trade	Private	Dealer
2 Dr SE 4WD Ext Cab SB	4338	5495	6908
2 Dr SE Ext Cab SB	3678	4658	5856

Body Styles	TMV Pricing		
	Trade	Private	Dealer
2 Dr XE 4WD Ext Cab SB	3862	4891	6149
2 Dr XE Ext Cab SB	3045	3857	4849

Options	Price
AM/FM/CD Audio System	+123
Air Conditioning [Opt on XE]	+262
Aluminum/Alloy Wheels [Opt on XE]	+131

Options	Price
Automatic 4-Speed Transmission [Opt on 2WD]	+262
Compact Disc Changer	+144

1997 (cont'd)

No changes for 1997.

1996

Heading into the last year of the current body style, Nissan adds a driver-side airbag to improve safety. Four-wheel-drive models get a new five-spoke alloy wheel design.

Mileage Category: J

Body Styles	TMV Pricing		
	Trade	Private	Dealer
2 Dr SE 4WD Ext Cab SB	3481	4468	5832
2 Dr SE Ext Cab SB	3029	3888	5075

Options	Price
Air Conditioning [Opt on XE]	+232
Aluminum/Alloy Wheels [Opt on XE]	+116

Body Styles	TMV Pricing		
	Trade	Private	Dealer
2 Dr XE 4WD Ext Cab SB	3235	4154	5422
2 Dr XE Ext Cab SB	2575	3306	4315

Options	Price
Automatic 4-Speed Transmission [Opt on 2WD]	+233

1995

King Cab models received no major changes for the 1995 model year as Nissan is preparing to introduce a completely redesigned truck within the next few years.

Mileage Category: J

Body Styles	TMV Pricing		
	Trade	Private	Dealer
2 Dr SE V6 4WD Ext Cab SB	3021	3893	5347
2 Dr XE 4WD Ext Cab SB	2588	3335	4581
2 Dr XE Ext Cab SB	1922	2478	3404

Options	Price
Air Conditioning [Opt on XE]	+210

Body Styles	TMV Pricing		
	Trade	Private	Dealer
2 Dr XE V6 4WD Ext Cab SB	2905	3744	5143
2 Dr XE V6 Ext Cab SB	2257	2909	3995

Options	Price
Automatic 4-Speed Transmission	+210

Maxima

2004

Mileage Category: D

Body Styles	TMV Pricing		
	Trade	Private	Dealer
4 Dr SE Sdn	18047	19336	21484

Options	Price
18 Inch Wheels - Chrome [Opt on SE]	+1530
AM/FM/Cassette/CD Changer Audio System [Opt on SE]	+250
Automatic Stability Control [Opt on SL]	+900
Heated Front Seats [Opt on SE]	+250
Heated Front and Rear Seats [Opt on SE]	+400
Heated Steering Wheel	+120
Leather Seats [Opt on SE]	+900
Navigation System [Opt on SE]	+2000
Power Driver Seat w/Memory	+250
Power Heated Mirrors [Opt on SE]	+180

Body Styles	TMV Pricing		
	Trade	Private	Dealer
4 Dr SL Sdn	19232	20516	22657

Options	Price
Power Moonroof	+900
Power Passenger Seat [Opt on SE]	+200
Power Rear Window Sunshade [Opt on SE]	+400
Power Retractable Mirrors	+150
Power Tilt and Telescopic Steering Wheel	+180
Rear Spoiler [Opt on SE]	+250
Satellite Radio System	+400
Traction Control System [Opt on SE]	+300
Xenon Headlamps [Opt on SE]	+520

The Maxima has been fully redesigned for 2004. It now rides on the same underpinnings as the well-received Nissan Altima. This year's Maxima is longer, wider and more powerful than the previous version.

2003

Mileage Category: D

Body Styles	TMV Pricing		
	Trade	Private	Dealer
4 Dr GLE Sdn	14774	15999	18039
4 Dr GXE Sdn	13678	14811	16700

Options	Price
Aluminum/Alloy Interior Trim [Opt on SE]	+155
Automatic Climate Control [Opt on SE]	+121
Bose Audio System [Opt on SE]	+242
Front Side Airbag Restraints [Opt on SE]	+172
Heated Front Seats [Opt on GLE,SE]	+173
Leather Seats [Opt on SE]	+621
Limited Slip Differential [Opt on SE]	+275

Body Styles	TMV Pricing		
	Trade	Private	Dealer
4 Dr SE Sdn	14092	15260	17206

Options	Price
Navigation System [Opt on GLE,SE]	+1380
Power Driver Seat w/Memory [Opt on SE]	+142
Power Heated Mirrors [Opt on GLE,SE]	+142
Power Moonroof [Opt on GLE,SE]	+621
Power Passenger Seat [Opt on SE]	+228
Rear Spoiler [Opt on GLE,GXE]	+344
Traction Control System [Opt on GLE]	+206

Since the Maxima was updated last year and is scheduled for a redesign in 2004, there are no major changes in store for the family sedan in 2003. There's a Titanium Edition package available for the SE and side airbags are now standard on GLEs.

Nissan
Maxima

2002

The Maxima receives updates this year that make it less of a family sedan and more of an entry-level luxury sport sedan. Headlining this year's upgrades is a 3.5-liter V6 that produces a stunning 255 horsepower. For maximum performance, sport-tuned SE models now combine this engine with a standard six-speed manual transmission. Other changes include revised exterior styling, additional feature content and an optional GPS navigation system.

Mileage Category: D

Body Styles	TMV Pricing		
	Trade	Private	Dealer
4 Dr GLE Sdn	12102	13243	15146
4 Dr GXE Sdn	11273	12337	14109

Options	Price
Bose Audio System [Std on GLE]	+210
Compact Disc Changer [Std on GLE]	+300
Front Side Airbag Restraints	+150
Heated Front Seats	+150
Leather Seats [Std on GLE]	+540
Limited Slip Differential	+240
Navigation System	+1200

Body Styles	TMV Pricing		
	Trade	Private	Dealer
4 Dr SE Sdn	11325	12393	14173

Options	Price
Power Driver Seat w/Memory [Opt on SE]	+123
Power Heated Mirrors	+123
Power Moonroof	+540
Power Passenger Seat [Std on GLE]	+198
Rear Spoiler	+294
Traction Control System	+180

2001

A 20th Anniversary edition includes the 227-horsepower version of the standard 3.0-liter V6 from the Infiniti I30, as well as goodies like bronze-lensed headlight covers, a body kit, ersatz carbon-fiber interior trim, drilled metal pedals and a number of features normally optional on the SE. This special model also gets an exclusive color: Majestic Blue. A new Meridian package is optional on all Maximas, bundling side-impact airbags and a low washer fluid indicator with heated front seats and side mirrors, as well as special trunk lid trim. Adding optional traction control to the SE or GLE results in a Z Edition Maxima, for some zany reason.

Mileage Category: D

Body Styles	TMV Pricing		
	Trade	Private	Dealer
4 Dr GLE Sdn	10258	11845	13310
4 Dr GXE Sdn	9158	10576	11884

Options	Price
AM/FM/Cassette/CD Audio System [Opt on GXE]	+133
Aluminum/Alloy Wheels [Opt on GXE]	+133
Automatic 4-Speed Transmission [Std on GLE]	+266
Bose Audio System [Std on GLE]	+478
Chrome Wheels	+659
Compact Disc Changer	+244
Front Side Airbag Restraints	+133

Body Styles	TMV Pricing		
	Trade	Private	Dealer
4 Dr SE 20th Anniv Sdn	10685	12339	13865
4 Dr SE Sdn	9680	11178	12560

Options	Price
Heated Front Seats	+127
Leather Seats [Std on GLE]	+599
Power Driver Seat	+133
Power Moonroof	+478
Power Passenger Seat [Opt on SE]	+175
Rear Spoiler [Std on SE]	+255
Traction Control System	+159

2000

The Maxima has been (controversially) redesigned, providing more power, more room and more amenities to the luxury/performance sedan buyer. Key among the improvements is 222 horsepower from the standard V6, a boost in rear-seat legroom and an available 200-watt Bose audio system.

Mileage Category: D

Body Styles	TMV Pricing		
	Trade	Private	Dealer
4 Dr GLE Sdn	8725	10418	12077
4 Dr GXE Sdn	7291	8706	10092

Options	Price
AM/FM/Cassette/CD Audio System [Opt on GXE]	+190
Aluminum/Alloy Wheels [Opt on GXE]	+297
Automatic 4-Speed Transmission [Std on GLE]	+475
Bose Audio System [Std on GLE]	+428
Compact Disc Changer	+284
Front Side Airbag Restraints	+119
Heated Front Seats	+119

Body Styles	TMV Pricing		
	Trade	Private	Dealer
4 Dr SE Sdn	7941	9481	10991

Options	Price
Leather Seats [Std on GLE]	+536
Power Driver Seat	+119
Power Moonroof	+428
Power Passenger Seat [Opt on SE]	+121
Rear Spoiler [Std on SE]	+227
Traction Control System	+142

1999

Traction control is now available on models with automatic transmissions and, in addition to minor interior enhancements, four new colors debut. The SE trim level has been renamed SE-Limited (SE-L) and offers new standard features.

Mileage Category: D

Body Styles	TMV Pricing		
	Trade	Private	Dealer
4 Dr GLE Sdn	7119	8697	10339
4 Dr GXE Sdn	5621	6867	8163

Options	Price
AM/FM/Cassette/CD Audio System [Opt on GXE]	+143
Aluminum/Alloy Wheels [Opt on GXE]	+224
Antilock Brakes	+271
Automatic 4-Speed Transmission [Std on GLE]	+358
Bose Audio System [Std on GLE]	+323

Body Styles	TMV Pricing		
	Trade	Private	Dealer
4 Dr SE Limited Sdn	6474	7909	9403
4 Dr SE Sdn	6439	7866	9352

Options	Price
Compact Disc Changer	+215
Leather Seats [Std on GLE]	+404
Power Moonroof	+323
Power Passenger Seat [Opt on SE]	+130
Rear Spoiler [Opt on GLE,GXE]	+172

Mileage Category: D

Body Styles	TMV Pricing		
	Trade	Private	Dealer
4 Dr GLE Sdn	5918	7354	8973
4 Dr GXE Sdn	4865	6045	7375

Options	Price
AM/FM/Cassette/CD Audio System [Opt on GXE]	+118
Aluminum/Alloy Wheels [Opt on GXE]	+185
Antilock Brakes	+224
Automatic 4-Speed Transmission [Std on GLE]	+297
Bose Audio System	+267

Body Styles	TMV Pricing		
	Trade	Private	Dealer
4 Dr SE Sdn	5452	6774	8265

Options	Price
Compact Disc Changer	+178
Leather Seats [Opt on SE]	+334
Power Moonroof	+267
Rear Spoiler [Std on SE]	+127

1998

Side-impact airbags are added to the optional equipment lists of the SE and GLE models. Sterling Mist is a new color choice for this sporty sedan.

Body Styles	TMV Pricing		
	Trade	Private	Dealer
4 Dr GLE Sdn	4698	6080	7769
4 Dr GXE Sdn	3759	4865	6216

Options	Price
Aluminum/Alloy Wheels [Opt on GXE]	+163
Antilock Brakes	+198
Automatic 4-Speed Transmission [Std on GLE]	+314
Bose Audio System	+235

Body Styles	TMV Pricing		
	Trade	Private	Dealer
4 Dr SE Sdn	4070	5268	6732

Options	Price
Compact Disc Changer	+157
Leather Seats [Opt on SE]	+294
Power Moonroof	+235

1997

The Nissan Maxima gets a new grille, headlights, bumpers and taillights. New alloy wheels and foglights on the SE, new wheel covers on the GXE and new aluminum wheels on the GLE round out the changes.

Body Styles	TMV Pricing		
	Trade	Private	Dealer
4 Dr GLE Sdn	4053	5245	6892
4 Dr GXE Sdn	3118	4035	5302

Options	Price
Aluminum/Alloy Wheels [Opt on GXE]	+145
Antilock Brakes	+176
Automatic 4-Speed Transmission [Std on GLE]	+233
Bose Audio System	+186

Body Styles	TMV Pricing		
	Trade	Private	Dealer
4 Dr SE Sdn	3429	4438	5832

Options	Price
Compact Disc Changer	+139
Leather Seats [Opt on SE]	+261
Power Moonroof	+209

1996

All new for 1995, the excellent Maxima receives few changes for 1996. A four-way power passenger seat is available, a new center console cupholder will hold a Big Gulp and two new colors grace the Maxima's decidedly dull flanks. Taillights are as ugly as ever.

Body Styles	TMV Pricing		
	Trade	Private	Dealer
4 Dr GLE Sdn	3300	4236	5795
4 Dr GXE Sdn	2767	3551	4858

Options	Price
AM/FM/Cassette/CD Audio System [Std on GLE]	+84
Aluminum/Alloy Wheels [Opt on GXE]	+131
Antilock Brakes	+159
Automatic 4-Speed Transmission [Std on GLE]	+210

Body Styles	TMV Pricing		
	Trade	Private	Dealer
4 Dr SE Sdn	2986	3832	5242

Options	Price
Bose Audio System [Std on GLE]	+168
Leather Seats [Std on GLE]	+236
Power Moonroof	+189
Rear Spoiler [Std on SE]	+90

1995

Wow, what a beauty. The redesigned Maxima bows with an aerodynamic shape and a lengthened wheelbase. The new Maxima is available as a budget-minded GXE, sporty SE or luxurious GLE. All Maximas get the 190-horsepower engine previously exclusive to the SE.

Murano
2004

Mileage Category: M

Body Styles	TMV Pricing		
	Trade	Private	Dealer
4 Dr SE AWD SUV	22639	24131	26617
4 Dr SE SUV	21483	22974	25460

Options	Price
AM/FM/Cassette/CD Changer Audio System	+250
Bose Audio System	+650
DVD Entertainment System	+1720
Heated Front Seats	+250

Body Styles	TMV Pricing		
	Trade	Private	Dealer
4 Dr SL AWD SUV	21953	23445	25931
4 Dr SL SUV	20797	22288	24774

Options	Price
Leather Seats	+850
Luggage Rack	+200
Navigation System	+2000
Power Adjustable Foot Pedals	+300

Nissan
Murano/Pathfinder

2004 (cont'd)

SE models now include a manual-shift mode for the CVT, and satellite radio pre-wiring is standard on all models. The standard driver seat now features 10-way power adjustment.

Options	Price
Power Driver Seat w/Memory	+250
Power Heated Mirrors	+150
Power Moonroof	+900
Power Passenger Seat	+200

Options	Price
Satellite Radio System	+400
Trailer Hitch	+580
Xenon Headlamps [Opt on SL]	+250

2003

Not satisfied with the current crop of crossover SUVs? Nissan rolls out the newest car-based SUV, the Murano. It boasts a powerful V6 engine, distinct styling.

Mileage Category: M

Body Styles	TMV Pricing		
	Trade	Private	Dealer
4 Dr SE AWD SUV	20704	22104	24438
4 Dr SE SUV	19637	20966	23180

Body Styles	TMV Pricing		
	Trade	Private	Dealer
4 Dr SL AWD SUV	20171	21535	23808
4 Dr SL SUV	19107	20400	22554

Options	Price
18 Inch Wheels - Chrome	+828
AM/FM/Cassette/CD Changer Audio System	+155
Automatic Stability Control	+293
Bose Audio System	+242
Camper/Towing Package	+365
Heated Front Seats	+242
Leather Seats	+587
Luggage Rack	+117

Options	Price
Navigation System	+1380
Power Adjustable Foot Pedals	+173
Power Driver Seat w/Memory	+142
Power Moonroof	+621
Power Passenger Seat	+176
Tire Pressure Monitoring System	+121
Traction Control System	+173
Xenon Headlamps [Opt on SL]	+190

Pathfinder
2004

The LE models are now called Platinum Editions and include electroluminescent gauges, aluminum door sill plates and special dark wood trim. Rounding out the minimal changes for this year are three new exterior colors -- Canteen, Luminous Gold and Platinum.

Mileage Category: M

Body Styles	TMV Pricing		
	Trade	Private	Dealer
4 Dr LE Platinum 4WD SUV	20589	21797	23811
4 Dr LE Platinum SUV	18906	20110	22116

Body Styles	TMV Pricing		
	Trade	Private	Dealer
4 Dr SE 4WD SUV	17379	18578	20575
4 Dr SE SUV	16134	17328	19317

Options	Price
Automatic Climate Control [Opt on SE]	+250
Bose Audio System [Opt on SE]	+250
Compact Disc Changer [Opt on SE]	+150
DVD Entertainment System	+1600
Front Side Airbag Restraints [Opt on SE]	+300
Front and Rear Head Airbag Restraints [Opt on SE]	+350
Garage Door Opener [Opt on SE]	+150

Options	Price
Heated Front Seats [Opt on SE]	+200
Leather Seats [Opt on SE]	+900
Power Driver Seat [Opt on SE]	+225
Power Moonroof [Opt on SE]	+950
Power Passenger Seat [Opt on SE]	+225
Satellite Radio System	+400
Trailer Hitch	+450

2003

All 2003 Pathfinders will offer optional satellite radio, with a choice of XM or Sirius services. The LE model receives a standard leather-appointed interior, while SE models feature restyled wheels. Both models also feature a new four-spoke steering wheel and electronic rear-hatch window release. For safety, there is a new Vehicle Dynamic Control Package that bundles Vehicle Dynamic Control (VDC), traction control and a tire-pressure monitoring system. Two items no longer offered are the manual transmission and the optional navigation system. Guess you have to buy a map.

Mileage Category: M

Body Styles	TMV Pricing		
	Trade	Private	Dealer
4 Dr LE 4WD SUV	16413	17784	20069
4 Dr LE SUV	15827	17149	19353

Body Styles	TMV Pricing		
	Trade	Private	Dealer
4 Dr SE 4WD SUV	15005	16259	18348
4 Dr SE SUV	14355	15554	17553

Options	Price
Automatic Stability Control	+293
Bose Audio System [Opt on SE]	+138
Compact Disc Changer [Opt on SE]	+311
DVD Entertainment System	+1104
Fog Lights [Opt on SE]	+138
Front Side Airbag Restraints [Opt on SE]	+207
Heated Front Seats [Opt on SE]	+138
Leather Seats [Opt on SE]	+621

Options	Price
Power Driver Seat [Opt on SE]	+179
Power Moonroof [Opt on SE]	+621
Power Passenger Seat [Opt on SE]	+179
Satellite Radio System	+275
Tire Pressure Monitoring System	+121
Traction Control System	+173
Trailer Hitch	+289
VCR Entertainment System	+897

For the latest vehicle information, visit www.edmunds.com

2002

Mileage Category: M

Body Styles	TMV Pricing		
	Trade	Private	Dealer
4 Dr LE 4WD SUV	14590	15999	18347
4 Dr LE SUV	13397	14690	16846

Options	Price
Automatic 4-Speed Transmission [Opt on SE 4WD]	+600
Bose Audio System [Std on LE]	+120
Compact Disc Changer [Std on LE]	+270
DVD Entertainment System	+960
Fog Lights [Std on LE]	+120
Front Side Airbag Restraints	+180
Heated Front Seats [Std on LE]	+120
Leather Seats	+540

Body Styles	TMV Pricing		
	Trade	Private	Dealer
4 Dr SE 4WD SUV	12766	13999	16053
4 Dr SE SUV	12288	13475	15452

Options	Price
Limited Slip Differential [Opt on LE]	+150
Navigation System	+1200
Power Driver Seat	+156
Power Driver Seat w/Memory [Opt on LE]	+132
Power Moonroof [Std on LE]	+540
Power Passenger Seat	+156
Trailer Hitch	+240
VCR Entertainment System	+780

The 2002 Nissan Pathfinder receives only minor refinements. These include a new front grille, steering wheel and a revised audio system with new faceplate and faster functioning in-dash six-disc CD changer. The SE trim, now the base Pathfinder since the XE has been dropped, features a new titanium-accented step rail and roof rack with integrated air dam, body-color bumpers and fender flares, new 16-inch aluminum-alloy wheels and new seat cloth. Not to be outdone, the luxurious LE has 17-inch aluminum-alloy wheels as standard equipment this year.

2001

Mileage Category: M

Body Styles	TMV Pricing		
	Trade	Private	Dealer
4 Dr LE 4WD SUV	12169	14013	15716
4 Dr LE SUV	11518	13264	14876
4 Dr SE 4WD SUV	11545	13295	14911

Options	Price
Automatic 4-Speed Transmission [Opt on SE]	+532
Compact Disc Changer	+382
Front Side Airbag Restraints	+160
Leather Seats	+478
Limited Slip Differential	+132

Body Styles	TMV Pricing		
	Trade	Private	Dealer
4 Dr SE SUV	10763	12394	13900
4 Dr XE 4WD SUV	11652	13418	15048
4 Dr XE SUV	10779	12412	13920

Options	Price
Navigation System	+1063
Power Driver Seat [Opt on SE]	+120
Power Moonroof	+478
Power Passenger Seat [Opt on LE,SE]	+120
Trailer Hitch	+207

A long overdue 250-horsepower V6 engine debuts for 2001, making Pathfinder the most powerful SUV in its class. An interior freshening and more standard goodies, as well as snazzy options like an in-dash navigation system and an entertainment system for rear-seat occupants, are new for 2001. Also added to the LE's options list this fall is the handy All-mode automatic 4WD system from the Infiniti QX4.

2000

Body Styles	TMV Pricing		
	Trade	Private	Dealer
4 Dr LE 4WD SUV	9915	11645	13341
4 Dr LE SUV	9294	10916	12505
4 Dr SE 4WD SUV	9343	10973	12570

Options	Price
Automatic 4-Speed Transmission [Opt on SE]	+475
Compact Disc Changer	+333
Exterior Spare Tire Carrier [Opt on SE]	+142
Front Side Airbag Restraints	+143
Heated Front Seats	+143
Leather Seats	+428

Body Styles	TMV Pricing		
	Trade	Private	Dealer
4 Dr SE SUV	8675	10189	11673
4 Dr XE 4WD SUV	8966	10530	12064
4 Dr XE SUV	8263	9705	11118

Options	Price
Limited Slip Differential	+118
Power Door Locks [Opt on XE]	+119
Power Driver Seat	+147
Power Moonroof	+428
Power Windows [Opt on XE]	+136
Trailer Hitch	+185

After a substantial update in the middle of the 1999 model year, the Pathfinder soldiers into the new millennium without change. However, rumor has it that later in 2000 the Pathfinder will get a massive power upgrade.

1999

Mileage Category: M

Body Styles	TMV Pricing		
	Trade	Private	Dealer
4 Dr LE 4WD SUV	8614	10328	12112
4 Dr LE 4WD SUV (1999.5)	8182	9810	11505
4 Dr LE SUV	7804	9357	10973
4 Dr LE SUV (1999.5)	7595	9106	10679
4 Dr SE 4WD SUV	7669	9195	10783
4 Dr SE Limited 4WD SUV (1999.5)	7733	9272	10873

Options	Price
AM/FM/Cassette/CD Audio System [Std on LE]	+126
Automatic 4-Speed Transmission [Opt on SE,XE]	+358
Bose Audio System [Std on LE]	+161

Body Styles	TMV Pricing		
	Trade	Private	Dealer
4 Dr SE Limited SUV (1999.5)	7354	8817	10340
4 Dr XE 4WD SUV	6974	8362	9807
4 Dr XE 4WD SUV (1999.5)	7578	9086	10655
4 Dr XE SUV	6410	7685	9013
4 Dr XE SUV (1999.5)	7052	8455	9915

Options	Price
Leather Seats [Opt on LE,SE]	+323
Power Moonroof	+323
Trailer Hitch	+140

Only the LE trim level sees change in 1999, with new body-color fender flares and SE-style alloy wheels, tires and tubular step rails.

1998

The only changes to the 1998 Pathfinder include chrome bumpers for the XE model, the addition of air conditioning to XE and SE standard equipment lists and additions to the XE Sport Package equipment.

Mileage Category: M

Body Styles	TMV Pricing		
	Trade	Private	Dealer
4 Dr LE 4WD SUV	6609	8117	9817
4 Dr LE SUV	6127	7524	9100
4 Dr SE 4WD SUV	5757	7070	8551

Options	Price
AM/FM/Cassette Audio System	+116
Automatic 4-Speed Transmission [Std on LE]	+297
Bose Audio System [Opt on SE]	+178

Body Styles	TMV Pricing		
	Trade	Private	Dealer
4 Dr XE 4WD SUV	5191	6375	7710
4 Dr XE SUV	4803	5899	7135

Options	Price
Leather Seats [Opt on SE]	+267
Power Moonroof	+267
Trailer Hitch	+116

1997

Changes to the 1997 Nissan Pathfinder include storage pockets added at all doors, a new exterior color and an available Bose sound system.

Mileage Category: M

Body Styles	TMV Pricing		
	Trade	Private	Dealer
4 Dr LE 4WD SUV	5950	7418	9212
4 Dr LE SUV	5372	6697	8316
4 Dr SE 4WD SUV	4946	6166	7657

Options	Price
Air Conditioning [Std on LE]	+262
Automatic 4-Speed Transmission [Std on LE]	+262
Bose Audio System [Opt on SE]	+157

Body Styles	TMV Pricing		
	Trade	Private	Dealer
4 Dr XE 4WD SUV	4440	5535	6873
4 Dr XE SUV	4118	5134	6375

Options	Price
Leather Seats [Opt on SE]	+235
Power Moonroof	+235

1996

Outstanding new Pathfinder debuts with dual airbags and great interior styling. Engine output is up, but the Pathfinder is still not going to win any drag races. The new interior is open, airy and much more comfortable than most of its competitors.

Mileage Category: M

Body Styles	TMV Pricing		
	Trade	Private	Dealer
4 Dr LE 4WD SUV	4820	6082	7824
4 Dr LE SUV	4460	5627	7239
4 Dr SE 4WD SUV	4125	5204	6695

Options	Price
Air Conditioning [Std on LE]	+232
Automatic 4-Speed Transmission [Std on LE]	+233

Body Styles	TMV Pricing		
	Trade	Private	Dealer
4 Dr XE 4WD SUV	3645	4599	5917
4 Dr XE SUV	3283	4143	5330

Options	Price
Leather Seats [Opt on SE]	+209
Power Moonroof	+209

1995

Mileage Category: M

Body Styles	TMV Pricing		
	Trade	Private	Dealer
4 Dr LE 4WD SUV	3569	4592	6297
4 Dr LE SUV	3239	4168	5715
4 Dr SE 4WD SUV	3075	3957	5426

Options	Price
Air Conditioning [Std on LE]	+210
Automatic 4-Speed Transmission [Std on LE]	+210

Body Styles	TMV Pricing		
	Trade	Private	Dealer
4 Dr XE 4WD SUV	2608	3355	4601
4 Dr XE SUV	2470	3178	4359

Options	Price
Leather Seats [Opt on SE]	+189

A two-wheel-drive version of Nissan's ancient sport-utility is now available in LE flavor.

Pickup

1997

Mileage Category: J

Body Styles	TMV Pricing		
	Trade	Private	Dealer
2 Dr STD Std Cab SB	2377	3011	3786
2 Dr XE 4WD Std Cab SB	3313	4196	5276

Options	Price
AM/FM/CD Audio System	+123
Air Conditioning	+262
Aluminum/Alloy Wheels	+131

Body Styles	TMV Pricing		
	Trade	Private	Dealer
2 Dr XE Std Cab SB	2703	3423	4304

Options	Price
Automatic 4-Speed Transmission [Opt on XE Std Cab]	+262
Compact Disc Changer	+144

The Value Truck package on XE models is now a no-cost option. It includes air conditioning, aluminum-alloy wheels, a tachometer, trip meter and an AM/FM/cassette stereo. All two-wheel-drive models with the Value Truck also get upgraded all-season tires and intermittent wipers. Two new exterior colors -- Autumn Sunburst and Starfire Blue Pearl -- have been added to the color palette.

1996

Nissan adds a driver-side airbag to improve safety. Four-wheel-drive models get a new five-spoke alloy wheel design.

Mileage Category: J

Body Styles	TMV Pricing		
	Trade	Private	Dealer
2 Dr STD Std Cab SB	1898	2437	3181
2 Dr XE 4WD Std Cab SB	2639	3387	4421

Options	Price
Air Conditioning	+232
Aluminum/Alloy Wheels	+116

Body Styles	TMV Pricing		
	Trade	Private	Dealer
2 Dr XE Std Cab SB	2146	2755	3596

Options	Price
Automatic 4-Speed Transmission [Opt on XE Std Cab]	+233

1995

Nissan compact pickups received no major changes for the 1995 model year in anticipation of a completely redesigned truck for 1996.

Mileage Category: J

Body Styles	TMV Pricing		
	Trade	Private	Dealer
2 Dr STD Std Cab LB HD	1877	2419	3322
2 Dr STD Std Cab SB	1474	1900	2610

Options	Price
Air Conditioning	+210

Body Styles	TMV Pricing		
	Trade	Private	Dealer
2 Dr XE 4WD Std Cab SB	2279	2938	4035
2 Dr XE Std Cab SB	1763	2272	3121

Options	Price
Automatic 4-Speed Transmission [Opt on XE]	+210

Quest

2004

The 2004 Quest is an all-new minivan from Nissan that features distinctive styling, innovative features and a powerful V6.

Mileage Category: P

Body Styles	TMV Pricing		
	Trade	Private	Dealer
4 Dr S Pass Van	16634	17762	19641
4 Dr SE Pass Van	21184	22380	24372

Options	Price
Aluminum/Alloy Wheels [Opt on S]	+500
Camper/Towing Package	+540
DVD Entertainment System	+1500
Front Side Airbag Restraints [Opt on SL]	+350
Heated Front Seats [Opt on SL]	+150
Leather Seats [Opt on SL]	+1300

Body Styles	TMV Pricing		
	Trade	Private	Dealer
4 Dr SL Pass Van	17697	18790	20612

Options	Price
Navigation System [Opt on SE, SL]	+1950
Park Distance Control (Rear) [Opt on S, SL]	+200
Power Passenger Seat [Opt on SL]	+200
Running Boards	+550
Satellite Radio System	+400

2002

This is likely the last year for the Quest before it is discontinued. As such, changes for 2002 are minimal. These include revised 16-inch alloy wheel designs for the GXE and SE, new exterior colors and revised option packages.

Mileage Category: P

Body Styles	TMV Pricing		
	Trade	Private	Dealer
4 Dr GLE Pass Van	12259	13528	15642
4 Dr GXE Pass Van	10331	11400	13181

Options	Price
AM/FM/CD Audio System [Opt on GXE]	+129
Air Conditioning - Front and Rear [Opt on GXE]	+375
Automatic Dimming Rearview Mirror	+125
Captain Chairs (4) [Opt on GXE]	+450
Child Seat (1) [Opt on GXE]	+138
Fog Lights [Opt on GXE]	+240
Heated Front Seats [Std on GLE]	+119
Leather Seats [Std on GLE]	+630
Luggage Rack [Opt on GXE]	+135

Body Styles	TMV Pricing		
	Trade	Private	Dealer
4 Dr SE Pass Van	11069	12215	14124

Options	Price
Power Driver Seat [Std on GLE]	+180
Power Moonroof	+510
Power Passenger Seat [Std on GLE]	+180
Rear Wind Deflector	+120
Running Boards	+324
Trailer Hitch	+264
Two-Tone Paint	+180
VCR Entertainment System	+420

2001

Despite the company's decision to kill the Quest after a short 2002 model run, Nissan imbues the 2001 Quest minivan with a raft of minor improvements. Styling front and rear is freshened, and redesigned alloy wheels debut on all models. The entry-level GXE gains a rear stabilizer bar, while the sporty SE receives acceleration-sensitive strut valving and a strut tower brace. New interior gauges and fabrics spice things up, and a 130-watt Super Sound system is standard on SE and GLE. Luxury GLE models also get an in-dash six-CD changer and a wood 'n' leather steering wheel. An optional overhead family entertainment system replaces the former floor-mounted model, though that rather archaic unit can still be specified for SE and GLE Quests equipped with a sunroof. Front seatbelts now have pre-tensioners for improved occupant protection, and crash test scores are up this year, as well.

Mileage Category: P

Body Styles	TMV Pricing		
	Trade	Private	Dealer
4 Dr GLE Pass Van	10259	12027	13659
4 Dr GXE Pass Van	8569	10046	11409

Options	Price
AM/FM/Cassette/CD Audio System [Opt on GXE]	+186
Air Conditioning - Front and Rear [Opt on GXE]	+345
Captain Chairs (2) [Opt on GXE]	+398
Child Seat (1) [Opt on GXE]	+122
Fog Lights	+202
Leather Seats [Opt on SE]	+583
Power Driver Seat	+165

Body Styles	TMV Pricing		
	Trade	Private	Dealer
4 Dr SE Pass Van	9307	10912	12393

Options	Price
Power Moonroof	+452
Power Passenger Seat [Opt on SE]	+175
Running Boards	+281
Trailer Hitch	+154
Two-Tone Paint	+159
VCR Entertainment System	+372

2000

A stabilizer bar is now standard on the GLE model while new titanium-colored accents have been added to the 16-inch SE and 15-inch GXE alloy wheels. The SE gets auto on/off headlights and all Quests now come with a video entertainment system at no extra cost.

Mileage Category: P

Body Styles	TMV Pricing		
	Trade	Private	Dealer
4 Dr GLE Pass Van	8032	9704	11343
4 Dr GXE Pass Van	6790	8203	9588

Options	Price
AM/FM/Cassette/CD Audio System [Opt on GXE]	+204
Air Conditioning - Front and Rear [Opt on GXE]	+308
Compact Disc Changer	+284
Fog Lights	+166
Leather Seats [Opt on SE]	+521

Body Styles	TMV Pricing		
	Trade	Private	Dealer
4 Dr SE Pass Van	7495	9054	10583

Options	Price
Power Driver Seat	+145
Power Moonroof	+404
Power Passenger Seat [Opt on SE]	+145
Running Boards	+237
Trailer Hitch	+137

1999

Nissan redesigns its minivan for 1999 and adds a new SE trim level, standard driver-side sliding rear door and a more powerful engine.

Mileage Category: P

Body Styles	TMV Pricing		
	Trade	Private	Dealer
4 Dr GLE Pass Van	6794	8429	10131
4 Dr GXE Pass Van	5850	7258	8723

Options	Price
AM/FM/Cassette/CD Audio System	+153
Air Conditioning - Front and Rear [Opt on GXE]	+233
Compact Disc Changer [Std on GLE]	+215
Leather Seats [Std on GLE]	+393

Body Styles	TMV Pricing		
	Trade	Private	Dealer
4 Dr SE Pass Van	6044	7498	9012

Options	Price
Power Driver Seat	+130
Power Moonroof	+305
Power Passenger Seat [Opt on SE]	+130

1998

Mileage Category: P

Body Styles	TMV Pricing		
	Trade	Private	Dealer
3 Dr GXE Pass Van	4952	6407	8047

Options	Price
AM/FM/Cassette/CD Audio System [Opt on XE]	+127
Air Conditioning - Front and Rear [Opt on XE]	+215
Antilock Brakes [Opt on XE]	+224
Captain Chairs (4) [Opt on XE]	+178

Body Styles	TMV Pricing		
	Trade	Private	Dealer
3 Dr XE Pass Van	4500	5822	7313

Options	Price
Compact Disc Changer	+178
Leather Seats	+325
Power Moonroof	+252

No changes to the 1998 Quest.

1997

A few new colors are the only changes to the 1997 Quest.

Mileage Category: P

Body Styles	TMV Pricing		
	Trade	Private	Dealer
3 Dr GXE Pass Van	3956	5386	7133

Options	Price
Air Conditioning - Front and Rear [Opt on XE]	+189
Antilock Brakes [Opt on XE]	+198
Captain Chairs (4) [Opt on XE]	+157

Body Styles	TMV Pricing		
	Trade	Private	Dealer
3 Dr XE Pass Van	3495	4759	6303

Options	Price
Compact Disc Changer	+157
Leather Seats	+287
Power Moonroof	+223

1996

Substantial upgrades include dual airbags, integrated child safety seats, side-impact protection meeting 1997 passenger car standards, revamped fabrics, new colors, freshened styling and a cool in-dash six-disc CD changer. The Quest is still in the hunt.

Mileage Category: P

Body Styles	TMV Pricing		
	Trade	Private	Dealer
3 Dr GXE Pass Van	3418	4810	6733

Options	Price
Air Conditioning - Front and Rear [Opt on XE]	+168
Antilock Brakes [Opt on XE]	+176

Body Styles	TMV Pricing		
	Trade	Private	Dealer
3 Dr XE Pass Van	2755	3879	5430

Options	Price
Compact Disc Changer	+139
Leather Seats	+255

1995

GXE models get standard captain's chairs for second-row occupants. The Extra Performance Package is renamed the Handling Package. No other significant changes for the Quest.

Mileage Category: P

Body Styles	TMV Pricing		
	Trade	Private	Dealer
3 Dr GXE Pass Van	2500	3642	5545

Options	Price
AM/FM/Cassette/CD Audio System [Opt on GXE]	+90
Air Conditioning - Front and Rear [Opt on XE]	+152
Antilock Brakes [Opt on XE]	+159

Body Styles	TMV Pricing		
	Trade	Private	Dealer
3 Dr XE Pass Van	2124	3095	13

Options	Price
Leather Seats	+231
Power Moonroof	+179
Power Sunroof	+137

Sentra

2004

Mileage Category: E

Body Styles	TMV Pricing		
	Trade	Private	Dealer
4 Dr 1.8 S Sdn	8286	9306	11006
4 Dr 1.8 Sdn	7227	8256	9970
4 Dr 2.5 S Sdn	9608	10630	12332

Options	Price
AM/FM/CD Audio System [Opt on 1.8 non-S]	+350
Air Conditioning [Opt on 1.8 non-S]	+900
Antilock Brakes [Opt on SE-R]	+320
Automatic 4-Speed Transmission [Opt on 1.8]	+800

Body Styles	TMV Pricing		
	Trade	Private	Dealer
4 Dr SE-R Sdn	10383	11457	13247
4 Dr SE-R Spec V Sdn	11057	12169	14021

Options	Price
Cruise Control [Opt on 1.8 S]	+140
Front Side Airbag Restraints [Opt on SE-R]	+250
Power Moonroof [Opt on 2.5 S, SE-R]	+700
Rear Spoiler [Opt on 1.8 S, 2.5 S]	+360

For 2004, the Sentra receives some exterior changes that include new front and rear fascias and a revised hood. Inside, the Sentra gets a new trip computer, which is standard on the SE-R, Spec V and 2.5 S. There is also an upgraded Rockford Fosgate stereo. The Sentra SE-R Spec V gets a new Brembo brake package, seats from the Skyline, new interior fabric and two new exterior colors -- Volcanic Orange and Sapphire Blue.

2003

Mileage Category: E

Body Styles	TMV Pricing		
	Trade	Private	Dealer
4 Dr 2.5 Limited Edition Sdn	8769	9737	11350
4 Dr GXE Sdn	7593	8441	9854
4 Dr SE-R Sdn	9648	10713	12488

Options	Price
AM/FM/CD Audio System [Opt on XE]	+242
Air Conditioning [Opt on XE]	+552
Aluminum/Alloy Wheels [Opt on GXE]	+173
Antilock Brakes [Opt on GXE,SE-R,SE-R Spec V]	+469
Automatic 4-Speed Transmission [Opt on GXE,SE-R,XE]	+552
Fog Lights [Opt on GXE]	+124

Body Styles	TMV Pricing		
	Trade	Private	Dealer
4 Dr SE-R Spec V Sdn	10265	11398	13287
4 Dr XE Sdn	6610	7348	8578

Options	Price
Front Side Airbag Restraints [Opt on GXE,SE-R,SE-R Spec V]	+173
Power Moonroof [Opt on 2.5 Ltd Ed,SE-R Spec V]	+483
Premium Audio System [Opt on GXE]	+224
Rear Spoiler [Opt on 2.5 Ltd Ed,GXE,XE]	+248
Rockford Fosgate Audio System [Opt on SE-R Spec V]	+275

For 2003, there is a new 2.5 Limited Edition trim, which includes GXE front fascia styling, the 165-horsepower QR25 4-cylinder engine, standard automatic transmission, standard Antilock Braking System (ABS) and side-impact supplemental airbags. The Sentra CA model is no longer available as all 1.8-liter engine-equipped Sentra XE and GXE models sold with California emission specifications offer zero evaporative emissions and meet SULEV (Super Ultra Low Emission Vehicles) standards. Other changes this year include a new power steering ratio for XE and GXE, a revised six-speed manual transmission for SE-R Spec V model and a new bright yellow exterior paint color for the SE-R and SE-R Spec V.

2002

Mileage Category: B

Body Styles	TMV Pricing		
	Trade	Private	Dealer
4 Dr CA Sdn	6978	7900	9436
4 Dr GXE Sdn	6668	7549	9017
4 Dr SE-R Sdn	7780	8822	10559

Options	Price
AM/FM/CD Audio System [Opt on XE]	+210
Air Conditioning [Opt on XE]	+480

Body Styles	TMV Pricing		
	Trade	Private	Dealer
4 Dr SE-R Spec V Sdn	8363	9483	11350
4 Dr XE Sdn	5680	6431	7682

Options	Price
Aluminum/Alloy Wheels [Opt on GXE]	+150
Antilock Brakes	+408

Beloved by compact car enthusiasts, the Nissan Sentra SE-R returns after a seven-year hiatus. The Sentra SE is no longer available, though Nissan has created additional options packages for the GXE to make it similar to the SE.

2002 (cont'd)

Options	Price
Automatic 4-Speed Transmission	+480
Compact Disc Changer	+240
Front Side Airbag Restraints	+165

Options	Price
Power Moonroof	+420
Rear Spoiler [Opt on GXE]	+132
Rockford Fosgate Audio System	+270

2001

After last year's redesign, the 2001 Sentra is carrying over unchanged in XE, GXE, SE and super-ultralow emission California trims.

Mileage Category: B

Body Styles	TMV Pricing		
	Trade	Private	Dealer
4 Dr CA Sdn	5923	7242	8460
4 Dr GXE Sdn	5532	6763	7900

Body Styles	TMV Pricing		
	Trade	Private	Dealer
4 Dr SE Sdn	6227	7613	8893
4 Dr XE Sdn	4795	5863	6849

Options	Price
AM/FM/Cassette Audio System [Opt on XE]	+160
Air Conditioning [Opt on XE]	+425
Aluminum/Alloy Wheels [Std on SE]	+318
Antilock Brakes	+362
Automatic 4-Speed Transmission	+425

Options	Price
Compact Disc Changer	+212
Front Side Airbag Restraints	+160
Power Moonroof	+319
Rear Spoiler	+180

2000

The Sentra has been completely overhauled for the 2000 model year. A better ride, more powerful engines and a new enviro-friendly version top the bill, and we likes what we sees.

Mileage Category: B

Body Styles	TMV Pricing		
	Trade	Private	Dealer
4 Dr GXE Sdn	4623	5803	6960
4 Dr SE Sdn	5305	6659	7986

Body Styles	TMV Pricing		
	Trade	Private	Dealer
4 Dr XE Sdn	3834	4812	5770

Options	Price
AM/FM/Cassette Audio System	+143
Air Conditioning [Opt on XE]	+380
Aluminum/Alloy Wheels [Std on SE]	+284
Antilock Brakes	+323
Automatic 4-Speed Transmission	+380

Options	Price
Compact Disc Changer	+190
Front Side Airbag Restraints	+119
Power Sunroof	+262
Rear Spoiler	+161

1999

Fresh front-end styling, a Limited Edition Option Package for GXE models and some new paint colors constitute the changes for 1999.

Mileage Category: B

Body Styles	TMV Pricing		
	Trade	Private	Dealer
4 Dr GXE Sdn	3807	4866	5969
4 Dr SE Limited Sdn	4119	5265	6458

Body Styles	TMV Pricing		
	Trade	Private	Dealer
4 Dr SE Sdn	4042	5167	6337
4 Dr XE Sdn	3217	4112	5044

Options	Price
AM/FM/Cassette/CD Audio System	+170
Air Conditioning [Opt on XE]	+287
Aluminum/Alloy Wheels [Opt on GXE]	+215
Antilock Brakes	+271

Options	Price
Automatic 4-Speed Transmission	+287
Power Moonroof	+197
Rear Spoiler [Opt on GXE,XE]	+121

1998

A new Sentra SE debuts, sporting the same 140-horespower engine and styling cues found in the 200SX SE-R coupe. Other changes include an exterior freshening that features new front and rear fascias.

Mileage Category: B

Body Styles	TMV Pricing		
	Trade	Private	Dealer
4 Dr GLE Sdn	3231	4239	5375
4 Dr GXE Sdn	3023	3967	5031
4 Dr SE Sdn	3300	4329	5490

Body Styles	TMV Pricing		
	Trade	Private	Dealer
4 Dr STD Sdn	2336	3065	3887
4 Dr XE Sdn	2644	3470	4401

Options	Price
AM/FM/Cassette/CD Audio System [Std on GLE]	+141
Air Conditioning [Opt on STD]	+238
Antilock Brakes	+224

Options	Price
Automatic 4-Speed Transmission	+238
Compact Disc Changer	+166
Power Moonroof	+163

1997

The base model is now simply called "Base" instead of S. Nissan works to quiet the Sentra's interior by using a bigger muffler and reducing the number of suspension-mounting points.

Mileage Category: B

Body Styles	TMV Pricing		
	Trade	Private	Dealer
4 Dr GLE Sdn	2604	3559	4726
4 Dr GXE Sdn	2410	3293	4373

Body Styles	TMV Pricing		
	Trade	Private	Dealer
4 Dr STD Sdn	1896	2591	3441
4 Dr XE Sdn	2123	2902	3853

1997 (cont'd)

Options	Price
AM/FM/CD Audio System	+123
Air Conditioning [Opt on STD]	+195
Antilock Brakes	+198

Options	Price
Automatic 4-Speed Transmission	+210
Compact Disc Changer	+146
Power Moonroof	+144

1996

Prices have crept up, making the Sentra a hard sell against the Neon, Prizm and Cavalier. Still, you may be able to find a good deal on a former rental vehicle. We've seen tons of them at the Alamo rental lots.

Body Styles	TMV Pricing		
	Trade	Private	Dealer
4 Dr GLE Sdn	1850	2643	3739
4 Dr GXE Sdn	1795	2565	3628

Mileage Category: B

Body Styles	TMV Pricing		
	Trade	Private	Dealer
4 Dr STD Sdn	1346	1923	2719
4 Dr XE Sdn	1533	2191	3099

Options	Price
Air Conditioning [Opt on STD]	+173
Antilock Brakes	+176

Options	Price
Automatic 4-Speed Transmission	+186

1995

An all-new Sentra is released featuring aero styling and a stubby trunk. The 1995 Sentra is available only as a four-door sedan, the two-door model now being called the 200SX. Increased interior space is the most noticeable feature of the redesign. The engines remain unchanged from previous models.

Body Styles	TMV Pricing		
	Trade	Private	Dealer
4 Dr GLE Sdn	1404	2097	3252
4 Dr GXE Sdn	1303	1948	3022

Mileage Category: B

Body Styles	TMV Pricing		
	Trade	Private	Dealer
4 Dr STD Sdn	1023	1529	2372
4 Dr XE Sdn	1194	1784	2767

Options	Price
Aluminum/Alloy Wheels	+126
Antilock Brakes	+159

Options	Price
Automatic 4-Speed Transmission	+168

Titan
2004

Body Styles	TMV Pricing		
	Trade	Private	Dealer
4 Dr LE 4WD Crew Cab SB	23640	25148	27662
4 Dr LE 4WD Ext Cab SB	21537	23012	25472
4 Dr LE Crew Cab SB	21375	22872	25368
4 Dr LE Ext Cab SB	19475	20951	23410
4 Dr SE 4WD Crew Cab SB	20714	22227	24748
4 Dr SE 4WD Ext Cab SB	18610	20086	22545

Mileage Category: K

Body Styles	TMV Pricing		
	Trade	Private	Dealer
4 Dr SE Crew Cab SB	18449	19949	22450
4 Dr SE Ext Cab SB	16548	18023	20482
4 Dr XE 4WD Crew Cab SB	19650	21164	23689
4 Dr XE 4WD Ext Cab SB	17281	18756	21215
4 Dr XE Crew Cab SB	17385	18887	21390
4 Dr XE Ext Cab SB	15219	16694	19152

The Titan is an all-new full-size truck from Nissan. It was designed to compete head-on with the best-selling half-ton trucks from Ford, GM and Dodge.

Options	Price
17 Inch Wheels [Opt on 4WD]	+350
Bed Extender	+240
Bed Liner [Opt on XE, SE]	+320
DVD Entertainment System [Opt on SE, LE Crew]	+1450
Fog Lights [Opt on XE, SE 4WD]	+150
Front Side Airbag Restraints	+400
Front and Rear Head Airbag Restraints	+450
Navigation System [Opt on LE]	+1850
Off-Road Suspension Package [Opt on 4WD]	+200

Options	Price
Overhead Console [Opt on XE]	+120
Park Distance Control (Rear) [Opt on LE]	+350
Power Adjustable Foot Pedals [Opt on SE]	+180
Power Moonroof [Opt on LE Crew]	+900
Privacy Glass [Opt on XE Ext]	+130
Sliding Rear Window [Opt on XE Ext]	+150
Split Front Bench Seat [Opt on SE]	+190
Trailer Hitch [Opt on SE, LE]	+500

Xterra
2004

Body Styles	TMV Pricing		
	Trade	Private	Dealer
4 Dr SE 4WD SUV	15952	16953	18623
4 Dr SE S/C 4WD SUV	16709	17717	19398
4 Dr SE S/C SUV	15708	16718	18400
4 Dr SE SUV	14783	15776	17431

Mileage Category: M

Body Styles	TMV Pricing		
	Trade	Private	Dealer
4 Dr XE SUV	11447	12348	13849
4 Dr XE V6 4WD SUV	13537	14438	15939
4 Dr XE V6 SUV	12307	13208	14709

Options	Price
AM/FM/CD Changer Audio System [Opt on XE V6]	+375
Alarm System [Opt on XE V6]	+120
Automatic 4-Speed Transmission [Opt on XE V6]	+1000

Options	Price
Automatic Dimming Rearview Mirror [Opt on XE, XE V6]	+220
Cruise Control [Opt on XE, XE V6]	+200

For 2004, 17-inch alloy wheels are now standard on non-supercharged SE models, and 16-inch, four-spoke alloys are standard on the XE-V6.

2004 (cont'd)

Options	Price
Fog Lights [Opt on XE V6]	+225
Front and Rear Head Airbag Restraints	+500
Intermittent Wipers	+145
Keyless Entry System [Opt on XE, XE V6]	+180
Leather Seats [Opt on SE]	+999
Limited Slip Differential (Rear) [Opt on XE V6]	+249
Moonroof [Opt on SE]	+349
Painted Wheels [Opt on XE V6]	+300

Options	Price
Power Door Locks [Opt on XE, XE V6]	+120
Power Windows [Opt on XE, XE V6]	+330
Rockford Fosgate Audio System [Opt on XE V6]	+300
Side Steps [Opt on XE]	+300
Steering Wheel Radio Controls	+125
Tilt Steering Wheel [Opt on XE]	+150
Trailer Hitch	+349

2003

Though the Xterra was updated just last year, Nissan has made further changes for 2003. Mechanically, the V6 has received a slight increase in power, and a stability control system (Nissan's VDC) will be a new option. Also for 2003, Xterra XE V6 models come with standard 16-inch alloy wheels and tubular step rails, and four new exterior colors are available, including Atomic Orange and Camouflage (limited and late availability). Inside, a driver seat-height and lumbar adjuster has been added to V6 models and a new roof headliner net (on nonsunroof models) and luggage side net have also been added, along with new metal ceiling tie-down hooks. A "rugged" leather package is now offered for the SE trim. Other refinements include a 300-watt rating for the Rockford Fosgate-powered eight-speaker audio system, an available tire-pressure monitoring system and Electronic Brakeforce Distribution. A heavy-duty alternator and dual 12-volt power outlets located in the engine compartment are also standard on SE trim.

Mileage Category: M

Body Styles	TMV Pricing		
	Trade	Private	Dealer
4 Dr SE 4WD SUV	14403	15606	17611
4 Dr SE S/C 4WD SUV	14803	16040	18101
4 Dr SE S/C SUV	14186	15371	17347
4 Dr SE SUV	13414	14535	16403

Body Styles	TMV Pricing		
	Trade	Private	Dealer
4 Dr XE SUV	10457	11330	12786
4 Dr XE V6 4WD SUV	12412	13449	15177
4 Dr XE V6 SUV	11375	12325	13909

Options	Price
AM/FM/CD Changer Audio System [Opt on XE V6]	+259
Alarm System [Opt on XE V6]	+138
Automatic 4-Speed Transmission [Opt on XE V6]	+690
Automatic Dimming Rearview Mirror [Opt on XE,XE V6]	+151
Automatic Stability Control [Opt on SE]	+293
Cruise Control [Opt on XE,XE V6]	+128
Fog Lights [Opt on XE V6]	+155
Front and Rear Head Airbag Restraints	+344
Keyless Entry System [Opt on XE,XE V6]	+117
Leather Seats [Opt on SE]	+690
Limited Slip Differential [Opt on XE V6]	+173

Options	Price
Moonroof [Opt on SE]	+241
Power Door Locks [Opt on XE,XE V6]	+155
Power Mirrors [Opt on XE,XE V6]	+128
Power Windows [Opt on XE,XE V6]	+176
Rockford Fosgate Audio System [Opt on XE V6]	+207
Side Steps [Opt on XE]	+207
Tilt Steering Wheel [Opt on XE]	+117
Tire Pressure Monitoring System [Opt on SE]	+121
Traction Control System [Opt on SE]	+173
Trailer Hitch	+241

2002

Nissan's popular Xterra SUV receives a variety of updates for the 2002 model year. Front-end styling is updated, and the bulged hood hides a newly optional supercharged V6. Inside, there are revised gauges, seat fabrics, climate controls, two additional power points and a bigger glovebox. Also standard are dual-stage front airbags, rear child-seat anchors, variable intermittent front windshield wipers, a rear window wiper and a foot-operated parking brake. In terms of options, a new in-dash six-disc CD changer is available on XE Xterras and standard on SE models. Nissan has also made the sunroof optional instead of standard. Finally, as a tribute to dedicated Xterra owners, an Enthusiast Package is available only on XE V6 four-wheel-drive models. It includes ceiling tie clamps, a first aid kit, a tilt steering wheel, foglights, front tow hooks, map lights, a limited-slip differential, manually locking hubs and rubber floor mats.

Mileage Category: M

Body Styles	TMV Pricing		
	Trade	Private	Dealer
4 Dr SE 4WD SUV	12177	13353	15313
4 Dr SE S/C 4WD SUV	12825	14063	16127
4 Dr SE S/C SUV	11829	12971	14874
4 Dr SE SUV	11194	12275	14077
4 Dr XE S/C 4WD SUV	12073	13239	15182

Body Styles	TMV Pricing		
	Trade	Private	Dealer
4 Dr XE S/C SUV	11088	12158	13942
4 Dr XE SUV	8724	9566	10971
4 Dr XE V6 4WD SUV	10336	11334	12998
4 Dr XE V6 SUV	9433	10344	11861

Options	Price
Alarm System [Opt on XE V6]	+120
Aluminum/Alloy Wheels [Opt on XE V6]	+240
Automatic 4-Speed Transmission	+600
Automatic Dimming Rearview Mirror	+132
Brush Guard	+354
Fog Lights [Opt on XE V6]	+120

Options	Price
Limited Slip Differential [Opt on XE V6]	+150
Moonroof [Opt on SE]	+210
Power Door Locks [Opt on XE,XE V6]	+135
Power Windows [Opt on XE,XE V6]	+153
Side Steps [Opt on XE,XE V6]	+180
Trailer Hitch	+210

2001

SE models come with titanium interior accents as well as a premium audio system boasting 100 watts of peak power and an in-dash six-disc CD changer. New steering wheel-mounted audio controls can be used to operate this system. New colors, including one called Gold Rush, and restyled 16-inch alloy wheels round out the changes.

Mileage Category: M

Body Styles	TMV Pricing		
	Trade	Private	Dealer
4 Dr SE 4WD SUV	11143	12832	14391
4 Dr SE SUV	10260	11814	13249
4 Dr XE SUV	7862	9054	10154

Body Styles	TMV Pricing		
	Trade	Private	Dealer
4 Dr XE V6 4WD SUV	9473	10909	12235
4 Dr XE V6 SUV	8552	9849	11046

Options	Price
AM/FM/Cassette/CD Audio System	+160
Aluminum/Alloy Wheels [Std on SE]	+318
Automatic 4-Speed Transmission	+532
Automatic Dimming Rearview Mirror	+116

Options	Price
Brush Guard	+324
Compact Disc Changer	+233
Fog Lights [Std on SE]	+120
Limited Slip Differential [Std on SE]	+133

Options	Price
Power Door Locks [Std on SE]	+120
Power Windows [Std on SE]	+136

Options	Price
Side Steps [Opt on XE,XE V6]	+160
Trailer Hitch	+186

Mileage Category: M

Body Styles	TMV Pricing		
	Trade	Private	Dealer
4 Dr SE 4WD SUV	9464	11114	12731
4 Dr SE SUV	8648	10155	11633
4 Dr XE SUV	6689	7855	8998

Body Styles	TMV Pricing		
	Trade	Private	Dealer
4 Dr XE V6 4WD SUV	8222	9655	11061
4 Dr XE V6 SUV	7305	8579	9827

2000

A truck-based mini-SUV, the athletic new Xterra competes with several smaller vehicles built on car platforms.

Options	Price
AM/FM/CD Audio System [Opt on XE]	+119
Aluminum/Alloy Wheels [Std on SE]	+284
Automatic 4-Speed Transmission	+475
Camper/Towing Package	+119

Options	Price
Compact Disc Changer	+309
Limited Slip Differential [Std on SE]	+119
Power Windows [Std on SE]	+121

Oldsmobile
Achieva/Alero

Achieva

1998

Mileage Category: C

Body Styles	TMV Pricing		
	Trade	Private	Dealer
4 Dr SL Sdn	1880	2597	3405

Oldsmobile limited sales of the Achieva to fleets for 1998, so if you're considering one, it's probably a former rental car.

1997

Side-impact standards are met, and standard equipment lists are enhanced. Series II Coupe gets new alloy wheels, and the lineup has been simplified.

Mileage Category: C

Body Styles	TMV Pricing			Body Styles	TMV Pricing		
	Trade	Private	Dealer		Trade	Private	Dealer
2 Dr SC Cpe	1427	2142	3016	4 Dr SL Sdn	1364	2048	2883

Options	Price
Power Moonroof	+118

1996

Substantial upgrades make the Achieva palatable for 1996. A new interior with dual airbags, standard air conditioning, a new base engine, daytime running lights, a theft-deterrent system and optional traction control make this Oldsmobile an excellent value in the compact class.

Mileage Category: C

Body Styles	TMV Pricing			Body Styles	TMV Pricing		
	Trade	Private	Dealer		Trade	Private	Dealer
2 Dr SC Cpe	934	1521	2332	4 Dr SL Sdn	974	1587	2434

Options	Price
Automatic 4-Speed Transmission	+156

1995

Fewer options and powertrains are available; SOHC and high-output Quad 4 engines are gone. Standard engine makes 150 horsepower this year, up from 115 in 1994. A V6 is optional. Air conditioning is standard.

Mileage Category: C

Body Styles	TMV Pricing			Body Styles	TMV Pricing		
	Trade	Private	Dealer		Trade	Private	Dealer
2 Dr S Cpe	597	1047	1796	4 Dr S Sdn	569	998	1713

Options	Price	Options	Price
Air Conditioning	+89	Power Moonroof	+79
Automatic 4-Speed Transmission	+124		

Alero

2004

As the Olds brand heads into the sunset, the Alero receives only minor changes. Sport Red is a new exterior color, and the six-speaker stereo has been downgraded to four speakers.

Mileage Category: C

Body Styles	TMV Pricing			Body Styles	TMV Pricing		
	Trade	Private	Dealer		Trade	Private	Dealer
2 Dr GL Cpe	8368	9211	10615	4 Dr GL Sdn	8368	9211	10615
2 Dr GLS Cpe	9955	11013	12777	4 Dr GLS Sdn	9414	10425	12111
2 Dr GX Cpe	7939	8821	10291	4 Dr GX Sdn	7584	8427	9831

Options	Price	Options	Price
3.4L V6 OHV 12V FI Engine [Opt on GL]	+715	Rear Spoiler [Opt on GL, GLS]	+200
AM/FM/Cassette/CD Audio System [Opt on GL, GLS]	+145	Satellite Radio System	+325
Antilock Brakes [Std on GLS]	+200	Sport Suspension [Opt on GLS]	+250
Power Moonroof [Opt on GL, GLS]	+700	Traction Control System [Std on GLS]	+200

2003

Any music lovers out there? For 2003, the Alero expands its scope of available sounds by offering XM Satellite Radio as an option. It's the only Oldsmobile to do so.

Mileage Category: C

Body Styles	TMV Pricing			Body Styles	TMV Pricing		
	Trade	Private	Dealer		Trade	Private	Dealer
2 Dr GL Cpe	7373	8253	9720	4 Dr GL Sdn	7301	8173	9626
2 Dr GLS Cpe	8635	9665	11382	4 Dr GLS Sdn	8348	9344	11004
2 Dr GX Cpe	6829	7644	9003	4 Dr GX Sdn	6624	7415	8732

For the latest vehicle information, visit www.edmunds.com

Options	Price
3.4L V6 OHV 12V FI Engine [Opt on GL]	+312
Antilock Brakes [Std on GLS]	+354
Power Driver Seat [Opt on GL]	+159

Options	Price
Power Moonroof [Opt on GL,GLS]	+336
Satellite Radio System	+169

2002

The biggest news for the 2002 Alero is an all-new four-cylinder engine on GX and GL1 models. Redesigned 15-inch wheels, a revamped interior console and two new exterior colors round out this year's changes.

Mileage Category: C

Body Styles	TMV Pricing		
	Trade	Private	Dealer
2 Dr GL Cpe	5784	6597	7951
2 Dr GLS Cpe	6868	7833	9441
2 Dr GX Cpe	5474	6244	7526

Body Styles	TMV Pricing		
	Trade	Private	Dealer
4 Dr GL Sdn	5711	6514	7851
4 Dr GLS Sdn	6742	7689	9268
4 Dr GX Sdn	5294	6038	7277

Options	Price
3.4L V6 OHV 12V FI Engine [Opt on GL]	+317
Aluminum/Alloy Wheels [Opt on GX]	+144

Options	Price
Power Moonroof	+288

2001

A five-speed manual transmission is now available with the four-cylinder engine; an eight-speaker premium sound system is now standard on the GLS (optional on GL); and a refined ABS system and 16-inch wheels are now standard on the GLS.

Mileage Category: C

Body Styles	TMV Pricing		
	Trade	Private	Dealer
2 Dr GL Cpe	4670	5745	6737
2 Dr GLS Cpe	5585	6870	8056
2 Dr GX Cpe	4438	5459	6402

Body Styles	TMV Pricing		
	Trade	Private	Dealer
4 Dr GL Sdn	4572	5623	6594
4 Dr GLS Sdn	5472	6731	7893
4 Dr GX Sdn	4268	5250	6156

Options	Price
3.4L V6 OHV 12V FI Engine [Opt on GL]	+241

Options	Price
Power Moonroof	+239

2000

A performance suspension is newly optional on GL models. The four-cylinder gets a composite intake manifold, while all models benefit from the addition of three rear-shelf anchors for child safety-seat restraints. If glitz is your thing, you can now opt for a new gold package on GL and GLS versions.

Mileage Category: C

Body Styles	TMV Pricing		
	Trade	Private	Dealer
2 Dr GL Cpe	3507	4470	5413
2 Dr GLS Cpe	4264	5434	6581
2 Dr GX Cpe	3216	4099	4964

Body Styles	TMV Pricing		
	Trade	Private	Dealer
4 Dr GL Sdn	3388	4318	5229
4 Dr GLS Sdn	4338	5529	6696
4 Dr GX Sdn	3100	3951	4785

Options	Price
3.4L V6 OHV 12V FI Engine [Opt on GL]	+238
Aluminum/Alloy Wheels [Opt on GL,GX]	+124
Automatic 4-Speed Transmission [Opt on GL,GX]	+140

Options	Price
Leather Seats [Opt on GL]	+281
Power Moonroof	+203

1999

Oldsmobile has dropped the slow-selling Achieva in favor of this new clean-sheet design patterned after the successful Intrigue midsize sedan. Available in both two- and four-door configurations with three well-equipped trim levels, the Alero represents a quantum leap forward over previous small Olds models.

Body Styles	TMV Pricing		
	Trade	Private	Dealer
2 Dr GL Cpe	2983	3920	4895
2 Dr GLS Cpe	3391	4456	5564
2 Dr GX Cpe	2632	3459	4320

Body Styles	TMV Pricing		
	Trade	Private	Dealer
4 Dr GL Sdn	2779	3651	4559
4 Dr GLS Sdn	3628	4766	5951
4 Dr GX Sdn	2671	3509	4382

Options	Price
3.4L V6 OHV 12V FI Engine [Opt on GL]	+188
Leather Seats [Opt on GL]	+222

Options	Price
Power Moonroof	+160

Aurora
2003

Mileage Category: H

Body Styles	TMV Pricing		
	Trade	Private	Dealer
4 Dr 4.0 Sdn	14956	16185	18233

Options	Price
17 Inch Wheels - Chrome	+416
Automatic Climate Control (2 Zone) - Driver and Passenger	+195

Options	Price
Bose Audio System	+260
Compact Disc Changer	+239

Oldsmobile
Aurora

2003 (cont'd)

The V6 has been dropped in the final year of production making the Aurora one of the few V8-only sedans on the market. Two new exterior colors -- Bordeaux Red and Steel Blue -- have also been added for the Aurora's going-away party.

Options	Price
Heated Front Seats	+179
Navigation System	+538
Power Moonroof	+622

Options	Price
Power Passenger Seat	+125
Special Factory Paint	+286

2002

A navigation radio supplements the OnStar system for easy-to-follow driving directions. Three new exterior colors debut along with chrome exhaust tips.

Mileage Category: H

Body Styles	TMV Pricing		
	Trade	Private	Dealer
4 Dr 3.5 Sdn	10644	11779	13670

Options	Price
17 Inch Wheels - Chrome [Opt on 4.0]	+355
Automatic Climate Control (2 Zone) - Driver and Passenger [Opt on 3.5]	+166
Automatic Stability Control [Opt on 3.5]	+155
Bose Audio System	+222
Chrome Wheels	+355

Body Styles	TMV Pricing		
	Trade	Private	Dealer
4 Dr 4.0 Sdn	11823	13082	15181

Options	Price
Compact Disc Changer	+204
Heated Front Seats	+153
Navigation System	+731
Power Moonroof	+485
Special Factory Paint	+175

2001

Oldsmobile has redesigned the Aurora, plopping its flagship sedan onto a more rigid but still front-drive platform. Remaining stylish and contemporary, Aurora is more conventional in appearance but overall, remains an enticing package. Both 3.5 V6 and 4.0 V8 versions are available, each equipped with a full load of luxury accoutrements.

Mileage Category: H

Body Styles	TMV Pricing		
	Trade	Private	Dealer
4 Dr 3.5 Sdn	8166	9671	11060

Options	Price
Automatic Stability Control [Opt on 3.5]	+145
Bose Audio System	+184
Chrome Wheels	+294
Compact Disc Changer	+169

Body Styles	TMV Pricing		
	Trade	Private	Dealer
4 Dr 4.0 Sdn	9265	10972	12548

Options	Price
Heated Front Seats	+127
Power Moonroof	+402
Special Factory Paint	+145

1999

Mileage Category: H

Body Styles		TMV Pricing		
		Trade	Private	Dealer
4 Dr STD Sdn		5108	6412	7769

Options	Price
Chrome Wheels	+197
Delco/Bose Audio System	+205

Options	Price
OnStar Telematics System	+245
Power Moonroof	+270

It's the status quo again in Auroraville, except this year Olds has added two more hydraulic engine mounts (for a total of three) to better isolate engine vibrations. Other than that, a few new colors have been added (Galaxy Silver, Copper Nightmist and Dark Bronzemist).

1998

Status quo in Auroraville, but second-generation airbags have been added.

Mileage Category: H

Body Styles		TMV Pricing		
		Trade	Private	Dealer
4 Dr STD Sdn		3945	5254	6729

Options	Price
Chrome Wheels	+171
Delco/Bose Audio System	+177

Options	Price
OnStar Telematics System	+212
Power Moonroof	+212

1997

Larger front brakes, an in-dash CD player for the Bose sound system, a tilt-down right-hand exterior mirror for backing assistance, an integrated rearview mirror compass and a three-channel garage door opener are added this year.

Mileage Category: H

Body Styles		TMV Pricing		
		Trade	Private	Dealer
4 Dr STD Sdn		3075	4215	5609

Options	Price
Chrome Wheels	+152
Delco/Bose Audio System	+158

Options	Price
Power Moonroof	+189

1996

Daytime running lights are added, and looking through the backlight won't make your eyes water from distortions anymore. We knew it was only a matter of time before some goofball decided chrome wheels and a gold package would look great on the otherwise classy Aurora. The new Oldsmobile? What's that? When do we get the fake convertible roof, guys?

Mileage Category: H

Body Styles	TMV Pricing		
	Trade	Private	Dealer
4 Dr STD Sdn	2328	3309	4665

Options	Price	Options	Price
Chrome Wheels	+128	Power Moonroof	+160
Delco/Bose Audio System	+133		

1995

World-class V8 front-drive luxury sedan features cutting-edge styling, dual airbags, ABS and traction control.

Mileage Category: H

Body Styles	TMV Pricing		
	Trade	Private	Dealer
4 Dr STD Sdn	1736	2543	3887

Options	Price	Options	Price
Delco/Bose Audio System	+105	Power Moonroof	+127

Bravada

2004

In its last year of production, the Bravada receives satellite radio as its only notable new option.

Mileage Category: M

Body Styles	TMV Pricing			Body Styles	TMV Pricing		
	Trade	Private	Dealer		Trade	Private	Dealer
4 Dr STD AWD SUV	18372	19729	21989	4 Dr STD SUV	17387	18744	21004

Options	Price	Options	Price
Automatic Load Leveling [Opt on AWD]	+375	Heated Front Seats	+250
Bose Audio System	+495	Polished Aluminum/Alloy Wheels	+495
Compact Disc Changer	+295	Power Adjustable Foot Pedals	+150
DVD Entertainment System	+1295	Power Sunroof	+800
Front Side Airbag Restraints	+350	Special Factory Paint	+165

2003

Oldsmobile quietly added a two-wheel-drive model to the Bravada lineup last year, making it a bit more attractive to those who don't need the foul weather capability of all-wheel drive. This year 2WD Bravadas get standard traction control while AWD versions now feature a coil spring rear suspension. The previously standard air-spring setup is still an available option on AWD models. Side airbags have also been moved from the standard equipment package to the options list while the standard 4.2-liter engine has been given a 5 horsepower bump.

Mileage Category: M

Body Styles	TMV Pricing			Body Styles	TMV Pricing		
	Trade	Private	Dealer		Trade	Private	Dealer
4 Dr STD AWD SUV	16398	17748	19999	4 Dr STD SUV	15756	17054	19216

Options	Price	Options	Price
Automatic Load Leveling [Opt on AWD]	+195	Front Side Airbag Restraints	+182
Bose Audio System	+258	Heated Front Seats	+130
Compact Disc Changer	+153	Polished Aluminum/Alloy Wheels	+258
DVD Entertainment System	+520	Power Moonroof	+416

2002

Olds brings out a new Bravada that's dramatically improved over its predecessor. A roomier interior, refined suspension, unique style and an all-new inline six packing more power than most competitors' V8s highlight the changes made to Oldsmobile's luxury ute.

Mileage Category: M

Body Styles	TMV Pricing			Body Styles	TMV Pricing		
	Trade	Private	Dealer		Trade	Private	Dealer
4 Dr STD AWD SUV	13895	15221	17430	4 Dr STD SUV	13011	14252	16319

Options	Price	Options	Price
17 Inch Wheels	+199	DVD Entertainment System	+441
Bose Audio System	+219	Power Sunroof	+355
Compact Disc Changer	+131	Traction Control System	+197

2001

Mileage Category: M

Body Styles	TMV Pricing		
	Trade	Private	Dealer
4 Dr STD AWD SUV	8898	10386	11759

2001 (cont'd)

In the last model year before the long-awaited redesign, Oldsmobile adds a few goodies to distract us. Once a dealer-installed option, the OnStar communications system is now a factory-installed option. The Bravada's already comfortable seating is enhanced by new standard equipment such as an eight-way power passenger seat and memory control for the driver seat. A new option group includes the towing package, OnStar and white-letter tires. Previously available only with a package, the Platinum Edition (two-tone paint treatment) is now a stand-alone option. Those longing for a more understated green can now select Sage Green as an exterior color.

Options	Price
Bose Audio System	+182
Compact Disc Changer	+145

Options	Price
OnStar Telematics System	+255
Power Moonroof	+294

2000

GM's OnStar communications system is now available as a dealer-installed option, and a new cargo management system is expected sometime this year. Special color treatments include a new Jewelcoat Red option that features a deep red base color finished with a red-tinted final top coat in place of the usual clearcoat. There's also a Platinum Edition option that adds pewter-colored lower body cladding.

Mileage Category: M

Body Styles	TMV Pricing		
	Trade	Private	Dealer
4 Dr STD AWD SUV	6497	7778	9034

Options	Price
Bose Audio System	+154
Compact Disc Changer	+123

Options	Price
OnStar Telematics System	+279
Power Moonroof	+234

1999

In the wake of last year's restyle, Bravada sees feature refinements for '99. The driver-side airbag has been redesigned into a mini-module to permit a clearer view of the instruments, while the turn signal stalk now provides a flash-to-pass feature. A telltale warning lamp has been added to alert the driver when the tailgate lift glass is ajar. And an anti-theft alarm system is now standard. There's also an option package that combines a driver-side memory seat and a power passenger-side seat, as well as sound system upgrades across the board.

Mileage Category: M

Body Styles	TMV Pricing		
	Trade	Private	Dealer
4 Dr STD AWD SUV	5224	6421	7666

Options	Price
Bose Audio System	+122
OnStar Telematics System	+190

Options	Price
Power Moonroof	+185

1998

Front styling is revised, and new body-side cladding alters the Bravada's profile. Inside, dual second-generation airbags are housed in a new dashboard. A heated driver-side exterior mirror is newly standard, while heated front seats have been added to the options roster. Battery rundown protection and a theft-deterrent system are new standard features.

Mileage Category: M

Body Styles	TMV Pricing		
	Trade	Private	Dealer
4 Dr STD AWD SUV	4403	5544	6830

Options	Price
Power Moonroof	+160

1997

Bravada drops the split-tailgate arrangement at the rear in favor of a top-hinged liftgate with separately lifting glass. So, tailgate parties aren't as convenient, but loading cargo sure is easier. Also new to the options list is a power tilt and slide sunroof. Included with the hole in the roof are a mini-overhead console, a pop-up wind deflector and a sun shade. Rear disc brakes replace the former drums, combining with the front discs to provide better stopping ability.

Mileage Category: M

Body Styles	TMV Pricing		
	Trade	Private	Dealer
4 Dr STD AWD SUV	3508	4576	5882

Options	Price
Power Moonroof	+143

1996

Nice truck, but how many luxury SUVs do we really need? Only a few things about the Bravada differentiate it from the Chevy Blazer and GMC Jimmy: the seats, front styling, trim -- and the price tag.

Mileage Category: M

Body Styles	TMV Pricing		
	Trade	Private	Dealer
4 Dr STD AWD SUV	3056	4080	5494

Cutlass

1999

Mileage Category: C

Body Styles	TMV Pricing		
	Trade	Private	Dealer
4 Dr GL Sdn	3360	4415	5513

Body Styles	TMV Pricing		
	Trade	Private	Dealer
4 Dr GLS Sdn	3666	4818	6016

Options	Price
Power Moonroof	+160

No changes to Oldsmobile's fresh-in-'97 bread-and-butter sedan, except for two new colors, Bronze Mist and Dark Cherry, and the addition of a Gold Package.

Mileage Category: C

Body Styles	TMV Pricing			Body Styles	TMV Pricing		
	Trade	Private	Dealer		Trade	Private	Dealer
4 Dr GL Sdn	2596	3587	4705	4 Dr GLS Sdn	2815	3888	5099

Options	Price
Power Moonroof	+127

1998

No changes to Oldsmobile's fresh bread-and-butter sedan, except for the addition of second-generation airbags.

Mileage Category: C

Body Styles	TMV Pricing			Body Styles	TMV Pricing		
	Trade	Private	Dealer		Trade	Private	Dealer
4 Dr GLS Sdn	2153	3231	4548	4 Dr STD Sdn	1908	2863	4030

1997

Oldsmobile retires the Ciera and introduces the Cutlass, based on the same platform as Chevy's new Malibu. Cutlass is more upscale that its Chevrolet counterpart, offering a slightly more powerful V6 engine on all models, and a sunroof option, standard leather interior and larger wheels on the GLS.

Cutlass Ciera

Mileage Category: D

Body Styles	TMV Pricing			Body Styles	TMV Pricing		
	Trade	Private	Dealer		Trade	Private	Dealer
4 Dr SL Sdn	1232	1863	2734	4 Dr SL Wgn	1331	2013	2955

1996

Best-seller prepares for retirement at the end of the year, receiving badge revisions, some additional standard equipment and an improved optional V6 engine.

Mileage Category: D

Body Styles	TMV Pricing			Body Styles	TMV Pricing		
	Trade	Private	Dealer		Trade	Private	Dealer
4 Dr SL Sdn	844	1348	2187	4 Dr SL Wgn	973	1552	2517

Options	Price	Options	Price
3.1L V6 OHV 12V FI Engine [Opt on Sdn]	+103	Automatic 4-Speed Transmission [Opt on Sdn]	+114

1995

Offered in a single trim level this year. Rear defroster and cassette player are standard. Brake/transmission shift interlock is new.

Cutlass Supreme

Mileage Category: D

Body Styles	TMV Pricing			Body Styles	TMV Pricing		
	Trade	Private	Dealer		Trade	Private	Dealer
2 Dr SL Cpe	1894	2798	3903	4 Dr SL Sdn	2086	3082	4300

Options	Price	Options	Price
Leather Seats	+151	Power Moonroof	+132

Alloy wheels and a power trunk release are added to the standard equipment list, while coupes gain side-impact protection that meets federal safety standards. The 3.4-liter, DOHC V6 engine is dropped from the options list.

1997

1996

The convertible has been retired. The sedan and coupe enjoy their last year in production, receiving engine upgrades for 1996.

Mileage Category: D

Body Styles	TMV Pricing			Body Styles	TMV Pricing		
	Trade	Private	Dealer		Trade	Private	Dealer
2 Dr SL Cpe	1512	2285	3353	4 Dr SL Sdn	1602	2422	3555

Options	Price	Options	Price
3.4L V6 DOHC 24V FI Engine	+116	Leather Seats	+128

Mileage Category: D

Body Styles	TMV Pricing			Body Styles	TMV Pricing		
	Trade	Private	Dealer		Trade	Private	Dealer
2 Dr S Cpe	965	1539	2495	4 Dr S Sdn	965	1539	2495
2 Dr STD Conv	1457	2324	3768				

Options	Price	Options	Price
3.4L V6 DOHC 24V FI Engine	+92	Power Moonroof	+89
Leather Seats [Opt on S]	+101		

1995

Redesigned dashboard equipped with dual airbags debuts. Single trim level offered this year. Front bench seat is no longer available. Front seatbelts are mounted to door pillars instead of doors. Air conditioning, power windows, power locks, tilt steering and cassette player are standard on all models.

Oldsmobile
Eighty-Eight/Intrigue

Eighty-Eight
1999

Mileage Category: G

Body Styles	TMV Pricing			Body Styles	TMV Pricing		
	Trade	Private	Dealer		Trade	Private	Dealer
4 Dr 50th Anniv Sdn	5028	6275	7572	4 Dr STD Sdn	4268	5326	6428
4 Dr LS Sdn	4633	5782	6977				

Options	Price	Options	Price
Leather Seats [Opt on LS]	+203	Power Moonroof	+256
OnStar Telematics System	+245		

The Eighty-Eight gets two new exterior colors, Champagne and Evergreen, and the LS model gets the option of white-stripe 16-inch tires. Oh, wait. Oldsmobile is celebrating the nameplate's golden anniversary with a special 50th Anniversary Edition Eighty-Eight. It has 16-inch aluminum wheels fitted with 215/65SR blackwalls, a highly contented leather interior package and special badging finished in, what else? Gold.

1998
Virtually nothing, unless you find a new fuel cap, better access to rear seatbelts, new ABS wheel-speed sensors and a couple of new colors intriguing. Second-generation airbags are standard.

Mileage Category: G

Body Styles	TMV Pricing			Body Styles	TMV Pricing		
	Trade	Private	Dealer		Trade	Private	Dealer
4 Dr LS Sdn	3703	4727	5882	4 Dr STD Sdn	3395	4334	5393

Options	Price
Leather Seats	+212

1997
Side-impact protection is upgraded to federal safety standards, interiors are improved and new Oldsmobile logos adorn the body.

Mileage Category: G

Body Styles	TMV Pricing			Body Styles	TMV Pricing		
	Trade	Private	Dealer		Trade	Private	Dealer
4 Dr LS Sdn	2730	3760	5018	4 Dr STD Sdn	2508	3453	4609

1996
Royale designation dropped, and the Eighty-Eight gets fresh Aurora-inspired styling front and rear. Standard equipment levels go up, and daytime running lights are added.

Mileage Category: G

Body Styles	TMV Pricing			Body Styles	TMV Pricing		
	Trade	Private	Dealer		Trade	Private	Dealer
4 Dr LS Sdn	2190	2990	4094	4 Dr LSS Sdn	2580	3522	4822
4 Dr LSS S/C Sdn	2670	3644	4990	4 Dr STD Sdn	1950	2661	3644

Options	Price
Power Moonroof	+166

1995
Engine upgraded to 3800 Series II status, and supercharged 3.8-liter V6 is a new option on LSS models. New onboard navigation system called Guidestar was a $1,995 option, originally available only in California.

Mileage Category: G

Body Styles	TMV Pricing			Body Styles	TMV Pricing		
	Trade	Private	Dealer		Trade	Private	Dealer
4 Dr LS Sdn	1486	2085	3083	4 Dr LSS Sdn	1621	2275	3364
4 Dr LSS S/C Sdn	1754	2462	3641	4 Dr STD Sdn	1322	1855	2744

Options	Price	Options	Price
Compact Disc Changer	+83	Leather Seats [Std on LSS]	+101

Intrigue
2002

Mileage Category: D

Body Styles	TMV Pricing			Body Styles	TMV Pricing		
	Trade	Private	Dealer		Trade	Private	Dealer
4 Dr GL Sdn	7994	9115	10984	4 Dr GX Sdn	7478	8527	10274
4 Dr GLS Sdn	9103	10379	12506				

Options	Price	Options	Price
Automatic Stability Control	+264	Heated Front Seats [Opt on GL]	+120
Bose Audio System [Opt on GL]	+122	Leather Seats [Opt on GL]	+366
Chrome Wheels [Opt on GL,GLS]	+233	Power Moonroof [Opt on GL]	+332

LATCH child-seat anchors and two new colors are added, along with a standard CD player. GLS models receive additional standard equipment that includes a two-tone leather interior, sunroof and a HomeLink system. This is the last year for the Oldsmobile Intrigue.

2001

The Intrigue receives only minor changes for 2001, including two new exterior colors and a standard air filtration system. The OnStar driver assistance system is now standard on GLS models while Precision Control System equipped models receive exterior "PCS" badging.

Body Styles	TMV Pricing		
	Trade	Private	Dealer
4 Dr GL Sdn	6144	7649	9038
4 Dr GLS Sdn	6725	8372	9892

Options	Price
AM/FM/Cassette/CD Audio System [Opt on GL,GX]	+165
Automatic Stability Control	+219
Bose Audio System	+184
Chrome Wheels	+220

Mileage Category: D

Body Styles	TMV Pricing		
	Trade	Private	Dealer
4 Dr GX Sdn	5634	7014	8287

Options	Price
Compact Disc Changer	+169
Leather Seats [Opt on GL]	+366
Power Moonroof	+275

2000

All Intrigues get restyled six-spoke 16-inch alloy wheels in either silver argent paint or chrome, and the option of adding Oldsmobile's Precision Control System (PCS). The full-function traction-control unit that's standard on the GL and GLS is now available on the GX. Retained accessory power becomes standard, and GL buyers can opt for the revised heated seats on the GLS.

Body Styles	TMV Pricing		
	Trade	Private	Dealer
4 Dr GL Sdn	4626	6049	7444
4 Dr GLS Sdn	4911	6422	7903

Options	Price
AM/FM/Cassette/CD Audio System [Opt on GL,GX]	+140
Automatic Stability Control	+186
Bose Audio System [Opt on GL,GLS]	+133
Chrome Wheels	+187

Mileage Category: D

Body Styles	TMV Pricing		
	Trade	Private	Dealer
4 Dr GX Sdn	4145	5421	6671

Options	Price
Compact Disc Changer	+143
Leather Seats [Opt on GL]	+310
Power Moonroof	+234

1999

Last year, Oldsmobile dumped the stodgy Cutlass Supreme for the Intrigue; a suave, sophisticated sporty sedan designed to take on the best of the imports. For '99 Olds is dumping the 3800 Series II V6 that powers the Intrigue for an all-new, 24-valve 3.5-liter twin-cam V6. Until production of the 3.5-liter (a design based on the Aurora V8) can be ramped up to meet the Intrigue build schedule, the new 215-horsepower engine will come standard only in the new top-line GLS model, and optional in the base GX and mid-line GL series. Full function traction control is now available in models equipped with the new power plant. Minor feature revisions, one new color and new badging rounds out the changes this year.

Body Styles	TMV Pricing		
	Trade	Private	Dealer
4 Dr GL Sdn	3415	4571	5774
4 Dr GLS Sdn	3611	4834	6106

Options	Price
Chrome Wheels	+148
Leather Seats [Opt on GL]	+246

Mileage Category: D

Body Styles	TMV Pricing		
	Trade	Private	Dealer
4 Dr GX Sdn	3173	4247	5365

Options	Price
Power Moonroof	+185

1998

Oldsmobile dumps the stodgy Cutlass Supreme for the Intrigue; a suave, sophisticated, sporty sedan designed to take on the best of the imports. Too bad refinement issues exist. Second-generation airbags are standard equipment.

Body Styles	TMV Pricing		
	Trade	Private	Dealer
4 Dr GL Sdn	2746	3773	4931
4 Dr GLS Sdn	3059	4203	5494

Options	Price
Chrome Wheels	+128
Leather Seats [Opt on GL]	+212

Mileage Category: D

Body Styles	TMV Pricing		
	Trade	Private	Dealer
4 Dr STD Sdn	2276	3127	4087

Options	Price
Power Moonroof	+148

LSS

1999

Body Styles	TMV Pricing		
	Trade	Private	Dealer
4 Dr S/C Sdn	5805	7244	8742

Options	Price
Chrome Wheels	+148

Mileage Category: G

Body Styles	TMV Pricing		
	Trade	Private	Dealer
4 Dr STD Sdn	4749	5926	7152

Options	Price
Power Moonroof	+256

The LSS gets two new exterior colors (Champagne and Evergreen) for '99. Olds has also upgraded the standard radio to an AM/FM stereo cassette with CD player and seek-scan, auto tone control, digital clock and power antenna.

1998

New colors, improved ABS, a revised electrochromic rearview mirror, second-generation airbags and a redesigned fuel cap are the major changes for 1998.

Body Styles	TMV Pricing		
	Trade	Private	Dealer
4 Dr S/C Sdn	4559	5820	7242

Mileage Category: G

Body Styles	TMV Pricing		
	Trade	Private	Dealer
4 Dr STD Sdn	4047	5166	6428

1998 (cont'd)

Options	Price		Options	Price
Chrome Wheels	+128		Power Moonroof	+212

1997

Minor changes accompany Oldsmobile's euro-flavored sedan into 1997. The center console and shifter are new, and other interior upgrades have been made. New, more prominent badging has been added to the exterior. Finally, the final-drive ratio has been changed to 2.93-to-1 from 2.97-to-1.

Mileage Category: G

Body Styles	TMV Pricing			Body Styles	TMV Pricing		
	Trade	Private	Dealer		Trade	Private	Dealer
4 Dr S/C Sdn	3472	4571	5914	4 Dr STD Sdn	3307	4353	5631

Options	Price
Power Moonroof	+189

Ninety-Eight

1996

Mileage Category: H

Body Styles	TMV Pricing		
	Trade	Private	Dealer
4 Dr Regency Elite Sdn	2561	3640	5131

Options	Price
Power Moonroof	+177

Supercharged engine dropped from this model, and daytime running lamps have been added. Don't expect a 1997 Ninety-Eight.

1995

Engine upgraded to 3800 Series II status. Alloy wheels are standard. Flash-to-pass is new standard feature.

Mileage Category: H

Body Styles	TMV Pricing			Body Styles	TMV Pricing		
	Trade	Private	Dealer		Trade	Private	Dealer
4 Dr Regency Elite S/C Sdn	1864	2728	4169	4 Dr Regency Elite Sdn	1769	2590	3958

Options	Price
Power Moonroof	+140

Regency

1998

Mileage Category: H

Body Styles	TMV Pricing		
	Trade	Private	Dealer
4 Dr STD Sdn	4191	5582	7150

Options	Price
Power Moonroof	+212

Minor changes this year. The ABS is upgraded, it's easier to get at the rear seatbelts, colors are revised and the "unleaded fuel only" label is removed from the inside of the fuel door.

1997

New name for an old concept. Look closely...see the old Eighty-Eight before 1996's restyle? Regency takes over where the Ninety-Eight left off, satisfying traditional Oldsmobile buyers.

Mileage Category: H

Body Styles	TMV Pricing		
	Trade	Private	Dealer
4 Dr STD Sdn	3401	4662	6204

Options	Price
Power Moonroof	+189

Silhouette

2004

Mileage Category: P

Body Styles	TMV Pricing		
	Trade	Private	Dealer
4 Dr GL Pass Van Ext	12911	14260	16507
4 Dr GLS AWD Pass Van Ext	17293	18777	21249
4 Dr GLS Pass Van Ext	14550	15899	18146

Options	Price
AM/FM/CD Changer Audio System	+295
Camper/Towing Package [Opt on GL]	+195
Chrome Wheels	+695

Body Styles	TMV Pricing		
	Trade	Private	Dealer
4 Dr Premiere AWD Pass Van Ext	18306	19790	22262
4 Dr Premiere Pass Van Ext	15473	16822	19070

Options	Price
Heated Front Seats [Opt on GLS]	+275
Power Dual Sliding Doors [Opt on GLS]	+350
Power Sliding Door [Opt on GL]	+450

Largely unchanged for 2004, the Silhouette now offers standard keyless entry on all trim levels and optional luggage roof rails.

2003

Body Styles	TMV Pricing		
	Trade	Private	Dealer
4 Dr GL Pass Van Ext	11485	12501	14193
4 Dr GLS AWD Pass Van Ext	15899	17305	19648
4 Dr GLS Pass Van Ext	12690	13812	15682

Options	Price
AM/FM/CD Changer Audio System	+153
Chrome Wheels	+362

Body Styles	TMV Pricing		
	Trade	Private	Dealer
4 Dr Premiere AWD Pass Van Ext	16874	18366	20853
4 Dr Premiere Pass Van Ext	14092	15338	17414

Options	Price
Power Dual Sliding Doors [Opt on GLS]	+182
Power Sliding Door [Opt on GL]	+234

For 2003, traction control and 16-inch wheels are now standard on two-wheel-drive models.

2002

Mileage Category: P

Body Styles	TMV Pricing		
	Trade	Private	Dealer
4 Dr GL Pass Van Ext	9380	10352	11972
4 Dr GLS AWD Pass Van Ext	13378	14764	17075
4 Dr GLS Pass Van Ext	10823	11945	13815

Options	Price
Air Conditioning - Front and Rear [Opt on GL]	+244
Aluminum/Alloy Wheels [Opt on GL]	+131
Chrome Wheels	+308
Compact Disc Changer	+131

Body Styles	TMV Pricing		
	Trade	Private	Dealer
4 Dr Premiere AWD Pass Van Ext	14218	15692	18148
4 Dr Premiere Pass Van Ext	11621	12826	14833

Options	Price
Park Distance Control (Rear) [Opt on GL]	+122
Power Dual Sliding Doors [Std on Premiere]	+155
Power Sliding Door [Opt on GL]	+199

Despite the fact that the Silhouette is headed to the graveyard with the rest of Oldsmobile's lineup, there are still minor changes on tap for the 2002 model. The Versatrak AWD system will now be available on GLS and Premiere models coupled with special 16-inch aluminum wheels. The standard front airbags are now dual-stage units that deploy according to the severity of the crash, and Premiere models equipped with the onboard video system get a DVD player in place of a standard VCR.

2001

Mileage Category: P

Body Styles	TMV Pricing		
	Trade	Private	Dealer
4 Dr GL Pass Van Ext	7376	8693	9909
4 Dr GLS Pass Van Ext	8326	9813	11186

Options	Price
Air Conditioning - Front and Rear [Opt on GL]	+165
Chrome Wheels	+255

Body Styles	TMV Pricing		
	Trade	Private	Dealer
4 Dr Premiere Pass Van Ext	9276	10932	12461

Options	Price
Power Sliding Door [Opt on GL]	+165

Oldsmobile is giving minivan buyers good reason to shop the Silhouette for 2001, even if General Motors issues a death sentence for the brand. All models get freshened styling, a touring suspension package with self-leveling suspension and an air inflation kit, fold-flat second-row captain's chairs, improved sound-deadening insulation and standard OnStar communications. Upscale GLS and Premiere models have two-tone leather seating, a rear parking aid, an integrated universal garage door opener, 16-inch wheels with an available chrome finish, power-sliding driver door, in-dash CD changer, third-row captain's chairs, stowable third-row seat, wood grain accents, eight-way power front seats and dual-zone A/C as either optional or standard. The Premiere also gets an updated onboard entertainment system with a larger video screen.

2000

Mileage Category: P

Body Styles	TMV Pricing		
	Trade	Private	Dealer
4 Dr GL Pass Van Ext	5445	6612	7756
4 Dr GLS Pass Van Ext	6126	7439	8726

Options	Price
Air Conditioning - Front and Rear [Opt on GL]	+140
OnStar Telematics System [Opt on Premiere]	+279

Body Styles	TMV Pricing		
	Trade	Private	Dealer
4 Dr Premiere Pass Van Ext	6977	8472	9938

Options	Price
Power Sliding Door [Opt on GL]	+140

Olds has canned its 112-inch wheelbase GS, meaning all 2000 Silhouettes (GL, GLS and Premiere) are now extended-length (120-inch wheelbase) seven-passenger models. The traction-control system has been improved, and heated front seats are available in leather. There's also a redesigned instrument cluster with dual trip odometers, as well as upgraded radios, interior lighting and electrical system functions.

Oldsmobile
Silhouette

1999

Olds is headlining its Premiere Edition, a loaded-up model that debuted in mid-'98 with a standard integrated video entertainment system in back. But other news for 1999 includes a horsepower and torque increase for Silhouette's 3.4-liter V6, plus the addition of a theft-deterrent system and heated outside rearview mirrors as standard equipment. And if four new exterior colors (Sky, Ruby, Silvermist and Cypress) weren't enough, then consider the availability of a new Gold Package (but only if you must).

Mileage Category: P

Body Styles	TMV Pricing		
	Trade	Private	Dealer
4 Dr GL Pass Van Ext	4409	5556	6750
4 Dr GLS Pass Van Ext	4869	6136	7454

Options	Price
Leather Seats [Opt on GS]	+234

Body Styles	TMV Pricing		
	Trade	Private	Dealer
4 Dr GS Pass Van	4656	5867	7127
4 Dr Premiere Pass Van Ext	5300	6679	8114

Options	Price
OnStar Telematics System [Opt on Premiere]	+245

1998

Side-impact airbags are standard for front seat passengers, and Oldsmobile is building more short-wheelbase vans with dual sliding doors. Front airbags get second-generation technology, which results in slower deployment speeds. Midyear, a Premiere Edition debuted, loaded with standard features including a TV/VCR setup in back.

Mileage Category: P

Body Styles	TMV Pricing		
	Trade	Private	Dealer
4 Dr GL Pass Van Ext	3411	4466	5655
4 Dr GLS Pass Van Ext	3815	4994	6323

Options	Price
Leather Seats	+186

Body Styles	TMV Pricing		
	Trade	Private	Dealer
4 Dr GS Pass Van	3509	4594	5817
4 Dr Premiere Pass Van Ext	4351	5696	7213

Options	Price
OnStar Telematics System [Opt on Premiere]	+212

1997

Completely redesigned, the new Silhouette comes in several trim levels and two sizes, each with a healthy load of standard equipment.

Mileage Category: P

Body Styles	TMV Pricing		
	Trade	Private	Dealer
3 Dr GL Pass Van Ext	2859	3872	5111
3 Dr GLS Pass Van Ext	3108	4209	5554

Options	Price
Leather Seats	+165

Body Styles	TMV Pricing		
	Trade	Private	Dealer
3 Dr STD Pass Van	2559	3465	4573
3 Dr STD Pass Van Ext	2753	3728	4920

Options	Price
Power Moonroof	+132

1996

Mileage Category: P

Body Styles	TMV Pricing		
	Trade	Private	Dealer
3 Dr STD Pass Van	2050	2856	3969

Options	Price
Leather Seats	+140

New 180-horsepower, 3.4-liter V6 makes the Silhouette even better able to imitate Japan's bullet train.

1995

The 3.1-liter V6 engine is dropped in favor of the more powerful 3.8-liter V6.

Mileage Category: P

Body Styles	TMV Pricing		
	Trade	Private	Dealer
3 Dr STD Pass Van	1428	2084	3178

Options	Price
Leather Seats	+110

Acclaim/Breeze

Acclaim

Mileage Category: C

Body Styles	TMV Pricing		
	Trade	Private	Dealer
4 Dr STD Sdn	650	1139	1954

Options	Price
3.0L V6 SOHC 12V FI Engine	+95

Last year for Acclaim.

Breeze

Mileage Category: C

Body Styles	TMV Pricing		
	Trade	Private	Dealer
4 Dr STD Sdn	3316	4359	5382

Options	Price	Options	Price
2.4L I4 DOHC 16V FI Engine	+171	Automatic 4-Speed Transmission	+399
AM/FM/CD Audio System	+133	Compact Disc Changer	+143
Aluminum/Alloy Wheels	+260	Power Sunroof	+264
Antilock Brakes	+258		

New colors and child-seat tether anchorages update the Breeze for 2000.

Mileage Category: C

Body Styles	TMV Pricing			Body Styles	TMV Pricing		
	Trade	Private	Dealer		Trade	Private	Dealer
4 Dr Expresso Sdn	2522	3454	4424	4 Dr STD Sdn	2493	3414	4372

Options	Price	Options	Price
2.4L I4 DOHC 16V FI Engine	+130	Automatic 4-Speed Transmission	+302
Aluminum/Alloy Wheels	+197	Power Sunroof	+200
Antilock Brakes	+218		

1999

Power windows, locks and mirrors, along with floor mats and a driver seat height adjuster are now standard on the Breeze. In addition, the suspension has been revised for a more pleasant ride.

Body Styles	TMV Pricing			Body Styles	TMV Pricing		
	Trade	Private	Dealer		Trade	Private	Dealer
4 Dr Expresso Sdn	2045	2922	3911	4 Dr STD Sdn	2006	2866	3835

Options	Price	Options	Price
Aluminum/Alloy Wheels	+156	Automatic 4-Speed Transmission	+240
Antilock Brakes	+173	Power Sunroof	+159

1998

Availability of a 2.4-liter engine brings 150 horsepower and 167 pound-feet of torque, and that's just what the Breeze needs to live up to its name. Both engines can meet California emissions regulations, and new engine mounts help make them quieter. An Expresso package adds some aesthetic changes, a power sunroof is now optional and there are six new colors to choose from.

Body Styles	TMV Pricing		
	Trade	Private	Dealer
4 Dr STD Sdn	1622	2410	3372

Options	Price	Options	Price
Aluminum/Alloy Wheels	+158	Automatic 4-Speed Transmission	+197
Antilock Brakes	+175		

1997

Plymouth is inching the Breeze up-market in both price and content. This year sees a fairly sizable price hike and the addition of luxury options such as an in-dash CD changer. Changes to the standard equipment list bring a nicer center console, improved basic stereos and increased-flow rear-seat heater ducts.

Mileage Category: C

Body Styles	TMV Pricing		
	Trade	Private	Dealer
4 Dr STD Sdn	1171	1859	2810

1996

The Breeze is introduced this year as Chrysler Corporation's bargain-basement midsize sedan. Nicely equipped with air conditioning and a decent stereo, the Breeze has a surprising amount of interior room.

Breeze/Grand Voyager

1996 (cont'd)

Options	Price
Antilock Brakes	+138
Automatic 4-Speed Transmission	+155

Options	Price
Power Sunroof	+127

Grand Voyager

2000

Mileage Category: P

Body Styles	TMV Pricing		
	Trade	Private	Dealer
4 Dr SE Pass Van Ext	5091	6377	7637

Body Styles	TMV Pricing		
	Trade	Private	Dealer
4 Dr STD Pass Van Ext	4771	5977	7159

Options	Price
3.3L V6 OHV 12V FI Engine	+369
AM/FM/Cassette/CD Audio System [Opt on SE]	+238
Air Conditioning - Front and Rear [Opt on SE]	+323
Aluminum/Alloy Wheels [Opt on SE]	+158
Antilock Brakes [Opt on SE]	+258

Options	Price
Camper/Towing Package	+159
Captain Chairs (4) [Opt on SE]	+255
Infinity Audio System [Opt on SE]	+274
Power Driver Seat [Opt on SE]	+116
Sunscreen Glass [Opt on STD]	+171

The Expresso trim level is discontinued, and Plymouth changes some of the standard features and options on base and SE models. Notably, base models now come with a cassette player. This is the last year for the Grand Voyager, as Chrysler begins dismantling the Plymouth division. Fortunately, the van's demise shouldn't pose much of a problem for shoppers, as the Dodge Grand Caravan gives you the same product with slightly different styling.

1999

SE models get body-color door and liftgate handles, as well as a body-colored front grille. All models add a cargo net between the front seats, and you can now get built-in child seats with the second-row captain's chairs.

Mileage Category: P

Body Styles	TMV Pricing		
	Trade	Private	Dealer
4 Dr Expresso Pass Van Ext	4163	5438	6766
4 Dr SE Pass Van Ext	3877	5065	6302

Body Styles	TMV Pricing		
	Trade	Private	Dealer
4 Dr STD Pass Van Ext	3592	4693	5838

Options	Price
3.3L V6 OHV 12V FI Engine	+280
AM/FM/Cassette/CD Audio System [Opt on SE]	+180
Air Conditioning [Opt on STD]	+121
Air Conditioning - Front and Rear [Opt on Expresso,SE]	+245
Antilock Brakes [Opt on STD]	+218

Options	Price
Camper/Towing Package	+121
Captain Chairs (4) [Opt on Expresso,SE]	+194
Infinity Audio System [Opt on Expresso,SE]	+208
Sunscreen Glass [Opt on SE,STD]	+130

1998

Plymouth adds an Expresso trim level; intended to offer both style and value, this van has body-color door handles and silver exterior accents, and comes with privacy glass, keyless entry and a CD player. In other news, all Grand Voyagers get depowered, next-generation front airbags, adjustable front head restraints and new seat fabric. The four-speed automatic transmission receives upgrades for durability, and it can now be paired with the 3.0-liter V6 (which is LEV-certified in California). Other minor changes include an easy-entry feature for the left-hand captain's chair (in the second row) on vans with the left-hand sliding door, revised built-in booster seats and grocery bag hooks on the rear seat backs.

Mileage Category: P

Body Styles	TMV Pricing		
	Trade	Private	Dealer
4 Dr Expresso Pass Van Ext	3036	4098	5295
4 Dr SE Pass Van Ext	2895	3906	5047

Body Styles	TMV Pricing		
	Trade	Private	Dealer
4 Dr STD Pass Van Ext	2541	3428	4429

Options	Price
AM/FM/Cassette/CD Audio System [Opt on Expresso,SE]	+143
Air Conditioning - Front and Rear [Opt on Expresso,SE]	+195

Options	Price
Antilock Brakes [Opt on STD]	+173
Captain Chairs (4) [Opt on Expresso,SE]	+153

1997

Changes for 1997 include updated transmission software, an upgraded antilock brake system and an enhanced accident response system that unlocks the doors and turns on the interior lights if the front airbags deploy. Additionally, Plymouth has made improvements to the cabin insulation (to reduce noise and vibration) and cassette stereo units. Standard lighting elements now include front map lights and liftgate flood lamps; a cargo bay power point is also part of the deal. New options include an eight-way power driver seat and an overhead console with a trip computer, compass and outside temperature display. A Rallye decor package is available on SE models -- it includes a roof rack, tinted glass, alloy wheels and various silver accents and decals. Rounding out the changes are new wheel covers for the base model.

Mileage Category: P

Body Styles	TMV Pricing		
	Trade	Private	Dealer
3 Dr SE Pass Van Ext	2357	3270	4386

Body Styles	TMV Pricing		
	Trade	Private	Dealer
3 Dr STD Pass Van Ext	2062	2861	3837

Options	Price
3.3L V6 OHV 12V FI Engine	+292
AM/FM/Cassette/CD Audio System [Opt on SE]	+144
Air Conditioning - Front and Rear [Opt on SE]	+197
Antilock Brakes [Opt on STD]	+175

Options	Price
Captain Chairs (4) [Opt on SE]	+144
Premium Audio System [Opt on SE]	+167
Sliding Driver Side Door	+138

1996

The Grand Voyager is completely redesigned for 1996, and Chrysler's minivan designers and engineers have substantially improved upon the original formula: Interior comfort is top-notch, engines are more powerful (though you can no longer get the torquey 3.8-liter V6), and the available left-hand sliding door is an industry first.

Mileage Category: P

Body Styles	TMV Pricing		
	Trade	Private	Dealer
3 Dr SE Pass Van Ext	1914	2738	3876

Options	Price
3.0L V6 SOHC 12V FI Engine	+140
3.3L V6 OHV 12V FI Engine [Opt on SE]	+163
Air Conditioning - Front and Rear [Opt on SE]	+155

Body Styles	TMV Pricing		
	Trade	Private	Dealer
3 Dr STD Pass Van Ext	1671	2391	3385

Options	Price
Antilock Brakes	+138
Captain Chairs (4) [Opt on SE]	+136
Premium Audio System [Opt on SE]	+131

1995

Mileage Category: P

Body Styles	TMV Pricing		
	Trade	Private	Dealer
3 Dr LE AWD Pass Van Ext	1647	2430	3736
3 Dr LE Pass Van Ext	1497	2209	3396
3 Dr SE AWD Pass Van Ext	1427	2107	3241

Options	Price
AM/FM/Cassette/CD Audio System [Opt on SE]	+88
Air Conditioning - Front and Rear	+119
Antilock Brakes [Opt on SE]	+106

Body Styles	TMV Pricing		
	Trade	Private	Dealer
3 Dr SE Pass Van Ext	1322	1952	3001
3 Dr STD Pass Van Ext	1243	1835	2821

Options	Price
Captain Chairs (4) [Opt on LE,SE]	+88
Leather Seats [Opt on LE]	+112
Premium Audio System [Opt on SE]	+101

Changes this year are minimal. ABS is now standard on LE models. SE models can be equipped with a snazzy Rallye package designed for those trying to disguise the fact that they are driving a minivan -- it includes two-tone paint treatment, tinted glass and 15-inch alloy wheels. Lastly, the four-speed automatic transmission benefits from engineering refinements.

Neon

2001

Mileage Category: B

Body Styles	TMV Pricing		
	Trade	Private	Dealer
4 Dr Highline LX Sdn	4407	5759	7007

Options	Price
Air Conditioning	+513
Aluminum/Alloy Wheels	+182
Antilock Brakes	+349
Automatic 3-Speed Transmission	+308
Compact Disc Changer	+192

Body Styles	TMV Pricing		
	Trade	Private	Dealer
4 Dr Highline Sdn	4089	5345	6504

Options	Price
Cruise Control	+115
Front Side Airbag Restraints	+179
Leather Seats	+338
Power Moonroof	+305
Power Windows	+131

Side-impact airbags and leather seats are now available in Plymouth's economy car. A center shoulder belt for the rear seat and an internal emergency trunk release further improve this Plymouth's safety consciousness. A Sun and Sound or a Value/Fun option group is available this year, each of which includes a sunroof. New interior and exterior options for the Neon pump some life into this fading brand.

2000

Everything's new inside and out, as the second-generation Neon grows up, not old. A totally redesigned suspension and steering system, low-speed traction control and a complete exterior redesign head up the notable changes.

Mileage Category: B

Body Styles	TMV Pricing		
	Trade	Private	Dealer
4 Dr Highline Sdn	2713	3794	4854

Options	Price
AM/FM/CD Audio System	+150
Air Conditioning [Std on LX Sdn]	+380
Aluminum/Alloy Wheels	+155
Antilock Brakes	+319

Body Styles	TMV Pricing		
	Trade	Private	Dealer
4 Dr LX Sdn	3051	4268	5460

Options	Price
Automatic 3-Speed Transmission	+228
Compact Disc Changer	+190
Power Moonroof	+226

1999

Mileage Category: B

Body Styles	TMV Pricing		
	Trade	Private	Dealer
2 Dr Competition Cpe	1822	2700	3613
2 Dr Expresso Cpe	2155	3192	4272
2 Dr Highline Cpe	1933	2863	3831

Options	Price
Air Conditioning [Std on Comp Cpe,Expresso]	+288
Aluminum/Alloy Wheels	+118
Antilock Brakes	+242

Body Styles	TMV Pricing		
	Trade	Private	Dealer
4 Dr Competition Sdn	1839	2726	3649
4 Dr Expresso Sdn	2212	3276	4383
4 Dr Highline Sdn	1965	2911	3896

Options	Price
Automatic 3-Speed Transmission	+192
Compact Disc Changer	+144
Competition Package	+288

Nothing changes for '99.

1999 (cont'd)

Options	Price
Power Moonroof	+172

1998

California and other emission-regulating states get an LEV (Low Emission Vehicle) engine calibration. Also changed this year are ABS, a new ignition key lock and the addition of four new colors.

Mileage Category: B

Body Styles	TMV Pricing		
	Trade	Private	Dealer
2 Dr Competition Cpe	1320	2109	2998
2 Dr Expresso Cpe	1483	2369	3368
2 Dr Highline Cpe	1387	2216	3151
4 Dr Competition Sdn	1373	2194	3120

Body Styles	TMV Pricing		
	Trade	Private	Dealer
4 Dr Expresso Sdn	1436	2294	3262
4 Dr Highline Sdn	1399	2235	3177
4 Dr Style Sdn	1644	2626	3734

Options	Price
Air Conditioning [Opt on Competition,Highline]	+229
Antilock Brakes	+173
Automatic 3-Speed Transmission	+152

Options	Price
Competition Package	+229
Power Moonroof	+136

1997

The 1997 Neons are made quieter with the addition of a structural oil pan. Other changes include new optional radios, a new seat fabric, new wheels and wheel covers and a few new paint colors.

Mileage Category: B

Body Styles	TMV Pricing		
	Trade	Private	Dealer
2 Dr Expresso Cpe	1112	1906	2876
2 Dr Highline Cpe	1026	1759	2655
2 Dr STD Cpe	960	1645	2482

Body Styles	TMV Pricing		
	Trade	Private	Dealer
4 Dr Expresso Sdn	1152	1974	2978
4 Dr Highline Sdn	1109	1900	2867
4 Dr STD Sdn	983	1685	2543

Options	Price
Air Conditioning [Opt on STD]	+231
Antilock Brakes	+175
Automatic 3-Speed Transmission	+154

Options	Price
Compact Disc Changer	+115
Competition Package	+131
Power Moonroof	+138

1996

Antilock brakes are optional across the line, and base models get more standard equipment for 1996. A value-packed Expresso package is aimed at 20-something first-time buyers. A base coupe is newly available, and all Neons are supposedly quieter than last year. A power moonroof joins the options list, and a remote keyless entry system with panic alarm is available.

Mileage Category: B

Body Styles	TMV Pricing		
	Trade	Private	Dealer
2 Dr Highline Cpe	756	1394	2276
2 Dr STD Cpe	718	1324	2160
2 Dr Sport Cpe	849	1566	2557

Body Styles	TMV Pricing		
	Trade	Private	Dealer
4 Dr Highline Sdn	820	1510	2463
4 Dr STD Sdn	727	1341	2189
4 Dr Sport Sdn	856	1576	2571

Options	Price
Air Conditioning	+182
Antilock Brakes	+138

Options	Price
Automatic 3-Speed Transmission	+122
Competition Package	+331

1995

The all-new Neon is introduced as Plymouth's entry in the compact car class. Roomy, cute and quick are three of the best adjectives we can find for this car. The Neon is available in coupe and sedan body styles in three trim-levels. Safety equipment includes standard dual airbags, optional antilock brakes and an optional integrated child seat.

Mileage Category: B

Body Styles	TMV Pricing		
	Trade	Private	Dealer
2 Dr Highline Cpe	493	994	1828
2 Dr Sport Cpe	604	1217	2239
4 Dr Highline Sdn	557	1122	2063

Body Styles	TMV Pricing		
	Trade	Private	Dealer
4 Dr STD Sdn	447	899	1652
4 Dr Sport Sdn	588	1185	2180

Options	Price
Air Conditioning	+141
Antilock Brakes [Std on Sport]	+106

Options	Price
Automatic 3-Speed Transmission	+94
Leather Seats	+77

Prowler

2001

Mileage Category: F

Body Styles		TMV Pricing		
		Trade	Private	Dealer
2 Dr STD Conv		25731	28557	31166

Get your Plymouth Prowler while you can. After 2001 it becomes the Chrysler Prowler. Sure, it will be the identical car, but that powerful Plymouth Prowler alliteration will be gone forever! You can get these in Copper Metallic and a silver/black combination this year. New adjustable damper shocks are offered as standard equipment.

Prowler

2000

Mileage Category: F

Body Styles	TMV Pricing		
	Trade	Private	Dealer
2 Dr STD Conv	23124	25955	28730

Options	Price
Special Factory Paint	+570

Prowler Purple is discontinued, replaced by Prowler Silver for 2000. Chrome wheels are standard, as is a new leather shift boot and speed-sensitive volume for the stereo.

1999

Mileage Category: F

Body Styles	TMV Pricing		
	Trade	Private	Dealer
2 Dr STD Conv	20622	23478	26450

Options	Price	Options	Price
Chrome Wheels	+288	Special Factory Paint	+288

A brand-new 3.5-liter engine under the hood creates performance more fitting a hot rod. Also new for '99 is one more color option: Prowler Yellow.

1997

Mileage Category: F

Body Styles	TMV Pricing		
	Trade	Private	Dealer
2 Dr STD Conv	18732	21281	24397

Plymouth brings a hot-rod-style show car to market. Although the Prowler's V6 kicks out a respectable 214 horsepower, it comes only with a four-speed automatic transmission. More show than go, some enthusiasts will lament the Prowler's lack of a V8 and manual gearbox.

Voyager

2000

Mileage Category: P

Body Styles	TMV Pricing			Body Styles	TMV Pricing		
	Trade	Private	Dealer		Trade	Private	Dealer
3 Dr STD Pass Van	4038	5060	6061	4 Dr SE Pass Van	5016	6285	7529

Options	Price	Options	Price
3.0L V6 SOHC 12V FI Engine [Opt on STD]	+304	Antilock Brakes [Std on SE]	+258
3.3L V6 Flex Fuel OHV 12V FI Engine [Opt on STD]	+369	Camper/Towing Package	+159
3.3L V6 OHV 12V FI Engine	+369	Captain Chairs (4)	+255
7 Passenger Seating [Opt on STD]	+143	Infinity Audio System	+274
AM/FM/Cassette/CD Audio System	+238	Power Driver Seat	+116
Air Conditioning [Opt on STD]	+159	Sliding Driver Side Door [Opt on STD]	+226
Aluminum/Alloy Wheels	+158	Sunscreen Glass [Std on SE]	+171

The Expresso trim level is discontinued. A new option package that Plymouth calls "T-Plus" allows buyers to pick up the 3.0-liter V6, cruise control, a tilt steering wheel and power windows, mirrors and locks, all for about $20,000. Base models now come standard with a cassette player. Note that this is your last opportunity to get a Plymouth-badged Voyager, as Chrysler dismantles its value-oriented division -- all future Voyagers will be badged as Chryslers.

1999

Mileage Category: P

Body Styles	TMV Pricing			Body Styles	TMV Pricing		
	Trade	Private	Dealer		Trade	Private	Dealer
3 Dr STD Pass Van	2952	3857	4798	4 Dr SE Pass Van	3794	4956	6166
4 Dr Expresso Pass Van	3978	5196	6464				

Options	Price	Options	Price
3.0L V6 SOHC 12V FI Engine [Opt on STD]	+231	Camper/Towing Package	+121
3.3L V6 OHV 12V FI Engine	+280	Captain Chairs (4)	+194
AM/FM/Cassette/CD Audio System [Opt on SE]	+180	Infinity Audio System	+208
Air Conditioning [Opt on STD]	+121	Sliding Driver Side Door [Opt on STD]	+172
Antilock Brakes [Opt on STD]	+218	Sunscreen Glass [Std on Expresso]	+130

SE models get body-color door and liftgate handles, as well as a body-colored front grille. All models add a cargo net between the front seats, and you can now get built-in child seats with the second-row captain's chairs.

1998

Mileage Category: P

Body Styles	TMV Pricing			Body Styles	TMV Pricing		
	Trade	Private	Dealer		Trade	Private	Dealer
3 Dr STD Pass Van	2266	3058	3952	4 Dr SE Pass Van	2702	3647	4713
4 Dr Expresso Pass Van	2870	3873	5005				

Options	Price	Options	Price
3.0L V6 SOHC 12V FI Engine [Opt on STD]	+176	Antilock Brakes [Opt on STD]	+173
AM/FM/Cassette/CD Audio System [Opt on SE]	+143	Captain Chairs (4)	+153

Plymouth adds an Expresso trim level; intended to offer both style and value, this van has body-color door handles and silver exterior accents, and comes with privacy glass, keyless entry and a CD player. In other news, all Voyagers get depowered, next-generation front airbags, adjustable front head restraints and new seat fabric. The four-speed automatic transmission receives upgrades for durability, and it can now be paired with the 3.0-liter V6 (which is LEV-certified in California). Other minor changes include an easy-entry feature for the left-hand captain's chair (in the second row) on vans with the left-hand sliding door, revised built-in booster seats and grocery bag hooks on the rear seat backs.

1998 (cont'd)

Options	Price
Sliding Driver Side Door [Opt on STD]	+136

1997

Changes for 1997 include updated transmission software, an upgraded antilock brake system and an enhanced accident response system that unlocks the doors and turns on the interior lights if the front airbags deploy. Additionally, Plymouth has made improvements to the cabin insulation (to reduce noise and vibration) and cassette stereo units. Standard lighting elements now include front map lights and liftgate flood lamps; a cargo bay power point is also part of the deal. New options include an eight-way power driver seat and an overhead console with a trip computer, compass and outside temperature display. Finally, base models get new wheel covers.

Mileage Category: P

Body Styles	TMV Pricing		
	Trade	Private	Dealer
3 Dr SE Pass Van	2223	3084	4136

Options	Price
3.3L V6 OHV 12V FI Engine	+341
AM/FM/Cassette/CD Audio System	+144
Antilock Brakes [Std on SE]	+175
Automatic 3-Speed Transmission [Opt on SE]	+121

Body Styles	TMV Pricing		
	Trade	Private	Dealer
3 Dr STD Pass Van	1900	2636	3536

Options	Price
Captain Chairs (4)	+144
Premium Audio System [Opt on SE]	+167
Sliding Driver Side Door	+138

1996

The Voyager is completely redesigned for 1996, and Chrysler's minivan designers and engineers have substantially improved upon the original formula: Interior comfort is top-notch, engines are more powerful and the available left-hand sliding door is an industry first.

Mileage Category: P

Body Styles	TMV Pricing		
	Trade	Private	Dealer
3 Dr SE Pass Van	1805	2582	3656

Options	Price
3.0L V6 SOHC 12V FI Engine	+140
3.3L V6 OHV 12V FI Engine	+163
Antilock Brakes [Opt on STD]	+138

Body Styles	TMV Pricing		
	Trade	Private	Dealer
3 Dr STD Pass Van	1529	2187	3096

Options	Price
Captain Chairs (4)	+136
Premium Audio System [Opt on SE]	+131

1995

Mileage Category: P

Body Styles	TMV Pricing		
	Trade	Private	Dealer
3 Dr LE Pass Van	1465	2162	3323
3 Dr SE Pass Van	1252	1848	2840

Options	Price
Antilock Brakes [Std on AWD,LE]	+106
Captain Chairs (4)	+88

Body Styles	TMV Pricing		
	Trade	Private	Dealer
3 Dr STD Pass Van	1097	1619	2490

Options	Price
Premium Audio System [Opt on STD]	+101

Changes this year are minimal. ABS is now standard on LE models. SE models can be equipped with a snazzy Rallye package designed for those trying to disguise the fact that they are driving a minivan -- it includes two-tone paint treatment, tinted glass and 15-inch alloy wheels. The four-speed automatic transmission benefits from engineering refinements, while the base model is no longer available with a manual transmission. A natural gas version of the 3.3-liter V6 is available in limited numbers this year.

Aztek
2004

Mileage Category: L

Body Styles	TMV Pricing		
	Trade	Private	Dealer
4 Dr STD AWD SUV	11662	12779	14640

Options	Price
17 Inch Wheels	+500
AM/FM/CD Changer Audio System	+400
AM/FM/CD/MP3 Audio System	+125
Air Conditioning - Front and Rear	+165
Alarm System	+200
Antilock Brakes [Opt on 2WD]	+680
Camper/Towing Package	+450
Center Console	+150
Cruise Control	+250
DVD Entertainment System	+1100
Front Side Airbag Restraints [Opt on 2WD]	+300
Heads-Up Display	+425

Body Styles	TMV Pricing		
	Trade	Private	Dealer
4 Dr STD SUV	10285	11402	13263

Options	Price
Heated Front Seats	+180
Leather Seats	+640
OnStar Telematics System	+770
Overhead Console	+200
Power Driver Seat	+250
Power Moonroof	+285
Power Passenger Seat	+200
Privacy Glass	+225
Refrigerator	+600
Satellite Radio System	+325
Steering Wheel Radio Controls	+120
Trip Computer	+150

An MP3 player is newly available, as are new five-spoke aluminum wheels. A rally appearance package that includes chrome exhaust tips, a body-colored front grille and a lowered suspension is now available, but can only be had with black, orange or gray exterior paint.

2003

For 2003, the Aztek offers a few new high-tech options like a DVD-based entertainment system and XM Satellite Radio. You'll also find additional wheel styles, a tire pressure-monitoring system and a new "luxury appointment group" for top-of-the-line models.

Mileage Category: L

Body Styles	TMV Pricing		
	Trade	Private	Dealer
4 Dr STD AWD SUV	10886	11971	13780

Options	Price
17 Inch Wheels	+167
AM/FM/CD Changer Audio System	+167
Antilock Brakes [Opt on 2WD]	+385
Camper/Towing Package	+207
DVD Entertainment System	+567
Front Side Airbag Restraints [Opt on 2WD]	+170
Heads-Up Display	+241
Heated Front Seats	+156
Leather Seats	+368

Body Styles	TMV Pricing		
	Trade	Private	Dealer
4 Dr STD SUV	9433	10373	11940

Options	Price
OnStar Telematics System	+269
Power Driver Seat	+136
Power Moonroof	+136
Power Passenger Seat	+136
Satellite Radio System	+184
Tinted Glass	+122
Tire Inflation System	+156
Traction Control System	+170

2002

After a chilling reception from consumers in its first year, Pontiac is attempting to salvage the Aztek with a slight makeover that includes a monotone exterior and a new rear spoiler. Inside, numerous amenities that were optional on last year's model are now standard equipment.

Mileage Category: L

Body Styles	TMV Pricing		
	Trade	Private	Dealer
4 Dr STD AWD Wgn	9025	10072	11817

Options	Price
17 Inch Wheels	+243
AM/FM/CD Changer Audio System	+144
AM/FM/Cassette/CD Audio System	+207
Camper/Towing Package	+178
Heads-Up Display	+207
Leather Seats	+414

Body Styles	TMV Pricing		
	Trade	Private	Dealer
4 Dr STD Wgn	8308	9272	10878

Options	Price
OnStar Telematics System	+338
Power Driver Seat	+117
Power Moonroof	+316
Power Passenger Seat	+117
Temperature Controls - Driver and Passenger	+170

2001

Pontiac brings forth a new so-called Sport Recreation Vehicle, blending attributes of a station wagon, minivan, SUV and Pumbaa the talking pig (from "The Lion King") into an "interesting" offering.

Mileage Category: L

Body Styles	TMV Pricing		
	Trade	Private	Dealer
4 Dr GT AWD Wgn	7978	9358	10632
4 Dr GT Wgn	7755	9097	10335

Options	Price
AM/FM/CD Changer Audio System	+124
AM/FM/Cassette/CD Audio System	+136
Camper/Towing Package	+153

Body Styles	TMV Pricing		
	Trade	Private	Dealer
4 Dr STD AWD Wgn	7646	8968	10189
4 Dr STD Wgn	7100	8328	9462

Options	Price
Captain Chairs (4)	+126
Heads-Up Display [Opt on GT]	+116
Power Moonroof	+273

Pontiac
Bonneville

Bonneville
2004

The supercharged SSEi version of Pontiac's luxury tourer is no more, but a V8-powered GXP model makes its debut later in the model year. This most performance-oriented of Bonnevilles, the GXP, gets more streamlined styling (less cladding, that is) and comes with 18-inch wheels, a sport-tuned suspension, leather/suede seats and a Monsoon sound system. Aside from that, chrome wheels are now available on the SE model.

Mileage Category: G

Body Styles	TMV Pricing		
	Trade	Private	Dealer
4 Dr GXP Sdn	21500	22820	25019
4 Dr SE Sdn	13874	14913	16645

Options	Price
AM/FM/Cassette/CD Audio System	+150
Aluminum/Alloy Wheels [Opt on SE]	+375
Automatic Climate Control (2 Zone) - Driver and Passenger [Opt on SE, SLE]	+365
Chrome Wheels [Opt on SE, SLE]	+595
Compact Disc Changer	+595
Front Side Airbag Restraints [Opt on SE, SLE]	+350
Garage Door Opener	+150
Heads-Up Display [Opt on SSEi]	+325
Heated Front Seats	+295

Body Styles	TMV Pricing		
	Trade	Private	Dealer
4 Dr SLE Sdn	16803	18052	20133

Options	Price
Leather Seats [Opt on SE, SLE]	+305
Power Moonroof	+1100
Power Passenger Seat [Opt on SE, SLE]	+250
Rear Spoiler [Opt on SE]	+225
Satellite Radio System	+325
Special Factory Paint	+750
Split Front Bench Seat	+150
Traction Control System [Opt on SE]	+175

2003

The Bonneville gets only minor changes for 2003. Base SE models now sport newly styled 16-inch steel wheels and a standard AM/FM/CD stereo, while all models can be upgraded with optional XM Satellite Radio. Previously standard side airbags are now optional on SE and SLE models.

Mileage Category: G

Body Styles	TMV Pricing		
	Trade	Private	Dealer
4 Dr SE Sdn	11208	12148	13714
4 Dr SLE Sdn	13465	14594	16476

Options	Price
17 Inch Wheels - Chrome [Opt on SLE, SSEi]	+337
Aluminum/Alloy Wheels [Opt on SE]	+212
Automatic Climate Control (2 Zone) - Driver and Passenger [Opt on SE, SLE]	+207
Compact Disc Changer	+337
Front Side Airbag Restraints [Opt on SE, SLE]	+198
Heads-Up Display [Opt on SSEi]	+184

Body Styles	TMV Pricing		
	Trade	Private	Dealer
4 Dr SSEi S/C Sdn	16524	17909	20218

Options	Price
Heated Front Seats	+167
Leather Seats [Opt on SE, SLE]	+450
OnStar Telematics System [Opt on SE]	+394
Power Moonroof	+623
Power Passenger Seat [Opt on SE, SLE]	+136
Satellite Radio System	+184

2002

Only subtle changes are on tap for the 2002 Bonneville. Most notable on the list are new front and rear fascias for the base SE model, while new exterior badging and dual exhaust tips debut on the SLE and SSEi models. Newly styled 17-inch wheels, three new exterior colors, LATCH child-seat anchors, an improved Monsoon sound system and redesigned cupholders round out the changes.

Mileage Category: G

Body Styles	TMV Pricing		
	Trade	Private	Dealer
4 Dr SE Sdn	9503	10439	11998
4 Dr SLE Sdn	11047	12135	13949

Options	Price
17 Inch Wheels - Chrome [Opt on SLE, SSEi]	+290
Automatic Climate Control (2 Zone) - Driver and Passenger [Opt on SE]	+219
Compact Disc Changer	+290
Heated Front Seats [Opt on SSEi]	+144

Body Styles	TMV Pricing		
	Trade	Private	Dealer
4 Dr SSEi S/C Sdn	13794	15153	17417

Options	Price
Leather Seats [Std on SSEi]	+414
OnStar Telematics System [Opt on SE]	+207
Power Moonroof	+526
Power Passenger Seat [Std on SSEi]	+258

2001

Heated seats are available on the SE and SLE, and Ivory White is a new color for the year. OnStar telematics with a one-year membership is optional on the SE but comes standard with the SLE and SSEi.

Mileage Category: G

Body Styles	TMV Pricing		
	Trade	Private	Dealer
4 Dr SE Sdn	7740	9003	10169
4 Dr SLE Sdn	8674	10089	11395

Options	Price
17 Inch Wheels - Chrome	+250
Automatic Climate Control (2 Zone) - Driver and Passenger [Opt on SE]	+157
Compact Disc Changer	+250
Heated Front Seats	+124

Body Styles	TMV Pricing		
	Trade	Private	Dealer
4 Dr SSEi S/C Sdn	11647	13548	15302

Options	Price
Leather Seats [Std on SSEi]	+357
OnStar Telematics System	+199
Power Moonroof	+453
Power Passenger Seat [Std on SSEi]	+138

2000

Brand-new from the ground up, Pontiac's flagship sedan moves onto a stiffer platform with rakish styling and high-tech goodies such as an integrated chassis control system.

Mileage Category: G

Body Styles	TMV Pricing		
	Trade	Private	Dealer
4 Dr SE Sdn	5982	7193	8380
4 Dr SLE Sdn	6623	7964	9278

Options	Price
AM/FM/CD Audio System	+121
Aluminum/Alloy Wheels [Opt on SE]	+123
Chrome Wheels	+225
Compact Disc Changer	+225
Leather Seats [Std on SSEi]	+322

Body Styles	TMV Pricing		
	Trade	Private	Dealer
4 Dr SSEi S/C Sdn	9077	10915	12716

Options	Price
OnStar Telematics System	+339
Power Driver Seat [Opt on SE]	+116
Power Moonroof	+371
Power Passenger Seat [Std on SSEi]	+116

1999

Body Styles	TMV Pricing		
	Trade	Private	Dealer
4 Dr SE Sdn	4591	5695	6844
4 Dr SLE Sdn	4986	6184	7430

Options	Price
Chrome Wheels	+178
Leather Seats	+254

Body Styles	TMV Pricing		
	Trade	Private	Dealer
4 Dr SSE Sdn	6350	7875	9463
4 Dr SSEi S/C Sdn	6413	7954	9558

Options	Price
OnStar Telematics System	+297
Power Moonroof	+293

GM's dealer-installed OnStar mobile communications system is available.

1998

Second-generation airbags are standard, the SE comes with a standard deck lid spoiler, and the SSE gets more standard equipment. New colors freshen the aging Bonneville.

Mileage Category: G

Body Styles	TMV Pricing		
	Trade	Private	Dealer
4 Dr SE Sdn	3584	4591	5726
4 Dr SLE Sdn	4292	5498	6858

Options	Price
Chrome Wheels	+160
Leather Seats	+228

Body Styles	TMV Pricing		
	Trade	Private	Dealer
4 Dr SSE Sdn	5058	6478	8080
4 Dr SSEi S/C Sdn	5419	6941	8657

Options	Price
OnStar Telematics System	+267
Power Moonroof	+263

1997

Changes for 1997 are few. Supercharged Bonnevilles get a new transmission, a new Delco/Bose premium sound system is optional on the SSE, and the EYE CUE heads-up display has a new motorized adjustment feature. Two new exterior colors, a new interior color and a new interior fabric visually liven up the aging Bonneville.

Mileage Category: G

Body Styles	TMV Pricing		
	Trade	Private	Dealer
4 Dr SE S/C Sdn	3373	4526	5935
4 Dr SE Sdn	2744	3682	4828

Options	Price
Chrome Wheels	+147
Electronic Suspension Control [Opt on SE]	+117

Body Styles	TMV Pricing		
	Trade	Private	Dealer
4 Dr SSE Sdn	3868	5190	6806
4 Dr SSEi S/C Sdn	3943	5292	6940

Options	Price
Leather Seats	+192
Power Moonroof	+242

1996

The Series II V6 has been supercharged for 1996, pumping out 240 horsepower. Styling front and rear has been tweaked, and daytime running lights debut.

Mileage Category: G

Body Styles	TMV Pricing		
	Trade	Private	Dealer
4 Dr SE S/C Sdn	2203	3131	4413
4 Dr SE Sdn	1921	2731	3849
4 Dr SLE Sdn	2517	3577	5041

Options	Price
Chrome Wheels	+125
Leather Seats	+164

Body Styles	TMV Pricing		
	Trade	Private	Dealer
4 Dr SSE S/C Sdn	2777	3946	5561
4 Dr SSE Sdn	2755	3915	5518

Options	Price
Power Moonroof	+206

1995

Base engine is upgraded to 3800 Series II status, gaining 35 horsepower in the process. SE models with the SLE package can be ordered with the supercharged 3.8-liter V6. Computer Command Ride is made available on SE models.

Mileage Category: G

Body Styles	TMV Pricing		
	Trade	Private	Dealer
4 Dr SE S/C Sdn	1551	2321	3603
4 Dr SE Sdn	1378	2062	3202

Body Styles	TMV Pricing		
	Trade	Private	Dealer
4 Dr SSE Sdn	1858	2781	4319
4 Dr SSEi S/C Sdn	2013	3012	4677

1995 (cont'd)

Options	Price
Leather Seats	+139
Power Moonroof	+174

Options	Price
Special Seats [Opt on SSE]	+209

Firebird

2002

Entering its last year of production, the Firebird gets few changes for 2002. Power mirrors and a power antenna are now standard on all models, and Bright Silver Metallic replaces Blue-Green Chameleon on the color palette.

Mileage Category: E

Body Styles	TMV Pricing		
	Trade	Private	Dealer
2 Dr Formula Hbk	12914	13968	15725
2 Dr STD Conv	13181	14257	16049
2 Dr STD Hbk	9177	9926	11174

Body Styles	TMV Pricing		
	Trade	Private	Dealer
2 Dr Trans Am Conv	16773	18142	20423
2 Dr Trans Am Hbk	13276	14360	16166

Options	Price
17 Inch Wheels [Opt on Trans Am]	+365
5.7L V8 OHV 16V FI w/Ram Air Engine [Opt on Trans Am]	+1193
Automatic 4-Speed Transmission [Opt on STD Hbk]	+316
Chrome Wheels	+290
Compact Disc Changer	+290

Options	Price
Leather Seats [Std on Trans Am]	+280
Limited Slip Differential [Opt on STD]	+173
Power Driver Seat [Opt on STD Hbk]	+131
T-Tops - Glass [Std on Trans Am]	+484
Traction Control System	+122

2001

For 2001, V8-equipped Formula and Trans Am receive five more horsepower and five more pound-feet of torque, new exterior and interior colors join the palette and the Ram Air Formula is dropped from the lineup.

Mileage Category: E

Body Styles	TMV Pricing		
	Trade	Private	Dealer
2 Dr Formula Hbk	10428	11870	13201
2 Dr STD Conv	10846	12346	13730
2 Dr STD Hbk	7561	8606	9571

Body Styles	TMV Pricing		
	Trade	Private	Dealer
2 Dr Trans Am Conv	13956	15886	17667
2 Dr Trans Am Hbk	11201	12751	14181

Options	Price
Automatic 4-Speed Transmission [Opt on STD]	+342
Chrome Wheels	+250
Compact Disc Changer	+250
Leather Seats [Std on Trans Am]	+241
Limited Slip Differential	+126

Options	Price
Monsoon Audio System [Opt on STD Hbk]	+138
Power Windows [Opt on STD Hbk]	+124
Ram Air Performance Package	+1321
T-Tops - Glass [Std on Trans Am]	+418
T-Tops - Solid	+417

2000

New wheels, exterior and interior colors and engine revisions for improved emissions and better throttle response on manual transmission-equipped cars top the list of Firebird changes for 2000.

Mileage Category: E

Body Styles	TMV Pricing		
	Trade	Private	Dealer
2 Dr Formula Hbk	9068	10500	11903
2 Dr SLP Firehawk Hbk	12455	14422	16350
2 Dr STD Conv	9427	10915	12374

Body Styles	TMV Pricing		
	Trade	Private	Dealer
2 Dr STD Hbk	6599	7641	8662
2 Dr Trans Am Conv	11647	13486	15288
2 Dr Trans Am Hbk	9790	11335	12850

Options	Price
17 Inch Wheels - Chrome [Opt on Trans Am]	+303
5.7L V8 OHV 16V FI w/Ram Air Engine	+890
AM/FM/Cassette/CD Audio System	+125
Automatic 4-Speed Transmission [Opt on STD]	+309
Chrome Wheels	+225

Options	Price
Compact Disc Changer	+225
Leather Seats [Std on Trans Am]	+218
Monsoon Audio System [Opt on STD Hbk]	+125
Ram Air Performance Package	+568
T-Tops - Glass [Std on Trans Am]	+377

1999

Electronic traction control is now available on all models, with a bigger gas tank and an oil life monitor standard. A Torsen limited-slip rear axle comes with V8 models (and V6 cars with the performance package), while an eight-speaker Delco/Monsoon sound system goes into the convertible. A power-steering cooler is now available for V8s, and a Hurst shifter is optional on the six-speed manual transmission. The Ram Air WS6 package now sports dual outlet exhaust, and two new exterior colors debut, Pewter and Medium Blue Metallic. The 30th anniversary Trans Am sports an extroverted paint scheme that features two blue stripes running over the hood and deck lid.

Mileage Category: E

Body Styles	TMV Pricing		
	Trade	Private	Dealer
2 Dr Formula Hbk	7404	8845	10344
2 Dr STD Conv	7673	9166	10719
2 Dr STD Hbk	5258	6281	7345

Body Styles	TMV Pricing		
	Trade	Private	Dealer
2 Dr Trans Am Conv	9373	11196	13093
2 Dr Trans Am Hbk	7776	9289	10863

Options	Price
17 Inch Wheels [Opt on Formula, Trans Am]	+158
5.7L V8 OHV 16V FI w/Ram Air Engine	+581
Automatic 4-Speed Transmission [Opt on STD]	+244
Chrome Wheels	+178
Compact Disc Changer	+178

Options	Price
Leather Seats [Std on Trans Am]	+172
Ram Air Performance Package	+448
Special Leather Seat Trim [Opt on Trans Am]	+274
T-Tops - Glass [Std on Trans Am]	+297

Mileage Category: E

1998

Firebirds get a minor restyle that is most evident from the front end. Also on tap for Formula and Trans Am models is a detuned Corvette engine making 305 horsepower without Ram Air induction. Base models can be equipped with a new Sport Appearance Package, and two new exterior colors debut. Second-generation airbags are standard.

Body Styles	TMV Pricing		
	Trade	Private	Dealer
2 Dr Formula Hbk	6065	7387	8878
2 Dr STD Conv	6245	7606	9141
2 Dr STD Hbk	4353	5302	6372

Body Styles	TMV Pricing		
	Trade	Private	Dealer
2 Dr Trans Am Conv	7940	9670	11621
2 Dr Trans Am Hbk	6403	7799	9373

Options	Price
17 Inch Wheels [Opt on Formula,Trans Am]	+223
5.7L V8 OHV 16V FI w/Ram Air Engine	+700
Automatic 4-Speed Transmission [Opt on STD]	+219
Chrome Wheels	+160
Compact Disc Changer	+160

Options	Price
Leather Seats [Std on Trans Am]	+174
Performance/Handling Package	+316
Premium Audio System [Opt on Trans Am Hbk]	+115
T-Tops - Glass [Std on Trans Am]	+267
Traction Control System	+121

Mileage Category: E

1997

Body Styles	TMV Pricing		
	Trade	Private	Dealer
2 Dr Formula Conv	5739	7155	8886
2 Dr Formula Hbk	4925	6141	7627
2 Dr STD Conv	5383	6712	8336

Body Styles	TMV Pricing		
	Trade	Private	Dealer
2 Dr STD Hbk	3498	4362	5417
2 Dr Trans Am Conv	6243	7783	9666
2 Dr Trans Am Hbk	5028	6269	7786

Options	Price
17 Inch Wheels [Opt on Formula,Trans Am]	+206
5.7L V8 OHV 16V FI w/Ram Air Engine	+590
Automatic 4-Speed Transmission [Opt on STD]	+195
Chrome Wheels	+147

Options	Price
Compact Disc Changer	+147
Leather Seats	+199
Performance/Handling Package	+290
T-Tops - Glass	+246

Pontiac upgrades the Firebird in several ways for 1997. Performance freaks will appreciate the addition of Ram Air induction to the options list of the Formula and Trans Am convertibles. Audiophiles will be blown away by the newly optional 500-watt Monsoon sound system. Luxury intenders can get power seats swathed in leather this year. Safety-conscious buyers will find daytime running lights. Additional cosmetic and comfort items keep the fourth-generation Firebird fresh for its fifth year.

Mileage Category: E

1996

A new standard V6 makes 40 more horsepower than the old one. The LT1 V8 also makes more power, particularly when equipped with Ram Air induction. A new color livens up the exterior, as if it needed it.

Body Styles	TMV Pricing		
	Trade	Private	Dealer
2 Dr Formula Conv	4737	6067	7904
2 Dr Formula Hbk	3681	4715	6142
2 Dr STD Conv	4058	5197	6771

Body Styles	TMV Pricing		
	Trade	Private	Dealer
2 Dr STD Hbk	2798	3584	4669
2 Dr Trans Am Conv	5110	6546	8528
2 Dr Trans Am Hbk	3794	4860	6332

Options	Price
17 Inch Wheels [Opt on Formula,Trans Am]	+175
5.7L V8 OHV 16V FI w/Ram Air Engine	+502
Automatic 4-Speed Transmission [Opt on STD]	+166

Options	Price
Compact Disc Changer	+125
Leather Seats	+169
T-Tops - Glass	+204

1995

Traction control is added as an option on Formula and Trans Am. Trans Am GT is dropped from lineup. Californians get a 3.8-liter V6 equipped with an automatic transmission on base models instead of the 3.4-liter V6. The new engine meets strict emissions standards in that state, and makes 40 additional horsepower.

Body Styles	TMV Pricing		
	Trade	Private	Dealer
2 Dr Formula Conv	3553	4627	6418
2 Dr Formula Hbk	2765	3602	4997
2 Dr STD Conv	3292	4288	5949

Body Styles	TMV Pricing		
	Trade	Private	Dealer
2 Dr STD Hbk	2036	2653	3680
2 Dr Trans Am Conv	4301	5603	7773
2 Dr Trans Am Hbk	3127	4073	5650

Options	Price
Air Conditioning [Std on Trans Am,Conv]	+89
Automatic 4-Speed Transmission	+141
Leather Seats [Opt on Formula,STD]	+102

Options	Price
Premium Audio System	+77
T-Tops - Glass	+173
T-Tops - Solid	+116

Pontiac
Grand Am

Grand Am

2004

An upgraded four-speaker sound system is now standard on SE models, while an MP3 player is standard on uplevel GT models and optional on all others except the base SE.

Mileage Category: C

Body Styles	TMV Pricing		
	Trade	Private	Dealer
2 Dr GT Cpe	10171	11105	12662
2 Dr GT1 Cpe	10728	11662	13218
4 Dr GT Sdn	10171	11105	12662
4 Dr GT1 Sdn	10728	11662	13218

Options	Price
3.4L V6 OHV 12V FI Engine [Opt on SE1]	+715
AM/FM/CD/MP3 Audio System [Opt on SE1, SE2, GT]	+200
Aluminum/Alloy Wheels [Opt on SE]	+375
Antilock Brakes [Opt on SE, SE1]	+200
Automatic 4-Speed Transmission [Opt on SE, SE1]	+850
Chrome Wheels [Opt on SE1, SE2, GT, GT1]	+650
Cruise Control [Opt on SE]	+250

Body Styles	TMV Pricing		
	Trade	Private	Dealer
4 Dr SE Sdn	8116	9084	10698
4 Dr SE1 Sdn	8957	9892	11450
4 Dr SE2 Sdn	9970	10905	12462

Options	Price
Leather Seats [Opt on GT, GT1, SE2]	+465
Power Mirrors [Opt on SE]	+180
Power Moonroof [Opt on GT, SE1, SE2]	+700
Power Windows [Opt on SE]	+250
Rear Spoiler [Opt on SE, SE1, SE2]	+225
Satellite Radio System	+325
Traction Control System [Opt on SE, SE1]	+200

2003

A new trim level has been added -- SE2 -- that offers buyers more standard equipment and additional options, while the SE coupe is no longer available. All SE sedans now feature cleaner styling thanks to less body cladding and smoother front and rear fascias. XM Satellite Radio is an available option on all models, while the OnStar communications system is now standard on all models except the base SE.

Mileage Category: C

Body Styles	TMV Pricing		
	Trade	Private	Dealer
2 Dr GT Cpe	8717	9690	11312
2 Dr GT1 Cpe	9202	10229	11941
4 Dr GT Sdn	8747	9723	11350
4 Dr GT1 Sdn	9230	10261	11978

Options	Price
16 Inch Wheels - Chrome	+368
3.4L V6 OHV 12V FI Engine [Opt on SE1]	+405
Aero Kit [Opt on GT, GT1]	+705
Aluminum/Alloy Wheels [Opt on SE]	+170
Antilock Brakes [Opt on SE, SE1]	+385
Automatic 4-Speed Transmission [Opt on SE, SE1]	+482

Body Styles	TMV Pricing		
	Trade	Private	Dealer
4 Dr SE Sdn	7045	7832	9144
4 Dr SE1 Sdn	7799	8669	10119
4 Dr SE2 Sdn	8640	9605	11211

Options	Price
Cruise Control [Opt on SE]	+142
Leather Seats [Opt on GT, GT1, SE2]	+326
Power Moonroof [Opt on GT, SE1, SE2]	+397
Power Windows [Opt on SE]	+144
Rear Spoiler [Opt on SE, SE1, SE2]	+127
Satellite Radio System [Opt on GT, GT1, SE1, SE2]	+184

2002

Base model SEs get a new 2.2-liter four-cylinder engine, while GTs get newly styled 16-inch wheels. All models receive a console upgrade and two new exterior colors.

Mileage Category: C

Body Styles	TMV Pricing		
	Trade	Private	Dealer
2 Dr GT Cpe	7041	8031	9680
2 Dr GT1 Cpe	7451	8498	10242
2 Dr SE Cpe	5778	6590	7942
2 Dr SE1 Cpe	6266	7147	8614

Options	Price
3.4L V6 OHV 12V FI Engine [Opt on SE1]	+348
Aluminum/Alloy Wheels [Opt on SE]	+146
Automatic 4-Speed Transmission [Opt on SE, SE1]	+402
Chrome Wheels	+290

Body Styles	TMV Pricing		
	Trade	Private	Dealer
4 Dr GT Sdn	7070	8063	9719
4 Dr GT1 Sdn	7481	8532	10282
4 Dr SE Sdn	5806	6622	7981
4 Dr SE1 Sdn	6295	7179	8653

Options	Price
Cruise Control [Opt on SE]	+117
Leather Seats [Opt on GT, GT1]	+280
Monsoon Audio System [Opt on SE1]	+139
Power Moonroof [Std on GT1]	+316

2001

For 2001, the Grand Am gets audio improvements, a wheel upgrade and revised paint choices.

Mileage Category: C

Body Styles	TMV Pricing		
	Trade	Private	Dealer
2 Dr GT Cpe	5689	6975	8162
2 Dr GT1 Cpe	5967	7315	8559
2 Dr SE Cpe	4350	5334	6241
2 Dr SE1 Cpe	4877	5979	6996

Options	Price
3.4L V6 OHV 12V FI Engine [Opt on]	+275
Aluminum/Alloy Wheels [Opt on SE, SE1 Cpe]	+206
Automatic 4-Speed Transmission [Opt on SE, SE1]	+346

Body Styles	TMV Pricing		
	Trade	Private	Dealer
4 Dr GT Sdn	5803	7115	8325
4 Dr GT1 Sdn	6120	7502	8777
4 Dr SE Sdn	4456	5462	6392
4 Dr SE1 Sdn	4980	6106	7146

Options	Price
Chrome Wheels	+271
Leather Seats	+199
Monsoon Audio System [Opt on SE1]	+143

For the latest vehicle information, visit www.edmunds.com

2001 (cont'd)

Options	Price
Power Moonroof [Std on GT1]	+250

Mileage Category: C

Body Styles	TMV Pricing			Body Styles	TMV Pricing		
	Trade	Private	Dealer		Trade	Private	Dealer
2 Dr GT Cpe	4320	5494	6644	4 Dr GT Sdn	4411	5608	6782
2 Dr GT1 Cpe	4554	5791	7003	4 Dr GT1 Sdn	4705	5983	7236
2 Dr SE Cpe	3361	4273	5168	4 Dr SE Sdn	3462	4402	5323
2 Dr SE1 Cpe	3658	4652	5625	4 Dr SE1 Sdn	3801	4833	5844
2 Dr SE2 Cpe	3968	5045	6100	4 Dr SE2 Sdn	4362	5546	6707

Options	Price	Options	Price
3.4L V6 OHV 12V FI Engine [Opt on]	+248	Leather Seats	+180
Automatic 4-Speed Transmission [Opt on SE,SE1]	+297	Power Moonroof [Std on GT1]	+225
Chrome Wheels	+244		

2000

Grand Am gets engine improvements, interior upgrades (including a revamped center console), new exterior appearance packages and revised paint choices.

Mileage Category: C

Body Styles	TMV Pricing			Body Styles	TMV Pricing		
	Trade	Private	Dealer		Trade	Private	Dealer
2 Dr GT Cpe	3458	4620	5829	4 Dr GT Sdn	3524	4707	5939
2 Dr GT1 Cpe	3665	4896	6178	4 Dr GT1 Sdn	3829	5115	6453
2 Dr SE Cpe	2727	3643	4596	4 Dr SE Sdn	2841	3794	4786
2 Dr SE1 Cpe	3074	4107	5181	4 Dr SE1 Sdn	3121	4169	5259
2 Dr SE2 Cpe	3158	4218	5322	4 Dr SE2 Sdn	3517	4698	5928

Options	Price	Options	Price
3.4L V6 OHV 12V FI Engine [Opt on SE1]	+196	Power Moonroof [Std on GT1]	+178
Leather Seats	+164		

1999

New for 1999, the Grand Am offers a host of standard and optional equipment as well as a completely redesigned exterior.

Mileage Category: C

Body Styles	TMV Pricing			Body Styles	TMV Pricing		
	Trade	Private	Dealer		Trade	Private	Dealer
2 Dr GT Cpe	2364	3304	4363	4 Dr GT Sdn	2490	3478	4593
2 Dr SE Cpe	2199	3071	4054	4 Dr SE Sdn	2222	3103	4096

Options	Price	Options	Price
Automatic 4-Speed Transmission	+217	Power Moonroof	+160
Leather Seats	+147		

Second-generation airbags are newly standard, and option groups are simplified.

1998

Mileage Category: C

Body Styles	TMV Pricing			Body Styles	TMV Pricing		
	Trade	Private	Dealer		Trade	Private	Dealer
2 Dr GT Cpe	1855	2685	3698	4 Dr GT Sdn	1820	2633	3627
2 Dr SE Cpe	1743	2523	3476	4 Dr SE Sdn	1703	2464	3394

Options	Price	Options	Price
Automatic 4-Speed Transmission	+200	Power Driver Seat	+147
Leather Seats	+172	Power Moonroof	+147

1997

Very minimal changes this year as Pontiac concentrates on Grand Prix and Trans Sport launches. Air conditioning is now standard. Also, three new colors are added.

Mileage Category: C

Body Styles	TMV Pricing			Body Styles	TMV Pricing		
	Trade	Private	Dealer		Trade	Private	Dealer
2 Dr GT Cpe	1289	1982	2939	4 Dr GT Sdn	1367	2102	3116
2 Dr SE Cpe	1194	1836	2723	4 Dr SE Sdn	1188	1826	2709

Options	Price	Options	Price
AM/FM/Cassette/CD Audio System	+126	Leather Seats	+146
Air Conditioning [Opt on SE]	+175	Power Moonroof	+125
Automatic 4-Speed Transmission	+168		

1996

New styling, a new base engine, dual airbags and body-mounted seatbelts.

Pontiac
Grand Am/Grand Prix

1995

Base engine upgraded to a 150-horsepower version of the Quad 4. High-output Quad 4 motor is dropped from the GT, which now uses the same standard and optional power plants as the SE. Variable-effort power steering is a new option on GT models, rear suspensions are redesigned and SE models get restyled wheel covers and alloy wheels.

Mileage Category: C

Body Styles	TMV Pricing			Body Styles	TMV Pricing		
	Trade	Private	Dealer		Trade	Private	Dealer
2 Dr GT Cpe	799	1334	2227	4 Dr GT Sdn	821	1372	2291
2 Dr SE Cpe	709	1186	1980	4 Dr SE Sdn	760	1269	2118

Options	Price	Options	Price
Air Conditioning [Opt on SE]	+148	Leather Seats	+98
Automatic 3-Speed Transmission	+80	Power Moonroof	+106
Automatic 4-Speed Transmission	+142		

Grand Prix

2004

The Grand Prix underwent a redesign for 2004, but those familiar with the big sedan will find its blend of performance and comfort hasn't changed much.

Mileage Category: D

Body Styles	TMV Pricing			Body Styles	TMV Pricing		
	Trade	Private	Dealer		Trade	Private	Dealer
4 Dr GT1 Sdn	11128	12268	14169	4 Dr GTP S/C Sdn	13328	14489	16424
4 Dr GT2 Sdn	12226	13383	15310				

Options	Price	Options	Price
16 Inch Wheels [Opt on SE]	+400	Leather Seats [Opt on GT, GTP]	+515
17 Inch Wheels - Chrome [Opt on GTP]	+595	OnStar Telematics System [Opt on GT, SE]	+695
AM/FM/CD Changer Audio System [Opt on GT2, GTP]	+200	Polished Aluminum/Alloy Wheels	+495
Aluminum/Alloy Wheels [Opt on GT1, GT2]	+400	Power Driver Seat [Opt on SE]	+350
Antilock Brakes [Opt on GT, SE]	+200	Power Moonroof [Opt on GT, GTP]	+895
Automatic Stability Control [Opt on GTP]	+350	Tire Pressure Monitoring System [Opt on GT1]	+200
Front and Rear Head Airbag Restraints [Opt on GT2, GTP]	+395	Traction Control System [Opt on GT, SE]	+200
Heads-Up Display [Opt on GT, GTP]	+450	Trip Computer [Opt on GT]	+150
Heated Front Seats [Opt on GT]	+150		

2003

Mileage Category: D

Body Styles	TMV Pricing			Body Styles	TMV Pricing		
	Trade	Private	Dealer		Trade	Private	Dealer
4 Dr GT Sdn	9752	10836	12643	4 Dr SE Sdn	8739	9710	11330
4 Dr GTP S/C Sdn	11690	12989	15155				

Options	Price	Options	Price
16 Inch Wheels [Opt on SE]	+170	Heated Front Seats [Opt on GT]	+156
16 Inch Wheels - Chrome [Opt on GT, GTP]	+198	Leather Seats [Opt on GT, GTP]	+368
Antilock Brakes [Opt on GT, SE]	+385	OnStar Telematics System [Opt on GT, SE]	+394
Bose Audio System [Opt on GT, GTP]	+195	Power Moonroof [Opt on GT, GTP]	+368
Heads-Up Display [Opt on GT, GTP]	+184	Special Interior Trim [Opt on GT, GTP]	+173

The Grand Prix coupe has been dropped from the lineup, leaving the SE, GT and GTP sedans as the remaining models. SE versions now come standard with an AM/FM/CD stereo, rear reading lamps and a ski pass-through, while all Grand Prix models now offer a standard overhead console with vanity mirrors and assist handles. A new Limited Edition package for GT and GTP models is available; it includes a new rear spoiler, special wheels, embroidered floor mats, blue foglamps, a monotone lower fascia, unique badging and door sill plates, white-faced gauges and special seats with leather inserts and blue stitching. ABS brakes are now optional on SE and GT models.

2002

A 40th Anniversary option package can be added to GT and GTP coupes and sedans. SE and GT models also gain additional standard equipment.

Mileage Category: D

Body Styles	TMV Pricing			Body Styles	TMV Pricing		
	Trade	Private	Dealer		Trade	Private	Dealer
2 Dr GT Cpe	8236	9314	11110	4 Dr GTP S/C Sdn	10134	11460	13671
2 Dr GTP S/C Cpe	9713	10984	13102	4 Dr SE Sdn	7067	7992	9533
4 Dr GT Sdn	8268	9350	11153				

Options	Price	Options	Price
16 Inch Wheels [Opt on SE]	+146	Leather Seats [Opt on GT, GTP]	+253
Bose Audio System [Opt on GT]	+192	OnStar Telematics System [Opt on GT]	+207
Chrome Wheels [Opt on GT, GTP]	+314	Power Driver Seat [Opt on SE]	+117
play [Opt on GT]	+158	Power Moonroof [Opt on GT, GTP]	+316

Mileage Category: D

2001

Body Styles	TMV Pricing		
	Trade	Private	Dealer
2 Dr GT Cpe	6548	7993	9326
2 Dr GTP S/C Cpe	8190	9995	11662
4 Dr GT Sdn	6613	8072	9418

Options	Price
Aluminum/Alloy Wheels [Opt on SE]	+124
Bose Audio System	+155
Chrome Wheels	+271
Heads-Up Display [Opt on GT]	+116

Body Styles	TMV Pricing		
	Trade	Private	Dealer
4 Dr GTP S/C Sdn	8391	10241	11949
4 Dr SE Sdn	5735	6999	8167

Options	Price
Leather Seats	+199
OnStar Telematics System	+199
Power Driver Seat [Std on GTP]	+128
Power Moonroof	+240

The Grand Prix receives only minor changes for 2001 including a Special Edition appearance package on GT and GTP models and optional 16-inch three-spoke aluminum wheels. The OnStar system is now available on GTP models while SE models receive a slight front-end revision.

Mileage Category: D

2000

Body Styles	TMV Pricing		
	Trade	Private	Dealer
2 Dr GT Cpe	5262	6657	8025
2 Dr GTP S/C Cpe	6491	8212	9898
4 Dr GT Sdn	5270	6668	8037

Options	Price
3.8L V6 OHV 12V FI Engine [Std on GT]	+157
Bose Audio System	+150
Compact Disc Changer	+174
Leather Seats	+180

Body Styles	TMV Pricing		
	Trade	Private	Dealer
4 Dr GTP S/C Sdn	6424	8126	9795
4 Dr SE Sdn	4503	5697	6868

Options	Price
OnStar Telematics System [Opt on GT,GTP]	+339
Power Driver Seat [Opt on GT,SE]	+116
Power Moonroof	+216

Improvements to the base 3.1-liter V6 net a gain of 15 horsepower, as well as improved durability, reduced noise and lower emissions. A limited run (2,000 coupes) of Daytona Pace Car replicas will be built, featuring unique exterior and interior details. Also new are a revised anti-theft system, five-spoke silver-painted wheels, three new exterior colors and Cyclone cloth upholstery.

Mileage Category: D

1999

Body Styles	TMV Pricing		
	Trade	Private	Dealer
2 Dr GT Cpe	4149	5335	6568
2 Dr GTP S/C Cpe	4893	6290	7745
4 Dr GT Sdn	4233	5441	6699

Options	Price
3.8L V6 OHV 12V FI Engine [Std on GT]	+124
Bose Audio System	+119
Compact Disc Changer	+138

Body Styles	TMV Pricing		
	Trade	Private	Dealer
4 Dr GTP S/C Sdn	5179	6659	8199
4 Dr SE Sdn	3654	4699	5786

Options	Price
Leather Seats	+164
OnStar Telematics System [Opt on GT,GTP]	+297
Power Moonroof	+170

The Grand Prix gets more muscle for '99 with low-restriction air-induction components giving the naturally aspirated 3.8-liter V6 five more horsepower, to 200. This engine is standard on the GT (sedan and coupe) and optional on the SE sedan. A traction control indicator and on/off button are now standard on GTP models. Minor revisions are in order inside, with front-door courtesy lamps and a six-speaker sound system now standard, and an eight-speaker Bose audio unit and OnStar mobile communications system optional. Outside, a rear deck spoiler is standard on the GT model, and two colors have been added to the 1999 exterior paint chart.

Mileage Category: D

1998

Body Styles	TMV Pricing		
	Trade	Private	Dealer
2 Dr GT Cpe	3447	4658	6023
2 Dr GTP S/C Cpe	3511	4745	6136
4 Dr GT Sdn	3398	4591	5936

Options	Price
Compact Disc Changer	+160
Leather Seats	+147

Body Styles	TMV Pricing		
	Trade	Private	Dealer
4 Dr GTP S/C Sdn	3940	5324	6884
4 Dr SE Sdn	3010	4067	5259

Options	Price
Power Moonroof	+153

Supercharged GTP models get traction control, and new colors are available inside and out. Second-generation airbags debut as standard equipment.

Mileage Category: D

1997

Body Styles	TMV Pricing		
	Trade	Private	Dealer
2 Dr GT Cpe	2538	3615	4931
2 Dr GTP S/C Cpe	2790	3975	5423
4 Dr GT Sdn	2660	3790	5171

Options	Price
Compact Disc Changer	+147
Leather Seats	+136

Body Styles	TMV Pricing		
	Trade	Private	Dealer
4 Dr GTP S/C Sdn	3167	4512	6156
4 Dr SE Sdn	2207	3145	4291

Options	Price
Power Moonroof	+159

Pontiac redesigns the Grand Prix for 1997, giving buyers slick new styling, a longer and wider wheelbase and supercharged V6 power on GTP models. Traction control, antilock brakes, dual airbags and side-impact protection are standard. Optional is a built-in child safety seat.

Pontiac
Grand Prix/GTO/Montana

1996

Mileage Category: D

Body Styles	TMV Pricing			Body Styles	TMV Pricing		
	Trade	Private	Dealer		Trade	Private	Dealer
2 Dr GTP Cpe	1788	2717	4000	4 Dr GT Sdn	1764	2680	3946
2 Dr SE Cpe	1638	2488	3662	4 Dr SE Sdn	1512	2297	3381

Options	Price	Options	Price
Antilock Brakes [Opt on SE]	+159	Power Moonroof	+136
Leather Seats	+146		

Minor trim and powertrain improvements to the only car in GM's stable that still has those stupid door-mounted seatbelts. Do yourself a favor. Wait for the 1997 GP.

1995

Brake/transmission shift interlock is added. GT coupe dropped in favor of GTP Package. GT sedan continues. Variable-effort steering is added to GTP and GT. New alloys debut on GT and GTP. Coupes can be equipped with a White Appearance Package, which includes color-keyed alloys and special pinstriping. Floor consoles are redesigned on models with bucket seats.

Mileage Category: D

Body Styles	TMV Pricing			Body Styles	TMV Pricing		
	Trade	Private	Dealer		Trade	Private	Dealer
2 Dr GTP Cpe	1270	2010	3244	4 Dr GT Sdn	1227	1942	3135
2 Dr SE Cpe	1165	1843	2973	4 Dr SE Sdn	1014	1606	2593

Options	Price	Options	Price
Antilock Brakes [Opt on SE]	+134	Leather Seats	+124
Compact Disc Changer	+82	Power Moonroof	+101

GTO

2004

Mileage Category: F

Body Styles	TMV Pricing		
	Trade	Private	Dealer
2 Dr STD Cpe	19996	21576	24210

Options	Price
6-Speed Transmission	+695

The GTO is an all-new rear-wheel-drive performance car from Pontiac. Although it is new to the U.S. market, it is based on a car sold by GM's Australian subsidiary, Holden, under the Monaro nameplate.

Montana

2004

Versatrak all-wheel drive is now an available option on all models as is a CD/MP3 player and XM Satellite Radio. Front and side impact airbags are now standard. Pontiac has decided not to offer separate Value and base trim levels this year; the lineup now consists of a base model and the highline MontanaVision. Note that ABS and second-row captain's chairs are now optional rather than standard on base models.

Mileage Category: P

Body Styles	TMV Pricing			Body Styles	TMV Pricing		
	Trade	Private	Dealer		Trade	Private	Dealer
4 Dr Montanavision Pass Van Ext	15008	16313	18487	4 Dr STD Pass Van	11650	12767	14629
4 Dr STD AWD Pass Van Ext	15399	16704	18878	4 Dr STD Pass Van Ext	12899	14016	15878

Options	Price	Options	Price
AM/FM/CD Changer Audio System [Opt on MontanaVision, STD Ext]	+395	Performance/Handling Package [Opt on EXT non-AWD]	+425
AM/FM/CD/MP3 Audio System	+225	Power Driver Seat [Opt on STD]	+250
Air Conditioning - Front and Rear [Opt on STD Ext]	+450	Power Heated Mirrors [Opt on STD non-AWD]	+150
Alarm System	+200	Power Passenger Seat [Opt on Ext]	+275
Aluminum/Alloy Wheels [Opt on STD non-Ext]	+325	Power Sliding Door	+435
Antilock Brakes [Opt on STD non-AWD]	+950	Privacy Glass [Opt on STD non-AWD]	+120
Automatic Load Leveling [Opt on EXT non-AWD]	+200	Rear Air Conditioning Controls [Opt on STD Ext]	+200
Captain Chairs (4) [Opt on STD non-AWD]	+200	Rear Audio Controls [Opt on STD]	+150
Chrome Wheels [Opt on Ext]	+800	Rear Spoiler [Opt on STD Ext]	+200
DVD Entertainment System [Opt on STD AWD]	+1500	Rear Window Defroster [Opt on STD non-AWD]	+150
Heated Front Seats [Opt on Ext]	+195	Rear Window Wiper [Opt on STD non-AWD]	+160
Leather Seats [Opt on Ext]	+900	Satellite Radio System	+325
Leather Steering Wheel [Opt on STD]	+120	Special Factory Paint	+150
OnStar Telematics System	+200	Traction Control System [Opt on non-AWD]	+195
Park Distance Control (Rear) [Opt on EXT]	+285	Trip Computer [Opt on STD non-AWD]	+200

2003

The Montana gets only a few minor upgrades for 2003. The most notable change is the addition of an extended-length version of the Special Value van with a 60/40-split bench second-row seat as standard. More available free flow options also give the Value van a greater range of equipment.

Mileage Category: P

Body Styles	TMV Pricing		
	Trade	Private	Dealer
4 Dr Montanavision AWD Pass Van Ext	15166	16671	19179
4 Dr Montanavision Pass Van Ext	12995	14284	16433
4 Dr STD AWD Pass Van Ext	13690	15048	17312
4 Dr STD Pass Van	10142	11149	12826

Body Styles	TMV Pricing		
	Trade	Private	Dealer
4 Dr STD Pass Van Ext	10999	12090	13908
4 Dr Value Pass Van	10009	11002	12657
4 Dr Value Pass Van Ext	10872	11951	13749

Options	Price
Air Conditioning - Front and Rear [Opt on STD,Value]	+255
Aluminum/Alloy Wheels [Opt on STD,Value]	+142
Antilock Brakes [Opt on Value]	+538
Compact Disc Changer [Opt on MontanaVision,STD]	+224
Leather Seats [Opt on MontanaVision,STD]	+467
OnStar Telematics System [Opt on MontanaVision,STD]	+241

Options	Price
Park Distance Control (Rear) [Opt on MontanaVision,STD]	+227
Power Driver Seat [Opt on STD,Value]	+136
Power Dual Sliding Doors [Opt on MontanaVision,STD]	+198
Power Sliding Door [Opt on STD]	+198
Sport Package [Opt on MontanaVision,STD]	+1456

2002

Pontiac's big news for the Montana this year is the availability of the Versatrak all-wheel-drive system. Also debuting this year on the Montana is the Thunder Sport package and a very cool DVD entertainment system.

Mileage Category: P

Body Styles	TMV Pricing		
	Trade	Private	Dealer
4 Dr Montanavision AWD Pass Van Ext	12592	14054	16491
4 Dr Montanavision Pass Van Ext	10693	11935	14004
4 Dr STD AWD Pass Van Ext	11331	12647	14840

Body Styles	TMV Pricing		
	Trade	Private	Dealer
4 Dr STD Pass Van Ext	9357	10443	12254
4 Dr Value Pass Van	8618	9619	11288

Options	Price
7 Passenger Seating [Opt on STD]	+477
Air Conditioning - Front and Rear [Opt on STD Ext]	+316
Aluminum/Alloy Wheels [Opt on STD]	+122
Chrome Wheels [Opt on Ext]	+268
Compact Disc Changer [Opt on Ext]	+144
Leather Seats [Opt on Ext]	+389
OnStar Telematics System [Std on Montanavision]	+207

Options	Price
Park Distance Control (Rear) [Opt on STD]	+195
Power Driver Seat [Opt on STD Ext]	+117
Power Dual Sliding Doors [Opt on Ext]	+170
Power Passenger Seat [Opt on Ext]	+117
Power Sliding Door [Opt on STD Ext]	+170
Rear Spoiler [Opt on Ext]	+134
Touring Suspension [Opt on Ext]	+146

2001

Updated styling and more feature content top the list of changes to the Montana for 2001, but perhaps most importantly, GM has figured out how to provide buyers with a third-row seat that flips and folds to create a flat load floor in extended-length models. New standard features include OnStar communications, power windows, a CD player and remote keyless entry. A rear parking aid sensor, power driver-side sliding door and an in-dash six-disc CD changer are new options. When you buy the available TV/VCP setup, you get a larger screen for 2001.

Mileage Category: P

Body Styles	TMV Pricing		
	Trade	Private	Dealer
4 Dr Convenience Pass Van Ext	7595	9126	10540
4 Dr STD Pass Van	6981	8389	9688
4 Dr STD Pass Van Ext	7158	8602	9934
4 Dr Sport Pass Van	7270	8736	10090

Body Styles	TMV Pricing		
	Trade	Private	Dealer
4 Dr Sport Pass Van Ext	7730	9289	10728
4 Dr Value Pass Van	6552	7873	9093
4 Dr Vision Pass Van Ext	8178	9827	11349

Options	Price
Air Conditioning - Front and Rear	+189
Aluminum/Alloy Wheels	+117
Compact Disc Changer	+124

Options	Price
Leather Seats	+493
Park Distance Control (Rear) [Opt on Convenience]	+168

2000

The 2000 Montana boasts improvements to its V6 and antilock brakes, an upgraded electrical system, a revised instrument cluster and radios, a quieter climate-control blower motor, the option of heated leather seats, reading lamps and oil-life monitoring as well as new paint schemes.

Mileage Category: P

Body Styles	TMV Pricing		
	Trade	Private	Dealer
4 Dr STD Pass Van	4854	6128	7376
4 Dr STD Pass Van Ext	5381	6793	8177

Body Styles	TMV Pricing		
	Trade	Private	Dealer
4 Dr Vision Pass Van Ext	5659	7144	8599

Options	Price
AM/FM/Cassette/CD Audio System	+139
Air Conditioning - Front and Rear	+170
Leather Seats	+377
OnStar Telematics System [Opt on STD]	+339

Options	Price
Power Sliding Door	+170
Power Windows	+123
Sport Suspension	+353

Pontiac
Montana/Sunfire

1999

The entire line gets a name change this year, from Trans Sport to Montana (the name pulled from '98's sporty trim package). Regular-wheelbase models come with one or two sliding doors, while extended wheelbase vans get two only with a right-side power-sliding door option. Side-impact airbags are standard, as are 15-inch 215-70R white-letter puncture sealant tires. New two-tone paint jobs are available and four new exterior colors are offered, as are options for front-row leather seats and an overhead video system. Better still, a special sport performance package adds cast-aluminum wheels, traction control and a specially tuned sport suspension for soccer dads (and moms) who are sport sedan wanna-bes.

Mileage Category: P

Body Styles	TMV Pricing		
	Trade	Private	Dealer
3 Dr STD Pass Van	3623	4757	5938
4 Dr STD Pass Van	3939	5172	6455

Options	Price
Air Conditioning - Front and Rear	+135
Leather Seats	+297
OnStar Telematics System	+297

Body Styles	TMV Pricing		
	Trade	Private	Dealer
4 Dr STD Pass Van Ext	4177	5484	6845

Options	Price
Power Sliding Door	+135
Sport Suspension [Opt on 4 Dr]	+278

Sunfire

2004

The Sunfire remains largely unchanged for 2004. Dual exhaust outlets are no longer available as a package option, but a CD/MP3 player with RDS and equalizer now comes with the Sun and Sound package.

Mileage Category: B

Body Styles	TMV Pricing		
	Trade	Private	Dealer
2 Dr STD Cpe	6468	7196	8411

Options	Price
AM/FM/CD Audio System [Opt on STD]	+250
Aluminum/Alloy Wheels [Opt on STD]	+400
Antilock Brakes [Opt on STD]	+600
Automatic 4-Speed Transmission [Opt on STD]	+800
Chrome Wheels [Opt on STD]	+400
Cruise Control [Opt on STD]	+250
Front Side Airbag Restraints [Opt on STD]	+400

Body Styles	TMV Pricing		
	Trade	Private	Dealer
2 Dr Special Value Cpe	4961	5571	6587

Options	Price
Keyless Entry System [Opt on STD]	+165
OnStar Telematics System [Opt on STD]	+380
Power Moonroof [Opt on STD]	+485
Sport Suspension [Opt on STD]	+295
Tilt Steering Wheel [Opt on STD]	+150
Traction Control System [Opt on STD]	+200

2003

The Sunfire gets a refresh this year that adds new front and rear fascias, a revised sport suspension and four new wheel styles. The 2.2-liter Ecotec four-cylinder is now the only engine offered, as the GT model has been dropped from the lineup. Base model Sunfires no longer come with standard ABS brakes, but it remains an available option. On the inside, there's a 60/40-split folding rear seat, an upgraded interior seat fabric and new options like side-impact airbags, XM Satellite Radio and the OnStar system.

Mileage Category: B

Body Styles		TMV Pricing		
		Trade	Private	Dealer
2 Dr STD Cpe		5468	6265	7593

Options	Price
16 Inch Wheels	+184
AM/FM/CD Audio System	+142
Aluminum/Alloy Wheels	+184
Antilock Brakes	+385
Automatic 4-Speed Transmission	+459
Cruise Control	+142

Options	Price
Front Side Airbag Restraints	+212
OnStar Telematics System	+241
Power Door Locks	+125
Power Moonroof	+280
Power Windows	+135
Satellite Radio System	+184

2002

All models get a tilt steering wheel and an electric trunk release as standard equipment. Three new exterior colors debut, while the three-speed automatic transmission gets dropped from the lineup.

Mileage Category: B

Body Styles	TMV Pricing		
	Trade	Private	Dealer
2 Dr GT Cpe	5710	6632	8169
2 Dr SE Cpe	4744	5511	6789

Options	Price
2.2L I4 DOHC 16V FI Engine [Opt on SE]	+219
AM/FM/CD Audio System [Opt on SE]	+117
Automatic 4-Speed Transmission	+394

Body Styles	TMV Pricing		
	Trade	Private	Dealer
4 Dr SE Sdn	5084	5906	7276

Options	Price
Power Moonroof [Opt on Cpe]	+270
Power Windows	+124

2001

A standard rear spoiler and a new exterior color are the only new additions to the Sunfire for 2001. The GT convertible is no longer available, leaving the sedan and coupe versions as the only available body styles.

Mileage Category: B

Body Styles	TMV Pricing		
	Trade	Private	Dealer
2 Dr GT Cpe	4467	5644	6731
2 Dr SE Cpe	3680	4650	5546

Options	Price
2.4L I4 DOHC 16V FI Engine [Std on GT]	+189
AM/FM/CD Audio System	+134
Aluminum/Alloy Wheels [Opt on SE]	+124

Body Styles	TMV Pricing		
	Trade	Private	Dealer
4 Dr SE Sdn	3790	4787	5708

Options	Price
Automatic 4-Speed Transmission	+340
Power Moonroof	+250
Power Windows	+121

For the latest vehicle information, visit www.edmunds.com

2000

Redesigned front and rear fascias for a sportier appearance, a new five-speed manual transmission and the availability of the premium Monsoon audio system lead Sunfire's upgrade list for 2000. There are also restyled rocker-panel moldings, new wheels and exterior colors, as well as a revised instrument panel cluster, floor console and upholstery.

Mileage Category: B

Body Styles	TMV Pricing		
	Trade	Private	Dealer
2 Dr GT Conv	4254	5544	6809
2 Dr GT Cpe	3527	4597	5646

Options	Price
2.4L I4 DOHC 16V FI Engine [Std on GT]	+170
AM/FM/CD Audio System	+121
AM/FM/Cassette/CD Audio System	+121

Body Styles	TMV Pricing		
	Trade	Private	Dealer
2 Dr SE Cpe	2830	3688	4529
4 Dr SE Sdn	2860	3728	4579

Options	Price
Automatic 3-Speed Transmission	+201
Automatic 4-Speed Transmission [Std on Conv]	+307
Power Moonroof	+225

1999

After Sunfire coupes got a rear spoiler last year, this year it's the sedan's turn, only as an option. The top-line 2.4-liter twin-cam engine is revised to improve breathing, including new fuel injectors, injection rails, exhaust manifold and catalytic converter. Fern Green Metallic is added to the paint color chart.

Body Styles	TMV Pricing		
	Trade	Private	Dealer
2 Dr GT Conv	3360	4553	5795
2 Dr GT Cpe	2633	3568	4540

Options	Price
2.4L I4 DOHC 16V FI Engine [Std on GT]	+135
Air Conditioning [Std on GT]	+248
Automatic 3-Speed Transmission	+176

Body Styles	TMV Pricing		
	Trade	Private	Dealer
2 Dr SE Cpe	2106	2854	3632
4 Dr SE Sdn	2135	2892	3681

Options	Price
Automatic 4-Speed Transmission [Std on Conv]	+262
Power Moonroof	+178

1998

All coupes have a rear spoiler, a new six-speaker sound system is available, the base four-cylinder gets some additional low-end punch and Topaz Gold Metallic is added to the paint color chart. Second-generation airbags are added as standard equipment.

Mileage Category: B

Body Styles	TMV Pricing		
	Trade	Private	Dealer
2 Dr GT Cpe	2229	3122	4129
2 Dr SE Conv	2676	3748	4956

Options	Price
2.4L I4 DOHC 16V FI Engine [Opt on SE]	+121
Air Conditioning [Std on GT,Conv]	+223
Automatic 3-Speed Transmission	+158

Body Styles	TMV Pricing		
	Trade	Private	Dealer
2 Dr SE Cpe	1678	2350	3108
4 Dr SE Sdn	1744	2443	3230

Options	Price
Automatic 4-Speed Transmission [Opt on GT,SE]	+226
Power Moonroof	+160

1997

SE convertible gets a higher level of standard equipment, including an automatic transmission. Coupes get a new front seatbelt guide loop, and a new Sports Interior trim debuts called Patina/Redondo cloth.

Mileage Category: B

Body Styles	TMV Pricing		
	Trade	Private	Dealer
2 Dr GT Cpe	1663	2388	3272
2 Dr SE Conv	2126	3051	4182

Options	Price
Air Conditioning [Std on Conv]	+205
Automatic 3-Speed Transmission	+136

Body Styles	TMV Pricing		
	Trade	Private	Dealer
2 Dr SE Cpe	1355	1945	2667
4 Dr SE Sdn	1382	1984	2718

Options	Price
Automatic 4-Speed Transmission [Std on Conv]	+205
Power Moonroof	+147

1996

Traction control, remote keyless entry and steering wheel radio controls are newly available. Old Quad 4 engine dumped in favor of new 2.4-liter twin-cam engine. Two new paint choices spiff up the exterior.

Mileage Category: B

Body Styles	TMV Pricing		
	Trade	Private	Dealer
2 Dr GT Cpe	1340	2005	2924
2 Dr SE Conv	1659	2484	3624

Options	Price
Air Conditioning [Std on Conv]	+168
Automatic 3-Speed Transmission [Std on Conv]	+116

Body Styles	TMV Pricing		
	Trade	Private	Dealer
2 Dr SE Cpe	1067	1597	2329
4 Dr SE Sdn	1092	1634	2384

Options	Price
Power Moonroof	+125

1995

All-new replacement for aged Sunbird comes in SE coupe or sedan, and GT coupe trim levels. An SE convertible debuted midyear. Dual airbags, ABS, tilt steering and tachometer are standard. Base engine is a 2.2-liter four-cylinder good for 120 horsepower. GT models get a 150-horsepower Quad 4 engine, which is optional on SE. Order the four-speed automatic transmission and you'll get traction control.

Mileage Category: B

Body Styles	TMV Pricing		
	Trade	Private	Dealer
2 Dr GT Cpe	941	1537	2530
2 Dr SE Conv	1107	1809	2979

Options	Price
2.3L I4 DOHC 16V FI Engine [Opt on SE]	+116
Air Conditioning	+142

Body Styles	TMV Pricing		
	Trade	Private	Dealer
2 Dr SE Cpe	706	1153	1898
4 Dr SE Sdn	725	1185	1953

Options	Price
Automatic 3-Speed Transmission [Std on Conv]	+98
Power Moonroof	+106

Trans Sport

1998

Mileage Category: P

Body Styles	TMV Pricing		
	Trade	Private	Dealer
3 Dr STD Pass Van	2999	4048	5231
4 Dr Montana Pass Van	3402	4592	5934

Options	Price
Air Conditioning - Front and Rear	+121
Captain Chairs (4)	+141
Leather Seats	+354

Body Styles	TMV Pricing		
	Trade	Private	Dealer
4 Dr Montana Pass Van Ext	3575	4826	6236
4 Dr STD Pass Van Ext	3355	4529	5852

Options	Price
Premium Audio System	+148
Sliding Driver Side Door [Opt on 3 Dr]	+117

Short-wheelbase models get the dual sliding doors and power-sliding door options. Side-impact airbags are standard, and a white two-tone paint job is new. Second-generation airbags are standard for front-seat occupants.

1997

Pontiac redesigns the Trans Sport.

Mileage Category: P

Body Styles	TMV Pricing		
	Trade	Private	Dealer
3 Dr SE Pass Van	2631	3757	5134

Options	Price
Captain Chairs (4)	+130
Leather Seats	+260

Body Styles	TMV Pricing		
	Trade	Private	Dealer
3 Dr SE Pass Van Ext	2712	3873	5292

Options	Price
Power Moonroof	+172

1996

Mileage Category: P

Body Styles		TMV Pricing		
		Trade	Private	Dealer
3 Dr SE Pass Van		1871	2816	4121

Options	Price
7 Passenger Seating	+148

Options	Price
Leather Seats	+183

A 180-horsepower, 3.4-liter V6 replaces weak base engine as well as the optional 3.8-liter V6. Front air conditioning is standard equipment for 1996.

1995

A brake/transmission shift interlock is added. New overhead console includes outside temperature gauge, compass and storage bin.

Mileage Category: P

Body Styles		TMV Pricing		
		Trade	Private	Dealer
3 Dr SE Pass Van		1364	2104	3336

Options	Price
3.8L V6 OHV 12V FI Engine	+142
Air Conditioning	+80
Air Conditioning - Front and Rear	+80

Options	Price
Automatic 4-Speed Transmission	+124
Leather Seats	+155

Vibe

2004

All-season tires are now included with the 17-inch aluminum wheels, and XM radio is now available as part of the "Moon and Tunes" package. A dealer-installed supercharger will be available for the base engine starting later in the model year.

Mileage Category: L

Body Styles	TMV Pricing		
	Trade	Private	Dealer
4 Dr GT Wgn	12215	13310	15134
4 Dr STD AWD Wgn	12428	13523	15347

Options	Price
17 Inch Wheels [Opt on GT, STD 2WD]	+440
Aluminum/Alloy Wheels [Opt on STD 2WD, STD AWD]	+440
Antilock Brakes [Opt on STD 2WD]	+500
Automatic 4-Speed Transmission [Opt on STD 2WD]	+850
Compact Disc Changer	+325
Cruise Control	+180
Keyless Entry System	+165

Body Styles	TMV Pricing		
	Trade	Private	Dealer
4 Dr STD Wgn	10410	11505	13329

Options	Price
Navigation System	+1650
Power Door Locks	+225
Power Moonroof	+700
Power Windows	+280
Premium Audio System	+150
Satellite Radio System	+325

2003

Mileage Category: L

The Vibe is an all-new model in Pontiac's lineup designed to combine the best attributes of an SUV, a station wagon and a small van. Thankfully, the result is rather attractive and hip, not to mention utilitarian.

Body Styles	TMV Pricing		
	Trade	Private	Dealer
4 Dr GT Wgn	10503	11550	13294
4 Dr STD AWD Wgn	11220	12338	14202

Options	Price
17 Inch Wheels [Opt on GT,STD 2WD]	+227
AM/FM/CD Changer Audio System	+184
Alarm System	+184
Aluminum/Alloy Wheels [Opt on STD 2WD,STD AWD]	+249
Antilock Brakes [Opt on STD 2WD]	+385
Appearance Package	+184

Body Styles	TMV Pricing		
	Trade	Private	Dealer
4 Dr STD Wgn	9491	10437	12013

Options	Price
Automatic 4-Speed Transmission [Opt on STD 2WD]	+462
Front Side Airbag Restraints	+198
Navigation System	+907
Power Moonroof	+280
Power Windows	+127

911

2004

Cabriolet versions of the C4S and Turbo models join the lineup along with the GT3 and a 40th Anniversary model. A mechanical rear differential lock is a new option for Carrera coupes, while the options list for the Carrera 4S adds a new Aerokit, two new types of 18-inch wheels and the Porsche Ceramic Composite Brake system (PCCB). Turbo models get a new tachometer and additional 18-inch wheel options. Finally, the GT2 model receives a boost in power along with brake and chassis upgrades.

Mileage Category: F

Body Styles	TMV Pricing		
	Trade	Private	Dealer
2 Dr Carrera 4 AWD Conv	66667	70312	76388
2 Dr Carrera 40th Anniv Edition Cpe	71150	74795	80869
2 Dr Carrera 4S AWD Conv	73778	77423	83497
2 Dr Carrera 4S AWD Cpe	66204	69849	75925
2 Dr Carrera Conv	62351	65815	71587
2 Dr Carrera Cpe	53387	56852	62627

Body Styles	TMV Pricing		
	Trade	Private	Dealer
2 Dr Carrera Targa Cpe	59106	62570	68343
2 Dr GT2 Turbo Cpe	160033	167239	179249
2 Dr GT3 Cpe	83449	88496	96907
2 Dr Turbo AWD Conv	105634	110499	118607
2 Dr Turbo AWD Cpe	97975	102119	109025

Options	Price
18 Inch Wheels - Sport Classic [Opt on Carrera, Targa, 4]	+2940
18 Inch Wheels - Sport Techno [Opt on 4S, Turbo]	+2860
18 Inch Wheels - Turbo Look [Opt on Carrera, Targa, 4]	+1435
Aero Kit [Opt on Turbo]	+7980
Alloy and Carbon Gearshift Knob	+735
Aluminum and Leather Gearshift Knob	+885
Aluminum and Wood Gearshift Knob	+735
Automatic 5-Speed Transmission [Opt on non-GT2, GT3, Anniv]	+3420
Automatic Dimming Rearview Mirror [Opt on Carrera, Targa, 4, 4S]	+145
Automatic Dimming Sideview Mirror(s) [Opt on Carrera, Targa, 4, 4S]	+200
Carbon Interior Trim	+1625
Carbon and Leather Steering Wheel [Opt on non-Anniv]	+1535
Cruise Control [Opt on GT2, GT3]	+570
Headlight Washers [Opt on Carrera, Targa, 4, 4S]	+300
Heated Front Seats [Opt on non-Anniv, GT3]	+410

Options	Price
Leather and Wood Steering Wheel [Opt on non-GT2, GT3, Anniv]	+1535
Metallic Paint [Opt on Carrera, Targa, 4, 4S, GT3]	+825
Navigation System [Opt on non-GT2, GT3]	+2680
Painted Wheels [Opt on non-Anniv]	+1550
Park Distance Control (Rear) [Opt on non-GT2, GT3, Anniv]	+530
Power Driver Seat w/Memory [Opt on Carrera Cpe, Targa]	+800
Rain Sensing Windshield Wipers [Opt on Carrera, Targa, 4, 4S]	+225
Rear Window Wiper [Opt on Cpe, non-GT2, GT3, Turbo]	+345
Special Factory Paint [Opt on non-Anniv]	+2245
Special Leather Interior Trim [Opt on non-GT2, GT3, Anniv]	+1410
Sport Seats [Opt on Carrera, Targa, 4]	+400
Sport Suspension [Opt on Carrera, Targa, 4]	+705
Traction Control System [Opt on Carrera, Targa]	+1235
Wood Interior Trim	+1625
Xenon Headlamps [Opt on Carrera, Targa, 4, 4S]	+1090

2003

Porsche finally puts a standard CD player in the 911. Five horsepower are mysteriously lost in non-Turbo 911s, meaning output is "only" 315 horses now.

Mileage Category: F

Body Styles	TMV Pricing		
	Trade	Private	Dealer
2 Dr Carrera 4 AWD Conv	61724	64360	68754
2 Dr Carrera 4S AWD Cpe	58572	61074	65244
2 Dr Carrera Conv	56655	59075	63109
2 Dr Carrera Cpe	49330	51438	54950

Body Styles	TMV Pricing		
	Trade	Private	Dealer
2 Dr Carrera Targa Cpe	54768	57108	61007
2 Dr GT2 Turbo Cpe	148664	154557	164379
2 Dr Turbo AWD Cpe	90474	94060	100037

Options	Price
18 Inch Wheels [Opt on Carrera, Carrera 4, Carrera Targa]	+1176
18 Inch Wheels - Sport Classic [Opt on Carrera, Carrera 4, Carrera Targa]	+2410
18 Inch Wheels - Sport Design [Opt on Carrera, Carrera 4, Carrera Targa]	+2410
18 Inch Wheels - Sport Techno [Opt on Carrera 4S, Turbo]	+1484
18 Inch Wheels - Turbo Look [Opt on Carrera, Carrera 4, Carrera Targa]	+1176
Aero Kit [Opt on Carrera, Turbo]	+6541
Aluminum and Carbon Gearshift Knob	+721
Aluminum and Leather Gearshift Knob	+725
Aluminum and Wood Gearshift Knob	+721
Aluminum/Alloy Interior Trim	+885
Automatic 5-Speed Transmission	+2803
Automatic Dimming Rearview Mirror	+201
Automatic Dimming Sideview Mirror(s)	+246
Bose Audio System	+652

Options	Price
Carbon Door Sill Insignia	+639
Carbon Interior Trim	+1332
Carbon and Leather Steering Wheel	+1258
Color To Sample Paint	+2861
Compact Disc Changer	+586
Cruise Control [Opt on GT2 Turbo]	+467
Heated Front Seats	+336
Hi-Fi Audio System	+680
Leather and Wood Steering Wheel	+988
Luggage Rack	+328
Metallic Paint	+676
Metallic Paint To Sample	+2861
Navigation System	+2156
Painted Wheels	+1270
Park Distance Control (Rear)	+434
Performance/Handling Package	+11467
Power Driver Seat w/Memory	+410
Rain Sensing Windshield Wipers	+184

Options	Price
Rear Wind Deflector	+205
Rear Window Wiper	+283
Special Factory Paint	+676
Special Interior Trim	+1434
Special Leather Interior Trim	+984
Special Leather Seat Trim	+324

Options	Price
Sport Chassis [Opt on Carrera,Carrera 4,Carrera Targa]	+578
Sport Seats [Opt on Carrera, Carrera 4,Carrera Targa]	+328
Traction Control System [Opt on Carrera,Carrera Targa]	+1012
Xenon Headlamps	+893

2002

For those zealots who feel that a 911 Turbo isn't quite enough, Porsche rolls out the new-for-'02 GT2. Standard 911s receive new front-end styling and a bump in engine size (from 3.4 liters to 3.6) and power (from 300 horsepower to 320). Other 911 updates include a real glovebox, the option of a Bose stereo, a single cupholder and a gaggle of new wheels. Open-air versions were not overlooked when they were making improvements; the Cabriolet finally gets a glass rear window and the Targa model returns after a four-year hiatus.

Mileage Category: F

Body Styles	TMV Pricing		
	Trade	Private	Dealer
2 Dr Carrera 4 AWD Conv	54441	56886	60961
2 Dr Carrera 4S AWD Cpe	52436	54791	58715
2 Dr Carrera Conv	51749	54074	57948
2 Dr Carrera Cpe	44346	46338	49658

Body Styles	TMV Pricing		
	Trade	Private	Dealer
2 Dr Carrera Targa Cpe	49751	51986	55710
2 Dr GT2 Turbo Cpe	138283	143934	153352
2 Dr Turbo AWD Cpe	85330	88798	94578

Options	Price
18 Inch Wheels	+1007
18 Inch Wheels - Sport Classic	+2121
18 Inch Wheels - Sport Design	+2121
18 Inch Wheels - Turbo Look	+1740
AM/FM/CD Audio System	+266
Advanced Design Package	+3333
Advanced Technic Package	+2463
Aero Kit	+5693
Arctic Silver Interior Package	+654
Automatic 5-Speed Transmission	+2607
Automatic Dimming Rearview Mirror [Std on GT2]	+266
Automatic Dimming Sideview Mirror(s) [Std on GT2]	+209
Automatic Stability Control [Opt on 2WD]	+608
Carbon Door Sill Insignia	+589
Carbon Interior Trim	+1212
Carbon and Leather Steering Wheel	+1155
Color To Sample Paint	+2630
Compact Disc Changer	+543
Cruise Control [Opt on GT2]	+319

Options	Price
Dark Wood Package	+1596
Design Package	+1505
Heated Front Seats	+315
Light Wood Package	+1596
Luggage Rack	+300
Metallic Paint	+1695
Navigation System	+2691
Painted Instrument Dials	+642
Painted Wheels	+133
Park Distance Control (Rear)	+399
Power Driver Seat w/Memory [Std on Turbo]	+228
Rain Sensing Windshield Wipers	+266
Rear Wind Deflector	+228
Special Factory Paint	+627
Special Interior Trim	+1319
Special Leather Seat Trim	+3724
Sport Chassis	+524
Traction Control System [Opt on 2WD]	+327
Xenon Headlamps	+608

2001

After a one-year hiatus, the 911 Turbo model makes its much anticipated return and brings with it 415 tire-shredding horsepower. All 911s get electric engine cover and trunk releases, improved interior lighting and improved trunk carpet. A new optional audio system includes a bass box, there are optional "Turbo Look 1" wheels, a self dimming day/night rearview mirror and a new three-spoke steering wheel with colored Porsche crests.

Mileage Category: F

Body Styles	TMV Pricing		
	Trade	Private	Dealer
2 Dr Carrera 4 AWD Conv	48391	52359	56022
2 Dr Carrera 4 AWD Cpe	43610	47669	51415
2 Dr Carrera Conv	46517	50332	53854

Body Styles	TMV Pricing		
	Trade	Private	Dealer
2 Dr Carrera Cpe	39483	42721	45710
2 Dr Turbo AWD Cpe	73518	79014	84088

Options	Price
18 Inch Wheels - Sport Classic [Opt on Cpe]	+1856
18 Inch Wheels - Sport Design	+1856
18 Inch Wheels - Turbo Look [Opt on Non-Turbo]	+830
AM/FM/CD Audio System	+209
Aero Kit	+5714
Arctic Silver Interior Package	+2149
Automatic 5-Speed Transmission	+2386
Automatic Dimming Rearview Mirror	+481
Automatic Dimming Sideview Mirror(s)	+192
Automatic Stability Control [Opt on Carrera]	+558
Carbon Interior Trim	+1451
Carbon and Leather Steering Wheel	+823
Color To Sample Paint	+2390
Compact Disc Changer	+492
Dark Wood Package	+5435
Design Package	+2362

Options	Price
Digital Audio System [Opt on Turbo]	+401
Heated Front Seats	+265
Hi-Fi Audio System [Opt on Carrera]	+419
Leather Seats [Std on Turbo]	+2243
Luggage Rack	+272
Maple Burr Package	+4256
Metallic Paint	+1538
Metallic Paint To Sample	+2390
Navigation System	+2470
Park Distance Control (Rear)	+363
Power Driver Seat w/Memory [Opt on Carrera]	+530
Power Passenger Seat [Opt on Carrera]	+530
Rain Sensing Windshield Wipers	+244
Rear Window Wiper	+234
Special Factory Paint	+1538
Sport Chassis [Opt on Carrera Cpe]	+481

2001 (cont'd)

Options	Price
Sport Suspension	+481

Options	Price
Traction Control System [Opt on Carrera]	+290

2000

A new exhaust system bumps horsepower from 296 to 300. Already featured on Carrera 4 models, two-wheel-drive Carreras now get an electronic drive-by-wire throttle and optional PSM stability control. All models receive an upgraded interior console and materials. The formerly optional charcoal odor filter is now standard. There are two new standard and one new optional exterior colors.

Mileage Category: F

Body Styles	TMV Pricing		
	Trade	Private	Dealer
2 Dr Carrera 4 AWD Conv	42427	46559	50610
2 Dr Carrera 4 AWD Cpe	39831	43711	47515

Options	Price
18 Inch Wheels - Sport Classic [Opt on Cpe]	+1706
18 Inch Wheels - Sport Design [Opt on Carrera Cpe]	+1538
18 Inch Wheels - Turbo Look	+763
AM/FM/CD Audio System	+192
Aero Kit [Opt on Carrera Cpe]	+4080
Automatic 5-Speed Transmission	+1980
Automatic Dimming Rearview Mirror	+346
Automatic Dimming Sideview Mirror(s)	+170
Compact Disc Changer	+430
Digital Audio System [Opt on Carrera]	+716
Heated Front Seats	+244
Leather Interior Trim [Opt on Carrera Cpe]	+1213
Limited Slip Differential [Opt on Carrera]	+740

Body Styles	TMV Pricing		
	Trade	Private	Dealer
2 Dr Carrera Conv	42078	46177	50194
2 Dr Carrera Cpe	35580	39046	42443

Options	Price
Metallic Paint	+490
Navigation System	+2049
Power Driver Seat w/Memory	+463
Power Passenger Seat	+463
Rain Sensing Windshield Wipers	+225
Rear Window Wiper	+205
Special Factory Paint	+945
Special Interior Trim [Opt on Carrera Conv]	+237
Special Leather Seat Trim [Opt on Carrera Conv]	+908
Sport Seats	+454
Traction Control System [Opt on Carrera]	+530
Trip Computer	+167

1999

Everything just got better with the totally redesigned 911, internally named the 996. The 911 Coupe, Cabriolet and Carrera 4 (available as either a coupe or cabrio) are all available for the 1999 model year.

Mileage Category: F

Body Styles	TMV Pricing		
	Trade	Private	Dealer
2 Dr Carrera 4 AWD Conv	38025	42384	46920
2 Dr Carrera 4 AWD Cpe	33198	37004	40966

Options	Price
18 Inch Wheels - Sport Classic [Opt on Cpe]	+1572
18 Inch Wheels - Sport Design [Opt on Cpe]	+1343
18 Inch Wheels - Turbo Look	+704
AM/FM/CD Audio System	+160
Aero Kit [Opt on Cpe]	+3388
Automatic 5-Speed Transmission	+1644
Automatic Dimming Rearview Mirror	+287
Compact Disc Changer	+357
Digital Audio System	+340
Hardtop Roof	+6156
Heated Front Seats	+202
Hi-Fi Audio System	+355

Body Styles	TMV Pricing		
	Trade	Private	Dealer
2 Dr Carrera Conv	36311	40473	44805
2 Dr Carrera Cpe	30965	34515	38210

Options	Price
Leather Interior Trim [Opt on Carrera Cpe]	+1007
Limited Slip Differential [Opt on Carrera]	+616
Metallic Paint	+407
Navigation System	+2095
Power Driver Seat w/Memory	+450
Power Passenger Seat	+450
Rain Sensing Windshield Wipers	+207
Rear Window Wiper	+170
Special Factory Paint	+785
Special Leather Seat Trim	+882
Traction Control System [Opt on Carrera]	+440
Trip Computer	+139

1998

The current-generation 911 goes the way of the dodo at year's end, replaced by the next evolutionary step toward the perfect driving machine.

Mileage Category: F

Body Styles	TMV Pricing		
	Trade	Private	Dealer
2 Dr Carrera 4 AWD Conv	35094	39346	44141
2 Dr Carrera 4S AWD Cpe	33030	37032	41544
2 Dr Carrera Conv	32397	36322	40749

Options	Price
17 Inch Wheels - Targa	+523
18 Inch Wheels - Sport Classic	+1492
AM/FM/CD Audio System	+177
Aero Kit [Opt on S Cpe]	+3218
Automatic 4-Speed Transmission	+1834
Automatic Dimming Rearview Mirror	+252
Compact Disc Changer	+457
Hardtop Roof [Opt on Cabriolet]	+5844
Heated Front Seats	+325

Body Styles	TMV Pricing		
	Trade	Private	Dealer
2 Dr Carrera S Cpe	28736	32217	36143
2 Dr Carrera Targa Cpe	30144	33796	37914

Options	Price
Hi-Fi Audio System [Opt on S Cpe]	+337
Leather Interior Trim [Opt on S Cpe]	+1382
Leather Seats	+742
Limited Slip Differential [Std on Carrera 4S, AWD]	+602
Metallic Paint	+1894
Power Driver Seat w/Memory	+427
Power Passenger Seat	+247
Rain Sensing Windshield Wipers	+197
Rear Window Wiper	+201

Options	Price
Special Factory Paint	+746
Special Leather Seat Trim [Opt on S Cpe]	+1364
Sport Chassis [Opt on S Cpe]	+378

Options	Price
Traction Control System [Opt on 2WD]	+602
Trip Computer	+247

Mileage Category: F

1997

The only change to this year's Porsche 911 is the availability of a Porsche-engineered child seat that will deactivate the passenger airbag when it is in place.

Body Styles	TMV Pricing		
	Trade	Private	Dealer
2 Dr Carrera 4 AWD Conv	32977	36158	40046
2 Dr Carrera 4S AWD Cpe	30596	33548	37156
2 Dr Carrera Conv	30461	33400	36991
2 Dr Carrera Cpe	26732	29311	32463

Body Styles	TMV Pricing		
	Trade	Private	Dealer
2 Dr Carrera Targa Cpe	28326	31719	35865
2 Dr Turbo AWD Cpe	53827	58572	64372
2 Dr Turbo S AWD Cpe	81269	88433	97189

Options	Price
17 Inch Wheels - Cup Design [Opt on Carrera Cpe]	+667
17 Inch Wheels - Targa [Opt on Carrera Cpe]	+502
AM/FM/CD Audio System	+146
Aero Kit [Opt on Cpe - Carrera, Carrera 4S]	+2513
Automatic 4-Speed Transmission	+1432
Automatic Dimming Rearview Mirror [Std on Turbo S]	+242
Compact Disc Changer	+439
Digital Audio System [Opt on Turbo]	+619
Hardtop Roof	+5619
Heated Front Seats [Std on Turbo S]	+267
Hi-Fi Audio System [Opt on Cpe - Carrera, Carrera 4S]	+502

Options	Price
Limited Slip Differential [Opt on Targa, RWD]	+579
Metallic Paint [Std on Turbo, Turbo S]	+1821
Pearlescent Metallic Paint [Opt on Cpe - Carrera, Carrera 4S]	+4805
Power Driver Seat	+271
Power Passenger Seat	+271
Rain Sensing Windshield Wipers	+189
Rear Window Wiper [Std on Turbo, Turbo S]	+165
Special Factory Paint	+717
Special Leather Interior Trim	+834
Trip Computer [Std on Turbo, Turbo S]	+203

1996

Trick Targa model joins the lineup, and power is up in midrange revs. New Carrera 4S model provides Turbo looks without Turbo price or performance. Bigger wheels are standard across the line, as well as Litronic headlights. New stereos and exterior colors compliment one new interior color this year. Remote keyless entry system gets an immobilizer feature.

Body Styles	TMV Pricing		
	Trade	Private	Dealer
2 Dr Carrera 4 AWD Conv	29955	32890	36944
2 Dr Carrera 4 AWD Cpe	26801	29878	34128
2 Dr Carrera 4S AWD Cpe	26980	30078	34356
2 Dr Carrera Conv	27297	30432	34761

Body Styles	TMV Pricing		
	Trade	Private	Dealer
2 Dr Carrera Cpe	23961	26712	30512
2 Dr Carrera Targa Cpe	26989	30088	34368
2 Dr Turbo AWD Cpe	47578	52562	59444

Options	Price
17 Inch Wheels - Spoke [Opt on Carrera, Targa]	+721
18 Inch Wheels - Technology Design	+891
AM/FM/CD Audio System	+142
AM/FM/Cassette/CD Audio System	+247
Automatic 4-Speed Transmission	+1772
Compact Disc Changer	+366
Digital Audio System [Opt on Turbo]	+933
Heated Front Seats	+260
Hi-Fi Audio System [Opt on Carrera 4S]	+418
Leather Seats [Std on Turbo]	+694

Options	Price
Limited Slip Differential [Opt on 2WD]	+563
Metallic Paint	+465
Pearlescent Metallic Paint	+4676
Power Driver Seat	+251
Power Passenger Seat	+251
Rear Window Wiper [Std on STD]	+160
Spoke Wheels	+649
Steering Wheel Package	+544
Trip Computer	+197

Mileage Category: F

1995

This year the optional Tiptronic automanual transmission allows driver to change gears either with the console-mounted gear selector as before or via buttons mounted on the steering wheel.

Body Styles	TMV Pricing		
	Trade	Private	Dealer
2 Dr Carrera 4 AWD Conv	26700	30050	35633
2 Dr Carrera 4 AWD Cpe	23713	26689	31648

Body Styles	TMV Pricing		
	Trade	Private	Dealer
2 Dr Carrera Conv	24511	27586	32712
2 Dr Carrera Cpe	21612	24324	28843

Options	Price
AM/FM/CD Audio System	+128
Automatic 4-Speed Transmission	+1350
Chrome Wheels [Opt on Carrera Conv]	+463
Compact Disc Changer	+272
Digital Audio System	+889
Heated Front Seats	+154
Hi-Fi Audio System [Opt on Conv]	+399

Options	Price
Leather Seats	+632
Limited Slip Differential [Opt on 2WD]	+469
Metallic Paint	+310
Pearlescent Metallic Paint	+3666
Power Driver Seat	+185
Power Passenger Seat	+185
Rear Window Wiper	+129

Porsche
911/928/968/Boxster

1995 (cont'd)

Options	Price		Options	Price
Steering Wheel Package	+468		Trip Computer	+106

928

1995

Mileage Category: F

Body Styles	TMV Pricing		
	Trade	Private	Dealer
2 Dr GTS Hbk	23871	26844	31799

Options	Price		Options	Price
Heated Front Seats	+248		Leather Seats	+846

This year the optional Tiptronic automanual transmission allows the driver to change gears either with the console-mounted gear selector as before or via buttons mounted on the steering wheel.

968

1995

After this year, and like its 928 sibling, the 968 dies a quiet death.

Mileage Category: F

Body Styles	TMV Pricing			Body Styles	TMV Pricing		
	Trade	Private	Dealer		Trade	Private	Dealer
2 Dr STD Conv	13228	14888	17655	2 Dr STD Cpe	10777	12129	14382

Options	Price		Options	Price
17 Inch Wheels - Spoke [Opt on Conv]	+444		Leather Seats	+597
AM/FM/CD Audio System	+128		Limited Slip Differential	+193
Automatic 4-Speed Transmission	+1061		Metallic Paint	+289
Compact Disc Changer	+534		Power Driver Seat	+174
Heated Front Seats	+193		Power Passenger Seat	+174
Hi-Fi Audio System	+240		Special Factory Paint	+251

Boxster

2004

For 2004, the Boxster S adds a sports exhaust system to the options list. The Boxster and Boxster S are also available in two new colors -- Atlas Gray and Carmon Red.

Mileage Category: F

Body Styles	TMV Pricing			Body Styles	TMV Pricing		
	Trade	Private	Dealer		Trade	Private	Dealer
2 Dr S Anniv Edition Conv	42163	44399	48126	2 Dr STD Conv	30101	32294	35949
2 Dr S Conv	36357	38865	43044				

Options	Price		Options	Price
17 Inch Wheels - Sport Classic [Opt on STD, S]	+1305		Heated Front Seats [Opt on STD, S]	+410
18 Inch Wheels - Sport Design [Opt on STD, S]	+2940		Leather Interior Trim [Opt on STD, S]	+2980
18 Inch Wheels - Turbo Look [Opt on STD, S]	+1435		Leather and Wood Steering Wheel [Opt on STD, S]	+1535
Aero Kit [Opt on STD, S]	+6350		Metallic Paint [Opt on STD, S]	+825
Aluminum Gearshift Knob [Opt on STD, S]	+735		Navigation System	+2680
Aluminum and Carbon Gearshift Knob [Opt on STD, S]	+735		Painted Wheels [Opt on STD, S]	+1550
Aluminum and Leather Gearshift Knob [Opt on STD, S]	+800		Park Distance Control (Rear) [Opt on STD, S]	+530
Aluminum and Wood Gearshift Knob [Opt on STD, S]	+735		Power Driver Seat w/Memory [Opt on STD, S]	+800
Aluminum/Alloy Interior Trim [Opt on STD, S]	+820		Rain Sensing Windshield Wipers [Opt on STD, S]	+275
Automatic Dimming Rearview Mirror [Opt on STD, S]	+215		Rear Wind Deflector [Opt on STD, S]	+235
Automatic Dimming Sideview Mirror(s) [Opt on STD, S]	+215		Roll/Light Bar [Opt on STD, S]	+535
Automatic Stability Control [Std on Anniv]	+925		Special Factory Paint [Opt on STD, S]	+3070
Carbon Interior Trim [Opt on STD, S]	+1625		Special Interior Trim [Opt on STD, S]	+3760
Carbon and Leather Steering Wheel [Opt on STD, S]	+1535		Sport Design Package [Opt on STD, S]	+1395
Compact Disc Changer	+715		Sport Suspension [Opt on STD, S]	+705
Cruise Control	+570		Traction Control System [Std on Anniv]	+1235
Hardtop Roof [Opt on STD, S]	+2345		Trip Computer [Std on Anniv]	+280
Headlight Washers [Opt on STD]	+300		Xenon Headlamps [Std on Anniv]	+1090

2003

Minor visual updates, including revised front and rear fascias and gray (versus the previous yellow) tint for the turn signal lenses, along with a boost in output keep the Boxster relevant in the face of faster, more refined rivals.

Mileage Category: F

Body Styles	TMV Pricing		
	Trade	Private	Dealer
2 Dr S Conv	34052	36533	40669

Options	Price
17 Inch Wheels [Opt on STD]	+1012
17 Inch Wheels - Sport Classic [Opt on S]	+1070
18 Inch Wheels	+1176
18 Inch Wheels - Sport Classic	+2410
18 Inch Wheels - Sport Design	+2410
18 Inch Wheels - Turbo Look	+1176
Aero Kit	+5205
Alarm System [Opt on STD]	+369
Aluminum Gearshift Knob	+602
Aluminum and Carbon Gearshift Knob	+602
Aluminum and Leather Gearshift Knob	+656
Aluminum and Wood Gearshift Knob	+602
Aluminum/Alloy Interior Trim	+672
Automatic 5-Speed Transmission	+2631
Automatic Dimming Rearview Mirror	+184
Automatic Dimming Sideview Mirror(s)	+225
Bose Audio System	+1332
Carbon Door Sill Insignia	+639
Carbon Interior Trim	+1332
Carbon and Leather Steering Wheel	+1258
Color To Sample Paint	+3537
Compact Disc Changer	+586
Cruise Control	+467

Body Styles	TMV Pricing		
	Trade	Private	Dealer
2 Dr STD Conv	27753	29775	33146

Options	Price
Hardtop Roof	+1922
Heated Front Seats	+336
Hi-Fi Audio System	+680
Leather and Wood Steering Wheel	+1258
Luggage Rack	+385
Maple Burr Package	+3643
Metallic Paint	+676
Metallic Paint To Sample	+3537
Navigation System	+2156
Painted Wheels	+1270
Park Distance Control (Rear)	+434
Power Driver Seat w/Memory	+279
Rain Sensing Windshield Wipers	+287
Rear Wind Deflector	+307
Roll/Light Bar	+439
Special Factory Paint	+676
Special Leather Interior Trim	+1648
Special Leather Seat Trim	+299
Sport Chassis	+578
Sport Design Package	+1143
Traction Control System	+1012
Trip Computer	+230
Xenon Headlamps	+893

2002

The Boxster stands pat for '02.

Mileage Category: F

Body Styles	TMV Pricing		
	Trade	Private	Dealer
2 Dr S Conv	30388	32842	36932

Options	Price
17 Inch Wheels - Boxster Design	+935
17 Inch Wheels - Sport Classic	+980
18 Inch Wheels - Sport Classic	+2044
18 Inch Wheels - Sport Design	+2044
18 Inch Wheels - Turbo Look	+912
AM/FM/CD Audio System	+266
Aero Kit	+4781
Aluminum/Alloy Interior Trim [Opt on STD]	+1056
Arctic Silver Interior Package	+551
Automatic 5-Speed Transmission	+2440
Automatic Dimming Rearview Mirror	+171
Automatic Dimming Sideview Mirror(s)	+209
Automatic Stability Control	+935
Bose Audio System	+836
Carbon Door Sill Insignia	+589
Carbon Interior Trim	+555
Carbon and Leather Steering Wheel	+1155
Color To Sample Paint	+3249
Compact Disc Changer	+543
Cruise Control	+437
Design Package	+1262

Body Styles	TMV Pricing		
	Trade	Private	Dealer
2 Dr STD Conv	24450	26424	29714

Options	Price
Hardtop Roof	+1744
Heated Front Seats	+315
Luggage Rack	+353
Maple Burr Package	+3340
Metallic Paint	+627
Metallic Paint To Sample	+3249
Navigation System	+2691
Painted Instrument Dials	+509
Park Distance Control (Rear)	+372
Power Driver Seat w/Memory	+228
Power Passenger Seat	+570
Rain Sensing Windshield Wipers	+266
Special Factory Paint	+627
Special Leather Interior Trim	+1512
Special Leather Seat Trim	+1820
Sport Chassis	+524
Sport Design Package	+1049
Traction Control System	+935
Trip Computer	+342
Xenon Headlamps	+648

Porsche

Boxster

2001

Minor interior changes are in store for 2001. The Boxster S' thicker roof lining has migrated to the regular Boxster. Both cars now feature a hidden cell phone antenna, a gauge cluster design similar to the 911's, improved interior lighting and better dashboard material quality. Porsche has also added a new button to the ignition key to control the driver seat and outside memory function. In terms of optional equipment, the sophisticated Porsche Stability Management system is now available for the Boxster and Boxster S.

Mileage Category: F

Body Styles	TMV Pricing		
	Trade	Private	Dealer
2 Dr S Conv	26946	30221	33245

Options	Price
18 Inch Wheels - Sport Classic	+1856
18 Inch Wheels - Sport Design	+1856
18 Inch Wheels - Turbo Look [Opt on S]	+1908
AM/FM/CD Audio System	+209
Aero Kit	+4343
Arctic Silver Interior Package	+2149
Automatic 5-Speed Transmission	+2240
Automatic Dimming Rearview Mirror	+481
Automatic Dimming Sideview Mirror(s)	+192
Automatic Stability Control	+848
Carbon Door Sill Insignia	+534
Carbon Interior Trim	+3035
Center Console	+499
Compact Disc Changer	+551
Cruise Control	+372
Dark Maple Interior Package	+3035
Design Package	+1799
Digital Audio System	+820

Body Styles	TMV Pricing		
	Trade	Private	Dealer
2 Dr STD Conv	22009	24686	27157

Options	Price
Hardtop Roof	+1601
Heated Front Seats	+265
Leather Seat Package	+1654
Litronic Headlamps	+747
Luggage Rack	+321
Metallic Paint	+2100
Navigation System	+2470
Painted Instrument Dials	+460
Painted Wheels	+119
Park Distance Control (Rear)	+363
Power Driver Seat w/Memory	+530
Power Passenger Seat	+530
Rain Sensing Windshield Wipers	+244
Special Factory Paint	+562
Sport Design Package	+1130
Sport Suspension	+481
Traction Control System	+848
Trip Computer	+298

2000

The big news for 2000 is the Boxster S. This more powerful version of the Boxster features a bigger engine that generates 250 horsepower. The regular Boxster (if you can call it that) also gets a horsepower boost in 2000, going from 201 to 217. Both models feature upgraded interior materials and new exterior colors.

Mileage Category: F

Body Styles	TMV Pricing		
	Trade	Private	Dealer
2 Dr S Conv	24389	27538	30624

Options	Price
17 Inch Wheels - Boxster Design	+740
17 Inch Wheels - Sport Classic [Opt on STD]	+1601
18 Inch Wheels - Sport Classic	+1706
18 Inch Wheels - Sport Design	+1706
18 Inch Wheels - Turbo Look [Opt on S]	+1754
AM/FM/CD Audio System	+192
AM/FM/Cassette/CD Audio System	+367
Aero Kit [Opt on S]	+3604
Automatic 5-Speed Transmission	+1860
Automatic Dimming Rearview Mirror	+344
Automatic Dimming Sideview Mirror(s)	+170
Compact Disc Changer	+507
Cruise Control	+342
Digital Audio System [Opt on STD]	+716
Hardtop Roof	+1398

Body Styles	TMV Pricing		
	Trade	Private	Dealer
2 Dr STD Conv	19197	21676	24105

Options	Price
Heated Front Seats	+244
Luggage Rack	+152
Metallic Paint	+490
Navigation System	+2049
Rain Sensing Windshield Wipers	+225
Rear Wind Deflector	+224
Roll/Light Bar	+314
Special Factory Paint	+490
Special Leather Interior Trim	+1213
Special Leather Seat Trim	+287
Sport Package	+1286
Technic Sport Package	+1182
Tonneau Cover	+769
Traction Control System	+530
Trip Computer	+274

1999

The Boxster is slowly adding features and options. This year, a Classic Package includes metallic paint and all-leather seats, and adds special highlights to the interior. The gas tank is increased from a 12.5- to a 14.1-gallon capacity, and gas-discharge Litronic headlights are optional. All the features in the Sport Package are individually optional this year, and 18-inch wheels are now available.

Mileage Category: F

Body Styles		TMV Pricing		
		Trade	Private	Dealer
2 Dr STD Conv		17694	20092	22588

Options	Price
17 Inch Wheels - Boxster Design	+748
18 Inch Wheels - Sport Classic	+2417
18 Inch Wheels - Sport Design	+748
AM/FM/CD Audio System	+160
AM/FM/Cassette/CD Audio System	+304
Automatic 5-Speed Transmission	+1545
Automatic Dimming Rearview Mirror	+286
Compact Disc Changer	+421

Options	Price
Cruise Control	+284
Digital Audio System	+340
Hardtop Roof	+1162
Heated Front Seats	+202
Hi-Fi Audio System	+355
Metallic Paint	+407
Power Driver Seat w/Memory	+450
Rear Wind Deflector	+186

Options	Price
Roll/Light Bar	+260
Special Factory Paint	+407
Special Leather Interior Trim	+1007
Special Leather Seat Trim	+1199

Options	Price
Sport Package	+1584
Technic Sport Package	+982
Traction Control System	+440
Trip Computer	+227

1998

Side airbags are standard for 1998.

Mileage Category: F

Body Styles	TMV Pricing		
	Trade	Private	Dealer
2 Dr STD Conv	16365	18577	21071

Options	Price
17 Inch Wheels - Boxster Design	+710
17 Inch Wheels - Sport Classic	+1366
AM/FM/CD Audio System	+152
AM/FM/Cassette/CD Audio System	+289
Alarm System	+294
Automatic 5-Speed Transmission	+1465
Automatic Dimming Rearview Mirror	+271
Compact Disc Changer	+399
Cruise Control	+270
Hardtop Roof	+815

Options	Price
Heated Front Seats	+192
Metallic Paint	+387
Rear Wind Deflector	+176
Roll/Light Bar	+247
Special Leather Interior Trim	+937
Special Leather Seat Trim	+1116
Sport Package	+1504
Technic Sport Package	+932
Traction Control System	+418
Trip Computer	+215

1997

This all-new roadster is introduced to compete in the revitalized midpriced sports car category. The Boxster features a 2.5-liter six-cylinder engine, a five-speed manual or five-speed Tiptronic transmission and a power top that closes in an impressive 12 seconds.

Mileage Category: F

Body Styles	TMV Pricing		
	Trade	Private	Dealer
2 Dr STD Conv	15356	17381	19856

Options	Price
17 Inch Wheels - Boxster Design	+683
17 Inch Wheels - Sport Classic	+1314
AM/FM/CD Audio System	+146
AM/FM/Cassette/CD Audio System	+278
Aero Kit	+693
Alarm System	+283
Automatic 5-Speed Transmission	+1408
Automatic Dimming Rearview Mirror	+261
Compact Disc Changer	+384
Cruise Control	+259
Hardtop Roof	+783

Options	Price
Heated Front Seats	+391
Leather Seats	+887
Metallic Paint	+371
Roll/Light Bar	+131
Special Factory Paint	+371
Special Leather Seat Trim	+1060
Sport Package	+1393
Tonneau Cover	+392
Traction Control System	+381
Trip Computer	+207

Cayenne
2004

Mileage Category: O

Body Styles	TMV Pricing		
	Trade	Private	Dealer
4 Dr S Tiptronic AWD SUV	46339	48575	52301
4 Dr Tiptronic AWD SUV	34202	36063	39164

Body Styles	TMV Pricing		
	Trade	Private	Dealer
4 Dr Turbo Tiptronic AWD SUV	68356	71342	76318

A V6-powered Cayenne joins the lineup as the new entry-level model.

Options	Price
18 Inch Wheels - Turbo Look [Opt on S]	+150
19 Inch Wheels	+850
20 Inch Wheels	+1960
Automatic Climate Control [Opt on non-S, Turbo]	+550
Automatic Climate Control (4 Zone)	+1690
Automatic Dimming Rearview Mirror	+200
Automatic Dimming Sideview Mirror(s)	+240
Automatic Load Leveling [Std on Turbo]	+1200
Automatic On/Off Headlights	+300
Carbon and Leather Steering Wheel	+1200
Comfort Seats [Opt on non-Turbo]	+1290

Options	Price
Compact Disc Changer	+715
Electronic Suspension Control [Opt on S]	+2000
Garage Door Opener	+150
Headlight Washers [Std on Turbo]	+800
Heated Front Seats [Std on Turbo]	+350
Heated Front and Rear Seats [Opt on non-Turbo]	+660
Heated Steering Wheel [Opt on non-Turbo]	+130
Keyless Ignition System	+995
Locking Differential (Rear)	+1830
Luggage Rack	+450
Metallic Paint [Opt on non-Turbo]	+495

2004 (cont'd)

Options	Price
Navigation System [Opt on non-Turbo]	+1700
Painted Wheels	+2400
Park Distance Control (Front and Rear) [Std on Turbo]	+990
Power Moonroof	+900
Power Rear Liftgate [Opt on S, Turbo]	+500
Running Boards	+2450

Options	Price
Skid Plates	+400
Special Leather Seat Trim [Opt on non-Turbo]	+3200
Trailer Hitch	+590
Wood Gearshift Knob	+345
Wood Steering Wheel	+290
Xenon Headlamps [Std on Turbo]	+700

2003

We would've never imagined it, but Porsche jumps onto the SUV gravy train. The Cayenne, with a choice of two potent V8s and an available active suspension, promises performance that's more like a 911 than an SUV.

Mileage Category: O

Body Styles	TMV Pricing		
	Trade	Private	Dealer
4 Dr S 4WD SUV	39965	41995	45378

Body Styles	TMV Pricing		
	Trade	Private	Dealer
4 Dr Turbo 4WD SUV	62662	65844	71148

Options	Price
19 Inch Wheels	+697
20 Inch Wheels	+1607
Aluminum/Alloy Interior Trim [Opt on S]	+811
Automatic Climate Control (4 Zone)	+1385
Automatic Dimming Rearview Mirror	+287
Automatic Dimming Sideview Mirror(s)	+225
Automatic Load Leveling [Opt on S]	+2623
Comfort Seats [Opt on S]	+1057
Compact Disc Changer	+586
Heated Front Seats [Opt on S]	+393
Heated Front and Rear Seats [Opt on S]	+787
Keyless Ignition System	+816

Options	Price
Metallic Paint [Opt on S]	+406
Navigation System [Opt on S]	+2238
Off-Road Suspension Package	+2336
Park Distance Control (Front and Rear) [Opt on S]	+811
Power Driver Seat w/Memory	+295
Power Moonroof	+902
Power Rear Liftgate	+287
Special Leather Seat Trim	+324
Sport Seats [Opt on S]	+1057
Tire Pressure Monitoring System	+484
Trailer Hitch	+484
Xenon Headlamps [Opt on S]	+738

Mileage Category: H

Body Styles	TMV Pricing		
	Trade	Private	Dealer
2 Dr Aero Turbo Conv	30281	32158	35286
2 Dr Arc Turbo Conv	28519	30396	33525
4 Dr Aero Turbo Sdn	21209	22914	25756

Options	Price
16 Inch Wheels [Opt on Arc, Linear]	+500
17 Inch Wheels [Opt on Linear]	+1000
Automatic 5-Speed Transmission	+1250
Automatic Climate Control [Opt on Linear]	+150
Automatic Dimming Rearview Mirror [Opt on non-Linear]	+120
Compact Disc Changer	+250
Fog Lights [Opt on Linear]	+150
Headlight Washers	+150

Body Styles	TMV Pricing		
	Trade	Private	Dealer
4 Dr Arc Turbo Sdn	18907	20379	22833
4 Dr Linear Turbo Sdn	16530	18018	20499

Options	Price
Heated Front Seats	+350
Metallic Paint	+500
OnStar Telematics System [Std on Aero]	+699
Park Distance Control (Rear) [Opt on non-Linear]	+200
Power Driver Seat [Opt on Linear]	+300
Rain Sensing Windshield Wipers [Opt on non-Linear]	+220
Tire Pressure Monitoring System [Opt on Linear]	+445
Xenon Headlamps [Opt on non-Linear]	+550

For 2004, the 9-3 convertible has been given the same full makeover the sedan received last year. The convertible is available in Arc and Aero models and equipped only with the 210-horsepower engine. The highline Vector sedan has been renamed the Aero, and the midlevel Arc sedan now comes standard with a five-speed manual transmission, rather than a six-speed. Bi-xenon headlights are a stand-alone extra on all 9-3s, while rear parking assist is now available as a non-package option on the sedan. The Sport Wheel Package for the Linear and Arc now includes a tire-pressure monitor.

2003

Mileage Category: H

The 2003 9-3 is an all-new design from top to bottom. It rides on a new platform, has new engines and an interior that's considerably more modern than the previous version.

Body Styles	TMV Pricing		
	Trade	Private	Dealer
2 Dr SE Turbo Conv	21664	23444	26410
4 Dr Arc Turbo Sdn	15997	17297	19464

Options	Price
16 Inch Wheels [Opt on Linear]	+332
17 Inch Wheels [Opt on Arc, Linear, SE]	+498
AM/FM/CD Changer Audio System [Opt on Arc, Linear, Vector]	+196
Aero Kit [Opt on SE]	+395
Aluminum/Alloy Interior Trim [Opt on SE]	+262
Automatic 4-Speed Transmission [Opt on SE]	+830
Automatic 5-Speed Transmission [Opt on Arc, Linear, Vector]	+830
Automatic Climate Control (2 Zone) - Driver and Passenger [Opt on Linear]	+130
Heated Front Seats	+315

Body Styles	TMV Pricing		
	Trade	Private	Dealer
4 Dr Linear Turbo Sdn	14004	15155	17073
4 Dr Vector Turbo Sdn	19121	20675	23264

Options	Price
Metallic Paint	+332
Park Distance Control (Rear) [Opt on Arc, Vector]	+216
Power Driver Seat [Opt on Linear]	+216
Power Moonroof [Opt on Arc, Linear, Vector]	+797
Rain Sensing Windshield Wipers [Opt on Arc, Vector]	+116
Rear Spoiler [Opt on SE]	+216
Sport Seats [Opt on SE]	+166
Sport Suspension [Opt on Arc, Linear]	+166
Xenon Headlamps [Opt on Arc, Linear, Vector]	+232

2002

Mileage Category: F

Body Styles	TMV Pricing		
	Trade	Private	Dealer
2 Dr SE Turbo Conv	17596	19211	21902
2 Dr Viggen Turbo Conv	21395	23265	26382
2 Dr Viggen Turbo Hbk	17554	19089	21646

Options	Price
17 Inch Wheels [Opt on SE Conv]	+440
Automatic 4-Speed Transmission [Opt on SE]	+640
Automatic Climate Control [Opt on SE Hbk]	+120
Heated Front Seats [Opt on SE]	+253
Metallic Paint	+253
Power Driver Seat w/Memory [Opt on SE Hbk]	+120

Body Styles	TMV Pricing		
	Trade	Private	Dealer
4 Dr SE Turbo Hbk	10876	11874	13536
4 Dr Viggen Turbo Hbk	17622	19162	21728

Options	Price
Power Passenger Seat [Opt on SE Hbk]	+141
Premium Audio System [Opt on SE Hbk]	+173
Rear Spoiler [Opt on SE Conv]	+173
Special Leather Seat Trim [Opt on SE Hbk]	+472
Sport Suspension [Opt on SE Conv]	+157

The base 9-3 three- and five-door models have been replaced by a value-priced SE five-door. High-performance Viggen models get a new interior color and a carbon-fiber instrument panel.

2001

Mileage Category: H

The base convertible has been dropped for this year while all other models get two new colors. The OnStar telematics system and traction control are now standard.

Body Styles	TMV Pricing		
	Trade	Private	Dealer
2 Dr SE Turbo Conv	14736	17124	19329
2 Dr Turbo Hbk	7915	9197	10380
2 Dr Viggen Turbo Conv	18050	20801	23340

Body Styles	TMV Pricing		
	Trade	Private	Dealer
2 Dr Viggen Turbo Hbk	14535	16750	18794
4 Dr SE Turbo Hbk	9643	11206	12648
4 Dr Turbo Hbk	8241	9576	10808

2001 (cont'd)

Body Styles	TMV Pricing		
	Trade	Private	Dealer
4 Dr Viggen Turbo Hbk	14669	16905	18969

Options	Price	Options	Price
Automatic 4-Speed Transmission	+540	Metallic Paint	+202
Heated Front Seats	+202	Power Moonroof [Opt on STD]	+517
Leather Seats [Std on SE,Viggen,Conv]	+607	Power Passenger Seat [Opt on SE Conv]	+157

2000

The base model gets restyled 15-inch alloy wheels, while the SE version gains performance enhancements and increased horsepower. The sporty 9-3 Viggen offers even more power, and is available as a five-door or convertible in addition to the coupe. All engines are now LEV compliant and GM's OnStar "Telematics" System becomes optional across the model lineup.

Mileage Category: H

Body Styles	TMV Pricing		
	Trade	Private	Dealer
2 Dr SE HO Turbo Conv	11185	13441	15653
2 Dr Turbo Conv	10959	13170	15338
2 Dr Turbo Hbk	5870	7054	8215
2 Dr Viggen Turbo Conv	13104	15483	17815

Body Styles	TMV Pricing		
	Trade	Private	Dealer
2 Dr Viggen Turbo Hbk	11550	13646	15700
4 Dr SE HO Turbo Hbk	7175	8623	10042
4 Dr Turbo Hbk	6262	7525	8763
4 Dr Viggen Turbo Hbk	11499	13586	15631

Options	Price	Options	Price
Automatic 4-Speed Transmission	+453	Leather Seats [Std on SE HO,Viggen,Conv]	+416
Compact Disc Changer	+170	Metallic Paint	+132
Heated Front Seats	+140	OnStar Telematics System	+338
Heated Front and Rear Seats	+196	Power Moonroof [Opt on STD]	+434

1999

Saab changed the car's name to the 9-3, giving it a mild exterior freshening to boot. Around midyear, a high-output version of its 2.0-liter turbo four-cylinder (making an amazing 200 horsepower) becomes the standard engine in the uplevel SE five-door and SE Convertible models equipped with a manual transmission. All SEs also get new five-spoke 16-inch alloy wheels. All five-speed manual 9-3s get revised gearbox ratios and a numerically higher (4.05-to-1) final drive ratio for better off-the-line feel. A revised 9-3 interior headliner provides more padding for increased protection in the event of a crash. And five-door SE variants add an integrated driver-seat armrest and a centrally located cupholder that swings out from the instrument panel.

Mileage Category: H

Body Styles	TMV Pricing		
	Trade	Private	Dealer
2 Dr SE HO Turbo Conv	8597	10363	12201
2 Dr SE Turbo Conv	8504	10253	12074
2 Dr Turbo Conv	6114	7371	8679
2 Dr Turbo Hbk	5030	6063	7139

Body Styles	TMV Pricing		
	Trade	Private	Dealer
2 Dr Viggen Turbo Hbk	9192	10837	12550
4 Dr SE HO Turbo Hbk	5372	6476	7626
4 Dr SE Turbo Hbk	5334	6431	7572
4 Dr Turbo Hbk	5101	6149	7240

Options	Price	Options	Price
Automatic 4-Speed Transmission	+316	Heated Front and Rear Seats	+143
Compact Disc Changer	+137	Leather Seats [Std on SE,SE HO,Viggen,Conv]	+370
Ground Effects [Opt on Conv]	+153	Power Moonroof [Opt on STD]	+316

9-5
2004

Mileage Category: I

Body Styles	TMV Pricing		
	Trade	Private	Dealer
4 Dr Aero Turbo Sdn	27630	29260	31977
4 Dr Aero Turbo Wgn	28179	29790	32476
4 Dr Arc Turbo Sdn	23065	24548	27020

Body Styles	TMV Pricing		
	Trade	Private	Dealer
4 Dr Arc Turbo Wgn	23531	25014	27486
4 Dr Linear Turbo Wgn	20951	22474	25011

For 2004, the Linear model is available only as a wagon. Arc models drop their 200-horsepower V6 and standard automatic transmission in favor of a 220-hp, four-cylinder turbo and a five-speed manual; an automatic remains optional. The Arc also picks up lower body cladding and is eligible for a 17-inch sport wheel package. Bi-xenon headlights are now offered as a stand-alone option on Arc and Aero models. Ventilated front seats, previously standard on the Arc, are now optional. Additionally, Aero models get a more aggressive lower body kit.

Options	Price	Options	Price
17 Inch Wheels [Opt on Arc]	+750	OnStar Telematics System [Std on Aero]	+699
Automatic 5-Speed Transmission	+1350	Park Distance Control (Rear) [Opt on Arc, Aero]	+245
Automatic Dimming Rearview Mirror [Opt on Arc]	+120	Power Moonroof [Opt on Linear]	+945
Automatic Dimming Sideview Mirror(s) [Opt on Arc, Aero]	+300	Rain Sensing Windshield Wipers [Opt on Arc, Aero]	+200
Climate Controlled Seats (Front) [Opt on Linear]	+500	Ventilated Seats (Front) [Opt on Arc, Aero]	+995
Headlight Washers [Opt on Linear]	+250	Xenon Headlamps [Opt on Arc, Aero]	+550
Metallic Paint	+500		

2003

After last year's extensive round of improvements, the 9-5 received only minor upgrades for 2003. All five-speed automatic-equipped models now have the Sentronic manual-shift feature with steering wheel-mounted controls. Ventilated sport seats are now optional on the Aero, while electronic stability control is now standard on all models.

Mileage Category: I

Body Styles	TMV Pricing		
	Trade	Private	Dealer
4 Dr Aero Turbo Sdn	20301	22019	24881
4 Dr Aero Turbo Wgn	20659	22407	25320
4 Dr Arc 3.0t Turbo Sdn	19516	20875	23139

Body Styles	TMV Pricing		
	Trade	Private	Dealer
4 Dr Arc 3.0t Turbo Wgn	21325	22838	25360
4 Dr Linear 2.3t Turbo Sdn	17071	18516	20923
4 Dr Linear 2.3t Turbo Wgn	17462	18940	21403

For the latest vehicle information, visit www.edmunds.com

2003 (cont'd)

Options	Price
Automatic 5-Speed Transmission [Opt on Aero,Linear]	+897
Automatic Dimming Rearview Mirror [Opt on Linear]	+123
Automatic Dimming Sideview Mirror(s)	+199
Harman Kardon Audio System [Opt on Linear]	+365
Metallic Paint	+332

Options	Price
Park Distance Control (Rear)	+163
Power Driver Seat w/Memory [Opt on Linear]	+149
Rain Sensing Windshield Wipers	+133
Ventilated Seats (Front) [Opt on Aero]	+661
Xenon Headlamps	+299

2002

Although it looks similar to last year's model, the 2002 9-5 has undergone extensive changes. There are now three distinct models, each with its own look and feature content. A new five-speed automatic transmission is available on all models, while the top-of-the-line Aero gets more power. Revisions to both the steering and suspension systems increase performance, while a new electronic stability control system and adaptive front airbags improve safety.

Mileage Category: I

Body Styles	TMV Pricing		
	Trade	Private	Dealer
4 Dr Aero Turbo Sdn	14796	16443	19189
4 Dr Aero Turbo Wgn	15005	16675	19459
4 Dr Arc 3.0t Turbo Sdn	14752	16394	19130

Body Styles	TMV Pricing		
	Trade	Private	Dealer
4 Dr Arc 3.0t Turbo Wgn	15022	16694	19480
4 Dr Linear 2.3t Turbo Sdn	12892	14326	16717
4 Dr Linear 2.3t Turbo Wgn	13202	14671	17119

Options	Price
Automatic 4-Speed Transmission [Std on Arc]	+640
Automatic Stability Control [Opt on Linear]	+211
Harman Kardon Audio System [Opt on Linear]	+173
Heated Front and Rear Seats [Opt on Linear]	+293

Options	Price
Metallic Paint	+253
Park Distance Control (Rear) [Opt on Aero,Arc]	+131
Xenon Headlamps	+240

2001

Entry-level models get more horsepower from the turbo four-cylinder while all models get the OnStar telematics system, turbo gauges and two new colors.

Body Styles	TMV Pricing		
	Trade	Private	Dealer
4 Dr 2.3t Turbo Sdn	11025	12919	14667
4 Dr 2.3t Turbo Wgn	11166	13083	14853
4 Dr Aero Turbo Sdn	12673	14849	16857

Body Styles	TMV Pricing		
	Trade	Private	Dealer
4 Dr Aero Turbo Wgn	12764	14956	16980
4 Dr SE V6t Turbo Sdn	12107	14186	16106
4 Dr SE V6t Turbo Wgn	12326	14442	16396

Options	Price
Automatic 4-Speed Transmission [Std on SE V6t]	+540
Harman Kardon Audio System [Opt on 2.3t]	+292
Heated Front and Rear Seats	+268

Options	Price
Leather Seats [Opt on 2.3t]	+360
Metallic Paint	+202
Ventilated Seats (Front)	+448

2000

Saab debuts the high-performance 9-5 Aero Sedan and Wagon with 230 horsepower. Entry-level sedans and wagons sport new 16-inch 10-spoke alloy wheels, and all SE versions offer a turbo V6 and auto-dimming rearview mirror. The 9-5 Wagon Gary Fisher Edition offers a sportier exterior design and a Saab Limited Edition Gary Fisher mountain bike. A sunroof and traction-control system (TCS) have been added to the standard equipment list.

Body Styles	TMV Pricing		
	Trade	Private	Dealer
4 Dr 2.3t Turbo Sdn	8265	9888	11479
4 Dr 2.3t Turbo Wgn	8416	10070	11691
4 Dr Aero Turbo Sdn	10415	12461	14466
4 Dr Aero Turbo Wgn	10728	12834	14899

Body Styles	TMV Pricing		
	Trade	Private	Dealer
4 Dr Gary Fisher Edition Turbo Wgn	9816	11745	13636
4 Dr SE V6t Turbo Sdn	9911	11858	13766
4 Dr SE V6t Turbo Wgn	9911	11858	13766

Options	Price
Automatic 4-Speed Transmission [Std on SE V6t]	+453
BBS Wheels	+623
Harman Kardon Audio System [Opt on 2.3t]	+246
Heated Front and Rear Seats	+196
Leather Seats [Opt on 2.3t]	+510

Options	Price
Metallic Paint	+132
OnStar Telematics System	+338
Power Driver Seat w/Memory [Opt on 2.3t]	+225
Ventilated Seats (Front)	+359

1999

Saab's replacement for the 9000 line of cars is called the 9-5. Available as a sedan with a turbocharged four-cylinder or turbocharged V6 engine, the 9-5 is designed to compete against conventional cars like the BMW 5 Series and Infiniti I30.

Mileage Category: I

Body Styles	TMV Pricing		
	Trade	Private	Dealer
4 Dr 2.3t Turbo Sdn	6506	8038	9632
4 Dr 2.3t Turbo Wgn	6829	8436	10109
4 Dr SE 2.3t Turbo Sdn	6963	8602	10307

Body Styles	TMV Pricing		
	Trade	Private	Dealer
4 Dr SE V6t Turbo Sdn	7772	9601	11505
4 Dr V6t Turbo Wgn	7859	9708	11633

Options	Price
Automatic 4-Speed Transmission [Std on SE V6,V6 Turbo Wgn]	+316
Heated Front and Rear Seats	+143
Leather Seats [Opt on STD,STD Turbo Wgn]	+370

Options	Price
Power Moonroof [Opt on STD]	+316
Ventilated Seats (Front)	+282

Saab
900

900

1998

Mileage Category: H

Body Styles	TMV Pricing		
	Trade	Private	Dealer
2 Dr S Conv	4969	6281	7760
2 Dr S Turbo Hbk	4101	5183	6404
2 Dr SE Turbo Conv	5749	7266	8977

Options	Price
Automatic 4-Speed Transmission	+213
Leather Seats [Std on SE,Conv]	+246

Body Styles	TMV Pricing		
	Trade	Private	Dealer
2 Dr SE Turbo Hbk	4260	5384	6652
4 Dr S Hbk	4158	5255	6492
4 Dr SE Turbo Hbk	4496	5682	7020

Options	Price
Power Moonroof [Opt on S]	+213

The Saab 900 three-door hatchback gets the same turbocharged engine as the SE models this year. Other changes include the addition of body-color front and rear bumpers.

1997
No changes this year.

Mileage Category: H

Body Styles	TMV Pricing		
	Trade	Private	Dealer
2 Dr S Conv	4256	5450	6909
2 Dr S Hbk	3498	4479	5678
2 Dr SE Talladega Turbo Conv	5049	6466	8198
2 Dr SE Talladega Turbo Hbk	3998	5119	6489
2 Dr SE Turbo Conv	4888	6260	7936
2 Dr SE Turbo Hbk	3736	4784	6064

Options	Price
Automatic 4-Speed Transmission [Std on SE V6]	+182
Leather Seats [Opt on S Hbk]	+212

Body Styles	TMV Pricing		
	Trade	Private	Dealer
2 Dr SE V6 Conv	5062	6482	8218
4 Dr S Hbk	3590	4597	5827
4 Dr SE Talladega Turbo Hbk	4122	5279	6692
4 Dr SE Turbo Hbk	4068	5209	6604
4 Dr SE V6 Hbk	4216	5399	6845

Options	Price
Power Moonroof [Opt on S]	+182

1996
The popular Saab 900 SE five-door is available this year with the turbocharged four-cylinder engine. An automatic transmission is now optional on turbos. V6 models come only with an automatic. Adjustable driver's lumbar support is now standard on all 900 models.

Mileage Category: H

Body Styles	TMV Pricing		
	Trade	Private	Dealer
2 Dr S Conv	3620	4701	6194
2 Dr S Hbk	2849	3700	4874
2 Dr SE Turbo Conv	4238	5503	7251
2 Dr SE Turbo Hbk	3361	4365	5751

Options	Price
Automatic 4-Speed Transmission [Opt on S,SE]	+164
Leather Seats [Std on SE,SEV6,Conv]	+193

Body Styles	TMV Pricing		
	Trade	Private	Dealer
2 Dr SE V6 Conv	4469	5804	7648
4 Dr S Hbk	2907	3775	4974
4 Dr SE Turbo Hbk	3463	4497	5926
4 Dr SE V6 Hbk	3551	4612	6077

Options	Price
Power Moonroof [Opt on S]	+164

1995
Daytime running lights (DRLs) are now standard on the 900. A new convertible 900 appears, and all 900 models get a new three-spoke steering wheel and an anti-theft alarm.

Mileage Category: H

Body Styles	TMV Pricing		
	Trade	Private	Dealer
2 Dr S Conv	3050	3945	5437
2 Dr S Hbk	2318	2998	4132
2 Dr SE Turbo Conv	3304	4274	5890
2 Dr SE Turbo Hbk	2897	3748	5165

Options	Price
Automatic 4-Speed Transmission	+137
Leather Seats [Std on SE,SE,Conv]	+162

Body Styles	TMV Pricing		
	Trade	Private	Dealer
2 Dr SE V6 Conv	3396	4392	6052
4 Dr S Hbk	2270	2936	4047
4 Dr SE V6 Hbk	2608	3373	4648

Options	Price
Power Moonroof [Opt on S]	+137

9000

1998

Mileage Category: I

Body Styles	TMV Pricing		
	Trade	Private	Dealer
4 Dr CSE Turbo Hbk	4235	5458	6837

Options	Price
Automatic 4-Speed Transmission	+197

No changes to the aging 9000.

1997

Mileage Category: I

No changes to this aging model.

Body Styles	TMV Pricing		
	Trade	Private	Dealer
4 Dr Aero Turbo Hbk	4085	5326	6843
4 Dr CS Turbo Hbk	3117	4064	5221
4 Dr CSE Anniv Turbo Hbk	3822	4983	6402

Options	Price
Automatic 4-Speed Transmission [Std on CSE V6]	+188
Leather Seats [Opt on CS]	+280

Body Styles	TMV Pricing		
	Trade	Private	Dealer
4 Dr CSE Turbo Hbk	3746	4884	6274
4 Dr CSE V6 Hbk	3987	5198	6678

Options	Price
Power Moonroof [Opt on CS]	+202

1996

The 9000 sedans are dropped, leaving only the hatchback body style. Cupholders for rear-seat passengers, new upholstery for the CS and new three-spoke alloy wheels for the CS and CSE round out the major developments for this year's model.

Body Styles	TMV Pricing		
	Trade	Private	Dealer
4 Dr Aero Turbo Hbk	3251	4259	5651
4 Dr CS Turbo Hbk	2686	3520	4671

Options	Price
Automatic 4-Speed Transmission [Opt on CS,CSE]	+172
Leather Seats [Opt on CS]	+251

Body Styles	TMV Pricing		
	Trade	Private	Dealer
4 Dr CSE Turbo Hbk	3221	4219	5597
4 Dr CSE V6 Hbk	3235	4239	5625

Options	Price
Power Moonroof [Opt on CS]	+204

1995

Saab adds a light-pressure turbo and a V6 to its large-car engine roster. V6 cars come only with an automatic transmission. Daytime running lights (DRLs) become standard on all 9000s this year.

Body Styles	TMV Pricing		
	Trade	Private	Dealer
4 Dr Aero Turbo Hbk	2705	3583	5045
4 Dr CDE Sdn	2555	3384	4766
4 Dr CS Turbo Hbk	2206	2922	4114

Options	Price
Automatic 4-Speed Transmission [Opt on S,SE]	+130
Leather Seats [Std on SE,SE V6,Conv]	+213

Body Styles	TMV Pricing		
	Trade	Private	Dealer
4 Dr CSE Hbk	2531	3352	4721
4 Dr CSE Turbo Hbk	2393	3170	4464

Options	Price
Power Moonroof [Opt on S]	+153

ION

2004

Saturn has upgraded the Ion with new fabrics, improved plastics and a new radio with MP3 and satellite radio capability. The electric steering has been revised for improved feel at highway speeds, while the sedan's five-speed automatic and the coupe's CVT have been recalibrated for improved gear selection and response. Finally, Saturn has installed additional sound-deadening material to reduce cabin noise. A Special Edition version of the sedan provides black exterior paint, distinctive 16-inch wheels and a two-tone interior.

Mileage Category: B

Body Styles	TMV Pricing		
	Trade	Private	Dealer
4 Dr 1 Sdn	5737	6644	8156
4 Dr 2 Cpe	8177	9103	10645
4 Dr 2 Sdn	7725	8632	10144

Options	Price
AM/FM/CD Audio System [Opt on 1]	+290
Air Conditioning [Opt on 1]	+960
Aluminum/Alloy Wheels [Opt on 2]	+375
Antilock Brakes	+200
Automatic 5-Speed Transmission	+900
Automatic Dimming Rearview Mirror [Opt on 2, 3]	+200
Cruise Control [Opt on 2]	+195
Front and Rear Head Airbag Restraints	+395
Keyless Entry System [Opt on 2]	+200

Body Styles	TMV Pricing		
	Trade	Private	Dealer
4 Dr 3 Cpe	8988	9913	11455
4 Dr 3 Sdn	8533	9440	10952

Options	Price
Leather Seats [Opt on 3]	+700
OnStar Telematics System [Opt on 2, 3]	+695
Power Mirrors [Opt on 2]	+180
Power Sunroof [Opt on 2, 3]	+725
Power Windows [Opt on 2]	+250
Premium Audio System [Opt on 2, 3]	+290
Rear Spoiler [Opt on 2, 3]	+250
Traction Control System	+200

2003

After 12 long years in production, Saturn is finally retiring its aging S-Series sedan and coupe in favor of the all-new Saturn Ion sedan and innovative quad coupe.

Mileage Category: B

Body Styles	TMV Pricing		
	Trade	Private	Dealer
4 Dr 1 Sdn	4928	5647	6845
4 Dr 2 Cpe	6877	7880	9551
4 Dr 2 Sdn	6709	7687	9317

Options	Price
AM/FM/CD Audio System [Opt on 1]	+238
AM/FM/CD Changer Audio System [Opt on 2,3]	+410
AM/FM/Cassette/CD Audio System [Opt on 1,2]	+307
Air Conditioning [Opt on 1]	+579
Aluminum/Alloy Wheels [Opt on 2]	+226
Antilock Brakes	+422
Automatic 5-Speed Transmission [Opt on Sedans]	+543
Automatic Dimming Rearview Mirror [Opt on 2,3]	+121
Continuously Variable Transmission [Opt on Coupes]	+739

Body Styles	TMV Pricing		
	Trade	Private	Dealer
4 Dr 3 Cpe	7815	8792	10420
4 Dr 3 Sdn	7364	8438	10227

Options	Price
Cruise Control [Opt on 2]	+142
Front and Rear Head Airbag Restraints	+238
Leather Seats [Opt on 3]	+479
OnStar Telematics System [Opt on 2,3]	+419
Power Moonroof [Opt on 2,3]	+437
Power Windows [Opt on 2]	+148
Premium Audio System [Opt on 2,3]	+175
Traction Control System	+121

ION Red Line

2004

Mileage Category: E

Body Styles	TMV Pricing		
	Trade	Private	Dealer
4 Dr S/C Cpe	11764	12866	14702

The Ion Red Line is a new performance-enhanced version of the standard quad coupe. Upgrades include a supercharged 200-horsepower engine, a tightened suspension, four-wheel disc brakes and 17-inch wheels.

L300
2004

Mileage Category: D

Body Styles	TMV Pricing		
	Trade	Private	Dealer
4 Dr 1 Sdn	7659	8783	10655
4 Dr 1 Wgn	8417	9485	11264
4 Dr 2 Sdn	9943	11067	12939

Body Styles	TMV Pricing		
	Trade	Private	Dealer
4 Dr 2 Wgn	10645	11740	13564
4 Dr 3 Sdn	10535	11630	13454
4 Dr 3 Wgn	11164	12231	14010

Options	Price
AM/FM/CD Changer Audio System [Opt on 2]	+250
Automatic Dimming Rearview Mirror [Opt on 2, 3]	+150
Chrome Wheels [Opt on 3]	+650
DVD Entertainment System [Opt on 2]	+995

Options	Price
Leather Seats [Opt on 2, 3]	+1295
OnStar Telematics System [Opt on 2, 3]	+695
Power Driver Seat [Opt on 2]	+325
Power Sunroof [Opt on 2]	+725

All L-Series sedans and wagons have been renamed "L300" this year, but both the 2.2-liter, four-cylinder engine and the 3.0-liter V6 are still available. The four-cylinder motor gets a five-horsepower increase this year for a total of 140. A five-speed manual transmission is no longer available with this engine. All L300s now include such standard equipment as head curtain airbags, ABS, heated mirrors, a six-speaker CD stereo and a tilt steering wheel. An auto-dimming rearview mirror with compass is optional, and Saturn is giving those who purchase a loaded sedan or wagon the option of getting a DVD entertainment system or OnStar telematics at no extra cost.

L-Series
2003

Mileage Category: D

Body Styles	TMV Pricing		
	Trade	Private	Dealer
4 Dr L200 Sdn	7518	8412	9901
4 Dr L300 Sdn	8994	10064	11846

Body Styles	TMV Pricing		
	Trade	Private	Dealer
4 Dr LW200 Wgn	8535	9549	11240
4 Dr LW300 Wgn	9436	10558	12427

Options	Price
16 Inch Wheels - Chrome	+151
AM/FM/Cassette/CD Audio System	+307
AM/FM/Cassette/CD Changer Audio System	+479
Aluminum/Alloy Wheels [Opt on L200,LW200]	+241
Automatic 4-Speed Transmission [Opt on L200]	+482
Automatic Climate Control	+121
DVD Entertainment System	+934

Options	Price
Heated Front Seats	+151
Leather Seats	+479
Luggage Rack [Opt on LW200,LW300]	+133
OnStar Telematics System	+419
Power Driver Seat	+196
Power Moonroof	+437
Premium Audio System	+121

Saturn's L-Series sedan and wagon receive a significant exterior and interior freshening for 2003. Both front and rear fascias have been redesigned for a new look. Front-end restyling includes clear wraparound headlamps with chrome trim, optional foglamps with chrome bezels integrated into the new fascia, a larger grille with a new Saturn badge and a raised hood. The rear end sports new taillamps and a revised fascia with additional chrome trim. No more black rocker panels and lower fascias -- the whole car is now offered with body-color trim. The interior now features brushed nickel-finish trim plates, silver faceplates in the instrument cluster and European-style upholstery. Ride and handling has been improved by adjusting spring rates; optional 16-inch wheels and tires should help, too.

2002

Mileage Category: D

Body Styles	TMV Pricing		
	Trade	Private	Dealer
4 Dr L100 Sdn	5649	6460	7811
4 Dr L200 Sdn	5934	6785	8204
4 Dr L300 Sdn	7017	8024	9701

Body Styles	TMV Pricing		
	Trade	Private	Dealer
4 Dr LW200 Wgn	6766	7737	9355
4 Dr LW300 Wgn	7505	8582	10376

Options	Price
AM/FM/Cassette/CD Audio System	+255
AM/FM/Cassette/CD Changer Audio System	+398
Aluminum/Alloy Wheels [Std on 300]	+175
Automatic 4-Speed Transmission [Std on 300]	+406

Options	Price
Heated Front Seats	+125
Leather Seats	+398
Power Driver Seat	+163
Power Moonroof	+363

Safety enhancements are the big news for 2002. All Saturn L-Series models now feature standard head curtain airbags, antilock brakes and traction control. Other enhancements include four-wheel disc brakes (on all models except L100), automatic headlamps, LATCH child seat anchors and post airbag-deployment signals. A DVD entertainment system will be available later in the year along with the OnStar communications system. New options packages add even more value with features like an in-dash six-disc CD changer and automatic climate control. New 15-inch alloy and 16-inch chrome wheels round out the upgrades.

2001

Mileage Category: D

Body Styles	TMV Pricing		
	Trade	Private	Dealer
4 Dr L100 Sdn	4354	5383	6333
4 Dr L200 Sdn	4822	5961	7013
4 Dr L300 Sdn	5508	6810	8012

Body Styles	TMV Pricing		
	Trade	Private	Dealer
4 Dr LW200 Wgn	5453	6742	7931
4 Dr LW300 Wgn	6089	7528	8857

Saturn has addressed safety concerns by making front and rear head curtain airbags optional on all trim levels. All sedans are now equipped with a three-point seatbelt in the rear center seat, but this feature is still not available in wagons. Sedans also will get an emergency trunk release handle. New colors include Cream White, Bright Silver, Silver Blue and Straight Shade Black. Bright White, Silver, Silver Plum and Blackberry have been discontinued.

2001 (cont'd)

Options	Price
AM/FM/CD Audio System	+166
AM/FM/Cassette/CD Audio System	+215
Aluminum/Alloy Wheels [Opt on 200]	+148
Antilock Brakes	+295
Automatic 4-Speed Transmission [Opt on L100,L200]	+362

Options	Price
Front and Rear Head Airbag Restraints	+166
Leather Seats	+335
Power Driver Seat	+137
Power Sunroof	+306

2000

The L-Series is a new midsize line of sedans and wagons that was developed for Saturn customers moving up from the smaller cars. Offered in three trim levels, with two engines and manual or automatic transmissions (depending on model), the L-Series is based on the European-market Opel Vectra platform, and consequently carries a distinct import feel.

Mileage Category: D

Body Styles	TMV Pricing		
	Trade	Private	Dealer
4 Dr LS Sdn	3586	4579	5552
4 Dr LS1 Sdn	3772	4816	5840
4 Dr LS2 Sdn	4365	5574	6760

Body Styles	TMV Pricing		
	Trade	Private	Dealer
4 Dr LW1 Wgn	4178	5335	6470
4 Dr LW2 Wgn	4721	6028	7310

Options	Price
AM/FM/CD Audio System	+146
AM/FM/Cassette/CD Audio System	+188
Aluminum/Alloy Wheels [Opt on LS1,LW1]	+129
Antilock Brakes	+258

Options	Price
Automatic 4-Speed Transmission [Opt on LS,LS1]	+317
Leather Seats	+293
Power Driver Seat	+120
Power Sunroof	+267

S-Series

2002

New aluminum 15-inch wheels and four new exterior colors are the only notable changes for 2002.

Mileage Category: B

Body Styles	TMV Pricing		
	Trade	Private	Dealer
3 Dr SC1 Cpe	4978	5807	7189
3 Dr SC2 Cpe	5902	6883	8519
4 Dr SL Sdn	3956	4614	5711

Body Styles	TMV Pricing		
	Trade	Private	Dealer
4 Dr SL1 Sdn	4694	5474	6774
4 Dr SL2 Sdn	5170	6030	7463

Options	Price
AM/FM/CD Audio System [Std on SC]	+198
AM/FM/Cassette/CD Audio System	+255
Air Conditioning [Std on SC2,SL2]	+413
Aluminum/Alloy Wheels	+175
Antilock Brakes	+350
Automatic 4-Speed Transmission	+431

Options	Price
Cruise Control	+118
Front and Rear Head Airbag Restraints	+163
Leather Seats	+398
Power Sunroof	+363
Power Windows [Std on SC2]	+123

2001

The S-Series sees no change from last year, save for optional head curtain airbags.

Mileage Category: B

Body Styles	TMV Pricing		
	Trade	Private	Dealer
3 Dr SC1 Cpe	4134	5245	6272
3 Dr SC2 Cpe	4897	6214	7430
4 Dr SL Sdn	3315	4207	5030

Body Styles	TMV Pricing		
	Trade	Private	Dealer
4 Dr SL1 Sdn	3843	4877	5832
4 Dr SL2 Sdn	4285	5438	6502
4 Dr SW2 Wgn	4572	5801	6937

Options	Price
AM/FM/CD Audio System	+166
AM/FM/Cassette/CD Audio System	+215
Air Conditioning [Opt on SC1,SL,SL1]	+348
Aluminum/Alloy Wheels	+148
Antilock Brakes	+295

Options	Price
Automatic 4-Speed Transmission	+362
Front and Rear Head Airbag Restraints	+137
Leather Seats	+335
Power Sunroof	+306

2000

Saturn has redesigned the body panels and cockpit of its S-Series SL Sedan and SW Wagon this year. GM's OnStar communications system will now be available as a dealer-installed option across the Saturn line.

Mileage Category: B

Body Styles	TMV Pricing		
	Trade	Private	Dealer
3 Dr SC1 Cpe	3255	4242	5209
3 Dr SC2 Cpe	3713	4840	5944
4 Dr SL Sdn	2679	3491	4287

Body Styles	TMV Pricing		
	Trade	Private	Dealer
4 Dr SL1 Sdn	3011	3924	4819
4 Dr SL2 Sdn	3301	4302	5283
4 Dr SW2 Wgn	3488	4545	5582

Options	Price
AM/FM/CD Audio System	+146
AM/FM/Cassette/CD Audio System	+188
Air Conditioning [Opt on SC1,SL,SL1]	+304

Options	Price
Aluminum/Alloy Wheels	+129
Antilock Brakes	+258
Automatic 4-Speed Transmission	+317

Options	Price
Leather Seats	+293
Power Sunroof	+267

Options	Price
Premium Audio System [Opt on Cpe]	+129

1999

Mileage Category: B

Body Styles	TMV Pricing		
	Trade	Private	Dealer
2 Dr SC1 Cpe	2501	3389	4314
2 Dr SC2 Cpe	2782	3771	4800
3 Dr SC1 Cpe	2533	3432	4368
3 Dr SC2 Cpe	2828	3833	4879
4 Dr SL Sdn	2080	2819	3588

Body Styles	TMV Pricing		
	Trade	Private	Dealer
4 Dr SL1 Sdn	2377	3222	4100
4 Dr SL2 Sdn	2545	3450	4391
4 Dr SW1 Wgn	2522	3417	4348
4 Dr SW2 Wgn	2684	3638	4630

Options	Price
AM/FM/CD Audio System	+135
Air Conditioning [Std on SC2,SL2,SW2]	+295
Antilock Brakes	+239

Options	Price
Automatic 4-Speed Transmission	+264
Leather Seats	+272
Power Sunroof [Opt on SC,SL]	+248

Starting in the late fall of 1998, all coupes will be fitted with a rear-access door on the driver side designed to provide easier entry to the backseat. Drum brakes replace the rear discs previously available on SC2s and SL2s equipped with ABS. Engines benefit from engineering upgrades that improve fuel economy and reduce noise, vibration and emissions. Finally, the SC2 gets new plastic wheel covers and a new optional alloy wheel design.

1998

Mileage Category: B

Body Styles	TMV Pricing		
	Trade	Private	Dealer
2 Dr SC1 Cpe	2040	2910	3890
2 Dr SC2 Cpe	2202	3140	4199
4 Dr SL Sdn	1626	2319	3101
4 Dr SL1 Sdn	1918	2736	3659

Body Styles	TMV Pricing		
	Trade	Private	Dealer
4 Dr SL2 Sdn	2081	2969	3970
4 Dr SW1 Wgn	1951	2783	3720
4 Dr SW2 Wgn	2123	3027	4047

Options	Price
AM/FM/CD Audio System	+123
Air Conditioning [Std on SC2,SL2,SW2]	+269
Antilock Brakes	+218

Options	Price
Automatic 4-Speed Transmission	+241
Leather Seats	+248
Power Sunroof [Opt on SC,SL]	+226

All models get reduced-force front airbags, and sedans and wagons get new seat fabrics. The SC2, SL2 and SW2 are equipped with new headrests, and the optional alarm system now has a programmable passive arming feature. On the mechanical side, structural upgrades to the engine blocks and transmission case housing are said to reduce noise and increase durability. Additionally, the automatic transmission's programming has been tweaked to reduce hunting on hills and improve shift quality. And Saturn says that revised shock absorbers on all cars provide a smoother ride. Restyled alloy wheels and plastic wheel covers round out the changes.

1997

Mileage Category: B

Body Styles	TMV Pricing		
	Trade	Private	Dealer
2 Dr SC1 Cpe	1704	2551	3587
2 Dr SC2 Cpe	1723	2579	3625
4 Dr SL Sdn	1345	2012	2827
4 Dr SL1 Sdn	1601	2397	3369

Body Styles	TMV Pricing		
	Trade	Private	Dealer
4 Dr SL2 Sdn	1684	2521	3544
4 Dr SW1 Wgn	1659	2484	3491
4 Dr SW2 Wgn	1716	2568	3610

Options	Price
AM/FM/CD Audio System	+116
Air Conditioning	+245
Antilock Brakes	+205

Options	Price
Automatic 4-Speed Transmission	+221
Leather Seats [Opt on SC2,SL2,SW2]	+233
Power Sunroof [Opt on SC,SL]	+212

Coupes get a new look inside and out for 1997. No longer stubby in appearance, all coupes adopt the longer wheelbase used by the sedans and wagons, as well as their softer, rounder styling cues. The SC1 and SC2 are now virtually identical in appearance (the SC2's body-color door handles being one of the few differences); both have exposed headlamps and standard daytime running lights. In other news, all models pick up a low-fuel indicator light and can be equipped with a single in-dash CD player. And Saturn has again taken measures to reduce engine noise and vibration.

1996

Mileage Category: B

Body Styles	TMV Pricing		
	Trade	Private	Dealer
2 Dr SC1 Cpe	1254	2029	3099
2 Dr SC2 Cpe	1350	2185	3339
4 Dr SL Sdn	1031	1667	2545
4 Dr SL1 Sdn	1161	1879	2870

Body Styles	TMV Pricing		
	Trade	Private	Dealer
4 Dr SL2 Sdn	1272	2058	3144
4 Dr SW1 Wgn	1210	1958	2990
4 Dr SW2 Wgn	1279	2069	3160

Options	Price
Air Conditioning	+217
Antilock Brakes	+183
Automatic 4-Speed Transmission	+196

Options	Price
Compact Disc Changer [Opt on Cpe]	+147
Leather Seats [Opt on SC2,SL2,SW2]	+208
Power Sunroof [Opt on Cpe,Sdn]	+190

Sedans and wagons get new exterior styling -- resulting in a softer, rounder appearance -- along with redesigned rear seats and standard daytime running lights. Traction control is now available on cars equipped with a manual transmission. Finally, both engines now use sequential-port fuel injection in place of multiport injection.

Saturn
S-Series/VUE

1995

SC1 coupes receive new high-back front seats, while all coupes get new front-end treatments and revised wheel covers.

Mileage Category: B

Body Styles	TMV Pricing		
	Trade	Private	Dealer
2 Dr SC1 Cpe	940	1598	2695
2 Dr SC2 Cpe	1071	1820	3069
4 Dr SL Sdn	662	1126	1899
4 Dr SL1 Sdn	835	1420	2395

Options	Price
Air Conditioning	+183
Antilock Brakes	+155
Automatic 4-Speed Transmission	+165

Body Styles	TMV Pricing		
	Trade	Private	Dealer
4 Dr SL2 Sdn	997	1695	2857
4 Dr SW1 Wgn	884	1502	2532
4 Dr SW2 Wgn	1003	1704	2873

Options	Price
Compact Disc Changer	+124
Leather Seats [Opt on SC2,SL2,SW2]	+175
Power Sunroof [Opt on Cpe,Sdn]	+160

VUE

2004

A new 3.5-liter V6 replaces the previous 3.0-liter unit. Larger 17-inch wheels and tires are now standard on the V6 AWD model and optional on the front-wheel-drive version. Antilock brakes are standard on all V6 models. The interior has been upgraded to reduce noise and now incorporates metallic and leather trim. The front seats now have seatbelt pre-tensioners and dual-stage front airbags. New entertainment choices include MP3-compatible CD players, satellite radio and a rear-seat DVD entertainment system (late availability).

Mileage Category: L

Body Styles	TMV Pricing		
	Trade	Private	Dealer
4 Dr STD AWD SUV	12017	13193	15152
4 Dr STD SUV	10152	11328	13287

Options	Price
17 Inch Wheels [Opt on V6 non-AWD]	+300
18 Inch Wheels [Opt on V6 non-AWD]	+1500
AM/FM/CD Audio System [Opt on STD]	+290
AM/FM/CD Changer/MP3 Audio System	+650
Alarm System [Opt on STD]	+200
Aluminum/Alloy Wheels [Opt on STD]	+400
Antilock Brakes	+300
Automatic Dimming Rearview Mirror [Opt on STD]	+120
Automatic On/Off Headlights [Opt on STD]	+150
Continuously Variable Transmission [Opt on STD]	+2085
Cruise Control [Opt on STD]	+200
Fog Lights [Opt on STD]	+170
Front Head Airbag Restraints	+395

Body Styles	TMV Pricing		
	Trade	Private	Dealer
4 Dr V6 AWD SUV	16322	17661	19893
4 Dr V6 SUV	14500	15776	17902

Options	Price
Heated Front Seats	+245
Keyless Entry System [Opt on STD]	+180
Leather Seats	+575
OnStar Telematics System	+695
Power Driver Seat	+350
Power Mirrors [Opt on STD]	+180
Power Sunroof	+725
Power Windows [Opt on STD]	+355
Premium Audio System	+295
Satellite Radio System	+325
Sport Suspension [Opt on V6]	+495
Traction Control System [Opt on STD]	+300

2003

New last year, the Vue gets only minor changes for 2003. V6 models are now available with front-wheel drive, while a new options package bundles together heated leather seats and a leather-wrapped steering wheel. A new optional audio system includes a subwoofer, 180-watt amplifier and six door-mounted speakers.

Mileage Category: L

Body Styles	TMV Pricing		
	Trade	Private	Dealer
4 Dr STD AWD SUV	11166	12202	13928
4 Dr STD SUV	9568	10456	11935

Options	Price
AM/FM/CD Audio System [Opt on STD]	+238
AM/FM/Cassette/CD Audio System	+307
AM/FM/Cassette/CD Changer Audio System	+479
Alarm System [Opt on STD]	+151
Aluminum/Alloy Wheels [Opt on STD]	+241
Antilock Brakes	+422
Continuously Variable Transmission [Opt on STD]	+739
Front and Rear Head Airbag Restraints	+238

Body Styles	TMV Pricing		
	Trade	Private	Dealer
4 Dr V6 AWD SUV	12760	13943	15915
4 Dr V6 SUV	12323	13466	15371

Options	Price
Keyless Entry System [Opt on STD]	+115
Leather Seats	+479
OnStar Telematics System	+419
Power Door Locks [Opt on STD]	+130
Power Moonroof	+437
Power Windows [Opt on STD]	+154
Premium Audio System	+178
Traction Control System [Opt on STD]	+121

2002

The Vue is an all-new sport-utility vehicle in Saturn's lineup, designed to compete on the lower end of the scale with models like the Ford Escape and Honda CR-V.

Mileage Category: L

Body Styles	TMV Pricing		
	Trade	Private	Dealer
4 Dr STD AWD SUV	9105	10042	11604
4 Dr STD SUV	7842	8650	9996

Options	Price
AM/FM/CD Audio System [Std on V6]	+198
AM/FM/Cassette/CD Audio System	+255

Body Styles	TMV Pricing		
	Trade	Private	Dealer
4 Dr V6 AWD SUV	11156	12304	14218

Options	Price
AM/FM/Cassette/CD Changer Audio System	+398
Alarm System [Std on V6]	+125

Options	Price
Aluminum/Alloy Wheels [Std on V6]	+200
Antilock Brakes	+350
Continuously Variable Transmission [Std on STD 4WD]	+613
Front and Rear Head Airbag Restraints	+198

Options	Price
OnStar Telematics System	+348
Power Sunroof	+363
Power Windows [Std on V6]	+128

Scion
xA/xB

xA

2004

Mileage Category: B

Body Styles		TMV Pricing		
		Trade	Private	Dealer
4 Dr STD Hbk		9962	10720	11983

Options	Price	Options	Price
AM/FM/CD Changer Audio System	+395	Front Side Airbag Restraints	+300
Alarm System	+259	Front and Rear Head Airbag Restraints	+350
Aluminum/Alloy Wheels	+665	Luggage Rack	+250
Automatic 4-Speed Transmission	+800	Rear Spoiler	+335
Fog Lights	+350		

In an effort to get buyers under 30 into its dealerships, Toyota launches an all-new division called Scion. The brand will eventually grow to three models, but for now two are offered; one of these is a small but well-equipped five-door hatchback called the xA. Scion will use a no-haggle sales strategy and give buyers ample opportunity to customize their xAs, drawing upon a list of over three dozen dealer-installed options.

xB

2004

Mileage Category: L

Body Styles		TMV Pricing		
		Trade	Private	Dealer
4 Dr STD Wgn		11278	12219	13787

Options	Price	Options	Price
AM/FM/CD Changer Audio System	+395	Fog Lights	+350
Alarm System	+429	Luggage Rack	+250
Aluminum/Alloy Wheels	+665	Rear Spoiler	+335
Automatic 4-Speed Transmission	+800		

In an effort to get buyers under 30 into its dealerships, Toyota launches an all-new division called Scion. The brand will eventually grow to three models, but for now two are offered, one of these a boxy, attention-getting vehicle called the xB. Scion will use a no-haggle sales strategy and give buyers ample opportunity to customize their xBs, drawing upon a list of over three dozen dealer-installed options.

Baja

2004

Mileage Category: J

Body Styles	TMV Pricing		
	Trade	Private	Dealer
4 Dr Sport AWD Crew Cab SB	15474	16577	18416

Options	Price
Alarm System	+250
Automatic 4-Speed Transmission	+800
Automatic Dimming Rearview Mirror	+200
Bed Extender	+301
Compact Disc Changer [Opt on Sport]	+525

Body Styles	TMV Pricing		
	Trade	Private	Dealer
4 Dr Turbo AWD Crew Cab SB	17337	18478	20379

Options	Price
Leather Seats [Opt on Turbo]	+1300
Premium Audio System	+267
Tonneau Cover	+495
Trailer Hitch	+346

A Turbo model joins the lineup, and true to its name, it comes with a turbocharged version of the base engine good for 210 horsepower and lots more fun. In other news, a revised suspension raises the Baja's ground clearance to 8.2 inches, and all models get new medium gray interior trim.

2003

Mileage Category: J

Body Styles	TMV Pricing		
	Trade	Private	Dealer
4 Dr STD AWD Crew Cab SB	15397	16564	18510

Options	Price
Alarm System	+131
Automatic 4-Speed Transmission	+553
Automatic Dimming Rearview Mirror	+127
Bed Extender	+135

Body Styles	TMV Pricing		
	Trade	Private	Dealer
4 Dr Sport AWD Crew Cab SB	14142	15214	17001

Options	Price
Compact Disc Changer	+311
Premium Audio System	+185
Trailer Hitch	+138

The Baja is all new for 2003. It's similar to the Subaru Outback, but it has an open cargo bed. Certainly a niche vehicle, it should appeal to people with active lifestyles, especially those who ski or surf.

Forester

2004

Mileage Category: L

Body Styles	TMV Pricing		
	Trade	Private	Dealer
4 Dr X AWD Wgn	14688	15916	17962
4 Dr XS AWD Wgn	16231	17459	19505

Options	Price
Aluminum/Alloy Wheels [Opt on X]	+659
Automatic 4-Speed Transmission	+800
Automatic Dimming Rearview Mirror	+162
Brush Guard	+301

Body Styles	TMV Pricing		
	Trade	Private	Dealer
4 Dr XT Turbo AWD Wgn	17964	19229	21338

Options	Price
Leather Seats [Opt on XS, XT]	+1750
Power Moonroof [Opt on XS, XT]	+800
Rear Spoiler	+353
Trailer Hitch	+295

Noting Forester fans' desire for more power, Subaru adds a turbocharged XT model to the lineup. The XT is essentially a loaded XS with a 210-hp engine replacing the 165-hp motor.

2003

Mileage Category: L

Body Styles	TMV Pricing		
	Trade	Private	Dealer
4 Dr X AWD Wgn	12799	13900	15736

Options	Price
Alarm System	+138
Aluminum/Alloy Wheels [Opt on 2.5 X]	+449
Automatic 4-Speed Transmission	+553
Automatic Dimming Rearview Mirror	+127
Brush Guard	+204
Compact Disc Changer [Opt on 2.5 X]	+311

Body Styles	TMV Pricing		
	Trade	Private	Dealer
4 Dr XS AWD Wgn	13963	15165	17167

Options	Price
Leather Seats [Opt on 2.5 XS]	+519
Power Moonroof [Opt on 2.5 XS]	+553
Premium Audio System	+138
Rear Spoiler	+242
Trailer Hitch	+204

Subaru's well-regarded Forester crossover sport-ute has been completely redesigned to be an even more enjoyable addition to your family. Engineers have given the tall wagon more interior room, a stiffer body structure, a revised chassis and more standard feature content -- all while keeping exterior dimensions the same and reducing the curb weight by 90 pounds.

2002

Mileage Category: L

Body Styles	TMV Pricing		
	Trade	Private	Dealer
4 Dr L AWD Wgn	10661	11711	13462

Options	Price
AM/FM/CD Audio System [Std on S]	+221
Aluminum/Alloy Wheels [Std on S]	+365
Automatic 4-Speed Transmission	+490
Brush Guard	+230
Compact Disc Changer [Std on S]	+319
Front Side Airbag Restraints [Opt on S]	+151

Body Styles	TMV Pricing		
	Trade	Private	Dealer
4 Dr S AWD Wgn	12032	13217	15192

Options	Price
Leather Seats	+429
Power Moonroof [Opt on S]	+398
Premium Audio System	+164
Rear Spoiler	+181
Rear Wind Deflector	+174
Trailer Hitch	+181

Subaru's mini-SUV/tall wagon gains three new standard features: a cargo area cover, daytime running lights and an intermittent mode for the rear wiper. Other changes include a new color for the Forester S' lower body cladding (from Titanium Pearl to Graystone Metallic) and the option of leather seating for S models equipped with the Premium package and automatic transmission.

2001

The 2001 Forester receives slight alterations to the front and rear fascias, a new Premium Package and upgrades to the interior.

Mileage Category: L

Body Styles	TMV Pricing		
	Trade	Private	Dealer
4 Dr L AWD Wgn	8902	10320	11628

Options	Price
AM/FM/CD Audio System	+235
Aluminum/Alloy Wheels	+333
Automatic 4-Speed Transmission	+447
Brush Guard	+210
Compact Disc Changer	+385
Front Side Airbag Restraints [Opt on S]	+140

Body Styles	TMV Pricing		
	Trade	Private	Dealer
4 Dr S AWD Wgn	10039	11636	13111

Options	Price
Keyless Entry System	+125
Leather Seats	+724
Power Moonroof [Opt on S]	+364
Premium Audio System	+559
Rear Spoiler	+165
Trailer Hitch	+165

2000

Forester L gets standard cruise control and Forester S receives a viscous limited-slip rear differential at base price increases of $100.

Mileage Category: L

Body Styles	TMV Pricing		
	Trade	Private	Dealer
4 Dr L AWD Wgn	7875	9233	10565

Options	Price
AM/FM/CD Audio System	+206
AM/FM/Cassette/CD Audio System	+206
Aluminum/Alloy Wheels	+292
Automatic 4-Speed Transmission	+393

Body Styles	TMV Pricing		
	Trade	Private	Dealer
4 Dr S AWD Wgn	8708	10211	11684

Options	Price
Brush Guard	+184
Compact Disc Changer	+339
Leather Seats	+440
Trailer Hitch	+145

1999

Forester's engine makes more torque and the automatic transmission has been improved. L and S models have longer lists of standard equipment and two new colors are available.

Mileage Category: L

Body Styles	TMV Pricing		
	Trade	Private	Dealer
4 Dr L AWD Wgn	6986	8317	9703
4 Dr S AWD Wgn	7655	9113	10631

Options	Price
AM/FM/CD Audio System	+162
AM/FM/Cassette/CD Audio System	+162
Aluminum/Alloy Wheels [Std on S]	+229

Body Styles	TMV Pricing		
	Trade	Private	Dealer
4 Dr STD AWD Wgn	6979	8309	9694

Options	Price
Automatic 4-Speed Transmission	+308
Compact Disc Changer	+265
Leather Seats	+422

1998

Subaru attacks the mini-SUV market head-on with the Forester, which actually constitutes an SUV body on an Impreza platform with a Legacy engine under the hood. The most carlike of the mini-utes, Forester is also the most powerful. Airbags remain the full power variety, despite new rules allowing lower deployment speeds.

Mileage Category: L

Body Styles	TMV Pricing		
	Trade	Private	Dealer
4 Dr L AWD Wgn	6186	7364	8692
4 Dr S AWD Wgn	6561	7810	9219

Options	Price
AM/FM/CD Audio System	+138
Aluminum/Alloy Wheels [Std on S]	+195
Automatic 4-Speed Transmission	+262

Body Styles	TMV Pricing		
	Trade	Private	Dealer
4 Dr STD AWD Wgn	6064	7218	8520

Options	Price
Compact Disc Changer	+226
Leather Seats	+359

Impreza

Impreza

2004

Body Styles	TMV Pricing		
	Trade	Private	Dealer
4 Dr Outback Sport AWD Wgn	13555	14685	16568
4 Dr RS AWD Sdn	13604	14769	16711
4 Dr TS AWD Wgn	12236	13333	15160

Body Styles	TMV Pricing		
	Trade	Private	Dealer
4 Dr WRX Turbo AWD Sdn	17171	18527	20788
4 Dr WRX Turbo AWD Wgn	16827	18183	20444

Options	Price
Aluminum/Alloy Wheels [Opt on TS]	+540
Automatic 4-Speed Transmission	+800
Automatic Dimming Rearview Mirror [Opt on Outback, WRX]	+183
Compact Disc Changer [Opt on Outback, RS, TS]	+520
Fog Lights [Opt on RS, TS]	+299
Heated Front Seats [Opt on WRX Sdn]	+250

Options	Price
Power Heated Mirrors [Opt on WRX Sdn]	+150
Power Moonroof [Opt on WRX Sdn]	+800
Premium Audio System	+267
Rear Spoiler	+300
Trailer Hitch [Opt on Outback, TS]	+295

For 2004, all Imprezas sport revised front and rear fascias -- gone are the oddball circular headlamps in favor of a more mainstream wedge-shaped design. In addition, all models get upgraded suspension struts (to improve ride quality and steering response), Electronic Brakeforce Distribution, a collapsible pedal system, revised gauges and a new stereo faceplate. The WRX and Outback Sport receive projector beam foglights. Inside, WRX models have new sport seats, a central tachometer and darker gray faux metal accents. The TS wagon, Outback Sport and RS sedan add an in-glass antenna, active front head restraints, central power door lock switch and multireflector halogen headlights. Further, the TS now has four-wheel disc brakes. The RS sedan's keyless entry system now has an audible confirmation feature, and keyless entry is now standard on the TS. Finally, the WRX sedan is now available with a Premium Package that includes a sunroof, trunk spoiler, heated mirrors, heated front seats and a wiper de-icer.

2003

Body Styles	TMV Pricing		
	Trade	Private	Dealer
4 Dr Outback Sport AWD Wgn	12012	13159	15070
4 Dr RS AWD Sdn	12144	13303	15235
4 Dr TS AWD Wgn	10868	11906	13635

Body Styles	TMV Pricing		
	Trade	Private	Dealer
4 Dr WRX Turbo AWD Sdn	15422	16891	19339
4 Dr WRX Turbo AWD Wgn	14617	16009	18328

Options	Price
Alarm System	+138
Aluminum/Alloy Wheels [Opt on TS]	+373
Automatic 4-Speed Transmission	+553
Automatic Dimming Rearview Mirror [Opt on Outback, WRX]	+127
Compact Disc Changer [Opt on Outback, RS, TS]	+311
Fog Lights [Opt on RS, TS]	+207

Options	Price
Keyless Entry System [Opt on TS]	+124
Performance/Handling Package [Opt on WRX]	+554
Premium Audio System	+185
Rear Spoiler	+248
Trailer Hitch [Opt on Outback, TS]	+204

As the Impreza was redesigned just last year, not much changes for 2003. Convenience has been improved; keyless entry is now standard equipment on the 2.5 RS, TS Sport Wagon and Outback Sport. For the WRX, Subaru will offer a standard rear spoiler on the sedan (though you can still get the car without, if you want) and Sonic Yellow is available as an exclusive WRX color.

2002

Body Styles	TMV Pricing		
	Trade	Private	Dealer
4 Dr Outback Sport AWD Wgn	10871	11934	13705
4 Dr RS AWD Sdn	11040	12120	13920
4 Dr TS AWD Wgn	9731	10682	12268

Body Styles	TMV Pricing		
	Trade	Private	Dealer
4 Dr WRX Turbo AWD Sdn	14457	15832	18124
4 Dr WRX Turbo AWD Wgn	13132	14381	16462

Options	Price
Aluminum/Alloy Wheels [Opt on TS]	+322
Automatic 4-Speed Transmission	+490
Fog Lights [Std on Outback Sport, WRX]	+183
Premium Audio System	+164

Options	Price
Rear Spoiler [Opt on Sdn]	+215
Rear Wind Deflector [Opt on Wgn]	+174
Trailer Hitch [Opt on Wgn]	+181

Subaru completely redesigns the Impreza and brings a high-performance turbocharged WRX variant into the fold to offer enthusiasts the opportunity to drive a powerful, all-wheel-drive sport sedan without breaking the bank. All Imprezas benefit from improvements in performance, refinement and safety. Along with the Impreza's trip upmarket come revised trim levels consisting of two sedans (WRX and 2.5 RS) and three wagons (WRX, Outback Sport and 2.5 TS Sport Wagon). The coupe body style has been dropped.

Impreza

2001

RS models get carbon-fiber patterned interior trim, a CD player and embroidered floor mats.

Mileage Category: B

Body Styles	TMV Pricing		
	Trade	Private	Dealer
2 Dr L AWD Cpe	7841	9381	10802
2 Dr RS AWD Cpe	9483	11345	13064
4 Dr L AWD Sdn	8036	9613	11069

Body Styles	TMV Pricing		
	Trade	Private	Dealer
4 Dr L AWD Wgn	8250	9869	11363
4 Dr Outback Sport AWD Wgn	8939	10693	12313
4 Dr RS AWD Sdn	9246	11060	12735

Options	Price
AM/FM/CD Audio System	+187
Aluminum/Alloy Wheels [Opt on L]	+294
Automatic 4-Speed Transmission	+447
Fog Lights [Opt on L]	+133

Options	Price
Keyless Entry System	+125
Leather Seats	+724
Luggage Rack	+134
Premium Audio System	+458

2000

For 2000, Subaru introduces the new Impreza 2.5 RS Sedan, a cross between an aggressive driver's car and a sedan. More standard equipment comes on the 2.5 Coupe and Sedan while the L model remains unchanged. The Outback Sport receives some exterior design changes. All Impreza models now come with 24-hour roadside assistance.

Mileage Category: B

Body Styles	TMV Pricing		
	Trade	Private	Dealer
2 Dr L AWD Cpe	5830	7178	8499
2 Dr RS AWD Cpe	7001	8620	10206
4 Dr L AWD Sdn	5814	7159	8477

Body Styles	TMV Pricing		
	Trade	Private	Dealer
4 Dr L AWD Wgn	6202	7636	9042
4 Dr Outback Sport AWD Wgn	6461	7955	9420
4 Dr RS AWD Sdn	7560	9309	11024

Options	Price
AM/FM/CD Audio System	+206
AM/FM/Cassette/CD Audio System	+206
Aluminum/Alloy Wheels [Opt on L,Outback]	+270

Options	Price
Automatic 4-Speed Transmission	+393
Luggage Rack	+117
Rear Spoiler [Std on RS,Cpe]	+172

1999

More horsepower, more torque and a more efficient automatic transmission are the big news this year. Multireflector halogen headlights are new and Outback Sport gets a revised grille. The 2.5 RS gets silver alloy wheels, a new front bumper, white gauge faces and more torque, as well as an upgraded leather-wrapped steering wheel and shift knob. Two new colors are available for 1999.

Mileage Category: B

Body Styles	TMV Pricing		
	Trade	Private	Dealer
2 Dr L AWD Cpe	4433	5617	6850
2 Dr RS AWD Cpe	5508	6978	8509
4 Dr L AWD Sdn	4806	6089	7424

Body Styles	TMV Pricing		
	Trade	Private	Dealer
4 Dr L AWD Wgn	5071	6425	7834
4 Dr Outback Sport AWD Wgn	5138	6510	7939

Options	Price
AM/FM/CD Audio System	+162
Aluminum/Alloy Wheels [Std on RS]	+225

Options	Price
Automatic 4-Speed Transmission	+308
Rear Spoiler [Opt on Sdn]	+135

1998

Impreza gets a new dashboard and revised door panels. The entry-level Brighton coupe is dropped, and the high-end 2.5RS coupe is added. No depowered airbags here.

Mileage Category: B

Body Styles	TMV Pricing		
	Trade	Private	Dealer
2 Dr L AWD Cpe	3465	4638	5960
2 Dr RS AWD Cpe	4280	5728	7360
4 Dr L AWD Sdn	3607	4828	6204

Body Styles	TMV Pricing		
	Trade	Private	Dealer
4 Dr L AWD Wgn	3666	4907	6306
4 Dr Outback Sport AWD Wgn	4217	5644	7253

Options	Price
AM/FM/CD Audio System	+138
Aluminum/Alloy Wheels [Std on RS]	+192
Automatic 4-Speed Transmission	+262

Options	Price
Leather Seats	+377
Rear Spoiler [Opt on Sdn]	+115

1997

Imprezas receive a facelifted front end that includes a Hemi-size hood scoop. A new Outback Sport Wagon debuts, with over six inches of ground clearance, foglights and a slightly raised roof. LX model disappears, which means only the Outback is equipped with ABS. Power and torque for both Impreza engines are up for 1997, and some new colors are available. HVAC controls are revised.

Mileage Category: B

Body Styles	TMV Pricing		
	Trade	Private	Dealer
2 Dr Brighton AWD Cpe	2013	2856	3886
2 Dr L AWD Cpe	2511	3563	4849
4 Dr L AWD Sdn	2607	3699	5033

Body Styles	TMV Pricing		
	Trade	Private	Dealer
4 Dr L AWD Wgn	2662	3777	5140
4 Dr Outback Sport AWD Wgn	3046	4322	5882

Options	Price
Aluminum/Alloy Wheels	+150

Options	Price
Automatic 4-Speed Transmission	+180

1996

The formerly optional 2.2-liter engine is standard across the board, except in the new budget-minded Brighton AWD Coupe. A new grille accompanies the bigger engine, and a five-speed is available as well.

Mileage Category: B

Body Styles	TMV Pricing		
	Trade	Private	Dealer
2 Dr Brighton AWD Cpe	1389	2111	3109

Body Styles	TMV Pricing		
	Trade	Private	Dealer
2 Dr L AWD Cpe	1721	2618	3856

Body Styles	TMV Pricing		
	Trade	Private	Dealer
2 Dr LX AWD Cpe	2097	3189	4696
4 Dr L AWD Sdn	1771	2692	3965
4 Dr L AWD Wgn	1786	2715	3998

Options	Price
Aluminum/Alloy Wheels [Std on LX AWD Cpe]	+134
Antilock Brakes [Opt on L]	+173
Automatic 4-Speed Transmission [Opt on L ,Outback,Cpe]	+184

Body Styles	TMV Pricing		
	Trade	Private	Dealer
4 Dr LX AWD Sdn	2123	3227	4752
4 Dr LX AWD Wgn	2219	3374	4969
4 Dr Outback AWD Wgn	2098	3190	4697

Options	Price
Compact Disc Changer	+126

1995

An Impreza coupe and an Outback wagon are added to Subaru's subcompact line of cars in an attempt to broaden their appeal with sporting and outdoor enthusiasts. Top-of-the-line LX model is introduced, replacing the LS trim level, with a 2.2-liter engine taken from the Legacy. Unfortunately it is available only with an automatic transmission.

Mileage Category: B

Body Styles	TMV Pricing		
	Trade	Private	Dealer
2 Dr L AWD Cpe	1356	2154	3483
2 Dr L Cpe	1168	1854	2998
2 Dr LX AWD Cpe	1594	2531	4092
2 Dr STD Cpe	1012	1608	2602
4 Dr L AWD Sdn	1356	2154	3483
4 Dr L AWD Wgn	1365	2169	3509
4 Dr L Sdn	1168	1854	2998
4 Dr L Special Edition AWD Sdn	1378	2188	3539

Options	Price
AM/FM/CD Audio System	+79
Air Conditioning [Opt on L AWD Cpe,STD]	+151
Aluminum/Alloy Wheels [Std on LX AWD Sdn]	+111

Body Styles	TMV Pricing		
	Trade	Private	Dealer
4 Dr L Special Edition Sdn	1219	1935	3129
4 Dr L Special Editition AWD Wgn	1396	2217	3584
4 Dr LX AWD Sdn	1583	2514	4065
4 Dr LX AWD Wgn	1675	2660	4302
4 Dr Outback AWD Wgn	1565	2485	4018
4 Dr Outback Special Edition AWD Wgn	1396	2217	3584
4 Dr STD Sdn	1012	1608	2602

Options	Price
Antilock Brakes [Opt on L]	+143
Automatic 4-Speed Transmission [Std on L Spec Edition,LX]	+168

Impreza WRX STi
2004

Mileage Category: E

Body Styles	TMV Pricing		
	Trade	Private	Dealer
4 Dr Turbo AWD Sdn	23446	24841	27167

Options	Price
Automatic Dimming Rearview Mirror	+183

The WRX STi is an all-new ultrahigh-performance version of the WRX. With its larger engine, driver-controlled all-wheel-drive system and track-ready suspension, it represents the ultimate in affordable all-wheel-drive performance.

Legacy
2004

Mileage Category: D

Body Styles	TMV Pricing		
	Trade	Private	Dealer
4 Dr GT AWD Sdn	17033	18132	19963
4 Dr GT AWD Wgn	17619	18717	20547
4 Dr L 35th Anniv Edition AWD Sdn	13790	14864	16654

Options	Price
Alarm System	+190
Aluminum/Alloy Wheels [Opt on L]	+540
Automatic 4-Speed Transmission	+800
Automatic Dimming Rearview Mirror	+186

Body Styles	TMV Pricing		
	Trade	Private	Dealer
4 Dr L 35th Anniv Edition AWD Wgn	14505	15579	17369
4 Dr L AWD Sdn	13270	14344	16134
4 Dr L AWD Wgn	13724	14798	16588

Options	Price
Compact Disc Changer [Opt on L, L SE]	+525
Premium Audio System [Opt on L, L SE]	+267
Rear Spoiler	+299

Subaru celebrates its 35 years of U.S. sales by offering a 35th anniversary special edition of the Legacy L sedan and wagon. Included are all the usual features found on L models, along with the addition of a 35th anniversary logo on the front fenders, 16-inch alloy wheels, a six-way power driver seat, leather-wrapped steering wheel, a sunroof and embroidered floor mats. In other news, all Legacys get new red burl interior trim, while ebony-patterned interior trim is available on GT models.

Subaru
Legacy

2003

For 2003, Subaru has added standard equipment and slightly altered available trim levels. The previous Legacy GT and GT Limited models have been consolidated into one 2.5 GT series, with all GT Limited equipment now standard. The new 2.5 GT's optional four-speed automatic now comes with a Sportshift manual mode. To fill the void created by the GT consolidation, Subaru has created an L Special Edition Package that adds several features from the 2.5 GT. Base L models now come with a standard CD player and keyless entry. 2.5 GTs have an upgraded sound system with an in-dash six-disc CD changer. Finally, all Legacys receive slightly freshened front-end styling.

Mileage Category: D

Body Styles	TMV Pricing		
	Trade	Private	Dealer
4 Dr 2.5 GT AWD Sdn	13276	14557	16691
4 Dr 2.5 GT AWD Wgn	13814	15146	17367
4 Dr L AWD Sdn	11170	12247	14043

Options	Price
Alarm System	+131
Aluminum/Alloy Wheels [Opt on L]	+363
Automatic 4-Speed Transmission	+553
Automatic Dimming Rearview Mirror	+127

Body Styles	TMV Pricing		
	Trade	Private	Dealer
4 Dr L AWD Wgn	11530	12642	14496
4 Dr L Special Edition AWD Sdn	11381	12479	14309
4 Dr L Special Edition AWD Wgn	11626	12748	14617

Options	Price
Compact Disc Changer [Opt on L,L SE]	+311
Premium Audio System [Opt on L,L SE]	+185
Rear Spoiler	+204

2002

Only minor changes are in store for Subaru's midsize Legacy sedan and wagon. GT Limiteds receive a standard All-Weather Package that includes heated front seats, heated outside mirrors and a windshield wiper de-icer. GT models now have larger front brakes, a new ignition switch illumination ring, standard floor mats and wood grain-patterned door switch trim. Other upgrades for all Legacys include a dome light off-delay and an internal trunk release (sedans only).

Mileage Category: D

Body Styles	TMV Pricing		
	Trade	Private	Dealer
4 Dr GT AWD Sdn	11490	12649	14581
4 Dr GT AWD Wgn	11975	13183	15195
4 Dr GT Limited AWD Sdn	12447	13702	15794

Options	Price
AM/FM/CD Audio System [Opt on GT,L]	+221
Aluminum/Alloy Wheels [Opt on L]	+322
Automatic 4-Speed Transmission	+490
Compact Disc Changer [Opt on GT,GT Limited]	+306

Body Styles	TMV Pricing		
	Trade	Private	Dealer
4 Dr L AWD Sdn	9522	10482	12083
4 Dr L AWD Wgn	9885	10882	12544

Options	Price
Fog Lights [Opt on L]	+159
Premium Audio System	+165
Rear Spoiler	+181

2001

The Brighton model is stricken from the Legacy lineup. All 2001 Legacys comply with low-emission vehicle (LEV) standards and come with standard 24-hour roadside assistance. Legacy L models now include an ambient temperature gauge, a dual-mode digital trip odometer and a fixed intermittent rear wiper with washer on the wagons. GT models feature a power moonroof, six-way power driver seat, limited-slip rear differential and multireflector halogen foglights.

Mileage Category: D

Body Styles	TMV Pricing		
	Trade	Private	Dealer
4 Dr GT AWD Sdn	9709	11214	12604
4 Dr GT AWD Wgn	10254	11845	13313
4 Dr GT Limited AWD Sdn	10675	12330	13857

Options	Price
AM/FM/CD Audio System	+235
Aluminum/Alloy Wheels [Opt on Brighton,L]	+294
Automatic 4-Speed Transmission	+447
Compact Disc Changer	+278

Body Styles	TMV Pricing		
	Trade	Private	Dealer
4 Dr L AWD Sdn	8189	9458	10630
4 Dr L AWD Wgn	8494	9810	11025

Options	Price
Fog Lights [Opt on Brighton,L]	+145
Premium Audio System	+559
Rear Spoiler	+165

2000

Subaru's Legacy is completely redesigned for the new millennium.

Mileage Category: D

Body Styles	TMV Pricing		
	Trade	Private	Dealer
4 Dr Brighton AWD Wgn	6611	7910	9184
4 Dr GT AWD Sdn	8058	9642	11194
4 Dr GT AWD Wgn	8368	10013	11625

Options	Price
AM/FM/CD Audio System	+206
AM/FM/Cassette/CD Audio System [Opt on L Wgn]	+206
Aluminum/Alloy Wheels [Opt on Brighton,L]	+292
Automatic 4-Speed Transmission	+393
Compact Disc Changer	+244

Body Styles	TMV Pricing		
	Trade	Private	Dealer
4 Dr GT Limited AWD Sdn	8612	10305	11964
4 Dr L AWD Sdn	6785	8119	9427
4 Dr L AWD Wgn	6934	8298	9634

Options	Price
Fog Lights [Opt on Brighton,L]	+137
Leather Seats [Std on GT Limited]	+455
Luggage Rack [Opt on Wgn]	+136
Power Moonroof [Opt on L]	+443
Rear Spoiler [Opt on GT Sdn,L Sdn]	+145

1999

Mileage Category: D

Body Styles	TMV Pricing		
	Trade	Private	Dealer
4 Dr 30th Anniv AWD Sdn	6654	8170	9747
4 Dr Brighton AWD Wgn	4900	6015	7176
4 Dr GT AWD Sdn	6293	7726	9218
4 Dr GT AWD Wgn	6707	8234	9823
4 Dr GT Limited 30th Anniv AWD Sdn	6742	8277	9875

Body Styles	TMV Pricing		
	Trade	Private	Dealer
4 Dr L AWD Sdn	5357	6576	7845
4 Dr L AWD Wgn	5709	7009	8362
4 Dr Limited 30th Anniv AWD Sdn	7477	9179	10951
4 Dr Outback AWD Wgn	6156	7558	9017
4 Dr Outback Limited 30th Anniv AWD Wgn	7074	8685	10361

Options	Price
AM/FM/CD Audio System [Std on GT Limited 30th,Outback Limited 30th,SUS]	+162
AM/FM/Cassette/CD Audio System [Opt on Outback]	+162
Aluminum/Alloy Wheels [Opt on Brighton,L]	+229
Automatic 4-Speed Transmission	+308

Options	Price
Compact Disc Changer	+191
Dual Power Moonroofs [Opt on Outback 30th]	+347
Leather Seats [Opt on 30th Anniversary,GT,Outback]	+433
Power Moonroof [Opt on L]	+347

Subaru celebrates 30 years of selling cars in the United States by adding special editions to the Legacy lineup. The L sedan and wagon are available with a package of goodies that includes power moonroof, alloy wheels, rear spoiler or roof rack, body-color trim, power antenna and seat height adjuster. New colors include Sandstone Metallic and Winestone Pearl. The 2.5GT Limited is newly available with a manual transmission, while all 2.5GT, Limited and Outback models receive standard remote keyless entry.

1998

Mileage Category: D

Body Styles	TMV Pricing		
	Trade	Private	Dealer
4 Dr Brighton AWD Wgn	3551	4513	5598
4 Dr GT AWD Sdn	4822	6129	7603
4 Dr GT AWD Wgn	4850	6165	7647
4 Dr GT Limited AWD Sdn	5493	6981	8660

Body Styles	TMV Pricing		
	Trade	Private	Dealer
4 Dr L AWD Sdn	4179	5312	6589
4 Dr L AWD Wgn	4215	5357	6645
4 Dr Outback AWD Wgn	4658	5920	7343
4 Dr Outback Limited AWD Wgn	5435	6908	8569

Options	Price
AM/FM/CD Audio System [Std on Limited]	+138
AM/FM/Cassette/CD Audio System	+138
Aluminum/Alloy Wheels [Opt on Brighton,L]	+195
Automatic 4-Speed Transmission [Std on GT Limited]	+262

Options	Price
Compact Disc Changer	+163
Dual Power Moonroofs [Opt on Outback 30th]	+295
Leather Seats [Opt on GT,Outback]	+369
Spoke Wheels	+209

Prices remain stable while equipment is shuffled and the LSi model is dropped. All Legacy sedans and wagons, except the Outback, sport the grille and multireflector halogen lights found on the 2.5GT. A new Limited model joins the 2.5GT lineup, and a dual power moonroof package is available for the Outback Limited wagon. Outbacks get new alloy wheels, an overhead console and longer splash guards, while midyear Outback Limiteds with revised trim and added content were dubbed 30th Anniversary models. The cold weather package has heated windshield wiper nozzles this year instead of an engine block heater. The Brighton wagon's stereo loses half its wattage, Limited models have a standard CD player and the base Outback comes with a weatherband radio. Full power airbags continue, despite new government rules allowing automakers to install reduced force bags to better protect small adults.

1997

Mileage Category: D

Body Styles	TMV Pricing		
	Trade	Private	Dealer
4 Dr Brighton AWD Wgn	2589	3391	4371
4 Dr GT AWD Sdn	4055	5311	6845
4 Dr GT AWD Wgn	4160	5448	7022
4 Dr L AWD Sdn	3249	4255	5484
4 Dr L AWD Wgn	3467	4540	5851

Body Styles	TMV Pricing		
	Trade	Private	Dealer
4 Dr LSi AWD Sdn	4432	5804	7481
4 Dr LSi AWD Wgn	4692	6144	7919
4 Dr Outback AWD Sdn	4095	5363	6913
4 Dr Outback AWD Wgn	3995	5232	6743
4 Dr Outback Limited AWD Wgn	4370	5723	7377

Options	Price
Aluminum/Alloy Wheels [Opt on Brighton,L]	+153
Automatic 4-Speed Transmission [Std on LSi]	+206
Compact Disc Changer [Std on LSi]	+128

Options	Price
Leather Seats	+290
Spoke Wheels	+153

Front-wheel-drive models are given the ax as Subaru returns to its all-wheel drive roots. Power and torque are up marginally with the base 2.2-liter engine. The 2.5-liter motor (also stronger this year and now available with a manual transmission) is now the only engine mated to the Outback. L models gain cruise control, antilock brakes and power door locks as standard equipment. GTs get a manual transmission, larger tires and revised styling. The Outback lineup is expanded with the introduction of a Limited model, which includes a leather interior, new alloy wheels, fresh exterior colors and wood grain interior trim.

1996

Mileage Category: D

Body Styles	TMV Pricing		
	Trade	Private	Dealer
4 Dr Brighton AWD Wgn	2001	2733	3743
4 Dr GT AWD Sdn	3371	4603	6305
4 Dr GT AWD Wgn	3508	4791	6562
4 Dr L AWD Sdn	2482	3389	4641
4 Dr L AWD Wgn	2781	3798	5202
4 Dr L Sdn	2374	3242	4441

Body Styles	TMV Pricing		
	Trade	Private	Dealer
4 Dr L Wgn	2467	3369	4615
4 Dr LS AWD Sdn	3336	4556	6241
4 Dr LS AWD Wgn	3488	4764	6525
4 Dr LSi AWD Sdn	3581	4890	6698
4 Dr LSi AWD Wgn	3915	5347	7324
4 Dr Outback AWD Wgn	3300	4507	6173

Options	Price
2.5L H4 DOHC 16V FI Engine [Std on GT,LSi]	+166
AM/FM/Cassette/CD Audio System	+128
Aluminum/Alloy Wheels [Opt on L]	+134

Options	Price
Antilock Brakes [Opt on L]	+173
Automatic 4-Speed Transmission [Std on GT,LS,LSi]	+115

A new sport model debuts, with a larger, more powerful engine. The 2.5GT is available in sedan or wagon format. The luxury-oriented LSi model also gets the new motor. A knobby-tired, raised-roof Outback wagon appears, offering 7.3 inches of ground clearance and an optional 2.5-liter engine. Designed specifically for American consumers, the Outback provides a carlike ride with light-duty off-road ability.

Subaru
Legacy/Outback

1995

New sheet metal freshens the flanks of one of our favorite compact sedans and wagons. Unfortunately the turbocharged engine has been dropped, leaving the Legacy with a rather anemic 2.2-liter four-cylinder that produces a meager 135 horsepower. The value leader Brighton wagon is introduced for budding naturalists. It includes all-wheel drive, air conditioning and a stereo with cassette. The Outback Wagon is also introduced as an alternative to the burgeoning SUV market.

Mileage Category: D

Body Styles	TMV Pricing		
	Trade	Private	Dealer
4 Dr Brighton AWD Wgn	1543	2210	3321
4 Dr L AWD Sdn	1733	2481	3728
4 Dr L AWD Wgn	1998	2861	4298
4 Dr L Sdn	1566	2242	3368
4 Dr L Wgn	1669	2389	3589
4 Dr LS AWD Sdn	2175	3114	4678

Options	Price
AM/FM/CD Audio System	+79
AM/FM/Cassette/CD Audio System [Opt on L,LSi]	+79
Air Conditioning [Opt on STD]	+151
Aluminum/Alloy Wheels [Opt on Brighton,L,LSi]	+111
Antilock Brakes [Opt on L]	+143

Body Styles	TMV Pricing		
	Trade	Private	Dealer
4 Dr LS AWD Wgn	2299	3291	4944
4 Dr LSi AWD Sdn	2449	3507	5270
4 Dr LSi AWD Wgn	2541	3638	5466
4 Dr Outback AWD Wgn	2018	2889	4340
4 Dr STD Sdn	1391	1991	2992

Options	Price
Automatic 4-Speed Transmission [Std on LS,LSi]	+151
Compact Disc Changer	+94
Leather Seats	+213
Power Moonroof [Opt on L]	+170

Outback

2004

Subaru commemorates 35 years of selling cars in the U.S. by offering a 35th anniversary special edition of the Outback H6-3.0 wagon, though this amounts to little more than a new alloy wheel design and a fender-mounted badge. Red Burl interior trim is new for the Outback this year, and six-cylinder models get restyled 16-inch wheels. L.L. Bean and Limited models get a new brown leather covering on the shifter handle, brake handle and steering wheel.

Mileage Category: D

Body Styles	TMV Pricing		
	Trade	Private	Dealer
4 Dr H6-3.0 35th Anniv Edition AWD Wgn	18198	19568	21853
4 Dr H6-3.0 AWD Sdn	19028	20378	22628
4 Dr H6-3.0 L.L. Bean Edition AWD Wgn	20895	22305	24655
4 Dr H6-3.0 VDC AWD Sdn	20980	22365	24672

Options	Price
Alarm System [Opt on STD, Limited Wgn]	+225
Automatic 4-Speed Transmission [Opt on STD, Limited Wgn]	+800
Automatic Dimming Rearview Mirror [Std on L.L. Bean]	+151

Body Styles	TMV Pricing		
	Trade	Private	Dealer
4 Dr H6-3.0 VDC AWD Wgn	21764	23134	25419
4 Dr Limited AWD Sdn	16987	18163	20123
4 Dr Limited AWD Wgn	17176	18350	20308
4 Dr STD AWD Wgn	14959	16034	17826

Options	Price
Rear Spoiler	+329
Trailer Hitch [Opt on Wgn]	+295

2003

Only minor changes have been made to the 2003 Subaru Outback. All models have freshened front-end styling and revised front struts. The struts feature internal rebound springs that are said to reduce body roll when cornering, as well as brake dive. In terms of features, the four-cylinder powered Outbacks gain the formerly optional All-Weather Package as standard equipment. The base Outback now has a standard CD player, and Outback Limiteds have an upgraded audio system with an in-dash six-disc CD changer. All six-cylinder Outbacks now have the OnStar communications system. Finally, the Outback H-6 3.0 VDC's premium McIntosh audio system has been fitted with an in-dash six-disc CD changer.

Mileage Category: D

Body Styles	TMV Pricing		
	Trade	Private	Dealer
4 Dr H6-3.0 AWD Sdn	16399	17624	19666
4 Dr H6-3.0 AWD Wgn	15807	16988	18956
4 Dr LL Bean AWD Wgn	17687	19008	21210
4 Dr Limited AWD Sdn	15302	16445	18350

Options	Price
Alarm System [Opt on H6,Limited,STD]	+131
Automatic 4-Speed Transmission [Opt on Limited,STD]	+346
Automatic Dimming Rearview Mirror	+127
Compact Disc Changer [Opt on H6,STD]	+311

Body Styles	TMV Pricing		
	Trade	Private	Dealer
4 Dr Limited AWD Wgn	15473	16629	18555
4 Dr STD AWD Wgn	13423	14425	16095
4 Dr VDC AWD Sdn	17809	19139	21356
4 Dr VDC AWD Wgn	18726	20124	22455

Options	Price
Premium Audio System [Opt on H6,STD]	+185
Rear Spoiler	+225
Trailer Hitch	+204

2002

Subaru has expanded the availability of its new 3.0-liter six-cylinder engine to the Outback sedan. The result is two additional sedan trim levels: 3.0-H6 and 3.0-H6 VDC. Minor upgrades to all trim levels this year include a dome light off-delay, an ignition switch illumination ring and wood grain-patterned door switch trim. Cars with the Vehicle Dynamics Control system now have a button to turn the system off, and sedans receive an internal trunk release. The automatic climate control system is upgraded with an air filtration system.

Mileage Category: D

Body Styles	TMV Pricing		
	Trade	Private	Dealer
4 Dr H6-3.0 AWD Sdn	14371	15471	17305
4 Dr L.L. Bean Edition AWD Wgn	15587	16781	18770
4 Dr Limited AWD Sdn	13621	14664	16401
4 Dr Limited AWD Wgn	13775	14830	16588

Options	Price
AM/FM/CD Audio System [Opt on STD]	+215

Body Styles	TMV Pricing		
	Trade	Private	Dealer
4 Dr STD AWD Wgn	11649	12542	14029
4 Dr VDC AWD Sdn	15665	16864	18863
4 Dr VDC AWD Wgn	16500	17763	19869

Options	Price
Automatic 4-Speed Transmission [Opt on STD,Limited Wgn]	+490

Options	Price
Compact Disc Changer	+306
Heated Front Seats [Opt on STD]	+184
Power Heated Mirrors [Opt on STD]	+123

Options	Price
Premium Audio System [Std on H6,LL Bean]	+169
Rear Spoiler	+199
Trailer Hitch	+181

2001

Two new models, the H6-3.0 L.L. Bean Edition and the H6-3.0 VDC, both featuring a more powerful 3.0-liter engine, join the happy Outback family. Braking is upgraded this year via larger front rotors with twin piston calipers.

Mileage Category: D

Body Styles	TMV Pricing		
	Trade	Private	Dealer
4 Dr L.L. Bean Edition AWD Wgn	13203	14899	16465
4 Dr Limited AWD Sdn	11691	13193	14580
4 Dr Limited AWD Wgn	11826	13345	14747

Body Styles	TMV Pricing		
	Trade	Private	Dealer
4 Dr STD AWD Wgn	9803	11062	12224
4 Dr VDC AWD Wgn	13927	15716	17367

Options	Price
AM/FM/CD Audio System [Opt on STD Wgn]	+202
Automatic 4-Speed Transmission [Opt on Wgn]	+447
Compact Disc Changer	+291
Heated Front Seats	+140

Options	Price
Premium Audio System	+559
Rear Spoiler	+165
Trailer Hitch	+165

2000

As with the Legacy platform it's based on, Subaru's hot-selling Outback is completely redesigned for the millennium.

Mileage Category: D

Body Styles	TMV Pricing		
	Trade	Private	Dealer
4 Dr Limited AWD Sdn	8943	10549	12124
4 Dr Limited AWD Wgn	9178	10827	12443

Body Styles	TMV Pricing		
	Trade	Private	Dealer
4 Dr STD AWD Wgn	7945	9372	10770

Options	Price
AM/FM/CD Audio System [Opt on STD Wgn]	+206
AM/FM/Cassette/CD Audio System	+206
Automatic 4-Speed Transmission [Opt on Wgn]	+393

Options	Price
Compact Disc Changer	+244
Heated Front Seats	+123
Trailer Hitch	+145

SVX
1997

Mileage Category: E

Body Styles	TMV Pricing		
	Trade	Private	Dealer
2 Dr L AWD Cpe	3662	4780	6147

Body Styles	TMV Pricing		
	Trade	Private	Dealer
2 Dr LSi AWD Cpe	4278	5584	7180

Options	Price
AM/FM/CD Audio System	+167

A body-color grille debuts, along with P215/55VR16 tires.

1996

The L model gets standard solar-reduction glass this year.

Mileage Category: E

Body Styles	TMV Pricing		
	Trade	Private	Dealer
2 Dr L AWD Cpe	2953	3991	5425

Body Styles	TMV Pricing		
	Trade	Private	Dealer
2 Dr LSi AWD Cpe	3393	4585	6230

Options	Price
AM/FM/CD Audio System	+149

1995

Dual airbags are extended to the base model.

Mileage Category: E

Body Styles	TMV Pricing		
	Trade	Private	Dealer
2 Dr L AWD Cpe	2142	2984	4387
2 Dr L Cpe	1785	2487	3657

Body Styles	TMV Pricing		
	Trade	Private	Dealer
2 Dr LS Cpe	1629	2269	3336
2 Dr LSi AWD Cpe	2678	3730	5484

Options	Price
AM/FM/CD Audio System	+123

Aerio

2004

Mileage Category: B

Body Styles	TMV Pricing			Body Styles	TMV Pricing		
	Trade	Private	Dealer		Trade	Private	Dealer
4 Dr LX AWD Sdn	9297	10173	11632	4 Dr SX AWD Wgn	9457	10333	11792
4 Dr LX Sdn	8335	9211	10670	4 Dr SX Wgn	8494	9370	10829
4 Dr S Sdn	7426	8302	9761				

Options	Price	Options	Price
Antilock Brakes	+350	Automatic Climate Control [Opt on S Sdn]	+450
Automatic 4-Speed Transmission [Std on AWD]	+800		

A 155-horsepower, 2.3-liter, four-cylinder engine; a seven-speaker stereo; and a driver-seat armrest are now standard on all Aerios. LX sedans (formerly called GS) and SX wagons now offer heated mirrors, foglights, a revised rear spoiler and an automatic climate control system on cars equipped with ABS. There's also a new 15-inch alloy wheel design.

2003

As the Aerio is a recent introduction to the market, there aren't that many changes for 2003. Suzuki has bumped the horsepower up by four to 145 and nudged the torque up one pound-foot to 135. Other additions include integrated cruise control buttons on the steering wheel, a three-point seatbelt and headrest for rear center seat and a new cloth design. The GS and SX models drop the rear-seat armrest, get a six-disc in-dash CD player and have the optional all-wheel-drive available.

Mileage Category: B

Body Styles	TMV Pricing			Body Styles	TMV Pricing		
	Trade	Private	Dealer		Trade	Private	Dealer
4 Dr GS AWD Sdn	7690	8686	10345	4 Dr SX AWD Wgn	7824	8837	10525
4 Dr GS Sdn	6812	7694	9163	4 Dr SX Wgn	6831	7715	9188
4 Dr S Sdn	6187	6988	8322				

Options	Price	Options	Price
Antilock Brakes [Opt on GS,SX]	+390	Automatic 4-Speed Transmission [Opt on S]	+573

2002

The Aerio is Suzuki's new compact car. Available in both sedan and wagon format, the Aerio boasts a powerful engine, distinctive styling and an affordable price.

Mileage Category: B

Body Styles	TMV Pricing			Body Styles	TMV Pricing		
	Trade	Private	Dealer		Trade	Private	Dealer
4 Dr GS Sdn	5511	6277	7553	4 Dr SX Wgn	5511	6277	7553
4 Dr S Sdn	5116	5826	7010				

Options	Price	Options	Price
Antilock Brakes	+307	Automatic 4-Speed Transmission	+452

Esteem

2002

Mileage Category: B

Body Styles	TMV Pricing			Body Styles	TMV Pricing		
	Trade	Private	Dealer		Trade	Private	Dealer
4 Dr GL Sdn	4167	4822	5914	4 Dr GLX Sdn	4500	5207	6385
4 Dr GL Wgn	4334	5015	6150	4 Dr GLX Wgn	4658	5391	6612
4 Dr GLX Plus Wgn	5865	6787	8323				

Options	Price
Automatic 4-Speed Transmission [Std on GLX Plus Wgn]	+452

Not much changes for the 2002 Esteem. The seat upholstery is new, and sedans now have an inside trunk release handle. Suzuki has changed with the trim levels, and last year's GLX+ and GLX Sport sedan trims are no longer available. Suzuki now offers a 24-hour roadside assistance program.

2001

Suzuki has equipped every model with an in-dash CD player. Stereo head units also get larger controls. Elsewhere, you will find gentle cosmetic changes: The front grille has been restyled, the seats are wrapped in a new fabric and floor mats are standard. Sky Blue Metallic is no longer available as an exterior color.

Mileage Category: B

Body Styles	TMV Pricing			Body Styles	TMV Pricing		
	Trade	Private	Dealer		Trade	Private	Dealer
4 Dr GL Sdn	3325	4220	5046	4 Dr GLX Sdn	3464	4396	5256
4 Dr GL Wgn	3352	4254	5086	4 Dr GLX Sport Sdn	4163	5283	6317
4 Dr GLX Plus Sdn	4455	5654	6761	4 Dr GLX Wgn	3560	4518	5403
4 Dr GLX Plus Wgn	4644	5893	7046				

Options	Price
Automatic 4-Speed Transmission	+393

2000

All Esteems get the 1.8-liter engine, starting with the September 1999 production run. GLX and GLX+ models receive 15-inch wheels and tires as standard equipment. Two new paint colors, Bluish Black Pearl and Cassis Red Pearl, replace Mars Red and Midnight Black.

Mileage Category: B

Body Styles	TMV Pricing		
	Trade	Private	Dealer
4 Dr GL Sdn	2195	2940	3670
4 Dr GL Wgn	2381	3191	3985

Options	Price
1.8L I4 DOHC 16V FI Engine [Opt on GL]	+158
Antilock Brakes	+215

Body Styles	TMV Pricing		
	Trade	Private	Dealer
4 Dr GLX Sdn	2480	3321	4146
4 Dr GLX Wgn	2575	3449	4305

Options	Price
Automatic 4-Speed Transmission	+316
Power Moonroof	+206

1999

A restyled front end with multireflector headlights and an overall smoother body distinguishes the 1999 Esteem line from its predecessors. Base GL models come with the 14-inch wheels that were standard on GLX models. Interior surfaces have been upgraded and a Clarion AM/FM cassette is available. An all-new 1.8-liter inline four that makes 122 horsepower.

Mileage Category: B

Body Styles	TMV Pricing		
	Trade	Private	Dealer
4 Dr GL Sdn	1640	2373	3136
4 Dr GL Wgn	1715	2480	3277

Options	Price
1.8L I4 DOHC 16V FI Engine	+122
Antilock Brakes	+184

Body Styles	TMV Pricing		
	Trade	Private	Dealer
4 Dr GLX Sdn	1803	2609	3448
4 Dr GLX Wgn	1876	2714	3586

Options	Price
Automatic 4-Speed Transmission	+244
Power Sunroof	+158

1998

A wagon adds diversity to the Esteem lineup.

Mileage Category: B

Body Styles	TMV Pricing		
	Trade	Private	Dealer
4 Dr GL SE Wgn	1291	2058	2923
4 Dr GL Sdn	1057	1685	2393
4 Dr GL Wgn	1106	1764	2505

Options	Price
Antilock Brakes	+161
Automatic 4-Speed Transmission [Opt on GL, GLX]	+214

Body Styles	TMV Pricing		
	Trade	Private	Dealer
4 Dr GLX SE Wgn	1399	2231	3170
4 Dr GLX Sdn	1165	1858	2639
4 Dr GLX Wgn	1213	1935	2750

Options	Price
Power Sunroof	+139

1997

No changes to the economical Esteem.

Mileage Category: B

Body Styles	TMV Pricing		
	Trade	Private	Dealer
4 Dr GL Sdn	743	1346	2084

Options	Price
Antilock Brakes	+147

Body Styles	TMV Pricing		
	Trade	Private	Dealer
4 Dr GLX Sdn	849	1538	2381

Options	Price
Automatic 4-Speed Transmission	+195

1996

New for 1996 are daytime running lights, standard air conditioning and body-color bumpers on the GL.

Mileage Category: B

Body Styles	TMV Pricing		
	Trade	Private	Dealer
4 Dr GL Sdn	565	1064	1752

Options	Price
Antilock Brakes	+128

Body Styles	TMV Pricing		
	Trade	Private	Dealer
4 Dr GLX Sdn	711	1337	2202

Options	Price
Automatic 4-Speed Transmission	+169

1995

The 1995 Esteem is Suzuki's entry in the subcompact car market. The Esteem has standard dual airbags and is available with antilock brakes but is saddled with a 1.6-liter engine.

Mileage Category: B

Body Styles	TMV Pricing		
	Trade	Private	Dealer
4 Dr GL Sdn	445	817	1438

Options	Price
Air Conditioning	+105
Antilock Brakes	+119

Body Styles	TMV Pricing		
	Trade	Private	Dealer
4 Dr GLX Sdn	532	978	1720

Options	Price
Automatic 4-Speed Transmission	+158

Forenza/Grand Vitara

Forenza

2004

Mileage Category: B

Body Styles	TMV Pricing		
	Trade	Private	Dealer
4 Dr EX Sdn	9440	10350	11866
4 Dr LX Sdn	8557	9467	10983

Options	Price
Antilock Brakes	+500

Body Styles	TMV Pricing		
	Trade	Private	Dealer
4 Dr S Sdn	7507	8417	9933

Options	Price
Automatic 4-Speed Transmission [Opt on S, LX]	+800

The Forenza is an all-new compact economy sedan from Suzuki.

Grand Vitara

2004

Mileage Category: L

Body Styles	TMV Pricing		
	Trade	Private	Dealer
4 Dr EX 4WD SUV	13380	14519	16418
4 Dr EX SUV	12397	13536	15435

Options	Price
Aluminum/Alloy Wheels [Opt on LX]	+500
Antilock Brakes [Opt on LX]	+500

Body Styles	TMV Pricing		
	Trade	Private	Dealer
4 Dr LX 4WD SUV	11646	12785	14684
4 Dr LX SUV	10778	11917	13816

Options	Price
Automatic 4-Speed Transmission [Opt on LX]	+1000
Cruise Control [Opt on LX 2WD]	+300

The Grand Vitara will be offered in LX and EX trims this year. The EX version gets new alloy wheels, a rear spoiler, foglights and a power sunroof. All models get a hard cover for the spare tire, revised taillights, heated sideview mirrors (excluding the 2WD LX model), body-colored door handles and a panic button on the keyless remote.

2003

For 2003, Suzuki has updated the dashboard and console for a higher quality look. Other additions this year include aluminum wheels, a seven-speaker stereo system with a CD player, adjustable center armrest with CD storage, an overhead console with reading lamps and storage compartments and a smaller rear headrest design for better reward visibility. Also of note: the Limited model has been dropped this year and last year's JLS and JLX models have been merged, leaving only one trim level for 2003.

Mileage Category: L

Body Styles	TMV Pricing		
	Trade	Private	Dealer
4 Dr STD 4WD SUV	8960	10050	11867

Options	Price
Aluminum/Alloy Wheels	+287
Antilock Brakes	+390

Body Styles	TMV Pricing		
	Trade	Private	Dealer
4 Dr STD SUV	8796	9866	11649

Options	Price
Automatic 4-Speed Transmission	+573

2002

For 2002, the Grand Vitara's model matrix has been simplified. The JLS (rear-wheel drive) and JLX (four-wheel drive) share most equipment, and the Limited Edition is available with either drive system. Hoping to better match the competition, Suzuki upped the V6's power for 2002, improving acceleration and throttle response. In terms of equipment, all Vitaras get the LATCH child seat system, 4WD vehicles now have heated side mirrors and optional heated seats, and the Limited Edition trim gains a leather-wrapped steering wheel and shift knob. Wrapping things up, Suzuki is now offering 24-hour emergency roadside assistance and towing for the duration of the vehicle's warranty to increase customer satisfaction.

Mileage Category: L

Body Styles	TMV Pricing		
	Trade	Private	Dealer
4 Dr JLS SUV	5741	6534	7856
4 Dr JLX 4WD SUV	6863	7812	9393

Options	Price
Aluminum/Alloy Wheels [Opt on JLS, JLX]	+226
Antilock Brakes [Opt on JLS, JLX]	+307

Body Styles	TMV Pricing		
	Trade	Private	Dealer
4 Dr Limited 4WD SUV	7787	8863	10656
4 Dr Limited SUV	7356	8372	10066

Options	Price
Automatic 4-Speed Transmission [Opt on JLS, JLX]	+452
Heated Front Seats [Opt on Limited 4WD]	+135

2001

Standard Grand Vitaras get redesigned front and rear bumpers and a restyled grille. New interior features include a redesigned AM/FM stereo with an in-dash CD player, adjustable front-seat armrests, redesigned head restraints, child seat-tether hooks and a new seat fabric. Top-of-the-line Grand Vitara Limiteds also get the improved stereo along with a tilt-and-slide power sunroof and new aluminum wheels.

Mileage Category: L

Body Styles	TMV Pricing		
	Trade	Private	Dealer
4 Dr JLS Plus SE 4WD SUV	6537	7900	9158
4 Dr JLS Plus SE SUV	6255	7559	8762
4 Dr JLS Plus SUV	5695	6883	7980
4 Dr JLS SUV	5080	6138	7115

Body Styles	TMV Pricing		
	Trade	Private	Dealer
4 Dr JLX 4WD SUV	5721	6913	8014
4 Dr JLX Plus 4WD SUV	6046	7307	8471
4 Dr Limited 4WD SUV	6669	8059	9343
4 Dr Limited SUV	6294	7606	8818

Options	Price
Automatic 4-Speed Transmission [Std on Limited]	+393

2000

The 2000 Limited Edition Grand Vitara comes with leather seats, privacy glass, foglamps, a hard spare tire cover, an armrest, gold emblems and a special black-and-white paint scheme. The spare tire cover on regular Grand Vitaras features a new design. The '99 model's base trim levels JS and JS+ have been renamed JLS and JLS+. A CD changer is standard equipment on JLS+ and JLX+ models.

Body Styles	TMV Pricing		
	Trade	Private	Dealer
4 Dr JLS SUV	4415	5422	6409
4 Dr JLX 4WD SUV	4724	5802	6858

Options	Price
Antilock Brakes [Opt on JLS,JLX]	+253
Automatic 4-Speed Transmission [Opt on JLS,JLX]	+316

Mileage Category: L

Body Styles	TMV Pricing		
	Trade	Private	Dealer
4 Dr Limited 4WD SUV	5399	6630	7837
4 Dr Limited SUV	5164	6342	7496

Options	Price
Compact Disc Changer [Opt on JLS,JLX]	+174

1999

The Grand Vitara is a completely new design from Suzuki and offers a standard V6 engine.

Body Styles	TMV Pricing		
	Trade	Private	Dealer
4 Dr JLX 4WD SUV	4007	5039	6114

Options	Price
Antilock Brakes	+195

Mileage Category: L

Body Styles	TMV Pricing		
	Trade	Private	Dealer
4 Dr JS SUV	3498	4400	5338

Options	Price
Automatic 4-Speed Transmission	+244

Samurai
1995

Mileage Category: L

Body Styles	TMV Pricing		
	Trade	Private	Dealer
2 Dr JL 4WD Conv	829	1185	1779

Options	Price
Air Conditioning	+102

The Samurai is retired this year with no changes.

Sidekick
1998

Body Styles	TMV Pricing		
	Trade	Private	Dealer
2 Dr JS Conv	1693	2314	3014
2 Dr JX 4WD Conv	2162	2954	3847
2 Dr JX SE 4WD Conv	2355	3218	4192
4 Dr JS SUV	2122	2899	3776
4 Dr JX 4WD SUV	2349	3210	4180

Options	Price
Air Conditioning [Opt on JS,JX]	+164
Antilock Brakes [Std on Sport JLX]	+161

Body Styles	TMV Pricing		
	Trade	Private	Dealer
4 Dr JX FLT 4WD SUV	2727	3727	4854
4 Dr Sport JLX 4WD SUV	2843	3884	5058
4 Dr Sport JS SUV	2364	3230	4207
4 Dr Sport JX 4WD SUV	2499	3415	4447
4 Dr Sport JX SE 4WD SUV	2770	3785	4930

Options	Price
Automatic 3-Speed Transmission	+142
Automatic 4-Speed Transmission	+226

A couple of new colors debut.

1997

A JS Sport 2WD model is added to the Sidekick lineup. It has a DOHC engine that makes 120 horsepower at 6,500 rpm. There are no changes to the rest of the Sidekick line.

Body Styles	TMV Pricing		
	Trade	Private	Dealer
2 Dr JS Conv	1448	2024	2728
2 Dr JX 4WD Conv	1863	2603	3507
4 Dr JS SUV	1808	2525	3401
4 Dr JX 4WD SUV	2053	2868	3864

Options	Price
Air Conditioning [Opt on JS,JX]	+162
Antilock Brakes [Opt on Sport JLX]	+147

Mileage Category: L

Body Styles	TMV Pricing		
	Trade	Private	Dealer
4 Dr Sport JLX 4WD SUV	2494	3484	4695
4 Dr Sport JS SUV	2076	2900	3907
4 Dr Sport JX 4WD SUV	2197	3069	4135

Options	Price
Automatic 3-Speed Transmission	+130
Automatic 4-Speed Transmission	+206

Suzuki
Sidekick/Swift

1996

Lots of changes to this mini SUV: the 16-valve, 95-horsepower engine is available across the board (except in the Sport), and dual airbags are housed in a revised instrument panel. New fabrics, colors and styling revisions update the Sidekick. All new for 1996 is a Sport variant, equipped with lots of exclusive standard equipment, a 120-horsepower twin-cam motor, a wider track, two-tone paint and a chrome grille.

Mileage Category: L

Body Styles	TMV Pricing		
	Trade	Private	Dealer
2 Dr JS Conv	1265	1788	2511
2 Dr JX 4WD Conv	1642	2322	3261
4 Dr JS SUV	1568	2216	3112

Options	Price
Air Conditioning [Opt on JS,JX]	+129
Antilock Brakes [Opt on JS,JX]	+128

Body Styles	TMV Pricing		
	Trade	Private	Dealer
4 Dr JX 4WD SUV	1809	2558	3592
4 Dr Sport JLX 4WD SUV	2155	3047	4278
4 Dr Sport JX 4WD SUV	1918	2712	3808

Options	Price
Automatic 4-Speed Transmission	+179

1995

The convertible model gets a new top.

Mileage Category: L

Body Styles	TMV Pricing		
	Trade	Private	Dealer
2 Dr JS Conv	1077	1540	2312
2 Dr JX 4WD Conv	1267	1812	2719
4 Dr JLX 4WD SUV	1530	2187	3282

Options	Price
Air Conditioning	+120
Automatic 3-Speed Transmission	+105

Body Styles	TMV Pricing		
	Trade	Private	Dealer
4 Dr JS SUV	1270	1816	2725
4 Dr JX 4WD SUV	1515	2166	3251

Options	Price
Automatic 4-Speed Transmission	+166

Swift

2001

Mileage Category: A

Body Styles	TMV Pricing		
	Trade	Private	Dealer
2 Dr GA Hbk	1575	2336	3038

Options	Price
Automatic 3-Speed Transmission	+255

Body Styles	TMV Pricing		
	Trade	Private	Dealer
2 Dr GL Hbk	1769	2623	3411

The 2001 Suzuki Swift remains mechanically unchanged. Suzuki has changed the exterior color options slightly: Bright White and Platinum Silver Metallic replace Polar White and Mercury Silver Metallic.

2000

The 2000 Suzuki Swift remains mechanically unchanged. Two new exterior colors -- Brilliant Blue Metallic and Catseye Blue Metallic -- are offered.

Mileage Category: A

Body Styles	TMV Pricing		
	Trade	Private	Dealer
2 Dr GA Hbk	1105	1828	2536

Options	Price
Air Conditioning [Std on GL]	+253

Body Styles	TMV Pricing		
	Trade	Private	Dealer
2 Dr GL Hbk	1166	1930	2679

Options	Price
Automatic 3-Speed Transmission	+206

1999

With the exception of some color changes, the Suzuki Swift remains unchanged for '99.

Mileage Category: A

Body Styles		TMV Pricing		
		Trade	Private	Dealer
2 Dr STD Hbk		825	1517	2238

Options	Price
Air Conditioning	+195

Options	Price
Automatic 3-Speed Transmission	+158

1998

Swift's engine makes nine more horsepower this year, and one more pound-foot of torque.

Mileage Category: A

Body Styles		TMV Pricing		
		Trade	Private	Dealer
2 Dr STD Hbk		689	1345	2084

Options	Price
Air Conditioning	+171
Antilock Brakes	+161

Options	Price
Automatic 3-Speed Transmission	+128

1997

New paint colors (Victory Red and Bright Teal Metallic) and new seat coverings are the only changes to the 1996 Swift.

Mileage Category: A

Body Styles	TMV Pricing		
	Trade	Private	Dealer
2 Dr STD Hbk	506	1085	1792

Options	Price	Options	Price
Air Conditioning	+156	Antilock Brakes	+147

1996

Two new colors and new seat fabrics.

Mileage Category: A

Body Styles	TMV Pricing		
	Trade	Private	Dealer
2 Dr STD Hbk	417	922	1620

Options	Price	Options	Price
Air Conditioning	+136	Antilock Brakes	+128

1995

The sedan is dropped and dual airbags are added. Antilock brakes become a much appreciated option. The two-door GT hatchback has also been dropped.

Mileage Category: A

Body Styles	TMV Pricing		
	Trade	Private	Dealer
2 Dr STD Hbk	331	709	1340

Options	Price	Options	Price
Air Conditioning	+126	Automatic 3-Speed Transmission	+86
Antilock Brakes	+119		

Verona
2004

Mileage Category: C

Body Styles	TMV Pricing			Body Styles	TMV Pricing		
	Trade	Private	Dealer		Trade	Private	Dealer
4 Dr EX Sdn	11891	12913	14617	4 Dr S Sdn	10154	11176	12880
4 Dr LX Sdn	10907	11929	13633				

Options	Price
Traction Control System [Opt on EX]	+500

The four-door, five-passenger Verona is an all-new midsize sedan in the Suzuki lineup. With a standard six-cylinder engine, automatic transmission and ample passenger and cargo room, it's designed to go head-to-head with class-leading vehicles like the Toyota Camry and Honda Accord.

Vitara
2004

Mileage Category: L

Body Styles	TMV Pricing			Body Styles	TMV Pricing		
	Trade	Private	Dealer		Trade	Private	Dealer
4 Dr LX 4WD SUV	9453	10444	12096	4 Dr LX SUV	8846	9837	11489

Options	Price	Options	Price
Aluminum/Alloy Wheels	+500	Automatic 4-Speed Transmission	+1000
Antilock Brakes	+500		

The Vitara two-door has been dropped. The Vitara four-door is upgraded with a V6 engine and comes with charcoal-colored bumpers and mud guards, a newly designed soft spare tire cover and new exterior colors.

2003

Besides the merging of the JLS and JLX trim levels, not much has changed for the Suzuki Vitara this year.

Mileage Category: L

Body Styles	TMV Pricing			Body Styles	TMV Pricing		
	Trade	Private	Dealer		Trade	Private	Dealer
2 Dr STD 4WD Conv	7080	8054	9676	4 Dr STD 4WD SUV	7460	8486	10195
2 Dr STD Conv	6916	7867	9452	4 Dr STD SUV	6970	7929	9526

Options	Price	Options	Price
Aluminum/Alloy Wheels	+287	Automatic 4-Speed Transmission	+573
Antilock Brakes	+390		

2002

The previous base-level Vitara JS and JX have been discontinued. The Vitara now comes only in fully equipped JLS (rear-wheel drive) and JLX (four-wheel drive) trim in either body style. Additionally, motivation for all Vitaras now comes from the 2.0-liter engine as the 1.6-liter has been dropped. Other changes for the new year include the addition of the LATCH child seat system, a new fender-mounted antenna, new donut-style headrests for better visibility and new exterior colors. Suzuki offers 24-hour emergency roadside assistance and towing for the duration of the vehicle's warranty to increase customer satisfaction.

Mileage Category: L

Body Styles	TMV Pricing		
	Trade	Private	Dealer
2 Dr JLS Conv	5218	6031	7387
2 Dr JLX 4WD Conv	5589	6461	7914

Options	Price
Aluminum/Alloy Wheels	+226

Body Styles	TMV Pricing		
	Trade	Private	Dealer
4 Dr JLS SUV	5493	6350	7778
4 Dr JLX 4WD SUV	5902	6822	8356

Options	Price
Automatic 4-Speed Transmission	+452

2001

All Vitara models get a restyled front grille, new seat fabric, a larger audio unit with an in-dash CD player and new exterior colors.

Mileage Category: L

Body Styles	TMV Pricing		
	Trade	Private	Dealer
2 Dr JLS Conv	4285	5380	6390
2 Dr JLX 4WD Conv	4915	6170	7329
2 Dr JS Conv	3672	4610	5476
2 Dr JX 4WD Conv	4416	5544	6586

Options	Price
Aluminum/Alloy Wheels	+196

Body Styles	TMV Pricing		
	Trade	Private	Dealer
4 Dr JLS SUV	4758	5974	7096
4 Dr JLX 4WD SUV	5197	6525	7751
4 Dr JS SUV	4438	5572	6618
4 Dr JX 4WD SUV	4998	6275	7454

Options	Price
Automatic 4-Speed Transmission	+393

2000

Four-door models receive a new luggage cover for 2000. The Vitara two-door JLS/JLX is equipped with air conditioning as standard equipment. There are three new paint colors, and four-wheel-drive models have a "4x4" sticker in the rear-quarter windows.

Mileage Category: L

Body Styles	TMV Pricing		
	Trade	Private	Dealer
2 Dr JLS Conv	3382	4335	5269
2 Dr JLX 4WD Conv	3863	4951	6017
2 Dr JS Conv	2668	3419	4156
2 Dr JX 4WD Conv	3443	4413	5363

Body Styles	TMV Pricing		
	Trade	Private	Dealer
4 Dr JLS SUV	3701	4743	5765
4 Dr JLX 4WD SUV	4401	5640	6855
4 Dr JS SUV	3476	4455	5414
4 Dr JX 4WD SUV	3927	5033	6117

Options	Price
Automatic 4-Speed Transmission	+316

1999

The Vitara is an all-new model that replaces the Sidekick as Suzuki's entry into the mini-SUV class.

Mileage Category: L

Body Styles	TMV Pricing		
	Trade	Private	Dealer
2 Dr JS 1.6 Conv	2205	2914	3651
2 Dr JS 2.0 Conv	2450	3236	4055
2 Dr JX 1.6 4WD Conv	2717	3591	4500

Options	Price
Air Conditioning	+195

Body Styles	TMV Pricing		
	Trade	Private	Dealer
2 Dr JX 2.0 4WD Conv	2900	3832	4803
4 Dr JS SUV	2810	3713	4653
4 Dr JX 4WD SUV	3111	4111	5152

Options	Price
Automatic 4-Speed Transmission	+244

X-90

1998

Mileage Category: L

Body Styles	TMV Pricing		
	Trade	Private	Dealer
2 Dr SE 4WD SUV	2611	3501	4504
2 Dr STD 4WD SUV	2484	3330	4285

Options	Price
Air Conditioning [Opt on STD]	+171
Antilock Brakes [Opt on STD]	+166

No changes this year.

Body Styles	TMV Pricing		
	Trade	Private	Dealer
2 Dr STD SUV	2159	2895	3724

Options	Price
Automatic 4-Speed Transmission	+203

1997

No changes to Suzuki's alternative to AWD vehicles.

Mileage Category: L

Body Styles	TMV Pricing		
	Trade	Private	Dealer
2 Dr STD 4WD SUV	1853	2581	3470

Options	Price
Air Conditioning	+156
Antilock Brakes	+147

Body Styles	TMV Pricing		
	Trade	Private	Dealer
2 Dr STD SUV	1592	2218	2982

Options	Price
Automatic 4-Speed Transmission	+185

1996

Based on Sidekick platform, this new concept features a two-seat cockpit, T-top roof, conventional trunk and available four-wheel drive.

Mileage Category: L

Body Styles	TMV Pricing		
	Trade	Private	Dealer
2 Dr STD 4WD SUV	1348	1859	2565

Options	Price
Air Conditioning	+136

Body Styles	TMV Pricing		
	Trade	Private	Dealer
2 Dr STD SUV	1127	1554	2144

Options	Price
Automatic 4-Speed Transmission	+161

XL-7

2004

Mileage Category: M

Body Styles	TMV Pricing		
	Trade	Private	Dealer
4 Dr EX 4WD SUV	15841	17215	19504
4 Dr EX III 4WD SUV	17032	18403	20688
4 Dr EX III SUV	15944	17311	19589
4 Dr EX SUV	14440	15780	18013

Options	Price
Antilock Brakes [Opt on LX, LX III 2WD]	+500

Body Styles	TMV Pricing		
	Trade	Private	Dealer
4 Dr LX 4WD SUV	13756	15135	17433
4 Dr LX III 4WD SUV	15245	16620	18912
4 Dr LX III SUV	14001	15368	17645
4 Dr LX SUV	12238	13578	15811

Options	Price
Automatic 5-Speed Transmission [Opt on LX 4WD]	+1000

The XL-7 receives minor updates to the exterior and equipment list. The Touring and Limited models have been renamed EX III and LX III. The front grille and bumper have been reworked, and the foglights, taillights and headlights all have a new look. The front-passenger airbags are now multistage, and there's a new panic button on the keyless remote. Lastly, the V6 engine gets two additional horsepower for a total of 185, and the automatic transmission is now a five-speed unit.

2003

For 2003, Suzuki has updated the Grand Vitara XL-7's dash and console with wood grain trim, chrome accents and a 12-volt accessory outlet. Other additions to the interior include a new seven-speaker system, integrated audio and cruise control buttons on the steering wheel, an adjustable center armrest with CD storage and smaller rear headsets for better rearward visibility. Suzuki has also changed some of its trim names for 2003. The previous "Standard" trim has now simply become the XL-7, while the "Plus" has become the XL-7 with the option of third-row seating. The "Touring" model has been dropped all together. The Limited model is now being offered with a six-disc in-dash CD changer. Finally, a Limited model with the third-row option is also available with climate control and a rear air conditioning switch.

Mileage Category: M

Body Styles	TMV Pricing		
	Trade	Private	Dealer
4 Dr Limited 4WD SUV	11223	12262	13994
4 Dr Limited SUV	10896	11905	13587

Options	Price
Aluminum/Alloy Wheels [Opt on Touring]	+287
Antilock Brakes [Opt on Touring]	+390
Automatic 4-Speed Transmission [Opt on Touring]	+573

Body Styles	TMV Pricing		
	Trade	Private	Dealer
4 Dr Touring 4WD SUV	10630	11614	13255
4 Dr Touring SUV	10307	11261	12851

Options	Price
Heated Front Seats [Opt on Limited]	+172
Third Seat	+430

2002

For 2002, the XL-7's 2.7-liter V6 engine has been upgraded to produce more power. Inside, all XL-7 models have gained features such as the LATCH child seat system, improved cargo floor design and new upholstery. All Standard and Plus models now offer optional ABS brakes, while the line-topping Limited Edition's interior gains woodgrain trim and a leather-wrapped steering wheel and shift knob. Suzuki offers 24-hour emergency roadside assistance and towing for the duration of the vehicle's warranty to increase customer satisfaction.

Mileage Category: M

Body Styles	TMV Pricing		
	Trade	Private	Dealer
4 Dr Limited 4WD SUV	9272	10190	11721
4 Dr Limited SUV	9054	9950	11444
4 Dr Plus 4WD SUV	8324	9148	10522
4 Dr Plus SUV	8026	8821	10146

Options	Price
Antilock Brakes [Std on Limited, Touring]	+307
Automatic 4-Speed Transmission [Std on Limited, Touring 2WD]	+452

Body Styles	TMV Pricing		
	Trade	Private	Dealer
4 Dr STD 4WD SUV	7900	8682	9986
4 Dr STD SUV	7433	8169	9396
4 Dr Touring 4WD SUV	8892	9772	11239
4 Dr Touring SUV	8814	9687	11142

Options	Price
Heated Front Seats [Opt on Limted 4WD]	+135

2001

The Suzuki XL-7 is an all-new midsize SUV based on a stretched Grand Vitara. It is the first in this class to offer third-row seating and a starting price of under $20,000.

Mileage Category: M

Body Styles	TMV Pricing		
	Trade	Private	Dealer
4 Dr Plus 4WD SUV	6763	7934	9014
4 Dr Plus SUV	6553	7686	8732
4 Dr STD 4WD SUV	6448	7564	8594

Options	Price
Automatic 4-Speed Transmission [Opt on Plus, Touring]	+393

Body Styles	TMV Pricing		
	Trade	Private	Dealer
4 Dr STD SUV	6080	7132	8103
4 Dr Touring 4WD SUV	7064	8286	9414
4 Dr Touring SUV	7003	8215	9333

Toyota
4Runner

4Runner

2004

A third-row seat is now optional on SR5 and Limited models. Black running boards are standard on SR5 and Sport models, and the optional navigation system now includes a rearview back-up monitor.

Mileage Category: M

Body Styles	Trade	Private	Dealer
4 Dr Limited 4WD SUV	26157	27651	30142
4 Dr Limited SUV	24515	26010	28501
4 Dr SR5 4WD SUV	21630	23125	25616

Options	Price
4.7L V8 DOHC 32V FI Engine	+350
AM/FM/Cassette/CD Changer Audio System	+450
Alarm System [Std on Limited]	+220
Automatic 5-Speed Transmission	+720
Automatic Dimming Rearview Mirror	+150
Compact Disc Changer	+570
DVD Entertainment System [Opt on SR5]	+1997
Front Side Airbag Restraints	+300
Front and Rear Head Airbag Restraints	+350
Garage Door Opener [Opt on SR5, Sport]	+125

Body Styles	Trade	Private	Dealer
4 Dr SR5 SUV	19988	21483	23975
4 Dr Sport Edition 4WD SUV	22525	24020	26511
4 Dr Sport Edition SUV	20883	22378	24870

Options	Price
JBL Audio System	+275
Leather Steering Wheel	+220
Luggage Rack [Opt on SR5]	+220
Navigation System	+2000
Power Sunroof	+900
Rear Audio Controls [Opt on SR5, Sport]	+150
Rear Spoiler	+200
Rear View Camera [Opt on Limited]	+200
Third Seat [Opt on SR5, Limited]	+735

2003

Toyota's popular midsize SUV has been completely redesigned this year. Though it stays true to its truck-based roots, it comes with many new upscale features, including an available V8 engine and an optional navigation system.

Mileage Category: M

Body Styles	Trade	Private	Dealer
4 Dr Limited 4WD SUV	23962	25719	28648
4 Dr Limited SUV	21578	23161	25800
4 Dr SR5 4WD SUV	19263	20676	23030

Options	Price
4.7L V8 SOHC 16V FI Engine	+717
AM/FM/Cassette/CD Changer Audio System	+151
Alarm System [Std on Limited]	+166
Front Side Airbag Restraints	+189
Front and Rear Head Airbag Restraints	+359
JBL Audio System	+321

Body Styles	Trade	Private	Dealer
4 Dr SR5 SUV	17600	18891	21043
4 Dr Sport Edition 4WD SUV	19889	21348	23780
4 Dr Sport Edition SUV	18432	19784	22037

Options	Price
Leather Steering Wheel	+166
Luggage Rack [Opt on SR5]	+166
Navigation System	+1434
Power Moonroof	+679
Rear Spoiler	+151

2002

Mileage Category: M

Body Styles	Trade	Private	Dealer
4 Dr Limited 4WD SUV	20432	22082	24832
4 Dr Limited SUV	18951	20481	23032

Options	Price
16 Inch Wheels [Opt on SR5]	+328
Leather Seats [Opt on SR5]	+579
Luggage Rack	+186
Power Sunroof	+562
Premium Audio System	+138

Body Styles	Trade	Private	Dealer
4 Dr SR5 4WD SUV	16904	18270	20545
4 Dr SR5 SUV	15346	16586	18653

Options	Price
Rear Heater	+117
Rear Wind Deflector	+148
Sport Package [Opt on SR5]	+1093
Sport Seats [Opt on SR5]	+197
Trailer Hitch	+121

Not much has changed this year for Toyota's truck-based 4Runner SUV. The SR5's optional Sport package has gained a front skid plate, floor mats and new tube step-up bars (optional). Handsome 15-inch alloy wheels are now standard, there's a new chrome package available, and Golden Pearl has been added to the Limited's selection of exterior colors.

2001

Mileage Category: M

Body Styles	TMV Pricing		
	Trade	Private	Dealer
4 Dr Limited 4WD SUV	16780	19017	21081
4 Dr Limited SUV	15653	17740	19666

Options	Price
AM/FM/Cassette/CD Changer Audio System [Opt on Limited]	+126
Aluminum/Alloy Wheels [Opt on SR5]	+261
Leather Seats [Opt on SR5]	+529
Power Sunroof	+513

Body Styles	TMV Pricing		
	Trade	Private	Dealer
4 Dr SR5 4WD SUV	14303	16210	17970
4 Dr SR5 SUV	13029	14765	16368

Options	Price
Running Boards [Opt on SR5]	+217
Sport Package [Opt on SR5]	+997
Sport Seats [Opt on SR5]	+179

Base models have been dropped, leaving Limited and SR5 trim levels equipped with a standard automatic transmission, Vehicle Skid Control (VSC), traction control and ABS with Electronic Brakeforce Distribution and BrakeAssist. All 4Runners have power door locks this year, as well as a prewired trailer hitch harness, a modified grille design and freshened taillights. New wheels for Limited and Sport debut, and a new premium 3-in-1 audio system with a CD changer is available. Revised sun visors with extensions and a HomeLink programmable transmitter come standard on Limited and can be ordered on SR5. Limited also gets a new color of wood trim, and standard front seat heaters. There's bad news for hard-core off-roaders -- the optional differential lock has been discontinued with the demise of the manual transmission. Three new colors replace two old ones on the color chart.

2000

Mileage Category: M

Body Styles	TMV Pricing		
	Trade	Private	Dealer
4 Dr Limited 4WD SUV	14407	16661	18870
4 Dr Limited SUV	13469	15576	17641
4 Dr SR5 4WD SUV	11766	13607	15412

Options	Price
AM/FM/CD Audio System	+221
AM/FM/Cassette/CD Audio System [Opt on STD,SR5 V6 2WD]	+387
Air Conditioning [Std on Limited]	+544
Alarm System [Std on Limited]	+177
Aluminum/Alloy Wheels [Std on Limited]	+229
Antilock Brakes [Opt on STD]	+376
Automatic 4-Speed Transmission [Opt on STD,SR5 V6 4WD]	+497
Compact Disc Changer	+366
Cruise Control [Opt on STD]	+138
Keyless Entry System [Opt on SR5]	+124
Leather Seats [Opt on SR5]	+464

Body Styles	TMV Pricing		
	Trade	Private	Dealer
4 Dr SR5 SUV	11127	12868	14574
4 Dr STD 4WD SUV	10938	12649	14326
4 Dr STD SUV	9871	11414	12927

Options	Price
Limited Slip Differential	+188
Power Door Locks [Opt on STD,SR5 V6 2WD]	+135
Power Moonroof	+450
Power Windows [Std on Limited]	+146
Privacy Glass [Opt on STD]	+172
Running Boards [Std on Limited]	+191
Sport Package	+770
Sport Seats	+157
Steel Wheels	+332
Tilt Steering Wheel [Opt on STD]	+135
Wide Tires And Wheels [Opt on SR5,STD]	+541

Optional color-coordinated fender flares are available on the SR5. An AM/FM/cassette/CD is now available on base models, and is standard on SR5 and Limited models. Daytime running lights are now included with the antilock brake package.

1999

Mileage Category: M

Body Styles	TMV Pricing		
	Trade	Private	Dealer
4 Dr Limited 4WD SUV	12415	14634	16944
4 Dr Limited SUV	11383	13418	15536
4 Dr SR5 4WD SUV	10288	12127	14041

Options	Price
AM/FM/CD Audio System [Std on Limited]	+171
AM/FM/Cassette/CD Audio System	+299
Air Conditioning [Std on Limited]	+420
Alarm System [Std on Limited]	+137
Aluminum/Alloy Wheels [Std on Limited]	+177
Antilock Brakes [Std on Limited,SR5]	+323
Automatic 4-Speed Transmission [Opt on STD,SR5 V6 4WD]	+385
Compact Disc Changer	+282
Leather Seats [Opt on SR5]	+534

Body Styles	TMV Pricing		
	Trade	Private	Dealer
4 Dr SR5 SUV	9259	10914	12636
4 Dr STD 4WD SUV	8980	10585	12255
4 Dr STD SUV	7828	9227	10683

Options	Price
Locking Differential	+145
Power Moonroof	+349
Power Windows [Std on Limited]	+203
Privacy Glass [Opt on STD]	+132
Running Boards [Std on Limited]	+147
Sport Package	+596
Sport Seats	+177
Steel Wheels	+256
Wide Tires And Wheels [Opt on SR5,STD]	+419

The 4Runner receives a number of upgrades this year, starting with a new and improved four-wheel-drive system equipped with a center differential and featuring a full-time 4WD mode in addition to the current two-high, four-high and four-low modes. New exterior features include a front bumper redesign, multireflector headlamps and an enhanced sport package with fender flares and a hood scoop on the SR5 model. Inside, a new center console/cupholder design will improve beverage-carrying capacity of the 4Runner and an automatic climate control system will be featured on the Limited models.

1998

Mileage Category: M

Body Styles	TMV Pricing		
	Trade	Private	Dealer
4 Dr Limited 4WD SUV	9725	11693	13913
4 Dr Limited SUV	9145	10996	13084
4 Dr SR5 4WD SUV	8325	10010	11911

Body Styles	TMV Pricing		
	Trade	Private	Dealer
4 Dr SR5 SUV	7668	9220	10971
4 Dr STD 4WD SUV	7010	8429	10029
4 Dr STD SUV	6262	7530	8959

For 1998, the Toyota 4Runner gets rotary HVAC controls, a new four-spoke steering wheel and revised audio control head units.

1998 (cont'd)

Options	Price
AM/FM/CD Audio System [Opt on SR5,STD]	+150
AM/FM/Cassette/CD Audio System	+263
Air Conditioning [Opt on SR5,STD]	+370
Alarm System	+120
Aluminum/Alloy Wheels [Opt on SR5,STD]	+156
Antilock Brakes [Opt on STD]	+284
Automatic 4-Speed Transmission [Opt on STD,SR5 4WD]	+338
Compact Disc Changer	+248

Options	Price
Leather Seats [Opt on SR5]	+470
Locking Differential	+122
Power Moonroof	+344
Power Windows [Opt on SR5,STD]	+174
Running Boards [Opt on SR5,STD]	+129
Sport Seats	+156
Steel Wheels	+226

1997

Toyota's SUV receives minor changes. The most noticeable is the addition of the 2WD Limited to the model lineup. SR5 models receive new interior fabrics.

Mileage Category: M

Body Styles	TMV Pricing		
	Trade	Private	Dealer
4 Dr Limited 4WD SUV	8324	10171	12429
4 Dr Limited SUV	7741	9460	11561
4 Dr SR5 4WD SUV	7299	8919	10900

Body Styles	TMV Pricing		
	Trade	Private	Dealer
4 Dr SR5 SUV	6725	8217	10041
4 Dr STD 4WD SUV	5835	7130	8713
4 Dr STD SUV	5316	6497	7940

Options	Price
AM/FM/CD Audio System	+129
AM/FM/Cassette/CD Audio System	+225
Air Conditioning [Opt on SR5,STD]	+316
Aluminum/Alloy Wheels [Opt on SR5,STD]	+133
Antilock Brakes [Opt on STD]	+242
Automatic 4-Speed Transmission [Opt on STD,SR5 4WD]	+289

Options	Price
Compact Disc Changer	+209
Leather Seats [Opt on SR5,STD]	+401
Power Moonroof	+294
Power Windows [Opt on SR5,STD]	+141
Sport Seats	+219
Steel Wheels	+193

1996

A new 4Runner with a potent V6, updated styling and more interior room debuts.

Mileage Category: M

Body Styles	TMV Pricing		
	Trade	Private	Dealer
4 Dr Limited 4WD SUV	7263	8974	11336
4 Dr SR5 4WD SUV	6414	7925	10012
4 Dr SR5 SUV	6078	7510	9487

Body Styles	TMV Pricing		
	Trade	Private	Dealer
4 Dr STD 4WD SUV	4902	6056	7650
4 Dr STD SUV	4408	5447	6881

Options	Price
AM/FM/Cassette/CD Audio System	+189
Air Conditioning [Opt on SR5,STD]	+266
Antilock Brakes [Opt on STD]	+204
Automatic 4-Speed Transmission [Opt on STD,SR5 4WD]	+244
Compact Disc Changer	+176

Options	Price
Leather Seats [Opt on SR5]	+338
Power Moonroof	+248
Sport Seats	+194
Steel Wheels	+162

1995

V6 models get new tape stripes.

Mileage Category: M

Body Styles	TMV Pricing		
	Trade	Private	Dealer
4 Dr Limited 4WD SUV	5511	6825	9016
4 Dr SR5 4WD SUV	4152	5142	6793

Body Styles	TMV Pricing		
	Trade	Private	Dealer
4 Dr SR5 SUV	4472	5539	7317
4 Dr SR5 V6 4WD SUV	4982	6170	8149

Options	Price
AM/FM/CD Audio System	+96
AM/FM/Cassette/CD Audio System	+168
Air Conditioning [Std on Limited]	+236
Alarm System	+77
Aluminum/Alloy Wheels [Opt on SR5]	+99
Antilock Brakes	+181
Automatic 4-Speed Transmission [Std on 2WD]	+216

Options	Price
Compact Disc Changer	+156
Leather Seats [Opt on SR5 V6]	+300
Power Moonroof	+196
Power Windows [Opt on 2WD,SR5 V6]	+76
Premium Audio System	+156
Running Boards	+79
Sport Seats	+99

Avalon

2004

Mileage Category: G

Electronic stability and traction control are now optional on base XL models.

Body Styles	TMV Pricing		
	Trade	Private	Dealer
4 Dr XL Sdn	18875	20023	21935

Options	Price
16 Inch Wheels	+150
Alarm System [Opt on XL]	+319
Aluminum/Alloy Wheels [Opt on XL]	+590
Automatic Dimming Rearview Mirror [Opt on XL]	+265
Heated Front Seats [Opt on XLS]	+150
Intermittent Wipers [Opt on XLS]	+125
JBL Audio System [Opt on XL]	+200
Keyless Entry System [Opt on XL]	+250

Body Styles	TMV Pricing		
	Trade	Private	Dealer
4 Dr XLS Sdn	22029	23176	25088

Options	Price
Leather Seats	+150
Navigation System [Opt on XLS]	+2000
Power Driver Seat [Opt on XLS]	+250
Power Moonroof	+900
Rear Spoiler	+569
Special Factory Paint	+220
Traction Control System	+650
Wood Interior Trim [Opt on XL]	+519

2003

Mileage Category: G

A few minor changes are in store for Toyota's large sedan. On the outside, you'll find freshened styling that consists of a new grille, new taillamps and redesigned bumpers. Inside, the 2003 Avalon has been upgraded with dual-stage airbags and ISO-FIX child safety seat anchor points. XLS models also have more features this year, including an autodimming driver-side mirror, rain-sensing wipers, a simulated wood-trimmed steering wheel and an optional navigation system.

Body Styles	TMV Pricing		
	Trade	Private	Dealer
4 Dr XL Sdn	16715	17836	19704

Options	Price
16 Inch Wheels	+291
AM/FM/Cassette/CD Changer Audio System [Opt on XLS]	+264
Alarm System [Opt on XL]	+241
Aluminum/Alloy Wheels [Opt on XL]	+340
Heated Front Seats [Opt on XLS]	+238
JBL Audio System [Opt on XL]	+223
Keyless Entry System [Opt on XL]	+132
Leather Seats [Opt on XL]	+642

Body Styles	TMV Pricing		
	Trade	Private	Dealer
4 Dr XLS Sdn	18897	20164	22276

Options	Price
Navigation System [Opt on XLS]	+1510
Power Driver Seat [Opt on XLS]	+181
Power Driver Seat w/Memory [Opt on XLS]	+155
Power Moonroof	+679
Power Passenger Seat [Opt on XLS]	+181
Special Factory Paint	+166
Split Front Bench Seat	+619
Traction Control System [Opt on XLS]	+491

2002

Mileage Category: G

Toyota has tinkered with the options packages, but otherwise left the Avalon alone. A new luxury package for the XL includes power leather-trimmed seats, 15-inch alloy wheels, remote keyless entry and a JBL audio system. There's also a Sport Luxury package that adds 16-inch alloy wheels and a rear spoiler in addition to the items in the luxury package.

Body Styles	TMV Pricing		
	Trade	Private	Dealer
4 Dr XL Sdn	14372	15503	17389

Options	Price
16 Inch Wheels	+266
AM/FM/Cassette/CD Changer Audio System [Opt on XLS]	+241
Aluminum/Alloy Wheels [Opt on XL]	+155
Automatic Stability Control [Opt on XLS]	+448
Heated Front Seats [Opt on XLS]	+217
JBL Audio System [Opt on XL]	+204
Keyless Entry System [Opt on XL]	+121
Leather Seats	+586

Body Styles	TMV Pricing		
	Trade	Private	Dealer
4 Dr XLS Sdn	16010	17270	19371

Options	Price
Pearlescent Metallic Paint	+152
Power Driver Seat [Opt on XL]	+166
Power Driver Seat w/Memory [Opt on XLS]	+145
Power Moonroof	+621
Power Passenger Seat	+166
Rear Spoiler [Opt on XL]	+172
Split Front Bench Seat	+566
Traction Control System [Opt on XLS]	+186

2001

Mileage Category: G

Two colors, Cognac Brown and Constellation Blue Pearl, are dumped for 2001, and an emergency trunk release has been added.

Body Styles	TMV Pricing		
	Trade	Private	Dealer
4 Dr XL Sdn	11852	13338	14709

Options	Price
AM/FM/Cassette/CD Changer Audio System [Opt on XLS]	+252
Aluminum/Alloy Wheels [Opt on XL]	+242
Automatic Stability Control [Opt on XLS]	+409
Heated Front Seats	+198
JBL Audio System [Opt on XL]	+227
Leather Seats	+535

Body Styles	TMV Pricing		
	Trade	Private	Dealer
4 Dr XLS Sdn	13815	15548	17147

Options	Price
Pearlescent Metallic Paint	+138
Power Driver Seat [Opt on XL]	+132
Power Driver Seat w/Memory [Opt on XLS]	+132
Power Moonroof	+573
Power Passenger Seat [Opt on XL]	+132
Split Front Bench Seat	+516
Traction Control System	+170

Toyota
Avalon

2000

Entering its second generation, the 2000 Avalon is roomier, more powerful and more technically advanced. The Kentucky-built Avalon features new styling inside and out, enhanced safety features, increased engine performance, and more comfort and convenience than its predecessor.

Mileage Category: G

Body Styles	TMV Pricing		
	Trade	Private	Dealer
4 Dr XL Sdn	9610	11037	12436

Options	Price
Alarm System [Opt on XL]	+220
Aluminum/Alloy Wheels [Opt on XL]	+213
Automatic Stability Control [Opt on XLS]	+359
Compact Disc Changer	+304
Heated Front Seats	+174
JBL Audio System [Opt on XL]	+199
Leather Seats	+470

Body Styles	TMV Pricing		
	Trade	Private	Dealer
4 Dr XLS Sdn	11683	13417	15117

Options	Price
Power Driver Seat [Opt on XL]	+133
Power Driver Seat w/Memory [Opt on XLS]	+134
Power Moonroof	+486
Power Passenger Seat [Opt on XL]	+133
Special Factory Paint	+122
Traction Control System	+149

1999

Mileage Category: G

Body Styles	TMV Pricing		
	Trade	Private	Dealer
4 Dr XL Sdn	6639	7864	9139

Options	Price
AM/FM/CD Audio System	+143
Alarm System [Opt on XL]	+170
Aluminum/Alloy Wheels [Opt on XL]	+164
Compact Disc Changer	+235
Heated Front Seats	+135

Body Styles	TMV Pricing		
	Trade	Private	Dealer
4 Dr XLS Sdn	7844	9291	10798

Options	Price
Leather Seats	+363
Power Driver Seat [Opt on XL]	+178
Power Moonroof	+385
Power Passenger Seat [Opt on XL]	+178
Traction Control System	+128

After a body makeover and safety improvements (side airbags) last year, the Avalon heads into '99 with only minor updates. Daytime running lights with auto-off color-keyed foglamp covers and dual heated color-keyed power mirrors are new this year. A new three-in-one ETR/cassette/CD sound system is optional on the XL model and Lunar Mist Metallic replaces Golden Sand Metallic.

1998

The Avalon gets side-impact airbags, new headlights and taillamps, a new grille, a new trunk lid and pre-tensioner seatbelts with force limiters.

Mileage Category: G

Body Styles	TMV Pricing		
	Trade	Private	Dealer
4 Dr XL Sdn	5518	6591	7802

Options	Price
Alarm System [Opt on XL]	+120
Aluminum/Alloy Wheels [Opt on XL]	+164
Compact Disc Changer	+206
Heated Front Seats	+119

Body Styles	TMV Pricing		
	Trade	Private	Dealer
4 Dr XLS Sdn	6806	8131	9625

Options	Price
Leather Seats	+492
Power Driver Seat [Opt on XL]	+157
Power Moonroof	+368
Power Passenger Seat [Opt on XL]	+157

1997

More power, more torque and added standard features make the Avalon one of the most appealing full-size sedans

Mileage Category: G

Body Styles	TMV Pricing		
	Trade	Private	Dealer
4 Dr XL Sdn	4335	5265	6402

Options	Price
AM/FM/Cassette/CD Audio System	+196
Aluminum/Alloy Wheels [Opt on XL]	+139
Compact Disc Changer	+239
Leather Seats	+322

Body Styles	TMV Pricing		
	Trade	Private	Dealer
4 Dr XLS Sdn	5546	6735	8188

Options	Price
Power Bench Seat [Opt on XL]	+273
Power Driver Seat [Opt on XL]	+134
Power Moonroof	+315
Power Passenger Seat [Opt on XL]	+134

1996

No changes.

Mileage Category: G

Body Styles	TMV Pricing		
	Trade	Private	Dealer
4 Dr XL Sdn	3536	4362	5502

Options	Price
AM/FM/Cassette/CD Audio System	+203
Aluminum/Alloy Wheels [Opt on XL]	+118
Antilock Brakes [Opt on XL]	+265
Compact Disc Changer	+148

Body Styles	TMV Pricing		
	Trade	Private	Dealer
4 Dr XLS Sdn	4644	5728	7224

Options	Price
Leather Seats	+272
Power Bench Seat	+230
Power Moonroof	+265
Premium Audio System [Opt on XL]	+397

For the latest vehicle information, visit www.edmunds.com

Avalon/Camry

1995

Marginally larger than the Camry, the Avalon is a true six-passenger sedan set to conquer Buick LeSabre and Ford Crown Victoria. Dual airbags, power windows, power mirrors and power locks are standard. ABS is optional. Mechanicals are mostly Camry-based.

Mileage Category: G

Body Styles	TMV Pricing		
	Trade	Private	Dealer
4 Dr XL Sdn	2939	3582	4653

Options	Price
Aluminum/Alloy Wheels [Opt on XL]	+92
Antilock Brakes [Opt on XL]	+235
Compact Disc Changer	+132
Leather Seats	+204
Power Bench Seat [Opt on XL]	+204

Body Styles	TMV Pricing		
	Trade	Private	Dealer
4 Dr XLS Sdn	3839	4678	6077

Options	Price
Power Driver Seat [Opt on XL]	+99
Power Moonroof	+211
Power Passenger Seat [Opt on XL]	+99
Premium Audio System [Opt on XL]	+353

Camry

2004

For 2004, a new 3.3-liter V6 is standard on SE V6 models. Relative to last year's 3.0-liter V6, this engine offers 33 more horsepower and an additional 31 pound-feet of torque, boosting ratings to 225 and 240, respectively. Fortunately, Toyota has also boosted the 3.0-liter engine's output -- it now makes 210 hp and 220 lb-ft of torque in V6-equipped LE and XLE models. Both V6 engines come standard with a five-speed automatic transmission this year. In other news, a new trim has been introduced; the Limited Edition Camry comes in an exclusive crystal-white color, and offers a unique front grille, standard foglamps and champagne-color exterior badging.

Mileage Category: D

Body Styles	TMV Pricing		
	Trade	Private	Dealer
4 Dr LE Sdn	13481	14679	16675
4 Dr LE V6 Sdn	15914	17171	19267
4 Dr SE Sdn	14058	15256	17252

Options	Price
AM/FM/Cassette/CD Changer Audio System [Opt on LE, SE]	+200
Alarm System [Opt on LE, SE]	+359
Aluminum/Alloy Wheels [Std on V6]	+410
Antilock Brakes [Std on V6, XLE]	+300
Automatic 4-Speed Transmission [Opt on SE, LE]	+830
Automatic Dimming Rearview Mirror [Std on XLE]	+265
Automatic Stability Control [Opt on V6]	+650
Chrome Wheels [Opt on LE]	+899
Front Side Airbag Restraints	+300

Body Styles	TMV Pricing		
	Trade	Private	Dealer
4 Dr SE V6 Sdn	16648	17905	20001
4 Dr XLE Sdn	16027	17247	19279
4 Dr XLE V6 Sdn	18100	19357	21453

Options	Price
Front and Rear Head Airbag Restraints	+350
Heated Front Seats [Opt on SE, XLE]	+315
Leather Seats [Opt on SE, XLE]	+750
Navigation System [Opt on SE, XLE V6]	+920
Painted Wheels [Opt on LE]	+499
Power Adjustable Foot Pedals [Opt on V6, XLE]	+120
Power Moonroof [Std on SE, XLE V6]	+900
Rear Spoiler	+435

2003

Other than the added availability of power-adjustable pedals, the Camry is unchanged for 2003.

Mileage Category: D

Body Styles	TMV Pricing		
	Trade	Private	Dealer
4 Dr LE Sdn	11901	12856	14447
4 Dr LE V6 Sdn	14481	15644	17581
4 Dr SE Sdn	12431	13428	15091

Options	Price
AM/FM/Cassette/CD Changer Audio System [Opt on LE, SE]	+302
Alarm System [Opt on LE, SE]	+271
Aluminum/Alloy Wheels [Opt on SE, XLE]	+309
Antilock Brakes [Opt on LE, SE]	+513
Automatic 4-Speed Transmission [Opt on LE, SE]	+626
Automatic Stability Control [Opt on LE V6, SE V6, XLE V6]	+321

Body Styles	TMV Pricing		
	Trade	Private	Dealer
4 Dr SE V6 Sdn	15334	16565	18617
4 Dr XLE Sdn	14501	15665	17605
4 Dr XLE V6 Sdn	16351	17664	19851

Options	Price
Front Side Airbag Restraints	+189
Front and Rear Head Airbag Restraints	+359
Heated Front Seats [Opt on SE, SE V6, XLE, XLE V6]	+238
JBL Audio System [Opt on LE, SE]	+155
Leather Seats [Opt on SE, XLE]	+566
Power Moonroof [Opt on LE, LE V6, XLE]	+600

2002

One of America's favorite cars is all new for 2002. Toyota's design goals for the new Camry included larger interior packaging, reduced noise, more advanced safety features, better driving dynamics and, of course, a new standard of value.

Mileage Category: D

Body Styles	TMV Pricing		
	Trade	Private	Dealer
4 Dr LE Sdn	10082	10994	12513
4 Dr LE V6 Sdn	11792	12859	14636
4 Dr SE Sdn	10779	11754	13380

Options	Price
16 Inch Wheels [Opt on XLE, XLE V6]	+190
AM/FM/Cassette/CD Changer Audio System	+276
Aluminum/Alloy Wheels [Opt on SE]	+283
Antilock Brakes [Opt on LE, SE]	+469

Body Styles	TMV Pricing		
	Trade	Private	Dealer
4 Dr SE V6 Sdn	12536	13669	15558
4 Dr XLE Sdn	11811	12879	14660
4 Dr XLE V6 Sdn	13426	14641	16666

Options	Price
Automatic 4-Speed Transmission [Opt on LE, SE]	+573
Automatic Stability Control [Opt on V6]	+293
Front Side Airbag Restraints	+172
Front and Rear Head Airbag Restraints	+207

2002 (cont'd)

Options	Price
Heated Front Seats [Opt on SE V6,XLE,XLE V6]	+217
JBL Audio System [Std on XLE,XLE V6]	+141
Keyless Entry System [Std on XLE,XLE V6]	+128
Leather Seats [Opt on SE V6,XLE,XLE V6]	+517
Navigation System	+1345

Options	Price
Power Driver Seat [Std on XLE,XLE V6]	+193
Power Moonroof	+548
Spoke Wheels [Opt on SE,XLE]	+283
Traction Control System [Opt on V6]	+207

2001

Want air conditioning, power windows/locks/mirrors and variable intermittent wipers on the CE? Buy the Value Package. To get remote keyless entry or a power driver seat on the LE, you must buy a Value Package. A power moonroof and an in-dash six-disc CD changer require the Leather Value Package on XLE models. LE V6 models get daytime running lights standard, while JBL audio is optional on all LEs. The anti-theft system with engine immobilizer is restricted to XLE V6 models.

Mileage Category: D

Body Styles	TMV Pricing		
	Trade	Private	Dealer
4 Dr CE Sdn	7273	8297	9243
4 Dr LE Sdn	8223	9384	10455
4 Dr LE V6 Sdn	9278	10586	11793

Body Styles	TMV Pricing		
	Trade	Private	Dealer
4 Dr XLE Sdn	9347	10664	11880
4 Dr XLE V6 Sdn	10475	11951	13314

Options	Price
AM/FM/Cassette/CD Changer Audio System [Opt on XLE,XLE V6]	+252
Air Conditioning [Opt on CE]	+632
Aluminum/Alloy Wheels [Opt on LE,LE V6]	+242
Antilock Brakes [Opt on CE,LE]	+428
Automatic 4-Speed Transmission [Opt on CE,LE V6]	+503
Cruise Control [Opt on CE]	+157
Front Side Airbag Restraints	+157
JBL Audio System [Opt on LE,LE V6]	+182

Options	Price
Leather Seats	+581
Power Door Locks [Opt on CE]	+148
Power Driver Seat	+196
Power Moonroof	+629
Power Windows [Opt on CE]	+167
Traction Control System	+189
Two-Tone Paint	+126

2000

The Camry sedan receives minor updates for the 2000 model year. The exterior benefits from new front and rear styling. Camry LE models get 15-inch tires with new wheel covers while the XLE gets standard 16-inch tires. Four-cylinder models make three more horsepower than last year. Interior upgrades include an available JBL premium audio system, automatic climate control, larger buttons on the audio faceplate, imitation wood trim on XLE models, optional leather seats with driver-side power on LE models and new LE model seat fabric. The hood is now supported with struts and dampers.

Mileage Category: D

Body Styles	TMV Pricing		
	Trade	Private	Dealer
4 Dr CE Sdn	6064	7137	8189
4 Dr LE Sdn	6775	7974	9150
4 Dr LE V6 Sdn	7642	8995	10321

Body Styles	TMV Pricing		
	Trade	Private	Dealer
4 Dr XLE Sdn	7664	9020	10350
4 Dr XLE V6 Sdn	8286	9753	11190

Options	Price
AM/FM/Cassette/CD Audio System [Opt on CE]	+387
Air Conditioning [Opt on CE]	+555
Alarm System [Opt on CE]	+220
Aluminum/Alloy Wheels [Std on XLE,XLE V6]	+202
Antilock Brakes [Opt on CE,LE]	+376
Automatic 4-Speed Transmission [Opt on CE,LE V6]	+442
Compact Disc Changer	+304
Fog Lights	+220
Front Side Airbag Restraints	+138

Options	Price
JBL Audio System [Opt on LE,LE V6]	+160
Leather Seats	+511
Power Door Locks [Opt on CE]	+130
Power Driver Seat	+172
Power Mirrors [Opt on CE]	+124
Power Moonroof	+552
Power Windows [Opt on CE]	+146
Rear Spoiler	+193
Traction Control System	+166

1999

Two new audio systems are available and both include three-in-one ETR/cassette/CD features. Also available are daytime running lights with auto-off. Vintage Red Pearl, Sable Pearl and Woodland Pearl replace Sunfire Red Pearl, Ruby Red and Classic Green Pearl.

Mileage Category: D

Body Styles	TMV Pricing		
	Trade	Private	Dealer
4 Dr CE Sdn	4463	5440	6457
4 Dr LE Sdn	5451	6644	7886
4 Dr LE V6 Sdn	6089	7421	8808

Body Styles	TMV Pricing		
	Trade	Private	Dealer
4 Dr XLE Sdn	6175	7527	8935
4 Dr XLE V6 Sdn	6595	8039	9542

Options	Price
AM/FM/CD Audio System [Std on XLE,XLE V6]	+143
AM/FM/Cassette/CD Audio System	+299
Air Conditioning [Opt on CE]	+429
Alarm System [Std on XLE,XLE V6]	+170
Aluminum/Alloy Wheels [Std on XLE,XLE V6]	+155
Antilock Brakes [Opt on CE,LE]	+323
Automatic 4-Speed Transmission [Opt on CE]	+342

Options	Price
Compact Disc Changer	+235
Fog Lights	+170
Leather Seats	+394
Power Driver Seat	+132
Power Moonroof	+427
Rear Spoiler	+150
Traction Control System	+128

1998

Side-impact airbags debut. Depowered front airbags further enhance this car's ability to protect its occupants in a crash. An engine immobilizer feature is now part of the theft-deterrent package.

Mileage Category: D

Body Styles	TMV Pricing		
	Trade	Private	Dealer
4 Dr CE Sdn	3735	4628	5634
4 Dr CE V6 Sdn	4415	5468	6655
4 Dr LE Sdn	4682	5799	7059

Options	Price
AM/FM/CD Audio System [Std on XLE,XLE V6]	+126
AM/FM/Cassette/CD Audio System	+263
Air Conditioning [Std on XLE,XLE V6]	+378
Alarm System [Std on XLE,XLE V6]	+149
Aluminum/Alloy Wheels [Std on XLE,XLE V6]	+156
Antilock Brakes [Opt on CE]	+284
Automatic 4-Speed Transmission [Opt on CE,CE V6]	+301

Body Styles	TMV Pricing		
	Trade	Private	Dealer
4 Dr LE V6 Sdn	5050	6255	7614
4 Dr XLE Sdn	5419	6712	8169
4 Dr XLE V6 Sdn	5732	7101	8645

Options	Price
Compact Disc Changer	+206
Fog Lights	+150
Leather Seats	+347
Power Driver Seat	+116
Power Moonroof	+376
Rear Spoiler	+132

1997

Toyota plays the market conservatively with the all-new Camry, giving consumers exactly what they want; a roomy, attractive, feature-laden car with available V6 performance and the promise of excellent reliability as well as resale value. The Camry is the new standard for midsize sedans.

Mileage Category: D

Body Styles	TMV Pricing		
	Trade	Private	Dealer
4 Dr CE Sdn	3214	4066	5107
4 Dr CE V6 Sdn	3773	4774	5997
4 Dr LE Sdn	4017	5082	6384

Options	Price
AM/FM/Cassette/CD Audio System	+225
Air Conditioning [Opt on CE,CE V6]	+322
Alarm System [Std on XLE,XLE V6]	+116
Aluminum/Alloy Wheels [Std on XLE,XLE V6]	+133
Antilock Brakes [Opt on CE]	+242

Body Styles	TMV Pricing		
	Trade	Private	Dealer
4 Dr LE V6 Sdn	4325	5473	6875
4 Dr XLE Sdn	4265	5397	6780
4 Dr XLE V6 Sdn	4778	6045	7593

Options	Price
Automatic 4-Speed Transmission [Opt on CE]	+257
Compact Disc Changer	+177
Leather Seats	+297
Power Moonroof	+321

1996

Mileage Category: D

Body Styles	TMV Pricing		
	Trade	Private	Dealer
2 Dr DX Cpe	2786	3553	4611
2 Dr LE Cpe	2993	3817	4956
2 Dr LE V6 Cpe	3715	4738	6151
2 Dr SE V6 Cpe	4028	5136	6667
4 Dr Collector V6 Sdn	4837	6168	8005
4 Dr DX Sdn	2864	3652	4741
4 Dr LE Sdn	3211	4095	5315

Options	Price
AM/FM/CD Audio System	+124
AM/FM/Cassette/CD Audio System [Std on Collector V6]	+189
Air Conditioning [Opt on DX]	+272
Antilock Brakes [Std on XLE,XLE V6]	+204

Body Styles	TMV Pricing		
	Trade	Private	Dealer
4 Dr LE V6 Sdn	3847	4905	6367
4 Dr LE V6 Wgn	4089	5214	6768
4 Dr LE Wgn	3658	4666	6057
4 Dr SE V6 Sdn	4202	5359	6956
4 Dr XLE Sdn	3804	4851	6297
4 Dr XLE V6 Sdn	4328	5520	7165

Options	Price
Automatic 4-Speed Transmission [Opt on DX]	+216
Compact Disc Changer	+148
Leather Seats [Std on Collector V6]	+250
Power Moonroof	+270

The 1996 Camry remains virtually unchanged from last year's model. Minor engine adjustments mean that the four-cylinder is fully compliant with all on-board diagnostic standards, and is now certified as a transitional low emission vehicle power plant. Additionally, the interior of the DX line gets a new seat fabric, the LE Sedan is available with a leather package, and the Wagon can now be ordered with a power-operated driver seat.

1995

Front and rear styling is updated, ABS is standard on XLE model, and Camry now meets 1997 side-impact protection standards. DX wagon dumped from lineup.

Mileage Category: D

Body Styles	TMV Pricing		
	Trade	Private	Dealer
2 Dr DX Cpe	2098	2678	3645
2 Dr LE Cpe	2637	3364	4576
2 Dr LE V6 Cpe	2930	3740	5089
2 Dr SE V6 Cpe	3264	4165	5667
4 Dr DX Sdn	2316	2956	4022
4 Dr LE Sdn	2766	3530	4802

Options	Price
AM/FM/CD Audio System	+80
AM/FM/Cassette/CD Audio System	+168

Body Styles	TMV Pricing		
	Trade	Private	Dealer
4 Dr LE V6 Sdn	3053	3896	5301
4 Dr LE V6 Wgn	3128	3992	5432
4 Dr LE Wgn	2871	3663	4984
4 Dr SE V6 Sdn	3366	4296	5845
4 Dr XLE Sdn	2993	3820	5198
4 Dr XLE V6 Sdn	3461	4417	6011

Options	Price
Air Conditioning [Opt on DX]	+241
Aluminum/Alloy Wheels	+87

Toyota
Camry/Solara

1995 (cont'd)

Options	Price
Antilock Brakes [Std on XLE,XLE V6]	+181
Automatic 4-Speed Transmission [Opt on DX]	+192
Compact Disc Changer	+132
Leather Seats	+222

Options	Price
Power Moonroof	+240
Premium Audio System	+80
Rear Spoiler	+84
Third Seat	+82

Camry Solara

2004

The Camry Solara is all new for 2004. It features a sleek new design, a larger optional V6 and a revamped interior with additional features and a more upscale look.

Mileage Category: D

Body Styles	TMV Pricing		
	Trade	Private	Dealer
2 Dr SE Cpe	13043	14144	15978
2 Dr SE Sport Cpe	14035	15173	17070
2 Dr SE Sport V6 Conv	19568	21032	23473
2 Dr SE Sport V6 Cpe	16541	17773	19826

Body Styles	TMV Pricing		
	Trade	Private	Dealer
2 Dr SE V6 Cpe	15533	16896	19168
2 Dr SLE Cpe	16003	17188	19163
2 Dr SLE V6 Conv	22720	24102	26405
2 Dr SLE V6 Cpe	18561	19924	22196

Options	Price
17 Inch Wheels [Opt on SE, SE V6 Cpe]	+200
AM/FM/Cassette/CD Changer Audio System [Opt on SE Sport, SE V6]	+200
Alarm System [Opt on SE Sport Conv]	+479
Automatic 4-Speed Transmission [Opt on SE, SE V6 Cpe]	+830
Automatic Dimming Rearview Mirror [Opt on SE, SE V6 Cpe, SE Sport Conv]	+265
Automatic Stability Control [Opt on SLE V6]	+350
Front and Rear Head Airbag Restraints [Opt on Cpe]	+400

Options	Price
Heated Front Seats [Opt on SLE Cpe]	+350
Navigation System [Opt on SLE V6]	+1350
Power Driver Seat [Opt on SE, SE V6 Cpe, SE Sport Conv]	+120
Power Moonroof [Opt on non-SLE Cpe]	+900
Rear Wind Deflector [Opt on Conv]	+395
Special Factory Paint	+220
Traction Control System [Opt on SLE V6]	+300

2003

For 2003, the manual transmission is no longer available with the V6 engine.

Mileage Category: D

Body Styles	TMV Pricing		
	Trade	Private	Dealer
2 Dr SE Conv	17607	18857	20941
2 Dr SE Cpe	11858	12700	14104
2 Dr SE V6 Conv	18090	19374	21515

Body Styles	TMV Pricing		
	Trade	Private	Dealer
2 Dr SE V6 Cpe	13996	14991	16648
2 Dr SLE V6 Conv	20425	21876	24293
2 Dr SLE V6 Cpe	16387	17551	19491

Options	Price
16 Inch Wheels [Opt on SE V6]	+223
AM/FM/Cassette/CD Changer Audio System [Opt on SLE V6]	+151
Alarm System [Opt on SE,SE V6]	+362
Aluminum/Alloy Wheels [Opt on SE]	+189
Antilock Brakes [Opt on SE]	+513
Automatic 4-Speed Transmission [Opt on SE]	+604
Automatic Climate Control [Std on SLE]	+166
Front Side Airbag Restraints	+189
Heated Front Seats [Opt on SE V6,SLE V6]	+238

Options	Price
JBL Audio System [Opt on SE,SE V6]	+155
Keyless Entry System [Opt on SE,SE V6]	+140
Leather Seats [Opt on SE V6]	+660
Power Driver Seat [Opt on SE,SE V6]	+211
Power Moonroof [Opt on SE,SE V6,SLE V6]	+679
Rear Spoiler [Opt on SE,SE V6]	+162
Special Factory Paint	+166
Traction Control System [Opt on SLE V6]	+226

2002

More power is in store from a new 2.4-liter four-cylinder engine. On the outside, Toyota has added a redesigned front grille and bumper, new headlights and taillights and a bolder rear bumper. A new appearance package (only available on the SE Coupe) includes alloy center caps for the wheels, a three-spoke perforated leather-wrapped steering wheel and shift knob, black trim and Black Pearl emblems. Rounding out the changes are standard daytime running lights, optional seat heaters (coupes only) and a trunk-opener function for the keyless remote.

Mileage Category: D

Body Styles	TMV Pricing		
	Trade	Private	Dealer
2 Dr SE Conv	15542	16782	18848
2 Dr SE Cpe	10160	10970	12320
2 Dr SE V6 Conv	16485	17800	19991

Body Styles	TMV Pricing		
	Trade	Private	Dealer
2 Dr SE V6 Cpe	12139	13107	14720
2 Dr SLE V6 Conv	18071	19512	21914
2 Dr SLE V6 Cpe	12937	13969	15689

Options	Price
16 Inch Wheels [Opt on SE V6]	+204
AM/FM/Cassette/CD Changer Audio System [Opt on SLE V6]	+138
Aluminum/Alloy Wheels [Opt on SE]	+172
Antilock Brakes [Opt on SE]	+469
Automatic 4-Speed Transmission [Std on SLE V6]	+552
Front Side Airbag Restraints	+172
Heated Front Seats [Opt on V6 Cpe]	+217

Options	Price
JBL Audio System [Std on SLE V6]	+141
Keyless Entry System [Std on SLE V6]	+128
Leather Seats [Std on SLE V6]	+604
Pearlescent Metallic Paint	+152
Power Driver Seat [Std on SLE V6]	+193
Power Moonroof [Opt on Cpe]	+621
Rear Spoiler [Std on SLE V6]	+148
Traction Control System [Opt on SLE V6]	+207

For the latest vehicle information, visit www.edmunds.com

2001

Mileage Category: D

Body Styles	TMV Pricing		
	Trade	Private	Dealer
2 Dr SE Conv	13638	15362	16953
2 Dr SE Cpe	8871	9992	11026
2 Dr SE V6 Conv	15147	17061	18828

Options	Price
AM/FM/Cassette/CD Changer Audio System [Opt on SLE V6]	+126
Aluminum/Alloy Wheels [Opt on SE,SE V6]	+274
Antilock Brakes [Opt on SE]	+428
Automatic 4-Speed Transmission [Std on SLE V6,Conv]	+503
Front Side Airbag Restraints	+157
JBL Audio System [Opt on SE,SE V6]	+126

Body Styles	TMV Pricing		
	Trade	Private	Dealer
2 Dr SE V6 Cpe	10574	11911	13145
2 Dr SLE V6 Conv	16389	18460	20372
2 Dr SLE V6 Cpe	11462	12911	14248

Options	Price
Leather Seats [Opt on SE V6]	+566
Pearlescent Metallic Paint	+138
Power Driver Seat [Opt on SE,SE V6]	+245
Power Moonroof	+566
Rear Spoiler [Opt on SE,SE V6]	+135
Traction Control System	+189

Top-level SLE models can be equipped with a new JBL audio system, so long as you order leather upholstery. Option package fiddling makes it easier to equip a Solara the way you like. The anti-theft and engine immobilizer system is restricted to SLEs, while SEs now come standard with a six-speaker cassette stereo. Twilight Blue Pearl is replaced by Indigo Ink as an exterior color.

2000

Mileage Category: D

Body Styles	TMV Pricing		
	Trade	Private	Dealer
2 Dr SE Conv	11534	13275	14981
2 Dr SE Cpe	7482	8611	9717
2 Dr SE V6 Conv	12413	14287	16123

Options	Price
Alarm System [Opt on SE,SE V6]	+213
Aluminum/Alloy Wheels [Opt on SE,SE V6]	+240
Antilock Brakes [Opt on SE]	+376
Automatic 4-Speed Transmission [Std on SLE V6,Conv]	+442
Compact Disc Changer	+276
Front Side Airbag Restraints	+138
JBL Audio System [Opt on SE,SE V6]	+276

Body Styles	TMV Pricing		
	Trade	Private	Dealer
2 Dr SE V6 Cpe	8117	9342	10543
2 Dr SLE V6 Conv	13948	16053	18116
2 Dr SLE V6 Cpe	9646	11102	12529

Options	Price
Leather Seats [Opt on SE,SE V6]	+497
Power Driver Seat [Opt on SE,SE V6]	+215
Power Moonroof	+497
Rear Spoiler [Std on SLE V6,Conv]	+119
Special Factory Paint	+122
Traction Control System	+166

Solara four-cylinder models will achieve ultralow emission vehicle (ULEV) status. A convertible version is now offered for topless fun. SLE models get a JBL premium audio system as standard equipment, and an in-dash six-disc CD changer is optional. Two new exterior colors are offered.

1999

Mileage Category: D

Body Styles	TMV Pricing		
	Trade	Private	Dealer
2 Dr SE Cpe	5537	6654	7816
2 Dr SE V6 Cpe	6310	7582	8906

Options	Price
AM/FM/Cassette/CD Audio System [Std on SLE]	+119
Alarm System [Std on SLE]	+183
Aluminum/Alloy Wheels [Std on SLE]	+186
Antilock Brakes [Opt on SE]	+323
Automatic 4-Speed Transmission [Std on SLE]	+380
Front Side Airbag Restraints	+119

Body Styles	TMV Pricing		
	Trade	Private	Dealer
2 Dr SLE V6 Cpe	7694	9245	10860

Options	Price
JBL Audio System [Std on SLE]	+237
Leather Seats [Std on SLE]	+427
Power Driver Seat [Std on SLE]	+185
Power Moonroof	+427
Traction Control System	+142

This all-new coupe is based on the Camry platform. Designed jointly by the Toyota Motor Corporation in Japan and the Toyota Technical Center in Ann Arbor, Michigan, the Solara is targeted at consumers who want the style of a sports car but the room and comfort of a larger, more practical vehicle.

Celica

2004

Mileage Category: E

Body Styles	TMV Pricing		
	Trade	Private	Dealer
2 Dr GT Hbk	13430	14626	16620

Options	Price
Action Package	+1875
Alarm System	+450
Aluminum/Alloy Wheels [Opt on GT]	+385
Antilock Brakes	+300
Automatic 4-Speed Transmission	+700
Automatic Dimming Rearview Mirror	+295

Body Styles	TMV Pricing		
	Trade	Private	Dealer
2 Dr GTS Hbk	15664	16938	19062

Options	Price
Compact Disc Changer	+550
Cruise Control [Opt on GT]	+320
Front Side Airbag Restraints	+250
Keyless Entry System	+272
Leather Seats [Opt on GTS]	+660
Power Door Locks [Opt on GT]	+250

High-intensity discharge headlights are now optional on all Celica models.

Celica

2004 (cont'd)

Options	Price
Power Moonroof	+900
Power Windows [Opt on GT]	+500
Rear Spoiler	+435

Options	Price
Rear Window Wiper [Opt on GT]	+120
Xenon Headlamps	+515

2003

The Celica has been revised for 2003 with freshened front and rear styling. In front, the Celica gets a new bumper and fascia with a wider upper air intake. Newly available high-intensity discharge (HID) headlights complement the car's advanced styling, and redesigned rear lights echo the projector-style look. Inside, Toyota has redesigned the center dash cluster for improved legibility and added a standard JBL audio system to the GT-S model. A power antenna is now standard on JBL-equipped models. Finally, you can get two new colors: Solar Yellow and Zephyr Blue Metallic.

Mileage Category: E

Body Styles	TMV Pricing		
	Trade	Private	Dealer
2 Dr GT Hbk	12178	13173	14830

Options	Price
Alarm System	+301
Aluminum/Alloy Wheels [Opt on GT]	+291
Antilock Brakes	+513
Appearance Package	+1117
Automatic 4-Speed Transmission	+604
Cruise Control [Opt on GT]	+151
Front Side Airbag Restraints	+189
JBL Audio System [Opt on GT]	+396

Body Styles	TMV Pricing		
	Trade	Private	Dealer
2 Dr GT-S Hbk	14311	15479	17426

Options	Price
Keyless Entry System	+174
Leather Seats [Opt on GT-S]	+498
Power Door Locks [Opt on GT]	+170
Power Moonroof	+679
Power Windows [Opt on GT]	+185
Rear Spoiler	+328
Xenon Headlamps [Opt on GT-S]	+389

2002

No changes this year.

Mileage Category: E

Body Styles	TMV Pricing		
	Trade	Private	Dealer
2 Dr GT Hbk	10239	11185	12762

Options	Price
Aluminum/Alloy Wheels [Std on GT-S]	+266
Antilock Brakes	+469
Appearance Package	+1097
Automatic 4-Speed Transmission	+552
Cruise Control [Std on GT-S]	+138
Front Side Airbag Restraints	+172

Body Styles	TMV Pricing		
	Trade	Private	Dealer
2 Dr GT-S Hbk	12177	13302	15177

Options	Price
Leather Seats [Opt on GT-S]	+455
Power Door Locks [Std on GT-S]	+155
Power Moonroof	+621
Power Windows [Std on GT-S]	+169
Premium Audio System [Std on GT-S]	+228
Rear Spoiler	+300

2001

No changes this year.

Mileage Category: E

Body Styles	TMV Pricing		
	Trade	Private	Dealer
2 Dr GT Hbk	8691	10000	11208

Options	Price
Aluminum/Alloy Wheels [Opt on GT]	+242
Antilock Brakes	+428
Automatic 4-Speed Transmission	+440
Cruise Control [Opt on GT]	+126
Front Side Airbag Restraints	+157
Leather Seats	+683

Body Styles	TMV Pricing		
	Trade	Private	Dealer
2 Dr GT-S Hbk	10222	11761	13181

Options	Price
Power Door Locks [Opt on GT]	+142
Power Moonroof	+554
Power Windows [Opt on GT]	+154
Premium Audio System [Opt on GT]	+208
Rear Spoiler	+274

2000

The all-new 2000 Celica is considerably more performance-oriented than the previous model. Highlights include a sleek exterior, a 180-horsepower engine and six-speed gearbox for the GT-S, and sharp handling.

Mileage Category: E

Body Styles	TMV Pricing		
	Trade	Private	Dealer
2 Dr GT Hbk	7800	9086	10346

Options	Price
Alarm System	+235
Aluminum/Alloy Wheels [Opt on GT]	+240
Antilock Brakes	+376
Automatic 4-Speed Transmission	+387
Compact Disc Changer	+304
Front Side Airbag Restraints	+138

Body Styles	TMV Pricing		
	Trade	Private	Dealer
2 Dr GT-S Hbk	8782	10230	11650

Options	Price
Leather Seats	+599
Power Door Locks [Opt on GT]	+124
Power Moonroof	+486
Power Windows [Opt on GT]	+135
Rear Spoiler	+240

For the latest vehicle information, visit www.edmunds.com

Mileage Category: E

Body Styles	TMV Pricing		
	Trade	Private	Dealer
2 Dr GT Conv	8121	9685	11312

Options	Price
AM/FM/Cassette/CD Audio System [Std on Conv]	+235
Alarm System	+181
Aluminum/Alloy Wheels [Std on Conv]	+186
Antilock Brakes	+323
Automatic 4-Speed Transmission	+342

Body Styles	TMV Pricing		
	Trade	Private	Dealer
2 Dr GT Hbk	6732	8027	9375

Options	Price
Compact Disc Changer	+235
Leather Seats	+463
Power Moonroof	+376
Sport Suspension	+224

The Celica GT Sport Coupe has been discontinued along with the color Galaxy Blue Metallic.

Celica ST is eliminated. GT's get more standard features and one new color: Caribbean Green Metallic.

Body Styles	TMV Pricing		
	Trade	Private	Dealer
2 Dr GT Conv	6416	7833	9431
2 Dr GT Cpe	5450	6655	8013

Options	Price
AM/FM/CD Audio System	+162
AM/FM/Cassette/CD Audio System [Opt on Hbk]	+206
Alarm System	+159
Aluminum/Alloy Wheels [Std on Conv]	+164
Antilock Brakes	+284
Automatic 4-Speed Transmission	+338

Body Styles	TMV Pricing		
	Trade	Private	Dealer
2 Dr GT Hbk	5616	6857	8256

Options	Price
Compact Disc Changer	+206
Keyless Entry System	+149
Leather Seats	+407
Power Moonroof	+285
Rear Spoiler [Opt on Cpe]	+164
Sport Suspension	+197

GT Coupe is gone, and Fiesta Blue Metallic can be specified for cars equipped with black sport cloth interior.

Body Styles	TMV Pricing		
	Trade	Private	Dealer
2 Dr GT Conv	5198	6454	7989
2 Dr GT Hbk	4667	5795	7174
2 Dr GT Limited Edition Conv	5601	6954	8608

Options	Price
AM/FM/CD Audio System	+138
AM/FM/Cassette/CD Audio System [Opt on GT]	+241
Air Conditioning [Opt on GT,ST]	+322
Alarm System	+136
Aluminum/Alloy Wheels [Opt on GT,ST]	+139
Antilock Brakes	+242
Automatic 4-Speed Transmission	+257
Compact Disc Changer	+177

Body Styles	TMV Pricing		
	Trade	Private	Dealer
2 Dr ST Cpe	3800	4718	5841
2 Dr ST Hbk	4052	5031	6227
2 Dr ST Limited Edition Hbk	4431	5502	6810

Options	Price
Keyless Entry System	+127
Leather Seats	+348
Power Moonroof	+244
Premium Audio System [Opt on GT]	+273
Rear Spoiler [Opt on GT,ST]	+133
Sport Seats	+311
Sport Suspension	+160

Front and rear styling tweaks, a new spoiler, new wheel covers, two new colors and revised fabrics debut this year.

Mileage Category: E

Body Styles	TMV Pricing		
	Trade	Private	Dealer
2 Dr GT 25th Anniv Conv	4816	6097	7866
2 Dr GT Conv	4498	5695	7347
2 Dr GT Cpe	3741	4736	6111
2 Dr GT Hbk	3798	4809	6204

Options	Price
AM/FM/CD Audio System [Opt on GT,ST]	+116
AM/FM/Cassette/CD Audio System [Opt on GT]	+203
Air Conditioning [Opt on GT,ST]	+272
Alarm System [Opt on GT,ST]	+115
Aluminum/Alloy Wheels	+118
Antilock Brakes	+204

Body Styles	TMV Pricing		
	Trade	Private	Dealer
2 Dr ST 25th Anniv Hbk	3860	4886	6304
2 Dr ST Cpe	2913	3687	4757
2 Dr ST Hbk	3075	3893	5022

Options	Price
Automatic 4-Speed Transmission	+216
Compact Disc Changer	+148
Leather Seats	+225
Power Moonroof [Opt on GT,ST]	+206
Premium Audio System [Opt on GT]	+230

Toyota
Celica/Corolla

1995
GT Convertible returns to lineup, available in red, white, blue or black.

Mileage Category: E

Body Styles	TMV Pricing		
	Trade	Private	Dealer
2 Dr GT Conv	3686	4711	6418
2 Dr GT Cpe	2904	3711	5056
2 Dr GT Hbk	2996	3829	5216

Options	Price
AM/FM/CD Audio System	+103
AM/FM/Cassette/CD Audio System	+132
Air Conditioning	+241
Alarm System	+102
Aluminum/Alloy Wheels	+104
Antilock Brakes	+181
Automatic 4-Speed Transmission	+192
Compact Disc Changer	+132

Body Styles	TMV Pricing		
	Trade	Private	Dealer
2 Dr ST Cpe	2349	3001	4088
2 Dr ST Hbk	2647	3382	4606

Options	Price
Keyless Entry System [Opt on ST]	+95
Leather Seats	+260
Power Moonroof	+183
Premium Audio System [Opt on GT]	+204
Rear Spoiler	+99
Sport Seats	+232
Sport Suspension	+120

Corolla

2004

After a full redesign last year, the Corolla carries over unchanged for 2004.

Mileage Category: B

Body Styles	TMV Pricing		
	Trade	Private	Dealer
4 Dr CE Sdn	9169	10025	11451
4 Dr LE Sdn	10380	11242	12678

Options	Price
Alarm System [Opt on LE, S]	+319
Aluminum/Alloy Wheels	+390
Antilock Brakes	+300
Automatic 4-Speed Transmission	+800
Automatic Dimming Rearview Mirror	+150
Cruise Control	+120
Front Side Airbag Restraints	+250

Body Styles	TMV Pricing		
	Trade	Private	Dealer
4 Dr S Sdn	10276	11138	12575

Options	Price
Keyless Entry System [Opt on S]	+255
Leather Seats [Opt on LE]	+700
Power Door Locks [Opt on CE]	+295
Power Moonroof [Opt on S, LE]	+750
Power Windows [Opt on S]	+350
Rear Spoiler	+225

2003

Toyota's Corolla is all-new for 2003. Far removed from the original Corolla, this one is the biggest yet. It's also more luxurious. The return is more interior room, a more substantial feel and changes aimed at fixing the previous model's shortcomings. Though pricing has increased, Toyota has made more equipment standard in the hopes of keeping the Corolla's reputation for value intact.

Mileage Category: B

Body Styles	TMV Pricing		
	Trade	Private	Dealer
4 Dr CE Sdn	8346	9255	10770
4 Dr LE Sdn	8599	9535	11096

Options	Price
Alarm System [Opt on LE, S]	+241
Aluminum/Alloy Wheels [Opt on LE, S]	+294
Antilock Brakes	+513
Automatic 4-Speed Transmission	+604
Automatic Dimming Rearview Mirror [Opt on LE]	+170
Cruise Control	+189
Front Side Airbag Restraints	+189

Body Styles	TMV Pricing		
	Trade	Private	Dealer
4 Dr S Sdn	8418	9334	10861

Options	Price
Keyless Entry System [Opt on S]	+151
Leather Seats [Opt on LE]	+449
Power Door Locks [Opt on CE]	+223
Power Moonroof [Opt on LE, S]	+566
Power Windows [Opt on S]	+181
Rear Spoiler [Opt on S]	+208

2002

Pricing for optional value packages has been lowered for all trim lines.

Mileage Category: B

Body Styles	TMV Pricing		
	Trade	Private	Dealer
4 Dr CE Sdn	6365	7119	8376
4 Dr LE Sdn	7220	8076	9503

Options	Price
Air Conditioning	+414
Aluminum/Alloy Wheels [Opt on LE, S]	+252
Antilock Brakes [Opt on LE, S]	+469
Automatic 3-Speed Transmission [Opt on CE]	+286
Automatic 4-Speed Transmission [Opt on LE, S]	+562

Body Styles	TMV Pricing		
	Trade	Private	Dealer
4 Dr S Sdn	6775	7579	8918

Options	Price
Cruise Control [Opt on LE, S]	+172
Front Side Airbag Restraints	+172
Power Door Locks	+145
Power Moonroof [Opt on LE, S]	+493
Rear Window Defroster [Opt on CE, S]	+141

2001

Midgrade CE trim replaces entry-level VE, top-line LE replaces midgrade CE and a sporty new CE-based S model debuts. Front and rear lighting is restyled, and the fascia up front is tweaked and now includes a chrome-ringed grille. An internal trunk release has been added, along with a push-button fresh/recirculate control for the ventilation system. Two new colors replace an equal number of shades that are fading away.

Mileage Category: B

Body Styles	TMV Pricing		
	Trade	Private	Dealer
4 Dr CE Sdn	5445	6493	7461
4 Dr LE Sdn	6141	7323	8414

Options	Price
AM/FM/Cassette Audio System [Opt on CE,S]	+132
Air Conditioning	+597
Aluminum/Alloy Wheels	+230
Antilock Brakes	+428
Automatic 3-Speed Transmission	+261
Automatic 4-Speed Transmission	+513

Body Styles	TMV Pricing		
	Trade	Private	Dealer
4 Dr S Sdn	5737	6840	7859

Options	Price
Cruise Control	+157
Front Side Airbag Restraints	+157
Power Door Locks	+170
Power Moonroof [Opt on LE,S]	+450
Power Windows [Opt on LE,S]	+180
Rear Window Defroster [Opt on CE,S]	+129

2000

The Corolla receives increased performance from VVT-i engine technology. Horsepower jumps from 120 to 125. The Corolla also achieves low emission vehicle status this year.

Mileage Category: B

Body Styles	TMV Pricing		
	Trade	Private	Dealer
4 Dr CE Sdn	4781	5807	6813
4 Dr LE Sdn	4937	5997	7036

Options	Price
AM/FM/CD Audio System	+166
Air Conditioning [Std on LE]	+524
Alarm System	+220
Aluminum/Alloy Wheels	+229
Antilock Brakes	+376
Automatic 3-Speed Transmission	+332
Automatic 4-Speed Transmission	+442

Body Styles	TMV Pricing		
	Trade	Private	Dealer
4 Dr VE Sdn	4681	5686	6672

Options	Price
Compact Disc Changer	+304
Cruise Control	+119
Front Side Airbag Restraints	+138
Power Door Locks [Opt on CE]	+124
Power Moonroof	+406
Power Windows [Opt on CE]	+158
Rear Spoiler	+163

1999

The VE model features a deluxe AM/FM ETR four-speaker audio system as standard equipment. A Touring Package is standard equipment on the Corolla LE model. Five new exterior colors include Silver Stream Opal, Venetian Red Pearl, Dark Emerald Pearl, Aqua Blue Metallic and Twilight Blue Pearl.

Mileage Category: B

Body Styles	TMV Pricing		
	Trade	Private	Dealer
4 Dr CE Sdn	3801	4763	5765
4 Dr LE Sdn	4184	5243	6346

Options	Price
AM/FM/CD Audio System	+128
AM/FM/Cassette/CD Audio System	+192
Air Conditioning [Std on LE]	+406
Alarm System	+170
Aluminum/Alloy Wheels	+177
Antilock Brakes	+323

Body Styles	TMV Pricing		
	Trade	Private	Dealer
4 Dr VE Sdn	3683	4617	5589

Options	Price
Automatic 3-Speed Transmission	+256
Automatic 4-Speed Transmission	+342
Compact Disc Changer	+235
Power Moonroof	+315
Power Windows [Std on LE]	+122
Rear Spoiler	+126

1998

The Toyota Corolla is completely redesigned this year with a new engine, new sheet metal and a new standard for safety in compact cars: optional front passenger side-impact airbags.

Mileage Category: B

Body Styles	TMV Pricing		
	Trade	Private	Dealer
4 Dr CE Sdn	3119	4057	5115
4 Dr LE Sdn	3393	4411	5560

Options	Price
AM/FM/Cassette/CD Audio System	+169
Air Conditioning [Opt on VE]	+357
Alarm System	+150
Aluminum/Alloy Wheels	+156
Antilock Brakes	+284

Body Styles	TMV Pricing		
	Trade	Private	Dealer
4 Dr VE Sdn	2904	3774	4755

Options	Price
Automatic 3-Speed Transmission	+188
Automatic 4-Speed Transmission	+301
Compact Disc Changer	+206
Power Moonroof	+276

Toyota
Corolla/ECHO

1997

The Classic Edition (CE) debuts and the slow-selling DX Wagon gets the ax.

Mileage Category: B

Body Styles	TMV Pricing		
	Trade	Private	Dealer
4 Dr CE Sdn	2576	3424	4460
4 Dr DX Sdn	2538	3373	4392

Options	Price
AM/FM/Cassette/CD Audio System	+144
Air Conditioning [Std on CE]	+305
Aluminum/Alloy Wheels	+133
Antilock Brakes	+242

Body Styles	TMV Pricing		
	Trade	Private	Dealer
4 Dr STD Sdn	2419	3213	4184

Options	Price
Automatic 3-Speed Transmission	+160
Automatic 4-Speed Transmission	+257
Compact Disc Changer	+177
Power Sunroof	+191

1996

The Toyota Corolla heads into 1996 with redesigned front and rear fascias, three new colors, new wheel covers, an optional integrated child seat and a revised interior. Additionally, the five-speed manual transmission has been revised for a better feel and more positive gear engagement.

Mileage Category: B

Body Styles	TMV Pricing		
	Trade	Private	Dealer
4 Dr DX Sdn	2255	3026	4090
4 Dr DX Wgn	2401	3221	4354

Options	Price
Air Conditioning	+257
Antilock Brakes	+204
Automatic 3-Speed Transmission	+135

Body Styles	TMV Pricing		
	Trade	Private	Dealer
4 Dr STD Sdn	1997	2679	3621

Options	Price
Automatic 4-Speed Transmission	+216
Compact Disc Changer	+148
Power Sunroof	+161

1995

The 1.8-liter engine loses 10 horsepower to meet stricter emissions regulations but torque is up. DX models get new interior fabric.

Mileage Category: B

Body Styles	TMV Pricing		
	Trade	Private	Dealer
4 Dr DX Sdn	1874	2519	3593
4 Dr DX Wgn	1907	2562	3654

Options	Price
Air Conditioning [Std on LE]	+228
Aluminum/Alloy Wheels	+99
Antilock Brakes	+181
Automatic 3-Speed Transmission	+120

Body Styles	TMV Pricing		
	Trade	Private	Dealer
4 Dr LE Sdn	2121	2850	4065
4 Dr STD Sdn	1606	2158	3077

Options	Price
Automatic 4-Speed Transmission	+192
Compact Disc Changer	+132
Power Sunroof	+143
Premium Audio System [Opt on DX Wgn]	+96

ECHO

2004

The Echo is unchanged for 2004.

Mileage Category: A

Body Styles	TMV Pricing		
	Trade	Private	Dealer
2 Dr STD Cpe	7053	7724	8843

Options	Price
AM/FM/CD Audio System	+140
AM/FM/Cassette Audio System	+220
AM/FM/Cassette/CD Audio System	+290
Air Conditioning	+875
Alarm System	+499
Aluminum/Alloy Wheels	+499
Antilock Brakes	+340
Appearance Package	+1060
Automatic 4-Speed Transmission	+800
Compact Disc Changer	+589
Front Side Airbag Restraints	+250

Body Styles	TMV Pricing		
	Trade	Private	Dealer
4 Dr STD Sdn	7371	8187	9548

Options	Price
Intermittent Wipers	+200
Keyless Entry System	+175
Power Door Locks	+180
Power Steering	+450
Power Windows [Opt on SDN]	+350
Premium Audio System	+315
Rear Spoiler	+300
Rear Window Defroster	+175
Split Folding Rear Seat	+325
Tachometer	+120

Mileage Category: A

2003

For 2003, the Echo receives a new look with a redesigned front and rear fascia. The front bumper and fenders feature sharper and more prominent lines, a new chrome-slat grille and new headlamps with a distinctive bulb layout. Optional round foglamps accent the new front-end design. In the rear, a new trunk lid with chrome plate garnish, a new bumper and redesigned combination clear-lens taillights provide a more upscale look. A new Appearance Package adds aerodynamic body enhancements, including overfenders that blend into the front and rear underbody. A rear trunk spoiler incorporates the LED high-mounted stop lamp. The standard 14-inch wheels get a new wheel cover design, and, for the first time, the Echo can be had with optional 15-inch wheels. The new styling is topped off with five new colors.

Body Styles	TMV Pricing		
	Trade	Private	Dealer
2 Dr STD Cpe	6004	6853	8267

Options	Price
AM/FM/Cassette/CD Audio System	+181
Air Conditioning	+642
Alarm System	+377
Antilock Brakes	+513
Automatic 4-Speed Transmission	+604
Front Side Airbag Restraints	+189
Keyless Entry System	+132

Body Styles	TMV Pricing		
	Trade	Private	Dealer
4 Dr STD Sdn	6617	7442	8818

Options	Price
Power Door Locks	+136
Power Steering	+189
Power Windows [Opt on SDN]	+147
Rear Spoiler	+226
Rear Window Defroster	+132
Split Folding Rear Seat	+125

Mileage Category: A

2002

Toyota has left the Echo untouched for 2002.

Body Styles	TMV Pricing		
	Trade	Private	Dealer
2 Dr STD Cpe	5087	5860	7147

Options	Price
AM/FM/Cassette/CD Audio System	+186
Air Conditioning	+586
Antilock Brakes	+469
Automatic 4-Speed Transmission	+614
Front Side Airbag Restraints	+172

Body Styles	TMV Pricing		
	Trade	Private	Dealer
4 Dr STD Sdn	5380	6197	7559

Options	Price
Keyless Entry System	+121
Power Door Locks	+124
Power Steering	+172
Power Windows	+183
Rear Window Defroster	+141

Mileage Category: A

2001

In an effort to better protect occupants of this lightweight economy car, Toyota makes side airbags optional for 2001. Brilliant Blue Pearl is a new color.

Body Styles	TMV Pricing		
	Trade	Private	Dealer
2 Dr STD Cpe	4370	5414	6377

Options	Price
AM/FM/Cassette/CD Audio System	+170
Air Conditioning	+581
Antilock Brakes	+428
Automatic 4-Speed Transmission	+503

Body Styles	TMV Pricing		
	Trade	Private	Dealer
4 Dr STD Sdn	4704	5828	6865

Options	Price
Front Side Airbag Restraints	+157
Power Door Locks	+142
Power Windows	+167
Rear Window Defroster	+129

Mileage Category: A

2000

The 2000 Toyota Echo brings a new name and a fresh concept to the Toyota lineup. Designed to attract youthful buyers, the Echo features a roomy and comfortable interior, superb gas mileage and an affordable price.

Body Styles	TMV Pricing		
	Trade	Private	Dealer
2 Dr STD Cpe	3731	4732	5714

Options	Price
AM/FM/CD Audio System	+124
AM/FM/Cassette/CD Audio System	+149
Air Conditioning	+511
Aluminum/Alloy Wheels	+138
Antilock Brakes	+376

Body Styles	TMV Pricing		
	Trade	Private	Dealer
4 Dr STD Sdn	3947	5006	6044

Options	Price
Automatic 4-Speed Transmission	+442
Compact Disc Changer	+318
Power Door Locks	+124
Power Steering	+149

Highlander

2004

Mileage Category: M

Body Styles	TMV Pricing		
	Trade	Private	Dealer
4 Dr Limited AWD SUV	24169	25603	27992
4 Dr Limited SUV	22613	23966	26222
4 Dr STD AWD SUV	19474	20868	23191

Options	Price
Alarm System [Std on Limited]	+359
Aluminum/Alloy Wheels [Std on Limited]	+520

Body Styles	TMV Pricing		
	Trade	Private	Dealer
4 Dr STD SUV	18228	19582	21838
4 Dr V6 AWD SUV	21205	22639	25029
4 Dr V6 SUV	19386	20766	23065

Options	Price
Automatic Dimming Rearview Mirror [Std on Limited]	+265
DVD Entertainment System	+1770

2004 (cont'd)

For 2004, a larger 3.3-liter V6 replaces the 3.0-liter engine, resulting in 10 extra horsepower for a total of 230. Additionally, a fold-flat third-row seat (for two passengers) is now optional on base models and standard on the Limited. To keep the extra passengers content in back, a rear DVD entertainment system is available on Limited models. On the safety front, all Highlanders now come with an electronic stability control system and a tire-pressure warning system, while side curtain airbags for the first and second rows are optional across the board. Rounding out the changes are freshened exterior styling, new seat fabric, new instrument and door panel trim and a 5-hp boost for the base four-cylinder engine (now rated at 160).

Options	Price
Front Head Airbag Restraints	+650
Heated Front Seats	+440
Keyless Entry System [Opt on STD, V6]	+180
Leather Seats	+1400
Luggage Rack [Std on Limited]	+220
Navigation System [Opt on Limited]	+1700
Power Driver Seat [Std on Limited]	+250
Power Moonroof	+900

Options	Price
Privacy Glass [Std on AWD, Limited]	+200
Rear Spoiler [Std on Limited]	+200
Running Boards	+625
Side Steps	+459
Third Seat [Opt on V6, STD 2WD]	+850
Tonneau Cover [Opt on STD, V6]	+140
Trailer Hitch	+390

2003

There are no changes for the Highlander this year.

Mileage Category: M

Body Styles	TMV Pricing		
	Trade	Private	Dealer
4 Dr Limited AWD SUV	21703	23161	25590
4 Dr Limited SUV	20105	21456	23707
4 Dr STD AWD SUV	17757	18950	20937

Body Styles	TMV Pricing		
	Trade	Private	Dealer
4 Dr STD SUV	16778	17905	19783
4 Dr V6 AWD SUV	19113	20397	22536
4 Dr V6 SUV	17879	19080	21081

Options	Price
AM/FM/Cassette/CD Changer Audio System [Opt on Limited]	+151
Alarm System [Std on Limited]	+271
Aluminum/Alloy Wheels [Std on Limited]	+377
Camper/Towing Package	+121
Front Side Airbag Restraints	+189
Heated Front Seats [Opt on Limited]	+332
Keyless Entry System [Std on Limited]	+166
Leather Seats [Opt on Limited]	+808

Options	Price
Limited Slip Differential	+294
Luggage Rack [Std on Limited]	+166
Power Driver Seat [Std on Limited]	+294
Power Moonroof	+679
Privacy Glass [Std on Limited]	+234
Tinted Glass [Std on Limited]	+208
Traction Control System	+491
Trailer Hitch	+219

2002

Toyota's car-based Highlander SUV receives no changes this year.

Mileage Category: M

Body Styles	TMV Pricing		
	Trade	Private	Dealer
4 Dr Limited AWD SUV	19908	21193	23335
4 Dr Limited SUV	18952	20176	22216
4 Dr STD AWD SUV	16497	17562	19338

Body Styles	TMV Pricing		
	Trade	Private	Dealer
4 Dr STD SUV	15543	16547	18220
4 Dr V6 AWD SUV	17531	18650	20516
4 Dr V6 SUV	16603	17675	19462

Options	Price
AM/FM/Cassette/CD Changer Audio System [Opt on Limited]	+138
Aluminum/Alloy Wheels [Std on Limited]	+345
Automatic Stability Control	+448
Front Side Airbag Restraints	+172
Heated Front Seats [Opt on Limited]	+304
Keyless Entry System [Std on Limited]	+148
Leather Seats [Opt on Limited]	+738

Options	Price
Limited Slip Differential [Opt on 4WD]	+269
Luggage Rack [Std on Limited]	+152
Power Driver Seat [Std on Limited]	+269
Power Moonroof	+621
Privacy Glass [Std on Limited]	+214
Traction Control System	+448
Trailer Hitch	+200

2001

Based on the same platform as the Lexus RX 300, Toyota's new Highlander SUV represents the best blend of a station wagon, a minivan and a sport utility available on the market today. Available only with a V6 and an automatic transmission driving power to the front or all the wheels, Highlander will be sold in one trim level with a Limited package listed on the option sheet.

Mileage Category: M

Body Styles	TMV Pricing		
	Trade	Private	Dealer
4 Dr STD AWD SUV	14164	15745	17204
4 Dr STD SUV	13198	14671	16031

Body Styles	TMV Pricing		
	Trade	Private	Dealer
4 Dr V6 AWD SUV	15032	16710	18259
4 Dr V6 SUV	14247	15838	17306

Options	Price
AM/FM/Cassette/CD Changer Audio System [Opt on V6]	+252
Alarm System	+135
Aluminum/Alloy Wheels	+315
Automatic Climate Control	+157
Automatic Stability Control	+409
Camper/Towing Package	+182
Front Side Airbag Restraints	+157

Options	Price
Heated Front Seats	+277
Keyless Entry System	+138
Leather Seats	+639
Limited Slip Differential	+245
Luggage Rack	+138
Power Driver Seat	+245
Power Sunroof	+513
Privacy Glass	+195

Options	Price	Options	Price
Traction Control System	+535	Trailer Hitch	+182

2001 (cont'd)

Land Cruiser

2004

Mileage Category: O

Body Styles	TMV Pricing		
	Trade	Private	Dealer
4 Dr STD 4WD SUV	41602	43705	47210

Options	Price	Options	Price
DVD Entertainment System	+2097	Navigation System	+3350
Front Side Airbag Restraints	+300	Running Boards	+315
Front and Rear Head Airbag Restraints	+350	Trailer Hitch	+379
Luggage Rack	+250		

The optional navigation system is now available with a rearview backup camera that lets drivers see what's behind them when backing out of parking spaces.

2003

Mileage Category: O

Body Styles	TMV Pricing		
	Trade	Private	Dealer
4 Dr STD 4WD SUV	37236	39523	43336

Options	Price	Options	Price
Front Side Airbag Restraints	+189	Navigation System	+2264
Front and Rear Head Airbag Restraints	+302	Running Boards	+260
Luggage Rack	+166		

Mechanically, the 2003 Land Cruiser delivers five more horsepower via a new five-speed automatic transmission. On the outside, you'll find standard 17-inch wheels, optional 18-inch wheels, slightly freshened front-end styling and clear-lens rear turn signals. Inside, Land Cruiser features a new dashboard design, a power tilt and telescoping steering wheel, rear seat audio and steering wheel-mounted audio controls. There is also a new optional rear DVD entertainment system and available front- and second-row side curtain airbags.

2002

Mileage Category: O

Body Styles	TMV Pricing		
	Trade	Private	Dealer
4 Dr STD 4WD SUV	31181	33334	36923

Options	Price	Options	Price
Luggage Rack	+224	Rear Wind Deflector	+155
Navigation System	+1932	Running Boards	+238

Toyota's flagship SUV receives no changes this year.

2001

Mileage Category: O

Body Styles	TMV Pricing		
	Trade	Private	Dealer
4 Dr STD 4WD SUV	24977	27625	30070

Options	Price	Options	Price
Navigation System	+1888	Third Seat	+1425

A navigation system is optional (and plays DVD movies when the vehicle is not in motion). Standard equipment includes an electrochromic rearview mirror with compass and JBL audio with an in-dash six-disc CD changer. Each of the power windows now features one-touch up and down control. Three new colors replace Desert Bronze on the color chart, and the alloy wheels have a new chromelike finish.

2000

Mileage Category: O

Body Styles	TMV Pricing		
	Trade	Private	Dealer
4 Dr STD 4WD SUV	21111	23724	26286

Options	Price	Options	Price
Automatic Climate Control (2 Zone) - Front and Rear	+315	Running Boards	+428
Luggage Rack	+180	Third Seat	+627
Rear Wind Deflector	+138		

The Land Cruiser receives new standard equipment features, such as vehicle skid control and an Active TRAC electronic four-wheel-drive system with torque transfer capability. Additional standard equipment includes illuminated entry for the remote keyless-entry system, power tilt/slide moonroof and a leather interior. The optional third-row seat now includes rear air conditioning.

1999

Mileage Category: O

Body Styles	TMV Pricing		
	Trade	Private	Dealer
4 Dr STD 4WD SUV	16732	19166	21699

Options	Price	Options	Price
Air Conditioning - Front and Rear	+243	Locking Differential	+150
Leather Seats	+777	Luggage Rack	+139

No changes this year.

Land Cruiser

1999 (cont'd)

Options	Price
Power Moonroof	+451
Running Boards	+331

Options	Price
Third Seat	+539

1998

For 1998, the all-new Land Cruiser gets a more powerful V8 engine, standard ABS, an increase in structural rigidity, an improved suspension system, increased passenger and cargo room and several new colors.

Mileage Category: O

Body Styles	TMV Pricing		
	Trade	Private	Dealer
4 Dr STD 4WD SUV	14614	17200	20115

Options	Price
Leather Seats	+684
Locking Differential	+132
Power Moonroof	+445

Options	Price
Running Boards	+291
Third Seat	+459

1997

The Black Package is discontinued, but black becomes an available color choice. A 40th-anniversary package lets buyers outfit their Cruiser with leather and choose one of two unique paint schemes.

Mileage Category: O

Body Styles	TMV Pricing		
	Trade	Private	Dealer
4 Dr 40th Anniv Limited 4WD SUV	12227	14618	17540

Options	Price
AM/FM/CD Audio System	+144
AM/FM/Cassette/CD Audio System	+303
Alarm System	+124
Aluminum/Alloy Wheels	+169
Burlwood Dash	+178
Compact Disc Changer	+257
Keyless Entry System	+127

Body Styles	TMV Pricing		
	Trade	Private	Dealer
4 Dr STD 4WD SUV	10990	13138	15764

Options	Price
Leather Seats [Opt on STD]	+392
Power Driver Seat [Opt on STD]	+134
Power Moonroof	+304
Power Passenger Seat [Opt on STD]	+134
Running Boards	+223
Third Seat	+540

1996

The Black Package debuts, featuring black paint along with chrome mirrors and door handles.

Mileage Category: O

Body Styles	TMV Pricing		
	Trade	Private	Dealer
4 Dr STD 4WD SUV	8755	10608	13168

Options	Price
AM/FM/CD Audio System	+121
AM/FM/Cassette/CD Audio System	+255
Aluminum/Alloy Wheels	+142
Burlwood Dash	+150
Compact Disc Changer	+216

Options	Price
Leather Seats	+331
Power Moonroof	+320
Running Boards	+188
Third Seat	+455

1995

Redesigned dashboard carries dual airbags, and ABS is now standard. Revised grille carries Toyota logo rather than nameplate.

Mileage Category: O

Body Styles	TMV Pricing		
	Trade	Private	Dealer
4 Dr STD 4WD SUV	6891	8421	10970

Options	Price
AM/FM/Cassette/CD Audio System	+244
Aluminum/Alloy Wheels	+126
Compact Disc Changer	+192
Leather Seats	+360
Locking Differential	+84

Options	Price
Power Driver Seat	+99
Power Moonroof	+227
Power Passenger Seat	+99
Running Boards	+167
Third Seat	+404

Matrix
2004

Mileage Category: L

Body Styles	TMV Pricing		
	Trade	Private	Dealer
4 Dr STD AWD Wgn	12459	13469	15152
4 Dr STD Wgn	10721	11732	13415
4 Dr XR AWD Wgn	13404	14414	16096

Body Styles	TMV Pricing		
	Trade	Private	Dealer
4 Dr XR Wgn	11794	12804	14487
4 Dr XRS Wgn	13620	14630	16312

Options	Price
17 Inch Wheels [Opt on XR, XRS]	+150
AM/FM/Cassette/CD Audio System [Opt on XR, XR AWD]	+140
Alarm System	+319
Aluminum/Alloy Wheels [Std on XRS]	+250
Antilock Brakes [Opt on STD, XR FWD]	+300
Automatic 4-Speed Transmission [Opt on STD, XR FWD]	+800
Cruise Control [Opt on STD, XR]	+180

Options	Price
Fog Lights [Opt on XR]	+150
Front Side Airbag Restraints	+250
Keyless Entry System [Opt on STD]	+200
Navigation System [Opt on XRS]	+1350
Power Moonroof [Opt on XR, XRS]	+800
Power Windows [Opt on STD]	+240
Rear Window Wiper [Opt on STD FWD]	+180

Introduced last year, the Matrix carries over unchanged into 2004.

2003

Mileage Category: L

Body Styles	TMV Pricing		
	Trade	Private	Dealer
4 Dr STD AWD Wgn	11565	12600	14325
4 Dr STD Wgn	9958	10849	12334
4 Dr XR AWD Wgn	11851	12912	14679

Body Styles	TMV Pricing		
	Trade	Private	Dealer
4 Dr XR Wgn	10949	11929	13562
4 Dr XRS Wgn	12043	13120	14916

Options	Price
Alarm System	+241
Aluminum/Alloy Wheels [Opt on STD,XR]	+309
Antilock Brakes [Opt on STD,XR]	+513
Automatic 4-Speed Transmission [Std on AWD]	+604
Compact Disc Changer [Opt on XR,XRS]	+264
Cruise Control [Opt on STD,XR]	+189
Fog Lights [Opt on XR]	+204

Options	Price
Front Side Airbag Restraints	+189
Keyless Entry System [Opt on STD]	+151
Navigation System [Opt on XR,XRS]	+1162
Power Door Locks [Opt on STD]	+200
Power Moonroof [Opt on XR,XRS]	+566
Power Windows [Opt on STD]	+181
Rear Window Wiper [Opt on STD]	+136

The Matrix is an all-new model from Toyota. It offers sporty looks, enhanced cargo-carrying abilities and useful features not commonly found in small cars.

MR2
1995

Mileage Category: E

Body Styles	TMV Pricing		
	Trade	Private	Dealer
2 Dr STD Cpe	2962	3784	5155

Body Styles	TMV Pricing		
	Trade	Private	Dealer
2 Dr Turbo Cpe	4114	5256	7160

Options	Price
AM/FM/CD Audio System	+96
AM/FM/Cassette/CD Audio System	+100
Air Conditioning	+144
Antilock Brakes	+253
Automatic 4-Speed Transmission	+192

Options	Price
Compact Disc Changer	+156
Leather Seats	+240
Limited Slip Differential	+96
Sunroof	+91
T-Tops - Glass [Opt on STD]	+402

Final year for Mister Two. Several states lose Turbo model, which wouldn't pass emissions regulations. Base models with T-bar roof get power windows and locks standard.

MR2 Spyder

2004

Mileage Category: E

Body Styles	TMV Pricing		
	Trade	Private	Dealer
2 Dr STD Conv	17448	18706	20801

Options	Price	Options	Price
6-Speed Sequential Semi-Manual Transmission	+1000	Leather Seats	+660
Alarm System	+259	Limited Slip Differential (Rear)	+270

After undergoing extensive changes last year, the MR2's upgrade for 2004 comes in the way of a newly optional limited-slip differential.

2003

For 2003, Toyota gives the MR2 Spyder a bolder look in front with a new bumper and fascia, dual-bulb projector-style headlights and integrated standard foglamps. The side air intakes are revised and now color-keyed. In rear, the MR2 is distinguished by new combination lamps with cylindrical turn signals and reverse lights that mimic the dual-bulb look of the headlights. Further, the rear grille garnishes combines body-color vertical ribs and mesh to emphasize the midengine design. A larger oval chrome tailpipe puts the emphasis on performance capability, and a new power antenna contributes to the roadster's clean lines. Inside, instrument panel graphics have been revised, and there are new chrome trim accents. Additionally, the leather seating packages -- black or tan -- now include matching color convertible tops. Mechanically, an all-new six-speed sequential manual transmission (SMT) is optional, replacing last year's five-speed SMT. Toyota has also upped the rear wheels to 16 inches in diameter.

Mileage Category: E

Body Styles	TMV Pricing		
	Trade	Private	Dealer
2 Dr STD Conv	14297	15511	17533

Options	Price	Options	Price
6-Speed Sequential Semi-Manual Transmission	+1415	Leather Seats	+498
Alarm System	+195		

2002

The MR2 Spyder rolls into 2002 with a new Formula One-style five-speed manual transmission. The only other change is that the yellow cloth interior has been discontinued.

Mileage Category: E

Body Styles	TMV Pricing		
	Trade	Private	Dealer
2 Dr STD Conv	12242	13373	15259

Options	Price	Options	Price
5-Speed Sequential Semi-Manual Transmission	+931	Leather Seats	+455

2001

No changes this year.

Mileage Category: E

Body Styles	TMV Pricing		
	Trade	Private	Dealer
2 Dr STD Conv	10666	12271	13753

Options	Price
Leather Seats	+390

2000

Toyota revives the MR2 nameplate on a minimalist two-seat roadster, set to compete directly with the ever-popular Mazda Miata. Only 5,000 are being built and sold.

Mileage Category: E

Body Styles	TMV Pricing		
	Trade	Private	Dealer
2 Dr STD Conv	9617	11200	12753

Paseo

1997

Mileage Category: E

Body Styles	TMV Pricing			Body Styles	TMV Pricing		
	Trade	Private	Dealer		Trade	Private	Dealer
2 Dr STD Conv	3382	4199	5197	2 Dr STD Cpe	2787	3460	4283

Options	Price	Options	Price
AM/FM/CD Audio System	+147	Automatic 4-Speed Transmission	+257
Air Conditioning	+297	Compact Disc Changer	+224
Aluminum/Alloy Wheels	+133	Rear Spoiler	+133
Antilock Brakes	+242	Sunroof	+131

A convertible debuts. Coupes get dual-visor vanity mirrors, fresh door trim and rotary-heater controls.

1996

All-new Paseo looks like last year's car, but is much improved. It now meets 1997 passenger car safety standards, and has a split-fold rear seat.

Mileage Category: E

Body Styles	TMV Pricing		
	Trade	Private	Dealer
2 Dr STD Cpe	2302	2914	3760

Options	Price	Options	Price
AM/FM/CD Audio System	+124	Automatic 4-Speed Transmission	+216
Air Conditioning	+250	Compact Disc Changer	+189
Antilock Brakes	+204	Power Sunroof	+176

1995

Mileage Category: E

Body Styles	TMV Pricing		
	Trade	Private	Dealer
2 Dr STD Cpe	1799	2299	3132

Options	Price	Options	Price
AM/FM/CD Audio System	+110	Automatic 4-Speed Transmission	+192
Air Conditioning	+222	Compact Disc Changer	+168
Aluminum/Alloy Wheels	+99	Power Sunroof	+156
Antilock Brakes	+181	Rear Spoiler	+99

Several states with strict emissions laws get detuned Paseo for 1995.

Pickup
1995

Mileage Category: J

Body Styles	TMV Pricing			Body Styles	TMV Pricing		
	Trade	Private	Dealer		Trade	Private	Dealer
2 Dr DX 4WD Ext Cab SB	3298	4097	5428	2 Dr DX V6 4WD Std Cab SB	3257	4046	5362
2 Dr DX 4WD Std Cab SB	2983	3706	4911	2 Dr DX V6 Ext Cab SB	2788	3463	4588
2 Dr DX Ext Cab SB	2549	3167	4197	2 Dr SR5 4WD Ext Cab SB	4044	5024	6656
2 Dr DX Std Cab SB	2001	2486	3294	2 Dr SR5 Ext Cab SB	3179	3949	5233
2 Dr DX V6 4WD Ext Cab SB	3574	4440	5882	2 Dr STD Std Cab SB	1805	2242	2971

Options	Price	Options	Price
AM/FM/CD Audio System	+108	Automatic 4-Speed Transmission	+204
Air Conditioning	+192	Compact Disc Changer	+132
Antilock Brakes	+181	Sunroof	+86

All models get a color-keyed center-high-mount-stop-lamp and redesigned audio systems.

Previa
1997

Mileage Category: P

Body Styles	TMV Pricing			Body Styles	TMV Pricing		
	Trade	Private	Dealer		Trade	Private	Dealer
3 Dr DX All-Trac S/C AWD Pass Van	4476	5659	7105	3 Dr LE All-Trac S/C AWD Pass Van	5525	6984	8768
3 Dr DX S/C Pass Van	4032	5098	6401	3 Dr LE S/C Pass Van	5059	6395	8027

Options	Price	Options	Price
AM/FM/CD Audio System	+147	Compact Disc Changer	+224
AM/FM/Cassette/CD Audio System	+241	Keyless Entry System	+127
Air Conditioning - Front and Rear [Opt on DX]	+359	Leather Seats	+385
Aluminum/Alloy Wheels	+139	Moonroof [Opt on LE]	+129
Antilock Brakes	+253	Power Moonroof [Opt on LE]	+353
Captain Chairs (2) [Opt on LE]	+246	Premium Audio System [Opt on LE]	+273
Captain Chairs (4) [Opt on LE]	+279	Privacy Glass	+136

The 2.4-liter supercharged engine received numerous improvements to reduce noise, vibration and harshness. Non-ABS models get larger brakes while all models received revised wheel covers. Two new colors added: Glacier Green Metallic and Deep Violet Pearl.

1996

All Previas now have supercharged power.

Mileage Category: P

Body Styles	TMV Pricing			Body Styles	TMV Pricing		
	Trade	Private	Dealer		Trade	Private	Dealer
3 Dr DX All-Trac S/C AWD Pass Van	3763	4859	6373	3 Dr LE All-Trac S/C AWD Pass Van	4391	5671	7438
3 Dr DX S/C Pass Van	3384	4370	5731	3 Dr LE S/C Pass Van	4065	5249	6884

1996 (cont'd)

Options	Price		Options	Price
AM/FM/CD Audio System	+124		Compact Disc Changer	+189
AM/FM/Cassette/CD Audio System	+203		Dual Power Moonroofs [Opt on LE]	+399
Air Conditioning - Front and Rear [Opt on DX]	+303		Leather Seats	+514
Aluminum/Alloy Wheels	+118		Power Moonroof [Opt on LE]	+298
Antilock Brakes	+213		Premium Audio System [Opt on LE]	+230
Captain Chairs (2) [Opt on LE]	+207		Privacy Glass	+115
Captain Chairs (4) [Opt on LE]	+235			

1995

Seat back map pockets and an illuminated driver's visor vanity mirror are standard on all models.

Mileage Category: P

Body Styles	TMV Pricing				Body Styles	TMV Pricing		
	Trade	Private	Dealer			Trade	Private	Dealer
3 Dr DX All-Trac AWD Pass Van	2806	3624	4987		3 Dr LE All-Trac AWD Pass Van	3380	4364	6005
3 Dr DX All-Trac S/C AWD Pass Van	2951	3811	5245		3 Dr LE All-Trac S/C AWD Pass Van	3661	4728	6505
3 Dr DX Pass Van	2662	3438	4730		3 Dr LE Pass Van	3030	3913	5385
3 Dr DX S/C Pass Van	2761	3566	4907		3 Dr LE S/C Pass Van	3152	4070	5601

Options	Price		Options	Price
AM/FM/CD Audio System	+110		Dual Power Moonroofs [Opt on LE]	+354
AM/FM/Cassette/CD Audio System	+180		Leather Seats	+288
Air Conditioning - Front and Rear [Opt on DX]	+269		Moonroof	+96
Aluminum/Alloy Wheels	+104		Power Moonroof	+264
Antilock Brakes	+189		Premium Audio System [Opt on LE]	+204
Captain Chairs (2)	+125		Privacy Glass	+102
Compact Disc Changer	+168		Running Boards	+80

Prius

2004

The Prius is completely redesigned for 2004 with a larger overall size, more power, better mileage and even more available features.

Mileage Category: C

Body Styles		TMV Pricing		
		Trade	Private	Dealer
4 Dr STD Hbk		16934	18545	21230

Options	Price		Options	Price
AM/FM/CD Changer Audio System	+225		Front and Rear Head Airbag Restraints	+350
Alarm System	+350		Garage Door Opener	+120
Automatic Dimming Rearview Mirror	+265		Navigation System	+1800
Compact Disc Changer	+589		Rear Window Wiper	+180
Fog Lights	+150		Xenon Headlamps	+825
Front Side Airbag Restraints	+300			

2003

Mileage Category: B

Body Styles		TMV Pricing		
		Trade	Private	Dealer
4 Dr STD Sdn		15292	16850	19447

Options	Price		Options	Price
AM/FM/Cassette/CD Audio System	+204		Front Side Airbag Restraints	+287
AM/FM/Cassette/CD Changer Audio System	+362		Navigation System	+2421
Cruise Control	+189		Special Factory Paint	+140

The Prius, a hybrid-electric vehicle, is unchanged for 2003.

2002

Initially offered as a single specification with no factory options, Toyota's advanced gasoline/electric hybrid now offers a choice of several new options for 2002. These include a navigation system, cruise control, side airbags and daytime running lights. There are also two new colors: Brilliant Blue and Blue Moon Pearl.

Mileage Category: B

Body Styles		TMV Pricing		
		Trade	Private	Dealer
4 Dr STD Sdn		13567	15175	17856

Options	Price		Options	Price
AM/FM/Cassette/CD Audio System	+186		Front Side Airbag Restraints	+262
AM/FM/Cassette/CD Changer Audio System	+331		Navigation System	+2213
Cruise Control	+172			

2001

Toyota's Prius, a gas/electric hybrid that follows in the more expensive Honda Insight's footsteps, offers space for five adults coupled with class-leading fuel economy.

Mileage Category: B

Body Styles	TMV Pricing		
	Trade	Private	Dealer
4 Dr STD Sdn	11352	13538	15555

Options	Price	Options	Price
AM/FM/Cassette/CD Audio System	+170	Front Side Airbag Restraints	+239
AM/FM/Cassette/CD Changer Audio System	+302	Navigation System	+2018
Cruise Control	+157		

RAV4

2004

Mileage Category: L

Body Styles	TMV Pricing				Body Styles	TMV Pricing		
	Trade	Private	Dealer			Trade	Private	Dealer
4 Dr STD AWD SUV	14268	15448	17415		4 Dr STD SUV	12836	13976	15877

Options	Price	Options	Price
AM/FM/Cassette/CD Changer Audio System	+250	Leather Steering Wheel	+170
Aluminum/Alloy Wheels	+400	Luggage Rack	+220
Automatic 4-Speed Transmission	+1050	Power Heated Mirrors	+150
Automatic Dimming Rearview Mirror	+125	Power Sunroof	+900
Front Head Airbag Restraints	+680	Privacy Glass	+310
Garage Door Opener	+125	Rear Spoiler	+200
Heated Front Seats	+440	Side Steps	+800
JBL Audio System	+330	Special Factory Paint	+220
Keyless Entry System	+230	Trailer Hitch	+335
Leather Seats	+670		

Toyota has given the RAV4 a midcycle freshening for 2004. Notable improvements include a larger 161-horsepower, 2.4-liter, four-cylinder engine, a mild restyling that gives it a more aggressive appearance, and inside, a new steering wheel and instrument panel. Standard equipment has increased significantly, with stability and traction control, antilock brakes, air conditioning and a six-speaker stereo heading up the list. Multistage front airbags are also new this year, and side airbags for front occupants and full-length head curtain airbags are now optional.

2003

Already sporty-looking, the RAV4 compact SUV gets even sportier thanks to a new optional sport package that adds a new grille, a hood scoop, color-keyed door handles, heated exterior mirrors, tubular roof rack and gray-painted bumpers and overfenders. Inside, the package adds special sport fabric seats.

Mileage Category: L

Body Styles	TMV Pricing				Body Styles	TMV Pricing		
	Trade	Private	Dealer			Trade	Private	Dealer
4 Dr STD AWD SUV	12022	13137	14996		4 Dr STD SUV	11537	12607	14391

Options	Price	Options	Price
AM/FM/Cassette/CD Audio System	+283	Luggage Rack	+166
Air Conditioning	+743	Power Door Locks	+177
Aluminum/Alloy Wheels	+302	Power Moonroof	+679
Antilock Brakes	+513	Power Windows	+200
Automatic 4-Speed Transmission	+792	Privacy Glass	+234
Cruise Control	+166	Rear Spoiler	+151
Fog Lights	+125	Special Factory Paint	+166
Keyless Entry System	+174	Sport Package	+415
Leather Seats	+566	Tinted Glass	+132
Limited Slip Differential	+294		

2002

Toyota's mini-SUV receives just a couple cosmetic changes this year. Models ordered with the Quick Order package now have gray-painted bumpers and overfenders, and Toyota has added color-keyed bumpers and overfenders to the "L" package. There are also three new L package colors: Rainforest Pearl, Spectra Blue Mica and Pearl White (Natural White and Vintage Gold have been discontinued).

Mileage Category: L

Body Styles	TMV Pricing				Body Styles	TMV Pricing		
	Trade	Private	Dealer			Trade	Private	Dealer
4 Dr STD AWD SUV	10648	11769	13637		4 Dr STD SUV	9953	11000	12746

Options	Price	Options	Price
AM/FM/Cassette/CD Audio System	+345	Limited Slip Differential [Opt on 4WD]	+269
Air Conditioning	+680	Luggage Rack	+152
Aluminum/Alloy Wheels	+276	Power Door Locks	+166
Antilock Brakes	+469	Power Moonroof	+621
Automatic 4-Speed Transmission	+724	Power Windows	+190
Cruise Control	+152	Privacy Glass	+214
Keyless Entry System	+159	Rear Spoiler	+138
Leather Seats	+517	Side Steps	+172

2002 (cont'd)

Options	Price
Special Factory Paint	+152

Options	Price
Tinted Glass	+141

2001

Completely redesigned, RAV4 grows in size and gets a more powerful engine, along with edgy new styling.

Mileage Category: L

Body Styles	TMV Pricing		
	Trade	Private	Dealer
4 Dr STD AWD SUV	9684	11194	12588

Body Styles	TMV Pricing		
	Trade	Private	Dealer
4 Dr STD SUV	8958	10354	11642

Options	Price
AM/FM/Cassette/CD Audio System	+315
Air Conditioning	+620
Aluminum/Alloy Wheels	+252
Antilock Brakes	+428
Automatic 4-Speed Transmission	+598
Cruise Control	+157
Keyless Entry System	+138
Leather Seats	+472

Options	Price
Limited Slip Differential	+245
Luggage Rack	+138
Power Door Locks	+151
Power Sunroof	+513
Power Windows	+173
Privacy Glass	+195
Rear Spoiler	+126

2000

The RAV4 SUV remains largely unchanged for 2000. A new cupholder design and the extinction of the two-door RAV4 convertible are the big news for '00.

Mileage Category: L

Body Styles	TMV Pricing		
	Trade	Private	Dealer
4 Dr L Special Edition AWD SUV	9293	10812	12301
4 Dr L Special Edition SUV	8952	10414	11848

Body Styles	TMV Pricing		
	Trade	Private	Dealer
4 Dr STD AWD SUV	8131	9460	10763
4 Dr STD SUV	7371	8576	9757

Options	Price
AM/FM/CD Audio System [Opt on STD]	+249
AM/FM/Cassette Audio System [Opt on STD]	+193
AM/FM/Cassette/CD Audio System	+276
Air Conditioning [Opt on STD]	+544
Alarm System	+193
Aluminum/Alloy Wheels [Opt on STD]	+271
Antilock Brakes	+376
Automatic 4-Speed Transmission	+580
Compact Disc Changer	+332

Options	Price
Cruise Control [Opt on STD]	+138
Leather Seats	+414
Limited Slip Differential	+215
Luggage Rack	+138
Power Door Locks [Opt on STD]	+133
Power Moonroof	+450
Power Windows [Opt on STD]	+152
Privacy Glass [Opt on STD]	+172
Side Steps	+130

1999

Leather seats and color-keyed body cladding are now available as part of the "L Special Edition" package. Color-keyed mirrors and door handles can also be had this year and the spare tire is now a full-size steel wheel with a soft cover.

Mileage Category: L

Body Styles	TMV Pricing		
	Trade	Private	Dealer
2 Dr STD AWD Conv	6991	8390	9847
2 Dr STD Conv	6319	7584	8901
4 Dr STD AWD SUV	7049	8460	9928

Body Styles	TMV Pricing		
	Trade	Private	Dealer
4 Dr STD SUV	6395	7675	9007
4 Dr Special Edition AWD SUV	7264	8718	10231

Options	Price
AM/FM/CD Audio System	+192
AM/FM/Cassette Audio System [Opt on STD]	+150
AM/FM/Cassette/CD Audio System	+214
Air Conditioning [Opt on STD]	+420
Alarm System	+150
Aluminum/Alloy Wheels	+209
Antilock Brakes	+323

Options	Price
Automatic 4-Speed Transmission	+448
Compact Disc Changer	+256
Leather Seats	+321
Limited Slip Differential	+167
Power Moonroof	+349
Power Windows [Opt on STD]	+117
Privacy Glass [Opt on STD]	+132

1998

Toyota's mini SUV enters its third year of production with minor changes to the grille, headlights, taillamps and interior. Four-door RAV4s get new seat fabric. A late-year introduction of the new RAV4 convertible makes this sport-ute more appealing for those who live in the sunbelt.

Mileage Category: L

Body Styles	TMV Pricing		
	Trade	Private	Dealer
2 Dr STD AWD Conv	5749	6942	8288
2 Dr STD AWD SUV	5439	6568	7842
2 Dr STD Conv	5310	6413	7657
2 Dr STD SUV	5142	6210	7414

Body Styles	TMV Pricing		
	Trade	Private	Dealer
4 Dr L Special Edition SUV	5829	7039	8404
4 Dr STD AWD SUV	5593	6754	8064
4 Dr STD SUV	5147	6216	7421

Options	Price
AM/FM/CD Audio System	+169

Options	Price
AM/FM/Cassette Audio System	+132

For the latest vehicle information, visit www.edmunds.com

Options	Price
AM/FM/Cassette/CD Audio System	+188
Air Conditioning	+370
Alarm System	+150
Aluminum/Alloy Wheels	+184
Antilock Brakes	+284
Automatic 4-Speed Transmission	+413

Options	Price
Compact Disc Changer	+226
Leather Seats	+282
Limited Slip Differential	+141
Power Moonroof	+344
Spoke Wheels	+257

1997

New fabric debuts on the two-door RAV, and a sunroof is finally available on the four-door. Improvements have also been made by using sound-deadening material in the dash area, reducing engine noise in the passenger compartment.

Mileage Category: L

Body Styles	TMV Pricing		
	Trade	Private	Dealer
2 Dr STD AWD SUV	4792	5868	7182
2 Dr STD SUV	4233	5183	6344

Body Styles	TMV Pricing		
	Trade	Private	Dealer
4 Dr STD AWD SUV	4800	5877	7194
4 Dr STD SUV	4499	5509	6743

Options	Price
AM/FM/CD Audio System	+133
AM/FM/Cassette/CD Audio System	+160
Air Conditioning	+316
Alarm System	+124
Aluminum/Alloy Wheels	+157
Antilock Brakes	+242
Automatic 4-Speed Transmission	+337

Options	Price
Compact Disc Changer	+174
Leather Seats	+241
Limited Slip Differential	+121
Power Moonroof	+294
Spoke Wheels	+219
T-Tops - Solid	+144

1996

A new mini-ute based on passenger car mechanicals debuts this year. It's available as a two-door or four-door.

Mileage Category: L

Body Styles	TMV Pricing		
	Trade	Private	Dealer
2 Dr STD AWD SUV	4172	5091	6360
2 Dr STD SUV	3730	4552	5687

Body Styles	TMV Pricing		
	Trade	Private	Dealer
4 Dr STD AWD SUV	4308	5257	6567
4 Dr STD SUV	4013	4897	6117

Options	Price
Air Conditioning	+266
Aluminum/Alloy Wheels	+133
Antilock Brakes	+204
Automatic 4-Speed Transmission	+284

Options	Price
Compact Disc Changer	+148
Spoke Wheels	+185
Sunroof	+162
T-Tops - Solid	+121

Sequoia
2004

Mileage Category: N

Body Styles	TMV Pricing		
	Trade	Private	Dealer
4 Dr Limited 4WD SUV	32298	33815	36342
4 Dr Limited SUV	29608	31110	33612

Body Styles	TMV Pricing		
	Trade	Private	Dealer
4 Dr SR5 4WD SUV	26013	27546	30100
4 Dr SR5 SUV	23178	24694	27220

Power front seats and a rear air conditioner are now standard on the SR5 model, and the Limited now comes with a sunroof.

Options	Price
AM/FM/Cassette/CD Changer Audio System	+200
Aluminum/Alloy Wheels [Opt on SR5 2WD]	+500
Automatic Dimming Rearview Mirror	+125
Automatic Load Leveling	+360
DVD Entertainment System	+1770
Front Side Airbag Restraints	+250
Front and Rear Head Airbag Restraints	+250
JBL Audio System [Opt on SR5]	+265
Keyless Entry System [Opt on SR5]	+245
Leather Seats [Opt on SR5]	+1345

Options	Price
Luggage Rack [Opt on SR5]	+220
Power Moonroof [Opt on SR5]	+1000
Rear Audio Controls	+240
Rear Spoiler [Opt on Limited]	+200
Running Boards [Opt on SR5]	+650
Side Steps [Opt on SR5]	+399
Skid Plates [Std on 4WD]	+159
Styled Steel Wheels [Opt on SR5 2WD]	+330
Trailer Hitch [Opt on SR5]	+275

2003

For 2003, the eight-passenger Sequoia SUV features new 17-inch alloy wheels and tires and an inside rearview auto-dimming mirror as standard equipment on the top-of-the-line Limited grade, and as options on the SR5 model. A rear DVD entertainment system with two cordless headphones, and a load leveling rear suspension are new features available on both Sequoia models.

Mileage Category: N

Body Styles	TMV Pricing		
	Trade	Private	Dealer
4 Dr Limited 4WD SUV	29105	30920	33946
4 Dr Limited SUV	27344	29050	31894

Body Styles	TMV Pricing		
	Trade	Private	Dealer
4 Dr SR5 4WD SUV	24144	25650	28160
4 Dr SR5 SUV	21776	23134	25398

Sequoia/Sienna

2003 (cont'd)

Options	Price
17 Inch Wheels [Opt on SR5]	+415
AM/FM/Cassette/CD Changer Audio System	+151
Automatic Climate Control (2 Zone) - Driver and Passenger [Opt on SR5]	+430
Automatic Load Leveling	+272
DVD Entertainment System	+1336
Front Head Airbag Restraints	+189
Front Side Airbag Restraints	+189
JBL Audio System [Opt on SR5]	+389
Keyless Entry System [Opt on SR5]	+185

Options	Price
Leather Seats [Opt on SR5]	+868
Luggage Rack [Opt on SR5]	+166
Power Driver Seat [Opt on SR5]	+226
Power Moonroof	+755
Power Passenger Seat [Opt on SR5]	+226
Rear Spoiler [Opt on Limited]	+151
Running Boards [Opt on SR5]	+302
Tinted Glass [Opt on SR5]	+158
Trailer Hitch [Opt on SR5]	+287

2002

The Sequoia is virtually unchanged for 2002. SR5 models have two additional stand-alone options this year: keyless remote and front foglamps.

Mileage Category: N

Body Styles	TMV Pricing		
	Trade	Private	Dealer
4 Dr Limited 4WD SUV	26422	28157	31049
4 Dr Limited SUV	25206	26881	29672

Body Styles	TMV Pricing		
	Trade	Private	Dealer
4 Dr SR5 4WD SUV	22325	23808	26280
4 Dr SR5 SUV	20079	21413	23636

Options	Price
16 Inch Wheels [Opt on SR5]	+328
AM/FM/Cassette/CD Changer Audio System	+138
Automatic Climate Control (2 Zone) - Front and Rear [Opt on SR5]	+393
Front Head Airbag Restraints	+172
Front Side Airbag Restraints	+172
JBL Audio System [Opt on SR5]	+207
Keyless Entry System [Opt on SR5]	+169
Leather Seats [Opt on SR5]	+793
Luggage Rack [Opt on SR5]	+152

Options	Price
Power Driver Seat [Opt on SR5]	+207
Power Moonroof	+690
Power Passenger Seat [Opt on SR5]	+207
Rear Spoiler [Opt on Limited]	+138
Running Boards [Opt on SR5]	+276
Styled Steel Wheels [Opt on SR5]	+228
Tinted Glass [Opt on SR5]	+145
Trailer Hitch [Opt on SR5]	+262

2001

Toyota releases the Tundra pickup-based Sequoia, a full-size SUV that represents the first serious challenge to the Chevrolet Tahoe/Suburban, Ford Expedition and GMC Yukon from across either ocean.

Mileage Category: N

Body Styles	TMV Pricing		
	Trade	Private	Dealer
4 Dr Limited 4WD SUV	23219	25720	28028
4 Dr Limited SUV	21449	23759	25891

Body Styles	TMV Pricing		
	Trade	Private	Dealer
4 Dr SR5 4WD SUV	18993	21038	22926
4 Dr SR5 SUV	17117	18960	20661

Options	Price
AM/FM/Cassette/CD Changer Audio System	+126
Air Conditioning - Front and Rear [Opt on SR5]	+359
Aluminum/Alloy Wheels [Opt on SR5]	+315
Front Head Airbag Restraints	+157
Front Side Airbag Restraints	+157
Keyless Entry System [Opt on SR5]	+138
Leather Seats [Opt on SR5]	+786
Luggage Rack [Opt on SR5]	+138

Options	Price
Power Driver Seat [Opt on SR5]	+204
Power Passenger Seat [Opt on SR5]	+204
Power Sunroof	+632
Rear Spoiler	+126
Running Boards [Opt on SR5]	+252
Styled Steel Wheels [Opt on SR5]	+208
Trailer Hitch [Opt on SR5]	+239

Sienna

2004

Mileage Category: P

Body Styles	TMV Pricing		
	Trade	Private	Dealer
4 Dr CE Pass Van	17881	19303	21674
4 Dr LE AWD Pass Van	21829	23251	25622
4 Dr LE Pass Van	19052	20474	22845
4 Dr XLE AWD Pass Van	25060	26510	28926

Body Styles	TMV Pricing		
	Trade	Private	Dealer
4 Dr XLE Limited AWD Pass Van	29260	30706	33116
4 Dr XLE Limited Pass Van	27378	28826	31238
4 Dr XLE Pass Van	22125	23547	25918

Options	Price
17 Inch Wheels [Opt on XLE]	+400
8 Passenger Seating [Opt on LE, CE]	+150
AM/FM/Cassette/CD Changer Audio System [Opt on XLE]	+295
Alarm System [Opt on LE]	+249

Options	Price
Aluminum/Alloy Wheels [Opt on LE, CE]	+699
Automatic Dimming Rearview Mirror [Std on XLE Limited]	+199
Automatic Stability Control [Opt on XLE]	+600
DVD Entertainment System [Opt on non-CE]	+1450

2004 (cont'd)

The Sienna has been completely redesigned for 2004. Roomier and more powerful than before, Toyota's minivan entry now has the all-important fold-flat third-row seat, as well as a choice of seven- or eight-passenger seating (on lower level trims) and available all-wheel drive.

Options	Price
Front Side Airbag Restraints [Opt on LE, XLE]	+300
Front, Rear and Third Row Head Airbag Restraints [Opt on LE, XLE]	+450
Garage Door Opener [Opt on LE]	+120
Heated Front Seats [Opt on XLE]	+350
Leather Seats [Opt on XLE]	+630
Navigation System [Opt on XLE, XLE Limited]	+1680

Options	Price
Power Moonroof [Opt on XLE]	+900
Power Sliding Door [Opt on LE]	+495
Rear Spoiler	+200
Running Boards	+599
Traction Control System [Opt on XLE 2WD]	+600
Trailer Hitch	+415

2003

The Sienna carries into 2003 virtually unchanged. The right-hand power-sliding door is now available on CE models, as are captain's chairs. A complete redesign is due for 2004.

Mileage Category: P

Body Styles	TMV Pricing		
	Trade	Private	Dealer
4 Dr CE Pass Van	14091	15278	17255
4 Dr LE Pass Van	15592	16905	19094

Body Styles	TMV Pricing		
	Trade	Private	Dealer
4 Dr XLE Pass Van	16560	17954	20278

Options	Price
AM/FM/Cassette/CD Changer Audio System [Opt on XLE]	+302
Alarm System [Opt on CE,LE]	+233
Aluminum/Alloy Wheels [Opt on LE]	+359
Camper/Towing Package	+121
Captain Chairs (4) [Opt on CE,LE]	+245
Cruise Control [Opt on CE]	+136
Front Side Airbag Restraints	+189
Heated Front Seats [Opt on XLE]	+332
JBL Audio System [Opt on LE]	+245
Keyless Entry System [Opt on CE,LE]	+166

Options	Price
Leather Seats [Opt on XLE]	+868
Luggage Rack [Opt on CE,LE]	+166
Power Door Locks [Opt on CE]	+181
Power Driver Seat [Opt on LE]	+245
Power Dual Sliding Doors [Opt on LE,XLE]	+600
Power Moonroof [Opt on XLE]	+679
Power Sliding Door	+298
Power Windows [Opt on CE]	+204
Tinted Glass [Opt on CE]	+189
Traction Control System	+415

2002

Nothing major is in store for Toyota's minivan this year. The most significant change is the availability of a new "Symphony" special edition for LE models. This special edition includes items like keyless entry, a roof rack, captain's chairs for the first two rows (six-way power driver seat), a premium JBL audio system, power swing privacy glass, color-keyed heated power side mirrors, an overhead console with HomeLink and painted bumpers and cladding. There's also a new color this year exclusive to the Symphony: Lunar Mist Metallic. The base CE model's Extra Value package now includes a roof rack and keyless entry for no extra cost.

Mileage Category: P

Body Styles	TMV Pricing		
	Trade	Private	Dealer
4 Dr CE Pass Van	11636	12809	14765
4 Dr LE Pass Van	12768	14055	16200

Body Styles	TMV Pricing		
	Trade	Private	Dealer
4 Dr XLE Pass Van	13886	15285	17617

Options	Price
AM/FM/Cassette/CD Changer Audio System [Opt on XLE]	+276
Aluminum/Alloy Wheels [Opt on LE]	+328
Automatic Stability Control	+379
Captain Chairs (4) [Opt on LE]	+448
Cruise Control [Opt on CE]	+124
Front Side Airbag Restraints	+172
Heated Front Seats [Opt on XLE]	+304
JBL Audio System [Opt on LE]	+204
Keyless Entry System [Opt on CE,LE]	+128

Options	Price
Leather Seats [Opt on XLE]	+793
Luggage Rack [Opt on CE,LE]	+152
Power Door Locks [Opt on CE]	+166
Power Driver Seat [Opt on LE]	+224
Power Dual Sliding Doors [Opt on XLE]	+548
Power Moonroof [Opt on XLE]	+621
Power Sliding Door [Opt on LE,XLE]	+272
Power Windows [Opt on CE]	+186
Traction Control System	+379

2001

Like other minivans on the market, the 2001 Sienna can be equipped with an on-board entertainment system. Dual power-sliding doors are optional, and the safety-conscious will like the fact that side airbags and a stability control system are available. Sienna's smooth V6 makes more power and torque this year. A rear defroster is standard on all Siennas, while JBL audio, heated front seats and an electrochromic rearview mirror with integrated compass are optional on XLE models. Styling has been tweaked front and rear, four new colors replace four old colors and all Siennas come with a driver-side sliding door.

Mileage Category: P

Body Styles	TMV Pricing		
	Trade	Private	Dealer
4 Dr CE Pass Van	10292	11963	13506
4 Dr LE Pass Van	11481	13345	15065

Body Styles	TMV Pricing		
	Trade	Private	Dealer
4 Dr XLE Pass Van	12391	14403	16260

Options	Price
AM/FM/Cassette/CD Changer Audio System [Opt on XLE]	+324
Aluminum/Alloy Wheels [Opt on LE]	+299
Automatic Stability Control	+346
Captain Chairs (4) [Opt on LE]	+472
Child Seat (1) [Opt on LE]	+157
Front Side Airbag Restraints	+157

Options	Price
Heated Front Seats [Opt on XLE]	+277
Keyless Entry System [Opt on CE,LE]	+138
Leather Seats	+887
Luggage Rack [Opt on LE]	+138
Power Door Locks [Opt on CE]	+151
Power Dual Sliding Doors	+566
Power Moonroof	+554

2001 (cont'd)

Options	Price
Power Sliding Door	+249
Power Windows [Opt on CE]	+167

Options	Price
Traction Control System	+346

2000

New for Sienna are two exterior colors and various audio enhancements. All grades feature a standard AM/FM/cassette audio system. XLE models add a CD deck and offer an optional in-dash six-disc changer.

Mileage Category: P

Body Styles	TMV Pricing		
	Trade	Private	Dealer
3 Dr CE Pass Van	8169	9685	11171
4 Dr LE Pass Van	9612	11396	13144

Body Styles	TMV Pricing		
	Trade	Private	Dealer
4 Dr XLE Pass Van	10514	12466	14380

Options	Price
Air Conditioning - Front and Rear [Opt on CE]	+326
Alarm System [Opt on CE,LE]	+177
Aluminum/Alloy Wheels [Opt on CE,LE]	+262
Captain Chairs (2)	+138
Captain Chairs (4) [Opt on LE]	+492
Child Seat (1)	+138
Compact Disc Changer	+304
Keyless Entry System [Opt on CE,LE]	+122
Leather Seats	+779
Luggage Rack [Opt on CE,LE]	+122

Options	Price
Power Door Locks [Opt on CE]	+133
Power Moonroof	+486
Power Sliding Door	+218
Power Windows [Opt on CE]	+146
Privacy Glass [Opt on CE]	+199
Rear Spoiler	+157
Running Boards	+329
Sliding Driver Side Door [Opt on CE]	+218
Trailer Hitch	+160

1999

Entering its second full model year of production at Toyota's Kentucky plant, the Sienna minivan gets a right-side power-sliding door. An engine immobilizer system has been added to the keyless-entry security system and all Siennas will be equipped with daytime running lights. Selected models have a full-size spare tire and Woodland Pearl replaces Classic Green Pearl as an exterior color option.

Mileage Category: P

Body Styles	TMV Pricing		
	Trade	Private	Dealer
3 Dr CE Pass Van	6979	8387	9853
4 Dr LE Pass Van	8234	9896	11626

Body Styles	TMV Pricing		
	Trade	Private	Dealer
4 Dr XLE Pass Van	9106	10944	12857

Options	Price
AM/FM/CD Audio System [Opt on CE,LE]	+137
Air Conditioning - Front and Rear [Opt on CE]	+252
Alarm System [Opt on CE,LE]	+137
Aluminum/Alloy Wheels [Opt on CE,LE]	+203
Captain Chairs (4) [Opt on LE]	+380
Compact Disc Changer	+235
Leather Seats	+602

Options	Price
Power Moonroof	+376
Power Sliding Door	+169
Privacy Glass [Opt on CE]	+153
Rear Spoiler	+122
Running Boards	+254
Sliding Driver Side Door [Opt on CE]	+169
Trailer Hitch	+124

1998

A new minivan from Toyota brings some innovation to the family transport market. A powerful 194-horsepower V6 engine rests under the hood of all models. Safety equipment includes standard antilock brakes, low tire-pressure warning systems and five-mph front and rear bumpers. Sienna boasts outstanding crash test scores.

Mileage Category: P

Body Styles	TMV Pricing		
	Trade	Private	Dealer
3 Dr CE Pass Van	5855	7218	8755
3 Dr LE Pass Van	6367	7849	9521

Body Styles	TMV Pricing		
	Trade	Private	Dealer
4 Dr XLE Pass Van	7413	9138	11084

Options	Price
AM/FM/CD Audio System [Opt on CE,LE]	+120
AM/FM/Cassette/CD Audio System [Opt on LE,XLE]	+146
Air Conditioning - Front and Rear [Opt on CE]	+169
Alarm System	+149
Aluminum/Alloy Wheels [Opt on LE]	+229
Compact Disc Changer	+206

Options	Price
Leather Seats	+530
Power Moonroof	+368
Privacy Glass [Opt on CE]	+135
Running Boards	+224
Sliding Driver Side Door	+141

Supra

1998

Mileage Category: F

Body Styles	TMV Pricing		
	Trade	Private	Dealer
2 Dr STD Hbk	12729	14874	17293

Options	Price
AM/FM/Cassette/CD Audio System	+424
Automatic 4-Speed Transmission	+376
Compact Disc Changer	+313

Body Styles	TMV Pricing		
	Trade	Private	Dealer
2 Dr Turbo Hbk	22861	26712	31055

Options	Price
Leather Seats [Opt on STD]	+459
Power Driver Seat [Opt on STD]	+117
Targa Top - Solid [Opt on STD]	+1044

Variable Valve Timing with intelligence appears on the new Supra.

1997

Turbo models get the six-speed manual transmission back, but the bigger news details massive price cuts. Turbos with automatics are $12,000 less expensive than last year! All Supras commemorate the nameplate's 15th anniversary with a rear spoiler, premium sound and special badging. Despite price cuts, equipment levels are enhanced across the board.

Mileage Category: F

Body Styles	TMV Pricing		
	Trade	Private	Dealer
2 Dr STD Hbk	10946	12950	15399

Options	Price
AM/FM/CD Audio System	+160
AM/FM/Cassette/CD Audio System [Std on Turbo]	+362
Automatic 4-Speed Transmission [Std on Turbo]	+321

Body Styles	TMV Pricing		
	Trade	Private	Dealer
2 Dr Turbo Hbk	19663	23263	27662

Options	Price
Compact Disc Changer	+267
Leather Seats [Std on Turbo]	+392
Targa Top - Solid	+891

1996

Manual transmission Turbo models are history, thanks to stringent emission regulations.

Mileage Category: F

Body Styles	TMV Pricing		
	Trade	Private	Dealer
2 Dr STD Hbk	9764	11633	14213

Options	Price
AM/FM/Cassette/CD Audio System	+195
Automatic 4-Speed Transmission [Std on Turbo]	+270
Compact Disc Changer	+225
Leather Seats	+331

Body Styles	TMV Pricing		
	Trade	Private	Dealer
2 Dr Turbo Hbk	15843	18873	23058

Options	Price
Limited Slip Differential [Std on Turbo]	+152
Premium Audio System	+150
Rear Spoiler	+138
Targa Top - Solid	+751

1995

No changes.

Mileage Category: F

Body Styles	TMV Pricing		
	Trade	Private	Dealer
2 Dr STD Hbk	8537	10138	12807

Options	Price
AM/FM/CD Audio System	+173
AM/FM/Cassette/CD Audio System	+263
Automatic 4-Speed Transmission	+240
Compact Disc Changer	+200

Body Styles	TMV Pricing		
	Trade	Private	Dealer
2 Dr Turbo Hbk	12878	15294	19321

Options	Price
Leather Seats	+293
Limited Slip Differential [Opt on STD]	+123
Rear Spoiler	+112
Targa Top - Solid	+293

T100

1998

Mileage Category: K

Body Styles	TMV Pricing		
	Trade	Private	Dealer
2 Dr DX 4WD Ext Cab SB	6499	7805	9277
2 Dr DX Ext Cab SB	5320	6389	7595
2 Dr SR5 4WD Ext Cab SB	6799	8164	9704

Options	Price
AM/FM/Cassette Audio System [Std on SR5]	+143
Air Conditioning	+226
Aluminum/Alloy Wheels	+201
Antilock Brakes	+284

Body Styles	TMV Pricing		
	Trade	Private	Dealer
2 Dr SR5 Ext Cab SB	5753	6909	8212
2 Dr STD Std Cab LB	3856	4631	5504

Options	Price
Automatic 4-Speed Transmission	+338
Bucket Seats	+124
Running Boards	+174
Tonneau Cover	+141

No changes to Toyota's full-size truck.

Toyota
T100/Tacoma

1997

Two new colors debut and the optional wheel and tire packages are larger this year. Standard models get radio prewiring, midlevel models get fabric door trim panels and SR5 models get chrome wheel arches.

Mileage Category: K

Body Styles	TMV Pricing		
	Trade	Private	Dealer
2 Dr DX 4WD Ext Cab SB	5489	6713	8208
2 Dr DX Ext Cab SB	4714	5765	7049
2 Dr SR5 4WD Ext Cab SB	5784	7073	8649

Options	Price
AM/FM/CD Audio System	+147
AM/FM/Cassette Audio System	+122
AM/FM/Cassette/CD Audio System	+160
Air Conditioning	+193
Aluminum/Alloy Wheels	+172

Body Styles	TMV Pricing		
	Trade	Private	Dealer
2 Dr SR5 Ext Cab SB	4839	5917	7235
2 Dr STD Std Cab LB	3316	4055	4959

Options	Price
Antilock Brakes	+242
Automatic 4-Speed Transmission	+289
Premium Audio System	+134
Running Boards	+149
Tonneau Cover	+121

1996

Essentially a carryover, but DX models are scrapped. Regular cabs can't be equipped with cruise control anymore. A new shade of red is offered, and tan interiors are offered in a wider variety of trucks.

Mileage Category: K

Body Styles	TMV Pricing		
	Trade	Private	Dealer
2 Dr DX 4WD Ext Cab SB	4810	5908	7425
2 Dr DX Ext Cab SB	4006	4921	6185
2 Dr SR5 4WD Ext Cab SB	5133	6306	7926

Options	Price
AM/FM/CD Audio System	+124
AM/FM/Cassette/CD Audio System	+135
Air Conditioning	+244
Aluminum/Alloy Wheels	+163
Antilock Brakes	+204

Body Styles	TMV Pricing		
	Trade	Private	Dealer
2 Dr SR5 Ext Cab SB	4156	5106	6417
2 Dr STD Std Cab LB	3011	3699	4649

Options	Price
Automatic 4-Speed Transmission	+244
Chrome Wheels	+167
Power Sunroof	+135
Running Boards	+126

1995

The 1995 T100 adds an extended-cab body style to fill out this midsize truck's lineup. A much more powerful DOHC V6 engine is introduced this year as are four-wheel antilock brakes. The antilock brakes are available only on DX and Xtracab models equipped V6 engine.

Mileage Category: K

Body Styles	TMV Pricing		
	Trade	Private	Dealer
2 Dr DX 1 Ton Std Cab LB	3032	3778	5022
2 Dr DX 4WD Ext Cab SB	3893	4852	6449
2 Dr DX 4WD Std Cab LB	3733	4652	6183
2 Dr DX Ext Cab SB	3209	3999	5315
2 Dr DX Std Cab LB	2981	3715	4938

Options	Price
AM/FM/Cassette Audio System	+91
AM/FM/Cassette/CD Audio System	+120
Air Conditioning	+144
Aluminum/Alloy Wheels	+128

Body Styles	TMV Pricing		
	Trade	Private	Dealer
2 Dr SR5 4WD Ext Cab SB	4141	5160	6859
2 Dr SR5 Ext Cab SB	3245	4044	5376
2 Dr STD Std Cab LB	2369	2952	3924
2 Dr V6 Std Cab LB	2646	3297	4383

Options	Price
Antilock Brakes	+181
Automatic 4-Speed Transmission	+216
Running Boards	+111
Tonneau Cover	+90

Tacoma
2004

All models get standard Electronic Brakeforce Distribution, and V6 models can now be equipped with Vehicle Stability Control. Four-wheel-drive V6 models come with Active TRAC, a traction control system intended for off-road use, while 4x2 PreRunner models have traction control, plus a limited-slip rear differential.

Mileage Category: J

Body Styles	TMV Pricing		
	Trade	Private	Dealer
2 Dr Prerunner Ext Cab SB	12348	13429	15231
2 Dr Prerunner Std Cab SB	10456	11462	13139
2 Dr Prerunner V6 Ext Cab SB	13203	14303	16136
2 Dr S-Runner V6 Ext Cab SB	14906	16100	18089
2 Dr STD 4WD Ext Cab SB	14180	15369	17351
2 Dr STD 4WD Std Cab SB	12211	13217	14894

Options	Price
AM/FM/CD Audio System [Std on S-Runner]	+275
Air Conditioning [Std on S-Runner]	+475
Alarm System	+249
Aluminum/Alloy Wheels [Std on S-Runner]	+760
Automatic 4-Speed Transmission [Opt on STD]	+720

Body Styles	TMV Pricing		
	Trade	Private	Dealer
2 Dr STD Ext Cab SB	10977	12058	13860
2 Dr STD Std Cab SB	9111	10117	11794
2 Dr V6 4WD Ext Cab SB	14723	15937	17960
4 Dr Prerunner Crew Cab SB	13978	15215	17277
4 Dr Prerunner V6 Crew Cab SB	14582	15817	17876
4 Dr V6 4WD Crew Cab SB	17043	18291	20370

Options	Price
Bed Extender	+282
Bed Liner	+299
Chrome Bumpers	+180
Chrome Step Bumper [Opt on STD, Prerunner 2 Dr Std]	+299
Chrome Wheels	+580

Options	Price
Cruise Control	+250
Intermittent Wipers [Opt on STD, V6, Prerunner 2 Dr]	+150
Keyless Entry System [Std on S-Runner]	+200
Leather Steering Wheel	+120
Locking Differential [Opt on V6]	+340
Power Door Locks [Std on S-Runner]	+180
Power Driver Seat [Opt on V6, 4 Dr Prerunner]	+350
Power Mirrors [Std on S-Runner]	+160
Power Windows [Std on S-Runner]	+265

Options	Price
Running Boards	+315
Side Steps	+369
Sliding Rear Window	+160
Sport Seats [Opt on V6]	+500
TRD Off-Road Suspension Package [Opt on Prerunner, V6]	+830
Tilt Steering Wheel	+120
Trailer Hitch	+359

Mileage Category: J

Body Styles	TMV Pricing		
	Trade	Private	Dealer
2 Dr Prerunner Ext Cab SB	11459	12421	14023
2 Dr Prerunner Std Cab SB	9767	10586	11951
2 Dr Prerunner V6 Ext Cab SB	12469	13515	15257
2 Dr S-Runner V6 Ext Cab SB	13597	14738	16639
2 Dr STD 4WD Ext Cab SB	13007	14098	15916
2 Dr STD 4WD Std Cab SB	11289	12236	13815

Body Styles	TMV Pricing		
	Trade	Private	Dealer
2 Dr STD Ext Cab SB	10228	11086	12515
2 Dr STD Std Cab SB	8391	9095	10267
2 Dr V6 4WD Ext Cab SB	13595	14735	16635
4 Dr Prerunner Crew Cab SB	12961	14048	15859
4 Dr Prerunner V6 Crew Cab SB	13333	14451	16315
4 Dr V6 4WD Crew Cab SB	15590	16897	19076

2003

The Tacoma compact pickup is upgraded for 2003 with standard antilock brakes on all models. Additionally, child restraint system lower anchors have been added to the front passenger seat on Regular and Xtracab models, and to the rear outboard seats on Double Cab models.

Options	Price
Air Conditioning [Std on S-Runner]	+442
Alarm System	+188
Aluminum/Alloy Wheels [Std on S-Runner]	+574
Automatic 4-Speed Transmission [Opt on STD]	+543
Chrome Wheels	+438
Keyless Entry System [Std on S-Runner]	+132
Locking Differential [Opt on V6]	+257
Power Door Locks [Std on S-Runner]	+174

Options	Price
Power Windows [Std on S-Runner]	+200
Running Boards	+238
Sliding Rear Window	+121
Sport Seats [Opt on V6]	+189
Stepside Bed	+234
TRD Off-Road Suspension Package [Opt on Prerunner, V6]	+626

Mileage Category: J

Body Styles	TMV Pricing		
	Trade	Private	Dealer
2 Dr Prerunner Ext Cab SB	10631	11640	13321
2 Dr Prerunner Std Cab SB	8940	9788	11202
2 Dr Prerunner V6 Ext Cab SB	11656	12762	14606
2 Dr S-Runner V6 Ext Cab SB	11529	12623	14446
2 Dr STD 4WD Ext Cab SB	11833	12955	14826
2 Dr STD 4WD Std Cab SB	10557	11446	12927

Body Styles	TMV Pricing		
	Trade	Private	Dealer
2 Dr STD Ext Cab SB	9344	10231	11708
2 Dr STD Std Cab SB	7705	8436	9654
2 Dr V6 4WD Ext Cab SB	12467	13649	15620
4 Dr Prerunner Crew Cab SB	11560	12657	14485
4 Dr Prerunner V6 Crew Cab SB	12092	13240	15152
4 Dr V6 4WD Crew Cab SB	14123	15463	17697

2002

A moonroof is available now on PreRunners and S-Runners have color-keyed side badging.

Options	Price
AM/FM/Cassette/CD Audio System	+172
Air Conditioning [Std on S-Runner]	+404
Aluminum/Alloy Wheels [Std on S-Runner]	+524
Antilock Brakes	+469
Automatic 4-Speed Transmission [Std on Prerunner, V6 Crew]	+497
Chrome Wheels	+400
Locking Differential	+235
Luggage Rack [Opt on Crew Cab]	+152

Options	Price
Moonroof [Opt on Crew Cab, Ext Cab]	+276
Power Door Locks	+121
Power Windows	+138
Running Boards [Opt on Crew Cab]	+217
Sport Seats [Opt on V6]	+172
Stepside Bed	+214
TRD Off-Road Suspension Package [Opt on Prerunner, V6]	+573

Mileage Category: J

Body Styles	TMV Pricing		
	Trade	Private	Dealer
2 Dr Prerunner Ext Cab SB	9609	11032	12346
2 Dr Prerunner Std Cab SB	7818	8977	10046
2 Dr Prerunner V6 Ext Cab SB	10749	12237	13610
2 Dr S-Runner V6 Ext Cab SB	10411	11954	13378
2 Dr STD 4WD Ext Cab SB	10848	12456	13940
2 Dr STD 4WD Std Cab SB	9502	10910	12209

Body Styles	TMV Pricing		
	Trade	Private	Dealer
2 Dr STD Ext Cab SB	8320	9553	10691
2 Dr STD Std Cab SB	6772	7776	8702
2 Dr V6 4WD Ext Cab SB	11202	12861	14393
4 Dr Prerunner Crew Cab SB	10457	12006	13435
4 Dr Prerunner V6 Crew Cab SB	11024	12658	14165
4 Dr V6 4WD Crew Cab SB	12841	14743	16499

2001

Toyota releases the Double Cab. A new StepSide version is available, and the S-Runner sport truck debuts. Revised front styling and new alloy wheels give Tacoma a more rugged look. New exterior colors and option package content shuffling sum up the obvious changes for 2001.

2001 (cont'd)

Options	Price
AM/FM/Cassette/CD Audio System [Std on Limited]	+157
Air Conditioning [Std on Limited]	+315
Aluminum/Alloy Wheels [Std on Limited]	+233
Antilock Brakes	+428
Automatic 4-Speed Transmission [Opt on SR5 V6,STD]	+453
Chrome Wheels	+296
Locking Differential [Opt on Prerunner]	+214

Options	Price
Moonroof	+245
Power Door Locks [Std on Limited]	+145
Power Windows [Std on Limited]	+167
Running Boards	+198
Stepside Bed	+126
TRD Off-Road Suspension Package	+503

2000

Tacomas with four-cylinder engines and four-wheel drive achieve improved performance from an enhanced gear ratio. Base-grade Tacomas feature new designs for the interior fabric and exterior mirrors. Daytime running lights are now included with the antilock brake package. There are also two new colors as well as a color-keyed package for those who like the monochrome look.

Mileage Category: J

Body Styles	TMV Pricing		
	Trade	Private	Dealer
2 Dr Limited 4WD Ext Cab SB	12156	14077	15959
2 Dr Prerunner Ext Cab SB	8708	10085	11434
2 Dr Prerunner Std Cab SB	6683	7740	8775
2 Dr Prerunner V6 Ext Cab SB	8887	10292	11669
2 Dr SR5 4WD Ext Cab SB	9591	11107	12592
2 Dr SR5 Ext Cab SB	8377	9701	10999
2 Dr SR5 V6 4WD Ext Cab SB	9964	11539	13082

Body Styles	TMV Pricing		
	Trade	Private	Dealer
2 Dr SR5 V6 Ext Cab SB	8655	10023	11364
2 Dr STD 4WD Ext Cab SB	8777	10163	11522
2 Dr STD 4WD Std Cab SB	8396	9724	11025
2 Dr STD Ext Cab SB	7021	8131	9219
2 Dr STD Std Cab SB	5603	6488	7356
2 Dr V6 4WD Ext Cab SB	9162	10610	12030
2 Dr V6 Ext Cab SB	8310	9624	10912

Options	Price
AM/FM/CD Audio System	+376
AM/FM/Cassette/CD Audio System [Std on Limited]	+320
Air Conditioning [Opt on Limited V6,V6,Std Cab]	+544
Alarm System	+138
Aluminum/Alloy Wheels [Std on Limited]	+204
Antilock Brakes	+376
Automatic 4-Speed Transmission [Opt on SR5 V6,STD]	+401
Automatic Locking Hubs (4WD)	+133
Bed Liner	+165
Chrome Bumpers	+221
Compact Disc Changer	+332
Cruise Control [Opt on SR5 V6]	+138

Options	Price
Limited Slip Differential	+188
Off-Road Suspension Package	+729
Power Door Locks [Std on Limited]	+127
Power Steering [Opt on STD Std Cab]	+166
Power Windows [Std on Limited]	+146
Running Boards	+158
Styled Steel Wheels [Std on STD 4WD Std Cab]	+260
Sunroof	+215
TRD Off-Road Suspension Package	+442
Tilt Steering Wheel [Std on Limited]	+135
Tonneau Cover	+193
Trailer Hitch	+155

1999

Toyota adds new front seat belt pre-tensioners and force limiters. Optional on Xtra Cab models is an AM/FM four-speaker CD audio system while 4x4s get 15-by-7-inch steel wheels. The PreRunner adds a regular cab option to its model mix. Natural White, Imperial Jade Mica and Horizon Blue Metallic replace White, Copper Canyon Mica, Evergreen Pearl and Cool Steel Metallic as color options.

Mileage Category: J

Body Styles	TMV Pricing		
	Trade	Private	Dealer
2 Dr Limited 4WD Ext Cab SB	10529	12322	14188
2 Dr Prerunner Ext Cab SB	7416	8680	9994
2 Dr Prerunner Std Cab SB	5976	6993	8051
2 Dr Prerunner V6 Ext Cab SB	7428	8693	10009
2 Dr SR5 4WD Ext Cab SB	7529	8810	10144
2 Dr SR5 Ext Cab SB	6793	7950	9153
2 Dr SR5 V6 4WD Ext Cab SB	8583	10044	11564

Body Styles	TMV Pricing		
	Trade	Private	Dealer
2 Dr SR5 V6 Ext Cab SB	7149	8365	9631
2 Dr STD 4WD Ext Cab SB	7464	8735	10057
2 Dr STD 4WD Std Cab SB	7229	8459	9740
2 Dr STD Ext Cab SB	6000	7022	8086
2 Dr STD Std Cab SB	4636	5425	6246
2 Dr V6 4WD Ext Cab SB	7646	8948	10303
2 Dr V6 Ext Cab SB	7089	8295	9551

Options	Price
AM/FM/CD Audio System [Std on Limited]	+290
AM/FM/Cassette/CD Audio System	+248
Air Conditioning [Opt on Limited,STD,V6]	+420
Aluminum/Alloy Wheels [Std on Limited]	+158
Antilock Brakes [Opt on STD]	+323
Automatic 4-Speed Transmission [Std on Limited,SR5 2WD]	+309
Bed Liner	+127
Chrome Bumpers [Std on Limited]	+171
Compact Disc Changer	+256

Options	Price
Locking Differential	+145
Power Steering [Opt on STD 4 cyl]	+128
Running Boards	+122
Styled Steel Wheels	+201
Sunroof	+167
TRD Off-Road Suspension Package	+380
Tonneau Cover	+150
Trailer Hitch	+119
Wide Tires And Wheels	+201

1998

Mileage Category: J

Body Styles	TMV Pricing		
	Trade	Private	Dealer
2 Dr Limited 4WD Ext Cab SB	8522	10163	12015
2 Dr Prerunner Ext Cab SB	5926	7068	8355
2 Dr Prerunner V6 Ext Cab SB	6036	7198	8509
2 Dr SR5 4WD Ext Cab SB	6512	7766	9180
2 Dr SR5 Ext Cab SB	5263	6278	7421
2 Dr SR5 V6 4WD Ext Cab SB	7221	8611	10179
2 Dr SR5 V6 Ext Cab SB	5833	6956	8223

Body Styles	TMV Pricing		
	Trade	Private	Dealer
2 Dr STD 4WD Ext Cab SB	6116	7295	8624
2 Dr STD 4WD Std Cab SB	5939	7084	8375
2 Dr STD Ext Cab SB	4486	5349	6323
2 Dr STD Std Cab SB	3793	4524	5349
2 Dr V6 4WD Ext Cab SB	6640	7919	9361
2 Dr V6 Ext Cab SB	5535	6602	7805

Options	Price
AM/FM/CD Audio System	+256
AM/FM/Cassette Audio System [Opt on STD,V6]	+139
AM/FM/Cassette/CD Audio System	+218
Air Conditioning [Opt on Limited,STD,V6]	+370
Aluminum/Alloy Wheels [Std on Limited]	+139
Antilock Brakes	+284
Automatic 4-Speed Transmission [Std on Prerunner,Prerunner V6]	+282

Options	Price
Compact Disc Changer	+206
Locking Differential	+122
Sunroof	+147
TRD Off-Road Suspension Package	+334
Tonneau Cover	+132
Wide Tires And Wheels	+177

The 1998 four-wheel-drive Tacomas receive fresh front-end styling that makes them more closely resemble their two-wheel-drive brothers. A new option package appears for 1998 as well; the TRD Off-Road Package for extended cab models is offered. On the safety front, Toyota introduces a passenger-side airbag that can be deactivated with a cut-off switch, making the Tacoma somewhat safer for children and short adults. Toyota also offers a new Tacoma PreRunner for 1998, billing it as a two-wheel-drive truck with four-wheel-drive performance.

1997

Mileage Category: J

Body Styles	TMV Pricing		
	Trade	Private	Dealer
2 Dr SR5 4WD Ext Cab SB	5596	6878	8444
2 Dr STD 4WD Ext Cab SB	4585	5635	6918
2 Dr STD 4WD Std Cab SB	4346	5342	6559
2 Dr STD Ext Cab SB	3287	4040	4961

Body Styles	TMV Pricing		
	Trade	Private	Dealer
2 Dr STD Std Cab SB	2741	3370	4138
2 Dr V6 4WD Ext Cab SB	4987	6129	7526
2 Dr V6 4WD Std Cab SB	4517	5551	6816
2 Dr V6 Ext Cab SB	4297	5282	6485

Options	Price
AM/FM/CD Audio System	+147
AM/FM/Cassette/CD Audio System	+186
Air Conditioning	+316
Antilock Brakes	+242
Automatic 4-Speed Transmission	+257

Options	Price
Compact Disc Changer	+224
Power Sunroof	+125
Sunroof	+125
Wide Tires And Wheels	+146

The 1997 Tacoma receives several new value packages that make optioning the truck easier. A locking rear-wheel differential is now available on all 4WD models. Bucket seats can be had on all Xtracab Tacomas this year; not just the SR5. Two-wheel-drive models have new headlamps and a new grille that make the vehicle look more like the T100.

1996

Mileage Category: J

Body Styles	TMV Pricing		
	Trade	Private	Dealer
2 Dr SR5 4WD Ext Cab SB	4333	5454	7002
2 Dr STD 4WD Ext Cab SB	3001	3777	4849
2 Dr STD 4WD Std Cab SB	2793	3516	4515
2 Dr STD Ext Cab SB	2375	2989	3838

Body Styles	TMV Pricing		
	Trade	Private	Dealer
2 Dr STD Std Cab SB	1806	2273	2919
2 Dr V6 4WD Ext Cab SB	3130	3940	5059
2 Dr V6 4WD Std Cab SB	2966	3733	4793
2 Dr V6 Ext Cab SB	2732	3439	4415

Options	Price
AM/FM/CD Audio System	+124
AM/FM/Cassette Audio System [Std on SR5]	+153
Air Conditioning	+266
Antilock Brakes	+204

Options	Price
Automatic 4-Speed Transmission	+244
Compact Disc Changer	+189
Off-Road Suspension Package	+520

Regular Cab 4WD models can be equipped with a new Off-Road Package.

1995

Mileage Category: J

Body Styles	TMV Pricing		
	Trade	Private	Dealer
2 Dr SR5 4WD Ext Cab SB	3967	4928	6529
2 Dr STD 4WD Ext Cab SB	2578	3203	4244
2 Dr STD 4WD Std Cab SB	2552	3171	4202
2 Dr STD Ext Cab SB	2016	2504	3318

Body Styles	TMV Pricing		
	Trade	Private	Dealer
2 Dr STD Std Cab SB	1620	2013	2667
2 Dr V6 4WD Ext Cab SB	2595	3224	4271
2 Dr V6 4WD Std Cab SB	2547	3164	4192
2 Dr V6 Ext Cab SB	2509	3117	4131

Options	Price
AM/FM/CD Audio System	+110
AM/FM/Cassette Audio System	+89

Options	Price
Air Conditioning	+236
Aluminum/Alloy Wheels	+84

New compact pickup with a real name debuted in March, 1995. Optional four-wheel ABS, a driver airbag and potent new engines are highlights of the new design. Rack-and-pinion steering replaces the old recirculating ball-type on the old truck. Front seatbelts are height-adjustable.

1995 (cont'd)

Options	Price
Antilock Brakes	+181
Automatic 4-Speed Transmission	+174

Options	Price
Sunroof	+94

Tercel

1998

Mileage Category: A

Body Styles	TMV Pricing		
	Trade	Private	Dealer
2 Dr CE Cpe	2590	3447	4414

Options	Price
AM/FM/CD Audio System	+171
Antilock Brakes	+284

Options	Price
Automatic 3-Speed Transmission	+188
Compact Disc Changer	+226

For 1998, the Tercel is available exclusively as a two-door CE model with additional standard features like color-keyed grille and bumpers, rear seat headrests, AM/FM stereo with cassette, air conditioning, digital clock and power steering.

1997

Standard and DX trim levels are shelved in favor of CE trim for all Tercels. All models have upgraded cloth trim, new rotary heater controls, a trip odometer and a storage console. New wheel covers adorn standard 14-inch wheels.

Mileage Category: A

Body Styles	TMV Pricing		
	Trade	Private	Dealer
2 Dr CE Cpe	1707	2362	3162
2 Dr Limited Edition Cpe	2129	2945	3943

Options	Price
AM/FM/CD Audio System	+147
Air Conditioning	+297
Antilock Brakes	+242
Automatic 3-Speed Transmission	+160

Body Styles	TMV Pricing		
	Trade	Private	Dealer
4 Dr CE Sdn	2196	3038	4066

Options	Price
Automatic 4-Speed Transmission	+225
Compact Disc Changer	+193
Rear Spoiler	+160

1996

Base cars can be equipped with fabric seats, and a "Sports" package is available.

Mileage Category: A

Body Styles	TMV Pricing		
	Trade	Private	Dealer
2 Dr DX Cpe	1556	2222	3141
2 Dr STD Cpe	1264	1805	2551

Options	Price
AM/FM/CD Audio System	+124
Air Conditioning	+250
Antilock Brakes	+204
Automatic 3-Speed Transmission	+189

Body Styles	TMV Pricing		
	Trade	Private	Dealer
4 Dr DX Sdn	1701	2428	3433

Options	Price
Automatic 4-Speed Transmission	+192
Compact Disc Changer	+189
Power Sunroof	+135
Rear Spoiler	+135

1995

Redesigned, but based on 1991-1994 generation. Coupe and sedan body styles. Coupe available in Standard and DX trim; sedan comes in DX flavor only. Dual airbags are standard. Height-adjustable seatbelts are new. Car now meets 1997 side-impact standards. Engine is more powerful than before.

Mileage Category: A

Body Styles	TMV Pricing		
	Trade	Private	Dealer
2 Dr DX Cpe	1215	1736	2603
2 Dr STD Cpe	1078	1540	2311

Options	Price
AM/FM/CD Audio System	+110
AM/FM/Cassette Audio System	+84
Air Conditioning	+222
Antilock Brakes	+181

Body Styles	TMV Pricing		
	Trade	Private	Dealer
4 Dr DX Sdn	1249	1786	2681

Options	Price
Automatic 3-Speed Transmission	+120
Automatic 4-Speed Transmission	+168
Compact Disc Changer	+144

Tundra
2004

Mileage Category: K

Body Styles	Trade	Private	Dealer
2 Dr SR5 V8 4WD Std Cab LB	17197	18879	21682
2 Dr STD Std Cab LB	10552	11822	13939
4 Dr Limited V8 4WD Crew Cab SB	24585	26226	28962
4 Dr Limited V8 4WD Ext Cab SB	22557	24170	26858
4 Dr Limited V8 4WD Ext Cab Step SB	23097	24709	27396
4 Dr Limited V8 Crew Cab SB	22191	23839	26586
4 Dr Limited V8 Ext Cab SB	20055	21663	24344
4 Dr Limited V8 Ext Cab Step SB	20593	22201	24880

Body Styles	Trade	Private	Dealer
4 Dr SR5 V6 4WD Ext Cab SB	17802	19371	21988
4 Dr SR5 V6 Ext Cab SB	14836	16322	18799
4 Dr SR5 V8 4WD Crew Cab SB	21978	23627	26375
4 Dr SR5 V8 4WD Ext Cab SB	19940	21557	24252
4 Dr SR5 V8 4WD Ext Cab Step SB	20478	22094	24788
4 Dr SR5 V8 Crew Cab SB	19583	21241	24003
4 Dr SR5 V8 Ext Cab SB	17141	18725	21366
4 Dr SR5 V8 Ext Cab Step SB	17679	19264	21904

Options	Price
17 Inch Wheels [Opt on SR5]	+500
AM/FM/CD Changer Audio System [Opt on Crew, SR5 Ext]	+260
Air Conditioning [Opt on STD]	+985
Alarm System [Opt on SR5, Crew]	+220
Aluminum/Alloy Wheels [Opt on SR5, Limited]	+400
Automatic 4-Speed Transmission	+770
Automatic Dimming Rearview Mirror [Opt on non-Ext]	+150
Automatic Stability Control [Opt on SR5, Limited Crew]	+690
Bed Extender [Opt on non-Step]	+399
Bed Liner	+299
Captain Chairs (2) [Opt on Limited, Ext SR5]	+145

Options	Price
DVD Entertainment System [Opt on Crew]	+1770
Keyless Entry System [Opt on SR5 Crew]	+150
Leather Seats [Opt on Limited]	+1100
Power Driver Seat [Opt on Limited]	+250
Power Mirrors [Opt on SR5 non-Crew]	+120
Power Moonroof [Opt on Crew]	+1000
Power Windows [Opt on SR5 non-Crew]	+200
Rear Audio Controls [Opt on Crew]	+150
Skid Plates	+159
Tilt Steering Wheel [Opt on 2WD Std]	+245
Trailer Hitch	+330

The four-door Double Cab joins the Tundra lineup for 2004. The Double Cab rides on an extended wheelbase of 140.5 inches, and features a cargo bed equal in length to the Access Cab's while gaining 3.5 inches of depth.

2003

Toyota has expanded the Tundra's body style variety by adding a new StepSide model. Its distinctive styling includes flared rear wheel arches and special tail lamps. If you want to make the StepSide even sportier, there is a new sport suspension package available. All Tundras this year have a restyled front fascia, standard antilock brakes and a center console similar to the one found in the Sequoia SUV. For the top-line Limited trim, Toyota has added a power sliding rear window.

Mileage Category: K

Body Styles	Trade	Private	Dealer
2 Dr SR5 V8 4WD Std Cab LB	15039	16169	18051
2 Dr STD Std Cab LB	9484	10197	11384
4 Dr Limited V8 4WD Ext Cab SB	19278	20726	23140
4 Dr Limited V8 4WD Ext Cab Step SB	19556	21025	23474
4 Dr Limited V8 Ext Cab SB	17101	18386	20527
4 Dr Limited V8 Ext Cab Step SB	17494	18808	20998

Body Styles	Trade	Private	Dealer
4 Dr SR5 Ext Cab Step SB	15253	16399	18309
4 Dr SR5 V6 4WD Ext Cab SB	15485	16648	18587
4 Dr SR5 V6 Ext Cab SB	13388	14394	16070
4 Dr SR5 V8 4WD Ext Cab SB	16900	18170	20286
4 Dr SR5 V8 4WD Ext Cab Step SB	17311	18611	20778
4 Dr SR5 V8 Ext Cab SB	14925	16046	17914

Options	Price
17 Inch Wheels [Opt on Limited,SR5]	+298
AM/FM/Cassette/CD Changer Audio System [Opt on SR5]	+370
Air Conditioning [Opt on STD]	+743
Alarm System [Opt on SR5]	+188
Aluminum/Alloy Wheels [Opt on SR5]	+302
Automatic 4-Speed Transmission [Opt on V6]	+581
Camper/Towing Package [Opt on Limited,SR5]	+325
Chrome Wheels [Opt on SR5]	+166

Options	Price
Keyless Entry System [Opt on SR5]	+132
Leather Seats [Opt on Limited]	+642
Limited Slip Differential [Opt on Limited,SR5]	+208
Power Door Locks [Opt on SR5]	+162
Power Driver Seat [Opt on Limited]	+181
Power Mirrors [Opt on SR5]	+136
Power Windows [Opt on SR5]	+189
Tilt Steering Wheel [Opt on STD]	+185

2002

SR5 models have new 16-inch wheels, and a limited-slip differential is available on V8-powered trucks. No other changes are in store for Toyota's full-size pickup this year.

Mileage Category: K

Body Styles	Trade	Private	Dealer
2 Dr SR5 V8 4WD Std Cab LB	13380	14494	16350
2 Dr STD Std Cab LB	8791	9523	10742
4 Dr Limited V8 4WD Ext Cab SB	17078	18500	20869
4 Dr Limited V8 Ext Cab SB	15175	16577	18913

Body Styles	Trade	Private	Dealer
4 Dr SR5 V6 4WD Ext Cab SB	13766	14912	16822
4 Dr SR5 V6 Ext Cab SB	11927	12920	14575
4 Dr SR5 V8 4WD Ext Cab SB	14992	16325	18546
4 Dr SR5 V8 Ext Cab SB	13294	14401	16246

Tundra

2002 (cont'd)

Options	Price
16 Inch Wheels [Opt on SR5 V8 Ext Cab]	+224
AM/FM/Cassette/CD Changer Audio System [Opt on SR5]	+224
Air Conditioning [Opt on STD]	+680
Aluminum/Alloy Wheels [Opt on SR5]	+276
Antilock Brakes [Std on Limited]	+469
Automatic 4-Speed Transmission [Std on V8]	+531
Captain Chairs (2) [Opt on Limted,SR5]	+207
Chrome Wheels [Opt on SR5]	+304
JBL Audio System [Opt on SR5]	+152
Keyless Entry System [Opt on SR5]	+121

Options	Price
Leather Seats [Opt on Limited]	+586
Limited Slip Differential [Opt on V8]	+190
Power Door Locks [Opt on SR5]	+148
Power Driver Seat [Opt on Limited]	+176
Power Mirrors [Opt on SR5]	+124
Power Windows [Opt on SR5]	+172
Styled Steel Wheels [Opt on SR5]	+152
Tilt Steering Wheel [Opt on STD]	+169
Two-Tone Paint [Opt on Limited]	+252

2001

Newly optional on Limited is a package that matches the bumpers and tailgate handle to the body color. The TRD Off-Road package is now available on Access Cabs with a V8 engine, while models equipped with a V6 receive an upgraded alternator. A notepad holder is now optional on SR5 and Limited, while Base regular cab trucks lose their standard cassette player. Two new colors are available, filling slots left vacant by three old colors that have been discontinued.

Mileage Category: K

Body Styles	TMV Pricing		
	Trade	Private	Dealer
2 Dr SR5 V8 4WD Std Cab LB	11972	13659	15216
2 Dr STD Std Cab LB	7884	8995	10020
4 Dr Limited V8 4WD Ext Cab SB	14811	16898	18824
4 Dr Limited V8 Ext Cab SB	13562	15473	17237

Body Styles	TMV Pricing		
	Trade	Private	Dealer
4 Dr SR5 V6 4WD Ext Cab SB	12021	13715	15278
4 Dr SR5 V6 Ext Cab SB	10546	12032	13404
4 Dr SR5 V8 4WD Ext Cab SB	13779	15719	17510
4 Dr SR5 V8 Ext Cab SB	11885	13559	15105

Options	Price
AM/FM/Cassette/CD Changer Audio System	+126
Air Conditioning [Opt on STD]	+620
Aluminum/Alloy Wheels [Std on Limited]	+239
Antilock Brakes	+428
Automatic 4-Speed Transmission [Opt on SR5 V6,STD]	+484
Leather Seats	+566

Options	Price
Power Door Locks [Std on Limited]	+138
Power Driver Seat	+135
Power Windows [Std on Limited]	+157
Styled Steel Wheels [Std on SR5 V8,Ext Cab]	+138
Tilt Steering Wheel [Opt on STD]	+126
Two-Tone Paint	+230

2000

This is an all-new, full-size pickup truck designed to compete with the Ford F-150, Chevrolet Silverado 1500, GMC Sierra 1500 and Dodge Ram 1500. It features an optional V8 engine and can be ordered in a two- or four-door, regular- or extended-cab configuration.

Mileage Category: K

Body Styles	TMV Pricing		
	Trade	Private	Dealer
2 Dr SR5 V6 4WD Std Cab LB	9289	10841	12363
2 Dr SR5 V8 4WD Std Cab LB	10285	12004	13688
2 Dr STD Std Cab LB	6564	7661	8736
4 Dr Limited 4WD Ext Cab SB	12959	15124	17246
4 Dr Limited Ext Cab SB	10838	12649	14424

Body Styles	TMV Pricing		
	Trade	Private	Dealer
4 Dr SR5 V6 4WD Ext Cab SB	10485	12236	13953
4 Dr SR5 V6 Ext Cab SB	9466	11048	12599
4 Dr SR5 V8 4WD Ext Cab SB	11176	13043	14874
4 Dr SR5 V8 Ext Cab SB	10239	11949	13626

Options	Price
AM/FM/Cassette/CD Audio System [Std on Limited]	+138
Air Conditioning [Opt on STD]	+544
Aluminum/Alloy Wheels [Std on Limited]	+122
Antilock Brakes	+376
Automatic 4-Speed Transmission [Opt on SR5 V6,STD]	+464
Bed Liner	+166
Compact Disc Changer	+138
Cruise Control [Opt on SR5 V6]	+124
Leather Seats	+497

Options	Price
Power Door Locks [Std on Limited]	+122
Power Driver Seat	+119
Power Windows [Std on Limited]	+138
Split Front Bench Seat [Opt on SR5 V6 Std Cab]	+127
Spoke Wheels	+210
Styled Steel Wheels [Std on SR5 V8,Ext Cab]	+193
Tonneau Cover	+193
Trailer Hitch	+124
Two-Tone Paint	+180

Cabrio

2002

Mileage Category: E

Body Styles	TMV Pricing		
	Trade	Private	Dealer
2 Dr GL Conv	10198	11134	12693
2 Dr GLS Conv	11023	12035	13721

Body Styles	TMV Pricing		
	Trade	Private	Dealer
2 Dr GLX Conv	11900	12992	14812

Options	Price
Automatic 4-Speed Transmission	+559

Reflex Silver with a gray top and Flannel Gray interior will be added to the spectrum, and Marlin Blue will replace Batik Blue. An on/off switch will allow you to govern the electrochromic mirror. For the 2002 model year, all-new Volkswagen vehicles will come standard with an improved four-year/50,000-mile bumper-to-bumper warranty, up from two years/24,000 miles. In addition, Volkswagen offers a fully transferable limited powertrain warranty that covers five years or 60,000 miles.

2001

A top-of-the-line GLX trim level has been added to the existing lineup for 2001. All models get an anti "trunk entrapment" button to keep people from getting stuck in the cargo hold.

Mileage Category: E

Body Styles	TMV Pricing		
	Trade	Private	Dealer
2 Dr GL Conv	8850	10072	11200
2 Dr GLS Conv	9484	10794	12003

Body Styles	TMV Pricing		
	Trade	Private	Dealer
2 Dr GLX Conv	10152	11554	12848

Options	Price
Automatic 4-Speed Transmission	+494

Options	Price
Compact Disc Changer	+279

2000

Volkswagen's Cabrio gets minor equipment updates for the millennium.

Mileage Category: E

Body Styles	TMV Pricing		
	Trade	Private	Dealer
2 Dr GL Conv	7934	9174	10390

Body Styles	TMV Pricing		
	Trade	Private	Dealer
2 Dr GLS Conv	8377	9687	10971

Options	Price
Aluminum/Alloy Wheels [Opt on GL]	+182
Automatic 4-Speed Transmission	+431
Compact Disc Changer	+244

Options	Price
Heated Front Seats [Opt on GL]	+123
Power Windows [Opt on GL]	+125

1999

Volkswagen imparts new Euro-styling on the '99 Cabrios, making them more aerodynamic and adding twin headlights that show their elements through the lens. Cabrio interiors also receive makeovers.

Mileage Category: E

Body Styles	TMV Pricing		
	Trade	Private	Dealer
2 Dr GL Conv	6002	7202	8451
2 Dr GLS Conv	6632	7958	9339

Body Styles	TMV Pricing		
	Trade	Private	Dealer
2 Dr New GL Conv	6295	7553	8862
2 Dr New GLS Conv	6822	8186	9606

Options	Price
Air Conditioning [Opt on GL]	+345
Aluminum/Alloy Wheels [Opt on GL,New GL]	+149
Automatic 4-Speed Transmission	+352

Options	Price
Compact Disc Changer	+199
Front Side Airbag Restraints [Opt on GL,GLS]	+159

1998

Mileage Category: E

Body Styles	TMV Pricing		
	Trade	Private	Dealer
2 Dr GL Conv	4843	6017	7342

Body Styles	TMV Pricing		
	Trade	Private	Dealer
2 Dr GLS Conv	5414	6726	8206

Options	Price
Air Conditioning [Opt on GL]	+304
Aluminum/Alloy Wheels [Opt on GL]	+131
Automatic 4-Speed Transmission	+309

Options	Price
Compact Disc Changer	+175
Front Side Airbag Restraints	+140

The Highline trim designation is replaced by more sensible GLS nomenclature. New GLS model gets a power top, making the Cabrio easier to live with. Optional are side-impact airbags mounted inside the seats. Standard on both base and GLS are door pocket liners, a trunk cargo net and sport seats with height adjustment.

1997

Cabrio comes in two trim levels for 1997: Base and Highline. Base models are decontented versions of last year's car, priced a couple thousand dollars lower to entice young drivers. Highline models have standard alloy wheels, foglights and leather seats. Engines have a redesigned cylinder head resulting in quieter operation.

Mileage Category: E

Body Styles	TMV Pricing		
	Trade	Private	Dealer
2 Dr Highline Conv	4598	5765	7192

Body Styles	TMV Pricing		
	Trade	Private	Dealer
2 Dr STD Conv	4329	5428	6772

1997 (cont'd)

Options	Price
Air Conditioning [Opt on STD]	+251
Automatic 4-Speed Transmission	+255

Options	Price
Compact Disc Changer	+145

1996

Daytime running lights and new body-color side moldings alter the exterior appearance of the 1996 Cabrio. A new color scheme also livens things up. Central locking and unlocking switch is dash-mounted.

Mileage Category: E

Body Styles	TMV Pricing		
	Trade	Private	Dealer
2 Dr STD Conv	3639	4696	6156

Options	Price
Air Conditioning	+220
Aluminum/Alloy Wheels	+149
Automatic 4-Speed Transmission	+224

Options	Price
Compact Disc Changer	+127
Leather Seats	+327

1995

Dual airbags, ABS and 115-horsepower engine are standard on this Golf derivative. Manual top only.

Mileage Category: E

Body Styles	TMV Pricing		
	Trade	Private	Dealer
2 Dr STD Conv	2800	3617	4979

Options	Price
AM/FM/CD Audio System	+105
Air Conditioning	+180
Aluminum/Alloy Wheels	+78

Options	Price
Automatic 4-Speed Transmission	+184
Compact Disc Changer	+104
Leather Seats	+268

EuroVan

2003

Mileage Category: P

Body Styles	TMV Pricing		
	Trade	Private	Dealer
3 Dr GLS Pass Van	14713	15990	18117

Body Styles	TMV Pricing		
	Trade	Private	Dealer
3 Dr MV Pass Van	17348	18854	21363

Options	Price
Heated Front Seats	+281
Pearlescent Metallic Paint	+243

Options	Price
Power Moonroof	+703
Weekender Package [Opt on MV]	+2345

Volkswagen makes no changes to the EuroVan for 2003. Keep in mind that if you want a VW-branded minivan to go with the family Passat, the all-new Microbus isn't too far away -- it's supposed to arrive by the 2005 model year.

2002

The EuroVan saw many upgrades for 2001, including a more powerful 201-horsepower V6 engine. This year, VW equips its minivan with a stability control system (ESP) to improve handling in inclement weather and adds Emerald Green, Reflex Silver and Black Magic Pearl exterior color choices on the MV with the Weekender package.

Mileage Category: P

Body Styles	TMV Pricing		
	Trade	Private	Dealer
3 Dr GLS Pass Van	12455	13642	15620

Body Styles	TMV Pricing		
	Trade	Private	Dealer
3 Dr MV Pass Van	15316	16776	19208

Options	Price
Heated Front Seats	+255
Pearlescent Metallic Paint	+220

Options	Price
Power Sunroof	+638
Weekender Package [Opt on MV]	+2119

2001

The EuroVan sees many upgrades for the 2001 model year; chief among them is a more powerful 201-horsepower V6 engine. Refinements have also been made to the electronic stability control system. Other changes include a new premium stereo, single seats for second-row seating and standard integrated foglights.

Mileage Category: P

Body Styles	TMV Pricing		
	Trade	Private	Dealer
3 Dr GLS Pass Van	10761	12433	13975

Body Styles	TMV Pricing		
	Trade	Private	Dealer
3 Dr MV Pass Van	13189	15238	17129

Options	Price
Heated Front Seats	+226
Pearlescent Metallic Paint	+155

Options	Price
Power Sunroof	+565
Weekender Package	+1874

2000

During its second year back in the U.S., Volkswagen's EuroVan receives remote central locking, dark-tinted glass on the side and rear windows and a brake-wear indicator. The GLS model receives additional reading lights in the rear and captain's chairs instead of a bench seat in the second row.

Mileage Category: P

Body Styles	TMV Pricing		
	Trade	Private	Dealer
3 Dr GLS Pass Van	8681	10204	11696

Body Styles	TMV Pricing		
	Trade	Private	Dealer
3 Dr MV Pass Van	9247	10869	12458

Options	Price
Compact Disc Changer	+222
Heated Front Seats	+198

Options	Price
Metallic Paint	+135
Power Moonroof	+493

Options	Price
Weekender Package	+1637

Mileage Category: P

Body Styles	TMV Pricing		
	Trade	Private	Dealer
3 Dr GLS Pass Van	7839	9320	10862

Options	Price
Compact Disc Changer	+181
Heated Front Seats	+161

1999

After a five-year hiatus, the EuroVan passenger van returns to the U.S. with a six-cylinder engine, structural improvements and new safety features.

Mileage Category: P

Body Styles	TMV Pricing		
	Trade	Private	Dealer
3 Dr MV Pass Van	8325	9898	11535

Options	Price
Power Moonroof	+402
Weekender Package	+1334

1997

The Eurovan camper remains unchanged for the 1997 model year.

Mileage Category: P

Body Styles	TMV Pricing		
	Trade	Private	Dealer
3 Dr Campmobile Pass Van	5877	7282	8999

Options	Price
Compact Disc Changer	+145

1995

This Eurovan camper is an all-new model based on the extended wheelbase Eurovan. It features a 2.5-liter, five-cylinder engine with a standard five-speed manual and a four-speed automatic as an option. Winnebago Industries complete the camper conversion by adding a "pop-top" roof, a cooking range, sink, refrigerator, fresh water tank, power outlets and storage cabinets. Standard features include air conditioning, central locking, power windows and mirrors and cruise control.

Mileage Category: P

Body Styles	TMV Pricing		
	Trade	Private	Dealer
3 Dr Campmobile Pass Van	4095	5341	7417

Options	Price
Automatic 4-Speed Transmission	+178

Golf
2004

Mileage Category: B

Body Styles	TMV Pricing		
	Trade	Private	Dealer
2 Dr GL Hbk	9413	10308	11801
4 Dr GL Hbk	9530	10426	11919
4 Dr GL TDi Turbodsl Hbk	12517	13599	15401
4 Dr GLS Hbk	10908	11803	13295
4 Dr GLS TDi Turbodsl Hbk	14017	15098	16899

Options	Price
Automatic 4-Speed Transmission [Opt on GL, GLS]	+875
Automatic 5-Speed Transmission [Opt on TDi]	+1075
Automatic Stability Control	+280
Compact Disc Changer	+499
Heated Front Seats [Opt on GLS]	+150
OnStar Telematics System	+699

Like the Jetta and New Beetle, the Golf gets a revised and more powerful version of the 1.9-liter TDI engine. A Monsoon stereo is now standard on the GLS model and all Golfs get a new fuel cap warning light and seatbelt reminder.

2003

The most affordable Volkswagen gets a few equipment changes for 2003. Probably the biggest of these is the availability of stability control (VW's ESP) on all trim levels. In other news, base GL models now include a CD player, cruise control and power windows and mirrors. GLS models now come with a sunroof and alloy wheels, while seat heaters and the premium Monsoon sound system will be optional across the line. Finally, VW has increased the padding on the side curtain airbag system; the base 2.0-liter four-cylinder now meets ULEV standards; and the standard stereo head unit will get backlighting for the buttons.

Mileage Category: B

Body Styles	TMV Pricing		
	Trade	Private	Dealer
2 Dr GL Hbk	8500	9330	10715
2 Dr GL TDi Turbodsl Hbk	11365	12475	14325
4 Dr GL Hbk	8662	9508	10919
4 Dr GL TDi Turbodsl Hbk	11569	12699	14581
4 Dr GLS Hbk	9907	10875	12487
4 Dr GLS TDi Turbodsl Hbk	11973	13142	15090

Options	Price
Automatic 4-Speed Transmission	+615
Automatic Stability Control	+197
Monsoon Audio System	+229

2002

The speedy 1.8T four-door has been eliminated from the Golf lineup. A CD player now comes standard on the GLS model, and the GL trim level is available both in two- and four-door configurations. Mojave Beige joins the color spectrum. Also new for the 2002 model year, all Volkswagen vehicles come with an improved four-year/50,000-mile bumper-to-bumper warranty, up from two years/24,000 miles. In addition, Volkswagen offers a fully transferable limited powertrain warranty that covers five years or 60,000 miles.

Mileage Category: B

Body Styles	TMV Pricing		
	Trade	Private	Dealer
2 Dr GL Hbk	7133	7940	9284
2 Dr GL TDi Turbodsl Hbk	9664	10757	12578
4 Dr GL Hbk	7308	8134	9510
4 Dr GL TDi Turbodsl Hbk	9910	11031	12898
4 Dr GLS Hbk	8332	9275	10847
4 Dr GLS TDi Turbodsl Hbk	10057	11194	13090

Volkswagen
Golf

2002 (cont'd)

Options	Price
Aluminum/Alloy Wheels [Opt on GLS,GLS TDi]	+182
Automatic 4-Speed Transmission	+559

Options	Price
Monsoon Audio System [Opt on GLS,GLS TDi]	+207
Power Moonroof [Opt on GLS,GLS TDi]	+479

2001

All Golf models get head protection airbags, higher quality interior fabrics, clear side marker lights, a trunk entrapment release button and a revised cupholder design.

Mileage Category: B

Body Styles	TMV Pricing		
	Trade	Private	Dealer
2 Dr GL Hbk	6382	7575	8675
2 Dr GL TDi Turbodsl Hbk	7952	9437	10807
4 Dr GLS 1.8T Turbo Hbk	7706	9145	10472

Body Styles	TMV Pricing		
	Trade	Private	Dealer
4 Dr GLS Hbk	6994	8300	9507
4 Dr GLS TDi Turbodsl Hbk	8882	10540	12070

Options	Price
Aluminum/Alloy Wheels [Opt on GLS]	+155
Automatic 4-Speed Transmission	+494
Compact Disc Changer	+279

Options	Price
Heated Front Seats	+141
Monsoon Audio System	+183
Power Moonroof	+333

2000

For 2000, the big news is the availability of the 150-horsepower 1.8T engine on the Golf GLS. In addition, the Golf receives several equipment updates, including child-seat anchor points, sun visor extenders, a glare-reducing shade band on the windshield, a brake wear indicator light in the instrument cluster, a theft-repelling engine immobilizer and a tether for the fuel cap. All Golfs are now eligible for dealer-installed in-dash CD player; a dealer-installed CD changer is also available. Finally, GLS buyers can opt for a premium Monsoon sound system in lieu of the standard eight-speaker system.

Mileage Category: B

Body Styles	TMV Pricing		
	Trade	Private	Dealer
2 Dr GL Hbk	5081	6194	7285
2 Dr GL TDi Turbodsl Hbk	6236	7603	8942
4 Dr GLS 1.8T Turbo Hbk	6476	7896	9287

Body Styles	TMV Pricing		
	Trade	Private	Dealer
4 Dr GLS Hbk	5674	6917	8135
4 Dr GLS TDi Turbodsl Hbk	7067	8616	10135

Options	Price
Aluminum/Alloy Wheels	+135
Automatic 4-Speed Transmission	+431
Compact Disc Changer	+244

Options	Price
Heated Front Seats	+123
Monsoon Audio System	+145
Power Moonroof	+291

1999

Mileage Category: B

Body Styles	TMV Pricing		
	Trade	Private	Dealer
2 Dr New GL Hbk	3937	4927	5957
2 Dr New GL TDi Turbodsl Hbk	5047	6317	7638
4 Dr GL Hbk	3670	4593	5555

Body Styles	TMV Pricing		
	Trade	Private	Dealer
4 Dr New GLS Hbk	4535	5677	6867
4 Dr New GLS TDi Turbodsl Hbk	5823	7289	8815
4 Dr Wolfsburg Hbk	4318	5405	6537

Options	Price
AM/FM/Cassette Audio System [Opt on GL]	+195
AM/FM/Cassette/CD Audio System [Opt on Wolfsburg]	+120
Air Conditioning [Opt on GL]	+345
Antilock Brakes [Std on VR6]	+311

Options	Price
Automatic 4-Speed Transmission	+352
Compact Disc Changer	+199
Front Side Airbag Restraints	+159
Power Moonroof [Std on VR6]	+237

Volkswagen offers two generations of the Golf for sale in 1999. The third-generation Golf has been around since 1993, and it is a carryover for 1999. VW deletes the K2 model from the lineup and adds content to the upscale Wolfsburg, including cruise control, power windows (with one-touch operation) and heated power mirrors. Later in the model year, the company introduces a completely redesigned Golf with an improved version of the base inline four and an available turbodiesel four, which delivers up to 49 mpg on the highway. If you can hold out for a 2000 model, VW will offer a 150-hp 1.8-liter turbo for four-door hatchbacks.

1998

The Trek and Jazz models disappear for 1998, but the winter-enthusiast K2 model sticks around. Late in the model year, Volkswagen offers the upscale Wolfsburg Edition, which comes standard with sport seats; upgraded velour upholstery; silver/white-faced gauges; leather-wrapped steering wheel, hand brake and shift knob; the eight-speaker sound system with cassette player; air conditioning; a power moonroof; a cargo net; alloy wheels; a chrome exhaust tip and a roof-mounted antenna. And you can option the Wolfsburg with useful features like cruise control, power windows with one-touch operation and heated power mirrors. All Golfs get keyless entry, and side-impact airbags are now optional across the line. The four-speed automatic gets a new shift logic pattern, which should enhance shift timing.

Mileage Category: B

Body Styles	TMV Pricing		
	Trade	Private	Dealer
4 Dr GL Hbk	3031	3893	4864
4 Dr K2 Hbk	3179	4082	5100

Body Styles	TMV Pricing		
	Trade	Private	Dealer
4 Dr Wolfsburg Hbk	3476	4464	5579

Options	Price
AM/FM/Cassette Audio System [Opt on GL]	+171
Air Conditioning [Opt on GL,K2]	+304
Antilock Brakes	+274
Automatic 4-Speed Transmission	+309

Options	Price
Compact Disc Changer	+175
Front Side Airbag Restraints	+140
Power Moonroof [Opt on GL,K2]	+208

For the latest vehicle information, visit www.edmunds.com

1997

The Golf's 2.0-liter inline four engine is fitted with a redesigned cylinder head, resulting in smoother power delivery. Other changes include the addition of a cargo area light, a new high-mounted brake light and open-door warning reflectors for all doors. Memory Red is a new exterior paint choice. Later in the model year, Volkswagen releases special-interest K2, Trek and Jazz versions of the Golf. The K2 targets winter enthusiasts, and as such comes with the buyer's choice of skis or a snowboard; a roof rack to carry said gear; heated front seats, windshield washer nozzles and exterior mirrors; special cloth upholstery; silver-faced gauges; and an eight-speaker cassette stereo. The Golf Trek targets mountain bikers, and it comes with a 21-speed mountain bike and a bike rack for the roof; alloy wheels; sport seats; special cloth and carpeting; a leather-wrapped steering wheel; silver-faced gauges; and foglights. Finally, the Jazz is solely for those who fancy a Golf with a sound system, six-CD changer, velour upholstery and alloy wheels baked right in. Curiously, none of these special models are eligible for the basic GL model's optional antilock brakes.

Mileage Category: B

Body Styles	TMV Pricing		
	Trade	Private	Dealer
2 Dr GL Hbk	2478	3270	4238
4 Dr GL Hbk	2662	3511	4548
4 Dr Jazz Hbk	2689	3550	4602

Options	Price
AM/FM/Cassette Audio System [Opt on GL,Trek]	+142
Air Conditioning [Opt on GL,K2,Trek]	+251
Antilock Brakes [Opt on GL]	+226

Body Styles	TMV Pricing		
	Trade	Private	Dealer
4 Dr K2 Hbk	2695	3555	4606
4 Dr Trek Hbk	2751	3630	4703

Options	Price
Automatic 4-Speed Transmission	+255
Compact Disc Changer	+145
Power Moonroof [Opt on GL,K2,Trek]	+172

1996

Last year's two-door Golf Sport and GTI VR6 models become a separate nameplate called simply the GTI. Meanwhile, Volkswagen trims down the remaining Golf lineup, leaving only the four-door GL hatchback for 1996. Upgrades include a smoother shifting automatic transmission, new cloth upholstery, the addition of a glovebox, retractor locking seatbelts (for more secure child-seat installation), easier-to-use height adjustment for the front belts, a central locking switch on the dash and a warning tone to remind you that you've left the headlights on. Additionally, VW removes the Roman numeral "III" designation from the Golf's exterior badging and adds Catalina Blue as an exterior color.

Mileage Category: B

Body Styles	TMV Pricing		
	Trade	Private	Dealer
4 Dr GL Hbk	1884	2612	3619

Options	Price
AM/FM/Cassette Audio System	+124
Air Conditioning	+220
Antilock Brakes	+199

Body Styles	TMV Pricing		
	Trade	Private	Dealer
4 Dr TDi Turbodsl Hbk	2680	3717	5148

Options	Price
Automatic 4-Speed Transmission	+224
Compact Disc Changer	+127
Power Moonroof	+151

1995

Volkswagen doubles the number of trim levels in the Golf line: During the year, four-door models are offered in entry-level base and City trim, as well as midlevel Celebration trim; the GL remains the best-equipped four-door Golf. In addition, a two-door Sport model joins the lineup; it has distinctive styling cues like seven-spoke alloy wheels and blacked-out taillights, along with standard sport seats and a power sunroof. All Golfs meet 1997 side-impact standards, and the front seatbelts are now height-adjustable and equipped with pre-tensioners. Daytime running lights are standard across the line.

Mileage Category: B

Body Styles	TMV Pricing		
	Trade	Private	Dealer
2 Dr GL Hbk	1433	2009	2969
2 Dr Sport Hbk	1586	2257	3375
4 Dr Celebration Hbk	1396	1957	2893

Options	Price
AM/FM/Cassette Audio System [Opt on City,STD]	+102
Air Conditioning [Std on GTI VR6,GL,Sport]	+180
Antilock Brakes [Std on GTI VR6]	+163
Automatic 4-Speed Transmission	+184

Body Styles	TMV Pricing		
	Trade	Private	Dealer
4 Dr City Hbk	1230	1724	2547
4 Dr GL Hbk	1529	2143	3166
4 Dr STD Hbk	1387	1944	2872

Options	Price
Compact Disc Changer	+104
Power Moonroof [Std on GTI VR6,Sport]	+124
Premium Audio System [Opt on Celebration]	+79

GTI

2004

Mileage Category: E

Body Styles	TMV Pricing		
	Trade	Private	Dealer
2 Dr 1.8T Turbo Hbk	12467	13512	15254

Options	Price
17 Inch Wheels [Opt on 1.8T]	+400
Automatic 4-Speed Transmission [Opt on 1.8T]	+1075
Automatic Climate Control [Opt on VR6]	+365
Automatic Dimming Rearview Mirror [Opt on VR6]	+150
Automatic Stability Control [Opt on 1.8T]	+280
Compact Disc Changer	+449

Body Styles	TMV Pricing		
	Trade	Private	Dealer
2 Dr VR6 Hbk	14720	15799	17597

Options	Price
Heated Front Seats	+150
Leather Seats	+650
Monsoon Audio System	+340
OnStar Telematics System	+699
Power Moonroof	+900
Rain Sensing Windshield Wipers [Opt on VR6]	+190

The 237-hp makes its debut for 2004 complete with a six-speed manual transmission and 4Motion all-wheel drive. The GTI sports restyled 16- and 17-inch alloy wheels. There's also a new fuel cap warning light.

2003

VW's stability control system (ESP), which includes BrakeAssist, is now optional on the 1.8T model and standard on the VR6. A leather-wrapped three-spoke steering wheel, shift knob and hand brake are standard on both. Minor changes include increased padding for the head curtain airbags, backlighting for the buttons on the standard-issue stereo head unit, pinch protection for the sunroof's tilt function and upgraded wipers. Silverstone Gray replaces Matchstick Red on the exterior color list. Finally, it turns out that last year's special-edition 337 model was indeed special -- it's history for 2003.

Mileage Category: E

Body Styles	TMV Pricing		
	Trade	Private	Dealer
2 Dr 1.8T Turbo Hbk	11758	12701	14273
2 Dr 20th Anniv Edition Turbo Hbk	15062	16270	18284

Options	Price
17 Inch Wheels [Opt on 1.8T]	+281
Automatic 5-Speed Transmission [Opt on 1.8T]	+756
Automatic Climate Control [Opt on VR6]	+186
Automatic Stability Control [Opt on 1.8T,20th]	+197

Body Styles	TMV Pricing		
	Trade	Private	Dealer
2 Dr VR6 Hbk	13076	14125	15873

Options	Price
Leather Seats [Opt on 1.8T,VR6]	+563
Monsoon Audio System [Opt on 1.8T,VR6]	+229
Power Moonroof [Opt on 1.8T,VR6]	+643
Rain Sensing Windshield Wipers [Opt on VR6]	+141

2002

For the 2002 model year, the GLS and GLX trim levels are dropped. Instead, choose from the juiced-up 180-horsepower turbocharged inline four (that can be mated to a five-speed manual or a five-speed automatic transmission with Tiptronic) or the VR6 engine. The current 174-horsepower, 12-valve VR6 will be replaced with a 24-valve unit good for producing 200 horsepower in the spring of 2002. Later on, a special-edition model called the GTI 337 will arrive with a six-speed manual hooked up to the 180-horse 1.8T, as well as 18-inch wheels, 225/45VR18 performance rubber, a ground effects kit, genuine Recaro seats and red accents inside and out. All-new Volkswagen vehicles come standard with an improved four-year/50,000-mile bumper-to-bumper warranty, up from two years/24,000 miles. In addition, Volkswagen offers a fully transferable limited powertrain warranty that covers five years or 60,000 miles.

Mileage Category: E

Body Styles	TMV Pricing		
	Trade	Private	Dealer
2 Dr 1.8T Turbo Hbk	10437	11395	12991
2 Dr 337 1.8T Turbo Hbk	12857	14037	16003

Options	Price
17 Inch Wheels [Opt on 1.8T]	+255
6-Speed Transmission [Opt on VR6]	+945
Automatic 4-Speed Transmission [Opt on 1.8T]	+686
Automatic Climate Control [Opt on VR6]	+169

Body Styles	TMV Pricing		
	Trade	Private	Dealer
2 Dr VR6 Hbk	11705	12779	14568

Options	Price
Leather Seats	+447
Monsoon Audio System	+223
Power Moonroof	+511
Rain Sensing Windshield Wipers [Opt on VR6]	+128

2001

The GTI benefits from a new 16-inch wheel design (for the GLX), optional 17-inch wheels, multifunction steering wheel controls and a revised cupholder design. Later in the model year, all GTIs will get side curtain airbags to protect the heads of front and rear passengers (in addition to the regular side airbags for front occupants already offered).

Mileage Category: E

Body Styles	TMV Pricing		
	Trade	Private	Dealer
2 Dr GLS 1.8T Turbo Hbk	9091	10463	11729

Options	Price
Automatic 4-Speed Transmission [Opt on GLS]	+494
Compact Disc Changer	+279

Body Styles	TMV Pricing		
	Trade	Private	Dealer
2 Dr GLX VR6 Hbk	10132	11661	13072

Options	Price
Leather Seats [Opt on GLS]	+508
Monsoon Audio System [Opt on GLS]	+183

2000

Volkswagen introduces the GLS Turbo model powered by the company's superb 150-horsepower 1.8T power plant to bridge the gap between the weak 115-hp inline four in the regular GLS and the potent VR6 available only in the pricey GLX model.

Mileage Category: E

Body Styles	TMV Pricing		
	Trade	Private	Dealer
2 Dr GLS 1.8T Turbo Hbk	7662	8979	10269
2 Dr GLS Hbk	7162	8394	9601

Options	Price
AM/FM/CD Audio System	+135
Automatic 4-Speed Transmission	+431
Compact Disc Changer	+244

Body Styles	TMV Pricing		
	Trade	Private	Dealer
2 Dr GLX VR6 Hbk	8583	10059	11506

Options	Price
Heated Front Seats [Opt on GLS]	+123
Leather Seats [Opt on GLS]	+271
Monsoon Audio System [Opt on GLS]	+145

1999

Mileage Category: E

Body Styles	TMV Pricing		
	Trade	Private	Dealer
2 Dr New GLS Hbk	5317	6456	7643
2 Dr New GLX VR6 Hbk	6796	8253	9769

Options	Price
Automatic 4-Speed Transmission	+352
Compact Disc Changer	+199

Body Styles	TMV Pricing		
	Trade	Private	Dealer
2 Dr VR6 Hbk	6719	8159	9659

Options	Price
Front Side Airbag Restraints	+159
Leather Seats [Std on New GLX]	+221

Volkswagen offers two generations of the sporty Golf-based GTI for sale in 1999. The third-generation GTI has been around since 1995, and it is a carryover. VW drops the sluggish four-cylinder version and offers only the VR6. Later in the model year, the company introduces a completely redesigned GTI with a smoother body and improved versions of the base inline four and VR6.

1998

The GTI VR6 receives several cosmetic upgrades taken from the 1997 Driver's Edition. Among them are a chrome-tipped exhaust pipe, silver/white-faced instruments, embossed sill covers, leather-wrapped steering wheel, shift boot and hand brake lever, new Sport-Jacquard seat fabric and the aluminum ball shift knob. Exclusive to the VR6 for 1998 are the Speedline 15-inch alloys from the Driver's Edition and one-touch up power windows with pinch protection. All GTIs get standard remote keyless entry, and side-impact airbags are optional.

Body Styles	TMV Pricing		
	Trade	Private	Dealer
2 Dr STD Hbk	3882	4824	5885

Options	Price
Automatic 4-Speed Transmission	+309
Compact Disc Changer	+175

Mileage Category: E

Body Styles	TMV Pricing		
	Trade	Private	Dealer
2 Dr VR6 Hbk	5332	6625	8082

Options	Price
Front Side Airbag Restraints	+140
Leather Seats	+194

1997

For 1997, the GTI VR6 gets new alloy wheels and a revised suspension that has been lowered by 10mm and includes stiffer shock absorbers, springs and stabilizer bars. Meanwhile, the 115-horsepower inline four that powers the base GTI is fitted with a new cylinder head for smoother power delivery. A cargo area light is now standard in the base model, and both models get a new high-mounted center brake light and open-door warning reflectors for all doors. Late in the 1997 model year, Volkswagen offers a limited run of the GTI VR6 Driver's Edition, which comes with a special set of seven-spoke alloys; an even lower, stiffer suspension with progressive antiroll bars; red brake calipers; chrome-tipped exhaust pipes; special cloth upholstery and floor mats; silver-faced gauges; a round aluminum/rubber shift knob; red stitching on the leather-wraps for the steering wheel, hand brake and shift boot and deluxe door sill covers embossed with the "GTI" name.

Body Styles	TMV Pricing		
	Trade	Private	Dealer
2 Dr STD Hbk	3135	3930	4903
2 Dr VR6 Driver's Edition Hbk	4138	5189	6475

Options	Price
Automatic 4-Speed Transmission	+255
Compact Disc Changer	+145

Mileage Category: E

Body Styles	TMV Pricing		
	Trade	Private	Dealer
2 Dr VR6 Hbk	4046	5074	6329

Options	Price
Leather Seats	+161

1996

Last year's two-door Golf Sport and GTI VR6 models become a separate nameplate called simply the GTI, with respective base and VR6 trim levels. Like the Golf Sport, the base GTI will continue on with VW's 115-hp inline four but will get some additional content, including alloy wheels, bolstered sport seats, whip antenna and smoke-tinted taillights. Meanwhile, the GTI VR6 gets a black leather seating option. Both models will benefit from new cloth upholstery, the addition of a glovebox, retractor locking seatbelts (for more secure child-seat installation), easier-to-use height adjustment for the front belts, a central locking switch on the dash and a warning tone to remind you that you've left the headlights on. New exterior colors include Catalina Blue for the base GTI and Windsor Blue, Bright Surf Green and Sequoia Green for the GTI VR6.

Body Styles	TMV Pricing		
	Trade	Private	Dealer
2 Dr STD Hbk	2573	3320	4353

Options	Price
Automatic 4-Speed Transmission	+224
Compact Disc Changer	+127

Mileage Category: E

Body Styles	TMV Pricing		
	Trade	Private	Dealer
2 Dr VR6 Hbk	3420	4414	5787

Options	Price
Leather Seats	+141

1995

The GTI returns with a vengeance after taking two years off -- based on the current-generation Golf, this pocket rocket has Volkswagen's 2.8-liter VR6 stuffed under its hood. Output is rated at 172 horsepower and 173 pound-feet of torque; the company says the GTI VR6 can go from zero to 60 mph in seven seconds flat. As before, the VR6 rides on a sport-tuned version of the regular Golf suspension; a standard traction control system prevents its low-profile 205/50R15 Goodyear tires from slipping too much off the line. Standard equipment includes height-adjustable sport seats, a sunroof, a premium eight-speaker sound system and daytime running lights. The GTI meets 1997 side-impact standards, and its front seatbelts are height-adjustable and equipped with pre-tensioners.

Mileage Category: E

Body Styles	TMV Pricing		
	Trade	Private	Dealer
2 Dr VR6 Hbk	2682	3465	4770

Options	Price
Compact Disc Changer	+104

R32
2004

Mileage Category: E

Body Styles	TMV Pricing		
	Trade	Private	Dealer
2 Dr AWD Hbk	21294	23048	25971

Options	Price
Leather Seats	+950

Cloaked in a humble Golf body, the R32 offers 240 hp, all-wheel drive and an aggressive suspension setup.

Jetta

2004

For 2004, all Jetta models get an updated look, optional telematics and a new and more powerful 1.9-liter TDI engine (GL and GLS models only). The 2.0-liter engine is now PZEV-rated, and the GLX trim is no longer available. Also note that you can no longer get the 1.8T engine in GL trim. Besides that, the GLI sedan sports new 17-inch alloy wheels and the Cold Weather Package items (heated seats and washer nozzles) as standard, while the GLS features a standard Monsoon stereo. The wagons get a revised instrument cluster late in the model year, and the sedans get new metallic trim rings around the gauges.

Mileage Category: C

Body Styles	TMV Pricing		
	Trade	Private	Dealer
4 Dr GL 1.8T Turbo Sdn	11597	12525	14072
4 Dr GL Sdn	10511	11355	12760
4 Dr GL TDi Turbodsl Sdn	14386	15634	17715
4 Dr GL TDi Turbodsl Wgn	15104	16353	18434
4 Dr GL Wgn	11097	11940	13345
4 Dr GLI 1.8T Turbo Sdn	14462	15390	16936
4 Dr GLI VR6 Sdn	13266	14348	16150

Options	Price
Automatic 4-Speed Transmission [Opt on GL, GLS]	+875
Automatic 5-Speed Transmission [Opt on 1.8T, TDi]	+1075
Automatic Stability Control [Std on GLI VR6]	+280
Compact Disc Changer	+499
Heated Front Seats [Opt on GLS]	+150
Leather Seats [Opt on GLI VR6, GLS]	+600

Body Styles	TMV Pricing		
	Trade	Private	Dealer
4 Dr GLS 1.8T Turbo Sdn	12786	13714	15260
4 Dr GLS 1.8T Turbo Wgn	12977	13809	15195
4 Dr GLS Sdn	12099	12971	14424
4 Dr GLS TDi Turbodsl Sdn	15687	16935	19016
4 Dr GLS TDi Turbodsl Wgn	16408	17656	19736
4 Dr GLS Wgn	12110	12940	14324

Options	Price
Leather Steering Wheel [Opt on GLS]	+120
OnStar Telematics System	+699
Power Moonroof [Opt on GLI VR6]	+900
Rear Spoiler [Opt on non-GLI 1.8T Sdn]	+479
Sport Package [Opt on GLS 1.8T]	+800

2003

Volkswagen eliminates the GLX trim level for wagons -- this means that those who prefer the VR6 engine to the 1.8T engine will have to stick with the sedan. As a consolation, GLS wagons equipped with the 1.8T are eligible for a premium package, which bundles traditional GLX content like power seats, automatic climate control, an auto-dimming rearview mirror, rain-sensing wipers, wood interior trim and a trip computer. Additionally, VW has made the 1.8T available on both the GL sedan and wagon. GLs now have power windows and mirrors, cruise control and a CD player, while the GLS gets a standard sunroof and alloy wheels. All Jettas are available with stability control (ESP), heated seats and the Monsoon sound system. Other changes include a ULEV rating for the 2.0-liter four-cylinder, redesigned cupholders and backlit buttons on the standard stereo head unit.

Mileage Category: C

Body Styles	TMV Pricing		
	Trade	Private	Dealer
4 Dr GL 1.8T Turbo Sdn	10584	11461	12924
4 Dr GL 1.8T Turbo Wgn	11245	12178	13733
4 Dr GL Sdn	9235	10001	11278
4 Dr GL TDi Turbodsl Sdn	13220	14408	16388
4 Dr GL TDi Turbodsl Wgn	14062	15229	17173
4 Dr GL Wgn	9754	10564	11912
4 Dr GLI VR6 Sdn	12257	13273	14968
4 Dr GLS 1.8T Turbo Sdn	11560	12519	14118

Options	Price
17 Inch Wheels [Std on GLI]	+281
Automatic 4-Speed Transmission [Opt on GL,GLS,TDi]	+615
Automatic 5-Speed Transmission [Opt on 1.8T]	+756
Automatic Climate Control [Opt on GLS 1.8T Wgn]	+176
Automatic Stability Control [Std on GLI]	+197
Leather Seats [Opt on GLS,GLI]	+563

Body Styles	TMV Pricing		
	Trade	Private	Dealer
4 Dr GLS 1.8T Turbo Wgn	11696	12666	14283
4 Dr GLS Sdn	10741	11632	13116
4 Dr GLS TDi Turbodsl Sdn	14405	15600	17592
4 Dr GLS TDi Turbodsl Wgn	14665	15882	17910
4 Dr GLS Wgn	11006	11919	13441
4 Dr GLX VR6 Sdn	13844	14993	16907
4 Dr Wolfsburg Turbo Sdn	11217	12148	13699

Options	Price
Monsoon Audio System	+229
Power Driver Seat w/Memory [Opt on GLS 1.8T Wgn]	+193
Power Moonroof [Opt on GLI,Wolfsburg]	+643
Power Passenger Seat [Opt on GLS 1.8T Wgn]	+193
Sport Suspension [Opt on GLS 1.8T]	+193

2002

For 2002, the turbocharged four-cylinder engine receives 30 extra horsepower for a total of 180, which you can couple to a five-speed automatic with Tiptronic -- the 1.8T is now available for both sedans and wagons. In the spring of 2002, the Jetta GLX sedan's optional 12-valve 174-hp VR6 is replaced by a new 24-valve unit providing 200 ponies. A six-speed manual gearbox and the aforementioned five-speed automanual become available with the new VR6. Later on, the GLI sedan will appear -- it includes the new VR6, the six-speed and stability control without all the expensive GLX trimmings and replaces the manual-shift GLX. Other changes include the availability of the 1.9-liter turbodiesel engine for GL and GLS wagons. The GLS trim level is new to the wagon in 2002 -- previously, you had to step right up to the GLS model. A CD player is now standard on all GLS and GLX models, and all-new Volkswagen vehicles come with an improved four-year/50,000-mile bumper-to-bumper warranty, up from two years/24,000 miles. Volkswagen also offers a fully transferable limited powertrain warranty that covers five years or 60,000 miles. An on/off switch for auto-dimming rearview mirrors, a cruise control indicator light, a trunk escape handle for sedans and a new exterior color (Reflex Silver replaces Silver Arrow) complete the changes.

Mileage Category: C

Body Styles	TMV Pricing		
	Trade	Private	Dealer
4 Dr GL Sdn	8061	8783	9986
4 Dr GL TDi Turbodsl Sdn	11648	12691	14428
4 Dr GL TDi Turbodsl Wgn	12362	13469	15314
4 Dr GL Wgn	8783	9569	10879
4 Dr GLI VR6 Sdn	11356	12324	13936
4 Dr GLS 1.8T Turbo Sdn	10175	11086	12604
4 Dr GLS 1.8T Turbo Wgn	10529	11472	13045
4 Dr GLS Sdn	8876	9672	10997

Options	Price
16 Inch Wheels [Opt on GLS VR6]	+310
17 Inch Wheels	+255
2.8L V6 DOHC 24V FI Engine [Opt on GLX VR6 Sdn]	+798
Aluminum/Alloy Wheels [Opt on GLS,GLS 1.8T,GLS TDi]	+182
Automatic 4-Speed Transmission	+559

Body Styles	TMV Pricing		
	Trade	Private	Dealer
4 Dr GLS TDi Turbodsl Sdn	12430	13544	15400
4 Dr GLS TDi Turbodsl Wgn	12601	13730	15611
4 Dr GLS VR6 Sdn	10433	11367	12924
4 Dr GLS VR6 Wgn	11000	11985	13626
4 Dr GLS Wgn	9904	10791	12269
4 Dr GLX VR6 Sdn	12077	13159	14963
4 Dr GLX VR6 Wgn	12216	13310	15133

Options	Price
Automatic 5-Speed Transmission [Opt on GLX VR6 Sdn]	+559
Leather Seats [Std on GLX VR6]	+511
Monsoon Audio System [Std on GLX VR6]	+207
Power Moonroof [Std on GLX VR6]	+543
Sport Suspension	+128

2001

For 2001, improved cloth and velour interior materials come standard in the GL and GLS trim. Side curtain airbags that offer head protection for front and rear passengers are introduced this year, and steering wheel controls for the audio and cruise systems are available on GLS/GLX trim models. Optional 17-inch wheels and a sport suspension can be had on GLX models and GLS models with the 1.8T or VR6 engine. The Wolfsburg Edition returns as a limited-edition model in early 2001 -- standard features include sport suspension, bolstered sport seats and 16-inch BBS wheels. All models get redesigned cupholders and a trunk entrapment release button. A wagon arrives in the spring of 2001.

Mileage Category: C

Body Styles	TMV Pricing		
	Trade	Private	Dealer
4 Dr GL Sdn	7189	8152	9040
4 Dr GL TDi Turbodsl Sdn	10668	12096	13414
4 Dr GLS 1.8T Turbo Sdn	8817	9997	11086
4 Dr GLS Sdn	7907	8965	9943
4 Dr GLS TDi Turbodsl Sdn	11198	12696	14079
4 Dr GLS VR6 Sdn	9320	10568	11719

Options	Price
Aluminum/Alloy Wheels [Std on GLX VR6]	+161
Automatic 4-Speed Transmission	+494
Compact Disc Changer	+279

Body Styles	TMV Pricing		
	Trade	Private	Dealer
4 Dr GLS VR6 Wgn	9781	11090	12299
4 Dr GLS Wgn	8634	9789	10856
4 Dr GLS Wolfsburg Edition 1.8T Turbo Sdn	9111	10331	11457
4 Dr GLX VR6 Sdn	10624	12045	13358
4 Dr GLX VR6 Wgn	10764	12204	13534

Options	Price
Leather Seats [Std on GLX VR6]	+310
Monsoon Audio System [Std on GLX VR6]	+183
Power Moonroof [Std on GLX VR6]	+333

2000

VW's 2000 Jetta arrives with an optional turbocharged 1.8T engine on the GLS as well as minor equipment updates.

Mileage Category: C

Body Styles	TMV Pricing		
	Trade	Private	Dealer
4 Dr GL Sdn	5864	6822	7761
4 Dr GL TDi Turbodsl Sdn	8078	9397	10689
4 Dr GLS 1.8T Turbo Sdn	6932	8064	9174
4 Dr GLS Sdn	6683	7774	8844

Options	Price
AM/FM/CD Audio System	+123
AM/FM/Cassette/CD Audio System	+123
Aluminum/Alloy Wheels [Std on GLX VR6]	+141
Automatic 4-Speed Transmission	+431
Compact Disc Changer	+244

Body Styles	TMV Pricing		
	Trade	Private	Dealer
4 Dr GLS TDi Turbodsl Sdn	8351	9715	11052
4 Dr GLS VR6 Sdn	7748	9013	10254
4 Dr GLX VR6 Sdn	8077	9396	10689

Options	Price
Heated Front Seats [Std on GLX VR6]	+123
Leather Seats [Std on GLX VR6]	+394
Monsoon Audio System [Std on GLX VR6]	+145
Power Moonroof [Std on GLX VR6]	+291

1999

Mileage Category: C

Body Styles	TMV Pricing		
	Trade	Private	Dealer
4 Dr GL Sdn	4204	5022	5873
4 Dr GLX VR6 Sdn	6537	7808	9131
4 Dr New GL Sdn	5010	5984	6998
4 Dr New GL TDi Turbodsl Sdn	6572	7850	9180
4 Dr New GLS Sdn	5802	6931	8107

Options	Price
AM/FM/Cassette Audio System [Opt on GL,TDI]	+195
Air Conditioning [Opt on GL,TDI]	+345
Antilock Brakes [Std on GLX]	+311
Automatic 4-Speed Transmission	+352

Body Styles	TMV Pricing		
	Trade	Private	Dealer
4 Dr New GLS TDi Turbodsl Sdn	6767	8083	9453
4 Dr New GLS VR6 Sdn	6338	7571	8855
4 Dr New GLX VR6 Sdn	7056	8428	9857
4 Dr TDi Turbodsl Sdn	6162	7361	8608
4 Dr Wolfsburg Sdn	5004	5977	6990

Options	Price
Compact Disc Changer [Std on Wolfsburg]	+199
Front Side Airbag Restraints	+159
Leather Seats	+321
Power Moonroof [Std on GLX]	+237

Volkswagen offers two generations of the Jetta for sale in 1999. The third-generation Jetta has been around since 1993, and it is a carryover for 1999. VW deletes the GT, K2 and GLS models from the lineup, leaving only the GL, GLX, TDI and Wolfsburg models. Later in the model year, the company introduces a completely redesigned Jetta with a smooth new European body, improved versions of the base inline four and the VR6 and a simplified lineup of GL, GLS and GLX models. If you can hold out for a 2000 model, VW will offer a 150-hp 1.8-liter turbo for the GLS.

1998

The TDI has finally arrived. New wheel covers and colors are offered, while remote keyless entry makes it easier to lock and unlock the Jetta. GLX models have new one-touch up power windows with pinch protection.

Mileage Category: C

Body Styles	TMV Pricing		
	Trade	Private	Dealer
4 Dr GL Sdn	3262	4117	5080
4 Dr GLS Sdn	3994	5038	6216
4 Dr GLX VR6 Sdn	4985	6289	7760
4 Dr GT Sdn	3830	4832	5962

Options	Price
AM/FM/Cassette Audio System [Opt on GL,GT,TDI]	+171
Air Conditioning [Opt on GL,GT,TDI]	+304
Antilock Brakes [Std on GLX]	+274
Automatic 4-Speed Transmission	+309

Body Styles	TMV Pricing		
	Trade	Private	Dealer
4 Dr K2 Sdn	3785	4775	5892
4 Dr TDi Turbodsl Sdn	4898	6180	7626
4 Dr Wolfsburg Sdn	3928	4955	6113

Options	Price
Bose Audio System [Opt on GLS]	+133
Compact Disc Changer [Std on Wolfsburg]	+175
Front Side Airbag Restraints	+140
Leather Seats	+283

1998 (cont'd)

Options	Price
Power Moonroof [Std on GLX,Wolfsburg]	+208

1997

Wolfsburg models are gone, and the Jetta GT arrives sporting the look of the GLX without the VR6 engine. Trek gets alloy wheels. GL, GLS, Trek and GT run more quietly, thanks to a new cylinder head design.

Mileage Category: C

Body Styles	TMV Pricing		
	Trade	Private	Dealer
4 Dr GL Sdn	2418	3254	4277
4 Dr GLS Sdn	3140	4225	5552
4 Dr GLX VR6 Sdn	3543	4767	6262
4 Dr GT Sdn	2616	3519	4624

Body Styles	TMV Pricing		
	Trade	Private	Dealer
4 Dr Jazz Sdn	2623	3534	4646
4 Dr TDi Turbodsl Sdn	3057	4113	5404
4 Dr Trek Sdn	2675	3600	4731

Options	Price
AM/FM/Cassette Audio System [Std on GLS]	+142
Air Conditioning [Std on GLS,GLX]	+251
Antilock Brakes [Std on GLX]	+226
Automatic 4-Speed Transmission	+255

Options	Price
Compact Disc Changer	+145
Leather Seats	+233
Power Moonroof [Opt on GLX]	+172

1996

A new three-bar grille is added up front. GLX models get a firmer front suspension and new "Bugatti" style wheels. New colors sum up the changes.

Mileage Category: C

Body Styles	TMV Pricing		
	Trade	Private	Dealer
4 Dr City Sdn	1803	2540	3557
4 Dr GL Sdn	1875	2640	3697
4 Dr GLS Sdn	2333	3285	4599
4 Dr GLX VR6 Sdn	2842	4003	5605

Body Styles	TMV Pricing		
	Trade	Private	Dealer
4 Dr TDi Turbodsl Sdn	2363	3328	4660
4 Dr Trek Limited Edition Sdn	2046	2881	4033
4 Dr Wolfsburg Sdn	1993	2807	3931

Options	Price
AM/FM/Cassette Audio System [Std on GLS]	+124
Air Conditioning [Std on GLS,GLX]	+220
Antilock Brakes [Std on GLX]	+199
Automatic 4-Speed Transmission	+224

Options	Price
Compact Disc Changer	+127
Leather Seats	+205
Power Moonroof [Std on GLX,Wolfsburg]	+151

1995

The GL gets air conditioning, cruise control, power mirrors and a split-folding rear seat.

Mileage Category: C

Body Styles	TMV Pricing		
	Trade	Private	Dealer
4 Dr Celebration Sdn	1451	2142	3293
4 Dr City Sdn	1228	1813	2788
4 Dr GL Sdn	1468	2166	3329

Body Styles	TMV Pricing		
	Trade	Private	Dealer
4 Dr GLS Sdn	1724	2545	3914
4 Dr GLX VR6 Sdn	2202	3251	4999
4 Dr STD Sdn	1311	1935	2975

Options	Price
AM/FM/Cassette Audio System [Std on GL,GLS,GLX]	+102
Air Conditioning [Std on GL,GLS,GLX,STD]	+180
Antilock Brakes [Std on GLX]	+163
Automatic 4-Speed Transmission	+184

Options	Price
Compact Disc Changer	+104
Leather Seats	+168
Power Moonroof [Std on GLS,GLX]	+124

New Beetle
2004

Mileage Category: E

Body Styles	TMV Pricing		
	Trade	Private	Dealer
2 Dr GL Conv	13491	14682	16666
2 Dr GL Hbk	10232	11100	12546
2 Dr GL TDi Turbodsl Hbk	13600	14842	16912
2 Dr GLS 1.8T Turbo Conv	16244	17434	19416
2 Dr GLS 1.8T Turbo Hbk	12816	13780	15386

Body Styles	TMV Pricing		
	Trade	Private	Dealer
2 Dr GLS Conv	14527	15560	17281
2 Dr GLS Hbk	11226	12068	13472
2 Dr GLS TDi Turbodsl Hbk	15134	16375	18444
2 Dr Turbo S Hbk	14723	15785	17556

Options	Price
17 Inch Wheels [Opt on GLS 1.8T]	+400
Automatic 4-Speed Transmission [Opt on GL, GLS, GLS 1.8T Hbk]	+875
Automatic 6-Speed Transmission [Opt on Conv, TDi]	+1075
Automatic Stability Control [Std on GLS 1.8T, Turbo S,]	+280

Options	Price
Heated Front Seats [Opt on GLS]	+150
Leather Seats [Opt on GLS]	+550
Leather Steering Wheel [Opt on GLS]	+120
OnStar Telematics System [Opt on GL, GLS, Turbo S Hbk]	+730
Rear Wind Deflector [Opt on Conv]	+250

2004 (cont'd)

Options	Price
Ski Sack [Opt on GLS Conv]	+185
Sport Seats [Opt on GLS 1.8T Conv]	+200

Options	Price
Xenon Headlamps [Opt on GLS]	+600

For 2004, the New Beetle is no longer available in GLX trim. There's an improved TDI engine and restyled 16- and 17-inch wheels. Turbo S models get uniquely styled 17-inch wheels as a late-year addition. New safety features include head curtain airbags and upgraded head restraints. The Monsoon audio system is now standard on the GLS and new GDL headlights are optional. Later in the model year a fixed rear spoiler will replace the power-operated unit and a CD player with MP3 capability will be added. Convertibles get new exterior colors and color combinations. All Beetles get a new fuel cap warning light this year. TDI models can be equipped with a Direct Shift Gearbox (DSG), which is a six-speed manual transmission with electronic control of the clutch and gearshifting. It can be operated in full automatic mode, like a traditional automatic, or shifted manually like a Tiptronic.

2003

Mileage Category: E

Body Styles	TMV Pricing		
	Trade	Private	Dealer
2 Dr GL 1.8T Turbo Hbk	10922	11833	13351
2 Dr GL Conv	12705	13765	15531
2 Dr GL Hbk	9191	9958	11236
2 Dr GL TDi Turbodsl Hbk	12445	13482	15211
2 Dr GLS 1.8T Turbo Conv	14910	16153	18226
2 Dr GLS 1.8T Turbo Hbk	11508	12468	14068

Body Styles	TMV Pricing		
	Trade	Private	Dealer
2 Dr GLS Conv	13395	14512	16375
2 Dr GLS Hbk	10422	11291	12739
2 Dr GLS TDi Turbodsl Hbk	14030	15200	17149
2 Dr GLX 1.8T Turbo Conv	15785	17102	19297
2 Dr GLX 1.8T Turbo Hbk	12600	13651	15403
2 Dr Turbo S Hbk	13562	14589	16301

Options	Price
17 Inch Wheels [Opt on GLS 1.8T,GLX]	+281
Automatic 4-Speed Transmission [Opt on Hbk]	+615
Automatic 6-Speed Transmission [Opt on Conv]	+826
Automatic Stability Control	+197

Options	Price
Leather Seats [Opt on GLS]	+563
Monsoon Audio System [Opt on GL,GLS]	+229
Rear Wind Deflector [Opt on Conv]	+176
Ski Sack [Opt on Conv]	+130

Volkswagen makes the TDI and 150-horsepower 1.8T engines available on the base GL trim level. All GLs now come with power windows and cruise control, and the GL 1.8T and all GLS models get alloy wheels. Stability control (ESP), heated seats, and the Monsoon sound system will be available across the line. All models except the GL get a standard sunroof and a larger center console container, and the GL and GLS have new cloth upholstery. Note that last year's Sport model has been discontinued. All models have a more comfortable rear seat, a clock/temperature display on the rearview mirror and turn signals mounted on the outside mirrors. Finally, if you've been holding out for a Beetle convertible since 1998, your wait is almost over -- the first drop tops should arrive at the dealers just in time for, well, winter. The first ones will be 2.0 GL and GLS models in February 2003, 1.8T-equipped GLS and GLX models later in the spring.

2002

Mileage Category: E

Body Styles	TMV Pricing		
	Trade	Private	Dealer
2 Dr GL Hbk	8178	9036	10465
2 Dr GLS 1.8T Turbo Hbk	9644	10655	12340
2 Dr GLS Hbk	8576	9476	10975
2 Dr GLS TDi Turbodsl Hbk	11737	12967	15018

Body Styles	TMV Pricing		
	Trade	Private	Dealer
2 Dr GLX 1.8T Turbo Hbk	10636	11751	13609
2 Dr Sport 1.8T Turbo Hbk	9918	10957	12689
2 Dr Turbo S 1.8T Hbk	12362	13479	15341

Options	Price
16 Inch Wheels [Opt on GLS,GLS 1.8T]	+223
17 Inch Wheels [Opt on GLS 1.8T,GLX 1.8T]	+255
Automatic 4-Speed Transmission	+559
Heated Front Seats [Std on GLX,Turbo S]	+172
Leather Seats [Opt on GLS,GLS 1.8T,GLS TDi]	+543

Options	Price
Monsoon Audio System [Opt on GLS,GLS 1.8T,GLS TDi]	+207
Power Moonroof [Opt on GLS,GLS 1.8T,GLS TDi]	+511
Special Factory Paint [Opt on GLS]	+606

A Turbo S model debuts, motivated by a 180-horsepower version of VW's 1.8-liter turbo engine teamed with a six-speed manual gearbox. Other exclusives for the Turbo S include Electronic Stabilization Program (ESP), a slightly stiffer suspension, 17-inch "Delta X" alloy wheels, revised turn signals and foglights, a front spoiler, a redesigned rear bumper with Turbo S badging and brushed alloy interior accents. Additionally, a rear spoiler will deploy from the hatch when these special Bugs reach 45 mph. Exterior paint for the S is limited to Reflex Silver, Black, Red and Platinum Gray. Later in the year, a Sport model debuts -- it's essentially a GLS 1.8T with a five-speed manual, 17-inch wheels, leather interior and a Sport badge on the deck lid. Changes for the rest of the lineup are minor: New colors such as limited-edition Snap Orange and Riviera Blue further enhance the Beetle's eye-candy appeal, and 16-inch wheels with 205/55 tires are now standard across the board. For 2002, all-new Volkswagen vehicles come standard with an improved four-year/50,000-mile bumper-to-bumper warranty, up from two years/24,000 miles. In addition, Volkswagen offers a fully transferable limited powertrain warranty that covers five years or 60,000 miles.

2001

Mileage Category: E

Body Styles	TMV Pricing		
	Trade	Private	Dealer
2 Dr GL Hbk	6712	7797	8799
2 Dr GLS 1.8T Turbo Hbk	7865	9137	10311
2 Dr GLS Hbk	7017	8151	9199

Body Styles	TMV Pricing		
	Trade	Private	Dealer
2 Dr GLS TDi Turbodsl Hbk	9527	11067	12488
2 Dr GLX 1.8T Turbo Hbk	8611	10002	11286

Options	Price
Aluminum/Alloy Wheels [Opt on GLS]	+226
Automatic 4-Speed Transmission	+494
Compact Disc Changer	+282
Heated Front Seats [Opt on GLS]	+152

Options	Price
Leather Seats [Opt on GLS]	+480
Monsoon Audio System [Opt on GLS]	+183
Power Moonroof [Opt on GLS]	+452
Special Factory Paint [Opt on GLS,GLS 1.8T]	+536

You can order 17-inch alloy wheels a la carte for GLS 1.8T and GLX models, while high-intensity discharge headlights are optional on all GLS and GLX models. New standard features for the GLX include the Monsoon sound system (optional for GLS), rain-sensing wipers and a self-dimming rearview mirror. All-new Beetles benefit from larger exterior mirrors, redesigned cupholders and a trunk entrapment release button.

Volkswagen
New Beetle/Passat

2000
Several minor equipment upgrades, such as improved theft protection, debut on the 2000 New Beetle.

Mileage Category: E

Body Styles	TMV Pricing		
	Trade	Private	Dealer
2 Dr GL Hbk	5992	7061	8108
2 Dr GLS 1.8T Turbo Hbk	7078	8340	9578
2 Dr GLS Hbk	6287	7409	8509

Options	Price
Aluminum/Alloy Wheels [Opt on GL,GLS]	+153
Automatic 4-Speed Transmission	+431
Compact Disc Changer	+246
Heated Front Seats [Opt on GLS]	+133

Body Styles	TMV Pricing		
	Trade	Private	Dealer
2 Dr GLS TDi Turbodsl Hbk	7991	9417	10814
2 Dr GLX 1.8T Turbo Hbk	7776	9163	10523

Options	Price
Leather Seats [Opt on GLS]	+420
Power Moonroof [Opt on GLS]	+394
Special Factory Paint [Opt on GLS,GLS 1.8T]	+468

1999
A high-performance turbo model debuts this year. A small spoiler over the rear window is the only exterior telltale that the Bug next to you has the 150-horsepower 1.8-liter turbocharged inline four from the larger Passat sedan under the hood.

Mileage Category: E

Body Styles	TMV Pricing		
	Trade	Private	Dealer
2 Dr GL Hbk	5103	6198	7337
2 Dr GLS 1.8T Turbo Hbk	5918	7187	8508
2 Dr GLS Hbk	5286	6419	7598

Options	Price
Aluminum/Alloy Wheels [Opt on GLS]	+124
Automatic 4-Speed Transmission	+390
Compact Disc Changer	+223

Body Styles	TMV Pricing		
	Trade	Private	Dealer
2 Dr GLS TDi Turbodsl Hbk	6538	7939	9398
2 Dr GLX 1.8T Turbo Hbk	6077	7380	8736

Options	Price
Heated Front Seats [Opt on GLS]	+120
Leather Seats [Opt on GLS]	+380
Power Moonroof [Opt on GLS]	+357

1998
Volkswagen revives a legend using retro styling touches wrapped around Golf underpinnings.

Mileage Category: E

Body Styles	TMV Pricing		
	Trade	Private	Dealer
2 Dr STD Hbk	4056	5039	6148

Options	Price
Antilock Brakes	+284
Automatic 4-Speed Transmission	+373
Compact Disc Changer	+196

Body Styles	TMV Pricing		
	Trade	Private	Dealer
2 Dr TDi Turbodsl Hbk	4956	6156	7510

Options	Price
Heated Front Seats	+126
Power Moonroof	+349

Passat
2004

The big news for 2004 is the addition of a 2.0-liter diesel four-cylinder engine to the lineup late in the model year. The 4Motion all-wheel-drive system is a delayed option on 1.8T-equipped GLS models. Also note that the 2.8-liter V6 is no longer available on GLS models. The premium Monsoon stereo and Homelink are now standard on all GLS models, while wood trim has been added to the optional Leather Package. The ESP stability control system is now standard on the GLX. Rounding out the changes are restyled 15- and 16-inch wheels and new side mirrors with integrated turn signals.

Mileage Category: D

Body Styles	TMV Pricing		
	Trade	Private	Dealer
4 Dr GL 1.8T Turbo Sdn	13607	14635	16348
4 Dr GL 1.8T Turbo Wgn	14218	15245	16958
4 Dr GL TDi Turbodsl Sdn	17631	19491	22592
4 Dr GL TDi Turbodsl Wgn	18359	20219	23319
4 Dr GLS 1.8T Turbo 4Motion AWD Sdn	15636	17020	19328
4 Dr GLS 1.8T Turbo 4Motion AWD Wgn	16247	17631	19939
4 Dr GLS 1.8T Turbo Sdn	14566	15951	18260
4 Dr GLS 1.8T Turbo Wgn	15177	16562	18870

Options	Price
17 Inch Wheels [Opt on W8]	+750
6-Speed Transmission [Opt on W8]	+1500
Automatic 5-Speed Transmission [Opt on GL, GLS, GLX]	+1075
Automatic Stability Control [Opt on GL, GLS]	+280

Body Styles	TMV Pricing		
	Trade	Private	Dealer
4 Dr GLS TDi Turbodsl Sdn	18258	19906	22652
4 Dr GLS TDi Turbodsl Wgn	19522	21382	24481
4 Dr GLX V6 4Motion AWD Sdn	19289	20611	22813
4 Dr GLX V6 4Motion AWD Wgn	19899	21222	23428
4 Dr GLX V6 Sdn	17561	18877	21070
4 Dr GLX V6 Wgn	18173	19491	21687
4 Dr W8 4Motion AWD Sdn	21943	23228	25369
4 Dr W8 4Motion AWD Wgn	21821	23067	25144

Options	Price
Compact Disc Changer	+499
Heated Front Seats [Std on GLX, W8]	+325
OnStar Telematics System [Std on GLX, W8]	+699

2003

Mileage Category: D

Body Styles	TMV Pricing		
	Trade	Private	Dealer
4 Dr GL 1.8T Turbo Sdn	12269	13161	14646
4 Dr GL 1.8T Turbo Wgn	12707	13630	15168
4 Dr GLS 1.8T Turbo Sdn	12851	13784	15341
4 Dr GLS 1.8T Turbo Wgn	13368	14340	15958
4 Dr GLS V6 Sdn	13567	14553	16196
4 Dr GLS V6 Wgn	14551	15608	17371

Options	Price
17 Inch Wheels [Opt on W8]	+527
6-Speed Transmission [Opt on W8]	+1055
Automatic 5-Speed Transmission [Std on 4Motion]	+756
Automatic Stability Control [Opt on GLS,GLX]	+197

Body Styles	TMV Pricing		
	Trade	Private	Dealer
4 Dr GLX V6 4Motion AWD Sdn	17149	18310	20245
4 Dr GLX V6 4Motion AWD Wgn	17507	18779	20899
4 Dr GLX V6 Sdn	15480	16605	18480
4 Dr GLX V6 Wgn	15854	17006	18926
4 Dr W8 4Motion AWD Sdn	19143	20549	22893
4 Dr W8 4Motion AWD Wgn	19542	20978	23371

Options	Price
Heated Front Seats [Opt on GL,GLS]	+229
Leather Seats [Opt on GLS]	+668
Monsoon Audio System [Opt on GL,GLS]	+229
Sport Suspension [Opt on W8]	+193

For 2003, a base GL sedan and wagon are available. Think of the GL as a GLS 1.8T for buyers who don't require any extras like alloy wheels, leather upholstery, seat heaters or a sunroof. Meanwhile, alloy wheels and sunroof are now standard on GLS models. The 4Motion all-wheel-drive system will not be offered on GLS V6 models, forcing interested buyers to cross the 30-grand line; however, VW has made stability control (ESP) optional on all Passats (except the W8, which has this standard). Also this year, you'll be able to get W8 sedans and wagons with a six-speed manual transmission and a sport package that includes a firmer suspension and the requisite 17-inch wheels. Lastly, the standard stereo head unit gets backlighting for the buttons.

2002

Mileage Category: D

Body Styles	TMV Pricing		
	Trade	Private	Dealer
4 Dr GLS 1.8T Turbo Sdn	10917	11723	13064
4 Dr GLS 1.8T Turbo Wgn	11766	12634	14080
4 Dr GLS V6 4Motion AWD Sdn	13109	14076	15688
4 Dr GLS V6 4Motion AWD Wgn	13915	14941	16651
4 Dr GLS V6 Sdn	11909	12788	14252
4 Dr GLS V6 Wgn	12842	13789	15368

Options	Price
Aluminum/Alloy Wheels [Std on GLX V6,W8]	+223
Automatic 5-Speed Transmission [Std on 4Motion]	+686
Heated Front Seats [Std on GLX V6,W8]	+207

Body Styles	TMV Pricing		
	Trade	Private	Dealer
4 Dr GLX V6 4Motion AWD Sdn	15657	16812	18736
4 Dr GLX V6 4Motion AWD Wgn	15940	17116	19075
4 Dr GLX V6 Sdn	14062	15099	16828
4 Dr GLX V6 Wgn	14272	15324	17079
4 Dr W8 4Motion AWD Sdn	17024	18299	20423
4 Dr W8 4Motion AWD Wgn	17379	18681	20849

Options	Price
Leather Seats [Std on GLX V6,W8]	+606
Monsoon Audio System [Std on GLX V6,W8]	+207
Power Moonroof [Std on GLX V6,W8]	+638

The arrival of the 270-horsepower, all-wheel-drive W8 sedan and wagon disturbs the tranquility of the Passat lineup. Standard features in the W8 cars build upon the already impressive GLX equipment list, adding Electronic Stabilization Program with BrakeAssist, vented disc brakes all around (as opposed to solid discs in rear) xenon headlights with washers, wider 215/55R16 tires, an upgraded trip computer and extra chrome throughout the cabin. The rest of the Passats receive only minor upgrades for 2002, including a trunk escape release for the sedan, a cruise control indicator light and an on/off switch for the electrochromic mirror. In addition, all-new Volkswagens come standard with an improved four-year/50,000-mile bumper-to-bumper warranty, up from two years/24,000 miles. In addition, Volkswagen will offer a fully transferable limited powertrain warranty that covers five years or 60,000 miles.

2001

Mileage Category: D

Body Styles	TMV Pricing		
	Trade	Private	Dealer
4 Dr GLS 1.8T Turbo Sdn	8890	9976	10979
4 Dr GLS 1.8T Turbo Wgn	9448	10602	11667
4 Dr GLS V6 4Motion AWD Sdn	11053	12403	13649
4 Dr GLS V6 4Motion AWD Wgn	11227	12598	13864
4 Dr GLS V6 Sdn	9832	11032	12141
4 Dr GLS V6 Wgn	10601	11896	13092
4 Dr GLX V6 4Motion AWD Sdn	12947	14529	15988
4 Dr GLX V6 4Motion AWD Wgn	13105	14706	16184
4 Dr GLX V6 Sdn	11329	12713	13990
4 Dr GLX V6 Wgn	11594	13010	14317
4 Dr New GLS 1.8T Turbo Sdn	9196	10320	11356

Options	Price
Aluminum/Alloy Wheels [Std on GLX,AWD]	+198
Automatic 5-Speed Transmission [Std on 4Motion]	+607
Compact Disc Changer	+279
Heated Front Seats [Opt on GLS,GLS V6]	+183

Body Styles	TMV Pricing		
	Trade	Private	Dealer
4 Dr New GLS 1.8T Turbo Wgn	9628	10804	11889
4 Dr New GLS V6 4Motion AWD Sdn	11079	12432	13681
4 Dr New GLS V6 4Motion AWD Wgn	11254	12629	13899
4 Dr New GLS V6 Sdn	10111	11346	12486
4 Dr New GLS V6 Wgn	10782	12099	13315
4 Dr New GLX V6 4Motion AWD Sdn	13168	14777	16261
4 Dr New GLX V6 4Motion AWD Wgn	13286	14908	16406
4 Dr New GLX V6 Sdn	11392	12784	14069
4 Dr New GLX V6 Wgn	12185	13674	15048

Options	Price
Leather Seats [Opt on GLS]	+480
Monsoon Audio System [Opt on GLS]	+183
Power Moonroof [Opt on GLS]	+565

The 2001.5 Passat arrives with updated exterior styling, minor interior changes and a more powerful four-cylinder engine. New features for the 2001 model year -- standard front and rear side curtain airbags, optional steering wheel controls for audio and cruise control for GLS (standard on the GLX) and a standard trunk entrapment release button -- carry over into 2001.5 Passats.

Volkswagen
Passat

2000

The radio display and anti-theft system have been updated. A brake-wear indicator is now standard on all models.

Mileage Category: D

Body Styles	Trade	Private	Dealer
4 Dr GLS 1.8T Turbo Sdn	7491	8636	9758
4 Dr GLS 1.8T Turbo Wgn	7616	8780	9921
4 Dr GLS V6 4Motion AWD Sdn	8831	10181	11504
4 Dr GLS V6 4Motion AWD Wgn	8876	10233	11563
4 Dr GLS V6 Sdn	8265	9528	10767

Body Styles	Trade	Private	Dealer
4 Dr GLS V6 Wgn	8696	10025	11328
4 Dr GLX V6 4Motion AWD Sdn	9653	11129	12576
4 Dr GLX V6 4Motion AWD Wgn	9793	11290	12758
4 Dr GLX V6 Sdn	9026	10406	11758
4 Dr GLX V6 Wgn	9633	11105	12549

Options	Price
Aluminum/Alloy Wheels [Std on GLX,AWD]	+173
Automatic 5-Speed Transmission	+531
Compact Disc Changer	+244
Heated Front Seats [Opt on GLS,GLS V6]	+160

Options	Price
Leather Seats [Opt on GLS]	+468
Monsoon Audio System [Opt on GLS]	+145
Power Moonroof [Opt on GLS]	+493

1999

After promising the availability of all-wheel drive this year, Volkswagen, in a last-minute product change, has cancelled the Synchro all-wheel-drive option on all Passats for 1999 and will not be offering the GLS wagon with a V6 engine.

Mileage Category: D

Body Styles	Trade	Private	Dealer
4 Dr GLS 1.8T Turbo Sdn	6260	7453	8696
4 Dr GLS 1.8T Turbo Wgn	6676	7949	9275

Body Styles	Trade	Private	Dealer
4 Dr GLS V6 Sdn	7050	8395	9794
4 Dr GLX V6 Sdn	7338	8738	10194

Options	Price
Aluminum/Alloy Wheels	+140
Automatic 5-Speed Transmission	+432
Compact Disc Changer	+199

Options	Price
Heated Front Seats [Opt on GLS]	+130
Leather Seats [Opt on GLS]	+381
Power Moonroof [Opt on GLS]	+402

1998

An all-new Passat arrives wearing updated sheet metal over a stretched Audi A4 platform. Engine choices include a spunky turbocharged four or a silky V6.

Mileage Category: D

Body Styles	Trade	Private	Dealer
4 Dr GLS 1.8T Turbo Sdn	5081	6223	7511
4 Dr GLS 1.8T Turbo Wgn	5492	6727	8120

Body Styles	Trade	Private	Dealer
4 Dr GLS V6 Sdn	5524	6766	8166
4 Dr GLX V6 Sdn	5842	7156	8638

Options	Price
Automatic 5-Speed Transmission	+380
Heated Front Seats [Opt on GLS]	+115

Options	Price
Leather Seats [Opt on GLS]	+309
Power Moonroof [Opt on GLS]	+302

1997

Mileage Category: D

Body Styles	Trade	Private	Dealer
4 Dr GLX V6 Sdn	4024	5232	6709
4 Dr GLX V6 Wgn	4028	5237	6715

Body Styles	Trade	Private	Dealer
4 Dr TDi Turbodsl Sdn	3906	5079	6512
4 Dr TDi Turbodsl Wgn	3952	5139	6590

Options	Price
Antilock Brakes [Opt on TDI]	+226
Automatic 4-Speed Transmission	+259
Compact Disc Changer	+145

Options	Price
Leather Seats	+255
Power Moonroof	+250

GLS model vanishes from radar as Volkswagen prepares for launch of all-new Passat in mid-1997.

1996

Daytime running lights debut, two new colors are added to the palette, and a new price-leader GLS model powered by a 2.0-liter, 115-horsepower, four-cylinder engine is introduced. Midyear, a Turbo Direct Injection (TDI) diesel model appears in sedan and wagon form.

Mileage Category: D

Body Styles	Trade	Private	Dealer
4 Dr GLS Sdn	2257	3046	4136
4 Dr GLX V6 Sdn	2912	3932	5339
4 Dr GLX V6 Wgn	3018	4074	5534

Body Styles	Trade	Private	Dealer
4 Dr TDi Turbodsl Sdn	2911	3930	5336
4 Dr TDi Turbodsl Wgn	2980	4022	5462

Options	Price
Antilock Brakes [Std on GLX]	+199
Automatic 4-Speed Transmission	+228
Compact Disc Changer	+127

Options	Price
Leather Seats	+224
Power Moonroof	+219

1995

Reskinned for 1995, VW adds dual airbags, three-point seatbelts, and side-impact protection that meets 1997 safety standards. Climate control system gains dust and pollen filter. GLX is only trim level.

Mileage Category: D

Body Styles	Trade	Private	Dealer
4 Dr GLS Sdn	1526	2130	3136
4 Dr GLX V6 Sdn	2106	2939	4328

Options	Price
Antilock Brakes [Opt on GLS]	+163
Automatic 4-Speed Transmission	+187
Compact Disc Changer	+104

Body Styles	Trade	Private	Dealer
4 Dr GLX V6 Wgn	2221	3100	4566

Options	Price
Leather Seats	+184
Power Moonroof	+179

Phaeton
2004

The Phaeton is an all-new ultraluxury flagship sedan from Volkswagen.

Mileage Category: I

Body Styles	Trade	Private	Dealer
4 Dr Premiere Edition W12 Sdn	51235	54510	59968
4 Dr V8 Sdn	41157	43775	48140

Options	Price
Climate Controlled Seats (Rear)	+1300
Heated Steering Wheel	+140
Metallic Paint [Opt on non-Premiere]	+1000
Park Distance Control (Front and Rear)	+655
Pearlescent Metallic Paint [Opt on non-Premiere]	+1000

Body Styles	Trade	Private	Dealer
4 Dr W12 Sdn	59844	63118	68574

Options	Price
Power Trunk Closer [Opt on V8]	+495
Rear Air Conditioning Controls	+200
Special Factory Paint	+2000
Special Interior Trim [Opt on non-Premiere]	+500

Touareg
2004

The five-passenger Touareg is an all-new midsize SUV from Volkswagen. Designed to provide both excellent handling on pavement and a high level of off-road ability, the Touareg, despite its unibody design, is a real SUV, not a soft-roader. Alongside that, buyers can look forward to beautifully furnished cabins equipped with plenty of standard convenience and safety features.

Mileage Category: M

Body Styles	Trade	Private	Dealer
4 Dr V10 TDi Turbodsl AWD SUV	47569	50600	55653
4 Dr V6 AWD SUV	26357	27942	30584

Options	Price
19 Inch Wheels [Opt on V8, V10]	+1200
AM/FM/CD Changer Audio System	+650
Automatic Climate Control (4 Zone) [Opt on V8, V10]	+1200
Automatic Dimming Sideview Mirror(s) [Opt on V6]	+225
Automatic Load Leveling [Opt on V8]	+350
Electronic Suspension Control [Opt on V6, V8]	+300
Headlight Washers [Opt on V8]	+600
Heated Front and Rear Seats [Opt on V8, V10]	+350
Heated Steering Wheel [Opt on V8, V10]	+140
Leather Seats [Opt on V6]	+1420
Locking Differential	+550

Body Styles	Trade	Private	Dealer
4 Dr V8 AWD SUV	31581	33251	36035

Options	Price
Navigation System	+2000
OnStar Telematics System [Opt on V6, V8]	+699
Park Distance Control (Front and Rear)	+600
Power Driver Seat w/Memory [Opt on V6]	+200
Power Passenger Seat [Opt on V6]	+180
Power Passenger Seat w/Memory [Opt on V8, V10]	+200
Power Retractable Mirrors [Opt on V6]	+175
Power Tilt and Telescopic Steering Wheel [Opt on V8, V10]	+180
Trailer Hitch	+150
Xenon Headlamps [Opt on V6, V8]	+750

Volvo
850/940

850
1997

The Turbo is now known as the T-5. GLT models get a new engine that makes 22 more horsepower than last year, and peak torque at a low 1,800 rpm. Base and GLT models meet Transitional Low Emission Vehicle (TLEV) regulations this year.

Mileage Category: H

Body Styles	TMV Pricing		
	Trade	Private	Dealer
4 Dr GLT Turbo Sdn	4848	5976	7355
4 Dr GLT Turbo Wgn	5157	6358	7825
4 Dr R Turbo Sdn	5727	7060	8689
4 Dr R Turbo Wgn	6271	7731	9515

Options	Price
Automatic 4-Speed Transmission [Opt on STD]	+219
Automatic Load Leveling [Std on R]	+123
Leather Seats [Std on R]	+241
Power Driver Seat w/Memory [Opt on STD]	+123

Body Styles	TMV Pricing		
	Trade	Private	Dealer
4 Dr STD Sdn	4126	5086	6260
4 Dr STD Wgn	4402	5427	6680
4 Dr T5 Turbo Sdn	5164	6366	7835
4 Dr T5 Turbo Wgn	5465	6737	8291

Options	Price
Power Moonroof [Opt on STD]	+236
Power Passenger Seat w/Memory [Opt on GLT,STD]	+123
Third Seat [Opt on Wgn]	+125

1996

This year all Volvo 850s are equipped with front seat side-impact airbags, optional traction control (TRACS) and a life insurance policy that pays $250,000 to the estate of any occupant who loses their life in the 850 as the result of an accident.

Mileage Category: H

Body Styles	TMV Pricing		
	Trade	Private	Dealer
4 Dr GLT Sdn	3989	5029	6465
4 Dr GLT Wgn	4129	5205	6692
4 Dr Platinum Limited Edition Turbo Sdn	4842	6104	7847
4 Dr Platinum Limited Edition Turbo Wgn	5190	6542	8410
4 Dr R Turbo Sdn	4890	6164	7924

Options	Price
Automatic 4-Speed Transmission [Opt on GLT,STD]	+200

Body Styles	TMV Pricing		
	Trade	Private	Dealer
4 Dr R Turbo Wgn	5310	6694	8606
4 Dr STD Sdn	3592	4529	5822
4 Dr STD Wgn	3663	4617	5935
4 Dr Turbo Sdn	4221	5321	6841
4 Dr Turbo Wgn	4402	5549	7134

Options	Price
Leather Seats [Opt on GLT,STD]	+221

1995

Side airbags are standard on all 850 Turbos this year; optional on other 850s. All models get Turbo's rounded front styling.

Mileage Category: H

Body Styles	TMV Pricing		
	Trade	Private	Dealer
4 Dr GLT Sdn	2953	3793	5193
4 Dr GLT Wgn	3433	4408	6034
4 Dr STD Sdn	2672	3432	4698
4 Dr STD Wgn	2694	3460	4736

Options	Price
Aluminum/Alloy Wheels [Std on GLT,T5R,Turbo]	+78
Automatic 4-Speed Transmission [Std on T5R,Turbo]	+191
Compact Disc Changer	+88
Front Side Airbag Restraints	+108
Leather Seats [Std on T5R,Turbo Sdn]	+210

Body Styles	TMV Pricing		
	Trade	Private	Dealer
4 Dr T5R Turbo Sdn	3935	5054	6918
4 Dr T5R Turbo Wgn	4113	5282	7231
4 Dr Turbo Sdn	3525	4527	6198
4 Dr Turbo Wgn	3650	4687	6416

Options	Price
Power Driver Seat w/Memory [Opt on STD]	+107
Power Passenger Seat w/Memory [Opt on GLT,Turbo]	+107
Rear Spoiler [Std on T5R]	+75
Third Seat [Opt on Wgn]	+108

940
1995

Mileage Category: I

Body Styles	TMV Pricing		
	Trade	Private	Dealer
4 Dr STD Sdn	3262	4115	5537
4 Dr STD Wgn	3496	4410	5934

Options	Price
Leather Seats	+107
Power Driver Seat	+88

Body Styles	TMV Pricing		
	Trade	Private	Dealer
4 Dr Turbo Sdn	3474	4383	5897
4 Dr Turbo Wgn	3729	4705	6331

Options	Price
Power Moonroof	+176

Daytime running lights debut. Level I and Level II trims are dropped in favor of less confusing base and Turbo designations.

960

1997

Body Styles	TMV Pricing			Body Styles	TMV Pricing		
	Trade	Private	Dealer		Trade	Private	Dealer
4 Dr STD Sdn	5555	6909	8563	4 Dr STD Wgn	5974	7430	9210

Mileage Category: I

Automatic load leveling joins the options list for the wagon, while tailored leather seating is no longer available on the wagon.

1996

Body Styles	TMV Pricing			Body Styles	TMV Pricing		
	Trade	Private	Dealer		Trade	Private	Dealer
4 Dr STD Sdn	4819	6072	7802	4 Dr STD Wgn	5124	6456	8295

Mileage Category: I

This year all Volvo 960s are equipped with front seat side-impact airbags, a multistep power door locking system that increases driver safety when entering the vehicle in parking lots and a life insurance policy that pays $250,000 to the estate of any occupant who loses their life in the 960 as a result of a car accident.

1995

Body Styles	TMV Pricing			Body Styles	TMV Pricing		
	Trade	Private	Dealer		Trade	Private	Dealer
4 Dr STD Sdn	3441	4341	5842	4 Dr STD Wgn	3589	4528	6093

Mileage Category: I

Options	Price	Options	Price
Compact Disc Changer	+127	Leather Seats	+107

Substantially revised with new sheet metal and detuned powertrain. Horsepower is down to 181 from 201, thanks to emissions standards. Daytime running lights are added. The dashboard is softened with more curves and contours. Suspensions are revised, and larger tires are standard. Other new standard equipment includes remote locking, an alarm system, headlight wipers and washers and wood interior trim.

C70

2004

Body Styles	TMV Pricing			Body Styles	TMV Pricing		
	Trade	Private	Dealer		Trade	Private	Dealer
2 Dr HPT Turbo Conv	27603	29153	31736	2 Dr LPT Turbo Conv	26298	27848	30431

Mileage Category: F

Options	Price	Options	Price
17 Inch Wheels	+500	Trip Computer [Opt on LPT]	+210
Aluminum/Alloy Interior Trim [Opt on LPT]	+155	Wood Interior Trim [Opt on LPT]	+155
Automatic 5-Speed Transmission [Opt on HPT]	+1000	Wood Steering Wheel	+250
Automatic Dimming Rearview Mirror [Opt on LPT]	+150		

The only notable changes are two new interior colors -- Volcano Red and Linen White -- that include additional aluminum (red) or birchwood (white) dash inlays.

2003

Body Styles	TMV Pricing			Body Styles	TMV Pricing		
	Trade	Private	Dealer		Trade	Private	Dealer
2 Dr HT Turbo Conv	26140	27443	29615	2 Dr LT Turbo Conv	24735	25968	28023

Mileage Category: F

Options	Price	Options	Price
17 Inch Wheels	+361	Dolby Pro Logic Audio System [Opt on HT]	+434
Automatic 5-Speed Transmission [Opt on HT]	+723	Leather and Wood Steering Wheel [Opt on LT]	+181
Compact Disc Changer [Opt on LT]	+867	Trip Computer [Opt on LT]	+181

For 2003, the C70 is only available in convertible form. Slight power increases are in store for both powertrains, with the LT engine now making 196 horsepower, an enhancement of six, and the HT engine producing 245, a boost of nine ponies over last year's output. The headlamps and taillamps have a jeweled effect, and the front grille is darkened. A rainbow of new colors -- Maya Gold, Ruby Red and Titanium Grey -- burst onto the scene.

2002

Body Styles	TMV Pricing			Body Styles	TMV Pricing		
	Trade	Private	Dealer		Trade	Private	Dealer
2 Dr HT Turbo Conv	24196	25446	27529	2 Dr LT Turbo Conv	23114	24272	26203
2 Dr HT Turbo Cpe	19541	20734	22721				

Mileage Category: F

Options	Price	Options	Price
17 Inch Wheels	+242	Dolby Pro Logic Audio System [Opt on HT Conv]	+363
Automatic 5-Speed Transmission [Opt on HT]	+605	Trip Computer [Opt on LT Conv]	+151
Compact Disc Changer [Std on HT Conv]	+726		

Volvo will offer the C70 Coupe in just one trim level, and the contents of last year's SE model will come with it, including the unique sport grille, 17-inch wheels and tires, power sunroof, leather upholstery, trip computer, auto-dimming rearview mirror and special dash inlays. New standard features for all C70s include Volvo's stability and traction control system (STC), heated front seats and an emergency trunk release. Convertibles also get 17-spoke alloy wheels and ride on Z-rated 205/55R16 Pirelli tires. Genuine wood dash trim replaces the "wood effect" trim in the optional Touring Package for the C70 LPT convertible. Ash Gold is now an exterior color choice, while Turquoise Metallic and Venetian Red Metallic have been discontinued.

C70/S40

2001

Volvo has dropped the C70 Coupe light-pressure turbo (LPT), meaning only the high-pressure turbo coupe (HPT) is offered. A new five-speed automatic transmission is optional equipment. Exterior styling remains the same, but there are new 16-inch wheels for all models, with the 17-inch wheels still being optional. Simulated wood trim replaces the previous car's burled walnut wood trim. The coupe's previously standard equipment of the trip computer, auto-dimming rearview mirror, simulated wood trim, leather upholstery and sunroof are now part of the Grand Touring option package. The premium audio system is optional on the HPT coupe and standard on the HPT convertible.

Mileage Category: F

Body Styles	TMV Pricing		
	Trade	Private	Dealer
2 Dr HT Turbo Conv	19384	21416	23292
2 Dr HT Turbo Cpe	15284	16886	18364

Options	Price
Automatic 4-Speed Transmission [Opt on HT]	+534
Automatic Stability Control [Opt on Conv]	+294
Compact Disc Changer	+214
Dolby Pro Logic Audio System [Opt on LT]	+427

Body Styles	TMV Pricing		
	Trade	Private	Dealer
2 Dr LT Turbo Conv	18565	20511	22308
2 Dr SE HT Turbo Cpe	16533	18267	19867

Options	Price
Heated Front Seats	+125
Power Moonroof [Opt on LT Cpe]	+641
Traction Control System	+288
Trip Computer [Opt on LT]	+133

2000

Volvo introduces a high-pressure turbo (HPT) convertible and makes minor equipment changes to all C70s for 2000.

Mileage Category: F

Body Styles	TMV Pricing		
	Trade	Private	Dealer
2 Dr HT Turbo Conv	15297	17351	19365
2 Dr HT Turbo Cpe	12696	14401	16072

Options	Price
17 Inch Wheels - Spoke	+182
Automatic 4-Speed Transmission [Opt on HT]	+443
Automatic Stability Control	+250
Dolby Pro Logic Audio System [Opt on LT]	+273
Leather Seats [Opt on LT Cpe]	+489

Body Styles	TMV Pricing		
	Trade	Private	Dealer
2 Dr LT Turbo Conv	14681	16653	18585
2 Dr LT Turbo Cpe	12349	14007	15633

Options	Price
Power Moonroof [Opt on LT Cpe]	+546
Special Leather Seat Trim	+728
Spoke Wheels	+182
Traction Control System	+246

1999

Volvo offers a light-pressure turbocharged engine in the coupe. Both coupes and convertibles get a bit of new standard and optional equipment.

Mileage Category: F

Body Styles	TMV Pricing		
	Trade	Private	Dealer
2 Dr HT Turbo Cpe	10561	12264	14036
2 Dr LT Turbo Conv	12398	14397	16478

Options	Price
Automatic 4-Speed Transmission [Std on LT]	+349
Automatic Stability Control	+218

Body Styles	TMV Pricing		
	Trade	Private	Dealer
2 Dr LT Turbo Cpe	10250	11902	13622

Options	Price
Dolby Pro Logic Audio System [Opt on LT]	+212
Traction Control System	+193

1998

Modeled on the S70 chassis, the C70 shares sheet metal with the S70 from the windshield forward, and is powered by the same set of turbocharged power plants.

Mileage Category: F

Body Styles	TMV Pricing		
	Trade	Private	Dealer
2 Dr HT Turbo Cpe	9305	10825	12539

Options	Price
Automatic 4-Speed Transmission	+281
Compact Disc Changer	+130
Dolby Pro Logic Audio System	+190

Body Styles	TMV Pricing		
	Trade	Private	Dealer
2 Dr LT Turbo Conv	11302	13148	15230

Options	Price
Special Leather Seat Trim [Opt on LT]	+382
Spoke Wheels	+574
Traction Control System	+128

S40

2004

Mileage Category: D

Body Styles	TMV Pricing		
	Trade	Private	Dealer
4 Dr 2.4i Sdn (2004.5)	16629	17982	20238
4 Dr LSE Turbo Sdn	17494	18692	20688

Options	Price
16 Inch Wheels [Opt on Turbo]	+500
AM/FM/CD Changer Audio System [Opt on 2.4i, T5 Turbo]	+850
Automatic Climate Control [Opt on 2.4i]	+800
Automatic Dimming Rearview Mirror [Opt on 2.4i, T5 Turbo]	+150
Automatic Stability Control	+250
Child Seat (1) [Opt on Turbo, LSE Turbo]	+300

Body Styles	TMV Pricing		
	Trade	Private	Dealer
4 Dr T5 Turbo Sdn (2004.5)	19008	20396	22711
4 Dr Turbo Sdn	14891	16078	18057

Options	Price
Child Seats (2) [Opt on 2.4i, T5 Turbo]	+300
Garage Door Opener [Opt on 2.4i, T5 Turbo]	+130
Headlight Washers	+165
Heated Front Seats	+250
Leather Seats [Std on LSE Turbo]	+1050
Leather Steering Wheel [Opt on Turbo]	+125
Metallic Paint [Opt on non-LSE]	+450
Navigation System [Opt on 2.4i, T5 Turbo]	+1995

For the latest vehicle information, visit www.edmunds.com

2004 (cont'd)

Options	Price
Power Driver Seat [Opt on 2.4i, T5 Turbo]	+250
Power Driver Seat w/Memory [Opt on T5 Turbo]	+180
Power Moonroof [Std on LSE Turbo]	+800
Power Passenger Seat [Opt on T5 Turbo]	+165
Rain Sensing Windshield Wipers [Opt on 2.4i, T5 Turbo]	+210

Options	Price
Sport Package [Opt on 2.4i, Turbo]	+650
Traction Control System [Opt on Turbo, LSE Turbo]	+350
Trip Computer [Opt on 2.4i, Turbo]	+210
Xenon Headlamps [Opt on 2.4i, T5 Turbo]	+700

Volvo offers two generations of its S40 sedan for sale in 2004. The old S40 receives few changes this year; however, an upscale LSE trim version has been added. There are also minor revisions to the front fascia, and the audio system now comes pre-wired for a CD changer. Midway through the model year, an all-new S40 arrives as a 2004.5 model. Nothing is carried over from the previous S40. The new sedan is shorter in overall length but has a longer wheelbase -- this translates to better handling and more interior room. Whereas the previous S40 has only one drivetrain option, the new version has two engine and three transmission choices.

2003

Mileage Category: D

Body Styles	TMV Pricing		
	Trade	Private	Dealer
4 Dr Turbo Sdn	13123	14298	16255

Options	Price
16 Inch Wheels	+361
Automatic Stability Control	+307
Child Seat (1)	+217
Fog Lights	+126
Heated Front Seats	+192
Leather Seats	+687

Options	Price
Metallic Paint	+325
Power Driver Seat	+235
Power Moonroof	+687
Premium Audio System	+397
Rear Spoiler	+181
Traction Control System	+163

Output from the 1.9-liter turbocharged mill is bumped up by 10 to 170 horsepower. A CD player makes its way onto the standard features list, and the front fascia gets a slight freshening thanks to a black egg-crate grille and body-colored side molding and bumpers. Inside you'll find a new three-spoke steering wheel and a four-dial instrument cluster. The sport package adds front and rear spoilers, blackout headlamp surrounds and 16-inch wheels, and the premium package now includes a leather-wrapped hand brake handle and gearshift lever.

2002

Mileage Category: D

Body Styles	TMV Pricing		
	Trade	Private	Dealer
4 Dr Turbo Sdn	10622	11673	13427

Options	Price
AM/FM/Cassette/CD Audio System	+227
Automatic Stability Control	+272
Child Seat (1)	+181
Heated Front Seats	+151
Leather Seats	+575
Metallic Paint	+242

Options	Price
Power Driver Seat	+197
Power Moonroof	+575
Premium Audio System	+333
Rear Spoiler	+151
Traction Control System	+151

Minor equipment changes have been made to Volvo's S40 for 2002. A Premium package now makes it easier for base sedan buyers to purchase desirable options like a sunroof, CD player, power driver seat and faux wood trim. And a Premium Plus package adds leather upholstery and a leather-wrapped steering wheel to the mix. The Sport package now includes aluminum interior accents, sport seats and an exclusive instrument cluster -- you can also get these items a la carte. A new center console design incorporates two integrated cupholders. Rear passengers will also have two cupholders at their disposal when they fold down the center armrest. And the S40 now comes with the an emergency trunk release. New exterior colors include Bamboo Green and Dark Blue.

2001

Mileage Category: D

Body Styles	TMV Pricing		
	Trade	Private	Dealer
4 Dr SE Turbo Sdn	10525	12170	13689

Options	Price
AM/FM/Cassette/CD Audio System	+259
Automatic Stability Control	+294
Child Seat (1)	+160
Heated Front Seats	+133
Leather Seats	+481
Metallic Paint	+214

Body Styles	TMV Pricing		
	Trade	Private	Dealer
4 Dr Turbo Sdn	9023	10463	11793

Options	Price
Power Driver Seat [Std on SE]	+240
Power Moonroof [Std on SE]	+588
Premium Audio System [Std on SE]	+374
Rear Spoiler [Std on SE]	+133
Traction Control System	+133

Only a year after debuting them on U.S. shores, Volvo has updated the S40 and V40 for 2001. Both the sedan and wagon gain additional crash protection in the form of standard head-protection airbags, dual-stage front airbags and a new child seat-safety system. Under the hood, engine improvements have been made to increase power and lower emissions. There's also a new five-speed automatic transmission that takes the place of the previous four-speed. Other changes are found in the cabin, with new material colors, a redesigned center stack for better functionality, more durable front-seat materials and improved switchgear. Rounding out the S40 and V40's 2001 changes are restyled headlights, bumpers and fenders.

2000

Mileage Category: D

Body Styles	TMV Pricing		
	Trade	Private	Dealer
4 Dr Turbo Sdn	7480	8941	10373

Options	Price
Automatic Stability Control	+250
Compact Disc Changer	+225

Options	Price
Leather Seats	+409
Power Moonroof	+501

The S40 is Volvo's completely new entry-level sedan. Along with its wagon variant, the V40, this car rounds out Volvo's vehicle lineup. Safety, styling and comfort are its main attributes.

S60

2004

Last year's 2.4T model is now the 2.5T, with the same 208-horsepower engine as the AWD model. Bi-xenon headlights are a new option, while the sport package for the 2.5T includes speed-sensitive power steering.

Mileage Category: H

Body Styles	TMV Pricing		
	Trade	Private	Dealer
4 Dr 2.4 Sdn	16200	17515	19705
4 Dr 2.5T Turbo AWD Sdn	18802	20116	22305

Options	Price
AM/FM/CD Changer Audio System	+1200
Automatic 5-Speed Transmission [Opt on 2.4, T5]	+1000
Automatic Climate Control [Opt on 2.4]	+370
Automatic Dimming Rearview Mirror [Opt on 2.4T]	+180
Automatic Stability Control [Std on T5]	+350
Garage Door Opener [Std on T5 Turbo]	+200
Headlight Washers [Std on 2.5T AWD]	+165
Heated Front Seats	+250
Leather Seats	+600
Metallic Paint	+450

Body Styles	TMV Pricing		
	Trade	Private	Dealer
4 Dr 2.5T Turbo Sdn	17760	19073	21262
4 Dr T5 Turbo Sdn	20353	21694	23930

Options	Price
Navigation System	+1995
Power Driver Seat w/Memory [Opt on 2.4]	+280
Power Moonroof	+950
Power Passenger Seat [Std on T5]	+250
Rain Sensing Windshield Wipers	+135
Sport Package	+750
Telematics System	+835
Trip Computer [Opt on 2.4]	+195
Xenon Headlamps	+500

2003

A new high-performance model, the S60 R, will become available later in the year. Otherwise, minor changes are in store for Volvo's sport sedan for 2003. A leather-wrapped steering wheel, along with a stereo with a CD and a cassette deck, now grace the interior of the 2.4 and the 2.4T. The latter also gets foglights and wood dash trim in its standard equipment list. For the all-wheel-drive version, the 2.4 turbocharged engine receives a small bump in displacement and horsepower. Rain-sensing wipers and OnCall Plus (the telematics system) are available, and two new colors, Titanium Grey and Ruby Red, brighten the exterior.

Mileage Category: H

Body Styles	TMV Pricing		
	Trade	Private	Dealer
4 Dr 2.4 Sdn	13856	14839	16478
4 Dr 2.4T Turbo Sdn	16648	17830	19799

Options	Price
16 Inch Wheels [Opt on 2.4]	+325
17 Inch Wheels	+361
AM/FM/CD Changer Audio System	+867
Automatic 5-Speed Transmission [Opt on 2.4, T5]	+723
Automatic Climate Control [Opt on 2.4]	+150
Automatic Stability Control [Std on T5]	+502
Fog Lights [Opt on 2.4]	+145
Heated Front Seats	+192
Leather Seats	+759

Body Styles	TMV Pricing		
	Trade	Private	Dealer
4 Dr 2.5T Turbo AWD Sdn	17835	19101	21211
4 Dr T5 Turbo Sdn	18157	19446	21593

Options	Price
Metallic Paint	+325
Navigation System	+1370
Power Driver Seat w/Memory [Opt on 2.4]	+235
Power Moonroof	+650
Power Passenger Seat [Std on T5]	+235
Sport Suspension [Opt on 2.5T, T5]	+181
Telematics System	+603
Trip Computer [Opt on 2.4]	+181

2002

The big news is the arrival of the S60 2.4T AWD and its slick electronically controlled all-wheel-drive system. Additionally, all S60 models get Emergency Brake Assistance (EBA), enhanced traction control performance and improved throttle management, resulting in quicker response in everyday driving situations. Volvo's Dynamic Stability Traction Control (DSTC) system is now standard in T5 models and optional for the 2.4T AWD (starting in December 2001). Other model-specific changes include satellite controls on the steering wheel and rear cupholders for the base 2.4 model and a memory function for the power seats and mirrors in 2.4T and T5 models. The entire lineup gets revised rear headrests, ISO-FIX child restraint attachment points and an emergency trunk release handle.

Mileage Category: H

Body Styles	TMV Pricing		
	Trade	Private	Dealer
4 Dr 2.4 Sdn	12995	13891	15383
4 Dr 2.4T Turbo AWD Sdn	16602	17758	19685

Options	Price
AM/FM/CD Changer Audio System [Opt on T5]	+726
AM/FM/Cassette/CD Audio System [Std on T5]	+227
Automatic 5-Speed Transmission [Opt on 2.4, T5]	+605
Automatic Stability Control [Opt on 2.4T, 2.4T AWD]	+454
Heated Front Seats	+197
Leather Seats	+635
Metallic Paint	+242

Body Styles	TMV Pricing		
	Trade	Private	Dealer
4 Dr 2.4T Turbo Sdn	15387	16447	18214
4 Dr T5 Turbo Sdn	16797	17954	19883

Options	Price
Navigation System [Opt on T5]	+1146
Power Driver Seat [Opt on 2.4]	+197
Power Moonroof [Opt on 2.4]	+575
Power Passenger Seat [Opt on 2.4T, 2.4T AWD]	+197
Sport Suspension [Opt on T5]	+151
Trip Computer [Std on T5]	+151

2001

The S60 is Volvo's new sedan that takes the place of the discontinued S70 Sedan. Smaller than the S80 but bigger than the S40, Volvo has designed the S60 to be sporty as well as safe.

Mileage Category: H

Body Styles	TMV Pricing		
	Trade	Private	Dealer
4 Dr 2.4 Sdn	11650	13103	14444
4 Dr 2.4T Turbo Sdn	13216	14864	16385

Options	Price
AM/FM/CD Changer Audio System [Opt on T5]	+641
AM/FM/Cassette/CD Audio System [Opt on 2.4, 2.4T]	+259

Body Styles	TMV Pricing		
	Trade	Private	Dealer
4 Dr T5 Turbo Sdn	13401	15071	16613

Options	Price
Automatic 5-Speed Transmission	+534
Automatic Stability Control [Opt on 2.4, 2.4T]	+294

For the latest vehicle information, visit www.edmunds.com

Options	Price
Compact Disc Changer	+641
Heated Front Seats	+125
Leather Seats	+641
Metallic Paint	+214
Navigation System	+1335
Power Driver Seat [Opt on 2.4]	+264

Options	Price
Power Moonroof	+641
Power Passenger Seat [Opt on 2.4T]	+187
Sport Seats [Opt on T5]	+133
Sport Suspension [Opt on T5]	+133
Traction Control System	+294
Trip Computer [Opt on 2.4,2.4T]	+133

S60 R
2004

Mileage Category: H

Body Styles	TMV Pricing		
	Trade	Private	Dealer
4 Dr Turbo AWD Sdn	25082	26852	29803

Options	Price
18 Inch Wheels	+995
AM/FM/CD Changer Audio System	+1200
Automatic 5-Speed Transmission	+1250
Compact Disc Changer	+350
Heated Front Seats	+250
Metallic Paint	+450

Options	Price
Navigation System	+1995
Power Moonroof	+950
Premium Audio System	+695
Special Factory Paint	+600
Telematics System	+835

Volvo creates a 300-horsepower R version of its S60 sedan. Equipped with the company's Four-C suspension system, this is one Volvo you'll want to drive hard.

S70
2000

Mileage Category: H

Body Styles	TMV Pricing		
	Trade	Private	Dealer
4 Dr GLT SE Turbo Sdn	10810	12503	14162
4 Dr GLT Turbo Sdn	10546	12198	13817
4 Dr SE Sdn	10351	11972	13561

Body Styles	TMV Pricing		
	Trade	Private	Dealer
4 Dr STD Sdn	9000	10409	11790
4 Dr T5 Turbo Sdn	10877	12580	14250
4 Dr Turbo AWD Sdn	10883	12587	14258

Options	Price
AM/FM/Cassette/CD Audio System [Opt on AWD,GLT,STD]	+221
Automatic 4-Speed Transmission [Opt on T5]	+443
Automatic 5-Speed Transmission [Opt on SE,STD]	+443
Automatic Stability Control	+250
Leather Seats	+489

Options	Price
Power Driver Seat w/Memory [Opt on STD]	+225
Power Moonroof	+546
Power Passenger Seat [Opt on AWD,GLT]	+205
Rear Spoiler	+134
Traction Control System	+246

Engine improvements, a new transmission and equipment upgrades constitute the changes for the 2000 S70.

1999

Mileage Category: H

Body Styles	TMV Pricing		
	Trade	Private	Dealer
4 Dr GLT Turbo Sdn	9034	10600	12230
4 Dr STD Sdn	7907	9277	10703

Body Styles	TMV Pricing		
	Trade	Private	Dealer
4 Dr T5 Turbo Sdn	9541	11194	12915
4 Dr Turbo AWD Sdn	9547	11202	12924

Options	Price
AM/FM/Cassette/CD Audio System [Opt on AWD,GLT,STD]	+173
Automatic 4-Speed Transmission [Opt on STD,T5]	+349
Leather Seats	+385

Options	Price
Power Driver Seat w/Memory [Opt on STD]	+116
Power Moonroof	+429
Traction Control System [Opt on GLT,STD,T5]	+193

Volvo adds an all-wheel-drive model (S70 AWD) to the lineup and makes a number of performance, safety and styling upgrades. All cars benefit from a new engine management system and an improved brake system that includes four-channel ABS and Electronic Brakeforce Distribution (EBD). In terms of safety, S70s now include head-protecting side airbags and dual-stage deployment for the front airbags. Stability and traction control is now standard on the T5, and all other front-drive models are equipped with traction control. On the cosmetic side, all S70s receive a new grille emblem and body-color side moldings, mirrors, door handles and bumpers.

1998

Mileage Category: H

Body Styles	TMV Pricing		
	Trade	Private	Dealer
4 Dr GLT Turbo Sdn	6383	7742	9275
4 Dr GT Sdn	5748	6972	8353

Body Styles	TMV Pricing		
	Trade	Private	Dealer
4 Dr STD Sdn	5381	6528	7821
4 Dr T5 Turbo Sdn	7042	8542	10234

Options	Price
AM/FM/Cassette/CD Audio System [Std on T5]	+139
Aluminum/Alloy Wheels [Opt on STD]	+130
Automatic 4-Speed Transmission [Std on GLT]	+281

Options	Price
Leather Seats	+312
Traction Control System	+225

Volvo's 850 sedan gets a new name, new nose, body-color trim, stronger side-impact protection, more powerful turbo engines, redesigned interior and revised suspension.

Volvo
S80

S80
2004

The S80 received a minor refresh this year that includes a modified grille, additional chrome trim and a revised rear fascia for the exterior along with a new gauge cluster and door panels for the interior. Volvo's Four-C adjustable suspension is a new option on all trim levels. All-wheel-drive and front-wheel-drive versions of the 2.5T will be added midyear, but neither can be ordered in conjunction with the Four-C suspension. Finally, the T6 Premier replaces the T6 Elite as the top trim level.

Mileage Category: I

Body Styles	TMV Pricing		
	Trade	Private	Dealer
4 Dr 2.5T Turbo AWD Sdn	19773	21248	23707
4 Dr 2.5T Turbo Sdn	18859	20334	22792
4 Dr 2.9 Sdn	19042	20468	22844

Body Styles	TMV Pricing		
	Trade	Private	Dealer
4 Dr T6 Premier Turbo Sdn	25693	27304	29990
4 Dr T6 Turbo Sdn	23606	25079	27534

Options	Price
17 Inch Wheels [Std on T6]	+500
AM/FM/CD Changer Audio System	+350
Automatic Dimming Rearview Mirror [Opt on 2.5T]	+180
Automatic Stability Control [Std on T6]	+350
Electronic Suspension Control [Opt on T6, 2.9]	+795
Headlight Washers [Opt on T6 Turbo, 2.9, 2.5T FWD]	+200
Heated Front Seats [Std on T6 Premier, 2.5T AWD]	+250
Leather Seats [Std on T6]	+1045
Metallic Paint [Opt on non-T6 Premier]	+450
Navigation System	+1995

Options	Price
Park Distance Control (Rear)	+400
Pearlescent Metallic Paint	+600
Power Moonroof [Std on T6]	+950
Power Passenger Seat [Opt on 2.5T]	+300
Power Rear Window Sunshade [Opt on 2.9, T6 Turbo]	+550
Premium Audio System	+850
Refrigerator [Opt on T6 Premier]	+900
Telematics System [Opt on 2.9, 2.5T]	+835
Xenon Headlamps	+500

2003

Only minor changes are in store for Volvo's flagship sedan. Rain-sensing wipers and On-Call Plus telematics are newly available features, and two new colors, Titanium Grey and Ruby Red, dress up the exterior.

Mileage Category: I

Body Styles	TMV Pricing		
	Trade	Private	Dealer
4 Dr 2.9 Sdn	17468	18780	20966
4 Dr T6 Elite Turbo Sdn	23529	24954	27330

Body Styles	TMV Pricing		
	Trade	Private	Dealer
4 Dr T6 Turbo Sdn	20948	22520	25140

Options	Price
17 Inch Wheels [Opt on 2.9]	+361
Automatic Stability Control [Opt on 2.9]	+502
Compact Disc Changer	+723
Heated Front Seats [Opt on 2.9, T6]	+192
Leather Seats [Opt on 2.9]	+759

Options	Price
Navigation System	+1370
Pearlescent Metallic Paint	+434
Power Moonroof [Opt on 2.9]	+650
Refrigerator [Opt on T6 Elite]	+506
Telematics System [Opt on 2.9]	+603

2002

As a follow-up to the S80 T6 Executive, Volvo has released the T6 Elite, which combines the increased rear legroom, wider rear door openings and interior luxuries of the Executive with the convenience of a rear bench seat, thus providing room for five. Additionally, all S80s will get Emergency Brake Assistance (EBA), enhanced traction control performance and improved throttle management, resulting in quicker response in everyday driving situations. Other improvements include color-coordinated exterior trim (rather than the usual black moldings), an emergency release trunk release handle and the availability of a DVD-based navigation system and xenon headlamps. New exterior color choices are Pearl White and Black Sapphire. To commemorate the 75th anniversary of its first car, Volvo heightens comfort levels for rear-seat passengers with a special trim level. The car's wheelbase is the same, but special door hinges allow for a wider door opening in order to access a roomier rear seat. Executive leather upholstery and a sunshade are standard. A rear-seat entertainment system with dual 7-inch screens can play DVD, television or a video game. Another option is a refrigerator in the rear center armrest. The Special Edition S80 can be distinguished by the body-colored bumpers and moldings.

Mileage Category: I

Body Styles	TMV Pricing		
	Trade	Private	Dealer
4 Dr 2.9 Sdn	15567	16918	19169
4 Dr T6 75th Anniv Edition Turbo Sdn	19266	20938	23724

Body Styles	TMV Pricing		
	Trade	Private	Dealer
4 Dr T6 Executive Turbo Sdn	20119	21864	24774
4 Dr T6 Turbo Sdn	17135	18622	21100

Options	Price
17 Inch Wheels [Std on T6 75th]	+151
Automatic Stability Control [Opt on 2.9]	+454
Compact Disc Changer	+302
Heated Front Seats [Opt on 2.9, T6]	+197
Metallic Paint [Opt on 2.9, T6]	+242

Options	Price
Navigation System	+1146
Pearlescent Metallic Paint [Opt on T6]	+363
Power Rear Window Sunshade [Opt on T6]	+227
Refrigerator [Opt on T6 75th]	+423

2001

Volvo has added a new trim level, the luxurious S80 T6 Executive. Additional standard content for all trim levels comes in the form of leather seating, a luggage holder, remote retractable rear head restraints, memory position mirrors and Homelink. The 2.9 gets new 16-inch wheels and an auto-dimming rearview mirror as standard. All S80s get dual-stage airbags. The available Security Package for the S80 2.9 and T6 will now include the Interior Air Quality System (IAQS) which keeps the passenger cabin free from odors and pollutants.

Mileage Category: I

Body Styles	TMV Pricing		
	Trade	Private	Dealer
4 Dr 2.9 Sdn	12925	14881	16686
4 Dr T6 Executive Turbo Sdn	15702	18078	20271

Body Styles	TMV Pricing		
	Trade	Private	Dealer
4 Dr T6 Turbo Sdn	13737	15815	17733

Options	Price
Compact Disc Changer	+360
Fax Machine [Opt on T6 Executive]	+481
Heated Front Seats	+240

Options	Price
Metallic Paint	+214
Navigation System	+1335
Power Moonroof	+641

2001 (cont'd)

Options	Price
Power Rear Window Sunshade [Opt on T6]	+200

2000

The 2.9 and T-6 models go unchanged, save a few new colors and options.

Mileage Category: I

Body Styles	TMV Pricing		
	Trade	Private	Dealer
4 Dr 2.9 Sdn	9555	11304	13018

Options	Price
Automatic Stability Control	+501
Compact Disc Changer	+307
Heated Front Seats	+205

Body Styles	TMV Pricing		
	Trade	Private	Dealer
4 Dr T6 Turbo Sdn	11080	13108	15095

Options	Price
Leather Seats	+544
Navigation System	+1137
Power Moonroof	+546

1999

This long overdue redesign of the S90 counts several firsts to its credit: first with a transverse inline six, first with fully integrated GSM phone, first to carry an environmental specification (Europe only at introduction) and the S80 boasts the world's smallest manual transmission.

Mileage Category: I

Body Styles	TMV Pricing		
	Trade	Private	Dealer
4 Dr 2.9 Sdn	8643	10447	12324

Options	Price
Automatic Stability Control	+218
Compact Disc Changer	+268
Heated Front Seats [Opt on 2.9]	+161

Body Styles	TMV Pricing		
	Trade	Private	Dealer
4 Dr T6 Turbo Sdn	10090	12000	13989

Options	Price
Leather Seats	+427
Navigation System	+713
Power Moonroof	+429

S90
1998

Mileage Category: I

Body Styles	TMV Pricing		
	Trade	Private	Dealer
4 Dr STD Sdn	6531	8001	9659

Options	Price
AM/FM/Cassette/CD Audio System	+139

No changes this year.

1997

The 960 sedan is now known as S90.

Mileage Category: I

Body Styles	TMV Pricing		
	Trade	Private	Dealer
4 Dr STD Sdn	5721	7115	8819

V40
2004

Mileage Category: D

Body Styles	TMV Pricing		
	Trade	Private	Dealer
4 Dr LSE Turbo Wgn	18088	19303	21329

Options	Price
16 Inch Wheels [Opt on Turbo]	+500
Child Seat (1)	+300
Headlight Washers	+250
Heated Front Seats	+220
Leather Seats [Opt on Turbo]	+1200

Body Styles	TMV Pricing		
	Trade	Private	Dealer
4 Dr Turbo Wgn	15618	16833	18859

Options	Price
Metallic Paint [Opt on Turbo]	+450
Power Driver Seat [Opt on Turbo]	+250
Power Moonroof [Opt on Turbo]	+800
Sport Package [Opt on Turbo]	+650
Traction Control System	+380

The V40 remains largely unchanged for the 2004 model year although an upscale LSE trim version is added. There are also minor revisions to the front fascia, and the audio system now comes prewired for a CD changer, whereas last year's version required an owner to purchase that option.

Volvo
V40/V70

2003

Output from the 1.9-liter turbocharged mill is bumped up by 10 to 170 horsepower. A CD player makes its way onto the standard features list, and the front fascia gets a slight freshening thanks to a black egg-crate grille and body-colored side molding and bumpers. Inside you'll find a new three-spoke steering wheel and a four-dial instrument cluster. The sport package adds front and rear spoilers, blackout headlamp surrounds and 16-inch wheels, and the premium package now includes a leather-wrapped hand brake handle and gearshift lever.

Mileage Category: D

Body Styles	TMV Pricing		
	Trade	Private	Dealer
4 Dr Turbo Wgn	14161	15428	17540

Options	Price	Options	Price
16 Inch Wheels	+361	Metallic Paint	+325
Automatic Stability Control	+307	Power Driver Seat	+235
Child Seat (1)	+217	Power Moonroof	+687
Fog Lights	+126	Premium Audio System	+397
Heated Front Seats	+192	Rear Spoiler	+181
Leather Seats	+687	Traction Control System	+163

2002

Minor equipment changes are in store for Volvo's V40 in 2002. A Premium package now makes it easier for base wagon buyers to purchase desirable options like a sunroof, CD player, power driver seat and faux wood trim. And a Premium Plus package adds leather upholstery and a leather-wrapped steering wheel to the mix. The Sport package now includes aluminum interior accents, sport seats and an exclusive instrument cluster -- you can also get these items a la carte. A new center console design incorporates two integrated cupholders. Rear passengers will also have two cupholders at their disposal when they fold down the center armrest. New exterior colors include Bamboo Green and Dark Blue.

Mileage Category: D

Body Styles	TMV Pricing		
	Trade	Private	Dealer
4 Dr Turbo Wgn	11624	12793	14740

Options	Price	Options	Price
AM/FM/Cassette/CD Audio System	+484	Metallic Paint	+242
Automatic Stability Control	+181	Power Driver Seat	+197
Child Seat (1)	+181	Power Moonroof	+575
Fog Lights	+118	Rear Spoiler	+133
Heated Front Seats	+197	Traction Control System	+151
Leather Seats	+696		

2001

Only a year after debuting them on U.S. shores, Volvo has updated the S40 and V40 for 2001. Both the sedan and wagon gain additional crash protection in the form of standard head-protection airbags, dual-stage front airbags and a new child seat-safety system. Under the hood, engine improvements have been made to increase power and lower emissions. There's also a new five-speed automatic transmission that takes the place of the previous four-speed. Other changes are found in the cabin, with new material colors, a redesigned center stack for better functionality, more durable front-seat materials and improved switchgear. Rounding out the S40 and V40's 2001 changes are restyled headlights, bumpers and fenders.

Mileage Category: D

Body Styles	TMV Pricing		
	Trade	Private	Dealer
4 Dr SE Turbo Wagon	10965	12685	14272

Options	Price
AM/FM/Cassette/CD Audio System	+259
Automatic Stability Control	+294
Child Seat (1)	+160
Heated Front Seats	+133
Leather Seats [Std on SE]	+481

Body Styles	TMV Pricing		
	Trade	Private	Dealer
4 Dr Turbo Wgn	9753	11281	12692

Options	Price
Metallic Paint	+214
Power Driver Seat [Std on SE]	+240
Power Moonroof [Std on SE]	+588
Traction Control System	+133

2000

The S40 is Volvo's completely new entry-level sedan. Along with its wagon variant, the V40, this car rounds out Volvo's vehicle lineup. Safety, styling, and comfort are its main attributes.

Mileage Category: D

Body Styles	TMV Pricing		
	Trade	Private	Dealer
4 Dr Turbo Wgn	7450	8907	10335

Options	Price	Options	Price
Compact Disc Changer	+225	Power Moonroof	+501
Leather Seats	+409		

V70
2004

Mileage Category: H

Body Styles	TMV Pricing		
	Trade	Private	Dealer
4 Dr 2.4 Wgn	17037	18296	20395
4 Dr 2.5T Turbo AWD Wgn	20028	21285	23382

Options	Price
17 Inch Wheels [Opt on 2.5T]	+700
AM/FM/CD Changer Audio System	+1200
Automatic 5-Speed Transmission [Opt on 2.4, T5]	+1000
Automatic Climate Control [Opt on 2.4]	+350
Automatic Dimming Rearview Mirror [Std on T5]	+180
Automatic Stability Control [Std on T5]	+350

Body Styles	TMV Pricing		
	Trade	Private	Dealer
4 Dr 2.5T Turbo Wgn	18987	20245	22342
4 Dr T5 Turbo Wgn	21184	22468	24607

Options	Price
Child Seat (1)	+300
Garage Door Opener [Std on T5]	+200
Headlight Washers [Std on 2.5T AWD]	+220
Heated Front Seats	+150
Leather Seats	+495
Luggage Rack [Opt on 2.5T]	+180

For the latest vehicle information, visit www.edmunds.com

2004 (cont'd)

Options	Price
Metallic Paint	+450
Navigation System	+1995
Power Driver Seat w/Memory [Opt on 2.4]	+250
Power Moonroof	+950
Power Passenger Seat [Opt on 2.4T, 2.5T]	+200
Power Retractable Mirrors [Opt on 2.5T]	+180
Rain Sensing Windshield Wipers	+180

Options	Price
Rear Spoiler [Opt on 2.5T]	+200
Sport Package [Opt on non-2.4]	+775
Sport Seats	+550
Telematics System	+835
Third Seat	+1300
Traction Control System [Std on T5]	+345
Xenon Headlamps	+500

Last year's 2.4T model is now the 2.5T, with the same 208-horsepower engine as the AWD model. New option packages for the 2.5T include Convenience and Special Titanium trim packages -- both bundle a wide variety of desirable features, but the latter includes distinctive exterior cosmetic touches as well. Finally, bi-xenon headlights are now optional while the top-line Dolby audio system has been upgraded with more speakers and greater amplification.

2003

Mileage Category: H

Body Styles	TMV Pricing		
	Trade	Private	Dealer
4 Dr 2.4 Wgn	15401	16446	18188
4 Dr 2.4T Turbo Wgn	17769	18974	20984

Body Styles	TMV Pricing		
	Trade	Private	Dealer
4 Dr 2.5T Turbo AWD Wgn	18619	19882	21988
4 Dr T5 Turbo Wgn	19331	20642	22828

Options	Price
17 Inch Wheels [Opt on 2.5T]	+343
AM/FM/CD Changer Audio System	+867
Automatic 5-Speed Transmission [Opt on 2.4, T5]	+723
Automatic Stability Control [Std on T5]	+325
Child Seat (1)	+217
Child Seats (2)	+199
Heated Front Seats	+192
Leather Seats	+759
Metallic Paint	+325

Options	Price
Navigation System	+1370
Power Driver Seat w/Memory [Opt on 2.4]	+235
Power Moonroof	+683
Power Passenger Seat [Opt on 2.4T, 2.5T]	+246
Sport Seats	+199
Telematics System	+603
Third Seat	+361
Traction Control System [Std on T5]	+177
Trip Computer [Std on T5]	+181

A new high-performance model, the V70R, making 300 horsepower, will be available later in the year. A leather-wrapped steering wheel and an audio unit with a CD and cassette player grace the interior of the 2.4 and 2.4T. The latter also gets real wood trim. For the all-wheel-drive version, the 2.4 turbocharged engine receives a small bump in displacement and horsepower. Rain-sensing wipers and OnCall Plus (the telematics system) are available, and two new colors, Titanium Grey and Ruby Red, brighten the exterior.

2002

Mileage Category: H

Body Styles	TMV Pricing		
	Trade	Private	Dealer
4 Dr 2.4 Wgn	14084	15006	16543
4 Dr 2.4T Turbo Wgn	16637	17725	19539

Body Styles	TMV Pricing		
	Trade	Private	Dealer
4 Dr T5 Turbo Wgn	17977	19154	21115
4 Dr Turbo AWD Wgn	17405	18556	20474

Options	Price
AM/FM/Cassette/CD Audio System [Std on T5]	+227
Automatic 5-Speed Transmission [Opt on 2.4, T5]	+605
Automatic Stability Control [Opt on AWD]	+454
Child Seat (1)	+151
Child Seats (2)	+181
Compact Disc Changer [Opt on T5]	+726
Heated Front Seats	+160
Leather Seats	+635

Options	Price
Metallic Paint	+242
Navigation System	+1146
Power Driver Seat w/Memory [Opt on 2.4]	+209
Power Moonroof [Opt on 2.4]	+726
Power Passenger Seat [Opt on 2.4T, AWD]	+206
Sport Seats [Opt on T5]	+181
Third Seat	+514
Trip Computer [Std on T5]	+151

Like the rest of its platform mates (S60 and S80), the V70 gets emergency BrakeAssist, enhanced traction control performance and improved throttle management, resulting in quicker response in everyday driving situations. In addition, a V70 AWD model will be offered -- minus the armor and raised suspension of Volvo's Cross Country. Standard content has been increased, as well: All models get a cargo security cover; the 2.4T gets six-spoke alloy wheels and a leather gearshift knob; and the T5 gets Dynamic Stability and Traction Control (DSTC), special vinyl/cloth upholstery, leather wrappings on the steering wheel, hand brake and shift knob and aluminum mesh accents. Other new features include a DVD-based navigation system, xenon headlamps and an upgraded premium audio system. Cosmos Blue is now an exterior color choice. Finally, Volvo has plans to offer a limited number of special-edition V70s to commemorate the Volvo Ocean Race that begins in Fall 2001; these cars will come with leather upholstery, Ocean Blue exterior paint, silver body moldings, identifying badges and unique floor mats.

2001

Mileage Category: H

Body Styles	TMV Pricing		
	Trade	Private	Dealer
4 Dr 2.4M Wgn	12755	14105	15351
4 Dr 2.4T Turbo Wgn	14771	16335	17778

Body Styles	TMV Pricing		
	Trade	Private	Dealer
4 Dr T5 Turbo Wgn	15942	17630	19189
4 Dr XC Turbo AWD Wgn	17665	19535	21262

Options	Price
AM/FM/Cassette/CD Audio System [Std on T5]	+259
Automatic 5-Speed Transmission [Opt on 2.4, T5]	+534
Automatic Stability Control [Opt on 2.4, 2.4T]	+294
Child Seats (2)	+160
Compact Disc Changer	+534
Heated Front Seats	+125
Leather Seats	+641
Navigation System	+1335

Options	Price
Power Driver Seat w/Memory [Opt on 2.4]	+187
Power Moonroof	+641
Power Passenger Seat [Opt on 2.4T, XC]	+187
Premium Audio System [Std on T5]	+187
Sport Seats [Opt on T5]	+133
Third Seat	+534
Traction Control System [Opt on 2.4, 2.4T]	+294
Trip Computer [Std on T5]	+133

The Volvo V70 has been redesigned for 2001. Major changes include a new body structure, fresh styling, a revised interior and upgraded feature content. Safety figures prominently with the new V70 (as usual), but it is also more sporting than before, especially in T5 trim.

Volvo
V70/V70 R

2000

Engine improvements, a new transmission and equipment upgrades constitute the changes for these 2000 Volvos. The V70 AWD and V70 T-5 have been discontinued.

Mileage Category: H

Body Styles	TMV Pricing		
	Trade	Private	Dealer
4 Dr GLT Turbo Wgn	10514	12085	13625
4 Dr R Turbo AWD Wgn	13854	15923	17951
4 Dr SE Wgn	10316	11858	13368

Options	Price
AM/FM/Cassette/CD Audio System [Opt on GLT,Turbo,XC]	+221
Automatic 5-Speed Transmission [Opt on SE,STD]	+443
Leather Seats [Opt on GLT,STD,XC]	+489
Power Driver Seat w/Memory [Opt on STD]	+225

Body Styles	TMV Pricing		
	Trade	Private	Dealer
4 Dr STD Wgn	9189	10561	11906
4 Dr XC SE Turbo AWD Wgn	13208	15181	17115
4 Dr XC Turbo AWD Wgn	12636	14523	16373

Options	Price
Power Moonroof [Std on R,XC SE]	+546
Power Passenger Seat [Opt on GLT,XC]	+205
Rear Spoiler [Opt on GLT,STD]	+134
Traction Control System [Opt on GLT,SE,STD]	+246

1999

Volvo makes a number of performance, safety and styling upgrades to the V70 line. All cars benefit from a new engine management system and an improved brake system that includes four-channel ABS and Electronic Brakeforce Distribution (EBD). In terms of safety, V70s now include head-protecting side airbags and dual-stage deployment for the front airbags. Stability and traction control is now standard on the T5, and all other front-drive models are equipped with traction control. On the cosmetic side, all V70s receive a new grille emblem and body-color side moldings, mirrors, door handles and bumpers.

Mileage Category: H

Body Styles	TMV Pricing		
	Trade	Private	Dealer
4 Dr GLT Turbo Wgn	9446	11030	12679
4 Dr R Turbo AWD Wgn	12552	14656	16846
4 Dr STD Wgn	8385	9790	11253

Options	Price
AM/FM/Cassette/CD Audio System [Std on T5]	+173
Automatic 4-Speed Transmission [Opt on STD,T5]	+349
Automatic Load Leveling	+197
Leather Seats	+385

Body Styles	TMV Pricing		
	Trade	Private	Dealer
4 Dr T5 Turbo Wgn	9980	11654	13397
4 Dr Turbo AWD Wgn	10116	11812	13578
4 Dr XC Turbo AWD Wgn	11062	12917	14847

Options	Price
Power Driver Seat w/Memory [Opt on STD]	+116
Power Moonroof	+429
Traction Control System [Opt on GLT,STD,T5]	+193

1998

Volvo's 850 wagon gets a new name, new nose, body-color trim, stronger side-impact protection, more powerful turbo engines, redesigned interior and revised suspension. All-wheel-drive versions arrive to battle luxury SUVs.

Mileage Category: H

Body Styles	TMV Pricing		
	Trade	Private	Dealer
4 Dr GLT Turbo Wgn	7124	8642	10353
4 Dr GT Wgn	6551	7947	9520
4 Dr R Turbo AWD Wgn	9559	11595	13891
4 Dr STD Wgn	5747	6970	8350

Options	Price
AM/FM/Cassette/CD Audio System [Std on T5]	+139
Automatic 4-Speed Transmission [Std on AWD,GLT,R,XC]	+281
Automatic Load Leveling [Std on AWD,R,XC]	+158

Body Styles	TMV Pricing		
	Trade	Private	Dealer
4 Dr T5 Turbo Wgn	8056	9773	11708
4 Dr Turbo AWD Wgn	7577	9191	11011
4 Dr XC Turbo AWD Wgn	8662	10507	12588

Options	Price
Leather Seats [Std on R,XC]	+315
Power Moonroof [Opt on STD,XC]	+345
Traction Control System [Std on AWD,R,XC]	+225

V70 R

2004

Volvo creates a 300-horsepower R version of its V70 wagon. Equipped with the company's Four-C suspension system, which among other things can adjust the shock damping up to 500 times per second, this is one Volvo wagon you'll want to drive hard.

Mileage Category: H

Body Styles	TMV Pricing		
	Trade	Private	Dealer
4 Dr Turbo AWD Wgn	27072	28882	31898

Options	Price
AM/FM/CD Changer Audio System	+350
Automatic 5-Speed Transmission	+1250
Child Seat (1)	+300
Heated Front Seats	+150
Metallic Paint	+450
Navigation System	+1995

Options	Price
Power Moonroof	+795
Premium Audio System	+850
Rain Sensing Windshield Wipers	+200
Special Factory Paint	+600
Telematics System	+835

V90

1998

Body Styles	Mileage Category: I		
	TMV Pricing		
	Trade	Private	Dealer
4 Dr STD Wgn	6472	7929	9573

Options	Price	Options	Price
AM/FM/Cassette/CD Audio System	+139	Automatic Load Leveling	+142

Nothing changes on the V90.

1997

Body Styles	Mileage Category: I		
	TMV Pricing		
	Trade	Private	Dealer
4 Dr STD Wgn	5388	6701	8305

The 960 wagon is now the V90.

XC

2002

Body Styles	Mileage Category: H		
	TMV Pricing		
	Trade	Private	Dealer
4 Dr Turbo AWD Wgn	21113	22683	25299

Options	Price	Options	Price
AM/FM/Cassette/CD Audio System	+197	Metallic Paint	+242
Automatic Stability Control	+454	Navigation System	+1146
Child Seat (1)	+151	Power Passenger Seat	+169
Child Seats (2)	+181	Skid Plates	+121
Compact Disc Changer	+726	Special Factory Paint	+454
Heated Front Seats	+197	Third Seat	+514
Leather Seats	+696	Trip Computer	+121

Like the rest of its platform mates (S60, S80 and V70), the V70 XC (the Cross Country) will get Emergency Brake Assistance (EBA), enhanced traction control performance and improved throttle management, resulting in quicker response in everyday driving situations. Integrated child booster cushions, previously optional, have been added to the standard features list. Other new features include a DVD-based navigation system, an upgraded premium audio system, xenon headlamps and deep-tinted windows. Cypress Green Metallic is now an exterior color choice. A limited-edition model aimed at sailing enthusiasts, the Ocean Race Cross Country, will offer leather upholstery, exclusive Ocean Blue exterior paint, silver body molding, special exterior badging, an additional rear skid plate and unique floor mats.

XC70

2004

Body Styles	Mileage Category: H		
	TMV Pricing		
	Trade	Private	Dealer
4 Dr Turbo AWD Wgn	24665	26082	28443

Options	Price	Options	Price
AM/FM/CD Changer Audio System	+350	Power Moonroof	+1050
Automatic Dimming Rearview Mirror	+180	Power Passenger Seat	+250
Automatic Stability Control	+350	Premium Audio System	+850
Child Seat (1)	+300	Telematics System	+835
Garage Door Opener	+200	Third Seat	+1250
Leather Seats	+1200	Trip Computer	+150
Metallic Paint	+450	Xenon Headlamps	+500
Navigation System	+1995		

The XC70 remains unchanged except for the addition of bi-xenon headlights to the options list and a revised steering system.

2003

Body Styles	Mileage Category: H		
	TMV Pricing		
	Trade	Private	Dealer
4 Dr Turbo AWD Wgn	22320	23975	26732

The psuedo-SUV formerly known as Cross Country gets a new name this year, to align itself more seamlessly with Volvo's revised SUV nomenclature. Now called the XC70, this all-wheel-drive, luxury crossover vehicle can be equipped with dark tinted windows, rain-sensing wipers and a new telematics system named On-Call Plus. Crystal Green is the new color for 2003.

2003 (cont'd)

Options	Price
AM/FM/CD Changer Audio System	+867
Automatic Stability Control	+325
Child Seat (1)	+217
Child Seats (2)	+199
Leather Seats	+759
Metallic Paint	+325
Navigation System	+1370

Options	Price
Power Moonroof	+683
Power Passenger Seat	+246
Telematics System	+603
Third Seat	+361
Traction Control System	+177
Trip Computer	+181

XC90

2004

Changes are minimal for the XC90's second year on the market. All models get wheel and tire upgrades -- 2.5Ts will wear 225/70R17 rubber and T6s will wear 235/65R17 rubber, but both get the same 17-inch "Neptune" wheels. Ice White is a new exterior color choice. Stand-alone options now include a wood steering wheel, aluminum dash inlays and a leather shift knob.

Mileage Category: O

Body Styles	TMV Pricing		
	Trade	Private	Dealer
4 Dr 2.5T Turbo AWD SUV	28393	30014	32716
4 Dr 2.5T Turbo SUV	27034	28655	31357

Options	Price
18 Inch Wheels	+400
Automatic Dimming Rearview Mirror [Opt on 2.5T]	+180
Automatic Load Leveling	+500
Garage Door Opener [Opt on 2.5T]	+150
Headlight Washers	+165
Heated Front Seats	+250
Leather Seats [Opt on 2.5T]	+700
Metallic Paint	+450
Navigation System	+1995
Park Distance Control (Rear)	+400

Body Styles	TMV Pricing		
	Trade	Private	Dealer
4 Dr T6 Turbo AWD SUV	32476	34134	36897

Options	Price
Power Moonroof [Opt on 2.5T]	+750
Power Passenger Seat [Opt on 2.5T]	+200
Power Retractable Mirrors [Opt on T6]	+220
Premium Audio System	+300
Rain Sensing Windshield Wipers	+210
Rear Air Conditioning Controls	+150
Third Seat	+300
Wood Steering Wheel	+325
Xenon Headlamps	+500

2003

Volvo throws in its hat into the luxury SUV ring with the XC90, a vehicle that offers an impressive list of safety and comfort features.

Mileage Category: O

Body Styles	TMV Pricing		
	Trade	Private	Dealer
4 Dr 2.5T Turbo AWD SUV	26367	28011	30752
4 Dr 2.5T Turbo SUV	25332	26912	29545

Options	Price
17 Inch Wheels [Opt on 2.5T]	+361
18 Inch Wheels [Opt on T6]	+271
AM/FM/CD Changer Audio System [Opt on 2.5T]	+199
Air Conditioning - Front and Rear	+488
Automatic Dimming Rearview Mirror [Opt on 2.5T]	+145
Automatic Load Leveling	+253
Dolby Pro Logic Audio System	+361
Heated Front Seats	+192
Leather Seats [Opt on 2.5T]	+759

Body Styles	TMV Pricing		
	Trade	Private	Dealer
4 Dr T6 Turbo AWD SUV	29971	31670	34502

Options	Price
Metallic Paint	+325
Navigation System	+1370
Park Distance Control (Rear)	+289
Power Moonroof [Opt on 2.5T]	+683
Power Passenger Seat [Opt on 2.5T]	+246
Power Retractable Mirrors [Opt on T6]	+181
Third Seat	+361
Xenon Headlamps	+361

Instructions:

Each vehicle in this book has a Mileage Category listed in its information. To determine the effect of the vehicle's mileage on its price, look up the mileage category in the rows along the left side of this table. Then find the vehicle's year along the top. Where the row and column meet, the average mileage range for that category and year is shown at the top of the box.

If the vehicle's mileage is less than the lower number in the mileage range, multiply the difference between the mileage and the lower number by the amount shown at the bottom of the box, and add to the price.

If the vehicle's mileage is greater than the higher number, multiply the difference by the amount shown and then subtract from the price.

Important: The mileage adjustment is not to exceed 50 percent of the vehicle's adjusted trade-in value!

Mileage Category	2004	2003	2002	2001	2000	1999	1998	1997	1996	1995
A, B, G	8,400-11,000	21,300-24,600	34,300-38,600	46,800-52,400	58,900-65,900	70,400-78,400	83,600-92,700	91,000-106,000	99,900-110,300	108,100-119,200
	+/- 7 cents	+/- 6 cents	+/- 6 cents	+/- 6 cents	+/- 5 cents	+/- 5 cents	+/- 4 cents	+/- 4 cents	+/- 3 cents	+/- 3 cents
C, D, E	8,100-10,600	20,800-24,000	33,400-37,500	45,600-51,000	57,300-63,900	68,600-76,000	81,800-90,200	89,100-98,100	98,000-108,000	106,300-117,100
	+/- 7 cents	+/- 7 cents	+/- 6 cents	+/- 6 cents	+/- 6 cents	+/- 5 cents	+/- 5 cents	+/- 4 cents	+/- 4 cents	+/- 3 cents
F	5,700-7400	15,200-17,300	24,200-27,200	33,300-37,100	42,400-47,000	51,400-56,800	61,800-68,900	68,200-75,800	76,300-84,100	83,800-92,200
	+/- 10 cents	+/- 9 cents	+/- 9 cents	+/- 8 cents	+/- 8 cents	+/- 7 cents	+/- 6 cents	+/- 6 cents	+/- 6 cents	+/- 5 cents
H	7,400-9,900	19,900-22,900	31,500-35,700	42,900-48,600	54,600-61,400	66,600-73,900	81,100-89,000	89,800-97,900	100,600-109,100	109,800-119,100
	+/- 8 cents	+/- 8 cents	+/- 7 cents	+/- 7 cents	+/- 7 cents	+/- 6 cents	+/- 5 cents	+/- 5 cents	+/- 4 cents	+/- 4 cents
I	9,900-12,600	19,000-22,300	30,600-35,000	42,100-47,200	53,300-59,300	64,100-71,000	77,300-85,000	85,300-93,200	96,100-103,800	106,400-114,000
	+/- 10 cents	+/- 9 cents	+/- 9 cents	+/- 9 cents	+/- 8 cents	+/- 8 cents	+/- 7 cents	+/- 7 cents	+/- 6 cents	+/- 6 cents
J, L, O, P	6,900-9,300	20,200-23,700	32,700-37,300	44,975-50,900	59,600-64,100	68,400-76,600	81,475-90,725	88,700-98,500	97,700-108,200	106,300-117,400
	+/- 8 cents	+/- 7 cents	+/- 7 cents	+/- 7 cents	+/- 6 cents	+/- 6 cents	+/- 5 cents	+/- 5 cents	+/- 5 cents	+/- 4 cents
K, M, N, Q	8,500-11,100	21,300-25,100	34,300-39,400	47,000-53,600	59,500-67,600	71,500-80,900	85,450-96,325	93,400-105,000	103,100-115,800	112,000-125,700
	+/- 7 cents	+/- 7 cents	+/- 7 cents	+/- 6 cents	+/- 6 cents	+/- 6 cents	+/- 5 cents	+/- 5 cents	+/- 4 cents	+/- 4 cents
R	3,100-4,200	7,700-8,900	12,300-13,600	17,200-18,700	22,300-24,100	27,300-29,500	33,600-36,300	37,400-40,300	42,100-45,400	46,900-50,500
	+/- 13 cents	+/- 12 cents	+/- 12 cents	+/- 11 cents	+/- 11 cents	+/- 10 cents	+/- 9 cents	+/- 9 cents	+/- 8 cents	+/- 8 cents

Certified Used Vehicle Programs

Introduction

Studies show that sales of certified used cars have increased dramatically since 2000. For many people, certified used cars have become affordable alternatives to new cars. "Factory Certified" refers to used cars that are offered for sale by your local dealer with the support of the vehicle's original manufacturer, with warranties that extend beyond the initial coverage. The original manufacturer of the vehicle is using their dealer network to inspect the car, determine if it is worth certifying, then offering support for the vehicle for a period of time beyond the original warranty. The certified warranty protection typically takes effect when the original warranty expires and, like a new car warranty, offers coverage for a certain number of years or miles, whichever comes first. Used cars sold with third-party warranties are sometimes advertised as "certified" but are not truly factory certified because the authority and expertise of the vehicle's manufacturer do not stand behind the "warranty" in any way. In fact the term "warranty" may be misleading as third-party warranties are really extended service contracts. A true warranty offers coverage that is included in the original purchase price; check out our "Understanding Extended Warranties" article for more information on aftermarket service contracts.

The downside to third-party service contracts is that they often obligate the customer to pay for needed repairs up front, then wait for a reimbursement check; some require the payment of a deductible that can vary from $50 to $400. In addition, there is always the risk that the insurance company or other underwriter of the service contract is not around to honor the warranty when a claim is made — this risk is much less when the responsible party is a vehicle manufacturer.

In many cases, a customer who purchases a certified used car will become eligible for benefits that a new car customer enjoys. Perks such as service loan cars, shuttle pick-up and drop-off service, roadside assistance, free maintenance and low-rate "incentive" loans can be one of many reasons to choose a certified used car over a less expensive used car bought from a private party or generic used car lot. Even if a specific perk is not part of the official certified program, you can sometimes negotiate additional features with your local dealer. Many certified programs will even offer longer warranties at an additional cost, but the real value lies in the factory-provided coverage that would be included in the purchase price of the car you're considering. Because some cars have a longer initial warranty when the car is purchased new, they therefore represent a better candidate as a certified used car — in other cases, buying a certified used car will net the customer a longer warranty than if he or she bought that same car new. The attraction to certified used vehicles is clear — new car benefits at a used car price.

Many programs offer perks not directly related to the vehicle itself. For example, some certified programs offer services such as trip routing, and trip interruption protection. Trip interruption protection is a feature that will reimburse the owner of a certified used car for incidental costs such as car rental, lodging, meals and out-of-town repair expenses should he or she become stranded due to a warranted mechanical breakdown when traveling out of town — usually an owner must be at least 100 miles from home in order to use the service. The rules and dollar amounts vary from brand to brand, so check with your local dealer for the specific details.

Each manufacturer runs its own certification program, and has different criteria for what kinds of cars will be accepted. In some cases, buying a certified used car will net the customer a longer warranty than if he or she bought the car new. Here is a breakdown of what each brand offers when purchasing a certified used car or truck.

Acura

Acura will only sell vehicles that are 6 years old or less, with less than 80,000 miles. Acura Certified includes:

- Warranty terms are 1 year/12,000 miles plus balance of new car warranty.
- 24-hour roadside assistance.
- No deductible.
- 3 day return/exchange program.
- Special financing available.
- Carfax vehicle history report.
- Dealer certification required.

Audi

Certified used Audis are covered under the Audi Assured program. Audi Assured includes:

- 300-point inspection with condition report

Certified Used Vehicle Programs

- Balance of new vehicle warranty
- Limited two-year warranty or total of 100,000 miles, whichever comes first
- $50 deductible
- The remaining portion of free scheduled maintenance (if any)
- 24-hour roadside assistance (provided by AAA)
- Trip interruption service which provides up to $500 per day if you become stranded due to warranty-covered breakdown
- Audi Assured warranty is transferable for $150 fee

BMW

BMW Certified used cars must be five years old or less with less than 60,000 miles. BMW Certified used vehicles include:

- Multipoint inspection
- Balance of new car warranty
- Limited two-year/50,000-mile warranty — but not to exceed 100,000 miles or six years
- $50 deductible
- 24-hour roadside assistance
- Special financing through BMW

Buick

Certified used Buick vehicles are covered under the GM Certified program. GM Certified used vehicles must be less than five years old, and have less than 60,000 miles. GM Certified used vehicles include:

- 108-point inspection, and restored to factory standards through reconditioning process
- Three-day or 150-mile return/exchange program

If a GM vehicle is still in the three-year/36,000-mile warranty period, the warranty is extended to 39 months or 39,000 miles; if it's out of its warranty, the warranty period is three months or 3,000 miles bumper to bumper and no deductible.

Cadillac

Cadillac cars and trucks are covered under a program that is similar to GM Certified, but it offers a few more features as Cadillac is a luxury brand. Certified Cadillacs must be four years old or newer and/or have less than 50,000 miles. Certified Cadillacs include:

- 110-point inspection
- Limited warranty that extends the new car warranty to six years or 100,000 miles from date first sold
- No deductible
- 24-hour roadside assistance for the full term of the warranty
- Trip interruption protection
- Special GM financing rates
- Six months free OnStar and personal calling for eligible vehicles model year 1999 and newer
- Transferable warranty

Chevrolet

Certified used Chevrolet vehicles are covered under the GM Certified program. GM Certified used vehicles must be less than five years old, and have less than 60,000 miles.

GM Certified used vehicles include:

Certified Used Vehicle Programs

- 108-point inspection, and restored to factory standards through reconditioning process
- Three-day or 150-mile return/exchange program

If a GM vehicle is still in the three-year/36,000-mile warranty period, the warranty is extended to 39 months or 39,000 miles; if it's out of its warranty, the warranty period is three months or 3,000 miles bumper to bumper and no deductible.

Chrysler

Chrysler vehicles must pass a history check before they can be certified, and only five-star dealers can sell certified Chrysler cars. Certified Chrysler cars include:

- 125-point inspection
- Limited powertrain warranty of eight years/80,000 miles from original date of purchase
- 24-hour roadside assistance
- Trip interruption protection
- Rental car reimbursement if car is out of service for more than a day

Dodge

Dodge vehicles must pass a history check before they can be certified, and only five-star dealers can sell certified Dodge cars and trucks. Certified Dodge vehicles include:

- 125-point inspection
- Limited powertrain warranty of eight years/80,000 miles from original date of purchase
- 24-hour roadside assistance provided by Cross Country Motor Club
- Trip interruption protection
- Rental car reimbursement if car is out of service for more than a day

Ford

Ford calls its certified program "Quality Checked." Certified Ford cars and trucks must be five years old or newer and have less than 50,000 miles. All Quality Checked Fords include:

- 115-point inspection
- Six-year/75,000-mile limited powertrain warranty from original date of purchase
- 24-hour roadside assistance
- Travel expense reimbursement of up to $500 per day for up to three days related to vehicle breakdown
- Destination expense assistance of up to $75 to cover cost of taxi or rental car to reach your destination
- Rental car reimbursement of up to $28 per day for up to five days if vehicle requires overnight repairs
- Warranty ID card

GMC

Certified used GMC trucks are covered under the GM Certified program. GM Certified used vehicles must be less than five years old, and have less than 60,000 miles. GM Certified used vehicles include:

- 108-point inspection, and restored to factory standards through reconditioning process
- Three-day or 150-mile return/exchange program

If a GM vehicle is still in the three-year/36,000-mile period, the warranty is extended to 39 months or 39,000 miles; if it's out of its warranty, the warranty period is three months or 3,000 miles bumper to bumper and no deductible.

Certified Used Vehicle Programs

Honda

Honda Certified Used cars include:

- 150-point inspection
- Vehicle history report
- Seven-year/100,000-mile powertrain warranty from date first sold*
- Additional 12-month/12,000-mile warranty
- No deductible

*Insight battery covered for eight years/80,000 miles.

Hummer

Hummer does not offer a certified used vehicle program at this time.

Hyundai

Hyundai certified protection cars must be less than four years old or have less than 48,000 miles. Hyundai certified vehicles include:

- 120-point inspection
- Extended limited warranty to six years/75,000 miles or five years/60,000 miles depending on age
- No deductible
- 24-hour roadside assistance
- Warranty is transferable

Infiniti

Infiniti certified used vehicles must be newer than six model years with various mileage restrictions. Infiniti certified vehicles include:

- 128-point inspection
- Balance of new car warranty
- One-year/12,000-mile warranty
- No deductible
- 24-hour roadside assistance for one year
- Service loan car for 12 months or 12,000 miles
- Trip interruption reimbursement up to $500 for breakdowns more than 100 miles from home

Isuzu

Isuzu does not offer a certified used vehicle program at this time.

Jaguar

Select Edition is what Jaguar calls its certified used cars and the vehicle must be four years old or newer with less than 50,000 miles. Each Select Edition Jaguar includes:

- 120-point inspection
- Carfax history report backed up with its $10,000 guarantee
- New car warranty extended to six years/100,000 miles

Certified Used Vehicle Programs

- Free scheduled maintenance for model year 2001 and newer for the remainder of new car warranty period
- No deductible
- 24-hour roadside assistance for two years or 50,000 miles
- Special financing available through Jaguar
- Complimentary subscription to *Jaguar Magazine*

Jeep

Jeep vehicles must pass a history check before they can be certified, and only five-star dealers can sell certified Jeep cars. Certified Jeep vehicles include:

- 125-point inspection
- Eight-year/80,000-mile warranty from the date new car was first sold
- 24-hour roadside assistance provided by Cross Country Motor Club
- Trip interruption protection
- Rental car reimbursement if car is out of service for more than a day

Kia

Kia does not offer a certified used vehicle program at this time.

Land Rover

Land Rover vehicles must be six years old or newer and have less than 75,000 miles to be certified. Certified Land Rover vehicles include:

- 97-point inspection
- Balance of new car warranty plus one year or 12,000 miles
- No deductible
- 24-hour roadside assistance for one year or 12,000 miles
- $35 fee to transfer warranty
- Special financing available

Lexus

All benefits and services enjoyed by new Lexus customers are offered to Lexus Certified Pre-Owned customers. Lexus Certified vehicles include:

- 128-point inspection
- Three-year/100,000-mile total vehicle limited warranty
- No deductible
- 24-hour roadside assistance
- New car finance terms
- Complimentary loaner car for qualified repairs
- Reimbursement for meals, lodging and rental car if a breakdown occurs
- Complimentary first oil and filter change

Lincoln

Lincoln certified cars are called Premier Certified and only Lincoln cars from the current model year or four prior model years are eligible for certifi-

Certified Used Vehicle Programs

cation, so long as they have less than 50,000 miles. Premier Certified Lincoln vehicles include:

- 141-point inspection
- Six-year/75,000-mile limited powertrain from the date the car was first sold
- Service can be obtained in any Ford, Mercury or Lincoln dealership
- 24-hour roadside assistance
- Complimentary first Motorcraft oil and filter change
- Warranty ID card

Mazda

Only Mazda vehicles that are less than five years old with less than 50,000 miles qualify for Mazda's Pre-owned program. Mazda Pre-owned benefits include:

- 100-point inspection
- Balance of new car warranty plus one-year/12,000-mile warranty
- Limited warranty honored by all Mazda dealers in the U.S. and Canada
- 24-hour roadside assistance
- Warranty is transferable

Mercedes-Benz

Mercedes-Benz certified cars are referred to as Starmark vehicles. Mercedes-Benz automobiles that are less than nine years old and/or have less than 90,000 miles are eligible for the Starmark program. Starmark vehicles include:

- 132-point inspection
- Seven-day/500-mile exchange
- Balance of new car warranty plus one year or total of 100,000 vehicle miles
- No deductible
- Roadside assistance with no limit on years or mileage
- Transferable warranty
- Special financing available

Mercury

Mercury vehicles must be newer than model year 1997 and have less than 50,000 miles in order to qualify for Mercury's certified used program. Certified used Mercury vehicles include:

- 115-point inspection
- Balance of new car warranty
- Six-year/75,000-mile powertrain warranty from date vehicle was first sold
- $100 deductible
- 24-hour roadside assistance

Mini

MINI does not offer a certified used vehicle program at this time.

Certified Used Vehicle Programs

Mitsubishi

Mitsubishi does not offer a certified used vehicle program at this time.

Nissan

Nissan certified used vehicles must be between six months and five model-years old, or with a mileage of 6,000 to 72,000. Nissan certified vehicles include:

- 128-point inspection
- 72-month or 100,000-mile warranty from date car was first sold
- Balance of new car warranty
- 24-hour roadside assistance
- No deductible

Oldsmobile

Certified used Oldsmobiles are covered under the GM Certified program. GM Certified used vehicles must be less than five years old, and have less than 60,000 miles.

- 108-point inspection, and restored to factory standards through reconditioning process
- Three-day or 150-mile return/exchange program

If a GM vehicle is still in the three-year/36,000-mile period, the warranty is extended to 39 months or 39,000 miles; if it's out of its warranty, the warranty period is three months or 3,000 miles bumper to bumper and no deductible.

Pontiac

Certified used Pontiac vehicles are covered under the GM Certified program. GM Certified used vehicles must be less than five years old, and have less than 60,000 miles.

- 108-point inspection, and restored to factory standards through reconditioning process
- Three-day or 150-mile return/exchange program

If a GM vehicle is still in the three-year/36,000-mile period, the warranty is extended to 39 months or 39,000 miles; if it's out of its warranty, the warranty period is three months or 3,000 miles bumper to bumper and no deductible.

Porsche

Porsche refers to its certified used program as "Porsche Approved." Porsche Approved vehicles must be eight years old or newer, or have less than 100,000 miles to qualify for certification. Only certain parts of the vehicle are covered and the Carrera GT is excluded from the Porsche Approved program. Certified Porsches include:

- 100-point inspection
- Balance of new car warranty
- Vehicles that are still under the original warranty get a limited warranty for a total of six years or 100,000 miles from the original in-service date
- Vehicles that are outside of the new vehicle warranty period receive a limited warranty for a maximum of two years or 100,000 miles from the original in-service date
- No deductible
- Limited warranty

For the latest vehicle information, visit www.edmunds.com

- Warranty transferable to individuals only
- Roadside assistance for one year

Saab

Saab vehicles must have less than 60,000 miles or be newer than model year 1998 in order to qualify for Saab's certified pre-owned program. Also, any used car with frame, fire or flood damage is immediately disqualified from the Saab certified program. Certified Saab cars include:

- 110-point inspection
- Carfax vehicle history report
- Balance of new car warranty
- 72-month/100,000-mile limited warranty from date car was first sold
- 24-hour roadside assistance

Saturn

Saturn is the only carmaker to certify other brands as part of its certified used program. Therefore it is possible to buy a "Saturn Certified" used car that might not be a Saturn. What Saturn dealers are really selling here is service — all Saturn Certified vehicles, regardless of brand, are offered with Saturn's no-haggle, no-pressure sales experience. A "Premium Certified" vehicle is a used Saturn that is certified while a car with only the "Certified" designation is a vehicle of any make other than Saturn. A Premium Certified Saturn must be less than four model-years old or have less than 60,000 miles. A Certified vehicle (any brand) has no mileage or age restrictions. Here is what the respective programs include:

- 150-point inspection*
- 100-point inspection**
- Three-day money-back guarantee
- 30-day/1,500-mile trade-in allowance*
- 12-month/12,000-mile limited warranty*
- 90-day/3,000-mile powertrain warranty**
- No deductible
- 24-hour roadside assistance*

*"Premium Certified" only

**Saturn "Certified" only

Scion

Only Scion vehicles that are less than five years old with less than 65,000 miles qualify for Scion's Certified Pre-Owned program. Scion's Pre-Owned benefits include:

- 160-point inspection
- Six-year/100,000-mile limited powertrain warranty from date car was first sold
- 24-hour roadside assistance
- Vehicle history report

Subaru

Subaru does not offer a certified used vehicle program at this time.

Certified Used Vehicle Programs

Suzuki

Suzuki does not offer a certified used vehicle program at this time.

Toyota

While Toyota doesn't spell out the exact terms required for a vehicle to qualify for its certified used program, it does say "...only the best of the best are chosen to be Toyota Certified Used Vehicles." Toyota Certified vehicles include:

- 128-point inspection with vehicle history report
- Vehicle reconditioned to Toyota standards
- Limited six-year/100,000-mile powertrain warranty from date car was first sold
- 24-hour roadside assistance during warranty period
- Special financing available through Toyota

Volkswagen

VW's certified pre-owned vehicles must be newer than five years old, or have less than 75,000 miles. Any certified pre-owned VW with an original new car warranty in place must be in service for at least 12 months. Certified pre-owned Volkswagens include:

- 112-point inspection
- Balance of new car warranty including five-year/50,000-mile powertrain warranty
- Two-year/24,000-mile limited warranty
- No deductible
- 24-hour roadside assistance with no mileage limit (provided by AAA)

Volvo

Only Volvo vehicles newer than model year 1999 (with mileage limit) can qualify for the Volvo certified pre-owned program. Volvo certified cars include:

- 130-point inspection
- Balance of new car warranty
- Six-year/100,000-mile warranty from date vehicle was first sold
- 24-hour roadside assistance
- Trip routing service
- Trip interruption allowance for qualified breakdowns

Used Car Deals: Program Cars, Rental Cars & Salvage Titles

By Philip Reed

Here at Edmunds.com, we get a lot of questions about buying cars from three sources:

- "Program cars" — also known as finance, factory or executive cars
- Used cars from rental car lots
- Used cars with salvage titles

In our eternal quest for deals on wheels, we decided to take a closer look at these cars. Can you get a good deal from these sources? Will they make solid, dependable transportation?

For the inside scoop, we talked with two executives from Automobile Consumer Services Corp. (ACS), Larry Lovejoy, chief operating officer, and Tarry Shebesta, president. Together, these two gentlemen have several decades of experience buying and selling cars. For an additional perspective, we also talked with John Mallette, owner of Face Lift Inc., an auto body shop in Long Beach, Calif.

Program Cars

Program cars have been owned by the manufacturer and given to employees for a short time to use for company business. The idea is to have a Ford employee, for example, drive a late-model Ford to advertise the company's product. These cars are maintained by the factory and usually sent to auction before the odometer turns 10,000 miles. The cars are sold to Ford dealers at closed auctions and then put up for sale on the car lot advertised as "program cars."

"Dealers like these cars because they can get them at low prices and then sell them at a good profit," Lovejoy said. "Besides that, they always get the service they need because they can work on them in their own shops."

Lovejoy said these cars can be a great deal for the average buyer. They have been well-maintained, so in essence you are buying a nearly new car with no worries about mechanical problems. Furthermore, some dealers might extend the warranty for the full term or you can drive it under the balance of the warranty.

So how would the average consumer go about buying a program car? Just call used car dealers or check the ads. "Dealers are proud to advertise program cars."

However, knowing what to pay for the car is a problem because "You have no idea what the dealer paid for it," Lovejoy said. However, he added, you should never pay more than invoice for such a car. Or you could consider assigning a certain value per mile the car was driven and deducting that amount from the invoice price. For example, lease cars that are over mileage are charged 15 cents a mile.

"The deals are there," Shebesta said. Three years ago, "I bought a finance car from a dealer I know. It was a '98 BMW 328i, with 3,740 miles on it and I got it for $1,400 below invoice."

Bob Sykes, a video producer who lives in the Los Angeles area, wanted to buy an Infiniti QX4, but didn't want to pay the $36,000 sticker price. Instead, he was shown an executive car, with 14,000 miles on it, by the salesman at the dealership. He was able to buy the one-year-old car for $25,000.

"I looked up the price on Edmunds.com to get an idea what they were going for," Sykes said. "I feel I got a great deal. But there were a few negatives: They had let the registration expire so I had to get it reregistered after only three months and that was a $700 hit. Also, it needed new brakes. But still, I'm going to look for a similar deal my next time buying a car."

Former rental cars sometimes turn up on used car lots advertised as "program cars." This will be revealed if you run a vehicle identification number check using a company called Carfax. For a modest monthly fee, you can run the VIN numbers of cars you are considering buying. The Carfax report will tell you who the previous owner was, whether the car has a salvage title and if there are any outstanding recalls on the vehicle.

Rental Used Car Lots

Both Lovejoy and Shebesta see nothing wrong with buying used vehicles that have been used as rental cars. The oft-cited criticism of former rental cars is that the drivers who rent them abuse them. That might be true in a few cases, Lovejoy said. But there are other benefits to offset that argument.

"Those (rental) companies take good care of the cars," Lovejoy said. "And the rental car agencies buy them right to begin with — at net, net, net numbers (invoice price minus the hold back, minus the advertising costs and the like). But for peace of mind, you would probably like to have a third-party inspection because not all rental cars are alike — there are some plums and some peaches."

Salvage Title Cars

Mention to a prospective buyer that the car has a salvage title, and they run in terror. Still, others have owned these cars and driven them for years. What is a salvage title and can these cars ever be a smart buy?

When a car has been severely damaged (either in an accident, or because of a flood or theft) the insurance company estimates how much it will cost to fix. At some point, the cost of repairs is more than the car is worth. Therefore, the car is often sold to a salvage company and used for parts. To protect future buyers, the car is given a salvage title.

In some cases, the salvage company, or an enterprising body shop, might fix up the car and try to sell it. Naturally, the price of the car will be below similar models' because it has a salvage title. The danger is that the car was improperly repaired. The biggest problem is with the alignment of the wheels — if the frame has been bent, it is difficult and expensive to straighten. A bent frame will cause abnormal tire wear and improper handling characteristics.

"Some states require (totaled) vehicles to be branded as salvage cars," Lovejoy said. "But if it is sold in another state, and re-titled, it can be sold to Mrs. Jones as a straight-up used car. She doesn't know it has been cut together from pieces of different cars."

Both Lovejoy and Shebesta advised extreme caution when considering the purchase of a car with a salvage title.

"Keep in mind that if you buy a salvage title car, the chances of selling it to someone else and recouping your money are very slim," Lovejoy said. "If you buy a salvage title car, you might want to count on keeping it until the wheels fall off."

John Mallette, from Face Lift Inc., also advised buyers to be cautious. However, he added, "sometimes it works when you're dealing with a theft recovery where there was little damage. You might save $3,000, $4,000, $5,000. But you will lose that right off the top when you go to sell it."

Other Markets

If you are looking for savings, Lovejoy and Shebesta said buyers might save big-time by going to a repossession or donation auction. You can't test-drive a car there, but you can start it up and shift through the gears to make sure the transmission is working. If you go this route, Lovejoy advised that you bring a mechanically inclined friend to look it over.

Mallette said his best buys have come from spotting cars with "For Sale" signs in the window. "I like cars that people are trying to get out of," he said. "Like if a kid is going off to college, I might be able to get that car cheap. And chances are, it's a little Toyota Corolla or something. People are always looking for a car in that price range."

When buying an older used car, Mallette always takes the car to a mechanic for an inspection. "I still spend the $50 to take it to a mechanic. Not because this person might be trying to get over with me. He might say it's in great shape but he might not know that something's wrong with it."

Before taking it to a mechanic, Mallette pre-examines the car himself. He looks at the transmission fluid (does it smell burned and look brown rather than pink?) the engine oil (beware of a car who's oil has a metallic look) the color of the antifreeze (it should be green) and the fan and timing belt. Finally, he checks to see how much gunk is built up on the inside of the exhaust pipe — a heavy deposit might indicate worn valves or piston rings.

As a closing note, Shebesta steered prospective buyers back to the old favorite: buying from a private party. When you buy a very old car, the most important factor is how it has been serviced. Only the previous owner can tell you the car's recent history.

The View from the Dealer's side of the Desk

By Philip Reed

Consumers can learn how better to approach the trade-in process by considering the transaction from the dealership's point of view. With this in mind, we posed a number of commonly asked questions to three experts in the used car business. There was a difference of opinion among these industry insiders, but there was also a lot of valuable information that will certainly help car shoppers.

One of our experts is Bill Weismann, a dealer from Orlando, Fla., who buys 25 to 30 cars a week. To raise the consumer's understanding of the trade-in process, he started an Edmunds.com Town Hall topic called Real World Trade-in Values. If you want an idea of what a dealer will give you for your car, post the information in this Town Hall topic, and he will give you a price.

Another expert is Kenneth Mills, a car salesman with eight years of experience, who currently sells Hondas. He wrote to Edmunds.com concerned about some of the information we printed about trade-ins. We asked him to help readers by giving us the dealer's perspective on the trade-in process. He replied at length to a number of questions, and his edited responses are listed below.

Finally, we have tapped the expertise of an Edmunds.com data analyst who spent a number of years working as a used car manager for a national franchise.

What is the biggest misconception consumers have about trading in their cars?

Mills: The amount of money that dealers make on them. Most dealers shoot for a gross profit per unit of between $1,200 and $1,800. Also, many people believe that if a book says their car is worth a certain figure, that we automatically give it to them. If the book is right, of course, we do. Used car values are merely opinions.

Weismann: The shopper will search the Internet sites looking for trade-in values. Naturally, they will believe the highest number. Trouble is, in the real world, the trade is often worth much less to a dealer. Why would they pay $10,000 for a car that goes begging at the auctions for $7,500? That Neon or Hyundai will rot on the lot and the dealer knows it.

Edmunds: A lot of consumers don't understand that the amount their trade-in will bring is in relation to a number of things: what day of the month it is, the product mix on the lot, the inventory mix. If a dealer already has five white Camrys on the lot, and you want to trade in a white Camry, they won't give you much for your car. If they're light on that car, or they're one or two cars short of making a bonus, they might step up.

How do you evaluate a trade-in and assign a price to it?

Mills: The used car manager will generally drive the car a mile or so, look at the paint to see if it has had body damage, and use the Black Book as a guide [The Black Book is used more in the Southeastern states]. The real trick is to buy the car right, or you might be looking at a wholesale loss in 60 days. A good used car manager knows which cars will bring top dollar and which ones won't.

Weismann: Right away, I might know roughly what it's worth unless it's purple or something. I don't use the Black Book or Kelley, but I watch the Manheim [auction prices] like a hawk. I write down the VIN [vehicle identification number] and mileage. I automatically Carfax it [run a Carfax vehicle history report on the car]. I catch a lot of problems that way. Then I take a look at the body by doing a general walk-around. I look for paint-work. If it looks like the car's been hit, I pop the hood. I look at the fluid levels, then take a quick spin around the block. Next, I look at the interior, the headliner and check to see if it was a smoker's car. I also look at the tires, check the tranny.

Edmunds: A lot of it is curb appeal. But condition of the paint and mileage is so critical. If there's 100,000 miles on a domestic, it's different than that kind of mileage on a German highline.

Trading In Your Used Car

Do you recommend that consumers trade in? Or should they sell on their own?

Weismann: It depends on what they've got. If you bought right in the first place, you might have something to trade in that will bring a good price.

Mills: Heck, yes. It is quick and doesn't cost you as much as you might think, especially if you drive the right kind of car. Also, many states (all the ones I have worked in) give you credit for your trade when figuring sales tax. For instance, let's say you are buying a $20,000 car, and have a $12,000 trade. The sales tax in my state is 6 percent on cars. You will pay taxes on $8,000 in most states, instead of $20,000, for a savings of $720.

When a dealer gives a customer a figure for a trade-in, is there some wiggle room there? Or is that a firm price?

Weismann: Usually not a lot of wiggle room. Some dealers might hit the guy low and work it from there. But I usually won't bump more than once.

Mills: If the purchase price on the new car has been negotiated, it is somewhat firm. If you are not getting enough, ask the dealer if it is his bid or from a wholesaler. If it is his, ask him to make some calls. This will often net a little more. If it is a wholesale bid, ask him to try to raise the wholesaler. Sometimes, he can. Also, if you are trading the same kind of car the dealer sells, and your car is very nice, you may be able to get more because they want it for the lot.

What can consumers do to make sure they get a fair price for their trade-ins?

Weismann: They need to be well aware of what they have. And what [the dealer] is looking for. What we're looking at is totally different than what they are looking at. If they have had paint work on a highline car, it slaughters [the trade-in value]. It's amazing how many consumers don't know how much difference that makes.

Mills: First, take your car, especially if it is old, to [someone who can tell you the wholesale value of the car — what the car would sell for at a dealers' auction]. Also, make sure that you are dealing apples to apples. What I mean is that a Ford dealer may say he is giving you more, when he is just discounting the car he is selling you. If you tell him your trade value is important, he will try to satisfy you there. On the other hand, if a Honda or Toyota dealer offers you less, that doesn't mean you are actually getting less for your car. Ask them what the "Actual Cash Value" is.

Edmunds: Use the research tools available to you on the Internet. Check Edmunds.com TMV®, but also look at the asking prices listed on AutoTrader.com. And keep in mind how important curb appeal is when trading in.

Is there anything else you think the consumer should know?

Mills: The hardest thing for customers is their emotional attachment to their cars. Everyone thinks his or her trade is the nicest one we have seen, which it may be. There is still a limit to how much the car is worth.

Also, the value of your car has nothing to do with the payoff [the amount still owed to the bank]. Many customers feel that we should give them their payoff for their cars. The two are unrelated. If you are upside-down [owe more than the car is worth] as they call it, don't worry. Most people who have a payoff are. If you can still make the new car affordable, do it. If not, you can use cash to get out, or keep the car a little longer.

Buying a Used Car for Under $3000

By Philip Reed

Paying less than $3,000 for a used car is about the least you can spend for wheels that are still pretty reliable. But shopping in this category presents some special challenges, as you'll see in the steps we've outlined below. Be sure to follow our quick guide to get great deals on good wheels.

1. Review Edmunds.com and other consumer publications for recommendations of good used cars. Compile a "target list" of three to five cars to shop for. These cars should have strong reliability ratings and be widely available. Check the True Market Value Price, or TMV (http://www.edmunds.com/tmv/used/index.html), of these vehicles.

2. Decide what, if any, options you want and what colors you would like. But keep in mind that every time you pick a "must-have" feature, or color, you have narrowed the list of cars to choose from. This might make your search more difficult. Also, consider shopping lesser known car brands to get better prices.

3. Consider getting a Carfax subscription for a month ($24.99, www.carfax.com). You can get the vehicle identification number (VIN) of prospective cars and run a Carfax vehicle history report on each car before you even go to inspect it. Among other things, Carfax will tell you if the car has been in a serious accident, had the odometer rolled back or a salvage title issued.

4. Get $3,000 in cash from your bank and keep it readily—and safely—at hand. Cars in this price range are usually paid for in cash (or a cashier's check) and they sell quickly. You need to be ready to buy the car on the spot if it looks good. Keep in mind you will need some money to register the car and pay sales tax on it.

5. Tell all your friends and co-workers you are looking for a good used car. You might be able to buy a car from a friend or a friend of a friend. (Note: Some people advise not to buy from friends for fear a lemon will break up a good relationship. We haven't found this to be a problem.)

6. Look for cars on Edmunds.com and other online classified ads, on eBay and in the local papers. Also, keep your eyes open for cars with "For Sale" signs in the window. Pay attention to cars being advertised for as much as $4,000 because you might be able to bargain them down to your target price.

7. When you find one of your target cars, run a Carfax report if the VIN is available. Call the owner and ask the questions listed on the following page.

8. Inspect the car and test-drive it. See the checklist on page 621. If time allows, and the owner approves it, take the car to a mechanic to have it inspected.

9. Negotiate your best price. Keep in mind that most private parties set their asking price about 20-percent above the actual figure at which they expect to sell their car. Dealers will set the "asking price" even higher than 20-percent above the anticipated transaction price.

10. Pay for the car and transfer the title into your name. Contact your state's department of motor vehicles to complete the necessary paperwork. Make sure to remember to start insurance on your new car.

Used Car Question Sheet

By Philip Reed and John DiPietro

Dealership/Name of Owner: _____

Phone: _____ Make/Model: _____ Year: _____

Mileage: _____ Why Low? High? _____

Exterior Color: _____ Smog: _____

Interior Color: _____ Leather: _____ Cloth: _____

Number of doors: _____ Engine: _____

Transmission: Auto: _____ Manual: _____

Is there a salvage title? _____ Do you have the title: _____

Are you the first owner? _____ Is it a trade in? _____ Lease return? _____

Have any major parts been replaced? _____

Are any repairs needed? _____ Has it been in an accident?: _____

Options/Add-ons: _____

Is there anything else I need to know: _____

Asking price: _____

Copy this checklist and take it to the dealership with you when you are test-driving prospective vehicles. *There is a detachable copy of this list in the back of this book.*

Make/Model:	Good	Fair	Poor
General Impressions			
Exterior: styling, finish, paint, body panel gap tolerances			
Interior: upholstery and ergonomics			
Materials quality: plastics and leather			
Interior			
Ease of entry to front and backseats			
Headroom in front and backseats			
Legroom in front and backseats			
Comfort of seats			
Layout of controls			
Visibility out front, side and rear windows (in convertible, check with top up and down)			
Effective mirrors, both inside and out			
Storage space			
Trunk space			
Convenience features, cupholders			
Drivetrain, Handling and Braking			
Acceleration			
Passing			
Hill climbing			
Engine noise			
Transmission: smooth shifting			
Transmission: downshift without hesitation			
Cornering			
Suspension			
Braking			
General Driving Impressions			
Wind and road noise			
Rattles and squeaks			
Stereo performance			
Safety Features			
Airbags: driver, passenger, side torso, head curtain			
Antilock brakes (ABS)			
Traction control			
Stability control			

Edmunds.com
Strategies for Smart Car Buyers

By the Editors at Edmunds.com and Philip Reed

Revised edition available February 2005

Strategies that guide consumers through the process of buying or leasing new and used cars, including all-new material to help consumers avoid the latest sales traps.

This book outlines proven buying scenarios, clearly explaining the consumer's course of action in simple terms. The complex and sometimes frightening process of car buying is demystified in a comprehensive guide that covers:

- How to choose the right car
- Getting a used car bargain
- Avoiding the pitfalls of leasing
- The acclaimed investigative series, "Confessions of a Car Salesman"
- Financing section detailing crucial contract dos and don'ts
- Commentary throughout text from undercover car salesman Chandler Phillips
- Edmunds' latest consumer tool: "Smart Car Buyer"
- Bonus section: "Verbal Self Defense" avoiding sales language pitches and traps
- New section: "Safely Navigating eBay Auctions"

"A brand name car buyers trust." —*The Wall Street Journal*

A trusted automotive resource since 1966, Santa Monica, California-based Edmunds.com is now the Internet's pioneer and leader in providing free third-party automotive information, tools and services for consumers. Edmunds.com empowers, educates and engages readers by providing them with straightforward information on all aspects of buying, selling and owning a vehicle.

Subscription Order Form

Please cut out or copy this page to order subscriptions to Edmunds.com Buyer's Guides.

All prices are in United States dollars.

2005 New Cars & Trucks Buyer's Guide 1 issue per year	**Pay Only** (includes Shipping & Handling)	**Quantity**
United States	**$13.70**	
Canada	**$14.70**	
International	**$16.70**	

2005 Used Cars & Trucks Buyer's Guide 1 issue per year	**Pay Only** (includes Shipping & Handling)	**Quantity**
United States	**$13.70**	
Canada	**$14.70**	
International	**$16.70**	

Make check or money order payable to:

Edmunds.com, Inc.
PO Box 338
Shrub Oaks NY 10588
USA

For more information or to order by phone, call (914) 962-6297. Please pay through an American bank or with American currency.
Rates subject to change without notice.

Name ______________________________

Company/Library ______________________________

Address ______________________________

City ____________________ State/Province ____________

ZIP/Postal Code ____________ Country ____________________

Telephone ______________________________

Credit Card # ____________________ Exp. Date ____________

Cardholder Name ______________________________

Signature ______________________________